The Good Food Guide® *1992*

The Good Food Guide® *1992*

Edited by Tom Jaine

Which? BOOKS

Published by Consumers' Association and Hodder & Stoughton

Which? Books are commissioned and researched by
The Association for Consumer Research and published by
Consumers' Association,
2 Marylebone Road, London NW1 4DX and
Hodder and Stoughton,
47 Bedford Square, London WC1B 3DP

Cover illustration by Nadine Wickenden
Typographic design by Tim Higgins
Maps by Bartholomew, A Division of
HarperCollins Publishers

British Library Cataloguing-in-Publication Data
A catalogue record for this book is available
from the British Library.

Thanks for choosing this book . . .

If you find it useful, we'd like to hear from you. Even if it doesn't live up to your expectations or do the job you were expecting, we'd still like to know. Then we can take your comments into account when preparing similar titles or, indeed, the next edition of the book. Address your letter to the Publishing Manager at Consumers' Association, FREEPOST, 2 Marylebone Road, London NW1 4DX.

We look forward to hearing from you.

Photoset in Linotron Meridien Medium
by Tradespools Ltd, Frome, Somerset
Printed and bound in The Netherlands
by Rotatie Boekendruk B.V., Krommenie

Contents

Introduction Tom Jaine p 7
The Editors p 9
Forty years on Christopher Driver p 10
What *The Good Food Guide* has meant to me p 14
The top-rated restaurants p 18
Restaurants with outstanding wine cellars p 19
County restaurants of the year p 20
The *Guide*'s longest-serving restaurants p 21
How to use this *Guide* p 22

Restaurants

London p 27
England p 139
Scotland p 465
Wales p 521
Isle of Man p 561
Channel Islands p 563
Northern Ireland p 565
Republic of Ireland p 571

County round-ups p 595

Features

Of women, waiters and the single table Elizabeth Carter p 621
Educating the palate Joanna Blythman p 625
Inspectors of floors and walls Tom Jaine p 628
Musical meals Tom Jaine p 631
What to drink in 1992 p 634
Your rights in restaurants p 642

General lists p 647
The Good Food Club 1991 p 653
Alphabetical list of entries p 665
Maps p 675
Report forms p 703

A new service to keep readers up to date

From December 1991 *The Good Food Guide* will offer a recorded telephone message giving details of restaurant sales, closures, chef changes and so on, since this edition was published. Telephone 071-224 4597 to hear the latest information.

Introduction

The Good Food Guide celebrates 40 years of publication. The *Guide* is independent; it is the voice of the consumer, not the catering industry. It does not even have that symbiotic relationship with the industry that may be witnessed in similar publications – it has no sponsors, no recruitment among ex-managers, no part in the industry's internal politics. Of course, without restaurants there would be no book, but the *Guide*'s *raison d'être* is the customer. Its reports come from customers, its inspectors are customers. *The Good Food Guide* is a hand that feeds restaurants; those restaurateurs who bite it should remember this. It is good that the customer should have a voice; that she or he can vote articulately, not just with the feet.

The Good Food Guide is affirmative. It is not a survey of every eating-place in the kingdom; rather it is a list of those found most acceptable by our readership. As editor, I and my predecessors have ever been rent by the urge to list as many places as possible, to cover the map, but the *Guide* cannot fill its pages with sentences like 'This is very bad, but it is the best in Leek.' The County round-up at the end of the book helps fill out the gaps; even so, none of the comments would reflect that judgement. It contains practical and, we hope, good places that are indeed 'useful in the area'.

The Good Food Guide has always operated through the Royal Mail. Each year more than 10,000 reports of a meal are received from readers. There are report forms at the end of this book, with more available on request, and the postage is paid by Consumers' Association. We do not rely merely on this information, and we are skilled at recognising reports from relatives and other caring supporters of ambitious restaurants. Double-checks are carried out by inspectors, who are sent to report on potential entrants, restaurants about which we have had conflicting reports, and places that have changed ownership or chef. The inspectors are consumers and have had long experience in paying the bill for themselves. They are unpaid volunteers.

The system prospers only if people write to us. As consumers become less ready to pen a letter – the Post Office's business increases as a result of junk mail and computer print-out, not hand-written *billets doux* – we value all the more the reports we receive. Despite the growing reluctance to put things in writing, reports have not reduced in number, and they are invariably acknowledged; I urge you to carry on writing.

There are a number of new features in this year's edition. We have signalled quiet (no music) dining-rooms; we have tried to single out those places that close credit card slips and deal properly with the service charge, i.e. include it in the net price, do not demand any extra gratuity and state this practice clearly on menus and bills; we have refined the marking system; we have noted each instance of the clear marking on menus of explicitly healthy eating alternatives; and we now indicate whether a restaurant is a new entry (i.e. did not appear in the last edition).

In response to the sharp operators who have tried to con money out of restaurateurs by using our illustrious title, Consumers' Association has registered *The Good Food Guide* as a trade mark. We hope that this will help preserve the good name of the *Guide* and act as a stick with which we can beat those who use it to take advantage of consumers. Please let us know if you spot or suspect an abuse.

The year 1991 was one of recession and restaurants have suffered as much as any kind of business. The dividend to the consumer has been a preoccupation with value, more perhaps than with profit, as competition has sharpened. Before too many cheers are heard, and some should certainly be raised, any fool will understand that businesses cannot run for long at a loss. Prices need to be at least realistic. If restaurant meals seem overpriced, it is worth considering them in the context of other retail activities. Fine cooking is produced by the sweat of many brows, will count for little if not based on excellent ingredients, and may often, despite an apparently high price, be cheap in real terms for the investment of time and money it represents.

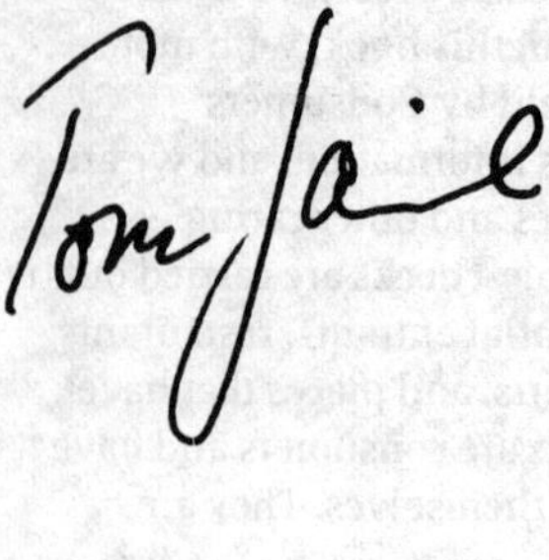

The Editors

Raymond Postgate *1951–70 editions*

The founder. Journalist, classicist, historian, socialist and crime noveiist. His idea for *The Good Food Guide* was born out of the dreadful standard of eating in post-war Britain. Although it took much of his time, he never wished to be merely 'Public Stomach Number 1' and certainly never aspired to being some highfalutin gourmet. His intention was to bring good food to more people than ever before.

Christopher Driver *1971–82 editions*

Journalist, poet, commentator and historian. A worthy successor to Postgate, Christopher Driver had been Features Editor of *The Guardian*. He brought to the *Guide* a nagging desire for high quality – essential when the restaurant business was mushrooming – and ability to express a variety of opinions concisely and with deadly accuracy.

Drew Smith *1983–9 editions*

Journalist. If there was ever a danger that the *Guide* would be identified with the middle-class elite gorging at troughs too expensive for the rest of us, Drew Smith was the populist antidote. His editions positively bristled with ideas that made the *Guide* appear more accessible, at a time when food was becoming a mass preoccupation.

Tom Jaine *1990 edition to current one*

Here yesterday, still here today. An historian and restaurateur by trade, he assumes the mantle of defender of consumers' interests in the eternal struggle over tablecloth and hot-plate with enthusiasm, bringing to his task the insights and understanding of someone who has also served on the *other* side of the swing-doors.

Forty years on

Christopher Driver

It is natural and proper that survivors of that blissful dawn in 1950, when they could eat and drink after a full decade of rationing, should look back nostalgically at the shoots of dormant cooking (British as well as Mediterranean) and congratulate themselves on their own minor contribution to post-war reconstruction. True, it seems unlikely that the first *Good Food Guide* (1951–2) should have been exhibited at the Festival of Britain in May 1951, only two months after it had been published. In spite of the editorial *cachet* of Raymond Postgate, historian and novelist, and other familiar names that were appended to inn recommendations (Clough Williams Ellis, Honor Balfour, John Arlott, Graham Hutton, Naomi Mitchison, for example); and in spite of the Festival's conception 'in a spirit of fun', as Sir Hugh Casson has recalled, the celebration and criticism of food would still have counted as sheer frivolity.

After all, it took at least a further 20 years to persuade BBC executives that the topic deserved serious attention on any medium or channel. The founders of Consumers' Association in 1957–8, courageous social inventors that they were, would have scorned the whole notion that a mere eating guide might come to be consulted in drawing-rooms and even public libraries in advance of a middle-class holiday, let alone establish itself for 40 years – a span of time as long as the *Guide Michelin* itself could then boast. Yet by the mid-1960s *The Good Food Guide* had come to symbolise a climate of feeling reminiscent of the equally sensual 1660s. From the parodied *Guide* entry that opens Kingsley Amis's novel *The Green Man* (1969) onwards, Raymond and his myriad correspondents became a gift to their fellow scribes. Day-by-day perusal of people's experiences told successive editors that 'all human life was there' in catering, and on both sides of the dining-room swing-doors: greed, rage, pretence, cupidity, lasciviousness. At the time, libel and other types of discretion modified the published entries; besides, as Raymond wrote in the leader launching the Club (20 May 1950): 'The only useful action is not to start on the unending task of condemning sin, but to reward merit.'

This did not prevent Raymond Postgate and his successors from comparing the excellent with the less good and even the intolerable, sometimes in the same restaurant on the same day. The classic example of this concerns the comet-like career of the north Soho restaurant, Lacy's, as depicted in the 1973 edition. It had been launched by a fine chef, Bill Lacy, and his wife Margaret Costa, an equally fine food writer who worked hard for Raymond's *Guide* over two decades. The quotes and commentary pro and con enraged some, amused others and reminded me (as they should remind any would-be restaurateur today) that in catering, as in opera, you may buy the best cast in the world but consistently precise ensemble is something else: 'Worth the 1,000-mile round trip from Edinburgh for sardines in mustard sauce, venison with black cherries and chestnuts, and hot fruit salad – my wife purred through every mouthful. The tastes of the many vegetables offered remained distinct throughout, so well had they been cooked.' 'When I complained gently about a barely eatable duck the waiter said that a "drunken woman customer" had similarly complained some days previously.'

I recall that entry because there were over 60 reports, many of them eloquent in either direction, and it took me a full day to assimilate the file and condense some 5,000 words to under 500.

The power of the *Guide*, from the earliest years, could be frightening. Most of that power derived, and still derives, from the collective anonymity of the *Guide*'s contributors. But the individual voice of the writer/editor mattered also. To a food historian (a specialism that did not exist when the *Guide* began) there is an oddity about uppercrust British catering between the wars – indeed, between 1910 and 1950. There were many great restaurants in London (Boulestin, for example), and in the country there were splendid inns for the intrepid motorist of the time (John Fothergill's Spread Eagle at Thame could be matched elsewhere, even if his personality could not). But there was no great restaurant critic nor any powerful institution (such as a newspaper or motoring organisation) that tried to judge actual cookery, year by year. We are luckier than we know with the *Guide*.

The *Guide* itself is old enough now to have its own continuities and discontinuities, its deaths and entrances, its amusements and asperities (there were always plenty of those with Raymond and his circle, not to mention their successors). Alas, much of the archive – including thousands of commissioned inspectorial reports which got so many slatternly or avaricious restaurants and hotels despatched to the fourth circle of the Inferno – has been destroyed or distributed: the sheer weight of paper (about 15,000 reports per annum) was too much for CA's stacking shelves. But some of the flavour of the times and exchanges should be shared with a new generation.

For instance, only this year a BBC interviewer was astonished to hear from me that Raymond found it necessary to ensure that a place was dropped from the *Guide* as soon as it was reliably reported that a landlord was operating a 'whites-only' policy. My interviewer was too young to know that race discrimination laws had to be fought for step by step by people of Raymond's calibre. A *Guide* reader had expressed his own reluctance 'to feed in the British counterpart of a Kaffir hut'. Raymond's reply must have spoilt his correspondent's breakfast: 'I would ask you not to report to us in the future. There are degrees of loutishness which prove a man to be incapable of judgement even on the matter of food and drink.'

The present editor does not have this kind of problem – I hope. But it is amusing to realise that in the 1960s, as in the 1990s, the correspondence included readers who wanted us to do something about wallpaper 'music' in restaurants and about the predicament of unaccompanied women (or mothers with young children) who were treated in one hotel after another with chilly dislike or outright hostility. And but for restaurateurs from the 'ethnic minorities', as a different generation calls them, we might still be fighting another British restrictive practice noted by an American in 1958: 'the all-too-common habit of finding the oven and refrigerator doors locked tightly at 8 or 9 o'clock. "We don't do dinner after 8 o'clock, Sir" is the most maddening phrase in Britain. I congratulate you on your stand.'

The last words should belong to Raymond Postgate, writing to his fellow Good Food Club members in August 1951, when the critical success of the first *Guide* (Cassell, 5 shillings) was assured but while the finances were tenuous in the extreme – as they remained until the late Peter Goldman, as director of Consumers' Association, held a capacious umbrella over the Club.

> Apart altogether from members' reports on existing entries, there are now three hundred entirely new recommendations; there are also a large number of very flattering letters which show how much the *Guide* was needed and how pleased members are to have it. The vast majority of the entries were wholly reliable. Perhaps two per cent seem to have been unjustified, which is an almost incredibly low margin of error.
>
> It has not been 'roses all the way' of course. One restaurateur telephoned in a fury because he was not praised as lavishly as he thought he should be. Another, reading that his wines were described as not very cheap, had the impudence to send a solicitor's letter. The 'Public Relations Officer' for a chain of hotels did not allow his managers to answer our standard enquiries, but substituted his own list of recommendations and his own eulogies and sent them in; afterwards he expressed indignation that I had not sent him proofs of the book for his approval; there is much to be done before all the hotelkeepers in this country accept the idea that they ought to be servants of the public and not dictators to it.
>
> The financial basis of the Club is very tenuous, especially as we have taken no advertisement. If it is to continue independent of the trade (and that is the only basis on which it is worth continuing) this can only be done by the activities of the members themselves. Even if I had the stomach of Gargantua and the purse of Midas I could not possibly test all the recommendations that come in. I should be dead at the end of the year. I should have had to eat five full meals every day in different inns and have

stayed in 400 different towns; and at that the work would have been scamped. You are one of those who have helped in the past and have indicated your willingness to help in the future. I am writing to ask if you are prepared to go on.

The proof has been the pudding.

What *The Good Food Guide* has meant to me

Andrew Lloyd Webber

I had an extraordinary piece of *Guide* déjà vu the other night. We had finished the first day of rehearsals for *Joseph and the Amazing Technicolor Dreamcoat.* I took my wife to Cibo (having read the *The Good Food Guide* review). I realised after 10 minutes that Cibo is on the site of The Gun Room restaurant in which, in 1968, the music master of Colet Court School suggested I write *Joseph* for an end-of-term concert.

When I was first invited to the Savile Club I headed straight for the library to see if by any chance there was a copy of Raymond Postgate's first *Good Food Guide.* There was. I sat spellbound. The pub in my village which was, in 1971, already a fast-food establishment, appeared in the first edition. Now I have a virtually complete collection of all the *Guides* and it is almost like a diary for me. How well I remember my first Italian dinner when I was 14 at the Portofino in Camden Passage and my first 7/6d lunch at Carlo's Place in the Fulham Road, both discovered thanks to the *Guide.* A few year's later I wrote the tune of *Jesus Christ Superstar* on a table napkin at Carlo's and for years I went there every time before I had an opening night, until I wrote *Jeeves*!

The *Guide* has had a huge bearing on my view of food. I suspect I was a later convert than some to new ways of cooking because I lived in Italy for most of my school holidays. But once the *Guide* pointed me in certain directions I realised that both it and *Gault-Millau* were on to something. It was the *Guide* which sent me to the inappropriately named Oxfam House to discover Raymond Blanc for the first time. And it has also sent me on quests it would take an advanced degree in sociology to understand. The *Guide* has conviction and verve. However much professional chefs bitch about the 'amateur nature' of its critics and comments, it's great to have a professionally edited guide in which we amateurs can share our thoughts about what we pay for.

I am devoted to *The Guide Food Guide* and I suspect there are many others like me who are unavailable for at least a week after publication. So here's to the next 40 years and the evening receptionist (now my wife) at Hintlesham Hall in 1981 who was easily the most delightful thing about the place. I now understand she worked there to subsidise her then embryonic career in three-day eventing. Mr Carrier, you shouldn't have let her slip!

Chris Patten

I can still recall the pleasant shock of discovering, 20 years ago, that Madame Barraterro's Hotel du Midi at Lamastre was exactly as Elizabeth David described it in *French Provincial Cooking*. Her book became, then and there, one of the most important gazetteers to the modest hedonism of my life. It shares pride of place with the red *Michelin Guide* for France and *The Good Food Guide*.

The achievement of the *Guide* is that it has done more than any person or institution to make increasingly available in this country what French lorry drivers take for granted – a good meal and a decent bottle of wine. (Unfortunately, the bill is still a lot higher over here.) The *Guide* has secured this triumph in the best possible way. It has unleashed the tastes and literary talents of a more widely travelled public against the previously implacable indifference of most of the catering industry. If ever there was a vindication of consumer power, this was it.

For many of my generation at Oxford, the *Guide* first led us to the Elizabeth, especially when parents were paying. Settled in London, I courted my wife in what used to be called The Singing Chef in Connaught Street. Elsewhere in London, the *Guide* helped me find two of the best wine lists at Mijanou and the Tate Gallery. Mijanou, incidentally, has always done just about the best-value lunch in town, and their Christmas pudding ice-cream is definitely *vaut le détour*. Of the restaurants in and around my home city, Tarts in subterranean Bath has recently deserved its place, and Homewood Park at Hinton Charterhouse continues to provide impeccable food in comfortable and unthreateningly elegant surroundings.

Taking children out to eat has meant that nowadays we pore over the entries about ethnic restaurants with special interest. We have been long-time fans of the New World, in London's Chinatown, where large numbers of growing girls with handsome appetites have been feasted for a song down the years.

There are one or two things I miss from old Guides. I particularly liked the section inserted for Plantagenets about eating in and around the French Channel ports. That is how we discovered La Huîtrière in Boulogne, a tiny restaurant attached to a fishmonger's. I have eaten the skate in black butter there a number of times, but have never quite had the time or the gumption for the plateau de fruits de mer.

Thanks partly to the *Guide* then, we eat better in Britain than we ever did before our taste-buds were properly mobilised. But there are still new frontiers and high streets to conquer. I recently visited another Elizabeth David discovery – the Auberge at Inxent in the Vallée de la Course. Now, when we can get, in Sussex or Sunderland, salty pancakes, trout, chicken and an omelette surprise like the ones we ate at Inxent for such a bargain-basement price, the *Guide*, its editor and its readers really will be able to rest on their – or rather our – collective laurels!

Michael Meyer

I first heard of the *Guide* in 1953 through Hugh Carleton Greene, brother of the novelist Graham Greene. We were playing cricket at Great Missenden for a BBC side, and after the game Hugh suggested that we should dine at an inn which had been taken over by a retired solicitor named Gerard Harris in a nearby village, Aston Clinton. In the then tiny dining-room of the Bell we ate wonderfully well ('main dishes of meat between 5/- and 8/6, of fish 3/6 to 5/6', the 1952–3 Guide reminds me), and when I asked Hugh, 'How on earth did you find this place?', he explained about the Good Food Club. Gerard Harris later told me that without it a place such as his, off the beaten track, could never have got off the ground.

I met Raymond Postgate at the Savile Club and soon became one of his inspectors, receiving £3 towards the expense of each meal for two. I was also co-opted as assistant editor and had to write about a third of the entries in Raymond's style. My brightest moment came when *The Sunday Times*, praising 'Mr Postgate's inimitable manner of writing', quoted an entry which had been knocked up by me. In those early years, all the office work was done by Raymond, his wife Daisy (George Lansbury's daughter) and me from their home in Hendon. I was always greeted by the opening of some special bottle from his cellar. One morning, soon after the present Queen's accession, he announced: 'Today I'm offering you a madeira specially bottled for the Queen's coronation.' This did not sound too enticing, and when I replied 'How nice', Raymond said: 'You haven't asked me which queen.' The bottle was from 1837 and was remarkable, like a kind of not-too-sweet butterscotch, heavily alcoholised.

It is hard now to imagine how totally the *Guide* changed eating out in Britain. After the Second World War many ex-servicemen had invested their demob gratuities in starting restaurants, mainly in rural areas, but there was no way except advertising and word of mouth by which they could become known. In 1949 Raymond hit on the brilliantly simple notion of inviting readers of a new weekly magazine called *The Leader*, founded by Edward Hulton and edited by Stephen Potter, to send him details of good eating-places throughout the country and to report on those named by others. So the Good Food Club came into being, and when after a few issues *The Leader* closed, the publisher Cassell suggested that Raymond should put his findings into an annual book. The first 10 or so editions were pocket-sized and priced at 5 shillings for around 300 pages.

Before 1939 there were virtually no serious restaurants in London outside Mayfair and Soho, bar a couple in the Strand. I don't recall one in Kensington, Chelsea, Hampstead or Islington. People in search of a meal out came into the centre of London as automatically as they did for a theatre. The only way to learn of new places was through friends. Those venturing outside their home area of the country had no idea where to eat. The distrust among the general public of *any* foreign food seems scarcely credible today. Raymond said that the two things which most changed this were national service and cheap holidays abroad. Even if only one in ten soldiers or tourists developed a taste for garlic or curry, lasagne or sauerkraut, this meant that there was a large new public wanting something more than roasts, grills or pies. And for this public, and those who sought to meet its needs, the *Guide* filled a gap which had seemed unbridgeable.

In 1963 Consumers' Association offered to take over the *Guide*, which meant that Raymond at last had proper office facilities, including the unimaginable luxury of a secretary. The operation had become too much for the house at Hendon. But ah! Those early, glorious, chaotic days.

The top-rated restaurants

Mark 5 for cooking

London

Chez Nico, W1
Le Gavroche, W1
Tante Claire, SW3

Scotland

Altnaharrie Inn, Ullapool

Mark 4 for cooking

London

Alastair Little, W1
L'Arlequin, SW8
Bibendum, SW3
Capital Hotel, SW3
Cavaliers, SW8
Clarke's, W8
Connaught, W1
Four Seasons, Inn on the Park, W1
Greenhouse, W1
Harveys, SW17
Oak Room, Le Meridien Hotel, W1
Le Soufflé, Inter-Continental Hotel, W1
Sutherlands, W1

England

Adlard's, Norwich
Arkle, Chester Grosvenor Hotel, Chester
Carved Angel, Dartmouth
Croque-en-Bouche, Malvern Wells
Gidleigh Park, Chagford
Lettonie, Bristol
Mallory Court, Bishop's Tachbrook
Manleys, Storrington
Le Manoir aux Quat' Saisons, Great Milton
Morels, Haslemere
Oakes, Stroud
Old Manor House, Romsey
Old Vicarage, Ridgeway
L'Ortolan, Shinfield
Le Poussin, Brockenhurst
Restaurant 19, Belvedere Hotel, Bradford
Seafood Restaurant, Padstow
Sharrow Bay, Ullswater
Le Talbooth, Dedham
Waterside Inn, Bray
White Moss House, Grasmere
Winteringham Fields, Winteringham

Scotland

Airds Hotel, Port Appin
Champany Inn, Linlithgow
Kinnaird House, Dunkeld
Peat Inn, Peat Inn
La Potinière, Gullane

Wales

Plas Bodegroes, Pwllheli
Walnut Tree Inn, Llandewi Skirrid

Restaurants with outstanding wine cellars

marked in the text with a 🍷

London

Au Jardin des Gourmets, W1
Bibendum, SW3
Boyd's, W8
Capital Hotel, SW3
Clarke's, W8
Gilbert's, SW7
Leith's, W11
Mijanou, SW1
Odette's, NW1
192, W11
190 Queensgate, SW7
Pollyanna's, SW11
RSJ, SE1

England

Adlard's, Norwich
Angel Inn, Hetton
Beetle & Wedge, Moulsford
Bell, Aston Clinton
Bridgefield House, Spark Bridge
Brookdale House, North Huish
Carved Angel, Dartmouth
Cobwebs, Leck
Corse Lawn House Hotel, Corse Lawn
Croque-en-Bouche, Malvern Wells
Crown, Southwold
Dundas Arms, Kintbury
Epworth Tap, Epworth
Fountain House, Dedham
Fox and Goose, Fressingfield
French Partridge, Horton
George, Stamford
Gidleigh Park, Chagford
Gravetye Manor, East Grinstead
Hambleton Hall, Hambleton
Harvey's Cathedral Restaurant, Lincoln
Hope End, Ledbury
Manor, Chadlington
Old Beams, Waterhouses
Old Manor House, Romsey
Old Post Office, Clun
Old Vicarage, Ridgeway
Old Vicarage, Witherslack
Pool Court, Pool in Wharfedale
Porthole Eating House, Bowness-on-Windermere
Read's, Faversham
Redmond's, Cleeve Hill
Röser's, St Leonards
Seafood Restaurant, Padstow
Sir Charles Napier Inn, Chinnor
Summer Lodge, Evershot
Le Talbooth, Dedham
Thornbury Castle, Thornbury
Three Lions, Stuckton
Village Restaurant, Ramsbottom
White Horse Inn, Chilgrove
White Moss House, Grasmere

Scotland

Airds Hotel, Port Appin
Ard-Na-Coille Hotel, Newtonmore
Braeval Old Mill, Aberfoyle
Cellar, Anstruther
Champany Inn, Linlithgow
Cross, Kingussie
Knipoch Hotel, Oban
Peat Inn, Peat Inn
La Potinière, Gullane
Ubiquitous Chip, Glasgow
Vintners Rooms, Edinburgh

Wales

Cemlyn, Harlech
Meadowsweet Hotel, Llanrwst
Penhelig Arms Hotel, Aberdovey
Plas Bodegroes, Pwllheli
Walnut Tree Inn, Llandewi Skirrid

County restaurants of the year

Our indulgence. The restaurants listed below are not invariably the best (highest rated) in their respective counties, but they are the ones that have caught the eye this year, engendered most excitement, or generally seemed laudable enterprises. Not all counties have an award winner.

England

Berkshire Royal Oak, Yattendon
Cornwall Café Volnay, Porthoustock
Cumbria White Moss House, Grasmere
Devon Horn of Plenty, Tavistock
Dorset Summer Lodge, Evershot
East Sussex Black Chapati, Brighton
Essex Le Talbooth, Dedham
Gloucestershire Marsh Goose, Moreton-in-the-Marsh
Hampshire Le Poussin, Brockenhurst
Hereford & Worcester Poppies, The Roebuck, Brimfield
Hertfordshire Hanbury Manor, Thundridge
Kent Cheevers, Tunbridge Wells
Lancashire Heathcote's, Longridge
Leicestershire Stapleford Park, Stapleford
Lincolnshire Harry's Place, Great Gonerby
Norfolk Garbo's, King's Lynn
North Yorkshire Melton's, York
Oxfordshire Bath Place Hotel, Oxford
Somerset Langley House Hotel, Langley Marsh
South Yorkshire Resturant Peano, Barnsley
Suffolk Fox and Goose, Fressingfield
Surrey Partners West Street, Dorking
Tyne & Wear Forsters, East Boldon
West Midlands Carl's, Trinity House Hotel, Coventry
West Sussex South Lodge, Lower Beeding
West Yorkshire Hansa's, Leeds
Wiltshire George & Dragon, Rowde

Scotland

Dumfries & Galloway Well View, Moffat
Highland Altnaharrie Inn, Ullapool
Lothian La Potinière, Gullane
Strathclyde Buttery, Glasgow
Tayside Murrayshall Hotel, Scone

Wales

Gwynedd Ye Old Bulls Head Inn, Beaumaris
Powys Llangoed Hall, Llyswen

The *Guide's* longest-serving restaurants

Forty years on and the *Guide* has seen many restaurants come and go. Some, however, have stayed the course with tenacity. Although all in the following list fall short of forty years' entry, some are nudging it. (Qualification for this list is that the restaurant must be in each edition of the *Guide* subsequent to its first entry.)

Connaught Hotel, W1	39 years
Gay Hussar, W1	35 years
Porth Tocyn Hotel Abersoch, Gwynedd	35 years
Gravetye Manor, East Grinstead, West Sussex	31 years
Sharrow Bay, Ullswater, Cumbria	31 years
Dundas Arms, Kintbury, Berkshire	29 years
Box Tree, Ilkley, West Yorkshire	27 years
French Partridge, Horton, Northamptonshire	27 years
Walnut Tree Inn, Llandewi Skirrid, Gwent	27 years
Butley-Orford Oysterage, Orford, Suffolk	25 years
Chez Moi, W11	23 years
Pool Court, Pool in Wharfedale, West Yorkshire	23 years
Rothay Manor, Ambleside, Cumbria	23 years
Sundial, Herstmonceux, East Sussex	23 years
Le Gavroche, W1	21 years
Summer Isles Hotel, Achiltibuie, Highland	21 years
Timothy's, Perth, Tayside	21 years

How to use this *Guide*

All the entries in this year's *Guide* have been rewritten between April and August. The information on which they are based is from reports sent in by readers over the last year and confirmed by anonymous inspection. No entry is based on a single nomination. In every case readers and inspectors have been prepared to endorse the quality of the cooking, the dining-room and the value for money.

The rating system grades restaurants, on the basis of their cooking only, from 1 to 5. This takes no account of elegance, ambience, service and value than it does of food and cooking. The marks take into account the perception of the *Guide* and its reporters, and signify the following:

1 **Competent cooking** Restaurants that achieve a satisfactory standard, endorsed by readers as worthy of the *Guide*.

2 **Good cooking** Restaurants that produce good food in most departments, though some inconsistencies may have been noted. They please most readers much of the time.

3 **Very good cooking** The kitchen achieves consistent quality, rarely disappointing in any department. Seldom faulted by *Guide* reporters.

4 **Excellent cooking** Restaurants with a high level of ambition and achievement. Generally, they delight.

5 **The best** These may excite debate, not as to whether the cooking is good, but whether it is better than their peers'.

* An asterisk next to a mark signifies that the *Guide* and its readers are of the opinion that the restaurant is a particularly fine example within its numeric classification.

The *Guide* office is reliant on proprietors for price information. Each year owners are asked to mark on a questionnaire the cost, for autumn of that year, of any set meals, and also the lowest and highest à la carte prices for each course. Our computer then adds the quoted price for coffee, service, and half a bottle of house wine per head. For à la carte prices it calculates the strict average cost. In practice, however, most people do not eat an 'average' meal, but may have drinks before the meal, drink a more expensive wine, and choose at least some top-flight dishes. The result can be a bill much higher than expected. Also, prices are likely to rise during the currency of the *Guide*. To try and satisfy everyone, the *Guide* continues, in the prices below the entry, to give the average cost of three-course meals as calculated by computer and double-checked. However, above the entry, the cost quoted gives the lowest such price, and the highest such price *inflated by 20 per cent* to bring some realism to bear on the likely upper limit.

How to read a *Guide* entry

CANTERBURY Kent [1] map 3 [2]

▲ *Mary's Kitchen* [3] [4] **NEW ENTRY** [5]

16 Elwood Avenue, Canterbury CT41 4RX [6]
CANTERBURY (0227) 7770666 [7] COOKING 2 [9]
behind Scala Cinema [8] COST £19–£24 [10]

(main text) [11] CELLARMAN'S CHOICE [12]

CHEF: Mary Smith PROPRIETORS: Mary and David Smith [13] OPEN: Mon to Sat [14] CLOSED: Aug [15] MEALS: 12 to 2, 7 to 9 [16] PRICES: £13 (£19), Set D £15 (£20). [17] Cover £1. Minimum £5 L. Net prices, card slips closed. [18] Unlicensed, but bring your own: corkage £1. [19] CARDS: Access, Amex, Diners, Visa [20] SEATS: 72. 4 tables outside. Private parties: 26 main room, 10 private room. [21] Car-park, 40 places. Vegetarian meals. [22] Heatly eating options. [23] Children's helpings. No children under 10. [24] Jacket and tie. [25] No-smoking area. [26] Wheelchair access (2 steps; also WC). [27] No music. [28] Air-conditioned. One sitting [29] Fax: (0227) 7770777. [30] ACCOMMODATION: 14 rooms, all with bath/shower. B&B £20 to £40. [31] Children welcome. [32] Pets welcome. [33] Afternoon teas. [34] Garden. Swimming-pool. Tennis. Air-conditioned. TV. Phone. Scenic. Doors closed at 11.30. Confirm by 6 [*Which? Hotel Guide*] [35]

1 The town and county (in the London section, restaurants are listed alphabetically by name rather than geographically).

2 The map number. The maps are at the end of the *Guide*.

3 The name of the restaurant. ▲ by the name denotes that it offers accommodation too.

4 The glass symbol denotes a wine list that is good, well above the ordinary. The symbol of a bottle indicates a truly outstanding wine list.

5 If a restaurant is new to the *Guide* this year (did not appear as a main entry in the last edition) NEW ENTRY appears opposite its name.

6 The restaurant's address and post code.

7 The restaurant's telephone number, including its STD code.

8 Any special directions in case the restaurant is difficult to find.

9 The *Guide*'s mark, out of five, for cooking quality, ranging from 1 for competent cooking to 5 for the best. See page 22 or the inside front cover for a full explanation.

10 This is the price range for three-course meals, based on our computer's calculation of an average three-course meal, including coffee, wine and service, according to prices provided by the proprietor. The top figure, however, has been inflated by 20 per cent to reflect (i) that many readers do not eat an 'average' meal and are therefore shocked when, with extra drinks and some top-range dishes, the bill rises well beyond the average price, and (ii) likely price rises that will come into play during the life of the *Guide*.

11 The text is based on reports sent in by readers during the last *Guide* year, confirmed by commissioned, anonymous inspections.

12 Some entries conclude with a CELLARMAN'S CHOICE. This is a wine, usually more expensive than the house wine, that the restaurateur assures us will be in stock during 1992, and recommends as suitable for the kind of food served, if you do not want to order the house wine.

13 The names of the chef and the owner, so that any change in management will be instantly detectable.

14 The days of the week the restaurant is open.

15 Annual closures.

16 The times of first and last orders for meals. It is always advisable to book before going to a restaurant. If you book and then cannot go, please remember to phone the restaurant to cancel.

17 These are average prices for three-course meals, giving the à la carte price and variations for set lunch (L) and dinner (D) where applicable. The initial price represents the prices on the main menu; the second price, in brackets, is the real cost when the extras of house wine, coffee and service (at 10% unless otherwise specified) have been added.

18 Net prices indicates that the prices given on a menu and on a bill are inclusive of VAT and service charge, and that this practice is clearly stated on menu and bill. Card slips closed indicates that the total on the slips of credit cards is closed when handed over for signature. When a fixed service charge is added to the bill the percentage is specified. When service is not mentioned, it is at the discretion of the customer.

19 A restaurant is unlicensed but customers may bring their own alcoholic drinks on to the premises. Any corkage charge is indicated.

20 The credit cards accepted by the restaurant.

21 Not all restaurants will take private parties. The maximum number of people in a party is given.

22 Many restaurants claim to cater for vegetarians but do not include suitable dishes on their menus as a matter of course. It is always advisable to explain, when booking, if you do not eat meat.

23 Healthy eating options indicates that a restaurant marks on its menu, in words and/or using symbols, low-fat dishes or other healthy eating choices.

24 Some restaurants and hotels are not keen on children in the dining-room. Where it says children welcome or children's helpings, this indicates that they don't mind. Any limitations on age are specified.

25 Jackets and ties are compulsory in very few restaurants and this is specified; otherwise it is indicated if smart dress is preferred.

26 Any no-smoking arrangements as given to us by the restaurants.

27 Wheelchair access means that the proprietor has confirmed that the entrance is 33 inches wide and passages four feet across. Where there are steps it will say so. If it says 'also WC', then the owner has told us that the toilet facilities are suitable for disabled people. The *Guide* relies on proprietors giving accurate information on wheelchair access. If you find the details in the *Guide* are inaccurate, please tell us.

28 Dining-rooms where live and recorded music will never be played. Where a restaurant has told us that music may be played we indicate this.

29 The restaurant serves a single sitting at a specific time.

30 Fax number when available.

31 The price for rooms as given to us by the hotels. The first price is for one person in a single room of single occupancy of a double, the second is the upper price for two people in a double room. When a price is for dinner, bed and breakfast it is indicated as D,B&B.

32 Children are welcome in the accommodation. Any age limitations are specified.

33 Pets are welcome in the hotel.

34 Teas are served to non-residents.

35 [*Which? Hotel Guide*] denotes that this establishment is also listed in the 1992 edition of our sister guide to over 900 hotels in Britain.

London

Adams Café **NEW ENTRY** map 10

77 Askew Road, W12 9AH COOKING 1
081-743 0572 COST £12

By day this is a modest café serving English breakfasts, mixed grills and boiled bacon and cabbage, by night the mood is transformed by candlelight, Tunisian bric-à-brac, carefully drapped cloths and Arab background music. While the café-feel is never wholly banished from seating, tables and counters, these offer a softer setting for the same kitchen's Mediterranean and Tunisian dishes. The speciality is couscous and four variations are offered, including a vegetarian one, but gargoulette, a spicy Tunisian lamb casserole, slow-cooked to an intense, memorable flavour, is worth exploring. Among the first courses, chorba, a thick, terracotta-coloured lamb soup stands out, or there are the various briks of egg, tuna, seafood or vegetables. Service by Frances Boukraa is discreet, and everything runs quietly. Mint tea makes an appropriate finish. A place that offers fair value and a happy atmosphere. Go prepared: it is unlicensed and credit cards are not accepted.

CHEF: Abdel Boukraa PROPRIETORS: Abdel and Frances Boukraa OPEN: Mon to Sat, D only CLOSED: bank hols MEALS: 7.30 to 10.30 PRICES: £9 (£10). Cover 75p. Unlicensed, but bring your own: no corkage SEATS: 36. Private parties: 36 main room. Vegetarian meals. Children welcome. Wheelchair access. Music

Alastair Little 🍷 map 14

49 Frith Street, W1V 5TE COOKING 4
071-734 5183 COST £27–£53

It's small – a shop front on Frith Street. It's bare – no tablecloths, curtains, carpet, nor even linen napkins. It's relaxed – eat a single course in the dug-out bar below, don't expect flunky service, just intelligent attention. It's creative – 'the most interesting and tempting menu we encountered in this country'. And it's very good, if thought expensive by some. The money is not begrudged on account of the food, rather 'the disjunction between food and atmosphere', or trappings. Most readers find this natural approach refreshing, and only occasionally vitiated by too much clatter and noise. The menu changes meal by meal, the longest section being first courses, though invention does not flag thereafter. A very regular visitor reflects: 'This penchant for Italian food (and Japanese, it should be added) is being joined by an enthusiasm for Pekinese cooking and the use of pigeon. The restaurant continues as both hothouse and experimental workshop rolled into one, often invigorating and still unique. If there is a homogeneous quality to a number of the cold first courses, maybe it is from the overuse of Colonna Extra Virgin Olive oil; my other criticism would be the variability of desserts, but savouries have held their own, day in, day out.' The principal characteristic of cooking here might be robustness, certainly deployment of 'contrasting textures and flavours that are strong or fairly strong' yet have variety and subtlety enough to stimulate, not overpower. A catalogue of success would read long. Here are some dishes that have pleased: two terrines with onion marmalade; tortilla of griddled salmon with spicy Mexican garnishes; steamed turbot, king prawns and scallops with soy sauce (a winner this); many risottos, for instance with cuttlefish and prawns; sweetbreads with spring vegetables; beef stew with Chinese greens (and soy again, 'a wondrous dish'); sticky toffee pudding; tiramisù; and always excellent crème brûlée. Criticisms sometimes mention overfacing quantity, other times techniques that need discretion more than generosity, such as fish in batter – 'a dish for heroes' is a hungry person's description; 'too much' is another's. In so individual a place disasters do occur, exacerbated by the lack of protective flannel in surroundings and service. Give it a try. There are four dozen wines on the ever-changing wine list, even-handed in its geographical preferences. Half a dozen 'specials' ease the choice while prices show sensible and fair range from decent Minervois at £10 to a Chassagne 1988 for a relatively modest £32.

CHEFS: Alastair Little and Juliet Peston PROPRIETORS: Mercedes Andre-Vega, Kirsten Pedersen and Alastair Little OPEN: Mon to Sat, exc Sat L CLOSED: bank hols MEALS: 12.30 to 3, 6 to 11.30 PRICES: £32 (£44), Set L £18 (£27) to £23 (£32) CARDS: Access, Visa SEATS: 38. Private parties: 8 main room, 14 private room. Vegetarian meals. Children's helpings. Wheelchair access (2 steps)

Alba

NEW ENTRY map 11

107 Whitecross Street, EC1Y 8JH — COOKING 2
071-588 1798 — COST £28

Hard by the Barbican, this Georgian terraced house hides within it a fresh-scrubbed bar and dining-room with pink-washed walls, tiled floors, metal seats (that are more comfortable than you may fear), lots of pot-plants and a team of people who gain many friends through being 'friendly, talkative, gesticulative, welcoming and above all full of enthusiasm'. Alba serves Piedmontese food (truffles if you are lucky). It also runs a line of old-hat Italian: veal with marsala, fillet with green peppercorns and so on, which should be ignored in favour of the daily specialities. The team is so enthusiastic that the image of the dish may sometimes excite more than its reality, but good reports have come for the bresaola (not just beef, but also venison and horse); the fresh pasta, especially the *panzerotti alle noci*, twists of pasta filled with ricotta and spinach, in a walnut and cream sauce; fresh grilled red mullet; mussels in white wine; and a thick chocolate cake layered with crème caramel. The cover charge gets you grissini – and ciabatta on good days. There is a service charge too. Old Italy dies hard, and can excite resentment when the enthusiasm is for some reason lacking. Although not in the same league as the lists found at the 'newish' wave of London Italian restaurants, the wines are all Italian, fairly priced and many good names are scattered about. House Italian is £6.90.

CHEF: Armando Liboi PROPRIETOR: Rudi Venerandi OPEN: Mon to Fri MEALS: 12 to 3, 6 to 11 PRICES: £16 (£23). Cover 80p. Service 10%. Card slips closed CARDS: Access, Amex, Visa SEATS: 45. Private parties: 70 main room. Vegetarian meals. Children's helpings. Wheelchair access (1 step). Music

Al Hamra

map 13

31–33 Shepherd Market, W1Y 7RJ — COOKING 2*
071-493 1954 and 6934 — COST £31–£47

Readers approve of the cheerful bustle of this Mayfair restaurant. 'People wandering in and out on the off-chance of a table. The doorman and maître d' embracing acquaintances and regulars, trying to fit everyone in. The staff are very friendly, the place bright and vibrant.' Al Hamra maintains its reputation as one of the best Lebanese eating-places in the capital, largely because of its excellent hot and cold meze. From a long list, readers have highlighted sujuk (spicy Lebanese sausages), foul moulaka (fried broad beans with garlic, coriander and olive oil) and makdous batinjan (baby aubergines stuffed with walnuts and spices). Main courses rely heavily on the chargrill, and there are also daily specials such as bamia (okra with meat and rice) and kibbeh labanieh with shish barak (crushed wheat and minced lamb cooked in yoghurt with little parcels of pasta filled with minced lamb and onion). Boneless marinated chicken grilled on skewers has been recommended. The £2.50 cover charge pays for the olives and a cornucopia of raw vegetables left on the table, but not for the bread. To drink there is Iyran yoghurt, Turkish coffee and mint tea, as well as a minimal wine list. House wine is £11.

CHEF: Hassan Mardani PROPRIETORS: R. Nabulsi and H. Fansa OPEN: all week CLOSED: 25 Dec and 1 Jan MEALS: noon to midnight PRICES: £15 (£31), Set L £21 (£35), Set D £25 (£39). Cover £2.50 CARDS: Access, Amex, Diners, Visa SEATS: 73. 4 tables outside. Private parties: 80 main room. Vegetarian meals. Children's helpings. Wheelchair access. Music

Anna's Place

map 11

90 Mildmay Park, N1 4PR — COOKING 2
071-249 9379 — COST £25

The view out of the shop-front on Mildmay Park is not enlivening; better to press through to the room at the back, or in fine weather the garden, where there is more space. Anna's Place is Swedish and its reasonable prices as well as its consistent welcome make it popular. When Anna herself is there, she may take you dish by dish through the menu, but this routine – so often bruited as the Unique Selling Point – is by no means the point. Some good dishes include the biff Strindberg (a sort of Swedish Stroganoff, the meat tenderised by a marinade, cut by accompanying pickled cucumber), the mild gravlax (better when the mustard sauce is remembered) and sill tallrik (marinated herrings good enough to reconcile one who had been brought up on St John's Wood pickled fish to their finer points). Less good may be the lack of strong flavour in some of the sauces and the heavy puddings, or a rhubarb brûlée that fails to deliver the needed sourness in the fruit to cut the richness. Caraway rolls start the Baltic mood. The nice short wine list has decent makers at fair prices.

CHEFS: Ross Mason and Derek Blanch PROPRIETOR: Anna Hegarty OPEN: Tue to Sat CLOSED: 2 weeks Christmas and Easter MEALS: 12.15 to 2.15, 7.15 to 10.45 PRICES: £15 (£21). Service 10% SEATS: 52. 5 tables outside. Private parties: 12 main room. Vegetarian meals. Children's helpings. Wheelchair access. Music

Arirang NEW ENTRY map 13

31–32 Poland Street, W1V 3DB COOKING 1
071-437 6633 COST £22–£36

The oldest Korean restaurant in London is hidden discreetly behind a dark plate-glass window at the Oxford Street end of Poland Street. The décor is plain and austere, the clientele mainly Korean or Japanese, the latter being fond of this type of cooking; Arirang is also cheaper than most Japanese restaurants in London. Korean cooking is robust peasant stuff, with none of the haute cuisine subtleties that marks the Japanese style. Oil, garlic and chillis are used copiously. The more interesting food tends to be that chosen from the list of specials such as marinated beef or squid in hot-sweet sauce, rather than the bulkier dishes of rice and noodles. A central burner is installed at each table for table-cooked food such as bulgogi or ansim. Both kim-chee (preserved cabbage pickle – 'fiery and good') and kosaree namul (bracken stalks – 'very soft and sweetly flavoured') make authentic starters. A good place to try simple Korean food designed to suit Korean rather than Western taste buds. House French is £6.90.

CHEF: Wan Yong Song PROPRIETOR: Yong Dhuk Bai OPEN: Mon to Sat CLOSED: 25 Dec and 1 Jan MEALS: 12 to 3, 6 to 11 PRICES: £16 (£23), Set L and D £16.50 (£22) to £23.50 (£30). Service 10%. Card slips closed CARDS: Access, Amex, Carte Blanche, Diners, Visa SEATS: 110. Private parties: 60 main room, 40 private room. Vegetarian meals. Children welcome. Wheelchair access. Music. Air-conditioned. Fax: 071-287 4190

L'Arlequin map 10

123 Queenstown Road, SW8 3RH COOKING 4
071-622 0555 COST £26–£61

The Delteils must have taken psychiatric advice when choosing the colour for their pair of dining-rooms on the Queenstown Road. The rooms calm the spirit, promote conversation without excessive conviviality and are cool, comforting vessels for considered hospitality and most sophisticated cooking. The danger is that the kitchen is too sophisticated. It does not fall into the hackneyed trap of over-decoration or overloading the plate with a mish-mash of flavours, but it does appear to draw back from pronounced tastes, even when the menu may imply otherwise. A main dish of loin of rabbit with mustard and cabbage might excite the peasant heart in any breast. In the event, a heaped tablespoon of refined spring cabbage was covered by a fan of thin, tender slices of rabbit – as tame in taste as it must have been in life – and the mustard in a cream sauce was evident only by the grains. The guts had flown. There was sophistication, too, in a 'persillé de homard et ris de veau', the terrine lined with strips of carrot, the whole lubricated by a tomato coulis. If you were to close your eyes, the components would be very difficult to identify. The point of such clever dishes should be comparison and contrast, not bland homogeneity. Much better, more like the Delteil style that we have applauded, were a half-dozen croûtons, each topped by diced tomato and a plump slice of scallop. A green-brown pistou sauce, exactly balanced between under- and over-statement, gave every mouthful life and pleasure. The textures, too, were finely judged. Many reports this year have made similar comments. They must be taken in the context of the price: the experience is pleasurable, but so much money may require a more dynamic emphasis on bursting flavours. Accounts do not raise questions of competence: this is a very even and consistent team, though one reader thought the petits fours akin to his daughter's efforts at kindergarten. Service is impeccable, as are specifics such as the bread rolls, and other generalities not yet mentioned. A book might be written on the intensity of the chocolate orange marquise, or the light hot soufflés or exact crème brûlée. The damage to wallets is minimised by eating the short set-price lunch. This may have the drawback of repetition: 'To find tomato, of which I am not unduly fond, cropping up (unannounced on the menu) as an integral part of the pre-starter, starter and main course was a little unexpected,' wrote a reporter. The spread of the wine list is not good, by either cost or type. Prices are very high and although some consideration is given for those who do not want to pay too much, there is almost nothing in the middle range. Choice of growers and shippers, especially among the low-priced wines, is by no means inspired. House wine may start at about £8.

CHEF: Christian Delteil PROPRIETORS: Mr and Mrs Christian Delteil OPEN: Mon to Fri CLOSED: 1 week winter, 3 weeks Aug MEALS: 12.30 to 2, 7.30 to 10.30 PRICES: £45 (£51), Set L £19.50 (£26). Net prices, card slips closed CARDS: Access, Amex, Diners, Visa SEATS: 45. No children under 5. Jacket and tie. No pipes in dining-room. Wheelchair access (also WC). Music. Air-conditioned. Fax: 071-498 7015

Les Associés NEW ENTRY map 10

172 Park Road, N8 8GY COOKING 2*
081-348 8944 COST £22–£34

One waits, one serves wine, one cooks: these are the three associates, all Frenchmen. They hold court in a former chippie, done out with style, with good pictures, ample room for each table and decent place-settings. Les Associés has been described as a 'superior bistro'. That might be true in France, but here, it is a *very* superior bistro that can provide a terrine of salmon studded with scallop coral; a scallop salad with a 'mound of saladings from *mâche* to strawberries'; fresh asparagus and a sauce mousseline flavoured with orange and ginger; confit of duck with sarladaise potatoes; breast of duck with pears; lamb cutlets with cumin; and tarte Tatin or chocolate marquise. These are all cooked and served with style, the kitchen evidently enjoying working with spices, for instance in monkfish with ginger and orange, as well as in classics such as chartreuse of snails or frogs' legs with garlic and parsley. The effect of the recession on Crouch End means that the partners are contemplating cooking simpler food so as to charge less. There is also talk of Gilles Charvet retreating to Oxfordshire to start a restaurant on his own. Either move may be to the detriment of London. The wine list is French-centred, with the best from the northern Rhône and Mâconnais. Prices are not low, but the house wines are good and cost £9.20.

CHEF: Gilles Charvet PROPRIETORS: Gilles Charvet, Dominique Chéhere and Didier Bertran OPEN: Tue to Sat, exc L Tue and Sat CLOSED: 10 days Christmas, 10 days Easter, Aug MEALS: 12.30 to 2, 7.30 to 10 PRICES: £20 (£28), Set L £13.95 (£22) CARDS: Access, Visa SEATS: 36. Car park. Vegetarian meals. Children's helpings L. Wheelchair access (also WC). Music

▲ *Auberge de Provence, St James's Court Hotel*

map 11

41 Buckingham Gate, SW1E 6AF — COOKING 3
071-821 1899 — COST £29–£73

The awnings over windows, which run the length of the vast Edwardian hotel, announce three restaurants: the Café Méditerranée, Inn of Happiness and Auberge de Provence. On such a grey Westminster street the Mediterranean touch seems wishful thinking, but a consultancy with and staff from L'Oustaù de Baumanière make it more real inside the Auberge, the flagship of the three. Full-fledged silver domery and battalions of waiters accompany high prices, though these are fair at lunchtime. The décor is all provençal: tiles, arches, random stone walls, wrought iron, simple wooden chairs (though, thankfully, thick cushions). The food has overtones of the south, but they are unduly refined by the time they get to the customer and lack the natural exuberance of the sort made famous by Roger Vergé in the '70s, who did manage to distil the sun and the light in a very sophisticated fashion. None the less, the cooking is not incompetent in dishes such as tender ravioli of chicken with minute 'ratatouille' vegetable dice in an accurately reduced chicken stock, or even a combination dish of sole fillets in oversalted saffron sauce and squid in a plain butter sauce with lashings of samphire. Fish may be the best thing to eat here. Puddings have got better. Service is very proper and very French. The wine list is long, but we were sent no copy for study. House wine is £10.50.

CHEF: Oliver Massart PROPRIETORS: TAJ International Hotels OPEN: Mon to Sat, exc Sat L MEALS: 12.30 to 2.30, 7.30 to 11 PRICES: £33 (£49), Set L £21.50 (£29) to £25 (£33), Set D £30 (£39) to £50 (£61) CARDS: Access, Amex, Diners, Visa SEATS: 80. Private parties: 40 main room. Vegetarian meals. Children welcome. Jacket and tie. Music. Air-conditioned. Fax: 071-630 7587 ACCOMMODATION: 390 rooms, all with bath/shower. Rooms for disabled. Lift. B&B £187 to £244. Children welcome. Baby facilities. Afternoon teas. Garden. Sauna. Air-conditioned. TV. Phone. Confirm by 6

Au Bois St Jean

map 11

122 St John's Wood High Street, NW8 7SG — COOKING 1
071-722 0400 — COST £17–£36

You get two floors of food here: the ground offering a bistro-style menu, the basement remaining a restaurant with live piano in the evening. The repertoire shows continuity with previous years: no complaints at duck in apricot and almond sauce, or wild duck with prunes and honey, lamb with shallots and chives, or veal with spinach and garlic. It is a sound neighbourhood place, and the staff are well-trained. People grouch at the supplements to an apparently fixed-price menu and the extra service charge making the apparent bargain more mainstream in cost, especially as the service charge is not mentioned on the bill itself even if it is on the menu. Desserts like strawberry tart or tarte Tatin end the meal. The unexciting wine list is wholly French and reliable. House wine is £7.45.

CHEF: Jean Claude Broussely PROPRIETORS: Bestmill Ltd OPEN: all week MEALS: 12 to 2.30, 6 to 11.30 PRICES: £16 (£25), Set L £9.95 (£17) to £12.95 (£20), Set D £17.75 (£26) to £21.75 (£30). Service 12.5%. Card slips closed CARDS: Access, Amex, Visa SEATS: 75. Private parties: 50 main room, 25 private room. Vegetarian meals. Children's helpings. Smart dress preferred. Music. Fax: 071-586 0410

Au Jardin des Gourmets 🍾

map 14

5 Greek Street, W1V 5LA
071-437 1816

COOKING 2
COST £23–£44

The Jardin celebrates its sixtieth birthday in 1991 and keeps an old-fashioned dark green and mirrored look, yet it has moved with the times sufficiently to offer one half of the restaurant as no-smoking. The satisfaction reported last year for Nicolas Picolet's modern French cooking has been qualified by the general feeling that the set-price menus at lunch and dinner offer fair value but occasional mistakes make the *carte* look pricey. Overcooked sweetbreads, undercooked vegetables and lacklustre flavours have been reported. Yet the menu, offering a much shorter choice of dishes like a vegetable terrine with lemon vinaigrette, fricassee of chicken with mushrooms, tomatoes and raspberry vinegar, or matelote of eel, may be satisfactory, especially in price (until drinks, wines and stiff service charge are added in). The welcome is often warm, perhaps warmer for old faithfuls, and delay only creeps in at the busiest of sessions. The wine list does make the visit worth it, though the man who was served the *wrong* half at £28 reasonably felt hard done by. Normally wine service is punctilious. The reports indicate how tight management, which is sometimes lacking here, is essential to the consistent success of a busy West End restaurant. Wines are a delight – clearly set out and a richly catholic selection. There is generous provision of half-bottles and fine clarets and burgundies, many with good age, are nicely balanced by many excellent but more modest wines. Pricing, particularly for W1, is fair throughout. House wine is £7.25. CELLARMAN'S CHOICE: Montagny premier cru 1989, Roy, £17.50; Gigondas, Grapillon d'Or 1986, £14.75.

CHEF: Nicolas Picolet PROPRIETORS: Au Jardin des Gourmets Ltd OPEN: Mon to Sat, exc Sat L MEALS: 12.30 to 2.30, 6.15 to 11.15 (11.30 Sat) PRICES: £25 (£37), Set L £14.50 (£23) to £17.50 (£26), Set D £16.95 (£25). Service 15%. Card slips closed CARDS: Access, Amex, Diners, Visa SEATS: 150. Private parties: 12, 14, 18 and 50 private rooms. Vegetarian meals. Children's helpings. No-smoking area. Wheelchair access. Music. Air-conditioned. Fax: 071-437 0043

🍾 *denotes an outstanding wine cellar;* 🍷 *denotes a good wine list, worth travelling for.*

Au Provençal

NEW ENTRY map 10

293–295 Railton Road, SE24 0JR — COOKING 1
071-274 9163 — COST £16–£38

This predominantly red, slightly dowdy, informal restaurant has Piaf-style music, or midweek live jazz-piano. It offers good value for some fair cooking in a place generally bereft of such things. Three set-price menus are on offer, and mixing and matching is possible. Though the relentless Frenchness is belied by such things as Rissoles Lucy, or 'puff pastry envelopes filled with Roquefort cheese and coriander, deep-fried and served with gooseberry relish', the cooking has delivered happy moments with a gâteau of chicken livers, a rough langoustine soup, sautéed chicken with couscous, fillet steak wrapped in bacon and topped with a kidney, or a 'cassoulet' of beans, lamb and small sausages. Some cooking is rough and ready, but the success rate is substantial – as are portions. Desserts have not had the same praise. A short French wine list has enough cheapies to go with the food and adequate house wines at £7.95. Au Provençal might do better to develop the vins de pays rather than négociants' bottles or very expensive burgundies.

CHEFS: Alan Gaunt and Colin Oxley PROPRIETORS: Alan and Debi Gaunt, Joanne and Colin Oxley OPEN: all week D, and Sun L MEALS: 12.30 to 5, 7 to 10.30 PRICES: Set Sun L £10.95 (£16), Set D £13.95 (£20) to £23.95 (£32). Card slips closed CARDS: Access, Visa SEATS: 54. Private parties: 36 main room. Vegetarian meals. Children's helpings. No-smoking area. Wheelchair access. Music

Bahn Thai

map 14

21A Frith Street, W1V 5TS — COOKING 2
071-437 8504 — COST £31

'The original home of true Thai food in London,' says a note on the menu, and Philip Harris' Soho restaurant generally proves its worth. Individual dishes are now marked on the menu with symbols indicating salads, vegetarian food and degrees of chilli heat. As ever, the repertoire is wide-ranging and challenging, with many specialities found nowhere else in Britain. Familiar items tend to draw most recommendations: starters such as spring rolls, fishcakes and butterfly king prawns with separate dipping sauces; curries including roast duck and chicken with coconut milk; and ground beef with chillies. But the kitchen also moves into the realms of marinated 'sashimi' prawns, spicy catfish salad with shredded green mango, scallops in light curry mousse, Thai-style dry-salt beef, and green papaya salad with sun-cured shrimps or salted baby crabs. Khai palo is stewed hard-boiled egg with pig's knuckle and trotters served with hot chilli and lemon sauce. There have been some indifferent reports concerning size of portions and quality of service, but a face-lift is promised and problems are said to be in the process of being sorted out. The wine list is intelligent and fairly priced; otherwise there are Thai beers and chrysanthemum tea. House French is £7.45.

See the back of the Guide *for an index of restaurants listed.*

CHEF: Penn Squires PROPRIETORS: Bahn Thai plc OPEN: all week CLOSED: some bank hols, some days Christmas and Easter MEALS: 12 to 2.45 (2.30 Sun), 6 to 11.15 (6.30 to 10.30 Sun) PRICES: £15 (£26). Cover 75p. Service 12.5%. Card slips closed CARDS: Access, Amex, Visa SEATS: 100. Private parties: 25 main room, 12, 35 and 50 private rooms. Vegetarian meals. Children welcome. No cigars/pipes in dining-room. Wheelchair access (also WC). Music. Air-conditioned. Fax: 071-439 0340

Bambaya

map 10

1 Park Road, N8 8TE
081-348 5609

COOKING 1
COST £24

'Relaxing' is how one happy customer put it when recommending Rosamund Grant's and Jenny Agada's cooking of Caribbean, African and black American food – with a bit of Asia thrown in for good measure. Fish or vegetarian dishes are the order of the day, whether Louisiana swordfish with mango sauce, creole king prawns with ginger and garlic or the ever-popular 'Stamp and Go' fishcakes of saltfish, with a warm chutney. The vegetarian dishes such as West African ochroe and vegetable stew or roti filled with spiced lentils are enjoyed too. Alcohol may be had, but mango juice or non-alcoholic cocktails such as Bambaya Surprise make a change.

CHEFS: Rosamund Grant and Jenny Agada PROPRIETORS: Bambaya Restaurant Ltd OPEN: all week, D only CLOSED: bank hols MEALS: 6.30 to 11 (10.30 Sun) PRICES: £12 (£20). Cover 50p. Service 10% for parties of 6 or more CARDS: Access, Amex, Visa SEATS: 45. Private parties: 45 main room. Vegetarian meals. Children's helpings. Wheelchair access. Music

Bayleaf Tandoori

NEW ENTRY map 10

2 North Hill, N6 4PU
081-340 1719 and 0245

COOKING 2
COST £14–£24

Readers have bemoaned the absence of this restaurant from recent editions of the *Guide*, insisting that it is well above the London average. The building once housed an Italian restaurant, and there are echoes of the past in the pale glass lamps and tiled floor of the comfortable, spacious dining-room. Indian paintings and music are tokens of its present incarnation. The menu is virtually a carbon-copy of Lal Qila (see entry), although prices are lower and there is more emphasis on fish dishes. Otherwise its menu is a classic new-wave selection of tandooris and curries. Aloo chat and murg chat are well-balanced ('mellow and zingy at the same time'), tandoori trout works well and chicken jalfrezi is spiked with plenty of fresh green chillies. Details such as sauces with onion bhajias, fresh and puffy nan bread and fried basmati rice are impressive, although some vegetable dishes can be rather dull. Flavours are both forthright and subtle, spicing is well judged, and the kitchen maintains its standards. A buffet lunch is offered on Sunday. To drink there are cocktails, Kingfisher beer, and a minimal list of 'curry house' wines. House French is £6.95.

CHEF: Hamid Ali PROPRIETORS: A.A. Khan, M.I. Chowdhury and Mrs N. Chowdhury OPEN: all week MEALS: 12 to 2.45, 6 to 11.15 PRICES: £11 (£20), Set L £8.95 (£14) CARDS: Access, Amex, Diners, Visa SEATS: 90. Private parties: 100 main room. Vegetarian meals. Children's helpings (Sun L only). Wheelchair access (also WC). Music

Bedlington Café

map 10

24 Fauconberg Road, W4 3JY
081-994 1965

COOKING 1*
COST £12–£20

'Tatty for a café, very tatty for a restaurant,' according to one reporter, this is a jewel, albeit rough-set. By day a café pure and simple, at night it draws in crowds for home-cooked Thai food. Bold, fresh and aromatic, the dishes make up a small menu, served in a small room for a small cost. Tables are crammed together, and lots of people want a seat. If you like chilli, then you will like the Bedlington. The off-licence for your own wine or beer is on the corner.

CHEF: Mrs P. Priyanu PROPRIETORS: Mr and Mrs Priyanu OPEN: all week, exc Sun L MEALS: 12 to 2, 6.30 to 9.30 PRICES: £9 (£13), Set L £10 (£12) to £12.50 (£14), Set D £12.50 (£14) to £15 (£17). Unlicensed, but bring your own: corkage 50p SEATS: 30. Private parties: 30 main room. Vegetarian meals. Children's helpings. No-smoking area. Wheelchair access (1 step). No music

Bibendum

map 12

Michelin House,
81 Fulham Road, SW3 6RD
071-581 5817

COOKING 4*
COST £36–£58

'Everyone should go here to have a look – and a meal. I saved for months to go myself. I have heard so many negative aspects – none of which could I find.' There's a testimonial, seconded by a report from elsewhere: 'One of the most welcoming restaurants I have had the pleasure of entering. The dining-room sparkled.' This is on the lofty first floor of the original Michelin building. It catches the light as excitingly as any Perpendicular clerestoried church. Tables are spaced to give privacy in the midst of life, save for the row of hugger-mugger twos that can give rise to speculation about rents per square inch. Simon Hopkinson's style of cooking, as developed here over three years, has deepened and become still more confident. Of course mistakes occur; and set against largely inelaborate settings and firmly expressive dishes, error becomes the more apparent. Joined to the end-cost of a meal, it will be resented. But which London kitchen lists 'lambs' balls' on a luncheon menu and then cooks them far better than any Middle Eastern chef in the capital? The rapidly evolving *carte* is substituted at lunchtime by a shorter fixed-price menu. Each gives ample choice from a repertoire that goes from fish and chips or plain asparagus with Parmesan, oil and lemon to confit of tuna with herbs, shallots and a bean salad or scallops with balsamic vinegar, meat juices and 'olive oil mash'. This is most emphatically not a mousse cuisine, nor one of stuffings, layerings, feuilletés or other culinary fandangos. Except for some of the strong flavours – chilli is not often given an outing, however – it is a wine merchant's dream; most of the dishes are simple perfection with fine wine.

Recommendations abound, and it is a measure of the variations in taste, and sometimes in the kitchen, that many outright approvals may be balanced by others' qualification. A list might include risotto primavera (or any risotto for that matter), spiced sausages and lentils with mustard fruits, clear fish soup, brains with black butter, salmon hollandaise, spiced and marinated beef with an oriental salad, sole with truffle sauce, lampreys à la bordelaise, and puddings like St Emilion au chocolat, chocolate soufflé, lemon tart ('not as tangy as the Roux'), and even vanilla ice-cream 'just like mother's'. Vegetables, for which you pay extra, are simple (good chips). Grouches that surface most often are about the service – sometimes lapsing under pressure – and the bill. Mistakes are more frequent than they need be, and not always corrected with style. Readers will learn with delight that the cover charge is no longer levied, but groan inwardly at the charge made for the second cup of espresso and the hefty 15 per cent service charge. It all adds to the cost, which the revised wine list goes further to moderate (sighs of relief) than it did last year. The declared change of heart on the wine buying, with greater emphasis on more moderately priced wine and a drift away from the French classics, is hard to detect; the list is still very expensive, although most reports enthuse about the quality of the wines. It is undoubtedly as fine a list of names as could be found anywhere: a page of Montrachets, eleven vintages of d'Yquem, seven of Latour – the youngest 1970 – and collections from Italy, Spain and the New World that would be the envy of many. But there is still virtually nothing below £15; thereafter, mark-ups discourage adventure, which is a pity. House wine is £8.50. CELLARMAN'S CHOICE: I Sistri, Chardonnay 1989, Barardenga, £31.50; Coudoulet de Beaucastel 1988, Perrin, £19.50. The Oyster Bar on the ground floor of the building, often very full indeed, is proposed by some as an entry in the *Guide* in its own right. The menu here has lengthened and improved. It affords very good, very expensive café eating, with style and panache though not exactly comfort.

CHEFS: Simon Hopkinson and Henry Harris PROPRIETORS: Paul Hamlyn, Sir Terence Conran and Simon Hopkinson OPEN: all week CLOSED: 26 Dec MEALS: 12.30 to 2.30 (3 Sat and Sun), 7 to 11.30 (10.30 Sun) PRICES: £32 (£48), Set L £24 (£36). Service 15%. Card slips closed CARDS: Access, Visa SEATS: 74. Children welcome. Children's helpings. No pipes in dining-room. Wheelchair access. Air-conditioned. No music. Fax: 071-823 7925

Billboard Café **NEW ENTRY** map 11

222 Kilburn High Road, NW6 4JP — COOKING 1*
071-328 1374 — COST £31

This warehouse with ventilation ducts and pop art posters as decoration is a small restaurant with a big atmosphere, perhaps from a sense of relief that Kilburn can deliver as much fun and food as Notting Hill. There is a happy mixture of drinkers and eaters enlivened, for once, by music (including live jazz a couple of times a week) and kept going by the tolerant yet effective ministrations of the staff. Although the chef is Greek, with Californian experience, it is Italy that provides the main inspiration for a menu with good fresh pasta, spicy sausages with spinach and mustards, a daily dish such as baby lamb chops with pesto, or breast of chicken with ricotta, basil and oregano stuffing and a topping of peppers. Late opening serves to emphasise its local identity. Some readers have considered the food misses its taste targets, given especially that the ingredients should result in high flavour, but they are in the minority. The wine list is very short, Italian, and enjoyed.

CHEF: Nasser Nateghi PROPRIETOR: Stelios B. Lambis OPEN: Mon to Sat, D only, and Sat and Sun L CLOSED: 25 and 26 Dec MEALS: 12 to 2.45, 6.30 to 12.45am PRICES: £16 (£26). Service 10%. Card slips closed CARDS: Access, Visa SEATS: 65. Private parties: 65 main room. Vegetarian meals. Children's helpings. No cigars/pipes in dining-room. Wheelchair access. Music. Air-conditioned

Bistrot 190

NEW ENTRY map 12

189 Queen's Gate, SW7 5EU COOKING 2*
071-581 5666 COST £29

189–190 Queen's Gate houses several activities, the most recent of which is this bistro, on the ground floor – right of the main hotel entrance – where Antony Worrall-Thompson shows he is not just a fancy chef but able to mix it with low-price, low-profit yet imaginative food: peasant cooking with a collar and tie. The room is handsome: plaster ceiling, lots of old pictures, dried flowers as a frieze, bare boards, fairly crowded with tables. There is no booking (unless you are a member of the 190 Club) and the hours are wonderfully long, from breakfast until late dinner, seven days a week. Understandably, it gets busy. The food is often good, the service is cheerful, and the prices are consumer-friendly. Echiré butter in baskets, good peasanty bread, and olives and radishes to nibble are included in the cover charge. The menu majors on dishes that are almost trite in the context of new-wave bistro/brasserie activities: bruschetta, wild mushroom ravioli, chargrilled vegetables with a mozzarella pizza, confit of duck, calf's liver, Toulouse sausages, lemon tart, chocolate cake and chocolate bread-and-butter pudding. Lamb shank with polenta and haricot beans, an extremely copious stew, is a signature dish. Cooking is cheerful, usually generous, and sometimes approximate. A place of such high turnover must expect misses as well as hits. This does not detract from its considerable popularity and success, though the robustness of seasoning, some say slap-happy, and artful casualness of delivery is too arch for some – as if they are playing at the bistro game. The wine list is short and 'merchant-sponsored' – they are certainly canny at 190; expect fair prices and interesting choices, depending on which merchant is doing the list in any one month.

CHEFS: Antony Worrall-Thompson and Clive O'Connor PROPRIETORS: 190 Queensgate plc OPEN: all week CLOSED: 25 and 26 Dec MEALS: 7am to 12.30am (11.30pm Sun) PRICES: £16 (£24). Service 12% CARDS: Access, Amex, Diners, Visa SEATS: 45. Private parties: 45 main room, 25 private room. Vegetarian meals. Children welcome. Music. Fax: 071-581 8172

Healthy eating options *in the details at the end of an entry signifies that a restaurant marks on its menu, in words and/or using symbols, low-fat dishes or other healthy eating choices.*

Blue Elephant

map 10

4–6 Fulham Broadway, SW6 1AA — COOKING 2
071-385 6595 — COST £34–£46

This is the most opulent of London's Thai restaurants. The impression created by bridges, ponds, fountains, much rushing water and vast quantities of plants is that of eating in a jungle: 'You can in some cases sit at a table and have to sweep the ferns from off your brow before speaking.' The menu takes its cue from the setting in its grandiloquence: 'The green sauce fiery as a volcano; the brown sauce sweet as a first kiss.' The food is generally liked, despite high prices – good fish in a spicy sauce, 'delicious' menam chicken soup, even praise for simple desserts such as fresh fruit and ice-cream. One reader, while satisfied with her meal, found the atmosphere 'smoky'. Another was disappointed to find the total on his credit card slip left open, on top of the 15 per cent service charge. House wine is £8.95.

CHEFS: Thaviseuth Pouthavong and Rungsan Mulijan PROPRIETORS: Blue Elephant Ltd OPEN: all week, exc Sat L CLOSED: 25 and 26 Dec MEALS: 12 to 2.30, 7 to 11.30 (10.30 Sun) PRICES: £26 (£38), Set L and D £25 (£34) to £28 (£37). Cover £1.50 (alc only). Service 15% CARDS: Access, Amex, Diners, Visa SEATS: 250. Private parties: 200 main room. Vegetarian meals. Children welcome. Smart dress preferred. Wheelchair access (2 steps; also WC). Music. Air-conditioned. Fax: 071-386 7665

Blueprint Café

NEW ENTRY map 11

Design Museum, Butlers Wharf, SE1 2YD — COOKING 2
071-378 7031 — COST £31

'I recommend the Café (which is a restaurant) strongly,' writes someone who has experienced the view from the terrace above the Design Museum. The Tower, Tower Bridge and river are majestic at any time, though the wind-whipped walks are more puritan than pleasant; go on a nice day. Given the Café's location and ownership, it is inevitable that people mention aspects of the design: the porthole into the kitchen, rubber table-mats, David Mellor cutlery and so on. In fact this is not intrusive – what Conran design is? – except that the chairs are not very comfortable. The cool of the place is matched by that of the staff, who are invariably pleasant. The repertoire here is predictably Italo-provençal-Californian: sun-dried tomatoes, plum tomatoes, thyme, basil, capers, olive oil, olives and rocket crop up through the menu; no criticism, this, just a guide to antecedents. The dishes themselves are not too unexpected either. Many are simple – a salad of beans, tomato and mustard dressing, say – but when execution is accurate, they give pleasure. Similarly, a main dish of chargrilled lemon sole with capers and sun-dried tomatoes managed to let through the flavour of the grill, not overcook the fish, nor overpower it with seasonings. Pastas are fresh. Not all the cooking has been of a standard: there are times when the pasta dishes have had little zip or life to them, and a busy lunch may bring many misfires. It is, however, an enjoyable excuse for crossing the river (you can boat it from the Tower Wharf) and must bring solace to those already living there. With the Museum, a Mellor shop and a Conran one too, Butlers Wharf will be paradise for one sort of modern man. A short, wide-ranging, modern wine list complements the food.

CHEFS: Rod Eccleston and Lucy Crab PROPRIETOR: Sir Terence Conran OPEN: all week, exc Sun D MEALS: 12 to 3 (3.30 Sun), 7 to 10.30 PRICES: £18 (£26). Service 12.5%. Card slips closed CARDS: Access, Visa SEATS: 120. 8 tables outside. Private parties: 100 main room. Vegetarian meals. Children's helpings. No pipes in dining-room. Wheelchair access (also WC). Music

Bombay Brasserie

map 12

140 Gloucester Road, SW7 4QH
071-370 4040

COOKING 1
COST £20–£42

Opinion remains divided about the merits of this fashionable and, some would say, opulent Indian restaurant. In the early days it drew much praise because the sheer quality of the food was beyond most people's 'curry house' expectations. Currently, however, there are complaints about basic inconsistencies and there is a feeling that the kitchen is resting on its laurels, which especially grates given the high prices. 'For many years this has been my favourite Indian restaurant,' writes a regular reporter. 'Standards have slipped, but it is still capable of producing very good food provided you order carefully.' The menu centres on the region around Bombay and the Punjab, with a few specialities from other parts of the subcontinent. A few of the more interesting items, such as Goan fish curry, have disappeared, making the choice less appealing. Murg makhani and rogan josh are still good; thalis are well-reported and rice is as up to the mark as it has always been. The main problem appears to be seafood: prawn curries have been 'worryingly inconsistent' and crab malabar has disappointed, although pomfret steamed in a banana leaf with mint chutney and fish tikka have been recommended. Service raises doubts: 'attentive and of a high standard,' say some; 'appalling,' comment others. Cocktails and Indian beers supplement a short, highly priced wine list. House French is £9.50.

CHEF: Udit Sarkhel PROPRIETORS: TAJ International Hotels OPEN: all week MEALS: 12.30 to 3, 7.30 to 12 PRICES: £22 (£35), Set L £13.50 (£20). Minimum £20 D CARDS: Access, Visa SEATS: 175. 25 tables outside. Vegetarian meals. Children's helpings. Music. Fax: 071-835 1669

Boucha's

NEW ENTRY map 11

3 North End Parade,
North End Road, W14 0SJ
071-603 0613

COOKING 2*
COST £30

The simplicity of the menu language – no messing with franglais here – and the anti-fuss approach belie the skill of the cooking. Ben Summerskill's tiny mirrored, pleated and ruched restaurant prides itself on Englishness and being a neighbourhood eating-place (with neighbourly prices). One reader enjoyed the single waiter's ability to serve yet 'maintain his charming manners and body movements'. A short *carte* shows the British is modern rather than bulldog traditional. So, 'fresh pasta pillow with a lentil and cumin filling on a coriander sauce' sits alongside rabbit casserole with raisins and herb dumplings. Reports speak of strong flavours that remain distinct while yet combining well: bubble and squeak with an apple and onion chutney; pork with red cabbage and cucumber in a honey and almond sauce ('though the cucumber did not add much'); duck with raspberry where the fruit 'was not decoration added at the last moment but part of the dish'. Puddings get more votes: a 'sensationally good' date and sponge pudding, called 'blind date', banana and prune ice-cream, and bread-and-butter spiked with ginger among others. Service is sensible and witty. The wine list is short and pitched low, with as much from beyond as within France. Halves are necessarily sparse. House wine is £7.50.

CHEF: Shane Gower PROPRIETOR: Ben Summerskill OPEN: Mon to Sat D CLOSED: 1 week Christmas MEALS: 7 to 10.30 PRICES: £16 (£25) CARDS: Access, Visa SEATS: 24. Private parties: 28 main room. Vegetarian meals. Children welcome. Smart dress preferred. No pipes in dining-room. Wheelchair access. Music

Boyd's 🍾

map 11

135 Kensington Church Street, W8 7LP
071-727 5452

COOKING 3
COST £22–£41

Competition is fierce around Kensington Church Street, but Boyd Gilmour is in confident mood. He now opens all week and has dispensed with some incidental costs and says that 'this saving has been passed back to the customer'. Most reporters agree that the restaurant still offers good value, given the area, and they have approved the simple green tables (without cloths at lunchtime) and the good, plain glasses and crockery. Lunch is a short, fixed-price menu; dinner is a *carte* with seven or eight choices at each stage. The style remains fashionable, modern, 1990s London – dictated by chargrilling, marinating, exotic vinaigrettes, trendy pulses and ravioli. This year's crop of enthusiastically reported dishes has included hot salmon mousse in filo pastry with finely chopped red and yellow peppers and tarragon; red onion tart with sour cream and pickled chilli dressing; cubes of chargrilled lamb on a bed of onion marmalade; and salmon poached in dill stock and dill butter. Vegetables are al dente, but 'meagre' and rather outmoded nouvelle miniatures. Some have felt that flavours are disappointing and that salads are 'no more than can be bought in a plastic bag from a supermarket'. But there is no disputing the brilliance of the sweets: 'sensational' hot pear and almond tart; 'delectable' three-tiered chocolate cake with raspberry coulis. A team of young, attentive staff delivers the goods. Even when Boyd Gilmour was out of action with a broken shoulder, there were no signs of faltering in the kitchen or out front. Within the succinct 100-odd-bottle wine list is a range as impressive in its geographical sweep as it is in its eye for quality. Prices are fair with sensible mark-ups at the higher reaches. Boyd's is upgraded to a bottle award for intelligence, generosity and brevity. House wines are from £8.85. CELLARMAN'S CHOICE: Vernaccia di San Gimignano, 'Terre di Tuffo' 1989, £22.50; Corbières, Dom. de la Fontsainte 1985, £10.25.

CHEF/PROPRIETOR: Boyd Gilmour OPEN: all week CLOSED: 2 weeks Christmas MEALS: 12.30 to 2.30, 7 to 11 PRICES: £25 (£34), Set L £14.50 (£22) CARDS: Access, Amex, Visa SEATS: 40. Private parties: 40 main room. Vegetarian meals. Children welcome. No music. Fax: 071-221 0615

Brady's

NEW ENTRY map 10

513 Old York Road, SW18 1TF — COOKING 1*
081-877 9599 — COST £20

Luke and Amelia Brady used to run the Old Black Lion in Long Melford, Suffolk. Brady's could not be more different, but aims even so at good value, good cooking and fresh ingredients. The setting is ready-distressed, but in the midst of an area of potential gentrification (wait now until the next boom). Prices are as recession-proof as they can be and the fish – cod, plaice or haddock in batter, and perhaps tuna, swordfish, salmon or sardines from the grill – is fresh. Batter is light and chips are 'crisp, slightly chunky and real'. Mushy peas put in an appearance for their fans. Traditional puddings include a nicely lemony treacle tart, even if with heavy pastry. Cream or custard is extra. Good coffee. The short wine card is really well chosen and cheap: Natter's Sancerre, Umani Ronchi's Verdicchio and so on. House white is £6.40.

CHEFS/PROPRIETORS: Luke and Amelia Brady OPEN: Tue to Sat CLOSED: Christmas to New Year MEALS: 12.15 to 2.30 (3 Sat), 7.15 to 11.30 (11 Tue) PRICES: £10 (£17). Service 10% SEATS: 45. Private parties: 25 main room. Children's helpings. Wheelchair access (1 step; also WC). Music

Bu San

map 11

43 Holloway Road, N7 8JP — COOKING 1*
071-607 8264 — COST £10–£29

'I put myself in the hands of the waiting staff, who seemed thrilled at the prospect,' writes one reader on trying Korean food for the first time. His party was not disappointed. Chef and proprietor Young Hyung Lee cooks a menu dominated by specialities from his homeland, plus a few idiosyncratic versions of Japanese classics such as sashimi, sunomono and sukiyaki. Dishes are adorned with astonishing arrangements of sculpted vegetables and fruit. Most dramatic of all is he mul chap tang bok um, a selection of fried seafood in a spicy hot sauce ('a baroque invention of dazzling scale, filling a quarter of the table'). Other praiseworthy items have included bulgogi cooked on a special gas burner, sizzling fried pork with chilli sauce, deep-fried chicken drumsticks in hot garlic sauce, and chunks of bean curd with vegetables in soy sauce. Kimchee, and fried beansprouts with sesame oil, spring onion and garlic are fine accompaniments. There are good-value set lunches. Drink tea, saké or ginseng brandy. House wine is £5.50. Plans are afoot to extend the tiny six-table dining-room.

CHEF: Young Hyung Lee PROPRIETORS: Young Hyung Lee and Tea Sun Lee OPEN: all week, exc L Sat and Sun CLOSED: 2 days Christmas, 1 Jan MEALS: 12 to 2.30, 6 to 11 PRICES: £15 (£24), Set L from £5.50 (£10) to £5.90 (£10), Set D £14.75 (£20) to £16.25 (£22). Service 10% SEATS: 26. Private parties: 31 main room. Vegetarian meals. Children's helpings. Music

See the back of the Guide *for an index of restaurants listed.*

Buzkash

NEW ENTRY map 10

4 Chelverton Road, SW15 1RH COOKING 1*
081-788 0599 COST £17–£30

Go through the door and Putney is replaced by Afghani carpets, cutlasses, ornaments and 'instruments of tyranny' according to one reader. The restaurant, like its sister Caravan Serai in Paddington Street W1 (see entry), seems run by an extended family of several generations and serves Afghan food of some quality in relaxed and hospitable surroundings. The informative menu appears never to change. Aficionados recommend the baking and the rice cookery (narengh chalaw has orange peel and almonds); ashak, a ravioli filled with leek with a lentil, lamb and yoghurt sauce; bonjon, a small stew of aubergines, green peppers and onions with yoghurt; and gosala gak, a kebab of moist marinated veal served with a dipping sauce of cherries, olive oil and pine kernels. Spicing is more delicate than in many Indian restaurants although there are obvious connections. The interest of Afghan cooking is how it takes from India on the one hand and from the ancient and refined Persian tradition on the other, in dishes such as poorshuda – poussin stuffed with rice and orange. Best to drink beer.

CHEF: Mr Padsha PROPRIETOR: Mr Natebkhail OPEN: all week, exc Sun L CLOSED: 25 and 26 Dec MEALS: 12 to 3, 6 to 11 (11.30 Fri and Sat) PRICES: £14 (£25), Set L £9.95 (£17). Cover 75p. Service 12.5%. Card slips closed CARDS: Access, Amex, Diners, Visa SEATS: 56. 9 tables outside. Private parties: 50 main room, 30 private room. Car park, 3 places. Vegetarian meals. Children welcome. No-smoking area. Music

Café du Marché

map 11

22 Charterhouse Square, EC1M 6AH COOKING 1
071-608 1609 COST £35

The imposing Smithfield Market built by Sir Horace Jones in 1866 stands on the site of a traditional meat market dating back much further, to the 1200s. Before sunrise it is vibrant, by day an empty hangar. For liveliness look instead to the Café du Marché, tucked down a nearby passageway, offering some people's idea of a little piece of France. It is possible to imagine that every neighbourhood in Paris has a bustling, informal and cheerful bistro like this. There is a set-price menu of bistro classics: soupe de poissons, brandade de morue, la petite marmite, rumpsteak de boeuf dijonnaise, and andouillette grillée à la mode. The menu upstairs in Le Grenier du Café is the same price, but with greater emphasis on grills. Some of the food can be predictable and handled unimaginatively, but overall the result is an assembly of unpretentious, straightforward cooking. Good reports of navarin of lamb, hake in chervil sauce and well-dressed, crisp salads contrast with others of poor fish soup and cloying, over-sweet desserts. The short, well-chosen wine list goes further afield than would the Paris equivalent. House wine is £11.

CHEF: Simon Cottard PROPRIETOR: C.K. Graham-Wood OPEN: Mon to Sat, exc Sat L MEALS: 12 to 2.30, 6 to 10 PRICES: Set L and D £18.50 (£29). Service 15%. Card slips closed CARDS: Access, Visa SEATS: 50. Private parties: 50 main room. Vegetarian meals. Children's helpings. No children under 2. No pipes in dining-room. Music

▲ *Capital Hotel* 🍷 map 12

Basil Street, SW3 1AT — COOKING 4
071-589 5171 — COST £25–£61

People have remarked on the solicitude of all the staff at this small luxurious hotel. 'They care,' they say – after we had mentioned hauteur in the last edition. There is no disagreement on the elegant calm of the dining-room, even if the window on the kitchen is thought as unlikely in this context as 'a perspex bonnet on a Bentley'. Nor is there much contest about Philip Britten's cooking, except that too many people's food seems to have arrived lukewarm at table. In style, it is calm British classicism, quite up to the fashionable mark, but not indulging in whimsy or wild modishness. The repertoire mobilised for the cheaper lunch menus, invariably thought a good deal, is in fact more fashionable, exploring braises and slow cookery – for instance cassoulet of duck with haricot beans – or Anglo-Italian crossover dishes such as sole, mussels and tomato bolognese, or a 'lasagne' of cod and leeks. Apart from these menus – two are offered each day – there is a seasonal *carte* of maybe eight choices at each course and a pair of five-course (plus coffee) set meals, one fish and one meat. Recommendations of dishes are legion, though outweighed perhaps by the popularity of lunch. They include lasagne of asparagus and smoked salmon; beignets of foie gras with an apple 'rissole' to cut the richness; broccoli timbale with julienne of salmon; ballotine of duck filled with foie gras and duck meat, with a ceps sauce; pot-roasted chicken with girolles; excellent French cheeses; and wonderful desserts. Most people go for the hot soufflés or the tarts; tarte Tatin is exemplary; raspberry, caramel or strawberry soufflés are first-rate. There is an aptness to the cooking here that people find reassuring; rare are the accusations of faulty techniques or lack of taste. The wine list suffered a hiccup at the beginning of the year when too many bottles were out of stock, but the cellar is a good one. Many stay with the 'Capital selection' on the first page, but further exploration will yield dividends among mature clarets and burgundies (clarets especially). Other regions and countries are summarily dealt with, but here and there there are spots of good value for the capital city, for instance the Loire. David Levin now has his own vineyards in the Loire which will be producing a Blanc de Blanc in 1991 and a Gamay in 1992 for house wines. The Blanc de Blanc is priced at £9.50. Value indeed.

CHEF: Philip Britten PROPRIETOR: David Levin OPEN: all week MEALS: 12.30 to 2.30, 7 to 11 PRICES: £41 (£48), Set L £20 (£25), Set D £46 (£51). Minimum £30. Net prices, card slips closed CARDS: Access, Amex, Carte Blanche, Diners, Visa SEATS: 35. Private parties: 6 main room, 4 and 24 private rooms. Car park, 12 places. Vegetarian meals. Children's helpings. No children under 4. Smart dress preferred. No pipes in dining-room. Wheelchair access (3 steps; also WC). Air-conditioned. Fax: 071-225 0011
ACCOMMODATION: 48 rooms, all with bath/shower. Rooms for disabled. Lift. B&B £157.50 to £190. Deposit: £175. Children welcome. Baby facilities. Pets welcome. Afternoon teas. Air-conditioned. TV. Phone

Restaurateurs justifiably resent no-shows. If you quote a credit card number when booking, you may be liable for the restaurant's lost profit margin if you don't turn up. Always phone to cancel.

Le Caprice

map 13

Arlington House,
Arlington Street, SW1A 1RT
071-629 2239

COOKING 3
COST £40

The equation of famous names and a full restaurant balanced with good food is not a common one, but at Le Caprice it works. The cooking is an urbane mix of internationally inspired dishes, with Italy heading the list. Thus grilled lamb cutlets with salsa verde come garnished with polenta, or perhaps there will be antipasti of baked vegetables, or grilled monkfish with caponata, or black risotto. Standards such as salmon fishcakes, smoked salmon with scrambled eggs, Caesar salad and grilled calf's liver are pitched exactly to the needs of a city-cool and figure-conscious clientele: comforting food in manageable proportions with no obligation to order a three-course meal. Above all, the cooking is good. Grilled rabbit with rosemary on a bed of finely chopped shallots, and roast breast of guinea-fowl on savoy cabbage with calvados jus followed up by drop scones with blueberries and cream and fresh raspberry and praline mille-feuille to finish, constituted one memorable meal. Readers have commented on the excellent chips served with some of the grills, the bread and good-quality butter, and the proper espresso. Book well in advance. Short and to the point, the wine list takes in classic regions with the same enthusiasm for Italy and Spain as for the New World. Price range is commendably wide with many decent bottles below £15, and mark-ups generally are not at all bad. House wine is £7.

CHEF: Mark Hix PROPRIETORS: C.J. Corbin and J.R.B. King OPEN: all week MEALS: 12 to 3, 6 to 12 PRICES: £22 (£33). Cover £1.50. Card slips closed CARDS: Access, Amex, Diners, Visa SEATS: 70. Vegetarian meals. No children under 5. Wheelchair access. Music. Air-conditioned. Fax: 071-493 9040

Caravan Serai

NEW ENTRY map 13

50 Paddington Street, W1M 3RQ
071-935 1208

COOKING 1*
COST £17–£31

This is a sister to Buzkash in Putney (see entry) and, although it gets fewer recommendations, on a par for its cooking of Afghan food – from the same menu indeed. It is worthy of note if only for the very economical lunch menu. See Buzkash for more details.

CHEF: M. Khan PROPRIETOR: Mr Natebkhail OPEN: all week, exc Sun L CLOSED: 25 to 26 Dec MEALS: 12 to 3, 6 to 11 (11.30 Fri and Sat) PRICES: £14 (£26), Set L £9.95 (£17) Cover 75p. Service 12.5%. Card slips closed CARDS: Access, Amex, Diners, Visa SEATS: 56. Private parties: 32 main room, 16 private room. Vegetarian meals. No-smoking area. Music

'The menu listed two trout. We said we could only manage one; an hour later we were still waiting, though happily with some very good cider. ''So sorry you've waited so long! We thought you'd each need two trout by now.'' We went back next night and had the same again...' On eating in Devon

Casale Franco

NEW ENTRY map 11

134–137 Upper Street, N1 1TQ — COOKING 2
071-226 8994 — COST £36

It may be tucked down an alley at the back of Upper Street and seat more than a hundred people, but there are queues at 7.30 for the pizza, pasta, chargrilled aubergines, calf's liver, shellfish fried in light and well-drained batter, good olive bread and heart-stopping espresso. No bookings are taken except for lunch (when the pizza oven is not lit). Messrs Pensa have a formula that appeals to the hearts, pockets and palates of all London. The pizza dough is first-rate, although some find the toppings less so. There are also some who think fish here is better than meat. However, this is more than just a pizza parlour, judging from the positive response to tagliatelle ai funghi or penne with four cheeses. The wine list is not exciting, though Italophiles recommend the Barbera d'Alla, Conterno Fantino and the Vino Nobile del Cerro. House Locorotondo from Apulia is £8.

CHEFS: Mario Pensa and Franco Pensa PROPRIETORS: Gisella and Franco Pensa OPEN: L Fri to Sun, D Tue to Sat MEALS: 12.30 to 2.30, 6.30 to 11.30 (11 Sun) PRICES: £19 (£30). Cover £1. Minimum £6.50 CARDS: Access, Visa SEATS: 126. 10 tables outside. Vegetarian meals. Children restricted. Wheelchair access. Music. Air-conditioned

Cavaliers 🍷

map 10

129 Queenstown Road, SW8 3RH — COOKING 4
071-720 6960 — COST £30–£67

The minimalist language of the menu may suggest extreme idiosyncrasy: 'red mullet, olives, basil; duck salad; lamb tapénade; sea bass, fennel, tomato; chocolate and raspberry desserts' reading almost parodically. In like manner, a report of sounds of verbal violence emanating from the kitchen only seconds before waiters emerge, wreathed in smiles and bearing food, gives frissons that this is another place to avoid if you fear a personality stalking the dining-room. In truth, it is not like this. Cavaliers seems an endearing restaurant, the more so as it has settled into handsomely refurbished premises behind a smart blue frontage on Queenstown Road; you enter by the side door, ringing the bell for admission. David Cavalier runs an impressive kitchen, but would it be more exciting if it were more accessible, both physically and financially? There seems to be some dilemma between charging the right price (up to a hefty £42 for a full dinner, before drinks) and getting the right level of business. Lunch, of course, is much cheaper than dinner; perhaps everything should be more even between the two meals. The style of cooking is accurate and happily much less ornate than it used to be. Thus a meal of fried scallops flavoured with lemon oil, on a bed of puréed asparagus in a light pastry case with a circlet of asparagus tips, followed by partridge casseroled in its own juices with tiny chopped vegetables (not so tiny that they lacked flavour) which was deftly carved at table, an orange soufflé, partnered by caramelised orange under spun sugar and an orange sorbet finished a memorable whole demonstrating tremendous economy and concentration. Recommendations have included ravioli of lobster, foie gras terrine, beef with red wine sauce, lobster thermidor, steak and kidney pudding with oysters (at lunch), oysters with spinach and caviare, and a saddle of lamb boulangère. A glass award for the wine list may be questionable when mark-ups press hard and when the expensive bulk of the list is unbalanced by decent mid-priced wines. Quality is fine though, especially in Burgundy, and there are interesting old Vouvrays. House wines are from £12. CELLARMAN'S CHOICE: Vouvray, Clos Naudin 1985, Foreau, £23; Savigny, 'Champ Chevrey' 1986, Tollot-Beaut, £30.

CHEF: David Cavalier PROPRIETORS: David and Susan Cavalier OPEN: Tue to Sat MEALS: 12.15 to 2, 7.15 to 10.30 (11 Sat if busy) PRICES: Set L £18.50 (£30), Set D £32.50 (£45) to £42 (£56) CARDS: Access, Amex, Diners, Visa SEATS: 50. Private parties: 50 main room. Children welcome. Smart dress preferred. Air-conditioned

Chanterelle

map 12

119 Old Brompton Road, SW7 3RN — COOKING 1
071-373 5522 and 7390 — COST £15–£29

From year to year Chanterelle appears in the *Guide*, approved by Kensington residents and visitors for serving them professionally, often amiably, and without charging too much. The repertoire for the three-course dinner, at a set price, includes poached-egg tart florentine; haddock, prawn and mussel pie; navarin of lamb; calf's liver with onion gravy; and baked rhubarb with almond cake or Atholl brose. Lunch is a bargain at almost half the price of dinner. Sunday lunch is a roast. Reports have remarked on the extreme variability of the cooking, but many readers are satisfied with the equation balancing value for money with quality. The all-French wine list is short and acceptable. House French is £6.80.

CHEF/PROPRIETOR: Fergus Provan OPEN: all week CLOSED: 4 days Christmas MEALS: 12 to 2.30, 7 to 11.30 PRICES: Set L £10 (£15), Set D £18 (£24). Service 12.5% for parties of 6 or more CARDS: Access, Amex, Diners, Visa SEATS: 45. 2 tables outside. Private parties: 10 main room. Children welcome. Smart dress preferred. No cigars in dining-room. Wheelchair access (2 steps). No music

Le Chausson

NEW ENTRY map 10

Ransome's Dock,
35–37 Parkgate Road, SW11 4NP — COOKING 2*
071-223 1611 and 924 2462 — COST £24–£36

Ransome's Dock is the last private dock in London. There is an intention to turn it into a marina; certainly, if Le Chausson does the catering, yacht owners would not be badly served. Sitting in the dining-room today – fake stone walls, soft-green table linen, windows looking out to the river – the visitor would not think the building was once an ice-cream factory. Eric Marin, a chef with high-powered names on his CV, seems to be pitching his menu at a price level well below the West End, or indeed its outposts in Queenstown Road, Battersea. This is as encouraging as the fair prices he asks for his daily set 'Market Menu'. The cooking often works, rather better in first courses than main ones, which have been dogged by less-than-perfect materials, an old-fashioned urge to dot the plate with odd (and not very good) vegetables, and some unsatisfactory saucing; otherwise the standard has been high.

Recommendations have included feuilleté of wild mushrooms and artichoke, celeriac soup with saffron and sliced scallops, smoked duck and ginger in filo pastry, lamb with a béarnaise, quail stuffed with a pepper mousse, the eponymous chausson (a Cornish pasty) stuffed with fresh raspberries (worth the wait) and simple passion-fruit mousse. Service is especially welcoming. If reliability can be improved, this is an encouraging re-drawing of London's restaurant map. Good properties and growers abound on the predominantly French wine list. California and Australasia are admitted, but the Italians, sadly, not. Within the confines of a 50-bottle list, including good half-bottles, determined effort is made to provide genuine choice in price as well as style. This is an excellent start. House wine is £9.50.

CHEF/PROPRIETOR: Eric Marin OPEN: Mon to Sat, exc Sat D MEALS: 12 to 2.45, 7 to 11 PRICES: £21 (£30), Set L and D £17 (£24) SEATS: 45. 4 tables outside. Private parties: 50 main room. Car park, 30 places D. Vegetarian meals. Children's helpings. Music. Air-conditioned

▲ *Chelsea Room, Hyatt Carlton Tower*

map 12

2 Cadogan Place, SW1 9PY — COOKING 3
071-235 5411 — COST £26–£68

The recession has the strangest effects. Just why Bernard Gaume's Chelsea Room, once London's leading gourmet hotel dining-room, should suddenly turn into a 'speciality fish restaurant', albeit with identical staff at front and back of house, has not been explained. The result is that the spacious suite of rooms and conservatory (no danger from eavesdropping here) has a menu of mainly fish. Endlessly modern recipes use coriander, black olives, endives, garlic and basil as flavourings where once mushrooms, white wine and a court bouillon, plus a few asparagus tips, were the boldest margins towards which a fish cook might stray. On the other hand the meat component of the *carte*, as in fish restaurants of yore, is plain and simple. A visit here confirms that the service is highly competent ('the head waiter must be worth millions to them'), the comfort level is high, and the cooking efficient but not exciting. It is reassuring that materials are first-rate. The sweet-trolley rears its ugly head here and is no more exciting than most. And as is too often found, though there is a full dessert menu with hot soufflés and the like, if the place is quiet or the hour late the staff simply fail to mention its existence. Some may be taken aback by the wine prices. No one expects first growths at bargain prices, but then there is little else available in the Chelsea Room. 'Australie' and 'Italie' have made tentative entries this year. Jean Quéro, for long the distinguished maître d'hôtel here, has left for a new post as we go to press. His absence will be felt.

CHEF: Bernard Gaume PROPRIETORS: Hyatt Hotels Ltd OPEN: all week MEALS: 12.30 to 2.45, 7 to 11 (10.30 Sun) PRICES: £40 (£57), Set L £23.50 (£26), Set D £29.50 (£39) CARDS: Access, Amex, Diners, Visa SEATS: 60. Private parties: 30 main room, 35 private room. Car park, 55 places. Children welcome. Jacket and tie. Wheelchair access. Music. Air-conditioned. Fax: 071-245 6570 ACCOMMODATION: 224 rooms, all with bath/shower. Lift. B&B £258.50 (doubles only). Children welcome. Baby facilities. Afternoon teas. Garden. Sauna. Tennis. Air-conditioned. TV. Phone. Scenic. Confirm by 6

Cherry Orchard

map 10

241–245 Globe Road, E2 0JD
081-980 6678

COOKING 1
COST £10–£18

Carnivores are easily converted to the vegetarian way of doing things in this happy, enthusiastically run co-operative. At lunchtime it is counter service; in the evening there are candles on the tables and waitress service. Menus change daily, ingredients are fresh and the kitchen shows some imagination and flair. Pâtés are made with olives and nuts, Greek salad is a regular fixture and main dishes might range from courgette croustade to stir-fried vegetables with pilau rice and peanut sauce. Vegetables and salads are abundant. To finish there are Loseley ice-creams or an over-the-top 'chocaholics' dream'. Unlicensed, but you can bring your own wine or choose from the vast range of teas and juices.

CHEFS: Jamie Lemone and Vajramala PROPRIETORS: Pure Land Co-operative OPEN: Tue to Sat CLOSED: Christmas week MEALS: 12 to 3, 6.30 to 10.30 PRICES: £8 (£10), D £12 (£15). Service 10% D. Unlicensed, but bring your own: corkage £1 CARDS: Access, Visa SEATS: 54. 6 tables outside. Private parties: 25 main room. Vegetarian and vegan meals. Children's helpings. No smoking. Wheelchair access (1 step). Music

Chez Liline

map 10

101 Stroud Green Road, N4 3PX
071-263 6550

COOKING 1*
COST £18–£38

Chez Liline has captured the hearts of the inhabitants of N4 to the extent that two sittings are necessary to cope with the Friday and Saturday night crowds. As the restaurant is Mauritian, fish is the thing, and more precisely shellfish and warm-water sea fish: vacqua, bourgeois, snapper and capitain. Flavourings owe allegiance to South East Asia – ginger, chilli, coriander and soy – with garlic, saffron, mustard and lemon nodding towards the French colonial influence. Despite the exotic provenance of the ingredients, the surroundings are very basic and attention to customers' comfort is not a high enough priority for some. It can be smoky. The fact that cigars are sold by the management does not help matters. Sweet dishes are not a strong point either. House wine is £7.50. Sylvain Ho Wing Cheong is mostly at the sister restaurant La Gaulette (see entry), so his role as chef is 'executif'.

CHEFS: Sylvain Ho Wing Cheong and Mario Ho Wing Cheong PROPRIETOR: Liline Ng Yu Tin OPEN: Mon to Sat MEALS: 12 to 2.30, 6.30 to 11 PRICES: £22 (£32), Set L and D £12 (£18) to £20 (£27). Minimum £10.95 SEATS: 52. Private parties: 52 main room. Vegetarian meals. Music

Chez Moi

map 10

1 Addison Avenue, W11 4QS
071-603 8267

COOKING 3
COST £21–£37

Down the Shepherd's Bush end of Holland Park is this long-standing favourite of local residents, the visiting business community and *Guide* readers alike. Younger generations might call the deep red and gilt-mirrored interior stuffy and old-fashioned, but it holds its charm, is not allowed to run to seed and gives the place its valid character. Service and welcome is also old-fashioned, making a nice contrast with the laid-back approach of modern Soho or Notting Hill. Richard Walton's menu keeps a foot in both camps. His carré of lamb has been a feature since the restaurant opened more than 20 years ago; other long runners are quail eggs with smoked salmon and sauce mousseline, tartare of salmon, and 'oursins' of scampi, prawn and scallop deep-fried in a fine vermicelli. On the other foot, market materials are offered with recipes that may reflect the travels of the owners, the enthusiasms of their staff or just 'quelque chose de différent'. Every year we get the odd dissentient voice, but the general run of opinion is that they know what they're doing at Chez Moi and do it well. It's the kind of place you can take anyone to. The wine list is very French and not exactly cheap, but allows space for affordable bottles and gives a fair outing to halves.

CHEF: Richard Walton PROPRIETORS: Richard Walton and Colin Smith OPEN: Mon to Sat, exc Sat L CLOSED: bank hols, Christmas to New Year MEALS: 12.30 to 2, 7 to 11 PRICES: £22 (£31), Set L £14 (£21). Card slips closed CARDS: Access, Amex, Diners, Visa SEATS: 45. Children's helpings. No pipes in dining-room. Wheelchair access. Air-conditioned. No music

Chez Nico 🍷

map 13

35 Great Portland Street, W1N 5DD
071-436 8846

COOKING 5
COST £43–£77

What is it one expects of a restaurant? Flavour? Taste? Accuracy of execution? Invention? Service? Ambience? All of these, and more: some amalgam which justifies the effort of getting there and paying for it. At Chez Nico you will certainly pay, but opinion is almost unanimous that it is worth it. The only doubt enters when the cheaper lunch is discussed; many have felt it is worth paying more to get more. This has become a problem with many of the best restaurants. People expect the earth and hope to get it at bargain prices – the bargain is still valid, but expectations have outrun the need for profit on the other side. The quality of Nico Ladenis' kitchen is such that it delivers more flavour than the kitchens of most of his peers, while still following the line of haute cuisine rather than diverging into gutsy peasant or bourgeois dishes. Taste and accuracy are there too, along with bags of invention. There is not much truck with wayward combinations, but the classic ingredients are deployed in ways that will not be met elsewhere. Thus a breast of chicken stuffed with morels, the entire flesh infused with intense fungal perfume, is accompanied by the drumstick coated in honey, rolled in rosemary and herbs then roasted to a crisp. The deep sweetness is overlaid with the wafting aromas of a provençal hillside – resinous and flowery at one time – which give strong accent (too strong?) to the dish. Food aside, the restaurant itself delivers good service, both attentive and knowledgeable, plenty of space between tables, and comfort. Then there is the light: the whole room is bathed in a rosy glow accumulated from shimmering reflections of silver, flowers and white napery in mirrors set as a dado rail. It is not a romantic place, but it shares the same faith in itself – unwillingness to hide its light – as does the cooking. The effect of this is that a meal here should be, and often is, actively pleasurable – and far more so than at many of its competitors. To rehearse the dishes that have been praised would be otiose and lengthy. We restrict comment to a plate of noodles with a wild mushroom and cep sauce. To each side were two small white chicken boudins (perhaps too salt) and a giant flat mushroom, cooked to crisp on the top, surmounted by a half-crown-size piece of foie gras. For once this was not for mere display and was economically judged enough not to overbalance the digestion. Textures, variety of tastes and intensity were exact. In the same way, a dish of sweetbreads and artichokes elicits the reflection from one reader: 'How does he achieve such flavour?' The materials themselves are not strong, yet Nico gets depth. Bread has moved on to tiny crusty white rolls, excellent and chewy. The long list of desserts gives rise to discussion. Perhaps there is no need for one: the petits fours are outstanding and the coffee robustly aromatic. A mistake was registered in a pear crumble infused with ginger, which was thought too desiccated; a layered chocolate mousse cake was almost too rich for its sauce and saved only by the mint sorbet served atop. Yet some of the fruit tarts, the lemon tart and the charlotte of apple, look and taste first-rate. One should not descant too much on price. Yes, it is dear to eat here. The existence of supplements on a fixed-price menu is regrettable. The wine list is much too expensive. But better, perhaps, to observe only that a master may reasonably charge what he thinks he is worth and the customer must make the choice. We may think a David Hockney too expensive but that does not mean we don't want to own it. Whether the master should adopt the same relativistic approach to wine pricing is another matter. Intelligence and very careful selection are much in evidence, but Pouilly Fumé at £40 a bottle? Some of the few halves seem to offer better value, but no full bottles are below £24.50. There are many over £50. CELLARMAN'S CHOICE: Chassagne Montrachet Morgeots 1988, Drouhin, £42; Côte Rôtie Brune et Blonde 1985, Guigal, £47.50.

CHEFS: Nico Ladenis and Paul Flynn PROPRIETORS: Nico and Dinah-Jane Ladenis OPEN: Mon to Fri CLOSED: 10 days Christmas, 3 weeks summer MEALS: 12 to 2.15, 7 to 11 PRICES: Set L £27.75 (£43) to £49 (£64), Set D £41 (£56) to £49 (£64). Net prices, card slips closed CARDS: Access, Diners, Visa SEATS: 48. Private parties: 48 main room, 12 private room. No children under 5. Smart dress preferred. No pipes in dining-room. Wheelchair access (1 step). Air-conditioned. No music. Fax: 071-436 0134

Chiang Mai — map 14

48 Frith Street, W1V 5TE — COOKING 1
071-437 7444 — COST £23–£32

Despite the competition among Thai restaurants in this quarter of Soho, Chiang Mai maintains rather than improves its standards. Visitors have found the décor 'rather jaded now', but the kitchen delivers a creditable version of northern Thai cooking with few compromises to Western tastes in the use of spices. Recommended dishes have included vegetarian spring rolls, hot-and-sour bamboo shoots, chicken curry with coconut cream, and pork with basil and peppers. Sticky rice and Thai noodles are excellent accompaniments. Portions can be rather small. Drink tea or Singha Thai beer. House French is £6.95.

CHEF/PROPRIETOR: Vatcharin Bhumichitr OPEN: all week MEALS: 12 to 3, 6 to 11.30 PRICES: £12 (£23), Set L and D £17 (£23) to £21 (£27). Service 10%. Card slips closed CARDS: Access, Amex, Visa SEATS: 60. Private parties: 12 main room, 20 and 25 private rooms. Vegetarian meals. Children welcome. Music

Chinon

map 10

25 Richmond Way, W14 0AS
071-602 4082

COOKING 3*
COST £55

This small restaurant, defended from the uninitiated by a complex one-way road system, produces very good food. Some have felt this is done defensively, even grudgingly if so much as a breath of a question is raised, but the quality is undeniable, the intent is serious. 'We had heard it was good, we thought it absolutely excellent, one of those places you could send any enthusiast for cooking with confidence' was one report. People have also noticed a serious price rise over the last year. The *carte* is short, even shorter when it is realised that dessert is no-choice, merely an *assiette du chef* of very high quality. One winter meal indicates the style and ambition. Thin-sliced huge scallops, chequered brown on one side, were arranged round a dariole of shredded and toothsome onion, courgettes, beans, peas, leek and cucumber; on top was a wafer of truffle and five grains of salmon caviare. The vegetable juices provided moistness; the shellfish was sweet, fresh and perfect. Then came pheasant breast sandwiching flavoursome boudin noir, held together with a layer of caul fat and roasted exactly. To one side sat a pile of haricots and bacon sitting on an oyster mushroom, with ceps sliced over the top, and a feuilleté of mixed wild mushrooms. The sauce was a light jus that captured the taste of all the main ingredients. Cheese was a thorough range, made up with fruit into a plate presented without enquiry as to preference; dessert was a plate of white chocolate mousse, a big brandy-snap bowl with cardamomed rice pudding, a tart filled with praline ice-cream capped by caramel stripes, and a warm slice of lemon tart. There was no choice, but what accuracy in flavours! Bread is imaginative. The short but decent wine list has plenty of half-bottles. House Duboeuf is £8.50.

CHEFS/PROPRIETORS: Barbara Deane and Jonathan Hayes OPEN: Tue to Sat, exc Sat L CLOSED: most bank hols MEALS: 12 to 2, 7 to 10 (11 Fri and Sat) PRICES: £34 (£46). Service 12%. Card slips closed CARDS: Access, Amex, Visa SEATS: 21. Private parties: 30 main room. Vegetarian meals. Children welcome. Smart dress preferred. Music

Christian's

map 10

1 Station Parade,
Burlington Lane, W4 3HD
081-995 0382 and 0208

COOKING 1
COST £24–£34

Christian's used to look like a greengrocer's, but the image has been tidied up with the addition of an eye-catching awning. The kitchen opens on to the tiny restaurant, allowing generous flashes of Christian Gustin in action. Chargrilling, the latest addition to the menu, keeps the repertoire up to date: chargrilled chicken with soy and spring onions complements roast salmon with herb sauce or a duck confit with onion compote. Execution is fair, if marred by inconsistency of concentration: a crudely made vegetable mille-feuille; bland carrot and coriander soup; an even blander game pâté with orange marmalade. Slow, sometimes amateur, service can exacerbate the problem ('skate was ordered but steak appeared'). But satisfied readers have reported on tender neck of lamb, a successful cassoulet and well-made ragoût of monkfish, salmon and scallops. Portions are generous, ingredients fresh, and on the whole the atmosphere and the cheery unstuffiness make this a successful neighbourhood restaurant. Coffee is disappointingly weak. The short wine list is entirely French and fairly priced. House wine is £6.35.

CHEF/PROPRIETOR: Christian Gustin OPEN: Tue to Sat, D only, and Sun L CLOSED: bank hols MEALS: 12.30 to 2.30, 7.30 to 10.45 PRICES: £20 (£28), Set Sun L £16.25 (£24). Service 15%. Card slips closed. CARDS: Access, Visa SEATS: 40. 4 tables outside. Private parties: 8 main room. Vegetarian meals. No cigars/pipes in dining-room

▲ *Churchill Hotel*

NEW ENTRY map 11

Portman Square, W1A 4ZX — COOKING **2**
071-486 5800 — COST £28–£40

The transformation of the coffee-shop and the old No.10 restaurant into The Restaurant at the Churchill is commendable, if only for the decision not to reproduce yet another country-house pastiche in a modern business hotel. Instead, modern wood panelling is cleverly off-set by vivid splashes of colour: paintings, plants, 'curtains like old school ties', urns overflowing with fruit, and dazzling, hand-painted flower-pots on each table. The décor is complemented by the menu, which is full of eclectic influences, from plain grills to tempura-fried jumbo prawns on black-bean ginger sauce, from bouillabaisse of halibut, snapper, mussels, clams and shrimp to florid-sounding 'Welsh leek pork sausages with curry split pea and mango tomato chutney'. There are often too many influences at work. Simpler ideas work best: oven-baked five-onion soup ('lusciously perfumed, slightly sweet and buttery'); guinea-fowl with mushroom fettuccine; herb-crusted halibut ('a good idea let down by the needless poor timing' of the waiting staff, but accessorised by no less than 13 different sorts of vegetable). With starters at around £4 and main courses around £11, the menu is good value. What it needs is practice and consistency. The wine list carries on the theme of contemporary fashions with an emphasis on New World wines, and its prices are far from greedy. House Californian is £8.

CHEF: Avner Samuel PROPRIETORS: Park Lane Hotels International OPEN: all week MEALS: 12 to 3, 6 to 11 PRICES: £22 (£33), Set L £17.95 (£28). Service 15%. Card slips closed CARDS: Access, Amex, Diners, Visa SEATS: 114. Private parties by arrangement. Car park, 60 places. Vegetarian meals. Children welcome. No-smoking area. Wheelchair access (also WC). Music. Air-conditioned. Fax: 071-486 1255 ACCOMMODATION: 450 rooms, all with bath/shower. Rooms for disabled. Lift. B&B £195 to £212. Children welcome. Afternoon teas. Tennis. Air-conditioned. TV. Phone

The Guide *always appreciates hearing about changes of chef or owner.*

Cibo

map 10

3 Russell Gardens, W14 8EZ
071-371 6271 and 2085

COOKING 2*
COST £42

A design- rather than comfort-led restaurant, Cibo has white walls, bumpy paintings, spotlit bundles of twigs and closely packed tables. Reports, despite a good first impression, have not been unanimously encouraging about the food. If you get the order right, you can come away with the impression of having eaten 'rustic and quite authentic north Italian food'. Gnocchi with fresh tomatoes and melted mozzarella; seafood risotto; calf's liver, kidneys and mushrooms; venison with garlic have all pleased. But on one occasion a platter of grilled fish was found to be not of the best, and a main-course fish and shellfish stew consisted of one langoustine, six mussels, two pieces of squid and a tiny piece of lobster. Popularity has provoked a surge in prices. The cost does little to reconcile people to variations though the enthusiasm and warm welcome from the staff makes it worth returning and trying again. We had no sight of the wine list this year, but it offers a mixed bag of Italians – some good, some boring. House wine is £7.25.

CHEF: Claudio Pecorari PROPRIETOR: Gino Taddei OPEN: all week, exc Sun D CLOSED: bank hols MEALS: 12 to 2.30, 7 to 11 PRICES: £26 (£35). Service 10% for parties of 5 or more CARDS: Access, Amex, Diners, Visa SEATS: 55. Private parties: 60 main room. Children's helpings. Music. Air-conditioned. Fax: 071-602 1371

Clarke's 🍷

map 11

124 Kensington Church Street, W8 4BH
071-221 9225

COOKING 4
COST £24–£46

This restaurant on two floors is next to the bread shop where wine, cheese, baked goods and a few other commodities can be bought. Clarke's bread is very good and the range is increasing, making it perhaps the most enterprising non-French bakers in London. In the restaurant, the large and airy basement is where to go for kitchen action while people-watchers claim the nobs stay upstairs. Who knows? Sally Clarke's formula is distinctive: a very short choice at lunchtime succeeded by a no-choice meal at dinner, the contents of which you can discover by a telephone call as the menus are fixed in advance. Much, but not all, of the meat and fish is chargrilled – thus the range of technique is not so dazzling as in other places. But at least the style works. This colours the tone of the repertoire. A lunch for two included a wild mushroom and celeriac risotto; chargrilled pigeon with salad, toasts and an orange dressing; and chargrilled halibut with olives and marjoram, together with cabbage and lentils. Another factor common to meals is Sally Clarke's love of salad leaves – and they come from a good source. One reader speculated that his main course of lamb with red wine jus and lots of bitter leaves, plus fennel, celery and mushrooms, had become, in concept at least, a first course of protein, salad and dressing. Unreserved acclamation comes for the British and Irish cheeses and for the desserts: 'I remember on my first visit the star turn was plum pancake with honey ice-cream; this time it was the prune ice-cream with honey waffle wafer and the brilliant simplicity of satsumas, mascarpone and shortbread.' Warm chocolate mousse with intense raspberry accompaniment, rhubarb tart and cinnamon ice-cream, and cranberry and clementine trifle are three other sweet courses memorable to happy readers. Chocolate truffles are pretty good too. Quantities are well-judged, mainly in favour of lightness; digestibility and value are good. Thus Clarke's remains the best and most sensitive exponent of modern American-influenced cooking – that interesting hybrid of French, Italian, Californian and directness. The Californian accent on the wine list is reinforced this year, with several wines otherwise unseen in Britain imported directly. France, though, continues to dominate with scrupulous care in selection; Italy has a brief but convincing showing in reds. Prices throughout are very fair, with much below £15. There is a range of interesting wines by the glass. House wine is £7.80.

CHEFS: Sally Clarke and Elizabeth Payne PROPRIETOR: Sally Clarke OPEN: Mon to Fri CLOSED: 2 weeks Aug, 10 days Christmas, 4 days Easter, bank hols MEALS: 12.30 to 2, 7 to 10 PRICES: Set L £20 (£24) to £24 (£28), Set D £34 (£38). Net prices, card slips closed CARDS: Access, Visa SEATS: 90. Private parties: 10 main room. Vegetarian meals. Children welcome. Wheelchair access. No music. Air-conditioned. Fax: 071-229 4564

▲ *Connaught* map 13

Carlos Place, W1Y 6AL COOKING 4
071-499 7070 COST £37–£85

The Gulf War may have caused the Grill Room to be deserted – hence, a party of seven was waited on by nine staff – but the Connaught will sail on regardless, convinced its tack will catch the wind in the end. The force of tradition catches people in the throat: the ornate lounges, the deferential welcome, the fine polish to the panelling, the menu that is understandable only to an Edwardian gourmet, and wave upon wave of service. It is excellently performed. That fashion has stood still may be a strength, but shows weaknesses as well: the hors d'oeuvre trolley could be rethought to advantage; the endless showing, carving, presentation and serving of something like a roast pheasant can be exhausting to the customer anxious to converse rather than spectate; the desserts, again from the trolley, have lost in many cases because they have been cold not warm, warm not hot. None the less, the traditional skills of haute cuisine live on and produce delights, whether they be oeufs de caille Maintenon; salmon quenelles in a pink champagne sauce; salmi of quail with truffles and a champagne sauce; or roast veal in pastry with a gratin of spinach and artichokes Mornay, and a fresh truffle gravy. These are done competently, even if too many say the truffles have less taste than they might. Old English cookery, such as grilled liver, roast game and the like, is given the full treatment. There is an element of regret in many reports this year. Perhaps too many people are dedicated followers of fashion to find the Connaught quite as charming as they once did. But its constituency will never really shrink away, so sail on, sail on. The wines leave people in ecstasy though the list, in truth, is not as wondrous as once it was. The restaurant is a good place to drink wine, if you can afford it. The service and glassware will reconcile any who would like a more adventurous choice.

▲ *This symbol means that accommodation is available.*

CHEF: Michel Bourdin PROPRIETORS: Savoy Hotel plc OPEN: Restaurant all week, Grill Room Mon to Fri CLOSED: Grill Room weekends and bank hols MEALS: 12.30 to 2.30, 6.30 to 10.15 (restaurant); 6 to 10.30 (Grill Room) PRICES: £48 (£71), Set L £24.45 (£37), Set D £26 (£39) to £52 (£68). Minimum £25 (Grill Room). Service 15%. Card slips closed CARDS: Access, Visa SEATS: 75. Private parties: 20 and 35 private rooms. No children under 6. Jacket and tie. No pipes in dining-room. Wheelchair access (also WC). No music. Air-conditioned ACCOMMODATION: 90 rooms, all with bath/shower. Rooms for disabled. Room prices on application. Lift. Afternoon teas. TV. Phone (*Which? Hotel Guide*)

Connolly's

map 10

162 Lower Richmond Road, SW15 1LY COOKING 1*
081-788 3844 COST £18–£25

Eamonn and Kate Connolly's restaurant is a converted shop close to Putney Common. Inside, the light room is brightened by splashes of yellow colour and a good selection of prints. Eamonn Connolly cooks a mixture of hearty, straightforward dishes, such as confit of duck with garlic sausage and beans, and lamb provençal, with more flamboyant, exotic combinations along the lines of smoked chicken with pickled bananas and breast of duck with mango sauce. Main courses come with a huge selection of fresh vegetables. Sweets have included decent tiramisù and cheesecake with a boozy sponge base. Coffee is accompanied by home-made truffles. Service is warm and friendly, even under pressure. Some have found Sunday lunch too popular for satisfaction, but others who visit at intervals are clear that the kitchen is improving. Around 20 modestly priced wines include house French at £8.50.

CHEF: Eamonn Connolly PROPRIETORS: Eamonn and Kate Connolly OPEN: all week, exc Sun D CLOSED: bank hols MEALS: 12 to 2.30 (1 to 4 Sun), 7 to 10.30 PRICES: Set L and D £10.95 (£18) to £13.95 (£21) CARDS: Access, Amex, Visa SEATS: 40. 6 tables outside. Private parties: 40 main room. Vegetarian meals. Children's helpings. No pipes in dining-room. Wheelchair access (1 step). Music

Cork & Bottle 🍷

map 14

44–46 Cranbourn Street, WC2H 7AN COOKING 1
071-734 7807 COST £23

Don Hewitson's wine bar celebrated 20 years of business in 1991 and goes into its third decade with new kitchens and extensive refurbishment. The customers, however, remain the same pleasing mixture of theatre-goers, trippers, office workers and lovers of wine (particularly of champagnes and New Zealand whites) always appreciative of the high spirits and welcome of the team here. Critics of the food there are: one mid-evening in the spring found a lacklustre collection of salads, no more pavlovas and not very good cheeses, but on better days standbys such as smoked trout pâté, mixed ham and cheese pie (extremely filling) and those pavlovas are well appreciated as accompaniments to a fast-changing, fair-priced and interesting collection of wines.

If a restaurant is new to the Guide *this year (did not appear as a main entry in the last edition)* NEW ENTRY *appears opposite its name.*

CHEF: Louie Egham PROPRIETOR: Don Hewitson OPEN: all week MEALS: 11am (noon Sun) to 10.30pm PRICES: £10 (£19). Card slips closed CARDS: Access, Amex, Diners, Visa SEATS: 60. Private parties: 20 main room, 20 private room. Vegetarian meals. Children restricted. Music. Air-conditioned. Self-service

La Croisette

map 11

168 Ifield Road, SW10 9AF
071-373 3694

COOKING 1
COST £24–£42

More French than France, this restaurant – reached by spiral staircase – specialises in fish. Part of the group encompassing Le Suquet (see entry), Le Quai St Pierre and La Bouillabaisse, its buying policies could not be impugned and the materials are good. Most of the ancillaries are not. Eat the simplest dishes to ensure satisfaction. Service needs improvement as well. House wine is £8.70. Although there is an acceptable deal for a fixed price, costs rise once on the *carte*. The best bet is still, perhaps, the *fruits de mer*. Lobsters can come small, and at high, high prices.

CHEF: Robin Bertrand PROPRIETOR: Pierre Martin OPEN: Tue to Sun, exc Tue L CLOSED: 25 Dec MEALS: 12.30 to 2.30, 7.30 to 11.30 PRICES: £20 (£29), Set L and D £16 (£24) to £26 (£35). Cover £1. Service 15%. Card slips closed CARDS: Access, Amex, Diners, Visa SEATS: 55. 3 tables outside. Private parties: 10 main room. Children welcome. Smart dress preferred. No pipes in dining-room. Music. Fax: 081-877 1937

Crowthers

map 10

481 Upper Richmond Road West, SW14 7PU
081-876 6372

COOKING 2
COST £20–£36

The setting for Crowthers is a converted shop on the main road through East Sheen, but the restaurant has a deliberately countrified domesticity. During the last year, Philip Crowther has added a few à la carte dishes to broaden the scope of his modern set menus and make prices more flexible. Culinary skill and pretty presentation show up well in tortellini of seafood with cream and basil sauce; Gruyère cheese ramekin with tomato and chervil; marinated tenderloin of pork in filo pastry; and ribs of Scotch beef with potato rösti and a shallot and red wine sauce. Reporters have also mentioned duck breast with limes, escalope of salmon with chive and saffron sauce, and roast quails stuffed with chicken liver pâté on a port and blackberry sauce. Ingredients are generally good, although sauces can be unbalanced – sometimes too strong, sometimes lacking flavour. Desserts have included gratin of fruits in hot sabayon sauce with passion-fruit sorbet and three-chocolate parfait in a raspberry coulis. Shirley Crowther is a pleasant hostess, but sometimes finds it difficult to cope with a full house. A short list of around 30 wines has some decent bottles from the New World. House French is £8.25.

CHEF: Philip Crowther PROPRIETORS: Philip and Shirley Crowther OPEN: Mon to Sat, exc L Mon and Sat MEALS: 12 to 2, 7 to 10 PRICES: £22 (£30), Set L £14 (£20) to £16.50 (£23), Set D £22 (£29) CARDS: Access, Amex, Visa SEATS: 32. Private parties: 32 main room. Vegetarian meals. Children welcome. Wheelchair access. Air-conditioned. Music. Fax: 081-876 0046

Diwana Bhel-Poori map 11

121 Drummond Street, NW1 2HL COOKING 1
071-387 5556 COST £6–£12

'Phenomenally popular,' writes one reporter, 'mainly because it offers pretty good value and lives on its reputation as the pioneering bhel poori house.' Opened in 1973, Diwana set the style and has spawned countless imitators. The view that it is 'the best Indian vegetarian food in London' overstates the case, but visitors are seldom disappointed. High points are the samosas, onion bhajias, bhel pooris, sev poori and aloo papri chat, while the de-luxe dosa has been reliably good. Three starter dishes are normally ample for one person, and it is worth leaving room for the home-made kulfi. Less impressive are the thalis, breads and main-course vegetable curries. This is a well-oiled, well-organised set-up, although some find it closer to new-age wholefood than the real thing, an opinion reinforced by the closely packed pine tables and benches, brown walls hung with ethnic wooden carvings, laid-back music and intense alternative conversations. A first-floor extension should ease the congestion and shorten the queues. Unlicensed, but there is lassi, fruit juice and mango milkshake to drink. A sister restaurant is at 50 Westbourne Grove W2, Tel: 071-221 0721.

CHEF: V.A. Qadir PROPRIETORS: the Patel family OPEN: all week CLOSED: 25 Dec MEALS: noon to 11.30 PRICES: £7 (£10), Set L and D £5 (£6). Unlicensed, but bring your own: no corkage CARDS: Access, Diners, Visa SEATS: 72. Vegetarian meals. Children welcome. Wheelchair access (1 step). Music. Fax: 071-383 0560

▲ *Dorchester* NEW ENTRY map 13

Park Lane, W1A 2HJ COOKING 3
071-629 8888 COST £34–£66

The Dorchester emerged from its builders' cocoon in time for Christmas 1990 and was almost immediately plunged into the gloom surrounding international tourism in the wake of the Gulf crisis. Refurbishment has had its effect on bedrooms and the creation of the new Oriental restaurant, but many of the features in parts familiar to readers have not been so radically changed as might be feared. The Grill Room's 'gold and floral patterns are sharper and brighter than before, giving a heightened state of vulgarity'. The Grill Room does not show culinary inspiration, though service is excellent and people enjoy the experience – good roast beef on Sundays. The news in the launch period was all about the Oriental, an extremely luxurious Cantonese restaurant with handsome antiques and wall-hangings and a calm unknown to any ethnic Chinese restaurants in Soho or Manchester. It is worth paying for this, and for the staff's enthusiasm. But pay you will and it is not certain that the food has the sparkle needed. On the plus side, it does have impeccable ingredients, some of which are uncommon, and concentrates on a single region, offering luxury dishes suitable for meals of this status. In this context there are some oddities, such as hot-and-sour soup and sweet-and-sour pork ('the soup was timid, the pork the soggiest I have had for years'). Far better to stick to the chef's fish specials of the day, or even lash out on luxuries such as dried scallops or abalone. Soup stocks are good. What may be missing are 'the bold colours, searing wok heat and gutsy flavours'. Desserts are a fair range and the tea ceremony is a delight. Lunch at a set price may be a good way to try this restaurant. The Terrace Room, smaller than it was, but with essentially the same decoration, still has its band – alas for the young, whoopee for those who remember the style. The food has gone out of style too – 'more plate than food' was one disconsolate comment. Nouvelle cuisine and the influence of Anton Mosimann have persisted here. Thus the excitement is low, and yet the quality is satisfactory. It needs more identity. The wine list at the Dorchester is very long and costly – even the New World bottles are pricey ones – but there is a range under £20 and there are a few half-bottles.

CHEFS: Willi Elsener (Grill and Terrace) and Simon Yung (Oriental) PROPRIETORS: Dorchester Hotel Ltd OPEN: Grill all week; Oriental Mon to Sat; Terrace Mon to Sat, D only CLOSED: 25 Dec Oriental MEALS: Grill 12.30 to 3, 6 to 11 (10.30 Sun); Oriental 12 to 2.30, 7 to 11; Terrace 7 to 11.30 PRICES: Grill £32 (£42), Set L £25 (£34), Set D £28 (£37); Oriental £31 (£47), Set L £25 (£34), Set D £30 (£39) to £35 (£44); Terrace £46 (£55), Set D £35 (£42) to £48 (£55). Net prices, card slips closed CARDS: Access, Amex, Diners, Visa SEATS: Grill 80, Oriental 77, Terrace 80. Private parties: 8 and 10 main rooms, 6, 10 and 12 private rooms. Vegetarian meals. Healthy eating options Grill and Terrace. Children's helpings. No children under 12 exc Grill. Jacket and tie. Wheelchair access (also WC). No music Oriental. Air-conditioned. Fax: 071-409 0114 ACCOMMODATION: 252 rooms, all with bath/shower. Rooms for disabled. Lift. B&B £211.50 to £253. Children welcome. Baby facilities. Afternoon teas. Sauna. Air-conditioned. TV. Phone

La Dordogne map 10

5 Devonshire Road, W4 2EU COOKING 2
081-747 1836 COST £36

The neat front in a side-street off Chiswick High Road gives on to a series of rooms holding a surprising number of people – sometimes too many for either comfort or efficiency. 'This is really a bistro masquerading as a restaurant' was the comment of one who found the food not up to the prices charged, though admitting that some surface attributes of 'restaurant' existed. A new chef has had little effect on the menu, which shows affinities with the Dordogne in too few of its run-of-the-mill Anglo-French dishes. If the cooking is accurate, this is no bad thing and a fillet of beef with a potato galette and a foie gras sauce can be a pleasing meal, preceded maybe by a robust fish soup or a tian of scallops on courgettes and tomatoes. Mistakes, however, can make for irritation. It would be good to see a more radical renewal of approach to save it from getting tired. It should be better. The wine list is best for exclusives from Bergerac and Cahors and for its Jurançon. House French is £9.90.

CHEF: Alain Chapon PROPRIETOR: Rachel Bitton OPEN: all week, exc L Sat and Sun MEALS: 12 to 2.30, 7 to 11 PRICES: £19 (£30). Cover £1. Service 10% CARDS: Access, Amex, Visa SEATS: 80. 6 tables outside. Private parties: 20 and 38 private rooms. Children restricted. Smart dress preferred. Wheelchair access. Music

'When asked if we were going to have dinner I said, "Yes, presuming that it will be excellent." "No, it is crap" was the answer.' On eating in Northumberland

Dragon's Nest

map 14

58–60 Shaftesbury Avenue, W1V 7DE — COOKING 1*
071-437 3119 — COST £18–£34

The most controversial Chinese restaurant in London continues to thrill, infuriate and baffle reporters. At its best there are few places that can challenge its authentic Szechuan cooking; at its worst it can seem unfriendly and not feel all that different from other venues in Soho Chinatown. 'Even some dishes tasted on successive nights can be quite different,' observes a regular visitor. The menu, printed on parchment pages in a little book, reads well but recommendations are thin on the ground. Sesame prawn toast, kidneys in chilli sauce, Szechuan duck with pancakes and plum sauce, and General Tsang's chicken have been enjoyed. One reported dish was ruined by excessive oil ('it sizzled everywhere, covering the tables and ourselves'). Some say the service has improved. Others disagree: one party of 40 had only two waiters and overpriced drinks added insult to injury; 'the staff did not want to be bothered to serve us' is yet another gripe. House wine is £8.

CHEF: M. Chang PROPRIETOR: P. Lam OPEN: all week CLOSED: Christmas MEALS: 12 to 2.45, 5 to 11.15 PRICES: £16 (£28), Set L and D £11.50 (£18) to £15 (£22) Minimum £10. Service 10% CARDS: Access, Amex, Diners, Visa SEATS: 150. Private parties: 70 main room, 40 private room. Children's helpings on request. Music. Air-conditioned

Eagle

NEW ENTRY map 11

159 Farringdon Road, EC1R 3AL — COOKING 1*
071-837 1353 — COST £25

Now that Fleet Street is dead, you have to resort to places like this former pub, next to *The Guardian* offices, to observe journalists legless or at their leisure. They are the main thing to look at, in a barely decorated warehouse of a room; other attractions are spread on the long bar. The food is breathlessly new-wave Italian and Mediterranean; it is cheap, somewhat rough and ready, but intelligently bought and definitely enjoyable. It has transformed the Eagle from something few people wanted or needed into a major social service: one on every street, please. Chargrilling figures in the vegetables, the T-bone steak Catalan-style, sardines with new potatoes and green salad and so on through a longish list. There are invariably pasta, a hearty soup, and often spiced sausages with good lentils. Owner-occupation gives The Eagle commitment, although the menu can be left almost blank half-way through lunch because food has run out. Try to smile and wait. There are good coffee, good beer, and wines that change from day to day. House French is £7.80.

CHEF: David Eyre PROPRIETORS: Michael Belben and David Eyre OPEN: Mon to Fri CLOSED: bank hols, 3 weeks from 22 Dec MEALS: 12.30 to 2.30, 6.30 to 10.30 PRICES: £14 (£21) SEATS: 40. 4 tables outside. Vegetarian meals. Children's helpings. Wheelchair access (1 step). Music

Report forms are at the back of the book; write a letter if you prefer.

Efes Kebab House

map 13

80 Great Titchfield Street, W1P 7AF — COOKING 1
071-636 1953 — COST £19–£24

This is a place for celebrations; Efes II (175–177 Great Portland Street, W1N 5FD, 071-436 0600) throws in Turkish music and belly-dancing for good measure in the evenings. The mood of large parties, and cheerfulness short of plate-throwing, is rarely broken by surliness or grouch on the part of the waiting staff and is encouraged by the generous portions of skewered meats (the title Kebab House is taken fairly literally) cooked as main courses or the reasonable, if run-of-the-mill, list of first courses. There are good pitta, good baklava and good flavours to the meats. It is crowded and very busy, particularly around lunchtime. Beer from Ephesus and a handful of Turkish wines supplement the summary wine list. House Italian is £6.75.

CHEFS/PROPRIETORS: K. Akkus and I. Akbas OPEN: Mon to Sat MEALS: noon to 11.30 PRICES: £10 (£19), Set L and D £14 (£19) to £15 (£20). Cover 60p. Minimum £5 CARDS: Access, Amex, Visa SEATS: 150. Private parties: 70 main room. Vegetarian meals. Children welcome. Air-conditioned

Eleven Park Walk

map 12

11 Park Walk, SW10 0AJ — COOKING 1
071-352 3449 and 8249 — COST £31

Whoever came up with the design concept of tiled floor, cream walls, lots of green plants and mirrors for Italian restaurants should have patented the idea and made a fortune. Park Walk fits smartly into this look. It is a cheerful restaurant, offering good service ('almost too good when the restaurant is empty,' according to one reporter) and a menu that blends old favourites and up-and-coming new ones – prosciutto with melon, fried calamari, calf's liver with polenta, and duck with black cherries. Even regional dishes are safely familiar: osso buco, bollito misto. Pasta dishes are carefully prepared, and spaghetti with lobster has been recommended. The tiramisù should be tried, especially with a cup of the excellent espresso. The mainly Italian wine list is reasonable as far as it goes. House wine is £7.

CHEF: Giancarlo Moeri PROPRIETORS: F. Zanellato, S. Movio, S. Livesi and C. Pulze OPEN: Mon to Sat MEALS: 12.30 to 3, 7 to 12 PRICES: £17 (£26). Cover £1.50. Service 15% for parties of 6 or more CARDS: Access, Amex, Visa SEATS: 100. Private parties: 100 main room. Vegetarian meals. Children's helpings. Wheelchair access (1 step). Music. Air-conditioned. Fax: 071-351 6576

Emile's

map 10

144 Wandsworth Bridge Road, SW6 2UH — COOKING 1
071-736 2418 — COST £23

Emile's has the feel of a successful bistro in full flow. The cosy ground floor has low-voltage lighting; candles provide illumination in the basement with its quarry-tile floor and bare brickwork. A short table d'hôte chalked on a blackboard supplements the *carte*. This is up-market bistro cooking which continues to offer value for money. A reporter notes that 'the liver is fantastic, starters are interesting and desserts mouthwatering'. Deep-fried Camembert with cranberry sauce, red snapper with sweet pimento sauce and beef Wellington line up alongside fillet of pork with apricot and herb stuffing, and marinated breast of duckling with ginger sauce. Steaks and grills are also available. Sweets are the likes of vanilla parfait, and pumpkin and almond tart with mango purée, or there are unpasteurised French cheeses. The short wine list is dominated by France and mark-ups are low. House wine is £6.50. There is a second branch at 96 Felsham Road SW15 1DQ, Tel: 081-789 3323 serving similar food at the same prices.

CHEF: Andrew Sherlock PROPRIETORS: Emil Fahmy and Andrew Sherlock OPEN: Mon to Sat, D only CLOSED: 25 Dec, 1 Jan, bank hols MEALS: 7.30 to 11 PRICES: £13 (£19), Set D £12.75 (£19). Minimum £7.20 CARDS: Access, Visa SEATS: 60. 12 tables outside. Private parties: 42 private room. Vegetarian meals. Children welcome. Wheelchair access (1 step). Music

English Garden

NEW ENTRY map 12

10 Lincoln Street, SW3 2TS COOKING 2*
071-584 7272 COST £21–£44

Curtain manufacturers must love the English Garden and its colleagues within the small group owned by Malcolm Livingstone. Here the curtains bulk large and flowing in a converted Chelsea terrace house with a handsome conservatory room at the back. The *prix fixe* lunch receives many plaudits for value and quality. One reader thinks the food here is what he would like to get in a restaurant in Devon or Gloucestershire: it is probably better. The style is recognisably British without arch nostalgia or straining for modern effect. Hence there are dishes such as spinach and Stilton soup; spinach and goats' cheese mousse with sorrel sauce; saddle of hare with red cabbage and redcurrants; Dover sole with smoked salmon sauce; treacle and apple tart with brandy sauce and clotted cream; and pineapple, almond and ginger salad in a gin syrup. Vegetables get mixed references and not all the cooking is without short-cuts, but service is effective – even welcoming to single women – and the ambience pleasing.

CHEF: Brian Turner PROPRIETOR: Malcolm Livingstone OPEN: all week CLOSED: 25 and 26 Dec MEALS: 12.30 to 2.30 (12 to 2 Sun), 7.30 to 11.30 (7 to 10 Sun) PRICES: £25 (£37), Set L £14.75 (£21) CARDS: Access, Amex, Diners, Visa SEATS: 60. Private parties: 30 main room, 30 private room. Vegetarian meals. Children welcome. Jacket and tie. Music. Air-conditioned

Faulkner's

map 11

424–426 Kingsland Road, E8 4AT COOKING 1
071-254 6152 COST £17

Nothing changes at one of London's best fish and chip shops. The place is clean, bright and simple; Ella Fitzgerald's voice may croon out of the speakers, the tea is strong and – this is the heart of the matter – the fish is fresh. Supplies depend on the boats. Prices seem high compared to a street-corner chippie, but this is real quality. Portions are massive and the range may include halibut and salmon, as well as skate, cod and haddock (on- or off-the-bone). Children's portions of filleted fish are available at half price. One inspector's advice is: 'Don't deviate from fish and chips into the realms of soup, mushy peas and bread rolls.' There is a minimal whites-only wine list, otherwise bring your own.

CHEF: Michael Webber PROPRIETORS: John Faulkner and Mark Farrell OPEN: Mon to Sat CLOSED: bank hols, 1 week Christmas to New Year MEALS: 12 to 2, 5 (4.30 Fri) to 10 (11.30am to 10 Sat) PRICES: £9 (£14). Minimum £2.50 SEATS: 65. Children welcome. No-smoking area. Music. Air-conditioned

La Fin de la Chasse

map 11

176 Stoke Newington Church Street, N16 0JL
071-254 5975

COOKING 1
COST £21–£34

At the sign of the hanging fox changes have taken place: a new chef has been installed, lunch abandoned. 'We now produce all our own food,' writes owner Robbie Richards, 'from the bread rolls through to the ice-cream.' The long and thin terraced house stretches through to a back yard with tables for summer dining. The *carte* is brief with a briefer set-priced menu: duck à l'orange and beef in madeira sauce are fairly standard fare. Cooking is generally sound although uneven patches have been reported. One meal produced a good rack of lamb, pink and succulent, but was accompanied by a timbale of vegetables overpowered by the addition of too much smoked bacon. Grilled goats' cheese, herb-encrusted on fried croûtons, has been a good beginning, but asparagus and oyster soup was found lacking in flavour. Incidentals such as the bread and vegetables are excellent. Service can be slow and not very attentive. Desserts are well executed: poached pear with a champagne sabayon, a délice of dark and white chocolate, strawberry sablé with home-made shortbread biscuits. House wine is £7.50.

CHEF: Jack Dominiczak PROPRIETORS: Robbie and Carol Richards OPEN: Tue to Sat, D only CLOSED: 2 weeks Christmas MEALS: 7 to 10.30 PRICES: £19 (£28), Set D £14.50 (£21). Cover £1. Service 10%. Card slips closed CARDS: Access, Amex, Diners, Visa SEATS: 40. 5 tables outside. Private parties: 14 main room. Vegetarian meals. Children's helpings. No-smoking area. Wheelchair access (1 step). Music

First Floor

NEW ENTRY map 11

186 Portobello Road, W11 1LA
071-243 0072

COOKING 1*
COST £30

Mighty trendy, it is sited above the Colville Arms, reached through a side door, via a gravel-strewn hallway sprouting giant plants and classic urns. More ruins, in the guise of old columns, are found upstairs alongside a fun mixture of striplights, spotlights, a chandelier, old and new furniture and dried flowers. The dining-room benefits from lots of natural light and has an appropriate view on to the upper chamber of the Saints' Tattoo Parlour. The menu, modern to the last, continues this sort of wild eclecticism. Consistency, however, is a problem. Well-received items have been goats' cheese, aduki bean and mint strudel, the flavouring of chilli, rosemary and mint, 'an explosion – way out'; bruschetta with grilled sardines, yellow pepper relish and tomatoes that could have done with a bit more of everything; John Dory with green beans, dill aïoli and grilled courgettes, made with excellent fish; roast pheasant and saffron; pecan pie; and lemon cheesecake. Cocktails are knock-out, but one diner who ordered two at the same time discovered there was only one shaker. A short but OK wine list has house wine at £7.50. As the *Guide* went to press a daytime weekday café menu (8.30am to 4pm) was introduced.

CHEFS: Alex Young and Pip Wylie PROPRIETORS: Peter Cross and Simon Rose OPEN: all week CLOSED: 25 and 26 Dec MEALS: 8am to 4pm (12.30 to 3.30 Sat and Sun), 7.30pm to 12.30am (11.30pm Sun) PRICES: £16 (£25). Service 12.5% CARDS: Access, Visa SEATS: 55. Private parties: 60 main room, 14 and 40 private rooms. Vegetarian meals. Children welcome. No cigars/pipes in dining-room. Music. Fax: 071-221 8387

Florians

map 10

4 Topsfield Parade,
Middle Lane, N8 8RP
081-348 8348

COOKING 1
COST £10–£29

Polenta, balsamic vinegar, pulses, wild mushrooms and olive oil are key ingredients at this rustic Italian regional food restaurant. The front is a café/wine bar; upstairs is a white dining-room full of light from a glass/plastic roof. The menu changes every two months, but marinating and chargrilling feature strongly. Reporters have praised the mussels, salt cod with polenta, cold chargrilled aubergines, peppers and courgettes. Lamb fillet with roasted shallots and white beans is typical of the menu. Other dishes – for example the salads or a baked filo packet of fresh crab and rocket – are more personal than Italian. Snacks, pizze and Italian sandwiches are served from noon through the day. The short, heady list of Italian regional wines is backed up by an impressive collection of grappa and some good Italian beers. House Sicilian is £7.50. Although the food can fail, the place has the secret of popularity; it's fun to eat here.

CHEF: Jillian Onisto PROPRIETORS: Franco Papa and Arnie Onisto OPEN: all week CLOSED: bank hols MEALS: 12 to 3 (3.30 Sun), 7 to 11 (10.30 Sun) PRICES: £15 (£24), Set L and D £5.50 (£10). Minimum £10 in restaurant CARDS: Access, Visa SEATS: 70. 4 tables outside. Private parties: 35 main room, 18 and 35 private rooms. Vegetarian meals. Children's helpings on request. Music

▲ *Four Seasons, Inn on the Park*

map 13

Hamilton Place, Park Lane, W1A 1AZ
071-499 0888

COOKING 4*
COST £29–£61

'The best hotel dining-room I've eaten in' was the enthusiastic response from a young but seasoned London campaigner. Many would agree with him at the moment. 'Dishes are aptly balanced between lightness and richness; the many humbler ingredients – a trademark of Bruno Loubet, even more than other chefs – are a welcome presence, though never handled with less than sophistication.' The dining-room itself, though not the rest of the hotel, is also on the sophisticated side of vulgarity; the view on a spring night is quite fun, the tables are well-spaced (though some have found a few badly sited ones too near the kitchen) and the service is never less than affable. With few exceptions, the waiting staff come in for unusual plaudits. That talent exists in the kitchen is better evidenced by the long *carte* than by the excellent-value, though rarely adventurous, limited-choice lunch menu. Influences abound. From the garden come lemon balm and vervain as well as more common herbs; from the spice box emerge ideas such as scallops poached in milk infused with mild curry spices; and from the 'terroir', roast saddle of rabbit with sun-dried tomatoes and braised vegetables. That urge to make something out of home cooking also appears, as in oxtail on a macaroni gratin. Occasionally a meal can slip into monotony, as did one apparently dominated by aniseed in an over-tarragoned sauce with the rabbit, in a liquorice sauce with venison (found by others to be an outstanding and perfectly balanced dish) and in a dessert of figs with a confit of fennel and parfait of vervain. Sometimes, too, either attention wanders, as in a brochette of scallops with a caricature sweet-and-sour sauce, or over-elaboration sets in to no effect, for example, turned vegetables were inapposite in a supposedly gutsy dish of rabbit, and little purées of chickpea next to a terrine of salt pork and foie gras (often well-liked) were devoid of interest, perhaps put there for visual effect. The general rule, however, is first-rate flavours: in turnip ravioli filled with wild mushrooms on a veal jus, and in grand pickled girolles with three sorts of duck – rillettes, a spicy tartare and simple foie gras; or in a salad of poached scallops with turnips and carrots with a flavour of goose fat in the dressing and even in an amuse-gueule of new potato filled with brandade of cod, a smidgeon of caviare and a coulis of tomato. This is cooking of great sophistication, rarely letting down expectations. The sweets trolley has been got rid of, leaving only cheese to be trundled about – this is worth a pause, even if refrigeration had got the better of a Brillat-Savarin one night. Desserts are often outstanding, surpassed only by the petits fours glacés. Here again are the intense flavours, in a white chocolate mousse smothered in dark chocolate sauce, a gratin of raspberries given edge by a lime cream, and a passion-fruit crêpe soufflé with mangoes seasoned with pepper, soaked in anis. Taste combinations in the final stage are always interesting. There is good espresso, and breads are acceptable. The wine list may not be quite the dearest in town, but a Collards Yates Chardonnay comes at precisely double the price listed at another good West End restaurant. There is no doubting the quality of what is on offer, with a claret list as long and fine as anywhere, and very strong showings from California and Italy. Limited economic relief can be found in a page of good wines offered by the glass, but the normal channels for thrift are closed with the lowest-priced Alsace at £18.50, young petits châteaux for £20 and Sancerre £29. What a pity!

The Guide *always appreciates hearing about changes of chef or owner.*

Card slips closed *in the details at the end of an entry indicates that the totals on the slips of credit cards are closed when these are handed over for signature.*

CHEFS: Bruno Loubet and Eric de Blonde PROPRIETORS: Inn on the Park OPEN: all week MEALS: 12.30 to 3, 7 to 10.30 PRICES: £45 (£51), Set L £22.50 (£29), Set D £40 (£47). Net prices, card slips closed CARDS: Access, Amex, Carte Blanche, Diners, Visa SEATS: 62. Private parties: 10 main room. Car park, 85 places. No children under 5. Jacket and tie. No pipes in dining-room. Wheelchair access (also WC). Music. Air-conditioned. Fax: 071-499 5572 ACCOMMODATION: 228 rooms, all with bath/shower. Rooms for disabled. Lift. B&B £233 to £286. Children welcome. Baby facilities. Afternoon teas. Air-conditioned. TV. Phone. Scenic. Doors close at midnight

Frith's

map 14

14 Frith Street, W1V 5TS — COOKING 2*
071-439 3370 and 734 7535 — COST £35

Frith's elicits marked reactions pro and con. These are quite genuine and underline how erratic the performance may be. Carla Tomasi pursues a brand of super-eclecticism, and a desire to present strong flavours in counterpoint rather than haute cuisine harmony. This can result in unbalanced dishes as well as an apparent misapprehension of textures. On the other hand, it is also beyond doubt that the food can work. One visitor, unimpressed by the surroundings, was immediately converted by spring rolls filled with minced and spiced chicken, served with a paste of tomato, mozzarella and black olives 'crammed with insinuating Mediterranean flavours'. These were followed by pork and venison sausages with red cabbage and pears on the one hand, braised hare with roasted garlic and walnuts on the other. The hare 'had been hung to the point of near-decomposition; it was exquisitely edible, dense and moist.' Vegetables were mashed potato, Chinese leaves with soy, and French beans. Desserts came in the guise of apple and blackberry shortbread pie with a calvados parfait and a chocolate truffle cake layered with almond shortbread and flavoured with ginger on a caramel sauce. On this occasion, the cooking had ideas and was matched by the skill to execute them boldly. From even this short description, readers will glean that it is not food for the light appetite. A certain heaviness of texture is also evident. But many other successes have been recorded in a large repertoire: roast leeks with tapénade and herbed shallots; a lavish and delectable vegetarian antipasto; quail with polenta studded with nuts (nuts are often found at Frith's); and basil tagliolini with red chilli pesto. Service can be so modern that it angers and has been called supercilious. Others are happy to be able to laugh a lot and not to be frowned at. The wine list, like the menu 'apparently written in Sanskrit', would qualify for an award had it been sent to us. A fast-moving and intelligent selection of wines from Italy as well as other countries (except France) is consumer-friendly in pricing. Carla Tomasi objects to our having likened her food to that of Sydney or California. 'I thought I was serving contemporary English cooking in a modern London restaurant.' Therein lies a doctorate on cultural exchange.

CHEF/PROPRIETOR: Carla Tomasi OPEN: Mon to Sat, exc Sat L CLOSED: 25 Dec, 1 Jan, 5 days Easter, bank hols MEALS: 1 to 2.30, 7.30 to 11.15 PRICES: £18 (£29) CARDS: Access, Visa SEATS: 81. 5 tables outside. Private parties: 40 main room. Vegetarian meals. Children's helpings. No cigars/pipes in dining-room. Wheelchair access. No music. Air-conditioned

Fung Shing

map 14

15 Lisle Street, WC2H 7BE — COOKING 2*
071-437 1539 — COST £17–£40

Lisle Street is awash with garbage and you have to pick your way along the narrow pavement, exotic fruit beneath your feet. In the midst of this, Fung Shing presents a smartish appearance. 'This is our preferred Cantonese restaurant and we have tried many others' is a common refrain of those attracted by the consistent standards of the kitchen, and by the service ('they are noticeably better at admitting to understand English than many of their rivals'). The menu is extensive, with the most interesting dishes contained in the 'special' section, notably crispy fried intestine and sizzling eel. Recent praise for stewed duck with yams, served in a heavy cast-iron pot, singled out the huge quantity of tea-coloured duck, skin fairly well separated from the meat, and plenty of soft-cooked bone. There has been enthusiasm too for Szechuan prawns in a sauce 'which was virtually colourless and extremely pure-tasting', meat-stuffed aubergines and deep-fried baby squid. The value-for-money equation is well met. Downstairs is a better place to sit than up. Although Chinese wines add interest to a pricey wine list, Tsing Tao beer makes a cheaper alternative. House French is £8.

CHEF: Fu Kwun PROPRIETORS: Traceflow Ltd OPEN: all week MEALS: noon to 11.45 PRICES: £25 (£33), Set L and D £11.50 (£17) CARDS: Access, Amex, Diners, Visa SEATS: 85. Private parties: 50 main room, 30 private room. Vegetarian meals. Children welcome. Music. Air-conditioned

Ganpath

map 11

372 Grays Inn Road, WC1 8BB — COOKING 1
071-278 1938 — COST £8–£14

It has been speculated that there have been changes in personnel here. 'It must be because they've put up wallpaper. This is not one of the more elegant Indian restaurants.' The cooking can still be good, though a wandering expert put it far lower than Ragam (see entry) and lacking its earlier individuality. However, masala vada, masala dosa, chicken dhansak, prawn bhuna, sag bhaji and onion bhajias have been approved of, even if sag gosht and bean and coconut bhaji have not. Keep an eye on it. The staff remain endearing and helpful; the bills remain low.

CHEF: S. Rajah PROPRIETOR: R. Sivanantham OPEN: all week, exc Sun L CLOSED: 25 and 26 Dec, bank hols MEALS: 12 to 3, 6 to 12 PRICES: £6 (£12), Set L £4.95 (£8). Service 10% alc only CARDS: Access, Visa SEATS: 59. Private parties: 60 main room. Vegetarian meals. Children's helpings. No-smoking area. Wheelchair access. Music

Several sharp operators have tried to extort money from restaurateurs on the promise of an entry in a guide book that has never appeared. The Good Food Guide *makes no charge for inclusion and does not offer certificates of any kind.*

La Gaulette map 13

53 Cleveland Street, W1 5PQ COOKING 2
071-580 7608 and 323 4210 COST £26–£49

This is Sylvain Ho Wing Cheong's second, but more central, Mauritian fish restaurant (see entry for Chez Liline). The menu changes daily and seasonally according to what is available at Billingsgate market and from specialist suppliers. Red snapper, dorade, vacqua, parrot fish, bourgeois and capitain, not to mention the more familiar wild salmon, mussels, prawns and lobster, are cooked with combinations of ginger, chilli, coriander, garlic, saffron and soy. The style owes allegiance to South East Asia, but French colonial influences lift it out of Chinese cooking, giving the distinctive signature that the chef calls Mauritian. When shellfish is offered with sauce, it is sometimes a battle to remember which sauce you ordered. Special gastronomic meals are available for groups. Downstairs is a cheaper wine bar where some of the same dishes are available. Seating is cramped and some wines are dear. House French is £10.95.

CHEF: Sylvain Ho Wing Cheong PROPRIETORS: Mr and Mrs Sylvain Ho Wing Cheong OPEN: Mon to Sat, exc Sat L CLOSED: bank hol Mons MEALS: 12 to 3, 6.30 to 11 PRICES: £28 (£41), Set L £17.95 (£26). Minimum £13.95 CARDS: Access, Amex, Diners, Visa SEATS: 70. Private parties: 40 main room, 30 private room. Vegetarian meals. Children welcome. Music

Le Gavroche 🍷 map 13

43 Upper Brook Street, W1Y 1PF COOKING 5
071-408 0881 and 499 1826 COST £38–£90

In the space of a few years, Le Gavroche has taken on institutional status. Some suggest its very immobility is stagnation, if not decline; others defend trusty conservatism. The large basement is comfortable and spacious; its green and bamboo decoration might be described as mature. A small reception and bar on the ground floor is useful for waiting, but regulars are whisked through with fair velocity. The *carte* is long and French. You may listen to its recitation and translation by rote from table to table. Though the repertoire changes, the classics persist and the style remains firmly as it was. At lunch there is a cheaper set menu, and at dinner a longer and dearer *menu exceptionnel*. Half a dozen daily specialities are the final gilding and can often represent the most interesting choices. It is worth noting that the most common cause for complaint is the food cooked for the apparently bargain lunch; this holds true for other expensive and celebrated restaurants. Perhaps the shine has gone off this particular feature of restaurant life (the profit motive having reasserted itself) or, perhaps, it is a reflection on the sort of people who order such meals – critical private money, not company purses. There are several people who defend Le Gavroche's own offering: 'We have it two or three times a year and are always greeted warmly; we like to think the staff like people who spend their own money. It is always, for us, not so much a meal as an experience.' The innate conservatism of the kitchen has not resulted in a decline into gross richness – though some people now observe an excess of salt in the seasoning – and the fine balance between quantity and digestive impact seems to have been more accurate than in past years. Some have disputed the composition of set meals, for instance the placing of a roast lobster, accompanied by too salty a bisque of a sauce, between a first-course roulade of salmon trout and dill and a main dish of duck with mushrooms and truffle. An evening that showed the best qualities of the restaurant opened with a first course of *huîtres Francine*, one of the Gavroche classics, composed of warm oysters atop small ethereal salmon quenelles, with cucumber strands, diced tomato flesh and the lightest of butter sauces. The dish was accurate, a variety of fresh and delicately complex tastes and textures, and served admirably as a beginning. To follow was roast teal of fine flavour, nice presentation and exact cooking, served with a medley of root vegetables and wild mushrooms with a truffle and port sauce precisely measured in its intensity and sweetness. The medallion of foie gras adorning the plate was the single instance of overkill, perhaps there to help justify the cost of £28.70. The cheese, in fine condition, came on three trays, arranged by type. After that was the simplest of desserts: a jellied terrine/cake of orange and grapefruit with a simple champagne sauce was more refreshing than a sorbet and done better than most versions across England. The service is a major operation. One guest noted that it was difficult to maintain conversation, so frequent were the discreet interventions; some lightness might, he thought, be an advantage. Another maintained that the staff are human under that cool veneer, and that a little repartee soon brings it out. As the staff persist in leaving credit card slips open even though service is included, humanity is the least one might expect after efficiency. For the price, one's hope is also that the cooking is nearly without fault. Generally, misjudgement and catastrophe have not been frequent topics for comment; more often it is the very evenness of culinary tone that is compared unfavourably by some to those with more verve. The wine list provides matter for regular debate. One reader with long memory noted that a Latour '61 was £430 more expensive than that at the Inn on the Park (£510). Without doubt the prices are high – too high. The arrangement of the list also makes it very difficult to see those bottles that are less than, say, £20 – that is, affordable in Gavroche terms. There are a surprising number of these, but it will take 15 minutes' close attention to winkle them all out.

CHEFS: Albert Roux and Michel Roux Junior PROPRIETORS: Le Gavroche Ltd OPEN: Mon to Fri CLOSED: 23 Dec to 2 Jan MEALS: 12 to 2, 7 to 11 PRICES: £63 (£75), Set L £29.50 (£38), Set D £55 (£63). Minimum £50 D. Net prices CARDS: Access, Amex, Carte Blanche, Diners, Visa SEATS: 60. Private parties: 80 main room, 20 private room. Vegetarian meals. No children under 6. Jacket and tie. No cigars/pipes in dining-room. Air-conditioned. No music. Fax: 071-409 0939

Gavvers

map 12

61–63 Lower Sloane Street, SW1W 8DH
071-730 5983

COOKING 3
COST £18–£34

There has been something of a turn-round here, at the Roux brothers' Lower Sloane Street outpost, once the Gavroche, now a good restaurant offering a set-price, short menu of French cooking to packed houses. Value? Certainly. Enjoyable? According to most reports. Well served? 'A charming young staff, brilliant, unobtrusive, but nothing ever missed.' The substance to the plaudits is a *carte* of four or five choices supplemented by specials, headed 'Albert

[Roux] préfère' and 'Michel [Roux] adore', and three *plats du jour*. The range goes from fast – John Dory with sesame seeds and cucumber – to slow – cassoulet, choucroute, garbure – the accent wholly French, down to Poilâne bread with the garbure and the resolutely French staff: 'She wanted to talk to us about Normandy.' Dishes that receive special comment include duck rillettes with a leek sauce; a fine mousseline of foie gras; ravioli of fruits de mer; a daube of venison; duck with a caper and blackcurrant sauce; gratin of pears with ginger ('positively sexy'); and croûtade de pommes, sauce caramel ('my wife is still talking about the pastry'). Ancillaries are generous and properly executed. Places like this may go through cycles of achievement, even when the management concept behind them remains the same. This year has been a good one for Gavvers. The Roux brothers are inescapable, although absent in person, and even crop up on the wine list and on the label of the calvados bottle. The rest of the wines can bump up the bill substantially and that sense of value, so encouraging in the rest of the operation, may be best preserved by trying the house wines at £10.60.

CHEF: Bruno Valette PROPRIETORS: Roux Restaurants Ltd OPEN: Mon to Sat, exc Sat L CLOSED: bank hols MEALS: 12 to 2.30, 7 to 11 PRICES: Set L £12.50 (£18) to £14.75 (£20), Set D £22.65 (£28) to £27.95 inc wine (£27.95). Net prices. Card slips closed CARDS: Access, Amex, Diners, Visa SEATS: 60. Children welcome. Wheelchair access. Air-conditioned. No music. Fax: 071-622 5657

Gay Hussar

map 14

2 Greek Street, W1V 6NB
071-437 0973

COOKING 2
COST £22–£38

'My first visit since the change of ownership,' wrote a reader in January 1991, 'and I could detect no difference from formerly. Even the old waiter is the same one.' It is a self-proclaimed Hungarian restaurant, but the kitchen takes the whole of central Europe for its inspiration. There is a sameness about the menu but regulars know what they like. The soups can be recommended, especially the jellied borsch, as well as pancake stuffed with goulash and served with creamed spinach, chicken paprika, and pike with beetroot and cabbage. Portions are enormous – 'They still have the peasant attitude that if you have a lot it must be good.' However, this is not always the case. Veal goulash can be dull, roast duck has been known to be too dry and Serbian chicken too fatty. Few readers manage to get to the dessert stage ('we normally have fruit' is a common refrain), but poppy seed strudel and fruit pudding have been endorsed. One regular from the old regime complained that dumplings with plum sauce are no longer available. The Hungarian and other Eastern European wines continue to give best value. Once past the food, the real attraction of this place is the setting – old Soho in aspic, with a most interesting collection of customers. Sit downstairs if you can. House wine is £8.

CHEF: Laslo Holecz PROPRIETORS: Magyar Restaurant Ltd OPEN: Mon to Sat MEALS: 12.30 to 2.30, 5.30 to 11 PRICES: £20 (£32), Set L £15 (£22) CARD: Amex SEATS: 70. Private parties: 20 main room, 12 private room. Children's helpings L. Smart dress preferred. Wheelchair access. Air-conditioned. No music

Gilbert's 🍷

map 12

2 Exhibition Road, SW7 2HF — COOKING 2
071-589 8947 — COST £20–£35

A visit that provoked enjoyment also prompted the comment, 'a theme of simplicity and strong flavours'. This small, and none too comfortable, place in a row of shops between the V & A and South Kensington tube station boasts a fine wine list (also mobilising strong flavours) and cooking that borrows from the world, with leanings towards French provincial for main courses, England for desserts, and that strange Euro-American consensus for first courses. Julia Chalkley manages accuracy ('the halibut with a rich cider cream sauce was bolstered with crunchy carrots and celery and was just right') and pungency ('chicken *à notre façon*, boned thighs with herb encrusted skin in tasty, thick tomato and liver-based sauce'). The short menus – one for lunch, one for dinner, one super-economy lunch – change regularly though there are long-runners, for example the chicken already mentioned. Crab soufflé, potted rabbit with prunes, ragoût of beef with prunes and cinnamon, English puddings, including a Derbyshire gooseberry tart, or a sticky toffee, good, strong cafetière and simple, toothsome fudge get fair reports. Ann Wregg is enthusiastic and hospitable, in a place that might sometimes appear more at home in a small East Anglian town than South Ken. It suffers from the same slightly unpredictable performance of small provincial spots where turnover does not admit a brigade of reliefs or back-ups. A sensible range of half-bottles, a wide selection of dessert wines and spirits and two pages of 'Fine Wines' show wine-buying at its most intelligent. Europe and the rest of the world are dealt with even-handedly and arranged mainly under grape varieties. The robust Sancerre of Jean-Max Roger is lined up with Cloudy Bay Sauvignon, and under the Cabernets the always fine Ch. Hanteillan is teamed with the rich Hawk Crest, Napa Valley. Only top-quality, but not necessarily top-money, growers are admitted to this exemplary, compact and fair-priced list. House wines from Sicily are £8.90. CELLARMAN'S CHOICE: Cabernet Sauvignon 1983, Jean Léon, £16.50; Washington State Salishan Chardonnay 1987, £18.75.

CHEFS: Julia Chalkley and Sue Breen PROPRIETORS: Julia Chalkley and Ann Wregg
OPEN: Mon to Sat, exc Sat L MEALS: 12.30 to 2, 7 (6 by arrangement during Proms) to 10.15 PRICES: Set L £13.50 (£20) to £16.50 (£23), Set D £18.50 (£25) to £21.50 (£29)
CARDS: Access, Amex, Visa SEATS: 32. 2 tables outside. Children welcome. Wheelchair access (2 steps). Air-conditioned. No music

Gopal's of Soho

map 14

12 Bateman Street, W1V 5TD — COOKING 2
071-434 1621 and 0840 — COST £16–£30

'Still the best of the nouvelle Indian restaurants in the West End' is a view held about this classy little Soho restaurant. The menu is distinctive, with some unfamiliar dish names and descriptions. As a result, newcomers often settle for the excellent thalis: the vegetarian version has been rated highly as 'a fine selection for a non-vegetarian restaurant'. Sometimes dishes do not match expectations – Goa murg, advertised as 'cooked in a hot sauce with coconut and rare spices' was actually timid. Even so, the kitchen usually delivers freshly flavoured, deeply spiced dishes and the menu has some unusual specialities including king prawns cooked with spring onions; achar gosht (hot lamb cooked in pickle masala); mutton Xacutti with coconut and vinegar; and steamed chicken cooked in a sealed pot with Hyderabadi herbs and spices. Baingan masala is an excellent vegetable dish and buttery pilau rice is fragrant with cumin seeds. The wine list, put together in consultation with David Wolfe, is worth pursuing; otherwise drink Kingfisher beer. House French is £6.95.

CHEF: N.P. Pittal PROPRIETORS: N.P. Pittal and Christine Mathias OPEN: all week CLOSED: 25 and 26 Dec MEALS: 12 to 3.15, 6 to 11.45 PRICES: £17 (£25), Set L and D £9.50 (£16) to £10.50 (£18). Cover £1 CARDS: Access, Amex, Diners, Visa SEATS: 48. Private parties: 50 main room. Vegetarian meals. Children's helpings. Wheelchair access (1 step). Music. Air-conditioned

Grahame's Seafare

map 13

38 Poland Street, W1V 3DA
071-437 3788 and 0975

COOKING 1
COST £29

Atmosphere alone makes this kosher fish restaurant worth a visit, especially for lunch, when it is advisable to book. 'One of the few restaurants where one can eat alone without the protection of a book,' according to one reporter, 'because watching and overhearing those on other tables is so entertaining. The mixture of ketchup, motherly waitresses and Muscadet is perfect for those with a taste for the bizarre.' Salmon, sole, halibut, plaice or haddock – fried in oil or grilled and steamed, or cooked in butter or milk on request (at a small extra charge) and served in enormous portions with nicely cut chips – are equal to the surroundings. Half a dozen sauced dishes, mainly of sole, complement the range. On an otherwise dull dessert menu, the apple strudel is judged to be better than the cheese blintzes. There is lemon tea but there are also half a dozen low-priced white wines, some in half-bottles, from £6.50.

PROPRIETOR: Chetin Ismet OPEN: Mon to Sat CLOSED: bank hols, Jewish New Year MEALS: 12 to 2.45, 5.30 to 9 (8 Fri and Sat) PRICES: £16 (£24). Card slips closed CARDS: Access, Amex, Visa SEATS: 86. Children's helpings. Wheelchair access (also WC). No music. Air-conditioned

Great Nepalese

map 11

48 Eversholt Street, NW1 1DA
071-388 6737

COOKING 1*
COST £15–£23

Last year's improved rating was perhaps too ambitious, creating expectations that the kitchen was unable to match. Even so, this cheerful restaurant 'continues to deliver the goods'. Gopal Manandhar's two sons now help in running the place, and the dining-room has been spruced up with new carpets and hand-carved Nepalese wood panels. Little else changes. The kitchen's output is full-flavoured, pungent at times, but always vividly spiced. High points are the Nepalese specialities: masco bara (deep-fried, black lentil pancakes), bhutuwa chicken, toriko sag and coriander pickle. Chicken tikka, mutton dhal and chicken masala are more distinctive than the usual curry-house offerings. The range of vegetables and pulses means that this is a promising venue for vegetarians. Boiled basmati rice is invariably good, and breads are fresh. The setting is useful for north London locals and commuters: 'It's a nice place to eat before taking the night-sleeper from Euston,' said one traveller. Drink lager or lassi; finish off with spiced tea or a shot of devastating Nepalese Coronation rum. House Italian is £5.75 a litre.

CHEF: Ishad Ali PROPRIETOR: Gopal Manandhar OPEN: all week CLOSED: 25 and 26 Dec MEALS: 12 to 2.45, 6 to 11.45 PRICES: £12 (£19), Set L and D £9.75 (£15). Minimum £5. Service 10%. Card slips closed CARDS: Access, Amex, Carte Blanche, Diners, Visa SEATS: 48. Private parties: 34 main room. Vegetarian meals. Children's helpings. Music

Greenhouse **NEW ENTRY** map 13

27A Hay's Mews, W1X 7RJ COOKING 4
071-499 3331 COST £38

'British food at its best. No mucking around of ingredients, just good quality, exact technique and a great chef. This is the first time I have eaten Gary Rhodes' food and I will return at the earliest opportunity. Forget the rather clubby, stiff atmosphere (only three women there one full lunchtime session) and the unexciting wine list, but go for the excellent food at more than fair prices.' Thus enthused one report. David Levin's restaurant, beneath a block of flats in a mews, is a greenhouse only in name, decorative splurge at the entrance and horticultural pictures on the walls, otherwise, there's a deliberately downbeat demeanour to the whole room. Conceived years ago as a place for good-value food – older readers may recall rack of lamb and ratatouille – it lost direction to some extent, but its new incarnation is as straight as a die. The menu is long and changes little from month to month. Cheap prices are bumped up by a cover charge and stiff vegetable costs, but faggots or fishcakes for £6.50 can hardly be dear in the heart of Mayfair. There are elements of other people's fashions in dishes such as carpaccio; vegetable broth with pasta, beans, tomatoes and basil; and red mullet with pasta and pesto, but British does seem best here. Examples include poached egg with sautéed potatoes, and black pudding, bacon and saladings; cod with parsley and lemon butter sauce; herrings with mustard sauce; boiled bacon and split peas; calf's liver with mash and onion gravy; plus a galaxy of *echt* British puddings, including a bread-and-butter version 'with cream/milk ratio of four to one'. Forget the concept and consider the taste: 'Braised oxtail came on a clear soup/sauce in a deep dish. It smelled sensational. The oxtail was covered with tiny pieces of carrot, courgettes, shallots and chives, its taste was perfect – just the correct richness, excellent quality of execution. My lips stuck together willingly from the richness of the meat – wonderful! Seasoning was exact, the tail was tender; the consommé was a nice foil to the near-overwhelming succulence of the meat.' An apple and almond tart was similarly acclaimed: 'sensational crisp pastry', 'flavourful apple sorbet', 'light and balancing sauce' – only the apples were too hard and lacking ripeness or savour. Service comes with a smile, even if the occasional roll is dropped. One reader was impressed by a willingness to compose a four-course meal and reduce quantities and price to fit the digestion – co-operation of a high order for a place so busy. Forget the wine list (at least it's cheap), but don't forget to order the fishcakes. House wines are £10.50 and there's Arkell's bitter.

CHEF: Gary Rhodes PROPRIETOR: David Levin OPEN: all week, exc Sat L and Sun D MEALS: 12 to 2.30, 7 to 11 PRICES: £20 (£32). Cover £1. Card slips closed CARDS: Access, Visa SEATS: 100. Private parties: 120 main room. Vegetarian meals. Children's helpings. Smart dress preferred. Wheelchair access (3 steps). No music. Air-conditioned. Fax: 071-225 0011

Gurkha Brasserie

NEW ENTRY map 10

756 Finchley Road,
Temple Fortune, NW11 7TH COOKING 1
081-458 6163 COST £8–£19

The sign outside says 'Indian and Nepalese cuisine', which sums up the intentions of this informal restaurant. Inside, the box-like dining-room has its share of prints of the Himalayas, photos of famous Gurkhas, and hand-embroidered artefacts on the walls. The menu has a modest selection of authentic Nepalese specialities, and these are the most successful dishes. Momo (steamed meat dumplings served with a garlicky tomato sauce), aloo ko acher (a cold dish of potatoes with spices, fresh coriander and ground cashews) and chow-chow (noodle soup with prawns) have been intriguing. Other more familiar Indian dishes such as tandoori chicken, fish masala and karahi lamb have been unremarkable. To finish there is kulfi or Nepalese sikarni. Service is friendly and the value for money is exceptional. Drink lager or lassi. House wine is £5.65.

CHEF/PROPRIETOR: Hari Kc OPEN: all week MEALS: 12 to 2, 6 to 12 (12.30am Fri and Sat) PRICES: £8 (£16), Set L £4.50 (£8), Set D £8.50 (£12). Service 10%. Card slips closed CARDS: Access, Amex, Visa SEATS: 32. Private parties: 35 main room, 35 private room. Vegetarian meals. Children's helpings. Music

Haandi

NEW ENTRY map 11

161 Drummond Street, NW1 2PB COOKING 1
071-383 4557 COST £10–£24

This most recent Indian arrival in Drummond Street, almost opposite Laurence Corner, is not exclusively vegetarian, and provides a useful alternative to the bhel poori tendency. Inside, black-framed windows, high-backed chairs and a tiled floor give an almost Japanese feel. The plain walls are discreetly hung with a few prints and the menu is varied, tipping its hat to the Gujarati tradition with dahi vada, ragara pattis (shallow-fried stuffed potato cakes), vegetable pakoras and a vegetarian thali. But the thrust is firmly carnivorous: tandooris, tikkas, Goan fish curry, murgh makhani and lamb pasanda all feature. Recommended dishes have included potato bonda (served with home-made fresh tomato and chilli sauce on request), chicken jeera spiked with cumin, brinjal bhaji and fresh-tasting pilau rice. Breads are up to the mark. Ingredients are fresh, spicing is distinctive. At lunchtime there is an excellent buffet notable for its range of vegetable dishes and pulses as well as a dazzling array of interesting pickles and chutneys. More reports, please.

CHEFS: Noor Mohammad and Mr Salim PROPRIETOR: Mr Nasir OPEN: all week CLOSED: 25 Dec MEALS: 12 to 2.30, 6 to 11.30 (12 Fri and Sat) PRICES: £9 (£17), Set L £5.50 (£10), Set D £9.75 (£15) to £14.25 (£20). Service 10% alc only. Card slips closed CARDS: Access, Amex, Diners, Visa SEATS: 50. Private parties: 50 main room. Vegetarian meals. Children welcome. Wheelchair access. Music

Harveys

map 10

2 Bellevue Road, SW17 7EG COOKING 4
081-672 0114 and 0115 COST £39–£76

'His cooking is superb. Escabèche of red mullet a dream of flavours mingling through perfectly trimmed fillets; terrine of langoustines very fresh, exactly constructed and a good tang of coriander; navarin of lamb, tapénade of lamb both composed with thought, neither over-garnished nor messed about; brilliant tarte Tatin of pears with the right amount of caramelly toffee soaking into delicious short pastry. Clos du Papillon (Savennières) at £16 was fairly priced.' Thus reported one seasoned diner of a lunch at Harveys. By day or night it is a pleasant room to eat in: simple in shape, done out in a restrained version of a Busby Berkeley filmset, with no heavy colours or oppressive detail. All seems steady in the kitchen. Reports concentrate on what have become classics of the repertoire: panaché of scallops, foie gras and ginger with Sauternes sauce; the tagliatelle of oysters; Bresse pigeon en crepinette with a thyme jus; or the lamb fillet with calf's kidneys and a tarragon jus. New and less familiar dishes appear, however, especially at lunch. This year very warm accounts have been had of ragoût of shellfish with leeks and truffles; an assiette of pork with spices, the meat from the pig's head, cooked with honey and ginger; and sea bass with caviare stuffing to name but three. Lightness is a feature of these dishes and much of the kitchen's output, flavours not being deadened through a burden of cream or butter, nor generally overseasoned with salt or coarsened by over-reduction. Nor are quantities outfacing. On the other hand, the use of spices is becoming more marked, recognition perhaps of the need for progress and experiment. Sweet dishes, by contrast with earlier courses, seem almost over-generous but get consistent plaudits: the pyramid of caramel hiding a mango sorbet on a praline ice-cream with a passion-fruit coulis; poached pear with pistachio cream; admirable lemon tart; chocolate soufflé; prune soufflé with armagnac; and feuilleté of strawberries. A man who ate his way through the menu, with a couple of guests, over two evenings, felt strongly that the fish cookery here was superior to the meat. His opinion has been echoed by less broad-brush sampling. There is an inconsistency about the running of the restaurant that sits ill with the generally steady performance of the kitchen. The service seems to suffer from mild indifference at times, yet is super-efficient at others. Thus, one party, half of whom turned up 20 minutes late, were peremptorily refused a table, while another was given an excellent vegetarian menu after prior negotiation. Similarly, while some praise the sommelier, others have had difficulty in pouring their own wine. 'Service is unsure and even nervous, so that the atmosphere is far from relaxing' was one verdict, echoed several times though certainly not invariably. The wine list is long and predominantly French, mark-ups can shock, but prices start at about £15. The kitchen may be quieter than it was, but the cult of personality lives here. Take the mood portrait of Marco Pierre White on the back of the menu echoing many such pictures in the press this year: should this influence what we choose?

CHEF/PROPRIETOR: Marco Pierre White OPEN: Mon to Sat MEALS: 12.30 to 2, 7.30 to 11.15 PRICES: Set L £24 (£39), Set D £46 (£63) CARDS: Access, Visa SEATS: 45. No children under 16. No pipes in dining-room. Air-conditioned

Hiders

map 10

755 Fulham Road, SW6 5UU
071-736 2331

COOKING 2
COST £19–£34

Rumours about imminent closure were completely unfounded – as one *Guide* reader noted: 'Darling, everyone who was anyone in Chelsea was there, as well as one M'Lord. There was much kissing of cheeks.' The food remains consistently good, although there have been grumbles about the increase in prices. Menus are a mix of classic European favourites, with a sprinkling of in-vogue ideas. Rack of lamb with a herb crust, salmon Stroganoff and calf's liver with sage share the bill with timbale of avocado mousse and horseradish, and veal sweetbreads coated in sesame seeds on a bed of taglioni with ginger sauce. Sweets are in similar style: crème brûlée, bitter chocolate charlotte with caramelised oranges, a trio of sorbets in a tulip basket set on a fruit coulis. A basic, undetailed wine list is written down one side of the menu. House French is £7.95.

CHEFS: Paul Duvall and Andrew George PROPRIETORS: Richard and Hilary Griggs OPEN: Mon to Sat, exc Sat L CLOSED: 1 week Christmas, bank hols MEALS: 12.30 to 2.30, 7.30 to 11.30 PRICES: £21 (£28), Set L and D from £12.95 (£19) to £14.95 (£21). Service 12.5% CARDS: Access, Visa SEATS: 60. Private parties: 50 main room, 50 private room. Children welcome. No pipes in dining-room. Wheelchair access. No music. Air-conditioned

Hilaire 🍷

map 12

68 Old Brompton Road, SW7 3LR
071-584 8993

COOKING 3
COST £27–£52

A pair of bow-fronted windows gives a fine view into this apparently small restaurant, and of the food being consumed by window-table diners. But appearances can be deceptive and those without a booking can find the charmingly diminutive place surprisingly enlarged as they are shown to the downstairs dining-room and to a table in a slightly cramped cubby-hole under the street. Bryan Webb's cooking is modern, offering an assortment of Mediterranean flavours interspersed with some classic ideas: minestrone with pesto; escabèche of red mullet with aubergine purée; fillet of lamb tapénade; roast turbot with potato purée and extra-virgin olive oil; osso buco with gremolata and risotto. Readers have enjoyed baked artichoke with goats' cheese, potato pancakes with foie gras; roast duck with cider, apples and celeriac chips; and brochette of monkfish, scallops and pancetta. A trio of chocolates at dessert stage has also been heavily endorsed. The daily menu offers a reasonable set-price lunch but prices climb alarmingly for the evening *carte*. Generous portions go some way to alleviate the high cost. Bread is interestingly varied. Service can be slow; one reader complained of a 40-minute wait for the first course, with only 12 for lunch and four staff serving. A catholic 'house selection' makes an encouraging start to the wine list and includes Bruno Paillard champagne at a fairly modest £28.50. Generally there is little concession to economy, although the selection is excellent throughout. Arrangements by wine style rather than country can throw up intriguing comparison; but here, rather unhelpfully, there is often no attempt to put wines into price order, which would be the only intelligent way to provide a hierarchy and thus aid choice. Prices are actually not at all bad, given the location, but they start from a rather high level. House wines are from £13.15. CELLARMAN'S CHOICE: California, Edna Valley Chardonnay 1988, £23; St Estèphe, Ch. Le Crock 1986, £19.85.

CHEF/PROPRIETOR: Bryan Webb OPEN: Mon to Sat MEALS: 12.30 to 2.30, 7 to 11.30
PRICES: £32 (£43), Set L £16.95 (£28) to £20.90 (£33), Set D £15.50 (£27) to £19.45 (£31)
CARDS: Access, Amex, Diners, Visa SEATS: 40. Private parties: 8 main room, 25 private room. Vegetarian meals. Children's helpings. No music. Air-conditioned

L'Hippocampe

NEW ENTRY map 14

63 Frith Street, W1V 5TA — COOKING 3
071-734 4545 — COST £24–£43

As the name and sassy piscine decoration – avoiding the heavy tastelessness of fishnets, lobster pots and aquaria – might lead you to expect, this is a fish restaurant. Tim Hughes is a chef turned fish cook, his previous track record – including Harveys (see entry), Snaffles, briefly, and Mortons House Hotel – giving hope of great things. This hope is often satisfied, as in a meal that included crab and potato pancake ('incredibly tender, with no hint of stodge'); baked scallops in the shell with a puff pastry lid and a Sauternes sauce; monkfish with tomato and tarragon ('sweetly fresh, with gentle aniseed flavour to the sauce'); and John Dory with shellfish ravioli and a langoustine sauce ('big gleaming flakes, and a sauce that was not over-reduced but left to sing its own flavours. As good an haute cuisine fish dish as I have had in recent years,' enthused the reporter). Other testimony bears this out. The contrary view does not impugn the skills of the chef, but reflects the difficulty of ensuring perfect materials in the face of fluctuating business. Other minus points have been the vegetables, a serious organisational failure, and desserts that are without lustre, but with very decent pastry. Meat is sometimes served, for instance, as an alternative main course on the absolutely bargain table d'hôte daily menu (also available in the evening if supplies last). L'Hippocampe is the sort of restaurant that needs encouragement – difficult to imagine when London is filled with such dross, apparently making money hand over fist. A predictable emphasis on whites is handled intelligently in the wine list. From decent Muscadet and Delegat's Sauvignon, the list goes through a gentle price gradient, taking in dry Jurançon at £15.60 and Montagny at £17.50; even the heights are priced modestly for W1, with Chardonnay Au Bon Climat at £25.15. Half-bottles are sparse. House wine is £8.50.

CHEF: Tim Hughes PROPRIETORS: Pierre and Kathleen Condou OPEN: Mon to Sat, exc Sat L CLOSED: 25 Dec to New Year, bank hols MEALS: 12.15 to 2.30, 6.15 to 11.15 PRICES: £27 (£36), Set L (and D if supplies last) £16 (£24) to £17.50 (£26) CARDS: Access, Amex, Visa SEATS: 40. Private parties: 15 main room. Children's helpings. No cigars/ pipes in dining-room. Wheelchair access. Music. Air-conditioned. Fax: 071-287 1027

Ikkyu

map 13

67 Tottenham Court Road, W1P 9PA
071 436-6169 and 636 9280

COOKING 2
COST £11–£26

The entrance – a couple of doors from Goodge Street tube station – hardly suggests a restaurant at all, but this 'cheap and cheerful' basement serves some of the most robust and best-value Japanese food in the West End. The pace can be hectic, particularly at lunchtime, when crowds pack in for set meals centring on sashimi, grilled fish, deep-fried dishes and teriyaki. In the evening the kitchen delivers something close to Japanese home cooking with wholesome hotpots, noodles and soups sharing the stage with sushi on the chaotically handwritten menu. Reporters have mentioned perfectly grilled fresh salmon, shrimp croquettes, squid with okra yakitori, and fried pork with slender green Japanese leeks. The menu also takes in rolled conger in seaweed, five-coloured fermented soya beans, boiled tofu with oyster hotpot, and rice with pickled plums in soup. Some find that the hustle and bustle is part of the attraction of the place; others complain about the disorganised service and severe language difficulties between staff and customers. Green tea is free, otherwise drink saké or Kirin beer.

CHEF: Y. Sato PROPRIETOR: M. Kawaguchi OPEN: Mon to Fri, and Sun D MEALS: 12.30 to 2.30, 6 to 10.30 PRICES: £16 (£22), Set L and D £6 (£11) to £7 (£13). Service 10% CARDS: Access, Amex, Diners, Visa SEATS: 65. Private parties: 30 main room, 12 private room. Vegetarian meals. Children welcome. Music. Air-conditioned

L'Incontro 🍷

map 12

87 Pimlico Road, SW1W 8PH
071-730 6327

COOKING 2
COST £25–£50

The style of this place seems undimmed, notwithstanding successive waves of designer-consciousness that have swept over London. The cooking, too, appears to stick to the same rather uneven course, though is more likely to satisfy than that of the sister restaurant, Santini. Perhaps 'the architect is more important than the chef' – a heretical view espoused by one of the high-profile restaurant designers this year – has some ludicrous truth at the bottom of it. The cooking has some of north-eastern Italy to it and fish, shellfish and polenta – and not a little pasta – are well in evidence. Shellfish seems better than white fish, liver better than many of the meat choices. Go for the style, the wine and be prepared to pay. It would be difficult to better L'Incontro for a sampling of Italian wines. The top names, Mascarello and Maculan, Conterno and Capezzana are here, older wines can be had for a price but many more modest wines are also on offer at around £12. A few French and Californian creep in. Half-bottles are noted by their virtual absence and the poor-sighted may have difficulty discerning this closely written list. House wine is £12.50. CELLARMAN'S CHOICE: Gavi Castello di Tassarolo 1989, £18.50; Venegazzù della Casa 1986, £19.50.

CHEFS: D. Minuzzo and I. Santin PROPRIETOR: G. Santin OPEN: all week MEALS: 12.30 to 2.30 (1 to 3.30 Sun), 7 to 11.30 (10.30 Sun) PRICES: £28 (£42), Set L £14.50 (£25). Cover £1.50. Service 12% alc only CARDS: Access, Amex, Diners, Visa SEATS: 65. Private parties: 30 private room. Vegetarian meals. Children's helpings. Wheelchair access. Music. Air-conditioned. Fax: 071-730 5062

Isohama

NEW ENTRY map 11

312 Vauxhall Bridge Road, SW1V 1AA — COOKING 1
071-834 2145 — COST £14–£48

A plain oblong room is divided by black wooden screens, with unexpected deep purple upholstery taking the austerity off the whole. Good, plain Japanese cooking with business-like but polite service gets most people through lunch at a happy canter. The longer menu is reserved for the evening, when the restaurant is felicitously placed for Victoria's theatres. Jellyfish in vinegar with cucumber strips and spinach is outstanding, salmon roe and vinegar rice are fresh and reviving and noodles are acceptable.

CHEF: Yukio Saito PROPRIETORS: Senko (UK) Ltd OPEN: Mon to Sat, exc Sat L MEALS: 12 to 2.30, 6 to 10.30 PRICES: £19 (£32), Set L £6.50 (£14) to £18 (£27), Set D £23 (£32) to £30 (£40). Service 10%. Card slips closed CARDS: Access, Amex, Diners, Visa SEATS: 35. Vegetarian meals. Children's helpings. Wheelchair access (1 step). No music. Air-conditioned

Ivy

map 14

1 West Street, WC2H 9NE — COOKING 2*
071-836 4751 — COST £44

'It's a good alternative to the Garrick Club' is unanswerable if you're not a member, but the remark captures two secrets of the Ivy's resounding success: famous people are seen there – stagey ones too – and the food is conservative. The linkage with the Caprice (see entry) is evident from some of the dishes and the owners' great skill in serving a discriminating market so well they seem to have it eating out of their hands. You might be entering a church when you push the door into the bar, but all thoughts of reverence may be banished in the pleasant, but not exactly cheerfully designed, restaurant. Some tables are better sited than others. The staff, a positive brigade, are well-trained and capable of rapid delivery and regular checking for lacks of bread and incidentals. The cooking should be good: the repertoire is simple and capable of endless repetition. After two hundred covers, perhaps the repetition gets too much for the Ivy, but the general opinion is one of satisfaction with salmon fishcakes, bubble and squeak, grilled lamb, tuna with tomato relish or even the simple pasta dish. Bang bang chicken is often enjoyed for its spiciness, even if carrot and coriander soup seemed to have its flavouring added as mere afterthought. Vegetables can mount up to a horrifying total, so order with forethought. Espresso is excellent; lemon tart, cold rice pudding (a mite solid) with prunes in armagnac and 'Coupe Caprice' of cinnamon ice-cream with fresh berries have pleased as desserts. The modern wine list is split between bottles under £20 and the conspicuous consumption specials. House wines are £7.

CHEFS: Nigel Davis and Nevil Wilkins PROPRIETORS: Jeremy King and Christopher Corbin OPEN: all week MEALS: 12 to 3, 5.30 to 12 PRICES: £26 (£37). Cover £1.50 CARDS: Access, Amex, Diners, Visa SEATS: 110. Private parties: 8 main room, 20 and 80 private rooms. Vegetarian meals. No children under 5. Wheelchair access. Air-conditioned. No music. Fax: 071-497 3644

Jade Garden

map 14

15 Wardour Street, W1V 3HA — COOKING 2
071-437 5065 — COST £16–£34

'A hard-core Cantonese place in the heartland of old Soho,' writes a keen supporter of this reliable and popular restaurant. Local competition is fierce but the kitchen holds up well, feeding a large and enthusiastic congregation. The spacious ground-floor dining area is dominated by a curving staircase leading to a balcony. Affordable dim-sum and one-plate meals are praised: paper-wrapped king prawns, stuffed bean curd rolls, sesame prawn toasts and mixed seafood fried noodles have all been good. The main menu is wide-ranging and recommended dishes span the full repertoire: hot-and-sour soup; crispy duck with pancakes; sizzling chicken with black-bean sauce; fried prawns with pickled ginger and pineapple; steamed pork with plum sauce; fried shredded beef with chilli. Lo-hon vegetables and special fried rice are decent accompaniments. House wine is £7.50.

CHEF: Raymond Bignold PROPRIETORS: L.S. and P.W. Man OPEN: all week CLOSED: 25 and 26 Dec MEALS: noon (11.30am Sat and Sun) to 11.30 PRICES: £15 (£28), Set L and D £9.50 (£16) to £17 (£24) CARDS: Access, Amex, Visa SEATS: 160. Private parties: 70 main room, 70 private room. Children welcome. Wheelchair access (1 step). Air-conditioned

Jin

NEW ENTRY map 14

16 Bateman Street, W1V 5TB — COOKING 1*
071-734 0908 and 0856 — COST £13–£31

Eric Wee opened London's first Korean restaurant in 1976. Now, a generation later, his son Tony has set up in Soho. His dining-room looks elegant, austere, almost Japanese, with black wooden tables and high-backed chairs, and cream-painted walls adorned with modern Korean paintings. 'Jin' means 'authentic' and early reports suggest that the kitchen is living up to its name. The menu is wide-ranging, with the emphasis on salads, pickles, vegetables and barbecued specialities cooked on a grill set into each table. Appetisers such as kim-chee (pickled cabbage), oei namul (cucumber in a vinegar and chilli dressing) and cold spiced spinach with sesame seeds have all been of the highest quality. Yuk whe – the Korean version of steak tartare – is flavoured with sesame oil, sugar and Asiatic pear juice; kim is a delicacy of toasted salted seaweed; stir-fried squid and vegetables come with a fiery sweet chilli sauce. 'Cooked at the table' dishes include not only the famous bulgogi but also ox tongue, belly pork and marinated prawns. Slices of chicken are grilled, dipped in a hot chilli and saké sauce, and finished with lemon juice: the result is 'sensational'. There are good-value set lunches. It is worth trying Korean barley tea or saké. House French is £7.50.

CHEF: Mr Ro PROPRIETOR: Tony Wee OPEN: all week, exc Sun L CLOSED: 25 and 26 Dec, 1 Jan MEALS: 12 to 3, 6 to 11 PRICES: £13 (£24), Set L £7.90 (£13) to £19.50 (£26), Set D £15.50 (£22) to £19.50 (£26). Service 12.5%. Card slips closed CARDS: Access, Amex, Carte Blanche, Diners, Visa SEATS: 80. Private parties: 50 main room. Vegetarian meals. Children welcome. Wheelchair access (1 step). Music. Air-conditioned

Joe's Café

map 12

126 Draycott Avenue, SW3 3AH
071-225 5269

COOKING 2
COST £31–£38

It certainly has style. Joseph Ettedgui's uncompromisingly modern café at fashionable Brompton Cross offers smart, if predictable, brasserie fare – ravioli of wild mushrooms, warm duck and rocket salad; escalope of salmon in sorrel sauce; steak pommes frites. It is also pricey. Reports praising the food give voice to a constant source of irritation provoked by a cover charge and 15 per cent service on top of maximum prices. Despite calling itself a café, it does not serve all-day food and it is disappointing to see only two half-bottles on the wine list. However, one reader reported requesting lunch at 3pm and 'was made to feel very welcome and served civilly'. There is a brunch menu. Reports have been much warmer this year; there seems to have been an improvement in both cooking and sense of hospitality. House wine is £10.80.

CHEF: Jerome Laugenie PROPRIETORS: Joseph Ltd OPEN: all week, exc Sun D CLOSED: 25 Dec and 1 Jan MEALS: 12 (11 Sun) to 3.30, 7.30 to 11.30 PRICES: L £19 (£31). D £20 (£32). Cover £1. Service 15%. Card slips closed CARDS: Access, Amex, Carte Blanche, Diners, Visa SEATS: 95. 2 tables outside. Private parties: 25 main room. Vegetarian meals. Children's helpings. Wheelchair access. Music. Air-conditioned

Kagura

NEW ENTRY map 10

356 Regent's Park Road, N3 2LJ
081-346 4846

COOKING 2*
COST £24–£70

This is a simple, elegant-looking place, part of the JA Centre, a few minutes' walk from Finchley Central tube station. It is done out in white, grey and black with clever use of alternating panels of dark mirror glass and mirror-polished metal. A small print adds one minute touch of colour. The repertoire is extensive, ranging from cheap snack lunches and bentou 'meal-boxes' to kaiseki banquets. The kitchen delivers food with finesse and the cooking is of a high order – sometimes delicate, sometimes with 'a distinct touch of earthiness'. Outstanding sashimi is presented on a wooden boat with a tray for dipping sauce on the 'fore-deck'. Salmon Oyako-Ae is a simple creation that must have inspired many Western versions of salmon tartare. Other fine dishes have included steamed and grilled eel with teriyaki sauce; sunomono (an appetiser of assorted fish and vegetables in vinegar sauce); crab meat with scrambled egg in wet rice; and fried tofu in a mustard-flavoured sauce. Soups such as miso and sansai soba with buckwheat noodles are well balanced and distinctive. Portions are generous and prices are very reasonable considering the quality of the food. Drink tea, saké or Japanese beer.

CHEF: Mr Shirahi PROPRIETORS: JA Centre OPEN: Sat and Sun L, Tue to Sun D MEALS: 11 to 2, 6 to 10 PRICES: £18 (£32), Set L £15 (£24) to £25 (£35), Set D £15 (£24) to £45 (£58). Service 12.5% CARDS: Access, Amex, Diner, Visa SEATS: 30. Vegetarian meals. Music. Air-conditioned

Kalamaras

map 11

76–78 Inverness Mews, W2 3JQ
071-727 9122

COOKING 2
COST £23

A dark, but never dismal, basement in a mews off Inverness Place. The simpler (unlicensed) Micro-Kalamaras (at number 66) is but a step away if the crowds press too close. This is popular eating, for its reasonable cost, cheerful flavours and range of Greek dishes (wider than many proto-Greek places in the capital). The menu is in Greek, a translation and explanation is offered by the efficient and open-hearted staff but assimilation – especially as not every dish is hackneyed – is not easy: 'If you don't speak Greek, take a Greek.' The printed menu is supplemented by daily specials and these may well include homespun, slow-cooking recipes that are worth trying – kid makes an occasional appearance, for instance. Some recommendations have been fried aubergine with garlic dip; excellent olives; salt- and sun-dried anchovies, grilled then served with olive oil and lemon; and baby lamb with spinach and onions. There is decent Greek coffee and a short Greek wine list. The red Boutari has been 'fruity, well-balanced and full'. House wines are from £6.65.

CHEF/PROPRIETOR: Stelios Platonos OPEN: Mon to Sat, D only CLOSED: bank hols MEALS: 7 to 12 PRICES: £12 (£19). Cover £1. Service 10%. Card slips closed CARDS: Access, Amex, Diners, Visa SEATS: 96. Private parties: 16 and 28 private rooms. Vegetarian meals. Children's helpings. Wheelchair access. Music. Air-conditioned

Kastoori

NEW ENTRY map 10

188 Upper Tooting Road, SW17 7ER
081-767 7027

COOKING 1
COST £13–£22

Dinash and Kanchan Tanki offer creative Gujarati cooking in an unprepossessing location. The simple brown and white dining-room is curiously adorned with plaster mouldings of cherubs as well as flowers on walls and tables. There is a willingness to offer more than the familiar range of bhel pooris and dosas – although these are generally good versions – and the owners are eager to produce special, unlisted dishes on request. Interesting starters include a variant of onion bhajia made with cassava (mogo) and dahi poori (crisp wheatflour shells filled with chickpeas, potato and a sour sambal sauce). Vegetable curries have been praised and breads are a great strength. A speciality is chana bhatura (chickpea curry with fried bhatura bread). Poppadums come with a selection of vivid home-made pickles and chutneys. Dishes can vary greatly in quality, although this may simply be a sign of teething troubles. Fresh flavours, generous portions and good value bring in the crowds, so booking is essential. To drink there is excellent lassi and a 'fairly basic' choice of wines. House wine is £6.75.

CHEF: Dinash Tanki PROPRIETORS: Dinash and Kanchan Tanki OPEN: all week, exc L Mon and Tue CLOSED: 25 Dec MEALS: 12.30 to 3, 6 to 10.30 (11 Fri to Sun) PRICES: £7 (£13), Set L and D £7.25 (£12) to £11.95 (£18). Minimum £5 CARDS: Access, Visa SEATS: 76. Private parties: 40 main room. Vegetarian meals. Children welcome. Wheelchair access. Music

Kensington Place 🍷 map 11

201 Kensington Church Street, W8 7LX COOKING 3*
071-727 3184 COST £20–£37

'The cooking at this place really is excellent,' writes one contented reader. 'We have enjoyed so many different dishes that it is difficult to think of one or two that stand out above the rest: perhaps the goats' cheese and chicken mousse and the spiced lamb with couscous. The careful choice of vegetables to go with each dish is excellent; wonderful bread and olives too.' The easy way out of describing this restaurant is to rehearse conflicting views: it takes people differently. Some feel ill at ease with the giant windows giving on to Kensington Church Street and the large space within bouncing noise like a squash court. But most people are happy to be here, for the atmosphere is a good one, the service is laid-back but caring and efficient, and the food is inventive. That it is almost constantly full must indicate that it succeeds somewhere. The daily menu runs a wide gamut of styles and influences. There are plenty of neo-Italian crostini, risottos and the like, plenty of simple brasserie dishes like grilled calf's liver with a beurre rouge and black pudding and apple, but a strong line too in the classical repertoire: partridge with salt pork and cabbage, roast grouse, pheasant on a bed of spinach or, when available, quince. Desserts may take in tarte Tatin, crème brûlée, and lemon tart: pastry work is good. A compendium of a report written after weekly visits through the year praised dishes such as foie gras with sweetcorn pancakes, cuttlefish with a light tomato sauce, and braised duck with Seville orange, but went on to add that things may vary according to the intensity of business (tarte Tatin may come cold or luke-warm) and that the restaurant's scale may mean tastes lack the intensity of long work. The reporter finishes, 'Rowley Leigh is inventive, eclectic and intelligent and we can eat here without an overdraft or a coronary check-up.' Many endorse the reasonable cost for the standard of food produced. A straightforward and succinct wine list contains carefully selected and fairly priced bottles, albeit with some vintages that look a little recent. House wine is £7.95. CELLARMAN'S CHOICE: New Zealand Sauvignon 1990, Collards, £16.75; St Joseph 1985, de Boisseyt, £19.

CHEF: Rowley Leigh PROPRIETORS: Nick Smallwood and Simon Slater OPEN: all week MEALS: 12 to 3.30, 6.30 to 11.45 (10.15 Sun) PRICES: £21 (£31), Set L £12.50 (£20). Card slips closed CARDS: Access, Visa SEATS: 90. Private parties: 90 main room. Children's helpings. Music. Air-conditioned. Fax: 071-229 2025

▲ *This symbol means that accommodation is available.*

Khun Akorn

map 12

136 Brompton Road, SW3 1HY
071-225 2688

COOKING 1
COST £18–£38

Down below there is Le Café Pingouin, which seems to be attempting an East/West mélange, but the wiser course may be to stick to straight Thai on the ground floor (there is no obvious connection between the two places save the Siamese-twin entrance). Khun Akorn is on the luxurious side, in tone and price, though the cooking is not so radical a departure from the general run of London Thai places. The level of spicing is acceptable; materials are put into relief by some effort in display and ornamentation. A standard Thai repertoire is given variety by a number of specials created at the Imperial Hotel, Bangkok, such as stir-fried crab claws, grilled trout marinated with soy, and the rather worrying-sounding salmon with a pink curry sauce – Thai cooking meets Western luxury ingredients. Service is amiably deferential. House wines are £8.80 and £9.

CHEFS: Mr Boontavee and Mr Dusit PROPRIETOR: Khun Akorn OPEN: Mon to Sat CLOSED: 25 and 26 Dec, 1 Jan MEALS: 12 to 3, 6.30 to 11 PRICES: £23 (£32), Set L £11.50 (£18) CARDS: Access, Amex, Visa SEATS: 60. Private parties: 65 main room. Vegetarian meals. Children's helpings on request. Music. Air-conditioned. Fax: 071-225 2680

Lal Qila

map 13

117 Tottenham Court Road, W1P 9HL
071-387 4570

COOKING 2
COST £17–£41

Over the years this has proved itself to be the most dependable Indian new-wave restaurant in central London. The elegant, dimly lit dining-room has hardly changed since the early days and a long-serving team of waiters provide smooth service. Equally, the unchanging menu now looks almost old-fashioned. But the kitchen rarely falters: tikkas, tandooris and kebabs are some of the best of their kind in London – crisply charred on the outside, succulent within; the Maharaja mixed grill has been excellent; curries are distinguished by fresh complex spicing and raw materials are good. Lamb pasanda is made with thin slabs of pungent, tender meat; karahi murg uses full-flavoured chicken. Vegetables are distinctive. Little potatoes are cooked with fresh fenugreek and ginger, baigan masala is made with the pulp of aubergines, and soft spinach is cooked in butter. Fragrant fried basmati rice is rich but ungreasy and randomly tinged with saffron. Prices are steep, but the recently introduced weekday lunchtime buffet offers a good-value alternative. To drink there are cocktails, Kingfisher beer and lassi, as well as a modest selection of wines. House French is £7.50.

CHEF: Ayub Ali PROPRIETORS: Ayub Ali, Enamul Haque and A. Kalam OPEN: all week MEALS: 12 to 3, 6 to 11.30 PRICES: £12 (£23), Set L £10 (£17) to £15 (£23), Set D £15 (£22) to £25 (£34). Service 15% CARDS: Access, Amex, Diners, Visa SEATS: 80. Private parties: 40 main room. Vegetarian meals. Children's helpings. Smart dress preferred. Music. Air-conditioned

Langan's Brasserie

map 13

Stratton Street, W1X 5FD
071-493 6437

COOKING 2*
COST £42

Nearly every report about a meal here comments on how pleasant a place it is to go: 'still welcoming even though very busy', 'electric atmosphere', 'bustling, exciting and fun', 'made to feel welcome despite the size of the place', 'a jolly place, splendid people to look at', 'I sat next to a one-time politician turned TV presenter – you can't have things all your own way'. The service thus assured, even if on occasion it is slow, how about the food? Another constant in reports is that too often it is not hot: well-flavoured but not hot. The brasserie is enormous: two floors of restaurant, a large bar, people scurrying everywhere. The glitterati stay at ground level, but there are few complaints about the Venetian room above – nice decoration, nice waiters, a lot of smokers. The menu gives ample choice: good brasserie dishes, old English favourites, Langan's long-runners like the spinach soufflé with anchovy sauce. You are given ample veg, too, a rarity nowadays, and desserts are enjoyed – treacle tart and custard being top of the pops. Roast game, roast beef, seafood salad, baked egg on cabbage and bacon hash, steaks and chateaubriands, medallions of venison with red wine and mushroom are the things people write home about. They are cooked to a standard and that is lifted by the ambience and locale. The wine list is mainly French and not overpriced for the area, though hardly exciting.

CHEFS: Richard Shepherd, Dennis Mynott and Roy Smith PROPRIETORS: Michael Caine and Richard Shepherd OPEN: Mon to Sat, exc Sat L CLOSED: bank hols MEALS: 12.30 to 3, 7 to 11.45 (8 to 12.45 Sat) PRICES: £22 (£35). Cover £1. Service 12.5%. Card slips closed CARDS: Access, Amex, Diners, Visa SEATS: 200. Private parties: 12 main room. Vegetarian meals. Children's helpings. Wheelchair access (1 step). Music. Air-conditioned

Launceston Place 🍷

map 12

1A Launceston Place, W8 5RL
071-937 6912

COOKING 2*
COST £20–£37

'I feel I can leave my slippers here,' comments a regular who likes the fairly priced set menu available alongside the *carte*. Older sister of Kensington Place (see entry), Launceston Place has pursued neighbour-friendliness at the expense of street-fashion and keeps its tables as full as its sibling's (expansion into the premises next door is imminent). Not that the food ignores fashion: smoked eel, potato salad and chives; faggots and lentils; split-pea soup; salmon fishcakes; oxtail; and Sunday joints of roast beef are sufficient pointers to the revival of mother's pride cookery, while a vegetable strudel with yoghurt and coriander or aubergine mille-feuille with tomato and Parmesan will satisfy the moderns. The standard of cooking has been more even this year, enhancing the utility of any neighbourhood spot, and service copes effectively with a complex space and exigent customers. The wine list is the right length – neither too long nor too short – and offers a catholic choice from the New and Old Worlds that includes Bruno Paillard champagne, Ch. Caronne-Ste-Gemme, Gaston Hochar's Ch. Musar, Rossignol Changarnier from Burgundy and the excellent Quenard Chignin, to name but some from this side of the globe. House wines, from Loron and Ch. les Rousseaux, are £7.95 and £9.50 respectively.

CHEF: Charles Mumford PROPRIETORS: Nick Smallwood and Simon Slater OPEN: all week, exc Sat L and Sun D MEALS: 12.30 to 2.30, 7 to 11.30 PRICES: £22 (£31), Set L and D £12.50 (£20) to £14.95 (£23) CARDS: Access, Visa SEATS: 55. Private parties: 25 main room, 14 private room. Vegetarian meals. Children's helpings L. No pipes in dining-room. Wheelchair access. No music. Air-conditioned

Laurent

map 11

428 Finchley Road, NW2 2HY — COOKING 1
071-794 3603 — COST £22

'We had just seen a great movie about Morocco, and here we were, not exactly "en souk" but probably the nearest to it in England,' wrote one reporter. Visitors love the vibrant atmosphere and good value of Laurent Farrugia's no-nonsense restaurant. He watches vigilantly, but benevolently, from the kitchen door as proceedings unfold, and occasionally joins in the action. The menu is built around three versions of couscous – big wholesome platters which can be bolstered with extra portions of spicy merguez sausages. Fiery harissa sauce accompanies every order. To start, there is only brique à l'oeuf; to finish there is a choice of crème caramel, crêpes Suzettes, ice-creams and sorbets. The house white (£7) is French, but check out the gutsy Algerian or Moroccan reds.

CHEF/PROPRIETOR: Laurent Farrugia OPEN: Mon to Sat CLOSED: first 3 weeks Aug MEALS: 12 to 2, 6 to 10.30 PRICES: £12 (£18). Minimum £6 CARDS: Access, Visa SEATS: 36. Private parties: 50 main room. Vegetarian meals. Children's helpings. No music

Leith's

map 11

92 Kensington Park Road, W11 2PN — COOKING 3
071-229 4481 — COST £39–£61

A reader from the country likes Leith's for the 'cossetting' service, for the fact that the vegetarian menu is much cheaper – as well it might be – than the seasonal *carte* for meat- and fish-eaters (priced according to the number of courses) and because 'they still treat you like royalty if you turn up in torn jeans'. The restaurant may have the psychological confidence to take all-comers induced by long survival. The house and dining-room impress: a constellation of down-lighters on the ceiling, trompe-l'oeil windows on the walls, a sense of comfort and solidity only momentarily dispelled by chairs on castors that can disconcertingly magnify sudden leg movements of the unsuspecting diner. The *carte* is supplemented by trolleys, hors d'oeuvre and dessert; so happy are they to dispense their mobile fare, it may be easy to forget there is a kitchen. It is best to stick with it. Cooking can be accurate, timely and sensitive in dishes such as marinated scallops with coriander and ginger dressing, red pepper mousse with grilled vegetables, layered rabbit and spinach, and brill with champagne and chive sauce. Desserts are trolley-borne save one, perhaps a hot soufflé or a cream tart – peach in the spring menu. As befits a place of this established character, trimmings are well drilled and competent. Bills will be high. The wine list shows a heart of an enthusiast beating behind a formal exterior. Classic regions receive fine treatment, but good Californians show a determination to push the boundaries. Prices reflect quality, and with five good 'house selections', a scatter of decent lower-priced wines and some half-bottles, economy of sorts can be achieved. House wines are £13.50. CELLARMAN'S CHOICE: Albariño, Lagar de Cevera, Rias Baixas 1990, £17.50; Washington State, Salishan Lot 1, Pinot Noir 1986, £23.50.

CHEF: Alex Floyd PROPRIETORS: Leith's Restaurant Ltd and Prue Leith OPEN: all week, D only CLOSED: 3 or 4 days Christmas, 2 days Aug bank hol MEALS: 7.30 to 11.30 PRICES: Set D £32.50 (£39) to £44 (£51). Net prices, card slips closed CARDS: Access, Amex, Diners, Visa SEATS: 85. Private parties: 24 main room, 10, 24 and 36 private rooms. Vegetarian meals. Children welcome. Wheelchair access (3 steps). No music. Air-conditioned

Los Remos map 11

38A Southwick Street, W2 1JQ COOKING 1
071-723 5056 and 706 1870 COST £18–£34

The sturdy basement tapas bar has its own entrance to distinguish it from the restaurant above, and generally footsteps are directed below. The efficient all-Spanish staff certainly understand the English concept of tapas as a Continental fast food for travellers from Paddington Station or other passers-by. Los Remos is a cheerful place with lively Spanish music on tape and a display of over 20 fresh-looking tapas ranged along the bar. Popular choices include meatballs, chicken in red Rioja sauce, grilled sardines, fried squid, jamon serrano and octopus with olive oil and paprika. Portions are generous. Wines are Spanish, heavily biased towards Rioja and less wide-ranging than one might expect, but presented proudly and clearly. The restaurant is less of a sure-fire winner than the tapas bar.

CHEF: Santiago Garcia PROPRIETOR: Roberto Lopez OPEN: Mon to Sat MEALS: 12 to 3, 7 to 12 PRICES: restaurant £17 (£28), tapas bar £9 (£18). Cover 50p. Service 10% CARDS: Access, Amex, Carte Blanche, Diners, Visa SEATS: restaurant 65, tapas bar 35. Private parties: 65 main room. Vegetarian meals. Children welcome. Music. Air-conditioned

Lou Pescadou map 11

241 Old Brompton Road, SW5 9HP COOKING 1
071-370 1057 COST £32

Lou Pescadou is the cheapest in a small chain of fish restaurants. The menu revolves around fresh fish and shellfish regularly supplied from Brittany: turbot, red mullet, plaice, skate, John Dory and monkfish, all simply cooked. Soupe au pistou, pasta, salads and omelettes, plus steak for meat-eaters, bolster the menu. Most prices are not high and portions are generous. Run-of-the-mill desserts (chocolate mousse, peach melba, apple tart) come in ample quantities. The no-booking policy can have its attractions or drawbacks depending on the time of day – waiting customers are parked in the small downstairs bar. This, combined with the cover charge and the 15 per cent service charge, can greatly bring up the bill. House wine is £8.50.

CHEF: David Laurent PROPRIETORS: Oakhelm Ltd OPEN: all week CLOSED: 2 weeks Christmas MEALS: 12 to 3, 7 to 12 PRICES: £17 (£27). Cover £1. Service 15%. Card slips closed CARDS: Access, Amex, Diners, Visa SEATS: 60. 8 tables outside. Private parties: 20 main room. Vegetarian meals. Children's helpings. Wheelchair access (1 step). No music

Mandalay

map 10

100 Greenwich South Street, SE10 8UN — COOKING 2
081-691 0443 — COST £16–£31

A Burmese restaurant is still a rarity; indeed, Gerald Andrews, who is of part-Burmese parentage, would say it is unique. His knowledge, imbibed at first hand and coupled with unquenchable enthusiasm, even missionary zeal, is of help if doubts exist as to what to order: this, of course, provided he is not deep in the kitchen; the staff, too, are equipped to advise. Flavours come from onion oil, tamarind, tomato, garlic, coriander and chillies. Though most of the dishes themselves are not over-hot, the soups and broths that come with them are liquid fire. Alternative mouthfuls give variety and potency to the cooking. The one-plate meals of meat or noodles in a soup, such as molinga (rice noodles in a fishy soup with onions in batter and much green coriander), are also very satisfactory. Try the duck hsi-byan, stir-fried cabbage and pun-ta-hkaw-swe. Beer goes well with the food but there are also some decent light white wines. House wine is £6.50.

CHEF/PROPRIETOR: Gerald Andrews OPEN: Tue to Sat, D only, and Sun L MEALS: 12.30 to 3, 7 to 10.30 PRICES: £16 (£26), Set Sun L £9.50 (£16). Minimum £9.50. Card slips closed CARDS: Access, Diners, Visa SEATS: 58. Private parties: 26 main room, 26 private room. Vegetarian meals. Children welcome

Mandarin Kitchen

map 11

14–16 Queensway, W2 3RX — COOKING 2
071-727 9012 and 9468 — COST £18–£38

The comments of one reader summarise accurately the feelings of others: 'We go here regularly for some of the best fish in London. It *smells* right as you go in, and is the nearest thing to some of the great, bustling, bourgeois restaurants of Hong Kong and Singapore. Soft-shell crabs in sesame seed, roast eel with chilli, mussels in black-bean sauce – though it could be a little stronger on the black beans – and superb barbecue duck with perfect strips of skin are some of the dishes we most frequently order. The service is charming, but the wine list is lacking Alsaces and Loires, so drink lager.' Fish is the thing, even if one reporter felt his table's sea bass was not as large as those of this neighbours – of such things is envy generated.

CHEFS: Kwong Wing Man and D.D. Ly PROPRIETORS: Stephen and Helen Cheung OPEN: all week MEALS: noon to 11.30 PRICES: £14 (£25), Set L £12 (£18) to £18 (£25), Set D £15 (£21) to £25 (£32) CARDS: Access, Amex, Diners, Visa SEATS: 110. Private parties: 110 main room. Vegetarian meals. Children welcome. Wheelchair access. Music. Air-conditioned

Mandeer

map 13

21 Hanway Place, W1P 9DG — COOKING 1
071-323 0660 — COST £8–£23

Some of the best Indian vegetarian food in central London is served in this dimly lit basement behind Tottenham Court Road. The owners are committed to additive-free, healthy food and at first glance the menu reads like a litany of new-age wholefoods: tofu, Loseley Park ice-creams and unpolished brown rice (often mixed with wholewheat and tahini). The cooking, however, is firmly rooted in the Gujarati tradition. Five popular thalis – including one for vegans and another without onions or garlic – are the mainstays, backed up by a familiar list of samosas ('the best on this planet'), bhajias, bhel pooris, dosas and vegetable curries. There are also several more unusual items such as kachori (deep-fried mung bean pastries), steamed patra (aravi leaves layered with chickpea paste) and puffed lotus seed savoury cooked with tomatoes, onions and soy sauce. Mater paneer, Bombay aloo, tarka dhal and breads have all been excellent. Sweets include carrot halva, mango kulfi and wild Himalayan apricots in Jaipur rosewater. Good-value lunches are served in the adjoining Ravi Shankar Hall. Drink lassi, fruit juice or Kingfisher beer. The short wine list now features organic wines. House French (organic) is £7.30.

CHEF: Mr Daudbhai PROPRIETORS: Mr and Mrs Patel OPEN: Mon to Sat CLOSED: bank hols MEALS: 12 to 3, 6 to 10 PRICES: £9 (£19), Set L £3 (£8) to £3.65 (£9), Set D £7.25 (£13) to £11.50 (£17). Minimum £7. Service 10%. Card slips closed CARDS: Access, Amex, Diners, Visa SEATS: 75. 15 tables outside. Private parties: 100 private room. Vegetarian meals. Children's helpings. No-smoking area. Music. Self-service L

▲ *Manzi's*

map 14

1–2 Leicester Street, WC2H 7BL — COOKING 1
071-734 0224 — COST £40

When the Manzi family set up business in 1928, the Soho eating scene was dominated by Europe and the Chinese invasion had yet to happen. Rooted in the past, it continues to belong to another age and sustains its near-legendary reputation as the archetypal old-style fish restaurant, although the whole place now seems fairly basic compared with some of its gentrified competitors. It is 'jolly fun' according to one reader. First-class cooking of good ingredients is usually the order of the day, the kitchen working best when it keeps things simple – as in Dover sole with chips and mange-tout. House white (£7.10) is the best match for the food.

CHEF: Vincenzo Frappola PROPRIETORS: the Manzi family OPEN: all week, exc Sun L CLOSED: 25 Dec MEALS: 12 to 2.30, 5.30 to 11.30 (6 to 10.30 Sun) PRICES: £23 (£33). Cover £1.50. Card slips closed CARDS: Access, Amex, Diners, Visa SEATS: 160. Private parties: 17 main room, 45 private room. No children under 7. Wheelchair access (2 steps). Music ACCOMMODATION: 16 rooms, all with bath/shower. Lift. B&B £40 to £62. Deposit: £20. Confirm by midnight

denotes an outstanding wine cellar; *denotes a good wine list, worth travelling for.*

Maroush III

map 11

62 Seymour Street, W1H 5AF — COOKING 2
071-724 5024 — COST £35

There seems to be a feeling that this branch of the Maroush empire is the best place to go for good-value authentic Lebanese meze, now that the slightly more up-market Maroush I has reopened. An entire meal can be built from the long list of hot and cold starters which range from hummus, tabouleh and stuffed vine leaves to falafel, sujuk (spicy Lebanese sausages) and chargrilled chicken wings with garlic and lemon sauce. Fresh tongues, raw liver and brains with a special dressing are more esoteric morsels. 'Try the kibbey nayab (puréed raw meat with crushed wheat, onions and spices) if you dare,' enthuses one supporter of the dish. Main courses are dominated by meaty chargrills, casseroles and dishes such as stuffed cabbage. A huge bowl of healthy raw vegetables begins the meal, and the supply of fresh pitta bread never falters. The manager and his team of waiters are most attentive. Lebanese house wine is £11.

CHEF: F. Ladkani PROPRIETOR: M. Abouzaki OPEN: all week CLOSED: 25 Dec MEALS: noon to midnight PRICES: £16 (£29). Cover £1.50. Card slips closed CARDS: Access, Amex, Diners, Visa SEATS: 60. 5 tables outside. Private parties: 60 main room. Vegetarian meals. Children welcome. Smart dress preferred. Music. Air-conditioned

Martin's 🍷

map 11

239 Baker Street, NW1 6XE — COOKING 3*
071-935 3130 and 0997 — COST £32–£52

There has been a change of administration at Martin's, hence the arrival of Herbert Berger (late of Keats, which has become a northern outpost of the Gay Hussar). This has done great things for the cooking at this most civilised of restaurants where the well-upholstered space seems to encourage soft conversation (not whispering) rather than the usual shouts now necessary in the hard-edged London fashionables. An inspection meal early in Herbert Berger's stint here showed an ability to meld flavours in dishes such as foie gras with green cabbage and Riesling, or lamb with a parsley crust and English mustard sauce. The tendencies are modern enough: tartare of salmon à la Raymond Blanc; warm salad of rocket, scallops, sea bass and red mullet with balsamic vinegar, Parmesan and garlic; corn-fed chicken with spring vegetables, more balsamic, and olive oil. Desserts reveal Berger's Austrian origins in poppy seed pancakes in a rum sauce with 'a lovely understated spice filling', or hot apple and almond Pithiviers with blackberry coulis. Even the petits fours have taken a step up. This is an encouraging start. It is to be hoped he will be persuaded to remain. From impeccable sources, the wine list is a model of clarity. Half-bottles are scattered through the range on the main list, but the house selection of a dozen interesting bottles all offered at £13.25 is good value – especially for NW1.

Report forms are at the back of the book; write a letter if you prefer.

CHEF: Herbert Berger PROPRIETORS: Martin Coldicott and Herbert Berger OPEN: Mon to Fri MEALS: 12 to 2, 7 to 10 PRICES: £31 (£43), Set L £21.50 (£32). Service 15%. Card slips closed CARDS: Access, Amex, Diners, Visa SEATS: 60. Private parties: 16 private room. Children welcome. Smart dress preferred. Wheelchair access (1 step). Music. Air-conditioned

Mayflower

NEW ENTRY map 14

68–70 Shaftesbury Avenue, W1V 7DF COOKING 2*
071-734 9207 COST £20–£36

This rather gloomy-looking set of rooms is said to be the unofficial canteen for the Taiwanese in London. Its menu has more of mainland China than many of the Hong Kong-influenced places in Chinatown, which may be one reason for its adoption by a nation of exiles. Not that Hong Kong and Canton do not figure in dishes such as deep- and stir-fried milk with crab and scallops. Some unusual dishes on the menu, well worth exploring, include steamed salt fish with minced pork, stuffed fish stomach with prawn and crab sauces, and fish lips with bone marrow. There are also good casserole and doufu dishes, for instance eel with garlic, mushrooms and roast pork, or peipa doufu: a mixture of vegetables. Service is cheerful, the place is full – signs of happiness and value.

CHEF: F. Chung PROPRIETOR: Patrick Tsang OPEN: all week, D only CLOSED: 23 to 25 Dec MEALS: 5pm to 4am PRICES: £16 (£30), Set D £12.50 (£20) to £15 (£23) CARDS: Access, Amex, Diners, Visa SEATS: 120. Private parties: 40 main room. Vegetarian meals. Children welcome. Music. Air-conditioned

Melati

map 14

21 Great Windmill Street, W1V 7PH COOKING 1
071-437 2745 COST £21–£26

The restaurant is deep in X-certificate Soho, its smart pine frontage contrasting with the tacky peep-show doorways nearby. Three levels of eating are full of tables jammed closely together, pine panelling and South East Asian knick-knacks. Service is casual, the music sounds like Singapore disco. Apart from the occasional late-afternoon lull, the place is normally bursting. The food is 'as uncompromising as ever', says one regular, perhaps with reference to the chilli-heat. Many dishes are recommended: excellent satays, including a vegetarian version with tofu, potent sup undang, beef rendang, deep-fried beef Melati-style and fried chicken in lemon sauce. Massive bowls of laksa soup are 'still the best in town'. For a cheap meal there are also one-plate noodle dishes such as mee goreng and char kway teow, as well as nasi ramas (a mixed bag of fried chicken, fish cutlets, vegetables and rice). To finish, try Sam's Triple – a Technicolor dessert with layers of puréed avocado, mango and pineapple. Drink Indonesian Bintang or Singapore Tiger beer. A second branch, Minang, opened recently at 11 Greek Street W1V 5LE, Tel: 071-434 1149 – reports, please.

The Guide *always appreciates hearing about changes of chef or owner.*

CHEFS: S. Alamsjah and H. Hasyim PROPRIETORS: M.C.W. Ong and S. Alamsjah OPEN: all week CLOSED: 25 Dec MEALS: noon to 11.30 (12.30 Fri and Sat) PRICES: £12 (£21), Set L and D for 2 inc wine £38 (£44) CARDS: Access, Amex, Diners, Visa SEATS: 120. Private parties: 50 main room. Vegetarian meals. Children welcome. Wheelchair access. Music. Air-conditioned

Meson Don Felipe

map 11

53 The Cut, SE1 8LF COOKING 1
071-928 3237 COST £24

One of the few success stories to emerge from the late-1980s rush to open Spanish-style tapas bars, Meson Don Felipe continues in its own lively way. It is frequently far too crowded to notice the décor, get anywhere near the display of tapas on the bar, or even read the daily specials on the blackboard, but the frenetic crush is all part of the fun. An all-Spanish staff cope with admirable cheerfulness under the circumstances since the layout – more bar than table space – adds further to the mêlée. This place is a boon to anyone using the Old and Young Vics and the South Bank complex, although the tapas can be a bit hit-and-miss. A printed list includes all the popular choices: squid in batter, garlic prawns, fried sardines, garlic mushrooms, Spanish omelette, meatballs, chicken in oil and garlic. 'Not great food, but good quality tapas at fair prices' sums it up. An espresso machine has now been installed, hooray! A reasonably priced Iberian wine list includes some decent half-bottles and half a dozen good sherries. House wine is £6.95.

CHEF: Juan Arteaga PROPRIETORS: Philip and Ana Diment OPEN: Mon to Sat, exc Sat L MEALS: 12 to 3, 5.30 to 11 PRICES: £12 (£20). Service 10%. Card slips closed CARDS: Access, Visa SEATS: 50. Private parties: 10 main room. Vegetarian meals. Children's helpings. Wheelchair access (also WC). Music. Fax: 071-386 0337

Le Mesurier

map 11

113 Old Street, EC1V 9JR COOKING 2
071-251 8117 COST £37

Gillian Enthoven opens her miniature restaurant, in a small terrace next to the church in Old Street, for weekday lunches and private parties in the evenings. If food and cooking occupy the ground floor, then it is architecture (the occupation of Mr Enthoven) above. Certainly, the spare white dining-room feels architect-designed, but not so much tricksy post-modernism as calm functionalism. A short menu of three choices at each course is changed every two weeks, and if Gillian Enthoven was ever characterised as being an 'Elizabeth David' sort of cook, it reads with less sense of tradition than that may imply. Cod with peanut, ginger and avocado sauce, and guinea-fowl in pastry with a lime sauce are two examples. First courses of oysters with cheese, cream and shallot sauce and an asparagus, mushroom and Gewurztraminer soup continue that theme. The best dessert is often a soufflé, for which Gillian has special affection; others think the affection justified. Service can be overtaken by numbers as can the cooking, occasionally, if orders fall inconveniently. There is a very brief wine list, with house Corney and Barrow at £8.

CHEFS: Gillian Enthoven and Loic du Pape PROPRIETOR: Gillian Enthoven OPEN: Mon to Fri L (D by arrangement only for minimum of 15) CLOSED: 1 week Christmas, 3 weeks Aug MEALS: 12 to 3, 6 to 11 PRICES: £22 (£31). Service 12.5%. Card slips closed CARDS: Access, Amex, Diners, Visa SEATS: 24. Private parties: 24 main room. Vegetarian meals. Children's helpings. No children under 5. Wheelchair access. No music L. Fax: 071-608 3504

Mijanou 🍷 map 12

143 Ebury Street, SW1W 9QN COOKING 3
071-730 4099 COST £26–£54

Mijanou may be petite but the portions here are for Gargantua. The generosity and the way the food is presented both convey a country restaurant in the city, an impression reinforced by the summer garden, albeit paved from edge to edge. For six months, the Blechs grappled with dry rot, opening again in spruced-up premises in the summer of '91. The ground-floor room has lost its fortune-teller's feel of strong, deep colours and looks much larger painted white. The downstairs, still resplendent with stained-glass and mirrors, is now used for coffee and drinks (and smoking) rather than dining. The menus, one for lunch and one for dinner, are set-price. Lunch, especially, constitutes fair value. Although everything is expressed in French and the pleasant staff is mostly French – as, indeed, is Sonia Blech herself – the food is not specifically French, provincial or otherwise. Indeed, the vein of invention running through and the enjoyment of sweet-and-sour combinations, for instance a 'carpaccio' of duck with melon and a melon and crème fraîche mousse, is more English than French. Generally, it is not simple cooking either: counterpoint and contrast are essential to the plate, just as they may be to the sauces, and this may cause a pleasant crowding of the surface with sensation. This can be compounded by a deliberate roughness of execution. The 'carpaccio' of duck was not beaten or sliced thin, and the vegetables à la grecque served with three sorts of marinated fish were in literal profusion. Come dessert, the crêpes soufflés come in a medium Le Creuset dish as two pancakes bursting with strawberry soufflé: a trencherman's paradise, but not the style of some refined West End franglais kitchen. Instead, here is a *bonne bourgeoise* knowing and delivering quality when she sees it. This is one reason why Mijanou is so beloved by its regulars; that and the sight of Sonia Blech beavering away in the kitchen halfway down the stairs. To succeed, this style of cooking needs to be bursting with moistness and flavour – hearty in fact as well as to the eye. It often is. For example, take one pre-closure meal: mousseline of wild mushrooms with wild rice, grilled salmon with asparagus and a ginger sauce, and a Swiss roll of vanilla and chocolate ice-creams wrapped around one another. If, however, there is inaccuracy, or blandness, then heartiness can seem more akin to lack of finish. This was so in a multi-flavoured dish of veal with artichoke, gnocchi and a red wine and tarragon sauce suffering from dryness in the meat. Ancillaries are acceptable and the wine list masterminded by the discreet yet ever-present Neville Blech is distinguished. The range is catholic, and only the best seem to have been considered, making choice very difficult: from Ch. Haut-Bailly in two vintages, to the youngest maker of Menetou-Salon, Alain Gogué, to Warren Winiarski, David Hohnen and Steve Kistler in the New World, and

Jean Léon or Francesco Giuntini in Spain and Italy. Even the notes are helpful and prices very fair. House selections start at £13 for Peter Sichel's Sirius. The Wine Treasury is the sales arm of this list and some of the bins can be bought by the case.

CHEF: Sonia Blech PROPRIETORS: Neville and Sonia Blech OPEN: Mon to Fri MEALS: 12.30 to 2, 7 to 11 PRICES: Set L £17 (£26) to £21 (£30), Set D £28 (£38) to £34.50 (£45) SEATS: 18. 4 tables outside. Private parties: 18 main room. Children welcome. No smoking. No music. Fax: 071-823 6402

Mr Kong

map 14

21 Lisle Street, WC2H 7BA COOKING 2
071-437 7341 COST £14–£26

This remains one of the better Cantonese restaurants in Soho Chinatown despite some difference of opinion. Queues testify to its popularity. The long menu is supplemented by an intriguing list of chef's specialities, including highly rated sautéed venison with ginger wine sauce; deep-fried crispy duck with yam paste; stewed lamb with dry bean curd sticks; and stuffed fish maw with abalone and prawn paste. Readers have spoken highly of the wun-tun soup, succulent fried squid with vegetables, fried intestines, crab with ginger and spring onion on a bed of crispy noodles, and fried bean curd with vegetables. Special fried rice has been 'quite the best tasted in a long time'. Those in favour of this restaurant say the the cooking has got verve, although occasional mishaps in the kitchen can cause disappointment. There is also some dispute about the atmosphere, especially downstairs: some find it claustrophobic, others prefer it to the ground-floor dining area. The 20-strong wine list includes saké and Taiwanese Shao Shing. House wine is £6.50.

CHEFS: S. Kong and Y. W.Lo PROPRIETORS: Edwin Chow, K. Kong, Y.W. Lo, W. Lee and M. Lee OPEN: all week CLOSED: 4 days Christmas MEALS: noon to 1.45am PRICES: £12 (£22), Set D £8.60 (£14) to £16 (£22). Minimum £7 after 8pm CARDS: Access, Amex, Diners, Visa SEATS: 120. Private parties: 50 main room, 40 private room. Children welcome. Wheelchair access. No music. Air-conditioned

Mitsukoshi

NEW ENTRY map 13

Dorland House,
14–16 Regent Street, SW1Y 4PH COOKING 2*
071-930 0317 COST £32–£82

Enter through the glass doors of the Mitsukoshi department store and find the basement restaurant, populated largely by Japanese customers who enjoy fair value and some delicate cooking over a wide range. A series of set meals is supplemented by daily specials. Highlights of visits here, apart from the sushi, have been crab and crab paste; salmon roe on minced mooli; the silkiest tofu with ginger and turnip pastes; sunamono; a perfect example of chawan mushi; and the dessert kuzukiri, arrowroot noodles with 'rock sugar' syrup, tasting like caramelised maple syrup. The staff work hard to keep abreast of the kitchen. If you drink saké you will be offered a choice of six different cups from which to drink. There is also a fair wine list, but soup and tea are included in meal prices.

CHEF: Mr Shimada PROPRIETOR: Mr Mitsukoshi OPEN: Mon to Sat CLOSED: Christmas, 18 to 26 Aug MEALS: 12 to 2.30, 6 to 10.30 PRICES: £18 (£32), Set L and D from £20 (£34) to £50 (£68). Service 15%. Card slips closed CARDS: Access, Amex, Diners, Visa SEATS: 50. Private parties: 50 main room, 20 and 10 private rooms. Children Sat only. Music. Air-conditioned

Miyama

map 13

38 Clarges Street, W1Y 7PJ COOKING 2*
071-499 2443 COST £21–£56

The menu seems less extensive than those of some Japanese restaurants, but ask for the à la carte list of seasonal specials. There is a teppanyaki bar at the front. Mr Miyama is said to cook here in the evenings and at his city branch – City Miyama, 17 Godliman Street EC4, Tel: 071-489 1937 – at lunchtimes. The cooking is extremely careful: deep-fried soft-shelled crabs, excellent noodles, interesting sushi and subtle sauces. Aubergine grilled with sweet soy bean paste is memorable. Service is deferential and efficient. House wine is £12 and champagnes are nearly half the price of those at Nakano in Beauchamp Place.

CHEFS: F. Miyama and T. Miura PROPRIETORS: F. Miyama, T. Miura and Y. Ishibashi OPEN: Mon to Sat, exc Sat L MEALS: 12.30 to 2.30, 6.30 to 10.30 PRICES: £22 (£40), Set L £9 (£21) to £32 (£47), Set D £28 (£43) to £32 (£47). Service 15%. Card slips closed CARDS: Access, Amex, Diners, Visa SEATS: 75. Private parties: 25 main room, 8 and 12 private rooms. Vegetarian meals. Children's helpings L. Jacket and tie. Wheelchair access (1 step; also WC). Music. Air-conditioned

Mon Petit Plaisir

map 11

33C Holland Street, W8 4LX COOKING 1
071-937 3224 COST £18–£34

'A small, friendly, non-threatening, almost deliberately old-fashioned bourgeois neighbourhood restaurant with food to match' is one reporter's verdict on this sibling of Mon Plaisir (see next entry). The food is dependable, 'not terribly exciting, but comforting to the palate and the wallet'. A short, regular *carte* is backed up by set lunches and dinners listed on a blackboard. Typical dishes are duck with green peppercorn sauce, tournedos Roquefort and grilled salmon with béarnaise sauce. Salade gourmande with smoked chicken, smoked duck breast and quails' eggs; roulade of salmon with chive sauce; breast of chicken with langoustines; and fillet of lamb cooked rare with sauce poivrade have all been enjoyed. The short list of around 20 French wines has a few half-bottles. House wine is £7.50.

CHEF: Christophe Hariot PROPRIETOR: Alain Lhermitte OPEN: Mon to Fri CLOSED: 4 days Easter, Christmas to New Year MEALS: 12 to 2.30, 7 to 10.30 PRICES: £19 (£28), Set L £13.50 (£18), Set D £15.95 (£20). Service 12.5% alc only. Card slips closed CARDS: Access, Amex, Diners, Visa SEATS: 36. 4 tables outside. Private parties: 20 main room. Children's helpings. No cigars/pipes in dining-room. Music. Air-conditioned

Mon Plaisir

map 14

21 Monmouth Street, WC2H 9DD
071-836 7243

COOKING 1
COST £14–£32

Alain Lhermitte's seminal French bistro evokes nostalgia and fond memories: 'reassuringly unchanged, interesting, as much fun as ever'; 'one could be in Paris'; 'my favourite restaurant' are comments. 'I dined here last night for the first time for nearly a decade. Everything was admirable, the soups terrific, the steaks correctly hung and cooked medium-rare, the tarte aux pommes excellent.' The kitchen works best with old-style bistro classics: slabs of herby terrine ('exactly what one would eat at a set meal in France'), chargrilled duckling with béarnaise, beef bourguignonne, lamb cutlets, raspberry tart and caramel soufflé have all been recommended. New potatoes and frites are spot-on, although vegetables can be overcooked. French bread and the cheeseboard rate well. More ambitious dishes such as monkfish with pepper sauce can be dull and popularity causes problems with smooth output. Service is normally congenial, although that, too, may become off-hand under pressure. There are some decent, drinkable wines on the French list. House wine is £7.50. At Mon Plaisir du Nord – The Mall, 359 Upper Street N1, Tel: 071-359 1932 – Alain Lhermitte has founded a third restaurant in the same format. Early reports show a need to do better.

CHEF: Michel Dubarbier PROPRIETOR: Alain Lhermitte OPEN: Mon to Sat, exc Sat L
MEALS: 12 to 2.30, 6 to 11.15 PRICES: £18 (£27), Set L £13.75 (£21) and Set pre-theatre D inc wine £13.75. Service 12.5%. Card slips closed CARDS: Access, Amex, Diners, Visa
SEATS: 95. Private parties: 26 main room, 30 private room. Vegetarian meals. Children's helpings. Wheelchair access. Music. Fax: 071-379 0121

Monkeys

map 12

1 Cale Street,
Chelsea Green, SW3 3QT
071-352 4711

COOKING 2*
COST £17–£49

The cream double frontage sits on Chelsea Green, a nice backwater to the King's Road. Monkeys – started by three wise ones, the story goes – is a distinguished example of the neighbourhood restaurant. It has been going a long time, people get to know about it, they like the intelligent, seemly, yet not overposh atmosphere, and they return. The cooking makes it worthwhile – Anglo-French, without fireworks, but rarely messing it up. A meal might progress through a salad of calf's liver, bacon and croûtons, or a lobster ravioli, to roast saddle of hare in pastry on a bed of spinach or lamb with tarragon, the lamb tasting of the grill, tender and pink, the sauce with body and flavour, finishing with a classic oeufs à la neige. Monkeys delivers, and at a price people can afford, The wine list often runs some good bin-ends; Tom Benham knows his cellar, even if his proclaimed 'smooth' house wine has been adjudged rough.

'As we entered, a very thin cat wandered by–this should have been a sign of what was to come.' On eating in Cumbria

CHEF: Tom Benham PROPRIETORS: Tom and Brigitte Benham OPEN: Mon to Fri CLOSED: 2 weeks Easter, 3 weeks in Aug MEALS: 12.30 to 2.30, 7.30 to 11 PRICES: £30 (£41), Set L £10 (£17) to £15 (£23), Set D from £19 (£27) to £30 (£39). Minimum £16.50 D CARDS: Access, Visa SEATS: 45. Private parties: 50 main room, 10 private room. Children welcome. No pipes in dining-room. No music. Air-conditioned

Le Muscadet

map 11

25 Paddington Street, W1M 3RF — COOKING 1
071-935 2883 — COST £35

'I can't help feeling very positive about Le Muscadet, although the food is not amazing,' writes a regular. Others, visiting the place for the first time, reiterate: 'The place was full and the lively atmosphere compensated for the food.' Not that the food is bad. The cooking, by an English chef, is decently French in style, though it lacks heart. For instance, 'some pieces of al dente apple lay chastely by the side of an intact-skinned black pudding. It was an excellent pudding but should have been on closer terms with the apple.' There were also correctly pink and tender lamb noisettes that proved to be disappointingly short of taste. Medallions of beef in a robust red wine and shallot sauce or perfectly cooked turbot and Dover sole have been reported as better bets. The cheese is undoubtedly the highspot of the menu ('a good variety in perfect condition and no meanness about the portions'). Service, although excellent, gets a slap on the wrist: 'I was rather disappointed to be presented with a blank total on my credit card voucher when 12.5 per cent had already been added.' There is an affordable French wine list. House Muscadet is £9.20.

CHEF: Donald Smith PROPRIETOR: François Bessunnard OPEN: Mon to Sat, exc Sat L MEALS: 12.30 to 2.30, 7.30 to 10.45 (10 Sat) PRICES: £20 (£29). Service 12.5% CARDS: Access, Visa SEATS: 35. Private parties: 40 main room. Children welcome. Smart dress preferred. Wheelchair access. Music. Air-conditioned

Museum Street Café

map 13

47 Museum Street, WC1 1LY — COOKING 3
071-405 3211 — COST £12–£25

'Run to eat there,' instructed someone from America relieved at finding good value and personal commitment (and a kindred approach to cooking) in this small room, that might once have been a bookshop, on the street leading up to the main gates of the British Museum. Though expansion is hoped for, the premises have remained the same small and austere dining-room – that indeed looks like a good café – with a counter at the back and kitchen beyond. Lunch is a short menu of maybe five main courses, a couple of firsts, four or five sweet things and cheese. Prices are affordable, the food is real and sometimes very distinguished even when at its simplest, for instance a lemon, fennel and vanilla custard – what flavours! Dinner revolves around a weekly menu which offers a choice of two dishes at each of the three courses. The chargrill and the bread oven are the essential tools of cooking here: the bread is first-rate, so are the substantial focaccias or pizzas, so is the rich chocolate cake. The majority of meats and fish are chargrilled: 'There was first an enticing raw-fish smell, then, after grilling, an even more blissful taste of salmon.' The reporter called the cooking 'ethical' – her main courses came without sauce or accompaniment save vegetables. There are, of course, some braised or fried dishes in the repertoire, sauces do figure, and the salads are invariably praised, including the dressing. Coffee is good; there is no licence; smoking is not allowed. A touch of asperity enters Gail Koerber's notes when observing how many people turn up late, are short on advised numbers or don't come at all. Booking, at night, is essential; it is not the sort of place for passing trade and a lost table is a lost living.

CHEFS: Gail Koerber and Mark Nathan PROPRIETOR: Mark Nathan OPEN: Mon to Fri MEALS: 12.30 to 2.30, 7.30 to 9.15 PRICES: Set L £10 (£12) to £15 (£17), Set D £18.50 (£21). Unlicensed, but bring your own: no corkage. SEATS: 22. Private parties: 22 main room. Vegetarian meals L with prior notice. Children's helpings with prior notice. No smoking. No music

Nakano

map 12

11 Beauchamp Place, SW3 1NQ — COOKING 2
071-581 3837 — COST £20–£73

Nakano is another Japanese restaurant that aims down-market and might be appealing to a less formal clientele than the first-generation pioneers. The menu, however, is more exciting than the quarry tiles, bleak white walls and plain tablecloths. Other than the usual set meals, there is a long list of dishes, including a score of 'chef's recommendations'. These include aubergine grilled with a topping of miso sauce and sesame, salmon skin with chilli and white radish, and deep-fried soft-shelled crab with rice vinegar. Presentation and service are with all the style that should be anticipated. Drink saké hot, on the rocks, or chilled.

CHEF: Mr Kikuchi PROPRIETORS: Meadowdawn Ltd OPEN: Tue to Sun, exc Sun L CLOSED: bank hols, 1 week Aug bank hol, 25 Dec and 1 Jan MEALS: 12.30 to 2.30, 6.30 to 11 PRICES: £20 (£40), Set L £8.50 (£20) to £18 (£30), Set D £26.50 (£43) to £42.50 (£61). Cover £2 D. Minimum £20 D. Service 15% CARDS: Access, Amex, Diners, Visa SEATS: 30. Private parties: 30 main room. Vegetarian meals. Children's helpings. Music. Air-conditioned. Fax: 071-357 7315

Neal Street Restaurant

map 14

26 Neal Street, WC2H 9PS — COOKING 2
071-836 8368 — COST £53

This remains an expensive restaurant; it also remains a most pleasant place to spend an evening. Unfortunately, the pictures, the cool comfort of the room and tables and the buzz of continuing business seem more reliable than the food. This continues to highlight wild mushrooms, Antonio Carluccio's speciality, many of which are interesting but not always of first quality. Though the menu may lead one to think of this as an Italian restaurant, many of the techniques and recipes are more international than that. In like fashion, the wine list does not explore the current wealth of Italy as well as it might. Despite these comments, some dishes – for example, a casserole of rabbit with wild mushrooms – may be outstanding. Techniques and tasting need more regularity, and the ordinary denizens of Covent Garden might welcome a reduction in the 15 per cent service charge and a slightly lower cost for not very good vegetables. The wine list answers if you wish to drink well, but you pay for it. House wine is from £9.

CHEF: M. Santiago Gonzalez PROPRIETOR: Antonio Carluccio OPEN: Mon to Fri CLOSED: Christmas to New Year and bank hols MEALS: 12.30 to 2.30, 7.30 to 11 PRICES: £30 (£44). Service 15%. Card slips closed CARDS: Access, Amex, Visa SEATS: 65. Private parties: 24 private room. Vegetarian meals. Wheelchair access. Air-conditioned. No music. Fax: 071-497 1361

Neshiko

map 11

265 Upper Street, N1 2UQ
071-359 9977

COOKING 2
COST £19–£76

The name 'Neshiko' holds many secrets. It refers to a small town in the south of Japan that was once the only place where foreigners were allowed during the three centuries Japan was closed to outsiders. It is also a pun: 'Loch Ness is Nesshi-ko (Ness Lake) in Japanese, as the owner told me gleefully,' comments one reporter. The Upper Street setting may not be home territory for a large Japanese community, but the menu delves and delivers some fascinating examples of home cooking for non-Japanese customers: nameko oroshi (small mushrooms with grated white radish) and ika natto (raw squid with 'brown, slimy, earth-tasting' fermented soya beans) are typical. Otherwise the menu, presented on pale parchment, runs the gamut of cooking styles and dishes. Deep-fried tofu in a 'golden coat' of powdered Japanese arrowroot, chunks of aubergine simmered in stock, and marinated salmon with a mild lemon dressing have all been good. Sushi was rather tired on one occasion. Here is a Japanese restaurant which sets out to cultivate Western custom; the atmosphere is relaxed rather than intimidating. The wine list includes saké and plum wine. House French is £8.95.

CHEF: Isao Murato PROPRIETORS: Kawab Ltd OPEN: Mon to Sat, exc Sat L CLOSED: 25 Dec to 1 Jan MEALS: 12 to 2.30, 6 to 11.30 PRICES: £18 (£32), Set L £10 (£19), Set D £28 (£38) to £50 (£63). Service 10%. Card slips closed CARDS: Access, Amex, Diners, Visa SEATS: 55. Private parties: 30 main room, 25 private room. Vegetarian meals. Children welcome. Smart dress preferred. Wheelchair access. Music

New World

map 14

Gerrard Place, W1V 7LL
071-734 0677 and 0396

COOKING 1
COST £12–£29

'A rock of reliability in an area where the chefs seem to indulge in a permanent game of musical chairs between restaurants.' For many this is the place to go for dim-sum: 'The paper prawns, glutinous rice and most of the meat dumplings are consistently good.' For some it is the noodle soup, the roast meats, especially sucking pig, and spare ribs in black-bean sauce. For the adventurous there are dishes such as chickens' feet. Prices are a plus. The contents of the trolley can be past their best at a late weekday lunch, at weekends they can be better. The place fills up quickly, despite its vast size, queues often form, and the kitchen responds accordingly. In the evening it is nothing special. For a Chinese restaurant the wine list is long. House wine is £6.05.

CHEFS: W.L. Wong, L. Diep and T.W. Man PROPRIETORS: New World Restaurant Ltd OPEN: all week MEALS: 11am to 11.45pm (11pm Sun) PRICES: £12 (£24), Set L and D from £6.60 (£12) CARDS: Access, Amex, Diners, Visa SEATS: 600. Private parties: 200 main room, 20, 80 and 100 private rooms. Vegetarian meals. Children welcome. Wheelchair access (also WC). Music. Air-conditioned

Nichol's

map 11

75 Fairfax Road, NW6 4NN — COOKING 2
071-624 3880 — COST £34

This restaurant has many of the ingredients that should go into a well-stirred pot: comfort, intelligent owners, kitchen skills in abundance, none too showy an approach to getting the food before the customer. There are some slips – a lack of distinct flavour or identity to cooking, a failure to welcome visitors as warmly as they might wish – but these are infrequent. It remains, however, a spiritually 'cool' operation. The menu is short, expression concise: meat or fish, and sauce – onion and mustard with lamb; mushroom and tarragon with guinea-fowl; thyme-flavoured beurre blanc with salmon. These sauces are light and usually well-judged. The Nichols are from New Zealand, and greater emphasis on fish from southern waters is expected this year. First courses may often include a tart (leek, celery and asparagus, or onion, for example) among the half-dozen options that surprise only a little, but impress by their flavours, for instance smoked trout with a celeriac mayonnaise. Pastry work and incidentals are praised, though they may be absent at lunchtime. The wine list is two-thirds Australasian, though it hardly has room to explore byways of that most exciting region. House wines are £8.95.

CHEF: David Nichol PROPRIETORS: Susan and David Nichol OPEN: all week, exc Sat L and Sun D MEALS: 12 to 3, 7 to 10 PRICES: £20 (£28). Service 10%. Card slips closed CARDS: Access, Amex, Visa SEATS: 45. 3 tables outside. Vegetarian meals. Children's helpings. Wheelchair access. Music. Air-conditioned

▲ *Nontas*

map 11

16 Camden High Street, NW1 0JH — COOKING 1
071-387 4579 — COST £18

A stalwart among tavernas, with rooms too, where decorative improvements in recent years have reduced the overcrowding of tables. Many people come for the fish kebab, the taramasalata that avoids the lurid pink that taverniks learn to dread, and the lamb 'that fell off the bone', just as it always does. Meze, for a minimum of two people, are also popular. Service is invariably obliging. House wine is £5.95 and there are a couple of dozen Greek bottles from which to choose.

CHEF: Nontas Vassilakas PROPRIETORS: Nontas and Helen Vassilakas OPEN: Mon to Sat MEALS: 12 to 2.45, 6 to 11.30 (snacks 8.30am to 11.30pm) PRICES: £10 (£15). Service 10% for parties of more than 6 CARDS: Access, Amex, Diners, Visa SEATS: 50. 10 tables outside. Private parties: 25 main room. Children welcome. Wheelchair access. Music. Fax: 071-383 0335 ACCOMMODATION: 12 rooms, all with bath/shower. B&B £32 to £49. No children under 12. Afternoon teas. Garden. TV. Phone. Doors close at 12.30am

Now & Zen

NEW ENTRY map 14

4A Upper St Martin's Lane, WC2 9EA COOKING 2
071-497 0376, 0377 and 0378 COST £41

Harry Yeung's snazziest and most recent Zen venture is in a trendy West End location between Soho Chinatown and Covent Garden. The décor is pure modern chic – sleek and white with an effective use of flowers to add colour – a Rick Mather design, as in the other Zen restaurants. A huge oval atrium connects the three levels around a designer fountain of inverted glass dishes. On the ground floor is a sushi bar; in the split-level basement are restaurant, kitchen and pianist. The long menu is modern, exotic and adventurous. To begin, deep-fried diced tofu with peppercorn salt and steamed Peking ravioli in chilli sauce have been perfectly cooked. The 'soup of the day' might be long-cooked pork and watercress with two kinds of almonds. Slices of deep-fried boneless chicken garnished with frills of Yunnan ham and caramelised walnuts is a Cantonese classic, improved by making the skin as crispy as Peking duck. Another speciality, pork spare ribs flavoured with star anise, soy and Chinkiang vinegar, and sautéed mixed vegetables in a taro nest, was finely executed but less exciting. The sheer authenticity of some dishes can sometimes be too much for Western palates. The restaurant seems 'destined to succeed', since the glitzy market it is pitching for is very different from that of nearby Chinatown. We hope it will prove to be more than a nine-day wonder. More reports, please.

CHEF: Michael Leung PROPRIETORS: Blaidwood Catering Ltd OPEN: all week MEALS: 12 to 3, 6.30 to 12 PRICES: £19 (£34). Cover £1 CARDS: Access, Amex, Diners, Visa SEATS: 200. Private parties: 100 main room, 30 private room. Vegetarian meals. Children welcome. Smart dress preferred. Wheelchair access (also WC). Music. Air-conditioned. Fax: 071-437 0641

▲ *Oak Room, Le Meridien Hotel* 🍷

map 13

21 Piccadilly, W1V 0BH COOKING 4
071-734 8000 COST £32–£67

The hotel, one of Norman Shaw's late works, is full Edwardian baroque down to the former open-air terrace for dancing and cocktails behind an imposing colonnade. The Terrace Garden, which is further up the building, is now a likeable but undistinguished restaurant-cum-coffee-shop, enjoyable for its conservatory setting. For serious eating, though, you must go to the Oak Room. Perhaps – the Ritz notwithstanding – this is London's most beautiful dining-room, even though it has been cut in half and its entrance from Piccadilly curtailed. The room retains magnificent proportions, and the atmosphere, despite the never-ending panelling, is light and airy: the oak has been stripped and limed and the Murano chandeliers float gently over the tables. Even with this backdrop and formal service in the grand style, it is possible to relax here. The partnership between Michel Lorain and David Chambers, consultant and executive respectively, has lasted as long as the restaurant in its current ownership and is very successful. Menus feature 'cuisine traditionelle' and 'cuisine créative', the product of Lorain's invention, while Chambers prepares a weekly and a daily menu. 'Traditionelle' is high on truffles, while 'créative' mobilises spices – cinnamon with foie gras and apple terrine, cloves with turbot on a bed of savoy cabbage, and bergamot tea with duck and endive – as well as indulging in variations of classics such as gazpacho with langoustines or pigs' trotters mixed with crab and basil. Lunch delivers particularly good culinary value; many rate it among the top three in London. One summer meal described by an inspector speaks of the pleasure this restaurant gives readers. 'The *crème d'asperges legère à la coriandre* is poured on to a soup plate which has three lobster quenelles previously placed in the centre. The soup has a little rough texture, just enough to relieve it from being bland, is just this side of being over-seasoned and tastes of a generous amount of asparagus and cream. A *blanc de bar à l'huile vierge parfumée* is a steamed sea bass sitting on an intense purée of celeriac and carrots. The root vegetables work well to contrast the softness of the fish. The *noisettes de chevreuil au poivre vert* comprises competently cooked pieces of venison, each piece interleaved with an endive, the meat tasting only faintly gamey. Puddings are all from the trolley and feature more predictable fruit salads and gâteaux. After tasting six different ones . . . they are pretty hit-or-miss. Why does a hotel of this calibre and resource not provide individually prepared desserts? Mind you, a nice touch is the feathering of raspberry coulis and cream by a straight-faced young waiter who then presents each guest with a different flower design for each pudding. Details, from amuse-gueules to the assortment of petits fours and breads, are first-rate, totally in keeping with the class of this establishment.' The wine list affords an excellent overview of classic French regions, with some of the better growers and properties. It is less satisfactory for the rest of the world, though the price range is useful. California is plumbed deeper than Australasia. Prices are in line with the location, but not as astronomical as some. There is drinking below £20 and house wines are £13.

CHEF: David Chambers PROPRIETORS: Meridien Hotels OPEN: Mon to Sat, exc Sat L MEALS: 12 to 3, 7 to 11.30 PRICES: £30 (£42), Set L £23 (£32), Set D £44 (£56) CARDS: Access, Amex, Diners, Visa SEATS: 50. Private parties: 8 main room. Children welcome. Jacket and tie. No pipes in dining-room. Wheelchair access (also WC). Music. Air-conditioned. Fax: 071-437 3574 ACCOMMODATION: 260 rooms, all with bath/shower. Rooms for disabled. Lift. B&B £175 to £215. Deposit: 1 night. Children welcome. Baby facilities. Afternoon teas. Swimming-pool. Sauna. Snooker. Air-conditioned. TV. Phone. Confirm 1 day ahead

---

'I do find it difficult to have my conversation interrupted by the query ''Is everything all right?''. I mutter an affirmative only to find that I have to answer the question again and perhaps even again. I also find that if I make anything but a positive comment then this is not well received.' On eating in Surrey

---

Odette's 🍷

map 11

130 Regent's Park Road, NW1 8XL — COOKING 3
071-586 5486 and 8766 — COST £38

This is a house of many chambers, yet in small compass, that manages ingeniously to satisfy a range of demands. The decoration – a hall of mirrors in the main dining-room, a dense miscellany of pictures everywhere else – creates an ambience at once elegant and informal, again an ingenious solution that has lasted. Change, however, is evident in the cooking with new chef Daniel Evans hot-footing it from Alastair Little (see entry) and imparting a vivid energy to the menu, the tastes and appearance of the food. There are obvious borrowings: a menu that changes at every meal; a love of Japanese inspiration; a bold adaptation of Italian materials and recipes; but such colonisation should benefit us all. The repertoire is large, only repeating itself spasmodically, but things like a 'triad of tuna (sashimi, tataki, tartare) with a selection of Japanese pickles'; little pizza of grilled vegetables, chicory, marinated goats' cheese and pesto; roast loin of monkfish wrapped in pancetta, with spring greens or feuilleté of lambs' sweetbreads and fillet with minted split green peas may be taken as paradigms. Execution and arrangement are bold, sometimes too copious, and a very long way from nouvelle cuisine. There is a certain evangelism for honesty of culinary purpose shining through. The conversion has extended to sourcing of materials – very fine fish and other French specialities through the now famous William Black, buyer in Boulogne and Paris to the quality – the imaginative speciality breads in rustic loaves (gone are the prissy micro-rolls) and the excellent petits fours. No wonder it attracts a loyal following. Al fresco dining is well-catered for with a garden room at the back and pavement tables in high summer. Cheaper and more informal food can be had in the amiable basement wine bar. It does not always work like clockwork, but Simone Green's calm control will quiet the most strenuous objections. With near-neighbour Bibendum – the wine merchant, not the restaurant – on hand it is no surprise to find good names such as Natter, Rolly Gassmann and Collard on the wine list. A major refurbishment has succeeded in bringing more wines, better arranged, with a broader sweep of quality and provenance. Six wines are available by the glass and a commendable range of half-bottles allows for variety and economy. Prices throughout are fair, with much below £15, as well as sound choices for the more extravagant. Odette's is promoted to a bottle for effort but, please, drop the alternative vintage notation. House wine is £8.90. CELLARMAN'S CHOICE: Mâcon-Péronne 1989, Dom. de Mortier, £15.75; Rothesay Bay Chardonnay 1989, £17.95.

CHEF: Daniel Evans PROPRIETOR: Simone Green OPEN: Mon to Sat, exc Sat L MEALS: 12.30 to 2.30, 7.30 to 11 PRICES: £22 (£32). Service 12.5%. Card slips closed CARDS: Access, Amex, Diners, Visa SEATS: 55. Private parties: 28 and 8 private rooms. Children welcome. No music

Net prices *in the details at the end of an entry indicates that the prices given on a menu and on a bill are inclusive of VAT and service charge, and that this practice is clearly stated on menu and bill.*

192

map 11

192 Kensington Park Road, W11 2ES COOKING 2
071-229 0482 COST £28

'The thing is the atmosphere,' begins one commentary that lists as minus points loud voices, heavy smoke and internecine warfare evident for those seated too near the kitchen. Other readers enter big credits for the informal coming and going of the upstairs bar, which feels like real life, the spare, now almost period-piece decoration, the daily-changing menu of creative modern dishes cooked by Maddalena Bonino, the generally amiable service (even if there is squabbling at the hotplate) and the excellent wines. Both wine bar and restaurant – exclusively the latter in the basement – continue to attract a strong body of support from the district and beyond. The cooking, offered on a *carte* of about a dozen choices in each course (more free-form at lunchtime), can be expressive in new-wave dishes such as chicken livers with sesame and a celeriac rémoulade; chillied pasta with sun-dried tomatoes and mussels; red mullet and couscous with a tomato and mint salsa; chicken with rhubarb chutney; and desserts which may be light (moussecake) or substantial (brownies). The main comment is unpredictability, coming perhaps from press of business rather than lack of commitment or skill. Generous provision of wines by the glass ('large' or 'standard') makes for experiment. The selection of wines is exemplary and catholic, the presentation brisk and the prices would be fair in the provinces, which makes them bargains in West London. A bottle is awarded this year for fine value and intelligent, succinct selection. House wines are from £8.

CHEFS: Maddalena Bonino and Josh Hampton PROPRIETORS: Anthony Mackintosh, Michael Chassay and John Armit OPEN: all week, exc Mon L MEALS: 12.30 to 3 (1 to 3.30 Sun), 7.30 to 11.30 (7 to 11 Sun) PRICES: £16 (£23). Card slips closed CARDS: Access, Amex, Visa SEATS: 75. 3 tables outside. Private parties: 10 main room, 30 private room. Children's helpings. No cigars/pipes in dining-room. Wheelchair access. Music. Air-conditioned. Fax: 071-727 7133

190 Queensgate

map 12

190 Queen's Gate, SW7 5EU COOKING 3*
071-581 5666 COST £21–£58

If you need to eat foie gras, this must surely be the place to try it. At least half a dozen of the dishes on the menu revolve around its texture and flavour. Other offal is also given fair mention: duck gizzards, calf's liver, lambs' kidneys, bone marrow – not offal, but the same sort of intention is in mind – and sometimes trotters. If you like simplicity, however, 190 should cede eminence to Simon Hopkinson's Bibendum (see entry), where the raw material will be susceptible to more direct appreciation. This house in Queen's Gate has a bar and bistro (see Bistrot 190 entry) on the ground floor, a hotel (under different ownership) on the floors above, and the main restaurant in the basement. When you enter, the feeling is very much that of a club. The bar is comfortable, large and relaxing. The restaurant is very much more elaborate – swagged, tented ceilings, large pictures, lots of lights, grand table settings – in sum, fitted for the cooking that will be offered. The initial impression of club is not so far adrift, for 190 is a club of food service professionals: chefs, managers and any assorted hangers-on that can be persuaded to pay the subscription. Members get a £5 discount on the menu price and a percentage discount elsewhere in the building. Cooking has remained extremely gutsy, overly complicated and enamoured either of layers of flavour or the juxtaposition of different tastes around the plate. Here, if three things can serve as well as one, be sure that three will be used. So a grilled fillet of mullet served atop a bed of roughly chopped tomato and basil cooked in the most flavoursome olive oil was surrounded by triangular crostini of brandade, tapénade and anchoïade. Puritans have said that the fish needed no more attention than the tomato mixture. Layering comes in a signature dish of Bresse pigeon, cabbage and foie gras, the theme continues into the desserts: lemon three ways. Dieters be warned. The success of the kitchen is often resounding, but there have been slip-ups, for instance, a leathery and salty cheese soufflé. Service, especially of wine, is intelligent and enjoyable though delays can occur: 'We arrived at 9.33 and were ushered hastily into the bar on the basis that our table was just being vacated...I fell asleep...At 10.15 we asked for a menu...At 10.30 we sat down at table, exhausted with hunger...The main courses arrived at about 11.15.' It was Murphy's Law that this reporter should have an ice-bucket spilled over his foot ('I declined the waitress's offer to dry my sock'). It is revealing that, even though passing through a blizzard of practical impediments, he judged the food very favourably. From Italy, Burgundy and Australia the sureness of selection displayed in the wine list shows enthusiasm and consideration. Mark-ups are not at all bad, if a little haphazard in places; there is still much good drinking under £15 and a decent range of halves. House wines are from £9.25. CELLARMAN'S CHOICE: Barossa Valley, Chardonnay 1988, Hill-Smith, £16.25; Ch. Sociando Mallet 1985, £26.45.

CHEFS: Antony Worrall-Thompson and Sebastian Snow PROPRIETORS: 190 Queensgate plc OPEN: Mon to Sat, exc Sat L CLOSED: 10 days Christmas, 2 weeks Aug, bank hols MEALS: 12 to 3, 7 to 11 PRICES: Set L £14.50 (£21) to £19 (£26), Set D £33.50 (£42) to £38.50 (£48) CARDS: Access, Amex, Diners, Visa SEATS: 70. Private parties: 80 main room, 25 private room. Children's helpings. Smart dress preferred. No music. Air-conditioned. Fax: 071-581 8172

Orso 🍷

map 14

27 Wellington Street, WC2E 7DA — COOKING 2
071-240 5269 — COST £37

A large, very trendily decorated basement restaurant that is reached from an undistinguished entrance just south of Covent Garden. It sits back to back with Joe Allen, its corporate parent, which does for fashionable American food much as Orso does for Italian: 'Had we been the two well-known film actresses at the next table who arrived after us and were served sooner, we would have been better off,' complained a reporter. Invariably busy – you will be pushed off your table for a second evening sitting – Orso is none the less convenient for matinée and pre-theatre meals. Sundays, too, are more manageable. The food is as fashionable as the waiting staff (the hairstyles are worth a visit) and can be excellent; so, too, can be the service – happy, friendly, speedy and keen. There is a dark side to this moon, however, too often reported for comfort.

Some of this may be venting of spleen for delays and overcrowding, but other instances of purely sloppy cooking are genuine enough. Even so, this place taught London about new-wave Italian and it is still worth reading the lesson. Eat the pasta, the little pizze, shellfish 'all succulent, fresh and perfectly cooked' with spaghetti, the risotto with arugula, grilled lamb with trivisano, the mascarpone and the salads, and drink the coffee. The brief and exclusively Italian wine list shows intelligence in its range and enthusiasm for top quality. A few older vintages remain. There is much very good drinking below £15 and prices throughout are fair. House wine is £9 a litre. CELLARMAN'S CHOICE: Galestro 1990, Antinori, £10.50; Valpolicella Classico 1989, Allegrini, £11.

CHEF: Martin Wilson PROPRIETORS: Orso Restaurants Ltd OPEN: all week CLOSED: 25 and 26 Dec MEALS: noon to midnight PRICES: £21 (£31) SEATS: 110. Vegetarian meals. Children welcome. No music. Fax: 071-497 2148

Osteria Antica Bologna

NEW ENTRY map 10

23 Northcote Road, SW11 1NG — COOKING 1*
071-978 4771 — COST £12–£24

In Italy an *osteria* is a small town or village inn where wine and simple dishes are traditionally served. In a bland Clapham shopping street this translates as a basically decorated café with close, small tables, hard uncomfortable chairs and benches and, as one reader put it, 'a naff exterior' – namely barrel ends and planks of wood. Yet reports have spoken well of the food and of the inexpensive Italian wine list. In keeping with the *osteria* theme, first courses are reminiscent of Spanish tapas: little dishes of sausage with black beans, bruschetta, crostini, all designed to be shared. Aurelio Spagnuolo was born in Sicily and raised in Bologna and his cooking reflects this in a mixture of northern and southern dishes. About half the menu is vegetarian, including a hearty soup of bread, cabbage and beans, and some polenta dishes. Pasta with swordfish and mint and black cuttlefish with aubergine owe more to modern Italian restaurant cooking and are not as well handled. The cooking can be erratic, especially the quality of ingredients. No one disputes the good value of it all, nor the necessity to book a table. House Italian is £6.20.

CHEF: Aurelio Spagnuolo PROPRIETORS: Rochelle Porteous and Aurelio Spagnuolo OPEN: all week, exc Sun D MEALS: Mon to Sat 11am to 11pm, Sun L 12 to 4 PRICES: £12 (£20), Set L £6.50 (£12) CARDS: Access, Visa SEATS: 70. Private parties: 40 main room. Vegetarian meals. Children welcome. Music. Air-conditioned

Panda Si Chuen

map 14

56 Old Compton Street, W1V 5PA — COOKING 1
071-437 2069 — COST £15–£24

This Szechuan restaurant has taken Panda into its name. Regular supporters complain that the name is more Szechuan than the cooking, the original fire of which has got as polished as the redecorated dining-rooms. Thus the kitchen has fallen to the assault of blandness and standardised menus. Yet tea-smoked duck, fish-fragrant aubergines with shredded pork and pelmeni with hot pepper sauce and garlic are unfamiliar enough for many and repay ordering. The rest of the repertoire is none the less well cooked and service is excellent.

CHEF: Ping Tzue PROPRIETOR: K. Chew OPEN: Mon to Sat MEALS: noon to 11.30 PRICES: £9 (£20), Set L £9 (£15), Set D £12 (£19) CARDS: Access, Amex, Diners, Visa SEATS: 60. Private parties: 40 main room, 15 private room. Vegetarian meals. Children welcome. Music. Air-conditioned

Il Passetto

map 13

230 Shaftesbury Avenue, WC2H 8EG — COOKING 1
071-836 9391 and 379 7962 — COST £31

The tallest pepper-mill is hardly out of place at this discreet, long-established restaurant, and the ebullient affability of owners and staff ensure a loyal following for what is hardly new-wave cookery but is at least fresh – witness the materials trundled up and down the room on trolleys. Seafood salad and bucattini pasta are the invariable diet of one pair of incorrigible supporters, and each will have his or her favourite from among the fresh pasta, veal or calf's offal dishes. The wines are Italian, with house at £7.95.

CHEF: Jesus Sanchez PROPRIETORS: Domenico Forcina and Jesus Sanchez OPEN: Mon to Sat, exc Sat L CLOSED: 25 and 26 Dec, bank hols MEALS: 12 to 3, 6 to 11.30 PRICES: £16 (£26). Cover £1 CARDS: Access, Amex, Diners, Visa SEATS: 46. Private parties: 50 main room. Children welcome. Wheelchair access. Music. Air-conditioned

Pizzeria Castello

map 11

20 Walworth Road, SE1 6SP — COOKING 1
071-703 2556 — COST £15

Some say that this is the best independent pizzeria in the capital; more feel that perhaps it was once, but is now no better than the local competition. The setting is certainly not in its favour: an unpromising building opposite the shopping centre on the Newington Butts roundabout is hardly an attractive prospect for many people. But the queues continue to form and the place is packed every night. Large, over-topped pizzas cooked in big ovens by the entrance are the main attraction; pasta dishes are less impressive. Service can be 'breathless'. Like the food, thc house wine (£5.20) is cheap and cheerful.

CHEF: Cicero Calogero PROPRIETORS: Renzo Meda and Antonio Proietti OPEN: Mon to Sat, exc Sat L MEALS: noon (5 Sat) to 11 PRICES: £8 (£12) CARDS: Access, Visa SEATS: 180. Private parties: 30 main room. Vegetarian meals. Children's helpings on request. Wheelchair access (also WC). Music. Air-conditioned

Pizzeria Condotti

map 13

4 Mill Street, W1R 9TE — COOKING 1
071-499 1308 — COST £24

This is one of the most elegant pizza houses around and ahead of most of its competitors. Condotti has links with the Pizza Express chain, which means that toppings are vivid, mozzarella cheese is standard and eggs are free-range. The back-up is an assortment of colourful salads, good garlic bread, ice-creams and cheesecake. Drink espresso coffee, ice-cold Italian Peroni beer or the house Chianti at £7.20.

CHEFS: Mahmoud Eskendry and Nacevr Hammami PROPRIETORS: Enzo Apicella and Peter Boizot OPEN: Mon to Sat MEALS: 11.30am to midnight PRICES: £11 (£20). Service 12.5% for parties of 6 or more CARDS: Access, Amex, Diners, Visa SEATS: 130. Private parties: 70 main room, 50 private room. Children's helpings. Wheelchair access (2 steps). No music. Air-conditioned

Poissonnerie de l'Avenue NEW ENTRY map 12

82 Sloane Avenue, SW3 3DZ COOKING 2
071-589 5774 COST £24–£42

If one says this long-established fish restaurant is popular with locals it may be condemned, in terms of inverse snobbery, to ghetto status. In fact, it offers an old-fashioned welcome and some very good fish in fairly plush surroundings, and even if sourcing does not have especial panache it knocks spots off some of the French-fish competition for politeness and consistency. Prices, for the area, are not high, though the cover charge helps boost the total if you are eating from the *carte*. The wine list is short and not very informative. House wines are £9.

CHEF: Fernando Tomassi PROPRIETOR: Peter Rosignoli OPEN: Mon to Sat CLOSED: 23 Dec to 3 Jan, 4 days Easter, bank hols MEALS: 12 to 3, 7 to 11.30 PRICES: £24 (£35), Set L £17.50 (£24). Cover £1.25 alc only. Card slips closed CARDS: Access, Amex, Diners, Visa SEATS: 90. 8 tables outside. Private parties: 24 private room. Children's helpings. Smart dress preferred. No-smoking area. Wheelchair access. Air-conditioned. No music. Fax: 071-581 3360

Pollyanna's map 10

2 Battersea Rise, SW11 1ED COOKING 1
071-228 0316 COST £25–£42

Artful design renders this super-cool to the eye: a long dining-room on a mezzanine stretching through broad blocks of light and shade created by clever paintwork and minimalist joinery. The nearest to 'polly' here is the blue parrot-fish usually offered as a main course. Norman Price runs an informative, accessible and amiable operation. The information concerns the wine list: all his own work. Accessibility and amiability come from the attitudes, helped by a change to fixed-price menus this year, as well as the good-value traditional Sunday lunches. Richard Aldridge, roasts apart, cooks with a modern palette and a sweet palate. Meals are not without fault and surprising sweetness can rear its ugly head, which may not help the wines. The style, evinced by dishes such as nage of monkfish or lamb with wild mushrooms and a madeira sauce, is modern, reinforced by that old English staple banoffi pie at dessert stage. The bottle award for the wine list is retained. Exclusively French, the selection is good and intelligent. As much weight is given to petits châteaux and modest Loires as it is to fine Alsaces from 1983 and the enviable range of top burgundies. Prices are a close and fair reflection of quality throughout. House wines are from £9.50. CELLARMAN'S CHOICE: St Romain 1987, Leflaive, £22.50; Graves, Ch. de France 1982, £17.50.

CHEF: Richard Aldridge PROPRIETOR: Norman Price OPEN: Mon to Sat, D only, and Sun L CLOSED: 4 days Christmas MEALS: 1 to 3, 7 to 12 PRICES: Set Sun L £14.95 (£25), Set D £19.95 (£30) to £24.50 (£35). Service 10%. Card slips closed CARDS: Access, Amex, Visa SEATS: 35. Private parties: 20 main room, 35 private room. Vegetarian meals. Children's helpings (Sun L only). Music

Poons

map 14

4 Leicester Street, WC2H 7BL
071-437 1528

COOKING 1
COST £16–£30

In its early days, this branch of the Poons mini-empire was considered rather swish. Today, compared with many of its gentrified neighbours, it looks and feels more like a café, with cramped, closely packed tables and queues of tourists and theatre-goers jostling for a place. When it is on form, the kitchen can deliver gutsy back-to-the-roots Cantonese dishes: not only the famous wind-dried specialities, but also one-plate meals, roast meats, hotpots and casseroles. Stewed spiced brisket chow-mein has been 'potently flavoured'; braised stuffed bean curd in gravy has had all the flavour of 'real peasant food – rustic, earthy, full-blooded'. Reporters have also praised wun-tun soup, crispy pork and stewed eel casserole, and duck with ginger. There is criticism that the cooking is uneven, 'uninspiring stuff' and that the décor is becoming increasingly tacky. Staff can also be off-hand, although one visitor spotted 'that rarest of sights in a Chinese restaurant – waiters with smiles and good humour!' Drink jasmine tea. House wine is £8.

CHEF/PROPRIETOR: W.N. Poon OPEN: Mon to Sat CLOSED: 25 Dec MEALS: noon to 11.30 PRICES: £13 (£25), Set L and D £9 (£16) to £13 (£25). Minimum £6 SEATS: 100. Private parties: 30 main room. Children welcome. Air-conditioned. Fax: 081-458 0968

Poons

NEW ENTRY map 14

27 Lisle Street, WC2H 7BA
071-437 4549

COOKING 2
COST £8–£14

Seasoned reporters agree that this original branch of Poons is still Soho's seminal Cantonese café. It is 'basically honest, a place to fill up with good, solid, mostly simple Chinese food'. The window is hung with famous wind-dried specialities – flattened ducks, sausages and Chinese bacon, as well as roast meats and offal. The downstairs room is cramped and functional; upstairs it seems almost posh by comparison, although the imitation wood panelling, bentwood chairs and plastic tablecloths are reminders that this place has few restaurant aspirations. The kitchen scores with fresh-tasting ingredients and spot-on authentic cooking. As well as the wind-dried foods, there are robust hotpots and casseroles, one-plate rice and noodle dishes and specialities such as stewed bean curd with crispy pork and shrimp paste, oil-soaked scallops, and fried beef with bitter cucumber. Reporters have been wholly won over by the char siu pork and roast duck, oyster hotpot with crispy pork, ginger and vegetables, deep-fried prawns with garlic and chilli and spicy Singapore noodles. Choi-sum greens with oyster sauce are outstandingly succulent. The décor may seem tatty, but the food more than compensates for that. Drink tea.

CHEFS: Mr B.T. Ly and Mr Chiu PROPRIETORS: Mr and Mrs Kit Chuen Chiu OPEN: all week CLOSED: Christmas MEALS: noon to 11.30 PRICES: £8 (£12), Set L and D £7 (£8). Minimum £2.20 SEATS: 40. Private parties: 30 main room. Vegetarian meals. Children welcome. No music. Air-conditioned

Quality Chop House

map 11

94 Farringdon Road, EC1R 3EA — COOKING 2*
071-837 5093 — COST £26

If you start by going downstairs to the lavatories, or walk straight down the aisle to visit the kitchen, you will view the clean tiling, stainless steel and mod cons of a late-twentieth-century restaurant: proof against the most violent health and safety inspection. Sit in the pine-settled booths, six places per slot, with a head-high shelf of bottled sauces at one end, anaglypta on walls and ceiling, and converted gas lamps on the walls and you may think yourself on a filmset for a First World War working-class drama. The customers may disabuse you of ragged-trousered thoughts: suits, American visitors, barely shaved chins of thinking *Guardian* journalists from across the road, young bloods appreciative of the plentiful revivalist cooking – huge bowls of chips, giant slices of calf's liver and bacon – all mingle in a happy and extremely busy throng. Charles Fontaine's idea of a decent place for simple cooking (good materials, accurate tastes) has worked. The tolerance of the waiting staff is infinite and eating here is free of hassle, even if the to and fro of parties is constant and may mean a shared booth if you go as a couple. There are occasions when time is too short to eat in peace before your window ('we need the table at 10') begins to close. Portions are giant: celeriac rémoulade, a pungent Caesar salad, corn beef hash, ribeye steak (regulars say the quality can vary), accurate omelettes, old-fashioned bread-and-butter pudding – the kitchen does not go in for namby-pamby interpretations. Good coffee, tea in bags. The wine list is short, but very reasonably priced.

CHEF/PROPRIETOR: Charles Fontaine OPEN: all week, exc Sat L MEALS: 12 to 3, 6.30 to 11.30 PRICES: £14 (£22) SEATS: 48. Vegetarian meals. Children's helpings. Wheelchair access. No music

Ragam

map 13

57 Cleveland Street, W1P 5PQ — COOKING 1*
071-636 9098 — COST £16

The simple, box-like dining-room is so cramped that 'you might find yourself tucked up at the far end, rubbing shoulders with a waiter folding napkins or reading a newspaper,' according to one reporter. Even so, the cooking 'puts to shame many of its illustrious competitors'. Main attractions from the vegetarian and carnivorous menu are south Indian dishes and specialities from the Kerala coast. Excellent masala dosa, uthappam, avial (mixed vegetables cooked with coconut, yoghurt and curry leaves) and kalan (a Kerala curry with sweet mango and spices) have been recommended. Meat curries show clean flavours, subtle spicing and a noticeable lack of the residual oil so characteristic of second-rate curry houses: sag josh, chicken malabar and lamb dupiaza have all been good. Breads are some of the best of their kind in London (chapatis, puris and parathas are made with proper skill), but be warned, they come in pairs and are the size of dinner-plates. Lemon rice and coconut rice are up to the mark. Service is casual, genuinely friendly and gracious. Italian house wine is £6.

CHEFS: J. Dharmaseelan and Mojid Ullah PROPRIETORS: J. Dharmaseelan, T. Haridas and S. Pillai OPEN: all week MEALS: 12 to 3, 6 to 11.30 PRICES: £7 (£13). Minimum £4. Service 10%. Card slips closed. CARDS: Access, Amex, Diners, Visa SEATS: 34. Private parties: 34 main room, 25 private room. Vegetarian meals. Children's helpings. Wheelchair access (also WC). Music. Air-conditioned

Rani

map 10

7 Long Lane, N3 2PR — COOKING 2
081-349 4386 and 2636 — COST £11–£28

Designed on clean bright lines, strong on red, with slightly utilitarian furnishings, Rani is one of the most authentic Indian vegetarian restaurants in London. This is largely because the owner's wife and mother do most of the cooking. Close attention to detail means that even the chutneys and pickles are made on the premises and the fresh flavours of these encapsulate the fine balance and style of the kitchen. An excellent range of breads and an imaginative selection of vegetable curries are backed up by bhel pooris, bhajias, masala dosai and papri chat. Spicing is authoritative and there is a real feel for texture and contrasts. One special dish is offered each day. The selection of home-made sweets is extensive; falooda must have been inspired by Barbara Cartland – all pink and frothy. Carrot halva, ras malai and gulab jamun have also been enjoyed. Service is friendly and attentive. No gratuities are accepted. Excellent lassi and Indian lager to drink. House French is £10 a litre.

CHEFS: Kundan Pattni and Sheila Pattni PROPRIETOR: Jyotindra Pattni OPEN: all week, exc Mon, Tue and Sat L CLOSED: 25 Dec MEALS: 12.30 to 2, 6 to 10.30 PRICES: £15 (£23), Set L £5 (£11) to £10 (£16), Set D from £7 (£13) to £17 (£23). Minimum £7. Net prices, card slips closed CARDS: Access, Visa SEATS: 90. Vegetarian meals. Children's helpings. No children under 6. No-smoking area. Music

Riva

NEW ENTRY map 10

169 Church Road, SW13 9HR — COOKING 3
081-748 0434 — COST £32

This small restaurant in a shopping parade at the bottom of Castelnau, the long street running south from Hammersmith Bridge, caused an almighty stir in the summer of 1990. Its opening seemed to be a gift to the massed scribblers of the capital – having had no Italian food like it since the River Café and Cibo (see entries). What was more, it wasn't too dear and everyone seemed happy and friendly – a most propitious opening. The promise has been fulfilled. Lots of opera, nice architectural prints, pale grey walls and an Italian ethnic staff are in the background. Andrea Riva was once heard confessing that he tended to employ people who had not been 'sullied' by prior English experience, though he himself is an old hand. The predictable things here are most enjoyable: grilled vegetables, black risotto, calf's liver with polenta, tiramisù ('I am now addicted,' wrote one reader of the tiramisù). Equally, there are good and less familiar items: goose carpaccio with pecorino and walnut dressing; red snapper with pine kernels; skate with butter-beans; and sweet gnocchi. Mistakes do occur: too much oil with vegetables, crystals in ice-cream and nugatory scallops with tagliatelle have figured, but the smooth is worth the rough. Exclusively Italian, the wines are mostly under £20. A single page of youthful vintages promises many exhilarating marriages with the food. Two fine dessert wines are available by the glass and grappe ('a vast selection from £3,' claims the wine list) are worth investigation. Greater depth, especially in the red wines, might merit a glass award. House wine is £7.20.

CHEF: Francesco Zanchetta PROPRIETOR: Andrea Riva OPEN: all week, exc Sat L CLOSED: Christmas, Easter, bank hols MEALS: 12 to 2.30, 7 to 11 (11.30 Fri and Sat, 9.30 Sun) PRICES: £18 (£27). Service 10%. Card slips closed CARDS: Access, Visa SEATS: 50. 2 tables outside. Private parties: 40 main room. Vegetarian meals. Children's helpings. No pipes in dining-room. Wheelchair access. Music. Air-conditioned

River Café 🍷

map 10

Thames Wharf Studios,
Rainville Road, W6 9HA
071-381 8824

COOKING 3*
COST £42

That this restaurant is invariably full – and booking can sometimes be like applying for a reference from the KGB – must say something about the quality of the Tuscan and north Italian food, even about the service and quality of welcome, which some find off-hand and even occasionally minatory. The British are not great followers of architectural fashion, so the fact that the Café is within the same block as Sir Richard Rogers' offices (and was designed by him) should be less of a draw than Rose Gray's or Ruthie Rogers' skills at the stove. Finding the Thames-side setting through a whirlpool of one-way streets is never easy; ask for directions. If the wind abates and the rain is not pressing, take in the view from the terrace. The room itself is basic in comfort, cramped for space and can be noisy. In the context of the usual disjunction between formalists who like hardware for their money and those who go to restaurants for the food and are prepared to pay for quality, intending visitors need to be of the second persuasion. They will find a menu that changes meal by meal and offers a half-dozen choices at each course. Desserts apart, the repertoire is exclusively Italian. The grill is important, but more techniques than that are mobilised for cooking main courses: liver and veal pan-fried, sea bass poached, shin of veal slowly braised, beef or partridge pot-roasted. Modes of assembly differ too. While some dishes are built around counterpoint and disposition of elements over a plate – prosciutto di San Daniele and Cavaillon melon, or a lamb salad where chargrilled lamb comes with a salsa verde, arugula, red chicory and chargrilled leeks – there are other things such as Bresse pigeon stuffed with thyme, served with port and crème fraîche and some braised Swiss chard, that reflect far more complex preparation. In all instances, though, the restaurant revolves around materials, one of the main characteristics of London new-wave in the late '80s. Indeed, such places as this have almost created a new generation of importers and wholesalers. Here fresh and other ingredients withstand examination. The Café also depends on preparation techniques steering a course between over-refinement and rough artlessness. One reader was struck at how a salsa verde with grilled turbot, and field and wild mushrooms, did just that. Desserts can be grand and chocolate oblivion cake has induced the correct consequence, but they do not always show the excitement of the first parts of a meal. Ice-creams and sorbets, though, are ace. If a course in Italian wine is needed, drink here. Ossie Gray's notes are really helpful about growers and estates. The choice is enviable, short enough not to outface, developing and yet upper-crust. House wine is £8.50.

CHEFS: Rose Gray and Ruth Rogers PROPRIETORS: Richard and Ruth Rogers, and Rose Gray OPEN: all week, exc Mon L, Sat D and Sun D CLOSED: bank hols MEALS: 12.30 to 3.15, 7.30 to 9.15 PRICES: £26 (£35). Service 12.5%. Card slips closed CARDS: Access, Visa SEATS: 80. 8 tables outside. Private parties: 70 main room. Car park, 30 places. Vegetarian meals. Children's helpings. Wheelchair access (also WC). No music. Air-conditioned

Rotisserie

map 10

56 Uxbridge Road, W12 8LP
081-743 3028

COOKING 1
COST £23

This is a reliable fixture of the Shepherd's Bush scene, near the tube station and close by the foot-bridge with a train on it. The long, narrow dining-room has plenty of space and light and the kitchen works to a well-tried formula. Business centres around a short, rarely changing menu dominated by the spit-roast and charcoal grill: corn-fed chicken, Scotch salmon, Barbary duck, rack of lamb, escalope of veal and calf's liver all receive the treatment. Ribs of beef are cooked spot-on and served with home-made béarnaise sauce. To start there are excellent spicy chicken wings, gravlax and merguez sausages, backed up by pasta and fashionable salads such as sautéed chicken liver with pancetta, new potatoes and balsamic vinegar. To finish there are ices and crème brûlée. 'Good and reliable with the simple things' sums it up. Like the menu, the wine list is short, sharp and to the point, taking in Argentina and Australia as well as France and Spain. House French is £7.50.

CHEF: Emanuel Schandorf PROPRIETOR: Karen Doherty OPEN: Mon to Sat, exc Sat L MEALS: 12 to 3, 6.30 (7 Sat) to 11 (11.30 Fri and Sat) PRICES: £12 (£19). Minimum £8 L CARDS: Access, Visa SEATS: 76. Vegetarian meals. Children welcome. Music

Royal China

map 10

3 Chelverton Road, SW15 1RN
081-788 0907

COOKING 2
COST £28–£41

Dazzling décor sets the tone for this impressive and chic Chinese restaurant. Black enamelled walls decorated with waves and birds, perspex-edged pillars and a black ceiling divided into squares by gold-coloured lines create a stunning impression. The menu is equally eye-catching, with its fancy names and florid descriptions. Hot and cold appetisers and the list of house specialities include some original ideas: yam prawns, deep-fried 'frilly' squid balls and marinated pork with jellyfish share the stage with sesame prawn toasts, Vietnamese spring rolls and Peking dumplings with chilli sauce. Elsewhere there are 'seven colour' bean curd soup, sautéed prawns with mango in a bird's nest, hot and spicy veal, and braised chicken breast in garlic sauce. Lobster is cooked six ways. Set meals include one for vegetarians. The wine list is strong on clarets; there is also a range of imported bottled beers. House French is £7.50.

CHEF: Simon Man PROPRIETORS: Ken Poon, Simon Man and Martin Man OPEN: all week CLOSED: 25 and 26 Dec MEALS: 12 to 2.30, 6.30 to 11 PRICES: £16 (£28), Set D £20 (£28) to £26 (£34) CARDS: Access, Amex, Diners, Visa SEATS: 70. Private parties: 70 main room. Vegetarian meals. Children welcome. Smart dress preferred. Wheelchair access. Music. Air-conditioned. Fax: 081-785 2305

RSJ

map 11

13A Coin Street, SE1 8YQ
071-928 4554 and 9768

COOKING 2
COST £20–£34

IPC, LWT, QEH, RFH, NFT, NT; the area is awash with acronyms. This one is for the steel joist that crosses the upstairs dining-room. All the others provide ample supplies of customers, as do departing trippers aiming for Waterloo, happy to pay none too much for very acceptable Anglo-French cooking. The hustle and bustle may abbreviate attentions from the front-of-house staff – some reporters have commented that knowledge of the excellent wine list is not always detailed – but no one criticises their cheery willingness or general efficiency. There is a set-price menu and a *carte* on offer. 'The menu changes often but some things are so good that we return for more, such as the chilled consommé encasing a lobster claw or the turbot with orange sauce.' A spring menu ranged over truffle and foie gras sausages (a bargain); hot smoked salmon; timbale of crab and sweetbread with a citrus salad; Dover sole with shellfish and salmon; maize-fed chicken with mushrooms and asparagus; walnut pear mousse; and amaretto parfait. Satisfaction can be measured by the number of RSJ fans, but even they have mentioned times when the tastes just miss the mark, that usually strong flavours are muted or undetectable. Equanimity is restored by the economy of it all and the fact that credit card slips are invariably closed. A new departure this year is a basement brasserie in converted wine cellars – a short card details confit of duck with lentils, cheese and sausage pasties, rillettes of pork (less rustic than their original) and beefburgers among a dozen options. Savennières, in the Loire valley, is not a name to rush to the front of even a wine-lover's vocabulary, but at RSJ no fewer than eight are listed. Chenin Blanc and Cabernet Franc are the grapes and this list does its best to run through their repertoires – old and new, sweet and dry – with carefully chosen burgundies from top growers Vocoret and Forest and a few excellent clarets and champagnes completing the picture. A bottle is awarded not simply for bravura, but as just reward for diligent work, missionary zeal and clarity of presentation. House wine is £8.95. CELLARMAN'S CHOICE: Sancerre 1989, Pellé, £14.25; Chinon, Vieilles Vignes 1989, Breton, £12.95.

CHEF: Ian Stabler PROPRIETOR: Nigel Wilkinson OPEN: Mon to Sat, exc Sat L CLOSED: 3 days Christmas MEALS: 12 to 2, 6 to 11 PRICES: £20 (£28), Set L and D £13.75 (£20) to £15.75 (£22). Service 10%. Card slips closed CARDS: Access, Amex, Visa SEATS: 60. Private parties: 40 main room, 20 private room. Children's helpings on request. Music. Air-conditioned

Rue St Jacques

map 13

5 Charlotte Street, W1A 1HP
071-637 0222

COOKING 3
COST £37–£60

Gunther Schlender's restaurant is as polished as his cooking: it glows in the down-lights against crimsons, gilts and greys, the setting of the silver, large plain glassware and white linen. A series of rooms exists, each pleasing, none very large. This is romantic, though often frequented by, and only affordable to, suits lunching suits. Service is as soigné as the rest. Two menus, one at lunch, the other at dinner, offer a wide choice, that at lunch being of simpler compositions and with fewer luxuries. Set-price, it has the courage not to charge supplements save for the beef with foie gras and truffles. The cooking shows loyalty to past fashions; it can sometimes, therefore, seem too refined for its own good – too much consideration of form at the expense of content. Fresh pasta with tomato was pretty and tender, but hardly flavourful; a guinea-fowl was nicely cooked but the sauce was an indeterminate reduction, its ingredients impossible to work out; a salad of cooked baby vegetables in saffron oil had rested in the fridge too long, the stronger pimentos chasing out lighter tastes during its sojourn; a strawberry mille-feuille proved to be of filo pastry, not puff, enhancing it for slimmers but reducing its variety of flavour. At the same time, this can be cooking of accuracy and some invention, delivering mainly classic flavours in sophisticated manner. It is also very rich. Favourable comment on such things as mussels with saffron and noodles, papillotes of smoked salmon with mayonnaise, John Dory with spices from the Far East, and sweetbreads with spinach and a vermouth butter sauce has been received. The wine list has the upper crust growers and properties, with little from outside France. There is an especially fine run of clarets and red burgundies. House wine is from £11.50.

CHEF: Gunther Schlender PROPRIETORS: Jessop and Boyce Restaurants OPEN: Mon to Sat, exc Sat L CLOSED: Christmas, Easter, bank hols MEALS: 12.15 to 2.30, 7.15 to 11 PRICES: Set L £23 (£37), Set D £29.50 (£44) to £35 (£50). Service 15%. Card slips closed CARDS: Access, Amex, Diners, Visa SEATS: 70. Private parties: 30 main room, 12, 14 and 24 private rooms. Vegetarian meals. Children's helpings on request. Jackets preferred. No pipes in dining-room. Wheelchair access (1 step). Music. Air-conditioned. Fax: 071-637 0224

Cellarman's Choice: a wine recommended by the restaurateur, normally more expensive than house wine.

County round-ups listing additional restaurants that may be worth a visit are at the back of the Guide, *after the Irish section. Reports on round-up entries are welcome.*

Sabatini

NEW ENTRY map 12

22 Brompton Road,
Knightsbridge Green, SW1X 7QN — COOKING 1
071-589 8772 and 581 3485 — COST £42

Occupying that expensive corner of Knightsbridge almost opposite Harrods means that Sabatini is not cheap. One reader wonders if it is the enormous number of solicitous waiters and other staff who account for the high prices. The place itself is tiny, the décor modern Italian trattoria – pale colours, floor tiles, lots of greenery and discreet ceiling lighting. Plate-glass mirrors help create an illusion of space. The menu lacks some sparkle. Fish dishes and first courses are a shade more inventive than the meats: monkfish with a lentil sauce, salmon with balsamic vinegar, grilled vegetables in garlic oil and granary tagliatelle served with duck ragoût stand out. What the kitchen lacks in imagination it makes up for in sound basic ingredients and careful cooking, though some lapses occur. A crisp, non-greasy dish of lightly battered strips of Dover sole and squid was marred by a cloying sweet-and-sour sauce, 'very fast-food' in style. Yet veal stuffed with leeks and Gorgonzola was carefully done, the strong cheese handled with care. Desserts, apart from a light tiramisù, are not exciting and espresso is surprisingly weak. The predominantly Italian wine list is short on information such as growers' names, but long on flowery and inaccurate prose. Prices are quite low. House Italian is £8.95.

CHEF: Roberto Magnani PROPRIETOR: John Layton OPEN: Mon to Sat MEALS: 12 to 3, 7 to 11.30 PRICES: £21 (£35). Cover £1.30. Service 10%. Card slips closed CARDS: Access, Amex, Diners, Visa SEATS: 100. Private parties: 100 main room. Vegetarian meals. Children's helpings. Music. Air-conditioned

Sabras

map 10

263 Willesden High Road, NW10 2RX — COOKING 1
081-459 0340 — COST £13–£23

Sabras began life as a neighbourhood café but has developed over the years into a highly respected Indian vegetarian restaurant. The long menu covers a lot of territory, although its heart is Gujarati. Farshan snacks such as samosas, kachoris and patra are served with a pair of home-made chutneys; there are cold pooris from Bombay's Chowpatty Beach, south Indian dosas and a formidable list of pulses and vegetable curries. Look for ravaiya (stuffed baby aubergines with bananas and potatoes), ugavela moong (home-sprouted mung beans with chillies and lemon), peppers stuffed with spices, and seasonal Indian vegetables such as karela, tindora and dudhi. Surati undhiu is an Indian winter extravaganza (served December to March) with unusual vegetables, including violet yams and mini broad beans, served with puris. The array of sweets takes in not only kulfi and halva, but also aam-ras (mango pulp) and puran poli (stuffed mini chapatis with sugar, nutmeg and cardamom). Recent reports suggest that the kitchen may be resting on its laurels: 'warmed-up and dried-out starters and one-dimensional curries on my last visit,' complains one regular visitor. To drink there are lassi and spiced tea, as well as beers from around the world and a few basic wines. House French is £5.50.

CHEFS/PROPRIETORS: Hemant and Nalinee Desai OPEN: all week, exc Mon L MEALS: 12.45 to 2.30, 6 to 10 (1 to 10 Sat and Sun) PRICES: £10 (£19), Set L and D £8.50 (£13) to £11 (£16). Service 12.5%. Card slips closed CARDS: Access, Visa SEATS: 32. Private parties: 32 main room. Vegetarian meals. Children welcome. No-smoking area. Wheelchair access. Music

St Quentin

map 12

243 Brompton Road, SW3 2EP
071-581 5131

COOKING 2
COST £19–£32

St Quentin gained a lot of friends when it celebrated 10 years of trading with 10 days of old prices for new food. For a decade, then, it has been a useful staging post to the V & A, Harrods or Brompton Oratory. It may seem strange to assert, but it is as much a local resource as a bistro in N6, foie gras notwithstanding. The set-price menus remain very fair value. Cooking of dishes such as a chicken liver parfait served with raisin bread, scallops with tarragon, quenelles of pike, crab with grapefruit, even that old standby omelette Norvègienne, has been thought acceptable, though other accounts will mention blandness as the consequence of too many people, a cause as well of occasional long waits for attention. Although it is partly owned by that most British of companies, the Savoy Group, and boasts an English chef, St Quentin remains resolutely French. House wine is £7.60.

CHEF: Stephen Whitney PROPRIETORS: St Quentin Ltd OPEN: all week MEALS: 12 to 3 (4 Sun), 7 to 12 (11.30 Sun) PRICES: £19 (£27), Set L £11.90 (£19), Set D £14.90 (£22). Service 12.5%. Card slips closed CARDS: Access, Amex, Diners, Visa SEATS: 85. Private parties: 25 private room. Children welcome. Air-conditioned. No music. Fax: 071-584 6064

▲ *Savoy Grill and River Restaurant*

map 14

Strand, WC2R 0EU
071-836 4343

COOKING 3
COST £37–£74

The Grill Room, on the left of the hotel entrance, has an independent life as a luxury establishment restaurant. David Sharland has proved a capable chef and the repertoire is as much appreciated for the traditional grills, roasts and British favourites on one side of the menu as for the haute cuisine on the other. Dishes such as guinea-fowl sautéed and served with a light vegetable broth, sole with leeks and chanterelles, brill à la niçoise, lobster consommé with its ravioli are abreast, but not ahead, of current developments and are executed to a very high standard. Service, appointments and price are everything we know, and may fear, of such well-entrenched institutions. Anton Edelmann's River Room, deep inside the hotel, with great views of the river from window tables and an orchestra come the evening, has to be more generalist in its approach. Here, too, British tradition can be essayed alongside haute cuisine, and reporters have been struck by the efficiency of the systems that can deliver exactly bought and exactly cooked food to so many people at once. Mistakes are inevitable, though never wholly vitiating the worth of this very steady hotel kitchen. The wine list offers a price range, but it does not measure up to the stocks of the more ambitious West End hotels making a pitch for culinary fame. There is concession to reality in the choice from outside France. Both restaurants have various fixed-price offerings that give opportunity to moderate the cost.

CHEFS: David Sharland (Grill) and Anton Edelmann (River Restaurant) PROPRIETORS: Savoy Hotel plc OPEN: Grill Mon to Sat, exc Sat L; River Restaurant all week, exc Sun L CLOSED: Grill Aug MEALS: Grill 12.30 to 2.30, 6 to 11.15; River Restaurant 12.30 to 2.30, 7.30 to 11.30 (10.30 Sun) PRICES: Grill £33 (£51), Set pre-theatre D £27 (£37); River Restaurant £43 (£62), Set L £24.50 (£38), Set D £29.50 (£43) to £41.30 (£56) CARDS: Access, Amex, Carte Blanche, Diners, Visa SEATS: Grill 80, River Restaurant 150. Children restricted L, 7 or over only D Grill. Jacket and tie. No pipes in dining-room. Wheelchair access. Music River Restaurant. No music Grill. Air-conditioned. Fax: 071-240 6040 ACCOMMODATION: 202 rooms, all with bath/shower. Rooms for disabled. Lift. B&B £185 to £210. Children welcome. Baby facilities. Afternoon teas. Air-conditioned. TV. Phone. Confirm by 6 (*Which? Hotel Guide*)

Simply Nico NEW ENTRY map 11

48A Rochester Row, SW1P 1JU COOKING 3
071-630 8061 COST £30–£41

The man himself *mange ici* on Saturdays. First conceived as a super-bistro – almost the first, and called Very Simply – it had a restricted menu, set prices and some emphasis on the grill. In the couple of intervening years, it has been redecorated, had oilcloth removed for table linen although the bare boards and close-set tables remain, and picked up a menu that is more restaurant than bistro. The set-price menus remain fair at any rate, even if ancillaries and drinks send bills soaring. There are moments when service is peremptory (too often this), or when intentions seem at odds with expectations. On the menu steak survives at a supplement, while new dishes include shin of veal braised in madeira, chicken stuffed with green peppercorns, garlic and ceps, and cod with pickled vegetables and garlic mayonnaise. Some of the desserts, along the lines of apple charlotte, pear crumble, armagnac parfait and crème brûlée instead of crème caramel, have been seen at Chez Nico. Most people enjoy it here even if noise can be a problem; they like the olives, the baguette and the butter; they take pleasure from a decent confit of duck with creamed mustard lentils, the stuffed chicken, the brochette of liver – though bacon was too fatty for one and the sauce too sweet – or the first course of warm escalope of salmon with herb mayonnaise. Fish soup is still a convincing colour, with strong Pernod overtones; a warm potato salad with more confit of duck has slightly sweet mustard sauce. An inspection meal found that main courses were imperfectly executed – elaboration was not matched by skill – but that chips still had a good flavour if not crispness. Old hands (not that old after all) hanker for a return to simplicity, feeling that the original idea was a good one. They also wish service was better. The wine list is good reason for a clash of expectations. There are four wines under £12, the rest are between £16.50 (one only) and £58. There are but four half-bottles. This is a contradiction.

All letters to the Guide *are acknowledged with an update on latest sales, closures, chef changes and so on.*

CHEF: Andrew Jeffs PROPRIETORS: Nico and Dinah-Jane Ladenis OPEN: Mon to Sat, exc Sat L CLOSED: 10 days Christmas, 4 days Easter, 3 weeks Aug MEALS: 12 to 2, 7 to 11 PRICES: Set L and D £23 (£30) to £27 (£34). Net prices, card slips closed CARDS: Access, Diners, Visa SEATS: 48. Private parties: 24 main room. Vegetarian meals. Children welcome. Smart dress preferred. No pipes in dining-room. Wheelchair access (1 step). Air-conditioned. No music. Fax: 071-436 0134

Singapore Garden Mayfair map 13

85 Piccadilly, W1V 9HD COOKING 1
071-491 2222 COST £19–£44

Reporters feel that this classy, plush venue has the edge on its Swiss Cottage original (see entry below). The décor is pure Mayfair – black marble floors, black chairs, exotic plants and an all-pervading air of luxury. The menu centres on Singapore, with a few detours into China and Malaysia. Seafood is a strong suit. Otherwise, there have been recommendations for turkey satay, mee goreng and other noodle dishes, beef rendang and baby okra with garlic. Also look for specialities such as chilli lobster, jellyfish salad and aromatic duck wrapped with yams. Staff are excellent but the £1 cover charge and 15 per cent service charge seem unjustifiable. Drink Tiger beer, or house wine at £9.90.

CHEF: Toh Kok Sum PROPRIETORS: Stephen Lim, David Tsai and Thomas Wong OPEN: all week CLOSED: Christmas week MEALS: 12 to 2.45, 6.30 to 11.30 (11 Sun) PRICES: £24 (£37), Set L £10.80 (£19), Set D £19.80 (£30) to £21.50 (£32). Cover £1. Minimum £12. Service 15% CARDS: Access, Amex, Diners, Visa SEATS: 90. Private parties: 80 main room, 10 private room. Vegetarian meals. Children welcome. Music. Air-conditioned

Singapore Garden Restaurant map 11

83–83A Fairfax Road, NW6 4DY COOKING 1
071-328 5314 COST £22–£31

Reports indicate that the cooking is better than ever at this spacious, plant-filled restaurant offering a lengthy menu of Chinese and Malaysian/ Singaporean dishes. Well liked locally, it has a large, regular clientele, especially in the evenings, and on Saturday nights there is live music. Recommendations have been for the steamed meat dumplings, prawn sambal, beef rendang, chilli beef and Singapore noodles. Fish seems to be a strong point. Desserts of ginger ice-cream and sago pudding with coconut milk and syrup are 'refreshing and different'. Service, even on a busy Saturday night, remains smiling. Apparently reasonable prices mount up with bits and pieces, plus steep service. House wine is £7.15, but Tiger beer is better with the food.

CHEF: Mrs S. Lim PROPRIETORS: the Lim family OPEN: all week MEALS: 12 to 2.45, 6 to 10.45 (11.15 Fri and Sat) PRICES: £14 (£26), Set D £14.85 (£22). Minimum £9. Service 12.5%. Card slips closed CARDS: Access, Amex, Diners, Visa SEATS: 100. Private parties: 60 main room, 60 private room. Vegetarian meals. Children welcome. Music. Air-conditioned

▲ *This symbol means that accommodation is available.*

Soho Soho NEW ENTRY map 14

11–13 Frith Street, W1V 5TS COOKING 1*
071-494 3491 COST £17–£35

'This is the nearest I think one can find to the sort of ordinary brasserie one goes to when in any large French city,' comments a reporter about this cheerful Soho venue. Some have found the orange and green plastic around the frontage 'aesthetically jarring', but the inside is clean, light and airy. The menu for the upstairs restaurant, a short *carte* of fixed dishes with half a dozen or so *plats du jour*, has a few fashionable touches such as lentils, polenta and olive bread, but the emphasis is happily French. To start there have been asparagus on a bed of salad leaves topped with shavings of Parmesan, and pissaladière adorned with fresh ingredients that 'spoke of themselves'. Centrepieces are the likes of leg of duck on a bed of braised white cabbage, fettucine with an intensely flavoured wild mushroom sauce, and a brave dish of salmon fillet braised in goose fat. Calf's liver has drawn high praise: 'It is properly sliced, it is eatable with a spoon, it is deliciously seasoned and cooked correctly with parsley in good butter.' To finish, a compote of fruit is served cold with crème fraîche and a puff pastry biscuit. The incidentals are impressive: real French bread, huge pots of unsalted butter, olives, almonds and good Dijon mustard – all included in the cover charge – plus decent coffee. Snacks are served in the downstairs bar. House French is £8.75. There is live music every night from 8.30pm in the Brasserie and Piano Bar.

CHEF: Tony Howarth PROPRIETORS: Neville Abraham and Laurence Isaacson OPEN: Mon to Sat, exc Sat L CLOSED: bank hols MEALS: 12 to 3, 6 to 11.30 (restaurant); 11.30 to 11 (wine bar) PRICES: £18 (£29), Set D (8pm to 9pm) £8.95 (£17). Cover £1. Service 12.5%. Card slips closed CARDS: Access, Amex, Diners, Visa SEATS: 80. Private parties: 50 private room. Vegetarian meals. Children welcome. No-smoking area. Music. Air-conditioned

Sonny's map 10

94 Church Road, SW13 0DQ COOKING 2
081-748 0393 COST £18–£30

An excellent place for large parties – fair-priced, spacious and willing. Couples may have to speak, not whisper, sweet nothings, and deals will have to be done at full volume. Some things never change – the stuffed cheetah in the first room, before you pass the bar and descend steps to the main dining area, subfusc decoration relieved by colour in the pictures, bare and echoing floors – but there is now a Sonny's grocery shop next door and there seem to be more tables in the front. The cooking can be excellent, very much in the modern bistro-café mode with the chargrill, a love of sausages and of piquant flavours in evidence. It may not invariably work – some people mention low temperatures in food that may wait before dispatch when busy, others have simply found food lacklustre – but the risk is worth it. A party of six, each of whom had different first and main courses, pronounced themselves entirely satisfied (save for chips staying too long in the fryer); others were equally impressed by the fair value of the set menu of two courses and coffee. Nearly everyone seems to have merguez sausages at some time, perhaps with potato and chive cakes, coriander and cumin chickpeas, or cabbage and bacon. The fish soup (thick and peppery, with not too much garlic) is also popular; salmon and tuna are favoured fish; calf's liver, rack of lamb and breast of chicken (perhaps wrapped in Parma ham and cabbage leaf) are popular meats; and sauces are of the butter/salsa/relish sort. Crème brûlée, a light sticky toffee pudding and chocolate walnut pie are mentioned desserts, though some have commented that this course is not as good as the rest. The cafetière coffee is fair. A set menu for Sunday lunch, this time getting as far as pudding too, is the answer to many Barnes domestic problems. Perhaps every London suburb could do with a place like this. The wine list is short, changes frequently, and takes a modern view of what is acceptable – as many bottles from outside as from within France. Prices are fair, there are usually sufficient halves, and Natter's Sancerre, João Pires' dry Moscato, Edna Valley Pinot Noir or Stags' Leap Cabernet, to cite one week's offering, are decent enough for any meal. House wine is £6.95. The arrival of new chef Nikki Barraclough in the summer of 1991 has already elicited reports of improvements in the kitchen.

CHEF: Nikki Barraclough PROPRIETOR: Rebecca Mascarenhas OPEN: all week, exc Sun D CLOSED: bank hols, 1 week Christmas MEALS: 12.30 to 2.30, 7 to 11 PRICES: £16 (£25), Set L and D £11.50 (£18), Set Sun L £13.50 (£19) CARDS: Access, Diners, Visa SEATS: 70. Private parties: 70 main room. Vegetarian meals. Children welcome. Smart dress preferred. Wheelchair access. Music. Air-conditioned

▲ *Le Soufflé, Inter-Continental Hotel*

map 12

1 Hamilton Place, W1V 0QY — COOKING 4
071-409 3131 — COST £36–£68

The designers have tried their best with this windowless room, and the deep moulded ceilings, cheerful yet calming primrose-to-cream papyrus finish to the walls, green carpet and deep banquettes are some compensation for lack of daylight. The staff help too: unremittingly concerned and eager, they are a good brigade. Peter Kromberg has been cooking here for more years than he might remember, but there are few signs of staleness to the menu. He produces dishes of great finesse, sometimes so great as to nearly miss their mark. He is also aware of current international trends (at least half his customers must be foreign businessmen or travellers) hence perhaps the section entitled 'cuisine de vie' which offers lighter food cooked in as complex a way as the rest of the menu. Soufflés are red hot, but that goes almost without saying. Otherwise, the Kromberg style appears to best effect in fish cookery – when it is applied to meat, the delicacy may translate into lack of courage. Following this line of argument, white meats, for instance a chicken breast with truffles and potato 'scales', may work better than others. A first course of langoustines, set on a bed of spinach with a circlet of fried courgettes and radiating spokes of orange, lemon, grapefruit and semi-dried tomato quarters was of immense sophistication and accuracy. It was sauced by a warm lemon dressing seasoned with pink peppercorns and a fugitive hint of leaf coriander. Readers speak in like terms of a pigeon and langoustine consommé, and a whole salmon stuffed with a turbot and spinach mousse, encased in the lightest pastry crust and served with a lobster and mushroom sauce. This may sound like too many flavours, but worked magnificently on the plate. The big cheese trolley may be too big if everyone eats soufflés; if soufflé is not your bag, there is a sweets trolley – and a good one for this form of presentation. Le Soufflé has a style and it is worth sampling it; it will be a costly experiment. The wine list won't help in this respect. It is almost better to keep to the short list at a single price, which is slipped into menus. The main range is, of course, impressive. House wines are £14.

CHEF: Peter Kromberg PROPRIETORS: Inter-Continental Hotels Group OPEN: all week, exc Sat L MEALS: 12 to 3.30, 7 to 11 PRICES: £39 (£57), Set L £25.50 (£36), Set D £43 (£55) CARDS: Access, Amex, Diners, Visa SEATS: 80. Private parties: 10 main room. Car park, 100 places. Vegetarian meals. Children welcome. Jacket and tie. Wheelchair access (also WC). Music. Air-conditioned. Fax: 071-493 3476 ACCOMMODATION: 467 rooms, all with bath/shower. Rooms for disabled. Lift. B&B £229 to £247. Children welcome. Baby facilities. Afternoon teas. Sauna. Air-conditioned. TV. Phone

Soulard

map 11

113 Mortimer Road, N1 4JY — COOKING 2
071-254 1314 — COST £19–£26

'The Dordogne in Dalston,' wrote one reader. 'Keep people going there, since this type of cooking in unpretentious surroundings deserves encouragement,' wrote another. Philippe Soulard must have excited a following loyal enough, for here he is, still going strong a few years later. The surroundings are surely unpretentious, but if it keeps prices down and cooking honest, so much the better. A short *carte* is supplemented by daily dishes listed on a blackboard, recited with gusto to each table. 'Every member of our party chose a different meal and each thought they had chosen the best.' The menu does not go so far as reproducing tourist France on the plate; it has absorbed more British influences than that in such dishes as tagliatelle with mint and vegetables, marinated salmon with blinis, lamb with honey and mint sauce, pear Belle-Hélène and crème brûlée. Portions are generous, with green salad and good frites. The style is all French, down to the last goodbye, as is the short wine list. House wine is £6.50.

CHEF: Christian Veronneau PROPRIETOR: Philippe Soulard OPEN: Tue to Sat, exc Sat L CLOSED: 2 weeks summer MEALS: 12 to 2, 7 to 10.30 PRICES: £15 (£21), Set L £13 (£19) to £16 (£22) CARDS: Access, Amex, Visa SEATS: 28. 9 tables outside. Private parties: 15 private room. Vegetarian meals. Children's helpings. No cigars in dining-room. Music

Sree Krishna

map 10

194 Tooting High Street, SW17 0SF — COOKING 1
081-672 4250 — COST £6–£14

The setting is inauspicious – a dimly lit dining-room decorated in shades of brown on the main road from Tooting to Wimbledon. A Buddha lit with fairy lights and prints of Indian deities catch the eye. The high points are the south Indian specialities and dishes from the Kerala Coast: dosas, dahi vada, iddly sambar (a steamed cake made from rice and black lentils) and avial (mixed vegetables with coconut, yoghurt and curry leaves) are typical. The kitchen also delivers good versions of onion bhajias, sag bhaji and vegetable korma. The restaurant is expanding its list of vegetable specialities, and there is a full complement of curries for meat-eaters. Drink lassi, Kingfisher beer or Indian Veena wine.

CHEF: Mullath Vijayan PROPRIETORS: T. Haridas and family OPEN: all week MEALS: 12 to 3, 6 to 12 PRICES: £6 (£12), Set L and D £2.50 (£6) to £4.90 (£9). Minimum £2.50. Service 10%. Card slips closed CARDS: Access, Amex, Diners, Visa SEATS: 120. Vegetarian meals. Children welcome. Wheelchair access (also WC). No music. Air-conditioned

Sri Siam

map 14

14 Old Compton Street, W1V 5PE — COOKING 2
071-434 3544 — COST £15–£30

A cluster of classy Thai restaurants is now entrenched in and around Old Compton Street. Sri Siam has lived up to its early promise. The kitchen shows its class with good ingredients and a generous use of fresh herbs. Spicing is carefully pitched, although there is fierce heat where it is needed. There are many recommendations from the wide-ranging menu: chicken satay, tom yum soups, chicken with lemon grass, 'red' and 'green' curries of different intensities, and fish steamed in a banana leaf and served with two sauces. One rare speciality is larb – a northern Thai dish of minced meat with ground roasted rice served on a salad with a hot-and-sour dressing. The restaurant also boasts a full vegetarian menu approved by the Vegetarian Society. Desserts are intriguing: nam kang sai is a bizarre combination of crushed ice with sweetcorn, lychees and grass jelly topped with rose syrup, vanilla ice-cream and roasted peanuts. Set lunches and dinners are good-value introductions to the cuisine. Singha Thai beer is pricey, but it suits the food; otherwise there is tea and house wine at £7.50. A second branch, Sri Siam City, is due to open at 85 London Wall, London EC2 – reports, please.

CHEF: Pong Chan PROPRIETORS: Thai Restaurants plc OPEN: all week, exc Sun L CLOSED: Christmas and New Year MEALS: 12 to 3, 6 to 11.15 (10.30 Sun) PRICES: £17 (£25), Set L £8.90 (£15), Set D £14.50 (£22). Service 12.5% CARDS: Access, Amex, Diners, Visa SEATS: 75. Private parties: 40 main room. Vegetarian meals. Children welcome. Wheelchair access. Music. Air-conditioned

Stephen Bull 🍷

map 13

5–7 Blandford Street, W1H 3AA — COOKING 3*
071-486 9696 — COST £41

In London, you pay your money and you take your choice. There are a few restaurants, not more than a dozen, where you know your hard-earned cash will buy a specific character of cooking not reproduced, or but in faint copies, elsewhere. Stephen Bull is one of these places. Reading the menu is sufficient proof that the mind behind the execution is working to its own set of rules. This should go some way towards mitigating practical error. The restaurant itself is stripped-down in decoration, still innocent of colour and relies for effect on geometry, mirrors and the play of light on surfaces. The theory is that meals should not be too dear; you pay for this in square footage, so as a trysting place at night it may be less successful than for a vigorous business lunch. A grudging report summarised reactions to the place thus: 'A meal replete with evidence of creativity and intellect, with scarcely a cliché in sight, demonstrably fairly priced and most efficiently served. Everything looked good and there was genuine choice. Stephen Bull has a fondness for the art of combination, which has suffered terrible abuse in recent years, but this meal showed much more thought.' Commendations of many dishes have been received: mushrooms stuffed with chicken and foie gras then crumbed and fried; Jerusalem artichoke mousse; black pudding and apple; red mullet with haricot beans and pimento; duck with lentils and cumin; pheasant with chestnuts; salmon barded with pork fat, with roasted shallots and a green pea sauce; better judged vegetables designed to the main dish; a filo roll of banana, passion-fruit and orange with a coconut ice-cream; saffron bread-and-butter pudding; a celebration of chocolate; and good cheeses (British), even if not everyone knows much about them. Criticisms come from people who like darker, cosier restaurants and from some who find a gap between execution and conception. The food is careful and does not rely on overstatement. But if the cook's palate is too reticent the result may be bland. There is also a tendency to prissiness in presentation. The food would often benefit if it was not turned too much. This is a London particular and should not be missed. With nine house wines chosen with such care, it is scarcely necessary to venture further, which could be a mistake, since the list thereafter has acquired depth and length; prices which would seem generous in a provincial setting are bargains for W1. Half-bottles show the same intelligent range. House wines are £9.50 to £12.95

CHEFS: Stephen Bull and John Bentham PROPRIETOR: Stephen Bull OPEN: Mon to Sat, exc Sat L CLOSED: 1 week Christmas MEALS: 12 to 2.30, 6 to 10.30 PRICES: £24 (£34). Card slips closed CARDS: Access, Visa SEATS: 60. Private parties: 50 main room. Vegetarian meals. Children's helpings. Wheelchair access (1 step). Air-conditioned

Sud Ouest

map 12

27–31 Basil Street, SW3 1BB — COOKING 1
071-584 4484 — COST £19–£47

For all its title, there is not much of the south-west of France to distinguish this place from the general run of Anglo-French restaurants in the capital. True, you get a mean cassoulet, it is reported, but for special order rather than a constant on the menu. Garlic may be too much for the *déraciné* customers of this backstreet to Harrods – though salt evidently is not. The vaguely distressed-cum-plain rustic decoration, enlivened with abstract paintings, provides a reasonable framework for country cooking – even more rustic is the crepuscular basement (lavatories in former coal-holes). Some readers have had excellent dinners comprising dishes like asparagus and mushroom salad with truffle oil dressing; mouclade with basil and curry sauce; scallops with parsley and garlic; magret of duck on cabbage and apple; lamb with garlic and shallots; and prune and armagnac mousse. The output of the kitchen may show a careful hand with sauces. The wine list has a few south-western items although they come at Harrods prices. House wines are from £8.50. The Café next door offers a cheap, fast, all-day alternative.

CHEF: David Shuttleworth PROPRIETOR: Martin Davis OPEN: Mon to Sat MEALS: 12.30 to 3, 7 to 11 PRICES: £28 (£39), Set L £10 (£19) to £12 (£21). Cover £1.50 CARDS: Access, Amex, Diners, Visa SEATS: 110. Private parties: 60 main room, 50 private room. Vegetarian meals. Children welcome. Wheelchair access (1 step). Music. Air-conditioned. Fax: 071-581 2462

Suntory

map 13

72 St James's Street, SW1A 1PH COOKING 3
071-409 0201 COST £25–£62

This is among the most aristocratic – plutocratic would be another word – Japanese restaurants in London. Costs are high, but the food, particularly the classical banquets and the sushi and sashimi work, can be exemplary. Raw materials are of the highest quality. There is a teppanyaki bar on the lower floor. Service, of course, matches location and status. The wine list gives free rein to profit, but house wine is £10.

CHEF: M. Hayashi PROPRIETORS: Suntory Ltd OPEN: Mon to Sat CLOSED: 25 Dec, 1 Jan, bank hols MEALS: 12 to 1.30, 7 to 9.30 PRICES: £45 (£52), Set L £20 (£25), Set D £40 (£45). Net prices, card slips closed CARDS: Access, Amex, Diners, Visa SEATS: 130. Private parties: 2 main room, 4, 7 and 14 private room. Children restricted. Air-conditioned. Fax: 071-499 7993

Le Suquet

map 12

104 Draycott Avenue, SW3 3AE COOKING 2
071-581 1785 and 225 0838 COST £36

The 'most genuinely French atmosphere in London' is one reason for this, the most sympathetic of Pierre Martin's small chain of fish restaurants, keeping a solid band of regular customers. The genuine Frenchness may extend to non-English speaking waiters and a certain rapid brusqueness of attention – until the waiters know you, that is – but this may be worth undergoing so as to eat the plateau de fruits de mer, the lobster from the live tank, and other fresh fish and shellfish on offer. The more complicated the cooking, the less likely it is to succeed. Vegetables and salad are wayward; desserts are not important. House wine is £8.70.

CHEF: Jean Yves Darcel PROPRIETOR: Pierre Martin OPEN: all week MEALS: 12.30 to 2.30, 7 to 11.30 PRICES: £21 (£30). Cover £1. Service 15% CARDS: Access, Amex, Diners, Visa SEATS: 50. 4 tables outside. Private parties: 16 private room. Vegetarian meals. Children welcome. Smart dress preferred. Wheelchair access. Music. Air-conditioned

Surinder's

map 11

109 Westbourne Park Road, W2 5QL COOKING 1
071-229 8968 COST £24

Value for money is a big plus at Surinder Chandwan's Notting Hill bistro. A short fixed-priced menu (with supplements for luxuries such as foie gras and oysters) deals in the likes of avocado and smoked fish mousse, jambon persillé, calf's liver, saddle of lamb, and tuna cooked with fines herbes. Fresh vegetables draw good reports. Occasionally there are disappointments, such as lobster thermidor with tough, leathery meat, or stodgy lemon syllabub, but the venue remains creditable. The dining-room is smartly decorated in peach with a polished wooden floor and original artwork by Surinder's wife on the walls. Service is always friendly and relaxed. A modest list of French and Italian wines offers reasonably priced drinking. House French is £7.95.

CHEF/PROPRIETOR: Surinder Chandwan OPEN: Tue to Sat, D only, and Fri L MEALS: 12 to 3.30, 7 to 11 PRICES: Set L and D £13.95 (£20). Service 10%. Card slips closed CARDS: Access, Amex, Visa SEATS: 45. Private parties: 45 main room, 40 private room. Vegetarian meals. Children welcome. Wheelchair access (2 steps). No music

Suruchi

map 11

18 Theberton Street, N1 0QX — COOKING 1
071-359 8033 — COST £7–£11

One of a clutch of south Indian vegetarian cafés that are springing up around London. The style is characteristic of the genre: cream and green colour schemes, lots of light, pine chairs and fresh flowers on the tables. Piped sitar music seems to have replaced soft classical sounds. The short menu offers excellent value, but standards can be variable. The high points from recent reports have been large samosas with excellent light pastry, aloo papri chat and first-rate aloo chana with poori (well-spiced chickpeas and potatoes accompanied by crisp hollow poori 'like large flying saucers'). Less impressive have been the dosas and kulfi ice-cream. Unlicensed, but you can bring your own or drink lassi, falooda or masala tea.

CHEF: Rafiq Uddin PROPRIETORS: Suruchi Partnership OPEN: all week MEALS: 12 to 2.30, 6 to 10.45 PRICES: £7 (£9), Set L and D £5.60 (£7). Unlicensed, but bring your own: no corkage CARDS: Amex, Visa SEATS: 40. Vegetarian meals. Children welcome. Wheelchair access (1 step). Music

Surya

map 11

59–61 Fortune Green Road, NW6 7DR — COOKING 1
071-435 7486 — COST £10–£19

The prevailing mood among London's new breed of Indian vegetarian restaurants is informality combined with a touch of sophistication. A small, but quite smart place, Surya is fashionably decorated in shades of green and white, with glass-topped tables and modern high-backed chairs. The menu is concise and accessible. Reporters have recommended crisp, crunchy bhel pooris, mater paneer, baigan bhartha (baked aubergines with tomato sauce) – and vegetable pilau with roast cashews and pistachios. Otherwise there are samosas, aloo bonda, masala dosa, various dhals, breads and home-made kulfi, plus an enterprising choice of daily specials, ranging from stuffed green chillies and kofta curry on Wednesday to kachori (lentil pastries) and banana, methi and tomato curry on Friday. Dishes are 'true in flavour', distinctive, clean-tasting and noticeably lacking in oil. Sunday lunch is a buffet. Service is very assured, helpful and friendly. Drink lassi, falooda (rose-flavoured milkshake) or Golden Eagle Indian beer. House French is £5.95.

CHEF: H. Tiwari PROPRIETOR: R.C. Tiwari OPEN: all week, D only, and Sun L CLOSED: 24 and 25 Dec MEALS: 12 to 2, 6 to 11 PRICES: £7 (£11), Set Sun L £4.95 (£10), Set D £6 (£11) to £11 (£16). Minimum £6. Service 10%. Card slips closed CARDS: Access, Amex, Diners, Visa SEATS: 34. Private parties: 20 private room. Vegetarian meals. Children's helpings (Sun L and early D, 6pm to 7pm). No children under 6 after 7pm. No-smoking area. Wheelchair access (1 step; also WC). Music

Sutherlands 🍷 map 13

45 Lexington Street, W1R 3LG COOKING 4
071-434 3401 COST £36–£62

The purposely downbeat exterior must by now be familiar to taxi-drivers, although the uninitiated can easily miss it. Behind the façade lies the long thin restaurant, rising a level towards the back and divided into three zones. It has been likened, especially in the case of the top-lit back room, to a shrine or temple. Some find its designer airs too much for them and wish for more light and a can of emulsion, but it makes its statement and makes it well. Restaurateurs have always known that it's the 'headline' price that counts with punters, hence the urge to keep it low and pile on the extras. Inevitably, then, many have commented on a price rise in the evening meal, now £38 for three courses, while in fact this is but an increase of £3.50 on last year, for the price then of £29 was for only two courses, another £6.50 being needed for dessert. It should also be noted that the recessionary lunch menu at £24.50 is a reduction on the cost of lunch in 1990. The restaurant has shown singleness of purpose: the cooking is still innovative, the service intelligent and civilised. There continue, doubtless unintended, to be longueurs of service and delivery from the kitchen, and occasionally a lack of assurance in the waiting staff that has not been seen before. However, the food is up to the mark, though a certain element of novelty may have sped away with time. There is no copyright in the kitchen. What were bright ideas, such as the tiny rolls in anything up to six flavours – the Parmesan, or mixed herb or caraway getting strong support this year – have cropped up in lots of places as bread gains fashionable notice. Recommendations have been many and various, but a winter meal for two may set a thousand scenes. First bite was a cube of saffron pilaff with haddock in a warm oil emulsion with sharp shreds of spring onion. One first course of noodles, wild mushrooms and cream was just good. The other, an oxtail broth, which came in a copper pan, to be poured over a ravioli of oxtail with a scattering of wild rice and vegetable dice, managed several textures, taste contrast between light clear broth and intense ravioli filling, and a bit of colour variation thrown in. Pheasant was cooked with root vegetables and served with a tarragon jus, salted just too much. The alternative was a tart of morels, spinach, mushroom and potato. This has been praised several times (at other meals artichoke has been in the list): great pastry, great flavours. There were cheeses, British and French, well-kept and interesting, then a pair of citrus sorbets before coffee and cubes of three sorts of chocolate, which left the reporter feeling short-changed as other tables seemed to have a more exciting choice. The meal exemplified the ability to think up good combinations and the confidence to present a package, with everything to design: no serendipity of extra vegetables here, or self-seasoning. Some comments surface about sauces which miss their mark, but overall blandness is not a fault. A purposeful and succinct wine list spreads its attention broadly: clarets, including some decent petits châteaux, fine red burgundies and carefully chosen Rhônes, Italians and New World bottles. Halves are particularly good. House wine apart, prices start at about £14 and thereafter climb very steeply. House wines are from £8.75. CELLARMAN'S CHOICE: Macon-Viré 1989, Bonhomme, £23.50; Blagny 1985, Leflaive, £32.50.

CHEF: Garry Hollihead PROPRIETORS: Siân Sutherland-Dodd, Garry Hollihead and Christian Arden OPEN: Mon to Sat, exc Sat L MEALS: 12.15 to 2.15, 6.15 to 11.15 PRICES: Set L £24.50 (£36) to £38 (£52), Set D £38 (£52). Service 12.5%. Card slips closed CARDS: Access, Carte Blanche, Visa SEATS: 45. Private parties: 45 main room, 20 private room. Vegetarian meals. Children's helpings on request. No cigars/pipes in dining-room. Wheelchair access. Air-conditioned. Fax: 071-287 2997

Tandoori Lane NEW ENTRY map 10

131A Munster Road, SW6 6DD COOKING 1
071-371 0440 and 4844 COST £19

'A real find in an unpromising street,' according to a reader. The long narrow dining-room is decorated in black and white, with black venetian blinds at the windows. The menu is a standard assortment of tandooris and curries, but ingredients are well chosen, dishes are carefully prepared and prices are reasonable. Light onion bhajias are freshly made and served with a lemon and mint sauce, prawn pooris are well-above average and chicken tikka masala has good meat in a delicate creamy sauce. King prawn delight is a speciality, cooked with cream, almonds and – unexpectedly – red wine. Among the vegetables, mater paneer has been outstanding. Breads and rice are up to the mark. Coffee arrives in a glass jar with a burner to keep it warm. The waiters in blue tunics are friendly. House wine is £6.95.

CHEFS: Abul Musabbir and Harun Miah PROPRIETORS: Mohammad Ismail, Mahmudul Hassan and Abul Khair OPEN: all week CLOSED: Christmas MEALS: 12 to 1, 6 to 11 PRICES: £10 (£16). Card slips closed CARDS: Access, Amex, Visa SEATS: 38. Vegetarian meals. No children under 7. Music. Air-conditioned

Tante Claire 🍷 map 12

68–69 Royal Hospital Road, SW3 4HP COOKING 5
071-352 6045 COST £29–£76

'I like the yellow chairs, but not the mustard walls of the Ladies,' says one reader who applauds the light, air and space of this simply elegant restaurant, redolent of '30s design, if no pastiche. Most agree. 'The service is remarkably good,' says another. That here is one of the most polished, yet not aloof, restaurant brigades in London is also agreed – even, in the end, by one who rang the bell at 12.30 (opening time) yet was not answered until 12.45. 'M. Koffmann is most pleasant, his kitchen impressive,' reported a third, one among many readers this year who had talked with a normally reticent chef and appreciated the encounter. Tante Claire continues to please mightily. Its lunch, for example, remains one of London's great bargains: totally inclusive, no culinary short-change – even, if possible, a more balanced and apposite composition than dinner. 'It was a symphony.' At night it is as expensive as any restaurant in this bracket, and the proceedings are surprisingly formal. Yet, it has been observed that here, of all the top restaurants, it is private money being spent, not merely the petty cash of corporate treasuries. Koffmann's cooking is not conservative, although elements of the repertoire run and run. He achieves depth of flavour and variety without over-complexity. A fulsome report of a summer lunch – better fun than Chelsea Flower Show – puts the experience into words: 'Our lunch was a virtuoso display of consistency from start to finish. Salade Gersoise features lamb's lettuce dressed in a light, but distinctly provençal, olive oil. It is topped with small slivers of buttery foie gras and thin slices of chicken giblets; at once both earthy and light. The *mousseline de saumon* is like a Zeppelin, pink in colour, the mousse texture like a cloud floating over a bed of carrot and ginger julienne. The salmon flavour just gently permeates, encouraged by the ginger and a most beautifully balanced, but deliberately sharp, beurre blanc loaded with shallots and fine vinegar. *Fillet de turbot rôti* is a sensational hunk of white fish roasted so it has a good brown colouring, its gleaming top sealing the juices within. The flesh of the fish retains a certain firmness, yet is moist. Timing is impeccable. To accompany, there is a bed of pasta with poppy seeds and a fulsome gravy, robust enough to counter the roasting technique. A *ballotine de volaille* is a tender breast of chicken stuffed with a mirepoix of finely chopped mushrooms and onions. Like those of the fish, the flavours are allowed to punch straight through and not be distracted by frivolities or garnishes. Other items like the array of canapés, the all-right petits fours and the joke portion of token vegetables are fine, but not as exciting. The cooking bravado is demonstrated with flair at the beginning and at the finale. Pierre Koffmann's bread is outstanding. The apple-walnut brown roll and the white one topped with poppy seed both have a wonderful real bread texture, fine crisp crusts and a yeasty aroma. On a par are desserts like *mille-feuille tièdes*: a couple of feuilletés each injected with a smear of crème pâtissière. The light, buttery flakiness of the pastry being spurred into action by an intense vanilla-flavoured custard is so simple. Equally the *gratin de fruits rouges* features an even lighter cream custard which has been quickly coloured under the grill before serving. The remarkable taste is the contrast between the slight brown skin of the custard versus the creamy texture of the custard and the slight sharpness of the strawberries and raspberries. This is Koffmann at his best.' The wine buyer feels no need to stray beyond France; within those confines a workmanlike task is achieved. As well as the predictable clarets and burgundies – good years, old vintages, fine growers – a refreshing canter around the French regions brings much of interest and at very moderate prices. Tante Claire is one of the few big names that makes a genuine effort to provide decent value as well as enthusiasm for the wine drinker. There is no house wine, but prices start at £11.30.

CHEF: Pierre Koffmann PROPRIETORS: Mr and Mrs Pierre Koffmann OPEN: Mon to Fri CLOSED: bank hols MEALS: 12.30 to 2, 7 to 11 PRICES: £53 (£63), Set L £23.50 (£29). Minimum £40 D. Net prices CARDS: Access, Amex, Diners, Visa SEATS: 38. Children welcome. Jacket and tie. Wheelchair access. Fax: 071-352 3257

Tatsuso

map 11

32 Broadgate Circle, EC2M 2QS — COOKING 2
071-638 5863 — COST £21–£95

Of the two sorts of Japanese restaurant in the UK – the cheap and the expensive – this falls into the second category. The front is walled with glass, through which you can watch the teppanyaki bar. Beyond and below is the large, sparsely furnished restaurant where a fairly standard menu and series of banquet menus are offered, though more interesting daily specials are available if you can elicit the information. Buying and cooking is very competent and pitched to City business. Service is immaculate, porcelain is exquisite and tradition is respected.

CHEFS: Mr Maehara and Mr Hirai PROPRIETORS: Terrii-Broadgate Ltd OPEN: Mon to Fri CLOSED: bank hols MEALS: 11.30 to 3, 6 to 9.30 PRICES: £23 (£38), Set L £13 (£21) to £60 (£72), Set D £15 (£24) to £65 (£79). Service 12.5% CARDS: Access, Amex, Diners, Visa SEATS: 130. Private parties: 30 main room, 6 and 8 private rooms. Vegetarian meals. Children welcome. Music. Air-conditioned

Thailand

map 10

15 Lewisham Way, SE14 6PP — COOKING 2
081-691 4040 — COST £32

Such is the charisma of this tiny Thai restaurant that hardly a report is received without 'what a find!' featuring prominently. 'The only problem is actually getting in' was the heartfelt cry from one who eats there regularly, 'since more and more people appear to be getting to know about it and it only seats 25.' Khamkhong Kambungoet is an ethnic Lao from the part of Thailand that was once Laos and her cooking, though Thai-dominated, has at its heart some unusual Laotian dishes. Portions remain generous, with consistency (especially in the face of increased popularity) a strong point. Of the starters, spicy soups – notably both the hot-and-sour chicken and the prawn – are outstanding, while spring rolls, Thai-style fishcakes and chicken satay are of a very high standard. A strong selection of noodles plus a 'particularly good' vegetable curry have also been singled out for praise. Her husband, Glaswegian Victor Herman, runs front-of-house with disarming charm and is presumably responsible for the 75 malt whiskies on offer. Thai beer or organic apple and orange juice are alternatives to the short wine list. House Sicilian is £6.95.

CHEF: Khamkhong Kambungoet PROPRIETORS: Victor and Khamkhong Herman OPEN: Tue to Sat, D only CLOSED: 25 and 26 Dec, 1 Jan MEALS: 6 to 10.30 PRICES: £20 (£27). Card slips closed CARDS: Access, Amex, Diners, Visa SEATS: 25. Private parties: 25 main room. Vegetarian meals. Children restricted. Music

The 1993 Guide *will be published before Christmas 1992. Reports on meals are most welcome at any time of the year, but are extremely valuable in the spring. Send them to* The Good Food Guide, *FREEPOST, 2 Marylebone Road, London NW1 1YN. No stamp is needed when posting in the UK.*

Thistells

NEW ENTRY map 10

65 Lordship Lane, SE22 8EP COOKING 1*
081-299 1921 COST £29

Thank old-time grocers David Greig for the impressive tiles (thistle motif) and fitting-out of this shop turned wine bar then restaurant. Sami Youssef is a legend in his own lifetime: first at Nico Ladenis in Lordship Lane, then L'Auberge (his own), then Thistells, which he and Mrs Youssef turned from wine bar to restaurant. Mrs Youssef remains the genius of front-of-house: 'She deserves gold stars,' according to one report, 'for her bedside manners with the punters', right down to the hint of expulsion as the lighting increases in intensity towards closing time. Sami Youssef offers a menu that mixes classical French bourgeois/bistro food with Middle Eastern dishes such as ful medames and those of his own invention like the strips of liver (lamb's or calf's) with cumin, coriander and lemon. England gets a peek at pudding-time – banoffi pie, even in Dulwich – with mixed reports. Cooking is knowledgeable: the watercress soup had depth and flavour, the sole with vermouth sauce extracted much flavour from the fish, the duck cassoulet was hearty and substantial even if the beans were barely cooked. The style of the place still remains half way a wine bar, though prices are more those of a restaurant. Bad days can intervene, but for SE22 this is a welcome return to the stove for all. House French is £6.80.

CHEFS: Sami Youssef and Myron Penaydo PROPRIETOR: Sami Youssef OPEN: all week, exc Sun D MEALS: 12 to 3, 7 to 10.30 PRICES: £15 (£24). Service 10%. Card slips closed CARDS: Access, Visa SEATS: 40. Private parties: 50 main room. Vegetarian meals. Children's helpings. Wheelchair access. Music

Topsy-Tasty

map 10

5 Station Parade, Burlington Lane, W4 3HD COOKING 1
081-995 3407 COST £15–£22

The Bedlington Café (see entry) finally produced this restaurant offspring to cope with the enthusiasm for Thai food that it had excited in the denizens of Chiswick. It is a large, bustling, noisy room serving mostly Thai, but also some Japanese, Vietnamese and Laotian, dishes. This is not the place for a lovers' tryst, unless before a walk in leafy suburban groves. Not every meal is a success, but the aromas of garlic, basil or lemon grass that waft, Bisto-like, under noses as dishes pass to table are sure indicators of emphatic, spicy and immediate cooking. Excellent value.

CHEF: Mr Boy PROPRIETOR: Mrs P. Priyanu OPEN: Mon to Sat, exc Mon L MEALS: 12 to 2.30, 6.30 to 11 PRICES: £11 (£16), Set D £12.50 (£15) to £15 (£18). Unlicensed, but bring your own: corkage 70p SEATS: 45. Private parties: 40 main room. Vegetarian meals. Children welcome. Music

'On my most recent visit, to my horror, a duo performed Sinatra standards (both performers looked over seventy years of age, and whether they'd survive the evening became a morbid fascination for the captive audience).' On eating in Cambridgeshire

La Truffe Noire

NEW ENTRY map 11

29 Tooley Street, SE1 2QF — COOKING **2***
071-378 0621 — COST £14–£50

East of London Bridge on Tooley Street stretch renovated warehouses interspersed with granite and glass office blocks all hugging the river. On the other side of the street, it is a different story: a Dickensian patch of warehouses, their façades ebony black from fumes of ages, decaying council blocks, railways and lorries. La Truffe Noire sits firmly in the land of the gentry and bankers – a pearl among commercial swine. It proclaims itself outside as a brasserie as well as restaurant; well, hardly, though there is a bar. It can produce good food, its named special ingredient featuring in a truffle soup and truffle ravioli. The last are outstanding: 'a long aftertaste of woods, undergrowth and autumn leaves, with a sauce of truffles and butter that is bold without intruding,' according to a reader. Otherwise, there is a mixture of menus, none too dear, which may be the justification for the brasserie description. The £9 brasserie menu is outstanding value, and the set-price restaurant menu delivers shellfish in pastry, monkfish with lentils, and lamb with aubergine caviare at fair prices too. Monkfish with Beaujolais and scallops with basil and a beurre blanc are other examples of fish that has been well-handled. The dessert stage has not received the same encomiums, nor the coffee and petits fours. The chef comes from a distinguished background (Bocuse) and can clearly do his stuff. Service, too, is exceptionally cheerful. The wine list seems altogether more ambitious than the location might indicate. But then there may be free-spending yuppies just around the corner. House wines are £8.

CHEF: Mr Lucas PROPRIETORS: Mr and Mrs M. Alam-Ahmed OPEN: Mon to Sat, exc Sat L CLOSED: bank hols MEALS: 12 to 3, 6.30 to 11 PRICES: £32 (£42), Set L and D £15 (£21) restaurant, £9 (£14) brasserie. Service 10%. Card slips closed CARDS: Access, Amex, Visa SEATS: 40. 25 tables outside. Private parties: 55 main room, 20 and 30 private rooms. Vegetarian meals. Children welcome. No cigars/pipes in dining-room. Wheelchair access. Music. Air-conditioned. Fax: 071-403 0689

▲ *Truffles, Portman Inter-Continental Hotel*

map 11

22 Portman Square, W1H 9FL — COOKING **2***
071-224 1383 — COST £28–£48

The framework is a fairly unprepossessing '60s tower-block on Portman Square. Although efforts have been made to humanise the dining-room with dark panelling, screens and booth arrangements, there is still that inescapable sense of hotel about it all. This is a pity, because it may scare off private customers who would welcome the chance to eat professionally cooked, classically oriented food which is not prohibitively expensive. The rub may be in teamwork. David Dorricott cannot be everywhere and not all elements of the meal will be of equal success. 'The sweets looked good, but were not as described. I was unable to taste chestnut in the mousse and the vanilla compote had a strong lemon flavour.' There is brunch on Sunday from noon to 4pm. The wine list is long and upper-crust in an international hotel way. Inflation has taken its toll, alas, but there are some bottles just under £15 and a fair choice of halves. House wines are £12.

CHEF: David Dorricott PROPRIETORS: Portman Inter-Continental Corporation OPEN: all week, exc Sat L CLOSED: 26 Dec MEALS: 12.30 to 2.30 (3 Sun), 7 to 10.30 PRICES: Set L £19.50 (£28) to £26.50 (£36), Set D £26.50 (£36) to £30 (£40). Card slips closed CARDS: Access, Amex, Diners, Visa SEATS: 75. Private parties: 160 private room. Vegetarian meals. Children's helpings. Wheelchair access (also WC). Music. Air-conditioned. Fax: 071-224 6295 ACCOMMODATION: 272 rooms, all with bath/shower. Rooms for disabled. Lift. B&B £166 to £215. Children welcome. Baby facilities. Afternoon teas. Garden. Tennis. Air-conditioned. TV. Phone. Confirm by 6

Tui map 12

19 Exhibition Road, SW7 2HE COOKING 1
071-584 8359 COST £34

Across the road from the V & A, Tui may give spice to a day devoted to art. It will certainly inject a little politeness into your world; the 12.5 per cent service charge may be thought payment for that. The cover charge – this is a traditional restaurant even if the decoration is coolly modern – does not appear to be justified by nibbles or crackers. The menu is short but well focused. The fish and shellfish dishes get most praise. The soups, including tom yum, are generous in quantity, freshly spiced with better-than-usual prawns in the tom yum goong. They are also dear, even if served in a steamboat. Some readers find the best atmosphere at the lower level. House French is £7.25.

CHEFS: Mr and Mrs Kongsrivilai PROPRIETOR: Ekachai Thapthimthong OPEN: all week CLOSED: bank hols and 25 Dec MEALS: 12 to 2.30 (12.30 to 3 Sun), 6.30 to 11 (7 to 10.30 Sun) PRICES: £20 (£28). Cover 75p. Service 12.5% CARDS: Access, Amex, Diners, Visa SEATS: 52. Private parties: 12 main room. Vegetarian meals. Children welcome. Smart dress preferred. No cigars/pipes in dining-room. Wheelchair access. No music. Fax: 071-352 8343

Tuk Tuk map 11

330 Upper Street, N1 2XQ COOKING 1
071-226 0837 COST £18

A cheerful café-restaurant that offers one-plate meals in generous quantity, with food of the kind that tuk tuk drivers (those who clatter round Bangkok on motorised tricycles) might stop to eat at street-corner stands. The difference is that here the food is never so chilli-hot, though sweetness rears its ugly head often enough. Noodle dishes (pahd kai ohb and pahd taie – with chicken or seafood) have been especially enjoyed and the tom yum kung (hot-sour soup with prawns and rice) will set you up. Busy times can be disarrayed. Drink the beers.

CHEF: Khodsavanh Phongphongsavat PROPRIETOR: Stephen Binns OPEN: Mon to Sat, exc Sat L CLOSED: 25 and 26 Dec, 1 Jan, bank hols MEALS: 12 to 3, 6 to 11 PRICES: £10 (£15). Service 10%. Card slips closed CARDS: Access, Amex, Visa SEATS: 100. 2 tables outside. Private parties: 60 main room. Vegetarian meals. Children welcome. Wheelchair access. Music

Turner's

map 12

87–89 Walton Street, SW3 2HP
071-584 6711

COOKING 3
COST £26–£52

The restaurant itself always comes in for praise as a relaxing room in which to sit – better towards the window – though a minority feel constrained by lower ceilings and closer tables than are found generally in this price bracket. What attracts is that the interior is untrammelled by decorative overkill. The same might be said of Mr Turner's unforced, naturally hospitable welcome. It brings regular return customers. The style of the kitchen is modern classical: a salad of flaked salmon with cucumber, a perhaps almost inevitable *salade tiède* of pigeon breast, then guinea-fowl with lime, duck with a calvados sauce, or fillet of veal wrapped in cabbage. Desserts can be simple yet refreshing, more British than the savoury courses: gooseberry mousse, lemon parfait, hot apple tart with bilberries. After an interregnum, a new chef has been brought on so that Brian Turner can resume his inside-out role of chef-proprietor. This should steady service, which has come in for criticism. A reader's comment that the food is 'good, but hardly exceptional or exciting' echoes the feelings of others. Quantities continue to be restrained, though prices are never low. House wines are from £14.

CHEFS: Brian Turner and Peter Brennan PROPRIETOR: Brian J. Turner OPEN: all week, exc Sat L CLOSED: 25 to 31 Dec (exc New Year's Eve D) MEALS: 12.30 to 2.30, 7.30 to 11 (10 Sun) PRICES: £34 (£43), Set L £15.75 (£23) to £18.50 (£26), Set D £23.50 (£31) to £29.50 (£37). Net prices, card slips closed CARDS: Access, Amex, Diners, Visa SEATS: 52. Private parties: 22 private room. Children's helpings (Sun L only) Smart dress preferred. Wheelchair access (2 steps). Music. Air-conditioned. Fax: 071-584 4441

Upper Street Fish Shop

map 11

324 Upper Street, N1 2XQ
071-359 1401

COOKING 1
COST £13

'First-rate. Great atmosphere. Not the world's cheapest chippy, but we shall return!' That is a reader's view no doubt shared by the crowds who regularly pack into the Conways' splendid venue. Red and white is the colour scheme inside and out, with check tablecloths and decorative flourishes provided by old clocks, luxuriant greenery and artwork. The place is split down the middle by a long counter, so take-away queues are screened off from sit-down customers. Alan Conway chooses the fish and supervises the frying; Olga Conway provides spirit and, often, conversation. Cod, skate, haddock and plaice are cooked to a turn with perfect batter and served with a heap of ungreasy chips. In addition there are specials such as 'milky' fish soup, fish lasagne, halibut in white sauce and poached fresh salmon. Old-fashioned home-made sweets have their devotees.

CHEF: Alan Conway PROPRIETORS: Alan and Olga Conway OPEN: Mon to Sat, exc Mon L CLOSED: bank hols MEALS: 12 to 2 (3 Sat), 5.30 to 10 PRICES: £10 (£11). Unlicensed, but bring your own: no corkage SEATS: 50. Children's helpings. Wheelchair access. No music. Air-conditioned

Veeraswamy

NEW ENTRY map 13

99–101 Regent Street, W1R 8RS
071-734 1401

COOKING 1
COST £22–£52

London's most famous and oldest surviving Indian restaurant was opened in 1927 by one Edward Palmer and the daughter of the Nizam of Hyderabad. The East-West connection lives on. At the door is an Indian commissionaire in full military regalia, who escorts diners to the dusky pink and grey first-floor dining-room. It feels like part of some large hotel or an 'elegant version of an Indian government guesthouse'. The well-constructed menu is overtly regional, with a strong vein of vegetarian dishes. From the north-west frontier there are tandooris (including scallops); alu tikki is a snack from the streets of Delhi; sev puri is from Bombay; there are also Bengali fish, Keralan kadai gosht and fiery Goan chicken. Readers have praised dahi barrha (lentil dumplings in spiced yoghurt), achar gosht with pickle masala, and Kashmiri chicken with a vivid green, fruity sauce. Rice is basmati or brown. Vegetables are intriguing: spinach with lotus roots; colocasia with mango and pomegranate; puréed mustard leaves; potatoes with fenugreek. Prices are high, but the cooking is honest, delicate and more than competent. Service is professional. Lunch is a self-service buffet. The wine list is 'needlessly ambitious' but there are also lassi and Kingfisher beer. House French is £11.50.

CHEF: V. Subramanium PROPRIETORS: Key West Club OPEN: Mon to Sat MEALS: 12 to 2.30, 6 to 11.30 PRICES: £23 (£40), Set L £12.50 (£23), Set D £12 (£22) to £30 (£43). Minimum £10. Service 15% CARDS: Access, Amex, Diners, Visa SEATS: 140. Private parties: 50 main room, 40 private room. Vegetarian meals. Children welcome. Smart dress preferred. No music. Air-conditioned

Villandry Dining Room

NEW ENTRY map 13

89 Marylebone High Street, W1M 3DE
071-224 3799 and 487 3816

COOKING 2
COST £31

In a few short years, Jean-Charles Carrarini established his food shop Villandry as a place worth crossing town for to buy, at a price, distinctive and top-quality French and Italian groceries, French wine, and fresh cheeses, butter, bread and vegetables brought direct from Paris on a Wednesday, while not disregarding some English produce. Encouraged by success, he has opened a room behind the shop, furnished it in varnished woods, which give a Sunday school look, and here serves lunches cooked by Gina Caridia, once at Ballymaloe House in Ireland (see entry, Shanagarry). Sandwiches may still be bought in the shop. The daily menu always has a soup, a few salads and perhaps three hot dishes. The cooking is not complex or high-falutin, but there can be no better mushroom omelette cooked at midday (*champignons de Paris*, of course) nor many places that offer a lunch of chanterelles on lusciously buttery fried bread. The pasta is good, the Irish smoked salmon superlative. Desserts have been less successful, but still a street ahead of any British lunch café in walking distance. Coffee is first-rate, as is the butter. Bread from Max (brother of Lionel) Poilâne may be used in the menu dishes but, alas, is not that doled out in baskets. The wine list is interesting, though a Vosne Romanée at

£35 may raise a wry smile, however good. The cheaper bottles (never very cheap) are from growers unfamiliar to British shippers and therefore worth a try.

CHEF: Gina Caridia PROPRIETORS: Jean-Charles and Rosalind Carrarini OPEN: Mon to Sat, L only (D by arrangement for parties of 15 or more) MEALS: 12.30 to 2.30 PRICES: £19 (£26). Net prices, card slips closed CARDS: Access, Visa SEATS: 36. Private parties: 40 main room, 40 private room. Vegetarian meals. Children's helpings. No smoking. Wheelchair access. Air-conditioned

Wakaba

map 11

122A Finchley Road, NW3 5HT COOKING 2*
071-722 3854 COST £15–£44

'Definitely one of London's better Japanese restaurants' was the verdict on this stylish place frequented by the upwardly mobile. The slick high-tech interior has echoes of Tokyo, with its severe, starkly white walls, glowing multi-coloured panels, curving windows and pillars, and a sushi bar at one end. The quality of the sushi is outstanding, largely because the fish is impressively fresh, 'glossy and colourful'. Watching the sushi chef is part of the dramatic spectacle of eating here. Other highlights are the unusual appetisers ('skilfully and lovingly made in the tradition of food-as-art') and presented on a black wooden fan-shaped plate: tiny 'coins' of beef wrapped around asparagus, a tiny slab of rolled omelette, an oblong of pork set in agar-agar, a single deep-fried prawn to be eaten whole and other delicacies. The menu deals in all the categories of Japanese cooking, with a bias towards meat. Yosenabe (Japanese-style bouillabaisse), deep-fried tofu with a soy-based sauce, and takiawase (simmered seasonal vegetables in dashi stock sauce) have all been well executed. The room is bare of sound absorption, so expect a noisy night rather like a university refectory in full cry. Drink green tea, saké or beer.

CHEF/PROPRIETOR: Minoru Yoshihara OPEN: Mon to Sat CLOSED: 1 week Aug, 5 days Christmas, 4 days Easter MEALS: 12 to 2.30, 6.30 to 11 PRICES: £28 (£33), Set L £10 (£15) to £13.50 (£18), Set D from £23 (£28) to £32 (£37). Minimuum £16. Net prices CARDS: Access, Amex, Diners, Visa SEATS: 55. Private parties: 60 main room. Vegetarian meals. Children restricted. Wheelchair access (also WC). Air-conditioned

Wiltons

map 13

55 Jermyn Street, SW1Y 6LX COOKING 2
071-629 9955 COST £52

A paradigm of a British restaurant – and we do not mean the type established during the last war – offering comfort within fairly constrained surroundings and a clientele that serves as a study in its own right. The fish and game is reason for coming here, and the best is the simplest. 'Without doubt its fried and grilled plaice is the finest you could eat anywhere. The dressed crab is outstanding, and the sea bass in dill was excellent and exactly cooked. Service is impeccable and you are always given a warm welcome. I would give them high marks but the chips, in contrast to the plaice, are the worst I have ever been presented with.' Thus speaks an habitué. You will pay dearly for the wine and the food is hardly cheap. House wine is £12.50.

CHEF: Ross Hayden PROPRIETORS: Wiltons (St James's) Ltd OPEN: Mon to Sat, exc Sat L CLOSED: 2 weeks Aug MEALS: 12 to 2.30, 6 to 10.30 PRICES: £28 (£43). Cover £1. Minimum £12.50 CARDS: Access, Amex, Diners, Visa SEATS: 90. Private parties: 20 main room, 16 private room. Children welcome. Jacket and tie. No cigars in dining-room. Wheelchair access (1 step). Air-conditioned. No music. Fax: 071-495 6233

Wódka

map 12

12 St Alban's Grove, W8 5PN — COOKING 2
071-937 6513 — COST £31

A backwater south of the mainstream of Kensington High Street is home to this relaxed – though the seats are too hard to be exactly relaxing – Polish restaurant that might have been a butcher's shop in a previous incarnation: tiles and pine panelling now overlaid by cool grey coloration and spare furniture. A seat in the room downstairs – glass-throwing can be done in private – is not as enviable as a seat at ground level. The menu revolves round Poland, but a light Poland, not one of school sauces thickened with paste. It can be enjoyable: the cold sorrel soup would have been better for less thickening, or served hot; pierogi are sometimes blistered in the oven but delicious when soft, filled with spinach and cream cheese; calf's liver with horseradish and beetroot is good, with a zippy flavour from the horseradish; dauphinois potatoes, not exactly Polish, are excellently made. The spareness of the cooking, often a quality, can sometimes mean boredom. Blinis are satisfactory and the black sausage has its supporters. Vodka is available in plenty of forms, but the wines are carefully chosen, New World as well as French. House wine is £7.70.

CHEF: Tony Rowe PROPRIETOR: Jan Woroniecki OPEN: all week, exc L Sat and Sun CLOSED: Bank hols MEALS: 12.15 to 2.30, 7 to 11 PRICES: £19 (£26) CARDS: Access, Amex, Diners, Visa SEATS: 60. Private parties: 10 main room, 30 private room. Vegetarian meals. Children welcome. Music. Fax: 071-376 1571

Yoisho

NEW ENTRY map 13

33 Goodge Street, W1P 1FD — COOKING 1*
071-323 0477 — COST £28

The owner of this unpretentious little restaurant (and that sounds like James Thurber's wine-tasting notes) is by profession a travel agent who felt Japanese food was too expensive in London. Here, therefore, value is good and the best items to eat are the homely dishes rather than Japanese haute cuisine. 'The noodles were the best I've ever eaten,' said a hitherto uncomprehending fan of the film *Tampopo*. The soups and stocks are good. He also extolled the virtues of the braised dishes such as potato with pork and shitake mushrooms with egg. Service is ultra rapid, everything arriving at once, so order little and often if you care about cooling.

CHEF: Mr Takayama PROPRIETOR: Mr Watanabe OPEN: Mon to Sat, exc Sat L CLOSED: bank hols MEALS: 12.30 to 2, 6 to 10.15 PRICES: £15 (£23). Minimum £8 SEATS: 74. Private parties: 74 main room. Children welcome. Music. Air-conditioned

Zen W3

map 11

83 Hampstead High Street, NW3 1RE — COOKING 1
071-794 7863 and 7864 — COST £31

Like other restaurants in the Zen chain, this chic venue provokes extreme reactions. 'Fantastic! Some of the best Chinese food I have eaten' is one view. Another is 'bland, unexciting and poor value for money. Our local take-away does a lot better for a fraction of the cost.' The menu is a modern-sounding assemblage of healthy, evolved dishes, spicy salads, steamed fish and lightning-fried meat. Despite a few exotic titles – 'Future Shock' is bean curd in peppercorn salt – much of the cooking is conventional, and dishes do not always live up to expectations: sautéed shredded beef with bean skins 'comprised a heap of glutinous jelly-like material with a few microscopic pieces of meat and half a dozen frozen peas'. But there has been high praise for the quality and freshness of the mixed hors d'oeuvre, crispy aromatic duck with pancakes, king prawns with black-bean sauce and braised duck fillet in lemon sauce. The kitchen also deals in Peking ravioli with chilli sauce, steamed wild salmon, grilled chicken breast with coriander sauce, and sea-spice aubergines. Service is generally up to the mark. Fifty wines are dominated by good vintages from reliable French growers. House French is £8.50.

CHEF: Michael K.S. Leung PROPRIETORS: Blaidwood Ltd OPEN: all week CLOSED: 25 to 27 Dec MEALS: noon to 11.30 (11 Sun) PRICES: £14 (£26). Service 12.5% CARDS: Access, Amex, Diners, Visa SEATS: 135. Private parties: 100 main room, 24 private room. Vegetarian meals. Children welcome. Smart dress preferred. Wheelchair access (2 steps). Music. Air-conditioned

ABBERLEY Hereford & Worcester map 5

▲ *Elms Hotel* NEW ENTRY

Abberley WR6 6AT
GREAT WITLEY (0299) 896666
on A443 between Worcester and Tenbury Wells, 2m W of Great Witley

COOKING 3
COST £22–£44

This exceptionally handsome country house was long a fixture in *The Good Food Guide*. Its absence, as private owners were succeeded by a corporation, was regretted. Today, in the hands of Queens Moat Houses, it seems to be undergoing a renaissance: new kitchens, much refurbishment of public rooms built originally by a pupil of Sir Christopher Wren (and architect of the Guildhall in Worcester) and recruitment of a new chef. Early reports have been satisfactory, both as to the motivation of the serving staff and the quality of the food. This is not a place straining for effect; indeed, it is country-careful in listing, for one dinner, a set of first courses running through carrot and orange soup; terrine of chicken, spinach and mushrooms; avocado with mussels and prawns; a salad of lamb and almonds with a raspberry vinaigrette; smoked salmon; and ogen melon with pernod and ginger. These were done with discrimination and accuracy. Main courses, under domes, continue the theme, though the *carte* does have more unfamiliar braised dishes such as ox liver in ginger wine and rabbit with stout. The British cheese is good. The heavily laden sweets trolley seems another sign that tradition is being left unruffled. The potential for this place, however, is great, as is the setting. May the Elms recover from its past disease. Ambition and enthusiasm in the cellar are less marked than in the kitchen: the wines provide reasonable geographic range but, with few bottles below £15, value is not a feature. House wine is £11.

CHEF: Michael Gaunt PROPRIETORS: Queens Moat Houses plc OPEN: all week, exc Sat L (by arrangement only) MEALS: 12.30 to 2, 7.30 to 9.30 PRICES: £26 (£37), Set L £14.95 (£22), Set D £22 (£30). Card slips closed CARDS: Access, Amex, Diners, Visa SEATS: 70. Private parties: 42 main room, 12 and 30 private rooms. Car park, 60 places. Vegetarian meals. Children's helpings on request. Jacket and tie. No cigars/pipes in dining-room. Wheelchair access (1 step; also WC). No music. Fax: (0299) 896804 ACCOMMODATION: 25 rooms, all with bath/shower. B&B £82 to £97. Children welcome. Baby facilities. Afternoon teas. Garden. Tennis. TV. Phone. Scenic

▲ *This symbol means that accommodation is available.*

ABINGDON Oxfordshire map 2

▲ *Thame Lane House*

1 Thame Lane, Culham,
Abingdon OX14 3DS COOKING **2**
ABINGDON (0235) 524177 COST £22–£35

This guesthouse is at the head of the lane to the European School on the Abingdon to Dorchester road. It offers simple, honest and real French cooking at a fair price, combined with enthusiastic and friendly hospitality and explanations from Marie-Claude Beech. Although non-residents have to book a day in advance, they will be offered a short menu of French bourgeois cooking – civet of hare, mouclade, gigot of lamb boulangère – tempered with simpler modern dishes such as avocado, mango and lime salad, or assiette du pêcheur with raspberry vinegar. Tastes are true, the civet was gamey with a vengeance, the sorbets are satisfactorily piercing; technique is sound. This is a tiny restaurant, the sort we need thousands of, giving genuine and individual service. A short wine list is French bar one Bulgarian, with some decent bottles, including twin vintages of Ch. Méaume, La Tour Figeac and Fieuzal.

CHEF: Marie-Claude Beech PROPRIETORS: Michael and Marie-Claude Beech OPEN: all week, exc Sun D CLOSED: 2 weeks Jan MEALS: 12.30 to 1, 7 to 8.30 PRICES: Set L £16 (£22) to £22.50 (£29), Set D £16 (£22) to £22.50 (£29). Net prices, card slips closed CARDS: Access, Visa SEATS: 16. Private parties: 16 main room. Car park, 8 places. Children's helpings on request. No children under 3. Smart dress preferred. No smoking in dining-room. No music ACCOMMODATION: 5 rooms, 1 with shower. B&B £26 to £49. Deposit: £10. No children under 3. Garden. TV. Doors close at 11.30. Confirm by 6.30

ALDEBURGH Suffolk map 3

▲ *Austins*

243 The High Street, Aldeburgh IP15 5DN COOKING **1**
ALDEBURGH (0728) 453932 COST £16–£34

The long blue awning on a pink frontage, with a wrought-iron balcony across the first floor, gives this hotel a seaside air. Within, theatricals and musicals are in evidence from the playbills and photographs on the walls. Austins provides a good touring base and a dining-room that shimmers with cleanliness, excellent service and fair, if old-fashioned, cooking. The menu may not at times (in winter months when custom is unpredictable) read excitingly, but the range of materials improves as the sun rises high in the sky. A meal that began with a twice-baked Gruyère soufflé on a simple tomato and tarragon sauce continued with breast of duck with cherries and three-mustard sauce, before a finale of meringue with four home-made ice-creams. It showed good elements (the soufflé, the pear sorbet and melon ice-cream) as well as bad (a meagre portion of overcooked duck and a solid meringue), just as another meal had an excellent chicken breast stuffed with herbs and cream cheese, but a dry coulibiac of salmon. Supporters of Austins stress the quality of the welcome and the acceptability of the kitchen. The wine list is short and fairly priced. House wines are from £6.25.

CHEF: Julian Alexander-Worster PROPRIETORS: Robert Selbie and Julian Alexander-Worster OPEN: Tue to Sun D, Wed and Sun L (other days by arrangement) CLOSED: first 2 weeks Feb MEALS: 12.30 to 2, 7.30 to 11 PRICES: £19 (£28), Set L £10.50 (£16). Cover £1 CARDS: Access, Amex, Visa SEATS: 30. Private parties: 30 main room. Children's helpings. No cigars/pipes in dining-room. Fax: (0728) 453668 ACCOMMODATION: 7 rooms, all with bath/shower. B&B £48 to £68.50. Children welcome. TV. Phone. Scenic. Doors close at 1am. Confirm by midday (*Which? Hotel Guide*)

Regatta

171–173 High Street, Aldeburgh IP15 5AN — COOKING 1
ALDEBURGH (0728) 452011 — COST £18–£26

Restaurant and wine bar are Siamese twins: two halves of one premises but with two front doors. The atmosphere has been described by one inspector as 'living-room-cum-bistro', but the linen is starchy. The maritime mural is worth its place and there are some good pieces of furniture. Each half of the operation offers its own menu. A restaurant meal in springtime that included tomato and apple soup, crab terrine with avocado sauce, guinea-fowl with grapes and hazelnuts, ragoût of seafood, lemon tart, and orange terrine exemplifies the repertoire and on this occasion showed the cooking in a fair light: reasonably solid, though a bit short on stand-up flavour, with no homogeneity to the guinea-fowl sauce and its trimmings. There were also poor desserts and pastry work. Standards have been very up and down this year; perhaps expansion (to other towns) has been costly. When Regatta is on form, the welcome is generous and civilised. The wine list is fair-priced and good. The range of half-bottles and a concentration on decent mid-priced wines world-wide make for enjoyment. House wine is £6.25.

CHEFS: K. Child and Sara E. Fox PROPRIETORS: Peter G.R. Hill and Sara E. Fox OPEN: all week MEALS: 12 (12.30 Sun) to 2.30, 7 to 10.15 PRICES: restaurant £16 (£22), wine bar £13 (£18). Card slips closed CARDS: Access, Visa SEATS: 90. 4 tables outside. Private parties: 50 main room. Vegetarian meals. Children's helpings. Wheelchair access (2 steps). Music

ALNWICK Northumberland — map 7

John Blackmore's

1 Dorothy Foster Court, Narrowgate,
Alnwick NE66 1NL — COOKING 3
ALNWICK (0665) 604465 — COST £31

John Blackmore's restaurant down a narrow alley and close to the castle offers antiquity amid comfortable modern furnishings and embellishments. Such is the charm of this tiny place that as the Blackmores turn more and more people away, they resist the commercial urge to introduce two sittings. Service remains unhurriedly attentive. Generous portions with lavish saucing epitomise the kitchen's style. One couple chose sweetbreads in sage and port sauce; hot trout mousse with vermouth sauce; fillets of beef with kidney, liver and bacon and leek sauce; and noisettes of lamb with mint and cream sauce.

Mousses appear with regularity – making up three out of six first-course possibilities in one diner's experience. Another reader, choosing a trio of vegetable mousses, was however disappointed by over-sweet and highly peppered carrot and broccoli mousse which tasted only of garlic. Some dishes are complicated, as in sautéed monkfish, broccoli and mushrooms with a lobster sauce, glazed with sauce hollandaise; or even baked suprême of chicken served on noodles with king prawns and a smoked salmon sauce. They are not overworked, however, and the freshness and quality of the ingredients does come out. 'No flannel, no flambés,' as one reader commented. Desserts are lavish and are best summed up by two non-pudding eaters who enjoyed 'a delicious crème brûlée and perfect summer pudding'. More imagination could be applied to the wine list but there is at least a fair selection of half-bottles. House French is £6.20.

CHEF: John Blackmore PROPRIETORS: John and Penny Blackmore OPEN: Tue to Sat, D only CLOSED: Jan MEALS: 7 to 9.30 PRICES: £18 (£26). Card slips closed CARDS: Access, Amex, Diners, Visa SEATS: 25. Private parties: 30 main room. Vegetarian meals. Children's helpings. Smart dress preferred. No smoking. Wheelchair access (1 step). Music

AMBLESIDE Cumbria map 7

▲ *Kirkstone Foot Country House Hotel*

Kirkstone Pass Road, Ambleside LA22 9EH COOKING 1
AMBLESIDE (053 94) 32232 COST £21–£29

New owners have taken over this long-established country hotel – a complex that has holiday flats and cottages in the grounds. Little has changed. Staff and management have been retained, and the kitchen is still run by Jane Cross. Her five-course dinners are built round a well-tried formula of English hotel cooking, with generous portions, a bedrock of classical ideas, plus a few modern touches – mostly among the starters. One good June meal began with a gratin of prawns and pimento before cream of tomato soup with fresh wholemeal mini-loaves. Main courses usually feature a roast as well as a vegetarian option, such as casseroled vegetables served in a cheese and potato nest. Desserts are displayed on an ample trolley. The cheeseboard might benefit from one or two local representatives. Meals begin with plenty of Melba toast and end with coffee and home-made chocolates. Standards are generally consistent, although there are discrepancies, and slack service occasionally disrupts the civilised atmosphere of the dining-room. A wide-ranging, reasonably priced wine list has a strong Australian contingent and many half-bottles. House Duboeuf is £6.50.

All details are as accurate as possible at the time of going to press, but chefs and owners often change, and it is wise to check by telephone before making a special journey. Many readers have been disappointed when set-price bargain meals are no longer available. Ask when booking.

CHEFS: Jane Cross and Valerie Walker PROPRIETORS: Frank Norfolk and Pauline Norfolk OPEN: all week, D only CLOSED: Jan to early Feb MEALS: 7.30 for 8 PRICES: Set D from £16 (£21) to £18.25 (£24). Card slips closed CARDS: Access, Visa SEATS: 50. Private parties: 10 main room. Car park, 30 places. Vegetarian meals. Children's helpings on request. No children under 7. Jacket and tie. No smoking in dining-room. Wheelchair access (also WC). Music. One sitting. Fax: (053 94) 31110 ACCOMMODATION: 16 rooms, all with bath/shower. D,B&B £37 to £95. Deposit: £20. Children welcome. Baby facilities. Afternoon teas. Garden. Fishing. TV. Phone. Scenic

▲ *Rothay Manor* 🍷

Rothay Bridge, Ambleside LA22 0EH COOKING 2
AMBLESIDE (053 94) 33605 COST £15–£37

The Nixons' elegant, civilised and eminently likeable Lakeland country house has lost none of its distinct Englishness. Tradition looms large in the Regency-style dining-room with waitresses in mob caps and pinnies, while the kitchen keeps faith with the past. Soups, terrines, high-quality roasts, home-made jellies and relishes and home-baked breads and biscuits set the tone of the menu. Dinner is five courses, with suggested wines for each course; a cheaper two-course option is also available. Reporters have praised the watercress and potato soup, goujons of sole with home-made tartare sauce, roast pork and passion-fruit mousse. Occasionally there are quibbles about lack of flavour and poor value for money, but votes are generally in favour. Inexpensive buffet lunches and splendid afternoon teas are available. The wine list offers fine range and good quality. Classic French regions show well with a refreshing gaggle of individual growers from Burgundy; Southern France, the Rhône, Portugal and Australia all have very commendable sections; Italy fares less well. Prices are reasonable, with much under £15, and there are good halves. House wine is £7.50. CELLARMAN'S CHOICE: New Zealand, Hawkes Bay Sauvignon Blanc 1989, Delegat's, £12; Bourgogne Rouge 1984, Vallet, £9.20.

CHEFS: Jane Binns and Colette Nixon PROPRIETORS: the Nixon families OPEN: all week CLOSED: last 3 weeks Jan, first week Feb MEALS: 12.30 to 2 (12.45 to 1.30 Sun), 8 to 9 PRICES: buffet L £9 (£15), Set Sun L £12.75 (£18), Set D £18 (£24) to £24 (£31) CARDS: Access, Amex, Diners, Visa SEATS: 70. Private parties: 12 main room, 30 private room. Car park, 30 places. Vegetarian meals. Children's helpings. Smart dress preferred. No smoking in dining-room. Wheelchair access (also WC). No music. Air-conditioned. Fax: (053 94) 33607 ACCOMMODATION: 18 rooms, all with bath/shower. Rooms for disabled. B&B £61 to £106. Deposit: £50. Children welcome. Baby facilities. Afternoon teas. Garden. Fishing. TV. Phone. Scenic. Doors close at midnight. Confirm by noon (*Which? Hotel Guide*)

Sheila's Cottage

The Slack, Ambleside LA22 9DQ COOKING 2
AMBLESIDE (053 94) 33079 COST £18–£32

The original cottage tea-room was probably the best of its kind in the Lake District. Nowadays the place also functions as a fully-fledged restaurant. The transition has not been an easy one. The décor is welcoming, with its pastel colour schemes, flowers, pine furniture and drawings of Cumbrian rural life on the walls. The food is generally of a high standard, but there have been reports of poor service. There are often long delays (despite a deliberate attempt at streamlining) and the waitresses have been noticeably lacking in the basic skills of their trade. A new team in the kitchen can deliver the goods and reporters have praised the quality of ingredients, well-balanced flavours, robust sauces and gravies, and generous portions of unadorned vegetables. Baking is the high point: admirable breads and rolls, tea-breads and pastries. A meal in December produced Stilton pâté with oatcakes, salmon with cream and chive sauce, beef with peppercorn sauce, chestnut mousse and the renowned sticky toffee pudding. Light lunches feature platters of seafood, Cumbrian ham with home-made damson chutney, and Swiss specialities. Set afternoon tea is a popular tourist attraction. Teas, cordials and house lemonade supplement a short, well-chosen wine list. House French is £8.50.

CHEFS: Peter Barnsley, Jane Sutherland and Heather Doherty PROPRIETORS: Stewart and Janice Greaves OPEN: all week, exc D Mon and Sun CLOSED: 2 weeks Jan MEALS: 12 to 2.30 (2 Sun), 3 to 5 and 7 to 9.30 PRICES: £19 (£27), Set L £12.50 (£18) SEATS: 65. Private parties: 47 main room. Children's helpings L. No smoking. Wheelchair access. Music. Air-conditioned. Fax: (053 94) 34488

AMERSHAM Buckinghamshire map 3

King's Arms NEW ENTRY

30 High Street, Old Amersham HP7 0DJ COOKING 1
AMERSHAM (0494) 726333 COST £19–£38

Old Amersham is at the bottom of the hill, the new town is at the top. The King's Arms is emphatically old: all that half-timbering makes it a copy-book example of the 'Olde English Inn'. Perhaps because John Jennison was once an inspector for the *Michelin Guide*, the food on offer, in a dining-room as replete with beams as the rest of the place, has an eye to current expectations (or those of 10 years ago). Dishes such as crab with ginger grapefruit and endive, a house pâté or terrine – be it turkey and hazelnut, game or smoked salmon – chicken breast stuffed with almond mousseline with a calvados sauce, and calf's liver with sweet glazed parsnips, are typical examples. Three to four times a year a plateau de fruits de mer is laid on. A full range of desserts, not forgetting old-English ones, are sometimes compiled in rather modern ways. Execution can lack bravura and seasoning, and lunch is a better deal than the full-price dinner, but this is useful for the area and the welcome from staff and owner is genuine. Wines are fairly priced and adequate. House wine is £7.40.

CHEF: Gary Munday PROPRIETOR: John Jennison OPEN: Tue to Sun, exc Sun D CLOSED: Christmas, 1 day after bank hols MEALS: 12.30 to 2, 7 to 9.30 PRICES: £23 (£32), Set L £12 (£19). Minimum £13.50 D CARDS: Access, Amex, Diners, Visa SEATS: 30. Private parties: 48 main room, 12 private room. Car park, 25 places. Vegetarian meals. Children welcome. No cigars/pipes in dining-room. No music

If a restaurant is new to the Guide *this year (did not appear as a main entry in the last edition)* NEW ENTRY *appears opposite its name.*

ASHBOURNE Derbyshire map 5

▲ *Callow Hall*

Mappleton Road, Ashbourne DE6 2AA COOKING 1
ASHBOURNE (0335) 43403 COST £17–£41

Alterations continue at this former home of a corset manufacturer, with the Spencers building new kitchens and reallocating rooms to eating, drinking or smoking (the dining-room is now no-smoking). Readers enjoy the location with its trees, grass, brooks and rivers, the richly coloured dining-room, and the welcome from the Spencers themselves – though wishing staff could be more experienced. A *carte* is offered at the same time as a five-course menu, each sharing many dishes. Between them they cover a fair range of materials, fish especially, until the sweets trolley, when the mechanics of service and presentation mean a certain lack of change or variety. The cooking of dishes such as chicken with baby sweetcorn and raisins, guinea-fowl with apple and celeriac, or brill with pink peppercorn cream sauce, is approved, though complexity is evidently not a hallmark. A few readers have commented that made dishes such as terrines or mousses have little to lift their taste into the memory bank. The mainly French wine list is fairly priced and includes an interesting slate of Bordeaux as well as excellent growers in Burgundy, Sancerre and the Rhône. There may be fewer hocks and mosels, but they too are worth exploring. House wine is £6.75.

CHEF: David Spencer PROPRIETORS: David and Dorothy Spencer OPEN: Mon to Sat D, and Sun L (other days by arrangement) MEALS: 12.30 to 2.30, 7.30 to 9.30 PRICES: £26 (£34), Set L £12.50 (£17), Set D £23.50 (£30). Card slips closed CARDS: Access, Amex, Diners, Visa SEATS: 80. Private parties: 50 main room, 40 private room. Car park, 70 places. Vegetarian meals. Children's helpings (Sun L only). No smoking in dining-room. No music. Fax: (0335) 43624 ACCOMMODATION: 12 rooms, all with bath/shower. D,B&B £86 to £161. Children welcome. Baby facilities. Garden. Fishing. TV. Phone. Scenic. Doors close at 11.30 (*Which? Hotel Guide*)

ASTON CLINTON Buckinghamshire map 3

▲ *Bell*

Aston Clinton HP22 5HP COOKING 2*
AYLESBURY (0296) 630252 COST £27–£64

There have been mixed experiences at this long-established inn where dining is a full-dress experience: service so impeccably correct that for one reader, it carried 'unobtrusiveness to the point where [the service] was incapable of detection'; orchestrated dome-lifting; a lengthy and elaborate menu, even if suspended in the face of a quiet midwinter Saturday. Visitors who splash out may wonder where the £100 disappeared, but there is a vein of good value in the set-price meals that elicits much praise. Baked eggs with morels and a rich fungal sauce, thick strips of pink beef with onion confit, and a cream mousse decorated with chocolate and mandarin orange confirmed the good opinion of the place held by a visitor, last there 40 years ago, who recognised the old bar with joy amid a flood of boyhood memories. A sense of sufficient simplicity is left far behind with the full *carte*, which might be a testament of recent culinary trends: poached cannon of lamb on a coriander and lentil sauce; scallops on crab croûtons with a red pepper sauce; 'lasagne' of salmon; carpaccio of lamb with tapénade, and so on; much couched in surprising prose ('a froth of chocolate captured in a dark chocolate case'). Although the flavours and combinations are new-wave, the presentation is old-hat nouvelle cuisine, exciting protestations of meagre portions and regrets at the workaday mixtures of beans and mange-tout as vegetable accompaniment. There are comments, too, on sufficient disappointing nights to invite speculation about consistency: 'The menu noted the absence of an established pastry chef. I wished I had not been the guinea-pig for the new one.' The setting for the cooking in a 'new' dining-room, with bench seating many would like trashed, is old English, perhaps a fitting spot therefore for trying the remarkable wine list with prices and quality to match. There are decent bottles under £15, albeit rather few; the emphasis is on France, pedigree and age. Good Rhône and Provence, Alsace and a few good petits châteaux are best value; beyond France, quality is paramount with Volpaia Chianti, Heitz Zinfandel and Moss Wood Cabernet Sauvignon, but mark-up pushes hard. 'Wines of the week', modestly priced, are printed with the menu.

CHEF: Kevin Cape PROPRIETORS: the Harris family OPEN: all week MEALS: 12.30 to 2, 7.30 to 10 PRICES: £38 (£53), Set L and D £17.35 (£27) to £35 (£46) CARDS: Access, Amex, Visa SEATS: 100. Private parties: 20 and 200 private rooms. Car park, 250 places. Children welcome. Smart dress preferred. No smoking in dining-room. Wheelchair access (also WC). Fax: (0296) 631250 ACCOMMODATION: 21 rooms, all with bath/shower. Rooms for disabled. B&B £92 to £107. Children welcome. Baby facilities. Pets welcome. Afternoon teas. Garden. TV. Phone. Scenic. Doors close at 12.30am (*Which? Hotel Guide*)

AYLESBURY Buckinghamshire map 2

▲ *Hartwell House*

Oxford Road, Aylesbury HP17 8NL
AYLESBURY (0296) 747444 COOKING 3
on A418, 3m S of Aylesbury COST £29–£65

Historic House Hotels are showing estimable determination in finishing this project, with the final phase of sports and conference facilities as well as extra rooms expected to be complete by the end of 1991. The house, the bedrooms and the gardens are a remarkable achievement of restoration, improving as it all mellows. A visit on a summer's day is a required minimum. For one, it will be cheaper than dinner from the *carte*. This, for food that can be at best tactful and sometimes faulty (though we now receive much less comment of this sort), comes at a stunningly high price. Though not cheap, the set-price menu is the wisest option. The menu also has a greater sense of actuality and verve to its recipes, though a set of first courses offering leek and potato soup, terrine of chicken and vegetables, and grilled monkfish with courgettes and tomato butter sauce or duck foie gras at a supplement, shows little adventure or imagination. Competent cooking does seem apparent, however, even if one is paying for the paintwork. There are few changes on the wine front, with high prices similar to those of last year. Nevertheless, the few offerings there are below about £15 show careful selection: Basedow Semillon, several good

Alsaces and a clutch of modest clarets. Older vintages and pedigree names, many from beyond the classic areas, are the main business of this list. House wine is £11.

CHEF: Aidan McCormack PROPRIETORS: Historic House Hotels Ltd OPEN: all week CLOSED: 24 to 26 Dec, exc to residents MEALS: 12.30 to 2, 7.30 to 9.45 PRICES: £44 (£54), Set L £19 (£29), Set D £32.50 (£43). Minimum £32.50 D. Net prices, card slips closed CARDS: Access, Amex, Diners, Visa SEATS: 60. Private parties: 30 main room, 16 and 30 private rooms. Car park, 70 places. Vegetarian meals. No children under 8. No pets. Jacket and tie. No cigars/pipes in dining-room. Wheelchair access (also WC). Music. Fax: (0296) 747450 ACCOMMODATION: 32 rooms, all with bath/shower. Rooms for disabled. Lift. B&B £98.50 to £316. No children under 8. Afternoon teas. Garden. Swimming-pool. Sauna. Fishing. TV. Phone. Scenic (*Which? Hotel Guide*)

Pebbles 🍷

Pebble Lane, Aylesbury HP20 2JH — COOKING 3
AYLESBURY (0296) 86622 — COST £23–£49

This cottage of a restaurant on a footpath off Kingsbury Square, leading down to the church, is too small to accommodate the burly frame of its chef-proprietor. Some supporters would aver that he needs a larger kitchen and more staff to allow his considerable talents full flight. Accounts of meals here through the year show an unpredictability brought on by staff numbers and expected business; in other words the recession bites. One correspondent's Saturday night limited-choice menu failed to coincide in either scale or price with details supplied to the *Guide* office. Alternatively, a spring meal, entered into with some trepidation by one reader, produced this result: 'An appetiser of proper French onion soup was followed by a warm salad of salmon in a thinnish hollandaise sauce flavoured with coriander, without detriment to the salmon. The main course was fallow deer, neither overhung nor overdone, but served *à point* in a poivrade sauce, happily neither thickened nor over-peppered. On the rim of the plate were shallots, morels, cherry tomatoes and a modest galette of potato. The sweets were an excellent chocolate marquise tempered with a delicate lemon sorbet and surrounded with grated almonds; and nougat glacé with redcurrant and raspberry coulis.' It can be done; it may be wise to hold a watching brief. Informative notes on a few selected Bordeaux properties reveal the true preoccupation of the wine list; fine vintages range from petits châteaux to first growths, affording good choice. Burgundy is represented by several smaller domaines and Deiss dominates Alsace. Italian wines barely get a look-in but the Americans and Australasians are a fine choice. There is much below £15; thereafter prices are erratic but offer some good-value drinking. CELLARMAN'S CHOICE: Gewurztraminer Réserve 1985, Deiss, £14.25; Ch. Cissac 1970 (half-bottle), £22.50.

CHEF/PROPRIETOR: Jeremy Blake O'Connor OPEN: Tues to Sun, exc Sun D MEALS: 12 to 2.15, 7.15 to 10.30 PRICES: Set L £13 (£23), Set D £29.50 (£41) CARDS: Access, Amex, Visa SEATS: 32. Private parties: 24 main room. Vegetarian meals. Children's helpings. Smart dress preferred. No cigars/pipes in dining-room. Wheelchair access. Music

BABBACOMBE Devon map 1

Table

135 Babbacombe Road,
Babbacombe TQ1 3SR COOKING 3*
TORQUAY (0803) 324292 COST £34–£44

'What makes Table special is neither décor nor location. The secret is excellent raw materials cooked with a marvellous sense of balance,' commented one reporter after a memorable visit to this little gem of a restaurant in a dreary suburban street. 'Boy, can Trevor Brooks cook!' exclaimed another. Trevor Brooks' track record, including stints at Inverlochy Castle and Hambleton Hall (see entries), shows in a vivid, modern, fixed-price menu. There are classic undercurrents, but ingredients are up-to-the-minute: pulses, seaweed, filo pastry, olive oil. Some visitors would welcome a more regularly changing repertoire, but this is a modest enterprise run by a young couple who have to work within limits. This means a meal is sometimes slow, even if worth the wait. Fish soup with aïoli and Parmesan draws many votes. It is an intense but delicate brew which derives its quality from the seven different fish used in its preparation. Elsewhere, there is praise for confit of duck with a green lentil sauce that 'took the richness from the meat', and soft marinated scallops in pastry with coriander and seaweed. A sorbet often appears before centrepieces such as free-range poulet noir with specks of truffle and leeks on a bed of noodles, sea bass with two sauces, and tournedos of beef with a green peppercorn and horseradish crust. Desserts occasionally disappoint, but most reporters rate them stunning: a brandy-snap basket of Grand Marnier ice-cream with spiced oranges and caramel sauce, and praline feuilleté with chocolate and ginger sauce have both been first-rate. A board of local cheeses often includes some rarities. Bread and rolls are made on the premises, using flour from Crowdy Mill, Harbertonford and everyone mentions the petits fours. The 30-strong wine list is developing and has been boosted by a new selection of half-bottles. House white is £9.

CHEF: Trevor Brooks PROPRIETORS: Trevor Brooks and Jane Corrigan OPEN: Tue to Sun, D only MEALS: 7.30 to 9.30 PRICES: Set D £25 (£34) to £28 (£37). Card slips closed SEATS: 20. Private parties: 21 main room. No children under 10. Music

BAGSHOT Surrey map 3

▲ *Latymer, Pennyhill Park Hotel*

College Ride, Bagshot GU19 5ET COOKING 3
BAGSHOT (0276) 71774 COST £24–£60

No doubt the astronomic prices, the over-stated decoration and sheer fanciness and flounce of the place (who, for instance, can take seriously a menu that offers 'steamed salmon and monkfish enrobed together on a cucumber and dill essence'?) will put off many people who take their pleasures more simply than south-east country club (with golf, clay-pigeon shooting and a Roman-style swimming-pool) operations. That said, David Richards can cook excellently, arranges the food inventively, and manages to let the flavours cut through the apparent complication and multiplication of elements in dishes such as terrine of crab in a lobster jelly; fillet of venison with apricot and chestnut stuffing on a poivrade sauce; and banana and pineapple fritters on three fruit coulis and spun sugar. The service, too, is as enthusiastic and willing as the setting will allow. The sort of place for the older family on a weekend outing – make sure granny is paying. And avoid generous gestures with the wine list; careful scanning will reveal a few bottles below £15, but this is essentially a list of classics with prices to match. House wine is £12.95.

CHEF: David Richards PROPRIETORS: Pennyhill Park Ltd OPEN: all week, exc Sun L MEALS: 12.30 to 2.30, 7.30 to 10.30 PRICES: £35 (£50), Set L £22 (£24) to £40 (£44) CARDS: Access, Amex, Diners, Visa SEATS: 60. Private parties: 30 and 40 private rooms. Car park, 150 places. Vegetarian meals. Children's helpings on request L. Children over 10 D. Jacket and tie. No cigars/pipes in dining-room. Music (occasionally). Fax: (0276) 73217 ACCOMMODATION: 76 rooms, all with bath/shower. B&B £123 to £226. Children welcome. Baby facilities. Afternoon teas. Garden. Swimming-pool. Sauna. Tennis. Fishing. Golf. TV. Phone. Scenic

BAKEWELL Derbyshire map 5

Green Apple

Diamond Court, Water Street,
Bakewell DE4 1EW COOKING 1
BAKEWELL (0629) 814404 COST £15–£30

Roger Green is a larger-than-life chef-proprietor who wanders dining-room as well as kitchen. He is keen on green materials and won't allow smoking anywhere (except outside on the terrace when it's not raining). He offers food for all: take-aways, cheap lunches, more elaborate dinners. The dinners are not long but they draw on many influences, Middle Eastern as well as mainstream European. It is hard to be sure of cooking systems in a place that announces frozen New Zealand oysters, thawed on receipt of your order, are 'just as good as fresh', but no doubt it is Bakewell's most enterprising spot. A short wine list is sensibly compiled and not too dear. House wines from Berry Bros and Rudd are £9.95.

CHEFS: Roger Green, Nick Andrews, Pam Wain and Alison Ray PROPRIETORS: Roger and Judith Green OPEN: summer all week, exc D Sun to Tue; winter Mon to Sat L, Thur to Sat D MEALS: 12 to 2, 7 to 9.30 PRICES: L £8 (£15), Set D £12 (£20) to £17 (£25). 4% charge for credit cards CARDS: Access, Diners, Visa SEATS: 50. 8 tables outside. Private parties: 50 main room. Vegetarian meals. Children's helpings. No smoking. Wheelchair access. Music

'Trying to get further quantities of bread, butter, mineral water etc. was a bit like trying to flag down a taxi in the rush hour.' On eating in London

Restaurateurs justifiably resent no-shows. If you quote a credit card number when booking, you may be liable for the restaurant's lost profit margin if you don't turn up. Always phone to cancel.

BARNET Hertfordshire map 3

Mims

63 East Barnet Road, Barnet EN4 8RN COOKING 2
081-449 2974 and 447 1825 COST £23–£35

Mims, in a parade of shops where it can easily be missed, gives the impression of summer – all green and white with rather uncomfortable wrought-iron chairs. The menu is a surprise, far removed from its East Barnet location: stuffed squid with salsa, roast rabbit with pink peppercorns and roast monkfish with tomato, garlic and coriander speak of more exotic parts. There is a strong classical French influence behind the inventive, new-wave cooking – an indication of Ali Al-Sersy's training at the hands of the Roux brothers. A report on a winter dinner for four, preceded by a spread of assorted home-made breads and two kinds of butter, ran out of superlatives: 'delightful' watercress soup, 'absolutely heavenly' cream cheese and spinach pancakes, steamed monkfish in a 'delicate' sauce and duck with confit both pronounced 'excellent' while 'the sweets were a revelation'. Another report praised the calf's liver with onion and dill. Not all readers agree, for there seems to be the occasional bad night, judging from dissenting reports that complain of slovenly service and of dishes not quite as they should be. The wine list is short and not too dear. House wine is £8.25.

CHEF: Ali Al-Sersy PROPRIETORS: M. Abouzahrah and Ali Al-Sersy OPEN: Tue to Sun, exc Sat L CLOSED: 1 week Christmas MEALS: 12 to 3, 6.30 to 11 (noon to 10.30 Sun) PRICES: L £17 (£23), Set D £17 (£25) to £20.50 (£29) CARDS: Access, Visa SEATS: 50. Private parties: 50 main room. Car park, 6 places D only. Children welcome L and Sun. No cigars/pipes in dining-room. Wheelchair access (1 step). Music

Wings

6 Potters Road, New Barnet EN5 5HW COOKING 1
081-449 9890 COST £31

Elegant and suburban Wings does not look like a Chinese restaurant. Even the attentive but unobtrusive service is unlike that encountered in the various Chinatowns. The menu, though, offers all the popular Peking and Szechuan favourites: sizzling dishes, crispy duck with pancakes, and a fair amount of seafood. Consistent and reliable cooking draws a regular following. Both crab with ginger and with black-bean sauce have been praised for freshness while the Szechuan set dinner is good value for money. Other choices range from Kungpo chicken and crispy beef with chilli and carrots to a Wings' special of steamed halibut. Note the cover *and* high service charge. House wine is £6.45.

CHEF: Ho Yuen Wan PROPRIETOR: Pak Wah Tse OPEN: all week, exc Tue Jan to Nov MEALS: 12 to 2.30, 6 to 10.30 PRICES: £14 (£26). Cover 85p. Service 15%. Card slips closed CARDS: Access, Amex, Diners, Visa SEATS: 80. Private parties: 40 main room. Vegetarian meals. Children welcome. Wheelchair access. Music

BARNSLEY South Yorkshire map 5

Armstrongs

NEW ENTRY

6 Shambles Street, Barnsley S70 2SQ COOKING 1
BARNSLEY (0226) 240113 COST £29

'It's interesting that Barnsley – famed for its chop and other hearty offerings for mining folk – can support a place like this,' comments a Yorkshire inspector. Times change. 'Café Bar' says a sign above the panelled double doors of this town-centre restaurant described by a reader as 'chic, stylish and arty, without going over the top'. The ground-floor dining area, complete with prints, plants and a piano, has a mirrored bar at one end and a curving staircase leading to the privacy of the upstairs balcony. Nick Pound worked with Stephen Bull at Lichfields during the '80s. Puff pastry cases, ravioli, warm salads, fruit sauces, parfaits and brandy-snap baskets figure prominently, although there are more substantial stalwarts such as lamb stew to assuage northern appetites. Dishes can lack zest, but reporters have liked boned quail stuffed with mushrooms; apple and celeriac soup; fillets of sole with shellfish sauce; and roast breast of duck with orange and onion confit. The best-selling iced butterscotch meringue cake has been called a 'beautiful creation'. Staff are well-organised and the atmosphere buzzes. The wine list has around 80 bottles including four house wines from £7.45.

CHEFS: Nick Pound, Ron Widdowson and Lee Hammond PROPRIETOR: Nick Pound
OPEN: Tue to Sat, exc Sat L CLOSED: 2 weeks Aug, bank hols MEALS: 12 to 2, 7 to 10
PRICES: £17 (£24) CARDS: Access, Visa SEATS: 60. Private parties: 40 main room, 18 and 40 private rooms. Vegetarian meals. Children welcome. Wheelchair access. Music

Restaurant Peano

COUNTY RESTAURANT OF THE YEAR

NEW ENTRY

102 Dodworth Road, Barnsley S70 6HL COOKING 2*
BARNSLEY (0226) 244990 COST £14–£31

'Our restaurant is not typical of this area,' write the Peanos of their Victorian pile one mile from junction 37 of the M1. Indeed, this is emphasised by the decorative style of traditional Victorian overlaid with bold modern functionalism. Michael Peano, ex-Fischer's of Baslow and Waterside Inn (see entries), is half-Italian, half-German and this blend of influences and cultures is strongly reflected in his short, simple menus. Pasta is made on the premises and appears in the guise of ravioli of lobster, and tagliatelle with tomato sauce and pesto, or as an accompaniment to a saddle of lamb with kidneys. A recent report admired assertive flavours in dishes such as timbale of aubergine mousse with ratatouille and red snapper with basil and tomato vinaigrette. One reader was taken with a dish of tender, succulent pink lamb laid on a bed of wafer-thin potatoes salted just enough to complement the meat. Ingredients are well bought, including pasta and polenta flour imported from Italy. Incidentals, including vegetables and home-made bread, are carefully considered. Desserts do not let the side down. A modest but sure hand is shown in the choice of 30-odd wines, divided equally between France and Italy. Prices are very fair, and there are some fine Italians. This is an encouraging start.

CHEF: Michael Peano PROPRIETORS: Michael and Tracey Peano OPEN: Tue to Sun, exc Sun D MEALS: 12 to 2 (2.30 Sun), 7 to 9.30 PRICES: £18 (£26), Set L £9 (£14) to £11 (£16) CARDS: Access, Visa SEATS: 45. Private parties: 45 main room. Car park, 35 places. Vegetarian meals with prior notice. Children's helpings. Wheelchair access (also WC). Music

BARNSTAPLE Devon map 1

▲ *Lynwood House*

Bishops Tawton Road,
Barnstaple EX32 9DZ
BARNSTAPLE (0271) 43695
on A377, between town centre and ring road

COOKING 1
COST £35

One way or another, the Roberts family seems set for many years yet at Lynwood House. Gradually a new generation – Adam, Matthew and Christian – is taking over. In the restaurant the emphasis is on fish, some local and some, like the smoked salmon, imported from Scotland. Such a static menu hardly changes from year to year, which is never very encouraging, especially for locals, unless the dishes are definitive versions. It is unfortunate that reports have suggested that even the Lynwood pot ('various fish on a bed of rice in a rich wine and cream sauce') is not all it's cracked up to be. Praise has been warm for the friendly welcome – in most instances, at least – and for dishes such as 'flimsey' of prawns in a pastry case on a pool of cream sauce with accompanying salad, and an excellent fish stew. Praline ice-cream with butterscotch sauce *and* meringue is indicative of the serious nature of dessert here. Although this is a sound local resource, and the best place in the district to eat fish or shellfish, perhaps more radical change would provide a fillip to standards and invention. The didactic wine list presents a decent range of French wines at fair prices and a clutch from other countries as well. House wine is £6.75.

CHEFS: Ruth and Adam Roberts PROPRIETORS: John, Ruth, Adam, Matthew and Christian Roberts OPEN: all week, exc Sun L MEALS: 12 to 2, 7 to 10 PRICES: £21 (£29) CARDS: Access, Visa SEATS: 70. Private parties: 70 main room, 24 and 70 private rooms. Car park, 40 places. Vegetarian meals. Children's helpings. No smoking in dining-room. Wheelchair access (also WC). No music. Fax: (0271) 79340 ACCOMMODATION: 5 rooms, all with bath/shower. B&B £47.50 to £67.50. Children welcome. TV. Phone. Confirm by 6 (*Which? Hotel Guide*)

Prices quoted in the Guide *are based on information supplied by restaurateurs. The figure in brackets below an entry is the average for a three-course meal with service, coffee and half a bottle of house wine, as calculated by computer. The prices quoted at the top of an entry represent a range, from the lowest average meal price to the highest; the latter is inflated by 20 per cent to take account of the fact that very few people eat an average meal, and also that prices are likely to rise during the year of the* Guide.

BARWICK Somerset map 2

▲ *Little Barwick House*

Barwick, nr Yeovil BA22 9TD
YEOVIL (0935) 23902
off A37, taking second left opposite Red House Pub

COOKING 2*
COST £28–£36

Plenty, good cheer and a sense of belonging seem to be the hallmarks of this family business. The Colleys' daughter helps out on busy nights. The house is newly decorated but remains 'homely'. Veronica Colley's style of cooking does not change radically: substantial, honest, British and with a strong emphasis on game and meats, though a vegetarian menu stands ready for proffering. Christopher Colley is a positive host and does the carving; seconds are not stinted. A short menu is supplemented by daily extras, often game and roast meats, and salmon once the season begins. Crème caramel seems addictive to some readers, although other desserts – often creamy or dressed up by meringue – are enjoyed by everyone. The wine list is a success story; short it may be, but everything is selected with purpose and prices make extravagance worthwhile and affordable. A little more depth and a glass award may be merited.

CHEF: Veronica Colley PROPRIETORS: Mr and Mrs C. Colley OPEN: Mon to Sat, D only MEALS: 7 to 9 PRICES: Set D £19.90 (£28) to £21.90 (£30). Card slips closed CARDS: Access, Amex, Visa SEATS: 40. Private parties: 50 main room. Car park. Children's helpings. No music ACCOMMODATION: 6 rooms, all with bath/shower. B&B £62 to £103. Deposit: £20. Children welcome. Pets welcome. Garden. TV. Phone. Scenic. Doors close at 11 (*Which? Hotel Guide*)

BASLOW Derbyshire map 5

▲ *Fischer's at Baslow Hall* 🍷

Calver Road, Baslow DE4 1RR
BASLOW (0246) 583259

COOKING 3
COST £24–£48

Baslow Hall, an imposing house of Derbyshire stone, in large gardens and approached by a long tree-bordered drive, was built in 1907. Three of the ground-floor rooms are converted for dining, decorated with vivid carpets and print fabrics (a little strident for some tastes). Max Fischer's repertoire is wide. He is aware of modern trends without compromising his own classical inclinations; clarity of taste is all important. Visitors have been uniformly impressed by the accuracy and finesse of the cooking. One who had the 'no choice' menu writes: 'A first course of fresh salmon interlaced with asparagus was superb. This was followed by an amazing concoction: slices of aubergine stacked with layers of chopped kidney and herby cheese, the whole coated with a fine vinaigrette. Quite the best thing I have tasted for a long time.' Others have praised the calf's liver with ginger and lime, escalope of salmon with basil sauce, and roast partridge served with pasta and crunchy red cabbage. Only very occasional lapses have been reported: a seafood platter with a bland saffron sauce; venison medallions heavily sauced and with a fierce peppery taste; a poor selection of cheeses. Desserts such as prune tartlet served with pistachio ice-cream and rum sauce and a trio of chocolate delicacies show confident flavours at work. Details are often good, especially home-made bread. Service, under the direction of Susan Fischer, is pleasant and cheerful. The fair-priced wine list shows good sense and is not overlong. It spurns neither decent low-priced bottles nor the more exalted and shows good range, although it is still very tentative beyond Europe. There is an intelligent spread of halves. The wine service is good and considerate. House wines are from £9. CELLARMAN'S CHOICE: Chablis, premier cru Côte de Léchet 1986, Defaix, £24; Margaux, Ch. Notton 1980, £17.

CHEF: Max Fischer PROPRIETORS: Max and Susan Fischer OPEN: all week, exc Mon L and Sun D MEALS: 12 to 1.30 (2 Sun), 7 to 9.30 (10 Sat) PRICES: Set L £17.50 (£24) to £18.50 (£25), Set D £28.50 (£36) to £31.50 (£40) CARDS: Access, Amex, Visa SEATS: 35. Private parties: 35 main room, 10 and 25 private rooms. Car park, 60 places. Children's helpings L. No children under 10. No smoking in dining-room. Wheelchair access (also WC). No music ACCOMMODATION: 6 rooms, all with bath/shower. B&B £62.50 to £107.50. Garden. TV. Phone. Scenic (*Which? Hotel Guide*)

BATH Avon map 2

Beaujolais NEW ENTRY

5A Chapel Row, Queen Square,
Bath BA1 1HN COOKING 1
BATH (0225) 423417 COST £15–£30

While competitors come and go, the Beaujolais carries on forever, even surviving fire, in 1991, which put its new extension into the garden out of action. Jean-Pierre Augé reckons lasting popularity comes from the evenings being 'very informal, the décor being very erotic – it does break the ice if the customer is a bit stiff'. This is a fine Gallic view of the Brits. The informality (who knows about eroticism?) is an essential element in the appeal of the Beaujolais. Food standards fluctuate but, on form, the kitchen's output is a decent standard of bistro cookery, cheerfully served. Caramelised onion tart; a warm spinach and goats' cheese mousse; veal chop with onion, mushrooms and bacon; and a thin, crinkly steak, beurre maître d'hôtel, just as would be served in ten thousand Routiers, are examples of the product. The decent, short wine list has lots of Duboeuf and some nice Loire choices. House wines are from £7.50.

CHEFS: Jean-Christophe Carras and Geraldine Fauld PROPRIETORS: Jean-Pierre Augé and Phillipe Wall OPEN: Mon to Sat CLOSED: bank hol Mons MEALS: 12 to 2, 7 to 10.30 (11 Sat) PRICES: £18 (£25), Set L £8.50 (£15). 10% service on parties of 5 or more CARDS: Access, Visa SEATS: 80. 5 tables outside. Private parties: 50 main room, 25 private room. Vegetarian meals. Children's helpings L. No-smoking area. Wheelchair access. Music

The Guide *relies on feedback from its readers. Especially welcome are reports on new restaurants appearing in the book for the first time.*

Chikako's NEW ENTRY

Theatre Royal, Sawclose,
Bath BA1 1ET COOKING 1
BATH (0225) 464125 COST £17–£30

This Japanese restaurant, complete with a side room equipped for traditional eating, occupies the same building as Bath's Theatre Royal. (Entry is gained from a footway skirting the theatre and a monster building site.) Chikako's has long been part of the Bath community. The usual range of Japanese dishes and cooking styles is offered: sukiyaki, teppanyaki, light and generous tempura, as well as good noodle and rice dishes such as boiled eel with a sweet sauce. First courses, such as spinach with sesame seeds, are limited in range but made from good materials. Service is friendly, informative and charming. Language is not a difficulty. There is a short list of wines, as well as Suntory beer and saké. House wine is £6.90.

CHEF: Chikako Cameron PROPRIETORS: Chikako's (TRB) Ltd OPEN: all week, D only CLOSED: 25 Dec MEALS: 6 to 11 PRICES: £14 (£21), Set D £10.30 (£17) to £18 (£25). Service 10%. Card slips closed CARDS: Access, Diners, Visa SEATS: 60. Private parties: 40 main room, 16 private room. Vegetarian meals. Children's helpings. Music. Air-conditioned

Garlands

7 Edgar Buildings, George Street,
Bath BA1 2EE COOKING 2
BATH (0225) 442283 COST £22–£36

Garlands, set on a broad pavement that surveys the length of Milsom Street, the city's main shopping promenade, is a nice refuge from the perpetual hustle of carrier bags and car parking that Bath seems to have become. The dining-room feels bright and fresh, night and day, a mood enhanced by the cheerful attentions of Joanna Bridgeman, who has taken more of a role front-of-house than hitherto. Tom Bridgeman's repertoire is modern mainstream: salmon with a tarragon cream or Gressingham duck on an orange and Dubonnet sauce with soured cherries might be preceded by a terrine layered with red mullet, sole and salmon or a filo parcel filled with chicken and hazlenut mousseline on a curry sauce. His execution veers from the very acceptable to the unprepared. Were he to steady up, the place would be much more reliable. Comments have mentioned food too cool, yet no press of business to justify the oversight; a first course of quail in a tartlet where the limbs remained unboned; poor vegetables; characterless bread; and a general lack of seasoning to give point of flavour. Yet the intentions are nearly so very good and certainly local correspondents feel that the performance is improving. The wine list is not long, but it is fairly chosen, even if two halves ordered for a single meal (and there is not a lot of choice) turned out to be different vintages from those listed. House wines are £9.50.

CHEF: Tom Bridgeman PROPRIETORS: Tom and Joanna Bridgeman OPEN: all week, exc Mon L CLOSED: 25 to 27 Dec MEALS: 12.15 to 2.15, 7 to 10.30 PRICES: £21 (£30), Set Sun L £13.50 (£22) CARDS: Access, Amex, Visa SEATS: 30. Private parties: 14 main room. Vegetarian meals. Children welcome. No cigars/pipes in dining-room. Wheelchair access. Music

▲ *Priory Hotel*

Weston Road, Bath BA1 2XT — COOKING 3
BATH (0225) 331922 — COST £32–£48

It is regrettable that Select Country Hotels, the owners, are in receivership, and that the resulting insecurity may affect the day-to-day running of this sound hotel. Meanwhile, it continues to trade with an eye to eventual sale, staff and management remain the same, and Michael Collom's output has not disappointed his customers. The hotel itself is *rus in urbe*, a country house in style and approach in the satellite suburb/village of Weston. New additions giving more bedroom space are well enough in keeping with the early Victorian Bath stone house, and the gardens (no park here) are pleasing. Cooking, too, has that conservatively modern country-house feel. It scores through generally accurate rendition, though never straying too far from the refined sensibilities of its clientele (often tourists on a grand tour) in dishes such as lamb with ratatouille; guinea-fowl with shallots, apples, mushrooms, apple and bacon; and smoked chicken with quails' eggs in a pastry case with béarnaise sauce. There is more adventure in the fish: crab in a pancake with a light chilli sauce or sea bass with Japanese spices. Wine prices are high. There are many fine names here. The wines are resolutely classic, French and expensive, with barely a nod to the New World, Italy and Spain. There are some good half-bottles. House wine is £12.50.

CHEF: Michael Collom PROPRIETORS: Select Country Hotels OPEN: all week MEALS: 12.30 to 2, 7 to 9.30 PRICES: £31 (£40), Set L £20.50 (£32), Set D £28 (£40). Card slips closed CARDS: Access, Amex, Diners, Visa SEATS: 64. Private parties: 40 main room, 22 and 40 private rooms. Car park, 25 places. Vegetarian meals. Children welcome. Smart dress preferred. No smoking in dining-room. Wheelchair access. No music. Fax: (0225) 448276 ACCOMMODATION: 21 rooms, all with bath/shower. B&B £96.70 to £152.40. Deposit: 1 night (overseas clients). Afternoon teas. Garden. Swimming-pool. TV. Phone. Scenic. Doors close at 11.30

▲ *Royal Crescent Hotel* — NEW ENTRY

16 Royal Crescent, Bath BA1 2LS — COOKING 2
BATH (0225) 319090 — COST £28–£60

In the middle of Bath's most famous street, almost unreachable by car (but far more exciting to go on foot), the Royal Crescent Hotel occupies a role somewhere between museum and tourist trap. Recommendation of such places is always difficult: the cost is high, standards vary too often. However, this year reports of meals at the hands of Michael Croft, the long-standing chef, have been more than satisfactory. A plus point is the dining-room; it occupies a perfect dower house. A minus point is the use of drinking glasses that might have come from the local petrol station. The cooking is 'solid modern without excesses', and may include poached egg in oyster mushrooms and red wine sauce, mussel soup in saffron and curry spices (heavy on curry, short on mussels), delicate timbale of chicken livers and foie gras, or pigeon with caramelised turnip and madeira sauce ('well-executed but not intensely gamey and earthy as might be expected'). Desserts are passable and so are petits fours. Prices might cause a stop and a midday visit is probably the best bet; the restaurant looks better in daylight and red mullet, pigeon and partridge are interesting ingredients at the set-lunch prices. If only the cooking were more consistent and the hotel were a more personal enterprise, this place could be distinguished. The long and not cheap wine list, with house wines starting at £17, might explain why the hotel is filled with rich 'American tourists or the sort of English who speak in very loud voices'.

CHEF: Michael Croft PROPRIETORS: Queens Moat Houses plc OPEN: all week MEALS: 12.30 to 2, 7 to 9.30 (10 Sat) PRICES: £34 (£50), Set L £17 (£28) to £21 (£32), Set D £25 (£37). Card slips closed CARDS: Access, Amex, Diners, Visa SEATS: 70. 8 tables outside. Private parties: 70 main room, 45 and 48 private rooms. Car park, 10 places. Vegetarian meals. Children's helpings on request. No children under 7 D. Smart dress preferred. No cigars/pipes in dining-room. Wheelchair access (1 step). Music. Fax: (0225) 339401
ACCOMMODATION: 44 rooms, all with bath/shower. Lift. B&B £100 to £138. Children welcome. Baby facilities. Afternoon teas. Garden. TV. Phone. Scenic (*Which? Hotel Guide*)

Tarts 🍷

8 Pierrepont Place, Bath BA1 1JX — COOKING **2**
BATH (0225) 330280 and 330201 — COST £16–£34

Tablecloths and refurbishment have long rid this basement restaurant of the description 'bistro'. So, too, remarked one reporter, have the prices; this seems an unkind cut, especially in the light of the 'recession special' menu, which offers excellent value and has had the benefit, says John Edwards, 'of making the restaurant full again'. The printed menu is supplemented by a long list of daily specials which combine well the familiar and adventurous. There has been a certain tilt towards the Orient, following recruitment of a chef with Pacific experience, evinced by the appearance of sushi, sashimi and teriyaki – for instance, a lamb teriyaki marinated in ginger, honey, soy and garlic. The small touches of imagination carry through to European foods. An egg Benedict is done with a duck egg, and kid makes a welcome showing in a roast saddle with a tarragon jus and in a salad with artichokes, celeriac, carrots and asparagus. Readers stress the amiability of the service: 'We said we were going on to a concert and the timing was expertly and discreetly managed.' The intelligent, fair-priced wine list displays careful selection, not overbalanced by the enthusiasm for Rioja (a fine range of older Reservas). House wines are from £7.80. CELLARMAN'S CHOICE: Hawkes Bay Chardonnay 1989, Delegat, £15; Brouilly, Ch. des Tours 1990, £16.

CHEF: Michel Lemoine PROPRIETOR: John Edwards OPEN: Mon to Sat CLOSED: 3 days Christmas MEALS: 12 to 2.30, 6.45 to 10.45 (11 Fri and Sat) PRICES: L £15 (£22), D £20 (£28), Set L and D (exc Sat D) £9 (£16) to £11.50 (£19). Service 10% for parties of 6 or more CARDS: Access, Visa SEATS: 50. Private parties: 22 main room, 8 and 12 private rooms. Vegetarian meals. Children welcome. No cigars/pipes in dining-room. Music

Woods **NEW ENTRY**

9–13 Alfred Street, Bath BA1 2QX COOKING 1*
BATH (0225) 314812 COST £16–£32

This large restaurant has two zones. That nearest the front is available for brasserie-style food, served quickly. The other, heavily themed towards horse racing, David Price's obsession, is a bustling restaurant offering a series of set-price menus, a 'happy menu' for the first hour of the evening and a blackboard of daily specials. The style is idiosyncratic, with a whiff of the Pacific rim: chicken with tamari, ginger and chillies; lamb and almond casserole with cardamom and apricots; gambas with bean sprouts and scallops with lemon butter in filo parcels. On the *carte*, desserts – headed by banoffi pie – are aptly termed 'cholesterol corner'. Not every dish sings as loud a song of flavour as might be expected, but one reader wrote, 'I enjoyed the filo parcels which I normally loathe for poor execution; the venison was nicely cooked with a racy sauce; the chocolat St Emilion was superb.' Crudités are on the table for whiling away the time before ordering. Bread is only moderate, as is the coffee. Vegetables show an equal love of flavourings: red cabbage with cumin, courgettes with dill. Service is friendly and enthusiastic. Music is 'loud and horrid'. A wine list with fair spread has house wines at £7.80.

CHEF: Mary Jane Alley PROPRIETORS: David and Claude Price OPEN: Mon to Sat CLOSED: 24 to 29 Dec MEALS: restaurant 12 to 2.15, 6.30 to 10.15; brasserie 11 to 11 (Sat 11 to 3) PRICES: £17 (£24), Set L £10 (£16) to £17 (£24), Set D £10 (£16) to £19.95 (£27) CARDS: Access, Visa SEATS: 70. 8 tables outside. Private parties: 70 main room, 38 private room. Vegetarian meals. Children's helpings. No cigars or pipes in dining-room. Wheelchair access (2 steps; also WC). Music. Fax: (0225) 443146

BATTLE East Sussex map 3

▲ *Powdermills* **NEW ENTRY**

Powdermill Lane, Battle TN33 0SP COOKING 2
BATTLE (042 46) 5511 COST £19–£35

The name refers to gunpowder and to the time when this area close to Battle Abbey was the centre of the gunpowder industry. Powdermills is a Georgian house undergoing a major transformation. Gazebos, urns and statues of Greek gods fill the garden, while the interior has been done out to suggest gentrified rusticity. The marble-floored Orangery restaurant is a prestigious setting for Paul Webbe's modern cooking. He was chef at La Vieille Auberge in Battle and has brought many ideas with him, including a full set menu for vegetarians. Ingredients are top drawer, but results are sometimes too complex and too rich. Even so, the kitchen has produced some fine things: timbale of asparagus set in a purée of yellow peppers decorated with 'the prehistoric shapes of wild mushrooms'; breast of Barbary duck with roasted shallots, smoked bacon and tarragon; dark chocolate mousse with vanilla sauce. Reporters have also praised chunky fish soup with toasted brioche; roast saddle of venison with cassis sauce and caramelised pears; and glazed Bramley tart with a calvados butterscotch sauce. The modestly priced wine list has much from France, but also a few bottles from Sussex vineyards. House French is £7.50. (Visitors should note that there is a restricted menu and a different chef on Mondays.)

CHEF: Paul Webbe PROPRIETORS: Douglas and Julie Cowpland OPEN: all week, exc Sun D MEALS: 12 to 2.30, 6.30 to 9.30 PRICES: £21 (£29), Set L £13.50 (£19), Set D £14.50 (£20) CARDS: Access, Visa SEATS: 60. 3 tables outside. Private parties: 80 main room, 20 private room. Car park, 50 places. Vegetarian meals. Children's helpings (L and high teas only). No children under 12 D. Smart dress preferred. Wheelchair access (also WC). Music. Fax: (042 46) 4540 ACCOMMODATION: 15 rooms, all with bath/shower. B&B £35 to £95. Children welcome. Baby facilities. Pets welcome. Afternoon teas. Garden. Swimming-pool. Fishing. TV. Phone. Scenic. Doors close at midnight. Confirm by 8 (*Which? Hotel Guide*)

BEAMINSTER Dorset map 2

▲ *Bridge House*

Prout House, Beaminster DT8 3AY COOKING 2
BRIDPORT (0308) 862200 COST £18–£35

This thirteenth-century priest's house has been converted to a secular lodging and Peter Prinkster has added conservatory and extra bedrooms round a courtyard. The leitmotifs, however, of bare, warm stone, beams and large fireplaces span the centuries with effortless ease. Staff health problems have caused ups and downs over the last 12 months and there have been days when the serving staff have not coped any better than the kitchen. Wendy Mathews' accession to the stoves has meant a return to a certain stability. Peter Pinkster's intentions were always good taste through simplicity and fine materials. Menus do not, therefore, stun by invention: salmon is pan-fried with butter and lemon and served straight forth; Scotch fillet is done with a herb butter, no more. When everything is just so this is highly satisfactory, but the smallest deficiencies are easily detected. A good, light menu is offered in the conservatory: pancakes, salads and a handful of grills. Dinner is set-price, with a short choice of around five dishes at each course, cheese and coffee included. Not everything is plain, for example, quail with grapes and walnuts, and a stir-fry of chicken, prawns and mushrooms. A fine apple crumble at dessert stage and good coffee and truffles also get mentions. The wine list is intelligently succinct with many fine names from across the globe. Prices are all very fair. House wine is £7.25. CELLARMAN'S CHOICE: Sylvaner 1989, Zind-Humbrecht, £10.25; Rioja Tinto 1987, CVNE, £11.75.

CHEFS: Peter Pinkster and Wendy Mathews PROPRIETOR: Peter Pinkster OPEN: all week CLOSED: 23 to 30 Dec MEALS: 12.30 to 2, 7 to 9 (9.30 Sat) PRICES: conservatory L and D £12 (£18), Set D £22.85 (£29). Card slips closed CARDS: Access, Amex, Diners, Visa SEATS: 42. 3 tables outside. Private parties: 24 main room, 18 private room. Car park, 22 places. Vegetarian meals. Children's helpings with prior notice. No smoking in dining-room. Wheelchair access. No music ACCOMMODATION: 14 rooms, all with bath/shower. Rooms for disabled. B&B £35 to £92. Deposit: £10. Children welcome. Pets welcome. Afternoon teas. Garden. TV. Phone. Scenic. Doors close at 11. Confirm by 6 (*Which? Hotel Guide*)

'Unfortunately, the pieces of chicken were overwhelmed by a glutinous lava of over-thickened sauce with surface tension already forming.' On eating in Hampshire

BECKINGHAM Lincolnshire map 6

Black Swan

Hillside, Beckingham LN5 0RF COOKING 3
NEWARK (0636) 626474 COST £29

Reports continue to praise the competency of the kitchen, the good value and the warm (though one summer night it was thought lugubrious) welcome. A *carte* is now offered instead of the set-price menus, offering some five first courses and eight main. A meal eaten by regulars began with saffron seafood soup and pheasant and tarragon pâté in a pastry envelope, followed by a pigeon tart with wild mushrooms and spring onions on a caraway-seed sauce and baked guinea-fowl on a bed of aubergine purée with a star anise sauce. The verdict: 'We were not disappointed.' Imagination combines with an awareness of what are fashionable combinations: loin of lamb served on a casserole of lamb sweetbreads, haricot beans and lentils on a red wine sauce, chicken breast filled with spinach mousse, served on a spicy satay sauce. The cheeseboard comes in for criticism: 'an unimaginative selection of supermarket cheeses'; 'Cheeses always tend to disappoint. Why do English restaurants try to major on French cheeses when we have such a choice of good English cheeses?' Desserts on the other hand are good, especially the soufflés. This is not surprising as Anton Indans spent some time at Peter Kromberg's Le Soufflé at the London Inter-Continental (see entry). The wine list offers a couple of dozen reasonably priced reds and whites backed up by a few burgundies of some class, still fairly priced. House wine is £6.50.

CHEF: Anton Indans PROPRIETORS: Anton and Alison Indans OPEN: Tue to Sun, exc Sun D MEALS: 12 to 2, 7 to 10 PRICES: £17 (£24) CARDS: Access, Visa SEATS: 30. Private parties: 24 main room, 12 private room. Car park, 9 places. Children's helpings L. No smoking. Wheelchair access (also WC). Music

BERWICK-UPON-TWEED Northumberland map 7

Funnywayt'mekalivin'

41 Bridge Street,
Berwick-upon-Tweed TD15 1ES COOKING 2*
BERWICK-UPON-TWEED (0289) 308827 and 86437 COST £25

'Unique', 'just like home', 'unusual and relaxing': epithets come easily to reporters of Elizabeth Middlemiss's four-nights-a-week operation (other times only by advance booking). In new and more spacious (as well as luxurious) premises, she serves a four-course menu, with choice only for pudding, at a set time. As the place is often full, reservation is necessary. Vegetarians are catered for. To start, there is soup (pear and pea, tomato and mint), a soufflé or perhaps a small tart, then a meat or fish course, maybe chicken with a white wine sauce or pork with prunes, a salad or vegetables, including good dauphinoise potatoes, then a couple of puddings and often Teviotdale cheese. Coffee is included in the price. Elizabeth Middlemiss aims to preserve the joys of the dinner party and have lots of fun and atmosphere; the wonder is that she succeeds and cooks good, natural food as well. The move to new premises as the *Guide* goes to press has brought with it a licence and very slightly increased prices. House wines are from £6.50.

CHEF/PROPRIETOR: Elizabeth Middlemiss OPEN: Wed to Sat, D only (other nights and L by arrangement for parties of 8 or more) MEALS: 8 PRICES: Set D £17.50 (£21). Net prices, card slips closed CARDS: Access, Visa SEATS: 28. Private parties: 28 main room. Vegetarian meals. No children under 8. No smoking during meal. Music. One sitting

BEXHILL East Sussex map 3

Lychgates

5A Church Street, Old Town,
Bexhill TN40 2HE COOKING 2
BEXHILL (0424) 212193 COST £16–£29

Lychgates is a white clapperboard Georgian house hard by the church. The restaurant is devoted to good value, lunch bringing a two-course set menu of limited choice while in the evening three- and five-course menus increase the range and price. The menu is spelled out in franglais, reflecting the kitchen's solidarity with its British roots as in turnip and beetroot soup or a steak, kidney and oyster pie, alongside a fashionable eclecticism. Hence Dover sole is marinated in lime with chilli, olives and tomato and the range of flavours found in sauces runs a cosmopolitan gamut: lime, lemon, honey, mustard, chilli. These multiply in a single dish, but John Tyson often has the necessary dexterity to produce dishes such as pot-roast baby chicken with lemon, lemon balm and mustard, and duck with honey, thyme and cream. Correctly cooked vegetables – about half a dozen – come in English proportions. Much, but not all, opinion is favourable. The eclecticism is sometimes more enthusiastic than accurate. John Tyson is said to have gone to Mallorca 'for inspiration'. 'Why, therefore,' asks a reader, 'does his gazpacho taste like no other, apparently with a cream base?' Service can be slow. The wine list is enthusiastic, with a standard selection complemented by a short list of seven or so wines chosen to match the menu of the week. House wine is £8.45.

CHEF: John Tyson PROPRIETORS: John and Sue Tyson OPEN: Tue to Sat, exc L Tue and Sat MEALS: 12.30 to 2, 7.15 to 10.30 PRICES: Set L £10 (£16), Set D from £17.25 (£24) CARDS: Access, Visa SEATS: 26. Private parties: 18 main room. Vegetarian meals. Children's helpings. No children under 8 D. No cigars/pipes in dining-room. Wheelchair access

BILLESLEY Warwickshire map 2

▲ *Billesley Manor* 🍷

Billesley B49 6NF
STRATFORD-UPON-AVON (0789) 400888 COOKING 2
off A422, 2m W of Stratford-upon-Avon COST £24–£52

Oak panelling inside, stone mullions out, large gardens, a health centre and facilities for conferences are all part of the scene. 'The reproduction of Rembrandt's *Night Watch* over the fireplace did not increase my admiration for the strikingly original taste of owners Queens Moat Houses,' said one reporter.

Mark Naylor has been chef here for six years and more, a steadiness that should be applauded. The customers have benefited from continuity; even on Mark Naylor's day off the brigade is well enough trained to produce a very passable dinner. There is a *carte* and table d'hôte; the latter may be more adventurous, and cheaper. Cooking is accurate and does not go in for needless elaboration: a hot raspberry soufflé was not oversweetened, nor was its coulis spoiled by meddling. Materials seem well chosen: a filo parcel of crab was well-baked and fresh; bread is bought in, but very palatable. Those serving may be wearing suits (as should be the male customers) but are anxious to please and not hoity-toity. This is a chain that has got it right. A catholic selection of a hundred wines, due attention to vintages and the likes of Ch. d'Issan and Ch. Gloria and Burgundians Dujac and Tollot-Beaut encourage confidence. Pricing this year hits harder at the top end – Veuve Clicquot n.v. at £37 – but there is much reliable drinking around £15. An intelligent range of half-bottles is offered. House wine is £9.50. CELLARMAN'S CHOICE: Chardonnay Portico dei Leoni 1986, £22; Ch. Maucamps 1986, £19.50.

CHEF: Mark Naylor PROPRIETORS: Queens Moat Houses plc OPEN: all week MEALS: 12.30 to 2, 7.30 to 9.30 (10 Fri and Sat) PRICES: £32 (£43), Set L £17 (£24), Set D £25 (£33). Card slips closed CARDS: Access, Amex, Diners, Visa SEATS: 75. 6 tables outside. Private parties: 8 main room, 100 private room. Car park, 150 places. Vegetarian meals. Children's helpings. No children under 12. Jacket and tie. No cigars/pipes in dining-room. No music. Fax: (0789) 764145 ACCOMMODATION: 41 rooms, all with bath/shower. B&B £99 to £125. Children welcome. Baby facilities. Afternoon teas. Garden. Swimming-pool. Tennis. TV. Phone. Scenic. Doors close at 1am. Confirm by 6

BIRDLIP Gloucestershire map 2

▲ *Kingshead House* 🍷

Birdlip GL4 8JH COOKING 2
GLOUCESTER (0452) 862299 COST £20–£37

'The Knocks are more interested in providing an excellent meal than sumptuous or chintzy surroundings,' said one visitor who noticed the dining chairs didn't match. This is a quibble in the context of this handsome old house, notably co-operative service from Warren Knock and enthusiastic cooking by his wife. 'Aubergine, cheese and mushroom filo pastry parcels with a red pepper sauce' were outstanding, well-matched by an almond tart for pudding; terrine of lobster and sole was chunky, each flavour discernable; koulibiac in delicate pastry went down well. Desserts, especially fruit gratins, are also welcomed. Organic produce, from a Birdlip farm, is used where possible, and it is noted that even when meat is said to be 'hard work' it comes out well for flavour. Judy Knock's style is consistent at the moment: identifiably English, with French country overtones, it avoids too many daring combinations while keeping taste-buds alert with piquancy and edge to many of the flavourings – though the bread has sometimes lacked salt. This is a pleasantly relaxed operation, where criticism rarely surfaces. Modest prices, all-embracing range and a very decent selection of half-bottles are the hallmarks of the intelligent wine list. Quality is assured from the simplest to the grandest – a decent 1986 Côte de Blaye at the bottom end and the sound and excellent 1982 Marquis de Terme scaling the heights at a reasonable £28. There are no flashy first growths at matching prices here. House wines are from £8.50. CELLARMAN'S CHOICE: Mâcon Chaintré, Dom. des Granges 1989, M. Cognard, £12.50; Barbera d'Asti Superiore 1982, Pavese, £10.75.

CHEF: Judy Knock PROPRIETORS: Judy and Warren Knock OPEN: Tue to Sun, exc Sat L and Sun D CLOSED: 25 and 26 Dec, 1 Jan MEALS: 12.30 to 2, 7.30 to 10 PRICES: Set L £13 (£20) to £14.50 (£21), Set D £21.50 (£28) to £23.50 (£31). Service 10% and card slips closed for parties of 6 or more CARDS: Access, Amex, Diners, Visa SEATS: 32. 2 tables outside. Private parties: 36 main room. Car park, 12 places. Vegetarian meals. Children's helpings. No cigars/pipes in dining-room. Wheelchair access (1 step). Music ACCOMMODATION: 1 room, with bath/shower. B&B £35 to £50. Deposit: £10. Pets by arrangement. Garden. Scenic. Doors close at midnight. Confirm by 6

BIRKENHEAD Merseyside map 5

Beadles

15 Rosemount, Oxton,
Birkenhead L43 58G COOKING 1
051-653 9010 COST £25

Since 1977, Roy Gott's restaurant in a converted shop has been a godsend to the Wirral. One habitué, returning from abroad, commented that it was 'good to see that they were still trying after all these years'. The menu is a short Anglo-French *carte*, with a few unexpected flourishes, some good game and daily fish dishes. Typically, there might be home-made boudin blanc with pear chutney, calf's liver with star anise glaze, and beef fillet with balsamic vinegar and tea sauce. Desserts are in the mould of chocolate marquise and brandy-snap baskets filled with home-made ice-creams. Roy Gott is an enthusiast, reciting dishes in every detail and advising on the eclectic wine list. Most bottles are £10 or under. House French is £6.

CHEF: Bea Gott PROPRIETORS: Roy and Bea Gott OPEN: Tue to Sat, D only CLOSED: Aug MEALS: 7.30 to 9 PRICES: £15 (£21). Service 10% for parties of 6 or more SEATS: 34. Private parties: 30 main room. Vegetarian meals. Children welcome. Wheelchair access. Music

Rondelle

11 Rose Mount, Oxton,
Birkenhead L43 5SG COOKING 3
051-652 8264 COST £34

'Rondelle has not changed since it opened,' says a regular visitor. 'Its good points are still good, its bad points still bad.' Few would dispute Mark Wilkinson's culinary talents, or his ability to watch, learn and absorb ideas from his peers. After trips to kitchens in London, he brings it all back home to the Wirral. Most reporters are mightily impressed with his efforts. The cooking is modern British, centring on a short *carte* with six choices at each stage. Recommendations are many: mussels in herb and curry sauce; goats' cheese wrapped in smoked salmon with miniature salad leaves; saddle of venison with timbale of cabbage; best end of lamb with balsamic sauce; steamed brill with aniseed and lemon sauce; chocolate marquise with orange sauce and prunes. The range of breads, the 'fearsome array of cheeses', and countless petits fours show the aspirations of the kitchen. That is the good news. The bad news is that the place should improve its poor interior, scrappy handwritten menus and service. A local supporter warns: 'I can see that before long Mark will be enticed away to a more impressive establishment. It will be a great pity for our area.' The affordable wine list has three dozen wines with House French at £6.50.

CHEF: Mark Wilkinson PROPRIETORS: Harry Wilkinson and Mark Wilkinson OPEN: Tue to Sat, D only and Sun L (other days L by arrangement) MEALS: 12 to 2, 7 to 9.30 (10.15 Sat) PRICES: £20 (£28). Card slips closed CARDS: Access, Visa SEATS: 30. Private parties: 36 main room. Vegetarian meals. Children's helpings. No children under 6. Smart dress preferred. No pipes in dining-room. Wheelchair access (1 step). Music

BIRMINGHAM West Midlands map 5

Adil

148–150 Stoney Lane,
Sparkbrook, B11 8AJ COOKING 1
021-449 0335 COST £12

Birmingham has many Indian centres, but Sparkhill and Sparkbrook lay claim to being the focus of the balti industry. Adil was probably the first to gain a reputation beyond its neighbourhood, and continues to draw enthusiastic reports. Kashmiri baltis are characterised by the fact that dishes are cooked and served in shallow cast-iron pans like flattened woks. Adil offers a vast choice of around 70 baltis, from chicken with vegetables to mince with bitter melon. Vegetables are particularly good, exploiting the range of exotic produce sold in local Indian greengrocers. Freshly made breads (the proper accompaniment) are outstanding. The décor is functional: 'Although the menus under the glass table-top remind you of a '50s fish and chip shop, that is about as near to European taste you'll find here.'

CHEF: Mr Ashraf PROPRIETOR: Mr Arif OPEN: all week MEALS: noon to midnight PRICES: £7 (£10). Unlicensed, but bring your own: no corkage CARDS: Access, Visa SEATS: 70. Private parties: 50 private room. Vegetarian meals. Children welcome. No music

Chung Ying

16–18 Wrottesley Street, B5 6RT COOKING 2
021-622 5669 and 1793 COST £14–£29

As the Arcadian Shopping and Leisure Complex takes shape and new money pours into Birmingham's Chinese Quarter, the Chung Ying goes from strength to strength. Its reputation as perhaps the best Cantonese restaurant in the neighbourhood remains unchallenged. Around 40 dim-sum show the sharpness and vigour of the kitchen: deep-fried squid with a sweet-and-sour sauce, plump Shanghai dumplings with vinegar dip, stuffed green pepper and grease-free paper-wrapped prawns have all been excellent. Roughly formed beef balls are steamed with succulent Chinese mushrooms. Freshness and vivid flavours are the key. Fish is a high point: reporters have praised king prawns with ginger and spring onion and sweet-and-sour deep-fried fish. Other memorable dishes from the gargantuan 300-strong menu have ranged from beef with ginger and spring onion to more esoteric Cantonese specialities, including stewed belly-pork with yams and stuffed crispy duck with crabmeat sauce. Massive one-plate rice, noodle and soup dishes are perfect for a quick meal. Fast, pleasant service. House wine is £7.20 a litre or drink tea.

CHEF/PROPRIETOR: Siu Chung Wong OPEN: all week MEALS: noon to midnight (11 Sun) PRICES: £12 (£22), Set L and D £8 (£14) to £17 (£24). Service 10% CARDS: Access, Amex, Diners, Visa SEATS: 200. 48 tables outside. Private parties: 100 main room, 100 private room. Car park, 10 places. Vegetarian meals. Children welcome. Smart dress preferred. Music. Air-conditioned

Days of the Raj

51 Dale End, B4 7LS — COOKING 2
021-236 0445 — COST £12–£28

The restaurant is tucked away, almost unnoticed, beneath the back of a Tesco store in a street of multi-storey car parks close to the law courts. Inside, the bar and first-floor dining-room are decorated in a flamboyant version of Indian new wave that verges on overkill. Pink is the dominant colour, furniture is bamboo and rattan, and there are faded sepia photographs of colonial India on the walls. The cooking is a refined version of north Indian and Punjabi, with the emphasis on subtly flavoured specialities from the tandoori oven. There is much eulogising about fresh oriental herbs on the menu, and dishes are noticeably enhanced with coriander. Old-style anglicised curries are absent from a repertoire that takes in karahi gosht, Goan king prawn, lamb badam pasanda and nargesi kofta (balls of minced lamb 'treated with egg, onion, tomatoes and herbs in a process of slow-steaming'). Accompaniments such as vegetables and breads are varied and interesting. Lunch is a buffet. Drink lassi, lager or the house wine at £6.95.

CHEF: Rashpal Sunner PROPRIETOR: Balbir Singh OPEN: all week, exc L Sat and Sun CLOSED: L bank hols MEALS: 12 to 2.30, 7 (6 Fri and Sat) to 11.30 PRICES: £12 (£21), Set L £6.45 (£12) to £7.95 (£14), Set D £11 (£17) to £16 (£23). Minimum £7.50 CARDS: Access, Amex, Diners, Visa SEATS: 120. Private parties: 100 main room, 30 private room. Vegetarian meals. Children's helpings with prior notice. Smart dress preferred. Wheelchair access (also WC). Music. Air-conditioned

Henrys

27 St Pauls Square, B3 1RB — COOKING 1
021-200 1136 — COST £19–£31

Reporters consider that this expansive restaurant in Birmingham's jewellery quarter is smarter and more relaxed than Henry Wong's original venue in Harborne. The 100-dish-strong menu is clearly tailored to Western palates, with recommendations for aromatic crispy duck, sizzling oysters with ginger and spring onion, and fried mixed vegetables in a crispy bird's nest. The kitchen also deals with satays, loin of lamb with chilli and pepper, fried scallops with cashews, and lemon chicken. Vegetarians might look for deep-fried aubergines, or sweet-and-sour water chestnuts. Portions are generous. Drink tea, saké, Chinese wine or house French at £7.50.

CHEF: C.W. Choi PROPRIETORS: Henry Wong and C.W. Choi OPEN: Mon to Sat CLOSED: 1 week Aug MEALS: 12 to 2, 6 to 11 (11.30 Fri and Sat) PRICES: £14 (£26), Set L and D from £12 (£19) CARDS: Access, Amex, Diners, Visa SEATS: 100. Vegetarian meals. Children welcome. Music

Maharaja

23–25 Hurst Street, B5 4AS — COOKING 1
021-622 2641 — COST £13–£24

Since the mid-'70s this tiny little dining-room has maintained its reputation as one of the most consistent Indian restaurants in central Birmingham. In recent years it has been given a fashionable look, with pink colour schemes and cane chairs. The menu is still entrenched in classic north Indian and Punjabi cooking, using freshly mixed and ground spices to give sauces a distinctive intensity. Recent reports have praised chicken bhuna masala, rogan josh and vegetable biriani. Tandoori mixed grill comes with a fiery mint and yoghurt dressing; onion kulcha is an excellent bread. Service is friendly and unhurried. House wine is £6.25.

CHEF: Bhupinder Waraich PROPRIETOR: N.S. Batt OPEN: Mon to Sat MEALS: 12 to 2.30, 6 to 11.30 PRICES: £12 (£18), Set L £8.50 (£13) to £12.50 (£17), Set D £9.75 (£14) to £15.50 (£20). Minimum £7 CARDS: Access, Amex, Diners, Visa SEATS: 65. 18 tables outside. Private parties: 30 main room. Vegetarian meals. Children welcome. Wheelchair access. Music. Air-conditioned

▲ *Sir Edward Elgar Restaurant, Swallow Hotel*

12 Hagley Road, Five Ways, B16 8SJ — COOKING 3
021-452 1144 — COST £22–£44

The Swallow Hotel has made its nest at Five Ways, in a former office block. It comes complete with an Ancient Egyptian leisure club and two restaurants: Lily Langtry's and Sir Edward Elgar's. The list of food in the latter is hidden amid a short biography of the composer and an extract from his *Enigma Variations*. Idris Caldora continues to run the kitchen here, with food that carries its taste through all the flounce of a luxury international dining-room. The set-price and shorter menu of the day, the price depending on how many courses are taken, is reckoned better value than the *carte*. Whichever is chosen, it will come topped and tailed with impressive waves of canapés, appetisers and petits fours. The repertoire is confined to well-tried ingredients: main dishes stray as far as rabbit, but not into offal; the methods are stove-top speedy, not mother's pride peasant cooking. Chicken livers with roasted courgettes and tomato, warm scallops with French bean salad in a saffron dressing, roast lamb with basil-flavoured juices and wild rice, and maize-fed chicken with foie gras and a lemon thyme sauce have been found satisfactory. Desserts, too, deserve mention, even if strawberries in mid-winter are a response to the demands of hotel planners rather than natural cooking. The wine list has a fair number of halves, and a lot of prestige bottles. To counterbalance that, the Italian section is worth a look, though the New World selection is no more than adequate. House wines are from £10.50.

CHEF: Idris Caldora PROPRIETORS: Swallow Hotels OPEN: all week, exc Sat L MEALS: 12.30 to 2.30, 7.30 to 10.30 PRICES: £30 (£37), Set L and D £17 (£22) to £29 (£34). Card slips closed CARDS: Access, Amex, Diners, Visa SEATS: 50. Private parties: 5 private rooms. Car park, 90 places. Vegetarian meals. Children's helpings. Jacket and tie. No-smoking area. Wheelchair access (also WC). Music. Air-conditioned. Fax: 021-456 3442 ACCOMMODATION: 98 rooms, all with bath/shower. Rooms for disabled. Lift. B&B £97.50 to £120. Children welcome. Baby facilities. Pets welcome. Afternoon teas. Swimming-pool. Steam-room. Air-conditioned. TV. Phone. Confirm by 6 (*Which? Hotel Guide*)

Sloans 🍷

27–29 Chad Square, Hawthorne Road,
Edgbaston, B15 3TQ — COOKING 3
021-455 6697 — COST £21–£46

Squeezed between an Augustus Barnett and a ladies' hairdresser, this restaurant – L-shaped, split-level, 'pinkish' – belies its location in a shopping precinct. What's more, Roger Narbett cooks very well, carrying the torch for Anglo-French style in a city that needs more good restaurants. Mr Narbett senior directs the young and willing front-of-house staff. 'His eyes are everywhere; sometimes they have a far-away air, speculating, perhaps, on villas in the sun,' wrote one reader who reckoned such luxuries deservedly earned. A winter meal for two – blizzards outside but a full house within – ran from a ballotine of chicken, foie gras, wild mushrooms and pistachios, and a mussel and thyme soup; through escalope of salmon, covered with a layer of smoked salmon and served with fried scampi and a beurre noisette, and turbot dusted with paprika then grilled, with fresh noodles, asparagus tips and a lemon grass sauce; to a finish of hot lime soufflé. Each main course sounds as though it has one element too many, and a sharper butter sauce would apparently have alleviated the sinking richness of the salmon dish. The other comment was that neither the thyme, as in the mussels, nor the lemon grass, in the turbot, were very much in evidence. Otherwise, the meal was excellently produced with the lime soufflé the perfect end ('all passages in ear, nose and throat zinged and sang'). The *carte* offers eight dishes at each course, and there is a shorter fixed-price menu for midday. Although fish is often singled out for praise, meat – almost inevitably accompanied by mushrooms at some seasons – is there in abundance. A house selection of a dozen French regional wines between £8.75 and £12.75 affords an encouraging start to the predominantly French wine list. Classic areas are well represented with good growers and sound vintages. Prices are neither high nor especially low. There are Zind-Humbrecht Alsaces and excellent Rhônes, and many well-chosen half-bottles. House wines are from £8.75. CELLARMAN'S CHOICE: Jurançon, Dom. Cauhapé 1989, £12.75; Chinon, Clos de Danzay 1985, Druet, £17.75.

CHEF: Roger Narbett PROPRIETORS: John and Roger Narbett OPEN: Mon to Sat, exc Sat L CLOSED: bank hols, 1 week after Christmas MEALS: 12 to 2, 7 to 10 (10.30 Sat) PRICES: £25 (£38), Set L £15 (£21) to £16 (£22). Service 10% for parties of 10 and more CARDS: Access, Amex, Visa SEATS: 62. Private parties: 80 main room. Car park, 80 places. Vegetarian meals. No children under 6. Smart dress preferred. No-smoking area. Wheelchair access (1 step; also WC). Music. Air-conditioned. Fax: 021-454 4335

BIRTLE Greater Manchester map 5

▲ *Normandie* 🍷

Elbut Lane, Birtle BL9 6UT COOKING 3
061-764 3869 and 1170 COST £25–£41

The view, when not in cloud or rain, is stunning and is one of the attractions of this hotel and restaurant that has come a long way since it started life as a drovers' inn. It is run in a calm but decisive manner by Gillian Moussa and her son Max, who leave the kitchen under Pascal Pommier's control. The intention is seriously French. There is much to delight on the short-choice seasonal menu, which is backed up by a more limited fixed-price daily menu. A satisfied spring diner reported a meal of a delicate globe artichoke bavarois with light tempura vegetables and a subtle dressing; a navarin of seafood containing excellent quality red mullet, brill, monkfish and scallop; roast rack of Welsh lamb with a provençal crust, served with a tarragon juice; and iced hazelnut nougat with kumquat coulis. A light touch is evident, in both the balance of the menu and its execution. A summer gazpacho was pronounced finely judged, while a regular customer reports on the continued excellence of the home-baked bread and good selection of cheeses. Occasional grouses have included criticism of a 'too heavy' fish terrine served fridge-cold, and of tough, dry partridge – but too few occur to mar the general impression of satisfaction. Tipping is not encouraged. Many excellent wines with high mark-up and more modest wines at very approachable prices are offered on the wine list. There are many fine bottles below £15 or thereabouts – a straight Bourgogne from Mongeard-Mugneret at £15.80, Lehmann Shiraz at £12.80 and a clutch of petits châteaux – and some good halves. House French is £8.50. CELLARMAN'S CHOICE: Rosemount Semillon/Chardonnay 1989, £11.40; Ch. Chambert-Marbuzet, St Estèphe 1983, £28.25.

CHEF: Pascal Pommier PROPRIETORS: Gillian Moussa and Max Moussa OPEN: Mon to Sat, exc L Mon and Sat CLOSED: 26 Dec to first Sun in Jan and 1 week Easter MEALS: 12 to 2, 7 to 9.30 PRICES: £28 (£34), Set D £18.50 (£25). Card slips closed CARDS: Access, Amex, Diners, Visa SEATS: 60. Private parties: 70 main room. Car park, 60 places. Vegetarian meals. Children's helpings with prior notice. Smart dress preferred. No cigars/pipes in dining-room. Wheelchair access. Music. Fax: 061-764 4866 ACCOMMODATION: 24 rooms, all with bath/shower. Rooms for disabled. Lift. B&B £55 to £79. Children welcome. Baby facilities. TV. Phone. Confirm by noon

---

'The tables were crammed together but fortunately my neighbour resembled Gina Lollobrigida's daughter.' On eating in London

BISHOP'S TACHBROOK Warwickshire map 2

▲ *Mallory Court*

Harbury Lane,
Bishop's Tachbrook CV33 9QB
LEAMINGTON SPA (0926) 330214 COOKING 4
off A452, 2m S of Leamington Spa COST £33–£61

An immaculate Edwardian house whose very designed interior speaks of comfort and cosseting. It is a member of Relais & Châteaux. But appearances can be deceptive; a regular visitor complains 'there is no recognition that we have ever previously crossed the threshold'. A feeling reiterated by another: 'Nobody seemed to be in charge, or to extend personal greeting, which rather clouded the country-house hotel image the place is obviously cultivating.' The kitchen, working along similarly luxurious lines, is more successful in achieving its aims. Allan Holland has been cooking consistently for several years and the change in mark reflects this. Reports have stressed the accuracy and finesse of his cooking. A meal last winter included quenelles of pike with crayfish sauce ('a faultless version of a classic dish'); provençal fish soup; and fillet of sea bass stuffed with sea bass mousseline and served on a bed of fine pasta with red pepper coulis and delicate ratatouille. This last was 'an elegant, simple but technically tricky dish with good strong flavours of the south'. Other readers have reported excellent canapés and petits fours; a first-course mille-feuille of crisp potato and turnip rösti filled with sautéed slivers of foie gras; and crab with avocado, pink grapefruit and ginger followed by monkfish and saffron potatoes as part of a late summer lunch. Thus Allan Holland is able to put on the high-strut with dishes of complexity and depth or, equally, to 'produce the simplest and most polished lunch I have been fortunate to eat'. French and British cheeses are well-kept, and good desserts include a hot caramel soufflé with an armagnac and prune ice-cream. It may be no coincidence that readers seem almost to prefer the deceptive simplicity to the layers of elaboration. The wine list is French in bulk, but some useful price-levellers are brought in from other countries. Prices are firm but not outrageous. The order in which clarets and burgundies are listed seems to follow no course of logic. The choices, however, are sound and often distinguished. House wines are from £8.50.

CHEF: A.J.G. Holland PROPRIETORS: A.J.G. Holland and J.R. Mort OPEN: all week MEALS: 12.30 to 1.45, 7.30 to 9.30 (10 Sat) PRICES: Set L £24.50 (£33), Set D £42.50 (£51). Net prices, card slips closed CARDS: Access, Visa SEATS: 50. Private parties: 50 main room. Car park, 50 places. No children under 12. Jacket and tie. No cigars/pipes in dining-room. Fax: (0926) 451714 ACCOMMODATION: 10 rooms, all with bath/shower. B&B £105 to £195. No children under 9. Afternoon teas. Garden. Swimming-pool. Tennis. TV. Phone. Scenic

Healthy eating options *in the details at the end of an entry signifies that a restaurant marks on its menu, in words and/or using symbols, low-fat dishes or other healthy eating choices.*

BLACKPOOL Lancashire map 5

September Brasserie NEW ENTRY

15–17 Queen Street, Blackpool FY1 1PU COOKING 2*
BLACKPOOL (0253) 23282 COST £18–£32

Has Blackpool at last got a decent restaurant? This brasserie above a ladies' hairdressers is the brainchild of Michael Golowicz. The hair is the preserve of Pat Wood, who also helps in the brasserie in the evenings. Inside are carefully set tables, a semi-open kitchen and views directly on to the open sea. The cooking, which is good, appeals to two markets: lunchtime and evening. The lunch menu on the blackboard is especially cheap yet still includes interesting dishes from good materials. 'Organics' are sought wherever possible. Michael Golowicz's background comes out in his 'specialities': lots of vodkas, home-cured herrings with shallots and olive oil, and loin of cold boar with redcurrant and vodka sauce. The short evening *carte* may contain success and failure at one and the same meal. For instance, a dish of linguine was too innocent of sauce to give any interest, while a rice pudding with prune purée seemed in desperate need of the single cream in a jug to one side to give lubrication. Yet execution of wild boar stuffed with cheese and air-dried ham, with a cranberry sauce, and breast of goose with a calvados sauce and apple purée, was beautifully carried off. Generosity coupled to apposite sauce-making surfaced in a seafood gratin of crab, scallops, squid and sea urchin. Vegetables, too, are ably handled. And if the rice pudding didn't quite work, no such delinquency showed in a treacle tart and its pastry. Service is refreshingly effective and friendly. The wine list is short, but each bottle seems a good one particularly as all of them are organics. This place deserves to succeed.

CHEF: Michael Golowicz PROPRIETORS: Michael Golowicz and Pat Wood OPEN: Tue to Sat CLOSED: 2 weeks summer, 2 weeks winter MEALS: 12 to 3, 6.30 to 9.30 PRICES: L £11 (£18), D £18 (£27). Card slips closed CARDS: Access, Amex, Carte Blanche, Diners, Visa SEATS: 34. Private parties: 30 main room. Vegetarian meals. Children's helpings. Music

BLACKWATER Cornwall map 1

Long's

Blackwater TR4 8HH COOKING 2*
TRURO (0872) 561111 COST £16–£35

The conversion from tin-mining company headquarters to smart restaurant is striking, with a turquoise and peach colour scheme mirrored by Ann Long's picture-book modern style of cooking. Her daily-changing *carte* offers some five choices and each dish can show many flavours at work: best end of lamb spread with spinach and basil pesto, cooked in puff pastry and served on a red wine sauce, turbot fillets with a grilled herb crust served on cardamom sauce and an ink sauce, duck breast wrapped in bacon on a madeira sauce and a plum purée. When on form the kitchen gives great satisfaction: 'We thoroughly enjoyed very imaginative cooking' and 'The general enthusiasm for food and drink was infectious as we tasted and guessed the components of each course' were two comments. Equally, dishes can be overworked and promised flavours not apparent: a crab and courgette terrine with a basil-flavoured sauce, seemingly innocent of basil, and a ballotine of goose and slices of pork fillet 'flavourless and slightly tough'. The dedication to wrapping everything up can also fail on technique: 'meat should be browned to seal it before being wrapped in pastry – it wasn't. Filo pastry was soggy.' There is encouragement to try more than one dessert, none designed for the weight-conscious: blackcurrant crumble, crème brûlée with prunes, oatmeal meringue and chocolate mousse sum it up. Sunday lunch remains a set-price bargain. The short fair-priced wine list is idiosyncratic; three Israeli wines and a short flight of decent clarets, a Gevrey-Chambertin of Rousseau and the excellent Colegiata of Toro jostle with wines of less precise provenance. House wine is £7.20.

CHEF: Ann Long PROPRIETORS: Ian and Ann Long OPEN: Wed to Sat, D only, and Sun L CLOSED: 4 weeks during winter MEALS: 12.30 to 1.45, 7.30 to 10 PRICES: £19 (£29), Set Sun L £11.25 (£16). Card slips closed CARDS: Access, Amex, Visa SEATS: 30. Private parties: 10 main room, 10 and 12 private rooms. Car park, 20 places. Children's helpings. No children under 12. Smart dress preferred. Wheelchair access (also WC). No music

Pennypots

Blackwater TR4 8EY — COOKING 2*
REDRUTH (0209) 820347 — COST £32

A comment such as 'the most improved restaurant in the area' suggests that Kevin Viner is continuing to cook with flair and professional acumen without allowing his ideas to get out of control. Ingredients, especially fish, are top-quality and the cooking can be mightily impressive. A piece of sea bass comes with mini-courgettes (and flowers) stuffed with sea trout mousse on an orange and cream sauce; mussels are steamed in their own juices with garlic, tomato and basil; plump scallops are served in a salad with fresh coriander and butter sauce plus a 'ribbon' of deep-fried vegetables. Reporters regularly extol the intensely flavoured crab bisque. Elsewhere, freshly picked morels have appeared as an accompaniment to sautéed fillet steak with madeira sauce. Sweets are minor miracles of artifice, adorned with spun-sugar cages, 'necklaces of blackcurrants' and herb flowers. Details such as the home-baked bread, pre-prandial nibbles and petits fours are worthy of a serious restaurant. The very cottagey dining-room is an apt backdrop for Jane Viner's unfussed, informal service. Forty reasonably priced wines include a decent showing of half-bottles. House French is £6.50.

CHEF: Kevin Viner PROPRIETORS: Kevin and Jane Viner OPEN: Tue to Sat, D only (Sun D July to Sept) MEALS: 7 to 10 PRICES: £20 (£27). Card slips closed CARDS: Access, Amex, Diners, Visa SEATS: 30. Private parties: 18 main room, 12 private room. Car park, 10 places. Vegetarian meals. Children's helpings on request. No smoking before 10pm. Wheelchair access (1 step). Music

The Guide *relies on feedback from its readers. Especially welcome are reports on new restaurants appearing in the book for the first time.*

BLANDFORD FORUM Dorset map 2

▲ *La Belle Alliance*

White Cliff Mill Street,
Blandford Forum DT11 7BP COOKING 1
BLANDFORD FORUM (0258) 452842 COST £16–£32

A tough year has none the less seen the Davisons in a flurry of decoration and expansion (an extra bedroom for guests) in this late-Victorian house on the Shaftesbury road; Blandford's baroque is nearer the centre. Flowers give a festive outline to the house which, despite its name, is profoundly English in character, as are the cooking and the enthusiastic attentions of Lauren Davison and her young staff. Smoked salmon wrapped round crab and prawns with a cucumber mayonnaise, a 'symphony' of salmon and scallops with ginger and spring onions, quail with madeira sauce and red cabbage, pineapple with hot caramel and a coconut sorbet, and a hot crumble are some dishes from a spring menu that would defy a Frenchman but serve as markers of current country restaurant fare in England. The place excites much enthusiasm, from people who feel that Philip Davison's cooking has improved over the years and from others who like the elements of special event fostered by the style and ambience, though these are less sophisticated than in grander, broader-acred places. The wine list is short, but soundly based: Dezat from Sancerre, Bossard's Muscadet, a white Monthélie from Garaudet, reliable Brown Bros or Firestone from the New World. House wine is £8.95.

CHEF: Philip Davison PROPRIETORS: Lauren and Philip Davison OPEN: Tue to Sat, D only, and Sun L; bank hol Sun and Mon D MEALS: 7 to 9.30 (10 Sat) PRICES: Set L £11.50 (£16), Set D £15.50 (£20) to £22.50 (£27). Net prices, card slips closed CARDS: Access, Amex, Visa SEATS: 32. Private parties: 36 main room. Car park, 14 places. Children by arrangement. No smoking in dining-room. Wheelchair access. Music. Fax: (0258) 480053 ACCOMMODATION: 6 rooms, all with bath/shower. B&B £48 to £62. Children by arrangement. Baby facilities. Pets welcome. TV. Phone. Scenic. Doors close at midnight. Confirm by 6

BOLLINGTON Cheshire map 5

Mauro's

88 Palmerston Street,
Bollington SK10 5PW COOKING 2
BOLLINGTON (0625) 573898 COST £19–£26

Good fresh pasta dishes are a popular choice in this family-run restaurant. Signora Mauro has been seen supervising the kitchen (it is on view from the dining-room) in the absence of her husband, yet she is still able to emerge, calm and unruffled, to deliver food to the table. The menu has plenty of Anglo-Italian staples on it but the daily specials, often either pasta or fish, may be the preference of many. One reporter who reluctantly gave the excellent trolley of antipasti a miss was well pleased instead with a simple gratin of mushrooms with a fresh tomato and basil sauce, followed by home-made cheese and ham ravioli; another found fresh noodles with mushrooms followed by breast of chicken stuffed with pâté and garlic butter exactly cooked and sufficiently pungent. Vegetables – for example deep-fried fennel, spinach with cream, and battered courgettes – are generously supplied. Desserts, trolley-borne, pass through the obvious cheesecakes and soft fruit to a popular coffee-soaked chocolate sponge, tiramisù and caramel oranges. Coffee is not expensive. The wine list is exclusively Italian save for a couple of champagnes. Mastroberardino, Antinori, Lungarotti and Fedrigotti are some of the good makers. House Italian is £7.10 and a strong finish may be assured by the good range of grappas. Sunday lunch (note there are special children's rates) is a new departure.

CHEF/PROPRIETOR: V. Mauro OPEN: Tue to Sun, exc Sat L and Sun D MEALS: 12 to 2, 7 to 10 PRICES: £15 (£22), Set Sun L £13.85 (£19) CARDS: Access, Amex, Visa SEATS: 50. Vegetarian meals. Children's helpings. Wheelchair access (also WC). Music

BOTALLACK Cornwall map 1

Count House

NEW ENTRY

Botallack TR19 7QQ
PENZANCE (0736) 788588
off B3306, 1m N of St Just,
300 yds down cliff road

COOKING 1*
COST £32

'It is to my mind the best kind of unpretentious family restaurant, set in a most beautiful, if barren, part of the country. The interior is uniquely magical, reminiscent of eating in tucked-away places in the Mediterranean,' writes one supporter of the Ashtons' conversion overlooking the Atlantic. Part of the magic comes from the new conservatory, a mass of flowering plants – bougainvillaea and Albertine roses in May – as a setting for Helen Ashton's food. She worked for a while with Jeremy Ashpool at the King's Head, Cuckfield (see entry), and there are echoes of his style in her vivid flavourings and seasonal ingredients. Dinner is a short *carte* with half a dozen choices at each stage, and most dishes are pointed up with forthright accompaniments. The following have been recommended: salad of smoked quail with gooseberry vinaigrette; red mullet with hot lime and ginger dressing; lamb fillet marinated in yoghurt, garlic and mint with lemon butter sauce; braised poussin with whisky sauce. Timbale of smoked trout wrapped in smoked salmon has been 'ambrosial'. Vegetables are spot-on, but highly priced. To finish, home-made honey ice-cream and strawberry oatmeal meringue are more interesting than toffee pudding. Sometimes the ideas don't quite work, but the overall effect is winning. The wine list is short and sharp, but only the house wine (£7.50) is in single figures.

CHEF: Helen Ashton PROPRIETORS: Helen and Graham Ashton OPEN: Tue to Sun, exc Sun D, Apr to Oct; Thurs to Sat and Sun L, Nov to Mar MEALS: 12.30 to 2, 7 to 9.45 PRICES: £17 (£27), light L from £2.20. Service 10%. Card slips closed CARDS: Access, Amex, Visa SEATS: 64. Private parties: 50 main room. Car park, 30 places. Children's helpings (Sun L only). No children under 5 D. Wheelchair access. Music

If a restaurant is new to the Guide *this year (did not appear as a main entry in the last edition)* NEW ENTRY *appears opposite its name.*

BOTLEY Hampshire map 2

Cobbett's

15 The Square, Botley SO3 2EA COOKING 1
BOTLEY (0489) 782068 COST £19–£41

Charles and Lucie Skipwith have been in residence at their beamed Tudor cottage since 1974 and continue to please visitors with their brand of French cooking. They describe the décor in their dining-room as 'tastefully mid-Channel'; reporters see it as a cross between cottagey and luxurious. The kitchen delivers a mix of modern and provincial dishes, ranging from marinated raw salmon with tomato and basil sorbet, and braised guinea-fowl with raspberry vinegar sauce to rillettes of pork, fillet of beef with tarragon sauce and pigeon breasts with a burgundy sauce. Fish is fresh from the south coast boats. Desserts such as charlotte of red fruits are much appreciated. Bread rolls, nibbles and petits fours are home-made. The adjoining 'bistrot' dining-room is open for one-course lunches: 'This is to combat the recession,' say the Skipwiths, 'although it has met with little appreciation.' Ironically the main dining-room is usually full, even though prices are by no means cheap. The short wine list seldom moves far from the major French growing regions. House wine is £9.20.

CHEFS: Lucie Skipwith and Peter Hayes PROPRIETORS: Charles and Lucie Skipwith OPEN: Mon to Sat, exc L Mon and Sat MEALS: 12 to 2, 7 to 10 PRICES: £22 (£34), Set L £10.50 (£19) to £12.50 (£21), Set D £20 (£27), Snacks from £5.50 CARDS: Access, Amex, Visa SEATS: 40. Private parties: 50 main room, 8 and 14 private rooms. Car park, 15 places. Vegetarian meals. Children's helpings. Smart dress preferred. No cigars/pipes in dining-room. Wheelchair access. Music

BOUGHTON LEES Kent map 3

▲ *Eastwell Manor*

Eastwell Park, Boughton Lees TN25 4HR COOKING 3
ASHFORD (0233) 635751 COST £26–£56

The park (half a county it looks like) is farmed now, but none the less makes an impressive setting for this giant baronial pile, built this century. As a hotel, it is still quaintly formal: jacket and tie, please. Mark Clayton's background, in kitchen terms, is baronial itself and his cooking shows its breeding in skills and in purchasing, though desserts are said by some to need a drop of polish (not, however, by the happy eaters of hot ice-cream, deep-fried in batter). The canapés, perhaps marinated salmon, a lamb pâté with green peppercorns or fish tartlet with chives, raise expectations for either the *carte* or the set-price menu, which has a slightly less exciting daily choice. Recommendations have included marinated fish with three sauces: orange with monkfish, tarragon with smoked haddock, tomato with salmon; a pigeon salad, with the breast roast and the leg braised, on a decent set of leaves; duck breast on leeks and bacon with marbled blackcurrant sauce; beef with mushroom tartlets and roast garlic, or with a shallot confit; and crisply grilled red mullet with pesto-flavoured potato purée and a langoustine sauce. Service is improving and the hope must be that Queens Moat Houses does not abandon its policy of allowing Mark Clayton his liberty. The recession is a testing time. Wines here score high on quality but low, for the customer, on economy. Prices starting at £14 rise very steeply and thwart adventure. House wine is £14.

CHEF: Mark Clayton PROPRIETORS: Queens Moat Houses plc OPEN: all week MEALS: 12.30 to 2, 7.30 to 9.30 (10 Sat) PRICES: £34 (£47), Set L £16.50 (£26), Set D £24.50 (£35) CARDS: Access, Amex, Diners, Visa SEATS: 70. Private parties: 50 main room, 40 private room. Car park, 100 places. Vegetarian meals. Children's helpings. No children under 7. Jacket and tie. No cigars/pipes in dining-room. Wheelchair access (2 steps; also WC). Fax: (0233) 635530 ACCOMMODATION: 23 rooms, all with bath/shower. Rooms for disabled. Lift. B&B £90 to £150. Children welcome. Baby facilities. Pets welcome (small dogs only). Afternoon teas. Garden. Tennis. Fishing. Snooker. TV. Phone. Scenic. Confirm by 6 (*Which? Hotel Guide*)

BOURNEMOUTH Dorset map 2

Sophisticats

43 Charminster Road,
Bournemouth BH8 8UE COOKING 2
BOURNEMOUTH (0202) 291019 COST £31

John Knight's and Bernard Calligan's restaurant has proved a life-saver for many a south coast holidaymaker, and is consistently well reported. The setting is a converted shop, the décor dotted with cat ornaments and motifs. Accessible, slightly old-fashioned dishes with cosmopolitan overtones make up the long menu. Freshness, high-quality ingredients and neat presentation are hallmarks of the cooking. Smoked chicken with avocado and grilled cheese, kidneys and bacon in red wine, veal with tarragon, and crisp roast duck with cherries have all been recommended. Javanese steak is another favourite, and the restaurant has a decent line in fresh fish – monkfish thermidor has been good. Vegetables are abundant. Stars among the sweets are the hot soufflés (the lime and chocolate version was 'quite the best dessert we have ever had', according to one reporter), and the igloo pudding (home-made brandy and meringue ice-cream adorned with huge blueberries). Service is friendly and welcoming. Best bets on the modest list of 50 wines are the 'special interest' bottles at the end. House French is £6.95.

CHEF: Bernard Calligan PROPRIETORS: John Knight and Bernard Calligan OPEN: Tue to Sat, D only CLOSED: 2 weeks Feb, 1 week July, 2 weeks Nov MEALS: 7 to 9.30 PRICES: £17 (£26) SEATS: 32. Private parties: 12 main room. Vegetarian meals. Children welcome. Wheelchair access (also WC). Music

'The highlight of the evening was upon us. To accompany the main dishes, a selection of nine root vegetables was given to us and we had to guess what they were. The winner would receive a bottle of wine (of the management's choice). The excitement was terrific as we waded through boring earthy vegetables overcooked to the point of wateriness and mush. Who could tell and who cared? However, I can report that I got six right out of the nine (with some contention over whether swede and swede turnip were different).'
On eating in the Highlands

BOWNESS-ON-WINDERMERE Cumbria map 7

Porthole Eating House

3 Ash Street,
Bowness-on-Windermere LA23 3EB — COOKING 2
WINDERMERE (053 94) 4293 — COST £40

'In spite of the cramped tables, it is one of the most "fun" restaurants I've been in. Enthusiastic and amused attention from everyone.' Nineteen years in and still going, Gianni and Judy Berton's idiosyncratic Anglo-Italian restaurant draws the crowds. Michael Metcalfe remains loyal to the stoves, cooking dishes from a basic printed menu supplemented by weekly specialities. Ignore the first. The second may encompass Italian recipes: bresaola, even a decent spag. bol., or sometimes an item from Aunt Ancilla's repertoire; but more likely it will be a modern restaurant confection: vegetarian tortelloni, seafood maize pancake with tarragon, an interpretation of veal kidney agrodolce. Ice-creams, trifle and sticky toffee pudding complete the picture. What can be a good board of British cheese may be eaten with the single-rise brown bread. Variations in reports come not so much from poor cooking as from the feeling that the choices on offer on a single evening are not as exciting as they might be. Unusually, a flight of 'older and finer' clarets (price on application), together with champagnes, is tucked away at the conclusion of the wine list. Headed by ranges of Italian and Spanish at affordable prices, this offers a refreshing approach that puts these and many fine Rhônes and Alsaces before the classics. California and Australia get a good showing. House wine is £9 a litre.

CHEF: Michael Metcalfe PROPRIETORS: Judy and Gianni Berton OPEN: all week, D only, exc Tue (L parties by arrangement) CLOSED: mid-Dec to mid-Feb MEALS: 6.30 to 11 PRICES: £24 (£33). Card slips closed CARDS: Access, Amex, Diners, Visa SEATS: 40. 6 tables outside. Private parties: 24 main room, 24 private room. Vegetarian meals. Children's helpings. Music

BOX Wiltshire map 2

▲ *Clos du Roy at Box House*

Box SN14 9NR — COOKING 3
BATH (0225) 744447 — COST £21–£54

This austerely handsome rectory stands on the verge of the old London road through Box, with Brunel's London railway tunnel not far distant. Accounts of meals taken here have fluctuated wildly in the past year, the reason being, perhaps, Philippe Roy's involvement in his 'hotel project' at the expense of his cooking. Whatever the reason may be, a recent inspection showed that he can cook with style and panache and that, though ever willing to mobilise the full palette of techniques, he is simplifying and deepening some of his attributes of style. Thus, a terrine of pigeon with pistachio was well set off by a strong raspberry vinaigrette and its own elements: panada, pistachio, breast and mousse of mushrooms gave variety of taste and texture. A feuilleté of fish with excellent puff pastry was conservatively sauced with a herb decoction; it would have been better on a hot plate. A cassolette of turbot and salmon came with an oyster and saffron sauce, again showing judgement; as did a ballotine of mallard on a mango sauce so well reduced and balanced that it was impossible to sort out its constituents. Vegetables continue to show a tendency to aimless elaboration. But austerity was almost the note of a black chocolate mousse with passion-fruit coulis. It would be good if this place could settle down. Calm reigns over the wine list, prices remaining stuck as high or higher than in London, although names are unmistakably of good pedigree. Fine Loire moelleux comes from close to Philippe Roy's home territory; a collection of grand clarets, excluding 1970 but including over-priced 1984, might indicate less sureness of hand. House wines are from £13.

CHEF: Philippe Roy PROPRIETORS: Philippe and Emma Roy OPEN: Tue to Sun MEALS: 12 to 2.30, 7 to 10 PRICES: Set L £12.50 (£21) to £15.50 (£24), Set D £22.50 (£31) to £36.50 (£45). Net prices, card slips closed CARDS: Access, Amex, Diners, Visa SEATS: 55. Private parties: 28 main room, 15 and 30 private rooms. Car park, 50 places. Vegetarian meals. Children's helpings. No-smoking area. Wheelchair access (1 step; also WC). No music. Fax: (0225) 743971 ACCOMMODATION: 9 rooms, all with bath/shower. B&B £70 to £95. Children welcome. Baby facilities. Pets welcome. Afternoon teas. Garden. Swimming-pool. Fishing. TV. Phone. Scenic. Doors close at 12.30. Confirm by noon (*Which? Hotel Guide*)

BRADFIELD COMBUST Suffolk map 3

▲ *Bradfield House*

Sudbury Road,
Bradfield Combust IP30 0LR COOKING 2
SICKLESMERE (0284) 386301 COST £16–£28

The Ghijbens' restaurant-with-rooms is a pink-painted, half-timbered house with a delightful, expansive garden at the back. Reports suggest the kitchen rarely disappoints or over-reaches itself, and correlate prices with consistent quality. Much of the menu has a domestic English feel: country broth, tenderloin of pork with apricot and hazelnut stuffing, rack of lamb with an artichoke tartlet filled with redcurrant jelly. Elsewhere, there have been recommendations for fish soup with croûtons, poached salmon with courgette and spinach sauce, and breast of guinea-fowl with apples and calvados. Vegetables continue the English theme, while sweets look to France for inspiration, as in chocolate marquise and meringues with fresh fruit and raspberry coulis. 'The warm service and pleasant country-house atmosphere add to the good feeling of the place,' writes one contented visitor. The carefully chosen wine list has some quality wines at affordable prices, as well as a decent showing of half-bottles. House French is £6.85.

CHEFS/PROPRIETORS: Roy and Sally Ghijben OPEN: Wed to Sat, D only, and Sun L MEALS: 12 to 1.45, 7 to 9.45 PRICES: £18 (£23), Set L £11.75 (£16). Net prices, card slips closed CARDS: Access, Visa SEATS: 36. 2 tables outside. Private parties: 24 main room, 16 private room. Car park, 12 places. Children's helpings (Sun L). No children under 5. No pipes in dining-room. Wheelchair access (1 step; also WC). Music ACCOMMODATION: 4 rooms, all with bath/shower. B&B £40 to £70. Deposit: 10%. Children welcome. Baby facilities. Garden. TV. Phone. Scenic. Doors close at midnight. Confirm by 6

▲ *This symbol means that accommodation is available.*

BRADFORD **West Yorkshire** map 5

Bharat

502 Great Horton Road,
Bradford BD7 4EG
BRADFORD (0274) 521200

COOKING 1
COST £10–£25

Great Horton Road is a long hill climbing out of the town in a predominantly Muslim area. The restaurant is in a two-storey building that receives a mixed reaction from readers: 'A bit like a warehouse,' says one; 'More comfortable than most Indian restaurants in Bradford,' comments another. The menu doesn't stray far from the familiar output of tandooris and curries, although petisse and pathra are unexpected starters. Otherwise, there is a well-tried assortment ranging from kurmas, dhansaks and birianis to meat kofta, chicken jeera and lamb tikka. Readers have liked the whole tandoori trout, and king prawn puri served on a first-rate nan. Other dishes have been little more than average. Drink Kingfisher beer or house wine at £5.75 a litre.

CHEFS: Mahendra H. Parmar and Mohan Mistry PROPRIETORS: Mohan and Jantilal Mistry OPEN: Tue to Sun, exc Sun L MEALS: 12 to 2, 6 to 12 PRICES: £10 (£21), Set L £5.95 (£10), Set D for 2 £22.50 (£31). Card slips closed CARDS: Access, Amex, Diners, Visa SEATS: 48. Private parties: 48 main room. Car park, 8 places. Vegetarian meals. Children's helpings. No-smoking area. Wheelchair access. Music. Air-conditioned

▲ *Restaurant 19, Belvedere Hotel* 🍷

North Park Road, Bradford BD9 4NT
BRADFORD (0274) 492559

COOKING 4
COST £38–£48

The wedding-cake character of the dining-rooms certainly makes a better frame than the darkening lines of late-Victorian Bradford for celebratory eating. Staying is possible too and overnight visitors confirm the quality of the handful of rooms, worth visiting if only to make stately progress down the staircase. This restaurant is exceptional for the city. The partners show absolute dedication, in the face sometimes of lukewarm appreciation, and continue to develop an ambience in which they manage to welcome people by name, even if they only visit twice a year, and to motivate a young team of workers. A four-course menu (soup at second) includes complex cooking: ravioli of crab and lobster on a bed of spinach followed by a tart of foie gras with onion was a combination that engraved itself on the memory of a summer transient. A winter menu produced appetisers of turmeric-flavoured kebabs, smoked salmon in filo and strong cheesy quiche. The first course was saddle of hare with beetroot and wild mushrooms, then came leek and haddock soup before red mullet, salmon, scallops, lobster and monkfish with tagliatelle and too little sauce; the fish may have been in very fine condition but it needed more than a lubricating squeeze of lemon. Rhubarb and ginger pie with rhubarb ice-cream was the dessert, though ginger won over the rhubarb. Food tends to be arranged vertically on the plate and some reporters have questioned the lack of vegetables in identifiable quantities (it depends on the dish). The most enthusiastic diners enjoy Stephen Smith's mobilisation of flavours; the lukewarm suggest that some dishes show signs of unreconstructed nouvelle cuisine. No one questions the gentle politeness of Robert Barbour's service. The intelligent wine list commences with a 'house selection' of a dozen wines, described as 'typical of their region...and very good value for money'. Good petits châteaux and soundly chosen bottles from the Rhône and Alsace are complemented by modest showings from the USA, New Zealand and Australia, which indicate an unstuffy approach. There is much decent drinking around or below £15.

CHEF: Stephen Smith PROPRIETORS: Stephen Smith and Robert Barbour OPEN: Tue to Sat, D only MEALS: 7 to 9.30 (10 Sat) PRICES: Set D £28 (£38) to £30 (£40) CARDS: Access, Amex, Visa SEATS: 40. Private parties: 10 main room. Car park, 16 places. Children welcome. No pipes/cigars in dining-room. Music ACCOMMODATION: 4 rooms, all with bath/shower. B&B £60 to £70. No children under 8. TV. Phone. Doors close at midnight. Confirm by 4.30 (*Which? Hotel Guide*)

BRAITHWAITE Cumbria map 7

▲ *Ivy House*

Braithwaite CA12 5SY COOKING 1
BRAITHWAITE (059 682) 338 COST £26

The hotel is as dark green as its name suggests, and the colour carries through to the first-floor dining-room. Dining seems to happen early; 7pm is sometimes urged as an ideal time – perhaps walkers get hungry – but in fact the evenings are more relaxed than the indicated hours seem to imply. In like manner, the cooking is more assured than are the menus, which with dishes such as peach with herbs and cream cheese coated with a curry mayonnaise, or duck breast with cherries and madeira sauce, may not strike immediately as being at the cutting edge of modernity. A menu that featured dill in three out of six main dishes was also a mite unbalanced. But mackerel with gooseberry sauce, veal with a rum sauce and an ending of sticky toffee pudding was a meal that worked extremely well, was freshly cooked and tasted as if thought had gone into the making. The service and enthusiastic hospitality of the Shills also won praise. The wine list is adequate. House wines are from £5.95.

CHEF: Wendy Shill PROPRIETORS: Nick and Wendy Shill OPEN: all week, D only MEALS: 6.30 to 7.30 PRICES: Set D £16.95 (£22). Card slips closed CARDS: Access, Amex, Diners, Visa SEATS: 36. Private parties: 10 main room. Car park, 19 places. Vegetarian meals. Children's helpings. No smoking in dining-room. Music. Fax: (076 87) 78338 ACCOMMODATION: 12 rooms, all with bath/shower. D,B&B £43 to £49. Deposit: £20. Pets by arrangement. TV. Phone. Scenic. Doors close at 11.30. Confirm by 4.30 (*Which? Hotel Guide*)

All entries in the Guide *are rewritten every year, not least because restaurant standards fluctuate. Don't trust an out-of-date* Guide.

See the back of the Guide *for an index of restaurants listed.*

BRAMLEY Surrey map 3

Le Berger

4A The High Street, Bramley GU5 0HB
BRAMLEY (0483) 894037

COOKING 2
COST £25–£59

Another restaurant suffering 'Surrey sickness', an ailment that causes high prices and an inability to deliver consistent performance. The outside may be unassuming but everything sparkles within. Peter Hirth offers a complicated menu but can Surrey justify charges of £21 for a dish of venison, when the other two courses and coffee may cost another £20? You have to be very good to earn this. And is there any sense in running a *carte* like this in parallel with a table d'hôte which is not expensive at all? Many have come away thinking the cheaper set-price menu has not had enough effort and commitment. Yet repeated inspection shows that good food can be produced: duck liver parfait, Stilton soufflé, escalope of salmon with a leek sauce, and a mixture of fish and shellfish, each cooked to a turn, with a simple sauce for once actually enlivened by dice of tomato flesh. Lime tart managed a full flavour in filling and sauce, and a chocolate dariole spiked with orange was heavy from richness, not improper materials. The French wine list is short and has a ludicrous price spread for its length: this is another sign of Surrey sickness. House wines start at £9.75.

CHEF/PROPRIETOR: Peter Hirth OPEN: Tue to Sat CLOSED: 2 weeks Jan, bank hols MEALS: 12.30 to 2, 7 to 9.30 PRICES: £35 (£49), Set L and D £13.50 (£25) to £16.50 (£28). Card slips closed CARDS: Access, Amex, Diners, Visa SEATS: 24. 2 tables outside. Private parties: 15 main room. Children welcome. Jacket and tie. No-smoking area

BRAMPTON Cumbria map 7

▲ *Farlam Hall*

Brampton CA8 2NG
HALLBANKGATE (069 77) 46234
on A689, 2m from Brampton (not at Farlam village)

COOKING 3
COST £33–£41

The favourite sport of children at this small Relais & Châteaux is to rush out with breakfast toast and feed the ducks in the pond at the bottom of the lawn, which rises to skirt the walls of the handsome eighteenth-century house. Perhaps because the Quinions remain together as a family act, the hotel does not share that occasional snootiness which informs other members of this prestigious group. None the less, a sense of theatre is fully indulged, from the simultaneous sitting for dinner to the quasi-Victorian uniforms of the staff. Luxuries are not deployed; this is not a foie gras and caviare shop. The set-price menu offers a short choice of sound materials with sauces: quail, venison and pork masquerading as veal in a piccata milanese. Fillet of lemon sole comes with coconut and banana and a prawn brandy sauce. There is a profusion of vegetables, and there are English puddings and English cheeses: good stuff. The meal can be a bit of a procession, but that's what comes of simultaneous service. The wine list is fair-priced and adequate but not exciting. House wine is £8.50.

CHEF: Barry Quinion PROPRIETORS: the Quinion and Stevenson families OPEN: all week, D only CLOSED: Feb MEALS: 8 PRICES: Set D £25.50 (£33) to £27 (£34). Card slips closed CARDS: Access, Visa SEATS: 40. Private parties: 30 main room. Car park, 30 places. No children under 5. Smart dress preferred. Wheelchair access. No music. One sitting. Fax: (069 77) 46683 ACCOMMODATION: 13 rooms, all with bath/shower. D,B&B £90 to £190. No children under 5. Pets by arrangement. Afternoon teas. Garden. TV. Phone. Scenic. Doors close at midnight. Confirm by 2 (*Which? Hotel Guide*)

BRAY Berkshire map 2

Waterside Inn 🍷

Ferry Road, Bray SL6 2AT COOKING 4*
MAIDENHEAD (0628) 20691 COST £32–£84

Waterside is *grande luxe,* from the valet parking to the riverside terrace beneath drooping willow, to coffee and petits fours in a summer-house on the bank. Now there is an electric launch too; it can be hired for a picnic outing or merely a trip for an aperitif. Not all the restaurant is pitched towards the river; there is a large and comfortable lounge on the entrance side and the rear of the dining-room compensates for its lack of view with 'French glitz and artificial foliage'. One reporter's view is that 'it is no longer in the vanguard of innovation, but its absolute mastery of classic techniques, razor-sharp service and all-round excellence place it high in the pantheon of British restaurants.' This year's experiences would tend to bear this out. The razor-sharp service can be blunted if too many commis are detailed to your table, and it has been noted that the credit card slip is left open even though the menu and bill state service included (perhaps that is how it is kept well honed?). The food offered is certainly classic: '*quenelle de brochet, ravioles de homard tièdes truffés sauce vierge, médaillons de boeuf et poêlée de foie gras sauce périgourdine*' sound like entries from *Larousse Gastronomique*. But as is found in most places of this stature, the food offers plenty of individual touches, from the double set of complimentary items – for example, the hot appetiser once was homely haddock with sliced new potatoes – to the waiter suggesting (correctly) the order in which to eat the cheeses from the Philippe Olivier selection. Some dishes that have pleased, including those from the very fair value set-price lunch menu, have been a vol-au-vent of snails in a butter sauce infused with puréed parsley; eggs en cocotte with asparagus and truffle on a madeira sauce; layered salmon and turbot on a light butter sauce with courgette and carrot ribbons; fillet of veal with vegetables and a madeira sauce – the veal cooked exactly enough to elicit full flavour and succulence; baby lamb with thyme and a mint hollandaise; tarte Tatin (of course); a fine fruit salad with lemony crème anglaise; and crème brûlée with passion-fruit. It can be very popular – at Sunday lunch, for instance – and latecomers may have less choice from the cheaper menu than they bargained for. The wine list is long and hardly cheap. Germany is the only wine-producing country other than France admitted to exist. There is some consideration for bottles under £20 and there are lots of halves. The classics are exciting to behold; the regional choice is less enlivening, even if affordable.

CHEF: Michel Roux PROPRIETORS: Roux Waterside Inn OPEN: Tue to Sun, exc Tue L CLOSED: 25 Dec to mid-Feb, Sun D end Oct to mid-Apr MEALS: 12 to 2, 7 to 10 PRICES: £57 (£70), Set L £23.50 (£32) to £49.50 (£58), Set D £37 (£45) to £49.50 (£58). Minimum £30. Net prices CARDS: Access, Carte Blanche, Diners, Visa SEATS: 80. Private parties: 80 main room, 8 private room. Car park, 30 places. Vegetarian meals. Children restricted. Smart dress preferred. No cigars/pipes in dining-room. Wheelchair access (2 steps; also WC). Air-conditioned. Fax: (0628) 784710

BRIDPORT Dorset map 2

Will's

NEW ENTRY

4–6 Barrack Street,
Bridport DT6 3LY
BRIDPORT (0308) 27517

COOKING 2
COST £25

Will Longman's modest restaurant feels rather like a '70s café transformed to suit the needs of the '90s. The atmosphere is relaxed and informal, the décor is all fresh flowers, old pine tables and chairs and Canadian maple floors. The weekly-changing menu is dictated by fresh seasonal ingredients, and fish is a strong point: shellfish soup, scallops on a bed of leeks, and sea bass with fennel sauce have all been good. Readers regularly mention chargrilled monkfish steaks with spicy tomato sauce. The kitchen has also delivered very good smoked trout and cream cheese soufflé, pungent Toulouse sausage in cider with onions, and fillet of pork braised with plums, brandy and cream sauce. Vegetables, supplied by a local organic farm where possible, are cooked al dente. To finish there are fruity sorbets and locally made ice-creams, as well as excellent lemon tart. Each month, the restaurant stages gastronomic evenings from different parts of the world. The short wine list has plenty of decent drinking around £10. House French is £6.95.

CHEF: William Longman PROPRIETORS: William Longman and Robyn Huxter OPEN: Tue to Sat, D only; also Mon D bank hols and summer CLOSED: 2 weeks end Oct to early Nov MEALS: 7 to 9.45 (10.15 Sat) PRICES: £15 (£21) CARDS: Access, Visa SEATS: 30. Private parties: 30 main room. Vegetarian meals. Children's helpings. Wheelchair access (2 steps; also WC). Music

BRIGHTON East Sussex map 3

Black Chapati

COUNTY RESTAURANT OF THE YEAR

NEW ENTRY

12 Circus Parade, New England Road,
Brighton BN1 4GW
BRIGHTON (0273) 699011

COOKING 2
COST £28

The name is bizarre. In fact, everything about this idiosyncratic Indian restaurant is unlikely. Black venetian blinds and a starkly elegant black and white dining-room set the tone, but the mood is casual. Chef Stephen Funnell is, according to a reporter, 'an English jackdaw who snatches ideas from the entire subcontinent'. The results can be a revelation – varied, light and subtle, with clear but robust flavours. A short menu is supplemented by daily specials, on Sundays there is a buffet, and invention shows right across the range. To start, there might be steamed sea bass with mint and cucumber yoghurt or rich yellow fish soup served with slices of fried garlicky bread with roasted fennel and cumin seeds, alongside onion bhajis, vegetable samosas made with filo pastry, and shish kebab. Main courses may include Sri Lankan beef curry, Hyderabadi chicken (a free-range bird) with almonds, and Goanese duckling – fanned-out slices of breast on a pomegranate sauce. Shikar vindaloo is not the usual curry-house firewater, but the real thing, made from pork marinated in hot spices and coconut vinegar. Incidentals are impressive: home-made chutneys, steamed rice, vegetables and sweets such as coconut egg custard. Menu explanations are clear and honest. To drink there are Breton cider, French bière de garde and a minimal list of carefully chosen wines. House French is £6.95.

CHEFS: Stephen Funnell and Lauren J. Alker PROPRIETORS: Black Chapati Ltd OPEN: Tue to Sun, exc Tue L and Sun D CLOSED: 1 week Christmas MEALS: 12.30 to 1.30 (1 to 3.30 Sun), 7 to 10.30 PRICES: £14 (£23). Service 10%. Card slips closed CARDS: Access, Amex, Visa SEATS: 30. 2 tables outside. Private parties: 30 main room. Vegetarian meals. No children after 9. Wheelchair access. Music

Food for Friends

17A–18 Prince Albert Street,
The Lanes, Brighton BN1 1HH — COOKING 1
BRIGHTON (0273) 736236 — COST £7–£10

This informal, unpretentious vegetarian café remains the best in The Lanes for food and for offering very good value for money. Counter service, no bookings, long queues and shared tables do not deter. Breakfast has home-baked organic bread, pain au chocolat and croissants. Careful buying, increasingly of organic produce, provides the basis for some imaginative meals: carrots, onions and spinach in filo pastry with a white wine and parsley sauce; stir-fried vegetables with tofu; falafels with tsatsiki and chilli sauce. A heavy-handedness has been noted in some of the dishes, either in execution (a bland, soggy vegetable quiche, for example), or in the rushed serving during a busy lunch when pakoras were slopped on to plates and dhal poured unceremoniously over the top. But on the whole portions are generous and the food is fresh tasting. The range of salads is inventive and cakes and desserts are well made. To drink there are herbal and other teas, beer and house French wine at £4.15.

CHEFS: Karen Samuel and Philip Taylor PROPRIETORS: Simon Hope and Jeremy Gray OPEN: all week MEALS: 9am to 10am PRICES: £5 (£8), Set L and D from £4 (£7) SEATS: 50. Vegetarian meals. Children's helpings. No-smoking area. Wheelchair access. Music. Fax: (0273) 571363

Langan's Bistro

1 Paston Place, Brighton BN2 1HA — COOKING 2*
BRIGHTON (0273) 606933 — COST £19–£32

Peter Langan's legacy lives on, away from the capital, in this admirable sibling of the great Stratton Street brasserie (see London entry). The gallery of prints and drawings, the short handwritten daily-changing menu and the loyalty to fresh market ingredients are instantly recognisable. Reliability, rather than innovation, is the strength of the place. Reporters speak fondly of the mushrooms stuffed with snails and garlic, warm duck salad, crab and fennel soup, rack of lamb with roasted garlic, and delicate poached salmon. 'Food is cooked accurately and treated with respect,' comments a regular visitor. The choice of mainly cold sweets does not quite match the rest of the repertoire. Service is highly praised. House wine is £6.75.

CHEF: Mark Emmerson PROPRIETORS: Coq d'Or Restaurants Ltd OPEN: Tue to Sun, exc Sat L and Sun D CLOSED: first 2 weeks Jan, last 2 weeks Aug MEALS: 12.30 to 2.30, 7.30 to 10.30 PRICES: £20 (£27), Set L £13.50 (£19). Cover 75p. Service 10%. Card slips closed CARDS: Access, Amex, Diners, Visa SEATS: 48. Vegetarian meals. Children welcome. Music. Air-conditioned

▲ *La Noblesse, Hospitality Inn*

Kings Road, Brighton BN1 2GS — COOKING 3
BRIGHTON (0273) 206700 — COST £26–£58

A good suggestion from our readers was a management buy-out by the kitchen and subsequent removal of La Noblesse, lock, stock and barrel, to a new home. Richard Lyth is a fine chef whose work is hampered by sloppy hotel management and, on occasion, poor restaurant service. Other parts of the hotel have not been recommended. The setting is expense account territory, but the food is more serious. Materials are carefully bought and recipes on both *carte* and *menu gourmande* sufficiently inventive. An example of the second began with a complimentary dish of smoked salmon with a herb sauce; the bread was 'hot, sweet and good'. A straightforward first course with accurately cooked scallops and scampi on a bed of salad leaves (inventive leaves, too) preceded a slice of turbot with a carrot and saffron sauce and a herb crust topping; duck with cinnamon sauce and oyster mushrooms in cream, which came with an enriching accompaniment of duck foie gras; vegetables built in to the main dishes – not many, but felt to be well judged; good French cheese (mostly unidentifiable to the waiter) and an anticlimactic caramelised pineapple with (absent) green peppercorns and vanilla ice-cream. The coffee did not impress, even if the candelabra of mignardises was sensational. Others have had equally satisfactory experiences from the ample *carte*. Wine prices are high; the management's attitude is reflected in an unambitious list which relies heavily on big-name négociants. Bottles from fringe areas and the New World may be the best bets.

CHEF: Richard Lyth PROPRIETORS: Mount Charlotte Investments plc OPEN: Mon to Sat, exc Sat L MEALS: 12 to 2.30, 7 to 10.30 PRICES: £34 (£48), Set L £15.95 (£26), Set D Mon to Fri £21.95 (£32), Set D Sat £31 (£42). Card slips closed CARDS: Access, Amex, Diners, Visa SEATS: 45. Private parties: 45 main room. Car park, 60 places. Vegetarian meals. Children welcome. No pipes in dining-room. Wheelchair access (also WC). Air-conditioned. Music. Fax: (0273) 820692 ACCOMMODATION: 204 rooms, all with bath/shower. Rooms for disabled. Lift. B&B £110 to £130. Children welcome. Baby facilities. Pets welcome. Afternoon teas. Swimming-pool. Sauna. Tennis. Air-conditioned. TV. Phone. Scenic. Confirm by 2

BRIMFIELD Hereford & Worcester map 2

▲ *Poppies, The Roebuck* 🍷

COUNTY RESTAURANT OF THE YEAR

Brimfield SY8 4WE
BRIMFIELD (058 472) 230

COOKING 3
COST £41

There is a great distinction between bar and restaurant: the one dark panelling and tradition, the other light and air, bold fabrics, comfortable cane chairs and a pale colour scheme. Providentially, the food comes from the same talented hands, though prices in the bar are substantially lower. As the recession has skimmed off the cream of restaurant clientele, so has Carole Evans put more effort into the bar and lounge meals. No one should complain; her cooking is exemplary. There is a strong line in fish, be it from Loch Fyne (langoustines with mayonnaise) or the south coast (lemon sole with lime and caper butter – in the bar – or brill with mustard cream sauce – in the restaurant). Carole Evans enjoys fruit flavours in savoury dishes: chutneys, citrus tastes and astringent accents are often deployed, but as important are the aromas of herbs (though not so often spices) and the classic combinations of mushroom, onion, red wine and other alcohols in dishes like calf's liver with Dubonnet and orange, lobster with saffron potatoes, and chicken with cider pie (another bar dish). Desserts are more numerous than first and main courses: interesting ice-creams (lemon balm and ewes' milk); a strong vein of British recipes (bread-and-butter pudding, 'Poppies Pond Pud', the longstanding poppy seed parfait with fresh dates); excellent meringues with summery sorbets. There is a full and descriptive list of British cheeses ensuring full information if the staff are caught out. On the wine list, half-bottles have come into greater favour this year, with a good range of price and style. Selection throughout the list is excellent, but whether or not the French classic regions attract a premium mark-up, the best buys are towards the end of the list where Spain, Italy and robust and interesting Australians and Californians make their mark. Any list including Paillard champagne, Beaucastel Châteauneuf and Isole e Olena Chianti shows enthusiasm and knowledge. House wine is £10.50.

CHEF: Carole Evans PROPRIETORS: John and Carole Evans OPEN: Tue to Sat CLOSED: 2 weeks Feb, 25 and 26 Dec MEALS: 12 to 2, 7 to 10 PRICES: £27 (£34). Net prices, card slips closed CARDS: Access, Visa SEATS: 40. Private parties: 40 main room. Vegetarian meals. Children welcome. No-smoking area. Wheelchair access ACCOMMODATION: 3 rooms, all with bath/shower. B&B £35 to £65. No children under 10. TV. Phone. Scenic. Doors close at 12.30am. Confirm by 6 (*Which? Hotel Guide*)

BRISTOL Avon map 2

Bistro Twenty One

21 Cotham Road South, Kingsdown,
Bristol BS6 5TZ
BRISTOL (0272) 421744

COOKING 2
COST £31

Alain Dubois' popular venue continues to thrive and as a result he has recently refurbished and extended the place to double the seating capacity. Visitors come here to enjoy the good-value food and to soak up the cheerful atmosphere

– although the music can sometimes be more 'foreground' than 'background'. The menu is a mix of old and new bistro: French onion soup, coq au vin, grilled Dover sole, sweet and savoury pancakes, as well as fillet of turbot with saffron sauce, guinea-fowl with juniper berries, and best end of lamb with honey and ginger sauce. Reporters have been impressed with the high quality and presentation of many dishes, including crab and mango mayonnaise, poussin with walnut sauce, sirloin steak with mushroom and cream sauce, and dark and white chocolate mousse. Ingredients are generally good, although on one reported occasion mussels were 'the size of peas'. Service is excellent. The well-chosen wine list is dominated by France. House French is £6.75.

CHEF/PROPRIETOR: Alain Dubois OPEN: all week, exc Sat L and Sun D MEALS: 12 to 2.30, 6.30 to 11.30 PRICES: £19 (£26) CARDS: Access, Visa SEATS: 80. Private parties: 30 main room, 30 private room. Vegetarian meals. Children's helpings. Wheelchair access. Music

Jameson's

30 Upper Maudlin Street,
Bristol BS2 8DJ COOKING 1
BRISTOL (0272) 276565 COST £14–£30

'It appears to be a Victorian house with all the rooms knocked through. We were sitting in what must have once been the conservatory. Although music played, Sinatra had thoughtfully been semi-strangled so it intruded little.' The reasons why this reader could hear the music only with difficulty were the press of business – this place is popular – and the proximity of main road and traffic lights. Value is the order of the day here for dishes like rillettes of pork with hot ciabatta bread; tabbouleh; endive, chicken liver and cashew-nut salad; duck with almonds and kumquats; red mullet in a parcel with fennel; and double chocolate mousse or hot banana strudel. Not everything works perfectly (the cooking is more redolent of bistro than restaurant) but the standard is maintained, the food is hot and the vegetables are generous. Redecoration has coincided with a rearrangement of menus and hours. The *plat du jour*, with a first course thrown in, is especially reasonable. Service is well appreciated. The wine list, headed by Avery's house Clochemerle at £7.95 a litre, offers fair prices and a decent choice.

CHEFS: Ian Leitch and Carole Jameson PROPRIETORS: Carole and John Holmes OPEN: all week, exc Sat L and Sun D MEALS: 12 to 2.30 (4 Sun), 6 to 11 PRICES: £17 (£25), Set L £12.50 inc wine (£14), Set D £13.95 (£21) to £16.90 (£25). Card slips closed CARDS: Access, Visa SEATS: 70. Private parties: 35 main room. Vegetarian meals. Children's helpings. Wheelchair access (2 steps). Music. Fax: (0272) 241596

County round-ups listing additional restaurants that may be worth a visit are at the back of the Guide, *after the Irish section. Reports on round-up entries are welcome.*

Several sharp operators have tried to extort money from restaurateurs on the promise of an entry in a guide book that has never appeared. The Good Food Guide *makes no charge for inclusion and does not offer certificates of any kind.*

Lettonie 🍷

9 Druid Hill, Stoke Bishop,
Bristol BS9 1EW — COOKING 4
BRISTOL (0272) 686456 — COST £23–£41

Martin Blunos is of Latvian origin, hence the name of the restaurant and the reason for some of the pictures, but his cooking is full-flood modern European, showing few signs of the tilt towards the Mediterranean of many fashionable London places. The dining-room is still mildly shop-like, but seats are comfortable, tables are decently dressed and the food itself is fairly remarkable for its setting. Thus, reports of meals are marked by an element of surprise on the part of the writers. One such meal began with first-rate very white bread and a complimentary celeriac soup (the complimentary dish may be quite elaborate, for instance a whole fillet of sole with good butter sauce) before scallops baked in the shell (sealed with pastry) with light butter sauce and strips of vegetables, and a dish of smoked cod tortellini with a Sauternes sauce. Main dishes have included a signature composition of pig's trotter stuffed with sweetbreads on a madeira sauce ('the skin as thin and tender as a chicken's'), and lamb on a lentil purée, with a rösti, onion marmalade and thyme gravy. The arrangement of this lamb showed Martin Blunos' affection for the conventions of nouvelle cuisine inasmuch as it was surrounded by a proliferation of tiny vegetables (the baby aubergines were especially noteworthy). Desserts of a poached apple with a glazed almond and rosemary sabayon, and pear mousse with ginger – plus half a poached pear for good measure – show invention continuing to the very end. This is very accomplished cooking. Some people would like to see more of the chef, so that they can at least thank him, but that would work to the detriment of other people's dinners. A largely French wine list includes some good red Rhônes, is not overpriced and is adequate for the task in hand. It is an intelligently succinct, catholic selection of wines, with most kept at fair prices. Burgundies are from smaller growers and several interesting Bordeaux petits châteaux. House wines are from £9.25. CELLARMAN'S CHOICE: St Véran, Cuvée Prestige 1988, Lassarat, £17; St Emilion, Ch.Pipeau 1986, £19.60.

CHEF: Martin Blunos PROPRIETORS: Martin and Siân Blunos OPEN: Tue to Sat CLOSED: 2 weeks Aug, 1 week Christmas, bank hols MEALS: 12.30 to 2, 7 to 9.30 PRICES: Set L £13.95 (£23) to £23.95 (£34), Set D £23.95 (£34) CARDS: Access, Amex, Visa SEATS: 24. Private parties: 16 main room. Vegetarian meals. Children's helpings on request. Wheelchair access (1 step). No music

Markwicks 🍷

43 Corn Street, Bristol BS1 1HT — COOKING 3*
BRISTOL (0272) 262658 — COST £20–£38

'We were great fans of the Markwicks when they were at Bistro Twenty One, but as this restaurant is not open on a Saturday it has taken all this time to visit them in Corn Street. I regret the wasted years,' wrote a reader. Corn Street is in the old mercantile centre of Bristol. Markwicks, once a safety deposit, is surrounded by banks, life companies and building societies. Parking is not easy. The long vaulted room is flanked by two smaller spaces, one still equipped with grilles and locks against robbers. Conversion to restaurant, particularly the small bar that greets you on entry, has been successful. Stephen Markwick cooks and Judy Markwick is a capable hostess: 'Even if it's full there are no long waits and the staff are always pleasant and helpful.' At lunch there is a short set-price menu to supplement the *carte*, which runs to a half-dozen choices in each course. Lunch constitutes good value. Stephen Markwick remains faithful to a style that has not gone overboard for neo-Italianism or Californian simplicity. Sauces are good and substantial and flavourings depend on classic combinations or their derivatives. This makes for well-rounded dishes. A summer lunch – crab bisque; salmon, scallops, monkfish and hake in saffron sauce decorated with lobster eggs; and a grape tart – showed the merits of simplicity coupled with generosity. There is no mimsy or loss of impact of dishes by over-multiplication of elements. Recommendations extend to crab tart with crisp pastry and a delicate moist filling; fish soup, herby and light; mussels marinière; guinea-fowl in a smooth velvet sauce of apples and calvados; tender venison with cranberry and apple purée; sweetbreads with apples and calvados; veal with creamed spinach; and partridge with shallot and red wine sauce. Vegetables are good and are varied between fish and meat, so at least they do not send out red cabbage with brill, a fault too often met in otherwise decent restaurants. Sweet things are variable: a rum pudding served hot did not get a lot of help from its accompanying poached pear, but a warm hazelnut and apple tart was worth the wait. Pancakes are firm favourites. Occasionally, flavours are heightened too far through over-seasoning. This is consistent, assured and popular cooking, using good materials in a sane fashion. France predominates on the sound, if bordering on the conservative, wine list. Good French country wines, among 150-odd bottles, show consideration to the pocket – including the reliable Sauvignon de Haut Poitou and excellent Mas de la Rouvière Bandol – as does a fair scatter of halves. Prices are reasonable throughout and there is little attempt to dazzle with exalted names. House wine is £8.50. CELLARMAN'S CHOICE: Pinot Grigio 1990, Jerman £23.50; St Joseph Réserve Personnelle 1985, Jaboulet Ainé, £17.50.

CHEF: Stephen Markwick PROPRIETORS: Stephen and Judy Markwick OPEN: Mon to Fri MEALS: 12 to 2, 7 to 10.30 PRICES: £26 (£32), Set L £14.25 (£20) to £16.25 (£22). Net prices, card slips closed CARDS: Access, Visa SEATS: 50. Private parties: 6 and 14 private rooms. Children's helpings. No music

Melbournes

74 Park Street, Bristol BS1 3AF — COOKING 1
BRISTOL (0272) 226996 — COST £11–£23

Fair cooking at fair prices on the steep street (once Bristol's finest) that runs from the cathedral green to the university tower at the top. The encouragement of bring-your-own wine, Australian-style, keeps costs down still further, though the short wine list on the reverse of the menu is both fairly chosen and cheap. The split-level restaurant is well packed and can be noisy on busy nights, but the bronzed (Australian, you see) waiters bustle fast and deliver efficiently. Food is bistro-style, betrayed by too great a reliance on cream in the sauces (squirted on top of mousses for puddings), but not incompetent.

Vegetables are fresh and simple. Tastes may be slightly muted, especially when masked by cream: a broccoli and Stilton soup, for instance, might have puzzled many a blind taster. House wine is £6.

CHEFS: C. Cowpe and M. Read PROPRIETORS: A. Wilshaw, N. Hennessy, C. Cowpe and M. Read OPEN: Tue to Sun, exc Sat L and Sun D CLOSED: week between Christmas and New Year MEALS: 12 to 2, 7 to 10.30 PRICES: Set L £6.50 (£11) to £10.50 (£16), Set D £11.75 (£17) to £13.75 (£19). Service 10%. Card slips closed. Licensed, also bring your own: no corkage CARDS: Access, Visa SEATS: 70. Private parties: 40 main room. Vegetarian meals. Children's helpings. No cigars/pipes in dining-room. Wheelchair access (1 step; also WC). Music

Muset

12–16 Clifton Road, Clifton,
Bristol BS8 1AF — COOKING 1
BRISTOL (0272) 732920 — COST £19–£25

The restaurant is difficult to find: strangers are advised to go along nearby Queens Road and ask for directions. Inside, it has been impressively refurbished and has three separate dining areas on different levels. It is invariably full, cheerful and buzzing with life. A big draw is, no doubt, the BYO policy: customers can bring their own wine (no beer or spirits), no corkage is charged and the restaurant provides glasses. The menu, backed up by blackboard specials, offers idiosyncratic bistro-style dishes. Chicken livers with ribbon pasta, confit of duck, and fillet of salmon with spicy crab sauce impressed an inspector more than the quality of the desserts. Others have mentioned avocado and smoked turkey with orange vinaigrette, a duo of pickled salmon and halibut, and suprême of chicken stuffed with goats' cheese and coriander sauce. Service is fast and efficient. As well as BYO, the restaurant has a creditable wine list with strong leanings towards the New World. House French is £5.95.

CHEF: D. Wheadon PROPRIETORS: A.J. Portlock and D. Wheadon OPEN: Mon to Sat, D only MEALS: 7 to 10.30 PRICES: Set D £12.95 (£19) to £15.40 (£21). Service 10%. Card slips closed. Licensed, also bring your own: no corkage. CARDS: Access, Visa SEATS: 130. Private parties: 30 main room. Children's helpings. No children under 10 after 8pm. Music. Air-conditioned

Orient Rendezvous

95 Queens Road, Clifton,
Bristol BS8 1LW — COOKING 1
BRISTOL (0272) 745202 and 745231 — COST £15–£28

There are many attractions beyond the food in this stylish Chinese restaurant, for instance, a dance floor with live entertainment till two in the morning, and an ambitious list of vintage clarets and burgundies. The rockery garden is complete with new fishponds and waterfalls, and outside eating is planned for the summer. The 100-dish menu has a strong showing of seafood and sizzling dishes ranging from crab with black-bean sauce and stewed scallops with vegetables to lamb in yellow-bean sauce. Specialities from Szechuan feature prominently: 'ocean-flavoured' squid, cold sliced pork with garlic, deep-fried shredded beef with chilli. Service has been described as 'first class'. House French is £6.50, and there are 25 beers from around the world.

CHEF: David Wong PROPRIETOR: Raymond Wong OPEN: all week CLOSED: 25 to 28 Dec MEALS: 12 to 2.30, 6.30 to 11.30 PRICES: £13 (£23), Set L £10 (£15), Set D £17.50 (£23). Service 10%. Card slips closed CARDS: Access, Amex, Diners, Visa SEATS: 165. Private parties: 150 main room, 8 to 30 private rooms. Car park, 25 places. Vegetarian meals. Children welcome. Smart dress preferred. Music. Air-conditioned

Rocinante's NEW ENTRY

85 Whiteladies Road,
Bristol BS8 2NT — COOKING 1
BRISTOL (0272) 734482 — COST £22

The music is loud (jazz or world), the place is bright, the art is fun, the cream floor tiles and painted furniture give it a Mediterranean feel and you can eat outside, if Bristol rain lets up, to give that Iberian feeling. Rocinante's is a tapas bar with extras, and has a proprietor who cares about organic farming, and not using alloys or other such things in the kitchen. Concern with supplies means the meat dishes, for instance, are a cut above the norm: excellent veal chop, skewers of lamb, and chicken with rice. The cooking varies from good to perfunctory. On a wide sampling, there were some signs of economising – either of effort or techniques – but warm approval was expressed for the coffee, the crème caramel, albondigas (spicy meat balls), grilled prawns with a not-very-garlicky aïoli, and the calamares. Service is willing and witty; wines may turn up as another year to that listed. A tapas bar with soul is a rare bird in England and this certainly has lots of soul.

CHEFS: Robin Huber and Barny Haughton PROPRIETOR: Barny Haughton OPEN: all week, exc Sun D (by arrangement only) MEALS: 12 to 3, 6 to 11 PRICES: £12 (£28). Minimum £7.50 (bookings only). Service 10% on parties of 6 or more CARDS: Access, Visa SEATS: 80. 6 tables outside. Private parties: 40 main room, 30 private room. Children's helpings. Wheelchair access (3 steps; also WC). Music

BROADHEMBURY Devon — map 1

Drewe Arms NEW ENTRY

Broadhembury EX14 0NF — COOKING 2*
BROADHEMBURY (040 484) 267 — COST £32

Broadhembury has probably been on a calendar cover. The Drewe Arms, at the start of the chestnut-lined church walk, fits the bill: low eaves, cream-washed walls either side of the broad entry. Inside is of a piece: interconnecting rooms, pine panelling, good old pub furniture, a big fireplace, a sense of English snug. The Burges kept a pub in East Anglia where Kerstin Burge showed her prowess at fish cookery, now displayed again. An infrastructure of bar food is vaulted over by a long blackboard of fresh fish plus beef and venison. Dory, turbot, lobster, sole and sea trout were the varieties on offer one day in May. First courses will usually include gravlax and prawns (Greenland or

Mediterranean) as well as a soup and, for instance, scallops with lime, cream and tarragon. This is fine, natural food cooked with sensitivity and directness. Reflecting on the perils of success, Kerstin Burge comments that 'foodies' expecting the (over-decorated) world for £15 a head are misdirected to come here. Desserts, such as treacle tart, hazelnut meringue and mincemeat meringue tart form a substantial last course. The wine list is a model of economy and sensible, world-wide selection.

CHEF: Kerstin Burge PROPRIETORS: Kerstin and Nigel Burge OPEN: all week (Sun D and Mon L limited menu only) MEALS: 12 to 2, 7 to 10 PRICES: £20 (£27) CARDS: Access, Visa SEATS: 24. 6 tables outside. Private parties: 24 main room. Car park, 8 places. Vegetarian meals. Children's helpings L. No pipes in dining-room. Wheelchair access (1 step; also WC). No music

BROADWAY Hereford & Worcester map 2

▲ *Collin House*

Collin Lane, Broadway WR12 7PB
BROADWAY (0386) 858354 COOKING 2
on A44, 1m NW of Broadway COST £22–£35

'Collin House remains very consistent indeed,' writes one reader. This is true of both the relaxed and unpretentious atmosphere and the cooking. John and Judith Mills have established a style over the years offering good, wholesome British traditional dishes in modern versions (not too modern). The style evolves slowly. Three years ago there was no double-baked Stilton and celery soufflé with watercress sauce on the menu, but the duck liver terrine with crab apple relish has remained fairly constant; the repertoire tends to remain stable from month to month with such things as mussels cooked with white wine and shallots; roast breast of duckling with honey, ginger and kumquat sauce; and a vegetarian choice of leek tart with basil and tomato sauce. The *carte* is short and priced according to the main course selection. Desserts are British and good: bread-and-butter pudding, treacle tart with ginger ice-cream, date sponge pudding with butterscotch sauce. Lunch is served in the bar, where poached salmon and prawns in a Mediterranean sauce made a 'most pleasant stop-over on the way home' for one reader. A short and intelligent wine list covers all areas including the New World. House French is £8.50.

CHEFS: Judith Mills and Mark Brookes PROPRIETORS: John and Judith Mills OPEN: all week, exc Sun D CLOSED: 5 days Christmas MEALS: 12 to 1.30, 7 to 9 PRICES: Set L £13.50 (£22), Set D £16.50 (£25) to £20 (£29). Card slips closed CARDS: Access, Visa SEATS: 24. 4 tables outside. Private parties: 32 main room. Car park, 25 places. Vegetarian meals. Children's helpings. No cigars/pipes in dining-room. Wheelchair access (1 step; also WC) ACCOMMODATION: 7 rooms, all with bath/shower. B&B £41 to £91. Deposit: £40. Children under 6 by arrangement. Garden. Swimming-pool. Scenic. Doors close at 11.30 (*Which? Hotel Guide*)

denotes an outstanding wine cellar; *denotes a good wine list, worth travelling for.*

Hunters Lodge

High Street, Broadway WR12 7DT — COOKING 2
BROADWAY (0386) 853247 — COST £18–£34

A substantial house that stands back from the main street, its stonework well covered by plant life. It is a useful place for visitors as well as being popular with a large body of regulars. Kurt Friedli is a sound, professional chef and Dottie manages front-of-house along well-tried and admired lines. Hunters Lodge is a well-fitting suit that satisfies those in search of egg mayonnaise as well as those looking for more ambitious dishes like boned and roast quail with port wine. Long-cooked recipes, a venison pie or boiled lamb with caper sauce, are as available as the sautéed and pan-fried. The repertoire is well-tried too, just as the service is silver (sometimes giving rise to cool food), and the desserts are laid out on the sideboard. 'Good honest cooking, with delightful proprietors, that gave me a meal of fresh pea soup, navarin of lamb, exactly cooked vegetables, then floating islands,' reports one who will revisit. The wine list includes sound bottles from Ch. Cissac and Millet in Bordeaux; Thévenin, Lamblin and Chanson in Burgundy; plus some specials from Germany and French classics. House wine is £7.

CHEF: Kurt Friedli PROPRIETORS: Kurt and Dottie Friedli OPEN: Tue to Sun, exc Sun D CLOSED: first 2 weeks Feb, first 2 weeks Aug MEALS: 12.30 to 2, 7.30 to 9.45 PRICES: £20 (£28), Set L £12.85 (£18), Set D £19 (£25) CARDS: Access, Amex, Diners, Visa SEATS: 55. 6 tables outside. Private parties: 35 main room, 22 small room. Car park, 20 places. Vegetarian meals. Children's helpings. No children under 8. No cigars/pipes in dining-room. Wheelchair access (also WC). Music

▲ *Lygon Arms* 🍷

Broadway WR12 7DU — COOKING 2*
BROADWAY (0386) 852255 — COST £29–£53

No one can deny the scale and beauty of the original building. It has, of course, grown: new wings for business conferences, extra bedrooms, and new buildings for a country club have been accumulated. Money and a certain taste are not lacking, but this is not Richard Rogers architecture. Dining takes place in the great hall – heraldic, stag-ridden, brassed and pewtered, yet strangely genteel. Clive Howe has developed a menu that explores the possibilities of British cooking – there are overtones here of Kit Chapman's work at the Castle in Taunton (see entry). On one summer menu, first courses included oxtail pie with pickled quail's egg, a tart of baked Cheshire cheese and apple, crab with beetroot and sour cream. Main courses continued the theme with lamb glazed with goats' cheese, basil and pine-kernels; salmon and barley pie with a dill sauce; and rabbit with apple and mustard sauce. Desserts are deeply traditional. The intelligence of this repertoire is that while it may be historical and relying on local materials, it is not reconstructionist, but a forward development. Execution is not always wholly satisfactory when, for example, a quiet lunch is overshadowed by a large function, but the performance of kitchen and service brigades has been sharpened. The wine list is 'grand hotel' in style but does not ignore the need for bottles under £15. House wine is £9.75.

CHEF: Clive Howe PROPRIETORS: The Savoy Group OPEN: all week MEALS: 12.30 to 2, 7.30 to 9.30 PRICES: £33 (£44), Set L £18.75 (£29), Set D £27.25 (£38). Card slips closed CARDS: Access, Amex, Carte Blanche, Diners, Visa SEATS: 90. Private parties: 90 main room, 20, 40 and 76 private rooms. Car park, 150 places. Vegetarian meals. Children's helpings. Smart dress preferred. No-smoking area. Wheelchair access (also WC). Music. Fax: (0386) 858611 ACCOMMODATION: 65 rooms, all with bath/shower. Rooms for disabled. B&B £105 to £135. Deposit: 1 night. Children welcome. Baby facilities. Pets welcome. Afternoon teas. Garden. Swimming-pool. Sauna. Tennis. Fishing. Golf. Snooker. TV. Phone. Scenic. Confirm by 6

BROCKENHURST Hampshire map 2

Le Poussin

COUNTY RESTAURANT OF THE YEAR

The Courtyard, Brookley Road,
Brockenhurst SO42 7RB COOKING 4
LYMINGTON (0590) 23063 COST £18–£42

Until spring 1991 Le Poussin was large and formal, with pink tablecloths, French waiters and rooms to let upstairs. Those premises having been sold to an Indian restaurateur, the Aitkens retained their long, narrow bar and, working as navvies and decorators for three months, transformed it into a smaller and prettier restaurant that they can run almost entirely on their own, though the kitchen 'team' is in fact a strong one. The change has several bonuses: a small car park, a splendid new kitchen, a charming outdoor courtyard with flowers, trellises and space for two or three small tables. The restaurant itself is intimate, friendly and unfussed, with plain white linen, prettily curtained windows and cream panelled walls hung with prints of poultry. Service is by the watchful Caroline Aitken, with her son Justin acting as a solicitous and newly schooled sommelier. In the kitchen, Alexander Aitken uses local produce wherever possible. In this part of England he has, after all, a splendid selection: fresh fish, shellfish and samphire from Hampshire's rivers and nearby seashore; game from the surrounding New Forest and local estates; strictly seasonal vegetables, salads and soft fruits from a friend's market garden up the road; wonderful offal from the nearest abattoir; and a staggering variety of wild fungi gathered with an enthusiasm bordering on fanaticism by the Aitkens themselves. The spirited cuisine is still outstanding. The dishes have texture and freshness of flavour often missing in places where the *mise en place* leaves the chef with nothing more to do than heat up food. Alongside this, the presentation is pretty without being fussed. A spring meal began with grilled scallops on a shell filled with rich leek purée, covered with a hair-fine, crisp mesh of julienned vegetables. This was followed by a little dome of Pithivier-marked pastry containing lambs' sweetbreads, surrounded by vegetables and yet more sweetbreads on a rich meat gravy. In conclusion, the famous 'array' of fruits and sorbets included a stunning elderflower and champagne sorbet. An option of wines by the glass chosen from the house selection – a glass with each course at £10 – might attract many, since the main list has an expensive look to it. While there is little choice below £15 the range thereafter is good, and prices are not at all bad value. Selection is sound and shows enthusiasm, with a run of six vintages of the unctuous Moulin du Touchais. House wines are from £8.95.

CHEF: Alexander Aitken PROPRIETORS: Alexander and Caroline Aitken OPEN: Tue to Sun, exc Sun D MEALS: 12 to 2, 7 to 10 PRICES: Set L £9.95 (£18) to £12.50 (£21), Set D £20 (£29) to £25 (£35) CARDS: Access, Visa SEATS: 25. Private parties: 25 main room. Car park, 6 places. Vegetarian meals. Wheelchair access. Music. Fax: (0590) 22912

BRUTON Somerset map 2

▲ *Claire De Lune*

2–4 High Street, Bruton BA10 0EQ COOKING 2
BRUTON (0749) 813395 COST £28

Bruton is beautiful, but not on the crest of every sophisticate's wave. A certain line of conservativism, therefore, runs through Thomas Stewart's menus as he cuts and trims to fit the needs of this constituency. At present the result is cooking that shows training and skill. If it also moderates waywardness, such a move back to basics can be of benefit to both sides of the hot-plate. It also offers good value, for both food and wine, and Kate Stewart's welcome is always appreciated. House wine is £7.95.

CHEF: Thomas Stewart PROPRIETORS: Thomas and Kate Stewart OPEN: Mon to Sat, D only (L by arrangement) MEALS: 7 to 10 (10.30 Sat) PRICES: £16 (£23) CARDS: Access, Visa SEATS: 40. Private parties: 40 main room. Children's helpings. Smart dress preferred. Wheelchair access (2 steps). Music ACCOMMODATION: 3 rooms, all with bath/shower. B&B £25 to £35. Children welcome. TV. Scenic. Doors close at 10

Truffles

95 The High Street, Bruton BA10 0AR COOKING 2
BRUTON (0749) 812255 COST £20–£30

A score of seats occupying two former weavers' cottage in a small, though prosperous, country town hardly sounds like a recipe for economic survival nowadays. But survive the Bottrills have – largely because customers are happily welcomed and Martin Bottrill knows his cooking. Seriousness may sometimes lurch into solemnity, the cottages can appear uncomfortably full (or hot), but value is fair and the cooking undeniably draws from more metropolitan inspiration than Bruton. A rough duck terrine had excellent open texture and strong flavour complemented by an onion marmalade; a fish medley with an oriental ginger sauce could have benefited from more ginger and panache; but the tropical fruit jellied compote with a passion-fruit cream sauce was a finely judged amalgam of sweet and tart. The monthly-changing menu offers half a dozen choices at each course: for example, sweet pepper mousse with smoked trout and asparagus; guinea-fowl stuffed with morels on a tarragon sauce; veal cutlet with lemon butter sauce; a chocolate meringue, sponge and mousse cake; and a yoghurt and honey bavarois. The flavours are even rather than strong; the cooking is short and not mother's pride new-wave stews or casseroles. Vegetarians get their own menu and special diets attention if a day's notice is given. The wine list is canny enough, especially generous with half-bottles, and bolstered by a quartet of second labels from prestigious Bordeaux châteaux. House Duboeuf is £7.25.

CHEF: Martin Bottrill PROPRIETORS: Martin and Denise Bottrill OPEN: Tue to Sat, D only and Sun L (weekday L and Sun and Mon D by arrangement) MEALS: 12 to 2, 7 to 9.30 PRICES: Set L £12.95 (£20), Set D £17.95 (£25) SEATS: 20. Private parties: 20 main room. Vegetarian meals. Children restricted. Smart dress preferred. Wheelchair access (1 step). No music

BUCKLAND Gloucestershire map 2

▲ *Buckland Manor*

Buckland WR12 7LY
BROADWAY (0386) 852626 COOKING 2
off A46, 1m SW of Broadway COST £27–£48

Change is rarely admitted to exist in Cotswold heritage hotels such as this: all gables, beams, honeyed stone and mullions, with a croquet lawn outside. Here, where there are new owners, the chef has survived the transition. The Vaughans have instituted a 'steady as she goes' policy: Americans would worry at too radical a shift from luxury, high prices and formality. The most noticeable improvement is that the menu has cast out French and reads instead as a matter-of-fact listing in English. Certainly Buckland is successful at what it aims to do in that Martyn Pearn's cooking is enjoyed: goats' cheese in filo, a salmon and sole terrine and another of duck foie gras, estouffade of sole and mussels, cod in white wine sauce, crème brûlée, lemon tart and chocolate marquise with vanilla sauce are successes mentioned. This is not mould-breaking stuff, but competently done. However, niggles are voiced at lack of finesse through the whole meal; at these prices, everything needs to be right. Customers have to wade through a lot of notes on the wine list. There are good petits châteaux, fine classified clarets of good years, reliable burgundies, excellent Loires and Alsaces, and many good Germans. Clarets are particularly strong in half-bottles, and prices throughout the list are reasonable. A pity it is not all a little clearer. House wine is £8.50.

CHEF: Martyn Pearn PROPRIETORS: Roy and Daphne Vaughan OPEN: all week MEALS: 12.30 to 1.45, 7.30 to 8.45 PRICES: £29 (£40), Set Sun L £17.50 (£27) CARDS: Access, Amex, Visa SEATS: 38. 6 tables outside. Private parties: 10 main room. Car park, 30 places. No children under 8. Smart dress preferred. No cigars/pipes in dining-room. Wheelchair access (also WC). Fax: (0386) 853557 ACCOMMODATION: 10 rooms, all with bath/shower. Rooms for disabled. B&B £135 to £240. No children under 12. Afternoon teas. Garden. Swimming-pool. Tennis. TV. Phone. Scenic (*Which? Hotel Guide*)

BURFORD Oxfordshire map 2

▲ *Lamb* NEW ENTRY

Sheep Street, Burford OX8 4LR COOKING 1
BURFORD (099 382) 3155 COST £9–£37

'Burford is a town of antique shops and objects that you don't want to buy but which vaguely tempt you. The Lamb, by contrast, is authentic.' A slur from an inspector on the traders of Burford this may be, but it is endorsement of the pub lunches at this handsome stone-built inn where every accoutrement of local colour was provided centuries ago. In the restaurant itself more formal meals are served. People speak fondly of the buffet supper on Sundays for good value and generous quantities. Dinner menus show an affection for what was once 'modern' cooking: fritters of smoked salmon and Brie on one occasion, the same mixture filling a breast of chicken on another; fillet stuffed with Stilton; dariole of sole filled with scallops; lamb en croûte. It is well enough done for no objection to be raised. More straightforward soups, and meats with sauces, do exist. Some of the desserts, like a home-made lemon meringue pie, have been excellent, while others have been roundly condemned as poor assemblies of various elements, or just for bad technique. The bar food contains good and bad: good soup, decent meat, fair smoked salmon, regrettable salad cream and mixture of vegetables and salad on a single plate. All reports agree that this is a good place to visit, romantic in the candlelight, and that the staff are eager to please. Wines are an adequate, conservative selection. There are a few half-bottles and much decent drinking can be had below £12. House wine is £7.50.

CHEFS: Pascal Clavaud and David Partridge PROPRIETORS: Richard and Caroline de Wolf OPEN: all week CLOSED: 25 and 26 Dec MEALS: 12 to 2, 7.30 to 9 PRICES: bar L £3.95 (£9), Set Sun L £15 (£22), Set D £19 (£26) to £24 (£31) CARDS: Access, Visa SEATS: 55. 8 tables outside. Private parties: 20 main room. Car park, 6 places. Children's helpings. No pipes in dining-room. Wheelchair access (1 step; also WC). No music ACCOMMODATION: 15 rooms, 14 with bath/shower. B&B £36 to £75. Children welcome. Baby facilities. Pets welcome. Garden. TV. Phone. Scenic. Doors close at 11 (*Which? Hotel Guide*)

BURGH LE MARSH Lincolnshire map 6

Windmill

NEW ENTRY

46 High Street, Burgh le Marsh PE24 5JT COOKING **2**
SKEGNESS (0754) 810281 COST £12–£24

'Chintz by the fire' was one person's shorthand description of this small restaurant that shares a car park with a fine, five-sailed windmill in the centre of the village. The mill supplies the flour for Tim Boskett's excellent brown cobs. Lincolnshire demands low and fair prices, so Sunday lunch is a palpable bargain and dinner prices are not high. Cooking is careful and tends towards reasonable simplicity, with art enough to maintain interest. Cheese beignets with tomato and onion purée, prawn and orange salad with a chervil vinaigrette, a 'balanced and well-textured' lamb bobotie, chicken that 'tasted of chicken' with mushroom and bacon in a cream sauce, and plentiful vegetables made a spring meal beyond criticism for wholesomeness, and it was well-finished by meringues, eclairs and Colombian coffee. Janette Boskett is a gentle hostess. The short wine list kicks off with four house selections by André Daguin, the Michelin-starred chef at Auch in south-western France. The price, £6, is typical of the rest of the two dozen bins.

CHEF: Tim Boskett PROPRIETORS: Tim and Janette Boskett OPEN: Tue to Sat, D only, and Sun L CLOSED: 1 week Christmas, first week Sept MEALS: 12 to 1.45, 7 to 9.15 PRICES: Set Sun L £6.95 (£12), Set D £11 (£15) to £15 (£20) SEATS: 50. Private parties: 40 main room. Car park, 40 places. Vegetarian meals. Children's helpings (Sun L only). No smoking preferred. Wheelchair access. Music

BURNHAM MARKET Norfolk map 6

Fishes'

Market Place, Burnham Market PE31 8HE COOKING 1
FAKENHAM (0328) 738588 COST £14–£28

As one letter-writer commented, Burnham Market has decent pubs, fair cafés, delis and food-shops, as well as this unassuming, sometimes overcrowded, otherwise nicely informal restaurant. It is run by 'a number of hard-pressed women' wrote another who appreciated their efforts to cope with busy summer crowds anxious to sample the good-value, set-price lunch menu. The menus are short and fishy – plus baked ham and smoked goose. They give a chance to eat fish plain (monkfish, salmon, Dover sole, skate and oysters) and fish messed about (crab gratin, lobster thermidor, smoked or cured salmon, oysters with Stilton or garlic). Salmon fishcakes are ever-popular. Salads, not vegetables, and baked potatoes are the accompaniments; 'Fishes' Temptation' is a baked potato with smoked salmon butter. When the cooking works it is a good balance of directness, value and fine materials. Complaint concerns those rushed and hectic summer sessions. Produce can be bought at the counter for 'cottage suppers'. The wine list may be short, but it has some reasonable bottles and is not expensive. House wine is £6.20.

CHEFS: Carole Bird, Gillian Cape and Paula Ayres PROPRIETOR: Gillian Cape OPEN: Tue to Sun, exc Sun D (Oct to June), and Mon bank hols CLOSED: Christmas and 3 weeks Jan MEALS: 12 to 2, 6.45 to 9 (9.30 Sat in summer) PRICES: £17 (£23), Set L £8.50 (£14) to £12 (£18) CARDS: Access, Amex, Diners, Visa SEATS: 48. Private parties: 30 main room. Children's helpings. Children under 5 before 8.30 D. Wheelchair access (1 step). No music

BURY ST EDMUNDS Suffolk map 3

Mortimer's

30 Churchgate Street,
Bury St Edmunds IP33 1RG COOKING 1
BURY ST EDMUNDS (0284) 760623 COST £26

A busy fish restaurant that has minimalist décor – very white except for the bright oilcloth table coverings and splashes of green plants – and exceedingly minimalist hours, so much so that the short opening times draw the most criticism; some feel that it is impossible to have a slow, quiet meal, that service is 'brisk' and one is 'consistently rushed'. Yet the fresh fish continues to draw praise and crowds. 'The fish was excellent and needed to be as it was central to the meal with very little else,' commented one winter diner. Fish soup (declared to be 'robustious'), grilled sardines and 'correctly cooked' potted shrimps vie with the smoked fish and Loch Fyne oysters as openers to a menu that has an old-fashioned feel to it – lemon sole bonne femme, brill vénitienne and halibut florentine. The menu differs little from that of the sister restaurant in Ipswich (see entry). Puddings are simple but well made, ranging from home-made sorbet to near perfect crème caramel. The wine list tells neither the year nor much about origin. House French is £7.25.

CHEF: Kenneth Ambler PROPRIETORS: Kenneth Ambler and Michael Gooding OPEN: Mon to Sat, exc Sat L CLOSED: bank hols and day after, 23 Dec to 5 Jan, 2 weeks Aug MEALS: 12 to 2, 7 to 9 (8.30 Mon) PRICES: £15 (£22) CARDS: Access, Amex, Diners, Visa SEATS: 60. Private parties: 8 main room. Children's helpings on request. No-smoking area/no pipes in dining-room. Wheelchair access (1 step). No music

CALSTOCK Cornwall map 1

▲ *Danescombe Valley Hotel* 🍷

Lower Kelly, Calstock PL18 9RY COOKING 3
TAVISTOCK (0822) 832414 COST £35

Martin and Anna Smith are individuals of strong, yet amiable, character, which is reflected in their hotel. It sits high over the Tamar; the view – viaduct, trees cascading down the Cotehele bank, meadows, a town stuck to a riverside slope, occasional tripper-boats charging upstream or downstream – is narcotic. It may be savoured from verandah or bedroom window. Evening meals are no-choice, and the restaurant is closed on Wednesdays and Thursdays. Outsiders are welcome, but only if there is room after residents have been accommodated. This is not a place for casual calling. The slight lack of compromise – the Smiths have worked out how to live an acceptable life and will not deviate – is tempered by a happy informality (first-name terms here) and self-deprecation. Anna Smith's repertoire has moved firmly away from the Elizabeth David/ French provincial style, with which she began, to a neo-Italian mode. The leitmotif is still the raw material. By definition this is local, which will be apparent from the main course, while the Italian influence will shine through brightest at first or last in the meal. Techniques mobilised are relatively simple, but good on pastry and cakes, and Anna Smith has not developed into a 'professional' cook. This preserves the freshness of the whole operation. A meal that began with aubergine terrine, had rack of lamb and herbs as main course, before an exemplary choice of local cheeses which gave place to panettone, then coffee. Residents need the benefit of an extra hour to travel through the long annotations on the wine list. It can be difficult to spot mention of the wines themselves, which is a pity, since selection, with due enthusiasm for Italy, is fine and prices are very kind. A glass of the bubbly Prosecco costs £2.25 and a bottle of South Australian Cabernet is £7.50. Half-bottles remain scanty. Tips are not expected or accepted.

CHEF: Anna Smith PROPRIETORS: Martin and Anna Smith OPEN: Fri to Tue, D only CLOSED: Nov to 2 April MEALS: 7.30 for 8 PRICES: Set D £25 (£29). Card slips closed CARDS: Access, Diners, Visa SEATS: 12. No children under 12. No smoking in dining-room. No music. One sitting ACCOMMODATION: 5 rooms, all with bath/shower. D,B&B £87 to £159. Deposit: £50. No children under 12. Garden. Scenic. Doors close at midnight. Confirm by 6 (*Which? Hotel Guide*)

Net prices *in the details at the end of an entry indicates that the prices given on a menu and on a bill are inclusive of VAT and service charge, and that this practice is clearly stated on menu and bill.*

CAMBRIDGE Cambridgeshire map 3

Midsummer House

Midsummer Common,
Cambridge CB4 1HA — COOKING 2*
CAMBRIDGE (0223) 69299 — COST £22–£52

The setting is pure Cambridge – a splendid Victorian house near the river and overlooking Midsummer Common. Inside, the house provides several options for mood and atmosphere. Some visitors like the discreet, subtly lit downstairs dining-room, others favour upstairs, where intimacy prevails. There is also a small bustling conservatory. Hans Schweitzer offers thoroughly modern set menus for lunch and dinner, and approved dishes are legion: tartare of salmon and tuna; warm salad of lamb's liver with winter leaves; game soup embellished with an ingenious ball of white turnip; gazpacho ('so thick with vegetables that a knife and fork could have been used'); roast rack of lamb with mushrooms and shallots; and feuilleté of shrimps and mussels with saffron sauce. Elsewhere there is exoticism in goats' cheese with spiced aubergine baked in filo pastry or tea-smoked salmon with lemon grass and wild rice. 'I have taken chefs to Midsummer House three times in the last two months, to learn about presentation and sweets,' comments an hotelier, 'since both are immaculate (notably an apple jalousie with vanilla and ginger ice-cream and butterscotch sauce).' The array of British and French cheeses is prodigious. Occasionally there are quibbles, but the consensus is that the kitchen is on the way up. First and last courses seem to be more satisfactory than main dishes; a tale familiar to many who frequent British restaurants. Efficiency and charm sum up the service. The wine cellar has increased its stock of halves. Prices can still be high. The range is world-wide, but the longest suit is claret. House wines are £9.50.

CHEF: Hans Schweitzer PROPRIETORS: Chris Kelly and Hans Schweitzer OPEN: all week, exc Sat L and Sun D MEALS: 12 to 1.30, 7.15 to 9 PRICES: Set L £15 (£22) to £22 (£29), Set D £22 (£29) to £34 (£43) CARDS: Access, Amex, Diners, Visa SEATS: 35. 2 tables outside. Private parties: 35 main room, 12 private room. Children's helpings on request. Smart dress preferred. Wheelchair access. No music

Twenty Two 🍷

22 Chesterton Road, Cambridge CB4 3AX — COOKING 2
CAMBRIDGE (0223) 351880 — COST £30

'I and two friends dined here while our husbands were at a college dinner.' The ladies made a wise choice. Chilled melon and ginger soup, and garlic mushrooms in filo pastry were good first courses, followed by skate with butter and capers, roast potatoes, cauliflower with pine kernels, and red cabbage. 'All were delicious.' Owners Michael and Susan Sharpe offer a short eclectic set menu, with a salad appearing after the first course. Other choices have been rack of lamb with apricot and mint, and fillet of pork with leeks, black olives and cream; there is always something interesting for vegetarians, such as hot vegetable strudel with red pepper sauce. Brandy-snap baskets with Grand Marnier ice-cream are a favourite pudding. Short and unassertive the wine list may be, but there is hardly a bottle on it which has not earned its place; prices are kept low, and the classic areas have to share space with the Rhône, Italy and carefully chosen New World wines. Pithy, apposite notes encourage enthusiasm. This has the makings of an excellent list. House wine is £7.50. CELLARMAN'S CHOICE: Laurent Perrier n.v., £19.50; Rioja Reserva 1984, Contino, £13.50.

CHEF: Michael Sharpe PROPRIETORS: Michael and Susan Sharpe OPEN: Tue to Sat, D only (L by arrangement) MEALS: 7.30 to 9.30 PRICES: Set D £18.50 (£25) CARDS: Access, Visa SEATS: 28. Private parties: 28 main room. Vegetarian meals. No children under 12. Music

CAMPSEA ASH Suffolk map 3

▲ *Old Rectory* 🍷

Campsea Ash IP13 0PU
WICKHAM MARKET (0728) 746524 COOKING 1
on B1078, 1m E of A12 COST £30

The Old Rectory is the idiosyncratic approach to catering writ large. In a country better provided with good restaurants it would co-exist with nearby eating-places, but would be known only to familiars who liked the approach. Here, there is little choice thus a wider and unprepared constituency. But the general public should realise that Stewart Bassett cooks a no-choice menu, provides only rudimentary service and runs a home for paying guests who either love it or hate it. He has taste and character; he also has a dog 'who tried to stick its nose in my friend's food'. The cooking, a cross between English old-fashioned and French country, can be excellent; it can also fail. No choice means no fall-back. An excellent wine list, with most bins in stock, gives solace. Such enterprises should be encouraged, but be sure to like it before you go.

CHEF/PROPRIETOR: Stewart Bassett OPEN: Mon to Sat, D only MEALS: 7.30 to 9 PRICES: Set D £18.50 (£25) CARDS: Access, Amex, Diners, Visa SEATS: 35. Private parties: 18 main room, 20 private room. Car park, 15 places. Vegetarian meals. Children's helpings on request. Wheelchair access ACCOMMODATION: 6 rooms, all with bath/shower. B&B £30 to £48. Deposit: £20. Children restricted. Garden. Doors close at midnight. Confirm by noon (*Which? Hotel Guide*)

CANTERBURY Kent map 3

George's Brasserie NEW ENTRY

71–72 Castle Street, Canterbury CT1 2QD COOKING 1
CANTERBURY (0227) 765658 COST £17–£37

Canterbury's neighbourhood restaurant, popular night and day, serves several markets (there is a crêperie next door too). The daily menu, which does not necessarily change every day, is fixed-price, with a longer and slowly changing *carte* to supplement choice. Cooking – lentil soup, pasta with smoked-salmon sauce, lamb with a herb crust, grilled squid with chilli, lemon and garlic – is cheerfully Continental with a Mediterranean tinge. It may sometimes be approximate. Other dishes, such as grilled pepper and aubergine with tomato and chilli, and pheasant with mushrooms, bread sauce and port gravy, have had endorsements. Service is certainly cheerful, occasionally muddled. House wines are £6.75.

CHEFS/PROPRIETORS: Simon Day and Beverley Holmes OPEN: all week, exc Sun D CLOSED: 25 Dec, 1 Jan MEALS: 11am to 10pm (10.30 pm Fri and Sat) PRICES: £22 (£31), Set L and D £10.80 (£17). Card slips closed CARDS: Access, Amex, Carte Blanche, Diners, Visa SEATS: 120. 15 tables outside. Private parties: 50 main room, 45 and 30 private rooms. Car park, 30 places D. Vegetarian meals. Children's helpings. No-smoking area. Wheelchair access (3 steps). Music. Fax: (0227) 451011

CARTMEL Cumbria — map 7

▲ *Aynsome Manor*

Cartmel LA11 6HH — COOKING 1
CARTMEL (053 95) 36653 — COST £14–£29

Beyond the utterly overtramped part of Lakeland, this handsome eighteenth-century building continues its career as an hotel under the control of the Varley family. It may be long practice that induces a certain mechanical feel in the service of the five-course dinners (at not too high a price). Three-quarters of an hour from beginning to end is going some. Forgetfulness may be the reason for approximate cooking in main dishes such as salmon with cucumber and tomato hollandaise (set like a custard) and pheasant in bacon with whisky and (rare) ginger sauce; or is it complaisance on the part of the customers, just as it may be they who encourage the heavy overload of cream on the sweets trolley? Perhaps Edwina Currie was not entirely adrift in her analysis of regional tastes. There are good names from a scattering of countries on the wine list. Prices throughout are fair. The offer 'We would be happy to help you make your selection' is worth acting on; there are gems tucked away. House wine is £7.

CHEFS: Tony Varley, Ian Simpson, Victor Sharratt and Chris Miller PROPRIETORS: Tony and Margaret Varley OPEN: Mon to Sat, D only, and Sun L CLOSED: 2 to 27 Jan MEALS: 1 (Sun), 7 to 8.15 PRICES: Set Sun L £9 (£14), Set D £17 (£24) CARDS: Access, Amex, Visa SEATS: 35. Private parties: 35 main room. Car park, 20 places. Children's helpings. No children under 5 D. Smart dress preferred. No smoking in dining-room. Wheelchair access. One sitting Sun L ACCOMMODATION: 13 rooms, 12 with bath/shower. D,B&B £49 to £98. Children welcome. Baby facilities. Pets welcome. Afternoon Tea. Garden. TV. Phone. Scenic. Doors close at 11.30

▲ *Uplands*

Haggs Lane, Cartmel LA11 6HD — COOKING 3
CARTMEL (053 95) 36248 — COST £19–£35

'The problem with eating in most country-house hotels is one of atmosphere, or rather the lack of it,' observes a reader. 'Uplands is different. It is more like a bistro, where conversation comes easily and naturally.' Even so, this off-shoot of Miller Howe lives up to its prestigious mentor and shows its pedigree. Short fixed-priced menus at lunch and dinner sometimes bear the John Tovey stamp, but Tom and Diana Peter have imposed their own individual style on the place.

Meals always feature a generous, heartwarming tureen of soup – celery and lovage, fennel and almond, parsnip and ginger, for example – plus a hot wholemeal loaf fresh from the oven. As the centrepiece there might be grilled Windermere char with watercress sauce, medallions of venison and blackcurrant and juniper sauce, or stuffed breast of chicken with mustard and tomato sauce. Sometimes there are flashes of flamboyance, as in poached fillet of sole stuffed with smoked salmon and mango with chive and Noilly Prat sauce; elsewhere the kitchen is staunchly traditional, delivering impeccable roast sirloin of beef with Yorkshire pudding. Main courses come with a harvest festival of vegetables: shredded beetroot with lime, carrots with coriander, broccoli cooked with sesame oil, even tiny minted new potatoes 'hardly bigger than marrowfat peas' have been outstanding. At dinner, the five-course feast might begin with hot salmon mousse wrapped in smoked salmon with watercress sauce or poached langoustines with tarragon sauce. To finish, there are delights in the shape of hot sticky toffee date pudding, tipsy trifle and chocolate brandy roulade with raspberries and Tia Maria. The wine list is short and sharp, with plenty of half-bottles and a generous showing from the Antipodes.

CHEF: Tom Peter PROPRIETORS: John J. Tovey and Tom and Diana Peter OPEN: Tue to Sun and Mon bank hols CLOSED: 1 Jan to 24 Feb MEALS: 12.30 to 1, 7.30 to 8 PRICES: Set L £13.30 (£19), Set D £22.40 (£29). Card slips closed CARDS: Access, Amex, Visa SEATS: 34. Private parties: 34 main room. Car park, 18 places. Vegetarian meals. No children under 8. No smoking in dining-room. Wheelchair access. Music ACCOMMODATION: 5 rooms, all with bath/shower. D,B&B £68 to £116. No children under 8. Pets welcome. Garden. TV. Phone. Scenic. Doors close at 11. Confirm by 3 (*Which? Hotel Guide*)

CHADLINGTON Oxfordshire map 2

▲ *Manor*

Chadlington OX7 3LX COOKING 1
CHADLINGTON (0608) 76711 COST £42

Both the manor itself and its setting are beautiful. The restoration is bold, even if some details in the bedrooms could still be worked on. Simple to a fault, the menu is short and performance mixed. Complaints are too frequent to endorse consistency, even in a meal composed of nettle soup, a salad of warm pigeon breasts, salmon with hollandaise and perhaps a lemon tart before cheese. However, there is approval for dishes such as tomato and mint soup, scallops with a mousseline sauce, venison patties, orange and honey salted duck, chicken with smoked bacon and Stilton, simple vegetables and prune and Armagnac ice-cream or a rich chocolate pavé. Service from David Grant is generally cheerful, and he knows about wine. Other staff have not been so well considered. 'You come here for the wine, the food is a small extra,' was one bibulous comment. 'Obsessive' inadequately describes a list that includes 44 vintages of Ch. Latour stretching back to 1924, and provides a slate of 10 English wines. Prices are very fair, with good petits châteaux and some fine Alsaces and Rhônes. Excellent half-bottles. House wine is £8.

CHEF: Chris Grant PROPRIETORS: David and Chris Grant OPEN: all week, D only MEALS: 7 to 9 PRICES: Set D £25.50 (£35). Card slips closed CARDS: Access, Visa SEATS: 24. Private parties: 6 and 10 private rooms. Car park, 16 places. Children welcome. No smoking in dining-room. Music ACCOMMODATION: 7 rooms, all with bath/shower. B&B £60 to £130. Children welcome. Garden. TV. Phone. Scenic. Doors close at 11

CHAGFORD Devon map 1

▲ *Gidleigh Park*

Chagford TQ13 8HH COOKING 4*
CHAGFORD (0647) 432367 COST £41–£71

The house could be Ascot, but the drive, the tumbling water, the hills and woods could only be Devon. To get the best out of it, sit of a summer's day on the terrace overlooking the nascent Teign, admire the gardener's graft and take another lunge at a glass from Avignonesi kept on the Cruvinet machine. If cold weather forces a retreat into the dining-rooms, there is a view here too. It is the way of country-house hotels that the atmosphere can be muted when couples outnumber parties, but it is not the fault of the service, described as 'the model balance of correct and polite but light and easy'. Nor is it the consequence of Shaun Hill's cooking which is enjoyable enough to provoke spontaneous cries shattering any modest hush. Two features struck people during the last year. The first is the quality of the underpinning: 'The consistent brilliance of the buttermilk or granary bread, the croissants and brioches, the walnut bread, and the scones at tea, the biscuits with early morning tea, the jam, the marmalade, the sausages...is incredible.' The second is Shaun Hill's own style of cooking: 'A rich set of ingredients is complemented by lightness of touch; complex combinations never muffle or confuse individual flavours.' Consider these dishes: scallops in a lentil and coriander sauce, giving a medley of zesty flavours riding over the solid earthy taste of lentils; red mullet with ginger, garlic and tomato; and Gressingham duckling with a Sauternes and thyme sauce, the duck meltingly soft, the skin supported by an almost-mousse of fat, yet still having the lightest layer of crispness, the herb in the sauce giving breath to the underlying sweetness. Then, there has been the corn-fed pigeon with a sweetbread sausage. The carved bird sits on top of root vegetables, with a stock and olive oil sauce; the sausage is packed tight so that the creamy sweetbreads burst out under pressure of the knife. Or, finally, venison noisettes piled, wigwam-style, on pieces of toast which absorb the game juices are complemented by crisp yet fondant foie gras of duck, and a scattering of roots and mushrooms; the sauce is clean yet strong, to counter the rich soft textures made from venison stock and madeira. Although the 'peasant' strand of modern cooking, exemplified by Italian influences, is strong here, it is combined with an easy familiarity with luxuries. A main dish such as the venison comes from the same stove as a spiced pheasant and lentil soup, 'drunk on Dartmoor in the middle of a snowstorm out of a paper cup'. Cheese – two storeys on a trolley – is always good, and desserts should not be forgone, whether you choose the warm rice pudding with caramelised bananas, apple tart with butterscotch sauce, hot rhubarb and ginger compote with a ginger ice-cream or banana and cognac soufflé. Menus are fixed-price, a short choice is supplemented by a no-option speciality meal for the whole table, and at lunch there is a two-choice meal at lower cost. The charity contribution added to the bill has been for the Chagford Recreational Trust this year; objection to the 40 pence levy may be made. The wine list, like the food, shows enthusiasm for Italy. It remains a remarkable collection, deep and broad, that alters each year with new acquaintance. Drink the good stuff: prices appear high at the start, but the dearer the bottle the better the value. The burgundies and the Rhônes appear to be from less adventurous sources than might be expected but this is amply compensated for by the American reds or the Italians. The Cruvinet gives eight wines by the (large) glass, all outstanding, so it is understandable that many do not progress from that to the full list. Breakfast is worth staying over for.

CHEF: Shaun Hill PROPRIETORS: Kay and Paul Henderson OPEN: all week MEALS: 12.30 to 2, 7 to 9 PRICES: Set L £32 (£41) to £42 (£51), Set D £42 (£51) to £50 (£59). Net prices, card slips closed CARDS: Access, Visa SEATS: 35. Private parties: 18 main room. Car park, 25 places. Children welcome. Smart dress preferred. No cigars/pipes in dining-room. Wheelchair access. Fax: (0647) 432574 ACCOMMODATION: 14 rooms and cottage, all with bath/shower. D,B&B £170 to £275. Children restricted. Pets welcome. Afternoon teas. Garden. Tennis. Fishing. TV. Phone. Scenic. Doors close at midnight (*Which? Hotel Guide*)

CHEDINGTON Dorset map 2

▲ *Chedington Court* 🍷

Chedington DT8 3HY
CORSCOMBE (0935) 891265 COOKING 2
off A356, 4m SE of Crewkerne COST £36

'This really has remained a country-house hotel, unlike so many of its competitors,' comments a visitor on the Chapmans' yellow-stone Victorian mansion, which has beautifully laid-out gardens at the back. Hilary Chapman has been joined in the kitchen by Christopher Ansell-Green; the overall style remains unchanged, although the fixed-price dinner menu now includes a vegetarian choice. The Chapmans care about sources and suppliers and make the point that chefs should be concerned about reducing the inhumane treatment of animals. Their meat and poultry comes mainly from the Real Meat Company and the Pure Meat Company, which deal only in free-range and naturally reared produce. A typical menu from April shows the Chapmans' approach: smoked-duck salad or cream of Jerusalem artichoke soup before casserole of monkfish with tomatoes and oregano; then roast boned quail with chicken and thyme stuffing or spinach and cream cheese pancake flamed in madeira. A trolley of sweets precedes the cheeseboard. The house is spotlessly maintained, but 'the most exceptional aspect is the modest pricing of rooms, food and wines – especially the wines'. An abundance of half-bottles and enthusiasm for good, mid-priced wines makes for economic drinking. There are many fine names on the list, but some editing (minor Rhônes and Beaujolais get a page each) would not be misplaced. Claret vintages are polarised – a few very old bottles, many from 1983 or even more recently, but little from the mid-years. House wine is £6.50. CELLARMAN'S CHOICE: Mercurey, Ch. de Chamirey 1988, £18.50; Brouilly, Ch. des Tours 1989, £13.

CHEFS: Hilary Chapman and Christopher Ansell-Green PROPRIETORS: Philip and Hilary Chapman OPEN: all week, D only MEALS: 7 to 9 PRICES: Set D £26.50 (£30). Card slips closed CARDS: Access, Amex, Visa SEATS: 30. 2 tables outside. Private parties: 32 main room, 40 private room. Car park, 20 places. Vegetarian meals. Children's helpings. Smart dress preferred. No cigars/pipes in dining-room. Wheelchair access (also WC). Music. Fax: (0935) 891442 ACCOMMODATION: 10 rooms, all with bath/shower. B&B £53 to £138. Deposit: £30. Children welcome. Baby facilities. Afternoon teas. Garden. Golf. Snooker. TV. Phone. Scenic. Doors close at midnight. Confirm by 6 (*Which? Hotel Guide*)

CHELTENHAM Gloucestershire map 2

Le Champignon Sauvage 🍷

24–26 Suffolk Road,
Cheltenham GL50 2AQ COOKING 2*
CHELTENHAM (0242) 573449 COST £23–£36

Set in a 'Chelsified' part of Cheltenham, this restaurant makes some pictorial capital out of its name, but do not worry that every dish will be full of fungi. Some are – salmon mousse with leeks and wild mushrooms – but David Everitt-Matthias describes himself as having 'a highly wrought style which judiciously balances a wealth of flavours and a multiplicity of ingredients. This is not pared-down simplicity but intelligent elaboration.' This needs a broader palette than mere mushrooms. Hence dishes feature like poussin with pistachio, almonds and pine kernels, each with its own sauce; and oysters and mussels with cream and coriander and a lobster ravioli. The mode encounters approval. A mille-feuille of kidneys, pork loin alternating with black pudding and a hot white-chocolate soufflé made one meal that raised no cavil; as did another rather simpler lunch of spinach soup with a float of garlic cream, cod with a tomato butter sauce and ratatouille, the large array of Olivier cheeses, and 'a pretty plateful' of caramel mousse with orange-zested sauce with supporters of blackberries, raspberries and praline. The bread is good. There is appreciation, too, for the service, even if the exact interpretation of 'last orders' helped one party from the music festival not a jot. Fine names are scattered liberally through the wine list – Rolly Gassmann in Alsace, Mongeard-Mugneret in Burgundy and a row of pedigree clarets. Australia and California are treated handsomely. Prices are kept within bounds; many bottles over £25 are matched by careful selection below £15, providing real choice within a limited compass. Half-bottles are thinly spread, but presentation is clear. House wine is £7.50. CELLARMAN'S CHOICE: Auxey-Duresses 1985, Duc de Magenta, £24.50; Fixin 1986, Mongeard-Mugneret, £21.90.

CHEF: David Everitt-Matthias PROPRIETORS: David and Helen Everitt-Matthias OPEN: Mon to Sat, exc Sat L MEALS: 12.30 to 1.30, 7.30 to 9.30 PRICES: Set L £17.50 (£23), Set D £21.50 (£30) CARDS: Access, Amex, Visa SEATS: 34. Private parties: 26 main room. Children welcome. Smart dress preferred. Wheelchair access (1 step; also WC). Music. Air-conditioned

Epicurean **NEW ENTRY**

Cleeveland House, Evesham Road,
Cheltenham GL52 2AH COOKING 3
CHELTENHAM (0242) 222466 COST £30–£82

The bust of Epicurus has moved from Stow-on-the-Wold to this Georgian hotel in Cheltenham, where it is ensconced on the ground floor. Everything else moved too, so a sense of déjà vu may hit as old hands see the upholstery, pictures and colour scheme all over again. It works very well – grey and yellow – in its new vessel, enhanced by good plasterwork. Certain people remark that this Epicurean, mark two, is flashier, perhaps to justify the excessively steep prices. Cheltenham has always been a home for apoplexy; the prices can but exacerbate the complaint. So, too, will the printing of the menu, which must have been conceived by a computer enthusiast with a new piece of software: it's guaranteed to induce astigmatism in five minutes. The menu, following fashion, says very little about the dishes it lists. One reporter likened many of McDonald's dishes to the produce of that other, better-known, McDonald's, not for their taste but for the apparently irrepressible urge to make little piles or sandwiches of everything. Hence 'roast pigeon with truffle, madeira jus' consisted of – taking it from the top – a slice of black truffle, a chicken and mushroom ravioli, two legs of pigeon, two breasts of pigeon, a layer of excellent, crisp-fried grated potato, and at the bottom, a bed of spinach surrounded by a pool of madeira sauce. This dish was first-class, save that the sauce contained undercooked lentils and the pigeon was nearly cooked too long (could this be because the pile takes so long to assemble?). The components tasted of what they were, not as common as it sounds, and held together as one whole. Other dishes, too, have been well-reported, for instance, a salad of sweetbreads sandwiched between three layers of fried grated potato surrounded by three mounds – lamb's lettuce, frisée and rocket – scattered with pine kernels. The sauce seemed to be of wild mushrooms and truffle in a stock base, cleverly mingled with the fine vinaigrette that dressed the leaves. This is complicated cookery that needs further work to make it *individual* cookery, when it may fully justify the prices. There have been comments, since the move, of very slow production – one meal lasting from booked arrival at 9pm to midnight – and of a lost edge to the cooking. This may be just the result of dislocation. Puddings, however, have not shown up well. Service is generally as keen as mustard. The wine list goes in for vertical stocks of claret and high prices. It is certainly classy but there is barely a bottle of anything under £20. The chutzpah of the pricing here invites comparison with Redmond's up the hill (see Cleeve Hill entry). Who will get the greatest renown? Or the greatest business? Perhaps a tasting menu of nine courses at £60 is the way to make a splash, but Mr McDonald must be sure he doesn't miss his footing. House wine is from £15.

CHEF: Patrick McDonald PROPRIETORS: Patrick and Claire McDonald OPEN: Tue to Sun, exc Sun D MEALS: 12.30 to 2.30, 7 to 10.30 PRICES: £45 (£61), Set L £20 (£30) to £55 (£68), Set D £30 (£41) to £55 (£68). Card slips closed CARDS: Access, Amex, Diners, Visa SEATS: 30. Private parties: 18 private room. Vegetarian meals. Children's helpings. Wheelchair access. No music

Mayflower

32–34 Clarence Street,
Cheltenham GL50 3NX COOKING 1
CHELTENHAM (0242) 522426 and 511580 COST £13–£32

A long life, more than 10 years, plus a growing reputation for comfortable surroundings and Cantonese and Szechuan cooking have made the Mayflower appear secure. However, a regular visitor from beyond the Cotswolds was distressed that his earlier reports were belied by liberal use of colouring, sugar and lacklustre ingredients. Variation in standards is a besetting problem but the Mayflower's consistency was once its strong point. The wine list is better than average, as is the food on good days. The wine-tasting notes are general rather than tied to Chinese dishes. House Mommessin is £6.50.

CHEF: H.S. Truong PROPRIETORS: the Kong family OPEN: all week, exc Sun L CLOSED: 25 to 28 Dec MEALS: 12 to 1.45, 5.45 to 10.45 (11.15 Fri and Sat) PRICES: £15 (£27), Set L £7 (£13) to £10 (£16), Set D from £14 (£20) CARDS: Access, Amex, Diners, Visa SEATS: 110. Private parties: 80 main room, 80 private room. Vegetarian meals. Children welcome. Wheelchair access (1 step). Music. Air-conditioned. Fax: (0242) 251667

CHESTER Cheshire map 5

Abbey Green 🍷

1 Rufus Court, Northgate Street,
Chester CH1 2JH COOKING 1*
CHESTER (0244) 313251 COST £13–£25

Abbey Green appears to be a building site, but persevere – the restaurant exists. It has gone through various changes in the past year, and is about to move to an adjacent building while the *Guide* is in the press. This may explain a certain unevenness in reports. None the less, enthusiasm abounds for generally inventive and well-flavoured vegetarian food. It takes in adaptations of oriental recipes as well as more orthodox pancakes and stuffed vegetables. One meal began with sweetcorn and dill soup 'with a spiciness behind the obvious flavours' that made it more interesting, continued with mushroom dumplings with a really strong flavour of mushrooms – never an obvious quality of restaurant mushroom dishes – and a nut pâté en croûte with port and plum sauce ('a combination I would not dare attempt that worked unreservedly,' according to one reporter). Other recommendations include spiced carrot koftas with lentil and orange sauce, a spinach roulade with chestnut, mushroom and leek filling, and the 'Abbey Platter' of several samples, if they do not overwhelm or cancel each other out. Many of the wines are signalled as 'organic'. A very wide geographical spread is offered; selection is as careful as ever and prices generous to a tee. Order with confidence. House wine is £6.50.

CHEF: Kevin Woods PROPRIETORS: Duncan Lochhead, Kevin Woods and Julia Dunning OPEN: Mon to Sat MEALS: 12 to 2.30, 6.30 to 10.15 PRICES: L £8 (£13), D £15 (£21). Card slips closed CARDS: Access, Visa SEATS: 55. 12 tables outside. Private parties: 8 main room, 24 private room. Car park, 20 places. Vegetarian meals. Children's helpings. No-smoking area. Wheelchair access. Music

▲ *Arkle, Chester Grosvenor Hotel* 🍷

Eastgate Street, Chester CH1 1LT — COOKING 4
CHESTER (0244) 324024 — COST £26–£60

Traffic engineers have made penetrating the envelope of Chester's old centre as frustrating as the medieval fortifications once made the infiltration of rampaging Welshmen. Park soon, and walk. The Grosvenor sits handsomely on one of the principal thoroughfares. Through the door and left is the Brasserie, a cheaper and quite stylish restaurant that never lives up to its looks, if reports are to be believed; straight on for the Arkle and the Library bar that acts as an alcoholic (and musical) antechamber. The ceilings are low, but the decorative urges are old-fashioned posh – lots of panelling and pillars. The nightwatchman of management who guards the entrance will insist on correct dress – for the bar as well as the restaurant. This may please the formally minded until exceptions (for reasons of grandeur, or fame, who knows?) are spotted lurking in corners. The insistence then becomes irksome. The Arkle, however, proves itself a thoroughly good restaurant: excellent service and fine cooking, as intelligent and aware as any in the region and inventive too. Reports confirm a willingness to deal with robust flavours – hare that was really gamey; a controlled enjoyment of complexity, as seen in fine 'cumulative' desserts like a trio of lemon – sorbet, hot pancakes and a délice – or of passion-fruit – ice-cream, sorbet and light warm soufflé; and a good appreciation of combinations like pheasant with apples and cloves, and quail with black pudding, pistachio and couscous. The menu is quite long, with a nightly set dinner in addition. If it has a fault, it may be the overloading of first courses with rich and luxurious ingredients. There are good supporters, such as the amuse-gueule, the trolley of bread ('We tried five sorts, all very fresh. The banana was our favourite,' ran one report), and the well-kept cheeses from Olivier, as well as good British truckles, including, for one reader, 'the best Cheshire I have ever eaten'. It is regrettable that the menu itself is written in French peppered with error. Arkle has proved not only a thoroughbred but a long-runner too. The intimidating wine list sets the scene with 40-odd champagnes, only to be followed by a page of white burgundies, with the modest Sauvignon de St-Bris at £17.50 one of the cheapest offerings. Clarets come in sets – the longest, Léoville-Barton, is eight vintages – and red burgundies are all from illustrious growers. The Rhône and Alsace receive relatively light treatment, while Spain is surprisingly long. For the rest of the world, quality is maintained, if limited in choice. Half-bottles there are, but £14 for the Sancerre pushes credibility. House wines are from £9.50. CELLARMAN'S CHOICE: Fixin Blanc 1986, Geoffroy, £29.50; Aloxe-Corton premier cru, Clos les Maréchaudes 1985, £34.

All details are as accurate as possible at the time of going to press, but chefs and owners often change, and it is wise to check by telephone before making a special journey. Many readers have been disappointed when set-price bargain meals are no longer available. Ask when booking.

CHEFS: Paul Reed and Simon Radley PROPRIETORS: Grosvenor Estate Holdings OPEN: Mon to Sat, exc Mon L CLOSED: Bank hols, 25 Dec to 1 Jan MEALS: 12 to 2.30, 7 to 10.30 PRICES: £38 (£50), Set L £16.50 (£26) to £20 (£30), Set D £37 (£48) CARDS: Access, Amex, Diners, Visa SEATS: 40. Private parties: 10 main room. Car park. Children's helpings. Jacket and tie. No cigars/pipes in dining-room, no smoking during meals. Wheelchair access (also WC). Music. Air-conditioned. Fax: (0244) 313068 ACCOMMODATION: 86 rooms, all with bath/shower. Rooms for disabled. Lift. B&B £123.50 to £192. Deposit: 1 night. Children welcome. Afternoon teas. Sauna. Golf. Air-conditioned. TV. Phone. Scenic

---

CHICHESTER West Sussex map 3

Thompsons **NEW ENTRY**

30A Southgate, Chichester PO19 1DR COOKING 1
CHICHESTER (0243) 528832 COST £21–£34

Chichester is often ill-served by restaurants, leaving theatre-goers hungry or in a hurry to drive too far for a decent table. Thompsons has lately been receiving comment as the best spot in town, the more so since new owners took over at the beginning of 1991 in this first-floor, pink Georgian dining-room with a very small street frontage. The worry might be that if Chichester does not keep it full, the long lunch and dinner menus will lose the bloom of freshness. First samplings are not without optimism, indicating good presentation and generous quantities. There is, however, a penchant for too many rich butter sauces, and the chicken stuffed with sweetbreads and truffles seemed to need an acid cut to its sauce to make it digestible. Seasonal menus reflect some nice ideas in the mainstream of fashion: snail and artichoke terrine; sweetbreads with an apricot coulis; gigot of lamb with lentils; or red gurnard with herbs and garlic. Desserts continue the ambition and there is a choice of four coffees at the end. Let's hope Chichester gives encouragement. Astute buying provides a concise and carefully balanced wine list; prices are fair throughout and good growers abound. House wines are £8.50.

CHEFS/PROPRIETORS: Elly and Jonas Tester OPEN: Mon to Sat, exc Mon L CLOSED: first 2 weeks Jan MEALS: 12.30 to 2, 7.30 to 11 PRICES: L £14 (£21), D £20 (£28) CARDS: Access, Visa SEATS: 45. Private parties: 60 main room. Vegetarian meals. Children's helpings. Music

---

CHILGROVE West Sussex map 3

White Horse Inn

Chilgrove PO18 9HX COOKING 1
EAST MARDEN (024 359) 219 COST £23–£36

This place is picture-book stuff: nestling in wooded slopes, wistaria-clad, with log fires, beams and an awful lot of old wine hither and yon. The White Horse, an inn since 1765, is a wine cellar with a restaurant. That some parity is allowed may be deduced from the joining of chef Neil Rusbridger in partnership with the Phillipses. Meals are set-price, lunch shorter and simpler than dinner, and they can be satisfactory as in mussel soup with saffron, a mildly curried mushroom pancake, good traditional partridge (though this could have been basted more regularly) and a recited list of sweet things, including very acceptable ice-creams. There are also bar meals, with some enjoyment of slow-cooking as in braised oxtail or silverside. Moments there are when nothing works quite as intended, and the staff come in for some criticism; but minor failings may be absorbed by a draught from Barry Phillips' remarkable wine list. If length alone wins awards then this list is the victor; its quality cannot be faulted and it scores high on value for money. Enthusiasm for the best is more than commendable, but when this becomes obsession and is thrown, uncontrolled and unedited, at the customer, then perhaps there should be a pause for thought. A bottle award it must be, but with a warning for the impatient, impecunious or poor-sighted to proceed no further than house wines, a commendable and fairly priced range from £7.95. CELLARMAN'S CHOICE: Savennières, Clos du Papillon 1989, Baumard, £16.50; St Emilion, Ch. Plaisance 1985, £10.95.

CHEF: Neil Rusbridger PROPRIETORS: Dorothea and Barry Phillips and Neil Rusbridger OPEN: Tue to Sat CLOSED: 3 weeks Feb, 1 week Oct MEALS: 12 to 2, 7 to 9.30 (10.30 during Chichester theatre season) PRICES: Set L £16 (£23), Set D £21 (£29) to £22.50 (£30). Service 10%. Card slips closed CARDS: Access, Carte Blanche, Diners, Visa SEATS: 65. Private parties: 30 main room, 12 and 30 private rooms. Car park, 100 places. Vegetarian meals. Children's helpings. No cigars/pipes until all diners are on coffee. Wheelchair access (also WC). Music. Air-conditioned. Fax: (024 359) 301

CHINNOR Oxfordshire map 2

Sir Charles Napier Inn

Sprigg's Alley, nr Chinnor OX9 4BX COOKING 1
RADNAGE (0494) 483011 COST £25–£41

Take the Sprigg's Alley lane off the Bledlow Ridge out of Chinnor, leaving bleak gravel pits and suburban country residences behind, and come to rest on a plateau above the Chiltern scarp to enjoy a former pub offering enterprising food, champagne on draught, informal surroundings and a garden full of assorted fowl and, sometimes, livestock. It is a great spot for a summer lunch with a walk to finish. There has often been a strong taste of exoticism in the cooking here, although most dishes mentioned this year have laid greater stress on meats – venison, wild goose, goose liver (not foie gras), cockerel, home-reared boar and home-smoked poultry. Exoticism, anyway, has been domesticated in the Britain of the '90s so there is not so much arrest to dishes like chicken with coriander, cardamom and yoghurt, and greater cause for comment may be cassoulet or braised knuckle of lamb with caper sauce: sure signs of new-wave slow cookery. Although the theory of the operation is not in question (even if the price is more firmly Home Counties than some can bear), the practice comes in for brickbats. Most concern the consequences of too much business: slow or slapdash service, food with lacks occasioned by a stretched kitchen. But people like the inn's informality, even if one found the contrast between suited clients and the denim shorts of the wine waitress too piquant for comfort. Coffee remains poor and the busy meals can be very slow, giving pause for thought about the service charge. The intelligently balanced, not over-long and enthusiastically put together wine list treats the rest of the world as evenly as it treats Europe. Growers and properties are exemplary – Juillot in Burgundy, Lehmann in Barossa, Champet's Côte Rôtie and well-aged Chianti Riserva from Badia. Clarets are finely chosen and Vouvrays a special enthusiasm. House wine is £7.75. CELLARMAN'S CHOICE: Margaret River, Chardonnay 1984, Leeuwin Estate, £26.75; Hawkes Bay, Cabernet-Merlot 1989, Vidals, £15.75.

CHEF: Batiste Tolu PROPRIETORS: the Griffiths family OPEN: Tue to Sun, exc Sun D MEALS: 12 to 2 (3 Sun), 7.30 to 10 (10.30 Fri and Sat) PRICES: £25 (£34), Set L £13.50 (£25), Set D £15.50 (£27). Service 12.5%. Card slips closed CARDS: Access, Visa SEATS: 65. 10 tables outside. Private parties: 45 main room, 25 and 45 private rooms. Car park, 60 places. Vegetarian meals. Children's helpings L. No children under 7 D. No cigars/pipes in dining-room. Wheelchair access. Music. Air-conditioned

CIRENCESTER Gloucestershire map 2

Tatyans

27 Castle Street, Cirencester GL7 1QD COOKING 1
CIRENCESTER (0285) 653529 COST £11–£30

Reporters rate this light, airy Chinese restaurant a cut above the provincial average. The main attraction is an all-purpose 60-dish menu that takes in satays, Singapore noodles and Hunan specialities as well as more familiar Pekinese and Szechuan items such as hot-and-sour soup, crispy aromatic duck and kung-po prawns. A healthy crop of recommended dishes has included mixed hot hors d'oeuvre, Hunan pork, crispy shredded beef with chilli, sizzling scallops with ginger and spring onion, and chicken with lemon sauce. Set lunches are excellent value. Service is attentive. Another plus is the short but well-chosen wine list. House wine is £7.50. As we went to press the owners were planning a new menu and wine list.

CHEFS: Y. Liang and T.S. Wong PROPRIETORS: Lookhot Ltd OPEN: all week, exc Sun L MEALS: 12 to 2, 6 to 10.30 PRICES: £14 (£24), Set L £6 (£11) to £10 (£15), Set D £14 (£21) to £18 (£25). Card slips closed CARDS: Access, Amex, Diners, Visa SEATS: 60. Private parties: 60 main room. Children welcome. Wheelchair access (1 step). No music

CLAYGATE Surrey map 3

Les Alouettes

7 High Street, Claygate KT10 0JW COOKING 3
ESHER (0372) 464882 COST £29–£46

Les Alouettes sits bang on a road junction in the centre of Claygate, a village ever wishing to declare UDI from Esher. (It is wisest to park next to the British Legion next door.) Well-furnished in pinks and greys, with a small mezzanine area to one side, the restaurant can be on the dark side, so the window end may be preferred. Michel Perraud cooks a resolutely haute cuisine menu. His background is the Roux brothers' Waterside Inn at Bray (see entry) and he shares in the Anglo-European culinary mainstream. The results can be successful; do not think they can ever be cheap. Glowing reports have been had of an aubergine mousse on a deep pink tomato butter sauce; langoustine and mango salad; smoked salmon with avocado and mushrooms, which may sound boring but was lifted by deft touches in the dressing; chicken accurately and simply done with spring vegetables; and salmon with coriander, basil, tomato and a fine olive oil vinaigrette. Lightness lifts the style, even if other dishes, such as scallops and langoustines, have come with too rich and too copious a butter sauce. Capacity to deal with humble as well as luxury ingredients comes through in a winter dish of oxtail with root vegetables. Professionalism in the kitchen, which normally produces a sound meal (if you are in tune with the principles of this style), is not always matched by that in the dining-room. People have felt patronised and not well looked after ('too many chiefs, and not enough Indians,' wrote one reporter). The cheese trolley and the desserts, among which crème brûlée, tarte Tatin and a terrine of sorbets stand out, are universally approved. The predominantly French wine list is well chosen, but with scarcely a bottle below £15 (house wine is £9) it offers no scope for economy. Over-enthusiastic pouring by the sommelier has irritated, as has the custom of removing the bottle to a side table.

CHEF: Michel Perraud PROPRIETOR: Steve Christou OPEN: Mon to Sat, exc Sat L CLOSED: 12 to 28 Aug MEALS: 12.15 to 2, 7 to 9.30 (10 Fri and Sat) PRICES: Set L £21 (£29) to £27 (£35), Set D £26 (£34) to £33 (£38). Service 12.5%. Card slips closed CARDS: Access, Amex, Diners, Visa SEATS: 75. Private parties: 85 main room. Children's helpings. Smart dress preferred. Wheelchair access (3 steps). Music. Air-conditioned. Fax: (0372) 468337

Le Petit Pierrot

4 The Parade, Claygate KT10 0NU — COOKING 2
ESHER (0372) 465105 — COST £20–£32

The Brichots' popular neighbourhood restaurant near the station finds favour with readers. Chef Jean-Pierre cultivates his French roots while catering for English palates. It is a formula that pays dividends. One couple's recommendations cover most of the menu: onion soup with port wine, terrine of duck and chicken with celeriac salad, roast duckling glazed with honey and toasted almonds, paupiette of crab and sole in asparagus sauce, duo of sorbets with exotic fruits, and tarte au citron. Others have liked the navarin of lamb with winter vegetables, and scallops with leeks, ginger and saffron sauce. Vegetables are varied and simply cooked. Annie Brichot is an attentive hostess, and Jean-Pierre often rounds off the evening with a tour of the tables. A short French wine list has house vin de pays at £7.95.

CHEF: Jean-Pierre Brichot PROPRIETORS: Jean-Pierre and Annie Brichot OPEN: Mon to Sat, exc Sat L MEALS: 12.15 to 2.30, 7.15 to 10.30 PRICES: Set L £14 (£20) to £17 (£23), Set D £19 (£27) CARDS: Access, Amex, Diners, Visa SEATS: 30. No children under 9. Smart dress preferred. Wheelchair access. Music. Air-conditioned

'The food itself was good but hardly very exceptional or exciting. I also thought the portions rather mean, and I am a person who does not like to leave a restaurant feeling as though I should be put on wheels and rolled home.' On eating in London

CLEEVE HILL Gloucestershire map 2

▲ *Redmond's*

Cleeve Hill, Cheltenham GL52 3PR COOKING 3*
CHELTENHAM (0242) 672017 COST £21–£43

High on Cleeve Hill, with a fine panorama across the lights on the plain to the hills beyond, Redmond's is good to visit night and day. The house itself is no scene-stealer but light, air and freshness have been brought to the interior by sympathetic modern furnishing and handsome pictures, and simple bedrooms (those with a view are best) are useful adjuncts to a distinguished restaurant. Some readers notice a slight chilliness in winter months, or sitting in the first room nearest the door when looking at menus. Redmond Hayward cooks a short menu of between three (lunch) and five (dinner) choices, always of fair value and especially so at lunch. Almost every dish has flavour contributors giving accent to the harmony: salmon with lemon and ginger sauce, breast of guinea-fowl with vanilla and orange sauce, red mullet with fennel and squid-ink sauce. This is in the full mainstream of neo-classical cooking; the accents are unexpected and there is an avoidance of that mellow euphony of classic haute cuisine, as well as of cream and dairy fats in much of the saucing. The same modernism has always been shown in desserts, too; for instance, an early use of spices in ice-creams. Meals have also been nicely balanced this year by a complimentary preliminary course – for instance, a spinach and salmon terrine or chicken with mushroom mousse, obviating the need for hot canapés with drinks, which are now offered with olives instead. Successes this year have included a leek and Gruyère tart with hazelnut dressing on the accompanying salad, a mille-feuille (rather like a poppadum, said one reader) of spinach and chicken and chicken liver (nearly overbalanced by liverishness), calf's liver with bacon sauce, terrine of ratatouille and Gressingham duck with sage. At the same time, there have been a number of mishits recorded, hence the adjustment of the rating. There has been a vein of suggestion that flavours have not been sufficiently developed, sometimes with reference to the combinations of strength and balance in a single dish, others in terms of absolute taste – a lemon tart only faintly citric, for example. There have also been some practical failures, be they in timing of service or in kitchen technique. The wine list continues to be one of the more intelligently succinct, fairly priced and exciting collections available. 'Buying wine in a restaurant ought not to be an expensive lottery,' writes Mr Hayward; and he is true to his word. House wine is £8.

CHEF: Redmond Hayward PROPRIETORS: Redmond and Pippa Hayward OPEN: all week, exc L Mon and Sat, and Sun D CLOSED: first week Jan MEALS: 12.30 to 2, 7.15 to 10 PRICES: Set L £16.50 (£21) to £18.50 (£23), Set D £30 (£34) to £32 (£36). Net prices, card slips closed CARDS: Access, Visa SEATS: 36. Private parties: 24 main room, 12 private room. Car park, 16 places. Children's helpings on request. No smoking in dining-room. No music ACCOMMODATION: 5 rooms, all with bath/shower. B&B £48 to £75. Garden. TV. Phone. Scenic. Doors close at midnight

See inside front cover for an explanation of the 1 to 5 rating system recognising cooking standards.

CLITHEROE Lancashire map 5

Auctioneer

New Market Street, Clitheroe BB7 2JW COOKING 2
CLITHEROE (0200) 27153 COST £16–£28

Clitheroe, famous as the place that signed the death warrant of the poll tax, can offer its visitors more than just political debate. Henk Van Heumen, in his quasi-bistro overlooking the cattle market, produces varied à la carte lunches and fixed-price four-course dinners at reasonable prices. Indeed, lunch is a bargain. A regular warns, however, that on the dinner menu 'there are an increasing number of very heavy supplements on both first and main courses'. Fish is well handled. A Good Friday lunch enjoyed after a drive through the Trough of Bowland offered a 'feast of fish': a symphony of seafood and a rainbow of sole, salmon and turbot were both distinguished by the fact that you could 'taste each fish and notice the different textures'; a 'gutsy' provençal fish soup preceded paupiettes of sole and salmon, Dutch apple pie and a raspberry crème brûlée to finish. Others have reported a pan-fried fillet of halibut served with grapes, banana and toasted almond flakes ('an outlandish combination which worked'), whereas a suprême of chicken stuffed with banana had the chicken taste losing to the over-powering fruit. First courses, including a hearty cream of lentil soup with bacon and a terrine of chicken livers that did not shirk the strong flavour of offal but balanced it with a fruity Cumberland sauce, have been praised. Vegetables are less interesting and service can be gauche despite the ministrations of the estimable Frances Van Heumen. Theme evenings celebrate French regional food and wine. The wine list is modestly priced with a decent selection of half-bottles. House French is £8.75. There is no connection between this restaurant and the Auctioneer in Preston.

CHEF: Henk Van Heumen PROPRIETORS: Henk and Frances Van Heumen OPEN: Tue to Sun MEALS: 12 to 1.30, 7 to 9.30 PRICES: midweek L £9 (£16), Set L £10.25 (£16), Set D £16.50 (£23). Minimum £5.75 CARDS: Access, Visa SEATS: 44. Private parties: 24 private room. Vegetarian meals. Children's helpings L. Smart dress preferred. Music

Brown's Bistro NEW ENTRY

10 York Street, Clitheroe BB7 2DL COOKING 1
CLITHEROE (0200) 26928 COST £29

Members of the Brown family share the duties in this modest restaurant spread over three floors. Check tablecloths, candles, bare pine floors and an abundance of wine bottles help create the bistro atmosphere. Menus and wines are listed on blackboards, and dishes change daily according to the produce available. Fish from Manchester market shows up well in dishes such as tiger prawns in garlic butter, scallops au gratin, and fillet of monkfish with lobster sauce. Otherwise, there might be chicken livers madeira; roast duckling with home-made sage and onion stuffing and a decent orange sauce; and fillet of lamb with blackcurrant sauce. Vegetables are generously supplied, but can be overcooked. Sweets are the likes of syrup sponge with custard and coffee and ginger mousse. The young staff are well-trained, friendly and efficient. The list of around a hundred reasonably priced wines centres on France, though Italy figures strongly too. House Burgundy is £6.

CHEFS: David and Ian Brown PROPRIETORS: David and Carole Brown OPEN: Mon to Sat, exc Sat L MEALS: 12 to 1.45, 7 to 10 PRICES: £18 (£24) CARDS: Access, Visa SEATS: 68. Private parties: 30 main room. Vegetarian meals. Children's helpings. Wheelchair access (2 steps; also WC). Music. Air-conditioned

CLUN Shropshire map 4

▲ *Old Post Office*

9 The Square, Clun SY7 8JA COOKING 2*
CLUN (058 84) 687 COST £21–£36

On one side there is a square, or broadening of the street, on the other a view from the conservatory windows of roofs, hills, stone and grass. People enjoy visiting the Old Post Office: the Arbuthnots make them welcome, they serve good breakfasts (croissants and home-made bread), to set you up for a tramp on Offa's Dyke, and enjoyable dinners. Baby leek terrine with a hazelnut sauce; scallops in a pastry basket with a dill sauce; fettucine of vegetables and mushrooms with sorrel sauce; quail stuffed with truffled pâté; veal with shallots and garlic and a wine sauce as well as a parsley purée; great English cheeses, all carefully described; 'luscious, squidgy' chocolate and plum gâteau; coffee and home-made florentines: all of these please, as does the cottagey feel to the old shop premises contrasted with the newer extension at the back. Richard Arbuthnot, having once mixed it in the wider world of restaurants, is not willing to sink into a backwater. His style is modern enough: aubergine, tomato and sheeps' cheese in layers with a basil sauce or roasted yellow pepper soup with Parmesan are dishes from Kensington High Street rather than the wilds of Powys over the border. His execution, which in the past has not always lived up to the conception of the dish in question, does seem to have steadied in this last year. Good Whittard teas feature as well as coffee. Arranging the wine list in order of price rather than by region results in juxtapositions that may nudge the cautious into unfamiliar territory. The opulent Cabernet Sauvignon from Rongopai in New Zealand is sandwiched by Ch. La Tour de By 1983, a reliable Haut Médoc, and a fragrant St-Aubin 1987, all within a pound of each other. Selection of wines is intelligent, with an eye for quality as well as value. Fine growers, a wide range and good half-bottles, along with clear presentation and fair prices, have contributed to the bottle award. House wines are from £7. CELLARMAN'S CHOICE: Fronsac, Ch. Rouet 1983, £13.75; Gaillac, Ch. Lastours 1987, £10.75.

CHEF: Richard Arbuthnot PROPRIETORS: Anne and Richard Arbuthnot OPEN: Wed to Sun, D only (Thur to Sun L by arrangement) CLOSED: 1 week after May and Aug bank hol, 24 Dec to 3 Jan, 22 Jan to 14 Mar MEALS: 12.30 to 1.30, 7.15 to 9.30 PRICES: L £12 (£21), D £22 (£30) CARDS: Access, Visa SEATS: 30. 2 tables outside. Private parties: 25 main room. Vegetarian meals. Children welcome. No cigars/pipes in dining-room. Music ACCOMMODATION: 2 rooms. B&B £21 to £42. Children welcome. Baby facilities. Scenic. Doors close at midnight. Confirm by 6 (*Which? Hotel Guide*)

COCKERMOUTH Cumbria map 7

Quince and Medlar

13 Castlegate, Cockermouth CA13 9EU COOKING 2
COCKERMOUTH (0900) 823579 COST £20

In a tall period house close by the castle is this vegetarian restaurant capable of distinguished cookery, and self-sufficient, save for the drinks and butter. Colin Le Voi draws from the full palette of kitchen technique for first courses that involve soufflés (smoked Westmorland cheese), mousses (dariole of fennel and orange) and fresh pasta (aubergine and pumpkin-seed ravioli). A certain weight, from pulses or grains, is more evident in the main courses: crisp sunflower-seed bread basket filled with courgettes and beansprouts, with sesame and soy sauce; aduki bean and artichoke casserole; and lentil and potato galette with cabbage and juniper and a red pepper sauce. Tastes are defined and separate though one reporter felt that perhaps more emphasis on *sauce* would assist digestion of main courses. Desserts give a chance for gross-out: hot bread-and-butter pudding, hot date and walnut sponge – bliss. Three dozen wines, modestly priced, give a good range of style and provenance. Much decent drinking can be had well below £12 and there are a few half-bottles. House French is £5.80.

CHEF: Colin Le Voi PROPRIETORS: Louisa and Colin Le Voi OPEN: Tue to Sun, D only
CLOSED: 3 weeks Feb MEALS: 7 to 9.30 PRICES: £12 (£17). Card slips closed
CARDS: Access, Visa SEATS: 26. Private parties: 14 main room. Vegetarian meals. Children restricted. Smart dress preferred. No smoking. Music

COGGESHALL Essex map 3

Baumann's Brasserie

4–6 Stoneham Street, Coggeshall CO6 1TT COOKING 2
COGGESHALL (0376) 561453 COST £16–£40

There is an Essex man who says this is 'one of the best cheap restaurants I know', and those who take the business lunch would concur about cheap and often agree about the quality too. The Brasserie is a restaurant really, though the sense of happy informality in the decoration (place-settings are not so informal) may be inspired by the given name. The *carte*, supplemented by a fixed-price table d'hôte morning and evening, reflects '80s fashion – so far avoiding *nouvelle paysannerie*, mother's pride and new-wave Italian – in dishes such as warm salad of smoked goose with a hazelnut dressing, filo tart of smoked haddock and mussels with a leek sauce, a vol-au-vent of lambs' sweetbreads with a caramelised orange sauce, excellent vegetables, appreciated sweet waffles and a lemon and lime cheesecake. There is an impression that the place (decoratively) develops, that the cooking has trimmed itself to fit its bill more exactly and the restaurant is a positive pleasure to be in. There is a well-balanced, short wine list. House wines are £7.75.

CHEFS: Mark Baumann and Doug Wright PROPRIETORS: Baumann's Brasserie Ltd
OPEN: Tue to Sun, exc Sat L and Sun D MEALS: 12.30 to 2 (2.30 Sun), 7.30 to 10
PRICES: £19 (£27), Set L £9.95 (£16), Set D £17.50 (£24) to £25 (£33). Card slips closed
CARDS: Access, Amex, Diners, Visa SEATS: 75. Private parties: 75 main room. Children's helpings. Music

---

COLCHESTER Essex map 3

Warehouse Brasserie

12 Chapel Street North,
Colchester CO2 7AT COOKING 1
COLCHESTER (0206) 765656 COST £20

This popular venue not far from the ABC cinema continues to pack them in. The style is flexible, the food eclectic, the value excellent. Order a couple of starters, a light main course or a full meal. A fixed monthly menu is supplemented by an enterprising choice of daily specials. Starters such as duck rillettes with pickles, or red pepper mousse with orange and chicory salad, might precede wild rabbit croquettes with sorrel sauce, chargrilled herrings with gooseberry sauce, or leg of veal with mustard and sour cream. There is always plenty for vegetarians, including home-made pasta. Reporters have been pleased with fish terrine, aubergine nut roast and the old-fashioned puddings. Service is generally pleasant. A short, affordable wine list has house French at £6.50.

CHEFS: Gerry Ford, Anthony Brooks and Stuart Motts PROPRIETORS: Gerry and Jane Ford OPEN: Mon to Sat MEALS: 12 to 2, 7 to 10 PRICES: £11 (£17) CARDS: Access, Visa SEATS: 75. Private parties: 20 main room. Vegetarian meals. Children's helpings. Wheelchair access (1 step). Air-conditioned. No music

---

COLERNE Wiltshire map 2

▲ *Lucknam Park*

Colerne SN14 8AZ COOKING 3
CORSHAM (0225) 742777 COST £30–£55

The house is a gallimaufry of post-Renaissance architectural styles all in honeyed stone, with flat lawns stretching towards the RAF station at Colerne. The main public rooms run across the principal façade. The dining-room, with repro eighteenth-century pictures, is the least satisfactory of these. The cooking, however, has come in for much praise. Michael Womersley offers an ambitious menu in as up-to-date a style as can be: thin escalopes of salmon just cooked and lying in an emulsion of oil, tomato and coriander; curried lobster bisque; wild mushrooms and tagliatelle; confit of spiced duck with pine-kernels. There is no denying the intentions, but the performance does not always match up if meals taken throughout the year are a guide. As the kitchen has picked up prizes, so has the sommelier. Awards from this *Guide* are handed out sparingly. The wine list, albeit resplendent with fine names and old and excellent vintages, is structured and priced to unnerve all but the wealthiest. There is little below £15 and modest, youthful clarets are well over £20.

CHEF: Michael Womersley PROPRIETOR: Christopher Cole OPEN: all week MEALS: 12.30 to 2, 7.30 to 9.30 PRICES: Set L from £19.50 (£30), Set D from £35 (£46). Card slips closed CARDS: Access, Amex, Diners, Visa SEATS: 75. Private parties: 75 main room, 10 to 25 private rooms. Car park, 70 places. Vegetarian meals. Children's helpings. Jacket and tie. No pipes in dining-room. Wheelchair access (also WC). Music. Fax: (0225) 743536
ACCOMMODATION: 42 rooms, all with bath/shower. Rooms for disabled. B&B £95 to £130. Children welcome. Baby facilities. Afternoon teas. Garden. Swimming-pool. Sauna. Tennis. Fishing. Golf. Snooker. TV. Phone. Scenic (*Which? Hotel Guide*)

CONSETT Co Durham map 7

Pavilion

NEW ENTRY

2 Station Road, Consett DH8 5RL COOKING 1
CONSETT (0207) 503388 COST £10–£32

'The standard of cooking would merit inclusion in the *Guide* regardless of location,' writes a local inspector. 'The fact that it is in Consett is a bonus.' The restaurant is in a huge, smart room above the Golden Dragon pub. This is a long way from Newcastle Chinatown, but the kitchen has built a reputation and booking is essential. The westernised Cantonese menu includes a few Pekinese dishes and some interesting chef's specials; unadvertised items, such as outstanding salt and chilli squid, can also be produced on request. The chefs care about freshness, presentation is impressive and the kitchen excels at spot-on deep-frying and vivid complex flavours. Mixed hors d'oeuvre have featured excellent sesame prawn toasts, deep-fried oysters, stuffed crab claws, and salt and pepper prawns speckled with tiny shavings of green chilli. Other recommended dishes have been stir-fried scallops with ginger and spring onion, grilled king prawns with tomato sauce, and baked crab with black-bean sauce. Service is friendly and courteous. Forty reasonably priced wines include house wine at £6.30.

CHEF: Wan Yip PROPRIETORS: the Yip family OPEN: all week D, Thur to Sat L CLOSED: 24 to 25 Dec, 1 Jan MEALS: 12 to 1.30, 6.30 to 10 (10.30 Sat) PRICES: £15 (£27), Set L £5.50 (£10), Set D £12 (£18) to £16.50 (£23) CARDS: Access, Amex, Diners, Visa SEATS: 100. Private parties: 100 main room. Vegetarian meals. Children welcome. Smart dress preferred. Music

CORSE LAWN Gloucestershire map 2

▲ *Corse Lawn House Hotel*

Corse Lawn GL19 4LZ
TIRLEY (045 278) 479 COOKING 3
on B4211, 5m SW of Tewkesbury COST £24–£48

The lawn is a long green to each side of the road. The house – originally Queen Anne with a coach-splash at its front door – has taken various additions in recent years to make quite a splash of brick itself, complete with swimming-pool and tennis court. The shift in emphasis from restaurant to hotel has prompted comments this year that value is not so good: a reflection, perhaps, of fluctuation in performance, rather than of the modest price rises for set meals. A stronger management team, reinforced by the Hines' son Giles, may help. The extensions, though done as an exercise in conservation architecture, mean the dining-room, for instance, is less organically part of a country house than in some comparable places, but Corse Lawn also benefits from the way in which it has a local presence as well as being a peaceful hang-out for the motoring classes. The bar is a lively spot, not country-house at all, and jeans and sweaters have been seen even in the dining-room. The bar menu is a junior version of the full *carte*. The tone of several reports shows that the food continues to be excellent: well-bought materials, well-conceived recipes, moving along established lines. However, it has been vitiated by details that can easily mar the experience: poor temperature control, over-stretched service, a failure of some dishes to deliver the flavour they advertised, and occasionally too small a portion. To balance this, there has been praise for vegetable cookery, especially of spinach, excellent sauces such as white wine and chanterelle with veal, wild mushroom with beef, cranberry with venison (a frequently encountered meat here), and port with pigeon (another regular, though toughness has been a problem). Long-staying guests find the comfort of the rooms impressive and the variety of food very adequate. On the wine list fine growers abound – Sauzet in Burgundy, Guigal and Avril on the Rhône, Capezanna in Tuscany – and half-bottles feature well. But choice of bottles below £12 is very limited and shows no great flair in selection; a choice of several wines by the glass is an option. House wines are £7.90. CELLARMAN'S CHOICE: Julienas 1988, Gobet £16.30; Montagny 1988, Vignerons de Buxy, £22.05.

CHEFS: Baba Hine and Tim Earley PROPRIETORS: Denis, Baba and Giles Hine OPEN: all week MEALS: 12.30 to 2, 7 to 10 PRICES: £27 (£40), Set L £15.95 (£24), Set D £23.50 (£33). Card slips closed CARDS: Access, Amex, Diners, Visa SEATS: 45. 8 tables outside. Private parties: 55 main room, 35 and 24 private rooms. Car park, 50 places. Vegetarian meals. Children's helpings. Wheelchair access (also WC). No music. Fax: (045 278) 840 ACCOMMODATION: 19 rooms, all with bath/shower. Rooms for disabled. B&B £60 to £100. Children welcome. Baby facilities. Pets welcome. Afternoon teas. Garden. Swimming-pool. Tennis. TV. Phone. Scenic. Doors close at midnight. Confirm by 6 (*Which? Hotel Guide*)

COSHAM Hampshire map 2

Barnards

109 High Street, Cosham PO6 3BB COOKING 2
COSHAM (0705) 370226 COST £17–£36

Despite Cosham High Street, not the Sunset Strip of the south coast, one reader is happy to drive a score of miles for David Barnard's sound cooking. Another comments, 'He does cook his heart out: good food, amateur service, modest premises; the best between Worthing and Portsmouth.' The last geographical flourish may be debated, but the message of genuine and often successful effort remains. The 'modest' surroundings are lifted by attention to the details of the table and linen, as well as the kindly ministrations of Mrs Barnard or her helpers. The menu is a monument of French – even bread-and-butter pudding is called 'pouding de pain et beurre'. That apart, it offers a short range of modern classical cooking: twice-baked soufflé; gravlax; omelette Arnold Bennett; duck with port and orange; or chicken with a walnut stuffing and

Stilton sauce. Set-price lunch is very fair value. Praise for the quality of the materials, especially the beef, is unstinted. The enjoyment for many comes from the evident commitment to handicraft – the bread, the ice-creams – as well as to cooking to order for a small audience: witness the apples, calvados, sultanas and spice wrapped in crisp pastry with a vanilla sauce. The wine list is very short and not overpriced. House wines are £7.50.

CHEF: David Frank Barnard PROPRIETORS: Mr and Mrs D.F. Barnard OPEN: Tue to Sat, exc Sat L MEALS: 12 to 2, 7.30 to 10 PRICES: £25 (£30), Set L £12.95 (£17). Net prices, card slips closed CARDS: Access, Visa SEATS: 20. Private parties: 20 main room. Children's helpings. Wheelchair access. No smoking during meals. Music

COVENTRY West Midlands map 5

▲ *Carl's, Trinity House Hotel*

COUNTY RESTAURANT OF THE YEAR

NEW ENTRY

28 Lower Holyhead Road,
Coventry CV1 3AU COOKING 2
COVENTRY (0203) 555654 COST £14–£35

At last, there is a serious restaurant in Coventry. Carl Timms, who made his name at Sloans (see entry) and Le Biarritz in Birmingham, has launched his latest venture in a hotel tucked away at the top of an inauspicious cul-de-sac not far from the city centre. Somewhat at odds with the setting and the cramped bar area, the dining-room tries to create a feeling of low-key luxury, with pale patterned wallpaper, sturdy dark wood chairs and pastel colour schemes. The serious effect is somewhat offset by the Muzak, complete with favourite TV themes. Timms' cooking is classic French by inclination, with a bedrock of fresh fish – the species ranging from hake, plaice and trout to salmon and scallops – and balanced sauces. Early reporters have been impressed by dishes: fillets of plaice in puff pastry, salmon with chervil butter and leeks, medallions of hake with mustard sauce, and monkfish with black peppercorn sauce highlight skilful handling and high-quality ingredients. Other recommendations are for fixtures of Timms' repertoire over the years: hot goats' cheese in flaky pastry, poached chicken with tarragon sauce, and white and dark chocolate parfait. Quibbles are few, although timing and technique occasionally go awry, and the bread ought to be improved. The set menus are excellent value, and there is a mini-menu for vegetarians. A short French wine list would benefit from some half-bottles. House wine is £7.95.

CHEF/PROPRIETOR: Carl Timms OPEN: all week, exc L Sat and Sun MEALS: 12 to 2, 7 to 10 (10.30 Sat) PRICES: £18 (£29), Set L £8.95 (£14), Set D £13.95 (£20). Card slips closed CARDS: Access, Visa SEATS: 30. Private parties: 30 main room. Vegetarian meals. Children's helpings. Smart dress preferred. Wheelchair access (1 step). Music ACCOMMODATION: 9 rooms, 2 with bath/shower. B&B £19 to £42. Garden. TV

The text of entries is based on unsolicited reports sent in by readers, backed up by inspections conducted anonymously. The factual details under the text are from questionnaires the Guide *sends to all restaurants that feature in the book.*

CRANLEIGH Surrey map 3

Restaurant Bonnet

High Street, Cranleigh GU6 8AE COOKING 2
CRANLEIGH (0483) 273889 COST £20–£36

Double yellow lines through Cranleigh can cause nightmares for potential visitors to this small restaurant that provides French cuisine *en plein Surrey*. Round the back, there is a municipal car park. The seasonal menu is cooked by Jean Pierre Bonnet and served by his wife and francophone staff ('They can't come from Surrey, not with this degree of professionalism,' opined one reporter). It offers the choice of house wine, aperitif and coffee included in the dinner price. Pastry seems a favourite: tarte aux pignons and gâteau marjolaine feature among the puddings; rabbit pie appears among main courses that also include stuffed pig's trotter, veal with watercress sauce and duck with wild mushrooms. Lunchtime value is appreciated, and dinner guests feel portions are generous enough in relation to the price. Maybe it is the offer of house wine in the cost of the meal that tilts the short wine list towards bottles at £15 and over. House wine is £8.50.

CHEF: Jean Pierre Bonnet PROPRIETORS: Jean Pierre and Ann Bonnet OPEN: Tue to Sun, exc Sat L and Sun D MEALS: 12 to 2, 7 to 10 PRICES: Set L £12.50 (£20) to £14.50 (£22), Set D £20.50 (£27) to £27 (£30). Card slips closed CARDS: Access, Amex, Visa SEATS: 50. Private parties: 35 main room. Children welcome. Smart dress preferred. No pipes in dining-room. Wheelchair access (1 step). Music

CROYDE Devon map 1

▲ *Whiteleaf at Croyde* 🍷

Croyde EX33 1PN COOKING 2
CROYDE (0271) 890266 COST £28

David and Florence Wallington's guesthouse has seen a welcome change this year; the granting of a restaurant licence means that non-residents can now sample David's cooking. He surprises with the scale and ambition of his work, divided between a standing menu and a daily list of specials. A strong traditional English influence sets the tone with earthy dishes of black pudding with apple, crusted rabbit casserole and steak and kidney pie. But Italian cooking is obviously a love and David adds zest to the menu with poached zampone (Italian sausage), gnocchi with tomato and Gorgonzola sauce, toasted polenta with feta cheese and tomato sauce and Venetian-style liver and onions, without losing balance. Soups, of which three are offered every night, are a strong point. Bread is home-made. Some find five courses heavy but three- and four-course menus are now offered. The wine list has a group of 1979 clarets, and fine growers in the Rhône. Rolly Gassmann Alsaces and enthusiasm for Italy give further encouragement. Mark-ups are reasonable. House wine is £7.50. CELLARMAN'S CHOICE: Barolo Riserva 1974, Borgogno, £24.50; St Joseph, Clos de l'Arbalestrier 1985, Florentin, £13.50.

CHEF: David Wallington PROPRIETORS: David and Florence Wallington OPEN: all week, D only MEALS: 7.30 to 8.30 PRICES: Set D £13.75 (£18) to £19.50 (£23). Minimum £13.75. Card slips closed CARDS: Access, Amex, Visa SEATS: 16. Car park, 10 places. Children's helpings. Smart dress preferred ACCOMMODATION: 5 rooms, all with bath/ shower. B&B £29 to £48. Deposit: £25. Children welcome. Baby facilities. Pets welcome. Garden. TV. Phone. Scenic. Doors close at midnight. Confirm by 7 (*Which? Hotel Guide*)

CROYDON Surrey map 3

34 Surrey Street

34 Surrey Street, Croydon CR0 1RJ COOKING 1
081-681 3316 and 686 0585 COST £18–£29

Exotic fresh fish done transatlantic style is the main business in Harry Coelho's and Randall Bertao's stylish restaurant complete with conservatory bar and live music. A note on the menu says 'availability of all seafood is subject to weather, season and fishing luck', but at least 10 species appear each day, from red snapper and barracuda to swordfish and monkfish. Such daily specials bolster a colourful, exotic menu that takes in deep-fried prawns with hoisin sauce, tagliatelle with smoked salmon, beef teriyaki and California-style chicken with avocado and lemon sauce. Chargrilling is a feature; dishes come with decent salads or fresh vegetables. There is New England seafood chowder to start, and pecan pie to finish. The transatlantic theme extends to the wine list, which has some drinkable Californians as well as bottles from France and Australia. House Bergerac is £6.60.

CHEFS: Steve Hughes, Skip Murray, Wayne Seaton and Robert Hughes PROPRIETORS: Harry Coelho and Randall Bertao OPEN: all week, exc Sat L and Sun D CLOSED: most bank hols, 25 Dec MEALS: 12 to 2.45, 7 to 10.45 (12.30 to 5.30 Sun) PRICES: £17 (£24), Set L £12.95 (£18). Service 12% for parties of 5 or more. Card slips closed when service added CARDS: Access, Amex, Diners, Visa SEATS: 80. Private parties: 80 main room, 40 and 50 private rooms. Vegetarian meals. Children's helpings. Wheelchair access (also WC). Music

CRUDWELL Wiltshire map 2

▲ *Crudwell Court*

Crudwell SN16 9EP COOKING 1
CRUDWELL (066 67) 355 and 7194 COST £26–£38

Crudwell Court has a pleasant, warm atmosphere. Wicker chairs and a pale green carpet give the dining-room a garden feel, enhanced by views of well-kept gardens. There has been guarded approval for the cooking. An inspection meal produced a good warm terrine of salmon and sole, fresh and light, surrounded by a moat of good buttery sauce, but breast of duck with cassis and blackcurrant sauce was unfortunately overcooked, even though the sauce was fruity and sharp. French lemon tart was 'stiff and tasteless'. Substantial English puddings, such as sticky toffee and bread-and-butter, are better executed. Other reporters have noted good soft herring roes in wine and cream, mushroom soup and rack of lamb glazed with honey, but have been disappointed by calf's liver in a madeira sauce ('not quite as good quality liver as I'd hoped for'). Incidentals are uneven: home-baked bread is excellent, butter good, but amuse-gueules and petits fours have been poor. The wine list offers a fair spread, a reasonable selection of halves, and is not excessively priced. House wine is £8.50.

CHEF: Chris Amor PROPRIETORS: Brian and Susan Howe OPEN: all week, exc Sat L MEALS: 12.30 to 1.45, 7.30 to 9.30 PRICES: Set L and D £17.50 (£26) to £22.95 (£32) CARDS: Access, Amex, Diners, Visa SEATS: 80. 6 tables outside. Private parties: 50 main room, 30 private room. Car park, 40 places. Children's helpings with prior notice. Smart dress preferred. Wheelchair access (also WC). No music. Fax: (066 67) 7853 ACCOMMODATION: 15 rooms, all with bath/shower. B&B £50 to £100. Deposit: £50. Children welcome. Baby facilities. Pets welcome. Afternoon teas. Garden. Swimming-pool. TV. Phone. Scenic. Doors close at midnight (*Which? Hotel Guide*)

CUCKFIELD West Sussex map 3

▲ *Jeremy's at the King's Head*

South Street, Cuckfield RH17 5VY COOKING 3
HAYWARDS HEATH (0444) 440386 COST £26–£31

The two rooms in a pub, operated by Jeremy Ashpool as a franchise, now have carpet, although the furniture and those who wait at table retain the same mixture of this and that which somehow determines the character and easy charm of the place. Jeremy is a fine cook, enthusiastic for strong flavour (often from herbs) and robust, inventive dishes such as these, eaten on one cold spring night: a salad of skate with hot fried herring roes; noodles with red peppers and fennel; duck with a pancake parcel of stir-fried vegetables, madeira sauce and apple; lamb with a lentil crust and a tarragon sauce. Execution is full of panache, although vegetables have not always been so luminescent, and a pear and almond tart that sat too long in the refrigerator paled by comparison with a full-flavoured prune and Armagnac ice-cream in which finesse of sweetening allowed other tastes to speak of themselves. Trimmings too – for example, the lentil tartlet served with the spring lamb – do not always have the consideration which might emanate from a larger kitchen brigade. The ambition seems worthwhile if the press of custom is anything to go by, especially since that can have its down-side in lengthy waits between courses. Jeremy might be thought a rough diamond, but the sparkle will seduce most comers. The wine list is the weak link; it lacks the conviction of the cooking although prices are fair.

CHEF: Jeremy Ashpool PROPRIETOR: Peter Tolhurst OPEN: Tue to Fri CLOSED: bank hols MEALS: 12.30 to 2, 7.30 to 10 PRICES: £17 (£26), Set D £17.95 (£26) CARDS: Access, Amex, Visa SEATS: 33. Private parties: 20 main room. Children welcome. Wheelchair access. No music ACCOMMODATION: 9 rooms, all with bath/shower. B&B £42 to £55. Children welcome. Baby facilities. Pets welcome. Garden. TV. Confirm by 6

County round-ups listing additional restaurants that may be worth a visit are at the back of the Guide, *after the Irish section. Reports on round-up entries are welcome.*

▲ *Ockenden Manor*

Ockenden Lane, Cuckfield RH17 5LD — COOKING 1
HAYWARDS HEATH (0444) 416111 — COST £23–£44

The manor grows from right to left – a reflection of its development through the sixteenth and seventeenth centuries – culminating in a tall stone block with mullioned windows looking across to Cuckfield church spire. Philip Guest cooks unpretentiously, even if aspects of service are in the 'grand hotel' style, and the dining-room is enjoyed for an evening out. There is a quietening of flavour in dishes reported: not so much fruit amongst the meat, and pleasant combinations as in smoked salmon with a lemon sauce and mint, duck with leeks and truffle, veal with ceps, and salmon with shallot sauce. The staff are welcoming, the surroundings comforting. Prices on the wine list are high, leaving little choice below £15. Quality and range are not in question, so it is a pity such high premiums discourage adventure.

CHEF: Philip Guest PROPRIETORS: Mr and Mrs H.N.A. Goodman OPEN: all week MEALS: 12.30 to 2, 7.30 to 9.15 PRICES: Set L £16.95 (£23) to £17.50 (£24), Set D £22.50 (£30) to £29.50 (£37). Card slips closed CARDS: Access, Amex, Diners, Visa SEATS: 50. Private parties: 45 main room, 75 private room. Car park, 40 places. Vegetarian meals. Children's helpings. Jacket and tie. No smoking in dining-room. Wheelchair access (also WC). Fax: (0444) 415549 ACCOMMODATION: 22 rooms, all with bath/shower. B&B £65 to £145. Deposit: £25 per person. Children welcome. Baby facilities. Afternoon teas. Garden. TV. Phone. Scenic. Doors close at 11.30. Confirm by 6 (*Which? Hotel Guide*)

DALLINGTON East Sussex — map 3

▲ *Little Byres*

Christmas Farm, Battle Road,
Dallington TN21 9LE — COOKING 3
BRIGHTLING (042 482) 230 — COST £35

The byres are the bedrooms and the barn – all brick and beams and crackling warm from a wood-burner – is the restaurant. Chris and Evelyn Davis do most of the work themselves, which gives the place its special character. One or two readers have detected battle fatigue which comes from having no staff and here and there a busy night takes the Davises by surprise. But enthusiasm remains intact: a passion for cooking simply, directly, with assertive flavours; a wish to improve and develop. Menus are set-price with a short flight of perhaps four choices at each course. Buying is on a short rein so choice is sometimes limited for late-comers. Exemplar dishes include a grilled rabbit sausage with thyme and garlic, served with an onion marmalade; loin of lamb in pastry with kidneys and field mushrooms; and caramelised apple tart – a disc of fine puff pastry covered edge to edge with slivers of apple. The push for flavour sometimes totters into stridency: 'an overdose of fennel seed made for not too successful an effort,' complained one reader. But successes there are too: the lamb is often mentioned, as is duck with wild mushrooms on a wild mushroom sauce ('generous, well-cooked (a little short of pink) and tasty duck immaculately presented'). There is a plethora of vegetables, usually appreciated, especially the oddities like onion squash hollowed out with its flesh puréed inside. Desserts (waits may be long) also have resounding echoes in reports: 'Roasted pears and cinnamon ice-cream went together perfectly; the pears seemed to have been macerated for a long time and roasted very slowly.' Vegetarians get a lot of effort put into their requirements if prior notice is given. There are good truffles at the end, tasty malty bread, though sometimes less good coffee. Music is classical and loud. The wine list is short and fairly priced. The Davises plan to move from their dependence on France and shorten still further their core list, but bolster it with more fine wines in small parcels. Advice usually needs to be sought from the kitchen if you are in doubt about the bottles.

CHEFS/PROPRIETORS: Chris and Evelyn Davis OPEN: Mon to Sat, D only MEALS: 7.30 to 9 PRICES: Set D £22.50 (£29). Card slips closed CARDS: Access, Visa SEATS: 35. Private parties: 40 main room, 20 private room. Car park, 18 places. Children's helpings. Wheelchair access (also WC). Music ACCOMMODATION: 5 rooms, all with shower. Rooms for disabled. B&B £30 to £40. Deposit: £25. Children welcome. Pets welcome. TV. Scenic. Confirm 2 days ahead (*Which? Hotel Guide*)

DARLINGTON Co Durham map 7

Victor's

84 Victoria Road, Darlington DL1 5JW COOKING 1
DARLINGTON (0325) 480818 COST £12–£29

Situated on the edge of the town centre, on the road that runs to the station, with a gridiron of pavement terraces off it, Victor's is not plush, but 'devoted to food'. Peter Robinson is a charming host and keeps the tables going almost single-handedly. The cooking suits this style: familiar, not over-ambitious, with an affordable fixed-price menu, which ensures a local following. Lambs' kidneys with a claret and grain mustard sauce, roulade of turkey with mushrooms and a basil sauce, and roast mallard with braised peas have all elicited praise. Starters can be less successful, for instance a dry and uninteresting chicken and mushroom terrine and a cream of pumpkin soup innocent of pumpkin flavour. Desserts such as honey and brandy ice-cream served in a home-made brandy basket and lemon mousse win general approval. Home-made bread, biscuits for cheese and petits fours show the kitchen's attention to small details. 'It fits the bill as a good-value local restaurant,' says a reader. The wine list is short with house wine at £7.

CHEFS: Peter and Jayne Robinson and Trudie Doig PROPRIETORS: Peter and Jayne Robinson OPEN: Tue to Sat MEALS: 12 to 2, 7 to 10.30 PRICES: Set L £7.50 (£12), Set D £18 (£24). Card slips closed CARDS: Access, Amex, Diners, Visa SEATS: 30. Private parties: 30 main room. Vegetarian meals. Children's helpings. Wheelchair access (2 steps). Music

The 1993 Guide *will be published before Christmas 1992. Reports on meals are most welcome at any time of the year, but are extremely valuable in the spring. Send them to* The Good Food Guide, *FREEPOST, 2 Marylebone Road, London NW1 1YN. No stamp is needed when posting in the UK.*

DARTMOUTH Devon map 1

▲ *Billy Budd's*

7 Foss Street, Dartmouth TQ6 9DW COOKING 1
DARTMOUTH (0803) 834842 COST £11–£31

'Happy' is a word that crops up regularly in reports about Gilly White's cheery bistro. The fun and good humour of the place is infectious. Keith Belt's light lunches are warmly recommended, as is the fixed-price evening menu. Regular fixtures continue to impress: twice-baked cheese soufflés topped with Parmesan, roast duck with apricot sauce, rack of lamb and sticky toffee pudding have lost none of their vigour. Fish dishes vary from day to day, depending on the local catch, and the freshness shows in seafood crêpes, fillet of hake baked with cheese and asparagus, and very classy turban of sole wrapped around a duxelle of mushrooms, with an embellishment of four whole scallops. Vegetables are generous and 'sympathetically cooked'. Good strong coffee comes with petits fours. Occasionally the kitchen has a bad night, resulting in quibbles like 'dry' salmon, 'stale' syllabub and 'nasty' bread-and-butter pudding. The short wine list is fair-priced. House French is £8.25.

CHEF: Keith Belt PROPRIETORS: Gilly White and Keith Belt OPEN: Tue to Sat CLOSED: Feb MEALS: 12 to 2, 7.30 to 10 PRICES: L £5 (£11), Set D £16.75 (£24) to £18.75 (£26). Minimum £16.75 D. Card slips closed CARDS: Access, Visa SEATS: 35. Private parties: 20 main room. Vegetarian meals with prior notice. Children's helpings. No children under 9 D. Smart dress preferred. Wheelchair access (1 step). Music ACCOMMODATION: 2 rooms (twins). B&B £29. Deposit: 10%. Children welcome. TV. Doors close at midnight. Confirm 4 weeks ahead

Carved Angel

2 South Embankment, Dartmouth TQ6 9BH COOKING 4
DARTMOUTH (0803) 832465 COST £27–£54

'How does Joyce Molyneux continue to do this in this small kitchen that ticks along like well-oiled clockwork?' enquired one customer who had enjoyed a memorable Sunday lunch. 'The choice, on all courses, proved a problem...the fairly ordinary-sounding avocado and melon salad with elderflower dressing actually looked quite wonderful as we saw it being prepared at a nearby table.' 'The food is very restrained,' commented another; 'There really is a great integrity about the ingredients, however, and about the place itself.' Indeed, the dedication to seasonal produce, most of it grown or reared locally, is greatly appreciated by regulars. 'I am sorry to say that we all had the same main course as it is only possible to have this dish at this time of year when the very tender, delicate, pink young rhubarb is still in season,' writes an enthusiast for the Dart salmon with rhubarb. The juxtaposition of restaurant and open-plan kitchen gives an interesting insight into the ordered working of the restaurant, with orders taken and produced with little commotion and then 'when the main courses are finished Joyce Molyneux draws a large bucket of hot water and scrubs the main preparation surface down with great gusto by herself'. Occasionally the harbour-front view can give an unwelcome glimpse of the boorish habits of the young British tourist, for the uncurtained large windows 'let us admire the river – but also lets the flotsam admire us'. Yet the close proximity to fishing boats does have its advantages: 'A plate of marinated fish was superb, with a variety of clean, separate flavours, all of which emphasised the freshness of the fish. The brill and salmon were particularly memorable and tasted of fresh sea,' ran one comment. Inspiration for dishes is drawn from many sources. The base is the French provincial cooking of Elizabeth David, yet the Molyneux style has evolved over the years by absorbing ideas from around the world, without compromising the quintessential Englishness which is her signature note. Recent reports have singled out for praise parsley noodles with Jarlsberg cheese, lemon and sour cream, and a chargrilled fillet steak with red wine, shallots and bone marrow. Desserts follow the same assured style, synthesising eclectic influences in a careful but not unadventurous balance of flavours, as in brown sugar meringues with pears and a red wine chocolate sauce, or iced lemon soufflé with raspberry purée which, according to one reporter, 'shocks you into summer' with its intensity of flavour. Prices may seem initially high for the unstuffy Devon coastal ambience, but there are no hidden extras (other than wine) and few regret the expense. Spaciousness in the dining-room is not matched in the closely typed layout of the wine list, which makes it difficult to tie price with wine. There is much decent drinking below £15, but the main thrust of the list is well over £20, with pedigree names, top-notch properties and correct vintages. The range of half-bottles is good. This is an intelligently balanced selection. House wine is £12. CELLARMAN'S CHOICE: Sauvignon Blanc 1988, Shaw & Smith, £18.50; St Joseph, Clos de l'Arbalestrier 1985, Florentin, £17.50.

CHEFS: Joyce Molyneux and Nick Coiley PROPRIETORS: Joyce Molyneux and Meriel Boydon OPEN: Tue to Sun, exc Sun D MEALS: 12.30 to 1.45, 7.30 to 9.30 PRICES: £34 (£40), Set L £21 (£27) to £25 (£31), Set D £34 (£40) to £39.50 (£45). Net prices SEATS: 30. Private parties: 30 main room, 15 private room. Children's helpings. Wheelchair access. No music

DEDHAM Essex map 3

▲ *Fountain House* NEW ENTRY

Dedham Hall, Brook Street,
Dedham CO7 6AD COOKING 1
COLCHESTER (0206) 323027 COST £20–£26

Fountain House has moved from East Bergholt to Dedham Hall. The setting – pastoral, fine natural gardens – is a tourist's dream. The furniture in some of the lounges may be 'saggy', as well as in short supply, but the house is a cracker. The cooking has not changed its spots. Simple to a fault, and even then not without error, it is *Good Housekeeping*'s Mrs Dinner-Party stuff, the desserts the best feature, with a general need for attention to materials and techniques, though price is fair. Yet the wine list is excuse enough for coming here. None of the enthusiasm (nor, it seems, the bottles) has been lost in the move. Classic French regions are allowed no more space than Alsace, Italy and the USA. From Cappezzana Carmignano to Cloudy Bay Sauvignon at £15 and Côte Rôtie, Les Jumelles, 1978 for £25, selection is rigorous but prices remain very fair throughout. There are many half-bottles. A place for happy vinous adventure.

House wine is £7.50. CELLARMAN'S CHOICE: Pinot Grigio 1989, Lageder, £11; Ch. Puygueraud 1986, £10.

CHEF: Wendy Anne Sarton PROPRIETOR: James F. Sarton OPEN: Tue to Sun, exc Sat L and Sun D CLOSED: 2 weeks end Feb MEALS: 12.30 to 2, 7.30 to 10 PRICES: Set L £14.50 (£20), Set D £16.50 (£22). Card slips closed CARDS: Access, Visa SEATS: 32. 3 tables outside. Private parties: 16 main room. Car park, 12 places. Vegetarian meals. Children's helpings. No cigars/pipes in dining-room. Wheelchair access. Music ACCOMMODATION: 12 rooms, 10 with bath/shower. B&B £38 to £57. Deposit: 20%. Children welcome. Garden. Scenic. Doors close at midnight. Confirm 1 day ahead

▲ *Le Talbooth*

COUNTY RESTAURANT OF THE YEAR

Gun Hill, Dedham CO7 6HP COOKING 4
COLCHESTER (0206) 323150 COST £28–£50

'My first glass of sherry was too warm; the second had an ice cube dropped in to cool it and was therefore diluted; the third had had time to chill in the refrigerator where the bottle should have been in the first place.' Thus do even efficient professional places commit solecisms. Professional Le Talbooth certainly should be; it has been in the same ownership for nigh on 40 years, aiming at the same up-market style of cooking and service. The framework, within which operate scores of foreign waiters, is quintessential eastern England: half-timbering, quiet flowing river, trees and verdure. The cooking is copy-book modern British: lamb comes with lentils; red mullet with a red wine sauce; foie gras with fried celeriac; pigeon with wild mushrooms, shallots and bacon, or perhaps with beansprouts, foie gras, lentil ravioli and roast shallots. At dinner, you pay for the setting: heavy curtains, good napery, unnecessary cut crystal glassware, vegetables delivered in individual copper pans, lots of service. At lunch, this seems a bargain, and the cooking is not noticeably simpler. Pleasure has often been noted, for example in a seafood chowder ('more like a fish stew with cream curry sauce'); a salad of duck breast; mussels in a 'copious and rich' sabayon; pheasant ('perhaps too young') with red and white cabbage and an excellent potato galette; turbot with ginger butter; bavarois of blackcurrant ('surprisingly bland'); and a very fine apricot parfait. Opinion seems at one that Steven Blake has moved on to a higher and better plane in the last year. One reader who had not visited Dedham for a decade was struck by the techniques and presentation: 'Skate and crab salad had as its base crabmeat at room temperature, the skate wing surmounted it and was warm from its cooking, a sherry dressing gave it force and piquancy. Sautéed sweetbreads took their balance from endives, though the sauce was slightly too reduced. The outstanding dish was lobster with a ravioli filled with lobster mousse on a shellfish butter sauce.' This last might have been three ways to kill a cat, but they melded into one. Desserts at this meal, particularly an apricot baba with candied fruits, were well up to standard. A useful 'personal selection' of wines below £14 heads the well-structured wine list. Thereafter a roll-call of classics at high but not unreasonable prices takes over. Petits châteaux creep in as do a few generic burgundies offering decent mid-priced drinking. Rhônes and Alsaces provide much happy hunting and prices on Loires seem to have eased a little this year. There are relatively few half-bottles, but nevertheless a good range. A very well structured list. House wine is £9.50. CELLARMAN'S CHOICE: Pinot Blanc 1989, St Helena, £15.50; Pauillac, Reserve de la Comtesse, 1985, £23.25.

CHEF: Steven Blake PROPRIETOR: Gerald M.W. Milsom OPEN: all week MEALS: 12.30 to 2, 7 to 9 (9.30 Sat) PRICES: £31 (£42), Set L £18.50 (£28), Set D £25 (£33). Service 10%. Card slips closed CARDS: Access, Visa SEATS: 70. Private parties: 70 main room; 24 private room. Car park, 70 places. Children welcome. Smart dress preferred. No cigars/pipes in dining-room. No music. Fax: (0206) 322752 ACCOMMODATION: 10 rooms, all with bath/shower. B&B £82.50 to £137.50. Rooms for disabled. Children welcome. Garden. TV. Phone. Scenic

DELPH Greater Manchester map 5

Honfleur, Cross Keys Inn NEW ENTRY

Huddersfield Road, Delph OL3 5RQ COOKING 1
SADDLEWORTH (0457) 874241 COST £15–£34

'Close your eyes and move back 20 years to the time when the three couples making up the Champeau family in England ran the Normandie at Birtle,' comments an inspector. 'They achieved a Michelin rosette for their very French cooking and scandalised Lancastrians by refusing to serve overcooked steak. Eventually they sold up and one couple moved to run the Cross Keys pub in Delph. Finally Jean-Pierre Champeau joined them and the Honfleur restaurant has been opened in an extension to the pub.' The menu is rooted in the pre-Bocuse period of rich Normandy cooking, heavy with cream and butter. 'Paquette' of seafood is wrapped in a lettuce leaf, and seafood vol-au-vent gets an Armoricaine sauce, although on one occasion the pastry was poor. Main courses are highlighted by good raw materials: duck breast with cream and cider sauce; noisettes of pink lamb with sauce choron. Vegetables in one report suffered from the age-old faults of overcooking and excessive butter. Apple tart may look inelegant, but it tastes good. Despite some quibbles, this is a very likeable place, refreshingly unfashionable, and plush without being pretentious. Good snacks are served in the bar. The wine list is short, mainly French and fairly priced. House wine is £8.10 a litre

CHEF: Jean-Pierre Champeau PROPRIETORS: Scottish & Newcastle Ltd OPEN: Tue to Sun MEALS: 12 to 2, 7.30 to 9.30 PRICES: £20 (£28), Set Sun L £9.50 (£15) CARDS: Access, Amex, Diners, Visa SEATS: 55. Private parties: 65 main room, 20 private room. Car park, 50 places. Vegetarian meals

DENT Cumbria map 7

▲ *Stone Close*

Main Street, Dent LA10 SQL COOKING 2
DENT (058 75) 231 COST £11–£17

A stone farmhouse, in a stone village with cobbled streets, now occupied by an all-day café that also serves as a B&B and evening restaurant (prior notice essential). The café card runs through filled granary rolls, home-made cakes, three-bean salad, home-roasted ham salad or decent gammon, while the evening menu is set-price with very limited choice: mushroom pâté, avocado dip and crudités, tomato and vegetable soup, spiced pork chops, stuffed aubergine, chocolate and fudge sponge or eighteenth-century apple and lemon tart were the possibilities on one deep-winter's day. Value is excellent, materials are genuine and cooking is often exact. Some people have found themselves cramped if both rooms are not used; others have said, 'Why is this so special?' The answer has to lie in the price, the kind attention, the modesty and the lack of short cuts. This is not haute cuisine, but good honest cookery. The wine list is on a blackboard and, true to form, shows interest and adventure in hunting out less expensive bottles that will none the less please. House wine is £6.60 a litre.

CHEFS: Patricia Barber and Hazel Haygarth PROPRIETORS: Graham Hudson and Patricia Barber OPEN: all week (prior notice for D) CLOSED: Jan and first 2 weeks Feb. Tea-shop closed mid-week Nov to mid-Mar MEALS: 10.30 to 5.15, 7.30 PRICES: £6 (£11), Set D £9.50 (£14), Snacks from £1.50 SEATS: 40. Private parties: 25 main room, 20 private room. Vegetarian meals. Children's helpings. No smoking during meals. Wheelchair access. Music. One sitting D ACCOMMODATION: 3 rooms. B&B £14.50 to £25. Deposit: £10. Children welcome. Baby facilities. Pets welcome. Afternoon teas. Scenic (*Which? Hotel Guide*)

DISS Norfolk map 6

▲ *Salisbury House*

84 Victoria Road, Diss IP22 3JG — COOKING 1
DISS (0379) 644738 — COST £25–£41

'The tranquillity of a Victorian country house in the heart of town,' murmurs the brochure though the town is no high-life Mecca, rather the paradigm of an English market town (according to Sir John Betjeman). The house, well provided with garden, devotes a series of English country-style rooms to eating and drinking. Barry Davies cooks in a manner that does not conflict with this, described by one reader as 'charming'. The menu, about half a dozen choices offered in each course, runs a familiar gamut of slices of smoked duck and orange on a nest of salad leaves; a country pâté with apricot and ginger sauce; best end of lamb in pastry with mint béarnaise; chicken stuffed with sweetbreads and pearl barley; and desserts like two-tone chocolate mousse, and prune and armagnac tart. What marks this place is the Davies' enthusiasm, communicated to their young staff. The wines are multifarious: more than 200 bins, almost exclusively French, with some good things (note the generous provision of halves) among some occasionally risky vintages – though, as Mr Davies comments, they can yield value. House French is £8.

CHEF: Barry Davies PROPRIETORS: Barry and Sue Davies OPEN: Tue to Sat, D only (Tue to Fri L by arrangement only) CLOSED: 1 week Christmas, 2 weeks July MEALS: 12.15 to 1.45, 7.30 to 9.15 PRICES: £19 (£27), Set L and D £17.50 (£25) to £25.75 (£34) CARDS: Access, Visa SEATS: 38. 3 tables outside. Private parties: 20 main room, 14 private room. Car park, 10 places. Children's helpings. No smoking in dining-room. Wheelchair access (1 step). Music ACCOMMODATION: 3 rooms, all with bath/shower. B&B £37 to £64. Children welcome. Baby facilities. Garden. TV. Scenic. Doors close at 11.30. Confirm by 9pm (*Which? Hotel Guide*)

DORCHESTER Dorset map 2

Mock Turtle **NEW ENTRY**

34 High West Street,
Dorchester DT1 1UP COOKING 1
DORCHESTER (0305) 264011 COST £15–£29

A deceptively small, narrow façade leads to a warren of small open-plan rooms. The décor is as much of a mélange as the descriptions of the dishes, and the owners clearly have ideas about restaurant food being very different from everyday fodder. Thus, there is frequently a fussy feel to dishes: a chicken breast is stuffed with crab and served with a tomato and saffron cream sauce, a chocolate cake is called choc-concoction gâteau. But the value is excellent and, above all, the cooking tries hard. Fish is a strength. A reporter enjoyed chargrilled local scallops on a bed of spring cabbage. Duck breast, served pink on a crème de cassis sauce with a blackcurrant tartlet was 'over-sweet and sticky', suffering from heavy-handedness, but was redeemed by a nicely timed, well-flavoured selection of vegetables. Bread is good quality, and service is friendly and hard-working. There are good home-made ice-creams and sorbets, especially banana ice-cream and passion-fruit sorbet. Simpler choices from the *carte* and dishes of the day tend to work best. Given the lack of other good options for local eating, it is hardly surprising that even latecomers may be unable to find a seat. Value extends to the wine list, which gives good geographic and economic spread. House New Zealand is £7.95.

CHEFS: Raymond Hodder and David Curtis PROPRIETORS: Raymond, Alan and Vivien Hodder OPEN: Mon to Sat, exc L Mon and Sat CLOSED: 26 and 27 Dec, 1 to 3 Jan MEALS: 12 to 2.30, 7 to 10.30 PRICES: Set L £8.95 (£15) to £11.95 (£18), Set D £13.95 (£21) to £16.95 (£24) CARDS: Access, Visa SEATS: 56. Private parties: 60 main room. Vegetarian meals. Children welcome. No cigars/pipes in dining-room. Wheelchair access (1 step). Music

DORCHESTER-ON-THAMES Oxfordshire map 2

▲ *George Hotel* 🍷

High Street,
Dorchester-on-Thames OX10 7HH COOKING 1
OXFORD (0865) 340404 COST £20–£42

The hotel sits firmly on the High Street, extending welcome to travellers much as it did when first built. The best bit, architecturally, is still the high, timbered dining-rooms where the food served is about as unhistoric as you can get. Traditionalists may stick to the daily menu at a set price, which will save a lot of money. But if mille-feuille of scallops and spinach with a lime butter sauce, or lamb smothered in goats' cheese, wrapped in filo, with tomato and rosemary sauce, is to your taste, they will be passably cooked. Desserts revolve around the ice-cream machine. The wine list is put together by an enthusiast who wishes, through a generous pricing policy, to spread that enthusiasm. Economy is as well catered for as extravagance. House wine is £8. CELLARMAN'S CHOICE: Montagny premier cru 1988, Roy, £17.25; Ch. Fourcas-Hosten 1982, £16.50.

CHEF: Neil Cordner PROPRIETORS: Neville and Griffin Ltd OPEN: all week
MEALS: 12.30 to 2, 7 to 9.45 (9 Sun) PRICES: £26 (£35), Set L £14 (£20), Set D £17 (£23)
CARDS: Access, Amex, Diners, Visa SEATS: 40. Private parties: 30 main room, 20 private room. Car park, 50 places. Vegetarian meals. Children's helpings. Smart dress preferred. Music. Fax: (0865) 341620 ACCOMMODATION: 18 rooms, all with bath/shower. B&B £62 to £76. Children welcome. Pets welcome. Afternoon teas. Garden. TV. Phone. Scenic. Confirm by 4 (*Which? Hotel Guide*)

DORKING Surrey map 3

Partners West Street

COUNTY RESTAURANT OF THE YEAR

NEW ENTRY

2, 3 and 4 West Street,
Dorking RH4 1BL
DORKING (0306) 882826

COOKING 3*
COST £20–£42

Andrew Thomason and Tim McEntire moved their restaurant from Sutton to Dorking, gutting then restoring a Tudor house in some luxury – and, when it comes to the lavatories, super-luxury. The beams and apparatus of Tudor houses have been overlaid by pastel shades of faux-marbre, button-backed banquettes and swagged curtains. Everything gleams. Through the glass, the heavy traffic can be watched as it trundles by. New premises mean new ambitions and the kitchen has risen to them. Pastry has been marked as especially good throughout the meal, and fish cookery, for example in scallop dishes, very exact – though one large, indeed generous, *nage* of a variety of white fish needed more verve to seasoning and saucing. Menus are set-price, but the dinner choice is of at least a half-dozen items in each course. Lunch, and various bargains, are shorter perforce. The style of presentation is modish, without excess, and the cooking has absorbed those lessons from the Mediterranean and California that we have all learned so furiously for the last three or four years, but its heart may lie more happily in the pastures of less assertive classical flavours. Saddle of rabbit with a rabbit liver mousse and guinea-fowl with a foie gras sauce are two examples of the latter, as is salmon, bass and scallops with a light hollandaise 'strong on chives'. Examples of the more modish have been ratatouille soup with mullet, a feuilleté of baby vegetables with a capsicum sauce and sea bass with peppers, aubergines and garlic. When the cooking is on form, it is refined and intelligent, muting over-strong flavours. The occasional danger is too much refinement. Desserts have been rightly praised for their sensible avoidance of too great complexity, yet depth of flavour. 'It would be hard to better this marquise', and 'I shall never venture to make a lemon tart again' have been comments. Wines are adequate if rather conservative in selection, and the list as a whole imparts a rather restrained enthusiasm. The house Entre-Deux-Mers has been criticised for thin acidity. Prices are fair. The old premises in Sutton have been turned into a brasserie: Partners Brasserie, 23 Stonecot Hill, Sutton SM3 9HB, Tel: 081-644 7743. The decoration has been lightened and the room enlarged, yet to call this a brasserie is ambitious. The cooking has yet to settle down, and prices are not very low, but it is a useful local resource that should gain its own momentum.

See the back of the Guide *for an index of restaurants listed.*

CHEFS: Tim McEntire, Paul Ager, Adrian Walton and Shane Whelen PROPRIETORS: Partners Restaurants plc OPEN: Tue to Sun, exc Sat L and Sun D MEALS: 12.30 to 2, 7.30 to 9.30 PRICES: Set L £13.25 (£20) to £19.50 (£26), Set D £16 (£23) to £26.95 (£35). Service 10%. Card slips closed CARDS: Access, Amex, Diners, Visa SEATS: 45. Private parties: 35 main room. Vegetarian meals. Children's helpings (Sun L only). No children under 5. No-smoking area. Wheelchair access (2 steps). No music

DORRINGTON Shropshire map 4

▲ *Country Friends*

Dorrington SY5 7JD
DORRINGTON (074 373) 707 COOKING 3
on A49, 5m S of Shrewsbury COST £22–£32

Dorrington is little more than a hamlet on the A49, and this half-timbered restaurant-with-rooms is very much its focal point. Charles and Pauline Whittaker continue to generate a great deal of interest from readers, who are firmly in favour of their distinctive brand of innovative cookery. This is a busy enterprise, producing everything itself, from breads, pasta and chutneys to the plum wine served as an aperitif. The restaurant *carte* is backed up by a simpler set menu and the style is consistent. Cheese soufflés appear among the starters and as savoury alternatives to the desserts; crab ravioli with curry sabayon may lack the consummate panache of Raymond Blanc, but it is well-balanced and flavoursome. Many dishes have been recommended: sautéed monkfish with pistou; skate in cider sauce with tomato and apple coulis; roast duck with corn syrup sauce and coriander mousse; chicken breast in puff pastry stuffed with courgettes and pine kernels; hot prunes with prune ice-cream; chocolate truffle cake. On most nights, the kitchen is in top gear, and timing and execution are spot-on, but there are occasional hiccups and ill-judged dishes. Vegetables also cause some controversy: although most visitors approve, some find the standard assortment dismally prepared and 'hopelessly out of tune' with the food on the plate. A blackboard menu of starters, snacks and sweets is served in the bar at lunchtime and on the rare occasions when the restaurant is quiet in the evening. At first glance, the wine list looks more substantial than it really is, with each vintage writ large on the page; but there is some good drinking to be had, especially among the clarets. House wines are from £8.35.

CHEFS: Charles Whittaker and Tim Greaves PROPRIETORS: Charles and Pauline Whittaker OPEN: Tue to Sat MEALS: 12 to 2, 7 to 9 (9.30 Sat) PRICES: £19 (£27), Set L and D £16 (£22) CARDS: Access, Visa SEATS: 40. Private parties: 45 main room. Car park, 40 places. Children welcome. Wheelchair access. No music ACCOMMODATION: 3 rooms, 1 with bath/shower. B&B £45. Garden (*Which? Hotel Guide*)

'Service is unattractive, hard-working. The restaurant manager is an elderly badly dressed, friendly man. The three girls serving food wore green dresses topped with frilly white aprons. One had an acne problem, one had a weight problem, one had a broken neck. The staff made Fawlty Towers *look stylish.'* On eating in Wales

DREWSTEIGNTON Devon map 1

▲ *Hunts Tor House*

Drewsteignton EX6 6QW COOKING 2
DREWSTEIGNTON (0647) 21228 COST £24

'Timbale of broccoli with fresh tomato sauce and a vinaigrette, followed by monkfish with a spicy white wine sauce, new potatoes, carrots and thin beans, Normandy apple flan, a platter of four local cheeses then coffee' was the first meal taken by early summer visitors. The next day they were offered smoked halibut as a first course, duck with ginger and soy as a main dish, praline mousse with a passion fruit coulis as a dessert. These are the sorts of things prepared by Sue Harrison in this comfortable moorland guesthouse, from which Castle Drogo is not far distant. There is no choice, but preferences can be readily accommodated as menus are not fixed until the day itself. There is no room for outsiders without prior arrangement, though residents can invite guests. Reports are unanimous about the care taken both inside and outside the kitchen. There are a couple of dozen decent wines, at fair prices, supplemented by Chris Harrison's alcoholic experiments: orange rum shrub, brandy lemon shrub and gin punch this year. House Duboeuf is £7.

CHEF: Sue Harrison PROPRIETORS: Sue and Chris Harrison OPEN: all week, D only (residents only) CLOSED: Nov to mid-Mar MEALS: 7.30 PRICES: Set D £16.50 (£20) SEATS: 8. Private parties: 12 main room, 8 private room. Vegetarian meals. No children under 14. No music. One sitting ACCOMMODATION: 4 rooms, all with bath/shower. D,B&B £45 to £83. Deposit: £20. No children under 14. Pets welcome. Scenic. Doors close at midnight. Confirm by 2

DULVERTON Somerset map 1

▲ *Ashwick House*

Dulverton TA22 9QD
DULVERTON (0398) 23868 COOKING 1
signposted from B3223 N of Dulverton COST £20–£33

The house of red brick, with steep roofs and dormer windows, sits above a lake wild with growth in the summer. From the terrace breakfasters, or quiet pre-dinner drinkers, can take in the peace, Richard Sherwood's Unique Selling Point. Unique too is the menu, a scroll written out for each party, of four courses with a choice of two dishes at each stage. Catering is mainly for residents, but outsiders are welcomed with prior warning. The traditions of English cooking are not forgotten in confections like rhubarb amber or bread-and-butter pudding, but the tide of restaurant culture has lapped these shores with apple and coriander soup, avocado mousse with a herb coulis, and prawns with cucumber, mushrooms and cream in a filo case. The wine list is short, French and from Averys. House wines are from £7.95.

The Guide *is totally independent, accepts no free hospitality, and survives on the proceeds from copies sold each year.*

CHEF/PROPRIETOR: Richard Sherwood OPEN: Tue to Sat, D only and Sun L MEALS: 12.15 to 1.15, 7.15 to 8.30 PRICES: Set L £12.50 (£20), Set D £19.50 (£28) SEATS: 30. 3 tables outside. Private parties: 30 main room. Car park, 30 places. No children under 8. Jacket and tie. No music ACCOMMODATION: 6 rooms, all with bath/shower. B&B £66 to £112. Deposit: £25. No children under 8. No pets. Afternoon teas. Garden. TV. Phone. Scenic. Doors close at 11. Confirm by 5 (*Which? Hotel Guide*)

EAST BOLDON Tyne & Wear map 7

Forsters

COUNTY RESTAURANT OF THE YEAR

NEW ENTRY

2 St Bedes, Station Road,
EAST BOLDON NE36 0LE
091-519 0929

COOKING 3*
COST £34

'If business stays as it is then I would hope to move to something bigger' is the optimistic note of Barry Forster, whose first mainland restaurant this is – he previously made a considerable reputation as chef at Longueville Manor in Jersey (see entry). Forsters is in 'a suburban shopping parade two-thirds of the way from Newcastle to Sunderland', as one London journalist put it, adding 'A peculiar disadvantage'. Barry Forster comes in fact from Newcastle, hence his return, having once worked at Fisherman's Lodge (see entry). The room (there is no messing with an ante-room) is pine-panelled and mildly chintzy. Front-of-house is ably tended by Sue Forster, which gives the whole place that advantageous feel of a family business. The style of cooking enjoys some input from local custom – beef au poivre – as well as reflecting current fashion – red mullet with tapénade and a red wine jus. Prices are praiseworthily fair. An early meal, taken soon after the last *Guide* went to press, included twice-baked Roquefort soufflé, salad of lobster and asparagus, filo pastry pizza with red mullet, salmon with chanterelle butter sauce, and white chocolate ice-cream – a good way of using this material, so sickly when served at room temperature. Later meals have shown that East Boldon is able to tap into national supply lines: Thai prawns, Scotch salmon, fish from Cornwall, fresh raspberries in May, wild mushrooms in abundance. Barry Forster's start has been auspicious: he should continue to do well. Wines do not match the ambition of the cooking, and few bottles rise above the adequate. House French is £7.10.

CHEF: Barry Forster PROPRIETORS: Sue and Barry Forster OPEN: Tue to Sat, D only MEALS: 7 to 10 PRICES: £20 (£28) CARDS: Access, Amex, Diners, Visa SEATS: 28. Private parties: 28 main room. Car park, 8 places. Vegetarian meals with prior notice. Children's helpings. Smart dress preferred. No pipes in dining-room. Music

---

If a restaurant is new to the Guide *this year (did not appear as a main entry in the last edition)* NEW ENTRY *appears opposite its name.*

An asterisk (*) after the 1 to 5 cooking mark at the top of an entry signifies that the Guide *and its readers think that the restaurant is a particularly fine example within its numeric classification.*

EASTBOURNE East Sussex map 3

Byrons

6 Crown Street, Old Town,
Eastbourne BN21 1NX — COOKING 2*
EASTBOURNE (0323) 20171 — COST £28

'Behind Safeway' was the laconic direction given by a helpful correspondent. Simon and Marian Scrutton probably antedate Safeway and certainly their restaurant is no mass-market clone capable of reproduction across the land. There are two small rooms, mildly uncomfortable in parts, though the psychological warmth of the place makes up for that, offering careful cooking that neither surprises by extravagant flashes of random inspiration nor bores by lack of consideration. A summer meal that was prefaced by black olives sprinkled with garlic and some miniature quiches went on to a spinach mousse with Parmesan sauce ('well-balanced, fresh and beautifully presented'), before a main course of free-range chicken stuffed with crab, wrapped in filo, with a hollandaise sauce – also reported earlier with a salmon mousse and béarnaise. Again, judgement and execution were good, and the dishes ably supported by a crisp ratatouille and other vegetables before a fine Bakewell tart. Desserts are quite creamy. The menu does not show signs of radical change – rather it presents variations on a theme. The wine list may be short and not always state the grower, but it has a nicely balanced range for a mere 28 bins. House wine is £7.80.

CHEF: Simon Scrutton PROPRIETORS: Simon and Marian Scrutton OPEN: Mon to Sat, D only (L by arrangement) CLOSED: 1 week Christmas MEALS: 7 to 10.30 PRICES: £18 (£23). Net prices, card slips closed CARDS: Amex, Diners, Visa SEATS: 22. Private parties: 10 main room, 10 private room. Vegetarian meals. Children welcome. No smoking during meals. Music

▲ *Mirabelle, Grand Hotel* — NEW ENTRY

Jevington Gardens,
Eastbourne BN21 4EQ — COOKING 2*
EASTBOURNE (0323) 410771 — COST £21–£50

The Grand, as the name suggests, is a large Victorian sea-front hotel – and the grandest in Eastbourne, if not on quite the same imposing scale as its Brighton equivalent. The Mirabelle restaurant, on the other hand (not the hotel's main restaurant), is coolly ultra modern in pale lemon, cream and grey, reflecting Keith Mitchell's modern style of cooking. Certainly he is inventive, but his *carte* displays a tendency for flavours to be piled on flavours, so that nothing seems to be simply done: a fresh crab bisque is infused with star anise and topped with a cream froth; oysters are lightly cooked in champagne sauce perfumed with lemon grass and served in their shells with salsify; loin of English lamb comes enrobed in chicken mousseline and savoy cabbage with a grain mustard sauce. But the kitchen's technique is up to the task. A recent meal included a main course of quail breasts baked in a butter puff pastry with a wild mushroom duxelle and madeira sauce and another, nearly as good, of braised veal with leeks and red pepper. To follow, poached pear with frangipane and a caramel sabayon was well made, but over-cluttered by a basket of unremarkable saffron ice-cream. There is only a small choice of fish – a shame as a fillet of grey mullet niçoise showed careful handling. The fixed-price dinner and lunch menus (the main course dictates the price paid) offer some simpler dishes and good value. Service is said to be friendly as well as efficient. The wine list is a hotel sort of collection; the house selection runs to six acceptable bottles from £11.50.

CHEFS: Keith Mitchell and Neil Wiggins PROPRIETORS: De Vere Hotels OPEN: Tue to Sat CLOSED: 1 to 15 Jan, 1 to 14 Aug MEALS: 12.30 to 2.30, 7 to 10.30 PRICES: £32 (£42), Set L from £13 (£21) to £16.50 (£24), Set D £19.50 (£28) to £26.50 (£35). Card slips closed CARDS: Access, Amex, Diners, Visa SEATS: 60. Private parties: 50 main room, 170 private room. Car park, 60 places. Vegetarian meals. Children's helpings. Jacket and tie. Wheelchair access. Music. Air-conditioned. Fax: (0323) 412233 ACCOMMODATION: 164 rooms, all with bath/shower. Rooms for disabled. Lift. B&B £90 to £170. Children welcome. Baby facilities. Pets welcome. Afternoon teas. Garden. Swimming-pool. Sauna. Snooker. TV. Phone. Scenic

EAST BUCKLAND Devon map 1

▲ *Lower Pitt*

East Buckland EX32 0TD
FILLEIGH (059 86) 243, changes to
(0598) 760243 in autumn 1991
off A361 at Stags Head, 3m NW of South Molton

COOKING 2
COST £29

The long farmhouse is difficult to find, but visitors can be sent a map in advance. Fourteen years on, a new conservatory dining-room is complete and the original dining area now acts as a comfortable lounge with low chairs. Suzanne and Jerome Lyons still take their cue in part from local producers: loin of pork from Heal Farm is pan-fried with Hancock's cider, sage and apple sauce. Tomatoes and mushrooms come direct from the growers. But flavours often come from further afield. Reporters have liked sautée of fresh prawns and mushrooms in garlic butter, spicy lamb with apricots and fresh coriander served with mint-flavoured yoghurt, and roast guinea-fowl and game casserole. Home-made butterscotch ice-cream steals the show from chocolate and brandy slice and banoffi pie in the dessert department. Jerome Lyons knows his wines and has developed a reasonably priced list bought mainly from Christopher Piper. A dozen house wines for less than £8 are boosted by an extended showing of half-bottles.

CHEF: Suzanne Lyons PROPRIETORS: Jerome and Suzanne Lyons OPEN: Tue to Sat, D only MEALS: 7 to 9 PRICES: £16 (£24). Card slips closed CARDS: Access, Visa SEATS: 34. Private parties: 34 main room, 18 private room. Car park, 25 places. No smoking in dining-room. Music. Fax: (0598) 760243 ACCOMMODATION: 3 rooms, all with bath/shower. B&B £50 to £95. Deposit: 10%. No children under 12. Garden. Scenic. Doors close at 11. Confirm by 6 (*Which? Hotel Guide*)

▲ *This symbol means that accommodation is available.*

EAST GRINSTEAD West Sussex map 3

▲ *Gravetye Manor*

Vowels Lane, East Grinstead RH19 4LJ
SHARPTHORNE (0342) 810567 COOKING 3
off B2110 at West Hoathly sign COST £33–£58

A thousand-acre haven of peace and beauty seems a fair enough description of the gardener William Robinson's creation at Gravetye. The house itself is sixteenth-century; the garden dates from the turn of the century. For the last 30 years, Peter Herbert has polished, furbished and improved on the original. The temptation is always to say that it's worth coming here for that alone, but justice to Mark Raffan's cooking forbids it. By the time the *Guide* is published, he will have moved on to join the Roux group, but with Stephen Morey – sous-chef 1988–90 – taking over, it seems likely that the kitchen will follow similar tracks. For the moment, the restaurant offers many options: a light luncheon; a full *carte*, but with first courses helpfully marked if they would be sufficient as light main dishes; and a set-price meal. Beware the prices, however. They may seem cheap, but VAT must be added: a prehistoric system, and seriously misleading to the unsuspecting or mathematically inept. Choice is generous on the *carte*, a bonus deriving from a busy dining-room. The style is modern country house: tradition is respected, especially in the set meals; luxuries are deployed with fair discretion; combinations are interesting – particularly in fish dishes such as cod on a rösti with a spiced capsicum dressing or sea bass with mushroomy noodles, courgette beignets and a port wine sauce – but at the same time tastes show decent restraint. This restraint may even be a fault, as in a lunch with horseradish sauce tasting more of cream; a pineapple and kirsch sorbet, those flavours difficult to descry, served with melon; and a 'very ordinary' plum crumble with 'the thinnest custard imaginable'. Such failings are not common and the following have all won approval: poached oysters on a bed of lamb's lettuce with an excellent vinaigrette; fricassee of lobster and langoustine; smoked venison with apple and celeriac and a good nutty dressing; a selection of three game – mallard, hare and venison – with a rich, dark red wine sauce; mallard with green lentils; a fine fruit terrine; and the constant three chocolate mousses. The vegetables are sometimes thought inept for delicate food; there are cavils at the dessert stage, and the coffee is on the light side. Service is manifold, as are the deep, comfortable seats that await the diner as he or she moves from room to room through the progress of an evening. This is an enchanting place, with a wine list to match. Five vintages of Bollinger RD stretching back to 1973 indicate the seriousness of the list. Prices are generally high but reflect good quality throughout. Vintages are top, growers pedigree and good ranges from the New World show some adventure. Alsaces are especially fine. There are marvellous magnums and many good halves. House wines from Louis Latour are £18. CELLARMAN'S CHOICE: Pouilly Fumé 1987, Ladoucette, £18; Volnay 1982, Latour, £27.

denotes an outstanding wine cellar; *denotes a good wine list, worth travelling for.*

CHEFS: Stephen Morey and Max Gnoyke PROPRIETORS: Peter Herbert and Leigh Stone-Herbert OPEN: all week CLOSED: 25 Dec D to non-residents MEALS: 12.30 to 1.45, 7.30 to 9.45 (10 Sat) PRICES: £29 (£48), Set L £19 (£33), Set D £22 (£36) SEATS: 50. Private parties: 10 main room, 20 private room. Car park, 30 places. No children under 7. Smart dress preferred. No smoking in dining-room. No music. Fax: (0342) 810080
ACCOMMODATION: 18 rooms, all with bath/shower. B&B £116 to £207. No children under 7. Garden. Fishing. TV. Phone. Scenic. Doors close at midnight (*Which? Hotel Guide*)

EDENBRIDGE Kent map 3

Honours Mill

87 High Street, Edenbridge TN8 5AU COOKING 3
EDENBRIDGE (0732) 866757 COST £25–£43

'There is nothing obviously false here, as in so many restaurants and pubs,' was the comment of one diner impressed by this conversion of a watermill in the centre of Edenbridge. (So genuine is the transformation that tall people should watch for injury from low-flying structural timber when negotiating the first-floor dining-room.) Although the cooking shows some ambition, it does not always have the technical assurance to carry the substantial fixed cost of a meal here – equally high at lunch or dinner unless you elect to eat but two courses – bearing in mind that not so far away, in the capital city, this price might get matchless invention and cookery. Having got beyond the menu, couched unnecessarily in French, readers have reported favourably on dishes as various as a casserole of snails and wild mushrooms (though suffering from over-thickened sauce), a warm salad of goats' cheese and bacon, scallops with saffron sauce, chicken stuffed with lobster with a lobster civet, lobster with spinach and pasta, duck with a slightly curried sauce and roast apples, roast pears with blackcurrant, prune and armagnac ice-cream with prunes soaked in brandy, floating islands and chocolate marquise. Skills are certainly apparent, even in the bread (on some days) and the petits fours, but so, too, are lapses: 'It was rather like Thursday night when you are peering in the fridge and decide to push all the leftovers into one stew,' was one report. Wines are all French and rather unambitious; selection is erratic, so go for a familiar name. Prices do not reflect quality fairly. House French is £9.25.

CHEF: Martin Radmall PROPRIETORS: Neville, Duncan and Giles Goodhew OPEN: Tue to Sun, exc Sat L and Sun D CLOSED: 2 weeks after Christmas, 2 weeks early June MEALS: 12.15 to 2, 7.15 to 10 PRICES: Set L £19.95 (£25) to £31.50 (£36), Set D £31.50 (£36). Net prices CARDS: Access, Visa SEATS: 38. Private parties: 20 main room. Children's helpings (Sun L only). No children under 12. No music

Prices quoted in the Guide *are based on information supplied by restaurateurs. The figure in brackets below an entry is the average for a three-course meal with service, coffee and half a bottle of house wine, as calculated by computer. The prices quoted at the top of an entry represent a range, from the lowest average meal price to the highest; the latter is inflated by 20 per cent to take account of the fact that very few people eat an average meal, and also that prices are likely to rise during the year of the* Guide.

EDGWARE **Greater London** map 3

Wing Ki

29 Burnt Oak Broadway,
Edgware HA8 5LD COOKING 1
081-205 0904 COST £11–£34

Wing Ki is one of the small number of Chinese restaurants with an extensive vegetarian section to its menu. Perhaps that is why, according to one report, it is 'frequently packed with members of the Indian community who know a good thing when they find it'. Wing Ki Yeung and his Irish wife Hannah have ever been responsive to customer demand, even to the extent of cooking for special diets whenever necessary. Crispy lamb in spiced sauce, Singapore noodles, stuffed aubergine with prawns, double-cooked beef and chicken in sea salt are recommended dishes. Chilli and garlic are almost universal components. The wine list is acceptable, short and inexpensive. House wine is £6.95.

CHEF: Wing Ki Yeung PROPRIETORS: Wing Ki and Hannah Yeung OPEN: Tue to Sun MEALS: 12 to 2.30, 6 to 11.30 PRICES: £16 (£28), Set L £6.50 (£11) to £7.50 (£12), Set D £15.50 (£21). Minimum £8 D. Card slips closed CARDS: Access, Visa SEATS: 60. Private parties: 65 main room. Vegetarian meals. Children before 8.45. Smart dress preferred. Music. Air-conditioned

ELY **Cambridgeshire** map 6

Old Fire Engine House 🍷

25 St Mary's Street, Ely CB7 4ER COOKING 1
ELY (0353) 662582 COST £28

One reader calls it a farmhouse. It's in the middle of the Close, so agriculture is fairly distant, but the message – quarry tiles, bare wooden tables, homely and usually happy staff (including one day one who, according to a reporter, 'looked dressed for going to do the garden') and tables outside for fine days – has essential truth. The menu is English, as is, emphatically, the cooking, sometimes with elements of old English (mittoon of pork, syllabub, local freshwater fish or eels) and a happy readiness to indulge in pies and casseroles, such as chicken with ginger and lemon pie or beef with Guinness and port. There have been more reports than in previous years of approximate and unsuccessful results. No one objects to the unpretentious mode of presentation, but one can take exception to lack of flavour, cool soups, tough meat and overly plain boiled veg – *à l'anglaise* with a vengeance. 'So pleasant an atmosphere, but to enjoy for that rather than the food,' was one subdued conclusion. There are no such reservations about the wine list: a model of clarity (even though notes verge on the verbose) and quality. You can order anything from the 70-odd main list with complete confidence; from the Gewurztraminer Bollenberg of Hartmann to Meursault from Jadot, and two top-class Tuscans with some age to them. Prices are modest: Goulet Champagne at £23 and a 1978 Gran Reserva Rioja at only £15. Spirits are good and there is a bin-end list for curiosities and bargains. House wines are £6. CELLARMAN'S CHOICE:

Chardonnay, Marqués de Casa Concha 1987, £8.25; Rioja, Viña Alcorta Reserva 1983, £10.50.

CHEFS: Ann Ford, Michael Jarman and Terri Kindred PROPRIETORS: Ann Ford and Michael Jarman OPEN: all week, exc Sun D CLOSED: 2 weeks from 24 Dec and bank hols MEALS: 12.30 to 2, 7.30 to 9 PRICES: £17 (£23) CARDS: Access, Visa SEATS: 36. 8 tables outside. Private parties: 36 main room, 22 private room. Car park, 8 places. Vegetarian meals with prior notice. Children's helpings. No-smoking area. No music

EMSWORTH Hampshire map 2

Spencers

NEW ENTRY

36 North Street, Emsworth PO10 7DG COOKING 2
EMSWORTH (0243) 372744 COST £28

Denis and Lesley Spencer set up their restaurant in premises formerly occupied by the original proprietors of 36 on the Quay (see entry below). The restaurant is on the upper floor of a cottage, which has odd corners, book-lined alcoves and real gaslights. Denis Spencer aims for consistent food without frills and changes his short fixed-price menu on the first Tuesday of each month. An inspection meal produced many good things: smoked duck breast and wild mushrooms in puff pastry with madeira sauce, 'delicately flavoured' grilled strips of smoked salmon with salad leaves, escalopes of monkfish with green peppercorn sauce, and apple ice-cream in a tulip biscuit with calvados sauce. The only real disappointment was a bland, unmemorable vegetarian dish of mixed green vegetables with tomato sauce. The cooking is essentially French, although there are cosmopolitan touches such as Chinese-style chilli pork. A modest, well-spread wine list is backed up by lesser-known wines of the month. House burgundy is £7.50.

CHEF: Denis Spencer PROPRIETORS: Denis and Lesley Spencer OPEN: Tue to Sat, D only (L by arrangement) CLOSED: 25 and 26 Dec MEALS: 7.30 to 10.30 PRICES: Set D £17 (£23) CARDS: Access, Visa SEATS: 45. Private parties: 24 main room, 10 and 11 private rooms. Vegetarian meals. Children welcome. Smart dress preferred. Music. Air-conditioned

36 on the Quay

The Quay, 47 South Street,
Emsworth PO10 7EG COOKING 2
EMSWORTH (0243) 375592 COST £29–£45

Richard Wicks continues to cook in this heavily curtained, rather ornate restaurant which has been given a little more air by conversion to semi-open plan – though this has raised noise levels to some sensitive ears. It is a full-dress restaurant in other ways: £6.50 for a Kir royale, silver domes covering food, menus in French (and English that may have ravioli 'nesting' in soup) and a properly dressed, if regrettably uninformed, staff. The expensive cooking may often be competent and enjoyable, though the witnesses are not unanimous, citing uncanny similarities of sauces on different dishes and failings in both taste and texture where fine judgement is essential.

'Restaurant' cooking is on show here. Too many first courses are pastes – pâtés, mousses, parfaits and the like – while main courses have some variety of texture, as well as interesting accompaniments -- couscous with peppers, potato with onion confit – even if mixed vegetables come in pastry caselets. Desserts have suffered from an excess of chocolate, though the summer pudding was a good one. The wine list is upper-crust French and expensive. House wines are £11.50.

CHEF: Richard Wicks PROPRIETOR: Raymond Shortland OPEN: Mon to Sat D, Tue to Fri L MEALS: 12 to 2, 7 to 11 PRICES: Set L £13.50 (£29), Set D £26.95 (£38). Card slips closed CARDS: Access, Amex, Visa SEATS: 42. Private parties: 32 main room, 10 private room. Car park, 8 places. Vegetarian meals. Children's helpings. No children under 5. Smart dress preferred. No cigars/pipes in dining-room. Music

EPWORTH Humberside map 5

Epworth Tap

9–11 Market Place,
Epworth DN9 1EU
EPWORTH (0427) 873333

COOKING 2
COST £20–£26

John and Helen Wynne's wine bar is an important place. Everything about it is genuine, and although it has been going for a long time neither of the Wynnes has lost enthusiasm. The Tap's survival may serve as a marker of our own commitment to fair feeding in Great Britain – not forgetting the drinking. 'This is excellent food and wine; the place is remarkable for its cleanliness, and for the courtesy of its staff. One can take people here from all walks of life with confidence that they will be served fresh food, decoratively, and that the vegetables will be crisp, not soggy,' comments one reporter. John Wynne advises of extension to the repertoire, citing salmon and spinach terrine, tagliatelle with home-made pesto, chicken with Pineau des Charentes and wild mushroom sauce, and a chocolate and amaretti terrine as examples. There are wine courses and special events such as a Tuscan Sunday lunch: four courses with exceptionally interesting wines at a knock-down price. Don't be intimidated by the length of the wine list; the absence of top-flight wines combined with a very fair mark-up allows experimentation without extravagance. Selection throughout is impeccable. Burgundy is especially favoured, but Italy and California receive fond and exemplary treatment.

CHEFS: Helen Wynne and Noreen Smith PROPRIETORS: Helen and John Wynne OPEN: Wed to Sat, D only (Sun L sometimes) MEALS: 7.30 to 10 (10.30 Sat) PRICES: £15 (£22), Set Sat D £14 (£20). Card slips closed CARDS: Access, Visa SEATS: 74. Private parties: 50 main room, 24 private room. Vegetarian meals. Children welcome. No-smoking area. Wheelchair access (3 steps). Music

All letters to the Guide *are acknowledged with an update on latest sales, closures, chef changes and so on.*

Cellarman's Choice: a wine recommended by the restaurateur, normally more expensive than house wine.

ERPINGHAM Norfolk map 6

Ark

The Street, Erpingham NR11 7QB COOKING 2
CROMER (0263) 761535 COST £14–£28

Sheila Kidd has firmly established herself over the years in this most rural of retreats. Indeed, so idyllic is the setting, so depopulated the surrounding villages, that one understands the Kidds' concern for lack of mid-week business. Accommodation is planned with mid-week bargain breaks firmly on the agenda. Regulars are consistent in their loyalty and praise for the generosity of the portions, the freshness of the ingredients and especially for Mrs Kidd's vastly assorted menus which draw on Elizabeth David for inspiration, brought up to date with some modern thinking. Thus, beef daube with walnuts rubs shoulders with a Moroccan lamb tagine. Satisfied readers have claimed they have never had a meal repeated in seven years, whilst recent newcomers to the Ark could not restrain their enthusiasm for the excellent quality of the accompanying vegetables. Marmalade ice-cream with walnut sauce, gooseberry cream tart or an old-English ratafia trifle represent a strong choice of puddings. A relaxed, unpretentious atmosphere complements the cooking. A succinct wine list has good bottles and is good value. House wine is £7.35.

CHEF: Sheila Kidd PROPRIETORS: Mike and Sheila Kidd OPEN: Wed to Fri and Sun L, Tue to Sat D MEALS: 12.30 to 2, 7 to 9.30 (10.30 Sat) PRICES: L £12 (£19), D £16 (£23), Set Sun L £10 (£14) SEATS: 32. Private parties: 38 main room. Car park, 15 places. Vegetarian meals. Children welcome. No smoking. Wheelchair access (also WC). No music

EVERSHOT Dorset map 2

▲ *Summer Lodge*

COUNTY RESTAURANT OF THE YEAR

Evershot DT2 0JR COOKING 2*
EVERSHOT (0935) 83424 COST £22–£43

A good deal of work has gone on over the year: rooms upgraded, kitchen enlarged, a bigger dining-room (in blue) with the incomparable flower arrangements that make the Lodge summer in winter. There has also been growth in staff with Tim Ford joining Roger Jones after a long stint at Sharrow Bay (see entry). The changes have had good effect: a better menu, a higher standard, a spirit of improvement. Fish is obviously enjoyed: lobster tartlet, John Dory, monkfish, brill, red mullet, and oysters with avocado bavarois are components of a small fish course. Soups and sauces too are showing profitable signs of work: a breast of chicken with port and truffle ('and you could taste the truffle') is a change from the pale emulsions that usually complement this meat; another comment was that 'they have always made good soups but now they have good stock pots these can be excellent'. The kitchen's output is set firmly in developments of the last decade: a liking for chutneys and relishes; a Mediterranean tinge to some of the dishes, not least in the home-made pasta; an accent on baking when it comes to desserts – pear Tatin or lemon tart for example, though Pithiviers has been thought heavy, and a caramel soufflé thought worthy of the best practitioners. The hotel has always been appreciated for its open welcome and the high motivation of the staff. It is encouraging to see a place prepared to take the gamble of radical upgrading in these difficult times. The same policy has been pursued in the wine cellar. Local loyalty brings six West Country wines on to an otherwise far from parochial list. Bordeaux petits châteaux and an abundance of 4me and 5me crus show a healthy respect for more modest wines, vintages are treated respectfully and prices, even of the older and grander, are approachable. Even-handedness is evident in intelligent selections from Italy, Australia and Spain. Half-bottles, listed separately, abound with many fine Sauternes/Barsac. Excellent spirits. A bottle is awarded for clarity, intelligence and generosity. House wines are from £8.45. CELLARMAN'S CHOICE: St-Véran, les Grandes Bruyères 1988, Luquet, £14.95; Monthélie 1988, Garaudet, £18.75.

CHEFS: Roger Jones and Tim Ford PROPRIETORS: Nigel and Margaret Corbett OPEN: all week CLOSED: 1 to 16 Jan MEALS: 12.30 to 1.30, 7.30 to 9 PRICES: £28 (£36), Set L £15.50 (£22), Set D £27.50 (£35). Card slips closed CARDS: Access, Visa SEATS: 48. 10 tables outside. Private parties: 28 main room. Car park, 30 places. Vegetarian meals. No children under 8. Wheelchair access (also WC). No music. Fax: (0935) 83005
ACCOMMODATION: 17 rooms, all with bath/shower. Rooms for partially disabled. B&B £65 to £190. No children under 8. Pets welcome. Afternoon teas. Garden. Swimming-pool. Tennis. TV. Phone. Scenic. Doors close at midnight. Confirm by 6 (*Which? Hotel Guide*)

EVERSLEY Hampshire map 2

New Mill

New Mill Road, Eversley RG27 0RA
EVERSLEY (0734) 732277 COOKING 2
off A327, ½m N of Eversley COST £24–£42

The mill workings still exist on view in the old part of the house, where low beams may slice the top off many a head. The restaurant occupies an extension, takes in the garden and has the advantage of ponds and water to build a calming vision of rural peace. Robert Allen comes from an elaborate background, in cooking terms. His food shows the result. There are many wrappings, fillings, mousses and terrines. Simpler food is available in the grill; the price is less stiff there too. The wine list is as elaborate as the food, and extremely thoroughbred. This shows in its prices as well. House wines start at £9.25.

CHEF: Robert Allen PROPRIETORS: New Mill Restaurants Ltd OPEN: all week MEALS: 12 to 2, 7 to 10 (12.30 to 8 Sun) PRICES: £28 (£35), Set L £19.50 (£24), Set D £25.50 (£30). Net prices, card slips closed CARDS: Access, Amex, Diners, Visa SEATS: 75. 4 tables outside. Private parties: 100 main room, 10 and 30 private rooms. Car park, 50 places. Vegetarian meals. Children's helpings. No-smoking area. Wheelchair access (2 steps; also WC). Music. Fax: (0734) 328780

The Guide *relies on feedback from its readers. Especially welcome are reports on new restaurants appearing in the book for the first time.*

EVESHAM Hereford & Worcester map 2

▲ *Cedar Restaurant, Evesham Hotel* 🍷

Cooper's Lane, Evesham WR11 6DA COOKING 2
EVESHAM (0386) 765566 COST £13–£26

The sparky trappings are but the gloss on a shrewd and genuinely enthusiastic operation. The Jenkinsons inject most of what they do with a cheerfulness that is infectious, and smiles come easily to readers who taste the lunchtime buffet ('salads in small bowls regularly replenished, not great buckets left to moulder') and see the modest bill. The hotel is close to the river, not far from Evesham's centre (a good base for touring), and is well-equipped – down to rubber ducks in the bathrooms and reading matter in the lavatories. Ian Mann remains an inventive chef – a sauce of tea and orange with pheasant, for instance – and a competent one ('How is his chicken liver parfait so much lighter than mine?'). Apart from the buffet, there are long menus that encourage experiment – 'wild boar unsuccessful, tempura successful,' reports John Jenkinson – and give room to long-standing favourites: crab cocotte; duck pâté with a kumquat and onion relish; kidneys with mustard sauce. Puddings and sweet things are always enjoyed, as are the service and the approach to children, tipping and music. The icing on the gingerbread has to be the wine list. Multi-volumed and multi-coloured, it turns its back resolutely on France. Brave or foolhardy, the magpie has spotted more than enough winners to satisfy all but the most stuffy. California and Australia, Spain and Italy show very strongly, New Zealand and Portugal not far behind. Curiosity is engaged by Tunisia, Peru and Romania. Prices throughout are fair. House wine is £6.80. CELLARMAN'S CHOICE: China, Tsing Tao, Chardonnay 1988, £12; New Zealand, Villa Maria, Cabernet Sauvignon 1988, £14.50.

CHEF: Ian Mann PROPRIETORS: the Jenkinson family OPEN: all week CLOSED: 25 and 26 Dec MEALS: 12.30 to 2, 7 to 9.30 PRICES: L buffet £6.20 (£13) to £14 (£19), D £18 (£22). Net prices, card slips closed CARDS: Access, Amex, Diners, Visa SEATS: 55. Private parties: 12 main room, 15 private room. Car park, 50 places. Vegetarian meals. Children's helpings. Wheelchair access (also WC). No music. Fax: (0386) 765443 ACCOMMODATION: 40 rooms, all with bath/shower. B&B £54 to £84. Children welcome. Baby facilities. Pets welcome. Afternoon teas. Garden. Swimming-pool. TV. Phone. Scenic. Doors close at midnight. Confirm by 6 (*Which? Hotel Guide*)

EYTON Hereford & Worcester map 2

▲ *Marsh* NEW ENTRY

Eyton HR6 OAG
LEOMINSTER (0568) 613952 and 611330 COOKING 1*
off B4361, 2m NW of Leominster COST £21–£36

The Marsh, a timbered house dating back to the fourteenth century, was rescued from dereliction by Martin and Jacqueline Gilleland, who have spent the last three years restoring it accurately under English Heritage's supervision. The results are worthwhile: a beautifully landscaped garden and discreet country-house hotel with a glorious Gothic hall. Jacqueline Gilleland's menu changes continually, depending on the best produce available, and there is pride in the home-grown herbs used. No fault has been found with a fresh crab salad, lamb noisette with aubergine charlotte or even a plain, but perfectly cooked, grilled Dover sole. Fish repeatedly stands out as well handled, with more complex brill and wild salmon in a butter sauce and lemon sole stuffed with crab in a chive sauce. Home-made bread is first-rate and desserts include cherry strudel with an almond sauce and good home-made caramel ice-cream with butterscotch sauce. With the kitchen still so young, one can expect increasing confidence. The wine list is not elaborate but is generous in its provision of half-bottles. House white is £9.50.

CHEF: Jacqueline Gilleland PROPRIETORS: Martin and Jacqueline Gilleland OPEN: all week MEALS: 12 to 2.30, 7 to 9.30 PRICES: Set L £16 (£21), Set D £24.75 (£30). Net prices, card slips closed CARDS: Access, Amex, Visa SEATS: 24. Private parties: 24 main room. Car park, 10 places. Children welcome. Smart dress preferred. No smoking in dining-room ACCOMMODATION: 5 rooms, all with bath/shower. B&B £74 to £100. Deposit: £15. Children in family suite only. Baby facilities. Garden. TV. Phone. Scenic. Confirm by 6

FAVERSHAM Kent map 3

Read's

Painter's Forstal, Faversham ME13 0EE
FAVERSHAM (0795) 535344 COOKING 3*
on Eastling road, 1m S of Faversham COST £21–£42

What people say about this place, even if likening it to a supermarket or 'a kind of run-down warehouse', is that the human warmth and sense of welcome are palpable: 'She (the waitress) was so caring and efficient that I asked her if she was one of the family owners.' Good habits can be transmitted to staff. Attitude counts for much, so appreciation for the children's prices and menus and the fair price for a good lunch menu is as gusty as for David Pitchford's cooking. If tired of endless restaurant short-order food, then come here for some slow cooking: oxtail with madeira, perhaps, or boiled beef and carrots with decent suet dumplings. David Pitchford is adept at both styles. Reporters comment on quality in raw materials, generosity, and the facility to put taste into made dishes, mousses and the like: bland is not a word to be used here. Dishes such as artichoke heart stuffed with wild mushroom mousse, three-fish quenelles, salmon on a lemon and chive sauce, grilled Dover sole with soft herring roes, and salmon with spinach and a champagne sauce have pleased as much as summer pudding, a cheesecake ('not to be confused with modern imposters') and a plate of chocolate desserts that was too much for one party, however delectable. This is good substantial cooking, with style and finesse. House wines with a pedigree are rare but at Read's the red comes from Cos d'Estournel, the white from Louis Latour. This sets the tone for the list, which is a fine collection with no duff vintages, growers of the quality of Sauzet and Rousseau in Burgundy, Clos du Val in California and Penfolds from South Australia, while Italy and Spain receive short but very select treatment with good, older wines. Splitting the 'regular' from the 'odd and unusual' may make life difficult for the customer, as may the generous spacing and notes. Read's gets a bottle award for sheer quality, range and fair prices. House wine is £10.50. CELLARMAN'S CHOICE: Chablis, Vaulorent 1987, Fèvre, £19; Côte Rôtie, Brune et Blonde 1983, Guigal, £25.

CHEF: David Pitchford PROPRIETORS: David and Rona Pitchford OPEN: Tue to Sat MEALS: 12 to 2, 7 to 10 PRICES: Set L £13.50 (£21), Set D £27.50 (£35). Card slips closed CARDS: Access, Amex, Diners, Visa SEATS: 60. 3 tables outside. Private parties: 60 main room, 12 private room. Car park, 30 places. Children's helpings. Wheelchair access (1 step; also WC). Music

FELSTED Essex map 3

Rumbles Cottage

Braintree Road, Felsted CM6 3DJ COOKING 2
GREAT DUNMOW (0371) 820996 COST £18–£31

Joy Hadley has been busy. She is establishing a third herb garden to feed her kitchen, and has substantially refurbished her country-cottage restaurant with new carpets, curtains and pictures. Customers approve of the new décor and her accomplished cooking. One Essex regular, who visits the place almost every month, provides a catalogue of approved dishes: eggs stuffed with Blue Cheshire cheese, lobster bavarois, pan-fried duck with pineapple and ginger sauce, poached cod with mussels, lychee cheesecake, and chocolate lime and hazelnut cluster. A sweet bavarois perfumed with lavender was 'a smash hit'. Joy Hadley also offers a 'guinea-pig menu' of new dishes (Tuesday to Thursday), which is an exercise in risk-taking. Failures can be dramatic and the promise of a club card and a badge hardly redeems the situation. Prices are laudable and a two per cent discount is offered to customers *not* paying by credit card. The wine list enables modest but affordable drinking. House wines are from £6.95. The owners are planning to open a second branch at 4 St James Street, Castle Hedingham, Essex – reports, please.

CHEF: E. Joy Hadley PROPRIETORS: E. Joy Hadley and M. Donovan OPEN: Tue to Sat, D only, and Sun L CLOSED: 3 weeks Feb MEALS: 12 to 2, 7 to 9 PRICES: £19 (£26), Set L and D £12.50 (£18) CARDS: Access, Visa SEATS: 46. Private parties: 24 main room, 8 and 10 private rooms. Vegetarian meals. Children's helpings. No-smoking area on request. Wheelchair access. No music

FLETCHING East Sussex map 3

▲ *Griffin*

Fletching TN22 3NS COOKING 1
NEWICK (0825) 722890 COST £17–£25

Edward Gibbon is buried in Fletching churchyard; nearby Sheffield Park, a National Trust property, was the home of his greatest friend. The Griffin perhaps harks back to earlier, Falstaffian, times: large log fires, the odd bit of exposed beam, in short olde worlde. But it has matchless views. Not so olde worlde, nor wholly English, is the menu: fresh pasta and wild mushrooms, salade niçoise, prawns with garlic butter, a variety of things from the grill, an enterprising bar menu and a set-price evening menu for dinner to supplement the *carte*. The cooking is more ambitious than that of most pubs, yet avoids the pitfalls of over-garnishing and poor, cheapskate, materials. There may be variation in accuracy through a single meal, but a resident at Sheffield Park was happy with two weeks' production and even more content to be there during a 'theme' weekend, in this instance Italy. A virtual absence of half-bottles on the mainly French wine list is compensated for by the availability of several wines, including that of the nearby Breaky Bottom, by the glass. Sound selection, intelligent spread and very fair prices make this a refreshing change from many pub wine lists. A 'connoisseur's corner' has been a success. House wine is £7.25.

CHEFS: Bridget Pullan, Ann Read and Victoria Luckin PROPRIETORS: Nigel and Bridget Pullan OPEN: all week, exc Sun D CLOSED: 24 Dec D, 25 Dec MEALS: 12 to 2.30, 7 to 9.30 (10 Fri to Sun) PRICES: £14 (£21), Set Sun L £10.95 (£17), Set D £13.95 (£20). Service 10%. Card slips closed CARDS: Access, Amex, Visa SEATS: 110. 6 tables outside. Private parties: 50 main room, 30 private room. Car park, 25 places. Vegetarian meals. Children's helpings. Wheelchair access (1 step). Music ACCOMMODATION: 4 rooms, all with bath/shower. B&B £30 to £65. Children welcome. Baby facilities. Garden. Tennis. Fishing. Golf. Snooker. TV. Scenic. Doors close at 11.30. Confirm by 6

FLITWICK Bedfordshire map 3

▲ *Flitwick Manor* NEW ENTRY

Church Road, Flitwick MK45 1AE
FLITWICK (0525) 712242 COOKING 2
off A5120, S of Flitwick COST £29–£59

'On such a perfect day, it was hardly possible to object to anything, and we drove back to London contented.' Whether you want a jaunt into the country or a local resource, Flitwick Manor, under new ownership for the past year, affords gracious surroundings in an ample setting. Cooking of such things as nettle cream soup with herb-scented gnocchi; asparagus mousse with morels in a Riesling sauce; monkfish wrapped in bacon, served with caramelised onions and a red wine sauce; calf's liver and onions and wild mushrooms in a red wine sauce; and walnut tart, poached pear and caramel ice-cream is careful and competent, but comes at steep prices for the area. Sometimes, home-made chocolates with coffee have been ecstatically reported.

CHEF: Duncan Poyser PROPRIETORS: Greentime Ltd OPEN: all week MEALS: 12 to 1.30, 7 to 9.30 PRICES: £35 (£49), Set L £19.50 (£29) CARDS: Access, Amex, Diners, Visa SEATS: 60. 6 tables outside. Private parties: 65 main room, 10 and 20 private rooms. Car park, 70 places. Vegetarian meals. Children's helpings. Smart dress preferred. No smoking in dining-room. Wheelchair access (also WC). Air-conditioned. No music ACCOMMODATION: 15 rooms, all with bath/shower. Rooms for disabled. B&B £78 to £98. Deposit: 50%. Children welcome. Baby facilities. Garden. Tennis. Fishing. Golf. Snooker. Air-conditioned. TV. Phone. Scenic

All entries in the Guide *are rewritten every year, not least because restaurant standards fluctuate. Don't trust an out-of-date* Guide.

FOWEY Cornwall map 1

Food for Thought

Town Quay, Fowey PL23 1AT COOKING 3
FOWEY (072 683) 2221 COST £20–£34

The former custom-house continues to elicit praise ranging from the cordiality of the owners and the picturesque quayside location to the excellent food. The cooking is confident and direct. Fresh fish is an obvious strength but it is well-matched by the quality of the meat dishes. Saddle of hare with a calvados sauce and tender lamb cutlets are as highly praised as the mussels, scallops, salmon, lemon sole, skate and the seafood gratin, in which, according to one diner, 'the lightness of the gratin allowed the taste of the individual pieces of fish to be appreciated'. Singled out for praise from an imaginative list of four courses have been fish soup (as much for the generous quantity as for the rouille), saffron tagliatelle with pesto and home-cured salmon with dill. Desserts usually include sticky toffee pudding ('voted a great success') and a rich crème brûlée with butterscotch sauce in a brandy-snap basket. 'A rare establishment to find in the depths of Cornwall, keeping to a high standard' was the accolade in one report. House Muscadet is £6.95.

CHEF: Martin Billingsley PROPRIETORS: Martin and Caroline Billingsley OPEN: Mon to Sat, D only CLOSED: Jan to early Feb MEALS: 7 to 9.30 PRICES: £19 (£28), Set D £14.50 (£20) CARDS: Access, Visa SEATS: 38. Private parties: 20 main room. No children under 5. Wheelchair access. No music

FRAMPTON ON SEVERN Gloucestershire map 2

Saverys

The Green, Frampton on Severn GL2 7EA COOKING 2
GLOUCESTER (0452) 740077 COST £28–£41

The longest village green in England stretches directly to the front door, drawing droves of tourists. These, attracted by the diminutive restaurant's traditional appeal, frequently displace regulars who then fire off occasional grumbles about being unable to get in. The cooking is based on sound raw materials which, in John Savery's hands, are translated into straightforward country dishes. These appear on a handwritten menu, five choices per course, chosen from a well-established repertoire. A recent meal produced a finely flavoured, if rather solid, terrine of chicken and hazelnuts with a well-made, roughly textured mango chutney; good-quality rack of lamb served pink as requested, but suffering ultimately from the English disease of too-hot plates, which rapidly turned the meat grey; a 'nicely timed and full of flavour' selection of vegetables; and strawberries soaked in peach liquor, in an almond biscuit basket, served with excellent home-made ice-cream. Niggles about lack of attention to small details – poor-quality nibbles brought to the table with the menu, weak coffee – could so easily be put right. The estimable Patricia Carpenter continues in her self-assured and friendly way to make all welcome. House wines are from £7.95.

CHEFS/PROPRIETORS: John Savery and Patricia Carpenter OPEN: Tue to Sat, D only (L by arrangement) MEALS: 7 to 9.15 PRICES: Set D £19.75 (£28) to £25.50 (£34). Card slips closed CARDS: Access, Visa SEATS: 26. Private parties: 26 main room. No children under 12. No pipes in dining-room. Wheelchair access. Music

---

FRESSINGFIELD Suffolk map 6

Fox and Goose

COUNTY RESTAURANT OF THE YEAR

Eye, Fressingfield IP21 5PB COOKING 3*
FRESSINGFIELD (037 986) 247 COST £22–£34

There's no stopping an addict. Ruth Watson, who clearly gets her highs in the kitchen, was no sooner out of Hintlesham Hall (see entry), a resounding success, than she bought this long-established restaurant deep in the Suffolk countryside. 'We were immediately captivated by the new sign, which shows a triumphant goose with a wilting fox in its beak,' reported a couple on their first visit since it was in the hands of the Clarke family. They detected little change in the essentials: still a country pub in feel, with domestic, not catering, intentions. The menu, a long, thin printed card with a short wine list on the reverse, shows a thoroughly modern approach to eating out. It is a London brasserie menu a long way from town, borrowing from China and Japan (Peking duck and tempura) as well as from Italy, France and old England. There is the same jeans-and-silk-shirt approach in listing beluga caviare at the same time as cod and chips. First courses can be increased in size to become main courses. Meals early in the life of the new regime have shown assurance in the kitchen in dishes such as the warm salmon salad niçoise, which combined generosity, good ingredients, and a decent dressing (the ideal in brasserie cooking), and the fish soup. Rump of lamb with broad bean and rosemary sauce showed more skill and finesse than the Peking duck, served here with a hoisin, rather than plum, sauce. Vegetables are good, and listed and priced individually. Puddings include blockbusters: roast caramelised bananas with ice-cream got very good notices, but classic British puddings get an outing here too. Likewise, Sunday roast is an event celebrated with full enthusiasm. The waiting staff may not be as enthusiastic or as knowledgeable as Mrs Watson, but early experiments will doubtless settle. A no-nonsense, four-dozen-long, closely printed wine list appears on the back of the menu; the most expensive bottle is £20.75 for a New Zealand Pinot Noir, but most wines are firmly below £12. Reliable, but not boring, such a list is a welcome change. The main list, opening with a formidable page of well-aged clarets at high but perfectly reasonable prices, should not intimidate; there are good bourgeois growths, fine Italians and Australasians at affordable prices as well as champagnes and fine burgundies. The utilitarian presentation is well and good, but makes for much page-turning. House wine is £7.50. CELLARMAN'S CHOICE: Pinot Grigio 1989, Collavini, £10.25; Chile, Viña Portal del Alto, Cabernet Sauvignon 1988, £9.25.

---

denotes an outstanding wine cellar; *denotes a good wine list, worth travelling for.*

CHEFS: Brendan Ansbro, Ruth Watson and Richard Cross PROPRIETOR: Ruth Watson
OPEN: Wed to Sun CLOSED: 2 weeks Christmas to New Year, 3 weeks end Sept
MEALS: 12 to 2.15, 7 to 9.30 PRICES: £19 (£28), Set Sun L £15 (£22). Card slips closed
SEATS: 50. Private parties: 36 main room, 20 private room. Car park, 30 places. No children under 10 D. No cigars/pipes in dining-room. Fax: (0379) 868107

GATESHEAD Tyne & Wear map 7

▲ *Eslington Villa Hotel* NEW ENTRY

8 Station Road, Gateshead NE9 6DR COOKING 2
091-487 6017 COST £16–£38

Gateshead is not a seed-bed of British cooking, but this hotel has played its part with style for some years now, and residential Gateshead has a certain élan even if the endless terraces do not. At night the Team Valley flashes and twinkles with many lights. The hotel, the dining-room with conservatory front looking over those lights, is comfortable 'country-house', 'middle-class and middle-aged' to one young blood, 'Munsteresque' to another (from America). The cooking is also slightly country-house, with plenty of modern influences in dishes such as warm timbale of courgette with poached seafood; chicken breast with prawns and buttered noodles; duck with orange, garlic and rosemary; and banana and clementine gratin with a kirsch sabayon. Presentation is as careful as was, for an inspection meal, the cooking of pork with barbecue sauce and bamboo shoots (to represent one strand) and ragoût of monkfish and prawns with a basil sauce. Service is young and willing. The wine list has a fair spread but is rather unevenly annotated. Prices are reasonable. House wines are £6.95.

CHEF: Allan O'Neill PROPRIETORS: Mr N. and Mrs M. Tulip OPEN: all week, exc Sat L and Sun D CLOSED: 23 Dec to 2 Jan, bank hols MEALS: 12 to 2, 7 to 10 PRICES: £24 (£32), Set L £10.95 (£16), Set D £18.50 (£24) CARDS: Access, Amex, Diners, Visa SEATS: 50. Private parties: 40 main room. Car park, 18 places. Vegetarian meals with prior notice. Children's helpings. Smart dress preferred. No smoking in dining-room. Wheelchair access (2 steps; also WC). Music. Fax: 091-482 2359 ACCOMMODATION: 14 rooms, all with bath/shower. Rooms for disabled. B&B £34.50 to £59.50. Children welcome. Pets welcome (small dogs in some rooms). Garden. TV. Phone. Scenic

---

GILLINGHAM Dorset map 2

▲ *Stock Hill House*

Wyke, Gillingham SP8 5NR COOKING 3*
GILLINGHAM (0747) 823626 COST £26–£42

The Hausers are a remarkable couple and their house shows it at almost every turn; just as the garden, still in the process of formation, is yet another monument to their indefatigable energy and deep-seated enthusiasm. Stock Hill House is early Victorian, on just the right scale for a small hotel; insulated from the hurry and scurry of the world by avenued drives and ample grounds. The decoration inside is arresting: intense colours, ornate furniture, flamboyant wallpapers, captivating items like the pair of rearing Indian ceremonial horses in the front hall. The place is stimulating. Even in winter there are flowers everywhere, from the porch to the innermost recess. Peter Hauser is Austrian and he does the cooking (and plays the zither, they say). His nationality may influence some of the cooking, but it is essentially that of someone who has been classically trained and is able to mobilise all the necessary techniques. Crab quenelles are light, as are meringues; consommés are clear; and herring is correctly cured. Peter enjoys cooking game – Dorset hare in red wine and mushroom sauce is a favourite of lovers of strong meat – and he is willing to pile on the substance: pot-pourri of lamb is roast loin, grilled liver and kidney, poached heart and tongue, with a cream mint sauce. The garden has its influence: nettle soup, the main ingredient taken from a patch that yields young leaves most of the year, is another excellent standby. A reader criticised our calling the cooking 'simple'; it is simple in so far as it avoids excess and over-complication, although some with light appetites may find it on the generous side. Desserts are an event, for the shape of the meringues or the lightness of the soufflés or the smooth texture of the parfaits. The Viennese Cardinal Schlangerl, alternate layers of meringue and sponge sandwiching a rich coffee mousse, on a coffee sauce, was 'pure indulgence' for one, but might sink another. The wine list is most remarkable for its selection of Rhônes and Loires from Yapp Brothers nearby. House wines are £9.75.

CHEF: Peter Hauser PROPRIETORS: Peter and Nita Hauser OPEN: Tue to Sun, exc Tue and Fri L and Sun D MEALS: 12.30 to 1.45, 7.30 to 8.45 PRICES: Set L £18.50 (£26), Set D £26.50 (£35). Card slips closed. CARDS: Access, Visa SEATS: 26. Private parties: 12 main room, 12 private room. Car park, 25 places. Children's helpings. No children under 7. Jacket and tie. No smoking in dining-room. No music. Fax (0747) 825628
ACCOMMODATION: 8 rooms, all with bath/shower. D,B&B £80 to £180. Deposit: £40. No children under 7. Garden. TV. Phone. Scenic. Doors close at midnight. Confirm by 8 (*Which? Hotel Guide*)

GLASTONBURY Somerset map 2

▲ *No.3*

3 Magdalene Street, Glastonbury BA6 9EW COOKING 1
GLASTONBURY (0458) 32129 COST £42

Hippies may come to Glastonbury for open-air delights. Others come to No.3, a small, highly decorated house providing accommodation and a restaurant well insulated from outside interference by a charming garden. Ann Tynan cooks a set-price menu offering half a dozen choices at each course. Her execution is careful, her recipes well tried in dishes such as lamb's liver Stroganoff, mushroom gratin, scallops in filo pastry with a prawn sauce, lamb in rosemary with a ginger and orange sauce, and magret with raspberry sweet-sour sauce. The old British love of inserting fruit at the most unlikely spots surfaces at every possible opportunity, as with a plate of smoked salmon with strawberries – something most of us could well avoid. Given that the service, on the surface, is provided by the proprietors' family, one visitor took it amiss that 'Service not included' had been added in manuscript to the bill. House Duboeuf is £9.

CHEF: Ann Tynan PROPRIETORS: John and Ann Tynan OPEN: Tue to Sat, D only CLOSED: Jan MEALS: 7 to 9 PRICES: Set D £26 (£35) CARDS: Access, Visa SEATS: 28. 2 tables outside. Private parties: 12 main room. Car park, 8 places. Children's helpings on request. No children under 5. Jacket and tie. No smoking in dining-room. No music ACCOMMODATION: 6 rooms, all with bath/shower. B&B £50 to £70. No children under 5. Garden. TV. Phone. Scenic. Doors close at 11.30. Confirm by 6

GLEMSFORD Suffolk map 3

Barretts 🍷

31 Egremont Street, Glemsford CO10 7SA COOKING 3*
GLEMSFORD (0787) 281573 COST £21–£41

The setting is a converted shop with a modest dining-room seating only 18; the restaurant, however, has high aspirations. Visitors are seldom disappointed. Nicholas Barrett's short menu is priced according to the number of courses. Light textures, faultless execution and spot-on accuracy are the hallmarks of his cooking. Starters such as marinated salmon with dill and cucumber dressing and warm smoked salmon with shredded cabbage show his talent for finding flavours that match well together. The litany of enthusiastically received main courses takes in wing of skate with capers and lemon, roast grouse with cassis sauce, and mignons of veal with garlic and mushrooms. His repertoire is eclectic, encompassing everything from straightforward pan-fried scallops with sweet shrimp sauce and calf's liver with bacon to more complex fillets of Dover sole steamed with crab and lemon sauce. Vegetables are faultless, cheeses are British. Puddings are dominated by 'dream' soufflés: mango, cinnamon with calvados sauce, vanilla with chocolate sauce poured into it at the moment of serving ('a dish of Elysian delight,' according to one regular reporter). Diane Barrett ensures that service is impeccable and succeeds in creating 'a standard of care and attention that few larger restaurants can emulate'. Sunday lunch centres round traditional roasts. The evenly priced wine list, supplied by Lay and Wheeler, is a model of clarity, has an eye for quality, and provides great range. It is intelligent and to the point. House wine is £8.50. CELLARMAN'S CHOICE: St Helena Pinot Blanc 1989, £13.95; Mount Edelstone Shiraz 1986, Henschke, £17.25.

CHEF: Nicholas Barrett PROPRIETORS: Nicholas and Diane Barrett OPEN: Tue to Sat, D only, and Sun L MEALS: 12 to 2, 7 to 9.30 PRICES: Set L £14.95 (£21), Set D £24.95 (£34). Card slips closed CARDS: Access, Visa SEATS: 18. Private parties: 12 main room. Car park, 10 places. Children's helpings (Sun L only). Wheelchair access. Music

Prices quoted in the Guide *are based on information supplied by restaurateurs. The figure in brackets below an entry is the average for a three-course meal with service, coffee and half a bottle of house wine, as calculated by computer. The prices quoted at the top of an entry represent a range, from the lowest average meal price to the highest; the latter is inflated by 20 per cent to take account of the fact that very few people eat an average meal, and also that prices are likely to rise during the year of the* Guide.

GLOUCESTER Gloucestershire map 2

Yeung's

NEW ENTRY

St Oswalds Road, Cattle Market,
Gloucester GL1 2SR
GLOUCESTER (0452) 309957

COOKING 1
COST £18–£36

'It reminded me,' says a reader, 'of restaurants on the outskirts of Las Vegas: a large detached single-storey building with fluorescent lights highlighting the name.' Yeung's exoticism extends to being so plant-filled, outside and in, that it could be mistaken for a garden centre. The restaurant specialises in Peking and Szechuan dishes, food of a sound quality. Steamed scallops ('fresh, succulent and sweet'), gota prawn (with ginger and garlic – 'an excellent rendition of this dish'), sliced pork with spring onions, and bean curd with minced pork show the restaurant's strengths. There is some flavour enhancement, but it is never too intrusive, though it is probably best to check for dishes without it. Service is helpful and willing. On the down-side, red-bean pancakes have been heavy-handed. Tea is decent but not free.

CHEF: C.H Voong PROPRIETORS: Henry and Ivy Soon, C.H. Voong and Peter Lee
OPEN: Mon to Sat, exc Mon L CLOSED: 25 and 26 Dec MEALS: 12 to 2.15, 6 to 11.15
PRICES: £11 (£20), Set L and D £12 (£18) to £22.50 (£30). Minimum £8. Service 10%.
SEATS: 100. Private parties: 50 main room. Vegetarian meals. Children welcome. Wheelchair access (also WC). Music. Air-conditioned

GOLCAR West Yorkshire map 5

Weavers Shed

Knowl Road, Golcar HD7 4AN
HUDDERSFIELD (0484) 654284

COOKING 1
COST £15–£32

This is a converted eighteenth-century cloth mill, the thick stone walls of which keep the air cool in summer and are now decently heated during the winter. 'I wonder,' wrote one customer, 'what will happen after the arrival of little McGunnigle.' The happy event has meant the temporary retirement of Kate McGunnigle while her sister-in-law steps into the breach. There is a strong vein of English cookery in dishes like Yorkshire batter pudding with onion and horseradish gravy, steak and kidney pie, and venison and hare pot with cream and sage; not to mention the trifle, steamed pudding and banana toffee tart (banoffi pie in all but name). This pleases most people, as do the fairly priced lunches, although criticism of lurid jelly in the trifle, miserly portioning of salmon and more beef than venison in a beef and venison casserole has been heard. A meal enjoyed began with filo parcels of Cotherstone cheese, followed by duck with apple and sage, ample vegetables and sticky toffee pudding. In most instances, the welcome is assured and enthusiastic. The wine list has some good bottles, most interest and value coming from outside France. Note the Jasnières from northern Touraine, Monticello Chardonnay from California, and CVNE's Rioja. House wine is £7.95.

CHEFS: Peter McGunnigle and Ian McGunnigle PROPRIETORS: Peter and Kate McGunnigle OPEN: Tue to Sat, exc Sat L CLOSED: first 2 weeks Jan, last 2 weeks July MEALS: 12 to 2, 7 to 9 (9.15 Sat) PRICES: £19 (£27), Set L £9.95 (£15) CARDS: Access, Amex, Visa SEATS: 70. Private parties: 40 main room, 30 private room. Car park, 40 places. Vegetarian meals. Children welcome. Smart dress preferred. Music

GORING Oxfordshire map 2

Leatherne Bottel

NEW ENTRY

Goring RG8 0HS COOKING 2
HENLEY (0491) 872667 COST £38

The setting, right on the Thames, and overlooking watermeadows and the Berkshire Downs in the distance, is enviable. Pretty gardens make the most of the location with tables and chairs for al fresco dining. Keith Read's cooking is accurate, very simple and relies as much on timing as skill, with salads and vegetables left to speak for themselves. The freshness and quality of ingredients are of prime importance; much is locally produced, even specially grown, while fresh fish comes from Cornwall. Soft herring roes are lightly dusted with granary breadcrumbs and lightly fried; pasta is 'cooked to perfection' and served with a pesto of wild mushrooms, black olives and a scattering of toasted pine kernels; fish soup comes heralded by 'a delicious aroma' and has a depth of colour that speaks of flavour; chargrilled mullet is served with coarsely chopped plum tomatoes and onion cooked in a liberal quantity of olive oil; best end of spring lamb is served with apple and mint noodles. Flavours are well handled, techniques up-to-date. Ancillaries such as home-made bread, butter and smoked garlic bread are very good indeed, but desserts are not a strong point. An adequate rather than exciting wine list affords fair range, and prices are not too bad. House wine is £9.50.

CHEF: Keith Read PROPRIETORS: Keith Read and Annette Bonnet OPEN: all week CLOSED: 25 Dec MEALS: 12.30 to 2 (2.30 Sat and Sun), 7 to 9.30 PRICES: £22 (£32). Card slips closed CARDS: Access, Amex, Visa SEATS: 60. 20 tables outside. Private parties: 20 main room, 12 and 20 private rooms. Car park, 40 places. Vegetarian meals. Wheelchair access. No music. Air-conditioned

GOUDHURST Kent map 3

Hughenden

The Plain, Goudhurst TN17 1AB COOKING 1
GOUDHURST (0580) 212065 COST £32

The transformation of this Grade II listed building and former tea-room next to the village pond has produced a beamed, chintzy, informal restaurant run by local farmer Michael Levett. Sarah Levett cooks a brief, fixed-price menu based on local produce; her style is straightforward. Although nothing is singly outstanding, food and service both please and, according to a number of readers, inspire a feeling of wellbeing. Fillet pork is cooked with peppers, fresh coriander, sherry and cream; best end of lamb roasted with a garlic and herb crust. Presentation is attractive and vegetables have been praised. A wide selection of home-made ice-creams and sorbets back up a list of desserts which range from chocolate roulade to sponge puddings. A thoughtful wine list, carefully annotated, provides a good geographical spread within a modest number of bins and there are some worthwhile choices under £10. House Duboeuf is £6.75.

CHEF: Sarah Levett PROPRIETORS: Sarah and Michael Levett OPEN: Tue to Sat, D only MEALS: 7.15 to 9.30 (9.45 Sat) PRICES: Set D £19.95 (£27). Service 10% for parties of 8 or more CARDS: Access, Visa SEATS: 35. Private parties: 40 main room. Children welcome. Smart dress preferred. No pipes in dining-room. Wheelchair access (also WC). Music

GRAMPOUND Cornwall map 1

Eastern Promise

1 Moor View, Grampound TR2 4RT COOKING 1
ST AUSTELL (0726) 883033 COST £21–£29

'It's all the same as ever,' comments a loyal supporter of this Chinese restaurant. 'The only change seems to be that the fish in the aquarium are even larger.' In fact, the wine list has been enlarged and traditional Chinese banquets are now laid on for special occasions. But the gist of the message is right: the kitchen is still delivering authentic cooking, although there are concessions to West Country palates in the mild spicing of some dishes. The menu runs the gamut of accessible Cantonese, Pekinese and Szechuan specialities and there are few disappointments: sesame prawn toasts, crunchy deep-fried 'seaweed', lemon chicken, sizzling squid with ginger and spring onion, and Szechuan lamb have all been enjoyable. A note on the menu says that 'almost all dishes are cooked with garlic, ginger and Chinese wine'. Philip Tse is an unfailingly affable host who deals happily with the crowds. Drink tea, Tsing Tao beer, saké or Chinese wine. House French is £5.90.

CHEF: Liza Tse PROPRIETOR: Philip Tse OPEN: all week, exc Wed, D only MEALS: 6 to 11 PRICES: £14 (£24), Set D £15.50 (£21) CARDS: Access, Amex, Diners, Visa SEATS: 64. Private parties: 40 main room, 24 private room. Car park, 25 places. Vegetarian meals. No children under 3. Music. Air-conditioned

GRASMERE Cumbria map 7

▲ *Lancrigg*

Easedale LA22 9QN COOKING 1
GRASMERE (096 65) 317 COST £24

A handsome house serving vegetarian food and accommodating vegetarian residents: perhaps they walk even more than omnivores, for there is often a welcome at tea-time, with fruit cake before the fire. Vegetarianism is not enough: the Whittingtons hold to organic materials in the kitchen as far as they are able. The cooking is surely enterprising, though lapses into inadequacy have been recorded, perhaps as a result of winter holidays or much building work. The general view is that dishes such as lentil and orange soup, potted cheese with herbs, a gougère with walnut and mushroom sauce, stuffed vine leaves with tahini and orange sauce, and puddings (the only point of choice in an otherwise set menu) such as lemon meringue pie with cardamoms or good old sticky toffee work well. Sometimes there are vegetables with the main course, or there is a range of salads. The hotel side of things has received some criticism. The wine list has an understandable preference for organics; this extends to beers, fruit beers and fruit juices. House wines are £6.50. A tea-barn serves light lunches from 12.30 to 2.

CHEF: Robert Whittington PROPRIETORS: Robert and Janet Whittington OPEN: all week, D only (L in tea-barn) MEALS: 7 PRICES: Set D £14.50 (£20). Card slips closed CARDS: Access, Visa SEATS: 25. Private parties: 30 main room. Car park, 16 places. Vegetarian meals. Children's helpings. No smoking in dining-room. Wheelchair access (also WC). Music. One sitting ACCOMMODATION: 15 rooms, 11 with bath/shower. Rooms for disabled. D,B&B £39.50 to £79. Deposit: £35. Children welcome. Baby facilities. Pets welcome. Afternoon teas. Garden. TV. Phone. Scenic. Confirm 1 week ahead

▲ *Michael's Nook* 🍷

Grasmere LA22 9RP — COOKING 3*
GRASMERE (096 65) 496 — COST £35–£54

The house, set on a hillside outside Grasmere, has bags of character and elegance in the drawing-room and bold scarlet and white dining-room. Furniture is antique: it is the antithesis of the current rash of blockboarded, veneered and varnished reproduction hotels. If you like cats, Mr Gifford will like you: the past and present menagerie of parrot, dog and cat is in evidence in picture or in the flesh. The current operation exudes professionalism, from the sophisticated menu to the wine list and the enthusiastic, yet informed, service. That an early breakfast was not up to scratch was perhaps an aberration. The menu, changing progressively from lunch to dinner, offers a short but ample choice, as well as the chef's 'recommended' dinner. There is also a 'gourmet's' menu, a long set dinner that exhibits restraint in quantity and careful variation in flavours and textures so that fatigue does not set in. A meal that included a vegetable 'mosaic' with avocado sauce, game consommé, salmon with mango and ginger noodles and some olive oil and soy sauce, and a banana parfait coated in chocolate with some caramelised banana and a custard showed off technique, mastery of tastes and a willingness to work even on a Lakeland February weekday lunch. Nor was the price excessive. Michael's Nook has struck a good vein. There are many good bottles on the wine list at around £12 or less – Vouvray from Brédif and the always reliable Trimbach Riesling 1985 balanced by pedigree clarets, burgundies and Rhônes. Selection is equally fastidious beyond Europe with Te Mata Hawke's Bay Cabernet Merlot and Moss Wood Margaret River Pinot Noir. There is an intelligent range of half-bottles, including five Chablis, and many interesting sherries by the glass. Wines are served lovingly with great attention to temperature. CELLARMAN'S CHOICE: Châteauneuf-du-Pape Blanc, Vieux Télégraphe 1989, £21.50; Graves, Ch. la Garde 1982, £16.95.

▲ *This symbol means that accommodation is available.*

CHEF: Heinz Nagler PROPRIETOR: Reg Gifford OPEN: all week, exc Sat L MEALS: 12.30 to 1, 7.30 to 8 (7.15 to 8.45 Fri and Sat) PRICES: Set L £26 (£35), Set D £35 (£45) CARDS: Access, Amex, Diners, Visa SEATS: 55. Private parties: 35 main room. Car park, 20 places. Vegetarian meals by arrangement. No children under 11. Smart dress preferred. No smoking in dining-room. No music. Fax: (096 65) 756 ACCOMMODATION: 14 rooms, all with bath/shower. D,B&B £148 to £340. No children under 8. Garden. Fishing. Golf. TV. Phone. Scenic. Doors close at 11.30 or by arrangement

▲ *White Moss House*

COUNTY RESTAURANT OF THE YEAR

Rydal Water, Grasmere LA22 9SE — COOKING 4
GRASMERE (096 65) 295 — COST £38

Reports speak loud and clear for themselves. 'Broccoli soup at a so-called gourmet Lakeland pub one lunch threw into brilliant relief the White Moss broccoli and basil soup that evening – with its superb texture and super-fine balance of flavours. New to us was roast breast of High Alston goose marinated in stout: a change from the duck everyone serves and enhanced, on this occasion, by the fine colour and sharp taste of passion-fruit sauce. The rack of Westmorland lamb roasted with parsley, sage, rosemary and thyme now comes with a warning, "Served pink unless otherwise requested". Only two of the 19 diners seemed to want to buck the challenge. In the event, it was about as rare and succulent as you're likely to get it.' The lamb was also remarked on by a more seasoned visitor (every year since 1986): 'The first time we have had it here; we all agreed it was the best main course yet served at our table.' The main point of this second report was that even if the structure of the meals and the style of Peter Dixon's cooking have remained the same (though one might note a perceptible lightening as full-fat dairy products are replaced by oils and yoghurts in many recipes), the variations of herbs, raw materials and interpretation are quite enough to keep interest alive. The pleasant stone-built house itself, once owned by Wordsworth, and sitting plumb-centre of the surrounding walking country, holds no novelties although the traffic is much quieter since lorries have been routed elsewhere. One guest bewailed the loss of a hundred conversations with passing pedestrians when confined indoors by rain and tempest. Peter Dixon cooks sensitively and accurately, mobilising flavour especially through herbs and careful choice of the best materials (look at the cheeses). Dinners start with soup; then comes a fish course, often a terrine or soufflé (the terrines voted the stronger, the soufflés the subtler vehicles of taste); meat and sauce – not leaden, blockbusting or crude – and excellent vegetables (try aubergine with sesame oil and four peppers) follow on; then a choice of three desserts, always one British and hot, followed by cheese and oat biscuits. The price is much less than that at fancier country houses. True, there is no choice, but few are those who protest. Sue Dixon manages the dining-room with gentle charm. An eye for bargains keeps the wine list well-replenished with older bottles, offered at very fair prices. With nearly 400 to choose from, each one a winner, the wines alone could justify a lengthy stay. Burgundies are particularly strong, but the Rhône, Alsace and Italy get good showings. The 1991 niggle about the lack of clarity in the list's layout still stands.

CHEF: Peter Dixon PROPRIETORS: Susan and Peter Dixon OPEN: Mon to Sat, D only CLOSED: end Nov to mid-Mar MEALS: 8 PRICES: Set D £25 (£32). Card slips closed SEATS: 18. 18 tables outside. Private parties: 18 main room. Car park, 10 places. No smoking in dining-room. Wheelchair access. No music. One sitting ACCOMMODATION: 7 rooms, all with bath/shower. D,B&B £148 (double rooms only). Garden. Fishing. TV. Phone. Scenic. Doors close at 11. Confirm by 6 (*Which? Hotel Guide*)

GRAYSHOTT Hampshire map 2

Woods Place

Headley Road, Grayshott GU26 6LB COOKING 1
HINDHEAD (0428) 605555 COST £23

'Having been here for exactly 10 years, we now feel there is time for a new challenge,' writes Dana Norrgren. So Woods has become Woods Place, with a more forceful rustic image than before: Liberty-style oilcloths have replaced linen, the cooking has been simplified and prices reduced. The menu is fairly restrained, but has a couple of dishes from the Norrgrens' home country of Sweden in each course. A May inspection reported favourably on pasta and smoked chicken in a creamy sauce; gravlax with mustard sauce; fillet of cod with a herb crust and 'a puddle of good old-fashioned parsley sauce'; 'beautifully cooked' calf's liver with light, creamy mashed potatoes; and Swedish meatballs – a mixture of lamb, pork and herbs, served with a fresh, tart sauce of lingonberries. The selection of raw materials is sound and presentation of the finished dish simple and uncluttered. Bread is home-baked; chips, served with an entrecôte steak, are excellent. On the other hand, desserts are not a strong point, and neither is the coffee. House wine is £6.50.

CHEF: Eric Norrgren PROPRIETORS: Eric and Dana Norrgren OPEN: Tue to Sat MEALS: 12 to 3, 7 to 10.30 PRICES: £13 (£19). Service 10%. Card slips closed CARDS: Access, Amex, Diners, Visa SEATS: 35. Private parties: 12 main room. Vegetarian meals. Children's helpings. Wheelchair access (also WC). Music

GREAT DUNMOW Essex map 3

▲ *Starr* 🍷

Market Place, Great Dunmow CM6 1AX COOKING 1
GREAT DUNMOW (0371) 874321 COST £27–£48

The inn is old, very old. That much is clear from the timbers exposed in the restaurant itself. More recent are the bedrooms to let in the former stable block. The menu is written on a blackboard that is paraded before, and explained to, each party. Fish is a strong point. There is an enjoyment of mixing fruit and meat, as in goose with plum or venison with raspberry; even turbot with red mullet quenelles gets rhubarb. First courses show off shellfish, as in scallops with fresh basil, crab with mango, and lobster roulade. The technical expertise in the kitchen can only just match the expectations aroused by the menu and prices therefore seem high. Bar snacks have been appreciated and so have the amiable staff. Lay and Wheeler provide the very good wine list; intelligent balance is shown both in spread of prices, all fair, and in geographical range.

House wines are from £8.95. CELLARMAN'S CHOICE: Semillon 1988, Henschke, £14.95; Cabernet Franc/Merlot 1987, Veritas, £12.75.

CHEF: Mark Fisher PROPRIETORS: Mr and Mrs B. Jones OPEN: all week, exc Sat L and Sun D CLOSED: 1 week Christmas MEALS: 12 to 1.30, 7 to 10 PRICES: Set L £18.50 (£27), Set D £18.50 (£27) to £31 (£40). Service 10% for parties of 6 or more CARDS: Access, Amex, Visa SEATS: 60. Private parties: 8 main room, 2 private room. Car park, 15 places. Vegetarian meals. Children's helpings. Wheelchair access (also WC). Music. Fax: (0371) 876337 ACCOMMODATION: 8 rooms, all with bath/shower. Rooms for disabled. B&B £60 to £110. Children welcome. Baby facilities. TV. Phone. Doors close at 9.30. Confirm by midnight

---

GREAT GONERBY Lincolnshire map 6

Harry's Place

COUNTY RESTAURANT OF THE YEAR

17 High Street, Great Gonerby NG31 8JS COOKING 3*
GRANTHAM (0476) 61780 COST £40–£54

Harry and Caroline Hallam run their place with no extra help: he cooks, she serves and they share the washing-up. Such constraints inevitably require a strict regime. The tiny, three-table dining-room is simply done out in pink and white with stripped pine and mirrors for contrast. Harry cooks for a maximum of 10 people at a sitting, reservations are essential and diners are expected to arrive on time. Sometimes this results in a severe, almost reverential atmosphere which may not appeal to everyone. But there is no denying the quality of the cooking. After 30 visits one reporter noted that the 'initial high standards of cuisine are getting better and better'. Food is cooked to order and there can be a long wait, but little pastries and plenty of freshly baked bread help to pass the time. Harry Hallam's technique and timing are spot-on, and there is an unpretentious generosity about his dishes. Pancake of Loch Fyne scallops with leeks, mushrooms and tarragon is not a gossamer crêpe, but a genuine bubbly aerated pancake, filled with 'sea-tasting' scallops, crunchy leeks and herbs, bound with a light sauce of fish stock and butter. Breast of free-range chicken with lemon thyme, white wine, bacon and calvados is roasted to perfection, carved off the bone in thick slices and served with a 'health-giving' sauce based on light olive oil and chicken stock; it comes with a pastry barquette filled with roasted sweet peppers. The repertoire also takes in sautéed Scarborough lobster with a gutsy cognac, tomato and basil sauce, loin of lamb with vintage cider and rosemary, and fillet of turbot baked with a herb crust. Sweets are dazzling: tarte citron is a classic and a Pithiviers of strawberries and raspberries is 'picturebook beautiful'. Like the menu, the wine list is minimal with only 19 choices. There is no house wine.

CHEF: Harry Hallam PROPRIETORS: Harry and Caroline Hallam OPEN: Tue to Sat (Sun and Mon by arrangement) CLOSED: 25 Dec, bank hols MEALS: 12.30 to 2, 7 to 9.30 PRICES: L £30 (£40), D £34 (£45) CARDS: Access, Visa SEATS: 10. Private parties: 10 main room; 4 private room. Car park, 4 places. Children's helpings on request. No smoking. No music

---

The Guide *always appreciates hearing about changes of chef or owner.*

GREAT MILTON Oxfordshire map 2

▲ *Le Manoir aux Quat' Saisons* 🍷

Church Road, Great Milton OX9 7PD COOKING 4*
GREAT MILTON (0844) 278881 COST £41–£96

Great Milton sits on the edge of a plain south of Oxford; Le Manoir occupies a honey-stone house on the edge of the village. From a super-restaurant, it has, over recent years, grown into a super-business: bedrooms and jacuzzi, bids for conference and meeting bookings, seats for nearly 100 in the restaurant, and gardens for herbs, flowers and vegetables. A visit is an event in which the meal is but an element. The success with which these extended goals have been met has been subject to debate through the year, and a certain consensus has emerged from reports that at present there is some disjunction between money and output and that, although technical faults are few, high expectations are not invariably satisfied. It may be reasonably objected that the expectations are not M. Blanc's fault. One problem has been the variability of harmony between food and service: the brigade of waiters does not always inspire confidence, though churlishness would never be suggested. 'Why was the "summer" menu offered me in November?' was the query of one reader with some idea of the calendar. The new development of the conservatory dining-room has been universally welcomed, save the noisy air-conditioning. It is the place to sit, surrounded by green inside and out, with lots more air and space than in the original dining-rooms. Drinks are taken in a good pair of rooms in the centre of the manor itself. These rooms may smell of stale tobacco, leaving people wondering why one is not cigar-free, but they give comfort for studying a long seasonal *carte*, a *menu gourmand*, a list of daily extras, and a *menu du jour* which offers the lunchtime bargain meal. It has been remarked before that tastes here are quiet, certainly never brash. It is not that they are deadened by cream, rather that the palette explored tends to classical understatement, even when exotics are utilised. This can result in disappointment to those, for example, now used to the Mediterranean new-wave and its forthright dishes spiked by chillies, spices and lots of basil and Parmesan. Rather, this is northern cooking. There are few olive oil-based sauces, though salad dressings are usually singled out for praise. Root vegetables (celeriac and turnip, beetroot and potato) are important adjuncts. Predictably, truffles and foie gras figure high on the list of ingredients. There is still surprising dependence on sabayons for sauces and on mousses of one sort or another in the composition of dishes: one *menu gourmand* had a mousse in every course, down even to an *amuse-bouche* of red pepper mousse at the very first. Yet meals can, of course, send reporters into rhapsodies with dishes like a terrine of leek and foie gras, the flavours complementary, the textures nicely contrasted; mille-feuilles of foie gras on potato and turnip galettes with a sherry sauce; red mullet on leaves of puff pastry and a sea-urchin scented sauce with strong accent given by provençal herbs; duck with ginger and coriander sauce; and pig's trotter filled with sweetbreads, calf's tongue with braised morels, fried kidneys and foie gras, a complex set of elements and methods combining into a light yet intense whole. Then there are desserts, such as cider mousse with vanilla-flavoured apple coulis; ginger and jasmine tea biscuit with a pepper and cardamom sauce; and pear on puff pastry with lime sorbet and vanilla sauce. These show the refinement to best advantage. The lunch menu is often appreciated for its relative cheapness though, with the inevitably restricted choice, the style may not suit your fancy that day; one reader felt that pot-au-feu was too 'bourgeois' yet did not want John Dory with baby onions and lardons of bacon. Eaters of this lunch often find the vegetables exiguous, especially the single potato provided with fish dishes. The event of eating here is given full support by ancillaries: good canapés; amuse-gueules almost always approved (though one of bresaola, aubergine and pepper in a sharp vinaigrette did not help the wine); bread surprisingly underseasoned; sensational petits fours; mineral water served free, although you pay if you ask for sparkling. The wine list is not chauvinist, though France gets the giant share, including many classics (though some would prefer a wider range of growers in Burgundy). The regional French wines are worth exploring and, for the place, affordable. There are also useful halves, though who could ever have enough of these when a complex meal may need much chopping and changing? House Sancerre is £22. The menu states that service is included, but nearly all our readers note that the credit card slip is left open.

CHEF: Raymond Blanc PROPRIETORS: Blanc Restaurants Ltd OPEN: all week CLOSED: 3 weeks from 22 Dec MEALS: 12.15 to 2.30, 7.15 to 10.30 PRICES: £62 (£80), Set L £26.50 (£41) to £59.50 (£74), Set D £59.50 (£74). Net prices CARDS: Access, Amex, Diners, Visa SEATS: 95. 4 tables outside. Private parties: 45 private room. Car park, 60 places. Vegetarian meals. Children's helpings. Smart dress preferred. No smoking in dining-room. Wheelchair access. Air-conditioned. No music. Fax: (0844) 278847 ACCOMMODATION: 19 rooms, all with bath/shower. Room for disabled. B&B from £184 for 2. Deposit: £150. Children welcome. Baby facilities. Afternoon teas. Garden. Swimming-pool. Tennis. TV. Phone. Scenic (*Which? Hotel Guide*)

GREAT MISSENDEN Buckinghamshire map 3

La Petite Auberge

107 High Street,
Great Missenden HP16 0BB — COOKING 1*
GREAT MISSENDEN (024 06) 5370 — COST £38

The Martels' tiny high-street restaurant is in cottagey premises once occupied by Frances and Gerald Atkins (see entry for Aberfeldy, Scotland). Inside, there are two dining areas which some have felt cramped, cold and colourless; the presence of just one smoker can affect everyone else in the restaurant. Home Counties reporters have spoken well of the food, which is based around a solidly French *carte* of hors d'oeuvre, meat and fish. Mousseline of red pepper with sharp tomato sauce, marinated salmon with dill sauce, fillets of John Dory with caramelised shallots, and duckling in red wine sauce have all been good. Fillet of beef with truffle sauce is a favourite, and scallops with saffron sauce appealed to one supporter. Glazed exotic fruits, lemon tart and nougat glacé are typical of the sweets. Flavours are pronounced, sauces are creamy. There is no house wine, but a short list of French bottles provides decent-value drinking.

CHEF: H. Martel PROPRIETORS: Mr and Mrs H. Martel OPEN: Mon to Sat, D only CLOSED: 25 Dec, Easter, bank hols MEALS: 7.30 to 10.30 PRICES: £23 (£32) CARDS: Access, Visa SEATS: 30. Private parties: 35 main room. Children welcome. Smart dress preferred. Wheelchair access. Music

GREAT YARMOUTH Norfolk map 6

Seafood Restaurant

85 North Quay, Great Yarmouth NR30 1JF COOKING 2
GREAT YARMOUTH (0493) 856009 COST £40

Great Yarmouth should have a good fish restaurant and this is it: a plush conversion of a Victorian pub, complete with live lobster tanks and cold cabinets for the display of the day's catch. Meat is on offer too – steak. The range is wide, the cookery is simple but fair: grilled, poached, in batter or 'saucey'. The infrastructure of the menu, starters, salads and so on, sometimes betrays the owners' Cypriot origins. Correct emphasis on white wines provides a strong suit of burgundies, but Alsace, Loire and New World wines are all chosen with the same intelligence. Prices are fair, albeit better value below £20. House wines are from £8.

CHEFS: Mark Chrisostomou and Gary Crompton PROPRIETORS: Christopher and Miriam Kikis OPEN: Mon to Sat, exc Sat L MEALS: 12 to 2, 7 to 10.45 PRICES: £25 (£33) CARDS: Access, Amex, Diners, Visa SEATS: 40. Private parties: 40 main room. Children's helpings. Smart dress preferred. Music

GRIMSTON Norfolk map 6

▲ *Congham Hall*

Lynn Road, Grimston PE32 1AH COOKING 3
HILLINGTON (0485) 600250 COST £19–£54

The house sits on flat ground – pure Norfolk – a sea of lawn punctuated by trees, shrubbery, fences and walls: the latter hiding and protecting the herb garden. 'The atmosphere and decoration strike a happy medium between the luxurious and comfortable', but there's no denying that it's handsome. The ability to do two things at once is noticed by others: 'The food was photo-worthy, but tasted good as well'; 'The staff were friendly and not over-zealous, avoiding the impression that one is doing them an honour by visiting.' Clive Jackson's cooking has pleased many readers. The set-price menu, reinforced by a long, no-choice, gastronomic 'Hobson's Choice' meal, changes periodically, though residents of a week felt they had nearly exhausted the possibilities available to them. An overall feeling is that cream gets into too many of the dishes or, a connected impression, that sauces can mask, and occasionally overpower, good ingredients. But there is some inventive cooking, well short of wildness, that includes a trio of smoked fish mousses on an oyster and vegetable stock sauce with herbs and truffle; an asparagus mousse in a leek parcel; pigeon breast on a corn pancake; turbot with spinach mousse; and three game meats with a juniper, thyme and orange sauce – too strong for some, very fine to others. Cheeses are approved – three warm cheeses with salad, for instance – as are many of the desserts such as the chocolate mint roulade, though not all the sorbets. Generally, a highly proficient kitchen, with a well-schooled team at the front-of-house. 'It's owner-occupied, and it shows.' An unambitious, decent and predictable wine list which continues to rely heavily on the big négociant names. House French is £9.25.

CHEF: Clive Jackson PROPRIETORS: Trevor and Christine Forecast OPEN: all week, exc Sat L MEALS: 12.30 to 2, 7.30 to 9.30 PRICES: Set L £13 (£19) to £15 (£22), Set D £30 (£38) to £36 (£45). Card slips closed CARDS: Access, Amex, Diners, Visa SEATS: 50. Private parties: 8 main room, 12 private room. Car park, 50 places. No children under 12. Jacket and tie. No smoking in dining-room. Wheelchair access. No music. Fax: (0485) 601191 ACCOMMODATION: 14 rooms, all with bath/shower. B&B £72 to £97. No children under 12. Garden. Swimming-pool. Tennis. TV. Phone. Scenic. Doors close at 11. Confirm by 6 (*Which? Hotel Guide*)

HALFORD Warwickshire map 2

Sykes House **NEW ENTRY**

Queen Street, Halford CV36 5BT COOKING 2*
STRATFORD-UPON-AVON (0789) 740976 COST £43

'We felt so much like personal guests that we didn't at first realise we were expected to go into the kitchen to discreetly pay the bill,' wrote a reader. The several reports received by the *Guide* enthuse about the hospitality of David Cunliffe, who cooks, and wife Peggy, who serves. Between them they do everything, from home-made appetisers and breads – caraway seed and buttermilk – to refreshing sorbets after the preliminary courses and petits fours with coffee. The form is a no-choice six-course menu; likes and dislikes are discussed over the telephone when booking (a minimum of 24 hours' notice). Portions are smallish and freshness is all-important, in the modern way. Thus the main course is presented with vegetables, but more are freshly cooked and served to arrive as you finish the first ration. Diners are staggered for the same reason. The style is English, with carefully sourced ingredients. A recent meal produced spring nettle broth; a potato galette with locally smoked salmon, soured cream and chive sauce ('excellent because it contained such very good raw materials'); Halford farm duckling with asparagus and wild mushroom sauce; a properly dressed mixed leaf salad with slivers of three English cheeses; and a white chocolate basket filled with buttered Seville oranges. House wines are from £7.95.

CHEF: David Cunliffe PROPRIETORS: David and Peggy Cunliffe OPEN: Wed to Sat D (reservations only); Mon to Tue D by arrangement MEALS: 7.30 to 8.15 PRICES: Set D £28.50 (£36). Card slips closed CARDS: Access, Visa SEATS: 24. Private parties: 12 main room, 12 private room. Car park, 14 places. Children welcome. Smart dress preferred. No smoking in dining-room. Wheelchair access (3 steps)

Card slips closed *in the details at the end of an entry indicates that the totals on the slips of credit cards are closed when these are handed over for signature.*

HAMBLETON Leicestershire map 6

▲ *Hambleton Hall* 🍷

Hambleton LE15 8TH
OAKHAM (0572) 756991 COOKING 3*
off A606, 3m SE of Oakham COST £27–£54

Rutland Water gives the lawns of Hambleton a fine outlook; its existence has the benefit of banishing through-traffic. Hambleton lives in its own world. The house has been decorated with great skill. It looks lived-in; one or two voices may echo 'too lived-in', but all salute the flower arrangements. The kitchen's script is presented as a seasonal *carte* with a daily four-course menu for those who can't cope with choice. Brian Baker likes certain dishes, and so do his customers. There are many points of similarity, even doppelgangers, on a summer menu of 1990 and a spring one of 1991. There is no harm in this, for Brian's repertoire contains some nice conceits: 'The underlying philosophy seems to be one of inventiveness within a conservative framework. It is not playful, nor are combinations frankly daring, yet there are lots of attractive ideas and nothing dull.' Luxury ingredients are mobilised with tact and usually with wit: an upturned mould of smoked salmon is filled with sliced, warm waxy potatoes bound with a mite of cream and egg and mixed with beluga caviare. A trimming of marinated cucumber gives edge; the caviare gives its salt to the potatoes; the smoked salmon lends richness. Excellent. Invention may falter if the profusion of upturned moulds is counted, but it will be noted in the popular first course of pea and mint mousse with mint, coriander and spring vegetables, or in the foie gras with mango and mint salsa and a slice of brioche. Main courses are no more hackneyed than the beginning of the meal, nor are desserts criticised as they were last year. On the contrary, fine pastry work, excellent soufflés, and willingness to handle simplicity – as in a sablé heart over just-cooked Dorset blueberries – have been noted. Some less positive comment does come about petits fours and canapés. Equally, the service, though never less than willing, is thought less soigné than the price of a meal (high) might deserve. The cooking seems steadier this year, and praise more general. Although the preoccupation of the wine list is fine bottles from the classic areas – white burgundies are especially strong – a nod to the New World, an intelligent range of halves and a careful selection of petits châteaux and good Loires make it possible to plot a more economical course. Prices start at £12 and rise steeply thereafter, but quality is assured throughout. House wines are from £14. CELLARMAN'S CHOICE: Semillon/Chardonnay 1989, Peter Lehmann, £14; Côtes du Rhône 1985, Guigal, £12.

CHEF: Brian Baker PROPRIETORS: Timothy and Stefa Hart OPEN: all week MEALS: 12 to 1.45, 7 to 9.30 PRICES: £33 (£43), Set L £17.50 (£27), Set D £35 (£45). Net prices, card slips closed CARDS: Access, Visa SEATS: 60. Private parties: 45 main room, 20 private room. Car park, 40 places. Vegetarian meals. Children's helpings. Smart dress preferred. No cigars/pipes in dining-room. Wheelchair access (also WC). Fax: (0572) 724721
ACCOMMODATION: 15 rooms, all with bath/shower. Rooms for disabled. Lift. B&B £105 to £225. No cigars/pipes in dining-room. Children welcome. Baby facilities. Pets welcome. Afternoon teas. Garden. Swimming-pool. Tennis. Fishing. Golf. TV. Phone. Scenic. Doors close at midnight (*Which? Hotel Guide*)

HARROGATE North Yorkshire map 5

Drum and Monkey

5 Montpellier Gardens,
Harrogate HG1 2TF COOKING 2
HARROGATE (0423) 502650 COST £20–£26

'Still struggling,' comments William Fuller laconically; struggling with the press of popularity, more like, for there is a steady stream of custom for the upstairs restaurant with its slate tables and red plush chairs, as well as for the enormous Victorian bar below. Fish is the thing – cheap or dear, plain or complicated – from lobster and prawns to soles, halibut and brill. There is not much dealing with cod, haddock or other lowlier inhabitants of the deep: to that extent, though people praise the 'French' feel of efficiency and bustle in the restaurant (but not the over-smoky atmosphere), it is an English style that is pursued here. Pacific oysters, salmon and spinach mousse, salmon and avocado 'délice', excellent granary bread, salmon trout with good hollandaise, sweet-and-sour prawn roulade, fresh raspberries and a brandy chocolate fudge cake were the components of a lunch (when a shorter menu operates than at dinner) that pleased in every particular save the boring new potatoes. There is a contingent that advocates the plain-cooked as better than the sauced dishes. Most are impressed by the capacity of the staff to control the flood of applicants. 'He said 30 minutes and, lo, the table was free in exactly that time.' The wines are not high-priced and the list is kept short. Sauvion Muscadet, Gisselbrecht Alsaces and Paillard champagne are good choices. House Duboeuf is £5.65.

CHEF: Patrick Laverack PROPRIETOR: William Fuller OPEN: Mon to Sat CLOSED: Christmas to New Year MEALS: 12 to 2.30, 7 to 10.15 PRICES: L £14 (£20), D £15 (£22). Card slips closed CARDS: Access, Visa SEATS: 48. Private parties: 8 main room. Children's helpings. Wheelchair access. No music

Millers

1 Montpellier Mews, Harrogate HG2 2TG COOKING 3
HARROGATE (0423) 530708 COST £25–£44

Simon Gueller has an impressive pedigree, and names Marco-Pierre White of Harveys, London (see entry) and the team from the Box Tree, Ilkley (see entry) as mentors and colleagues. This shows in his short, precise menus, which are mercifully free of purple prose: what you see is what you get. Dinner is fixed-price, lunch is a more affordable *carte* (although readers have been disgruntled by the fact that dishes may be withdrawn suddenly without prior warning and replaced with far less interesting offerings). Fresh fish shows up well in leek and lobster terrine, panaché of sole with scallops and langoustines, and confit of salmon with port wine and star anise. There is also a voguish fondness for fungi: wild mushrooms with fricassee of guinea-fowl, sirloin steak with truffles, pig's trotter stuffed with chicken and morels. Sweets are classical, ranging from oeufs à la neige to chocolate marquise and hazelnut ice-cream. While reporters are of one mind about the food, other details can irritate: 'nonchalant' wine service and a flippant, sometimes sarcastic attitude from the waiters. A list of around three-dozen wines has very few half-bottles and very little below £12. House wines are £8.50 and £11.95. Plans for a complete refurbishment of the restaurant are likely to include the provision of much-needed indoor toilet facilities.

CHEF: Simon Gueller PROPRIETORS: Simon and Rena Gueller OPEN: Mon to Sat, exc Mon D MEALS: 12 to 2, 7 to 10 PRICES: L £17 (£25), Set D £27.50 (£37) CARDS: Access, Diners, Visa SEATS: 24. Private parties: 30 main room. Vegetarian meals. Children's helpings on request. No pipes in dining-room. Wheelchair access (1 step; also WC)

HARROW Greater London map 3

Country Club

160 College Road,
Harrow-on-the-Hill HA1 1BH COOKING 1
081-427 0729 COST £17–£37

On the surface this place is no different from other suburban Chinese restaurants: crispy duck, sizzling dishes, a fair amount of seafood. Reports are mixed on the success of these dishes. The special set dinners are certainly best ignored. Mr Chu is one of the few Shanghai chefs in this country who trained in a Shanghai-Peking restaurant in Taiwan. There are Shanghai dishes on the menu but they are not marked as such: dumplings, spring rolls, sandpot soups, red-cooked Chinese cabbage pass unnoticed among the standard fare that caters to local community preferences. This is not a restaurant to drop into on spec. Instead, telephone a couple of days in advance and discuss a meal and then the entirely different repertoire of the Shanghai region will be opened up. House French is £6.50.

CHEF/PROPRIETOR: T.A. Chu OPEN: all week, D only MEALS: 6 to 11 PRICES: £17 (£23), Set D £11 (£17) to £24 (£31). Minimum £7 CARDS: Access, Visa SEATS: 55. Private parties: 50 main room, 14 private room. Children welcome. Music

HARWICH Essex map 3

▲ *Pier at Harwich* 🍷

The Quay, Harwich CO12 3HH COOKING 1
HARWICH (0255) 241212 COST £15–£38

Restaurant, bar, accommodation, fish and chip shop (The Ha'penny Pier) occupy a large verandahed house with prospect room at the top that overlooks the busy estuaries of Stour and Orwell. The restaurant is devoted to fish: from pie to salmon, from cod to halibut. Simple styles are on offer, but cheese sauces, salmon mousseline stuffings and the like have their place too. Reports have not been as content as hitherto, suggesting an overall lack of control in the kitchen. This is not formula food – the menu does change, fashions are slowly reflected – but it copes with large numbers, so systems of purchase and rules of cooking need rigorous imposition. The wine list is a generously intelligent canter across the world. Five white burgundies are nicely balanced with Alsaces, good Australians and French country wines, all very reasonably priced. There are decent half-bottles and a useful house selection. House wine is £7.50.

CELLARMAN'S CHOICE: Sonoma White 1988, Pedroncelli, £10.50; St Véran, Les Grandes Bruyères 1989, Luquet, £15.50.

CHEF: C.E. Oakley PROPRIETOR: G.M.W. Milsom OPEN: all week MEALS: 12 to 2, 6 to 9.30 PRICES: £22 (£32), Set L £8.50 (£15) to £10.50 (£17), Set D £16 (£22). Service 10%. Card slips closed CARDS: Access, Visa SEATS: 80. Private parties: 85 main room, 50 private room. Car park, 10 places. Children's helpings. Wheelchair access (2 steps). Music ACCOMMODATION: 6 rooms, all with bath/shower. B&B £45 to £72.50. TV. Phone. Scenic (*Which? Hotel Guide*)

HASLEMERE Surrey map 3

Morels 🍷

25–27 Lower Street, Haslemere GU27 2NY COOKING **4**
HASLEMERE (0428) 651462 COST £29–£52

An amuse-gueule here was described by a reader as 'baked Alaska with wild mushrooms and lentils'. This may typify Jean-Yves Morel's ability to adjust classics to his own ends. The restaurant generally provides quietly excellent food with sufficient interest to alert the mind as well as to stimulate the appetite. Some objection is made that the repertoire does not develop too radically, but reports don't reveal undue worry. The restaurant occupies cottages on a high pavement above a main road. Parking is terrible. The cool blue outside is taken up within and the succession of rooms shows design snap – in blues, creams and white – overlaying English vernacular architecture to great effect. Tables are well-set and well-spaced; the French waiting team is usually correctly efficient. A variety of interlocking menus are offered, depending on days of the week. Inevitably, prices are dearer at the weekend. The set-price lunch is very fair value, and those readers who have sampled across the board praise the effort that goes into the cheaper week-night menu as quite equal to that shown by the *carte* itself. Dishes that show some of the style include a tartare of smoked haddock with gazpacho dressing, a turret of the fish bound with a mayonnaise given texture-contrast from micro-diced cucumber and vivid colour from the dressing, or five tiny tarts of buttery pastry filled with a julienne of cucumber and soured cream, each one topped by a slice of cured salmon, or a fine puff pastry basket holding spears of asparagus, given a sauce Maltaise (orange hollandaise) made with blood oranges for colourful effect as well as taste. Usually, the cookery is light, though not stinting on butter. It does not shirk flavour however, as in a main-course of pork fillet with capers and saffron with a fine deep jus, or one of sweetbreads on a layer of spinach with almonds and a grand decoction of ceps, with a small puffball decorating the side of the dish. Nor does the cooking lack technique, remarked in a lamb fillet enveloped by a basil mousse – the lamb exactly pink, the mousse tender from outside to in. Among desserts the crème brûlée with sorbets is a firm favourite; so are any of the ices (which none the less may figure almost too frequently); so is the fine range of cheese (even if with no more than water biscuits); so, particularly, is the *grande assiette* of everything, which is the punter's friend on nearly every table – since, if for no other reason, the array of some half-dozen nibbles can be shared around. Coffee is strong, bread is decent, butter is matchless and vegetables are garden-fresh. The wine list is classic French with good growers, not a lot of adventure in the regions, but fine age among the clarets and burgundies at not too high a price. There are even enough halves for anyone. If Haslemere can support this, why is Surrey such a badlands for good, honest creative cookery?

CHEF: Jean-Yves Morel PROPRIETORS: Jean-Yves and Mary Anne Morel OPEN: Tue to Sat, exc Sat L CLOSED: 25 Dec, bank hols (exc Good Fri), 2 weeks end Feb, 2 weeks Sept/ Oct MEALS: 12.30 to 1.45, 7 to 10 PRICES: £31 (£43), Set L £17 (£29), Set D £20 (£32) CARDS: Access, Amex, Visa SEATS: 45. Private parties: 12 main room. Children's helpings. No cigars/pipes in dining-room. Wheelchair access (1 step). No music

HASTINGLEIGH Kent map 3

▲ *Woodmans Arms Auberge*

Hassell Street, Hastingleigh TN25 5JE
ELMSTED (023 375) 250

As the Guide *went to press this establishment closed.*

HATCH BEAUCHAMP **Somerset** map 2

Nightingales see under Taunton

NEW ENTRY

HAWORTH West Yorkshire map 5

▲ *Weavers*

15 West Lane, Haworth BD22 8DU COOKING 2
HAWORTH (0535) 643822 COST £18–£29

The interconnected dining-rooms and bar in this set of converted cottages are more full of bric-à-brac and objects than is the Brontë museum nearby. The ambience is lovable, as are the Rushworths. Their repertoire of cooking, usually called 'homely' without patronage, runs across a gamut of styles from traditional English to modern Anglo-French. The favourites are probably the traditional things, never easy to find done with panache, like Yorkshire pudding with gravy, 'Pennine pot-pie' (also called 'cow pie'), fisherman's pie and puddings such as 'Old School', sticky toffee or a substantial apple tart. The wine list is a catholic selection, fairly priced, of four dozen bins including very decent makers and bottles such as Jaboulet, Bruno Paillard, Peter Lehmann, Viña Ardanza and Toro Colegiata. House wines are £7.50. The 'early doors' menu written on a blackboard is a bargain for those who turn up at 7pm.

CHEFS/PROPRIETORS: Colin and Jane Rushworth OPEN: Tue to Sat, D only, and Sun L (Oct to Easter) CLOSED: 2 weeks July, 2 weeks Christmas MEALS: 12 to 1.30, 7 to 9 PRICES: £17 (£24), Set Sun L and D £12.50 (£18) CARDS: Access, Amex, Diners, Visa SEATS: 45. Private parties: 14 main room, 14 private room. Vegetarian meals. Children's helpings. Music. Air-conditioned ACCOMMODATION: 4 rooms, all with bath/shower. B&B £45 to £65. Deposit: £20. Children welcome. Air-conditioned. TV. Phone. Scenic. Doors close at midnight. Confirm 24 hours ahead

HAYDON BRIDGE Northumberland map 7

General Havelock Inn

Radcliffe Road, Haydon Bridge NE47 6ER COOKING 1
HAYDON BRIDGE (0434) 684376 COST £14–£31

Last year's rumours of sale or closure were unfounded, and the Clydes now say that they intend to stay put until they retire. Regulars mention that the bar meals are 'the best for miles around', but there is less consensus about full meals in the 'sometimes cold' dining-room. Prawns with lemon and cream cheese, baked fillet of plaice with parsley butter, and some stalwart English puddings such as apple pie have all been enjoyed. Others have found the cooking 'dull', the vegetables 'sad and low on quality', and overall 'poor value for money'. The set-price, four-course dinner menu doesn't stray far from the likes of avocado with spiced prawns and mussels, roast duck with redcurrant sauce, and spiced fillet of pork. House wine is £7.15.

CHEF: Angela Clyde PROPRIETORS: Ian and Angela Clyde OPEN: Wed to Sun, exc Sun D CLOSED: first 2 weeks Jan, last week Aug, first week Sept, second week Mar MEALS: 12 to 1.30, 7.30 to 9 PRICES: Set L £8 (£14) to £11 (£17), Set D £16 (£23) to £19 (£26) SEATS: 28. 4 tables outside. Private parties: 30 main room. Car park, 12 places. Vegetarian meals. Children's helpings. Wheelchair access (1 step; also WC). No music

---

HELFORD Cornwall map 1

▲ *Riverside*

Helford TR12 6JU COOKING 2
MANACCAN (032 623) 443 COST £42

This pair of cottages, a wall and a lane away from the creek that connects to the Helford river, is surrounded by small satellites, each housing a room or two. The Riverside reminds one of the 'cottage hotels' of pre-war days. Of course, it's done up to the mark for today and people enjoy the peace, the clean air and the light when they wake, as well as breakfast in the still of a summer's morning on the terrace. Eating more substantially is reserved for the evening, in the low and closely set dining-room of the big cottage. The Darrells are loquacious hosts and David Rayner beavers away in the kitchen, sometimes to good effect. Susan Darrell does the baking and jam-making. The menu is dear for Cornwall, nor is the set price innocent of supplements. Fish is obviously given pride of place, and this may be approached in a novel or emphatic way, with mixed results. Witch sole (or trout, or turbot) have been finished with rhubarb, and an orange sauce, or hake with a mustard mousse. Citrus flavourings are popular too, as in a brioche filled with scallops, pearl onions and ruby grapefruit. Meat dishes, perhaps three on a menu, show a liking for offal, lambs' sweetbreads and kidneys, calf's liver, and duck served with a plum, or sometimes plum and blackcurrant, sauce. Desserts are not always successful, but petits fours are enjoyed. A wine list was not sent this year, but it is reported to be extensive, with house wine from £7.60.

CHEFS: Susan Darrell and David Rayner PROPRIETOR: Susan Darrell OPEN: all week, D only; Sat and Sun L CLOSED: early Nov to mid-Feb MEALS: 12.30 to 2, 7.30 to 9.30 PRICES: Set D £28 (£35) SEATS: 35. 4 tables outside. Private parties: 30 main room. Car park, 12 places. Vegetarian meals. No children under 12 in dining-room (high tea provided). No pipes in dining-room. Wheelchair access (2 steps). No music ACCOMMODATION: 6 rooms, all with bath/shower. B&B £60 to £95. Deposit: £100. Children welcome. Baby facilities. Garden. TV. Scenic. Confirm by 6 (*Which? Hotel Guide*)

HEREFORD Hereford & Worcester map 2

Fat Tulip

The Old Wye Bridge,
2 St Martin's Street, Hereford HR2 7RE COOKING 1
HEREFORD (0432) 275808 COST £37

By the old bridge across the Wye, this flower has not yet drooped and died, but rather is continuing to offer dishes that sound adventurous to Herefordshire ears from a short menu that must also be quite expensive to Herefordshire eyes.

The cooking of dishes such as boned quail stuffed with calf's liver on a madeira sauce (venison liver was reported once), and mussels in puff pastry with a cream and saffron sauce, can have faults (too much salt for some people's taste) but has also proved satisfactory. It is not generally a 'refined' style. Ice-creams, locally made, are good, as can be the espresso. Service has sometimes seemed lacking, the more surprising on occasions when the restaurant is barely half-full. The wine list has some interesting items, including Pacherenc du Vic-Bilh, Brédif's Vouvray and Meursault Clos du Cromin. House wines – a Côteaux d'Ancenis, a Vouvray and two Riojas – are £8.50.

CHEF: Kevin Powles PROPRIETORS: Kevin and Susan Powles OPEN: Mon to Sat, exc Sat L MEALS: 12.15 to 1.45, 7.15 to 9.30 PRICES: £23 (£31). Card slips closed CARDS: Access, Amex, Visa SEATS: 35. Private parties: 20 main room. Children welcome. Wheelchair access (1 step). Music

HERSHAM Surrey map 3

La Malmaison

17 Queens Road, Hersham KT12 5ND COOKING 3
WALTON-ON-THAMES (0932) 227412 COST £19–£42

Amid generous space and quiet decoration, the dining-room overlooks a small courtyard rather than the high life of south-west suburban London. It confirms the self-sufficiency of this professional team: Jacques Troquet, once chef to a French ambassador, in the kitchen, emerging at the end of service to add his explanations to enquiries about the food, and his wife Lisa keeping a very firm hand on the front-of-house. The cooking shows a breadth of style and a capacity to add flavour that may not be expected in Hersham. There has, perhaps, been a greater emphasis on Mediterranean tastes and materials this year, reflecting the fashion of wider circles. Fish soup with garlic croûtons and rouille, aïoli garni with hake, red mullet with lime and fennel à la grecque, and turbot with shallots, mushrooms and a deep, dark sauce are some examples – Jacques evidently enjoys cooking fish. Modernity comes in again, even if not of the far south, with meat dishes like duck with cinnamon and grapefruit or pork with apples, apricots and caper sauce. Good cheese, good puddings and desserts have made reluctant visitors confirmed addicts. Special evenings, jazz nights even, enliven the daily round. The wine list is not too long, entirely French, and has difficulty offering enough half-bottles or a genuine range under £12; but spend more and the choice is fair. House French is £8.20.

CHEF: Jacques Troquet PROPRIETORS: Jacques and Lisa Troquet OPEN: Mon to Sat, exc Sat L MEALS: 12 to 2.30, 7 to 10 PRICES: £26 (£35), Set L £13.50 (£19) to £15.50 (£22), Set D £21.50 (£28). Service 10%. Card slips closed CARDS: Access, Amex, Diners, Visa SEATS: 40. 4 tables outside. Private parties: 55 main room, 12 private room. Healthy eating options. Children's helpings. Smart dress preferred. No smoking. Wheelchair access. Music

The text of entries is based on unsolicited reports sent in by readers, backed up by inspections conducted anonymously. The factual details under the text are from questionnaires the Guide *sends to all restaurants that feature in the book.*

HERSTMONCEUX East Sussex map 3

Sundial

Gardner Street, Herstmonceux BN27 4LA COOKING 2
HERSTMONCEUX (0323) 832217 COST £20–£54

A quarter-century of catering to the residents of Sussex has mellowed Giuseppe Bertoli, who now acts very much as solicitous host rather than 'chef on his piano' as in earlier years. The restaurant, too – tile-hung cottages with leafy open-air dining in summer – has mellowed, but not changed radically, its formula of international haute cuisine. Highly decorative, highly priced, except in the various set-price deals, and consistent in its intentions, this style pleases a sizeable body of customers, but will irritate others who are used to more recent conventions. A page of Italian wines remains the best bet on an otherwise rather overpriced and unbalanced list. A few vin de pays have been added this year. House wines are from £8.75.

CHEF: Giuseppe Bertoli PROPRIETORS: Laure and Giuseppe Bertoli OPEN: Tue to Sun, exc Sun D CLOSED: mid-Aug to Sept, 25 Dec to 20 Jan MEALS: 12.30 to 2 (2.30 Sun), 7.30 to 9.30 (10 Sat) PRICES: £32 (£45), Set L £11.50 (£20) to £15.50 (£24), Set D £24.50 (£34). Service 10%. Card slips closed CARDS: Access, Amex, Diners, Visa SEATS: 70. 8 tables outside. Private parties: 50 main room, 22 private room. Car park, 25 places. Vegetarian meals. Children's helpings. No smoking. Wheelchair access (also WC). Music

HETTON North Yorkshire map 5

Angel Inn

Hetton BD23 6LT COOKING 3
CRACOE (075 673) 263 COST £19–£30

Certain practical changes to the old taproom and cocktail bar have given more space to bar food and allow diners, who go straight to their tables for drinks and amuse-gueules, to have their table for the full evening: no more double sittings. Denis Watkins remarks on the growing popularity of the bar food, which he makes more brasserie-like by the year, and it has always been difficult for the *Guide* to know whether to spend more time recommending this or restaurant meals. The layout of the inn is complicated; corridors of service and access may give an insecurity of openness, but temperatures and togetherness are maintained by generous fires which work even in February snows. Occasionally reports suggest one more waiter should be hired or reflect that there was no sense of repose – but the place hums and bustles with people who want what is on offer, which cannot be bad. Both bar and dining-room offer fair value. The latter has a set-price menu of four or five printed seasonal choices, supplemented by daily specials. 'Moneybags' of seafood gain consistent plaudits, but other fish, perhaps queen scallops or tartare of salmon or fresh halibut, also get their own praise. Guinea-fowl is wrapped in Parma ham and savoy cabbage (shades of Alastair Little), and pigeon is chargrilled and sliced on to potato and carrot galette with wild mushroom sauce. Vegetables have become less 'saucy' according to some reports. Puddings continue to be excellent: 'autumn' pudding and sticky toffee again get frequent reference. This is the restaurant of an enthusiast, one might even say evangelist, of natural food and decent cooking and it should be encouraged. A wine dispenser has magnified the various delights obtainable here – Puligny-Montrachet, Wynns Chardonnay, Barolo are what you might expect by the glass. Enthusiasm for Italy is paramount but Burgundy is represented by excellent smaller growers, and a page of clarets has older vintages at very reasonable prices. There are good half-bottles. A simple approach and generously low mark-ups make this an exemplary list, and it receives a bottle award this year. House wine is £6.95. CELLARMAN'S CHOICE: Sauvignon de Touraine 1989, Marcedet, £9.85; Givry 'en Choué' 1987, Lespinasse, £15.10.

CHEFS: Denis Watkins and John Topham PROPRIETORS: Denis and Juliet Watkins and John Topham OPEN: Mon to Sat, D only, and Sun L CLOSED: 26 Dec, 1 Jan, 1 week Jan MEALS: 12.15 to 2, 7 to 9.30 PRICES: bar £13 (£19), restaurant Set L £15.50 (£21), Set D £18.80 (£25). Card slips closed CARDS: Access, Visa SEATS: 36. 15 tables outside. Private parties: 40 main room. Car park, 17 places. Children's helpings on request. Smart dress preferred. No pipes in dining-room. Wheelchair access (also WC). Music. Fax: (075 673) 363

HEXHAM Northumberland map 7

Black House **NEW ENTRY**

Dipton Mill Road, Hexham NE46 1RZ COOKING 2
HEXHAM (0434) 604744 COST £31

Apart from the gravelled, well-lit car park and the name board outside, the Black House has the appearance of a private residence: from without converted farm outbuildings, within a comfortable cross between a simple country cottage and the *Antiques Roadshow* – much decorative china and striking pieces of furniture. Hazel Pittock wisely keeps her monthly-changing menu short: six choices in each category. Plain steak was 'depressingly popular with the guests' one night, but the menu ranges more widely through the likes of beef olives, duck with orange, ginger and honey, feuilleté of salmon and prawns in champagne sauce and game pie. A vegetarian dish is always offered; a leek and Stilton pancake 'tasted better than it sounds' and even drew a gasp of envy. The cooking is sound and satisfying, and gets unanimous praise; quantities are generous, meats are well-chosen and the vegetables fresh (although sometimes cooked less well than others). The wine list has a heavy French emphasis; Italy, Germany and Spain get a nod and there is a glance at the New World. The price spread is fair, though prices are not bargain basement. House French is £7.75.

CHEFS: Hazel Pittock and Dawn Aston PROPRIETORS: Chris and Hazel Pittock OPEN: Tue to Sat, D only (L prior bookings only) MEALS: 7 to 9.30 PRICES: £19 (£26). Card slips closed CARDS: Access, Visa SEATS: 26. Private parties: 26 main room. Car park, 12 places. Vegetarian meals. Children restricted. Smart dress preferred. No smoking. Wheelchair access. Music

If a restaurant is new to the Guide *this year (did not appear as a main entry in the last edition)* NEW ENTRY *appears opposite its name.*

HIGH ONGAR Essex map 3

Shoes

The Street, High Ongar CM5 9ND COOKING 1
BRENTWOOD (0277) 363 350 COST £19–£36

This is a black and white, half-timbered former coaching-inn converted into a restaurant. Timber beams are the theme, with a vengeance, once the modern glazed doors are opened. That one person called it 'Tudorish' rather than Tudor speaks volumes for the effect of the conversion. Paul Spry's daily-changing menu is old-fashioned modern in avoiding upstanding flavours, lapsing often into sweetness and showing tendencies to fuss. It is, however, a useful prospect for Essex and would improve if a more robust approach was adopted. 'I cannot understand the fashion for polenta; this was like fried school semolina; the spinach was bland but looked pretty on the plate,' said one diner who also had duck breast with honey sauce which was 'mild, tender, thick-cut, without skin. I would have preferred strong, tender, thin-cut, with skin for flavour.' Others have mentioned the drawbacks of keeping things warm for too long before service or, alternatively, keeping cold dishes too long in the fridge. A steady and well-sourced wine list gives fair space to countries other than France and is thoughtfully provided with plenty of halves. The music irritates here. One meal was vitiated by a half-hour stint of trombone. Another diner requested a change of style but was told that the six-disc autochanger could not be meddled with. House French is £7.25.

CHEF: Paul Spry PROPRIETORS: L.A. Wootton, P.J. Gowan and Mrs D.C. Gowan OPEN: all week, exc Sat L and Sun D CLOSED: 1 week after Christmas MEALS: 12 to 2.30, 7.30 to 9.30 PRICES: £22 (£30), Set L £13.75 (£19) to £16.25 (£22) CARDS: Access, Visa SEATS: 60. Private parties: 40 main room, 40 and 20 private rooms. Children welcome. Smart dress preferred. Wheelchair access (1 step; also WC). Music

HINTLESHAM Suffolk map 3

▲ *Hintlesham Hall* NEW ENTRY

Hintlesham IP8 3NS COOKING 3
HINTLESHAM (047 387) 268 and 334 COST £27–£56

Hintlesham sails on. New owners have kept on the old staff so that to all appearances it remains the same. Customers who liked the edge of spiky personality introduced by Ruth Watson might wish to differ. Dining here is a luxurious experience (lunch is cheaper, though luxury is still pervasive). The dining-room is among the grandest, and coffee afterwards maybe taken in one of the Caroline rooms heavy with plaster and ornaments: remarkable. The food is more predictable: country-house English, with a few mistakes, and expensive. Is Ipswich ready for £50 a head? The long *carte*, at varying prices according to length of meal and time of the week, offers luxury ingredients at no extra cost; but it has not always delivered flavour in the marked fashion necessary to make it stand out from its peers. A winter meal included a salmon terrine with two-caviare sauce (the sauce better than the lumpish terrine); lambs' sweetbreads with morels, tomato and tarragon and fresh noodles; a filo basket with mussels and sole with a light mustard sauce; salmon with a lemon and coriander vinaigrette; calf's liver with a soubise and port sauce; beef fillet with a truffle sauce bound with foie gras ('this was very successful'); a suprême of halibut wrapped in lettuce, on a lentil and chive sauce; a chocolate fetishist's fantasy ('which I could have eaten again'); a lemon tart with lemon ice-cream; and apple mille-feuille with calvados sabayon. Ancillaries are what one would expect and the service is solicitous in the extreme. A regular luncher here stresses the value (comparative) and quality, even if coffee is £2.30 ('a second pot is happily provided', however). No expense has been spared on the assembly of the magnificent wine list; the customer is expected to contribute. Nothing is below £13, much is above £30. House recommendations sometimes provide a refuge for economy but not, alas, here. House wine is £13.95.

CHEF: Alan Ford PROPRIETORS: Hintlesham Hall Ltd OPEN: all week, exc Sat L MEALS: 12.15 to 1.45, 7 to 9.45 PRICES: Set L £17.50 (£27) to £19.50 (£29), Set D £29.50 (£39) to £37.50 (£47). Net prices, card slips closed CARDS: Access, Amex, Diners, Visa SEATS: 100. Private parties: 100 main room, 16, 40 and 81 private rooms. Car park, 100 places. Vegetarian meals. Children's helpings. No children under 10 D. Smart dress preferred. No smoking in dining-room. Wheelchair access (1 step; also WC). No music. Fax: (047 387) 463 ACCOMMODATION: 33 rooms, all with bath/shower. Rooms for disabled. B&B £80 to £160. Children welcome. Baby facilities. Garden. Sauna. Tennis. Fishing. Golf. Snooker. TV. Phone. Scenic (*Which? Hotel Guide*)

HOCKLEY HEATH West Midlands map 5

▲ *Nuthurst Grange*

Nuthurst Grange Lane,
Hockley Heath B94 5NL COOKING 2*
LAPWORTH (0564) 783972 COST £22–£55

'Here is a tale in which we really did cause some difficulties for a restaurant but which were coped with magnificently.' So begins an account of a Sunday lunch at Nuthurst Grange and reports concur that this well-upholstered hotel, within the motorway box that is now the Midlands, does not stint on welcome and energetic service. Nor does it stint on ingredients. Lunch, on that occasion, began with a selection of four sorts of fish in a dill cream sauce. Most dishes are complicated and come well ornamented. Dinner menus are at set prices and are of mounting elaboration. The most expensive (£35) is not cheap by any measure and would have to be better than reports suggest to constitute good value. Examples from it include asparagus and leek soup; cockles, prawns, mussels and lobster in white wine jelly with a mint cucumber mousse; lamb with a curried sauce; duck with prunes and armagnac; and excellent desserts, including puddings and cheeses. The wine list offers a fair range, in price and type, with some Mondavi Californians, burgundies from Parent, and Alsaces from Kuentz-Bas. House wines start at £9.55.

Dining-rooms where live and recorded music are not be played are signalled by No music *in the details at the end of an entry.*

CHEFS: D.L. Randolph and S. Wilkes PROPRIETORS: D.L. and D.A. Randolph OPEN: all week, exc Sat L MEALS: 12.30 to 2, 7 to 9.30 PRICES: Set L £13.50 (£22) to £17.50 (£26), Set D from £19.75 (£29) to £35 (£46). Card slips closed CARDS: Access, Amex, Diners, Visa SEATS: 50. 5 tables outside. Private parties: 60 main room. Car park, 40 places. Vegetarian meals. Children's helpings. No smoking in dining-room preferred. Wheelchair access (also WC). No music. Fax: (0564) 783919 ACCOMMODATION: 15 rooms, all with bath/shower. B&B £85 to £125. Children welcome. Baby facilities. Afternoon teas. Garden. TV. Phone. Scenic. Doors close at midnight

HOLDENBY Northamptonshire map 3

▲ *Lynton House*

Holdenby NN6 8DJ — COOKING 2*
HOLDENBY (0604) 770777 — COST £20–£34

In architectural terms, the stone ruins of Holdenby, the house built by Sir Christopher Hatton, Elizabeth I's favourite and Lord Chancellor, have more charm than this staringly red-brick former rectory on the road from Church Brampton to East Haddon. People do speak, however, in praise of Carol Bertozzi's cooking with an Italian tilt. It is quite formally, and very proudly, served by her husband Carlo and a small team. Although the outside of the house may have that raw Edwardian feel, the comfortable dining-room and conservatory are bedecked with flowers and the bedrooms are enjoyed as well. Dishes on the four-course set-price menu have Italian titles, but may be familiar in other guises. This does not mean that excellent lamb with a caramelised mint sauce, or venison with a red wine and berry sauce, are any less exactly cooked from good materials. As you might expect, home-made pasta, say cannelloni, is good. There is praise, too, for first courses of spinach and ricotta pancakes and Parma ham with sliced marinated aubergines, as well as for hazelnut meringue cake and good ice-creams to finish. Wines include a fair choice of Italian, but without vintage or other details. Sr Bertozzi would be happy to advise. House Corvo from Sicily is £10.75.

CHEF: Carol Bertozzi PROPRIETORS: Carlo and Carol Bertozzi OPEN: Mon to Sat, exc Mon and Sat CLOSED: Christmas, 2 weeks summer MEALS: 12.15 to 1.45, 7.15 to 9.45 PRICES: Set L £14.50 (£20), Set D £19.75 (£25) to £23.50 (£29). Net prices, card slips closed CARDS: Access, Visa SEATS: 45. Private parties: 55 main room, 20 private room. Car park, 30 places. Vegetarian meals. Children's helpings (Sun L only). No children under 6. Smart dress preferred. No cigars/pipes in dining-room. Wheelchair access. No music ACCOMMODATION: 5 rooms, all with bath/shower. B&B £58 to £68. No children under 6. Garden. Golf. TV. Phone. Scenic. Doors close at 12.30am. Confirm by 9 (*Which? Hotel Guide*)

'The small pieces of lamb contained some hidden bone which was OK but some had splintered and would have been dangerous if inadvertently swallowed in the dark dining-room. I had visions of asphyxia in yuppieland–stockbrokers using gold chains to remove the offending bone, while doctors searched my wallet in vain for a BUPA card.'
On inspecting in London

HOLT Norfolk map 6

Yetman's

37 Norwich Road, Holt NR25 6SA COOKING 2
HOLT (0263) 713320 COST £36

Inspired by the activities of Bernard and Carla Phillips at Moorings (see entry, Wells-next-the-Sea), Peter and Alison Yetman decided to open their own restaurant along the same lines. The emphasis is on well-chosen local ingredients, cooking that absorbs French and oriental influences into a modern English feel, carefree informality, and value for money. Organic vegetables and beef come from nearby farms and a fisherman travels to Lowestoft to procure fresh supplies direct from the boats. This translates into short dinner menus along the lines of salad of crab, avocado and home-smoked trout; leg of lamb roasted with garlic, cider and rosemary; sea bass baked with fennel, lemon grass and Pernod; and spinach gnocchi with spiced tomato, capsicum and almond sauce. Sweets might include rhubarb fool and apricot pancakes brûlée. Simpler (and cheaper) lunches are also served on Saturday and Sunday. Approved dishes have included crab chowder with fresh coriander; turbot baked with yoghurt, lime and ginger; fillet of beef with tarragon hollandaise; and French raspberry tart. The feeling is that this 'very pretty, very simple restaurant' is improving all the time. 'Bright, helpful, confident and competent waitresses–and Peter Yetman–add a great deal to the happy, "isn't life great?" atmosphere.' A well-spread wine list has 10 house wines, starting at £7.

CHEF: Alison Yetman PROPRIETORS: Alison and Peter Yetman OPEN: Wed to Sun D, Sat and Sun L MEALS: 12.30 to 2, 7.30 to 9 PRICES: £22 (£30) SEATS: 32. Private parties: 20 main room. Vegetarian meals. Children's helpings. No smoking. Wheelchair access (1 step). No music

HORNCASTLE Lincolnshire map 6

Magpies

NEW ENTRY

73–75 East Street, Horncastle LN9 6AA COOKING 1
HORNCASTLE (0507) 527004 COST £13–£28

'This is no place for faint-hearted appetites,' writes an inspector. Portions are generous, the restaurant may be called cosy, and the motherly waitresses are eager to ensure every mouthful is eaten. The Lees change their fixed-price menu every few weeks, although French onion soup is a standard fixture by popular demand. Gratin of leeks and bacon, potted prawns, rack of lamb with rosemary and fillet steak with béarnaise sauce show the style, while warm salad of monkfish and bacon, and breast of pigeon – fanned out in pink slices – with caramelised onions and red wine sauce add a more adventurous note. Excellent fresh vegetables are silver-served. To finish, lemon tart is a much safer bet than chocolate and rum cheesecake. The cooking can be a bit rough-and-ready, but generally it is well executed and certainly good value. In the absence of growers' names and vintages, any judgement on the short wine list has to rely on clarets and champagnes, where selection is good and prices fair.

CHEF: Matthew Lee PROPRIETORS: Joan, Matthew and Caroline Lee OPEN: Tue to Sat, D only, and Sun L CLOSED: 25 and 26 Dec, 2 weeks Oct or May MEALS: 12.30 to 2, 7.30 to 9.45 PRICES: £17 (£23), Set Sun L £8 (£13) CARDS: Access, Visa SEATS: 45. Private parties: 45 main room. Children's helpings (Sun L only). No children under 12, exc Sun. Smart dress preferred. Wheelchair access. Music

---

HORTON Northamptonshire map 3

French Partridge

Horton NN7 2AP COOKING 3
NORTHAMPTON (0604) 870033 COST £23–£29

One of the *Guide*'s marathon runners, this Georgian house extending into a barn and set by the road in a small Northampton village has been the locale for the Partridge family's hospitality for more years than some would like to recall. Mary Partridge supervises the front, father and son share the cooking. The ambience and decoration pre-date the 1990s. Old-fashioned virtues persist: fair value in the set-price, four-course menu with coffee; a certain substance to the cooking that makes few concessions to fashion, though by no means closing its eyes to the wider world, hence the offering on a single evening of Malayan-style baked chicken in coconut and citrus marinade and braised lamb shank with flageolets. The short menu has a choice of four dishes for first and main courses, an alternative fish or non-meat item in between, a run of half a dozen desserts, and a savoury to finish. Long-term residents have commented that their adrenalin sometimes remains unstimulated, but one reported 'the best meal we have ever had here, the richness of earlier times being replaced by more natural cooking'. Another enthused about all the menu's qualities even if he had trouble finding some of the ingredients proclaimed on it in the dishes themselves. Familiarity may breed disdain, but the Partridges are rarely complacent, hence the restaurant's continued popularity. Service is 'still adequate' though moving to well-rehearsed routines that at times may seem mechanical. The Partridges gain their bottle award not for length of wine list – only a few pages of clearly printed wines – nor for their glittering first growths with prices to match, but for good names (Ch. Hanteillan and Fourcas-Hosten in Bordeaux, Champet in Côte Rôtie) generally sound vintages and the catholic range, encompassing excellent New World wines as well as interesting and modestly priced wines from south-west France. Good half-bottles include several dessert wines. House wines are from £7.

CHEFS: David Partridge and Justin Partridge PROPRIETORS: David and Mary Partridge OPEN: Tue to Sat, D only CLOSED: 2 weeks Christmas and Easter, 3 weeks July to Aug MEALS: 7.30 to 9 PRICES: Set D £19.50 (£23) to £20.50 (£24). Net prices SEATS: 50. Private parties: 10 main room. Car park, 50 places. Children welcome. Wheelchair access

---

An asterisk (*) after the 1 to 5 cooking mark at the top of an entry signifies that the Guide *and its readers think that the restaurant is a particularly fine example within its numeric classification.*

HUDDERSFIELD West Yorkshire map 5

▲ *Lodge Hotel*

48 Birkby Lodge Road, Birkby,
Huddersfield HD2 2BG COOKING 1
HUDDERSFIELD (0484) 431001 COST £16–£31

Though the hotel is in a suburban setting, the large gardens give it a *rus in urbe* feel. The house boasts exceptional art nouveau interiors by the Manchester architect Edgar Wood and a dining-room in shades running from crimson to pink. The cooking is full-dress in presentation, complementing the napery, but honest intent is appreciated in reports of good home-made soups, serious Sunday roasts, and the lightest of mince pies made with filo pastry. Everyday menus stray from the more traditional, family Sunday lunch dishes into realms of steamed scallops, salmon and prawns on fried seaweed with a lemon grass sauce; a lobster, pheasant and dill sausage on sauce Nantua; Barbary duck with blackcurrant and orange sauce; and chicken with smoked salmon and artichoke mousse on a white wine sauce. The style is getting dated, but luckily it still pleases, especially when muddle and lack of flavour are avoided. The wine list offers a fair general selection, with a small 'connoisseur's section' at mainstream prices. House wines are £7.50.

CHEF: Richard Hanson PROPRIETORS: Kevin and David Birley OPEN: all week, exc Sat L and Sun D MEALS: 12 to 2, 7.30 to 9.45 PRICES: Set L £9.95 (£16), Set D £18.95 (£26). Card slips closed CARDS: Access, Amex, Visa SEATS: 60. 4 tables outside. Private parties: 24 main room, 20 and 24 private rooms. Car park, 40 places. Vegetarian meals. Children's helpings. Smart dress preferred. No smoking in half of dining-room. Wheelchair access (1 step; also WC). Music. Fax: (0484) 421590 ACCOMMODATION: 11 rooms, all with bath/shower. Rooms for disabled. B&B £50 to £60. Children welcome. Baby facilities. Pets (small) welcome. Afternoon teas. Garden. Snooker. TV. Phone. Scenic. Doors close at 1am. Confirm am before arrival

Paris II

NEW ENTRY

84 Fitzwilliam Street,
Huddersfield HD1 5BD COOKING 1
HUDDERSFIELD (0484) 516773 COST £13–£25

Not much change has been made to the premises that once housed Pisces, a fish restaurant. Paris II is an offshoot of Leeds' Paris (see entry) and operates on the same principle of fair prices, few frills and fresh food – a greater rarity than we would wish. The 'early bird' menu is excellent value, but so is the long *carte,* with lots of extra fish dishes written up on the blackboard. Frills are not so cut back that later diners don't get crudités, with a peppery cream-cheese dip, to nibble. First reports have praised the ingredients, especially the fish in dishes such as halibut with a competent hollandaise, or monkfish in tomato and lemon sauce with fresh chervil. There is less enthusiasm, however, for desserts, even if first courses of black pudding with mustard sauce and too sweet an apple purée or parfait of duck liver with too sweet a geranium jelly redressed the balance. As in Leeds, this is an excellent local resource whose philosophy is the right one. The wine list is different from the parent restaurant's but shows the same ability to select intelligently and price conservatively. House wines are £6.95.

CHEFS: David Rowley and David Rose PROPRIETORS: Martin Spalding, Steven Kendell and David Wheeler OPEN: Mon to Sat, exc Sat L MEALS: 12 to 2, 6 to 10.30 (Set D 6 to 7.30) PRICES: £15 (£21), Set L £6.95 (£13) to £8.95 (£15), Set D £11.95 inc wine (£14) CARDS: Access, Amex, Visa SEATS: 70. Car park, 20 places. Vegetarian meals. Children welcome. Music. Air-conditioned

HUNSTRETE Avon map 2

▲ *Hunstrete House* NEW ENTRY

Hunstrete BS18 4NS COOKING 2
KEYNSHAM (0761) 490490 COST £25–£48

If you pay large sums for a famous country-house hotel, it should be possible to maintain its standards and reputation, particularly if you keep the chef. So must the argument have gone when Clipper Hotels bought this low, almost rambling house from the Dupays, who had run it so successfully through the last decade and more. But readers will know only too well that this is not always the case; just as often, decline sets in. Signs are, however, that Hunstrete is still worth a visit. Robert Elsmore remains at the stove, the staff are willing and friendly, sometimes almost matey, and the house has a lot going for it – though one reader thought new paint and wallpaper would help it along. Elsmore's cooking is simple to a fault. A set menu of asparagus spears with truffle dressing, wild mushroom consommé, grilled salmon on a bed of spinach with new potatoes and thin apple tart with clotted cream, followed by some English cheese, was spare, sauceless and accurately cooked. But the assurance shown here evaporated in a dish of rack of lamb with sour cream and mashed potato, as boring as the crème caramel with a light biscuit which followed it. *Cuisine naturelle* needs a deal of invention to get it running, and the simplicity here too often skirts boredom. The trimmings of the evening are still considered, with ample scope for filling up on good hot canapés, handsome rolls or petits fours with weakish coffee. Keep wine ordering below about £15 and the reward will be good quality and fine value, as in Ch. Hanteillan 1986 at £14 and a Guigal Côtes du Rhône for £14.50. Thereafter, mark-ups push hard although there is no stinting on the quality.

CHEF: Robert Elsmore PROPRIETORS: Clipper Hotels OPEN: all week MEALS: 12.30 to 2.30, 7.30 to 9.30 PRICES: £29 (£40), Set L £15 (£25), Set D £29.50 (£40). Card slips closed CARDS: Access, Visa SEATS: 50. 6 tables outside. Private parties: 55 main room, 6 and 16 private rooms. Car park, 40 places. Vegetarian meals. No children under 9. Jacket and tie. No-smoking area. Wheelchair access (also WC). No music. Fax: (0761) 490732 ACCOMMODATION: 24 rooms, all with bath/shower. Rooms for disabled. B&B £95 to £150. No children under 9. Afternoon teas. Garden. Swimming-pool. Tennis. Fishing. Air-conditioned. TV. Phone. Scenic. Confirm by 6 (*Which? Hotel Guide*)

Net prices *in the details at the end of an entry indicates that the prices given on a menu and on a bill are inclusive of VAT and service charge, and that this practice is clearly stated on menu and bill.*

HURSTBOURNE TARRANT Hampshire map 2

▲ *Esseborne Manor* 🍷

Hurstbourne Tarrant SP11 0ER
HURSTBOURNE TARRANT (026 476) 444
on the A343, 1m N of Hurstbourne Tarrant
COOKING 2
COST £19–£49

Gents with neither will be provided with a jacket and tie to fit them for dining here. The food is full-dress too, as is the handsome late-nineteenth-century house with its seriously 1980s upholstery. Other aspects are usually thorough: for instance, the staff know about the cheeses – not so common an attribute. The content of the menus – five courses, with no choice in the middle, at a fixed price – veers from the utterly straight (melon and grapefruit with ginger) to the mildly interesting (smoked salmon with a lentil vinaigrette sauce, ham and parsley aspic with a new potato and shallot salad with capers). The fairly stiff price (but this is the South East and there are five courses) does allow fair use of luxuries – foie gras, smoked salmon, lobster – as constituents of dishes, and there are no surcharges. The level of performance is even enough to prompt a week-long resident to praise each and every dinner, even if vegetables have drawn comments about their inadequacy. The wine list has a fine selection from France, with younger growers from Burgundy shown well and good spreads of clarets and Rhônes. Italy and Spain, California and Australasia receive short but exemplary treatment. Prices seem to be pushing harder this year with very little on offer under £15. House wine is £12.

CHEF: Mark Greenfield PROPRIETORS: Michael and Frieda Yeo OPEN: all week MEALS: 12.30 to 2, 7.30 to 9.30 PRICES: Set L £11.50 (£19) to £15.50 (£23), Set D £31 (£41). Card slips closed CARDS: Access, Amex, Diners, Visa SEATS: 36. Private parties: 28 main room, 10 private room. Car park, 30 places. No children under 12. Jacket and tie. No cigars/pipes in dining-room. Wheelchair access. Music. Fax: (026 476) 473
ACCOMMODATION: 12 rooms, all with bath/shower. Rooms for disabled. B&B £80 to £107. No children under 12. Afternoon teas. Garden. Tennis. TV. Phone. Scenic. Doors close at midnight. Confirm by 6 (*Which? Hotel Guide*)

ILKLEY West Yorkshire map 5

Box Tree

29 Church Street, Ilkley LS29 9DR
ILKLEY (0943) 608484
COOKING 3*
COST £23–£54

The Box Tree continues to be called homely and cottagey, though its small rooms have seen some redecoration and the 'more sentimental' pictures are gradually being replaced. It continues, too, to present the same image and, sometimes, menu. One party was pleased to revisit for Sunday lunch after an absence of four years. They were pleased at the reasonable all-in price, and were able to eat the same things as on their first visit, such as crêpe Alfredo and breasts of wood pigeon. The *carte du jour*, sometimes expressed in a mish-mash of English and French – 'I couldn't find all the terms in my *Larousse*' – is more adventurous than the Sunday offering and a sight more modern. Hence, perhaps, the absence of words from a fusty *Larousse*. But while one reader found great satisfaction in a warm salad of red mullet and artichoke, baked fillet of turbot with leeks and a mustard sauce, and a delicious (if a mite rich) chocolate marjolaine, another was less impressed by an 'assiette of smoked salmon' that proved to be no more than smoked salmon and half a lemon. Similarly an 'assiette of lemon' without its promised soufflé was reduced to a lemon tart with lemon sorbet. A note of the perfunctory enters too many reports this year for comfort. The overall impression, however, is of a large and professional brigade capable of finesse and accuracy, and of food served without pomposity, though with the occasional flourish such as synchronised dome-lifting. Things which have impressed include elegant canapés and petits fours – several sorts of tuile; a plate of mussels with thin noodles and a saffron broth; poussin with lentils and robust tarragon sauce; a mille-feuille of calfs' sweetbreads with pistachio; the old favourite of strawberries with rose sorbet in a tuile basket; a fine elderflower sorbet; and small tartlets with crème pâtissière and poached fruit. Various ploys have been instituted to encourage business, from a supper club to free bottles of wine for regulars. The Box Tree deserves to survive. The cellar selection offers 20 decent wines at affordable prices, and fine wine and bin-end selections which make no concession to economy but do provide a good range of pedigree properties. There are good halves of dessert wines and a page of cognacs.

CHEF: Edward Denny PROPRIETOR: Eric Kyte OPEN: Tue to Sun, exc Sat L and Sun D CLOSED: 25 and 26 Dec, 1 Jan MEALS: 12 to 2.30 (Sun 12.30 to 2), 7.30 to 9.45 PRICES: Set L £12.50 (£23) to £14.75 (£28), Set D £24 (£36) to £32 (£45) CARDS: Access, Amex, Diners, Visa SEATS: 50. Private parties: 30 main room, 16 private room. Children welcome. Smart dress preferred. No cigars/pipes in dining-room. Wheelchair access

Sous le Nez 🍷 NEW ENTRY

19–21 Church Street, Ilkley LS26 9DR COOKING 1
ILKLEY (0943) 600566 COST £19–£29

The bistro downstairs is all hustle and bustle around rather small tables; the same food can be had on the floor above, in more elegant surroundings, though the timing is usually later in the evening. Sous le Nez's formula is a long daily menu, plus fish dishes listed on a blackboard and an 'early bird' set menu as at Paris (founded later) in Leeds (see entry). Sous le Nez en Ville (Quebec House, Quebec Street, Leeds) is set to do battle on the streets of Leeds itself. Reports praise the prices, the range and some of the cooking. Moules marinière were fresh and lively; deep-fried mushrooms with garlic and Stilton were decent examples of the breed. Duck with orange and bacon was passable – orange in flavour even if not caramelised enough – and lamb with shallots and wild mushrooms used good meat, correctly cooked. Desserts have shown more signs of mass production for high numbers. Prices and range on the no-nonsense wine 'sheet' should encourage experiment. There is a sound to excellent choice from a group of 1978 clarets, a 1985 Paillard champagne at a reasonable £30.95 and fine ranges of interesting south-western French and New World bottles. Italy, curiously, receives less attention. On the whole, this is an intelligent and generous list, presented with simple style. House wine is £7.95. CELLARMAN'S CHOICE: Branco Dry Moscato 1989, João Pires, £9.95; Barossa Valley, Shiraz 1987, Berri, £11.95.

CHEF: Ian Taylor PROPRIETOR: Robert Chamberlain OPEN: Mon to Sat MEALS: 12 to 2.30, 6 to 10.30 (11 Fri and Sat) PRICES: £16 (£24), Set L and D (served 6 to 7.30) £12.95 (£19). Service 10% on parties of 8 or more CARDS: Access, Amex, Visa SEATS: 100. Private parties: 50 main room, 20 private room. Vegetarian meals. Children's helpings on request. Children welcome. Smart dress preferred. Wheelchair access (1 step). Music

IPSWICH Suffolk map 3

Kinsella's

NEW ENTRY

19 St Peters Street, Ipswich IP1 1XF COOKING 2
IPSWICH (0473) 259 732 COST £20–£43

Kinsella's is enjoyably informal: you have to ring the doorbell to be admitted, drinks are taken in the owners' sitting-room and food is served in two small rooms on the ground floor where twelve people would constitute a crowd. This is an 'organic, free-range and wild food' restaurant. Craig Marchant writes: 'This effectively means that all meat used is free-range and additive-free, fish is never farmed, eggs are always free-range and our fruits and vegetables are organically grown when available. We have a conscious awareness of the source of all our foods.' This translates into a no-choice menu which changes weekly. Preferences and dislikes can be discussed when booking. The cooking is full of good ideas and food has a simple yet refined immediacy. Dishes commented on include a light cheese soufflé with a mustard cream sauce, skate with black butter, pheasant roasted with redcurrant and wine sauce, and citrus-marinated honey and herb roasted breast of chicken. British cheeses are included in the menu and only dessert brings a choice, perhaps a chocolate pot or a kiwi fruit pavlova. The home-baked Irish soda bread is proper as are the vegetables accompanying main courses. The wine list, long on words and pages, is an intelligently enthusiastic selection with very fair prices. Much is imparted in the notes, but brevity might ease the customers' task. There are many good French country wines. House wines are from £8.50.

CHEF: Vivienne Kinsella-Jaques PROPRIETORS: Craig Marchant and Vivienne Kinsella-Jaques OPEN: Tue to Sat, exc Sat L (L by arrangement day before) CLOSED: Maundy Thur to Easter Tue, 23 to 30 Dec, bank hols MEALS: 12 to 2, 7 to 8.30 PRICES: Set L £13.50 (£20) to £17 (£23), Set D £28.50 (£36). Card slips closed CARDS: Access, Visa SEATS: 18. Private parties: 10 main room, 8 and 10 private rooms. Vegetarian meals. No children under 12. Smart dress preferred. No smoking while others are eating. Music

Kwok's Rendezvous

23 St Nicholas Street, Ipswich IP1 1TW COOKING 1
IPSWICH (0473) 256833 COST £20–£28

Since 1980, Thomas and Lucia Kwok have run their Chinese restaurant as a family business, and are usually on hand to chat to customers. Their short, distinctive 50-dish menu is described as Pekinese, but Szechuan is the dominant inspiration. Tao-pan prawns braised with Szechuan bean sauce, cold sliced pork with chilli and garlic sauce, fiery General Tseng's chicken, deep-fried shredded beef, and lotus root with hot bean paste share the bill with sesame prawn toasts, Peking duck and quick-fried lamb with spring onion. Set meals are 'delicately presented'. Although personal, service is also correct. Even more remarkable is the wine list, which is a minor treasure of its kind: vintage champagnes, petits châteaux clarets and burgundies are backed up by good bottles from the Loire and Alsace that suit the food admirably. House French is £7.30.

CHEF: Thomas Kwok PROPRIETORS: Lucia and Thomas Kwok OPEN: Mon to Sat, exc Sat L (by arrangement) MEALS: 12 to 2, 7 to 10.30 PRICES: £11 (£20), Set L and D £13.95 (£21) to £15.95 (£23). Minimum £14.50 CARDS: Amex, Diners SEATS: 50. Private parties: 30 main room. Vegetarian meals. Children welcome. Smart dress preferred. Wheelchair access (2 steps; also WC). Music

Mortimer's on the Quay

Wherry Quay, Ipswich IP4 1AS — COOKING 1
IPSWICH (0473) 230225 — COST £26

'Unless you live in Ipswich you could still be looking for it,' grumbled one reader, perplexed at the one-way system and lack of signs. The dock-side setting among working wharves is 'fascinating', and the converted warehouse restaurant is unpretentious, light and airy. The menu is very similar to that of the sister restaurant at Bury St Edmunds (see entry). Fish dominates the list, and the freshest fish at that. Fillet of sole in a cream and tomato sauce, brill in breadcrumbs with a herb and horseradish sauce have both formed the mainstay of enjoyable meals only marred by comments on the sparsity of vegetables ('just new potatoes and a lettuce leaf'). However, good service, competent cooking and fair prices keep the place bustling and lively. The wine list lacks precision – few growers are given. House French is £7.25.

CHEF: Kenneth Ambler PROPRIETORS: Kenneth Ambler and Michael Gooding OPEN: Mon to Sat, exc Sat L CLOSED: bank hols and day after, 24 Dec to 5 Jan, 2 weeks Aug MEALS: 12 to 2, 7 to 9 (8.30 Mon) PRICES: £15 (£22) CARDS: Access, Amex, Diners, Visa SEATS: 60. Private parties: 8 main room. Children's helpings on request. Smart dress preferred. No-smoking area. Wheelchair access (1 step). No music

Singing Chef

200 St Helen's Street, Ipswich IP4 2RH — COOKING 1
IPSWICH (0473) 255236 — COST £17–£35

'Ipswich residents and visitors have a gem here which is insufficiently appreciated,' writes a local reporter. 'I confess to being a regular – I wish more people were. It would cheer up the chef and improve the food.' Sadly, lack of popular support and financial restraints have forced Kenneth Toyé to close at lunchtime and offer a fixed-price menu (including wine) as an inducement for diners on Tuesday and Wednesday. The restaurant has all the atmosphere of a genuine French bistro, with old-style provincial cooking to match. Fish soup with rouille is a perennial favourite; shellfish in saffron sauce is well reported, as are steaks. The kitchen also delivers the likes of bouillabaisse, shoulder of lamb stuffed with herbs, coq au vin and sautéed pork chops with white wine and grapes. There is a separate menu for vegetarians. Occasional hiccups, such as curdled crème brûlée, can let down the general level badly. The wine list is notable for its selection of single-estate champagnes. House burgundy is £8.50.

CHEFS: Kenneth Toyé and Jeannine Toyé PROPRIETORS: Cynthia and Kenneth Toyé OPEN: Tue to Sat, D only (Sun and Mon D, and L all week, for parties of 6 or more by arrangement) MEALS: 7 to 11 PRICES: £19 (£29), Set D Tue and Wed £14 (£17). Card slips closed CARDS: Access, Visa SEATS: 35. 4 tables outside. Private parties: 20 private room. Vegetarian meals. Children's helpings. No-smoking area. Wheelchair access (also WC). Music

IXWORTH Suffolk map 6

Theobalds

68 High Street, Ixworth IP31 2HJ COOKING 2
PAKENHAM (0359) 31707 COST £20–£40

A plain frontage in the village centre hides inglenook, beams, fine china and good furniture. 'Consistency is the word here. If Simon Theobald is off, the restaurant is closed,' writes one reporter who uses the restaurant every week and has never been let down. The kitchen's inspiration comes mainly from France, and this translates into a short menu priced on the main course. Lobster is served on a bed of noodles, wing of skate on a bed of spinach with white port sauce. Reporters have enjoyed lemon sole with mushroom sauce, medallions of venison with juniper berries, chicken breast stuffed with bacon and mushrooms, and spring lamb with rosemary. Twice-baked cheese soufflé is a regular fixture. There is no fading towards the finish, with excellent blackcurrant mousse, home-made ice-creams and traditional English cheeses. Service is very polished. The list of around 150 mostly French wines is notable for its wide selection of half-bottles. House wine is £8.95.

CHEF: Simon Theobald PROPRIETORS: Simon and Geraldine Theobald OPEN: Tue to Sun, exc Sat L and Sun D MEALS: 12.15 to 2, 7 to 10 PRICES: Set L £13.95 (£20), Set D £22.50 (£30) to £25.50 (£33) CARDS: Access, Visa SEATS: 36. Private parties: 36 main room. Children's helpings. No children under 8 D. No-smoking area. No music

JEVINGTON East Sussex map 3

Hungry Monk

Jevington BM26 5QF
POLEGATE (0323) 482178 COOKING 2
on B2105, between Polegate and Friston COST £31

The maze of interconnecting rooms in Sussex cottages continues to be enjoyed by an appreciative audience; thick walls and low ceilings, the crowding with furniture and things to look at, and the general bustle of it all as meal follows drink and coffee follows meal, each in a different spot, are cosily seductive. The blackboard menu, set-price, with a few supplements (why do salmon and venison carry no surcharge, while duck needs an extra £2.50?), offers a good choice of at least eight items per course. Fish is given a short run at the first course, but hardly stands up to the meat and other main dishes. This is one indicator of the cooking: robust, rich and substantial, a Sussex man's idea of food – none of that namby-pamby fish for dinner. Old favourites – especially among the puddings – crop up repeatedly in the steadily developing repertoire. There is an enjoyment of sweetness in savoury dishes: venison with cassis and shallot sauce, pork with apple and calvados, duck with passion-fruit and marsala, Brie with mango sauce. The Hungry Monk remains faithful to English restaurant cookery. Consistent application of a percentage mark-up gives moderate to good value at the lower end and rather poor value at the top of the unambitious wine list. There are good clarets, a nice clutch of English wines, mostly produced within a few miles of Jevington, and some half-bottles. House wines are from £7.70.

CHEFS: Claire Burgess and Thai La Roche PROPRIETORS: Nigel and Susan Mackenzie
OPEN: all week, D only, and Sun L (other days by arrangement for parties of 10 to 16)
MEALS: 12.15 to 2, 7 to 10 PRICES: Set L (Sun) and D £18.50 (£26). Service 12.5% on parties of 8 or more SEATS: 36. Private parties: 36 main room, 10 and 16 private rooms. Car park, 17 places. Vegetarian meals. Children's helpings. No children under 3. Smart dress preferred. No smoking. Music

KENDAL Cumbria map 7

Moon

129 Highgate, Kendal LA9 4EN COOKING 1
KENDAL (0539) 729254 COST £19

The 'Moon Run' in May was well attended by the fitter customers of this semi-vegetarian restaurant. Out of consideration for those who prefer sitting, a monthly Pudding Club has also been launched. The atmosphere is bistro; there are check tablecloths with yellow overlay, no place-settings until the order has been received, and a white candle is the only table decoration. Service can be perfunctory. Val Macconnell is not herself a vegetarian, which enables the Moon to have a foot in both dietary camps and follow a line of inventiveness through an open-minded repertoire. Many happy customers – and their existence may be measured by the sale of 5,000 copies of the Moon's recipe book – would agree with the reader who said, 'The flavours exceeded the expectations generated by the unpretentious presentation; certainly excellent value.' Chicken in tarragon cream, a delicate and good carrot, parsnip and tomato soup, greengage and ginger ice-cream and gooseberry, elderflower and ginger cheesecake have all been dishes showing an enthusiastic approach to fresh materials and high flavouring. It must also be said that sometimes flavours announced on the menu have not always got through to the plate. A beef, ginger (again) and mango casserole had moderate meat and the ginger and mango were difficult to ascertain. Perhaps a lack of finishing reduction was the explanation for it arriving at table in a soup bowl. As the *Guide* goes to press, the restaurant is open for Sunday brunch on a trial basis. The short wine list consists of a carefully chosen dozen-plus bottles. House wine is £6 a litre. There are good beers.

CHEF: Sharon Moreton and Val Macconnell PROPRIETOR: Val Macconnell OPEN: all week D, Thur to Sun L MEALS: 12 (11 Sun) to 2, 6 to 10 (10.30 Fri and Sat) PRICES: L £9 (£14), Sun L £11 (£15), D £11 (£16). Card slips closed CARDS: Access, Visa SEATS: 40. Private parties: 24 main room. Vegetarian meals. Children's helpings. No smoking. Wheelchair access. Music

KENILWORTH Warwickshire map 5

Restaurant Bosquet 🍷

97A Warwick Road, Kenilworth CV8 1HP COOKING 3
KENILWORTH (0926) 52463 COST £29–£43

An unprepossessing house on the main Kenilworth street leading east away from the castle towards Warwick. Inside is not a lot more exciting either: the restaurant is slightly 'front-room domestic' and the lavatory is in the owners' bathroom. Bernard Lignier has been cooking here for nine years; his style is emphatically French and leans towards complexity, involving ingredients like wild mushrooms and foie gras, and the wrapping up of food. This year has seen many compliments, for example, for a mousse of red mullet and langoustines wrapped in cabbage leaves with a lobster sauce, where the mousse was superb, though the cabbage leaves were too plentiful and the sauce rather too strong to be called subtle. The year has also seen brickbats, for a certain brutality of flavour – over-reduction, lack of balance between sauce and sauced – and for an approximate approach, as in over-iced ice-creams, burnt pastry and poor vegetables. This is unfortunate because Bernard Lignier's skills are great. A winter meal of guinea-fowl, langoustines and sweetbreads in filo pastry on a carrot and sweet wine sauce, followed by brill with lobster mousse on a lobster sauce, then a rather unseasonal raspberry mille-feuille was both finely judged and executed. Yet many are the regulars who find consistency all the year through. The service is slightly uncommitted and delivery of meals can be very slow even on nights when the dining-room is almost empty. Disarmingly hand-written and exclusively French, the list of 120-odd wines shows a sure hand. Its price range is wide: Provence, petits châteaux and good Rhônes provide much excellent drinking below £15. Beyond that, Hermitage from Chave, many fine clarets and pedigree burgundies demonstrate an insistence on the best. Enthusiasm may be curtailed by the relentless mark-up, but Alsaces are good value. House wines are from £9.50.

CHEF: Bernard Lignier PROPRIETORS: Bernard and Jane Lignier OPEN: Tue to Sat D; Tue to Fri L by arrangement CLOSED: last week July, first 2 weeks Aug MEALS: 12 to 2, 7 to 10 PRICES: £25 (£36), Set L and D £19 (£29) CARDS: Access, Amex, Visa SEATS: 28. Private parties: 30 main room. Vegetarian meals. Children welcome. No music

All details are as accurate as possible at the time of going to press, but chefs and owners often change, and it is wise to check by telephone before making a special journey. Many readers have been disappointed when set-price bargain meals are no longer available. Ask when booking.

KESWICK Cumbria map 7

▲ *Brundholme Country House Hotel*

Brundholme Road, Keswick CA12 4NL
KESWICK (076 87) 74495
from A66 roundabout take Keswick road, then first left after garage

COOKING 2
COST £30

The early nineteenth-century house was once described by Coleridge as being in a delicious situation. The setting may be spectacular, but the hotel is hard to find; directions should be sought. Public rooms are well furnished, in keeping with the style of the place. The bar and lounges have comfortable sofas and the dining-room is attractive and inviting. The fixed-price evening menu is supplemented by a *carte* devoted entirely to fish. The latter menu will be offered if you reserve in advance for lunch. Otherwise only a light bar lunch rather lacking in variety is available. The fish, noted for freshness, is confidently handled: steamed mussels interspersed with vegetables in a saffron sauce; fresh herb pancake stuffed with salmon, prawns and sole in a cream sauce; lemon sole stuffed with mushroom mousse with steamed vegetables and a cream and chervil sauce. The set menu might offer loin of Herdwick lamb or a sirloin of beef. Desserts are of the cold bavarois type but sticky date pudding features among occasional hot offerings. Good attention is paid to smaller details such as vegetables and cheeses. Inconsistencies in quality on the wine list rule out total confidence; Australia and New Zealand look good bets. Prices are fair. House Duboeuf is £6.90.

CHEFS: Ian Charlton and Steve Smith PROPRIETORS: Ian and Lynn Charlton
OPEN: all week, D only (L by arrangement) CLOSED: 23 Dec to 1 Feb MEALS: 7.30 to 8.45
PRICES: Set D £19 (£25) CARDS: Access, Visa SEATS: 50. Private parties: 55 main room, 55 private room. Car park, 25 places. Vegetarian meals. Children's helpings with prior notice. No children under 12. Smart dress preferred. No smoking in dining-room. Wheelchair access (also WC) ACCOMMODATION: 12 rooms, all with bath/shower. B&B £42 to £74. Deposit: £20. No children under 10. Pets welcome. Garden. Fishing. TV. Phone. Scenic. Doors close at 11.30. Confirm by 6 (*Which? Hotel Guide*)

KEYSTON Cambridgeshire map 6

Pheasant Inn 🍷

Keyston P18 0RE
BYTHORN (080 14) 241

COOKING 1
COST £35

A white-painted, seventeenth-century thatched building that functions as both pub and restaurant. Full meals are served in the tastefully rustic dining-room; a blackboard menu of simpler dishes and snacks is the main attraction in the bar. New chef Nick Steiger's track record has included stints at The Mirabelle in London and Gee's in Oxford. He cooks a short, modern *carte* with several choices at each stage like dariole of duck with a deep glossy cranberry sauce; smoked halibut with fresh tomato mousse; pigeon breasts in puff pastry with tarragon; fillet of brill with saffron; or roast rack of lamb with apple and rosemary jelly. To finish there is petit pot au chocolat with crisp brandy snaps or citrus lemon tart with Seville orange curd. Reports have been encouraging, although better bread and more careful balancing of flavours would improve the overall standard. The wine list shows a hotel group that not only allows fine and careful wine buying but also charges fair and sensible prices. Italy and New World vineyards are as well represented as the classic French. The bin-end list is a must for bargains. Nine good house wines are available by the glass and there is a decent spread of half-bottles. House French is £7.45.

CHEF: Nick Steiger PROPRIETORS: Poste Hotels Ltd OPEN: all week CLOSED: D 25 and 26 Dec MEALS: 12 to 2, 7 to 10 PRICES: £21 (£29). Card slips closed CARDS: Access, Amex, Diners, Visa SEATS: 100. 4 tables outside. Private parties: 30 main room, 30 private room. Car park, 50 places. Vegetarian meals. Children's helpings. Air-conditioned. No music

KILN PIT HILL Northumberland map 7

Manor House Inn

Carterway Heads DH8 9LX
EDMUNDBYERS (0207) 55268 COOKING 1
on A68, 2m S of Kiln Pit Hill COST £32

A dour-looking farmhouse on the side of the road, with a sign in the bar saying 'Well-behaved children are welcome before 8pm; badly behaved spoilt little monsters are not', is home to a creative pub and restaurant. Recommendations for the bar food have outnumbered those for the restaurant this year, doubtless because of the excellent value combined with the possibility of eating many of the same dishes. Salmon with ginger and currants, Mediterranean prawns in a garlic sauce, pasta, sweetcorn and mushroom gratin are mentioned kindly, as are the sticky toffee pudding and the lemon curd ice-cream (despite its ice crystals). 'A light in a culinary darkness' was one way of praising the kitchen. The short restaurant menu is nicely varied, with a welcome touch of spice in beef satay, crab cakes with piquant sauce, and duck with plums and ginger. A more critical reader felt the potential was there, although the overwhelming majority consider it realised and steadily improving. The wine list keeps prices realistic by including some useful regional wines from France and a handful from other countries. House wine is £6.20.

CHEFS: Jane and Elizabeth Pelly PROPRIETORS: Anthony, Jane and Elizabeth Pelly OPEN: Tue to Sat, D only CLOSED: Tue and Wed 2 Jan to 31 Mar MEALS: 7.30 to 10 PRICES: £18 (£27). Card slips closed CARDS: Access, Visa SEATS: 40. Private parties: 40 main room. Car park, 30 places. Vegetarian meals. No children under 12. Wheelchair access (1 step; also WC). Music

'I offered a credit card to pay the bill and when it was returned the bottom line of the voucher was not filled in. I filled it in myself and the waiter then explained that the 12.5 per cent service charge went to the restaurant and not the staff. Obviously, this explanation was intended to encourage me to provide an additional tip. It did not exactly surprise me because I had noticed the same waiter pull the same stunt with the table next to us and receive a £5 note.' On eating in London SW1

KING'S NORTON West Midlands map 5

▲ *Lombard Room*

NEW ENTRY

180 Lifford Lane,
King's Norton B30 3NT
021-451 3991 and 3992

COOKING 1
COST £21–£44

'I would recommend this restaurant,' says a reader, 'to any businessman wishing to impress clients.' Impress them by the gathering within one curtilage restaurant, motor museum and luxury hotel; impress by the grand piano 'with everything played at double speed'; and by the military precision of the waiters under the direction of Andrew Morgan, maître d'hôtel and brother of the chef. It is an emphatic sort of place: the prose on the menu will tell you that. For all the Lombard's embrace of thrusting convention – ties are de rigueur, mobile phones make it Lamont's Lament – the cooking is enthusiastic and mostly pleasant. For one diner, 'pot au feu of game (a soup) hit the balance perfectly', even if 'a melody of marinated exotic and seasonal fish' was more fishy marinade than delicate fish. Brochette of salmon and scallops seemed to have had too close acquaintance with chilli or cayenne, but other aspects of production were acceptable. The lunch menus are fair value and the location makes this a useful address. Four vintages of Leflaive Chevalier-Montrachet and seven La Lagune on the wine list are bound to impress, as do the prices. Unlike similar operations, the Lombard Room does not stop there: half-bottles are provided in abundance and there are many decent bottles below £15. Italy, Spain and the New World all have good showings. A page each of ports and cognacs confirms the allegiance of the list to familiar classics. House wine is £10.

CHEF: Anthony Morgan PROPRIETOR: J.A. Patrick OPEN: all week, exc Sat L and Sun D MEALS: 12 to 2.30, 7 to 10 PRICES: £27 (£37), Set L £12 (£21) to £15 (£24), Set D £18 (£25). Card slips closed CARDS: Access, Amex, Diners, Visa SEATS: 60. 10 tables outside. Private parties: 120 main room, 20, 40 and 120 private rooms. Car park, 230 places. Vegetarian meals. Children's helpings. Jacket and tie. No smoking in dining-room. Wheelchair access (also WC). Music. Air-conditioned. Fax: 021-433 3048
ACCOMMODATION: 10 rooms, all with bath/shower. Rooms for disabled. B&B £90 to £105. No children under 10. Afternoon teas. Garden. TV. Phone. Scenic. Confirm by 6

KING'S LYNN Norfolk map 6

Garbo's

COUNTY RESTAURANT OF THE YEAR

NEW ENTRY

7 Saturday Market Place,
King's Lynn PE30 5DQ
KING'S LYNN (0553) 773136

COOKING 2*
COST £30

The setting is a modest black and white building in the old town, opposite St Margaret's Church. Despite its cramped dining-room and functional fittings, this is a restaurant with serious intentions. Steve Aldis and Claire Shaw run the kitchen in tandem, producing their own breads, pasta, ice-creams, sorbets and chocolates. Ingredients are local but menus do not shrink from fashionable modern ideas. Pressed leek and asparagus terrine with truffle vinaigrette and fillet of brill with ravioli of mussels share the stage with stuffed leg of rabbit on a rich soupe au pistou. There is a strong vegetarian presence along the lines of parsnip and cashew-nut loaf in puff pastry with onion marmalade. Lentils appear as a bed for roast pheasant, pigeon and stuffed breast of corn-fed chicken. Casserole of local fish has included skate, coley, turbot, brill, mussels and a Dublin Bay prawn in a broth of 'excellent pedigree' with Gruyère cheese and aïoli. An inspection meal also yielded perfectly timed loin of lamb wrapped in tarragon mousse topped with fried celeriac. A blackboard of sweets may feature rhubarb and ginger pudding, or caramelised oranges with marmalade ice-cream. Thirty reasonably priced wines include house French at £7.95.

CHEFS/PROPRIETORS: Steve Aldis and Claire Shaw OPEN: Tue to Sat, D only MEALS: 7.30 to 10 PRICES: £18 (£25). Card slips closed CARDS: Access, Visa SEATS: 25. Private parties: 35 main room, 30 private room. Vegetarian meals. Children welcome. Music

Riverside

27 King Street, King's Lynn PE30 1HA — COOKING 1
KING'S LYNN (0553) 773134 — COST £22–£32

The restaurant forms part of the King's Lynn Arts Centre. Inside, the beams and bare bricks attest to the building's medieval origins. Menus are flexible and tailored to suit all pockets, with light lunches, salads, one-course meals and suppers as well as full dinners. Arbroath smokies with cream and cheese are a perennial favourite; poached halibut is a good lunch dish. The dinner menu concentrates on the likes of duck terrine with kumquat jelly, seafood pasta and steaks, backed up by more ambitious offerings such as breast of chicken stuffed with carrot and herb mousse with cheese fondue sauce. Desserts range from steamed puddings with custard to locally made sorbets and ice-creams. The short wine list has house French at £7.75.

CHEF: Dennis Taylor PROPRIETORS: Michael and Sylvia Savage OPEN: Mon to Sat MEALS: 12 to 2, 7 to 10 PRICES: L £15 (£22), D £19 (£27). Card slips closed CARDS: Access, Visa SEATS: 65. 24 tables outside. Private parties: 75 main room. Car park, 10 places. Vegetarian meals. Children's helpings. No smoking. Music

KINGSTON UPON THAMES Surrey — map 3

Ayudhya 🍷

14 Kingston Hill,
Kingston upon Thames KT2 7NH — COOKING 2
081-549 5984 and 546 5878 — COST £30

This is still one of the best Thai restaurants outside central London. Despite the recession, refurbishment has continued: the latest project is a decorative ceiling in the ground floor dining-room, and there are plans to give the exterior some authentic architectural features. Last year's experiment with set meals has been dropped, 'because we find most people prefer to order à la carte,' says chef/proprietor Somjai Thanpo (who is now using her maiden name). The full 75-dish menu is supplemented by around a dozen vegetarian specialities, such as stir-fried water spinach in black-bean sauce and vegetable soup with galangal and coconut milk. The full range of accessible Thai flavours and cooking styles is represented: satays and dim-sum, soups flavoured with lemon grass and kaffir lime leaves, fiery salads with lime and coriander dressings, curries of different 'colours', noodles and rice. Seafood is a strong suit: crispy fried pomfret with tamarind and chillies, steamed mussels with lemon grass and basil, and curried seafood mousse (a curious-sounding speciality topped with coconut cream and steamed on a bed of Chinese leaves). Home-made Thai sweets are supplemented by exotic fresh fruit and ice-creams. Careful attention is given to wines here; the range is catholic and prices are fair. House wines are £6.50.

CHEF/PROPRIETOR: Somjai Thanpo OPEN: all week, exc Sat L CLOSED: 25 and 26 Dec, 1 Jan, Easter Sun MEALS: 12 to 2.30 (3 Sun), 6.30 to 11 (11.30 Fri and Sat) PRICES: £14 (£25) CARDS: Access, Amex, Diners, Visa SEATS: 84. Private parties: 30 main room, 20 and 28 private rooms. Children welcome. Wheelchair access. Music

KINGTON Hereford & Worcester map 4

▲ *Penrhos Court* 🍷

Kington HR5 3LH COOKING 2
KINGTON (0544) 230720 COST £16–£41

Martin Griffiths (the man with the hammer) and Daphne Lambert (the woman with knives and chopping board) must feel a mixture of relief and disorientation as the project of restoring this wonderful timbered house comes to an end – if there are ever ends to such things. None the less, Penrhos Court now has rooms and the restaurant has moved from byre to reconstructed twelfth-century cruck hall with a brand new kitchen behind. Daphne Lambert will even have staff to help her. She has a great knowledge and enthusiasm for medieval food and cooking and puts on historic banquets during the year. The everyday menu is no exercise in nostalgia or scholarship, but a nicely composed short menu of some half-dozen choices. Self-sufficiency is the leitmotif: fine breads, herbs from the garden and decent local materials lifted by occasional luxuries like morels, served with amazing abandon with chicken and champagne cream sauce. The progress of the Court during the year will be interesting to watch. 'Daphne Lambert is a capable cook,' says a reader, and the new surroundings should give Daphne a more settled stage. Penrhos Court is a project that deserves to succeed. There is a short wine list, from Retsina to Meursault. Prices are fair. House wines are £9.

CHEF: Daphne Lambert PROPRIETORS: Martin Griffiths and Daphne Lambert OPEN: Wed to Sat, D only, and Sun L CLOSED: 25 and 26 Dec MEALS: 12.30 to 2, 7.30 to 10 PRICES: £25 (£34), Set Sun L £10 (£16) to £15 (£21), Set D £16 (£22) to £25 (£31) SEATS: 20. 10 tables outside. Private parties: 50 main room. Car park, 100 places. Children's helpings. Wheelchair access (1 step; also WC). Music. Fax: (0544) 230754 ACCOMMODATION: 19 rooms, all with bath/shower. Rooms for disabled. B&B £80 to £120. Deposit: 50%. Children welcome. Baby facilities. Afternoon teas. Garden. Fishing. TV. Phone. Scenic. Doors close at midnight

🍾 denotes an outstanding wine cellar; 🍷 denotes a good wine list, worth travelling for.

KINTBURY Berkshire map 2

▲ *Dundas Arms*

Station Road, Kintbury RG15 0UT
KINTBURY (0488) 58559 and 58263

COOKING 2
COST £24–£41

Its site is in its favour: close to canal, river, road and railway, it is an industrial archaeologist's dream. The pub side of the business pulls ever more of the weight, but the accommodation is popular and the calm green dining-room continues to produce mostly acceptable food. Set-price menus, morning and night, offer a half-dozen choices of relatively straightforward cooking: hence, meat or fish and sauce for main dishes. Fancy turns with mousses and stuffings are given no place, nor is there much more for braises or slow cookery. There are good gravlax and good game in season. Service attracts a mixed response. The wine list is austerely blunt in appearance. Press on and the rewards are great; the brief house wine list shows very astute knowledge, but that is only an introduction to fine selections of Australians, good Rhônes and very strong burgundies and clarets. Halves are less favoured, but prices on the whole are very fair. House wines are from £7.50. CELLARMAN'S CHOICE: New Zealand, Drylands Vineyard Sauvignon Blanc 1990, Collards £15; Dom. de Trévallon 1985, Dürrbach, £19.50.

CHEF/PROPRIETOR: David A. Dalzell-Piper OPEN: Tue to Sat CLOSED: Christmas to New Year MEALS: 12.30 to 1.30, 7.30 to 9.30 PRICES: £16 (£24), Set L £16 (£24), Set D £25 (£34) CARDS: Access, Amex, Visa SEATS: 50. 10 tables outside. Private parties: 22 main room. Car park, 40 places. Children's helpings. Smart dress preferred. No cigars/pipes in dining-room. Wheelchair access (2 steps; also WC). No music. Fax: (0488) 58568
ACCOMMODATION: 5 rooms, all with bath/shower. Rooms for disabled. B&B £55 to £65. TV. Phone. Scenic. Doors close at 11.30. Confirm by 6 (*Which? Hotel Guide*)

KIRKBY LONSDALE Cumbria map 7

▲ *Lupton Tower*

Lupton, Kirkby Lonsdale LA6 2PR
CROOKLANDS (044 87) 400
off A65, NW of Kirkby Lonsdale

COOKING 2
COST £24

This is one of the new breed of vegetarian hotels, and is highly rated by readers. The rambling building has a tower at one end and 'a lived-in eclectic look'. In the dining-room, there is 'a wonderful if slightly hushed atmosphere', with candlelight and elegant classical music adding to the romantic ambience. The style and lightness of Dorothy Smith's set-dinner menu, far removed from the lentil and wholemeal pastry school of vegetarian cooking, impress vegetarians and carnivores alike. Timbales, quenelles and vegetable moulds figure strongly. Meals might begin with minted melon balls in honey dressing or a roule filled with garlicky fromage frais tinged with coriander and orange. Soups such as cauliflower or parsnip and turnip come with excellent home-made bread. Main courses are along the lines of green vegetable terrine in beurre blanc, and rice pilaf with apricots and pine kernels served with marinated vegetables. Desserts continue the imaginative theme, as in chocolate and orange mousse with Grand Marnier or baked tangerine custard with apricot purée. The fixed price for four courses is remarkable value, as is the short wine list. House French is £6.50 a litre.

CHEF: Dorothy Smith PROPRIETORS: Mr and Mrs G.J. Smith OPEN: all week, D only CLOSED: Mon and Tue winter if no room bookings MEALS: 7.30 to 8 PRICES: Set D £15 (£20) SEATS: 32. 3 tables outside. Private parties: 28 main room, 12 private room. Car park, 16 places. Vegetarian meals only. Children's helpings. No smoking in dining-room. Wheelchair access (2 steps; also WC). Music ACCOMMODATION: 6 rooms, 4 with bath/shower. B&B £18.50 to £37. Deposit: £10. Children welcome. Pets by arrangement. Garden. Scenic. Doors close at 1am. Confirm by 4

KIRKHAM Lancashire map 5

Cromwellian

16 Poulton Street, Kirkham PR4 2AB COOKING 2
KIRKHAM (0772) 685680 COST £27–£37

'A friendly atmosphere, with an amiable proprietor who encouraged people out of their shells' was how a single visitor passing through a mid-winter Kirkham put it. The amiability is neither intrusive nor boring – it confirms the sense of cosiness in this small, beamed house where Josie Fawcett offers a monthly-changing, short menu with old favourites (for example, prawns and water-chestnuts in a pancake or a choux bun, with white wine sauce) featuring often in a well-practised repertoire. There is a certain generosity to the style: apple and pear pancakes ('very sweet and a lot of them') and often a robust zest to the flavourings, as in the salmon with ginger and brandied raisins wrapped in filo pastry, with a Vouvray sauce. Vegetables are plentiful. Vegetarians are always considered, even if Peter Fawcett observes that only some two per cent of his customers select the vegetarian option. A lot of work has been put into the wine list over the last 12 months. Predominantly French, but with fine examples from Spain and Australia, it has good range. A less tentative approach to Italy and Burgundy might merit a glass award. House wine is £7.95. CELLARMAN'S CHOICE: Chablis, premier cru la Forêt 1989, Vocoret, £19.95; Haut Médoc, Ch. St Saturnin 1982, £16.50.

CHEF: Josie Fawcett PROPRIETORS: Peter and Josie Fawcett OPEN: Tue to Sat, D only MEALS: 7 to 9.30 PRICES: Set D £19.95 (£27) to £22.95 (£31). Card slips closed CARDS: Access, Amex, Visa SEATS: 30. Private parties: 17 main room, 12 private room. Vegetarian meals. Children's helpings with prior notice. Wheelchair access. Music

KNUTSFORD Cheshire map 5

▲ *Belle Epoque*

60 King Street, Knutsford WA16 6DT COOKING 2
KNUTSFORD (0565) 633060 COST £38

'An old friend that is not only keeping well, but bursting with health,' writes a regular since the early days. The building is exceptional, in a remarkable main street. Go on a fine night and relish the bold stonework before absorbing the period interiors – perhaps more interesting in the bar areas than the slightly too chiaroscuro dining-room. Atmosphere by the bucketful is humanised by keen young staff and the bonhomie of both Mooneys. The Belle Epoque may evoke the art nouveau of the building but the cooking is all modern: wild mushroom risotto, langoustine ravioli, guinea-fowl sausage, calf's liver with pineapple sauce, pork fillet with bacon, leeks and sage, and a good English cheese board ('almost the size of anyone else's sweets trolley'). The cooking can be very successful, though it runs the risk of too long a menu, an approximate hand with seasoning or main flavourings, and a level of skill running just below that demanded by the prices. The Mooneys have constructed a seductive package, however; this is an enviable place to stay, good for weddings and small meetings, and as always it is enjoyable to be greeted with genuine enthusiasm as old friends and customers. Australia and California are dealt with more ambitiously than Burgundy in the generally sound and fairly priced wine list. A decent low-priced 'French selection' leads into fine clarets and choice Italians. House wines are from £8.50.

CHEFS: Graham Codd and David Mooney PROPRIETORS: Keith and Nerys Mooney OPEN: Mon to Sat, D only CLOSED: first week Jan MEALS: 7.30 to 10 PRICES: £21 (£32). Service 10%. Card slips closed CARDS: Access, Amex, Diners, Visa SEATS: 70. Private parties: 60 main room, 20, 60 and 80 private rooms. Vegetarian meals. No children under 10. No pipes in dining-room. Music. Fax: (0565) 634150 ACCOMMODATION: 7 rooms, all with bath/shower. B&B £35 to £50. No children under 10. Garden. TV. Scenic. Doors close at midnight. Confirm by 2 (*Which? Hotel Guide*)

LANGAR Nottinghamshire map 5

▲ *Langar Hall* **NEW ENTRY**

Langar NG13 9HG COOKING 1
HARBY (0949) 60559 COST £22–£40

This is not an easy place to find. Make for Langar church and look behind it. The house itself is quietly furnished and its scale domestic – soft cream colours, comfortable sofas, deep chairs and an air of faded elegance. A moated garden looks on to sheep-filled parkland. The kitchen produces dishes that are modern in style: lamb with a mild cream of garlic garnished with couscous; confit of duck leg with white kidney beans and tomato. Sauces are direct, and the meat is often of good quality. Local, if not home-grown, produce is a strength – herbs from the garden, carp from the medieval fishponds, Stilton cheese from Colston Bassett just down the road. One meal that pleased included a rich slice of duck and orange pâté, and fillet of salmon with an intensely flavoured and buttery Grand Marnier and orange sauce. A mango sorbet with mango sauce tasted emphatically of just that. Bread, vegetables and coffee draw good reports, as does the cheerful attention of Imogen Skirving. House wine is £7.75.

The Guide *office can quickly spot when a restaurateur is encouraging customers to write recommending inclusion – and sadly, several have been doing this in 1991. Such reports do not further a restaurant's cause. Please tell us if a restaurateur invites you to write to the* Guide.

CHEF: Frank Vallat PROPRIETOR: Imogen Skirving OPEN: Mon to Sat, D only, and Sun L (Mon to Sat L by arrangement) MEALS: 12 to 2.30, 7.30 to 9 PRICES: Set Sun L £15 (£22) to £17.50 (£25), Set D £19.75 (£28) to £25 (£33). Service 10% for parties of 8 or more. Card slips closed CARDS: Access, Amex, Visa SEATS: 30. Private parties: 30 main room, 4, 6, 8 and 10 private rooms. Car park, 30 places. Vegetarian meals with prior notice. Children restricted D. Wheelchair access (1 step). Music. Fax: (0949) 60145 ACCOMMODATION: 10 rooms, 9 with bath/shower. Rooms for disabled. B&B £48 to £95. Deposit: £20. Children welcome. Pets by arrangement. Garden. TV. Phone. Scenic. Confirm by 6 (*Which? Hotel Guide*)

LANGHO Lancashire map 5

▲ *Northcote Manor*

Northcote Road, Langho BB6 9BB
BLACKBURN (0254) 240555 COOKING **2***
on A59, 9m E of M6 exit 31 COST £19–£38

Northcote Manor is one of those solidly built Victorian mill-owner's houses that lends itself so well to conversion to a hotel. On a dull day it can look a bit dour and spartan but the welcome, and the food, belie these first impressions. A praised winter lunch ('the quality of the food prepared shone brightly') consisted of a shortcrust and fines herbes pastry case filled with seafood on a purée of leeks, émincé of pheasant in a mushroom sauce with rösti potatoes, and a spun-sugar basket of mixed fresh fruits with raspberry coulis. There can be an old-fashioned ring to the menu – chateaubriand with béarnaise sauce and pommes frites, venison with spätzli noodles, tournedos of beef with gratin potatoes – reflecting no doubt solid local tastes. This is lightened, however, by a modern approach – a breast of Goosnargh duckling is served on gingered leeks with chicken liver samosas and limequat dressing, or there is pan-fried sea bass and deep-fried skate served on a melée of vegetables with a fondue of chives. This is a kitchen that cooks carefully and to good effect. If selection of wines here seems uneven, pricing is bizarre. There are good wines and fair prices, not necessarily congruent but the dice are loaded in the customer's favour, especially for non-French bottles. House French is £7.85.

CHEF: Nigel Howarth PROPRIETORS: Craig J. Bancroft and Nigel Howarth OPEN: all week, exc Mon and Sun L MEALS: 12 to 1.30, 7 to 9 (10 Sat) PRICES: £22 (£32), Set L £12 (£19) to £14 (£21). Card slips closed CARDS: Access, Visa SEATS: 70. Private parties: 60 main room, 20 private room. Car park, 50 places. Children's helpings. Smart dress preferred. Music. Fax: (0254) 246568 ACCOMMODATION: 6 rooms, all with bath/shower. B&B £60 to £70. Deposit: £25. Children welcome. Afternoon teas. Garden. TV. Phone. Scenic (*Which? Hotel Guide*)

See inside front cover for an explanation of the 1 to 5 rating system recognising cooking standards.

An asterisk (*) after the 1 to 5 cooking mark at the top of an entry signifies that the Guide *and its readers think that the restaurant is a particularly fine example within its numeric classification.*

LANGLEY MARSH Somerset map 2

▲ *Langley House Hotel* 🍷

COUNTY RESTAURANT OF THE YEAR

Langley Marsh TA4 2UF COOKING 3*
WIVELISCOMBE (0984) 23318 COST £28–£38

The Wilsons are a husband and wife team who realise that small is beautiful and that the highest standards are achieved by doing as much as possible yourself: from the intense and characterful decoration of the interiors in this small country house – originating in the sixteenth century – to a walled garden that supplies fruit and vegetables. Anne Wilson manages the front-of-house. Though most people dine at the same time, eating a largely no-choice meal, 'there was constant service at the right time from beginning to end, when it unobtrusively faded away. This is difficult to get right and enjoyable to see carried off so well.' Peter Wilson is largely out of sight in the kitchen. A meal began with a fanned dessert pear marinated in walnut oil with a herb savoury Stilton cream that showed masterful simplicity. Next was black bream with scallions, soy and ginger: the fish next to a pile of briefly stir-fried scallions and vegetables, with a glossy and powerful sauce. Each element of fine taste, each complementing the other. For main course, duck with honey in an apple and thyme sauce with pink peppercorns was judged a subtle contrast of textures, with a conservative use of thyme and accompanied by an accurately cooked range of vegetables. Fine cheeses from Britain (mainly the south-west) are ordered at the start of the meal so they can be brought from the cold room to come up to temperature. Desserts such as elderflower syllabub and cranachan show the same wish to keep simple yet achieve complexity. Breakfast and tea confirm the serious intent. This is a fine small hotel. Good suppliers keep the wine list on an even keel: worthy names abound, but not at the expense of economy, with fair mark-ups and many decent half-bottles. A glass is awarded this year for enthusiasm constrained by intelligent brevity. House wines are from £7.50. CELLARMAN'S CHOICE: Rully 1988, Drouhin, £21.50; Vino Nobile di Montepulciano 1985, Avignonesi, £19.75.

CHEF: Peter Wilson PROPRIETORS: Peter and Anne Wilson OPEN: all week, D only (L by arrangement) MEALS: 8 to 9 PRICES: Set D £22.50 (£28) to £26.50 (£32). Card slips closed SEATS: 18. Private parties: 35 main room, 18 private room. Car park, 10 places. Vegetarian meals. No smoking in dining-room. Wheelchair access (also WC). No music. Fax: (0984) 24573 ACCOMMODATION: 8 rooms, all with bath/shower. B&B £59 to £90. Children welcome. Baby facilities. Pets welcome but not in public rooms. Afternoon teas. Garden. Fishing. TV. Phone. Scenic. Doors close at midnight. Confirm by 6 (*Which? Hotel Guide*)

LAVENHAM Suffolk map 3

▲ *Great House*

Market Place, Lavenham CO10 9QZ COOKING 2
LAVENHAM (0787) 247431 COST £19–£44

It may be a perfect English house in a calendar-picture English town, and bang opposite the market-cross into the bargain, but it's French-run and the food is French-cooked. The cooking is enjoyed for its vigour, though occasionally variable. A salad of mixed leaves with strips of beef in a mustard sauce, asparagus hollandaise, salmon and king prawns on shredded leeks, pork fillet with raisins and a port wine sauce, lamb noisettes with tarragon sauce, and decent apple tart and ice-creams all point to French country cooking. Good bread, good coffee. Children have been observed out of control here at Sunday lunch, but one man's control is another's liberty to be oneself. House wine is £12.50.

CHEF: Regis Crépy PROPRIETOR: John Spice OPEN: Tue to Sun, exc Sun D CLOSED: Jan MEALS: 12 to 2.30, 7 to 10.30 PRICES: £24 (£37), Set L £9.90 (£19) to £12.90 (£23), Set D £13.95 (£24) CARDS: Access, Amex, Visa SEATS: 65. 7 tables outside. Private parties: 50 main room, 30 private room. Vegetarian meals. Children's helpings. No cigars/pipes in dining-room. Music ACCOMMODATION: 4 rooms, all with bath/shower. B&B £50 to £78. Deposit: £20. Children welcome. Baby facilities. Pets welcome. Garden. TV. Phone. Scenic. Doors close at 1am. Confirm by midnight (*Which? Hotel Guide*)

LEAMINGTON SPA Warwickshire map 2

Les Plantagenêts NEW ENTRY

15 Dormer Place,
Leamington Spa CV32 5AA COOKING 2
LEAMINGTON SPA (0926) 451792 COST £19–£37

Two basement rooms in a restored Regency terrace house accommodate an unrepentantly French restaurant run by Remy Loth, from Vouvray; hence, apparently, a slight emphasis on dishes from Anjou, as well as the name of the place: Henry II was a Plantagenet and came from Anjou. The cooking, thoroughly mediated by English practice, is acceptable for the district and is offered through a short *carte* or set-price meal. Dishes such as smoked salmon with a blini and a leek mousse (very Angevin), kidneys and wild rice, pork with calvados and cream, and firm poached salmon with strong shellfish sauce have received approval, as has the French cheeseboard – generously sampled – and the simple desserts such as strawberry tartlet with crème fraîche, and mousses. The wine list takes in first growths (but 1973) and some fair Burgundy growers. Try the Muscadet or Gros Plant, both at £9.85.

CHEF/PROPRIETOR: Remy Loth OPEN: Mon to Sat, exc Sat L MEALS: 12.15 to 2.15, 7.15 to 10.15 PRICES: £22 (£31), Set L £12.50 (£19), Set D £17 (£22) CARDS: Access, Amex, Visa SEATS: 35. Private parties: 45 main room. Children welcome. Smart dress preferred. No-smoking area. Music. Air-conditioned

LECK Lancashire map 7

▲ *Cobwebs*

Leck, Cowan Bridge LA6 2HZ COOKING 3
KIRKBY LONSDALE (052 42) 72141 COST £38

Paul Kelly and Yvonne Thompson are young and certainly keen. This comes through every word they speak or write about their 'Country Guest House', which has sprouted a dining conservatory for more space and better views of the fells. It offers a dinner-party style of menu and occasional gourmet evenings, as well as having a remarkable cellar. The place thrives on self-sufficiency: bread, petits fours, everything done with genuine intent. The tilt to the cooking is English rather than classical: colourful and surprising 'split' soups that put two flavours in one bowl, for instance courgette and rosemary partnered by curried parsnip; and a slight sweetness favoured in first courses, for example, smoked chicken and mango salad, or in a main course of lamb fillet with kidney, apricot, and wild rice with rosemary and mustard sauce. Desserts, too, such as pineapple and coconut roulade or strawberry shortcake on a kiwi purée, demonstrate affiliations beyond the teaching of Escoffier. This is done with disarming and enjoyable style. Many like it, a few despite themselves. Although choice is restricted, just wait for the cheese: the slate of local varieties is immense – biscuits are home-made, of course. The wine list, bought with enthusiasm from impeccable sources and with very low mark-ups still in force, is an invitation to experiment. Pommery non-vintage at £20 or a Capezzana Riserva Chianti 1983 for £13 are bargains; also Pouilly Fumé of Ladoucette is offered at almost a quarter of the price asked in a well-known small restaurant in London. Clarets and burgundies are unevenly priced; 'price on application' is used too many times for comfort. Alsace and Australia are especially strong and there are good halves. House wine is £8.50. CELLARMAN'S CHOICE: Tokay, Vieilles Vignes 1989, Humbrecht, £13; Schinus Molle, Cabernet 1988, Crittenden, £11.50.

CHEF: Yvonne Thompson PROPRIETORS: Paul Kelly and Yvonne Thompson OPEN: Tue to Sat, D only CLOSED: end Dec to mid-Mar MEALS: 7.30 for 8 PRICES: Set D £25 (£32). Minimum £25. Card slips closed CARDS: Access, Visa SEATS: 20. Private parties: 16 main room. Car park, 15 places. No children under 12. Smart dress preferred. No smoking in dining-room. Music. One sitting ACCOMMODATION: 5 rooms, all with bath/shower. B&B £40 to £60. Deposit: 15%. No children under 12. Garden. Fishing. TV. Phone. Scenic. Doors close at 1am. Confirm by 6 (*Which? Hotel Guide*)

LEDBURY Hereford & Worcester map 2

▲ *Hope End*

Hope End, Ledbury HR8 1JQ
LEDBURY (0531) 3613
$^2/_3$m N of Ledbury, just beyond Wellington Heath

COOKING 3
COST £20–£42

'Primeval' was one visitor's description of the landscape surrounding the Hegartys' unique country hotel, once the childhood home of Elizabeth Barrett Browning. The Hegartys are defenders of an enduring tradition of cooking and horticulture; their solutions are constructive and successful. Thus, they are currently restoring the Georgian landscape garden and are adding a new orangery. Since 1979, they have maintained the eighteenth-century walled garden organically; they have rescued scores of old varieties from extinction and they are uncompromising in their support of local producers. Patricia's cooking is defined by the garden and by the British larder: home-baked bread, curds and yoghurt, vinegars, relishes and chutneys. This is the renewal of British food in action. The hotel is now open to residents seven days a week, the menu including a small choice at each stage, which allows for a regular vegetarian option such as cauliflower and sesame mould with peperonata. The formula remains intact: five stages with a little salad and British farmhouse cheeses before the sweet course. The alliance of the kitchen and the garden shows in the vivid use of herbs, which point up almost every dish. Soups remain a strong point: broad bean and lemon, mushroom and marjoram, sorrel and potato have all been recommended. Other praiseworthy offerings have included kidneys with wine and tarragon, wild salmon in aspic with chervil, spinach and ham tartlets, pulled and devilled chicken and casserole of lamb. The simplicity and freshness of the food can be deceptive, surprising those who are expecting complexity and elaboration. Prime, often unpasteurised, cheeses come with home-baked biscuits and apples from the orchard. Desserts show loyalty to the English tradition and a natural approach to healthy eating: summer pudding with seasonal fruits, quince ice-cream, upside-down apple cake, yoghurts and curd tarts. Patricia's devotion to the kitchen is matched by John Hegarty's knowledge and passion for the garden and his wine cellar, which is confined to France with only the briefest of flirtations with the rest of the world. As the wine list encompasses so many of the best producers of France (Juillot in Mercurey, and Meffre in Gigondas and Côtes du Rhône) and a fine bunch of clarets including petits châteaux, is it churlish to hope that John Hegarty might extend his enthusiasm to Italy? There are half-bottles in abundance, prices throughout the list are fair. House wine is £6. CELLARMAN'S CHOICE: Mâcon Viré 1988, Bonhomme, £13; Côtes de Bourg, Ch. La Graverie 1986, £11.

CHEF: Patricia Hegarty PROPRIETORS: John and Patricia Hegarty OPEN: Wed to Sun, D only (Mon to Tue D residents only) CLOSED: mid-Dec to mid-Feb MEALS: 7.30 to 8.30 PRICES: Set D £15.50 (£20) to £28.60 (£35). Card slips closed CARDS: Access, Visa SEATS: 24. Private parties: 6 main room. Car park, 10 places. No children under 12. Smart dress preferred. No smoking in dining-room. Wheelchair access (2 steps). No music. Fax: (0531) 5697 ACCOMMODATION: 9 rooms, all with bath/shower. Deposit £60. Garden. Phone. Scenic. Doors close at 11 (*Which? Hotel Guide*)

LEEDS West Yorkshire map 5

Bryans

9 Weetwood Lane, Headingley,
Leeds LS16 5LT COOKING 1
LEEDS (0532) 785679 COST £13

'Consistently good, even excellent' is how one reader described the very good fish and chips. 'I usually take overseas visitors to Bryans. It seems the only way of offering something uniquely British.' Many would agree that this is a more genuine experience than the tripperamas that some fish and chip shops have become. Haddock, whether 'jumbo' or 'baby', is always recommended.

CHEF: David Mitchell PROPRIETOR: Jan Fletcher OPEN: all week MEALS: 11.30am to 11.30pm (noon to 8.30 Sun) PRICES: £8 (£11). Minimum £2.43 SEATS: 140. Private parties: 100 main room. Car park, 50 places. Children's helpings. Wheelchair access. Music. Air-conditioned

Hansa's

COUNTY RESTAURANT OF THE YEAR

NEW ENTRY

72–74 North Street, Leeds LS2 7PN
LEEDS (0532) 444408

COOKING 1
COST £10–£16

This is an excellent Gujarati vegetarian restaurant in a row of converted shops away from the city centre. There are no pretensions to poshness here, just good honest home-cooking from Hansa Dabhi backed up by her female staff. The menu – adorned with colour photographs of dishes – is divided up into starters, specialities and main courses; there are also daily curries listed on a blackboard. Recommended dishes have included masala dosa, petis (crisp mixed vegetables embedded in mashed potato and deep-fried), grease-free deep-fried slices of aubergine, and valor ringan (Kashmiri 'runner beans' with aubergines in a tomato-based curry). Most dishes are accompanied by exemplary relishes and chutneys. There is also a wide choice of deep-fried bhajias and dhals, as well as good-value thalis. The choice of home-made sweets includes ice-creams, an Indian version of Knickerbocker Glory, an organic fruit cake and lapsi (bulgar wheat with syrup, cinnamon and sultanas) as well as shrikhand and ras malai. Service can be slow and haphazard under pressure. Drink lassi, lager or exotic fruit juice.

CHEF/PROPRIETOR: Hansa Dabhi OPEN: Tue to Sun, D only CLOSED: 25 and 26 Dec, 1 Jan MEALS: 6 to 10.30 (11.30 Fri and Sat) PRICES: £8 (£13), Set D £5.95 (£10) to £7.25 (£12). Service 10% for parties of 5 or more SEATS: 60. Private parties: 60 main room, 40 private room. Vegetarian meals. Children welcome. No-smoking area. Wheelchair access

Paris

36A Town Street, Horsforth,
Leeds LS18 4RJ
LEEDS (0532) 581885

COOKING 2
COST £14–£26

'A physical description would make mention of the dingy colour scheme – rag-rolling and all – that conspires to produce the effect of 20 years of nicotine stains; the bare floorboards; the round tables, with some booths for four round the edges; and the tree in the middle.' So went one report, but any implied criticism evaporated at discovering the 'early bird' menu for £11.95, including half a bottle of (moderate) house wine. Paris works successfully on a 'pile them high' principle and is a bonus for Leeds residents anxious to have fair cooking at fair prices. Occasionally, economy will out in small puddings and more green than white of leeks with a salmon dish, but quantities are not mingy and materials are decent. The style is French-inspired: no Italian influence here, though England may be admitted in the black pudding, steak pies or beef and horseradish. Service is friendly enough and the place fairly hums with large parties – a couple has to speak up. Given the throughput, this is a worthwhile and successful venture. The house wine may be no great shakes, but the wine list itself is an economical essay in vinous catholicity. There are some excellent bottles. House Duboeuf is £6.50. See entry under Huddersfield for a second branch of Paris.

CHEF: Steven Kendell PROPRIETORS: Martin Spalding and Steven Kendell OPEN: all week, D only MEALS: 6 to 10.30 (11 Fri and Sat) PRICES: £16 (£22), Set D £11.95 inc wine (£14) CARDS: Access, Amex, Visa SEATS: 86. Private parties: 16 main room. Vegetarian meals. Children welcome. Music

LEICESTER Leicestershire map 5

Bobby's

NEW ENTRY

154–156 Belgrave Road,
Leicester LE4 5AT
LEICESTER (0533) 660106 and 662448

COOKING 1
COST £5–£16

Leicester has one of the largest Asian communities in Britain, and Belgrave Road is one of its focal points – full of jewellers, sari makers, sweet centres and vegetarian cafés. Bobby's, an unassuming red-brick building on a street corner, combines a brilliant take-away with an informal dining-room (plus extra seating upstairs). The menu is fascinating, extraordinarily cheap and authentic. The list of 'farsan' snacks and starters is formidable, not only masala dosa, samosas, dahi vada and pakoras, but also kachori (deep-fried lentil balls), dhokla (deep-fried nuggets of chickpea flour with yoghurt, chillies and sesame seeds), mogo chips (cassava) and dhebra (millet flour with spinach and sesame seeds). Added to this are excellent-value thalis and vividly spiced curries such as aubergine and tomato and a dazzling array of sweetmeats. As an alternative to plain rice, try khichri (the precursor of kedgeree, a curious sticky porridge of mung beans and rice). Among the list of excellent breads look for thepla (a thin paratha flavoured with herbs and green chillies). There are few 'restaurant' trappings here: no cutlery on the tables, and no bill (simply take your place by the till in the take-away, and pay). Service is young, friendly and unfailingly courteous. Unlicensed, but there are lassi, falooda or mango juice to drink. More reports, please.

CHEF: Mrs M.B. Lakhani PROPRIETOR: Mr B.A. Lakhani OPEN: Tue to Sun MEALS: noon (11am Fri to Sun) to 10.30pm (11 Sat) PRICES: £8 (£13), Set L and D £3.99 (£5) to £6.25 (£7). Cover 40p. Unlicensed, but bring your own: no corkage CARDS: Access, Amex, Visa SEATS: 90. Private parties: 50 main room, 25 private room. Vegetarian meals. Children's helpings. No-smoking area. Music

Man Ho

NEW ENTRY

14–16 King Street, Leicester LE1 6RJ
LEICESTER (0533) 557700

COOKING 1
COST £12–£30

The setting is a pink and grey painted house in the shade of a horse-chestnut tree at the start of a leafy walk off King Street. John Lau has changed the name from Lai's to Man Ho and has transformed the interior. Gone is the subdued, almost French décor; in its place is a stylish dining-room with a grey ceiling and apricot walls hung with new-age 'fan' prints by William Gatewood. The menu makes few demands on the cooks or customers, but the kitchen knows its stuff: ingredients are fresh, timing is spot-on and many dishes show exemplary handling of the wok. Deep-fried king prawn 'cutlets', shredded duck-meat rolls, honey-roast pork, and spiced chicken with yellow-bean sauce and cashews have all been recommended. Stir-fried vegetables are excellent. A special menu served to one reader included memorable aromatic crispy duck, steamed scallops with ginger and spring onion, monkfish with snow peas and fried squid with salt and pepper sauce. An inspector was mightily impressed with the service: 'These waitresses, conversing happily in near-perfect English, are as sharp and friendly as any I've encountered in a Chinese restaurant.'

CHEF: Jeffery Chan PROPRIETOR: John Lau OPEN: all week CLOSED: 25 and 26 Dec MEALS: 12 to 2, 6 to 11.30 PRICES: £15 (£25), Set L £6.50 (£12), Set D from £12 (£18) to £13.50 (£20). Service 10% D. Card slips closed CARDS: Access, Amex, Diners, Visa SEATS: 100. Private parties: 60 main room, 40 private room. Vegetarian meals. Children welcome. Wheelchair access (3 steps). Music. Air-conditioned

Rise of the Raj

6 Evington Road, Leicester LE2 1HF — COOKING 1
LEICESTER (0533) 553885 — COST £14–£24

This pink and maroon restaurant is situated some way from the city centre, on the fringes of the prosperous suburb of Evington. The location means that visitors have found the place becalmed and disorganised at lunchtime while on form in the evening when the locals get home from work. The menu is a familiar Indian new-wave assortment of tandooris and curries with the likes of Madras and vindaloo as afterthoughts. Specialities such as murgh jalfrezi, lamb pasanda nawabi and king prawn masala are at the top of the range, otherwise there are dishes such as chicken tikka, karahi gosht and vegetable biriani. Thalis and the tandoori mixed grill are good value. Management is unchanged, but there have been staff problems, as one reader notes: 'The really good cooks and waiters go off to start their own restaurants, so extending the Bangladeshi/ Syhleti network.' To drink there are jazzy cocktails as well as Kingfisher beer and a handful of wines. House French is £5.50.

CHEFS: Abdul Bashir and Rouf Ullha PROPRIETOR: Abdul Bashir OPEN: all week MEALS: 12 to 2, 6 to 11.45 PRICES: £11 (£19), Set L £9 (£14), Set D £15 (£20). Minimum £7.95. Service 10% CARDS: Access, Amex, Diners, Visa SEATS: 70. Private parties: 40 main room, 45 private room. Vegetarian meals. Children's helpings. No children under 5. Smart dress preferred. Wheelchair access (2 steps). Music. Air-conditioned

LEIGHTON BUZZARD Bedfordshire — map 3

▲ *Swan Hotel*

High Street, Leighton Buzzard LU7 7EA — COOKING 1
LEIGHTON BUZZARD (0525) 372148 — COST £19–£35

'The vegetables were unremarkable, which is good, as it used to be the hallmark of small provincial hotels that vegetables were remarkably bad.' So went one report of a meal at this fine Georgian post-house on the High Street that has been properly maintained, decently embellished and serves as a useful local resource. Stephen McNally may produce a meal with oriental touches: start with lamb and lentils in pastry, continue with monkfish 'medals' stir-fried with cucumber and ginger in a lightly spiced butter sauce; or, he can cook trad Brit with the best of them for Sunday lunch. The tenor of reports is that not everything produced is faultless, but there are a sufficient number of enjoyable dishes to compensate for those that may be too bland, too tough, or too lacking in forthright texture. Everyone enjoys the airiness of the dining-room, the no-smoking policy and the willingness of the team. House wines from £8.25.

CHEF: Stephen McNally PROPRIETORS: Eric and Felicity Stephens OPEN: all week MEALS: 12 to 2, 7 (7.30 Fri) to 9.30 (10 Fri and 9 Sun) PRICES: £21 (£29), Set L £13.50 (£19) to £14.50 (£20), Set D £15 (£21) to £16.50 (£23). Card slips closed CARDS: Access, Amex, Diners, Visa SEATS: 80. 3 tables outside. Private parties: 80 main room, 40 and 40 private rooms. Car park, 10 places. Vegetarian meals. Children's helpings. No smoking in dining-room. Wheelchair access. Air-conditioned. Music. Fax: (0525) 370444 ACCOMMODATION: 38 rooms, all with bath/shower. B&B £67.50 to £80. Children welcome. Baby facilities. Afternoon teas. Air-conditioning. TV. Phone. Doors close at 11.30. Confirm by noon (*Which? Hotel Guide*)

LEWDOWN Devon map 1

▲ *Lewtrenchard Manor*

Lewdown EX20 4PN
LEWDOWN (056 683) 256 and 222
from A30 Okehampton to Launceston, turn left at Lewdown for 3/4m

COOKING 2
COST £21–£42

On the outside this is a splendid Elizabethan manor house, and the restored interior is the work of Sabine Baring-Gould (composer of 'Onward Christian Soldiers') an idiosyncratic Victorian who collected Tudor fine panelling and plasterwork. Some may call this pastiche gloomy (there is a propensity for heavy woodwork and bad nineteenth-century portraiture) but the building has a lot of character and the conversion to a hotel has been done with some panache. James Brown is now in charge of the kitchen. It is early days for him and he needs time to consolidate his style. Technique seems somewhat less assured, and the kitchen is a little more lacking in character than under his predecessor. One reported meal began with grilled scallops cooked with a lemon and ginger crumb. This was a good idea, nicely executed, and lifted by a delicious butter sauce; a drawback, however, was the burnt julienne of leeks. Roast breast of Gressingham duck ('juicy, full of flavour and beautifully pink') accompanied by a morel butter sauce had less character – technically competent but rather dull. The dessert was clumsy. A fondness for choux-paste swans and sugar-paste baskets for the petits fours could be discouraged to allow the kitchen more time to tighten things up. There is a surer hand on the mostly European wine list. It displays fondness for Spain with good older vintages, and draws on some good growers in Burgundy. Prices are fair and particular consideration is given to the selection below £15. There are good half-bottles. Were enthusiasm spread beyond Europe it could merit a glass award.

CHEF: James Brown PROPRIETORS: James and Sue Murray OPEN: all week, D only, and Sun L MEALS: 12 to 2.30, 7.15 to 9.30 PRICES: £29 (£35), Set Sun L £15 (£21), Set D £25 (£32). Card slips closed CARDS: Access, Amex, Diners, Visa SEATS: 40. Private parties: 8 main room, 16 and 50 private rooms. Car park, 50 places. No children under 8. Smart dress preferred. No smoking in dining-room. Wheelchair access. No music. Fax: (056 683) 332 ACCOMMODATION: 8 rooms, all with bath/shower. B&B £75 to £135. No children under 8. Pets by arrangement. Afternoon teas. Garden. Fishing. TV. Phone. Scenic. Doors close at midnight. Confirm by 6 (*Which? Hotel Guide*)

LEWES East Sussex map 3

Pailin NEW ENTRY

20 Station Street, Lewes BN7 2DB COOKING 1
LEWES (0273) 473906 COST £17–£23

Pailin does not overwhelm with exoticism, but it is a quiet, comfortable Thai restaurant, a place to be recommended for a reasonably priced and interesting meal. The cooking is firmly controlled; it is not of the highest order but there is a confidence about the execution which is reassuring. Thai cooking demands sound judgement in timing and flavouring and this Pailin manages consistently. The balancing tricks of sweet/sour, hot/fragrant, sharp/fresh are carried off well: a delicately but firmly flavoured chicken lemon soup, with lemon grass kept in control; pork spare ribs with a clearly flavoured sweet-and-sour sauce; spiced hot-and-sour rare beef salad, the hot spiciness complementing the warm-flavoured meat; prawn and crab hotpot showing fine balancing of spices and clear, fresh flavours; barbecued marinated chicken with sweet-sour plum sauce, hot, heavy but well balanced. Desserts are rather a non-event, coffee has been disappointing, so order jasmine tea instead. House French is £6.

CHEF: Rasamee Newman PROPRIETOR: Maitri Niyomthum OPEN: Mon to Sat CLOSED: 25 and 26 Dec MEALS: 12 to 2.30, 6.30 to 10.30 PRICES: £11 (£19), Set L and D £12 (£17) to £14.50 (£19). Card slips closed CARDS: Access, Amex, Carte Blanche, Diners, Visa SEATS: 40. Private parties: 25 main room, 15 private room. Vegetarian meals. Children's helpings. Music. Air-conditioned

LICHFIELD Staffordshire map 5

▲ *Swinfen Hall Hotel* NEW ENTRY

Swinfen, nr Lichfield WS14 9RS COOKING 1
LICHFIELD (0543) 481494 COST £19–£32

This glorious house built by Benjamin Wyatt in 1755 lay derelict for 40 years until 1986. Perhaps it was during this time that the name was hijacked by the neighbouring prison for young offenders. Some of the rooms, the entrance hall for instance, are impressive. Others, such as the panelled banqueting hall made ready for audio-visual presentation to 200 people, seem swamped by the conversion to hotel and inevitable conference centre (it is only 20 minutes to the NEC). The Edwardian part of the building is lavishly panelled and very heavy in feel. Staff do change here, and so do standards. The kitchen is currently in the hands of Steven Black, and some of the food – offered on a set-price menu with a half-dozen choices – can be workmanlike. Examples are a dish of langoustines on shredded vegetables with lime vinaigrette; good salmon but bland watercress sauce; excellent meats, although the sauce accompanying the lamb was over-reduced; decent vegetables; and a fine marquise. Not all finer techniques have been mastered – soufflés for one – but the present kitchen regime merits support. The setting may provoke over-ambition. The wine list is short and fairly priced.

CHEF: Steven Black PROPRIETORS: Mr V.J. and Mrs H.L. Wiser OPEN: all week, exc Sat L and Sun D CLOSED: 25 to 31 Dec MEALS: 12.30 to 2, 7.30 to 9 (9.30 Sat) PRICES: Set L £12.95 (£19), Set D £19.95 (£27). Card slips closed CARDS: Access, Amex, Visa SEATS: 60. Private parties: 80 main room, 28 and 120 private rooms. Car park, 110 places. Vegetarian meals. Children's helpings. Smart dress preferred. No smoking in dining-room. Wheelchair access. Music ACCOMMODATION: 19 rooms, all with bath/shower. B&B £65 to £95. Children welcome. Baby facilities. Afternoon teas. Garden. TV. Phone. Scenic. Confirm by 6 (*Which? Hotel Guide*)

LIFTON Devon map 1

▲ *Arundell Arms*

Lifton PL16 0AA
LIFTON (0566) 84666, changes to
(0566) 784666 in spring 1992 COOKING 1
on A30, 3m E of Launceston COST £18–£37

What was once an old inn complete with cockpit (now a tackle room) is now a luxurious sporting, especially fishing, hotel with atavistic touches – bare stone – but in the main furnished with much softness and great style. The dining-room, in particular, has the air of country house rather than country inn. This may have affected the kitchen's output, which can be grander in concept than execution. Although the Arundell is a welcome daytime haven for travellers weary of too many holidaymakers, as well as an evening delight for those whose legs have been made stiff from unremitting casting over a fast-running stream, the message is that simple means best. A salad of honey-glazed duck breast was given nice counterpoint with an onion chutney, but a croustade of wild mushrooms failed on most technical counts as well as flavour. A lime pie was a happy blend of sweet paste and a lime-zested custard; an ambitious chocolate cake was no more than acceptable. The *carte* is expensive for rural Devon, so better to stay with the short fixed-price menu. 'We make no service charge, and tips are not expected,' says the owner. The straightforward and reliable wine list has many good names, a decent range of halves and fair prices.

CHEF: Philip Burgess PROPRIETOR: Anne Voss-Bark OPEN: all week CLOSED: 4 days Christmas MEALS: 12.30 to 2, 7.30 to 9 PRICES: £25 (£31), Set L £13.50 (£18), Set D £22.25 (£27) CARDS: Access, Amex, Diners, Visa SEATS: 70. Private parties: 80 main room, 30 private room. Car park, 80 places. Vegetarian meals. Children's helpings. No smoking in dining-room. Music. Fax: (0566) 84494 (784494 from spring 1992) ACCOMMODATION: 29 rooms, all with bath/shower. B&B £51 to £81. Children welcome. Baby facilities. Pets welcome. Afternoon teas. Garden. Fishing. Golf. TV. Phone. Scenic. Doors close at 11.30

LINCOLN Lincolnshire map 6

Harvey's Cathedral Restaurant

1 Exchequergate, Castle Square,
Lincoln LN2 1PZ
LINCOLN (0522) 510333

COOKING 1
COST £13–£30

Bob Harvey's involvement in his new restaurant in Doddington (see County round-ups) has caused his face to be shown less frequently at this house at the historic central core of Lincoln. Family supervision, however, remains close. There are those who say that the paintwork, fixtures and fittings might be less historic with benefit to all, but these same reporters also feel that the cooking has taken a turn for the better. A variety of fair-value set menus complement the *carte*, and endorsements of things like pâtés, garlic mussels, potted cheese, roast meats and even a cassoulet have been received. Criticism there is, too, and standards do remain uneven. Sometimes lack of generosity is cited. Others say simply that no one bothered to see if the dish had flavour. Almost the same could be said of Troffs, the less gloomy bistro upstairs. The P.A.Y.D. – pay as you drink – policy is maintained; apart from a minimum 25 per cent of bottle price, what is leftover is not charged for. Generous, but one suspects there are few customers willing to leave much since choice here is fine and prices reasonable. A robust, if not rough and ready, approach manifests itself in the writing and presentation of the wine list, and, sadly, sometimes in the wine service, which may put the bottle award in doubt. House wine is £8.50.

CHEFS: Adrianne Harvey, Linda Wilson and Fiona Baldock PROPRIETORS: Adrianne and Bob Harvey OPEN: all week, exc Sat L and Sun D (Sat L by arrangement) CLOSED: Dec 26 MEALS: 12 to 2, 7 to 10 PRICES: £16 (£24), Set L £5.95 (£13), Set Sun L £7.50 (£15), Set D £16.95 (£25). Card slips closed CARDS: Access, Visa SEATS: 52. Private parties: 32 main room, 18 private room. Vegetarian meals. Children's helpings. Wheelchair access (3 steps; also WC). Music

Wig & Mitre

29 Steep Hill, Lincoln LN2 1LU
LINCOLN (0522) 535190 and 523705

COOKING 3
COST £22–£34

The theory behind this upstairs and downstairs pub is estimable: good food at all hours; good service at fair wages and discouragement of tips; eat what you will, even breakfast at tea-time, not what the owner thinks you should. 'Beating back the steakhouse chains' is Paul Vidic's interpretation of his aims in the kitchen; venison with glazed pear rather than T-bone and onion rings. That a bar meal of chilli con carne, with fresh chillies of course, and cod with a herb and garlic crust can be as good as a more elaborate affair of soufflé suissesse and panaché of mullet, bream, salmon and scallops with chives in more elaborate surroundings on the upper level is encouraging. Menus change constantly, cooking according to the markets, not to plans laid in managers' offices. Theory apart, the practice is satisfactory, even in hurried times. Service, too, is willing without unnecessary flounce, though some people would prefer more detail to their bills. The wine list, amply supplied with halves once you have cracked the layout, does have some good sources at affordable cost: Guigal, Vernay in Condrieu, Crochet's Sancerre, Viña Ardanza from Rioja Alta and Gaston Hochar's Ch. Musar from the Lebanon are examples. House wines are £8.35. A branch is planned for Leicester (Welford Place, 2 Welford Place, Leicester LE1 6ZH, Tel: (0533) 470758) as this *Guide* goes to press. Will the concept be capable of export?

CHEFS: Paul Vidic, Lino Poli, Peter Dodd and Simon Shaw PROPRIETORS: Valerie and Michael Hope OPEN: all week CLOSED: 25 Dec MEALS: 8am to 11pm PRICES: 'daily' menu £14 (£22), à la carte £20 (£28), Snacks from £2.50. Card slips closed CARDS: Access, Amex, Diners, Visa SEATS: 100. 6 tables outside. Private parties: 38 main room. Vegetarian meals. Children's helpings. Children restricted. No pipes in dining-room. Wheelchair access (1 step). No music. Fax: (0522) 532402

LIPHOOK Hampshire map 2

▲ *Nippon Kan, Old Thorns* **NEW ENTRY**

Longmoor Road, Liphook GU30 7PE COOKING 2
LIPHOOK (0428) 724555 COST £20–£58

Old Thorns describes itself as 'Golf course-Hotel-Restaurants'. Understandably, given the golfing emphasis, it is Japanese-owned and caters for many Japanese clients, for whom there is a Japanese restaurant. This is worth exploring. Two teppans dominate the room with extremely efficient air extraction over them. The menu offers a first page of teppanyaki for those sitting at the teppans (where you can watch the chef prepare and cook each dish). Of the five set menus, one is vegetarian. In addition there is a short *carte* of individual seafood, meat and vegetables. The dinner menu offers a longer *carte* and no less than 12 set menus. An inspection meal produced good gyuniku tataki – wafer-thin slices of beef served blue ('almost beef sashimi'); salmon roe on grated white radish; a 'subtle and delicate' fried chicken, Japanese-style; mussels steamed with saké; and sashimi of salmon, tuna, sea bass, ark-shell and yellow fish. Drink Japanese plum wine and green tea. The set lunch is excellent value.

CHEFS: Geoff Sutton and M. Hama PROPRIETORS: London Kosaido Co Ltd OPEN: all week MEALS: 12.30 to 2.30, 7 to 9.30 PRICES: £23 (£31), Set L £14.50 (£20) to £40 (£48), Set D £17.50 (£24) to £40 (£48) CARDS: Access, Amex, Diners, Visa SEATS: 50. Private parties: 50 main room. Car park, 200 places. Vegetarian meals. Children welcome. Jacket and tie. Fax: (0428) 725036 ACCOMMODATION: 33 rooms, all with bath/shower. B&B £78 to £98. Afternoon teas. Garden. Swimming-pool. Sauna. Tennis. Golf. TV. Phone. Scenic

All letters to the Guide *are acknowledged with an update on latest sales, closures, chef changes and so on.*

The Guide *relies on feedback from its readers. Especially welcome are reports on new restaurants appearing in the book for the first time.*

LITTLE WALSINGHAM Norfolk map 6

▲ *Old Bakehouse*

33 High Street,
Little Walsingham NR22 6BZ COOKING 2
WALSINGHAM (0328) 820454 COST £17–£30

People recommend the Bakehouse as a bed and breakfast stop and for its good value; residents, for instance, are well pleased by the bargain set meal available to them alone. There is quite a contrast between the low cellar bar with its Morris patterns and the main dining-room ('lofty and light with tables tactfully placed so others' conversations do not intrude'). Service is smooth, warmed by the Padleys' enthusiasm and willingness to talk about their craft. Chris Padley's cooking is stable, his style consistent. Cream sauces are enjoyed – mushrooms and bacon with brandy and cream, pork with prunes and cream, kidneys with orange, mustard and cream. Vegetables are copious and varied; at least half hit the bull each evening, but there are sometimes murmurs across the whole range. Certain particular dishes remain popular: leek and potato soup, those mushrooms, and the house pâté with nicely balanced port and orange sauce. Puddings are substantial and, again, often creamy. Comforting food, usually well-prepared, and plentiful, it is at moments regrettably overcooked, badly handled and felt to be out of touch with modern tastes. The wine list is adequate with good names at fair prices; there are many halves.

CHEFS/PROPRIETORS: Christopher and Helen Padley OPEN: Tue to Sat, D only, Apr to Nov; Wed to Sat, D only, Dec to Mar CLOSED: 3 weeks Jan to Feb, 2 weeks Oct to Nov, 1 week June MEALS: 7 to 9 PRICES: £18 (£25), Set D £11.50 (£17). Card slips closed CARDS: Access, Visa SEATS: 36. Private parties: 40 main room. Vegetarian meals. No children under 12. Smart dress preferred. No smoking in dining-room. Music ACCOMMODATION: 3 rooms, 2 with bath/shower. B&B £15.50 to £37. Deposit: £5. No children under 12. Scenic. Confirm by 6

LIVERPOOL Merseyside map 5

Armadillo 🍷

20–22 Matthew Street, L2 6RE COOKING 2*
051-236 4123 COST £29

Authentic Gallic-sounding cries emanate from the kitchen downstairs, but the Armadillo is fully part of the Liverpool scene. While one party had their car systematically burgled in the nearby multi-storey, they enjoyed a dinner including terrine of lentils and red peppers, squid stewed with ginger, good fresh grilled sole, and fillets of lamb with shallots wrapped with leeks. Vegetables were nicely cooked. Had they been at lunchtime or for the mid-week 'early supper', the economical spirits among them might have felt soothed by the fair pricing of the simpler, but still good, cooking and range of salads. 'They were freshly prepared, well-served, tasty and nourishing,' reports one reader who stayed in Liverpool after a day's shopping. The place is justifiably popular and the decoration shows it, but for 'a haven of relaxation' such as this, who cares? Value for food is more than matched by the wine list.

This has great range (not just in France), very useful notes, excellent growers and properties, and in some instances sensational prices. The Armadillo seems to be a public service.

CHEFS: John Scotland and Martin Cooper PROPRIETORS: Martin and Angela Cooper OPEN: Tue to Sat CLOSED: bank hols MEALS: 12 to 3 (12 to 5 Sat), 5 to 6.30 (Tue to Fri daytime menu), 7.30 to 10.30 PRICES: £18 (£24) CARDS: Access, Visa SEATS: 65. Private parties: 75 main room. Vegetarian meals. Children's helpings on request. Music. Air-conditioned

LIVERSEDGE West Yorkshire map 5

▲ *Lillibet's*

64 Leeds Road, Liversedge WF15 6HX COOKING 1
HECKMONDWIKE (0924) 404911 COST £15–£35

The substantial stone house is haven to a wide range of custom: 'One chap was in jeans and T-shirt and ties were the exception rather than the rule,' observed a reader. This makes a refreshing change from the image England projects of stuffed-shirt dining. The menu, a touch longer than last year, is priced according to main dish chosen, and includes a second course of soup or sorbet as well as coffee at the finish. It is fair value. Not much is left to speak for itself: full-dress cooking rather than modern understatement. Quail is stuffed with chicken mousse, lamb is topped with spinach and mushrooms before being wrapped in puff pastry, and pork is topped with tomato, herbs and mozzarella. Only duck is still 'au naturel' – though not always crisp, said one. The style is substantial, without grossness, and portions are generous. Desserts include meringues or pavlovas, often spoken well of, and good fresh fruit (more rarely seen than it used to be) as well as cooked dishes such as plums with a vanilla sauce. Refurbishment has improved the entrance and brightened bar and restaurant, as well as increased the number of bedrooms. Four dozen wines are supplemented by a blackboard list of extras: no crazed French chauvinism here, but an attempt to find value from all wine-producing countries. House wine is French and costs £7.95.

CHEF: Liz Roberts PROPRIETORS: Martin Roberts and Liz Roberts OPEN: Mon to Sat, D only (L by arrangement) CLOSED: 1 week between Christmas and New Year, 2 weeks end Aug MEALS: 12 to 1.45, 7 to 9.30 PRICES: Set L £9.50 (£15) to £11.50 (£17), Set D £16.75 (£23) to £22.50 (£29) CARDS: Access, Amex, Visa SEATS: 70. Private parties: 70 main room. Car park, 40 places. Vegetarian meals. Children's helpings. Music. Fax: (0924) 404912 ACCOMMODATION: 13 rooms, all with bath/shower. Rooms for disabled. B&B £43 to £65. Garden. TV. Phone. Doors close at midnight (*Which? Hotel Guide*)

'As we entered, a very thin cat wandered by – this should have been a sign of what was to come.' On eating in Cumbria

All details are as accurate as possible at the time of going to press, but chefs and owners often change, and it is wise to check by telephone before making a special journey. Many readers have been disappointed when set-price bargain meals are no longer available. Ask when booking.

LONGRIDGE Lancashire map 5

Heathcote's

COUNTY RESTAURANT OF THE YEAR

NEW ENTRY

104–106 Higher Road,
Longridge PR3 3SY
PRESTON (0772) 784969

COOKING 3*
COST £19–£40

Beside a road leading out of Longridge is a cottage, or rather three cottages knocked into one, where the inside is more prepossessing than the out. Walls and partitions have flown, but the two-level dining-room and bar still has a certain compartmental air – useful for no-smoke zoning, yet to be introduced. Money has been reserved for the things that matter, so the ceilings are Artex. But people like the jars of preserves and the chintz that give the place its character. Paul Heathcote is a young chef who has worked in prestigious spots – the Connaught, Sharrow Bay, Manoir aux Quat' Saisons (see entries) and, latterly, as head chef at the Courtyard in Broughton – and the presentation and style of cooking, as well as his commitment to success, show signs of his tutelage. The long printed menu, changed every couple of months, is long on descriptions. Prices, written in words, may shock some Lancashire folk, who will rush to take advantage of the fairly priced Sunday lunch. Mr Heathcote has wisely elected to begin as he means to go on. The cooking may sound and look over-sophisticated, but there is no absence of punchy flavours: black pudding, pig's trotter stuffed with onion and wild mushrooms, oxtail with cabbage, given a new angle by being smoked, chicken broth with (over-) herbed dumplings. Heathcote's terrines get rave reviews: leek and smoked duck with chervil butter sauce; his speciality of lamb fillet with wild mushrooms and new potatoes ('brilliant taste and texture, presentation full marks'); and the foie gras and leek with a truffle vinaigrette ('very melting liver, a smart salad round the rim of the plate, a very crumbly brioche'). Main dishes are also enjoyed, fish less so than meat, although lobster ravioli has been consistent. Approval has come for breast of duck on an apple and potato rösti, with honey and armagnac sauce, beef fillet with a red wine sauce, creamed mushrooms and shallots, and lamb cutlets with a herb crust and a cake of provençal vegetables. Desserts do not disappoint: marbled chocolate terrine, rich and dark; bread-and-butter pudding, even if over-decorated, 'the stuff of dreams'. The overload of trimming that can sometimes be seen surfaces again with the petits fours: good, but fewer sorts would probably mean better. Service is keen as mustard. Strangers to the region may very occasionally yawn as they comment 'another fancy place messing the food about', but a more realistic assessment includes the phrase, 'as good, perhaps better, than any I've eaten'. The North-West is fortunate Paul Heathcote was a stay-at-home. His determination to include bottles 'proudly showing the proprietor's name, as does my restaurant' is largely fulfilled. Careful and intelligent selection provide a good range of fair prices. More depth in Alsace and the Rhône, a few Italians and a better provision of halves would make a model list.

CHEF/PROPRIETOR: Paul Heathcote OPEN: all week D, L Fri and Sun MEALS: 12 to 2 (2.30 Sun), 7 to 9.30 PRICES: £24 (£33), Set L £12.75 (£19). Service 10%, max £15 CARDS: Access, Visa SEATS: 46. Private parties: 50 main room. Car park, 8 places. Vegetarian meals. Children welcome. Wheelchair access. Music

LOUGHBOROUGH Leicestershire map 5

Restaurant Roger Burdell

11–12 Sparrow Hill,
Loughborough LE11 1BT — COOKING 2*
LOUGHBOROUGH (0509) 231813 — COST £24–£35

The setting is an old manor house, elegantly done out in pastel shades. From the windows of the ground-floor bistro, where you can have a drink before eating, there are views of the nearby parish church; upstairs is the main dining-room, with a large stone fireplace, candles and shining silver on the tables. Here, Roger Burdell cooks a short fixed-price menu rooted firmly in classical tradition, as in warm onion and bacon tart, sautéed breast of chicken with watercress sauce and fillet of beef with shallots and madeira sauce. But there are more modern ideas too and they seem to work: warm salad of very rare pigeon breast with pine kernels and walnut dressing, marinated mixed raw fish, and mousseline-stuffed salmon in filo pastry with a wine sauce. Cheeses are 'traditionally made', and the pick of the sweets, according to one inspector, has to be the vanilla pudding with hot toffee sauce. Frills which some may associate with 'serious' eating are left out and service can be 'rather amateurish'. The wine list has a number of 'house recommendations' from £8.25.

CHEF/PROPRIETOR: Roger Burdell OPEN: Mon to Sat, exc Mon L MEALS: 12.30 to 2, 7.30 to 9.15 PRICES: Set D £17.50 (£24) to £21.50 (£29) CARDS: Access, Visa SEATS: 40. Private parties: 24 main room. Vegetarian meals. Children welcome. No cigars/pipes in dining-room. Music

LOUTH Lincolnshire map 6

Alfred's

Upgate, Louth LN11 9EY — COOKING 1*
LOUTH (0507) 607431 — COST £36

While waiting for their dinner one couple watched unflustered hands preparing it through the kitchen hatch; Rosemarie Dicker presents her dishes in a simple manner although the influences are modern. The handwritten menu changes monthly and offers four or five choices at each stage. Dishes steer a course between adventure and commercial good sense; steak always appears on the menu. Osso buco with root vegetables, parsley lemon and garlic, tuna fillets pan-fried in a hot chilli butter, calf's liver with a watercress and shallot sauce satisfy the chef and the more adventurous diner. A winter meal of smoked haddock mornay and fillet steak with celeriac showed sound buying of ingredients and care in execution. Desserts are well done; heavily endorsed has been a lemon tart with toasted banana. House wine is £7.95.

CHEFS: Rosemarie Dicker and Diane Willoughby PROPRIETORS: Paul and Rosemarie Dicker OPEN: Tue to Sat, D only (L Tue to Fri by arrangement) CLOSED: 25 Dec D, bank hols MEALS: 7 to 9.30 (10 Sat) PRICES: Set D £23.50 (£30). Card slips closed CARDS: Access, Visa SEATS: 45. Private parties: 50 main room, 50 private room. Vegetarian meals. Children's helpings. Wheelchair access (3 steps). Music

Ferns

NEW ENTRY

40 Northgate, Louth LN11 0LY — COOKING 1
LOUTH (0507) 603209 — COST £15–£32

This small restaurant, floral and pink in style, offers a simple menu based on fresh ingredients. The style is homely rather than inspired, and adapted to local tastes: prawn cocktail, and many roasts and grills for main courses. An unevenness in the quality of the cooking can give a varied meal: thick and creamy leek and potato soup and local mushrooms in an intense, well-judged sherry sauce, were followed by a disappointingly tasteless turkey escalope and a beef, beer and bacon pie, overwhelmed by the flavour of smoked bacon. Desserts put the meal back on course with a well-made brandy-snap basket, filled with an interesting selection of fruit, and a chocolate and hazelnut tart. 'Expertise will come' is the hopeful consensus on a boon in a poorly served area. Table d'hôte at £7.50 is excellent value. There is a short, all-organic wine list. House French is £9.95.

CHEF: Kim Thompson PROPRIETORS: Nick and Kim Thompson OPEN: Tue to Sat, D only MEALS: 7 to 9.30 PRICES: £18 (£27), Set D £7.50 (£15). Card slips closed CARDS: Access, Visa SEATS: 34. Private parties: 34 main room. Vegetarian meals. Healthy eating options. Children's helpings early evening. No children under 10 after early evening. Music

LOWER BEEDING West Sussex — map 3

▲ *South Lodge*

COUNTY RESTAURANT OF THE YEAR

Brighton Road, Lower Beeding RH13 6PS — COOKING 3*
LOWER BEEDING (0403) 891711 — COST £26–£58

Frederick Ducane Godman, explorer and botanist, left his mark on this late-Victorian country house, including the biggest (violently pink) rhododendron in England. Lavish refurbishment has not disguised the William de Morgan tiles, the ornate woodwork or the studied luxury of the original. Considering the prices for food and accommodation, luxury should be omnipresent. The talking point this year has been the arrival of chef Tony Tobin, last seen at Very Simply Nico in London (now Simply Nico, see entry), and the consequent transformation of standards – accompanied luckily by a tightening and improvement of service front-of-house. Marks of an apprenticeship *chez* Nico come through the classic menu, avoiding ludicrous combinations or unnecessary elaboration, which seems to lay great emphasis on sauces, often a mite sweet, or lacking an acidulated balancing ingredient that would lighten the impact. Buttery cooking lives on here. Good cooking too: a tripartite duck confit, fried foie gras on orange segments and leaf salad with pine-nuts was impressive (though buttery), as was a feuilleté of scallops with ginger and scallions, with more butter. The smokehouse is also enjoyed here: home-smoked cannon of lamb, done over sweet oak (tasting like something that sat over a collection of butts to one non-smoker), was a new variation on the theme, using excellent lamb – just as the fish, from London not the south coast, is of first-class provenance. Although the *carte* is the principal offering, the 'signature' menu is a fixed-price, no-choice alternative. Lunch is a comparative bargain though the price reduction is reflected in the relative tedium of the choice. South Lodge's potential is being tapped. Virtually every bottle on the mostly French wine list is over £15, fine enough quality, but not good value. House wine is £12.

CHEF: Anthony Tobin PROPRIETORS: Laura Hotels Ltd OPEN: all week MEALS: 12.30 to 2, 7.30 to 10 (10.30 Fri and Sat) PRICES: £35 (£48), Set L £15 (£26), Set D £25 (£37) to £32 (£45). Card slips closed CARDS: Access, Amex, Diners, Visa SEATS: 40. Private parties: 8 main room, 14, 45 and 80 private rooms. Car park, 100 places. Vegetarian meals. Children's helpings. Jacket and tie. No smoking in dining-room. Wheelchair access. No music. Fax: (0403) 891253 ACCOMMODATION: 39 rooms, all with bath/shower. Rooms for disabled. B&B £90 to £255. Children welcome. Baby facilities. Afternoon teas. Garden. Tennis. TV. Phone. Scenic. Confirm by 6

LOWER BRAILES Warwickshire map 2

▲ *Feldon House* 🍷

Lower Brailes OX15 5HW COOKING 2
BRAILES (060 885) 580 COST £24–£35

Allan and Maggie Witherick's Victorian house is a curiosity, and also a gem. Some would say that it is not like a restaurant at all, simply a private house which serves food to people who are prepared to book in advance and accept a no-choice set menu. The cooking is simple but deceptively accomplished. A party of four enjoyed a first-class lunch of warm salad of mushrooms with ham and croûtons, roast pheasant served with French beans, red cabbage and creamy potato purée, followed by fresh orange jelly with cream-filled meringue plus clove-flavoured apple ice-cream. Dinner guests are offered four courses along similar lines. A late winter menu, for example, consisted of lentil and orange soup, quenelles of smoked cod, Gressingham duck, and lemon meringue roulade. The wine list, now carefully annotated, is remarkable for its restraint; assembled by an enthusiast, it nevertheless rejects the encyclopaedic approach. In the compass of less than 50 entries 10 are interesting bin-ends and 11 are halves. Remarkable depth and intelligent and real choices are provided, all at reasonable prices. A glass award is given for refreshing lack of fuss, steady aim and sheer nerve. House French is £7.50. CELLARMAN'S CHOICE: Coopers Creek, Sauvignon Blanc 1990, £13.50; Chiroubles, Grosse Pierre 1988, Passot, £12.95.

CHEF: Allan Witherick PROPRIETORS: Allan and Maggie Witherick OPEN: all week, exc Sun D MEALS: 12.30 to 2, 7.30 to 8.30 PRICES: Set L £17.95 (£24), Set D £22.50 (£29). Card slips closed CARDS: Access, Visa SEATS: 14. Private parties: 10 main room, 4 private room. Car park, 9 places. Vegetarian meals. Children's helpings by arrangement. No music ACCOMMODATION: 4 rooms, all with bath/shower. B&B £30 to £56. No children under 14. Garden. TV. Phone. Scenic. Doors close at 11. Confirm 1 day ahead

Report forms are at the back of the book; write a letter if you prefer.

Cellarman's Choice: a wine recommended by the restaurateur, normally more expensive than house wine.

LYMINGTON Hampshire map 2

▲ *Provence* **NEW ENTRY**

Gordleton Mill Hotel, Silver Street,
Hordle, Lymington SO41 6DJ COOKING 3
LYMINGTON (0590) 682219 COST £19–£54

Under Jean-Pierre Novi this restaurant had an enviable reputation. He left, and it closed for extensive refurbishment – the dining-room was moved to take full advantage of views of water willows and the kitchen was reconstructed. Spring 1991 saw it open for business under a new chef, Jean Christophe Novelli, who has worked round here before. The new ambience is designed to appeal to visitors from Bournemouth and the rich south coast littoral; the cooking has more taste, although it suffers from an excess of ornament and 'finish', which detracts from Novelli's evident talent to deliver good flavours skilfully. Dishes are too robust to be described as nouvelle cuisine: ox tongue, braised pork knuckle and pig's trotter stuffed with wild mushrooms were three out of seven choices on a lunch menu. However, the methods do delight in those stuffings, sausages and fillings that were once all the rage: squid filled with avocado and crab, scallop sausages, lamb cutlets with a goats' cheese soufflé filling. Then to the puddings: again, trimmings and sugar cages to the fore, but again good food under the fandango. Novelli is keen on home-smoking and has already constructed his own smoke-hole. It may be hoped that this regime lasts as long as the previous one and that the food settles into a stronger groove. Sauces are good, materials inventive and service is improving. The Provence may be back. The exclusively French wine list is a neat balance of sound simple wines at very modest prices – Dom. du Tariquet at £10 and Gigondas by Meffre at £14.50, for example – and a fair scattering of very exalted names, especially from Burgundy, at matching prices. Mark-ups favour the bottles under £20 and unless extravagance is essential there is much at, or around, that price. There are good Alsaces and Rhônes and a range of halves. For an award, an exclusively French list should perhaps show greater adventure. House wines are from £10.

CHEF: Jean Christophe Novelli PROPRIETOR: William F. Stone OPEN: Tue to Sun, exc Sun D CLOSED: 7 to 21 Jan MEALS: 12 to 2.30, 7 to 10 PRICES: Set L £12 (£19) to £19.50 (£27), Set D £24 (£32) to £36 (£45) CARDS: Access, Amex, Visa SEATS: 40. 5 tables outside. Private parties: 30 main room, 15 private room. No children under 7. Jacket and tie D. No smoking in dining-room. Wheelchair access (1 step; also WC). Music. Air-conditioned. Fax: (0590) 683073 ACCOMMODATION: 7 rooms, all with bath/shower. B&B £57 to £120. Deposit: £50. No children under 7. Afternoon teas. Garden. TV. Phone. Scenic

All entries in the Guide *are rewritten every year, not least because restaurant standards fluctuate. Don't trust an out-of-date* Guide.

County round-ups listing additional restaurants that may be worth a visit are at the back of the Guide, *after the Irish section. Reports on round-up entries are welcome.*

LYMPSTONE Devon map 1

▲ *River House*

The Strand, Lympstone EX8 5EY — COOKING 2
EXMOUTH (0395) 265147 — COST £26–£47

An artist recommends this house lapped by the river Exe: 'The light was so beautiful on the water, I cannot remember the interior. The water under a full moon at high tide: a film set couldn't do it better. Hot hors d'oeuvre were served in the lounge as the tide came up and the champagne went down.' This puts the emphasis on the outdoors, which is viewed in comfort from behind large windows, either in the bar (nearest the water), or the dining-room. Shirley Wilkes cooks in the kitchen behind, her labours visible through a window on work. The variation in the menu is not so great from year to year and the style is much as it was four or more years ago, with perhaps more emphasis on vegetarian dishes and less on beef. Thus lemon sole stuffed with spinach and prawns, with a cheese sauce, quail with smoked oyster and herb stuffing, and pork with prune, cream and wine sauce come with platefuls of organic vegetables. Main courses precede substantial lemon roulades, almond tarts or banana pancakes. Michael Wilkes is enthusiastic in his welcome, waxes rhetorical in praise of the food and serves the wine from a serviceable list that is still not over-priced. Some feel that the food is quite expensive for the area.

CHEF: Shirley Wilkes PROPRIETORS: Mr and Mrs J.F.M. Wilkes OPEN: Tue to Sun, exc Sun D MEALS: 12 to 1.45, 7 to 9.30 (10.30 Sat) PRICES: L £16 (£26), Set L and D £28 (£34) to £32.50 (£39). Minimum £9.25 CARDS: Access, Amex, Visa SEATS: 35. Private parties: 25 main room, 14 private room. Vegetarian meals. Children's helpings. No children under 6. Smart dress preferred. No cigars/pipes in dining-room. No music ACCOMMODATION: 2 rooms, both with bath/shower. B&B £41 to £69. No children under 6. TV. Scenic

LYTHAM ST ANNE'S Lancashire map 5

▲ *C'est la Vie* — NEW ENTRY

Dalmeny Hotel, 19–33 South Promenade,
Lytham St Anne's FY8 1LX — COOKING 1
ST ANNE'S (0253) 712236 — COST £16–£36

The resort of Lytham St Anne's is indistinguishable these days from the suburbs of south Blackpool, but it is still noted for its gentility. Despite a go-ahead approach and modern façade distinguishing it from its promenade neighbours, the Dalmeny still recalls the traditional British seaside experience. It may not be to everyone's taste, but the basement restaurant is a good resource in an area not well-served by decent cooking. The emphasis is firmly on the quality of ingredients, bought from local farms and the fishing port, and the daily-changing set-price menu wisely tries not to be too ambitious or refined. One report endorsed pea, pear and watercress soup; pan-fried scallops on a bed of winter chicory with a mustard vinaigrette and a garlic hollandaise ('a good, coarse, refreshing starter with gutsy flavours'); a fricassee of teal, pheasant and duck; and noisette of lamb. Portions are over-generous, seasoning is erratic and, in particular, there is a tendency to oversalt. Vegetables tend to be run-of-the-mill and overcooked, and an offered cheese course produced only Cambazola. Desserts are competently handled. Service is efficient. The wine list favours France and is very reasonably priced. House wine is £6.75.

CHEF: Paul Caddy PROPRIETORS: the Webb family OPEN: all week, exc Mon L CLOSED: 24 to 26 Dec MEALS: 12 to 2, 7 to 9.30 PRICES: Set L £10.50 (£16) to £12.50 (£19), Set D £19.50 (£26) to £22.50 (£30). Card slips closed CARDS: Access, Visa SEATS: 50. Private parties: 50 main room, 20 private room. Car park, 100 places. Healthy eating options. Children's helpings. Smart dress preferred. No smoking in dining-room. Wheelchair access (also WC). Music. Air-conditioned. Fax: (0253) 724447 ACCOMMODATION: 104 rooms, all with bath/shower. Rooms for disabled. Lift. B&B £51.50 to £69.50. Deposit: £10. Children welcome. Baby facilities. Afternoon teas. Swimming-pool. Sauna. Fishing. Golf. Snooker. Squash. TV. Phone. Scenic. Confirm by 6

MACCLESFIELD Cheshire map 5

Topo's

15 Church Street, Macclesfield SK11 6LB COOKING 2
MACCLESFIELD (0625) 422231 COST £17–£34

It is difficult to categorise Topo's. Philip Wright is British and has a classical training. The menus mix Italian and French dishes and there is a pasta menu as a speciality item. The *carte* seems almost too long for its own good, but reporters commend Philip Wright's skill and his respect for ingredients – the new arrivals and oddities probably figuring on the blackboard of extras that supplements the printed sheets. The small scale of the place allows the chef-owner to do everything himself: a hollandaise was delayed because he was 'just whipping it up'. As one reader commented: 'What a find. The cooking is not refined but is honest and tastes of itself.' The same reporter was pleased to observe Philip Wright making several stops *à la* Keith Floyd to ensure cooking continued with brio. Wine prices are fair and a good range of bottles is provided on the list. A page of interesting Italians leads into generally sound selections from France. House wine is £9.50. CELLARMAN'S CHOICE: Riesling, la Decapole 1987, £11.85; Morellino di Scansano 1988, Mantellassi, £9.85.

CHEF/PROPRIETOR: Philip Wright OPEN: Tue to Sat CLOSED: 25 and 26 Dec, Good Fri L MEALS: 12 to 2, 7.30 to 10 PRICES: £19 (£28), Set L from £10.95 (£17), Set D from £12.25 (£19). Service 10%. Card slips closed CARDS: Access, Amex, Visa SEATS: 60. Private parties: 35 main room. Vegetarian meals. No children under 10. Smart dress preferred. Wheelchair access (1 step). Music

MAIDEN NEWTON Dorset map 2

Le Petit Canard

Dorchester Road, Maiden Newton DT2 0BE COOKING 2*
MAIDEN NEWTON (0300) 20536 COST £29

The Chapmans continue to plough their cosmopolitan furrow among the pastures and meadows of Dorset, where it goes down well though the food is in bold, if not stark, contrast to the cottagey building and decoration – ducks crop up in pottery, as well as on the menu. This changes monthly, runs to seven choices at each course and includes fairly up-to-the-minute items such as goats' cheese baked with thyme in radicchio leaves, fresh pasta with chargrilled vegetables and olive oil, chicken stuffed with wild-boar sausage, rum crêpe cake with espresso sauce, and raisin and walnut tart with a bourbon whiskey custard. Arrangement and style are in direct line from nouvelle cuisine, with modern improvements. As one reader commented, 'The food is never dull.' Nor is the wine list, which combines economy and taste with no false modesty about countries beyond France. The tasting notes are intelligent and, as the list is short, can be taken in at a sitting and be of some use. To supplement the core, there are more expensive bin-ends (i.e. small stocks) of decent clarets and burgundies. This is an intelligent restaurant that improves. House wine varies frequently.

CHEF: Geoff Chapman PROPRIETORS: Geoff and Lin Chapman OPEN: Tue to Sat, D only CLOSED: 1 week Feb MEALS: 7 to 9.15 PRICES: Set D £17.95 (£24) CARDS: Access, Visa SEATS: 28. Private parties: 28 main room. Vegetarian meals. No children under 8. No cigars/pipes in dining-room. Music

MALVERN WELLS Hereford & Worcester map 2

Croque-en-Bouche

221 Wells Road, Malvern Wells WR14 4HF COOKING 4
MALVERN (0684) 565612 COST £44

The *Guide* reports from year to year and it can be difficult to vary the approach, to suggest new lines of understanding. In the case of Croque-en-Bouche, Robin and Marion Jones have mapped out their route to happiness long since and have pursued it, with slight shift of emphasis here and there, with little deviation. They are self-reliant (no staff), self-sufficient (a productive garden), and self-financed (the prices charged could hardly bear the fluctuations in interest rates). The restaurant continues to offer a short weekly menu at fixed price that takes in the best in the classic bourgeois repertoire as well as looking further afield to the tastes, for example, of Japan. Readers have reported in glowing terms their appetisers of well-made sushi, and Robin Jones reports himself on Japanese salad dressings: one of sesame, the other oil-less and lightly cooked. This influence crops up again in the meals themselves: a vegetable stock flavoured with star anise, ginger and coriander, with pieces of salt cod; an oriental dish of monkfish judged 'ambrosial' by one reader, 'with a fine blend of flavours' from mizuno, seaweed, soy sauce and sherry vinegar. The Japan influence does not overpower the consistent production of dishes such as green pea and preserved duck soup ('our fourth favourite, after curried parsnip'), home-smoked salmon ('the applewood heavy but not excessive'), with a celeriac rémoulade or with home-pickled mackerel and sour cream, pot-roast partridge with mushrooms, venison eye-chops with a port and berry sauce, lamb stuffed with a parsley pesto, and toffee rice pudding with passion-fruit ice-cream, or chocolate mousse cake. The structure of the menu offers soup, then fish or vegetable entrée, main course with gratin of potato, salad (always exciting), British cheeses and a roll-call of desserts – who would miss pear, quince and apple tart with Prunelle de Bourgogne liqueur? Service continues to be by Robin Jones alone, seven tables done apace, the bar, the wine, the food and all. A strictish timetable may be imposed on the diners to ensure this runs without fault. Marion Jones does the cooking – even, this year, extending the self-sufficiency to breads. The wines need little introduction, but spare a thought for liqueurs. It is a matchless list of spiritous drink and well worth an economical exploration. The wine list defies criticism; this must now be one of the best annotated and most comprehensive collections in any restaurant, anywhere. Runs of vintages are found on every page – three years of Gigondas Les Pallières, eight of Marqués de Murrieta Rioja, six Sassicaia. Little of quality has escaped, and all is offered at prices that are generous to a fault. House wines are from £6.80. CELLARMAN'S CHOICE: Portico dei Leoni 1986, Castelli, £17.90; Rouge Homme, Cabernet 1986, £14.40.

CHEF: Marion Jones PROPRIETORS: Robin and Marion Jones OPEN: Wed to Sat, D only CLOSED: Sun before Christmas to Wed after New Year, 1 week July and Sept MEALS: 7.30 to 9.30 PRICES: Set D £31 (£37). Net prices, card slips closed CARDS: Access, Visa SEATS: 24. Private parties: 8 private room. No smoking. Wheelchair access. No music

Planters

NEW ENTRY

191–193 Wells Road,
Malvern Wells WR14 9HB COOKING 2
MALVERN (0684) 575065 COST £21–£26

Sandra tends the front-of-house; Chandra cooks. He is Sri Lankan and the cuisine ranges across Sri Lanka and South East Asia. 'Lucky Malvern, to have this as well as Croque-en-Bouche' was one apt comment. The large Edwardian house on the Ledbury road has a small bar and two dining-rooms, decorated in pinks and greys with sepia prints on the walls. Sandra is informed about the menu and will not let you over-order though choice can also be abdicated by taking the sampling 'Feast from the Menu'. The freshness and immediacy of the cooking, and the treatment of materials is best exemplified by *sayer tumis* or stir-fried vegetables ('each with identifiable taste and colourful presentation'). Other good things have been the Murtaba flat bread, mas badum (Sri Lankan pickled lamb), green beef curry, prawns with chilli, sambals, and the various satays to open meals. Desserts may go western: treacle tart and pavlova filled with exotic fruit. The wine list is short but inexpensive and includes some good makers like Guigal, Trimbach and Rosemount. House wines are £6.20.

CHEF: Chandra de Alwis PROPRIETOR: Sandra Pegg OPEN: summer Wed to Mon, winter Wed to Sat, D only CLOSED: 1 week Jan MEALS: 6.30 to 10.30 PRICES: £13 (£21), Set D £16.95 (£22). Service 10%. Card slips closed CARDS: Access, Visa SEATS: 40. Private parties: 40 main room. Vegetarian meals. Children welcome. Smart dress preferred. No cigars/pipes in dining-room. Wheelchair access (1 step). Music

'If you get upset by young stockbrokers complaining about how bad things are while drinking their third glass of champagne, perhaps best not to go here?'
On eating in Scotland

MANCHESTER **Greater Manchester** map 5

▲ *Armenian, Granada Hotel*

404 Wilmslow Road,
Withington, M20 9BM COOKING 2
061-434 3480 COST £25

There are some price rises, but otherwise the menu stays the same at this comfortable basement restaurant beneath the Granada Hotel. The sound Middle Eastern cooking takes in Armenia, to be sure, but spreads its wings towards North Africa and the Levant as well: a range of couscous – plentiful, fragrant and served with lots of fiery harissa; enough meze to keep the list-makers happy for a long time – tabouleh, baba-ganouge, kibbeh and kebabs – some Armenian in version, others mainstream Middle Eastern; even chicken tikka. There is a small range of desserts and good coffee. The wine list is summary; house wine is £6.95.

CHEFS: Mrs Minto and Mr Hovnanian PROPRIETORS: Hanni Al-Taraboulsy and Mr Jajoo OPEN: all week, D only MEALS: 6 to 10.30 (11 Fri and Sat) PRICES: £13 (£21) CARDS: Access, Amex, Diners, Visa SEATS: 50. Private parties: 65 main room. Vegetarian meals. Children's helpings. Music. Fax: 061-445 4902 ACCOMMODATION: 11 rooms, all with bath/shower. B&B £35 to £45. Children welcome. Baby facilities. TV. Phone. Confirm by 5

Café Istanbul

79 Bridge Street, M3 2RH COOKING 1
061-833 9942 COST £8–£22

Café Istanbul has developed from an ethnic haven for expatriate Turks into a buzzy Mancunian venue with trendy undertones: the restaurant has spread into the next-door building, the menu has been boosted by more fish and vegetarian dishes, and the wine list has been given a face-lift. It is still great value and great fun. Best bets on the menu are the meze – 18 starters, including hummus, stuffed vine leaves, fried carrots with garlic and yoghurt, shredded chicken with walnut sauce, pastries and meat balls. The mixed grill is heavy with protein, and the slow-cooked lamb on the bone with potatoes and tomato sauce reliably good. There is strong Turkish coffee and drinkable Turkish wine. House French is £5.80.

CHEF: Hasan Bicer PROPRIETOR: Sacit Onur OPEN: Mon to Sat CLOSED: 25 and 26 Dec MEALS: 12 to 3, 6 to 11.30 PRICES: £11 (£18), Set L £4.75 (£8). Service 10% for parties of 10 and over. Card slips closed when service charged CARDS: Access, Visa SEATS: 65. Private parties: 45 main room. Vegetarian meals. Children's helpings. Smart dress preferred. Wheelchair access (also WC). Music. Air-conditioned

The Guide *is totally independent, accepts no free hospitality, and survives on the proceeds from copies sold each year.*

Report forms are at the back of the book; write a letter if you prefer.

Koreana

Kings House,
40 King Street West, M3 2WY — COOKING 1
061-832 4330 — COST £11–£34

Another oriental gem among the tourists and the crowds of Chinatown, Koreana has stayed by its individual contribution, reinforced by Korean artefacts on the walls, waitresses in national costume and a menu full of classic Korean specialities such as bulgogi (marinated beef, chicken or ribs cooked at the table on a shield), mando (steamed dumplings in a soup), bindae tok (shallow-fried soy-bean pancake) and sliced fried fish with courgettes. There is a series of fair-value banquets, and spicing is as robust as it should be. Korean saké, jinro soju (a Korean liqueur), and ginseng and green tea are available. House French is £7.95.

CHEFS: Hyun K. Kim, H.S. Shin and C.S. Jeong PROPRIETORS: Koreana Restaurant Ltd OPEN: Mon to Sat, exc Sat L MEALS: 12 to 2.30, 6.30 to 10.30 (11 Sat) PRICES: £17 (£25), Set L £4.75 (£11) to £7.30 (£14), Set D £14 (£21) to £20 (£28). Card slips closed CARDS: Access, Amex, Diners, Visa SEATS: 80. Private parties: 100 main room. Vegetarian meals. Children welcome. Smart dress preferred. Music. Fax: 061-832 2293

Kosmos Taverna

248 Wilmslow Road, M14 6LD — COOKING 1
061-225 9106 — COST £16–£24

A Greek-Cypriot reader vouches for the authenticity of this much-liked taverna: 'Greeks could bring their relatives or friends without fear of disappointment.' The atmosphere and the excellent food attract a cosmopolitan crowd who relish the happy-go-lucky holiday mood of the place. Best value is the choice of three meze banquets (including one for vegetarians) for which the standard taverna favourites such as hummus, dolmades, falafels and kleftiko are supplemented by weekly specials with a regional flavour. Sofrito, from Corfu, is a casserole of beef with brandy, ouzo and red wine; from Pelion comes spetsofayi – spicy sausages with aubergines, peppers and tomato sauce; kaloyerros is strips of monkfish in batter with walnut and garlic sauce. From further afield there might be Persian lamb with dried lemons, kidney beans and seven different herbs. Reporters have also praised the fiery Kosmos dip, white bean soup, imam bayaldi, spanakopitakia and deep-fried baby squid. To finish, there are plenty of sweet Greek pastries. Some new Greek-Cypriot wines such as Robola and Calliga Rubis have been added to the promising list; there is also Cypriot Keo beer. House Italian is £3.80 for a half-litre carafe.

CHEF: Loulla Astin PROPRIETORS: Stewart and Loulla Astin OPEN: all week, D only, and Sun L CLOSED: 25 and 26 Dec MEALS: 6.30 (1 Sun) to 11.30 PRICES: £14 (£20), Set D £10 (£16) to £12 (£18) CARDS: Access, Visa SEATS: 80. Private parties: 40 main room. Vegetarian meals. Children's helpings. Wheelchair access (also WC). Music. Air-conditioned

See the back of the Guide *for an index of restaurants listed.*

Lime Tree

8 Lapwing Lane, West Didsbury, M20 8WS
061-445 1217 COOKING 1
2m from M56 exit 10 COST £16–£28

An inspector reflects on the success of the Lime Tree: 'It aims to provide moderately modern food at modest prices in a relaxed manner. When it started at Lapwing Lane four or five years ago, it succeeded on all three counts; now, I am not so sure about the first two. The atmosphere is still highly congenial and laid-back, but prices are not cheap except in comparison with London, and the menu has not moved on – modern has become conventional, favourites rather staid standards. Neither the inclusion of upwardly mobile components – wild mushrooms, gravlax – nor the use of French terms on the menu make up for laxity in the poorly trimmed escalopes, unsieved raspberry coulis, bought-in ice-cream from Walls, or a failure to taste everything before serving it to paying customers.' Things move on, but the Lime Tree, now extended to two branches, remains undyingly popular with Manchester. Meals may include chicken liver parfait, tortellini with cream, fragrant onion soup, scallops with dill cream, pigeon with wild mushrooms, duck with kumquat and passion-fruit sauce, and halibut with vermouth cream sauce. The reasons for success seem obvious. These dishes are more ambitious than mere bistro and prices are keen. Desserts seem more perfunctory than savoury dishes. The surroundings for eating benefit tremendously from the conservatory and, music apart, it does have the feeling of a place everyone is pleased to visit, shortcomings or no. The wine list is supplemented by bin-ends and specials; the main selection is adequate and cheap. The second branch in Rusholme (9–11 Wilmslow Road, Rusholme, M14 5TB, Tel: 061-225 7108), near the Whitworth Gallery, also deals in modern yet inexpensive cooking – even less expensive than the original. The marks of formula are there: the mixture of vegetables, unnecessary fruit trimmings to some main courses, and puddings which are no more successful than in the original branch. Black pudding is here too, as well as decent coffee.

CHEFS: Patrick Hannity, Simon Haywood and Alison Eason PROPRIETORS: Patrick Hannity and Robert Williams OPEN: all week, D only, and Sun L MEALS: 12 to 2, 6.30 to 10.30 PRICES: £16 (£23), Set Sun L £9.50 (£16) to £12.95 (£20) CARDS: Access, Visa SEATS: 80. Private parties: 50 main room. Vegetarian meals. Children's helpings (Sun L only). Wheelchair access. Music

Little Yang Sing

17 George Street, M1 4HE COOKING 1
061-228 7722 COST £10–£38

The dining-room has had a face-lift, with a new bar, modern carpets and venetian blinds, although it retains its closely packed tables and functional café-style fittings. Opening hours have been extended and Warren Yeung has installed a new chef. The main 170-dish menu does not stray far from the Cantonese tradition of dim-sum, hot-pots and casseroles, one-plate meals, and dishes such as braised brisket and steamed pork ribs with black-bean sauce. There is also a 'demi-veg' vegetarian seafood menu. When the kitchen is in gear it can shine brightly, and reporters have praised the immaculately crisp spring rolls and crab pastries, steamed beef balls with ginger and spring onion, and lightly battered chicken drumsticks with wu-nam sauce and deep-fried coconut milk balls. But the place is beginning to show some of the classic signs of a high-profile Chinese restaurant in decline: basic inconsistencies, a kitchen that seems to go to sleep at off-peak times, off-hand service and much pushing of easily assembled set banquets. There is dark Chinese beer. House French is £6.50.

CHEF: Auting Chung PROPRIETOR: Warren Yeung OPEN: all week MEALS: noon to 11.30 PRICES: £14 (£25), Set L £5.20 (£10) to £7.50 (£13), Set D £15 (£21) to £25 (£32). Service 10% CARDS: Access, Amex, Visa SEATS: 80. Private parties: 80 main room. Vegetarian meals. Children welcome. Music. Air-conditioned

Market Restaurant

Edge Street/104 High Street, M4 1HQ — COOKING 2
061-834 3743 — COST £29

'The restaurant is in its twelfth year and we're still enjoying it,' say the O'Gradys, and their enthusiasm shows. Some reporters remember the early days, when the place was simply 'good and cheap'; prices have risen since then, but the quality remains high. Menus are wide-ranging, and the kitchen tips its hat to some of the great culinary names of the past and present: Jane Grigson's curried parsnip soup; the Carved Angel nut roast with watercress stuffing and pimento sauce; Elizabeth Raffald's orange custard (from Manchester's most eminent Georgian recipe writer and housekeeper). One month's repertoire might encompass Thai fishcakes with chilli relish, fillet of pork with tapénade, chicken breast baked with yoghurt and ginger served with Basmati rice, and Greek orange and almond cake. The vegetarian tendency looms large with twice-baked red pepper soufflé, and home-made hazelnut noodles with mushroom sauce. Events in the popular Pudding Club and Starters Society have been extended to two nights every alternate month. The sensibly priced wine list has an ever-increasing organic contingent, while Peter O'Grady's CAMRA connections show in the fascinating list of bottle-conditioned Belgian beers. House French is £3.95 a half-litre.

CHEFS: Mary-Rose Edgecombe, Paul Mertz and Dawn Wellens PROPRIETORS: Peter O'Grady and Anne O'Grady OPEN: Tue to Sat, D only CLOSED: 1 week spring, 1 week Christmas, Aug MEALS: 6 (7 Sat) to 9.30 PRICES: £17 (£24). Card slips closed CARDS: Access, Amex, Diners, Visa SEATS: 40. Private parties: 40 main room, 25 private room. Vegetarian meals. Children welcome. Music

Mr Kuks

55A Mosley Street, M2 3HY — COOKING 1*
061-236 0659 — COST £16–£32

Stephen Kuk's long-established restaurant in the basement of a large office complex remains one of the few venues for authentic Pekinese cooking in a neighbourhood dominated by Cantonese establishments. The 160-dish menu covers the full range of accessible items, from hot-and-sour soup and smoked fish to moo-she pork with pancakes and Peking duck. There are also some Cantonese and Szechuan specialities, plus a good showing of dim-sum and one-plate rice and noodle dishes. Set meals and banquets are a major attraction. The list of more complex 'house specials' goes right to the heart of Pekinese cuisine: braised shark's fin in brown sauce, 'eight-jewel stuffing duck', oil-dripped chicken and assorted meat fire-pot. Onc couplc who visited on St Valentine's Day were provided with 'lovers' soup' (based on noodles and ham), an assortment of dim-sum, a whole lobster with ginger and spring onion, sliced honey chicken with a tangy lime sauce, and beef roll and black pepper accompanied by excellent fried rice. To finish, toffee milk-curd balls coated with sesame seeds were fresh, crisp and unusual. Service is attentive, but brusque at times. Chinese tea comes in western cups. House French is £7.

CHEF: Mr Lau PROPRIETORS: Stephen Kuk and Geoffrey Cohen OPEN: Tue to Sun, exc Sun L MEALS: 12 to 2.30, 6 to 11.30 PRICES: £15 (£25), Set L and D £10 (£16) to £20 (£27). Service 10% CARDS: Access, Amex, Diners, Visa SEATS: 95. Private parties: 95 main room. Vegetarian meals. Children's helpings. Music. Air-conditioned

▲ *Moss Nook*

Ringway Road, M22 5NA
061-437 4778
on B5166, 1m from Manchester Airport, M56 exit 5

COOKING 3
COST £22–£52

The fairly undistinguished brick house is now almost part of Manchester International Airport, but once through the door, according to one reporter, the atmosphere 'of the well-endowed dining area was claimed by one of my guests as typically French; it has a certain charm, and appealed to all of us because there was no music'. Comfort is a certain quality here, and substance when it comes to the food, even though there are traces of nouvelle cuisine – often thought the enemy of quantity – in Robert Thornton's capable cooking. Much satisfaction was had from a dinner that included a lobe of foie gras of duck, cooked accurately, with a sweet-sour sauce; a whole partridge, jointed and pan-fried (on a day when pheasant and good gamey duck were also on offer) with a raspberry sauce and a rather crowded plate of liver mousse, apple sauce as well as excellent vegetables. Potatoes, fondant and roast, came on separate dishes. The menu is quite long and is supplemented by various daily dishes and daily fixed-choice offerings (for the whole table only). Not only is there a complimentary soup served after the first course, but the complimentary appetiser is often a complete course in itself. Manchester gets a good deal, though prices are not low. The wine list concentrates mainly on France and Germany, with some help from further afield, and a page or two of fine wines for the adventurous. Many of the bottles have been carefully chosen – it's nice to see three Swiss wines on offer – and there are some that deserve a second look. Price range has been maintained, though house wines start at £9.75.

Several sharp operators have tried to extort money from restaurateurs on the promise of an entry in a guide book that has never appeared. The Good Food Guide *makes no charge for inclusion and does not offer certificates of any kind.*

CHEFS: Robert Thornton and Kevin Lofthouse PROPRIETORS: Pauline and Derek Harrison OPEN: Tue to Sat, exc Sat L CLOSED: 24 Dec for 2 weeks MEALS: 12 to 2, 7 to 9.30 (10 Sat) PRICES: £32 (£43), Set L £15.50 (£22), Set D £24 (£32). Card slips closed CARDS: Access, Amex, Visa SEATS: 50. 8 tables outside. Private parties: 10 main room. Car park, 50 places. Vegetarian meals. No children under 12. Smart dress preferred. No cigars/pipes in dining-room. No music. Air-conditioned. Fax: 061-498 8089 ACCOMMODATION: 1 room, with bath/shower. D,B&B £130. No children under 12. Garden. TV. Phone

Peppers

NEW ENTRY

63 Bridge Street, M3 3BQ
061-832 9393

COOKING 1
COST £11–£14

The consensus is that Peppers is a cut above the average for Manchester's Indian restaurants, especially in terms of value for money. Buffet meals are offered at remarkable prices. Gleaming metal chafing dishes, which dominate two sides of the downstairs dining-room, contain pilau rice, nan, poppadums, two meat curries and three vegetarian dishes together with a comprehensive display of Indian pickles and relishes. There is no service in the conventional sense; the welcome nevertheless is warm. Curries are prepared from fresh spices but there can be an element of sameness, particularly in the meat dishes. One reader found that a chicken korma and a gosht dopiaza were 'insufficiently differentiated from each other and from a sort of generalised all-purpose curry'. Dhal, pilau rice, aloo tikka and aloo palak have all been praised as has the kheer, an Indian rice pudding. House wine is £6.

CHEFS: Noor-Ul Hasan and Cemina Jafri PROPRIETOR: S.M. Hasan Jafri OPEN: Mon to Sat CLOSED: bank hols MEALS: 12 to 3, 6 to 11 (11.30 Fri and Sat) PRICES: Set L £5.50 (£11), Set D £6.50 (£12) CARDS: Access, Amex, Diners, Visa SEATS: 60. Private parties: 32 main room, 25 private room. Vegetarian meals. Children welcome. Music. Self-service

Quan Ju De

44 Princess Street, M1 6DE
061-236 5236

COOKING 1*
COST £10–£30

This is Beijing's ambassador to Manchester, where the duck, of course, is a speciality and one that is much enjoyed. There could be no greater contrast than that between the Victorian commercial buildings and cobbled paving of the Princess Street district and the cool modernity of this restaurant on an upper ground floor: space, light, paintings, glass screens, decent china. The spirit of Zen (see entries, London) has not quite got to Manchester, but it is having its effect in updating traditional Chinese restaurant decoration. There is even a pianist tinkling along on most evenings. The parts of the menu that get most praise are the first courses. A certain timorousness when it comes to spicing, for instance the beef with chilli, has been regretted, as has the continued absence of fresh fish and shellfish. However, the plate of hot starters – sesame prawn toasts, miniature spring rolls, fried seaweed with diced scallops, and spare ribs – met with much approval as did the pickled cucumbers, the excellent batter used in the 'three treasures' of peppers, mushrooms and courgettes, and grilled pork dumplings. Rice is well-handled; most desserts seem to be bought-in ices. Service can be rushed, but it is not rude. House French is £7.25.

CHEF: K.L. Zuo PROPRIETOR: Hoo Man Lau OPEN: all week CLOSED: bank hols MEALS: 12 to 2.30, 6 to 11 PRICES: £16 (£22), Set L £4.30 (£10) to £8.75 (£14), Set D £14.50 (£21) to £18.50 (£25). Service 10%. Card slips closed CARDS: Access, Amex, Visa SEATS: 120. Private parties: 90 main room, 30 private room. Vegetarian meals. Children welcome. Smart dress preferred. Music. Air-conditioned

Sanam

145–151 Wilmslow Road,
Rusholme, M14 5AW COOKING 1
061-224 1008 and 8824 COST £14

The Akhtar family's restaurant-cum-sweet centre has expanded dramatically and now seats 350. Some may find the surroundings bright and garish, but the kitchen rarely falters. Fresh, potent, authentic flavours put this place ahead of the local competition in Rusholme – otherwise known as Manchester's 'Curry Alley'. The menu features tandooris, birianis, dhansaks and the like, with a few odd specialities dotted here and there. Offal shows up in liver and kidney tikka, and karahi dil gurday (prepared with heart and kidney). There are also spiced lambs' brains and karahi quails. Sunday brings a special moghlai lamb biriani, as well as katlamma and puri chana served with semolina halva. Unlicensed, but there are mango milkshakes or jugs of lassi or Coke to drink. Take-aways are available.

CHEFS: Iftikhar Khan and Sultan Mahmood PROPRIETORS: Abdul Ghafoor Akhtar and Sons OPEN: all week MEALS: noon to midnight (1am Fri and Sat) PRICES: £10 (£12). Unlicensed CARDS: Access, Visa SEATS: 350. Private parties: 200 main room, 60 private room. Vegetarian meals. Children's helpings. Wheelchair access (also WC). Music. Air-conditioned. Fax: 061-256 2935

Siam Orchid

54 Portland Street, M1 4QU COOKING 1
061-236 1388 COST £10–£26

Distinctive purple-painted woodwork marks out this Thai restaurant. Despite some nods in the dining-room towards Thailand in the statues, pictures and orchids on the tables, it feels as routine and bleak as many of its Cantonese neighbours in Manchester Chinatown. The menu is accessible, and reporters have enjoyed steamed dim-sum, well-marinated chicken satay, squid salad with coriander dressing, and stir-fried beef with chillies and basil leaves. 'Steamed fish' is a whole lemon sole flavoured with ginger, spring onions and astringent preserved plums. This is creditable cooking, although there is a feeling that the results could be more distinctive and exciting.

CHEF: C. Sirisompan PROPRIETORS: C. Sirisompan and K. Sirisambhand OPEN: all week, exc Sat and Sun MEALS: 11.30 to 2.30, 6.30 to 11.30 (6 to 11.30 Fri and Sat, 5 to 11 Sun) PRICES: £12 (£22), Set L £5 (£10), Set D £7 (£12). Service 10% CARDS: Access, Visa SEATS: 55. Private parties: 55 main room. Children welcome. Music. Air-conditioned. Fax: 061-236 8830

Smithfield

NEW ENTRY

257 Barlow Moor Road,
Chorlton cum Hardy, M21 2GJ
061-862 9213

COOKING 1
COST £15–£24

This small restaurant is sited opposite Manchester's southern cemetery ('more like a tree-filled park in some places'). The cooking is 'modern British', so the range of flavours includes deep-fried Camembert, with too sweet a citrus sauce, lots of fruit sauces, a Stilton mousse in choux-pastry swans, as well as a range of traditional-sounding desserts ('the sponge was a mite close to school dinners for comfort'). Vegetarians get a fair crack of the whip. Prices are not high, and the revenue seems to go on fresh food rather than decoration. The Pattersons' open hospitality excites loyalty among their customers; loyalty to certain dishes, too, which seem long residents on a shortish menu. Four dozen wines are quite enough to complement the food, starting with house wines at £6.80.

CHEF: Xavier Patterson PROPRIETORS: Xavier and Rebecca Patterson OPEN: Tue to Sat, D only CLOSED: last 2 weeks Aug MEALS: 7 to 10.30 (11 Fri and Sat) PRICES: £14 (£20), Set D £9.80 (£15). Service 10% on parties of 6 or more CARDS: Access, Visa SEATS: 35. Private parties: 44 main room. Vegetarian meals. Children's helpings on request. Wheelchair access (1 step). Music

That Café

1031 Stockport Road,
South Levenshulme, M19 2TB
061-432 4672

COOKING 1
COST £18–£26

The ambience is 1930s, from bric-à-brac to music. Joe Quinn's idiosyncratic restaurant – where 'it doesn't seem to matter which staff are on duty, they are unfailingly calm, helpful and discreet' – is noted for sound value-for-money cooking. Vegetarian and meat dishes have equal prominence; hummus is lifted out of the ordinary by the addition of fresh orange, fish pâtés are notably light, while courgette roulade, rabbit in cream and tarragon ('the meat was excellent but a touch too much tarragon for me') and a 'simply done and enjoyed' salmon show the range of the short menu. Chocolate brandy mousse and rum and raisin cheesecake have both been praised. House French is £6.95.

CHEF: Joe Quinn PROPRIETORS: Joe Quinn and Stephen King OPEN: Tue to Sat, D only, and Sun L MEALS: 12 to 2.30, 7 to 10.30 PRICES: £15 (£22), Set D Tue to Thur only £11.95 (£18). Service 10% for parties of 8 or more CARDS: Access, Amex, Visa SEATS: 75. Private parties: 50 main room, 25 private room. Vegetarian meals. Children's helpings. Music (Sun L)

Tung Fong

2 Worsley Road, M28 4NL
061-794 5331

COOKING 1
COST £10–£40

A suburban half-timbered house is now occupied by an exile from Manchester's Chinatown, where Tony Ng was once at Hopewell City. It makes a spacious locale for professedly pan-regional Chinese cooking. The long menu has produced satisfactory dim-sum and char siu, and dishes such as prawns and garlic in a lotus leaf, crispy duck and salt and pepper ribs. However, the Szechuan fire seems to have been dulled by gentility and it is to be hoped that the newly arrived chef, Mr Chen, can introduce more vigour into spicing and seasoning.

CHEFS: K. Lee and Y.X. Chen PROPRIETORS: Tony Ng and Mrs C.K. Ng OPEN: all week, exc L Sat and Sun CLOSED: 25 Dec MEALS: 12 to 2, 5.30 to 11.30 PRICES: £12 (£23), Set L £4.30 (£10) to £7.50 (£14), Set D £13 (£19) to £25 (£33). Service 10%. Card slips closed CARDS: Access, Amex, Visa SEATS: 100. Private parties: 25 private rooms. Car park, 10 places. Vegetarian meals. Children welcome. Music

Woodlands

33 Shepley Road, Audenshaw, M34 5DJ — COOKING 2*
061-336 4241 — COST £21–£40

'What's a restaurant like this doing in Audenshaw?' The quip may sound unnecessarily dismissive but it does convey one reader's pleasure at the careful, professional cooking here. Others enjoy it too; there is a strong following of regulars. Inside the red-brick suburban villa, the surroundings are light and pleasing. A short bilingual menu stays short and has a structural continuity from season to season. Reporters have been struck by the satisfactory balance between plenty and restraint, and the good kitchen techniques, which have shown well in a dish of king prawns with crabmeat, and prawns fried in batter that was never too heavy and would have benefited only from a less buttery sauce. Admirable skills were shown, too, in Camembert baked in filo parcels with deep-fried vegetables and a good tomato sauce. Not everything is fried: brill stuffed with a fish mousse, and noisettes of lamb with two mint (or two tarragon) sauces are a couple of well-praised dishes. Puddings have been enjoyed, too. The sticky toffee was 'well beyond the nursery slopes of such things', and banana and toffee tart a homogeneous delight, even if bestarred with cream rosettes. Bread needs improving, but the service garners appreciation. The fair-priced wine list is brief but adequate. House wine is £8.25.

CHEF: William Mark Jackson PROPRIETORS: Mr and Mrs D. Crank OPEN: Tue to Sat, exc Sat L CLOSED: first week Jan. 1 week after Easter, 2 weeks Aug MEALS: 12 to 2, 7 to 9.30 (10 Sat) PRICES: £24 (£33), Set L £13.65 (£21), Set D £15.65 (£24). Card slips closed CARDS: Access, Visa SEATS: 36. Private parties: 22 main room, 14 private room. Car park, 12 places. Children's helpings. Smart dress preferred. No cigars/pipes in dining-room. Wheelchair access (3 steps). Music. Air-conditioned

Yang Sing

34 Princess Street, M1 4JY — COOKING 2*
061-236 2200 — COST £18–£25

The restaurant takes justifiable pride in the number of fellow restaurateurs who eat here; aficionados still claim the 'timing, seasoning and sharp flavours distance Yang Sing from the competition'. It is a massive business, stretching upwards into floors of banqueting rooms. The aim is to enquire about specials, and to study the vast menu closely to construct an interesting meal. It can be done. People are less impressed by the banquets. Dim-sum is on offer until 6pm and also has the edge on the rest of Chinatown, for variety as well as accuracy. Soup dumpling is an example of one dim-sum not often found, crabmeat balls an instance of 'everything being that bit fresher at Yang Sing'. One meal included lobster with ginger and spring onions, impeccably timed and with clear, intense flavours; Dover sole stir-fried with asparagus; pieces of roast duck with crisped skin intermixed with pineapple and slices of ginger; and impressive special fried rice with prawns and pork. All showed the qualities that stem from good practice and timely cooking. Staff do need close questioning if diners are to get the best out of the menu; for instance, to discover the freshest fish and most seasonal vegetables. Not everyone manages to achieve the easy relationship necessary to extract the information. House wine is from £6.35.

CHEF: Harry Yeung PROPRIETORS: Yang Sing Restaurant Ltd OPEN: all week CLOSED: 25 Dec MEALS: noon to 11 PRICES: £13 (£19), Set L and D £12.25 (£18). Service 10% CARDS: Access, Amex, Visa SEATS: 140. Private parties: 220 main room, 30 and 70 private rooms. Children welcome. Wheelchair access. Music. Air-conditioned. Fax: 061-236 5934

MANNINGTREE Essex map 3

Stour Bay Cafe

NEW ENTRY

39–43 High Street,
Manningtree CO11 1AH
COLCHESTER (0206) 396687

COOKING 1
COST £23

The ambience within the sixteenth-century building is anything but olde worlde: minimalist, stripped-down floors of polished wood, brick and cream-painted plaster walls, and mixed unpadded chairs – some punishingly uncomfortable – are thoroughly modern in their overall effect. The menu has a style that speaks of California: salsa, southern flavours, lots of grills and vegetables. Sherri Singleton, a fourth-generation Californian, tempers her cooking with English, French and oriental influences: fresh asparagus timbale with watercress sauce; brochette of salmon and monkfish marinated in lime, coriander and Thai seasonings. Fish is a speciality, often dominating the short *carte* with as many as five varieties. Whereas intentions are admirable, there are occasions when the performance has fallen short. Take one instance: mussels in pesto were tasteless specimens in a vast quantity of oil liquid containing an enormous amount of parsley. Equally, chicken of little character was accompanied by a runny orange sauce but with none of the advertised dill detectable. In contrast there was a satisfactory meal that included a nicely pink rack of lamb in a ginger crust, and a Jack Daniels tart, a variation of pecan pie. The majority of wines are New World and priced reasonably. House wine is £7.25.

CHEF: Sherri Singleton PROPRIETORS: David McKay and Sherri Singleton OPEN: Wed to Sun CLOSED: first 2 weeks Jan MEALS: 12 to 2.45, 7 to 9.30 (10 Fri and Sat) PRICES: £13 (£19) CARDS: Access, Visa SEATS: 75. Private parties: 60 main room, 15 private room. Vegetarian meals. Children's helpings. No-smoking area. Wheelchair access. Music

MARY TAVY Devon map 1

▲ *Stannary*

Mary Tavy PL19 9QB — COOKING 1*
MARY TAVY (0822) 810897 — COST £30

The building was once a truck shop where workers in the tin mine next door could exchange wage tokens for food. No such memory of grim economic necessity remains in the riot of greenery and Victoriana, complete with conservatory. The Stannary now serves vegetarian food – a luxury today that had different overtones then – using exclusively organic, free-range and decently farmed materials. Consciousness of the needs of special diets is very evident. Salt is not used, sugar rarely: flavours and edge are provided through fruits and vegetables adding piquancy or depth. There is, indeed, an amalgamation of the fruit and vegetable kingdoms more complete than in most places: mulled apple and tomato soup; a spicy passion-fruit dip; pecan parcel with an apricot gravy; or figs, beans and vegetables in a peanut and chilli sauce. Recipes are inventive and work very well, occasional heaviness being compensated for by many choices that have no undue elements of stodge: parcels of laver with sweetcorn stuffing; sweetcorn koftas; and the house speciality of stuffed mushrooms with a blue cheese sauce. Desserts include good ices and avoid stodge again by good light lemon cream with raspberry coulis, or pears with caramel covered in a meringue snow. Organic wines are not the only bottles stocked, but they are indicated in a short list that has a good catholic choice at fair prices. House wines are £6.80.

CHEF: Alison Fife PROPRIETORS: Michael Cook and Alison Fife OPEN: all week, D only (by arrangement winter) MEALS: 7 to 9.30 PRICES: £17 (£24). Minimum £10. Net prices, card slips closed CARDS: Access, Visa SEATS: 32. Private parties: 25 main room. Car park, 20 places. Vegetarian meals. Healthy eating options. Children welcome. No smoking in dining-room. Music. Fax: (0822) 810898 ACCOMMODATION: 3 rooms, all with bath/shower. B&B £18.50 to £37. Deposit: 20%. No children under 12. Garden. TV. Scenic

MASHAM North Yorkshire map 7

Floodlite

7 Silver Street, Masham HG4 4DX — COOKING 3
RIPON (0765) 689000 — COST £13–£29

Charles and Christine Flood run an unassuming restaurant in a substantial stone house a short walk away from the magnificent market square at Masham. The rooms may not excite ambitious interior designers, but a sight of the clean white linen, the well-set covers and the small flower arrangements on each table may be indication that the food is taken seriously. Charles Flood is a professional, who worked in Europe and around England before striking out on his own. He takes no short-cuts, and cooks what he announces as it should be cooked. This is bound to surprise anyone not knowing the past history of the restaurant; prices asked would lead one to expect no effort at all, so reasonable are they. Many classic recipes are in the repertoire – hollandaise sauces figure largely, for instance, but there are plenty of touches of spice and colour to satisfy the lover of variety. Especial care is taken with materials: hares are bought in large quantity, other game is plentiful, salmon is properly bought, and commodities like oysters and asparagus are freely offered in season. Accuracy of taste and cooking is very satisfactory: steak with a mushroom purée and a béarnaise; venison with pleurottes; duck with apple and tansy; mullet with citrus fruit; scallops with lobster sauce. They are dishes of quiet excellence. Desserts such as chocolate fudge cake, a variety of good ice-creams, and lemon meringue pie also please. There is pleasant arrangement, but no over-elaboration on the plate. Christine Flood and a helper are sympathetic hosts. This is an impressive and personal testament to real food and professionalism. There are very fairly priced wines. Good respectable names from across the globe are sound rather than exciting. House wine is £6.45.

CHEF: Charles Flood PROPRIETORS: Charles and Christine Flood OPEN: Tue to Sun, D; Fri to Sun L (other days by arrangement) MEALS: 12 to 2, 7 to 9.30 PRICES: £17 (£24), Set L £8.25 (£13). Card slips closed CARDS: Access, Visa SEATS: 36. Private parties: 28 main room. Vegetarian meals. Children's helpings on request. No-smoking area. Music

MATLOCK Derbyshire map 5

▲ *Riber Hall*

Matlock DE4 5JU
MATLOCK (0629) 582795 COOKING 1*
1m off A615 at Tansley COST £23–£41

An Elizabethan and Jacobean house set at the top of a steep lane that climbs from the village of Tansley to the top of the scarp above Matlock. As a hotel, the Hall garners compliments for willingness to please, its quiet and the four-postered bedrooms; as a restaurant, the Hall has cooking by Jeremy Brazelle that conforms to expectations of a certain degree of flounce and ornament but has solid achievement underpinning them. A fairly priced lunch menu and a set of vegetarian dishes are available as well as the *carte*. The repertoire may range from melon and mango salad with pine kernels, and a filo basket of calfs' brains and kidney with rosemary, to salmon on wilted lettuce with pistachio and asparagus, and a caramel cage of pineapple mousse with warm mango coulis to finish. Modern manners live on. The wine list is a very decent spread, from cheap to dear, covering French classics well and not forgetting Spain and the New World. Prices are not out of order.

CHEF: Jeremy Brazelle PROPRIETOR: Alex Biggin OPEN: all week MEALS: 12 to 1.30, 7 to 9.30 PRICES: £24 (£34), Set L £14 (£23) to £20 (£30). Card slips closed CARDS: Access, Amex, Diners, Visa SEATS: 42. Private parties: 34 main room, 14 private room. Car park, 50 places. Vegetarian meals. Children's helpings. No children under 12. Smart dress preferred. Fax: (0629) 580475 ACCOMMODATION: 11 rooms, all with bath/shower. B&B £76 to £90. Deposit: £35. No children under 12. Afternoon teas. Garden. Tennis. TV. Phone. Scenic (*Which? Hotel Guide*)

Report forms are at the back of the book; write a letter if you prefer.

MAWNAN SMITH Cornwall map 1

▲ *Nansidwell Country House* **NEW ENTRY**

Mawnan Smith TR11 5HU COOKING 2
FALMOUTH (0326) 250340 COST £18–£42

The house has a prospect of water as well as its own garden approach to an idyllic National Trust beach: in other words, it is a peach of a place. The house itself ('a concentrated effort not to be a country-house hotel but a country home,' according to one reporter) owes its character to the Robertsons, complete with dog (harmless). The staff, young and antipodean, are a delight. Tony Allcott, who has been cooking these last two years, spent time previously with Jean-Christophe Novelli (now at the Provence in Lymington, see entry). This still shows in his rather self-conscious decorative touches and arrangement of food on the plate; criticism has been levelled by some that the ability to arrange exceeds that to produce simple, flavoursome, light food. There is a *carte* which changes bi-monthly, and a daily set-price menu offering three alternatives. Some emphasis is laid on fish, and on the home-smoker used for salmon, trout and other things. A 'nouvellish' harkening for fruit pops up in savoury dishes such as raspberries with croûtons of chicken livers and with fillet steak. That apart, the repertoire is mainstream modern country house. An adequate wine list is fairly priced; over-reliance on the big Burgundy houses and inconsistency in annotation may be a cause for concern.

CHEF: Antony Allcott PROPRIETORS: Jamie and Felicity Robertson OPEN: all week MEALS: 12.30 to 2, 7 to 9 (9.30 if booked) PRICES: £23 (£32), Set L £10 (£18) to £25 (£34), Set D £20 (£29) to £26 (£35). Minimum £20 D CARDS: Access, Visa SEATS: 32. Private parties: 10 main room. Car park, 20 places. Vegetarian meals. Children's helpings. No children under 10 after 7.30. No cigars/pipes in dining-room, smoking after meal only. Wheelchair access (also WC). No music. Fax: (0326) 250440 ACCOMMODATION: 12 rooms, all with bath/shower. Rooms for disabled. B&B £76 to £120. Deposit: £100. Children welcome. Baby facilities. Pets welcome. Garden. Tennis. Fishing. Phone. TV. Scenic (*Which? Hotel Guide*)

MELMERBY Cumbria map 7

Village Bakery

Melmerby CA10 1HE COOKING 1
LANGWATHBY (0768 881) 515 COST £17

The Bakery is the centrepiece of an enterprise encompassing smallholding, craft gallery, food manufacturer (rum Nicky and Christmas pudding) and all-day café offering organic wholefood – meat, fish and vegetable – to hungry walkers, passing motorists and trippers. The epicentre may be the wood-fired Scotch oven, the chief product the excellent bread (not white), the rye being 'the best we have ever tasted', for one reporter, but the menu will satisfy from breakfast through to tea. Cumberland sausage, made from the Bakery's own free-range pork, Inverawe kippers, Lakeland char, a plate of North Country cheeses, and simple desserts are some of the things on offer. This year there have been reports of dilatory and none-too-happy service, and cooking that may miss the mark of lightness and accuracy. In general, however, this is a safe haven for cooking of intelligent honesty combined with invention. There are a few organic wines and cordials, ciders and beers.

CHEF: Diane Richter PROPRIETORS: Andrew and Lis Whitley OPEN: all week, daytime only CLOSED: Sun Jan and Feb MEALS: 8.30am to 5pm (L 12 to 2), Mon 8.30am to 2.30pm (snacks only), Sun 9.30am to 5pm PRICES: £9 (£14), Snacks from £1. Card slips closed CARDS: Access, Visa SEATS: 40. Private parties: 25 main room. Car park, 8 places. Vegetarian meals. Children's helpings. No smoking. Wheelchair access (1 step). No music. Fax: (0768) 881848

MIDDLE WALLOP Hampshire map 2

▲ *Fifehead Manor*

Middle Wallop SO20 8EG COOKING 2
ANDOVER (0264) 781565 COST £24–£44

The traffic whooshes by on its way to Salisbury Plain, but Fifehead turns its head to one side and affords some peace in a moving landscape. A venerable house, with modern additions, it has been done up by Margaret van Veelen in a style that stops short of inevitable country-house flounce. Hans de Gier has left the kitchen and there is some simplification in the choices on both the printed *carte* and the short daily menu. Cooking is adequate, but without fireworks in the recipes or bravura in the flavours. Asparagus with beurre blanc was excellently sauced but badly sourced; breast of duck 'suffused with orange' had so gentle a blush as to be undetectable; 'a gratin of fruits with a sorbet' comprised two slices of kiwi, some melon, apple, a piece of orange and a blackcurrant sorbet 'which might have been raspberry'. As in too many country places, the customer gets a degree of competence that puts a restaurant well ahead of its local rivals, but at a price that should buy more. The wine list is not long, but many of the choices are good and the prices not impossible. Ch. Hanteillan 1986 and Ch. Patache d'Aux 1985 are excellent bourgeois clarets, the Sancerre is from Vacheron, there are some pleasing Beaujolais, and there is a Gouges Nuits-St-Georges. House wine is £8.50.

CHEF: Mark Robertson PROPRIETOR: Margaret van Veelen OPEN: all week CLOSED: 1 week Christmas MEALS: 12 to 2.30, 7.30 to 9.30 PRICES: £28 (£37), Set L £17.50 (£24) to £19 (£26), Set D £23 (£30) to £26 (£33) CARDS: Access, Amex, Diners, Visa SEATS: 40. Private parties: 16 main room, 14 private room. Car park, 50 places. Children's helpings. Wheelchair access (also WC). No music. Fax: (0264) 781400 ACCOMMODATION: 16 rooms, all with bath/shower. Rooms for disabled. B&B £45 to £90. Children welcome. Baby facilities. Pets welcome. Afternoon teas. Garden. TV. Phone. Scenic. Doors close at midnight. Confirm by 6

The 1993 Guide *will be published before Christmas 1992. Reports on meals are most welcome at any time of the year, but are extremely valuable in the spring. Send them to* The Good Food Guide, *FREEPOST, 2 Marylebone Road, London NW1 1YN. No stamp is needed when posting in the UK.*

MIDHURST West Sussex map 3

Maxine's

Red Lion Street, Midhurst GU29 9PB COOKING 2
MIDHURST (073 081) 6271 COST £16–£28

A loyal following supports the de Jagers' intimate and atmospheric restaurant. 'After almost 10 years, I continue to be well pleased,' said one regular. The setting is a half-timbered house, with beams and wooden-backed chairs in the dining-room. Marti de Jager is always pleasant and efficient out front, while husband Robert cooks. The *carte* is short, concentrating on half a dozen options at each stage; there is also an excellent-value three-course set menu. Gravlax, warm goats' cheese salad with walnut dressing, fillet of lamb with tarragon and madeira sauce, and venison casserole show the style. Daily fish dishes are a bonus. Sunday lunch is a good roast. House French is £6.95.

CHEF: Robert de Jager PROPRIETORS: Robert and Marti de Jager OPEN: Wed to Sat, Sun L, bank hol weekends MEALS: 12 to 2, 7 to 10 PRICES: £19 (£24), Set L and D £10.95 (£16). Card slips closed CARDS: Access, Amex, Diners, Visa SEATS: 27. Private parties: 30 main room. Vegetarian meals. Children's helpings. No music

MILFORD ON SEA Hampshire map 2

Rocher's

69–71 High Street,
Milford on Sea SO41 0QG COOKING 3
LYMINGTON (0590) 642340 COST £17–£31

In this small seaside restaurant can be found very correct, classical cookery. Small wonder that many travel far to taste it. Even so, as one reader commented, 'an astonishing place in a town that is absolutely dead outside the holiday months; what do they do for customers in the winter?' They don't spend too much on staff or overheads, for one: the restaurant is simple, but comfortable, and it remains definitely 'family'. Customers are attracted by good value, especially the fixed-price Sunday lunch, as well as the generally assured cooking of dishes such as spinach and shallots in a puff pastry case; salmon with a red pimento butter sauce, or with a tarragon sauce; guinea-fowl with a caper sauce or a raspberry vinaigrette; duck with black cherries; and kidneys marchand du vin. Vegetables come as 'chef's sideplate'; desserts are light and best when freshly made rather than too cold from a refrigerator. Pastry work is excellent. It is rare that Alain Rocher is criticised for failing to deliver taste, or for misjudging timing or seasoning. Visitors never fail to warm to the atmosphere and the natural welcome. Chewton Glen (see New Milton entry), where the Rochers first worked in the district, is a benefactor of the general population. Exclusively French and strong on the Loire, the wine list has good names and decent vintages. Jadot from Burgundy and Jaboulet on the Rhône show a cautious but sound approach. Prices are fair. More adventure and a consistent listing of growers' names might merit a glass award. House wine is £7.95. CELLARMAN'S CHOICE: Cheverny Romorantin 1988, P. Tessier, £9.50; Chinon Rouge, Ch. de Ligré 1985, £11.50.

CHEF: Alain Rocher PROPRIETORS: Alain and Rebecca Rocher OPEN: all week D, exc Tue, and Sun L CLOSED: 2 weeks winter, 2 weeks summer MEALS: 12.15 to 2, 7 to 10 PRICES: £19 (£26), Set L £11.50 (£17). Card slips closed CARDS: Access, Visa SEATS: 30. Private parties: 30 main room. No children under 14. Smart dress preferred. No cigars/pipes in dining-room. Wheelchair access. Music

MOLLINGTON Cheshire map 5

▲ *Crabwall Manor* 🍷

Parkgate Road, Mollington CH1 6NE COOKING 2*
GREAT MOLLINGTON (0244) 851666 COST £20–£52

The Manor used to be a castellated red-brick house of medium dimensions. That house survives, but is almost overwhelmed by a ranch-style extension housing lots of new bedrooms. It is all in the finest possible taste. New bedrooms are well appointed, some superlative, though one 'superior double' suffered from kitchen noise on a putatively lazy Sunday morning. The danger in the dining-room is that intelligent cooking can be swamped by the greatly increased business; the car park is a sea of metal. Those of long acquaintance say the front-of-house has been sharpened up to cope, though complaints surface here, from the tone of attention to a single woman customer and stuffiness in the face of a jean-clad teenager, to repeated failures in principles and details of wine service. Certain constants stand out. First is the excellent value of Sunday lunch. The menu may lack some fireworks, but is none the less sound. Second, when on form the kitchen produces clear flavours, does not rely too heavily on cream or butter, and has taken on board that modern hybrid of tastes from Britain, Europe and the Orient. Third, the trimmings are generally well thought out though cutlery could be better chosen (and polished) and bread needs improvement. Dishes that have gained approval this year have included excellent confit of duck with couscous and a hot sauce, ravioli of salmon filled with a quenelle mixture and palpable chunks of the fish, parfait of chicken livers, salmon in a shallot butter sauce, crab gnocchi, a Chinese-style duck with port and soy sauce, and best end of lamb with leeks and herbs. Desserts get more comments about heaviness than they should, and other reports reflect too often that plates and food get to table too cold. The clear presentation and fine selection of wines go far beyond the boundaries of classic French areas. Some prices are high, but this is carefully balanced by a page of French country wines, good Alsaces and Loires and a steady eye on Australasia and the USA. There are good half-bottles, including a few Californians. Wine service and stock-keeping can be erratic. House wine is £9.75. CELLARMAN'S CHOICE: Mâcon Viré 1988, Bonhomme, £23; Mercurey, Ch. de Chamirey 1987, £26.

CHEF: Peter Mayoh PROPRIETOR: Carl Lewis OPEN: all week MEALS: 12 to 2, 7 to 9.30 PRICES: £28 (£43), Set L £13.50 (£20), Set D £23 (£31). Card slips closed CARDS: Access, Amex, Diners, Visa SEATS: 120. Private parties: 85 main room, 45 and 100 private rooms. Car park, 120 places. Vegetarian meals. Children's helpings. Jacket and tie. No cigars/pipes in dining-room. Wheelchair access (also WC). Music. Air-conditioned. Fax: (0244) 851400 ACCOMMODATION: 48 rooms, all with bath/shower. Rooms for disabled. B&B £94.70 to £120.70. Children welcome. Baby facilities. Afternoon teas. Garden. Snooker. TV. Phone. Scenic. Confirm 2 days ahead (*Which? Hotel Guide*)

MONTACUTE Somerset map 2

▲ *Milk House*

The Borough, Montacute TA15 6XB — COOKING 1
MARTOCK (0935) 823823 — COST £16–£32

A fine old house, sympathetically restored by the Duftons and dominated by giant fireplaces and the warm tones of the honeyed stone. There is an underlying philosophy to the food: that it should be organically reared or grown, that it should not be refined, and that its cooking should carry the smallest burden of fats, sugars and added 'impurities'. Special diets are enthusiastically catered for. Elizabeth Dufton's repertoire is timeless and rooted only in an English receptivity to influence, hence dishes like cress and sorrel pancake filled with braised and spiced mushrooms; *zewelswei*, an onion quiche in wholemeal pastry; lamb and red wine daube; spicy plum pudding; honey pie; hot chocolate, walnut and fudge pudding; and excellent home-made sorbets. The style is home-made in the best of senses, with limited artfulness, hence the comment 'tasty' repeated several times in reports. Bill Dufton's service is informally efficient, with plenty of opportunity for discussion. The value of the menu, bearing in mind the quality of materials, is very fair. A short list of wines includes many organics. House wines are from £8.75.

CHEF: Elizabeth Dufton PROPRIETORS: Elizabeth and William Dufton OPEN: Wed to Sat, D only, and Sun L (Wed to Sat L by arrangement) MEALS: 12 to 2, 7.30 to 9 PRICES: Set L £10 (£16) to £12.50 (£19), Set D £14.50 (£21) to £19.75 (£27). Card slips closed CARDS: Access, Visa SEATS: 24. 3 tables outside. Private parties: 24 main room, 24 private room. Vegetarian meals. Healthy eating options. Smart dress preferred. No smoking in dining-room. Wheelchair access. No music ACCOMMODATION: 2 rooms, both with bath/shower. D,B&B £98 (double room). Deposit: £10. No children under 12. Garden. Scenic. Doors close at midnight. Confirm by 4

MORETON-IN-MARSH Gloucestershire map 2

Marsh Goose

COUNTY RESTAURANT OF THE YEAR

NEW ENTRY

High Street,
Moreton-in-Marsh GL56 0AX — COOKING 3
MORETON-IN-MARSH (0608) 52111 — COST £19–£30

Restaurants in the Cotswolds are strange affairs. On the one hand, the Epicurean moves from Stow-on-the-Wold to Cheltenham in search of bright lights and more business; on the other, Marsh Goose steps into premises that have already been home to a succession of maybe five eating-houses (Sheridans the last), all of which seem to have thrown up their hands in despair. Yet the Marsh Goose appears, in its first year, to be resoundingly successful. Is it the cooking? Or is it the fact that its owners were once the very canny first developers of the Feathers at Woodstock (see entry) – another place that pitched price and standards exactly to the market? The Goose is not dear, emphatically cheap at lunch, and Sonya Kidney is doing a fine job of cooking food that impresses for its market buying (fish, meat and fowl), its freshness (vegetables), its invention (vegetables again, such as deep-fried fennel), its presentation ('nouvelle cuisine with generosity') and its fine flavours. A set-price dinner menu, with some supplements, includes a half-dozen choices at each turn, of modern British conception, such as grilled goats' cheese with asparagus, young spinach and shallot dressing; duck with thyme and lentils; chicken with a spinach, hazelnut and breadcrumb stuffing; rhubarb fool or blackcurrant parfait and an optional savoury at the end. Service, all dressed in bold bow-ties and waistcoats, is as fresh and unsullied as the cooking, yet does its job properly. There is a shop next door selling the restaurant's produce. The wine list is never a long book but covers the world without prejudice, offering some fine makers like Paillard, Fèvre, CVNE, Castle Hill in New Zealand and Torres from Chile, and sufficient halves. May the formula thrive. House Spanish wines are £7.80.

CHEF: Miss S.E. Kidney PROPRIETORS: Miss S.E. Kidney, Mr L. Brooke-Little and Mr G. Campbell-Gray OPEN: Tue to Sun, exc Sun D MEALS: 12.15 to 2.30, 7.30 to 9.45 PRICES: £12 (£19), Set D £18.90 (£25) CARDS: Access, Visa SEATS: 60. Private parties: 20 main room, 14 private room. Vegetarian meals. Children welcome. Children's helpings. Smart dress preferred D. Wheelchair access (also WC). No music

MORPETH Northumberland map 7

La Brasserie

59 Bridge Street, Morpeth NE61 1PQ COOKING 1
MORPETH (0670) 516200 COST £12–£35

There are audible sighs of relief at the existence of La Brasserie: 'useful in the area' and 'an oasis' are two comments. The upstairs dining-room, prettified by curtains and pictures, offers a very wide-ranging printed menu – too wide for aficionados of absolute slavery to the markets (what happens about all that fish in winter?) – covering, for example, prawns in filo pastry, turbot en papillote and escalope of venison with red wine and herbs. Service is cheerful, but not always highly trained. The wine list has a strong showing from Italy, proportionately speaking. Prices are not high. House wine is £7.90.

CHEF/PROPRIETOR: R.H. Wilkinson OPEN: Tue to Sun, exc Sun D MEALS: 11.30 to 2, 6.30 to 11 PRICES: £21 (£29), Set L £5.50 (£12) to £8.50 (£15), Set D £9.95 (£17) to £13.50 (£21). Card slips closed CARDS: Access, Amex, Diners, Visa SEATS: 50. Private parties: 30 main room, 50 private room. Car park, 6 places. Vegetarian meals. Children's helpings. Music

MOULSFORD Oxfordshire map 2

▲ *Beetle & Wedge*

Moulsford OX10 9JF COOKING 3
CHOLSEY (0491) 651381 COST £27–£52

Richard and Kate Smith took a plunge when they embarked on the purchase and conversion of this large, rambling riverside pub-hotel with enviable site and prospect. They had already had remarkable success at the Royal Oak, Yattendon (see entry), providing cross-over food that made the most of English and European tradition and serving it both exclusively in a restaurant and demotically in the bar. Wines, too, were red hot. Could they repeat – nay more, since they kept the Royal Oak – expand to double this formula? First reports, while conversion was under way, were in two minds. The ideas were there, but execution seemed overwhelmed by number and distracted by incompetence. This year, the Smiths surrendered the Royal Oak to capable successors and have concentrated their efforts here. It seems to be paying off. A restaurant and conservatory for gracious dining, a charcoal grill that provides much of the food, a boathouse bar and terrace for cheaper yet still imaginative eating. Numbers may still be daunting, but, insulated from the crowds, a meal here is progressively an enjoyable experience. Menus read well, and there are many regular fixtures from earlier repertoires: crab and avocado salad, sole with queen scallops, calf's kidney with black pudding and mustard sauce, venison with figs and chestnuts, apple and raspberry crumble. The kitchen proves its worth in delicious combinations such as pigeon breast, foie gras, wild mushrooms and asparagus in puff pastry, or chargrilled halibut on a bed of spinach with black noodles. Occasionally it may still falter; there have been complaints about beef fillet burned to a cinder, tough steaks, and overpriced sweets. The dessert price, however, includes coffee and petits fours, and the list is truly enticing: from plainer crumbles and rice pudding to bananas baked in rum and brown sugar served with passion-fruit ice-cream. Given time to settle to a pattern, this restaurant will be a distinguished addition to Thames-side jollifications. A predominantly French list put together by a wine enthusiast may dull customers' enthusiasm by mark-ups that push hard. A pity, since names and properties are fine, Alsaces are a good bet, and there is much decent-value drinking below £15. An absence of half-bottles is compensated for by the willingness to open a full bottle, for which pleasure you pay a small premium; an offer not to be refused. There are Adnams and Wadworths ales. House wine is £8.95. CELLARMAN'S CHOICE: Muscat d'Alsace 1988, Schlumberger, £17.50; Châteauneuf-du-Pape, Vieux Télégraphe 1987, £24.50. The most recent reports suggest that you are wisest to avoid the boathouse on high days and holidays. Numbers are very great here and the logistical skill needed to cope with them needs the mind of a Montgomery.

CHEF: Richard Smith PROPRIETORS: Richard and Kate Smith OPEN: all week, exc Sun D MEALS: 12.30 to 2, 7.30 to 10 PRICES: restaurant £34 (£43), Set Sun L £19.75 (£27); boathouse £17 (£27) CARDS: Access, Amex, Visa SEATS: 60. 16 tables outside. Private parties: 60 main room, 50 private room. Car park, 35 places. Vegetarian meals. Children's helpings. Smart dress preferred. No cigars/pipes in dining-room. Wheelchair access (also WC). Fax: (0491) 651376 ACCOMMODATION: 12 rooms, all with bath/shower. Rooms for disabled. B&B £65 to £75. Children welcome. Baby facilities. Pets by arrangement. Afternoon teas. Garden. Fishing. TV. Phone. Scenic. Confirm by 6 (*Which? Hotel Guide*)

Prices quoted in the Guide *are based on information supplied by restaurateurs. The figure in brackets below an entry is the average for a three-course meal with service, coffee and half a bottle of house wine, as calculated by computer. The prices quoted at the top of an entry represent a range, from the lowest average meal price to the highest; the latter is inflated by 20 per cent to take account of the fact that very few people eat an average meal, and also that prices are likely to rise during the year of the* Guide.

MOULTON North Yorkshire map 7

Black Bull

Moulton DL10 6QJ
DARLINGTON (0325) 377289
1m SE of Scotch Corner, 1m from A1

COOKING 2
COST £17–£38

'The tedium of the A1 back to London was broken by lunch at the Black Bull, which has brought a completely new association to Scotch Corner,' wrote one traveller. The Bull is a venue with several options: a Victorian-style seafood bar, 'Hazel' – the renovated Pullman carriage from the Brighton Belle – and the comfortable conservatory. There is a North Country generosity about the cooking and portions are huge. Massive grilled Dover sole, braised ox tongue with spinach and poached turbot with hollandaise come with vast platters of perfectly cooked vegetables. Those with stamina could move on to crème brûlée or crêpes Suzette. The kitchen tips its hat to more modern fashions with warm chicken liver salad and queenies, halibut and smoked salmon in filo pastry with sorrel butter, and poached chicken with asparagus in Riesling sauce. The owners are also wine merchants and offer a reliable, almost exclusively French list, including house wines from Georges Duboeuf at £7.25.

CHEF: Stuart Birkett PROPRIETORS: G.H. Pagendam and Mrs A.M.C. Pagendam OPEN: Mon to Sat CLOSED: 23 to 31 Dec MEALS: 12 to 2, 6.45 to 10.15 PRICES: £24 (£32), Set L £10.75 (£17) to £15 (£22). Card slips closed CARDS: Access, Amex, Visa SEATS: 100. 4 tables outside. Private parties: 30 main room, 10 and 30 private rooms. Car park, 80 places. No children under 7. Wheelchair access (also WC). No music. Fax: (0325) 377422

NAILSEA Avon map 2

La Cour

NEW ENTRY

120 High Street, Nailsea BS19 1AH
NAILSEA (0275) 857911

COOKING 1
COST £20–£30

The modern development towards the northern end of Nailsea, perhaps the West Country's longest town, is an odd home for a pair of French enterprises run by amiable rugby fan André Pierre Baqué. The restaurant is on the upper deck – reached by a vertiginous spiral staircase – above the Courtyard wine bar. A seasonal menu shows skills exercised with discretion in a winter meal of mussels with saffron cream, pink chicken livers with grapes and red wine, grilled bream on a bed of fennel and tarragon, pork fillet with mustard sauce, and apple pancakes with calvados. Small touches give encouragement: the canapés with the drinks, decent space between tables, the walnut bread with the simple cheeseboard; drinkable coffee and amiable service from graduates of French catering colleges. Concessions to English tastes are more marked in the wine bar, but even there, passable food may be had at economical prices. The wine list is short and there are only two half-bottles. House French is £8.50.

denotes an outstanding wine cellar; *denotes a good wine list, worth travelling for.*

CHEF: Marc Faussemagne PROPRIETOR: André Pierre Baqué OPEN: Tue to Sat, exc Sat L CLOSED: first week Jan MEALS: 12 to 2, 7 to 9.30 (10 Sat) PRICES: Set L and D £13 (£20) to £17.50 (£25). Service 10%. Card slips closed CARDS: Access, Visa SEATS: 36. Private parties: 42 main room. Vegetarian meals with prior notice. Children welcome. No-smoking area. Music

NAILSWORTH Gloucestershire map 2

Flynns

3 Fountain Street, Nailsworth GL6 0BL COOKING 3
NAILSWORTH (045 383) 5567 COST £21–£39

The restaurant is a flower-bedecked first-floor extension to the fish shop and deli below. 'It has no architectural merit unless one is enamoured of prefabricated Portakabin-type buildings,' according to one reader. Inside is a different story: colours, pictures and careful design have made an attractive space. Garry Flynn is a talented cook. He adapts classics from the masters – for example, his version of the Roux brothers' oysters on a salmon mousse with cucumber tagliatelle – and he imports spices and flavourings from the Far East familiar to him in his native Australia. His menus pack tremendous variety into a short list. Fish is always a strong point, whether it is brill sandwiched between salmon mousse and wrapped in laverbread, served with a basil sauce, or cod with a pesto crust, saffron sauce and fresh pasta. But meat is never forgotten, be it game, venison, or offal (oxtail has been very successful). Pasta is enjoyed – for instance, tortellini filled with scallop and bream mousse, and crab and ginger ravioli with grapefruit and mint. Lambs' kidneys with black pudding, madeira and spinach is another offal dish and venison has been offered marinated in soy and five-spice, with a green peppercorn sauce and sweet pickled vegetables and grapes. This is enquiring, yet assured, cookery. The success continues to the dessert stage. 'I suspect he (Garry Flynn) is one of the few who can make the humble banana look and taste so good,' commented one who had it wrapped in a pancake with orange and Cointreau sauce and a banana and gin ice-cream. The service by Deborah Reid is exemplary. The wine list, which has helpful notes, seems to draw much from Windrush Wines of Cirencester and thus features good properties from all over: Seaview, Hawk Crest, Moss Wood, Dom. de Nalys in Châteauneuf and Génot-Boulanger in Beaune. Although vegetarians seem to have no special dish on the menu, their diet is handled with imagination and enthusiasm on notification. House wines are £8.50.

CHEF/PROPRIETOR: Garry Flynn OPEN: Mon to Sat, exc Mon L MEALS: 12.30 to 2, 7 to 9 PRICES: £23 (£33), Set L £14.50 (£21). Card slips closed CARDS: Access, Visa SEATS: 30. Private parties: 45 main room. Car park, 5 places. Vegetarian meals. Children's helpings. No pipes in dining-room. No cigars during meals. No music

Healthy eating options *in the details at the end of an entry signifies that a restaurant marks on its menu, in words and/or using symbols, low-fat dishes or other healthy eating choices.*

NAYLAND Suffolk map 3

Martha's Vineyard 🍷

18 High Street, Nayland CO6 4JF COOKING 3
COLCHESTER (0206) 262888 COST £26

The Warrens continue as they began: a place that welcomes all sorts – suits and jeans; doesn't charge over the odds; doesn't set store by excess luxury or tricks of presentation; thinks about the food, cooking and wine; increasingly sets its face against indiscriminate smoking. Although unhappy at our use of the term 'nouvelle Dixie' to describe the cooking in last year's entry, Larkin Warren would at least admit to the prevalence of the American influence in the menus. It is not the parodic stuff of Brett Easton Ellis's *American Psycho*, but the unfamiliar emphases and combinations lift one far from dark green East Anglian horizons, sometimes towards the Far West, at others down to the Mediterranean. It is difficult to list a range of exemplar dishes that people have mentioned: pasta is a frequent candidate – tagliatelle with basil, pumpkin and guinea-fowl ravioli in a broth; vegetarian dishes are always intelligent – a filo frittata, for instance, with lots of fresh herbs; ribs – not spicy enough for some; or great fishcakes with watercress sauce. Desserts, excellent lemon tart and chocolate fudge cake, don't let the side down; nor does the bread, a different sort each day (baking in general is a strong point). Criticisms occasionally surface, the result perhaps of too many customers causing approximate cooking and flavouring. Prices have risen, but modestly. A fondness for Californian red wines does not stop at the eponymous bottles of Joseph Heitz. This succinct, but ambitious, range lists as many Californians as it does others under 'General', with France put firmly in place. Prices are fair with much interesting drinking under £15. Halves are rather limited, but a glass is awarded nevertheless for intelligence, brevity and excitement. House French is £7.25. CELLARMAN'S CHOICE: Rosso Conero 1988, Terrazze £14.75; Pinot Noir 1988, Saintsbury, £16.50.

CHEF: Larkin Warren PROPRIETORS: Christopher and Larkin Warren OPEN: Tue to Sat, D only CLOSED: 2 weeks summer, 2 weeks Christmas, 2 days Easter MEALS: 6.45 to 9 (9.30 Fri and Sat) PRICES: £15 (£22). Card slips closed CARDS: Access, Visa SEATS: 45. Private parties: 8 main room. Vegetarian meals. Children's helpings. No smoking. Wheelchair access. No music

NEWARK Nottinghamshire map 5

Gannets Bistrot NEW ENTRY

35 Castlegate, Newark NG24 1AZ COOKING 1
NEWARK (0636) 702066 COST £23

For around 12 years, Hilary and David Bower have run a thriving self-service café overlooking the River Trent. Now they have opened an upstairs bistrot with waitress service and tables for booking. The décor is all pine floorboards, mirrors and potted plants, with menus chalked on a blackboard. Gannets' reputation was built on its use of fresh ingredients and its enterprising mix of meat and vegetarian dishes. The bistrot follows suit. On the one hand there might be meaty, organic bangers and mash with onion sauce, Catalan pork casserole, free-range chicken and vegetable pie topped with wholemeal pastry, on the other there is mushroom, walnut and basil pâté, and spinach, hazelnut and aubergine bake. Salads are ever-present. Ice-creams (including a mincemeat version) are home-made; cheeses come from a quality local supplier. House French is £7.50 a litre.

CHEFS: Hilary Bower and Paul Godfrey PROPRIETORS: Hilary and David Bower
OPEN: Tue to Sat, exc Tue D CLOSED: Christmas week MEALS: 12 to 2.30, 6.30 to 9.30
PRICES: £13 (£19). Service 10%. Card slips closed CARDS: Access, Visa SEATS: 38.
Private parties: 38 main room. Vegetarian meals. Children welcome. No cigars/pipes in dining-room. Music

NEWCASTLE UPON TYNE Tyne & Wear map 7

Café Procope — NEW ENTRY

35 The Side, Quayside, NE1 3JE COOKING 1
091-232 3848 COST £18

Down on The Side, things don't change at Café Procope, even though there are new hands at the tiller. It is still laid-back in decoration ('money spent on the food rather than presentation' is the kind way of putting it), still a happy mix of young, student and old customers, and always with a world view of cooking. Hence a meal that included spanokopita (squid with chilli and sweet plum sauce), a Cuban dish (mujol asado con salsa esmerelda), an Israeli targenol be'paprika im orez and a Mexican lamb stew. Sweets are British and modern, including chocolate cheesecake. There are mistakes – the squid was chewy, had no chilli and tasted too sweet. But the Cuban mujol asado was big silvery chunks of grey mullet with potatoes and a spiced Caribbean marinade: excellent. Old standards like hummus and falafel get well done too. 'The "rough and readiness" of this café is compensated for by the interest of the food, which is above average. There are imperfections, but it is real food and home-cooked, even if not necessarily to everyone's taste,' was the summing up of one reader. There are lots of beers, and a few decent and inexpensive wines. House wines are £6.75.

CHEF: T. Fyffe PROPRIETORS: Mr N. Cornish, Mrs W. Cornish and Mr A. Dhanda
OPEN: all week CLOSED: bank hol Mons MEALS: 10.30am to 10.30pm (10pm Sun)
PRICES: £10 (£15), Snacks from £2.15. Service 12.5% for parties of 8 or more SEATS: 46.
Private parties: 50 main room. Vegetarian meals. Children welcome. Wheelchair access (also WC). Music. Air-conditioned

Courtney's — NEW ENTRY

5–7 The Side, NE1 3JE COOKING 2
091-232 5537 COST £19–£30

Newcastle is going through a good patch for restaurants. Courtney's is another benefit of the development of the Quayside area for entertainment rather than commerce and dockside life. Dark green outside, pale green and cream within, with the space cleverly handled on two levels and a very small bar area. The style of the place is brasserie-plus, the plus mainly coming from the blackboard with daily fish dishes and other extras. One diner praised the 'deceptive simplicity' after eating mahi-mahi (expressed from Hawaii via London) and halibut, both tasting ultra-fresh and exactly cooked on charcoal grill and in steamer. Vegetables, too, were plain but dealt with accurately – 'no microwave mush'. The first courses on the printed menu include brasserie/bistro standards like eggs Benedict (or a variation thereon) and fried mushrooms with boursin; and the desserts are sensibly limited so that service is swift and quality can be maintained. Service is also very informed, even didactic. This gives encouragement to waverers on the food side and to those who want to choose from the very short wine list that none the less is never hackneyed. House Duboeuf is £7.75.

CHEF: Michael Carr PROPRIETORS: Michael and Kerensa Carr OPEN: Mon to Sat, exc Sat L CLOSED: bank hols, exc Good Fri D MEALS: 12 to 2, 7 to 10.30 (10.45 Sat) PRICES: £18 (£25), Set L £13.95 (£19). Service 10% for parties over 6 CARDS: Access, Amex, Visa SEATS: 27. Private parties: 27 main room. Vegetarian meals. Children welcome. Children's helpings on request. No cigars/pipes in dining-room. Music

Dragon House

30–32 Stowell Street, NE1 4XQ COOKING 2
091-232 0868 COST £9–£35

Barry Yu's restaurant right in the heart of Newcastle's Chinatown continues to deliver some of the best food of its kind in the city. The main menu is a promising mix of Cantonese and Pekinese dishes, with a few specialities from Szechuan and Shanghai. Wafer-wrapped king prawns, crispy aromatic duck, stir-fried lamb with spring onion, and squid with garlic and chilli are typical. Some intriguing chef's recommendations include stuffed asparagus in crabmeat sauce, and oyster and roast pork hotpot. The restaurant also features an enterprising 'health and vegetarian' menu that goes beyond the usual Chinese offerings, with ocean soup (seaweed in vegetable stock), spicy aubergine hotpot, and deep-fried bean curd dumplings. Set dinners and banquets are good value, as are the weekday lunches. Book for the Sung Dynasty feast served on Sundays (noon to 3pm). House French is £6.

CHEF: Miky Yeung PROPRIETOR: Barry Yu OPEN: all week CLOSED: 25 Dec MEALS: 12 to 2, 6 to 11 PRICES: £16 (£29), Set L £4.75 (£9) to £6.50 (£10), Set D £13.50 (£18) to £17.50 (£23). Minimum £10.50 CARDS: Access, Amex, Carte Blanche, Diners, Visa SEATS: 150. Private parties: 70 main room. Vegetarian meals. Healthy eating options. Children welcome. Wheelchair access. Music. Air-conditioned

Fisherman's Lodge

Jesmond Dene, NE7 7BQ COOKING 3
091-281 3281 COST £20–£52

A Hansel and Gretel house in Jesmond Dene, Lord Armstrong's town park, although all thought of infantile kitsch is banished once the striking bar and dining-rooms are seen. The name denotes the speciality, though meats (or indeed vegetarian dishes) are to be found for a balanced choice. The menu makes no bones about surf 'n' turf, and the cooking is generally rich and substantial as well as making some play of ornament and visual conceits, not that this will be to the exclusion of simple preparations such as pan-fried baby halibut or lemon sole, oysters or gravlax or a delicately oak-smoked fillet of salmon with a cucumber butter sauce. The framework of the meal – befores and afters – is as generous and substantial as the cooking itself; and service is in keeping. The Lodge is an extremely successful restaurant that does not rest on its laurels – there is a continuous cycle of refurbishment – while its culinary style undergoes no serious revolution. The wine list spreads further afield than France, though white burgundy is the best section, and the page of Italians is worth pausing over, even if they might cause you to eat meat. Prices are very fair indeed. House wines are £9 a litre.

CHEF: Steven Jobson PROPRIETORS: Franco and Pamela Cetoloni OPEN: Mon to Sat, exc Sat L CLOSED: 25 to 28 Dec MEALS: 12 to 2, 7 to 11 PRICES: £32 (£43), Set L £14 (£20) to £15 (£21) CARDS: Access, Amex, Diners, Visa SEATS: 70. 3 tables outside. Private parties: 14 main room, 14 and 40 private rooms. Car park, 45 places. Children's helpings. No children under 6. Smart dress preferred. No smoking. Wheelchair access. Fax: 091-281 6410

Leela's

NEW ENTRY

20 Dean Street, NE1 1PG — COOKING 1*
091-230 1261 — COST £10–£32

A terrific transformation has taken place at this one-time pizza place on the road leading down to the quayside. In its new guise this restaurant now specialises in south Indian cooking with some dishes from other parts of the subcontinent. Kurikofe Paul cooks, while his wife Leela runs the front-of-house. The thrust of the menu is vegetarian, although meat and fish also feature. Dishes have bizarre names, although descriptions are more run-of-the-mill. Chammanthi are deep-fried flattened chickpea patties, parripu is really a creamy version of tarka dhal, while the extraordinarily titled Achinga Pattichular-thiathu is fresh green beans topped with soft fried onions, herbs and garlic. King prawn pappas, marinated in tamarind sauce and cooked with cream, were described by an inspector as 'the single most delicious thing I've eaten this year'. Accompaniments, breads and rice are first-rate, although some vegetable dishes have been disappointing. Sweets are westernised concoctions. Prices may seem high, but quality is compensation. A simpler menu is available at lunchtime. House wine is £7.90.

CHEF: Kurikofe Paul PROPRIETORS: Kurikofe and Leela Paul OPEN: Mon to Sat MEALS: 12 to 2.30, 5.30 to 11.30 PRICES: £16 (£27), Set L £4.95 (£10) to £9.95 (£15) CARDS: Access, Amex, Visa SEATS: 54. Private parties: 25 main room. Vegetarian meals. Children welcome. Music

An asterisk (*) after the 1 to 5 cooking mark at the top of an entry signifies that the Guide *and its readers think that the restaurant is a particularly fine example within its numeric classification.*

Rupali

6 Bigg Market, NE1 1UW — COOKING 1
091-232 8629 — COST £23

For 14 years Abdul Latif has kept Rupali at the forefront of Newcastle's Indian restaurants by a variety of marketing initiatives, fair cooking and good value (especially with the lunchtime specials and 'early eater' menu – two courses and a glass of wine for less than £6). The main *carte* is very wide indeed, taking in most Indian regions in a formulaic run through spring chicken, prawns, lamb and sometimes beef in several styles, but it does please a wide constituency. Breads are good; service and attention are excellent. House French is £6.25.

CHEF/PROPRIETOR: Abdul Latif OPEN: all week, exc Sun L MEALS: 12 to 2.30, 6 to 11.30 PRICES: £12 (£19). Card slips closed CARDS: Access, Amex, Diners, Visa SEATS: 54. Private parties: 50 main room. Vegetarian meals. Children's helpings. Music

21 Queen Street 🍷

21 Queen Street, Princes Wharf, NE1 3UG — COOKING 3*
091-222 0755 — COST £21–£49

Cars plunge, as if down a precipice, from the level of the station, hotels and broad streets of classical Newcastle to the wharves and crowding buildings of the riverside. The Tyne bridges soar overhead; on the water itself, a disco-bar boat is moored, lights flashing, a palpable image of the leisure and pleasure that has overrun this quarter since the coal and shipping trades moved on. Susan and Terence Laybourne's restaurant, even here, comes as a sassy surprise: no reproduction Victoriana, but cool peach/blue/grey modernity; understatement but also comfort; space, but also the feel of an owner-driven place (though one or two have wondered if the service is a touch too formalised). The food is of a piece with the image: modern, intelligent, directed by the enthusiasms of the chef, yet once or twice victim of technique over taste. The start of the meal, typically an *amuse-bouche* of a small cup of venison consommé, cheese straws and a crust topped with crab mousse and shredded cucumber, is another sign that the chef means business. Terence Laybourne's repertoire straddles most commodities: fish, game, meat and pastry work. Strongest successes have been registered with game, especially Kielder forest venison, and fish, as likely to be from Brixham as from the north-east. Less glittering has been the pastry work, though desserts such as hot lemon (or rhubarb) strudel and an apple tart cooked to order on the flakiest of thin discs have had supporters too. Ingredients and combinations are refreshingly different: for instance, a salad of smoked eel, endive and bacon; or soup of roasted yellow peppers with sage and Parmesan where each element seemed in (surprising) harmony. There is an affection for spices in things such as duck with oriental spices or scallops with Thai seasoning; and the pulses get a fair outing in borlotti beans with salt cod, and lentils with haddock and scallops. Vegetables remain a 'selection', some items – mashed parsnip, for instance – better than others. The assured kitchen usually achieves its aims, in an environment that cannot fail to give pleasure. Enthusiasm for the wines must be muted. Very good growers and properties abound – Paillard, Foreau, La Lagune – in this mainly French selection, but modest drinking is poorly served; choice below £15 is very restricted and the mark-up continues to push hard. Best value is probably in the Rhône. There are some dessert wines by the glass and several good half-bottles. The glass award is given on the strength of the intelligent selection of excellent wines; with food as good as this though, the customer should be entitled to a broader sweep, both geographic and economic. House wine is £9. CELLARMAN'S CHOICE: Pouilly Fumé, Ch. de Tracy 1989, £16.90; Chorey-lès-Beaune 1986, Tollot-Beaut, £19.30.

CHEF: Terence Laybourne PROPRIETORS: Susan and Terence Laybourne OPEN: Mon to Sat, exc Sat L CLOSED: 25 and 26 Dec, 1 Jan, bank hols MEALS: 12 to 2, 7 to 11 PRICES: £31 (£41), Set L £14.20 (£21) CARDS: Access, Amex, Diners, Visa SEATS: 50. Private parties: 50 main room. Children's helpings. Smart dress preferred. No pipes in dining-room. No music. Fax: 091-230 5875

NEW MILTON Hampshire map 2

▲ *Marryat Room, Chewton Glen Hotel* 🍷

Christchurch Road, New Milton BH25 6QS COOKING 3*
HIGHCLIFFE (0425) 275341 COST £26–£55

This utterly modernised, gabled, red-brick and green-shuttered house in the New Forest is serious luxury. You might guess it from the price of the set-dinner (though lunch is little more than half this), but visible proof surrounds the visitor. In Victorian times, the great palace hotels of London gave the newly rich a chance to hire upper-class style by the night. Chewton gives the late twentieth century a similar opportunity. Attention to detail is close and the staff are eagle-eyed: 'We were never made to feel like poor relations, even if we had come for lunch rather than the unaffordable dinner,' a reader comments. If last year's entry reflected improvements to the kitchen and dining arrangements, this year's must refer to the new health club – pillared swimming-pool and all. One disconsolate traveller felt the new facilities tended to dominate other aspects of the hotel – certainly, the menu now stresses healthy alternatives – and that there was less imagination evident in the cooking, as if physical jerks had drained the brain cells. This is, perhaps, too sweeping a comment, even if the majority of customers appear to plump for cold salmon on a day when the kitchen could have produced so many more original confections. Pierre Chevillard steers a passage between the refined and the earthy – thin-sliced tuna marinated in lime juice or confit of duck with lentils – as well as the conventional, fillet béarnaise, and the original, pigs' trotters rolled with breasts of quail. Cooking is precise, materials of the best quality and the hotel prides itself on being part of a European rather than merely English mainstream. When local demands, for instance on Mother's Day, impose their own crowds, a certain automation has been observed. None the less, this place must be a candidate for one of the most cosseted weekends available in the English countryside. The wine list impresses in length, pedigree and vintage; 15 vintages of Ch. Latour and a page of wines from

Romanée Conti set the tone. Quality is remarkable at the upper reaches; but below £15 selection is uneven with too many 'French bottled' appearing to imbue total confidence. Alsaces, petits châteaux and a range of French regional wines offer the most astute choice for the uncertain. House wines are from £11.75. CELLARMAN'S CHOICE: Fronsac, Ch. Mayne Vieil 1985, £15.35; Hawkes Bay, Chardonnay 1988, Te Mata, £28.30.

CHEF: Pierre Chevillard PROPRIETOR: Martin Skan OPEN: all week MEALS: 12.30 to 2, 7.30 to 9.30 PRICES: £37 (£46), Set L £20.50 (£26), Set D £38 (£44). Net prices, card slips closed CARDS: Access, Amex, Diners, Visa SEATS: 120. 6 tables outside. Private parties: 20 main room, 6 and 80 private rooms. Car park, 100 places. Vegetarian meals. Healthy eating options. Children's helpings. No children under 7. Jacket and tie. No cigars/pipes in dining-room. No music. Fax: (0425) 272310 ACCOMMODATION: 58 rooms, all with bath/shower. Rooms for disabled. B&B £155 to £375. Deposit: 1 night. No children under 7. Afternoon teas. Garden. Swimming-pool. Sauna. Tennis. Golf. Snooker. TV. Phone. Scenic. Doors close at midnight (*Which? Hotel Guide*)

NORTH HUISH Devon map 1

▲ *Brookdale House*

North Huish TQ10 9NR COOKING 3
GARA BRIDGE (054 882) 402 and 415 COST £43

The late-Victorian house stands at the bottom of a steep combe. It has been decorated by the Trevor-Ropers so as not to clash with its origins, to a degree of luxury that is never out of keeping with its (gentlemanly) scale. The restaurant and cooking are similarly well-judged; there is some thought of the guest who may want to eat a succession of meals here, so all is not power and weight. A set-price menu of half a dozen choices in each course changes on a rolling basis day by day. Terry Rich draws on tastes prevalent in many country houses as well as metropolitan restaurants: red mullet is served with ribbons of carrot and courgette and a warm olive oil dressing; oxtail is boned and wrapped in caul, then served with a grape and Sauternes sauce. These are balanced by hoary favourites: tartare of salmon; cured ham with melon and orange; sticky toffee pudding; lemon tart – all done well, with good materials, gathered from an impressive list of local suppliers, makers and growers. A springtime visit yielded high flavours in quail on a crisp potato-cake and first-rate lamb with ratatouille and a basil sauce. Vegetables, too, were accurately cooked. Not so impressive was a complete lack of seasoning in parsnip soup and a toppling into over-sweet in the sticky toffee pudding that needed cutting by a sharper orange sauce. English cheeses, mainly from the Ticklemore Cheese Shop in Totnes, were supplied to near excess and were for the most part in fine condition. Service, particularly when Charles or Carol Trevor-Roper are there, is punctual and knowledgeable. Fifteen 'recommended wines' priced by glass and bottle provide an intelligent and economical opening to the excellent wine list. Thereafter, wines are shown clearly under simple headings such as 'medium red', in price order, eschewing classification by region. Burgundians, Australians and Alsatians jostle together encouraging adventure. Even-handed selection allows excellent Italians alongside Californians. There is still a lack of half-bottles, but all praise to this otherwise robust and generous approach.

CELLARMAN'S CHOICE: California, Hawk Crest Chardonnay 1989, £13.95; Givry, en Choue 1987, Lespinasse, £17.95.

CHEF: Terry Rich PROPRIETORS: Charles and Carol Trevor-Roper OPEN: all week, D only MEALS: 7.30 to 9 PRICES: Set D £28 (£36) CARDS: Access, Visa SEATS: 24. Private parties: 16 main room. Car park, 15 places. No children under 10. No smoking in dining-room. Wheelchair access (also WC). No music ACCOMMODATION: 8 rooms, all with bath/shower. B&B £60 to £110. No children under 10. Garden. TV. Phone. Scenic. Doors close at midnight. Confirm by 6 (*Which? Hotel Guide*)

NORTHLEACH Gloucestershire map 2

Old Woolhouse

The Square, Northleach GL54 3EE COOKING 3
COTSWOLD (0451) 60366 COST £56

On a first visit, you may find the Old Woolhouse unsettling. There are only four tables, single diners are discouraged, bookings in general are often difficult to obtain and prices are not for those seeking a budget meal. The Astics have pursued their course with persistence. The repertoire hardly changes and is presented as a brief set-price menu. There is a choice of two first courses, one always fish, then meat accompanied invariably by gratin dauphinoise, followed by salad (never vegetables), then a St Marcellin cheese, then dessert. Classic saucing and traditional French flavours define the style: bream with Noilly Prat, veal kidney with mustard, and pork with armagnac. 'How can one go on turning out the same very limited repertoire year after year after year?' enquired one reader who found the sparkle missing after encountering old-fashioned overcooking of meat, a less than freshly made hot foie gras mousse, and mushrooms offered in three of five dishes that comprised the first and main courses of the menu. But there is still an enthusiastic following for this most French of restaurants with its personal, courteous service. The wine list is as individual as the restaurant, with most bottles over £25. No house wine, as such, but there is a bottle available for consumption by the glass, at a price.

CHEF: Jacques Astic PROPRIETORS: Jacques and Jenny Astic OPEN: Tue to Sat, D only (L and Sun and Mon D, by arrangement) CLOSED: Christmas MEALS: from 8.15 PRICES: Set D £35 (£47) SEATS: 18. Children welcome

Wickens

Market Place, Northleach GL54 3EJ COOKING 3
COTSWOLD (0451) 60421 COST £27–£36

Cotswold stone is firmly in evidence in this most English of restaurants. However, much of the front is modestly clothed in creeper, and the garden walls at the back are protected from the elements by the roof of the conservatory. Rough elements tamed well might be the theme of Christopher Wickens' cooking, not because he prettifies and fancies, but for the way he produces eloquent English farmhouse and bourgeois cooking. It is not revivalist, nor wholly chauvinist. Not everything served here has to be from a pre-war cookery book. Aubergines imam bayeldi sits happily next to braised hare and rabbit in Cumberland sauce. Nor is the cooking fancy, as may be judged from someone's less than kind comments that meals are 'school dinners'. The vast majority disagree and point instead to intelligent, fresh and inventive cooking that mobilises flavours and textures. A winter meal began with a rough terrine of pork served with elderberry and mustard vinaigrette, continued to a rabbit casserole with port, lots of onions and carrots – the gravy thick and savoury – and a lamb steak with a pear chutney sauce, the meat buoyed up by the faint acidity of the sauce. Vegetables, as often here, were good: garlic potatoes, carrots and orange, cauliflower and broccoli. Cheese includes a few British farmhouse examples, never too many and invariably in good fettle, with 'exceptional biscuits'. Joanna Wickens, otherwise being the mainstay of front-of-house, wields the spoon for desserts, which might more properly be described as puddings. Sticky toffee is 'light and substantially sticky', apple charlotte with lemon cream well-executed and lifted by the tang in the cream. The dinner menus follow a fixed-price format, with crudités, cheese and coffee built in, and the Wickens are now also opening for lunch, with cheaper dishes, even superior open sandwiches. This place is a social service. The wine list will always be explained by Christopher Wickens, a man who has thought out his whys and wherefores. Mainly from the English-speaking world, though no longer exclusively, the list has helpful notes and charitable prices. Most will drink the cheaper bottles, all well-chosen, but the 'French country' are higher class than the phrase implies, and there are some noble clarets and burgundies.

CHEFS/PROPRIETORS: Christopher and Joanna Wickens OPEN: Tue to Sat MEALS: 12.15 to 1.45, 7.20 to 9 PRICES: Set D £19.75 (£27) to £22 (£30) CARDS: Access, Amex, Visa SEATS: 36. Private parties: 22 main room. Children welcome. No smoking. Music

NORTHWICH Cheshire map 5

▲ *Nunsmere Hall* **NEW ENTRY**

Tarporley Road, Sandiway,
nr Northwich CW8 2ES
NORTHWICH (0606) 889100 COOKING 2*
off A49, 4m SW of Northwich COST £21–£66

It would be difficult to fault the setting: a red-stone house (not itself particularly beautiful, but redeemed by redecoration) built at the turn of the century on a wooded promontory that juts into a large lake. As the leaves turn in autumn, the first thought is of North America, not Cheshire. The McHardys are doing it thoroughly, and work in person – not surprising, perhaps, given Malcolm McHardy's background in hotels like the Mandarin Oriental. The chef is Paul Kitching, who trained with Ian McAndrew in Canterbury, then with Shaun Hill at Gidleigh Park (see entry). The restaurant is emphatically full-dress: a long *carte*, a tasting menu, a good yet cheaper lunch menu and materials reputedly shipped in from France and elsewhere (daily fish from Brixham). Reception of this new star has been fervent, though mostly reserved for the lunch offering, which is substantially less expensive than dinner. A more cynical visitor thought the menu writer should perhaps do some of the cooking; in other words the four-line descriptions excite the brain more than the food always stimulates the palate. Not that praise has been lacking for dishes such as 'ravioli of leek, ginger and apricot, bound with a mousseline of chicken, served with turned cucumber, topped with a deep-fried julienne of leek'; turbot with oysters on a 'deep concentration of tomato and tarragon'; lobster with lobster and mussel sauce; Bresse pigeon with wild mushrooms and potato purée, where the bird had taste even if too much texture; the lightest of hazelnut soufflés with an intense coffee ice-cream; and a tart of autumn berries with a champagne sabayon. Confusion, or lack of taste priorities, is one criticism, as in a duck confit with a raspberry sauce and a white truffle dressing, and a pork dish where the meat was nondescript against the prunes and sage sauce it came with. Vegetables come built into each main course, some ingrates think they are only 'garnish, not real vegetables at all'. Desserts and petits fours (the canapés are good too) are often approved, though even chocaholics have been defeated here by an excess of the magic bean. Coffee may be weak. The expectation should be a strengthening of the performance, so long as it is not overtaken by expansion (new rooms are being built) and extravagance – it is already expensive enough. Wine selection is inconsistent but prices are not; expect to pay a lot with Sancerre at £25 and virtually nothing below £15. Over-reliance on a few big names displays a lack of ambition. House wine is £9.50.

CHEF: Paul Kitching PROPRIETORS: Malcolm and Julie McHardy OPEN: all week MEALS: 12 to 2, 7 to 9.30 (10.30 Sat) PRICES: Set L £14.25 (£21) to £18.95 (£26), Set D £32.50 (£41) to £45 (£55). Card slips closed CARDS: Access, Amex, Visa SEATS: 40. 6 tables outside. Private parties: 42 main room, 24, 30 and 42 private rooms. Car park, 80 places. Vegetarian meals. No children under 12, exc L Sat and Sun. Jacket and tie. No smoking in dining-room. Wheelchair access (3 steps; also WC). Music. Fax: (0606) 889055 ACCOMMODATION: 32 rooms, all with bath/shower. Rooms for disabled. Children welcome. B&B £90 to £110. Afternoon teas. Garden. TV. Phone. Scenic

NORWICH Norfolk map 6

Adlard's

79 Upper St Giles, Norwich NR2 1AB COOKING 4
NORWICH (0603) 633522 COST £21–£46

It makes for interesting speculation to wonder how our better provincial restaurants – Adlard's and Oakes (see entry, Stroud), for example – would fare in London. Would their quiet devotion to flavour, executed with relative lack of pretension and served in a 'family' environment, survive in the capital's hothouse? Would they be viewed as exceptional, as the refreshing oases of quality and determination that Norwich and Stroud understand them to be? Adlard's is a green restaurant outside and in; the site is quite deep and allows a step up in level at the back, towards the kitchen, which creates pools of privacy as well as spots where you can find the staff discussing their next evening's plans. The interior is detailed in one report: 'uncluttered white china, floor-length emerald table-cloths covered in crisp white top cloths, emerald velvet walls, stark white paintwork, polished floor, and lovely fresh paintings on the walls, for once not for sale.' Mary Adlard is a fine hostess, and David Adlard may appear as plate-carrier, or for a chat at the end of service. Most people are struck by the simple depth of the sauces and the quality of the meats, which get more constant mention than fish. 'The duck with its own sausage had a sauce that tasted of duck; the sausage tasted of duck, the duck tasted of duck. It was not undercooked and therefore had more flavour, yet still maintained moistness and tenderness' was one report. Venison is an especial success. Another trait is the discreet quantities of food. In general, the judgement is correct, but there are accusations of parsimony, mostly over vegetables. The economy allows effect to be concentrated: thus, a small tartlet of ratatouille with lamb was thought by one diner to be 'so small that it would contribute nothing, but each forkful was fresh and strongly flavoured'. Intensity is an almost over-used point of reference: wild mushrooms in a mushroom reduction with tagliatelle was 'intense but not clogging'; fricassee of seafood with a lobster fumet was 'of great intensity with mussels, salmon and turbot'; intense, too, are the dauphinois potatoes that come with many main dishes, though some readers have remarked on first-rate puréed potatoes. Desserts, for instance apple tart with calvados and raisin ice-cream, or summer pudding bursting with tart berries so flavourful they overwhelmed the accompanying syllabub, are usually accorded equal praise. One quibble: coffee is adjudged weak on some nights. Nevertheless, Adlard's is a really good, steady centre of excellence – lucky Norwich. Go on Tuesday if you like bell-ringing (in the Catholic Cathedral) with your dinner. 'Bin Beginnings' set the tone for an intelligent wine list sensibly ranging in price. Every bottle is chosen with immense care. There is a generous provision of half-bottles. Spain and Italy receive fine treatment and vintages are good throughout. A bottle is awarded this year for continued concern for the customer's pocket without any diminution of quality. House French is £8. CELLARMAN'S CHOICE: Chauvigné Blanc 1988, Dom. Richou £13; Côtes du Rhône 1986, Guigal, £14.

CHEF: David Adlard PROPRIETORS: David and Mary Adlard OPEN: Tue to Sat, exc Sat L MEALS: 12.30 to 1.45, 7.30 to 9 PRICES: Set L £15 (£21) to £17 (£23), Set D £26.50 (£36) to £28 (£38). Card slips closed CARDS: Access, Visa SEATS: 40. Private parties: 40 main room. Children's helpings. Wheelchair access (also WC). No music

Brasted's

8–10 St Andrews Hill, Norwich NR2 1AD COOKING 1*
NORWICH (0603) 625949 COST £17–£42

One or two reports have gone overboard for the ambience: a tented dining-room, sofas and reading matter in the small bar, a definite sense of intimacy rarely broken by upsets of service from the basement kitchen. There is some emphasis on fish, though not to the exclusion of meats: an autumn meal which began with a mushroom and shallot crumble or gratin with a tarragon butter sauce was able to divide between lamb with honey and rosemary (handled wisely) and a plain but accurately grilled Dover sole. This is simple stuff, perhaps, but enlivened by mashed potatoes spiked with smoked salmon. Fish does command the advance troops of the first courses: scampi soup, fresh langoustines mayonnaise, salmon and spinach terrine and sweet-cured herring are the offerings of one day. The style of cooking is not elaborate, but shows sufficient care to satisfy, even if simplicity is equated with boredom by one who expected wild conceits to match the decoration. The wine list, which has at times been bolstered by an interesting miscellany of bin-ends ('We had a '69

Pommard but, alas, he had only one more bottle of it'), offers a useful range from France to New Zealand with a mixture of sources from English bottlings of old burgundy (Berry Bros) to the most fashionable such as Parent's Monthélie. House French is £8.25.

CHEF: Paul Chipperfield PROPRIETOR: John Brasted OPEN: Mon to Sat, exc Sat L MEALS: 12 to 2, 7 to 10 PRICES: £26 (£35), Set L £9.50 (£17) to £16.50 (£24) CARDS: Access, Amex, Diners, Visa SEATS: 22. Private parties: 14 main room. Vegetarian meals. Children welcome. Music. Fax: (0603) 766445

Greens Seafood

NEW ENTRY

82 Upper St Giles Street, Norwich NR3 1AQ
NORWICH (0603) 623733

COOKING 1
COST £23–£40

Dennis Crompton's modest seafood restaurant, in a quiet cul-de-sac not far from the city centre, has been a fixture of the Norwich scene since 1983 and readers have put forward a good case for its return to the listings. An inspection meal confirmed that this is a creditable venue and that the fish is of decent quality. Best bets on the short menu are dishes of the day, which depend on the catch: steamed sea bass wrapped in lettuce with vermouth sauce, and fillet of halibut coated with breadcrumbs and crab have been excellent. Other recommendations have included warm salad of assorted fish, Mediterranean prawns with a spicy Tabasco-laced dip, and 'splendid' grilled sole with garlic butter. Meat-eaters are offered fillet steak. Presentation is nouvelle, but portions are not. Sweets can be disappointing. The wine list has a good selection of reasonably priced whites to suit the food. House Muscadet is £9.20.

CHEF/PROPRIETOR: Dennis Crompton OPEN: Tue to Sat, exc Sat L CLOSED: 1 week Christmas, bank hols MEALS: 12.15 to 2, 7.15 to 10.45 PRICES: £25 (£33), Set L £16 (£23), Set D £25 (£33). Card slips closed CARDS: Access, Visa SEATS: 48. Private parties: 30 main room. Vegetarian meals. No cigars/pipes in dining-room. Music. Air-conditioned

Marco's

17 Pottergate, Norwich NR2 1DS
NORWICH (0603) 624044

COOKING 1
COST £23–£40

Marco Vessalio presides over his long-established Norwich institution with an open cheerfulness backed up by some sound cooking that has won him many regulars. Indeed, one visiting restaurateur writes: 'It is easy enough to cook an expensive cut of meat well, using the bones etc. to extract the jus for the sauce. Marco does this well enough, I imagine, but he excelled himself at a dish of stuffed pig's trotter – really a large portion of the leg of the pig filled with a pleasantly spicy sausage meat and served with a green sauce of capers, anchovies, watercress, garlic and parsley.' Others have been impressed by the gnocchi, tagliolini with Roquefort sauce and the pot-roasted venison. The kitchen is not afraid to offer offal, stews or odd cuts of meat along with the more popular cannelloni and chicken cacciatora. The home-made ice-creams – always a vanilla and a daily sorbet – elicit great praise. An all-Italian wine list includes house wine at £8.

CHEF/PROPRIETOR: Marco Vessalio OPEN: Tue to Sat CLOSED: 20 Aug to 20 Sept MEALS: 12.30 to 2, 7.30 to 10 PRICES: £23 (£33), Set L £17 (£23). Card slips closed CARDS: Access, Amex, Carte Blanche, Diners, Visa SEATS: 20. Private parties: 12 main room, 16 private room. Vegetarian meals. Children's helpings. Wheelchair access. Music

NOTTINGHAM Nottinghamshire map 5

Les Artistes Gourmands/ Café des Artistes 🍷

61 Wollaton Road, Beeston,
Nottingham NG9 2NG
NOTTINGHAM (0602) 228288

COOKING 2
COST £19–£31

Seven years after opening his restaurant on the outskirts of Nottingham, Eddy Keon continues to search for local producers and growers. Improvements in the city's wholesale market have ensured better supplies of fish, and brought fresh pasta produced by an Italian in nearby Long Eaton, and free-range geese from a farm near Grantham. Now the hunt is on for reliable sources of naturally reared meat. Organic vegetables and herbs are grown in the restaurant's own kitchen garden. All of this translates into a short menu of classic French cooking with inventive touches – as in a mille-feuille of chicken livers with a sauce made from Suze, a gentian liqueur from Jura. Chef Mark Ashmore has produced some impressive dishes: roulade of chicken and mushrooms with chive sauce; rack of lamb with garlic and tarragon sauce; salmon with orange sauce. Roast mallard is served with green lentils, smoked bacon and wild mushrooms. Presentation is nouvelle, but portions are not. To finish there are hand-crafted desserts and home-made ice-creams. Café des Artistes is run from the same kitchen, but offers cheaper dishes in bistro surroundings (including quiet French music) at the front of the restaurant. Children are encouraged: under-16s are offered their meals at £2 per foot of their height.

CHEF: Mark Ashmore PROPRIETOR: Eddy Keon OPEN: Mon to Sat CLOSED: 1 week Jan MEALS: 12 to 2, 7 to 10.30 PRICES: restaurant £19 (£26), Set L £15.90 (£21), Set D £19.90 (£26); café £13 (£19). Card slips closed CARDS: Access, Amex, Diners, Visa SEATS: 60. Private parties: 35 main room. Vegetarian meals. Healthy eating options. Children's helpings. No smoking. Wheelchair access. No music in restaurant

Loch Fyne Oyster Bar

17 King Street, Nottingham NG1 2AY
NOTTINGHAM (0602) 508481

COOKING 1
COST £23

Oysters in land-locked Nottingham sounds unlikely, yet this modest offshoot of the Loch Fyne Oyster Bar in Cairndow in Scotland (see entry) offers the real thing in an informal setting not far from the city centre. The full menu is available through the day, and the style is flexible: call in for a three-course meal, a snack or a cup of tea with home-made fruit loaf. Seafood is the main business and most items are air-freighted overnight from the parent company in Scotland. Loch Fyne oysters and queen scallops have been excellent, though one reporter found the mussels and langoustines rather tasteless. There are bowls of home-made soup, mixed seafood platters, salads of smoked fish and smoked chicken, plus a few hot dishes such as fried herrings with mustard sauce, baked trout and Arbroath smokies. This is an admirable enterprise, but there is a feeling that it could do better. A short, well-chosen wine list (including an organic Muscadet) suits the food. House French is £5.95. Much of the produce can be purchased from the shop counter.

CHEF: Judith Robb PROPRIETORS: Loch Fyne Oysters Ltd OPEN: Mon to Sat CLOSED: 25 Dec, bank hol Mons MEALS: 9am to 8.30pm PRICES: £14 (£19). Card slips closed CARDS: Access, Visa SEATS: 45. Private parties: 40 main room. Children's helpings. Wheelchair access. Music. Air-conditioned

Ocean City

100–104 Derby Road,
Nottingham NG1 5FB
NOTTINGHAM (0602) 475095

COOKING 1*
COST £10–£35

The popular view is that this sprawling restaurant still leads the field against increasingly strong competition in Nottingham's blossoming Chinese scene. The standard menu of around 150 items deals in Cantonese classics as well as fashionable ideas: sizzling dishes (including monkfish and oysters), specialities presented in hollowed-out fresh pineapples as well as edible birds' nests and a healthy showing of seafood. Sliced duck with plum sauce, deep-fried crispy squid, spicy minced beef with bean curd, and aubergines in black-bean sauce are typical dishes. In addition there is usually a list of more esoteric items, such as stewed belly pork with yams. At lunchtime, the choice of dim-sum and one-plate meals is a better bet than the westernised set menu. The kitchen generally maintains its high standards, although a recent report about 'cold' wun-tun soup, 'chewy' beef with ginger and spring onion and 'appalling service' suggest that the place may be losing some of its original sharpness. A well-spread list of around 40 wines includes a few curiosities such as lychee wine from Taiwan. House French is £6.50.

CHEF: Mr Ly PROPRIETORS: Dragon Wonder Ltd OPEN: all week CLOSED: 25 Dec MEALS: 12 to 3, 6 to 11.30 (noon to midnight Sat, noon to 10.30 Sun) PRICES: £13 (£24), Set L £5 (£10) to £11 (£17), Set D £11 (£17) to £22 (£29). Minimum £10 after 6pm CARDS: Access, Amex, Diners, Visa SEATS: 250. Private parties: 200 main room, 80 and 120 private rooms. Vegetarian meals. Children welcome. Wheelchair access (also WC). Music. Air-conditioned

Saagar

473 Mansfield Road, Sherwood,
Nottingham NG5 2DR
NOTTINGHAM (0602) 622014

COOKING 1
COST £10–£28

The second dining-room is still a prospect rather than actuality, but Saagar is popular enough to deserve more space and the service gracious enough to merit its popularity. Suburbs, and a video store, may be on the threshold but within Saagar the style is Regency and the cooking north Indian. Lamb from the tandoor, chicken pasanda and chicken tikka masala are among dishes singled out this year, but comments in favour of many others, and on the quality of ancillaries such as baking, are annual constants. House wine is £7 a litre.

CHEF: Amjaid Habib PROPRIETOR: Mohammed Khizer OPEN: all week CLOSED: 25 Dec MEALS: 12 to 2.30, 5.30 to 12.30am PRICES: £13 (£23), Set L £5 (£10), Set D £10 (£16) to £15 (£21). CARDS: Access, Amex, Visa SEATS: 45. Private parties: 45 main room. Car park, 6 places. Vegetarian meals. Children's helpings. No pipes in dining-room. Music. Air-conditioned

Sonny's

NEW ENTRY

3 Carlton Street, Hockley,
Nottingham NG1 1NL
NOTTINGHAM (0602) 473041

COOKING 1*
COST £13–£28

The most promising new venue in Nottingham is in a converted hamburger joint on the fringes of the Lace Market development. Vernon Mascarenhas worked at the original Sonny's in Barnes (see London entry) before taking over the Midlands off-shoot. The restaurant is white, inside and out, with white paintwork, white curtains and spherical white lampshades contrasting with bare black floorboards. The menu, in keeping with the décor, is an eclectic mix of up-to-the-minute café/brasserie ideas dominated by the chargrill. It is a world tour, taking in beancakes with crème fraîche, merguez sausages with potato and apple purée, deep-fried mozzarella with tomato and basil sauce, and entrecôte with roast red pepper butter. Pasta and fish dishes change daily and there are warm salads and jazzy risottos for vegetarians. Fish soup and sticky toffee pudding are best sellers. The kitchen has its limitations and there are occasional rough edges to the cooking, but this is exactly the kind of restaurant for a city in confident mood. Set lunches are good value. Service is laid-back and friendly. A modest global wine list offers decent drinking at affordable prices. House French is £6.95.

CHEF: Iain Broadbent PROPRIETORS: Mr V. Mascarenhas and Miss R. Mascarenhas OPEN: Mon to Sat CLOSED: 25 Dec, bank hols MEALS: 12 to 2.30 (3 Sat), 7 to 11 PRICES: £15 (£23), Set L £8.50 (£13), Set D £11 (£16). Service 10% for parties of 6 or more CARDS: Access, Visa SEATS: 70. Private parties: 70 main room. Vegetarian meals. Children's helpings. Wheelchair access. Music

OAKHILL Somerset map 2

▲ *Oakhill House*

NEW ENTRY

Bath Road, Oakhill BA3 5AQ
OAKHILL (0749) 840180

COOKING 2
COST £26

Launching themselves on to the sea of professional catering for the first time, the Coopers have taken this attractive country house – large gardens insulating it from traffic noise – and are in the process of redecorating it piecemeal to make a 'residential restaurant'. Floppy hats and a bowl of polished apples greet you surrealistically in the hall, the bar remains gloomy despite its log fire, but the dining-room – warm pinks and greys and rose-splashed fabrics – has a feel of what will come in its open-minded Englishness. Paul Cooper's forthright service is in tune with Marion Cooper's energetic modern cooking. Tastes are not minced, and Mediterranean and Middle Eastern influences abound in citrus marinades, subtle spicing, olives, goats' cheese, relishes and salsas. In the early months – they opened in spring 1991 – while supply sources were being encouraged and settled, quantities were not minced either. A daily menu, with three or four choices, might include merguez sausages brought home from France, fresh asparagus with fresh Parmesan, home-made pork and chicken sausages with green peppercorns and apple, fresh pasta with wild mushrooms, home-made honey ice-cream and poached pears, or a small choice of decent local and French cheeses. There have been signs of settling in: cool food because the timing had slipped, vegetables not suited to each main dish, but the jolt of turning from private to commercial cooking can be great. The wine list shows good beginnings with catholic choice from all over the world, easy prices, and lots of wines by the glass to compensate for lack of half-bottles. The notes will help everybody. House wine is £6.95.

CHEF: Marion Cooper PROPRIETORS: Paul and Marion Cooper OPEN: Tue to Sat, D only (L by arrangement) CLOSED: Jan MEALS: 7.30 to 9.30 PRICES: Set D £17.50 (£22). Net prices, card slips closed CARDS: Access, Visa SEATS: 20. 4 tables outside. Private parties: 50 main room, 20 and 50 private rooms. Car park, 30 places. Vegetarian meals. Children's helpings. No smoking in dining-room. Wheelchair access. No music. Fax: (0749) 840180 ACCOMMODATION: 5 rooms, all with bath/shower. B&B £40 to £90. Deposit: £20. Children welcome. Baby facilities. Garden. TV. Scenic

OLD BURGHCLERE Hampshire map 2

Dew Pond

Old Burghclere RG15 9LH
BURGHCLERE (063 527) 408 COOKING 3*
off A34, 3m W of Kingsclere COST £22–£38

'With the road almost closed by winter's first snowfall, the welcome was warm from attentive staff,' wrote one reporter. Spring and summer open up the landscape surrounding this small country house: Watership Down one way, Beacon Hill another, sheep everywhere. It's worth a trip for that alone, and for the Marshall family's most successful combination of hospitality and good cooking: everything done in-house, 'presentation an art form', cooking highly skilled, using classic techniques and combinations. 'The meats or fish, of high quality, are matched with an impeccable saucing technique giving a meal of utter consistency with clear, clean and direct tastes.' The fixed-price menu changes as time passes – not often enough for one regular visitor – and gives an adequate range of choice at a very fair price for the standard of execution. A first course of home-smoked salmon wrapping a light prawn mousse, on a salad of avocado and tomato with chives and red pepper, a breast of chicken with herbs and sherry sauce, venison (the game is good here) on savoy cabbage with shallots and a port sauce, and hazelnut and strawberry roulade are but a few of the dishes mentioned with enthusiasm. Dew Pond is a serious place. The shortish wine list takes in more than just France, though it could be developed in range and depth – or just variety of sources – to match the food's assurance. House Duboeuf is £8.

CHEF: Keith Marshall PROPRIETORS: Keith and Julie Marshall OPEN: Tue to Sat, exc Sat L CLOSED: 2 weeks mid-Aug, first 2 weeks Jan MEALS: 12 to 2, 7 to 10 PRICES: Set L £16 (£22) to £16.50 (£23), Set D £21 (£28) to £25 (£32) CARDS: Access, Visa SEATS: 40. Private parties: 50 main room, 25 private room. Car park, 25 places. Vegetarian meals. No children under 12. Smart dress preferred. Wheelchair access (also WC). No music

---

OLDBURY West Midlands map 5

▲ *Jonathans*

16–20 Wolverhampton Road,
Oldbury B68 0LH — COOKING 1
021-429 3757 — COST £31–£48

A living museum that is as ferociously twee in some of its habits as we have come to expect of British tourism: prices are expressed in old money, save that two shillings and sixpence actually means £2.60. (This reminded one person of a restaurant in south Devon, more French than the French, which priced everything in francs, except that 10 francs was really £10. Even the bill said it in francs.) Some people think Jonathans looks like a 'Birmingham roadhouse' but most rather like its generous pastiche. As for the food, bits of it may lack subtlety, most is far too complicated, but the basic cooking of the meats and fish is fair. Ignore the flim-flam on the menu, and enjoy the setting. Much is made of British cooking, and a lot is also made of sweet/sour combinations. Puddings are hearty and creamy and enjoyable. Wine prices are not too high and the list ranges widely. House wines are £6.90.

CHEFS: Jonathan Bedford and Graham Bradley PROPRIETORS: Jonathan Bedford and Jonathan Baker OPEN: all week MEALS: 12 to 2 (4 Sun), 7 to 10.30 PRICES: £30 (£40), Set D £24.90 (£31) CARDS: Access, Amex, Visa SEATS: 160. 10 tables outside. Private parties: 60 main room, 10, 18 30 and 120 private rooms. Car park, 10 places. Vegetarian meals. Children's helpings (Sun L). Children restricted. Smoking after meal only. Wheelchair access (also WC). Music. Fax: 021-434 3107 ACCOMMODATION: 26 rooms, all with bath/shower. Rooms for disabled. B&B £96 to £137. Deposit: 10%. Afternoon teas. TV. Phone. Confirm by 4

ORFORD Suffolk map 3

Butley-Orford Oysterage

Market Hill, Orford IP12 2LH — COOKING 1
ORFORD (0394) 450 277 — COST £24

The oysterage is in the middle of the village square. It is a simple, down-to-earth café-cum-restaurant on two floors, with the smokery at the back and a shop next door for home supplies. The Pinneys, mother and son, continue to ensure that their smoked salmon, mackerel, eel, trout and cod's roe together with oysters, crabs, lobsters and fresh fish are in as prime a condition as close proximity to smokehouse and sea allows. 'Keep it simple' is the secret of ordering here. Stick to the oysters, smoked fish and crabs and lobster, as anything with a sauce tends to be a let-down ('mussels, good, but juice while winey enough had been thickened with flour'), and salads can be disappointing. Service is homely and local, the wine list is short, well-judged and inexpensive, with plenty of halves.

CHEF: Joyce Knight PROPRIETORS: Mathilde Pinney and William Pinney OPEN: all week May to Oct; L all week and Fri and Sat D Nov to Apr MEALS: 12 to 2.15, 6 to 8.30 PRICES: £14 (£20) SEATS: 82. Private parties: 25 main room. Car park, 20 places. Children welcome. Wheelchair access (also WC)

OXFORD Oxfordshire map 2

Al-Shami

25 Walton Crescent, Oxford OX1 2JG COOKING 1
OXFORD (0865) 310066 COST £23

'The fact that it stays open till midnight makes it a welcome alternative to Indian and Chinese after the theatre,' comments one reporter about this friendly Lebanese restaurant. Other pluses are the value for money and the very obliging, relaxed service. The menu is dominated by three dozen hot and cold hors d'oeuvre, ranging from tabouleh and lamb's brain salad to falafels and arayes (minced meat with parsley grilled on Lebanese bread). Reporters have enjoyed ful medames and sujuq (spicy Armenian sausages). Main courses centre on chargrilled minced meat, lamb and chicken. Al Shami Kafta djaj is chicken marinated in 'home-made tomato purée, garlic paste, oil, cumin and herbs', according to the kitchen. Piles of uncut raw vegetables are left on the table to nibble while choosing, and there are sticky sweets from the trolley. The short wine list is mainly Lebanese, with Ch. Musar and araks much in evidence. House French is £6.50.

CHEF/PROPRIETOR: Mimo Mahfouz OPEN: all week MEALS: noon to midnight PRICES: £11 (£19). Cover £1. Service 10% for 6 or more SEATS: 40. Private parties: 60 main room. Vegetarian meals. Children welcome. Wheelchair access (also WC). Music. Fax: (0865) 311241

▲ *Bath Place Hotel*

COUNTY OF THE YEAR RESTAURANT

4–5 Bath Place, Oxford OX1 3SU COOKING 3
OXFORD (0865) 791812 COST £20–£38

Reservations of some sort have to be expressed about most restaurants in Oxford, but Bath Place appears to be the most consistent and satisfactory place to eat centrally. Tucked down a little pedestrian court off Holywell (parking, therefore, is a problem), it is a gathering of converted cottages: small rooms and low ceilings manage elegance and prettiness. Table settings are good too, all contributing to something that can, without patronage, be called 'charming'. Graham Corbett cooks a set-price meal with three or more choices in each course. Lunch remains good value and has not increased in price; dinner has reduced in cost. Presentation is nouvelle cuisine, as may be the quantities – though not for one happy eater, who wrote of 'sufficiency without bloat'. But the combinations of flavours have none of the waywardness we came to associate with the movement. Dishes such as chicken dariole wrapped in leeks, with oyster mushrooms and a Noilly Prat sauce, scallops with a salad and raspberry vinaigrette, fresh tagliatelle with bacon and mushrooms, cod with a salmon mousse and mustard sauce, and veal kidney with a port jus all show refinement and accuracy. Vegetables come on a side-plate. Desserts do justice to expectations: a tulip filled with chocolate pavé, or iced prune and armagnac soufflé with caramel sauce are par for the course. Very fair cheeses of half a dozen sorts, decent bread and strong coffee round out meals well. The wine list is mainly French, not overlong, but serviceable. House wine is from £9.50.

CHEF: Graham Corbett PROPRIETORS: the Fawsitt family OPEN: Tue to Sun, exc Sun D MEALS: 12 to 2, 7 to 10.15 PRICES: £22 (£32), Set L £12.95 (£20), Set D £21.95 (£29) CARDS: Access, Amex, Carte Blanche, Visa SEATS: 34. 4 tables outside. Private parties: 20 main room, 10 private room. Car park, 6 places. Vegetarian meals. No children under 10. Smart dress preferred. No cigars/pipes in dining-room. Music. Air-conditioned ACCOMMODATION: 10 rooms, all with bath/shower. B&B £70 to £100. Deposit: £25. No children under 10. TV. Phone. Scenic. Doors close at 10. Confirm by 10.30am (*Which? Hotel Guide*)

Cherwell Boathouse 🍷

Bardwell Road, Oxford OX2 6SR — COOKING 1
OXFORD (0865) 52746 — COST £23

The punts quant up and down or moor for a simple dinner, inside or out, in archetypical Oxford surroundings. Gerard Crowley's short weekly menus, at prices even state grants might afford, do not attempt haute cuisine, but they present fair ingredients more than adequately, taking in plenty of influences – Greek, British, French and Italian. A turnip soup, guinea-fowl with watercress sauce, fresh vegetables and port wine jelly might be one spring choice; asparagus with chive butter, cod plaki and sticky toffee pudding might be another. The glory lies in the wine list: 100 intelligently and enthusiastically selected wines which recognise no boundaries and display a fairness in price encouraging reciprocal adventure from the customer. Would that more wine bars could take to offering the likes of Menetou-Salon at £10 alongside Leflaive Chevalier Montrachet at £45 and Beaucastel 1981 for £16.50. House wine is £6. CELLARMAN'S CHOICE: Riesling, Muenchberg 1987, Ostertag, £12.50; Au Bon Climat, Pinot Noir 1987, £16.

CHEF: Gerard Crowley PROPRIETOR: Anthony Verdin OPEN: Tue to Sun, exc Sun D CLOSED: 4 days Christmas, L Oct to May MEALS: 12 to 2, 6.30 to 9.15 PRICES: Set L and D £14.50 (£19). Service 10% for parties of 6 or more. Card slips closed CARDS: Access, Amex, Diners, Visa SEATS: 50. 5 tables outside. Private parties: 50 main room. Car park, 12 places. Vegetarian meals. Children's helpings. Wheelchair access (1 step; also WC). No music

Healthy eating options *in the details at the end of an entry signifies that a restaurant marks on its menu, in words and/or using symbols, low-fat dishes or other healthy eating choices.*

15 North Parade

15 North Parade, Oxford OX2 6LX — COOKING 1
OXFORD (0865) 513773 — COST £18–£36

The restaurant now offers a 'Recession Special': any starter plus sweet and coffee for £10 maximum. There is also a pre- and post-theatre three-course menu and a flexible *carte* divided up into types – salads, chargrills, vegetarian and so on. Chef Stanley Matthews looks to California and the Mediterranean for inspiration, as well as re-vamping traditional British favourites. Chilli-marinated turkey with pineapple salsa and spinach gnocchi with blue cheese sauce appear alongside salmon fishcakes with parsley sauce and sticky toffee pudding. Soups are reliably good and readers have praised the spinach with feta cheese parcels, pot-roast pheasant and brill with herb butter sauce. Orange liqueur pancakes and chocolate mousse have been excellent finales. Some reporters have found dishes bland, 'bleak' and 'indifferent' but few dispute the quality of the short global wine list. House French is £8.

CHEF: Stanley Matthews PROPRIETOR: Georgina Wood OPEN: all week, exc Sun D MEALS: 12 to 2, 6.30 to 10.30 (theatre menu 6.30 to 7.15 and 9.30 to 10.30) PRICES: £22 (£30), Set Sun L £15.75 (£23), theatre menu £11.75 (£18). Card slips closed CARDS: Access, Visa SEATS: 55. Private parties: 55 main room. Vegetarian meals. Children's helpings. Wheelchair access (1 step; also WC). Music. Air-conditioned

Liaison

29 Castle Street, Oxford OX1 1LJ — COOKING 1
OXFORD (0865) 242944 — COST £19–£35

This is a multi-regional Chinese restaurant, cooking Malaysian satay as well as Szechuan chicken. Predictably, it is the more highly spiced dishes that get the votes, though some readers have observed too light a touch on seasonings when they should promise fire within. Not all, though: prawns stir-fried with garlic and chilli and sizzling scallops with green pepper, black bean and chilli were both well-executed, as was hoinam chicken ('sweet-and-sour chicken for grown-ups'), even if it suffered from being served tepid. From Sunday to Thursday, dim-sum are now served at lunchtime. Home-made brown bread ice-cream is an odd thing to find in a Chinese restaurant, but here it is. The service is attentive and not at all stand-offish. The wine list is adequate, with house wines at £6.50.

CHEF: Kok Leung Lam PROPRIETOR: Timmy Tsang OPEN: all week CLOSED: 3 days Christmas MEALS: 12 to 3 (4 Sun), 6.30 to 11.30 (12 Fri and Sat) PRICES: £13 (£19), Set D £14.25 (£21) to £22 (£29). Service 10% for parties of 5 or more CARDS: Access, Amex, Visa SEATS: 90. Private parties: 60 main room, 18 private room. Vegetarian meals. Children's helpings. Wheelchair access (2 steps). Music

The Guide *is totally independent, accepts no free hospitality, and survives on the proceeds from copies sold each year.*

Munchy Munchy

6 Park End Street, Oxford OX1 1HH — COOKING 1
OXFORD (0865) 245710 — COST £10–£19

Now established on the Oxford eating scene for 13 years, Munchy Munchy offers fewer surprises these days. A recent comment suggests it is increasingly a restaurant organised for the convenience of the chef and owners: there are no starters, a prohibition on the mixing of flavours from a range of ices for dessert and a peremptory 'one cheque only per bill'. Too speedy to be relaxing, it is at its best for a quick lunch or a pre-theatre/cinema meal. Ethel Ow's cooking of Indonesian and Malaysian food looks on paper an alluring mixture of fruit, spices and herbs, but on the plate it can be sweet and bland. Beef slices with coriander seeds and shrimp paste was more successful, deep and varied in flavour, but unfortunately not hot enough. A briskly served winter meal of chicken with turmeric, celery seeds, caraway and nutmeg and lamb with apple, cardamoms, mustard, fenugreek and paprika was better received. Arrive with your own wine.

CHEF: Ethel Ow PROPRIETORS: Tony and Ethel Ow OPEN: Tue to Sat CLOSED: 3 weeks Aug, 3 weeks Dec MEALS: 12 to 2, 5.30 to 10 PRICES: £9 (£16), Set L £8 (£10) to £12 (£14). Minimum £6. Service 10% for parties of 5 or more. Unlicensed, but bring your own: corkage 50p per person SEATS: 60. Private parties: 10 main room. No children under 6 Fri and Sat D. No-smoking area. Wheelchair access. No music

Restaurant Elizabeth

NEW ENTRY

84 St Aldate's, Oxford OX1 1RA — COOKING 2
OXFORD (0865) 242230 — COST £23–£38

The Elizabeth has been an Oxford institution since the '60s; it still keeps the feel of that era, both in decoration and culinary style – hence its popularity. Although the menu changes little, the daily specials afford the opportunity to step out a little. Game is Señor Lopez's favourite meat and good reports of simple fish dishes have been received as well as others for classics like quenelles in sauce Nantua. A gamey pumpkin soup, pheasant stuffed with crab and wrapped in pastry, plain roast game, game pie presented like a round Cornish pasty, and desserts like the famed crème brûlée and candied chestnuts in kirsch have all been liked. Apart from first-rate dauphinois, vegetables are not a strong point, nor is finesse in sauce-making, but the gravies pack a punch. The room, a strong green throughout, has a venerable feel and great outlook on to Christ Church meadow. The wine list is worthy of award, had a copy been submitted. Old clarets and Riojas are not priced exorbitantly, and are dealt with reverently.

CHEF: Salvador Rodriguez PROPRIETOR: Antonio Lopez OPEN: Tue to Sun CLOSED: 24 and 25 Dec MEALS: 12.30 to 2.30, 6.30 to 11 (7 to 10.30 Sun) PRICES: £25 (£32), Set L £14.95 (£23). Cover £1. Minimum £12. Net prices, card slips closed CARDS: Access, Amex, Diners, Visa SEATS: 40. Private parties: 40 main room, 20 private room. Vegetarian meals. Children welcome. No music

PADSTOW Cornwall map 1

▲ *Seafood Restaurant* 🍷

Riverside, Padstow PL28 8BY COOKING 4
PADSTOW (0841) 532485 COST £32–£61

A place as busy, as famous and as daring as this is bound to receive conflicting reports over a year. Some relate to those especially busy weeks when, unhappily, the failure rate may be a smidgeon higher. Others relate to specifics, for example leaden pastry work. Tellingly, what should appear on Rick Stein's annual report? A note that he, too, had felt pastry needed a boost; hence the arrival of David Pope, late of Well House, St Keyne (see entry) to reinforce this section. End of complaints. Readers also stress the happy informality of the restaurant. As you drive into Padstow, you fall over it, facing the main car park but affording visions of the estuary beyond the tarmac. Bright with white paint, colourful posters and pictures, plants and (for once) proper lighting, the Seafood can be noisy; it certainly is never pretentious or stuffy. The food is fish, of the freshest, cooked more imaginatively than just that 'good old plain fish', once the standby of fish restaurants. The chargrill is often in evidence; so is wine in the cooking, and so are herbs and spices in profusion. Worthy candidates for a culinary pantheon are too many to list, but note hake with tomato and parsley, lobster with herb butter, fried whitebait and grilled fresh pilchard, scallops with pesto, lemon sole with ginger and scallions, mussels stuffed with tomato, courgette and celery, prawns with coriander and chilli, smoked duck with preserved ginger, and ravioli of lobster with spinach. It is the freshness, the variety and the intelligence informing the recipes that makes all these and many more special. Puddings have also had good mentions: crème brûlée ice-cream with toffee sauce, bread-and-butter pudding and raspberry vacherin on a blackcurrant coulis are just three. Tarts will improve following the moves on pastry. Though prime fish may be dear here, the short set-price menu is excellent value for this standard of cooking. The rooms are always enjoyed, as are the breakfasts and the pasties from Stein's shop round the corner. A 'Short Wine List' provides many decent choices below £17. An emphasis on white wines is reflected in the main list of 200-plus bottles; greater enthusiasm for Australasia, California and Alsace could be afforded at the expense of white Bordeaux and the proliferation of more exalted burgundies. An intelligent firm hand is needed if the list is not to become a rag-bag of leftovers with little structure. Prices are fair, and the mark-up method is wise. House wine is £8.90. CELLARMAN'S CHOICE: Pouilly Fumé, Ch. de Tracy 1989, £17.50; Fleurie, La Madone 1988, M. Dudet, £15.85.

CHEF: Richard Stein PROPRIETORS: Richard and Jill Stein OPEN: Mon to Sat, D only MEALS: 7.30 to 9.30 (10 Sat) PRICES: £41 (£51), Set D £25 (£32) CARDS: Access, Visa SEATS: 75. Private parties: 24 main room. Children's helpings. Air-conditioned. No music. Fax: (0841) 533344 ACCOMMODATION: 10 rooms, all with bath/shower. B&B £29 to £97. Children welcome. Baby facilities. Pets welcome. Air-conditioned. TV. Phone. Scenic (*Which? Hotel Guide*)

PETWORTH West Sussex map 3

Soanes

Grove Lane, Petworth GU28 0HY
PETWORTH (0798) 43659
SE of Petworth. Take A285 S, signed Chichester; after 1m left to Pulborough road, then first left

COOKING 2
COST £20–£32

Carol and Derek Godsmark's restaurant is in an attractive converted farmhouse about half a mile outside the village. A modern conservatory makes 'a tactful addition' to the original building, while there is a restful feel to the dark blue/grey dining-room with its well-spaced tables and shelves of books. Carol Godsmark offers a choice of menus. The mainstay is a set-price two-course menu (with supplements for desserts and cheese). There is also a cheaper three-course menu on Wednesdays and Thursdays, and a popular Sunday lunch for families (with some novel price incentives for the young and old). Dishes are very attractively presented and the service, care and attention are excellent. However, the cooking may sometimes be uneven and rather studied: 'A little tossing of the chef's hat over the mill might contribute a little more flair,' comments an inspector. At its best the kitchen has delivered beautifully cooked Scotch salmon on puff pastry with velvety beurre blanc, roast rack of lamb with a full-flavoured tomato and tarragon sauce, chocolate Pithiviers with orange sauce, and apple tart with sultana and calvados cream. French cheeses are from Androuet. The sensibly priced 40-strong wine list has some fine burgundies and clarets. House Côtes du Rhône is £9. As the *Guide* went to press a brasserie-style lunch was planned for Tuesday to Friday.

CHEF: Carol Godsmark PROPRIETORS: Carol and Derek Godsmark OPEN: Wed to Sat D, L Tue to Fri and Sun MEALS: 12.30 to 2, 7.30 to 11 PRICES: Set L £17.50 (£22), Set D Wed and Thur £15 (£20), Set D Fri and Sat £21 (£27). Net prices, card slips closed CARDS: Access, Visa SEATS: 24. Private parties: 30 main room. Car park, 16 places. Children's helpings (Sun L only). Wheelchair access (2 steps). Music

PINNER Greater London map 3

La Giralda

66 Pinner Green, Pinner HA5 2AB
081-868 3429

COOKING 1
COST £11–£24

This long-established restaurant guarantees fair value and the most excellent Spanish wines from a long list too bulky to send to the *Guide*'s office. The food nods towards Spain in a revamped menu: gazpacho, pollo ajillo, entrecôte Santa Cruz and paella are examples. The set price allows free range over a long list of dishes and it gives consistent service to a large local following. The cooking may seem lacking in finesse, but materials are kept in good fettle simply by the scale of the business. The waiting staff are also long in service, and they cope admirably with bustle and queues. Do not expect elaborate ancillaries. House Rioja is £7.60.

CHEFS: David Brown and Derek Knight PROPRIETOR: David Brown OPEN: Tue to Sat MEALS: 12 to 2.30, 6.30 to 10.30 PRICES: Set L £5.50 (£11) to £9.50 (£16), Set D £13.50 (£20). Service 10%. Card slips closed CARDS: Access, Visa SEATS: 120. Private parties: 50 main room, 16 and 35 private rooms. Vegetarian meals. Children's helpings. Wheelchair access. No music. Air-conditioned. Fax: 081-868 1218

PITTON Wiltshire map 2

Silver Plough 🍷

NEW ENTRY

Pitton SP5 1DZ COOKING 1
FARLEY (072 272) 266 COST £16–£36

A village pub that has all the accoutrements – old beams, ancient furnishings, a pretty garden – plus better food and a better wine list than usual. Bar snacks, specials and the set-price dinner menu push back received ideas of pub cooking. The approach is up to date. Dishes range from simple cottage pie, to smoked sausage and black pudding with mustard, grilled field mushrooms with tapénade crostini, warm tart of Dorset Blue Vinney and Wiltshire ham, salmon on a bed of watercress and spinach, and a casserole of maize-fed chicken poached in its own broth with lentils and coriander. Execution varies. Fresh tuna steak and pigeon breasts have been over-cooked, steak has tasted bland, and a salad of avocado, feta and bacon has been crudely assembled. Poor attention to incidentals can irritate: stale, bought-in rolls and commercial wafers accompanying otherwise excellent home-made ice-cream. Perhaps the chef tries too hard, where a simplification of the menu (cutting down the number of dishes on offer) might help to tighten things up. There are interesting wines by the glass, otherwise the list of 100-odd bottles shows enthusiasm and intelligently astute selection. The many good bottles below £12 include Wynns Ovens Valley Shiraz; more extravagant such as Volnay Chevrets 1984 of Boillot at £27.75. All prices are fair. Half-bottles have good range. House wine is £8.50. CELLARMAN'S CHOICE: Savennières, Clos du Papillon 1988, Baumard, £12.15; Rioja 1986, Bodegas Ansabel, £9.95.

CHEF: J. Dockerty PROPRIETORS: Michael Beckett, P.K. Parnell and C.I. Manktelow OPEN: all week CLOSED: 25 Dec MEALS: 12 to 2, 7 to 10 (9.30 Sun and Mon) PRICES: £22 (£30), Set L from £9.50 (£16) to £12.95 (£20), Set D £16.45 (£24) to £19.45 (£28). Card slips closed CARDS: Access, Amex, Diners, Visa SEATS: 100. 14 tables outside. Private parties: 40 main room, 40 private room. Car park, 50 places. Vegetarian meals. Children's helpings L. Smart dress preferred. Music

PLUMTREE Nottinghamshire map 5

Perkins Bar Bistro

Old Railway Station, Plumtree NG12 5NA COOKING 2*
PLUMTREE (060 77) 3695 COST £25

Tony Perkins' conversion presents a solid, well-maintained front to both the railway station and conservatory addition. His food matches the care and attention he lavishes on the building: 'We set out to offer a wide variety of freshly cooked food at a fair, everyday price.' Traditional French cooking formed the background of Tony's training and the regularly changing snack and evening menus reflect this: piperade with croûtons, monkfish with rémoulade sauce, blanquette of lamb, poached salmon hollandaise. One frequent visitor enjoys the 'lively informal atmosphere', while other readers have been impressed by the generous quantities of 'tasty food of excellent quality'. Even that old standby, the wine glass full of prawns ('the Notts equivalent of crevettes roses'), has been singled out for freshness of taste and the generosity of the garlic mayonnaise. The wine list is unambitious, but there is a decent selection of half-bottles and four house wines (French and German) by the glass or bottle (£6.45).

CHEFS: Tony Perkins and Kevin Pole PROPRIETORS: Tony and Wendy Perkins OPEN: Tue to Sat CLOSED: 1 week Christmas MEALS: 12 to 2, 7 to 9.45 PRICES: £14 (£21) CARDS: Access, Amex, Visa SEATS: 90. 6 tables outside. Private parties: 24 main room. Car park, 60 places. Children welcome. Wheelchair access (1 step). Music

PLYMOUTH Devon map 1

Barretts of Princess Street

27 Princess Street, Plymouth PL1 2EX COOKING 1
PLYMOUTH (0752) 221177 COST £20–£31

The menu is the man: it carries on over several pages offering a variety of deals, meals and dishes to suit all occasions and times of day. Stephen Barrett likewise – ebullient, enthusiastic, anxious to be all things to all people – cooks in this moderne café-restaurant at the bottom of a moderne office block in the breezy wasteland (well, offices and space for harsh winds) behind the Theatre Royal in downtown Plymouth. Fair jazz plays on the tape machine, theatricals retreat here for recuperation and the cooking can be excellent, particularly of fish (the Barbican gives plenty of opportunity for fresh fish in small parcels) and game, Mr Barrett being keen on this latter. It can, alas, also misfire quite badly, due to faulty techniques in the kitchen. Best to keep it simple. In its favour, Barretts is the nearest thing to an all-day haven that Plymouth possesses. The wine list is similarly enthusiastic; Steve Barrett often writes on wine matters and his penchant for prose spills into the list. It changes frequently, catching the mood and fancy, and is worth exploring for New World as well as French bottles. House Dubeouf is £7.95.

CHEF: Stephen Barrett PROPRIETORS: Stephen Barrett and Geoffrey Rogers OPEN: Mon to Sat MEALS: 10.30am to 10.30pm PRICES: £19 (£26), Set L and D £12.95 (£20) to £18.75 inc wine (£22) CARDS: Access, Visa SEATS: 50. 6 tables outside. Private parties: 50 main room. Car park, 35 places. Vegetarian meals. Children's helpings. Music. Air-conditioned

The Guide *office can quickly spot when a restaurateur is encouraging customers to write recommending inclusion – and sadly, several have been doing this in 1991. Such reports do not further a restaurant's cause. Please tell us if a restaurateur invites you to write to the* Guide.

Chez Nous 🍷

13 Frankfort Gate, Plymouth PL1 1QA — COOKING 3*
PLYMOUTH (0752) 266793 — COST £34–£59

Frankfort Gate is a small pedestrian square in the modern part of Plymouth. Its most numerous inhabitants are the pigeons but, on sunny days, it almost has the bustle and life that the post-war planners intended. The high point is the shuttered front of Chez Nous, though its clean finish is no preparation for the restaurant itself. Inside, it remains firmly bistro, as it began: posters, bottles, roofed bar, tiny, firm-seated and very French, though Suzanne Marchal, who runs the front so well, is Plymouth through and through. Jacques Marchal is a fine cook, exercising restraint within a neo-classic style that presents food naturally yet imparts depth by well-made, if simple, sauces. His repertoire is consistent and works along accepted rather than wayward or even strongly inventive lines. This is the restaurant's strength, making it as near a single-star Michelin in provincial France as you might find. Another attraction is the quality of the materials, particularly the fish from Plymouth's Barbican. Meats, too, have been praised – the beef is always melting and full of flavour – and the micro-vegetables served here when the rest of Plymouth is dishing up giants are appreciated. Bread and butter remain weak points. Some dishes that mark the style are fresh snails with mushrooms, a ravioli of spinach and ricotta with pesto and fresh tomato coulis, pork loin with prunes, fillet of beef with bone marrow and a light port sauce, brill with wild mushrooms, scallops with ginger, and veal fillet with shitake. Good sight is essential to read the blackboard menu from the back of the room. This restaurant has never been cheap. The wine list is almost exclusively French with many decent bottles below £15 and a good range of halves. There are fine vintages and growers throughout. A glass is awarded this year. House wines are from £8. CELLARMAN'S CHOICE: Savennières, Clos du Papillon 1989, £14; Morey-St-Denis, En la Rue de Vergy 1986, Dom. Bruno Clair, £22.

CHEF: Jacques Marchal PROPRIETORS: Suzanne and Jacques Marchal OPEN: Tue to Sat CLOSED: first 3 weeks Feb and Sept, bank hols MEALS: 12.30 to 2, 7 to 10.30 PRICES: £35 (£49), Set L and D £24.50 (£34) to £35 (£45) CARDS: Access, Amex, Diners, Visa SEATS: 30. Private parties: 30 main room. Children welcome. Wheelchair access (also WC). Music. Air-conditioned

Yang Cheng

30A Western Approach, Plymouth PL1 1TQ — COOKING 1
PLYMOUTH (0752) 660170 — COST £11–£31

In the functional dining-room, with red flock wallpaper and simply laid tables, there is little to distract from the food. The kitchen will often cook special items not advertised on the menu, which centres on generous old-style Cantonese dishes: dim-sum, one-plate rice and noodles, roast meats and seafood. Ginger and garlic are not stinted. Readers praise deep-fried wun-tun, salt spare ribs, fried dumplings with vinegar dip, duck with pickled ginger and pineapple, and squid with green pepper and black-bean sauce. Service is helpful. Drink tea, saké or Great Wall Chinese white wine. House French is £6.

CHEF: K.Y. Wong PROPRIETORS: K.Y. Wong and K.S.L. Wong OPEN: Tue to Sun MEALS: 12 to 2.30 (3 Sun), 6 (6.30 Sun) to 11 PRICES: £14 (£24), Set L £6.30 (£11) to £8.30 (£14), Set D £10.30 (£16) to £19.80 (£26) CARDS: Access, Visa SEATS: 70. Private parties: 70 main room. Vegetarian meals. Children welcome. Music. Air-conditioned

POLPERRO Cornwall map 1

Kitchen

The Coombes, Polperro PL13 2RQ COOKING 1
POLPERRO (0503) 72780 COST £23–£41

The kitchen is almost so small (hot in summer, and cramped on busy nights) that readers have felt the cottage restaurant on the road down to the harbour does not do justice to the Batesons' careful cooking of local fish and shellfish – lobster and crab are the specialities. The menus are threefold: 'vegetarian', 'lobster' and 'kitchen', each at a set price, sharing a list of first and last courses. The approach is old-fashioned eclectic: nut roast rubbing shoulders with peperonata, crab with pink grapefruit, and hot bread pudding with local ice-cream. The execution is careful and materials often well bought. The repertoire evolves only slowly, but this must give a surge of welcoming familiarity to Polperro summer regulars. The short wine list is inexpensive. House French is £7.20.

CHEFS/PROPRIETORS: Ian and Vanessa Bateson OPEN: all week D only, exc Tue; Fri and Sat only in winter MEALS: 6.30 to 9.30 PRICES: Set D £15.90 (£23) to £26 (£34). Card slips closed CARDS: Access, Visa SEATS: 24. Private parties: 12 main room. Vegetarian meals. Children welcome. No cigars/pipes in dining-room. Wheelchair access. Music

POOL IN WHARFEDALE West Yorkshire map 5

▲ *Pool Court*

Pool Bank, Pool in Wharfedale LS21 1EH COOKING 3
LEEDS (0532) 842288 COST £23–£58

Pool Court impresses by its professionalism and continued appreciation of the art of hospitality: 'The children enjoyed the box of petits fours we were able to take away with us,' went one report. The house – sturdy stone, classical, well set in manicured grounds – is decorated to the last detail and maintained in like manner. There has been a lightening of style in the cooking. Spices, too, have been embraced with greater enthusiasm in dishes such as a ramekin of crab, leek and artichoke with a curry and vanilla oil; scallops with ginger and coriander; and vegetables cooked with cumin. Even the ice-creams have taken to liquorice. All this has been welcomed. A leap into high fashion has not meant that the English classics are ignored: grouse 'just right, tender but not overhung' in the season; fish 'fresh as can be – steamed turbot and sea bass, as well as salmon'. The menu is structured so that the main course fixes the price of the entire meal: a middle course of sorbet, soup or 'chef's choice', perhaps a parfait of duck liver, is built in. There is also the social service of a £10 set menu (no deviation allowed), which readers have reported to be dispensed without patronage or superciliousness by properly motivated staff; a mark, perhaps, of security induced by longevity in this most fluid of businesses. Selection throughout the catholic wine list is very sound. It is clear, even-handed and thankfully free of 'tasting notes'. The choice over £20 is carefully balanced by generous provision of half-bottles, a page of £8.95 'Everyday Wines', and many fine wines around the £15 mark. House wine is £16.45. CELLARMAN'S CHOICE: Tokay Reserve 1985, Trimbach, £17.50; Bourgogne, Hautes Côtes de Nuits 1986, Jean Gros, £19.90.

CHEF: David Watson PROPRIETOR: Michael W.K. Gill OPEN: Tue to Sat, D only (L by arrangement for parties of 10 or more) CLOSED: 2 weeks July to Aug, 2 weeks Christmas MEALS: 7 to 10 PRICES: Set D £10 (£23) to £33 (£48) CARDS: Access, Amex, Diners, Visa SEATS: 65. Private parties: 85 main room, 30 private room. Car park, 65 places. Vegetarian meals. Healthy eating options. Children's helpings. No cigars/pipes in dining-room. Wheelchair access. No music. Air-conditioned. Fax: (0532) 843115 ACCOMMODATION: 6 rooms, all with bath/shower. B&B £70 to £120. Garden. Air-conditioned. TV. Phone. Confirm by 6 (*Which? Hotel Guide*)

PORTHOUSTOCK Cornwall map 1

Café Volnay

COUNTY RESTAURANT OF THE YEAR

NEW ENTRY

Porthoustock TR12 6QW COOKING 2*
HELSTON (0326) 280183 COST £15–£24

When Messrs Chapman and Rye state they are 'in the centre of Porthoustock' – in a beamed, whitewashed cottage – visitors need fear no traffic lights, wardens or gyratory systems: Porthoustock has 16 houses around the cove and beach. What they may anticipate with some pleasure instead is an enjoyable meal unusual in its skill, verve and culinary style for this part of Cornwall. 'Two men fleeing the London catering jungle and operating with enthusiasm and determination' is how one reader described them. 'They already seem to be winning the support of the notoriously difficult Cornish.' Notwithstanding, it might be added, the very simple physical arrangements. But then, much may be endured for 'honest, flavoursome and obviously fresh food'. Enthusiasm Chapman and Rye must have; who else would serve Sunday brunches of Buck's Fizz and eggs Benedict (good hollandaise), or scrambled egg and smoked salmon on a February morning in this district? The repertoire is inventive: tandoori prawn filo parcels; leek and pear roulade; chicken breast with mozzarella and Parma ham; red mullet with tomato and oregano. The prices are generous in the extreme; the desserts improve from slow beginnings; the wine list is short and sensible. A wholly good thing. Book ahead.

CHEFS/PROPRIETORS: S.A. Chapman and C.N. Rye OPEN: summer Tue to Sun, D only, winter Wed to Sat, D only, and Sun brunch from 11am CLOSED: day following bank hols MEALS: 7 to 9 PRICES: £12 (£16), Set D £10 (£15) to £15 (£20) SEATS: 24. Private parties: 20 main room. Children's helpings with prior notice. No cigars during meals. Wheelchair access (2 steps; also WC). Music

All letters to the Guide *are acknowledged with an update on latest sales, closures, chef changes and so on.*

POUGHILL Cornwall map 1

▲ *Reeds*

Poughill EX23 9EL
BUDE (0288) 352841

COOKING 2
COST £28

'Mrs Jackson is a jewel; helpful, attentive, without intruding on one's thoughts or privacy. She maintains a spotless house, well-endowed with excellent original paintings, which is ever quiet and restful. Surrounding gardens have been worked on and will continue to improve. One of the delights was afternoon tea on the verandah, just this side of sleep as the bees, grasshoppers and buzzards made their presence felt. Food was good, vegetables fresh. Dinner menus were discussed each morning.' Thus wrote one visitor to this inimitable place feeding residents and the occasional, forewarning, outsider. Margaret Jackson cooks naturally, offers no choice in her dinners, but provides that facility of prior discussion. It is not guesthouse food: cutlet of salmon poached in Pineau des Charentes, followed by chicken wrapped in bacon with a red wine sauce, then a choice of three puddings – pears in lemon syrup, chocolate brandy cake and Grand Marnier soufflé. Just occasionally, slip-ups occur – perhaps induced by mid-winter blues. The wine list is very decent for the task, fortified by some old clarets from Mrs Jackson's own cellar. House Duboeuf is £6.50.

CHEF/PROPRIETOR: Margaret Jackson OPEN: Fri to Mon, D only CLOSED: 25 Dec
MEALS: 8 PRICES: Set D £19.50 (£23) SEATS: 10. Private parties: 10 main room. Car park, 10 places. No children under 16. Smart dress preferred. No music. One sitting
ACCOMMODATION: 3 rooms, all with bath/shower. B&B £37.50 to £65. Deposit: £10. No children under 16. Garden. Scenic. Doors close at midnight. Confirm by noon (*Which? Hotel Guide*)

POULTON-LE-FYLDE Lancashire map 5

▲ *River House* 🍷

Skippool Creek,
Thornton-le-Fylde FY5 5LF
POULTON-LE-FYLDE (0253) 883497
and 883307

COOKING 2*
COST £48

Opinions are divided on Bill Scott's long-standing restaurant. Some can't take the almost purposely run-down nature of the decoration – front door scratched by entering dogs, and countless objects of curiosity scattered hither and yon. Some have had inadequate meals, especially at the price; others have found everything perfect – good food, a fine host and picturesque decoration. The *carte* shows little affection for the ultra-fashionable, but there is a line of Japanese influence that lends variety, for instance salmon teriyaki or monkfish mikado. Experience and skill showed in the salmon: four fingers topped with black pepper on a julienne of peppers and onions with dark soy sauce was 'perfectly seasoned, lighter than it looked'. Seasoning is not always so accurate. Vegetables have needed salt, and a caramel sauce was overbalanced by sweetness. The enterprise is thoroughgoing: decent bread, very good supply lines for meat and fish, an unwillingness to serve the latter unless fresh off the boat. Sauces may tend to cream and portions are substantial. Good things are said of lamb with chicken-liver stuffing in a thin pastry case, soufflé suissesse, pleasant yet simple canapés, the quality of the beef in a chateaubriand, and desserts such as ticky-tacky – a version of sticky toffee pudding – and the sorbets and ice-creams. 'The place is brimful of character, the staff pleasant, the outlook romantic,' says a reader. The unevenness noticed this year is doubtless a passing phase; Mr Scott has great experience. Annotations on the wine list continue to be uneven. Where growers are shown, however, the choice is sound. Enthusiasm is evident in the range of Italian, Spanish and New World bottles. House wine is £10.50. CELLARMAN'S CHOICE: Frascati, Colle Gaio 1989, £19; Bandol, Dom. Tempier 1985, £16.

CHEF/PROPRIETOR: Bill Scott OPEN: Mon to Sat, exc Sat L MEALS: 12 to 2, 7.30 to 9.30 PRICES: £29 (£40) CARDS: Access, Visa SEATS: 40. Private parties: 40 main room. Car park, 20 places. Vegetarian meals. Children's helpings. Music ACCOMMODATION: 4 rooms, all with bath/shower. B&B £55 to £120. Children welcome. Baby facilities. Pets welcome. Garden. TV. Phone. Scenic. Confirm booking 2 days ahead (*Which? Hotel Guide*)

POWBURN Northumberland map 7

▲ *Breamish House*

Powburn NE66 4LL COOKING 1
POWBURN (066 578) 266 and 544 COST £19–£32

'It looks as if it were built for a vicar rather than a squire' was one way of saying that the house, and approach, is pleasing rather than grandiose. Inside, the house is more piecemeal, a 'comfortable' hotch-potch but without a lot of finesse. The food could be said to share that character. Some things on the single-service, limited-choice, set-price menu are well done, some more perfunctory. Reports mention good soups and sweet things, good local cheese (but packet biscuits) and good main materials; but there are mixed comments about sauces, and first courses may be designed for ease, not art. Vegetables are decent if not always apt for the choice of main dish. If the restaurant is filled with couples at tables for two, production can be metronomic and the atmosphere 'sepulchral'. The wine list includes some good things, and lots of half-bottles for those couples. Prices are fair. House wine is £9.90 a litre.

CHEFS/PROPRIETORS: Doreen and Alan Johnson OPEN: all week, D only, and Sun L CLOSED: Jan MEALS: 12.30 for 1, 7.30 for 8 PRICES: Set Sun L £12.50 (£19), Set D £19.50 (£27) SEATS: 30. Private parties: 22 main room. Car park, 30 places. Children by arrangement. Smart dress preferred. No smoking in dining-room. Wheelchair access (also WC). Music. One sitting. Fax: (066 578) 500 ACCOMMODATION: 11 rooms, all with bath/shower. B&B £41 to £62.50. Deposit: £25 per person. Children under 12 by arrangement. Pets welcome. Afternoon teas. Garden. TV. Phone. Scenic. Doors close at 11 (*Which? Hotel Guide*)

Cellarman's Choice: a wine recommended by the restaurateur, normally more expensive than house wine.

POWERSTOCK **Dorset** map 2

▲ *Three Horseshoes*

Powerstock DT6 3TF COOKING 1*
POWERSTOCK (030 885) 328 and 229 COST £16–£40

'I can be the only "fish restaurant" that has no menu when the weather turns bad,' writes Pat Ferguson when justifying his estimable refusal to use a freezer. Fish is definitely the main attraction at this village inn with a restaurant. The blackboard features as many as a dozen varieties: scallops with garlic butter, or with onions, wine and cream; seafood platters of mussels, scallops, oysters and cumin-flavoured monkfish; brill with a green sauce; fish soup with whole pieces of fish in the broth. Meat includes plenty of game – at those times of bad weather – but tends to be simply cooked so that Pat Ferguson can concentrate on getting out the fish. First and last courses may be simple and sometimes large. House wine is £6.95.

CHEF: Pat Ferguson PROPRIETORS: Pat and Diana Ferguson OPEN: all week MEALS: 12 to 2 (3 Sun), 7 to 10 PRICES: £25 (£33), Set Sun L £9.50 (£16) to £11.50 (£18), Set D £16.50 (£23) CARDS: Access, Amex, Diners, Visa SEATS: 50. Private parties: 50 main room, 20 and 24 private rooms. Car park, 30 places. Vegetarian meals. Children's helpings. Smart dress preferred. Smoking after meal only. Wheelchair access (also WC). Music
ACCOMMODATION: 4 rooms, 2 with bath/shower. B&B £24 to £44. Deposit: 1 night. Children welcome. Baby facilities. Pets welcome. Garden. Scenic. Doors close at midnight. Confirm by 6

PRESTBURY **Cheshire** map 5

▲ *White House*

New Road, Prestbury SK10 4DG COOKING 2
PRESTBURY (0625) 829376 COST £18–£42

'Simply Ryland's' is Ryland Wakeham's set-price menu introduced to cope with the recession's effect on his customers' pockets. The White House, and the linked accommodation at the Manor, is ever responsive, just as the main *carte* is marked up with dishes conforming to the reduced-fat requirements of 'spa cuisine'. The nicely converted farmhouse with conservatory in the centre of the village is busy with Cheshire folk pleased to essay a repertoire that is as reflective of current tendencies as any. Lobster with vanilla, toasted goats' cheese with tapénade, fish with aïoli, prawns and scallops on a red pepper vinaigrette, veal with coriander and vegetable spaghetti, and duck with lime and ginger are some examples that have elicited comment. This style is not usually delivered as 'simple peasantry' on the menu, but instead is interpreted in restaurant argot. Continued reliance on négociant wine cannot command total confidence, but the list is none the less decent, arranged by style of wine rather than region, with some good growers. Prices are fair. French is £9 a litre.

CHEF: Ryland Wakeham PROPRIETORS: Ryland and Judith Wakeham OPEN: Tue to Sun CLOSED: first week Jan and Aug MEALS: 12 to 2, 7 to 10 PRICES: £26 (£35), Set L £9.95 (£18) to £11.95 (£20), Set D £15.95 (£22) to £16.50 (£23). Card slips closed CARDS: Access, Amex, Diners, Visa SEATS: 75. 2 tables outside. Private parties: 70 main room, 20 and 40 private rooms. Car park, 16 places. Vegetarian meals. Healthy eating options. Children's helpings. Wheelchair access (also WC). Music. Fax: (0625) 828627 ACCOMMODATION: 8 rooms, all with bath/shower. Rooms for disabled. B&B £70 to £105. No children under 12. Garden. Sauna. TV. Phone. Scenic. Doors close at midnight. Confirm by midday

PRESTON Lancashire map 5

Auctioneer

ADT, Walton Summit, Bamber Bridge,
Preston PR5 8AA COOKING 1
PRESTON (0772) 324870 COST £14–£25

It looks, from the outside, like a large corrugated packing case with windows. It is above the car auction ring ('all G and H registration, no old bangers thank you,' writes one inspector) hence both name and tricking out of the menu: 'Lot 1, lobster bisque', 'job lot of vegetables', and so on. Inside, it is a different and more pleasant matter. Nigel Brookes is a character, and his aim is to give fair value for fair standards. The latter may cause haute cuisine eyebrows to be raised – chips with paella – but it leaves a large constituency happy. Sauces are reported as 'heavy-handed' on the one hand, or 'very tasty and rich'. Many of the ingredients are decent, though desserts are not a strong point. You buy your fillet steak, then bid for a sauce (at £1 extra), or you have 'millionaire's turkey' – lobster, turkey, a lobster sauce and rice. There is vigour and value here. The Brookes are happy and welcoming hosts. The wine list is just names – no dates, no makers – but not expensive. House wine is £7.50.

CHEF: Nigel Brookes PROPRIETORS: Nigel and Elizabeth Brookes OPEN: Mon to Sun L, exc Tue and Sat; Fri and Sat D MEALS: 12 to 2.30 (10.30 to 4 Mon and Wed), 7 to 10 PRICES: £15 (£21), Set L £8.95 (£14). Card slips closed CARDS: Access, Visa SEATS: 100. Private parties: 100 main room. Car park, 500 places. Vegetarian meals. Children's helpings. Music. Air-conditioned

PULBOROUGH West Sussex map 3

Stane Street Hollow

Codmore Hill, Pulborough RH20 1BG COOKING 3
PULBOROUGH (0798) 872819 COST £17–£34

The Kaisers run a well-loved restaurant: 'We have been coming here every fortnight for 10 years,' one correspondent told us. The location is perfect English, the cooking Swiss (in part), the service and welcome palpably warm. To complete the Hansel and Gretel illusion, hens and ducks lay eggs in the garden; vegetables, soft fruit and herbs are often home-grown; hams, salmon and chicken are home-smoked. There is a short, very reasonably priced lunch menu and a monthly à la carte that exhibits classical tendencies with a Swiss accent. Badische schneckensuppe, fisch knödels, kasseler fribourgeoise and zuger kirsch torte are examples of the latter and could be accompanied by the pair of Swiss wines on the list. Pastry is well handled, as usually are the vegetables – deft details enlivening what is at first sight a boring selection. There is no mincing of flavour; classic training it may be but informed by a wish to feed honestly and substantially. The wine list is mainly French bolstered by a few bottles from Germany and Italy. Some growers and properties are distinguished – Dujac and Clerget in Burgundy, Dagueneau in the Loire, Ch. Rahoul and Chasse-Spleen in Bordeaux – and prices are very fair.

CHEF: René Kaiser PROPRIETORS: René and Ann Kaiser OPEN: Wed to Sat, exc Sat L CLOSED: 2 weeks May and Oct, 24 to 26 Dec, 31 Dec and 1 Jan, 1 week Feb MEALS: 12.30 to 1.15, 7.30 to 9.15 PRICES: £19 (£28), Set L £8.25 (£17) SEATS: 35. Private parties: 24 main room, 16 private room. Car park, 14 places. Children's helpings. No smoking. No music

RAMSBOTTOM Greater Manchester map 5

Village Restaurant

16 Market Place, Ramsbottom BL0 9HT COOKING 3
RAMSBOTTOM (070 682) 5070 COST £31–£44

With its cobbled streets and stone cottages, Ramsbottom looks and feels like old Lancashire. Chris Johnson's and Ros Hunter's restaurant blends in with its surroundings and the kitchen takes its cue from the Englishness of the setting. Dinner is a six-course feast beginning at eight o'clock and often lasting through the evening. 'More and more we seem to be a place to celebrate a special occasion,' comments Chris Johnson. There is real knowledge, passion and commitment about this enterprise. Occasionally the mood can seem reverential and the pace as slow as a pilgrimage, but there is no doubting the quality of the cooking and the impeccable choice of raw materials. The cornerstones of the British larder are here in abundance: home-baked breads, hand-churned butter, relishes and 'tracklements', regional hams and unpasteurised farmhouse cheeses. Local growers supply organic vegetables. A typical menu might begin with Cumbrian air-dried ham with leeks and pear purée; then comes soup, such as nettle, or beef and onion. After this, there is fish – perhaps poached salmon with sorrel and ginger mayonnaise or halibut with lime mousseline sauce. Main courses are always impressively adorned: guinea-fowl with orange and Dijon mustard sauce, and cider and tarragon; fillets of beef and venison with redcurrant and Meaux mustard, and mango and horseradish. A plethora of five vegetables is the order of the day. Spot-on cheeses precede a trolley of sweets. Weaknesses seem to be concentrated towards the end of the extravaganza: most reporters find the desserts rather dull and heavy, and are bemused that the decaffeinated coffee is 'instant' when so much care is taken over the choice of ingredients elsewhere. Chris Johnson's eulogising is not to everyone's taste and some feel that 'he seems to be competing with the food to be the star of the show'. An evangelical approach to wine is much in evidence on the list; a relatively recent convert to the wine world, Chris Johnson is making up for lost time. The list (or rather lists) is perhaps irrelevant for most customers; carefully chosen glasses are offered with each dish for an all-in £10.50. The wine buff can request the cellar catalogue, a comprehensive if not pedantic volume of 1,000 bottles. Whichever route is taken, quality and value are assured.

CHEF: Ros Hunter PROPRIETORS: Ros Hunter and Chris Johnson (R.C.P.L. Ltd) OPEN: Wed to Sat, D only (Tue by arrangement) MEALS: 8 for 8.30 PRICES: Set D £23 (£31) to £28.50 (£37). Card slips closed CARDS: Access, Visa SEATS: 20. Private parties: 12 main room. No smoking. Music. One sitting

REDLYNCH Wiltshire map 2

▲ *Langley Wood*

Hamptworth Road, Redlynch SP5 2PB COOKING 2
ROMSEY (0794) 390348 COST £16–£28

One reader's report catches the tone of the place: 'We ate coq au vin, the best I've eaten outside France, real bourgeois cooking: hearty, meaty and generous. There were masses of vegetables, of which potatoes were the most delicious and the broccoli superb – crisp, lemony and buttered. My vegetarian daughter had vegetable paella which was excellent, so much so that it was finished by the rest of us. First courses were good but not amazing, whilst desserts were seriously good. We had three each, but the children went wild on hazelnut meringues, trifle, lemon mousse, a concoction called "chocolate disgusting", fruit salad and figs and apricots! The style is *very* simple and it is a relief not to have everything in matchsticks, decorated with blobs and leaves.' The Rosens' kingdom is well-loved, understated and bursts with genuine hospitality. The menus are not elaborate, tackle slow cooking with verve, and constitute very good value. Because Langley Wood is not sophisticated, those anxious for a night of suits, silver and candlelight may find it perplexing. Wines are not listed in great number, but they are good and cheap. The Sancerre may win the national challenge for economy. House wines are £5.25.

CHEF: Sylvia Rosen PROPRIETORS: David and Sylvia Rosen OPEN: Wed to Sat, D only and Sun L MEALS: 12.45 to 2, 7.30 to 11 PRICES: £17 (£23), Set L £12 (£16) CARDS: Access, Amex, Diners, Visa SEATS: 30. Private parties: 65 main room. Car park, 25 places. Vegetarian meals. Children's helpings. No cigars/pipes in dining-room. Wheelchair access (also WC). Music ACCOMMODATION: 3 rooms. B&B £15 to £30. Children welcome. Baby facilities. Pets welcome. Afternoon teas. Garden. Scenic

RICHMOND North Yorkshire map 7

▲ *Howe Villa*

Whitcliffe Mill, Richmond DL10 4TJ COOKING 2*
RICHMOND (0748) 850055 COST £18–£23

There is space for but a few outsiders if the rooms are full, so telephone first. Howe Villa is a good house ('the outside world falls away'), but reaching it may test tolerance of light industrial blight. Take the Leyburn and Reeth road out of Richmond and turn left at the Tyre Service Station. The cooking draws guests to the front door, and so does Anita Berry, of tireless energy and enthusiastic welcome. Her cooking is of a piece with the style of the place: fine domestic with good techniques and no unnecessary flounce. Although the premises are unlicensed, the Berrys will buy wine for you and they build a 'free' aperitif into the price of the meal. This consists of four courses, including cheese, but there is no choice at the main course. 'We had seven dinners. Each was excellent,' said one resident, who also noted, 'all guests had been before several times.' So, though menus may be short, the repertoire is carefully extended. Smoked fish in a rich cheese sauce, smoked trout mousse wrapped in smoked salmon, seafood pancake with a cheese sauce, chicken with tarragon, roast beef with Yorkshire served separately, loin of lamb boned and stuffed with orange and herbs are some of the good things. Desserts continue the quality – steamed chocolate pudding is notable, as is the bread-and-butter pudding – and cheeses are good Wensleydale or Coverdale. Long may Anita reign.

CHEF: Anita Berry PROPRIETORS: Tom and Anita Berry OPEN: all week, D only CLOSED: Dec and Jan MEALS: 7.30 to 8 PRICES: Set D £18 to £19. Unlicensed SEATS: 12. Private parties: 12 main room. Car park. Vegetarian meals. Children's helpings by arrangement. No children under 12. No smoking in dining-room. Music ACCOMMODATION: 4 rooms, all with bath/shower. D,B&B £80. Deposit: £20. No children under 12. Garden. TV. Scenic. Doors close at 11.30. Confirm by 6 (*Which? Hotel Guide*)

RIDGEWAY Derbyshire map 5

Old Vicarage

Ridgeway Moor, Ridgeway S12 3XW
SHEFFIELD (0742) 475814
off A616, on B6054 nearly opposite village church

COOKING 4
COST £25–£60

Sheffield, host to the 1991 World Student Games, might suggest a meal here to the *victor ludorum* to rebuild strength and health. He, or she, would find the late-Victorian house, hedged in by a leafy front garden, just outside the city and looking on to open fields. The interior is spacious, decorated for grace and comfort with a light touch that holds back from overload. A large dining-room leads on to a conservatory addition. Tessa Bramley has not stopped her development of ideas in the kitchen. Whereas once she might have been typed as an 'English' cook, reinterpreting the best of our mongrel tradition in the light of Elizabeth David and more recent cook-writers, she seems today to have absorbed the neo-Italian lesson, the oriental touch and the greater eclecticism enjoyed by many chefs here and in the New World. Ingredients still have priority: there are self-grown herbs, vegetables and fruit, and locally sourced meat and poultry, while rarer items are more widely searched for. But recent menus containing dishes such as devilled lambs' kidneys with bruschetta and plum tomato salad; beef fillet, lightly smoked over rosemary, on polenta with morel sauce; or chicken poached with saffron and cinnamon, served with spiced couscous, show loyalties beyond old England. These come from a dinner menu, perhaps of eight choices, priced according to the main dish chosen. At lunch, there is a *carte* of lighter dishes served in the garden-room, but travellers need not fear that the joys of the main menu will be denied them in daylight hours. Presentation and service is formal, occasionally halting, yet not striving for too much effect. The use of blossoms, herb sprigs and other small touches bring many dishes to life, imparting a stamp of personality. Desserts live up to earlier courses: lemon tart, chocolate pudding with fudge sauce and custard, even iced parfaits in a large tuile basket. The details add up. Over the last three or four years the Old Vicarage has moved from being a simple family enterprise that served really good food to being a 'professional restaurant'. Such transitions can sometimes be painful: the lessons of supervision and delegation may need learning anew. Perhaps there are moments when teacher was ignored and standards slip, so that the special is no more than ordinary. But usually, the student has absorbed the precepts and the results are fine indeed. A wine list has not been received this year. Let it suffice to say that we awarded a bottle in 1991, and reports continue to praise the quality and the service of the wines. House wine is £12.

CHEF: Tessa Bramley PROPRIETORS: Tessa and Andrew Bramley OPEN: Tue to Sat D, and Sun L (L Tue to Sat by arrangement) MEALS: 12.15 to 2.30, 7 to 11 PRICES: Set L and D £15 (£25) to £30 (£50) SEATS: 50. Private parties: 30 main room, 12 and 30 private rooms. Car park, 30 places. No children under 12. Smart dress preferred. No smoking. Music. Fax: (0742) 477079

RIPLEY Surrey map 3

Michels' 🍷

13 High Street, Ripley GU23 6AQ COOKING 3
GUILDFORD (0483) 224777 COST £29–£47

Ripley is the birthplace of Eric Clapton: a little-known fact. An infrequent visitor commented: 'The only thing that has changed about this village is the cooking and service at Michels'; these are much improved.' The decoration of the restaurant, too, has continued in its process of refurbishment: now it is all pale pink, with swathes of Colefax and Fowler, flowers, and enamelled elephants and cockerels 'exquisitely disposed'. A spring lunch confirmed the high form of the kitchen this year. An asparagus soup, fairly thin yet intensely flavoured, was followed by an aubergine and red pepper mousse, as good as the first course, in a moat of lemon and basil butter; gnocchi with goats' cheese, nicely accented by peppers and olives, were a welcome form of serving the cheese – another salad and warmed croûtons, and some will expire from boredom. Home-smoking has shown expertise over the oak chips, while a version of coq au vin with polenta reveals that slow cooking is as much embraced as fast. A light pastry filled with rhubarb cream, topped with frangipane and surrounded by a strawberry coulis, showed that novel desserts can still be conceived in a year when ideas seem at a premium. Lunches like this are very fair value, for skill, materials and ambience. Dinner is substantially more expensive. Careful selections on the succinct, mainly French, wine list include Rolly Gassmann Alsace and Rosemount Chardonnay. There are fair prices throughout and good half-bottles, though perhaps the list is a little unambitious. CELLARMAN'S CHOICE: Mâcon Viré 1988, Goyard, £16.15; Côtes du Rhône 1986, Guigal, £11.75.

CHEF: Erik Michel PROPRIETORS: Erik and Karen Michel OPEN: Tue to Sun, exc Sat L and Sun D MEALS: 12.30 to 2, 7.30 to 9.15 (9.45 Sat) PRICES: £29 (£39), Set D £20 (£29) CARDS: Access, Amex, Diners, Visa SEATS: 45. Children welcome

ROADE Northamptonshire map 3

Roadhouse Restaurant

16–18 High Street, Roade NN7 2NW COOKING 3
ROADE (0604) 863372 COST £19–£30

'A return after a leanish year makes one wonder why we have bothered to eat elsewhere' is the response that small country restaurateurs need, so long as the return is not so tardy next time. Chris Kewley steers his course in the kitchen, his wife Susan in the front-of-house – perhaps needing a tighter hand on the tiller when young, 'friendly rather than skilled' staff cannot answer questions from the curious. Another reporter identified how the Roadhouse 'underlines the UK problem of getting useful and sustained help in the kitchen' without enlarging the scope of the restaurant (i.e. its personality) to the point where the chef risks losing control. So this remains an individual, small, even 'cosy' operation. There is a short, six-choice *carte*, and periodic evenings are devoted to a single theme or maybe region or season, hence a salmon ballotine 'as light as a quenelle with intense flavour'; roast partridge with 'a rich lentil sauce that yet owed nothing to cream'; a dozen cheeses 'at their peak and interesting'; and an apple and almond tart that 'held its light almond crust firm to the end against a syllabub delicately flavoured with calvados with none of the kick to the palate one might have feared'. Here is a cook who can hold his own when circumstances allow him to, who can produce an asparagus feuilleté with beurre blanc, chicken stuffed with leeks in a tarragon sauce, and strawberries in a brioche with strawberry ice alongside the best of them, and who does not deliver impossibly rich food even if, generally, it is substantial. Some find the surroundings cramped rather than comfortable, but invariably well kept. Wines come from decent growers: Roty in Burgundy, Ch. Lynch-Bages in Bordeaux, Baumard in Savennières, Knappstein in South Australia. The list is not long, but adequate for the purpose. House wines are from £8.25.

CHEF: Christopher Kewley PROPRIETORS: Christopher and Susan Kewley OPEN: Tue to Sat, exc Sat L MEALS: 12.30 to 1.45, 7 to 10 PRICES: £20 (£25), Set L £14 (£19). Net prices, card slips closed CARDS: Access, Visa SEATS: 32. Private parties: 40 main room. Car park, 15 places. Children's helpings. Smart dress preferred. No music

ROCHFORD Essex map 3

▲ *Renoufs*

Bradley Way, Rochford SS4 1BU COOKING 1
SOUTHEND (0702) 544393 COST £12–£37

Derek Renouf has moved his restaurant, menu and all, into his hotel at Bradley Way. The original premises in South Street have been converted into a brasserie. It is too soon to report on the success of this latter development.

However, Derek Renouf has been cooking here for decades and there is no reason to suppose that new premises will cause him to alter his style, if he isn't changing his menu. This must be one of the few places in the UK that offers pressed duck à la Rouennaise. An inspection suggested that many of the dishes do not quite live up to their description; tastes may lack clarity, though good materials and classical French cooking should promote the opposite. However, Renoufs does have a strong local following and will provide a formal meal in traditional manner, pared down from some of the excesses of earlier years, at (just) affordable prices. There is not a lot of competition in East Essex. The wine list is long, with showcase selections from Dom. de la Romanée-Conti, Ch. Gilette, Duboeuf and others, as well as a number of slightly off-years. House wine starts at £9.20

CHEF/PROPRIETOR: Derek Renouf OPEN: all week, exc Sat L CLOSED: 26 to 30 Dec MEALS: 12.15 to 1.45, 7 to 10 PRICES: £21 (£31), Set L inc wine £11.50, Set D inc wine £13.50 to £19.50. Net prices, card slips closed CARDS: Access, Amex, Diners, Visa SEATS: 100. Private parties: 70 main room. Vegetarian meals. Children welcome. Wheelchair access (also WC). Music. Air-conditioned ACCOMMODATION: 24 rooms, all with bath/shower. Rooms for disabled. B&B £57.50 to £78. Children welcome. Baby facilities. Pets welcome. Garden. Air-conditioned. TV. Phone (*Which? Hotel Guide*)

ROMSEY Hampshire map 2

Old Manor House

21 Palmerston Street, Romsey SO51 8GF COOKING 4
ROMSEY (0794) 517353 COST £22–£51

You may eat kid here, often a sign of an enthusiastic chef, and Mauro Bregoli is that. Surroundings are posher, the service more formal, than the image of a burly Italian who smokes his meats, hunts his game, fishes his rivers and gathers his own fungi conjures up, but the Old Manor House manages to join the two traditions of country authenticity and *haute cuisine moderne* as well as most places in mainland Britain. The prices may act as truer indicators of poshness, though there is a real attempt to keep them within bounds at lunchtime. Markers of the dual inspiration are found in tagliarini with Parma ham, peas and cream; cotechino with lentils; bresaola; or risotto with truffles on the one hand; red mullet with carrot juice and saffron; duck with honey, lemon and 'three purées'; and breast of chicken filled with foie gras mousse on a sauce of Noilly Prat and cream on the other. Pasta, game, mushrooms of all sorts and cured meats are strong points, countered in some minds by a tendency to prissy display on the plate masking an occasionally lacklustre dish. More than one report has observed that sweet dishes, for instance the nougat glacé with raspberry coulis or with cherries, can be too sweet, and the impressive display of breads, cut to order at your table, may include novelty loaves that are thrown into the shade of staleness by the excellently fresh French baguettes. The Old Manor is impressively old and has stuck with old England rather than going Italian, but a breath of southern air may linger with aperitifs taken al fresco in the courtyard, while the syncopated lifting of domes by Continental waiters gives an authentic whiff of the new Community. Consideration for those not wishing to thumb their way through 30 pages of

900 wines is shown with 'choice of the house': 19 wines, fairly priced and offering a good range of style. Anyone daring to turn to page two will be drawn into a seemingly endless procession of the best names and superb vintages all clearly presented. France has star billing, but Mauro Bregoli by no means turns his back on his home country: Barolo, Barbaresco and 'super-Tuscans' occupy two pages. House wine is £8. CELLARMAN'S CHOICE: Cahors, Ch. la Caminade 1988, £13; Corbières, Ch. Etang des Colombes 1988, £17.

CHEF/PROPRIETOR: Mauro Bregoli OPEN: Tue to Sun, exc Sun D CLOSED: 24 Dec to 2 Jan MEALS: 12 to 2, 7 to 9.30 PRICES: Set L £14.50 (£22) to £21.50 (£30), Set D £33 (£42) CARDS: Access, Visa SEATS: 45. 6 tables outside. Private parties: 12 main room, 24 private room. Car park, 12 places. Children welcome. Smart dress preferred. No cigars/pipes in dining-room. No music

---

ROWDE Wiltshire map 2

George & Dragon

COUNTY RESTAURANT OF THE YEAR

NEW ENTRY

High Street, Rowde SN10 2PN COOKING 3
DEVIZES (0380) 723053 COST £15–£29

Sitting above a bend in the road through the village, this old pub – good back-to-back fireplaces from the sixteenth century – is the sort needed to spearhead change in eating and drinking habits in England. This is not to rubbish what used to be (though some would) but merely to remind us that we all eat out more now; for whatever reason, we spend less time in our own kitchens and depend more on outside resources. These, therefore, must be of better and higher standard than ever. Tim and Helen Withers are not just pandering here to middle-class invaders of 'real life', they are performing an essential service that should be encouraged. If it were, Tim Withers might be able to cook in a more professionally equipped kitchen for a start. The advantage to the customer is that you are offered fairly priced, fresh food cooked with imagination, and a memory that taste matters more than convenience. Try the fish soup, the home-made pasta, almost any of the fish dishes listed on the blackboard above the bar, the guinea-fowl with lime, venison and fruit pie, brown sugar meringues, or hazelnut shortbread. There is one room that is mostly restaurant and the bar-room keeps drinkers happy. Comfort is not great, it remains a pub, but any lack is made up by Helen Withers' cheerful assurance and the food itself. The wine list reminds you that this is a tied house, but the short choice is as good as can be mustered in these restrictive circumstances. House wine is £7.40.

CHEF: Tim Withers PROPRIETORS: Wadworth & Co OPEN: Tue to Sun, exc Sun D CLOSED: 25 to 26 Dec, 1 Jan MEALS: 12 to 1.45, 7 to 10 PRICES: £17 (£24), Set L £8.50 (£15). Card slips closed CARDS: Access, Visa SEATS: 35. 6 tables outside. Private parties: 20 main room. Car park, 17 places. Vegetarian meals with prior notice. Children's helpings. No children after 9pm. Wheelchair access (1 step; also WC). No music

---

Dining-rooms where live and recorded music are not be played are signalled by No music *in the details at the end of an entry.*

RUGBY Warwickshire map 5

▲ *Grosvenor Hotel*

Clifton Road, Rugby CV21 3QQ COOKING 1
RUGBY (0788) 535686 COST £19–£38

The hotel continues to change and expand with a new health club and swimming-pool adding to its attractions. After a spell away, setting up his own food wholesaling business, Richard Johnson is back in the kitchen and continues to offer creditable hotel cooking. Dishes are less 'fantastic' than before and ingredients are less exotic, according to long-term regulars, but this is a set-up that knows what its customers want. An unchanging 'Traditional Bill of Fayre' (duck terrine, steaks, poached salmon, calf's liver and bacon) is backed up by a daily fixed-price 'Gourmet Menu' which includes three courses plus a sorbet. Sautée of mushrooms with ham, spinach and 'wafer' pastry, stuffed roulade of sole with salmon and Noilly Prat sauce, lamb cutlets with minted hollandaise and redcurrant jus, and treacle sponge pudding show the style. Details such as bread and cheeses could be improved, service can be rather erratic and the clientele is largely expense-account, but the feeling is that the cooking is a cut above the local average. There are around 100 well-chosen and well-described wines. House French is £7.50.

CHEF: Richard Johnson PROPRIETORS: J. Hall and J. Hawes OPEN: all week, exc Sat L MEALS: 12 to 2, 7 to 10 PRICES: £23 (£32), Set L £11.95 (£19), Set D £17.95 (£26). Card slips closed CARDS: Access, Amex, Diners, Visa SEATS: 42. Private parties: 20 private room. Car park, 40 places. Children welcome. Smart dress preferred. No pipes in dining-room. Music. Fax: (0788) 541297 ACCOMMODATION: 21 rooms, all with bath/shower. B&B £67.50 to £77.50. Children welcome. Baby facilities. Afternoon teas. Swimming-pool. Sauna. TV. Phone

RYE East Sussex map 3

Landgate Bistro 🍷

5–6 Landgate, Rye TN31 7LH COOKING 2*
RYE (0797) 222829 COST £23

It may be noisy, even uncomfortable, but it has the hum of popularity. People come for lots of reasons: the staff are nice to children, the prices are none too high ('Having service included is a great bonus. I wish the same could be done for vegetables,' went one report), the materials are excellent, the food is nicely presented, and the cooking shows skill and panache. No wonder the bistro is full mid-week, even in winter. There is a view that locals are more convinced of its worth than strangers, but this should not disguise the many notes of satisfaction, such as this from one reporter: 'Asparagus soup was very good, based on a light chicken stock, and full of the proclaimed vegetable. The chicken quenelles and squid were as good as ever. Grilled sole was a proper size and accurately done. I had English calf's liver with sage, noting yet again the meaty texture and higher flavour compared to the Dutch. The chocolate option is now a chocolate truffle cake: actually a slice of mousse-like squish, a white layer between two brown, the edges darker still. Lemon and almond tart had a light lemony mousse over almond paste on a splendid light thin crust. My crème caramel was one of the better ones of recent years.' The repertoire does not pretend to haute cuisine, rather to immediacy. This may sometimes mean things are not as carefully finished as they might be, but they do taste as they began. Any restaurant offering Ch. Fourcas-Hosten 1982 at £15.50 and Tignanello 1985 for a mere £19 must be on an oenophile's list; selection is robust and prices remain outrageously fair. House wine is £6.90. CELLARMAN'S CHOICE: New Zealand, Hunter's, Marlborough Sauvignon Blanc 1990, £14.40; Gigondas, Dom. Les Pallières 1985, £15.

CHEF: Toni Ferguson-Lees PROPRIETORS: Nick Parkin and Toni Ferguson-Lees OPEN: Tue to Sat, D only MEALS: 7 to 9.30 PRICES: £14 (£19). Net prices, card slips closed CARDS: Access, Amex, Diners, Visa SEATS: 34. Vegetarian meals. Children's helpings. Music

SAFFRON WALDEN Essex map 3

Old Hoops

15 King Street, Saffron Walden CB10 1HE COOKING 1
SAFFRON WALDEN (0799) 22813 COST £31

The stairs to this restaurant almost overlooking the market may be dark, but how welcoming is the room and how encouraging the starched linen. Old Hoops is appreciated by a strong local following who like the fair prices and 'the knowledge that there are no extras lurking to sap the bill'. The repertoire is classically based, as it might be from one who learnt his trade and practised it in more formal metropolitan locales. The same dishes get endorsement from year to year: 'musselcress' soup, with watercress, potato, mussels and cream; chicken wrapped with filo, with a tarragon sauce; calf's liver, oregano, green peppercorns and blackcurrants. The range of puddings will finish anyone off – try the chocolate sponge flavoured with cinnamon, with a toffee sauce. Wines are none too dear, mainly French, with one or two good things. House wine is £6.95.

CHEF: Ray Morrison PROPRIETORS: Don Irwin and Ray Morrison OPEN: Tue to Sat CLOSED: 2 weeks summer MEALS: 12 to 2.15, 7 to 10 PRICES: £17 (£26) CARDS: Access, Amex, Diners, Visa SEATS: 40. Private parties: 40 main room. Children's helpings. Music

ST KEYNE Cornwall map 1

▲ *Well House* 🍷

St Keyne PL14 4RN
LISKEARD (0579) 42001 COOKING 3*
on B3254, 3m S of Liskeard COST £27–£44

The well at St Keyne was thought in the Middle Ages to cure blindness; the Well House today is better for dyspepsia and angst. Neat gardens surround it, lawns fall away to views of fields beyond and the public rooms and bedrooms are distinguished by their comfort rather than their grandeur. The dining-room is well arranged, tables not too close, the atmosphere lightened by less than traditional decoration. There have been chefs' musical chairs in the South West this year and the Well House's stoves are now the domain of David Woolfall, once at Teignworthy on Dartmoor and a worthy entrant to earlier editions of the *Guide*. The careful, modern cooking with attention to detail that Nicholas Wainford had secured from the previous occupant of the kitchen has not faltered with the changeover. The equally considered welcome and service, distinguished by thoroughness, continue from year to year, though they veer occasionally towards solemnity. A spring meal, taken from a daily-changing short menu, showed great craft. A leek and asparagus terrine ('with 40 shades of green in the marbled slice, [it] appeared to hold together by willpower alone') sat in a brilliant orange pool of pimento vinaigrette ('pungent but not overpowering'). A main course of guinea-fowl was tender, cooked to a moist flesh and crisp skin, with a dark green peppercorn sauce that may have been too strong, though never unpalatable. Vegetables were a 'chef's sideplate', but included thinnings from the carrot bed as well as excellent early potatoes. Cheeses, here on a piece of Cornish granite, are local and in fine condition. Desserts allow further displays of skill and management of flavour, as in a honey ice-cream with a warm gratin of raspberries and mango. Breads (breakfast and dinner), canapés, appetisers and petits fours are of the standard needed to confirm this as a distinguished kitchen. A steady gradient through the clarets from sound petits châteaux for around £12 to Ch. La Mission-Haut-Brion 1966 at £155, passing such delights as 1979 La Lagune, characterises the intelligent, mainly French, exclusively European, wine list, which offers good simple drinking as well as fair choice at more exalted levels. Half-bottles remain thinly scattered. House wine is £7.50. CELLARMAN'S CHOICE: Mâcon Lugny, Les Genevrières 1988, Latour, £14.25; Ch. Palmer 1979, £57.75.

CHEF: David Woolfall PROPRIETOR: Nicholas Wainford OPEN: all week MEALS: 12.30 to 2, 7.30 to 9 PRICES: Set L £21 (£27), Set D £24.95 (£32) to £29.70 (£37). Card slips closed CARDS: Access, Amex, Visa SEATS: 36. 5 tables outside. Private parties: 40 main room. Car park, 24 places. Vegetarian meals. No children under 8. Smart dress preferred. Wheelchair access (1 step). No music ACCOMMODATION: 10 rooms, all with bath/shower. B&B £60 to £105. Deposit: £25. Pets welcome. Afternoon teas. Garden. Swimming-pool. Tennis. TV. Phone. Scenic. Doors close at midnight (*Which? Hotel Guide*)

ST LEONARDS East Sussex map 3

Röser's

64 Eversfield Place, St Leonards TN37 6DB COOKING 3*
HASTINGS (0424) 712218 COST £22–£37

'We went in disbelief that such a serious restaurant could exist on the Hastings/St Leonards sea-front,' writes one visitor. She was completely won over by the food at the Rösers' remarkable venue. The setting is an unobtrusive terrace of Georgian buildings almost opposite the pier, with shiny wood panelling and a feeling of space inside. Dinner is now à la carte and lunch is an affordable fixed-price menu. There is a luxurious undercurrent to many of Gerald Röser's dishes: foie gras and chicken liver parfait with Beaumes de Venise jelly ('the first intense flavour took my breath away; so rich yet so delicious...'); pike soufflé with smoked salmon sauce and Beluga caviare. The precision and artistry shows in roast guinea-fowl, boned, carved and re-formed on the plate, with shallots, whole wild mushrooms and green coriander leaves arranged round the meat on top of a red wine sauce ('simply a masterpiece'). Other recommendations have included duck breast with raisins and champagne sauce, tournedos of salmon with chive sauce, and roast best end of Romney Marsh lamb with tarragon and rösti potatoes. One reporter with vegetarian leanings has enjoyed a plethora of specially created dishes: tempura of okra and aubergine in black-bean sauce; alexander buds pickled with ginger and fennel; flowering courgette filled with asparagus mousse. Procuring ingredients is a major preoccupation and visitors are encouraged to bring in any unusual local produce that they find. The kitchen maintains its high standards with impeccable desserts: chocolate mousse with coffee cream sauce; apple mille-feuille with calvados, creme patissière and butterscotch sauce. Cheeses are from Philippe Olivier and English farmhouse dairies. Canapés, petits fours, breads and butter all show the hallmarks of a high-quality enterprise. The long and serious wine list includes over a dozen grand and premier cru Chablis alone, and several 1983s at that, at prices that are both fair and sensible, with some older vintages looking especially good value. Alsace and Germany are well-favoured. Good low- and mid-priced wines are not ignored. House wine is £7.95. CELLARMAN'S CHOICE: Gewurztraminer Réserve Personnelle 1983, Hugel, £23; Aloxe-Corton 1986, Leflaive, £25.50.

CHEF: Gerald Röser PROPRIETORS: Gerald and Jenny Röser OPEN: Tue to Sat, exc Sat L MEALS: 12 to 2, 7 to 10 PRICES: £22 (£31), Set L £15.95 (£22). Net prices, card slips closed CARDS: Access, Amex, Diners, Visa SEATS: 40. Private parties: 20 main room, 40 private room. Vegetarian meals. Children welcome. No pipes in dining-room. Wheelchair access (2 steps). Music

ST MARGARET'S AT CLIFFE Kent map 3

▲ *Wallett's Court*

West Cliffe,
St Margaret's at Cliffe CT15 6EW — COOKING 2
DOVER (0304) 852424 — COST £23–£37

'Decoration here could be described as a study in exposed woodworm' was an almost waggish comment of one transient, whose colleague's more sober remark was: 'What an introduction to England and English cuisine for the many foreigners who appear here.' Chris and Lea Oakley have consolidated their remarkable conversion of this historic manor-farmstead into something much more professional than a B&B with evening meals. Yet the sense of personal involvement and struggle of the early years survives and gives it character. B&B monetary values have survived too, which makes it fairly priced. A short menu indicates a careful, rather than adventurous, hand in the kitchen, although meals become longer and more elaborate on Saturdays. The range of flavours is conservative, which makes the most commented-upon items the successful manipulation of sweet and sour in Cumberland sauce with smoked duck and a game pâté, and a compote of kumquats that has appeared variously with pan-fried venison and madeira sauce, with a salad of smoked goose, or a 'huntsman's' terrine. Decorated vegetables betray the professional origins (Le Poulbot in the City of London) of the chef. Puddings show less of a light hand than the savoury courses, but coffee is excellent. The wine list is adequate for its needs. House Bordeaux is £7.

CHEF: Chris Oakley PROPRIETORS: Chris and Lea Oakley OPEN: Tue to Sat, D only MEALS: 7 to 9 PRICES: Set D £17.50 (£23) to £25 (£31). Card slips closed CARDS: Access, Visa SEATS: 50. Private parties: 30 main room, 20 private room. Car park, 26 places. Vegetarian meals. Children's helpings. No music. Fax: (0304) 85343 ACCOMMODATION: 8 rooms, all with bath/shower. D,B&B £52.50 to £90. Children welcome. Baby facilities. Garden. Tennis. Billiards. TV. Phone. Scenic. Doors close at midnight. Confirm by 5 (*Which? Hotel Guide*)

ST MICHAEL'S ON WYRE Lancashire map 5

Mallards

Garstang Road,
St Michael's on Wyre PR3 0TE COOKING 1
ST MICHAEL'S (099 58) 661 COST £14–£31

John and Ann Steel's restaurant occupies the ground floor of a cottage. The walls are hung with plates and wines are kept in racks at the back of the dining-room. John Steel cooks a short menu of dishes with modern undertones. Reporters have enjoyed avocado salad with cashews and ceiery; chicken, leek and Stilton soufflé; and exactly timed loin of lamb with red wine and mint sauce. If supplies of the eponymous mallard run out, diners may be offered venison with orange and port sauce. Otherwise the menu takes in salmon roulade with asparagus sauce; king prawns with garlic, spring onions and pine kernels; and fillet of salmon and brill with Noilly Prat sauce. Generous helpings of vegetables have included 'exquisite' celeriac soufflés. The decent wine list has fair prices and improvements are in hand. Reservations are essential.

CHEF: John Steel PROPRIETORS: John and Ann Steel OPEN: Mon to Sat, D only, Sun L CLOSED: 2 weeks Aug, 1 week Jan MEALS: 12 to 2.30, 7 to 9.30 (10 Sat) PRICES: £18 (£26), Set Sun L £9.25 (£14). Card slips closed CARDS: Access, Visa SEATS: 24. Private parties: 36 main room. Car park, 20 places. Children's helpings. No smoking while others are eating. Wheelchair access. Music

SALISBURY Wiltshire map 2

Harper's

7 Ox Row, The Market Square,
Salisbury SP1 1EU COOKING 1
SALISBURY (0722) 333118 COST £12–£24

Adrian and Ann Harper will not be diverted from their crusade for quality, freshness and value for money. Their latest improvement is a one-course bistro menu, in which all dishes are under £5. The flexibility of the menus and the varied repertoire has produced a wholesome crop of recommendations: mushroom tartlet, fricassee of seafood, Sicilian fish soup, lambs' kidneys with Meaux mustard and madeira, a bowl of beefsteak casseroled with vegetables and herby dumplings. Sweets are liked: treacle tart, raspberry and white chocolate mousse, fig sue and Harper's 'luxury' bread-and-butter pudding. The setting, a first-floor room in a converted shop overlooking the market square, is decorated 'in the way such establishments *ought* to be but so rarely are in Britain,' according to a reader. An excellent, carefully considered wine list covers most major growers and regions. House French is £7.50. Strong local beers are also available.

CHEFS: Adrian Harper and Julie West PROPRIETORS: Adrian and Ann Harper OPEN: Mon to Sat CLOSED: 25 and 26 Dec MEALS: 12 to 2, 6.30 to 10 (10.30 Sat) PRICES: L £11 (£17), D £13 (£20), Set L £6.90 (£12), Set D £12.90 (£20), bistro menu from £3.70 CARDS: Access, Diners, Visa SEATS: 60. Private parties: 60 main room. Vegetarian meals. Children's helpings. Music. Air-conditioned

SCARBOROUGH North Yorkshire map 6A

Lanterna

33 Queen Street, Scarborough YO11 1HQ COOKING 2
SCARBOROUGH (0723) 363616 COST £28

A bright and cheery façade proclaims this little trattoria in a quiet side street off the town centre. The cork-walled interior, with shades of brown everywhere, contrasts strongly with outside and helps along the crowded, informal atmosphere. A sensibly limited menu offers popular predictables – spaghetti carbonara, scampi fritti, escalope Milanese, steak Diane – but they are carefully cooked and based on good-quality ingredients. There are good reports, too, of various fish dishes: queenies with a provençal sauce and 'crisp and tasty' strips of Dover sole fried in breadcrumbs. The wine list is short, in content as well as detail. Half of it is Italian. House Italian is £8.50 a litre.

CHEF: G. Arecco PROPRIETORS: Mr and Mrs G. Arecco OPEN: Tue to Sat, D only MEALS: 7 to 9.30 PRICES: £15 (£23). Card slips closed CARDS: Access, Visa SEATS: 36. Private parties: 36 main room. Vegetarian meals. No children under 2. Wheelchair access. Music

SEAFORD East Sussex map 3

Quincy's

42 High Street, Seaford BN25 1PL COOKING 1*
SEAFORD (0323) 895490 COST £22–£34

'If you separate technique from skilful flavouring, Ian Dowding does rather well,' according to one inspector. Mousses wobble, lamb is pink and juicy, fish not overcooked, chicken liver terrine nicely textured. But tastes in a ginger sauce for langoustines, and cinnamon in a seafood hotpot, thickening in a sauce for pheasant, and an overwhelming flavour of golden syrup in a lemon pudding made one reader question the kitchen work. Even so, Ian and Dawn Dowding's small restaurant is a useful resource for Seaford. The prices are not high, and the menu offers a wide choice from monkfish with lime butter sauce to new-wave chicken with lentils and smoked sausage, and lamb with aubergines and couscous, to old English steak, kidney and oyster. Puddings even allow for a choice of two hot things, and decent English cheese is available. Not all the wines listed are stocked (Murphy's law of choosing wine in restaurants) and the list is kept short and inexpensive. House wines are £6.75.

CHEF: Ian Dowding PROPRIETORS: Ian and Dawn Dowding OPEN: Tue to Sat, D only, and Sun L MEALS: 7.15 to 10, Sun 12 to 2 PRICES: Set Sun L and Tue to Sat D £14.95 (£22) to £20.95 (£28) CARDS: Access, Visa SEATS: 32. Private parties: 20 main room. Vegetarian meals. Children's helpings on request. Music

SHEFFIELD South Yorkshire map 5

Greenhead House

84 Burncross Road, Chapeltown,
Sheffield S30 4SF COOKING 2*
SHEFFIELD (0742) 469004 COST £31–£43

This smart stone cottage on the outskirts of Sheffield has a strong following of regulars. 'I have never had anything other than a good meal here and in more than half my visits the food, wine and service have been as good as any I have ever encountered,' writes one of them. Moral: book early for Saturday nights. The menu is monthly, four courses (soup at second), with a choice of four or five dishes at each. The cooking is sophisticated, including plenty of shellfish, such as the langoustines from the west coast of Scotland with a tomato jelly and a tapénade vinaigrette, and a crab tart with grilled scallops. But reports stress the even quality across the whole range of the meal, from small quiches with quail eggs as an appetiser, to the simple but well-cooked vegetables (even asparagus if you are in luck), and the coffee and petits fours included in the price of the meal. The welcome, service and ambience are also a constant of reports, lifting the quality of an evening here to a yet higher level. The wine list is supplemented by a couple of pages of bin-ends; the main range is an even choice of classic French regions with a few bottles from Spain. House wines are £8.75.

CHEFS: Neil Allen and Christine Roberts PROPRIETORS: Neil and Anne Allen OPEN: Tue to Sat, D only CLOSED: last 2 weeks Apr, last 2 weeks Aug, 24 to 31 Dec MEALS: 7.15 to 9 PRICES: Set D £24 (£31) to £28 (£36). Card slips closed CARDS: Access, Amex, Visa SEATS: 32. Private parties: 32 main room. Car park, 14 places. Children welcome. Wheelchair access. No music

▲ *Henfrey's Restaurant, Charnwood Hotel*

10 Sharrow Lane, Sheffield S11 8AA COOKING 2
SHEFFIELD (0742) 589411 COST £35–£56

This is a dynamic, ambitious enterprise. The owners have turned the original restaurant into a library and opened an entirely new dining-room. Their kitchen brigade has formidable credentials. What they deliver is food that is complex, light and accurate. It is a cuisine built of components – some might say too many. Even so, the 'gourmet menu' has produced fine things: 'tea-smoked' fillet of salmon; pigeon breast with pan-fried goose liver and rösti potatoes; medallions of lamb with soubise mousse and chartreuse of mushrooms on a jus of tarragon and watercress; gâteau of Brie with wild mushrooms; pear and lime mousse with poached pear and spun sugar. Prices are often much higher than anticipated and the style is jacket-and-tie formality. A short list of around 60 wines is notable for its range and quality, detail and typographical errors. It offers many fine growers world-wide, especially in Italy. Prices throughout are fair. A casual alternative to Henfrey's is the Brasserie Leo, serving dishes from the same kitchen – reports, please.

CHEF: Wayne Bosworth PROPRIETORS: Chris and Val King OPEN: Tue to Sat, D only MEALS: 7.30 to 10 PRICES: Set D from £23.75 (£35) to £34.20 (£47) CARDS: Access, Amex, Diners, Visa SEATS: 28. Private parties: 30 main room, 80 private room. Car park, 29 places. Vegetarian meals. Children welcome. Jacket and tie. No smoking in dining-room. Wheelchair access (also WC). Music. Air-conditioned. Fax: (0742) 555107 ACCOMMODATION: 26 rooms, all with bath/shower. Rooms for disabled. B&B £75 to £120. Children welcome. Baby facilities. Afternoon teas. Air-conditioned. TV. Phone. Confirm by 6

SHEPTON MALLET Somerset map 2

Blostin's

29 Waterloo Road,
Shepton Mallet BA4 5HH COOKING 2
SHEPTON MALLET (0749) 343648 COST £16–£31

Prices have hardly changed so that old friends may continue returning to this small, even 'cramped', restaurant where Nick Reed offers a set-price, short-choice menu bolstered by a few seasonal specialities. There are occasions when lack of room combines with heavy smoke, and the apparently compulsory staging-post of the bar before ordering induces some discomfort; but value has its way: 'We have paid far more for much, much less,' says one reader. The repertoire is not always wide: one year's salmon with 'creamy spinach' is this year's 'creamy leeks'; crab in filo becomes crab in wholemeal pastry. Supporters find the fish soup 'authentic', the mussels fat, and there is plenty of rich flavour to the duck with red wine and mushrooms before a 'sweet and gooey' sticky toffee pudding with butterscotch sauce. The Reeds are stayers; the welcome is invariably cheerful; enough adventure is provided (Nick Reed was once one of the few chefs willing to experiment with goat dishes) to enliven the consistency. The wine list includes the Australian Château Tahbilk as well as Nick Ryman's wines from Bergerac and a short but serviceable selection, topping with Ch. Siran and starting with a St-Pourçain, at fair prices. House wines at £6.75 are reckoned by some to be the best bet.

CHEF: Nick Reed PROPRIETORS: Nick and Lynne Reed OPEN: Tue to Sat, D only (L Tue to Fri by arrangement) MEALS: 12 to 2, 7 to 9.30 (10 Sat) PRICES: £19 (£26), Set L £9.95 (£16), Set D £12.95 (£19) to £13.95 (£20). Card slips closed CARDS: Access, Visa SEATS: 32. Private parties: 30 main room. Vegetarian meals. Children's helpings. Wheelchair access. Music

▲ *Bowlish House* 🍷 **NEW ENTRY**

Wells Road, Shepton Mallet BA4 5JD — COOKING 1
SHEPTON MALLET (0749) 342022 — COST £31

The wool merchants of Shepton Mallet did themselves proud on the housing side and Bowlish House is a much pedimented consequence. For many years it has been a restaurant-with-rooms, and the current owners, Bob and Linda Morley, have been here for the last four. 'The whole house was extremely well kept, and obviously cherished,' wrote one reporter who was beleaguered by wind and snow before finding safe haven amongst portraits, Crown Derby and central heating. The cooking, from a set-price menu offering half a dozen choices at each course, is self-taught and has shown steady improvement since the change in ownership. It may have lapses (some have criticised the meat for lack of tenderness, others the desserts for lack of oomph) but the general intentions are honest and mindful of the limitations of a one-cook kitchen, thus avoiding over-elaboration and mindless garnish. Bob Morley's ministrations front-of-house are discreet and to the point. The wine list is one for enthusiasts; Italy and Spain are given as much space as Burgundy and Bordeaux, which is always a good sign. Prices are fair. Ten house wines at £7.50 head the list with succinct, helpful notes. Half-bottles are limited. CELLARMAN'S CHOICE: Champagne Brut n.v., Granier, £19.25; Lerida, Abadia Reserva 1987, Raimat, £9.

CHEF: Linda Morley PROPRIETORS: Bob and Linda Morley OPEN: all week, D only (L by arrangement for groups) CLOSED: 1 week Feb, 1 week Oct MEALS: 7 to 9.30 (Sun 7 to 9) PRICES: Set D £19.50 (£26). Card slips closed CARDS: Access, Visa SEATS: 24. Private parties: 36 main room. Car park, 12 places. Vegetarian meals. Children welcome. No smoking during meals. Smart dress preferred. No music ACCOMMODATION: 4 rooms, all with bath/shower. B&B £48. Children welcome. Baby facilities. Pets welcome. Garden. TV. Doors close at midnight. Confirm by 6 (*Which? Hotel Guide*)

SHINFIELD Berkshire — map 2

L'Ortolan 🍷

The Old Vicarage, Church Lane,
Shinfield RG2 9BY — COOKING 4*
READING (0734) 883783 — COST £49–£85

The eponymous bunting is caged in a castellated rectory south of Reading. Around it, the garden improves, the car park grows, and the hum of the motorway can still be sensed in the quiet of the night. The double dining-room extends into a conservatory – the best spot to sit – which is balanced on the other side of the house by a new addition to extend the bar. The hard economic times have caused a variation in price-structure, with a mid-week evening menu at the same cost as lunch, but weekends remain bargain-free. Some readers have observed a difference in achievement between the full *carte* and the menu, always a problem where bargains are concerned. Considering how small the restaurant is, the choice is very wide – a signal of the kitchen's ambitions. John Burton-Race explores the classical palette of flavours in dishes demanding control so that tastes may be cleverly layered and interlaced. 'There is a lightness not to be confused with hesitancy, a sensitivity that gives subtlety' in most of the set-piece dishes. Those which have received good marks this year include a salad of crayfish and foie gras de canard; oysters touched by lime, served poached in their shells with watercress and cucumber; morels stuffed with a chicken mousse; asparagus with a broccoli mousse in a pastry case, with a truffle cream; calf's sweetbread and foie gras on a salad of chicory and lamb's leaves with walnuts and walnut dressing; John Dory with ceps and a truffle cream; duck with ginger and Sauternes, acidulated with peach juice, the leg served separately with a salad and a slice of foie gras; pig's trotter stuffed with chestnut and pheasant; and desserts such as the 'ivory tower' of white chocolate mousse and raspberries, enrobed with dark chocolate or kirsch parfait and pineapple sorbet between layers of coconut biscuit, or a plate of raspberry dishes from jelly to custard. The amount of foie gras and truffle nearly exceeds anywhere in the kingdom; they stamp their character across the repertoire and food can, therefore, be filling. The ancillaries, from hot delicacies with the drinks, to excellent bread, to those at the last gasp – that is, coffee and petits fours – are in tune with the rest of the operation. Service does not inspire the confidence of a central London place, though whether delays sometimes noted are the fault of the kitchen or the waiting staff is not evident. Christine Burton-Race makes a marvellously diffident yet informative hostess. Prices are high, made higher by supplements to the fixed-price (not an endearing feature) and mean that production must be faultless. The wine list, French with a few additions, includes lots of halves, but hardly a bottle below £20. Despite the compromises made due to the recession, it is this cost element of meals at places such as L'Ortolan that may cause their undoing. If any aspect of the meal is less than perfect, the ill-will generated by a three-figure bill is monumental.

CHEF: John Burton-Race PROPRIETORS: John and Christine Burton-Race OPEN: Tue to Sun, exc Sun D CLOSED: last 2 weeks Feb, last 2 weeks Aug MEALS: 12.15 to 2.15, 7.15 to 10.30 PRICES: Set L and D £29.50 (£49) to £49 (£71) CARDS: Access, Amex, Diners, Visa SEATS: 60. Private parties: 40 main room, 32 private room. Car park, 15 places. Children's helpings. Wheelchair access (2 steps). No music. Fax: (0734) 885391

SHIPTON GORGE Dorset map 2

▲ *Innsacre* **NEW ENTRY**

Shipton Gorge DT6 4LJ — COOKING 2
BRIDPORT (0308) 56137 — COST £12–£32

New owners Sydney and Lesley Davies have changed the name and the style of this converted Dorset farmhouse. It is no longer a 'farmhouse hotel', rather a 'restaurant-with-rooms'. Outside, there are orchards and a bucolic menagerie of sheep, pigs and goats. Inside, the place has been much improved to give a feel of well-ordered rusticity. A new brigade of cooks, headed by Simon Mazzei-Scaglione, has been spurred on to develop a distinctive repertoire based on local ingredients, including game, fish from the coast and Abbotsbury oysters. The cooking centres on a fixed-price dinner menu, with a cheaper two-course option in mid-week, and it reads well. One meal included tartlet of quails' eggs with asparagus; salmon steak, beaten paper-thin and served with lime and fennel vinaigrette; pork fillet filled with apricots and prunes; lamb cutlets with tarragon mousse; and hot toffee pudding baked to order with butterscotch sauce. Other reporters have noted fine flavours and sauces, and the venison ('so good that I had it two nights running'). Details such as decent bread and good coffee with home-made fudge and candied orange peel are encouraging signs for the future. Light lunches are served in the bar-lounge. The wine list is compatible with the menu and mark-ups are low. House New Zealand is £8.50.

CHEFS: Simon Mazzei-Scaglione and Amanda Buttle PROPRIETORS: Sydney and Lesley Davies OPEN: Tue to Sun, exc Sun D, and bank hol Mons CLOSED: 25 and 26 Dec, 1 week Nov MEALS: 12 to 1.45, 7 to 9.45 PRICES: light L from £2.20, Set L £8 (£12) to £12.50 (£17), Set D £16.50 (£21) to £22.50 (£27). Net prices, card slips closed CARDS: Access, Visa SEATS: 42. 8 tables outside. Private parties: 60 main room. Car park, 40 places. Vegetarian meals. Children's helpings. No smoking in dining-room. Wheelchair access (also WC). Music ACCOMMODATION: 7 rooms, all with bath/shower. B&B £45 to £66. Deposit: £20. Children welcome. Baby facilities. Pets welcome. Garden. TV. Scenic. Doors close at midnight. Confirm by 6 (*Which? Hotel Guide*)

SHIPTON-UNDER-WYCHWOOD Oxfordshire **map 2**

▲ *Lamb Inn*

High Street,
Shipton-under-Wychwood OX7 6DQ — COOKING 1
SHIPTON (0993) 830465 — COST £19–£29

A civilised Cotswold inn of some character quietly hugging the outskirts of the village. George Benham still reigns in the kitchen, producing set-price menus of roast spring lamb, venison cutlets, lemon sole and duck – dishes that are appreciated both for plain cooking and for generous portions. 'Good and fresh,' commented one August visitor on the quality of the ingredients used, 'which they need to be given the simplicity of the cooking.' 'The meal was good value and we enjoyed it,' summed up another, although a couple arriving on a Saturday night noted that the restaurant was so tiny 'that as many seemed to eat in the bar...with all that goes with such an area, i.e. smoke'. House wine is £7.

CHEF: George Benham PROPRIETORS: Vivien and Luciano Valenta OPEN: Mon to Sat D, Sun L CLOSED: Mon winter MEALS: 12.30 to 1.45, 7.30 to 9 PRICES: Set Sun L £12.50 (£19), Set D £17.50 (£24). Card slips closed CARDS: Access, Amex, Visa SEATS: 30. 8 tables outside. Private parties: 36 main room. Car park, 30 places. No children under 14. No smoking in dining-room. Wheelchair access (1 step). No music ACCOMMODATION: 5 rooms, all with bath/shower. B&B £68 double only. Deposit: £20. No children under 14. Garden. TV. Scenic. Doors close at 11. Confirm by 6

'The worst, however, was yet to come. We could not believe it when the waiters asked us to keep the cutlery from the first course to use for the main meal, but this actually happened. In a restaurant offering a basic menu at £15 per head, this is totally unacceptable. Still, as things turned out there was no point in keeping them anyway.' On eating in London

SHURDINGTON Gloucestershire map 2

▲ *Greenway*

NEW ENTRY

Shurdington GL51 5UG
CHELTENHAM (0242) 862352 COOKING 1
on A46, 2m S of Cheltenham COST £20–£43

The 'Green Way' from which the hotel takes its names was an ancient pre-Roman droveway, and, appropriately, the dining-room looks out towards a high ridge of hills dotted with sheep and solitary trees. But chef Edward Stephens worked at the Caprice (see entry, London) before taking over the kitchen in 1989 and his cooking is more modern city than countrified. Menus are coloured by florid descriptions: ragoût of mushrooms in pastry spiked with truffles; salad of warm globe artichoke with Parma ham and curly endive coated in virgin olive oil; loin of English lamb filled with spinach perfumed with rosemary. A lot of effort goes into the well-judged vegetables. Other results can be uneven and may sometimes be characterised as lacking spark. Incidentals such as nibbles and the chef's complimentary course need improving. Service is attentive without being obsequious. The list of around 200 wines emphasises champagnes and clarets. House vin de pays is £9.75.

CHEF: Edward Stephens PROPRIETOR: Tony Elliott OPEN: all week, exc Sat L CLOSED: 24 Dec to 6 Jan, L bank hols MEALS: 12 to 2, 7 to 9.30 (8.30 Sun) PRICES: Set L £13 (£20) to £16 (£23), Set D £28 (£36). Card slips closed CARDS: Access, Amex, Carte Blanche, Diners, Visa SEATS: 50. 4 tables outside. Private parties: 14 main room, 12 and 26 private rooms. Car park, 50 places. Vegetarian meals. No children under 7. Smart dress preferred. No cigars/pipes in dining-room. Wheelchair access (1 step; also WC). Music ACCOMMODATION: 18 rooms, all with bath/shower. Rooms for disabled. B&B £85 to £120. No children under 7. Garden. TV. Phone. Scenic. Doors close at 11.30 (*Which? Hotel Guide*)

SISSINGHURST Kent map 3

Rankins

The Street, Sissinghurst TN17 2JA COOKING 2
CRANBROOK (0580) 713964 COST £23–£36

'Always a pleasure,' comments a Kent reporter about Hugh and Leonora Rankin's beamed country restaurant. There is now the option of two menus: one is a short *carte*, priced according to the main course; the other is a more straightforward three-course fixed-price affair. Hugh Rankin's cooking is modern, drawing from the full range of European cooking, and shows some adventurous touches: salad of grilled peppers with capers, hard-boiled egg and anchovy; filo pastry cups with asparagus; ceviche of cod and prawns; dry-fried duck breast with braised red cabbage and green peppercorn sauce; chocolate marquise with orange sauce. Fish soup is powerful. Sauces with meat dishes are often very herby; those with fish are subtler. The pudding menu takes in exotic sorbets, fruit salad with a Cointreau and Muscat syrup, and English toffee and chocolate ice-creams. Sunday lunch follows the same theme, with the addition of a traditional roast. Service is consistently friendly. The short, fairly priced wine list of around 40 bins now has a wider choice of half-bottles. House French is £7.80.

CHEF: Hugh Rankin PROPRIETORS: Hugh and Leonora Rankin OPEN: Wed to Sat, D only, and Sun L MEALS: Sun L 12.30 (12 summer) to 1.30, 7.30 (6.30 summer) to 9 PRICES: £22.50 (£30), Set Sun L £15.50 (£23) to £18.95 (£27), Set D £19.95 (£28) CARDS: Access, Visa SEATS: 30. Private parties: 10 main room, 24 private room. Children's helpings (Sun L only). No children under 8. Smart dress preferred. Smoking after meal only. Music

SLAIDBURN Lancashire map 5

▲ *Parrock Head Hotel*

Slaidburn BB7 3AH
SLAIDBURN (020 06) 614 COOKING 1
1m NW of Slaidburn COST £17–£26

The long, low, starkly white building is set well outside picturesque Slaidburn, at a point where the land has risen to the bleak peat moor. Modern plate-glass windows afford fine sweeping views. Inside, there is no sign whatsoever of the farm Parrock Head used to be. Instead, deep sofas, flower arrangements and a beamed library proclaim an informal country-house style; service is by 'a covey of conscientious local ladies'. The kitchen produces food based on local ingredients and the menu, changed daily, is sensibly limited to a choice of four dishes for each of three courses. This will always include a soup, and perhaps some home-cured gravlax, to be followed by Lancaster guinea-fowl roasted with citrus fruits; a trio of beef, port and lamb set on a rösti potato with a red wine sauce; and lemon sole fillets stuffed with cream cheese and chive mousse with shrimp sauce. Masses of fresh vegetables have had to be 'crammed in on the table', but balanced the generosity of the main-course portions. It is a place worth knowing about in this remote moorland area; standards of cooking and hospitality are consistently maintained. A sensible wine list is arranged by weight and colour and adopts a catholic approach to world production. Prices are fair. House wine is £6.50.

CHEFS: Vicky Umbers and Paul Roberts PROPRIETORS: Vicky and Richard Umbers OPEN: all week, D only, and Sun L MEALS: 12.30 to 1, 7 to 8.30 PRICES: £16 (£22), Set Sun L £11.50 (£17) CARDS: Amex, Access, Visa SEATS: 32. Car park, 20 places. Vegetarian meals. Children's helpings. No smoking in dining-room. Wheelchair access ACCOMMODATION: 9 rooms, all with bath/shower. Rooms for disabled. B&B £35 to £58. Deposit: £10. Children welcome. Pets by arrangement. Afternoon teas. Garden. Fishing. Golf. TV. Phone. Scenic. Doors close at 11.30 (*Which? Hotel Guide*)

SOUTHAMPTON Hampshire map 2

Kuti's

70 London Road, Southampton SO1 2AJ COOKING 1
SOUTHAMPTON (0703) 221585 and 333473 COST £10–£24

This is a stylish venue for Indian food. The kitchen brigade has been joined by a chef from Veeraswamy in London (see entry) and the menu tries to offer a little more than standard curry-house fare. Bhel pooris, pakoras and vegetable samosas feature among the starters, while main courses are dominated by north

Indian tandooris and curries. Lamb pasanda, chicken jalfrezi and karahi dishes are specialities. There are also thalis and a well-reported lunchtime buffet. Start with chaas – a drink of diluted lassi, spiced, Bombay-style, with ginger, fresh coriander, cumin and dried mustard seeds. Finish with kulfi or ras malai. Indian beers include Kingfisher, Elephant and Golden Eagle. House wine is £5.85.

CHEFS: Anjab Ali, Kuti Miah and L. Khan PROPRIETOR: Kuti Miah OPEN: all week CLOSED: 25 Dec MEALS: 12 to 2.15, 6 to 11.30 PRICES: £10 (£20), Set L £6.50 (£10), Set D £11 (£15) to £15 (£20). Service 10% CARDS: Access, Amex, Visa SEATS: 66. Private parties: 30 main room. Car park, 10 places. Vegetarian meals. Children welcome. Smart dress preferred. Wheelchair access (also WC). Music. Air-conditioned

SOUTHEND-ON-SEA Essex map 3

Slassor's

145 Eastern Esplanade,
Southend-on-Sea SS1 2YD COOKING 1
SOUTHEND (0702) 614880 COST £25

Leslie Slassor works away in a tiny kitchen: 'One can only assume he trained in the galley of a submarine,' comments a reporter. 'Foods of the World,' reads a note at the top of the menu, but the Slassors' repertoire is essentially Anglo-French. The sea is a stone's throw away and fresh fish is a favourite choice – there might be queen scallops with tomato and saffron sauce, sea bream with prawns and cheese sauce, monkfish thermidor – but not the only one. The style is reassuringly, occasionally cloyingly, old-fashioned but there are modern ideas as well, such as fish soup with prawns and anise, pigeon breast with blackberry liqueur sauce, and black pudding with apples and calvados. The menu is backed up by blackboard specials. One customer with no doubts about the excellent cooking points out that the 'mini-sized' dining-room is better for communal spirit than private conversations. Sweets are built around ice-creams, meringues and alcohol. The restaurant is unlicensed, but you can bring your own wine.

CHEF: Leslie Slassor PROPRIETORS: Margaret and Leslie Slassor OPEN: Mon to Sat, exc Sat L (by arrangement) MEALS: 12 to 2, 7 to 9.30 PRICES: £17 (£21). Card slips closed. Unlicensed, but bring your own: corkage 75p CARDS: Access, Visa SEATS: 22. Private parties: 30 main room. Children's helpings. Music

SOUTH MOLTON Devon map 1

▲ *Whitechapel Manor* 🍷

South Molton EX36 3EG COOKING 3*
SOUTH MOLTON (0769) 572554 and 573377 COST £32–£50

There are now signs from the North Devon Link Road to take you into the foothills of Exmoor, where this most handsome house serves as hotel and restaurant. If attention can be torn away from the seventeenth-century screen in the hall, the early eighteenth-century woodwork throughout the ground floor and the sensitive conversion by the Shaplands, and turned towards food,

Thierry Leprêtre-Granet will cook a remarkably assured meal to satisfy the most demanding. As one visitor from the Midlands expressed it: 'I think John Shapland's local knowledge as a farmer and his fulfilled quest for the best ingredients amply supply the kitchen with the opportunity to demonstrate its not inconsiderable skills. The very small dining-room and remote location make this a surprising success.' Not that all materials come with Devon straw in their mouth; the London and international networks are milked for foie gras, cheese, mushrooms and the current fashionables. The principal menu offers a choice of five or six things at each course, and the repertoire is distinguished by its full use of a wide range of materials. For instance, two first courses one week were confit of quail with broad beans, garlic and tarragon, and calves' sweetbreads with braised green lentils and fried leeks. Seasoning here is gentle, and tastes achieve a quiet harmony. An autumn meal of buckwheat pancakes layered with spinach and crab, then loin of rabbit with lobster stuffing, followed by a hot plum soufflé contrasting with an iced plum sorbet, caused tremulation that the main course combination might not work, but it redeemed itself magnificently. The hope must be that the hotel will survive these difficult times so that depth of staffing can give absolute consistency to the performance. Canard Duchêne, a good, reliable champagne at £26.50, sets the tone on a wine list that combines decent selection and fair prices. Half-bottles are provided generously and real depth is given by older clarets and burgundies and skillfully chosen Italian bottles. This is an intelligent if slightly 'safe' list, which just merits a glass award this year. House wine is £12.50. CELLARMAN'S CHOICE: Cloudy Bay, Chardonnay 1989, £22; Auxey-Duresses 1982, Ampeau, £28.50.

CHEF: Thierry Leprêtre-Granet PROPRIETORS: John and Patricia Shapland OPEN: all week MEALS: 12 to 2, 7 to 8.45 PRICES: Set L £26 (£32), Set D £35.50 (£42). Net prices, card slips closed CARDS: Access, Visa SEATS: 20. Car park, 40 places. No children under 10. No smoking in dining-room. No music. Fax: (076 95) 3797 ACCOMMODATION: 10 rooms, all with bath/shower. B&B £60 to £85. Afternoon teas. Garden. TV. Phone. Scenic. Doors close at 11.30 (*Which? Hotel Guide*)

SOUTHSEA Hampshire map 2

Bistro Montparnasse

NEW ENTRY

103 Palmerston Road,
Southsea PO5 3PS
PORTSMOUTH (0705) 816754

COOKING 1
COST £20–£32

This once-upon-a-time steakhouse stands head and shoulders above Southsea's other places to eat. The strawberry-pink décor, hanging brass bowls with plants and bowed ceiling survive from previous regimes. There is a change of ruler, too, in the kitchen, hence the absence from last year's edition. Michael Weir comes from training at Ramore in Portrush, Drimcong in Moycullen and 36 on the Quay down the road at Emsworth (see entries). His work has kept the bistro its local primacy. A dinner of boned quail with caramelised shallots followed by a giant fillet of turbot with a leek cream sauce (too much cream, not enough leek) and a salad dressed earlier than it was ordered, showed essential skills, generosity and some judgement. Menus change monthly and have included sensibly simple yet appetising combinations such as a boudin of salmon mousse on a bed of cucumber and marjoram; smoked haddock on spinach with a chive sauce; pork with mushroom and rosemary; and braised rabbit with endives. Desserts may kick off with three hot dishes: a surprising burden to place on a one-man kitchen. A short wine list has house Duboeuf at £7.50.

CHEF: Michael Weir PROPRIETORS: Peter and Gillian Scott OPEN: Tue to Sat, D only CLOSED: bank hols MEALS: 7 to 10 PRICES: £17 (£27), Set D £12.50 (£20) to £14.50 (£22) CARDS: Access, Amex, Diners, Visa SEATS: 40. Private parties: 40 main room. Vegetarian meals. Children welcome. Children's helpings on request. No pipes in dining-room. Wheelchair access. Music

SOUTHWOLD Suffolk map 6

▲ *Crown* 🍷 **NEW ENTRY**

90 High Street, Southwold IP18 6DP COOKING 2
SOUTHWOLD (0502) 722275 COST £17–£29

'The Crown is the pub to the Swan's posh hotel' is one way of seeing it; 'the Crown does the young and rising, the Swan keeps to the old and sedentary' is another. The Crown was Simon Loftus' and Adnams' first full-flight excursion into catering and offered sharp cooking, as interesting in the bar as in the restaurant, as well as excellent wines. It was the toast of the county. It did go through bad times, however, with too many chefs and too many managers. It seems to have returned to form. Both bar and restaurant are doing well: quenelle of pike, sauce mousseline; warm salad of pigeon; toasted goats' cheese salad; pigeon breast flamed in Chartreuse; rack of lamb with basil and tomato sauce; magret with truffle sauce; lamb with sauce Choron – these are classic dishes and seem to be competently cooked. They lack the sparkle of the first edition of the Crown, but competence is worth seeking out. Desserts have not been so well noticed: 'pleasant, but no more' was the verdict on an all-round sampling. Through all the ups and downs, the service has remained excellent and the building itself a pleasure to visit. With three 'suggested wines' offered on each menu by the glass for an aggregate of £7.75 and many fine wines available separately by the glass, many customers will be content not to stray to the exceedingly good list. It could be expected that Adnam's, with a retail list second to none, would produce the goods in the restaurant. Style and generosity are the keynotes; the style extends broadly from good French country reds, through many fine burgundies of some age, and remarkable Italians and Californians. Generosity is manifested throughout, with mark-ups going very easy on the more exalted bottles. A place for pleasurable experiment.

All details are as accurate as possible at the time of going to press, but chefs and owners often change, and it is wise to check by telephone before making a special journey. Many readers have been disappointed when set-price bargain meals are no longer available. Ask when booking.

CHEF: Andrew Mallice PROPRIETORS: Adnams plc OPEN: all week CLOSED: second week Jan MEALS: 12.30 to 2, 7.30 to 9.45 (10 bar meals) PRICES: Set L £12.75 (£17) to £14.75 (£19), Set D £15.75 (£21) to £17.75 (£24), bar snacks £1.75 to £8.50. Card slips closed CARDS: Access, Amex, Visa SEATS: 25. 4 tables outside. Private parties: 18 main room, 25 and 45 private rooms. Car park, 20 places. Vegetarian meals. Children's helpings on request. No smoking in dining-room. Air-conditioned. No music. Fax: (0502) 724805 ACCOMMODATION: 12 rooms, all with bath/shower. B&B £33 to £52. Children welcome. Baby facilities with prior notice. Afternoon teas. Fishing. Golf. Air-conditioned. TV. Phone. Scenic. Doors close at midnight (*Which? Hotel Guide*)

▲ *Swan Hotel* 🍷

Market Place, Southwold IP18 6EG — COOKING 1
SOUTHWOLD (0502) 722186 — COST £17–£36

Standing on the small market-place of this picturesque seaside town, this refurbished hotel is the flagship of Adnams' Sole Bay Brewery. From the flagged entry, go one way to the bar, busy with lunches; go the other to the dining-room. The general opinion this year is that the Swan is running second to its sister, the Crown (see above). One cynical view is that 'the dining-room curtains, elaborately pleated, ruched and draped in an effect of stagey elegance, mirrored too closely the style of the food'. A more constructive comment was that first and last courses outshone the mains. 'Navarin of lamb had a slightly sickly sauce, the lamb had quietly changed into liver. The "julienne of game in a whisky and foie gras sauce" was so described in the morning; by evening it was listed as "in whisky and cream"; it materialised as just whisky. The game was only venison.' Three short menus – 'menu of the day', 'English classics' and 'the Swan dinner' – at three prices cater for the wide range of clientele that frequent the town, encompassing grilled cod on a prawn sauce, wild boar with a raspberry jus, and scallop and prawn ragoût with champagne and saffron sauce. Some things have been enjoyed: a seafood sausage, quenelles of smoked chicken, chocolate truffle cake, and fresh red fruit in a wine jelly. A dozen good house wines, all available by the glass, head a list directed at giving a fine range in price as well as provenance – good petits châteaux and New World varieties around £10 to Echézeaux and Penfolds Grange topping £50. Prices are all very fair. House wines are from £5.85 (£1.20 a glass). CELLARMAN'S CHOICE: Mâcon, Chardonnay 1989, Talmard, £10.05; Alto Mango, Vino da Tavola 1987, Giacosa, £16.50.

CHEF: David Goode PROPRIETORS: Sole Bay Hotels OPEN: all week MEALS: 12 to 2, 7 to 9.30 PRICES: Set L £12.50 (£17) to £18.50 (£24), Set D £15.95 (£21) to £24.50 (£30). Card slips closed CARDS: Access, Amex, Visa SEATS: 96. Private parties: 44 and 50 private rooms. Car park, 50 places. Children's helpings. No children under 5 after 7pm. Smart dress preferred. No smoking in dining-room. Wheelchair access (also WC). Fax: (0502) 724800 ACCOMMODATION: 45 rooms, all with bath/shower. Rooms for disabled. Lift. B&B £42 to £128. Deposit: £10. Children welcome. Baby facilities. Pets in garden-rooms only. Afternoon teas. Garden. TV. Phone. Scenic. Doors close at midnight (*Which? Hotel Guide*)

County round-ups listing additional restaurants that may be worth a visit are at the back of the Guide, *after the Irish section. Reports on round-up entries are welcome.*

SPARK BRIDGE Cumbria map 7

▲ *Bridgefield House*

Spark Bridge, Ulverston LA12 8DA
LOWICK BRIDGE (022 985) 239
4m N of Ulverston, off A5084 on back road leading to Coniston

COOKING 2
COST £26–£35

Hardly another house in sight contributes to relaxation for visitors. On the estate itself, however, David Glister is a whirlwind of activity with diggers, masons' trowels and blocks of stone. Landscaping and improvements continue apace during the day, then David Glister changes his rubber boots for a bow tie and takes charge of serving the meals his wife cooks. Readers speak highly of the quality of the welcome from two dedicated workers, but worry that the fine margin of profit and loss at quiet times makes the house a succession of pools of heat rather than a constant ocean of warmth. Bridgefield avoids grandeur in appointments (to a fault for some diners) and Rosemary Glister's cooking can sometimes err on the side of simplicity when menu descriptions and price may excite more high-falutin ideas. A dish of 'raspberries soaked in Drambuie in a toasted oatmeal and cream crunch' would have benefited from more raspberries (two were counted), less cream and some crunch. But soups, baking of things like Cheddar bannocks, sauces (for instance with lamb's kidney in madeira on toast as an end-of-meal savoury, or salmon with wine, ginger and vermouth) and inventive vegetables get warm praise. With a spread of fine New Zealand and Australian bottles and many less exalted Rhônes, Alsaces and petits châteaux from Bordeaux, there is much happy and good-value drinking below £20. Beyond this, the mark-up hits hard. Burgundy has yet to be infiltrated by smaller domaines. House wine is £9.20. CELLARMAN'S CHOICE: Coldstream Hills, Chardonnay 1988, Halliday, £18.50; Rioja Reserva, Contino 1984, £14.85.

CHEF: Rosemary Glister PROPRIETORS: David and Rosemary Glister OPEN: all week, D only MEALS: 7.30 for 8 PRICES: Set D £19 (£26) to £22 (£29). Card slips closed CARDS: Access, Visa SEATS: 20. Private parties: 24 main room. Car park, 10 places. Vegetarian meals. Children's helpings. Smart dress preferred. No smoking in dining-room. No music. One sitting. Fax: (022 985) 379 ACCOMMODATION: 5 rooms, all with bath/shower. B&B £37 to £74. Deposit: £20. Children welcome. Baby facilities. Pets welcome. Garden. Scenic. Confirm by 3

STADDLEBRIDGE North Yorkshire map 7

▲ *McCoy's*

The Tontine, Staddlebridge DL6 3JB
EAST HARLSEY (060 982) 671

COOKING 3*
COST £25–£55

Built from the first as an inn or roadhouse, beside what is now the A19, McCoy's is protected from traffic noise by double glazing. The original house is distinguished, the stables are enormous. As they are now, the buildings are idiosyncratic: the public rooms seem mainly furnished from second-hand warehouses, while the bedrooms, small but well-provided, are more conventional. On a good night, when the '30s or '40s music has struck the right mood and the dim lighting has promoted the suspension of daily reality, the atmosphere is memorable. The restaurant – more dim lighting and parasols down the centre line of tables – offers a menu that changes little from year to year. The main variables are the daily fish, and game in season. Some people wonder if such lack of development is good either for standards or for maintaining interest. Although some dishes like the ravioli of langoustine, lemon and truffle with lobster sauce seem in their way definitive, reports have suggested that the Bresse pigeon with cream, baby leeks, truffle, foie gras and port glaze does not invariably hang together as a dish. As might be surmised from these items, truffle and foie gras appear often and give the output here a particular character. It should also be admitted that the menu is a good one: not so large as to cause problems of freshness; offering a range of materials and finish; showing both a light touch with seasonings and indigestible elements, such as cream, and a modern tilt to composition that gives dishes interest. Desserts are also desirable: passion-fruit and nectarine soufflé, crêpes San Lorenzo, 'Choc-o-bloc Stanley' (the chocolate fondant that knocks spots off the competition), or a strawberry feuilleté. Cheese gets more varied reports. Coffee may be fine, though not the decaffeinated. The most troublesome area this year is service. Some reports express dissatisfaction: too laid-back to be caring, too absent to be efficient. (There has also been a comment about lack of finish in the rooms upstairs.) The wine list is not too long, with a choice of good, modern and fashionable growers from all round the world. It is arranged by weight and colour, with useful notes and house selections in each section: not full of cheap bottles, perhaps, but there is some consideration of range. Downstairs is the bistro. It occupies a large basement room, is loud, happy and popular, and pursues the bistro image down to 'paper napkins and railway buffet salts and peppers,' according to someone who evidently regretted not being in the restaurant. But the food is fair and honest and more characterful than that of most bistros in the region.

CHEFS: Tom and Eugene McCoy PROPRIETORS: Peter, Tom and Eugene McCoy OPEN: restaurant Tue to Sat, D only; bistro all week CLOSED: 25 and 26 Dec MEALS: bistro 12 to 2.30 (2 Sun), restaurant and bistro 7 to 10.30 PRICES: restaurant £34 (£46), bistro £18 (£25). Card slips closed CARDS: Amex, Access, Diners, Visa SEATS: 45. Private parties: 60 main room, 25 private room. Car park, 60 places. Vegetarian meals. Children's helpings. Music. Air-conditioned ACCOMMODATION: 6 rooms, all with bath/shower. B&B £75 to £95. Children welcome. Pets welcome. Garden. Air-conditioned. TV. Phone. Scenic

---

STAMFORD Lincolnshire map 6

▲ *George*

71 St Martin's, Stamford PE9 2LB COOKING 1
STAMFORD (0780) 55171 COST £27–£46

This old coaching-inn has long been a fixture – a favoured stop on the way north before motorways were conceived. Stamford is still a nodal point for road routes, but these days visits and pauses are more likely for rest, recreation and tourism. The restaurant sports a long seasonal menu and a terrace room thick with plants (the Garden Lounge) offers less formal cooking, sometimes with an

Italian tilt. Standards fluctuate more widely here than in the restaurant, which generally produces a steady quality. Roast meats borne on silver trolleys may be the most popular thing, but the range is wider than that: 'I like especially the sugar-baked ham and if I ring up the day before my visit, they usually provide it. This time, however, I was well satisfied with the calf's liver, simply fried with lemon and butter,' writes one who treasures the happy welcome from the staff as much as the bold cheeseboard with its whole Cheddar, whole Stilton and large wheel of Brie. The Garden Lounge offers 50 modestly priced, exclusively Italian wines. Maintaining intelligent selection and fair pricing, the main restaurant adds pedigree classic French and the New World. Very generous provision of halves and fine bin-ends encourage experiment. House wine is £7.95. CELLARMAN'S CHOICE: Tokay d'Alsace, Clos St-Urbain Rangen 1987, Zind-Humbrecht, £21; Crozes Hermitage 1988, Graillot, £14.45.

CHEFS: Chris Pitman and Matthew Carroll PROPRIETORS: Poste Hotels Ltd OPEN: all week MEALS: 12.30 to 2.30, 7.30 to 10.30 PRICES: restaurant £25 (£38), Garden Lounge £17 (£27). Card slips closed CARDS: Access, Amex, Diners, Visa SEATS: 85. 20 tables outside. Private parties: 90 main room, 16, 22 and 30 private rooms. Car park, 150 places. Vegetarian meals. Children's helpings. Jacket and tie. Wheelchair access (also WC). No music. Fax: (0780) 57070 ACCOMMODATION: 47 rooms, all with bath/shower. B&B £75 to £154. Children welcome. Baby facilities. Pets welcome. Afternoon teas. Garden. TV. Phone. Scenic. Confirm by 6 (*Which? Hotel Guide*)

STANDON Hertfordshire map 3

No.28 **NEW ENTRY**

28 High Street, Standon SG11 1LA COOKING 1
WARE (0920) 821035 COST £37

'Quality food in a gastronomically bleak area,' declared one reader appreciative of the Balls' new restaurant in the middle of the village high street. It occupies a handsome Edwardian house next to the Balls' successful catering company, which previously occupied the smaller restaurant premises. The transformation into a light, airy 18-seater restaurant has worked well, though the piped classical music can be too loud. The set-price menu is laudably short, just three choices per course, and the cooking has a fashionable, metropolitan air: dishes such as lobster ravioli and loin of venison on a rösti of artichoke with rhubarb and Dubonnet sauce nail the modernist colours to the mast. It is early days, but there is evident skill in the kitchen even if it is not yet fully into its stride. The lobster ravioli was served with spinach and a well-judged lobster sauce, which suffered only from under seasoning; the rhubarb and Dubonnet sauce, although well-made, was too fruity and tangy to blend in with the venison; fillets of John Dory on a nest of young broad beans with sorrel and purple sage sauce was satisfactory, as was a pear charlotte on a cassis sauce. The wine list is curiously uneven, but has real originality and interest if you pick and choose, especially among the Australasians, which include a Chardonnay, Redwood Valley Estate 1988 and Cabernet, Barossa Valley, Heggies Vineyard 1986. House wine is £7.50.

CHEFS: Adam Baldwin and Miranda Ball PROPRIETORS: Miranda and Trevor Ball OPEN: Tue to Sat, D only MEALS: 7 to 9.30 PRICES: Set D £27.50 (£31). Card slips closed CARDS: Access, Amex, Visa SEATS: 18. Private parties: 26 main room. Vegetarian meals. Children welcome. No smoking. Wheelchair access (1 step). Music. Fax: (0920) 822630

STAPLE CROSS East Sussex map 3

Olivers

Cripp's Corner, Staple Cross TN32 5RY COOKING 2
STAPLECROSS (0580) 830387 COST £16–£29

The building stands on the road from Hawkhurst to Hastings. The flock wallpaper does not necessarily chime the same note as the very genuine approach to cooking, but the overall mien is bright and cheerful. Lunches, except on Sunday, are no longer served, but the format of three set-price menus, each offering a choice of three, is preserved. The cheapest menu may have slivers of veal and beef with two sauces, while the next suggests feuilleté of rabbit and bacon with mustard sauce, and the dearest goes on to glazed breast of duck, 'enhanced' with celeriac and raisins. All constitute fair value, especially the cheapest. Desserts go on from there: passion-fruit délice, sultana sponge pudding, exotic fruits set in a vanilla mousse. The cooking is careful and not without skill. There are three dozen wines that do no disservice to either the food or the sense of value. House French is £6.50.

CHEF: Gary Oliver PROPRIETORS: Albert and Gary Oliver OPEN: Wed to Sun, D only, and Sun L CLOSED: first 3 weeks Jan MEALS: 12 to 1.30, 7 to 9.30 PRICES: Set L (Sun) and D £9.95 (£16) to £18.50 (£24) CARDS: Access, Visa SEATS: 36. Private parties: 45 main room, 18 private room. Car park, 20 places. No children under 5

STAPLEFORD Leicestershire map 6

▲ *Stapleford Park* 🍷

COUNTY RESTAURANT OF THE YEAR

NEW ENTRY

Stapleford, nr Melton Mowbray LE14 2EF COOKING 3
WYMONDHAM (057 284) 522 COST £31–£47

Clumps of trees in parkland, said to be the work of Capability Brown, are dwarfed by the expanse of hedge-free plain. Overhead, fighter planes swarm; this is RAF country. The house and crippled, but recovering, stables provide a remarkable exterior: their restoration is exemplary. So mellow is the stone in a golden setting sun that it might be honey poured from a pot. Within, there is a great mix of moods from the lofty first hall, the gloomy Victorian central saloon and quite dark but comforting public rooms, to the main dining-room with its excellent baroque wood carving. Designer bedrooms and all that stuff – sleep in a room done out in shirt fabric – are appreciated by most residents, though some doubt if they want a guided tour: it is not compulsory. On the other hand, the underlying jocularity that Bob Payton injects into running any business emerges for the visiting diner as enthusiasm on the part of staff and owners, which can't be bad. Meals may be served in a variety of places; the best is the old kitchen, pillared and almost monastic, but a nice contrast to the rest of the house. Into this carefully composed, almost film-set, Englishness have been dropped Rick Tramonto and Gale Gand, chefs from the USA, cooking old and new-wave American dishes. Having wrestled unsuccessfully with English country-house cooking, but always with an 'angle', Bob Payton's solution is to be welcomed. There is a weekday set-price choice, a *carte*, a lunchtime and an all-day menu. The latter will provide the hamburger. In keeping with the kitchen's style, novel breads, such as pesto, are delivered hot for each table of diners to slice themselves. Tastes are usually 'demonstrative' in things such as a minestrone, fresh pasta with queen scallops, juniper-scented gravlax, bouillabaisse, steak with horseradish mashed potatoes and a wild mushroom fricassee. Desserts from pecan pie to lots of ice-creams, are sweet and substantial. Service really is enthusiastic. People warmly praise Stapleford Park for a weekend, especially for the horsey and the gregarious. From the champagnes on, California vies with classic French on the wine list. Adventure is encouraged by clear presentation, a listing by wine style, which puts the Napa Valley alongside Pomerol, and prices, especially considering the surroundings, that are fair. There are decent house wines from £11.25. CELLARMAN'S CHOICE: Dry Creek, Chenin Blanc 1988, £15; Pomerol, Ch. Haut-Ballet 1983, £20.

CHEFS: Rick Tramonto and Gale Gand PROPRIETORS: Bob and Wendy Payton OPEN: all week MEALS: 12 to 2.30 (5 in lounges), 7 to 9 (10.30 Fri and Sat) PRICES: £27 (£39), light L from £4.25, Set D Sun to Thur £19.91 (£31). Card slips closed CARDS: Access, Amex, Diners, Visa SEATS: 150. 11 tables outside. Private parties: 70 main room, 16, 30, 40 and 150 private rooms. Car park, 200 places. Vegetarian meals. Children's helpings. No children under 10 unless accompanied by nanny. Smart dress preferred. No smoking in dining-room. Wheelchair access (also WC). Fax: (057 284) 651 ACCOMMODATION: 35 rooms, all with bath/shower. Rooms for disabled. Lift. B&B £120 to £280. Deposit: £50. No children under 10 unless accompanied by nanny. Pets welcome. Afternoon teas. Garden. Tennis. Fishing. TV. Phone. Scenic (*Which? Hotel Guide*)

STOKE-BY-NAYLAND Suffolk map 3

▲ *Angel Inn*

Stoke-by-Nayland CO6 4SA COOKING 1
COLCHESTER (0206) 263245 COST £21–£34

'The blackcurrant brûlée was one of the very best sweets we have had in a pub during the last decade.' Reporters' loyalties to this agreeable inn, which forms part of a series of converted Suffolk cottages, are firm. Votes are in favour of the bar food, which is exemplary: the blackboard menu has leanings towards steak and kidney pie, but also promises excellent fresh soups and dishes such as home-made rissoles with tomato and sweet pepper sauce. The adjoining restaurant favours more elaborate preparation, as in marinated breast of guinea-fowl with port sauce on a bed of baby leeks, and seems unnecessarily taken with filo pastry – found, for example, encasing baked scallops, or cauliflower served with tomato sauce. Adnams and Greene King beers are available on draught. House French is £7.

See the back of the Guide *for an index of restaurants listed.*

CHEF: Mark Johnson PROPRIETORS: Richard Wright and Peter Smith OPEN: Tue to Sun, exc Tue L and Sun D (all week bar meals) CLOSED: 25 and 26 Dec MEALS: 12 to 2, 6 to 9 PRICES: bar £15 (£21), restaurant £20 (£28) CARDS: Access, Amex, Diners, Visa SEATS: 40. Private parties: 26 main room. Car park, 20 places. Vegetarian meals. Children restricted. Wheelchair access (also WC). Music ACCOMMODATION: 6 rooms, all with bath/shower. B&B £39.50 to £51.25. Deposit: 50%. No children under 8. TV. Phone. Scenic. Doors close at 11.30 (*Which? Hotel Guide*)

STOKESLEY North Yorkshire map 7

▲ *Chapters* **NEW ENTRY**

27 High Street, Stokesley TS9 5AD COOKING 2
STOKESLEY (0642) 711888 COST £32

Alan Thompson has moved from his bistro in Bridge Road to this converted coaching-inn right in the centre of the village. Larger premises have allowed him more scope and he has been joined in the kitchen by David Brownless (formerly of Santoros, Yarm). Inside, the dining-room is strikingly modern with large terracotta flagstones and white louvred shutters at the windows. The menu shows influences from France and the Far East, with fish as a strong suit. Turbot might be steamed with a scallop mousse and fresh spinach or roasted with garlic, ginger, soy and spring onions. Dishes change each day, depending on the local markets. An inspection meal featured chicken and vegetable terrine with tomato and basil dressing; breast of duck on a bed of leeks with truffle-scented sauce; and hot pear and orange strudel with lime sauce. Other good dishes have included antipasti with scorched vegetables and goats' cheese, salmon with hollandaise sauce, and apple tart with caramel ice-cream. This is a skilful kitchen serving portions that are more than sufficient for North Country appetites, and Alan Thompson also has an eye for stylised presentation. An adequate list of around 30 wines includes house French at £7.75.

CHEFS: Alan Thompson and David Brownless PROPRIETOR: Alan Thompson OPEN: all week CLOSED: 25 Dec and 1 Jan MEALS: 12 to 2, 7 to 10 PRICES: £20 (£27), Snacks from £1.95 CARDS: Access, Amex, Diners, Visa SEATS: 64. 4 tables outside. Private parties: 50 main room, 24 private room. Vegetarian meals with prior notice. Children's helpings on request. Smart dress preferred. Wheelchair access (2 steps). Music ACCOMMODATION: 13 rooms, all with bath/shower. B&B £36 to £51. Children welcome. Baby facilities. Afternoon teas. Garden. TV. Phone

STON EASTON Somerset map 2

▲ *Ston Easton Park* 🍷

Ston Easton BA3 4DF COOKING 3
CHEWTON MENDIP (0761) 241631 COST £31–£50

'It was rather like being the guests of honour in a National Trust property,' commented one couple who arrived at Ston Easton on a wild, wet, windy April evening. It says a great deal about the Smedleys and their staff that this daunting Georgian mansion has a feeling of genuine warmth and class, rather than austere, stone-cold severity. Readers have endorsed last year's 'County Restaurant' accolade, and there is high praise for Mark Harrington's cooking. Much of the kitchen's success is due to impeccable ingredients: fruit, vegetables and herbs from the hotel's garden, well-hung meat, fish from the market. The menus are fixed-price, with several choices at each stage, and the style is modern, forward-looking and light, with a sprinkling of country-house luxuries such as foie gras and Beluga caviare. Vivid relishes and dressings embellish many of the starters: apple and sage chutney with pork and wild mushroom terrine; truffle vinaigrette with salad of calves' sweetbreads and asparagus; balsamic dressing with feuilleté of smoked salmon, Indian prawns and avocado. Recommendations for main courses show the range of Mark Harrington's repertoire: veal fillet in a Parmesan crust with tomato and basil noodles; chargrilled breast of Gressingham duck with caramelised shallots; ragoût of seafood ('five different varieties, a real delight'). Desserts are both cold (tulip Ston Easton – a famous assemblage of good sorbets and exotic fruit – or petit pot au chocolate) and hot (pecan pie or home-made crumpets with apple and cinnamon compote on warm plum sauce). Fine English cheeses and coffee with home-made sweetmeats complete the picture. Although grand names abound on the wine list, selection verges on the conservative, especially in Burgundy. Bottles from Italy and Spain are choice but it is California and the Antipodes which have recently caught the attention here and indicate vitality and intelligence in the wine buying. Prices are less high than might be expected; there is virtually nothing below £15 but the range just above is extensive and selection steady. House wine is £14.50. CELLARMAN'S CHOICE: House champagne bottled by Edward Sheldon, £30; Caillou Blanc de Ch. Talbot 1989, £19.

CHEF: Mark Harrington PROPRIETORS: Peter and Christine Smedley OPEN: all week MEALS: 12.30 to 2, 7.30 to 9.30 (10 Fri and Sat) PRICES: Set L £24 (£31), Set D £35 (£42). Net prices, card slips closed CARDS: Access, Amex, Diners, Visa SEATS: 40. 8 tables outside. Private parties: 40 main room, 14 and 22 private rooms. Car park, 40 places. Vegetarian meals. Children's helpings. No children under 12. Jacket and tie. No cigars/ pipes in dining-room. No music. Fax: (0761) 241377 ACCOMMODATION: 21 rooms, all with bath/shower. B&B £75 to £320. No children under 12. Pets by arrangement. Afternoon teas. Garden. Tennis. Snooker. TV. Phone. Scenic. Doors close at midnight. Confirm by 6 (*Which? Hotel Guide*)

STONHAM Suffolk map 3

Mr Underhill's 🍷

Stonham IP14 5DW
STOWMARKET (0449) 711206 COOKING 3
on A140, 300 yards S of junction with A1120 COST £26–£48

The recession is no fun, in town or country, and restaurants have had to tighten their belts along with the rest of us. Solace may be had from the thought that good places do generally survive; it is those without commitment, quality or any firm idea of what market they are pursuing that tend to drop like flies in a cloud of insecticide. Seen like this, Mr Underhill's is a survivor: this is tenth-anniversary year, and the Bradleys are showing not only rueful satisfaction at getting through yet another recession, but also happiness at their first real holiday since opening. The restaurant itself shows great panache and style in its fitting out – a positive taste is in evidence – and the approach to menus and repertoire is also consistent and bold. Intending hosts telephone to arrange a set menu – once agreement is struck there is no choice – and Chris Bradley may be cooking half a dozen different meals on any evening. The only permanent choice is at dessert: a slate of six or more is offered. This all has overtones of dinner parties of yesteryear, and the hostess going mad on a sideboard heavy with sweet after sweet. Some people even call the food here 'home cooking' but that undervalues it. Ancillaries are high-grade, and dishes such as tagliarini with lemon and Parmesan, salmon with chive beurre blanc, venison sauce poivrade, and lamb shank with polenta and Tuscan vegetables show attention to taste and style, as well as a true takeover of Italian influence since the Bradleys took that holiday. Desserts like strawberries in raspberry vinegar, tarte Tatin, creole coffee parfait and marinated apples have a sophistication light years beyond the cut-glass bowls of cream, mousses and custards. Judy Bradley is a fine hostess. The wine list is excellent. Enthusiasm is evident in recent additions from Austria, while New Zealand receives recommendation. A 'special selection' offers excitement, the main list reassurance, with fine French and Italian bottles. There are a few choice half-bottles. Prices are reasonable, especially below £20. House wines are from £8.75. CELLARMAN'S CHOICE: New Zealand, Kumeu River, Chardonnay 1989, £25.50; Côtes du Rhône 1988, Guigal, £9.75.

CHEF: Christopher Bradley PROPRIETORS: Christopher and Judy Bradley OPEN: Tue to Sat, D only, and Sun L (other L by arrangement) MEALS: 12.30 to 1.45, 7.30 to 8.45 PRICES: Set Sun L £17.50 (£26) to £25 (£35), Set D £25 (£35) to £30 (£40) CARDS: Access, Visa SEATS: 30. 6 tables outside. Private parties: 30 main room, 16 private room. Car park, 12 places. Vegetarian meals. Children's helpings with prior notice. Smoking after meal only. No music. Wheelchair access (also WC)

STONOR Oxfordshire map 2

▲ *Stonor Arms*

Stonor RG9 6HE COOKING 2
TURVILLE HEATH (049 163) 345 COST £25–£49

This extensively re-vamped and extended sixteenth-century building functions, despite the name and the inn sign, primarily as a 'two-tier restaurant' with accommodation. There are two eating areas: the informal 'bar' with its sporting antiques and Lloyd Loom furniture serves a flexible, all-week *carte;* the formal dining-room, adorned with comfortable seating, oil paintings and more antiques, offers a fixed-price three-course dinner menu (as well as Sunday lunch). Both areas have conservatories attached. Some readers have noted an improvement in standards; a few feel that the kitchen has lost some of its sharpness. The consensus, however, is still firmly in Stonor's favour. The catalogue of recent recommendations includes cream of wild mushroom soup ('with woodland intensity'), salad of avocado, bacon and quails' eggs, and steamed fillet of hake with an 'assertive' green mustard sauce. Simple dishes such as a plain grilled lemon sole have also been well reported. Desserts are a high point: poached pears with Pernod ice-cream, banana parfait with apricot sauce, baked apple charlotte, backed up by 'positively flavoured sorbets'. The wine list remains in fairly exalted territory with prices to match, despite economic relief provided by a few petits châteaux, some soundly chosen mid-priced burgundies and decent but limited Italian and New World wines. There are good and very fairly priced Loires. House wines are £8.25.

CHEF: Stephen Frost PROPRIETORS: Stonor Hotels Ltd OPEN: restaurant Mon to Sat, D only, and Sun L; 'bar' restaurant all week MEALS: 12 to 1.45, 7 to 9.30 PRICES: 'bar' restaurant £17 (£25), restaurant Set Sun L £19.95 (£26) to £23.95 (£31), Set D £28.50 (£36) to £33 (£41) CARDS: Access, Amex, Visa SEATS: restaurant 38, 'bar' restaurant 40. 6 tables outside. Private parties: 22 main room. Car park, 30 places. Children's helpings. Smart dress preferred in restaurant. No cigars/pipes in dining-room. Wheelchair access (also WC). Music. Fax: (0491) 638863 ACCOMMODATION: 9 rooms, all with bath/shower. Rooms for disabled. B&B £82.50 to £137.50. Children welcome. Garden. TV. Phone. Doors close at 11

STORRINGTON West Sussex map 3

▲ *Abingworth Hall*

Thakeham Road, Storrington RH20 3EF COOKING 2
WEST CHILTINGTON (0798) 813636 COST £23–£44

Abingworth is run with devotion by the Bulmans. An immaculate small hotel, from the lake and smooth, smooth lawns to the Edwardian house (though its origins may stretch further back than that), it is found two miles to the north of Storrington itself, on the B2139. A short set-price menu is offered together with a *carte* in the series of three dining-rooms; the cooking is sound with dishes on the conservative side of modern, which seems to suit customers, There has been acclamation for game in season and the English cheese selection. Less utterly traditional offerings have included a hot scallop mousse with crab and chive sauce, calf's liver with raspberry wine butter, lamb with wild mushrooms and madeira sauce, and carpaccio with tomato, lemon and chives. It is careful cooking, all done in-house, including the bread and petits fours. The wine list is sound. House wine is £7.80.

CHEF: Peter Cannon PROPRIETORS: Philip and Pauline Bulman OPEN: all week MEALS: 12.30 to 2, 7.15 to 9 PRICES: £28 (£37), Set L £17 (£23), Set D £28 (£35). Card slips closed CARDS: Access, Carte Blanche, Visa SEATS: 54. Private parties: 54 main room. Car park, 40 places. Children welcome. Smart dress preferred. No music. Fax: (0798) 813914 ACCOMMODATION: 21 rooms, all with bath/shower. Rooms for disabled. B&B £64 to £150. Deposit: £20. No children under 10. Garden. Swimming-pool. Tennis. Fishing. TV. Phone. Scenic. Doors close at 11

▲ *Manleys*

Manleys Hill, Storrington RH20 4BT COOKING 4
STORRINGTON (0903) 742331 COST £27–£52

'Immaculate' is the epithet used for the outside of the house, the largely pink, beamed interior, the monogrammed silverware and crockery, and the highly professional cookery of Karl Löderer. This may sometimes be too immaculate for its own good – if you love clear, strong, gutsy tastes – but his style has internal logic and he achieves the aims he sets himself. The one area that seems less than perfect is the service. Readers have noticed a lack of presence at the front-of-house, thus vitiating some of the kitchen's intentions. The long *carte* – maybe 10 or more main dishes offered – is made longer with detailed descriptions. Why, therefore, do the dishes not always match the descriptions, especially if the staff cannot explain the substitution of mange-tout by French beans? Technical expertise figures prominently in any description of a meal here: for instance the fine amuse-gueule of smoked salmon roundels filled with a rich and luscious mousse, cut to perfection by an acid dressing to the few accompanying leaves; or the caramelised flavour of the fresh, plump scallops in a warm butter stock sauce ('almost roasted in taste') that was absorbed by the fresh pasta and given texture and life by a filo money-bag filled with mushroom (but no bacon as stated on the menu). The skill may mask a certain timidity in flavours, so that a dish of venison with sweet-sour sauce really needed more support than ultra-fine potato croquettes and rather bland salsify. This meat, and others too, had been cooked a little past pink, but many who come here in fact eat fish, which is given greater stress than in many Sussex restaurants. A fillet of salmon marinated with ginger and spring onions, baked in filo pastry, with a plain butter sauce and mange-tout, shows the degree of skill. Puddings have always been a strong point – Salzburger Nockerln is a constant favourite – though the execution of the *cage défendu* was cleverer than that of the sorbets encased within the web of spun sugar and topped by a meringue bird. The Pithivier au chocolat demonstrated the fine hand with pastry work, as did the carefully made petits fours. This is a stronghold of culinary tradition that should attract many supporters in the South-East even if followers of new-wave Italian or mother's pride peasant cookery might feel at sea. The wine list is predominantly French, serious and expensive. There are decent house wines and a few interesting bargains. Mark-ups are high, growers superb, but then there is no intention to provide for economy here. House wine is £11.80.

CHEF/PROPRIETOR: Karl Löderer OPEN: Tue to Sun, exc Sun D, and Mon L CLOSED: first 2 weeks Jan MEALS: 12 to 2, 7 to 9.15 (10 Sat) PRICES: £31 (£43), Set L £18.60 (£27) to £24.50 (£33) CARDS: Access, Amex, Diners, Visa SEATS: 48. Private parties: 36 main room, 22 private room. Car park, 25 places. Children's helpings on request. No children under 7. Smart dress preferred. No cigars/pipes in dining-room. Wheelchair access (also WC). Music on request ACCOMMODATION: 1 double room with bath/shower. B&B £55 to £87. Afternoon teas. TV. Phone. Scenic

---

'Service is unattractive, hard-working. The restaurant manager is an elderly badly dressed, friendly man. The three girls serving food wore green dresses topped with frilly white aprons. One had an acne problem, one had a weight problem, one had a broken neck. The staff made Fawlty Towers *look stylish.'* On eating in Wales

Net prices *in the details at the end of an entry indicates that the prices given on a menu and on a bill are inclusive of VAT and service charge, and that this practice is clearly stated on menu and bill.*

STOURPORT-ON-SEVERN Hereford & Worcester map 5

Severn Tandoori

11 Bridge Street,
Stourport-on-Severn DY13 8UX COOKING 1
STOURPORT (029 93) 3090 COST £22

The Georgian façade gives way to a smart modern interior – no flock wallpaper is in evidence here at this predominantly north Indian restaurant. The emphasis is on the tandoor, but there is a strong following for old favourites such as rogan josh, chicken Kashmir and prawn dhansak. Patty shapta (a sweet pancake) and Indian ice-cream are a better bet than the English-inspired sweets. Drink lassi or lager. House wine is £7 a carafe.

CHEF: A. Audud PROPRIETORS: S.A. Quayum, M. Miah, A. Audud, Z. Ali and S.M. Meah OPEN: all week MEALS: 12 to 2, 6 to 11.30 PRICES: £12 (£18). Card slips closed CARDS: Access, Amex, Diners, Visa SEATS: 70. Private parties: 70 main room, 70 private room. Vegetarian meals. Children's helpings (weekend D only). No children under 4. Smart dress preferred. Wheelchair access (also WC). Music

STOW-ON-THE-WOLD Gloucestershire map 2

▲ *Wyck Hill House* **NEW ENTRY**

Burford Road,
Stow-on-the-Wold GL54 1HY
COTSWOLD (0451) 31936 COOKING 2
on A424, 2m SE of Stow-on-the Wold COST £15–£55

This large ochre-coloured, early eighteenth-century Cotswold mansion, on a hill with views of half England from the terraced lawns, got off to a halting start in the '80s. Since then, tighter management, further investment and redecoration (from hunting to floral themes in the dining-rooms) have allowed Ian Smith to settle in the kitchen and produce food of an acceptable standard. It may, however, be slightly old-fashioned (there's nothing worse than last year's modishness if you are a dedicated follower) or may dip below consistent excellence. The leitmotif of the cooking is either luxury ingredients (to justify the cost) or number, sheer multiplicity of elements, the value of which is undercut by repetition, for instance of a sauce, from one course to another. A warm salad of sweetbreads, wild mushrooms, French beans, bacon and mustard vinaigrette, already a fair assembly, had in fact two sauces, oyster mushrooms as well as morels and sweetbreads that tasted of not much. Prolixity may go to extremes when describing the vegetables: artful but not entirely necessary. At the same time, some of the cooking is very proficient indeed; it is greatly improved from a few years ago. The service too has loosened up and got better. The long and mainly French wine list makes some attempt in the 'Wyck Hill Selection' to help those unwilling to spend more than £15.

▲ *This symbol means that accommodation is available.*

CHEF: Ian Smith PROPRIETORS: Lyric Hotels OPEN: all week MEALS: 12.30 to 2, 7.30 to 9.30 (10 Sat) PRICES: Set L £8 (£15) to £14.95 (£23), Set D £30 (£39) to £36 (£46), Snacks from £8 CARDS: Access, Amex, Diners, Visa SEATS: 60. Private parties: 24 main room, 24 private rooms. Car park. 100 places. Vegetarian meals. Children's helpings. Jacket or tie. No smoking in dining-room. Wheelchair access (also WC). Music. Air-conditioned. Fax: (0451) 32243 and 30346 ACCOMMODATION: 30 rooms, all with bath/shower. Rooms for disabled. Lift. B&B £70 to £95. Children welcome. Baby facilities. Pets welcome. Afternoon teas. Garden. TV. Phone. Scenic. Confirm by 7pm (*Which? Hotel Guide*)

STRATFORD-UPON-AVON Warwickshire map 2

Sir Toby's

8 Church Street,
Stratford-upon-Avon CV37 6HB COOKING 1
STRATFORD-UPON-AVON (0789) 268822 COST £26

The Watkins' tiny restaurant is in a seventeenth-century building with oak beams and stone floors, within walking distance of the theatres. This is an industrious set-up, opening early for meals before the show and extending the home-made range to bresaola cured on the premises; pasta, sorbets and ice-creams; and home-smoked quail, chicken and loin of pork. Carl Watkins also gathers mushrooms from the wild. Joanna Watkins, who works away steadily in an open kitchen visible from the restaurant, can happily cope with both staunchly traditional ideas and more modern, exotically flavoured dishes. On the one hand she might offer rump steak with anchovy butter, treacle tart with custard, and savouries such as Welsh rarebit; on the other, baked avocado with spiced vegetables, coconut and sesame sauce, grilled skewers of lamb with cardamom rice, and lime soufflé. Fish shows up well, as in sliced scallops and salmon with fresh ginger, spring onion and home-made egg noodles. A useful eating-place in a town with few interesting restaurants. Two dozen wines provide plenty of choice and affordable drinking. House wine is £7.95 a litre.

CHEF: Joanna Watkins PROPRIETORS: Carl and Joanna Watkins OPEN: Tue to Sat, D only MEALS: 5.30 to 9.30 PRICES: £15 (£22). Card slips closed CARDS: Access, Amex, Visa SEATS: 40. Private parties: 30 main room, 18 private room. Vegetarian meals. Children's helpings. No pipes in dining-room. Wheelchair access (1 step). Music. Air-conditioned

STROUD Gloucestershire map 2

Oakes

169 Slad Road, Stroud GL5 1RG
STROUD (0453) 759950 COOKING 4
on B4070, 1/2m from Stroud COST £20–£52

'One of our favourites for the quality of the food and the warm, friendly welcome. It's like cocoa in bed, such a treat, but comforting and not excessive. You really feel cared for,' enthused one reader. Certain points are stressed by reports of meals in this small stone-built mock-Gothic house to one side of the not-very-exciting minor road out of Stroud (the tedious view gives more chance to concentrate on the food). First, the restaurant may not be fancy in its get up: 'Nothing over-fussy, polished floors and rugs, so a bit resonant, but it has its own character, not bland and pink' was one description. Second, the quiet yet attractive personalities of the Oakes themselves impress their customers: 'They appear to like children'; 'Caroline Oakes is equally charming to the famous and to teenage sisters having a birthday treat'; 'Caroline Oakes was particularly gracious and helpful'. A third point is the steady and relatively undemonstrative quality of the food. A salad of plaice and sole in goujons may be prettily arranged as a starfish, but talk of fancy decoration bulks small in relation to that of fine tastes and materials. The menu structure is a pair of fast-changing yet short fixed-price choices during the week, supplemented by a short (and not dear) *carte* at lunch and a separately priced *prix fixe* Sunday lunch. Mixing and matching between available menus is tolerated. New this year is an extra room converted for dining, which does not have outside views but affords the Oakes a chance to increase revenue in stringent times. Recommendations of satisfactory dishes are manifold. Lentil and herb soup, 'velvety' fish soup, smoked chicken and celeriac on a bed of lettuce dressed with hazelnut oil, home-made sausages (of duck once and then of venison), chicken stuffed with a chicken mousse and served with a madeira cream sauce, salmon on a bed of spinach with orange, shallot and tarragon dressing are some savoury items, served with good, yet fairly plain vegetables, and usually excellent rösti. Desserts show a good hand with pastry, especially in the apple tart served with a caramel sauce and sultana ice-cream. Individual bread-and-butter-pudding, Bakewell tart ('not quite a classic, but very light') and orange soufflé pancake with chocolate sauce ('the plate would have been licked had it not been so public') excite equal enthusiasm. Like all owners of small country places, the Oakes are feeling the financial cool, but good cooks do survive. For those for whom economy has no meaning, the wine list will disappoint. But for the rest of us, the intelligent, if unambitious, selection provides much decent drinking at modest prices. House wines are from £6.75. CELLARMAN'S CHOICE: New Zealand Blenheim Chardonnay 1989, Hunter's, £17.60; Ch. Musar 1982, £13.05.

CHEF: Christopher Oakes PROPRIETORS: Christopher and Caroline Oakes and Nowell and Jean Scott OPEN: Tue to Sun, exc Sun D MEALS: 12.30 to 1.45, 7.30 to 9.30 PRICES: L £15 (£20), Set Sun L £20.50 (£26), Set D £30 (£37) to £36 (£43). Card slips closed CARDS: Access, Visa SEATS: 40. Private parties: 30 main room, 10 private room. Car park, 12 places. Children's helpings. Wheelchair access. No music

STUCKTON Hampshire map 2

Three Lions 🍷

Stuckton Road, Stuckton SP6 2HF
FORDINGBRIDGE (0425) 652489 COOKING 3
1m off A338 at Fordingbridge COST £12–£42

Although the number of cooking-and-drinking, snacking-and-dining pubs is on the increase, the real brand leaders can still be listed on a small sheet of paper. This is one of them. Karl-Hermann Wadsack was once chef at Chewton

Glen (see New Milton entry) and has not forgotten his classical skills, even if cooking for a relatively simple environment that lacks frills. Yet the pub itself is described as 'splendid inside and out; despite the lateness of the season, flowers are everywhere; beautifully tidy outside and spotless within; the place looks – and is – welcoming'. The Wadsacks have a large clientele which gives rise to two sittings on busy nights (not always forewarned) and more smoke than the climate can absorb. But generally people crowd willingly into a bold and characterful set of rooms, gathering to read the long blackboard menus, happy to be served with dispatch, not haste. In the correct season, the things to go for are especially the fish and game: there are excellent sources of both. Avocado and seafood jambalaya, mussels marinière and fresh snails bourguignonne preceded one party's steak, kidney and oyster pie (with *plenty* of oysters) and pointed up the preoccupation here with freshness. Fish cookery shows some substantial tastes: a curry and coriander sauce with a mixture of white fish; shallot, coriander and mustard seed vinaigrette with wing of skate; and a Seychelles grouper with peppers, mushrooms and cucumber. The cheaper lunch menu includes more slow cooking than dinner: oxtail with madeira sauce; lamb knuckle with pickled beetroot; Westmorland tattiepot. A treasure chest for Hampshire, amply buttressed by the wine list managed by June Wadsack, who gives good space to Australia and California while showing fine ranges from Bordeaux, Burgundy, the Rhône and Germany. A tendency to the blockbuster school of wine lists is narrowly avoided; wonderful they may be, but perhaps five Gewurztraminer from Alsace is overdoing things. Any underlying logic to the order, especially of the clarets, remains obscure. But fine names and vintages abound, showing much evidence of intelligent buying across a wide price range. The mark-up is fair. House wine is £8.95. CELLARMAN'S CHOICE: Tokay d'Alsace Reserve 1988, G. Lorentz, £11.50; Ch. Fourcas-Hosten 1975, £28.

CHEF: Karl-Hermann Wadsack PROPRIETORS: Karl-Hermann and June Wadsack OPEN: Tue to Sat CLOSED: 3 weeks from 28 July, 22 Dec to 2 Jan MEALS: 12.15 to 1.30, 7.15 to 9 (9.30 Sat) PRICES: L from £5 (£12), D £22 (£35) CARDS: Access, Visa SEATS: 55. Private parties: 45 main room. Car park, 40 places. No children under 14. Wheelchair access. No music

STURMINSTER NEWTON Dorset map 2

▲ *Plumber Manor* 🍷

Sturminster Newton DT10 2AF
STURMINSTER NEWTON (0258) 72507
2m SW of Sturminster Newton, off A357 on Hazelbury Bryan road

COOKING 2
COST £23–£34

This is a family affair: the Prideaux-Brunes'. Richard 'knows his wine' and Brian 'works quietly in the background', producing food much appreciated by the hotel's supporters, made up largely of those who enjoy country life, sport and food that is proper yet reasonably simple. Thus the meats are good, presentation is not overworked, and game is excellent. The house is a quiet epitome of English country life, combining 'style with intimacy'. There is a short set-price menu running alongside an equally concise seasonal *carte*. The structure and main ingredients of these menus do not change so radically from month to month, though trimmings might. The overall feel is distanced from that of old country-house cooking by ideas such as melon with mango and kiwi sorbet plus a raspberry coulis, served as a first course. But the best bets remain venison, grouse, pheasant and well-bought lamb and beef. A trolley of sweet things is laden, not necessarily subtly. Strong burgundies – Juillot, Michelot and many more – are the highlights of a very decent wine list. There are many half-bottles and fair prices. A glass is awarded this year. House wine is £8.50.

CHEFS: Brian Prideaux-Brune and Mrs S. Baker PROPRIETORS: Richard, Alison and Brian Prideaux-Brune OPEN: all week, D only (L by arrangement only for parties of 10 or more) MEALS: 7.30 to 9.30 PRICES: Set D £18.50 (£23) to £24 (£28). Net prices, card slips closed CARDS: Access, Amex, Diners, Visa SEATS: 60. Private parties: 40 main room, 12 and 22 private rooms. Car park, 20 places. Vegetarian meals. Children welcome. Smart dress preferred. No cigars/pipes in dining-room. Wheelchair access. Music. Fax: (0258) 73370 ACCOMMODATION: 16 rooms, all with bath/shower. Rooms for disabled. B&B £55 to £120. No children under 12. Garden. Tennis. TV. Phone. Scenic (*Which? Hotel Guide*)

SUDBURY Suffolk map 3

Mabey's Brasserie

47 Gainsborough Street,
Sudbury CO10 7SS COOKING 2*
SUFFOLK (0787) 74298 COST £26

'It is fascinating to watch Robert Mabey at work,' says a reader. The dining booths, tightly packed together, afford privacy and a good view of the kitchen, though less so of the blackboard menu. It has obviously been fabricated to facilitate a fast-moving kitchen: first courses and desserts are prepared in advance and require only simple finishing-off during service. Main courses, involving a lot of chargrilling, are cooked to order. These can build up to a climax of activity, especially if everyone arrives at once. 'The roar as chip potatoes hit boiling fat was a comment on cooking under pressure.' A second result of the rush can be badly judged or timed food: soggy chips, different dishes identically sauced. However, most reports show that the food and the laid-back atmosphere are much enjoyed. A winter lunch included mushroom and garlic tartlet – 'Robert Mabey is a dab hand at garlicking his dishes' – a warm salad of bacon and calf's liver, grilled breast of pheasant served with red cabbage, a rich chocolate parfait and first-class, home-made vanilla ice-cream with caramel sauce. The menu can offer some imaginative interpretations, such as duck with honey and black pepper sauce. Stuffed courgette flowers appear in the right season. 'Big' chips are thick-cut and fried with the skins left on. Portions are generous, the cooking is enthusiastic. A short wine list, drawn mainly from Lay and Wheeler, offers fair prices. House wine is £6.50 (red) and £6.75 (white).

CHEFS: Robert Mabey and Laurance Clifford PROPRIETORS: Robert and Johanna Mabey OPEN: Tue to Sat MEALS: 12 to 2, 7 to 10 PRICES: £15 (£22) CARDS: Access, Visa SEATS: 35. Private parties: 40 main room. Vegetarian meals. Children's helpings. Wheelchair access (2 steps). Air-conditioned. No music

SURBITON Surrey map 3

Chez Max

85 Maple Road, Surbiton KT6 4AW COOKING 3
081-399 2365 COST £23–£35

Max Markarian's restaurant has a quiet professionalism about it. This comes as a plus-point in Surbiton. The decoration is along clean modern lines, with no overstatement, and no derogation from taste; the cooking is of a piece. The techniques are correct and though there may be occasional signs of slow business (refrigerated mousses) and though the kitchen goes in for few culinary pyrotechnics, the tastes are true. One report runs: 'We had a cheese soufflé on just-cooked fresh spinach with a cream sauce. The small individual soufflés were a triumph: light in texture, richly intense in flavour. Monkfish with lobster sauce was cooked plainly, with impressive restraint; the sauce had depth and authentic flavour. Fillet of lamb came with a rich reduction of meat juices given a terrific lift by fresh mint. The accompaniment was roast shallots in an exemplary case of filo pastry. Vegetables on a side-plate were simple, but competently done.' The menu, running to perhaps eight main courses (abbreviated at lunchtimes), has a certain continuity of repertoire, but gives fair rein to classic modern sauces (mango and lime with guinea-fowl, champagne with sole, honey and cloves with duck) and conservative ingredients. The desserts include a decent truffle cake, and a Tia Maria iced soufflé. Service, overseen by Mrs Markarian, is performed by charming young people from France. The chef can sometimes be spied through the square porthole in his kitchen door. One party was surprised to be asked for a deposit on an advance booking. The wine list is almost bereft of half-bottles; its strongest suit is claret, its weakest (from point of view of price range) red burgundy. An influx of new countries would give a better balance of price and taste. House wines are £9.75.

CHEF: Max Markarian PROPRIETORS: Mr and Mrs Max Markarian OPEN: Tue to Sat, exc Sat L MEALS: 12.30 to 2, 7.30 to 10 PRICES: £20 (£29), Set L £17.75 (£25), Set D £15 (£23) to £17.75 (£25). Minimum £12.50. Service 12.5%. Card slips closed CARDS: Access, Amex, Diners, Visa SEATS: 45. Private parties: 45 main room. No children under 7. No pipes in dining-room. Music

SUTTON COURTENAY Oxfordshire map 2

Fish at Sutton Courtenay **NEW ENTRY**

Appleford Road,
Sutton Courtenay OX14 4NQ COOKING 1
ABINGDON (0235) 848242 COST £32

'An unremarkable village pub serving unusually good food' is how one reader sums up this Victorian roadside hostelry. The décor holds few surprises, apart from some paintings of trout flies and a display of bottled fruits. The centre of attraction is the blackboard menu. Bruce Buchan changes his menu daily and is committed to fresh ingredients: fish is from Brixham, game is local and cheeses are farmhouse. This translates into a repertoire of English-inspired dishes with

French overtones and a few exotic flourishes. Excellent fresh mussels in a 'boozy wine sauce', smoked chicken consommé, lambs' kidneys with noodles, pigeon breast with wild mushrooms, and roast monkfish with garlic and tomato sauce have all been good. Crispy duck and five-spice salad has an authentic taste of the orient. First-rate puddings have included pears in a caramel sauce with almond ice-cream, and a glorious chocolate mousse. There are real ales and a better-than-average pub wine list of 30 well-chosen bins. House French is £7.50.

CHEF: Bruce Buchan PROPRIETORS: Bruce and Kay Buchan OPEN: all week, exc Tue D CLOSED: 4 days between Christmas and New Year MEALS: 12 to 2.15, 7 to 9.30 (10 Fri and Sat) PRICES: £20 (£27). Card slips closed CARDS: Access, Amex, Visa SEATS: 45. Private parties: 12 main room, 18 and 30 private rooms. Car park, 30 places. Vegetarian meals. Children's helpings. Smart dress preferred. Wheelchair access. Music

SWANAGE Dorset map 2

Galley **NEW ENTRY**

9 High Street, Swanage BH19 2LN COOKING 1
SWANAGE (0929) 427299 COST £32

The corner site struck one person as more of a lobster pot than a galley. Perhaps it was the plethora of fishing nets and endless piscine references in the decoration. Another reader extolled 'the gentle, relaxed atmosphere; no pushiness; no filling up of wine glasses; no games-playing with the credit card slips; no cover charge'. Nick Storer cooks fish, although meat occupies at least half the main-course entries on the overlong menu. The fish is of a fair standard: one reporter found the topping to her finger of monkfish 'smothered' with mushrooms and smoked bacon more flavourful than the fish itself; and you might question the need to serve halibut (a North Sea fish) in Swanage (turbot and brill country). There is a slight emphasis on 'healthy' eating: this seems to be reflected in a lack of salt in the seasoning rather than a denial of fats and oils, which were certainly in evidence in an otherwise satisfactory stir-fry of scampi with ginger and soy. Desserts could do with some work, though coffee is decent. Service is amiable and willing. A short wine list, arranged and bought with intelligence, kicks off with house white from the Côtes de Gascogne at £6.75.

CHEF: Nick Storer PROPRIETORS: N.D and M.G Storer OPEN: all week, D only CLOSED: 1 Jan to 1 Apr MEALS: 6.30 to 9.30 (10 Sat). Card slips closed PRICES: £20 (£27) CARDS: Access, Amex, Diners, Visa SEATS: 30. Private parties: 30 main room. Vegetarian meals. Children welcome. Music

If a restaurant is new to the Guide *this year (did not appear as a main entry in the last edition)* NEW ENTRY *appears opposite its name.*

All entries in the Guide *are rewritten every year, not least because restaurant standards fluctuate. Don't trust an out-of-date* Guide.

TAUNTON Somerset map 2

▲ *Castle Hotel* 🍷

Castle Green, Taunton TA1 1NF COOKING 3
TAUNTON (0823) 272671 COST £23–£56

It can never be easy taking over a kitchen from a chef whose name is a buzzword on the circuit. This is what Phil Vickery did when he replaced Gary Rhodes here in the autumn of 1990. His path was eased by his own experience – Gravetye Manor (see entry) and the Mount Somerset along the way – and by the involvement of Kit Chapman in menu-planning and development. Mr Chapman has always been an active restaurateur, with a brain to boot; hence many aspects of the previous regime survive, in particular the traditional (and cheap) English lunch menu. At the same time, the revisionist tendencies of Gary Rhodes and some of his brilliance at high flavour have been reduced on the *carte* itself. The hotel side of the business continues as before. There has been a move to stabilise prices, even to reduce those on the *carte*, perhaps by a reduction in the use of luxury ingredients, though not in the quality of local supplies. Regular users of the Castle have not been unhappy with the recent output of the kitchen. Certainly, it is more muted; while Rhodes served turbot on a bed of green vegetables and wild mushrooms cooked in goose fat with ginger, Vickery cooks brill with spinach and glazes it with a tomato and chive cream. Contrast also Vickery's duck liver parfait, served with celeriac and brioche, and Rhodes' duck foie gras, fried and served on a grape and leaf salad with celery and black pudding, or his foie gras terrine with langoustines and grapes in a Sauternes dressing. Small wonder some prices are lower. On form, Vickery does well; off his peak, the cooking too closely resembles grand-hotel food. There are good mentions though for skate on spinach and potato purée with a watercress sauce, cauliflower soup, salmon with caviare sauce, chicken stuffed with a herb mousse and served with a red pepper butter sauce, quail with rosemary sauce, sticky toffee pudding and a fine hot banana soufflé. Vegetables have had a mixed response, as have the ice-creams and sorbets, while the petits fours are plentiful and good. Service is smooth, except at a couple of tables, the location of which made the occupants feel they were at Waterloo owing to the pounding to and from the kitchen. It may also sometimes be slightly off-hand. The wine list has always been long and, in some respects, traditionalist in its choice of growers. However, it does stray to Greece as well as including a little from Italy and Spain, and there is a fancy showing from the New World. Best are its clarets. Prices are not impossible. There is a house selection of a couple of dozen bottles from £6.90.

CHEF: Phil Vickery PROPRIETORS: the Chapman family OPEN: all week MEALS: 12.30 to 2, 7.30 to 9 (9.30 Fri and Sat) PRICES: £37 (£47), set L £14.90 (£23), Set Sun L £16 (£24), Set D £22.50 (£31). Card slips closed CARDS: Access, Amex, Diners, Visa SEATS: 110. Private parties: 65 main room, 50 and 110 private rooms. Car park, 40 places. Vegetarian meals. Children's helpings with prior notice. Smart dress preferred. Wheelchair access (also WC). Fax: (0823) 336066 ACCOMMODATION: 35 rooms, all with bath/shower. Rooms for disabled. Lift. B&B £75 to £145. Children welcome. Baby facilities. Pets welcome (in bedrooms only). Afternoon teas. Garden. TV. Phone. Doors close at midnight. Confirm by 6 (*Which? Hotel Guide*)

Nightingales

NEW ENTRY

Bath House Farm, Lower West Hatch,
nr Taunton TA3 5RH
HATCH BEAUCHAMP (0823) 480392
and 480806 — COOKING 1
on A358, between Taunton and Ilminster — COST £24–£32

A small escalope of salmon with a walnut and orange salad, a choux bun filled with prawns, lemon sole layered over a mousseline on a saffron sauce, sirloin steak, soubise, and pommes de terre Anna, chocolate torte with strawberries, and an eclair filled with strawberry Chantilly was a spring meal eaten in this converted barn in the garden of Margaret and Jeremy Barlow's house. The welcome is always good – it's a home from home – and the cooking a careful version of good home entertaining. Nightingales keeps a local following, no doubt helped by the decent wine list with fair offerings from the New World as well as from France. House Clochemerle from Avery's is £7.25.

CHEFS: Margaret Barlow, Marie-Anne Owen and Sally Edwards PROPRIETORS: Jeremy and Margaret Barlow OPEN: Tue to Sat, D only MEALS: 7.30 to 10 (varies) PRICES: Set D £16.50 (£24) to £19.50 (£27). Card slips closed CARDS: Access, Visa SEATS: 40. 2 tables outside. Private parties: 46 main room. Car park, 25 places. Vegetarian meals. Children's helpings with prior notice. Children restricted. Wheelchair access (1 step; also WC). Music

---

TAVISTOCK Devon — map 1

▲ *Horn of Plenty*

COUNTY RESTAURANT OF THE YEAR

NEW ENTRY

Gulworthy, Tavistock PL19 8JD — COOKING 3
TAVISTOCK (0822) 832528 — COST £23–£48

The Horn of Plenty has changed hands, décor – including the welcome addition of a drawing-room – and chef. Although it is still early days, recent reports show no adverse effects; indeed, one reader, under the impression that the Stevensons were still there, reported, 'We were therefore very pleasantly surprised with the performance of the kitchen'. Peter Gorton has been exposed to Thai, Japanese and other oriental influences as well as those of the Mediterranean: provençal fish soup; home-made cannelloni filled with artichokes, mushrooms and asparagus; fillets of lemon sole with a coating of chopped prawns, scallops and fresh coriander, cooked in a tempura batter; or breast of duck in a piquant marinade with ginger-flavoured cabbage. The quality and freshness of ingredients used is first-class and timing and technique are accurate; saucing is simple and understated. Fish figures strongly, as in locally caught turbot filled with crabmeat and served with a langoustine sauce, and pan-fried salmon in a lemon and fresh herb marinade on a tomato and basil coulis. Just occasionally, flavours have been marred by complexity, showing a rare lack of judgement. Finely chopped bacon served with pan-fried scallops was too strong for the delicate seafood; the addition of red chilli to the shellfish with lemon sole in tempura batter was too powerful, masking the whole dish. Desserts include orange, chocolate and hazelnut parfait served with a light coffee cream and excellent sorbets. The wine list has sprung fully formed from careful plans of owner and suppliers. It is a well-chosen range, though not especially cheap. The prices are kept fair by some decent wines from Italy, Spain and the New World. House wines are from £8.

CHEFS: Peter Gorton and David Lewis PROPRIETORS: Elaine and Ian Gatehouse OPEN: all week, exc Mon L CLOSED: 25 and 26 Dec MEALS: 12 to 2, 7 to 9.30 PRICES: £30 (£40), Set L £12.95 (£19) to £16.80 (£23), Set D £22.50 (£29) CARDS: Access, Amex, Visa SEATS: 45. 6 tables outside. Private parties: 40 main room, 20 private room. Vegetarian meals. Children's helpings L. Wheelchair access (2 steps; also WC). No music ACCOMMODATION: 6 rooms, all with bath/shower. Rooms for disabled. B&B £51 to £78. Children welcome. Pets welcome. Garden. TV. Phone. Scenic (*Which? Hotel Guide*)

TEFFONT EVIAS Wiltshire map 2

▲ *Howard's House Hotel*

Teffont Evias SP3 5RJ COOKING 2
SALISBURY (0722) 716392 COST £21–£40

This is a good place to stay: attractive gardens, restful green decoration, log fires when necessary, 'and enough towels'. It is also a pleasing place to eat, once it has been located on a lane that branches away from the Hindon to Wilton road at the Black Horse. More help in the kitchen has given a greater breadth, especially with desserts and ancillaries. If sauces are the markers of a kitchen's approach, these are of this decade: lemon grass and ginger with sea bass; raspberry vinegar with brill; curry with chicken and mango; truffle gravy for pigeon. Reductions tend to be light. First courses show similar tendencies: quenelles of lobster and the quail stuffed with pesto and served with wild rice, tomato and an olive oil emulsion have been well reported. Desserts have demonstrated the competence intended by the accession of Claire Holloway. Toffee pecan pie with crème fraîche and baked tamarillos with saffron and honey ice-cream pleased one couple, while another found the apple feuilleté with calvados and cinnamon mousse equally satisfactory. With more consistency the wine list would be exemplary. Ambition, range and clarity are not lacking. But where over-reliance on big houses sets in – as in Burgundy and the Rhône – confidence in the list as a whole is shaken. There are good dessert wines. House wine is £9.25.

CHEFS: Paul Firmin and Claire Holloway PROPRIETORS: Paul Firmin and Jonathan Ford OPEN: all week, D only, and Sun L CLOSED: 24 to 31 Dec MEALS: 12.30 to 2, 7.30 to 10 PRICES: Set Sun L £14.50 (£21), Set D £25.50 (£33) CARDS: Access, Amex, Visa SEATS: 40. 4 tables outside. Private parties: 40 main room, 20 private room. Car park, 35 places. Vegetarian meals. Children's helpings (Sun L only). No cigars/pipes in dining-room. Wheelchair access. Music. Fax: (0722) 716820 ACCOMMODATION: 9 rooms, all with bath/shower. Rooms for disabled. B&B £50 to £78. Children welcome. Baby facilities. Pets welcome. Garden. TV. Phone. Scenic

The text of entries is based on unsolicited reports sent in by readers, backed up by inspections conducted anonymously. The factual details under the text are from questionnaires the Guide *sends to all restaurants that feature in the book.*

TETBURY Gloucestershire map 2

▲ *Calcot Manor* 🍷

Beverston, Tetbury GL8 8YJ COOKING 3*
LEIGHTERTON (0666) 890391 COST £19–£54

The hotel occupies an enlarged residential block of the original manor-farmhouse as well as converted farm buildings across the courtyard. Inside, the feeling is that of a comfortable country home, not an upwardly mobile country house. Ramon Farthing's cooking is perhaps more elaborate than that: 'technically accurate, well presented, low in animal fats and achieving a cross-fire of clear flavours' was one reader's verdict. This in dishes such as pigeon with shredded cabbage and bacon and a 'casserole' of lentils and chives; or pan-fried John Dory arranged round a pile of steamed potato slices moistened with sesame oil, shredded leeks and grapes, all sauced by a clear shellfish stock. Presentation and variety go into the vegetables too, so the usual selection is arranged round a mousse – once green bean, another time mushroom, spinach and celeriac. Small wonder then that cheeses are an impressive selection or that 'British puddings' should turn out to be a plate of micro-versions of lemon meringue pie, bread-and-butter pudding and sherry trifle with raspberry coulis. Failures in this complicated style do not often occur. Residents regret the menus do not change frequently. Others find the pricing system difficult to interpret. The high cost of a four-course evening meal was not mitigated for a child's simple meal. On the wine list, eight French country wines around £10 and some decent petits châteaux offer good and interesting drinking for those not wishing to explore the higher reaches. Mark-ups do not favour the top end, although pedigree and vintages are impeccable in the classic areas. Provence, Alsace and USA offer interest and, perhaps, better value. Half-bottles are limited. House wine is £9.45.

CHEF: Ramon Farthing PROPRIETORS: Brian and Barbara Ball OPEN: all week, exc Sun D MEALS: 12.30 to 2, 7.30 to 9.30 PRICES: Set L £12.75 (£19) to £17 (£24), Set D £29 (£37) to £36 (£45). Card slips closed CARDS: Access, Amex, Diners, Visa SEATS: 45. 3 tables outside. Private parties: 48 main room, 12 private room. Car park, 75 places. Vegetarian meals. Children's helpings L. Jacket and tie. No smoking in dining-room. Wheelchair access (also WC). Fax: (0666) 890394 ACCOMMODATION: 16 rooms, all with bath/shower. Rooms for disabled. B&B £95 to £140. No children under 12. Afternoon teas. Garden. Swimming-pool. Fishing. Golf. TV. Phone. Scenic (*Which? Hotel Guide*)

TEWKESBURY Gloucestershire map 2

▲ *Puckrup Hall* NEW ENTRY

Puckrup, nr Tewkesbury GL20 6EL COOKING 2
TEWKESBURY (0684) 296200 and 296150 COST £19–£35

This grand Regency mansion, formerly known as Tewkesbury Hall, stands in 40 acres of mature grounds between the Cotswolds and the Malvern Hills. Inside it is all high ceilings, oil paintings and large soft settees, with a spacious dining-room to match. Geoff Balharrie and his brigade produce well-presented modern dishes: wild mushroom ravioli on a bed of spinach with nutmeg and chive butter, breast of chicken stuffed with crab mousse ('the two flavours perfectly balanced'), hake and coriander quenelles with nettle and sorrel sauce, and warm apple and date tart all impressed a lunchtime visitor. The regularly changing evening *carte* moves into the complex realms of breast of guinea-fowl with lentil and shallot risotto, girolle mushrooms and a truffle reduction, and loin of Gloucester venison baked in pastry with chestnut and mint mousse served with sloe gin and rowanberry sauce. There are grills and flambés for the more conservative, and dishes such as aubergine fritters with yoghurt and plum sauce for vegetarians. The list of mostly British farmhouse cheeses reads well. Service is a model of professionalism. House wine is £8.25. More reports, please.

CHEF: Geoff Balharrie PROPRIETORS: Country Mansion Hotels OPEN: all week MEALS: 12.30 to 2, 7 to 9.30 (10 Sat) PRICES: Set L £13.25 (£19) to £15.25 (£21), Set D £22.50 (£29). Card slips closed CARDS: Access, Amex, Diners, Visa SEATS: 34. Private parties: 50 main room, 20 and 120 private rooms. Car park, 100 places. Vegetarian meals. Children's helpings. No children under 7. Jacket and tie. No smoking in dining-room. Wheelchair access (2 steps; also WC). Music ACCOMMODATION: 16 rooms, all with bath/shower. B&B £77.50 to £135. Children welcome. Baby facilities. Pets welcome. Afternoon teas. Garden. Fishing. TV. Phone. Scenic (*Which? Hotel Guide*)

THORNBURY Avon map 2

▲ *Thornbury Castle*

Castle Street, Thornbury BS12 1HH COOKING 3
THORNBURY (0454) 418511 COST £25–£44

The castle – the last one in England to be given a licence to crenellate – was never finished. The Duke of Buckingham lost his head too soon. Maurice Taylor would probably like to complete the job, but respect for history has meant adjustment, not destruction, in the process of creating a luxury hotel within the walls. Stairs can be vertiginous and access routes hard to remember, but they give character to the modern conversions of sumptuous bedrooms. Derek Hamlen continues to run the kitchen, with 'long-standing Thornbury favourites' providing apostolic succession from the days of Kenneth Bell, as does the suit of armour in the great hall. Recommendations of food such as fish soup nîmoise, spiced tomato soup, smoked Tay salmon, devilled crab with Parmesan, tournedos with mustard and thyme sauce and, more elaborately, a trio of game on a vegetable rösti with a blueberry and shallot sauce, show the cooking to be quiet rather than flash, well-judged rather than needlessly elaborate. Details such as two types of fudge and home-made chocolates, and a hot appetiser after cold canapés give encouragement, even if the dining-room chairs cause distress. One couple who stayed four days found inexplicable variation between one meal and the next, even with identical dishes. But in general the approval rate is high for willingness among the staff (gratuities are not expected), the welcome to solitary diners marooned in the northern hinterland of Bristol or the standard of a late-night supper of bread and cheese to one traveller speeding from rain-lashed Wales. With vineyards springing up in all corners of the country, Thornbury may not still be the only restaurant to claim its own wine. Thornbury Castle, Müller-Thurgau figures on a useful 'short list of wines under £15'. Thereafter, the unwary are in for a shock. Not on grounds of economy, for the prices throughout are generally fair, although erratic; rather because of the sheer length, quality and range of wines included. Italy remains dangerous territory for Thornbury, a reflection perhaps of the general out-of-date feeling. If the main list fails to satisfy, the 'proprietors' reserve' (24 hours' notice) may oblige. There are good sherries and half-bottles. House wines are from £9.95. CELLARMAN'S CHOICE: Fitou 1986, £15; Côtes du Rhône 1989, J.P. Brotte, £15.30.

CHEF: Derek Hamlen PROPRIETORS: Maurice and Carol Taylor OPEN: all week MEALS: 12 to 2, 7 to 9.30 (9 Sun) PRICES: Set L £17.75 (£25), Set D £25.50 (£34) to £29.50 (£37). Net prices, card slips closed CARDS: Access, Amex, Carte Blanche, Diners, Visa SEATS: 60. Private parties: 25 main room. Car park, 30 places. Vegetarian meals. No children under 12. Smart dress preferred. Music. Fax: (0454) 416188 ACCOMMODATION: 18 rooms, all with bath/shower. B&B £80 to £190. No children under 12. Afternoon teas. Garden. TV. Phone. Scenic (*Which? Hotel Guide*)

THORNTON-CLEVELEYS Lancashire map 5

▲ *Victorian House*

Trunnah Road,
Thornton-Cleveleys FY5 4HF COOKING 1*
CLEVELEYS (0253) 860619 COST £14–£27

The house is opposite the church (it was once indeed a convent) at the Thornton end of the twin settlement Thornton-Cleveleys. Some warning of the decorative theme is given in the name, and Mme Guérin dresses the Victorian part, too. The cooking, however, is traditional French, leavened by outside touches such as skewers of tiger prawns with breast of chicken, garlic and soya sauce. Reports praise the quiche, for example, as being 'true quiche' and 'far less outlandish than much "British" cooking today'. Skills and finesse are not invariably apparent, but the performance is generally steady. A four-course menu, with soups or sorbet at stage two, is offered at a set price with about eight choices at each course. Beginnings are simple – marinated herrings, pheasant terrine, Parma ham – main courses may extend to wrapping lamb in filo, coated with a leek and basil 'compote', or casseroled pheasant 'grand veneur'. The wine list is not long, all French, fairly priced and including some nicely chosen bottles, such as Laguiche Chassagne-Montrachet 1983 and Ch. Nenin 1982. Service is always amiable, from Mme Guérin or her helpers.

CHEF: Didier Guérin PROPRIETORS: Louise and Didier Guérin OPEN: Mon to Sat, exc Mon L CLOSED: last week Jan, first week Feb MEALS: 12 to 2, 7 to 9.30 PRICES: L £10 (£14), Set D £17.95 (£23). Net prices, card slips closed CARDS: Access, Visa SEATS: 65. 4 tables outside. Private parties: 40 main room. Car park, 20 places. Vegetarian meals. No children under 6. Smart dress preferred. Music. Fax: (0253) 865350 ACCOMMODATION: 3 rooms, all with bath/shower. B&B £39.50 to £67. Deposit: £10. No children under 6. Pets welcome. Garden. TV. Phone. Scenic. Confirm by 6 (*Which? Hotel Guide*)

Report forms are at the back of the book; write a letter if you prefer.

THRESHFIELD North Yorkshire map 7

Old Hall

Threshfield BD23 5HB — COOKING 1
SKIPTON (0756) 752441 — COST £19

The refurbished Victorian house looks more like a country residence than a roadside pub, with its oak panelling, shiny brass and secluded garden. There are no bookings: give your name to the bar staff and wait for a free table. Ian Taylor's blackboard menu draws the crowds and items are quickly depleted at peak times. The kitchen plunders the globe for inspiration: spicy peanut and pepper soup, chicken wings with Chinese sauce, and chicken tikka masala share the stage with cassoulet, carbonnade of beef and steamed salmon with dill sauce. Huge helpings satisfy Yorkshire appetites. Vegetables are 'nicely undercooked'. Occasional rogue specials, such as set-price lobster with salad and potatoes, offer exceptional value. To finish there might be summer pudding or Bavarian lemon torte. A minimal list of 18 wines includes house French at £8 a litre; alternatively there is well-kept Timothy Taylor's beer.

CHEFS: Rachel Mawer and Carl Gilbert PROPRIETOR: Ian Taylor OPEN: all week CLOSED: Mon, Jan to May MEALS: 12 to 2, 6.30 to 9.30 PRICES: £10 (£16) SEATS: 80. 4 tables outside. Private parties: 35 main room. Car park, 30 places. Vegetarian meals. Children's helpings. Wheelchair access (also WC). Music

THUNDRIDGE Hertfordshire map 3

▲ *Hanbury Manor*

COUNTY RESTAURANT OF THE YEAR

NEW ENTRY

Thundridge SG12 0SD — COOKING 3
WARE (0920) 487722 — COST £24–£66

The original house, Jacobean in style, was built in 1890. Do not expect an interior of high sensibility, rather lots of panelling and heavy detail. Massive and boring additions have been made to the whole; golf courses abound. This is a corporate conference paradise. It has style, however, if not that of the private country house beloved of England. The cooking has been the province of Albert Roux as consultant, who installed Rory Kennedy as chef. In the Zodiac Restaurant, the menu shows the spore of the Roux: soufflé suissesse and caneton Gavroche are verbatim, while other dishes show very strong similarities – for example, one might have been called papillote de saumon fumé Claudine by the change of two or so details. The menus combine this line of Roux with classics such as crêpes Suzette and more adventurous dishes. Exactitude in cooking is matched by that in seasoning: in red mullet with young spinach and bone marrow; or lobster roasted with garlic, thyme and spring vegetables, the flesh slipped out of the shell and replaced on a bed of mashed potato, the spring vegetables a masterpiece of timing and flavour. This is complex cooking, but here very successful. Service, silver domes and all, is elaborate and Gavroche-trained at the top. That it should be as perfect as that of the West End original is too much to expect, but it is more than adequate. It remains to be seen if Rory Kennedy can develop his own style. He certainly has the skills but first impressions are influenced by that uneasy sense of cloning.

The chance to experiment on the wine list is severely constrained by prices. Quality is not in doubt, but with Sancerre by Natter and 1985 Marqués de Murrieta white Rioja at £25 and £28 respectively a careful tread is dictated. Apart from a run of Ch. Latour, the young cellar has ground to make up on the vintage front. Clearly printed and carefully annotated, the list has a good feel – shame about the prices.

CHEF: Rory Kennedy PROPRIETORS: Poles Ltd OPEN: Mon to Sat, D only, and Sun L MEALS: 12 to 3, 7 to 11 PRICES: Set Sun L £17.50 (£24) to £21.50 (£28), Set D £17.50 (£24) to £48.50 (£55). Net prices, card slips closed CARDS: Access, Amex, Diners, Visa SEATS: 42. 12 tables outside. Private parties: 120 main room, 24, 32, 48, 104 and 120 private rooms. Car park, 150 places. Vegetarian meals. Children's helpings. Jacket and tie in Zodiac Restaurant. No cigars/pipes in dining-room. Wheelchair access (1 step; also WC). No music. Fax: (0920) 487692 ACCOMMODATION: 98 rooms, all with bath/shower. Rooms for disabled. Lift. B&B £110 to £125. Children welcome. Baby facilities. Small dogs allowed. Afternoon teas. Garden. Swimming-pool. Sauna. Tennis. Golf. Snooker. Air-conditioned. TV. Phone. Scenic. Confirm 2 weeks ahead (*Which? Hotel Guide*)

TIVERTON Devon map 1

Lowman **NEW ENTRY**

45 Gold Street, Tiverton EX16 6QB COOKING 2
TIVERTON (0884) 257311 COST £17–£31

The location beside the River Lowman provides the name. Since the Filmer-Bennetts count on some 30 local suppliers, the menu is peppered with locally made chutneys, cheeses, smoked salmon and clotted cream as well as Devon lamb. The menu is attractive both in price and choice. Dinner in January produced fresh scallops in white wine and cream sauce, poached egg in tomato and garlic sauce, steak and beer pie, and breast of chicken with grapes and white wine sauce. Readers have commented favourably on an admirable attempt at pigs' trotters Pierre Koffmann, stuffed with chicken breasts, sweetbreads, wild mushrooms and vegetables with a port sauce, although such dishes are not always within reach of Jane Hall's technique. Cooking on the whole is accurate, with time spent on presentation, and slips – notably, a lack of freshness in otherwise good home-made bread and in pastry – are occasional. The predominantly French wine list includes four Devon wines, some good burgundies and a decent selection of halves. House French is £6.65.

CHEF: Jane Hall PROPRIETORS: Jeremy and Elaine Filmer-Bennett OPEN: Tue to Sat CLOSED: Christmas to New Year MEALS: 12 to 2, 7 to 9 (9.30 Fri and Sat) PRICES: L £11 (£17), D £14 (£21), Set D £13.25 (£23) to £15.75 (£26). Card slips closed CARDS: Access, Visa SEATS: 40. 12 tables outside. Private parties: 40 main room, 20 private room. Vegetarian meals. Children's helpings. No-smoking area. Music

The 1993 Guide *will be published before Christmas 1992. Reports on meals are most welcome at any time of the year, but are extremely valuable in the spring. Send them to* The Good Food Guide, *FREEPOST, 2 Marylebone Road, London NW1 1YN. No stamp is needed when posting in the UK.*

TORQUAY Devon map 1

Capers

NEW ENTRY

7 Lisburne Square, Torquay TQ1 2PT COOKING 1
TORQUAY (0803) 291177 COST £41

Ian Cawley runs this unpretentious restaurant as an extension to his home and grows most of his own vegetables and herbs. There is nothing luxurious about the agreeable, apricot-painted dining-room and the kitchen stays within limits. The emphasis is on decent ingredients, simply cooked in the modern style, often with creamy but light sauces. Fresh fish from Torquay or Brixham dominates the short, regularly changing menu. Cold fillet of red mullet with tomato and coriander dressing, salmon in filo pastry with lime and ginger, and baked turbot with saffron and orange sauce have all been well reported. Fish soup comes with a forceful rouille and garlic croûtons. Otherwise the menu might take in grilled goats' cheese on brioche, wild rabbit pie or Gressingham duck braised with orange, tomato and almonds. Bread and rolls are baked on the premises, farmhouse cheeses come from the Totnes area. Sweets are the likes of Osborne pudding with Grand Marnier custard or brown sugar meringues filled with clotted cream. Snacks are available at lunchtime. A short list of affordable wine changes every three months. House French is £8.50.

CHEF/PROPRIETOR: Ian Cawley OPEN: Tue to Sat, exc Tue L MEALS: 12 to 1.30, 7 to 9.30 (10 Sat) PRICES: £25 (£34), L snacks from £3.50. Card slips closed CARDS: Access, Visa SEATS: 24. Private parties: 8 main room. Vegetarian meals with prior notice. Children's helpings. Music

▲ *Mulberry Room*

1 Scarborough Road, Torquay TQ2 5UJ COOKING 2
TORQUAY (0803) 213639 COST £11–£29

The fact that visitors are prepared to travel miles in the hope of getting a table says a great deal about Lesley Cooper's remarkable Victorian guesthouse on the fringes of Torquay's holiday district. She has been spurred on by success. Her lunchtime blackboard menus are becoming more ambitious, without a trace of fancy pretension: English asparagus with basil-scented mayonnaise, grilled herrings stuffed with rhubarb and allspice, and chicken with courgettes and coconut milk have joined the ranks alongside mushroom soup, moussaka and 'first-class' meringue pie. The secret is an honest, enterprising approach to home-cooking, but in tune with the times – a colour-coding system indicates low-fat and low-cholesterol dishes. Sunday lunch always features roast sirloin of Devon beef and a vegetarian dish plus, perhaps, farm chicken, local lamb or game. A splendid array of home-baked cakes and pastries are the stars of morning coffee and afternoon tea. The wine list is cheap and cheerful. House wine is £6 a carafe; there is also home-made sloe gin.

See inside front cover for an explanation of the 1 to 5 rating system recognising cooking standards.

CHEF/PROPRIETOR: Lesley Cooper OPEN: Wed to Sun, L only, and Sat D MEALS: 12.15 to 2.30, 7.30 to 9.30 PRICES: £13 (£18), Set L £7 (£11) to £8.50 (£13), Set D £16.50 (£21) to £18.50 (£24) SEATS: 30. 2 tables outside. Private parties: 40 main room. Vegetarian meals. Healthy eating options. Children's helpings. Wheelchair access (also WC). Music ACCOMMODATION: 3 rooms. B&B £16.50 to £33. Deposit: 10%. Children welcome. Afternoon teas. TV. Doors close at dusk. Confirm by dusk

TRESCO Isles of Scilly map 1

▲ *Island Hotel*

NEW ENTRY

Tresco TR24 0PU COOKING 1
SCILLONIA (0720) 22883 COST £8–£42

Tresco is a private island with no cars, no pollution, sweeping beaches and tropical gardens. 'Who wants to go to the Mediterranean?' Arrive in comfort by helicopter from Penzance or by open boat (clad against the elements) from St Mary's. The hotel sits rather incongruously in its magnificent surroundings: it has evolved over the years with much plate glass to maximise the view. Despite the lack of architectural cohesion, the quality of welcome and the comfortable interior are well spoken of. The strength of the kitchen is in the local fish; the morning catch could appear in the evening either filleted and poached with a light vermouth and dill sauce or deep-fried with tartare sauce. One guest commenting on the menu counted eight different varieties of fish ('local, caught by staff with nothing else to do on their days off'). Other endorsed dishes have included mushroom and herb soup, lobster bisque, scampi provençal, cassoulette of seafood and lobster thermidor. There are also plenty of meat, poultry and game dishes. House wine is £7.25.

CHEF: Mike Coombe PROPRIETOR: Robert Dorrien Smith OPEN: all week MEALS: 12 to 2, 7.15 to 9 PRICES: Set L £3.50 (£8) to £15 (£21), Set D £22.50 (£29) to £27.50 (£35). Card slips closed CARDS: Access, Amex, Visa SEATS: 130. 10 tables outside. Private parties: 40 main room. Vegetarian meals. Children's helpings. Smart dress preferred. Music ACCOMMODATION: 40 rooms, all with bath/shower. B&B £68.50 to £110. Deposit: 20%. Children welcome. Baby facilities. Afternoon teas. Garden. Swimming-pool. Tennis. Fishing. TV. Phone. Scenic

TRURO Cornwall map 1

▲ *Alverton Manor*

Tregolls Road, Truro TR1 1XQ COOKING 1
TRURO (0872) 76633 COST £16–£37

There is nothing immediately conventual about this hotel, save for the former chapel (to be converted into a banqueting suite) and the occasional mock-Gothic arched doorway. But convent it was, later converted quite plushly to secular use, with a good site looking over Truro and potentially good gardens. The stylish dining-room can be a touch sombre in the candlelight but is Truro's closest approach to luxury. Simon Jordan's cooking hankers for the '80s and the delights of careful arrangement, silver domes and reduced sauces. This can be its downfall, as in a meal when the same reduction infused two main courses, even if each had a different 'finish'. The *carte* is supported by a set menu, but adventure is advisable. Dishes such as a warm salad of pigeon breast with pimento; poussin with ginger, soy and garlic; lamb, either with lentil sauce or stuffed with a rosemary mousse, wrapped in spinach, and served on an oyster mushroom sauce, have been well reported. Desserts have not been so warmly received, and the waiting staff need instruction in cheese-mongering and details. Were the cooking to be bolder and less pretty, the hotel would be a model resort for Truro's citizens. Vintages are shown this year, but the wine list can still be coy when it comes to growers' names. Prices look fair, but it is difficult to be sure. Half-bottles are limited. House wines are from £5.20.

CHEF: Simon Jordan PROPRIETORS: Mr and Mrs J.J. Costelloe OPEN: all week MEALS: 12.15 to 1.45, 7.15 to 9.45 PRICES: £20 (£31), Set L £9.95 (£16), Set D £13.50 (£20). Card slips closed CARDS: Access, Amex, Diners, Visa SEATS: 50. 3 tables outside. Private parties: 35 main room, 25 and 35 private rooms. Car park, 70 places. Vegetarian meals. No children under 12. Smart dress preferred. No smoking during meals. Wheelchair access (also WC). Music. Fax: (0872) 222989 ACCOMMODATION: 25 rooms, all with bath/shower. Rooms for disabled. Lift. B&B £55 to £110. No children under 12. Afternoon teas. Garden. Snooker. TV. Phone. Scenic. Confirm by 6 (*Which? Hotel Guide*)

TUNBRIDGE WELLS Kent map 3

COUNTY RESTAURANT OF THE YEAR

Cheevers

56 High Street, Tunbridge Wells TN1 1XF COOKING 3
TUNBRIDGE WELLS (0892) 545524 COST £25–£35

Some people wish the menu here would show more rapid change; certainly Tim Cheevers works a small repertoire with care and adjustment only to details of supplies, but he cooks it very well and has impressed a growing clientele. For one reporter, the spare decoration of the restaurant, avoiding the giddy slopes of shimmering chintz or walls burdened with *trouvailles* and objects, is a recommendation in itself; for another, so is the accurate service; for a third, 'the duck with spring onions and ginger, a sort of Peking duck, was the best for several years' balanced as it was by a dark, sticky sauce with a fruited scent and zest. Vegetables, properly cooked, were felt to be redundant, even if they included Pink Fir Apple potatoes one October lunchtime. Dishes that continue to be praised are a two-tone crab mousse, wrapped in a spinach leaf; ravioli of mussels; good terrines; fresh fish, often one in pastry; lamb with mint and almond crust; venison with red wine and raisins; lemon tart with enjoyable pastry; and a white and dark chocolate mousse. Satisfaction seems to spring from assured technique, a comforting lack of fireworks and consistent performance with true flavours. The wine list has perhaps 50 bottles, with enough halves for most tastes. By no means all the choices come from France, and there is a nicely unhackneyed ring to the growers and properties. Prices rarely stray above £20. Drink Penshurst here, or Juillot's Mercurey, or Pelvillain's Cahors. House wines from Lamblin are £7.25.

CHEF: T.J. Cheevers PROPRIETORS: T.J. Cheevers, M.J. Miles and P.D. Tambini OPEN: Tue to Sat MEALS: 12.30 to 2, 7.30 to 10.30 PRICES: £17 (£25), Set D £22.50 (£29). Card slips closed CARDS: Access, Visa SEATS: 36. Private parties: 16 main room. Children welcome. No cigars/pipes in dining-room. Wheelchair access. No music

Sankey's

The Gate, 39 Mount Ephraim,
Tunbridge Wells TN4 8AA — COOKING 1
TUNBRIDGE WELLS (0892) 511422 — COST £34

'The old style' continues at Guy Sankey's unpretentious seafood restaurant, and the freshness of his fish still draws enthusiastic reports. Daily specials come 'direct from port'. Simple treatment seems to work best, but the kitchen also tries its hand with more ambitious work: steamed turbot with green peppercorn sauce, salmon en croûte, monkfish roasted with garlic. There is always an unchanging assortment of 'seafood bar classics' in the shape of native oysters, smoked wild salmon, Loch Fyne sweet-cured herrings, potted shrimps and stuffed clams. Home-made fishcakes and spaghetti with mussels are also available with snacks. Desserts are creamy, and the cheeseboard promotes 'The Best of the British Isles'. 'Poor fish soup and poor coffee' was the regretful assessment of one impressed by the quality of the produce, especially the scallops, and pleased by the welcome from one and all. Cidre bouché, natural Bière du Garde and German Weisse bier are alternatives to the workmanlike list of 40 wines. House French is £8. Guy Sankey is still campaigning for permission to open a downstairs wine bar within the restaurant.

CHEF: Eleuterio Lizzi PROPRIETOR: Guy Sankey OPEN: Mon to Sat CLOSED: bank hols MEALS: 12 to 2, 7 to 10 PRICES: £22 (£28). Net prices, card slips closed CARDS: Access, Visa SEATS: 60. 6 tables outside. Private parties: 8 main room, 30 private room. Children's helpings on request. No-smoking area. Music

Thackeray's House 🍷

85 London Road,
Tunbridge Wells TN1 1EA — COOKING 3*
TUNBRIDGE WELLS (0892) 511921 — COST £22–£48

Thackeray's House was Thackeray's house, and the building is tasteful compulsory revivalism owing to the laws against knocking monuments about too much. The ground floor is a restaurant, with space at a certain premium; round the corner is a separate entrance to the basement bistro, which continues to produce very good food at competitive prices. Customers will be relieved that Bruce Wass has never indulged in nostalgic cooking. Underpinning the menu is his professionalism, which means that each component has been thought about, carefully purchased and freshly cooked. There is a rigorousness of approach that shows on the plate in strong flavours avoiding stridency, and in direct presentation without lumpishness. It is, however, fairly uncompromising. The repertoire keeps up to date: bresaola is home-cured; there are first courses such as hot sea bass pâté with asparagus sauce and warm skate and scallop salad with ginger and soy vinaigrette; Mediterranean flavours are well explored, for instance in a main dish of John Dory and prawns with saffron; and classical depth and complexity is found in a two-fold dish of breast and ballotine of guinea-fowl with shitake mushrooms and basil. Vegetables are simple, yet given lifts of flavouring to take them beyond boredom; bread, canapés and petits fours are expert; cheese is British or Irish. The restaurant has always been among the more expensive in the district – for good reason – but a cheaper mid-week short menu has been introduced which represents good value. Sometimes there is a lapse into over-seriousness; this can be translated into a place that is not full of joy – which all good restaurants need to be. Service is leisurely, too slow sometimes for those who like a fast-paced meal. A dozen 'recommended wines' are kept below £12. Italy now takes first place in the very good list that follows – a few older vintages but mostly on the young side reflecting the recent determination to encourage more Italophiles. Classic areas are well chosen, if on the expensive side, and the New World has a page to itself. There are many good dessert wines and spirits and a sensible range of halves. House wine is £10.85. CELLARMAN'S CHOICE: Mâcon Peronne 1989, Rousset, £16.90; Gigondas, Les Pallières 1986, Roux, £19.40.

CHEF/PROPRIETOR: Bruce Wass OPEN: Tue to Sat CLOSED: 1 week Christmas MEALS: 12.30 to 2.30, 7 to 10 PRICES: £32 (£40), Set L £15.90 (£22) to £17.50 (£23), Set D £19.50 (£25) to £35 (£40). Net prices, card slips closed CARDS: Access, Visa SEATS: 35. Private parties: 40 main room. Children's helpings. No music

TWICKENHAM Greater London map 3

Cézanne

68 Richmond Road, Twickenham TW1 3BE COOKING 1
081-892 3526 COST £26

This plain – when it's cold, almost too plain – restaurant is going through a recession-induced identity crisis. Thus, things cost less (good) but there are also fewer interesting things (bad). Although we have had reports extolling gnocchi with pesto and fresh Parmesan, guinea-fowl satay, spinach and salmon in pastry with sour-cream sauce, and banana wrapped in filo with a butterscotch sauce, we have also heard regret at the 'snack-type' first courses, overcooked lamb, poorly bought beef, meagre vegetables and too-runny crème brûlée. Customers who are 'allergic to saxophones' (a new allergy to the *Guide*'s office, but understandable) also take exception to the endless music. Tim Jefferson's intentions are right; on paper they seem correct, and in the past they have been. But more rigorous control of their execution is needed to re-establish this as a good-value and inventive kitchen. House wine is £6.75.

CHEFS: Tim Jefferson and John Mackensie PROPRIETOR: Tim Jefferson OPEN: Mon to Sat, exc Sat L CLOSED: bank hols MEALS: 12.30 to 2, 7 to 10.30 (11 Fri and Sat) PRICES: £14 (£22). Card slips closed CARDS: Access, Amex, Visa SEATS: 38. Private parties: 40 main room. Vegetarian meals. Children's helpings. Wheelchair access. Music

McClements

12 The Green, Twickenham TW2 5AA COOKING 3
081-755 0176 COST £28–£49

John McClement is a chef of great skill who seems inhibited by his situation; this is a very small house on the Green, with an even smaller kitchen and staff. It may not reassure customers, just as it did not encourage one who had paid approaching £50 a head to find an ill-supplied lavatory and 'a pile of spare chairs on the landing giving an impression of a French village café'. That said, the proprieties of service are observed and the cook does all his own work. This can succeed to a high degree, as in a dish of warm oysters; a sea urchin soufflé; scallops with soy sauce and cream with a shredded shitake; black pudding, wrapped in pastry, with a mustard sauce and a nice trimming of a soft-boiled quail's egg; excellent raspberry mousse; chocolate praline ice-cream; and home-made petits fours such as warm pineapple tartlets, truffles and chocolate cups filled with Grand Marnier mousse. Main dishes, coincidentally perhaps, have not been so well reported, though some fish is imaginatively dealt with, as in turbot with chervil and tarragon (though too many chives). Duck with lime confit and juniper sauce to cut the richness also worked well. The wine list is an idiosyncratic mixture from Brown Bros Chardonnay at £22 to 1950 Ch. Peyreau at £130 or Ch. Lafite 1919 at £850. House wines are from £10.50.

CHEF/PROPRIETOR: John McClement OPEN: Mon to Sat, exc Sat L MEALS: 12 to 2.30, 7 to 10.30 PRICES: £30 (£41), Set L £18.50 (£28), Set D £18.50 (£28) to £28 (£39). Service 10%. Card slips closed CARDS: Access, Amex, Visa SEATS: 24. Private parties: 20 main room, 15 private room. Vegetarian meals. No children under 3. Smart dress preferred. Wheelchair access (also WC). Music. Fax: 081-890 1372

UCKFIELD East Sussex map 3

▲ *Horsted Place*

Little Horsted, TN22 5TS
UCKFIELD (0825) 75581 COOKING 3
2m S of Uckfield, on A26 COST £28–£52

This is an exceptional early Victorian Gothic pile to suit many occasions. Allan Garth has settled down in the kitchen and his cooking is more assured. There is a refreshing absence of showy techniques – no spun-sugar cages for the desserts, for instance – and ingredients are all good, without recourse to extravagance. A good meal comprised sautéed medallion of monkfish tail, cooked correctly and served on a bed of well-flavoured butter-beans alongside an oil and tomato sauce, its sweetness complementing the dry, butter-bean flavour; a handsome-looking terrine of provençal vegetables with refreshing tastes; calf's liver well balanced by its potato rösti and braised shallots; and medallions of venison, tender and of fine flavour, served with little contrasting mounds of chicken and herb quenelle. British cheeses are presented very grandly as whole cheeses on a heavy wicker basket. Invention continues at the dessert stage: carrot, hazelnut and apricot cake was 'a light, interesting upmarket version of health food nosh,' according to one reader. There is evidence of good teamwork between the kitchen and dining-room. The wine list is presented clearly, but without notes, and pricing is erratic. There are five house-selection wines from £11.95.

The Guide *always appreciates hearing about changes of chef or owner.*

CHEF: Allan Garth PROPRIETORS: Granfel Hotels OPEN: all week, exc Sat L CLOSED: 1 to 10 Jan MEALS: 12.30 to 2, 7.30 to 9.15 PRICES: Set L £16.50 (£28) to £20.50 (£32), Set D £30.50 (£43). Card slips closed CARDS: Access, Amex, Diners, Visa SEATS: 36. 10 tables outside. Private parties: 36 main room, 18 and 24 private rooms. Car park, 30 places. Vegetarian meals. No children under 7. Smart dress preferred. No smoking in dining-room. Wheelchair access (also WC). No music. Fax: (0825) 75459 ACCOMMODATION: 17 rooms, all with bath/shower. Rooms for disabled. Lift. B&B £120 to £310. No children under 7. Afternoon teas. Garden. Swimming-pool. Tennis. Golf. TV. Phone. Scenic. Doors close at 11. Confirm by 9

ULLSWATER Cumbria map 7

▲ *Sharrow Bay*

Howtown Road, Ullswater CA10 2LZ
POOLEY BRIDGE (076 84) 86301 and 86483
2m from Pooley Bridge on E side of lake, COOKING 4
signposted Howtown and Martindale COST £29–£53

'My nightmare is that I shall cross Pooley Bridge, drive down the lane and find that Sharrow has disappeared.' 'I would nominate Mr Sack and Mr Coulson for sainthood if I thought it would do any good.' Any comment about this late-Victorian country house strung along the side of Ullswater (with a further house down the lane for extra bedrooms in equal style) has to begin with overstatement. The place engenders strong feeling. For some, it is too good to be true, as if its only response to self-improvement could be more of the same; hence the lavishness and unchanging character. Another reader's reaction is 'the restaurant has the great virtue of being well-established so it runs like clockwork'. Such automation did not stop the same reader having her finest meal ever at Sharrow. Both lunch and dinner are set-price, stretching over five or six courses, with ample choice for the first course, main dish and dessert. The old-fashioned typed menus hide a lot of information, though the repertoire can be learned by heart by seasoned visitors (particularly for the first course). Cooking is classical in style, or conservative British. A pair of common factors link it with the manner developed at that more recent Lakeland institution, Miller Howe. One is scale. 'A long day's walking is essential to cope with their portions,' a reader wrote. A second is a degree of regimentation, albeit velvet-gloved; for many, dinner begins at the same time and courses come out in waves. The lounge, hardly large enough to take a full house at once, can have the atmosphere of an NHS waiting room. Although there is a tendency to plates loaded with myriad piles – even the fish course will often have two elements, fish and soufflé – there is a fine simplicity, in the meat cooking for instance, that appeals to the British palate and is generally well executed. Some regret that this spareness does not extend to the vegetables: too many, reports say, but then that is the British taste too. Desserts are another thing altogether. Proudly displayed where you enter the dining-room, the pastries, mousses, syllabubs and bavarois are invariably approved for technique and flavour. The food is good; it is in the best sense old-fashioned. It may suffer from numbers – for example, the fish course or even sorbet produced for everyone – but this almost pales beside the overall Sharrow 'experience'. The staff are well trained and know their tasks. The hosts are masters of their craft. The sense of well-being is palpable. If some find it self-congratulatory, it is surely not consciously so. Good range is offered by the wine list. There are decent petits châteaux, Italians and Australasians at affordable prices. In Burgundy especially, selection is conservative. House wine is £10.95.

CHEFS: Johnnie Martin, Colin Akrigg, Colin White, Philip Wilson and Robert Bond
PROPRIETORS: Francis Coulson and Brian Sack OPEN: all week CLOSED: Dec, Jan, Feb
MEALS: 1 to 1.45, 8 to 8.45 PRICES: Set L £23.50 (£29) to £28.50 (£34), Set D £38.50 (£44). Net prices SEATS: 65. Private parties: 10 main room. Car park, 30 places. Vegetarian meals. No children under 13. Jacket and tie. No smoking in dining-room.. Wheelchair access. No music. Fax: (076 84) 86349 ACCOMMODATION: 30 rooms, 25 with bath/shower. D,B&B £82 to £270. No children under 13. Afternoon teas. Garden. TV. Phone. Scenic. Doors close at midnight. Confirm by 11am (*Which? Hotel Guide*)

ULVERSTON Cumbria map 7

Bay Horse Inn and Bistro

Canal Foot, Ulverston LA12 9EL COOKING 3
ULVERSTON (0229) 53972 COST £18–£31

The Bay Horse canters on at a cracking pace; refurbishment in the winter of 1990–1, bedrooms planned for the spring of 1992. It still offers excellent value, in the bar or lounge and in the bistro, for cooking that mirrors the practice of chairman of the board John Tovey, though executed by resident director Robert Lyons. Its location, with fine views across Morecambe Bay, is marked by the Glaxo factory: 'bizarre' was the reaction of one visitor. The rapidly changing menu may be served in two evening sessions, one at 7.30 for 8, the next at 8.30 for 9, but production is not over-rapid and service is 'attentive without being invasive'. Ingredients sometimes surprise in their plethora, as in prawn and water-chestnut quiche on a kiwi and cucumber salad with a lemon and coriander dressing, or celery, apple and Stilton soup with walnuts and chives, but the Tovey school seems to bring these dishes off where less hardy spirits might cut something out of the recipe. The daring resurfaces with monkfish wrapped in Cumbrian air-dried ham after being marinated in yoghurt. It was cooked with apple and mushroom, then served with calvados cream sauce. The ham, a great idea, nearly dominated to the detriment of the whole. Recommendations come, however, for a whole range of things, from duck with a sauce of local fruits, veal marsala, or monkfish provençale, to pork with garlic, chestnuts and onions in a port wine sauce. Vegetables are exemplary; puddings work the English vein with profit; coffee comes free of charge after a full meal. The bar food is a bargain, provoking the comment: 'We have paid well into double figures for a dish of this quality.' The wine list is sound but the most fun is to be had from the New World list that comes as a supplement. This features more than 50 wines, all sensibly priced, including Schinus Molle, Wyndham Estate, Tisdall and Wirra Wirra Church Block from Australia, Cloudy Bay from New Zealand and Ch. St Michelle from Washington State. House wines are from £8.50.

CHEF: Robert Lyons PROPRIETORS: Robert Lyons and John J. Tovey OPEN: Mon to Sat, exc Mon L CLOSED: Jan and Feb MEALS: 12 to 1.30, 7 to 9 PRICES: £19 (£26), Set L £11.95 (£18). Minimum £7.50. Service 10% CARDS: Access, Visa SEATS: 30. 3 tables outside. Private parties: 28 main room. No children under 12. Smart dress preferred. No smoking. Wheelchair access (1 step; also unisex WC). Music. Air-conditioned

UNDERBARROW Cumbria map 7

Tullythwaite House

Underbarrow LA8 8BB COOKING 2
CROSTHWAITE (044 88) 397 COST £19–£35

Michael and Janet Greenwood's Lakeland home is off the beaten track, yet only three miles from Kendal. An enthusiasm for 'cottage economy' means that they are now growing more herbs and salad vegetables, and making herb jellies as well as producing their own breads, biscuits and petits fours. Dinner is a fixed-price, five-course menu, with centrepieces such as roast loin of wild venison with skirlie and rowan jelly, poached salmon with herb sauce and roast Gressingham duck with orange sauce. Framing this might be goujons of plaice with lemon and almonds and smoked haddock soup, then a pair of sweets along the lines of bramble mousse and brown-sugar meringue. Traditional cheeses come with home-made oatcakes. Service is very personal and unobtrusive. The house now has a refurbished sitting area and a gallery hung with pictures by local artists. The 100-strong wine list has a good showing of half-bottles. House wines are from £5.95.

CHEF: Janet Greenwood PROPRIETORS: Michael and Janet Greenwood OPEN: Wed to Sat, D only, and Sun L CLOSED: Feb MEALS: 12.30 for 1, 7 for 7.30 or 7.80 for 8 (by arrangement) PRICES: Set Sun L £13.95 (£19), Set D £22.95 (£29). Card slips closed CARDS: Access, Visa SEATS: 16. Private parties: 16 main room. Car park, 14 places. No children under 12. Smart dress preferred. No smoking. No music. One sitting

WADHURST East Sussex map 3

▲ *Spindlewood Hotel*

Wallcrouch, Wadhurst TN5 7JG
TICEHURST (0580) 200430
on B2099, between Wadhurst and Ticehurst COOKING 1
COST £20–£38

This late-Victorian house sits well back from the main road, above terraces of car park and carriage-sweep that plunge to bushy, blossomed gardens and duck-pond in the dell below – a peaceful English prospect. The house, perhaps once a large rectory, has a cream-painted, panelled dining-room and music that pursues you everywhere from one end of the meal to another. The hotel caters lovingly to the locality, the Fitzsimmons family being welcoming, long-memoried hosts. The menu changes steadily, but a veritable cornucopia may be tipped out when the day's fish is recited: some eight species on a good day, cooked as you will; perhaps the boat moors on the duck-pond. Favourable mention is made of boned quail wrapped in filo, with ginger and currants, plain grilled plaice of exemplary quality, a first-course hot mushroom cake, decent vegetables, and puddings that may include hot ginger sponge with orange sauce and vanilla ice. Do not, however, expect culinary fireworks. The wine list is short but deals in good makers, for instance Natter in Sancerre and Juillot in Mercurey. Prices are very fair. House wines are from £6.85.

CHEF: Harvey Lee Aram PROPRIETOR: R.V. Fitzsimmons OPEN: all week, exc L Mon bank hols CLOSED: 4 days Christmas MEALS: 12.15 to 1.30, 7.15 to 9 PRICES: Set L £14.95 (£20), Set D £19 (£25) to £26 (£32). Card slips closed CARDS: Access, Amex, Visa SEATS: 40. Private parties: 50 main room, 22 private room. Car park, 60 places. Vegetarian meals. Children's helpings. No cigars/pipes in dining-room. Music. Fax: (0580) 201132 ACCOMMODATION: 9 rooms, all with bath/shower. B&B £48 to £78. Children welcome. Baby facilities. Garden. TV. Phone. Scenic. Doors close at midnight. Confirm by 6

WALBERSWICK Suffolk map 6

Mary's

Manor House, Walberswick IP18 6UG COOKING 1
SOUTHWOLD (0502) 723243 COST £14–£22

Felicity and Rob Jelliff's cheerful seaside restaurant is a godsend for residents and holidaymakers alike. The dining-rooms are bedecked with nets, eel spears, model ships and maritime pictures, while fresh fish is the highlight of the simple menus. Rob obtains slip soles from the local boats and travels to Lowestoft twice a week for the rest of the catch. Felicity now has full control in the kitchen: 'We do not use bought-in puddings, but we do buy chips and potato croquettes without shame relative to our meal prices.' Otherwise it is good wholesome stuff, with lunches as the main attraction: reporters have feasted on hearty soups, spicy sausage casserole, steak and kidney pie, fresh vegetables and over-the-top creamy sweets. Cheeses come with home-baked Suffolk rusks. Morning coffee, afternoon tea and savoury high teas are greatly appreciated, and there are more ambitious evening meals on Friday and Saturday. Drinks include Hugh Rock's elderflower wine, James White's cider and apple juice, as well as milkshakes. The modest wine list from Adnams is, predictably, dotted with affordable gems. House wine is £5.90.

CHEF: Felicity Jelliff PROPRIETORS: Felicity and Rob Jelliff OPEN: Tue to Sun L, Fri and Sat D CLOSED: Mon to Thur Nov to Easter MEALS: 12 to 2, 7.15 to 9 PRICES: £9 (£14), Set D £13.50 (£18) SEATS: 45. 10 tables outside. Private parties: 25 main room, 20 and 25 private rooms. Car park, 20 places. Vegetarian meals. Children's helpings. No smoking. Wheelchair access (also WC). Music

WAREHAM Dorset map 2

▲ *Priory Hotel* NEW ENTRY

Church Green, Wareham BH20 4ND COOKING 1
WAREHAM (0929) 551666 COST £22–£52

An exceptional garden sweeps down to the river; then there is the prospect of watermeadows and, in the distance, the downs to each side of Corfe castle. The view from the mullioned windows of this former Benedictine priory is best appreciated in daylight, although the atmosphere of the dining-room itself is sufficient to deter those in the know from eating in the basement overflow, 'which is less nice'. When the latter is pressed into service reports have been critical of a hotel restaurant coping poorly under pressure, but readers are largely satisfied with the standard of cooking and service at other times. A lengthy *carte*, which incidentally proves that the art of flambéing at table is not yet dead, is supplemented by a short, daily-changing set-price lunch and dinner menu. Ravioli of chicken and mushrooms, lamb with sweetbreads and a broccoli and rosemary timbale, and escalope of veal with Gruyère cheese and madeira sauce have been enjoyed. Desserts from the trolley rely heavily on cream. Some inconsistency in pricing and selection of wines is continued. There are many fine bottles and much decent drinking can be had for under £12 (Italians are good value), but mark-ups are high. House wine is £8.50.

CHEF: Michael Rust PROPRIETORS: Stuart and John Turner OPEN: all week MEALS: 12.30 to 2, 7.30 to 10 PRICES: £31 (£43), Set L £11.95 (£22), Set D £22.50 (£29), Set Sat D £26.50 (£34). Card slips closed CARDS: Access, Amex, Diners, Visa SEATS: 68. 10 tables outside. Private parties: 44 main room, 22 and 44 private rooms. Car park, 20 places. Vegetarian meals. Children welcome. Smart dress preferred. Wheelchair access (also WC). Music. Fax: (0929) 554519 ACCOMMODATION: 19 rooms, all with bath/shower. Rooms for disabled. B&B £70 to £175. Afternoon teas. Garden. Fishing. TV. Phone. Scenic (*Which? Hotel Guide*)

WARWICK Warwickshire map 2

Fanshawe's

22 Market Place, Warwick CV34 4SL COOKING 1
WARWICK (0926) 410590 COST £28

A small, owner-occupied restaurant, well-surrounded by chintz and flowers, that attempts to offer a full service from open sandwiches to enthusiastically described main dishes – duck breasts 'burst', salmon 'swims', chicken breast 'crows with a fresh dill sauce' – for visitors to Warwick's market square. David Fanshawe's cooking is well above the average of most at such places and should be encouraged. Satisfaction with skewers of scallops, mushroom and bacon, grilled cod with a chervil butter, saddle of lamb with tomato and basil sauce, as well as desserts from home-made ice-creams to chocolate Malakoff has been reported. The short, fair-priced wine list has some refreshing choices: a Quincy rather than a Sancerre, a Bourgeuil rosé, a Couly-Dutheil Chinon, as well as a couple of English wines and an Israeli Cabernet Sauvignon from Edmond Rothschild. House wines are from £6.95.

CHEF: David Fanshawe PROPRIETORS: David and Susan Fanshawe OPEN: Tue to Sat CLOSED: 2 weeks Oct MEALS: 11.30 to 2, 6 to 10 PRICES: £16 (£23), Snacks from £2. Card slips closed CARDS: Access, Amex, Visa SEATS: 35. Private parties: 38 main room. Vegetarian meals. Children's helpings until 7.30pm. Wheelchair access (1 step). Music

The text of entries is based on unsolicited reports sent in by readers, backed up by inspections conducted anonymously. The factual details under the text are from questionnaires the Guide *sends to all restaurants that feature in the book.*

WATERHOUSES Staffordshire map 5

▲ *Old Beams*

Waterhouses ST10 3HW COOKING 3
WATERHOUSES (0538) 308254 COST £24–£46

Though Alton Towers is but 10 minutes away, the temptation to accelerate to 60 miles per hour in 2.8 seconds on the loop-the-loop should be resisted until lunch has been well digested. Old Beams, past its tenth anniversary in the hands of the Wallises, is an old inn, the village a watering spot on the coach road. The original building, old-beamed indeed, has been extended often, notably with a large conservatory, protected from the heat of the sun by blinds. This room is comfortable, a piano is sometimes played, and the food is much enjoyed. Reports this year have mentioned error: for instance, in vegetables hard rather than toothsome; pastry undercooked; sauces under-seasoned or anaemic. However, the whole often seems greater than the parts and the general impression is favourable with dishes that may include home-made pasta (rather dry and floury for one party) such as ravioli or tagliatelle or even one that is chocolate-flavoured for dessert. Combination dishes – a trio of game, rendezvous of fish, a mix of chicken and lobster with chicory sauce – are offered, and recipes come from a modern repertoire: mango and scallop with spiced dressing, and rhubarb and ginger mousse with a coconut sorbet. Long braises feature on most menus. Lunch is much cheaper than dinner. If one person thinks the cutlery tatty, another praises it for being antique; most are united in thinking Ann Wallis an energetic hostess, though service can be less than smooth. This place is an important local resource; the bedrooms over the road are also enjoyed – for the river as well as the thoughtful details. The best bit of breakfast, and a good bit of dinner, is the home-baked bread. Heavy with superlatives, the notes on the 100-plus wine list win on enthusiasm but little else. Pedigree names – Stags' Leap, Rousseau in Burgundy and many fine clarets – and good vintages speak for themselves. Prices accurately and fairly reflect quality with as many sound bottles below £12 as there are above £25. Half-bottles display a good range of price and style. Old Beams is upgraded to a bottle award this year. House wines are from £12.65. CELLARMAN'S CHOICE: Riesling 1987, Deiss, £14.20; Ch. Musar 1982, £13.25.

CHEF: Nigel J. Wallis PROPRIETORS: Nigel J. and Ann Wallis OPEN: Tue to Sun, exc Sat L and Sun D MEALS: 12 to 2, 7 to 10 PRICES: Set L £15.50 (£24), Set D £28 (£38). Card slips closed CARDS: Access, Amex, Diners, Visa SEATS: 50. Car park, 22 places. No children under 4. Wheelchair access (also WC). Music ACCOMMODATION: 6 rooms, all with bath/shower. Rooms for disabled. B&B £52 to £87. No children under 13. Garden. Fishing. TV. Phone. Scenic. Doors close at midnight. Confirm 48 hours ahead (*Which? Hotel Guide*)

The Guide *relies on feedback from its readers. Especially welcome are reports on new restaurants appearing in the book for the first time.*

All letters to the Guide *are acknowledged with an update on latest sales, closures, chef changes and so on.*

WATERMILLOCK Cumbria map 7

▲ *Rampsbeck Country House Hotel*

NEW ENTRY

Watermillock CA11 0LP
POOLEY BRIDGE (076 84) 86442 and 86688 COOKING 2*
on A592 Penrith to Windermere COST £22–£43

The white-painted villa takes advantage of views over Ullswater through large dining-room windows fully dressed by Laura Ashley plc. Andrew McGeorge cooks an old-fashioned modern menu of several choices for the food, but none for the price. It is old-fashioned in its wordy description and its propensity to multiply elements, to add stuffings, layers or mousses. The point worth making, however, is that at lunch, when dishes are cheaper, choice is smaller, and multiplication reduced, with the exception of the 11 different vegetables. A gutsy terrine of venison, hare and rabbit with pukka Cumberland sauce, a single yet generous smoked salmon salad, chicken chasseur ('rescuing that dish from all its trattoria-imposed indignities'), exactly cooked thick slices of calf's liver with piquant red wine sauce, and salmon on a bed of carrot and leek with a champagne cream sauce were all in estimable and direct style. A sticky toffee pudding and over-decorated chocolate mousse have showed sweet tastes dealt with well. The wine list is predictable and adequate but not cheap. House wines are £8.

CHEF: Andrew McGeorge PROPRIETORS: T.I. and M.M. Gibb, and M.J. MacDowall OPEN: all week CLOSED: early Jan to mid-Feb MEALS: 12 to 1.30, 7 to 8.45 PRICES: Set L £15.95 (£22), Set D £23 (£30) to £28.95 (£36). Card slips closed CARDS: Access, Visa SEATS: 40. Private parties: 60 main room, 20 private room. Car park, 35 places. Vegetarian meals. Children's helpings (L and early evening only). No children under 7 D. Smart dress preferred. No cigars in dining-room. Wheelchair access (2 steps)
ACCOMMODATION: 19 rooms, all with bath/shower. B&B £48 to £90. Deposit: £15. Children under 7 in parents' room only. Pets welcome. Afternoon teas. Garden. Fishing. TV. Phone. Scenic. Doors close at 11. Confirm by 6

WATH-IN-NIDDERDALE North Yorkshire map 7

▲ *Sportsman's Arms*

Wath-in-Nidderdale HG3 5PP COOKING 2*
HARROGATE (0423) 711306 COST £19–£37

The old stone inn, a couple of miles from Pateley Bridge, has made the change from pub to restaurant-with-rooms – although the bar remains for beer and lunchtime snacks. As if to emphasise the transformation, the dining-room is done out in shades of pink, with bentwood chairs and white crockery. It is pleasing 'but has no pretensions to graciousness', and visitors are often put off or distracted from their food by the near-freezing temperatures in the rooms. A dedicated kitchen team offers a short *carte* as well as a set-price menu including a half-bottle of wine and coffee. Ingredients are local where possible and the intentions are serious. Trio of game with wild mushrooms on a garlic, gin and juniper sauce, breast of duckling with bilberry and orange sauce, and poached salmon filled with scallops and glazed with sauce mousseline all arranged spaciously on large plates, show the style. The kitchen uses a lot of cream and butter. Readers have enjoyed warm salad of scallops and grapefruit with hazelnut dressing, pork in ginger and light curry sauce, and lobster in garlic butter. Everyone praises the vegetables, which are perfectly cooked and served generously in side dishes. Sweets have included excellent lemon strudel and chocolate roulade; there are also prime local and French cheeses in abundance. Occasional quibbles mar the overall picture. The well-spread wine list offers solace. House White is £7.50.

CHEF/PROPRIETOR: J.R. Carter OPEN: all week, exc Sun D MEALS: 12 to 1.45, 7 to 10 PRICES: £23 (£31), Set L £12 (£19) to £18 (£25), Set D £17.50 (£19) to £20 (£22). Card slips closed CARDS: Access, Amex, Diners, Visa SEATS: 45. 6 tables outside. Private parties: 60 main room. Car park, 50 places. Vegetarian meals. Children's helpings. Wheelchair access (also WC) ACCOMMODATION: 7 rooms, 2 with bath/shower. B&B £27 to £48. Children welcome. Baby facilities. Pets welcome. Garden. Fishing. TV. Scenic. (*Which? Hotel Guide*)

WATLINGTON Oxfordshire map 2

▲ *Well House*

34–40 High Street, Watlington OX9 5PY COOKING 1
WATLINGTON (049 161) 3333 COST £24–£35

The well is in the small bar of this intelligent conversion of a medieval brick and flint house, with bedrooms added in a new extension. The Crawfords have not been gripped by the Home Counties fury for high prices, making worrisome their comment that current anti-alcohol propaganda will have its effect on the prices they must charge for the food itself. Until prices do rise, value is very fair for careful yet imaginative cooking of dishes such as stir-fried smoked chicken with sesame, fish profiteroles with a coriander and yoghurt sauce, calf's liver with whisky and tarragon, sole with mushrooms and shallots, and good substantial desserts like a coffee gâteau or banoffi pie. Occasionally, elaboration gets the better of discretion as when, for instance, a piece of salmon is superfluously wrapped with a skate wing. Alan Crawford's attentions are genuine and concerned. As much attention is given to the modest as to the exalted in the fair-priced wine list, especially where clarets are concerned. Selection remains less assured elsewhere. There is a sensible range of half-bottles. House wine is £7.50.

CHEFS: Patricia Crawford and Brenda Jones PROPRIETORS: Patricia and Alan Crawford OPEN: Tue to Sun, exc Sat L and Sun D MEALS: 12.30 to 2, 7 to 9.15 (9.30 Sat) PRICES: £19 (£29), Set L and D £16.50 (£24). Card slips closed CARDS: Access, Amex, Diners, Visa SEATS: 40. 4 tables outside. Private parties: 45 main room. Car park, 15 places. Vegetarian meals. Children's helpings. Smart dress preferred. Wheelchair access (3 steps). No music ACCOMMODATION: 10 rooms, all with bath/shower. Rooms for disabled. B&B £37.50 to £62. Children welcome. Baby facilities. TV. Phone. Scenic. Doors close at 11.30. Confirm by 6 (*Which? Hotel Guide*)

WELLS Somerset map 2

Ritcher's

NEW ENTRY

5 Sadler Street, Wells BA5 2RR COOKING 2
WELLS (0749) 679085 COST £19–£28

Kate Ritcher and Nicholas Hart moved from their original premises in Coxley to this converted wine bar in the centre of Wells. On the ground floor is a bar with a spiral staircase leading to the pretty pink dining-room; there is also a cobbled courtyard for outdoor eating. The short menu deals in modern bistro food, with the emphasis on freshness, cheapness and accessibility. There are also cheap dishes and snacks aimed at lunchtime shoppers and business people. Spinach and Brie turnovers with béarnaise sauce, pan-fried chicken topped with smoked salmon and champagne cream, and strawberry torte with blackcurrant purée show the style. An meal of smoked chicken and salmon mousse with sauce grelais, followed by rack of lamb roasted with spinach and suet crust on a bed of root vegetables highlighted the quality of the raw materials, appetising flavours and attractive presentation. Some details such as the bread, butter and petits fours could be improved. The reasonably priced wine list has a strong contingent from Spain. House French is £7.45.

CHEF: Nicholas Hart PROPRIETORS: Nicholas Hart and Kate Ritcher OPEN: Mon to Sat CLOSED: bank hols MEALS: 12 to 2, 7 to 9.30 PRICES: £16 (£23), Set L and D £13.50 (£19), Snacks from £1.75. Card slips closed CARDS: Access, Visa SEATS: 24. 3 tables outside. Private parties: 24 main room. Vegetarian meals. Children's helpings L. No children under 10 D. Wheelchair access. Music

WELLS-NEXT-THE-SEA Norfolk map 6

Moorings

6 Freeman Street,
Wells-next-the-Sea NR23 1BA COOKING 3
FAKENHAM (0328) 710949 COST £18–£25

'I thought the voice sounded vaguely familiar' began one account of a returnee to the Norfolk coast who was overcome to find his former English teacher, Bernard Phillips, the proprietor of this 'friendly', 'packed', 'bustling', 'cheerful' restaurant where his wife Carla produces food that achieves freshness, fashionability and a certain taste of the genuine. Mr Phillips hunted through drawers, to revert to the first story, and came up with a class register – talk of food and times past. For this diner, the oriental fish soup ('clear, spicy and complex') will probably never taste the same again. That is a dish that draws inveterate praise, as does the orange-touched crab soup; the pan-fried fresh dabs; the samphire got in expressly to please a curious visitor; polenta with tomato and red pepper sauce; cockle pie; fresh sea bass; sole with port wine sauce; and pigeon with port and cream. This is cooking with guts and a willingness to live and cook together with one's locality. 'It's just like a good French local, except the vegetables are better' was the summary of someone who likes four veg with the main dish – certainly not a Frenchman. Moorings is rightly crowded on high days; the prices are very fair indeed. The press can be too close for some, but the new ban on smoking will improve the atmosphere. The wine list is not very long, but has an interesting set of choices, mostly French (though some Greek for enthusiasts), some hunted out by the Phillipses themselves. House wines are £6.25.

CHEFS: Carla Phillips and Jane Lee PROPRIETORS: Bernard and Carla Phillips OPEN: all week, exc Tue and Wed and Thur L CLOSED: 4 June to 22 June, 29 Nov to 14 Dec, 24 to 27 Dec MEALS: 12.30 to 2, 7.30 to 9 PRICES: Set L £12.10 (£18), Set D £15.10 (£21). Service 10% for parties of 8 or more SEATS: 40. Private parties: 40 main room. Vegetarian meals. Children's helpings. No smoking. Wheelchair access. No music

WEOBLEY Hereford & Worcester map 2

▲ *Jules Café*

Portland Street, Weobley HR4 8SB COOKING 2
WEOBLEY (0544) 318206 COST £17–£26

Outside is a fine timbered building that anyone would think of as pure Herefordshire; inside is a restaurant that keeps prices realistic by cutting down on the finery (and, latterly, luxury ingredients such as goose and salmon) but maintains honesty and imagination – spring flowers on the tables in January, for example. Cooking draws from a wide vegetarian and meat-eating repertoire. A lunch this year was of green-lipped mussels with a gratin topping of garlic, parsley and breadcrumbs, followed by a generous 'cassoulet' of barbary duck and pork with leeks, and a split pea and lentil bake with apple sauce that would have benefited from higher spicing. Hazelnut meringue, pistachio ice-cream and cold lemon soufflé were good too. Value is very fair. The wines do not seem to excite the Whitmarshes (i.e. a list may sometimes not even be offered) but, in keeping with their preferences in buying food, organics are given priority. Service warms to enthusiastic response but may remain silent-faced with formality. House wines are £7.50.

CHEFS/PROPRIETORS: Julian and Juliet Whitmarsh OPEN: all week CLOSED: 25 Dec, some winter Mons MEALS: 12 to 2, 7.15 to 9.30 PRICES: £11 (£17), £14 (£21), Set D £16 (£22) CARDS: Access, Visa SEATS: 36. Private parties: 30 main room. Vegetarian meals. Children's helpings. Wheelchair access. No music ACCOMMODATION: 3 rooms, 2 with bath/shower. B&B £18 to £30. Afternoon teas. Scenic. Doors close at 1am. Confirm by 6

WEST BAY Dorset map 2

Riverside Café and Restaurant

West Bay, Bridport DT6 4EZ COOKING 2*
BRIDPORT (0308) 22011 COST £26

It is not easy to find critics of this estimable venture in mass, yet individual, catering. The Watsons are jewels, described by one reader as continuing their 'good-natured struggle against the flood-tides of (now) up-market customers. The food is spectacularly good; yesterday, *palourdes* from Poole.' 'An unexpected pleasure,' wrote another; 'The relaxed chaos added to the atmosphere.' This chaos comes only from the sheer numbers who want to try the freshest of fish (from lobster to pilchard) cooked in the most natural styles, with first-rate chips and not-so-exciting salads. Ice-creams (Knickerbocker Glory, for example) will please young and old. The Riverside is a café, catering for all, yet rises to being a restaurant through love of good cooking and enthusiasm. For non-fish-eaters the café will provide burgers, sandwiches, snacks and simple grills. Good espresso and a short but sharp wine list. A remarkable place, but it is best to telephone before setting out. House wine is £8.95 a litre.

CHEFS: Janet Watson, Pam Townsend and Natalie Ansell Green PROPRIETORS: Janet and Arthur Watson OPEN: Tue to Sun, plus Mon in July, Aug, bank hols CLOSED: Dec to end Feb MEALS: 10.30 to 3.30, 6.30 to 8.30 (10.30 to 6 Sun) PRICES: £17 (£22). Service 10% for pre-booked table service. Card slips closed CARDS: Access, Amex, Visa SEATS: 80. 10 tables outside. Private parties: 70 main room. Vegetarian meals. Children's helpings. Wheelchair access (also WC). Music

WEST BEXINGTON Dorset map 2

▲ *Manor Hotel*

Beach Road, West Bexington DT2 9DF COOKING 1
BURTON BRADSTOCK (0308) 897616 COST £17–£28

The long sweep of Chesil Beach makes a fine prospect from this old house at the top of the village with a view down to the sea. All things to all men, the Manor does good bar food – excellent bread and cheese, an array of sweet things, even decent coffee – as well as full meals in the conservatory and dining-rooms. Cooking is substantial, with some good fish to be had, and service is generous – no report has ever mentioned stinting. The dinner menu is a set price, with at least a dozen choices, and has a pause for cheese. The style is robust bistro: an apple is peeled and cored, filled with crabmeat and given an avocado cream; rabbit is fried, sauced with mustard, onions, mushrooms and cream; and not only is there trifle, but summer pudding too – both will be served to you, if desired. The place gets busy on high days, but enthusiasm persists among owners and staff. The wine list has a fair range of bottles, with plenty of halves, and New World value is not forgotten. House wine comes from Eldridge Pope, as does most of the list, and costs £6.45.

CHEF: Clive Jobson PROPRIETORS: Richard and Jayne Childs OPEN: all week MEALS: 12 to 2, 7 to 10 (10.30 Sat) PRICES: Set L £12 (£17) to £14.50 (£19), Set D £17.95 (£23) CARDS: Access, Amex, Diners, Visa SEATS: 65. 18 tables outside. Private parties: 65 main room, 20 and 50 private rooms. Car park, 50 places. Vegetarian meals. Children's helpings. Music. Fax: (0308) 897035 ACCOMMODATION: 13 rooms, all with bath/shower. B&B £36 to £60. Deposit: £10. Children welcome. Baby facilities. Afternoon teas. Garden. TV. Phone. Scenic. Doors close at midnight. Confirm by 6 (*Which? Hotel Guide*)

County round-ups listing additional restaurants that may be worth a visit are at the back of the Guide, *after the Irish section. Reports on round-up entries are welcome.*

WEST MERSEA Essex map 3

▲ *Le Champenois, Blackwater Hotel*

20–22 Church Road,
West Mersea CO5 8QH COOKING 2
COLCHESTER (0206) 383338 and 383038 COST £23–£34

Mme Chapleo imposes her brand of Anglo-French hospitality on this ivy-clad row of houses quite close to the church. It proves popular. The *carte* is fundamental stuff: moules marinière, chicken liver pâté, mushrooms in garlic cream sauce, duck with orange and the like. But it is filled out by daily specials of fish, asparagus, venison and other more seasonal foods. The sweets trolley has been banished this year, which has given chef Roudesli greater liberty, well appreciated by regular customers. The wine list is an album of labels, with prices next to them. Largely French, of course, it includes examples from Ch. Rahoul, Georges Duboeuf and Louis Trapet in a canter round the regions. House wine from Duboeuf is £7.20.

CHEF: R. Roudesli PROPRIETOR: Monique Chapleo OPEN: all week, exc Tue L and Sun D CLOSED: 3 weeks Jan MEALS: 12 to 2, 7 to 10 PRICES: £20 (£28), Set L £17 (£23). Card slips closed CARDS: Access, Amex, Visa SEATS: 46. 3 tables outside. Private parties: 55 main room, 25 private room. Car park, 20 places. Vegetarian meals. Children's helpings. No cigars/pipes in dining-room. Smart dress preferred. Wheelchair access (also WC). No music ACCOMMODATION: 7 rooms, 4 with bath/shower. B&B £28 to £62. Deposit: £10. Children welcome. Baby facilities. Pets welcome. Afternoon teas. Garden. TV. Scenic. Doors close at 1am. Confirm by 9 (*Which? Hotel Guide*)

WETHERAL Cumbria map 7

Fantails

The Green, Wetheral CA4 8ET COOKING 2
CARLISLE (0228) 60239 COST £20–£31

Only one-and-a-half miles from a motorway junction (No. 42 on the M6), Fantails might qualify as a service station. For sure, you would eat better and cheaper here than in any of those dread granaries, butteries, harvests, or whatever. Light lunches, including Burmese spiced vegetables or filo parcels of cheese, might be designed for just such a stopover. The barn conversion at one end of the village green (the dovecote is there too) affords good views from its large bay windows. The Bowmans have maintained the impetus of their first two years in occupation. The *carte* offers permanent vegetarian options and a range of dishes that shows decent technique and a love, this year, of fungi: truffles with chicken on a bed of spinach, morels with lamb and a tarragon sauce, wild mushrooms with fillet of beef and on their own as a first-course feuilleté. Fruity desserts are bolstered by a 'chocolate fetishist's fantasy'. A pleasant restaurant, in a fine location, that serves its neighbourhood well. The fair-priced wine list is good, but perhaps leans a little heavily on négociants in Burgundy. The showing from Australasia is strong, and there are a fine dozen or so clarets. House wine is £7.25.

CHEF: Cameron Clarke PROPRIETORS: Jennifer and Bob Bowman OPEN: Mon to Sat MEALS: 12 to 2, 6.30 to 10 PRICES: £19 (£26), Set L and D £14.50 (£20), light L menu from £2.95. Card slips closed CARDS: Access, Visa SEATS: 75. Private parties: 50 main room, 12 and 25 private rooms. Car park, 25 places. Vegetarian meals. Children's helpings. Smart dress preferred. No-smoking area. Music

WETHERSFIELD Essex map 3

Dicken's 🍷

The Green, Wethersfield CM7 4BS COOKING 3
GREAT DUNMOW (0371) 850723 COST £21–£40

'I have often been subjected to meals in Essex for business reasons and until now I have never been able to finish a single course. In general, the good is atrocious, little better than school grub. Dicken's is light years ahead of the bunch,' wrote one reader. John Dicken remains on course for establishing a sound business based on good cooking of fresh ingredients. There is no special novelty about his recipes, except, being part of the current mainstream, that they are unusual in Essex. Spices feature often in dishes such as a salad of duck marinated in garam masala, or a tagliatelle and mussel fricassee with fennel and cumin. The use of strong flavours with fish is enjoyed, as in salmon with aubergine, tomato and basil vinaigrette sauce, or cod with brown butter, onion and artichoke. Meals have sometimes revealed unsatisfactory vegetables in too much butter and main courses lacking depth of flavour in either the meat or stock used for the sauce. Such failings seem infrequent, and when it comes to dessert, they seem absent altogether. There are a few other complaints: service could sometimes be faster and the minstrels' gallery in the old dining-room is 'a narrow shelf along which waitresses shuffle sideways,' according to one reporter who was marooned aloft with particularly unsalubrious neighbours. ('Below, it looked rather mellow' was his wistful close.) But there is good cooking here with every chance it will get better. The wine list, supplied by Lay and Wheeler and Reid Wines, is a model; it is succinct, offering a well-balanced range in quality and provenance, priced fairly throughout and with sufficient half-bottles. It merits a glass award this year. House wine is £7.50. CELLARMAN'S CHOICE: Tokay d'Alsace 1989, Schlumberger, £16.50; Keynton Estate, Shiraz/Cabernet 1987, Henschke, £15.25.

CHEF: John Dicken PROPRIETORS: John and Maria Dicken OPEN: Wed to Sun, exc Sat L and Sun D CLOSED: 2 weeks Feb MEALS: 12.30 to 2, 7.30 to 9.30 PRICES: £24 (£33), Set L £15.50 (£21) CARDS: Access, Visa SEATS: 45. Private parties: 35 main room, 20 private room. Car park, 11 places. Vegetarian meals. Children's helpings. Smart dress preferred. Wheelchair access (2 steps; also WC). No music

🍾 *denotes an outstanding wine cellar;* 🍷 *denotes a good wine list, worth travelling for.*

'Several of my Scottish meals this time prompt the thought that some restaurants hellbent on self-improvement have sent away for the John Cleese training films and been sent Fawlty Towers *by mistake. This was one such.'* On eating in Scotland

WHIMPLE Devon map 1

▲ *Woodhayes* **NEW ENTRY**

Whimple EX5 2TD COOKING 2
WHIMPLE (0404) 822237 COST £32

The Rendle family run this small Georgian country hotel very personally, yet avoid making guests feel that they are participating in a house-party. The operation is pitched mainly at residents: six tables in the dining-room match the number of bedrooms; non-residents may have to charm and cajole their way in for dinner. The house is dominated by floral prints and fabrics, dried-flower arrangements and heavily ruched curtains. Dinner runs to six courses, with no choice until the sweets. An appetiser, such as pear with Stilton and tarragon cream or smoked salmon mousse, precedes the soup (perhaps 'pale grassy green' lettuce and mint). Next there is fish: fillet of lemon sole with salmon mousseline and parsley sauce, or grilled brill with garden herbs. A sorbet is offered before the main course, which might be fillet of beef with red wine and shallots. For dessert, strawberry tartlette has been 'very nice and really rather restrained' for one reader. Cheese is normally a fine local farmhouse Cheddar. The kitchen scores heavily with its raw materials, spot-on timing and colourful presentation, but gets fewer marks for seasoning and flavour manipulation. The home-made bread is wonderful. A well-spread, good-value wine list has a decent showing of half-bottles. Ten house wines are all priced at £9.20.

CHEFS: Katherine Rendle and Michael Rendle PROPRIETORS: Katherine and Frank Rendle OPEN: all week, D only MEALS: 7.30 to 10 PRICES: Set D £22.50 (£27). Net prices CARDS: Access, Amex, Diners, Visa SEATS: 18. Private parties: 18 main room. Car park, 12 places. Vegetarian meals. No children under 12. No cigars/pipes in dining-room. Music ACCOMMODATION: 6 rooms, all with bath/shower. D,B&B £70 to £99. No children under 12. Afternoon teas. Garden. Tennis. TV. Phone. Scenic (*Which? Hotel Guide*)

WHITBY North Yorkshire map 6A

Magpie Café

14 Pier Road, Whitby YO21 3PU COOKING 1
WHITBY (0947) 602058 COST £11–£20

Every seaside town should support a café like the Magpie because it keeps faith with fresh ingredients and the virtues of home cooking. One family's experience sums it up: 'The Magpie serves only freshly landed fish (none is kept deep-frozen) so on occasion we may not always get our favourite halibut. Fish comes grilled or poached as well as fried. Salads are large and artistically presented. Bread and butter (brown and/or white) come automatically, as does tea (following the northern custom).' Fish and chips are the star of the show – everything from cod and haddock to turbot and monkfish, but crab and lobster also appear. Despite the rise in VAT and reduced fishing quotas, the owners manage to keep prices affordable, and have introduced some new features including a mixed fish platter and a 'weight-watchers' menu'. Desserts, jams, chutneys and chocolates are made on the premises. Expect to queue and share a table, even on the last day before winter closing; also arrive early if you want a window seat overlooking the harbour. There are excellent facilities for children. House white is £5.45.

CHEFS: Ian Robson and Alison McKenzie-Robson PROPRIETORS: Sheila and Ian McKenzie, Ian Robson and Alison McKenzie-Robson OPEN: all week, L only CLOSED: late Nov to Mar MEALS: 11.30 to 6.30 PRICES: £12 (£17), Set meals £6.35 (£11) to £9.75 (£14). CARDS: Access, Visa SEATS: 100. Private parties: 50 main room. Vegetarian meals. Healthy eating options. Children's helpings. No-smoking area. Air-conditioned. No music

Trenchers

New Quay Road, Whitby YO21 1DH — COOKING 1
WHITBY (0947) 603212 — COST £20

Tiffany lamps, ceiling fans and glass wall murals all contribute to the setting of this fish restaurant, glitzier than the cosy Magpie Café. There is good North Sea white fish, plus salmon and local crab. The lobster and scampi come from further afield. Steaks are chargrilled and sandwiches are available all day. There is a wine list, though it is light on some details and heavy on misspellings. House wine is £7.95 a litre.

CHEFS: Tim Lawrence and Gary Moutrey PROPRIETOR: Terry Foster OPEN: all week CLOSED: Christmas to mid-Mar MEALS: 11 to 9 PRICES: £12 (£17) SEATS: 150. Private parties: 150 main room. Vegetarian meals. Children's helpings. Wheelchair access. Music

WHITLEY BAY Tyne & Wear — map 7

Le Provençale

183 Park View, Whitley Bay NE26 3RE — COOKING 1
TYNESIDE (091) 251 3567 — COST £13–£34

Le Provençale is found on one of Whitley Bay's 'better' shopping streets, and has taken in next door, expanded its seating and enlarged the bar. The brown tones of the decoration, accented by floral cloths and wallpaper, give it a 'warm provincial' feeling which is enhanced by the extremely efficient, yet friendly, service of the large staff. A long, perhaps too long, *carte* (at very fair prices) runs most of the week, but Monday and Thursday are 'gourmet' nights when a set-price menu is in operation, on one theme or another. This shows Mr Guijarro on his mettle: a tart of mussels and spinach; a good seafood pancake; salmon with a prawn and saffron sauce; veal with olives, anchovies and capers; excellent beignets of apricot or a vanilla and chocolate charlotte demonstrate what he can achieve. The fact that the place is full on so many evenings may equally show that not many others in Whitley Bay do it so well or at so reasonable a cost. The wine list displays some ambition in range and is priced fairly. House wine is £6.90 a litre.

CHEF: Michael Guijarro PROPRIETORS: Mr and Mrs M. Guijarro OPEN: Mon to Sat D, Thur and Fri L CLOSED: 2 weeks summer MEALS: 12 to 2, 7.30 to 9.45 (7 to 10 Sat) PRICES: L £7 (£13), D £21 (£28), Set D £14.95 (£21) to £19.95 (£27) CARDS: Access, Amex, Diners, Visa SEATS: 52. Private parties: 52 main room. Children's helpings. No children under 7. Music. Air-conditioned

WICKHAM Hampshire map 2

▲ *Old House*

The Square, Wickham PO17 5JG — COOKING 2
WICKHAM (0329) 833049 — COST £37

It is a measure of the growth of Solent City, quondam dream of traffic and road planners of the '60s, that the Skipwiths have put double glazing into this handsome Georgian house on the square at Wickham. The restaurant itself is tucked away at the back, well insulated by both garden and heavy red curtains. Nicholas Harman continues to offer a short French *carte* that tastes a little more English than it sounds and may suffer from a lack of noble simplicity that allows bright flavours to shine through in dishes such as gigot of lamb with tomato and basil and sea bass with sorrel. Vegetables come at a stiff extra charge and it is particularly value for money that preoccupies readers who report on meals here. There is a very short wine list, with pride of place given to some clarets of 'personal importation'. The exercise of 'compare and contrast' if using the Old House as a staging-post to France via Portsmouth is a revealing one. House wines are £9.50.

CHEF: Nicholas Harman PROPRIETORS: Richard and Annie Skipwith OPEN: Mon to Sat, exc L Mon and Sat CLOSED: 2 weeks July to Aug, 10 days Christmas, 2 weeks Easter MEALS: 12 to 1.45, 7 to 9.30 PRICES: £22 (£31). Net prices, card slips closed CARDS: Access, Amex, Diners, Visa SEATS: 40. Private parties: 35 main room, 14 private room. Car park, 12 places. Children's helpings. No cigars/pipes in dining-room. Wheelchair access. No music. Fax: (0329) 833672 ACCOMMODATION: 12 rooms, all with bath/shower. B&B £75 to £95. Children welcome. Baby facilities. Garden. TV. Phone. Scenic. Doors close at midnight. Confirm by noon (*Which? Hotel Guide*)

WILLINGTON Co Durham map 7

Stile

97 High Street, Willington DL15 0PE — COOKING 1
BISHOP AUCKLAND (0388) 746615 — COST £23–£30

Paring down of the menu, and a new, laudable policy of changing it fortnightly have proved popular. 'One of the best meals we have had at Stile' was one enthusiastic recommendation. Although a winter diner reported a welcome as bland as his roast partridge, the wry observation 'Where else do you go to eat in the desert up here?' echoed the feeling of a more happily served couple. 'A nice, relaxed atmosphere, I hope this develops – we desperately need quality food in the Durham area,' reported a local. Pigeon breast (served pink) with juniper and pine kernel sauce, poached salmon and Barbary duck have all pleased. A couple of vegetarian dishes, perhaps stuffed sweet peppers with pine-nuts, and lentil and cider loaf, continue to feature. The fortnightly French dinners on a set menu have been joined by a more extensive, monthly 'gourmand' fixed-price menu, offering wines matched with food. The idiosyncratic wine list reveals real enthusiasm. Wines from Ch. Tayac, Côtes de Bourg, imported directly by the owners at reasonable prices, set the tone. House wine is £7.50 a litre.

CHEF: Jenny James PROPRIETORS: Mike Boustred and Jenny James OPEN: Tue to Sat, D only MEALS: 7 to 9.45 PRICES: £18 (£25), Special set D from £16.75 (£23). Card slips closed CARDS: Access, Visa SEATS: 50. Private parties: 34 main room, 18 private room. Car park, 14 places. Vegetarian meals. Children's helpings on request. No smoking. Wheelchair access (2 steps). Music

WILLITON Somerset map 2

▲ *White House Hotel* 🍷

Williton TA4 4QW COOKING 2*
WILLITON (0984) 32306 and 32777 COST £41

Guests and owners make similar points about this attractive house on the main road through the village. 'The rooms are modest but comfortable without the extras that add so much to cost with little benefit in terms of comfort,' says a guest. And Dick Smith questions the last edition's estimate of maximum price – 'people prepared to pay that might well be expecting at the very least a few flunkies around to open and close their car door'. This is not that sort of place; nor are prices, especially of wines, high. The lack of ceremony may contribute to a very quiet atmosphere – too quiet for some. Each night there is offered a five-course fixed-price menu, opening with a soup and proceeding through four or five choices for each principal stage, punctuated by a board of English cheeses. The style of cooking is emphatically that of the rediscovery of France during the early '60s. It depends successfully on excellent materials; its execution is without nonsensical elaboration, and in most reported meals the tastes are noticed and enjoyed. Dishes such as piperade basquaise, eggs en cocotte Lorraine, an armagnac- and thyme-flavoured duck liver pâté, tarragon chicken, hake baked with white wine and tomatoes, and fillet of beef béarnaise read attractively and to character. Only occasionally have they been known to fall down through lack of careful finish. A grilled marinated breast of pigeon served with a warm beetroot salad is a conceit less often remembered, yet much enjoyed. More such cooking should be encouraged. It has body enough to support the excellent and intelligent wine list, on which knowledge and enthusiasm abound. The house wines alone show real care in selection, while many good half-bottles and a page of bottles below £11 confirm a determination to give the customer a fair deal. Clearer presentation might encourage greater adventure. House wines are from £10. CELLARMAN'S CHOICE: Gewurztraminer, Herrenweg 1989, Zind Humbrecht, £14.60; Pesquera Reserva 1984, Fernandez, £23.

CHEF/PROPRIETORS: Dick and Kay Smith OPEN: all week, D only CLOSED: early Nov to mid-May MEALS: 7.30 to 8.30 PRICES: Set D £25 (£34) SEATS: 26. Private parties: 12 main room. Car park, 17 places. Children's helpings. No smoking while others are eating. Wheelchair access. No music ACCOMMODATION: 12 rooms, 10 with bath/shower. Rooms for disabled. B&B £26 to £68. Deposit: £25. Children welcome. Baby facilities. Pets welcome. TV. Phone. Doors close at 11.30. Confirm by 6

▲ *This symbol means that accommodation is available.*

WINCHCOMBE Gloucestershire map 2

Corner Cupboard Dining Room

Gloucester Street,
Winchcombe GL54 5LX COOKING 2
WINCHCOMBE (0242) 602303 COST £29

Christine Randle leases space from the Corner Cupboard, a pub on the main road through the village. Although there is a feeling of secrecy and seclusion about her tiny stone-walled dining-room, there is also a light, bright atmosphere, enhanced by colourful drawings and hand-thrown pottery on the tables. This is a small-scale, domestic set-up: Christine cooks almost single-handedly and focuses on a short four-course fixed-price menu. It is a simple format based on good raw materials and much of the work, such as butchering, is done in-house. The results are finely executed, but restrained. Warm chicken livers are served on a green salad with a good thick vinaigrette; slices of wild venison, cut from the top of the leg, are pan-fried and arranged on a stock-based sauce flavoured with cassis and blackcurrant. Otherwise there might be spinach roulade with salmon and smoked trout, roast guinea-fowl with a timbale of curried parsnips, or grilled monkfish with mustard and cucumber sauce. Sweets include home-made ice-creams. The details are impressive: well-judged sauces, plain fresh vegetables, locally baked bread, superb British farmhouse cheeses. Thirty modestly priced wines include house red at £7.95.

CHEF/PROPRIETOR: Christine Randle OPEN: Tue to Sat, D only MEALS: 7.30 to 9
PRICES: Set D £17.95 (£24) SEATS: 18. Private parties: 18 main room, 18 private room. Car park, 15 places. No children under 10. No smoking. No music

WINDERMERE Cumbria map 7

▲ *Gilpin Lodge* NEW ENTRY

Crook Road, Windermere LA23 3NE
WINDERMERE (053 94) 88818 COOKING 2
on the B5284, Kendal to Bowness road COST £20–£37

The house began life at the turn of the century as a solicitor's residence. Since 1988, the Cunliffes have transformed it into a country hotel set in 20 acres of grounds. Christine Cunliffe offers a daily fixed-price dinner menu running to five courses. A spring meal comprised gratin of fresh scallops and prawns, curried carrot and parsnip soup, and roast loin of lamb with leek and rosemary sauce with decorative nouvelle vegetables. The cooking is competent, if not aspiring to the height of nearby neighbours, and there have been good reports of pheasant pâté in puff pastry, smoked chicken and spinach pancakes, and venison with redcurrants. Boned quail might be stuffed with leek and chive mousse or a curious combination of wild mushrooms and smoked salmon mousse. The sweet menu is bolstered by an impressive list of dessert wines. Sticky toffee pudding has lived up to its name and home-made ice-creams have been excellent. Despite the well-ordered comfort of the place, some have found a rather 'frigid formality' to proceedings. The wine list is quietly enthusiastic;

excellent burgundies, an interesting page of Loires including some old Vouvrays, and a good range generally would be sufficient commendation, but fair mark-ups put many interesting bottles within affordable reach. House Côtes du Rhône is £8.50.

CHEFS: Christine Cunliffe and Chris Davies PROPRIETORS: John and Christine Cunliffe OPEN: all week, D only, and Sun L MEALS: 12.30 to 1.45, 7 to 8.45 PRICES: Set Sun L £12.75 (£20), Set D £22 (£31) CARDS: Access, Amex, Diners, Visa SEATS: 45. Private parties: 22 main room, 12 and 14 private rooms. Car park, 30 places. Vegetarian meals. No children under 9. Smart dress preferred. No smoking in dining-room. No music. Fax: (053 94) 88058 ACCOMMODATION: 9 rooms, all with bath/shower. B&B £45 to £106. No children under 9. Pets welcome. Garden. TV. Phone. Scenic. Doors close at midnight

▲ *Miller Howe*

Rayrigg Road, Windermere LA23 1EY
WINDERMERE (053 94) 42536 — COOKING 3*
on A592 between Windermere and Bowness — COST £50

The Howe is a typical Lakeland nineteenth-century stone house with later additions, the most recent of which is a conservatory where the crowds can take their aperitif in comfort (on a sunny day). There is little understatement in the decoration of the house, and the garden has cherubs everywhere. Although John Tovey has not been so much in evidence this year – ill health, and heavy commitments to books, television and teaching – nice touches endear customers new and old to the place. Anniversary and birthday cards and cakes, classical tapes in the bedrooms and rubber ducks for the bath do make a difference, it seems. Who can say if it is his absence that has brought a small rash of less enthusiastic comment about the staff and service: not always neat, not always considerate, sometimes patronising? Dinner is an event: a *coup de théâtre* if ever there was one. Guests have half an hour in the ante-rooms for drinks and a gander at the wine list, then it's on into the dining-room for the procession of dishes through four courses, choice only coming at the sweet time. 'I could almost hear the sheep dogs snapping at our heels as we were persuaded to our table,' said one of cynical cast of mind; but the formula is long-standing and the victims are willing, nay enthusiastic. Food at Miller Howe is characterised by profusion: leek and potato soup comes with toasted almonds and chopped chives and a savoury tartlet; roast pork is stuffed with Dijon mustard and rosemary, and served on a pear brandy purée with a rich gravy. Two vegetables are insufficient too: carrots with Pernod, swede with horseradish, spinach with garlic and orange, beans and sweetcorn with a honey-butter twirl, curried leek rings, baked savoury potato. The invention astonishes – and informs many other menus – but some readers find the tastes war against each other, especially when placed too close in little dollops on too small a plate. A periodic visitor made the point that it could be suggested the magic has subdued over the years, but at the same time, were this cooking found in a new restaurant, the existence of which no one took for granted, he would be faxing us reports in triplicate. John Tovey has set himself very high standards, and proved he can achieve them; so it only needs the smallest dereliction to bring upon his head extreme reaction. Reservations do exist. Long service has its hidden dangers, and the delivery of the meal in regimented form means there are sometimes delays, which gives a chance for resentment to set in. In sum, however, the consensus of reports is still firmly in favour. Enthusiasm for robust New World wines is confirmed by the strong recommendations provided at the foot of the menu; these invariably are Californian or Australian.

CHEFS: Ian Dutton and Curis Blaydes PROPRIETOR: John J. Tovey OPEN: all week, D only CLOSED: Dec to Feb MEALS: 8 for 8.30 (6.30 for 7 and 9 for 9.30 Sat) PRICES: Set D £32 (£42). Service 12.5%. Card slips closed CARDS: Access, Amex, Diners, Visa SEATS: 70. Private parties: 30 main room. Car park, 40 places. Vegetarian meals. No children under 12. Smart dress preferred. No smoking in dining-room. Music. Air-conditioned. Fax: (053 94) 45664 ACCOMMODATION: 13 rooms, all with bath/shower. D,B&B £90 to £240. No children under 12. Pets welcome. Afternoon teas. Garden. Air-conditioned. TV. Phone. Scenic. Doors close at 11. Confirm by midnight (*Which? Hotel Guide*)

Miller Howe Café

Lakeland Plastics Ltd,
Alexandra Buildings, Station Precinct,
Windermere LA23 1BQ — COOKING 2
WINDERMERE (053 94) 6732 — COST £17

A change of name from 'Kaff' to 'Café', and a redesigned menu herald a new phase for this admirable off-shoot of Miller Howe (see previous entry). Ian Dutton, head chef at John Tovey's hotel, has also taken control of the open-plan café kitchen. A short fixed menu of cakes, pastries, snacks and a few main dishes is supplemented by an extensive blackboard of specials. Echoes of Miller Howe are everywhere: excellent soups such as carrot and fennel; devilled mushrooms; cheese and herb pâté with orange and tomato salad; fine breads; sticky toffee pudding; special ice-creams. Local ingredients show up well in the Cumberland sausage made by a Windermere butcher, which is served with apple sauce and date chutney, Waberthwaite ham with Cumberland mustard, and scones with Lakeland cream. There are exotic touches too: South African bobotie is a fixture, or there might be beef marinated in port and Guinness, or cod with a mild onion and curry sauce. 'A real jewel, in a plastic setting' is one reporter's verdict. Recent refurbishment may help to ease the congestion and long queues that are the consequence of quality and year-round popularity: 'Only two tables were empty at 1.30 on a Tuesday in March. I dread to think what it gets like in summer,' observed one visitor. House French is £6.90 a litre.

CHEFS: Ian Dutton and William Tully PROPRIETORS: John J. Tovey and Ian Dutton OPEN: Mon to Sat, daytime only MEALS: 9am to 5pm PRICES: £9 (£14) SEATS: 40. 4 tables outside. Private parties: 40 main room. Car park, 60 places. Vegetarian meals. Children welcome. No smoking. Wheelchair access. Music. Fax: (053 94) 88300

All details are as accurate as possible at the time of going to press, but chefs and owners often change, and it is wise to check by telephone before making a special journey. Many readers have been disappointed when set-price bargain meals are no longer available. Ask when booking.

Roger's

4 High Street, Windermere LA23 1AF — COOKING 3
WINDERMERE (053 94) 4954 — COST £16–£34

Downstairs in the cosy, dimly-lit main restaurant life can be neighbourly on busy nights. There is a further room on the first floor, useful for small private parties. Roger Pergl-Wilson is a skilled cook who does not mince flavours: sauces such as the garlicky madeira gravy with lamb, and blackcurrant with goose are stock-based and powerful. Materials, too, show much quality. Lamb chops in blackcurrant sauce was the 'best lamb I have tasted for quite a while' for one reader. The repertoire, which has developed slowly over the years, has taken a leap forward with the introduction of fairly priced French regional menus. They come in two versions, 'rustique' and 'populaire', and may include chicken pie with salsify from the Périgord, or chicken with pine kernels, ceps and bacon from the Landes. Alena Pergl-Wilson continues as model hostess. The apparent modesty of this restaurant belies genuine cooking and consistent devotion to a demanding profession of the type which deserves continued support. The 100-bottle wine list continues to rely rather conservatively on big names in Burgundy, but elsewhere the selection shows enthusiasm and the prices are fair, with much genuine choice under £15. House French is £8.50.

CHEF: Roger Pergl-Wilson PROPRIETORS: Roger and Alena Pergl-Wilson OPEN: Mon to Sat (Sun bank hols), D only (L by arrangement) MEALS: 7 to 10 PRICES: £17 (£28), Set D from £10 (£16). Card slips closed CARDS: Access, Amex, Diners, Visa SEATS: 42. Private parties: 28 main room, 18 private room. Children's helpings. Wheelchair access. Music

WINKLEIGH Devon — map 1

Pophams

NEW ENTRY

Castle Street, Winkleigh EX19 8HQ — COOKING 2*
WINKLEIGH (0837) 83767 — COST £12

The first impression of this village corner shop, coffee-bar and café rolled into one, is the ingenuity with which the limited space has been used. Melvin Popham and Dennis Hawkes ring the changes with the positioning of tables, although 10 people is the maximum they can accommodate. The close quarters encourage chatty comments from neighbours and owners alike; this is off-putting, perhaps, to someone who wishes to be left strictly alone but in truth it creates a happy atmosphere of relaxation and enjoyment. The food has been enthusiastically received, its quality making apparently run-of-the-mill ideas quite out of the ordinary. Everything is home-made and stunning value to boot. The choice is sensibly limited: carrot soup, smoked trout pâté, chicken breasts stuffed with goats' cheese, vegetable lasagne and steak and kidney pudding have all been positively reported. Sticky toffee pudding is the heavily endorsed star of the desserts. Every village should have a place like this.

CHEF: Melvyn Popham PROPRIETORS: Melvyn Popham and Dennis Hawkes OPEN: Mon to Sat, daytime only MEALS: 9am to 3pm PRICES: £9 (£10). Card slips closed. Unlicensed, but bring your own: no corkage CARDS: Access, Visa SEATS: 10. Private parties: 8 main room. Vegetarian meals. No children under 14. No smoking. Music. Air-conditioned

WINTERINGHAM Humberside map 6

▲ *Winteringham Fields* 🍷

Winteringham DN15 9PF COOKING 4
SCUNTHORPE (0724) 733096 COST £20–£43

Winteringham was the site of the Roman ferry across the Humber to Brough. The Fields is an old farmhouse that envelops any who cross the threshold with both the warmth of the Schwabs' enthusiasm and the close domesticity of the interiors; it has been described by some as 'like a Swiss hotel', by others as 'nineteenth-century' – certainly the pine panelling, oak wainscot, cast-iron ranges, embossed wallpapers and well-packed feel give it a definite personality. The cooking is never English-farmhouse, though it commands much affection, as do the Schwabs and their well-motivated staff. Germain Schwab is Swiss and his origins are reflected partly on the wine list, and on the menu by his receptivity to pan-European movements. Semolina mille-feuille with scallops, langoustines and a lobster sauce, salmon pancake in a fish stock sauce, oyster soufflé with a citrus sauce, foie gras de canard, and calf's sweetbreads in a light stock and Sauternes sauce with orange zest and blackcurrants are first courses that show considerable assurance and technique. Main course dishes including halibut and salmon 'so fresh', pheasant with compote of apple, and tongue with a red wine sauce 'bourgeoise' continue the success. Space needs reserving for cheeses from the trolley, better than any for miles around even if mainly French, or for the desserts, which show Swiss skills in combinations like champagne biscuits marinated in hot wine, topped with an apricot soufflé. Even the vegetables – a spare modern selection – may include highlights, such as 'four spectacular sprouts'. This would do well anywhere, but on the Humber its presence causes ecstasy of discovery: 'I have at last found heaven.' The wine list is intelligently concise, and, this year, a model of clarity with many fine wines drawn even-handedly from around the world. The 'Patron's Reserve' of old and mostly famous clarets, with prices to match, is more than balanced by moderate provisions of decent, modest wines. Half-bottles are carefully chosen and interesting Swiss wines round off the list. House wine is £9.50. CELLARMAN'S CHOICE: Margaux, Ch. Paveil de Luze 1985, £20; Fendant du Valais 1989, J. Germanier, £17.50.

CHEF: Germain Schwab PROPRIETORS: Annie and Germain Schwab OPEN: Mon to Sat, exc L Mon and Sat CLOSED: first 2 weeks Jan, first week Aug MEALS: 11.30 to 1.30, 7 to 9.30 PRICES: £29 (£36), Set L £13.50 (£20) to £15 (£22). Card slips closed CARDS: Access, Visa SEATS: 40. Private parties: 14 main room, 10 private room. Car park, 16 places. Children welcome. Smart dress preferred. No smoking in dining-room. Wheelchair access (1 step; also WC). Music. Air-conditioned. Fax: (0724) 733898 ACCOMMODATION: 6 rooms, all with bath/shower. B&B £58 to £88. No children under 11. Afternoon teas. Garden. Air-conditioning. TV. Phone. Scenic. Doors close at midnight. Confirm by 6 (*Which? Hotel Guide*)

The Guide *is totally independent, accepts no free hospitality, and survives on the proceeds from copies sold each year.*

WITHERSLACK Cumbria map 7

▲ *Old Vicarage*

Witherslack LA11 6RS
WITHERSLACK (044 852) 381 COOKING 3*
off A590 COST £42

This old vicarage is run by two couples, now assisted by a named chef, and has been added to, improved, and turned by them into more and more of a professional hotel over the years. The formula, however, remains the original: a five-course dinner with a choice at pudding stage alone. The standards are high, and the style is emphatically British and occasionally substantial. Mousses exist, for instance a mousseline of sole with champagne and scallop sauce as a first course, but the roasts – duck, sucking pig, veal cushion, venison – come with stuffing rather than airy inserts, and rich sauces or gravies as well as excellent vegetables. Puddings, too, feature a brown Betty, steamed pudding or something else British alongside an effete bavarois, just as the cheeseboard is a celebration of northern dairies. Small wonder that there are recidivists. Cooking is usually *à point* and the presence of so many partners in the house – they usually take turn and turn about – means that the place runs along well-oiled and straight lines. For some people, this is exasperating, allowing no edge or spark, but the great majority would agree, as one reader put it, that 'this is like complaining that you can hear the clock ticking in a Rolls-Royce'. And as another comments: 'It's so full of nice touches: the serving of the crumble in a dish so you can serve yourself; the cafetière for one; the black pudding with Cumberland grill (breakfasts are fine); the individual jug of orange juice. If they had served only the brown bread and the wine we would insist on an entry. As it was, the roulade of smoked haddock and prawns, the lightest of cinnamon meringues weighted down with fresh redcurrant and then a cheese list of eight local things, made this the meal of the year.' The wine list too is even-handed in its provision of excellence from good to more modest bottles, its enthusiastic sweep across the globe catching some of the most ambitious wine-makers. The mark-up pushes hard over £25 but quality is evident throughout. There are good beers also. CELLARMAN'S CHOICE: Eden Valley Chardonnay 1989, Mountadam, £21; Beaune 1987, Joillot, £21.

CHEFS: Roger and Jill Burrington-Brown, Irene and Stanley Reeve and Stuart Harrison PROPRIETORS: Roger and Jill Burrington-Brown and Irene and Stanley Reeve OPEN: all week, D only MEALS: 7.30 for 8 PRICES: Set D £26 (£35). Card slips closed CARDS: Access, Amex, Diners, Visa SEATS: 35. Private parties: 18 main room. Car park, 25 places. Vegetarian meals. Children welcome. No smoking in dining-room. Music. One sitting. Fax: (044 852) 373 ACCOMMODATION: 13 rooms, all with bath/shower. Rooms for disabled. B&B £57 to £123. Children welcome. Pets welcome. Garden. Tennis. Fishing. Golf. TV. Phone. Scenic. Doors close at 11.30. Confirm by 6 (*Which? Hotel Guide*)

Several sharp operators have tried to extort money from restaurateurs on the promise of an entry in a guide book that has never appeared. The Good Food Guide *makes no charge for inclusion and does not offer certificates of any kind.*

WOBURN Bedfordshire map 3

Paris House

Woburn MK17 9QP
WOBURN (0525) 290692 COOKING 3
A4012, 1m SE of Woburn in Abbey grounds COST £23–£48

It is a wonderful setting for a restaurant: an extravagantly timbered house built for an International Exhibition in the nineteenth century and removed thence to parkland with deer and pheasants running wild. Paris House is a full-dress restaurant, one of the very few in the district. It also boasts a good first-floor room, with a round table to take 16, that gives wider views and privacy. Peter Chandler 'knows his fish': ragoût of salmon and monkfish, and mousseline of salmon and prawns with asparagus have been enthused about. Cooking is modern classical, as befits one who trained with the Roux brothers; thus there are good sauces, such as the tarragon and tomato with leg of lamb or oyster mushroom with breast of chicken. Raspberry soufflé is another firm favourite. One reader commented that the quality of the desserts was such that they were never too sweet (apart from *mucho* spun sugar). Service is French and formal, sometimes brusque, sometimes dilatory, usually appreciated. Peter Chandler appears after meals and his guided tour of the kitchens was valued by one café-proprietor. The wine list is expensive, though house wine is £9.50.

CHEF/PROPRIETOR: Peter Chandler OPEN: Tue to Sun, exc Sun D CLOSED: Feb MEALS: 12 to 2, 7 to 10 PRICES: Set L £16.50 (£23) to £29.50 (£38), Set D £29.50 (£38) to £32 (£40) CARDS: Access, Amex, Diners, Visa SEATS: 52. 3 tables outside. Private parties: 45 main room, 25 private room. Car park, 25 places. Vegetarian meals. Children's helpings. No children under 12 D. Smart dress preferred

WOODBRIDGE Suffolk map 3

Wine Bar 🍷

17 Thoroughfare, Woodbridge IP12 1AA COOKING 2
WOODBRIDGE (0394) 382557 COST £22

One report tells of a refusal to serve lunch at 2.05 despite lunchtime opening until 2.30. It continues: 'We wondered wherein lay the distinction between "atmosphere" and "unkempt".' This wine bar certainly has character: the wine list is creative; the food is interesting and is at wine bar prices; there are occasional clashes of personality. The cooking is worth noting. Among imaginative compositions have been sautéed lamb's liver with parsnip and pear cake and a lemon and thyme sauce; pigeon with mustard sauce and mushrooms; squid and prawns marinated in lime and oil, with coriander and chickpeas; and guinea-fowl two ways, the leg confit in duck fat, the breast with apple and apple cream sauce. It is worth living with the 'atmosphere', which most people find congenial, to sample them. With 18 interesting and modestly priced wines offered by the glass, there may be little need to investigate the list further. New World wines are explored thoroughly while clarets and burgundies are restricted to mid-priced bottles; the most extravagant, a Fixin at £14.65, is beaten by a Margaret River Pinot Noir from Western Australia for

£20. Mark-ups are really very kind. House wine is £6.50. CELLARMAN'S CHOICE: Gewurztraminer/Riesling 1988, Penfolds, £8.65; Côtes de Franc, Ch. Puyguerard 1986, £10.50.

CHEF: Sally O'Gorman PROPRIETORS: Sally O'Gorman and Richard Lane OPEN: Tue to Sat CLOSED: 25 and 26 Dec MEALS: 12 to 2.30, 7 to 11 PRICES: £13 (£18) SEATS: 50. Vegetarian meals. No children under 16. Music

WOODSTOCK Oxfordshire map 2

▲ *Feathers Hotel*

Market Street, Woodstock OX7 1SX COOKING 3
WOODSTOCK (0993) 812291 COST £25–£44

This free-range, eclectic and characterful hotel in the centre of Woodstock, gateway to Blenheim Palace, but worth a stop for its own sake, has proved itself over the past year. Various aspects of the accommodation and public rooms have been subject to a programme of refurbishment that leaves a pleasingly informal but finished compromise. Nick Gill, who kick-started the kitchen into a fine, gutsy style of haute cuisine without fuss yet full of original ideas, has been elevated to 'consultant' chef, with David Lewis in day-to-day charge. Ideas and witty presentation still exist, for instance in the plate of 'salmon, salmon and salmon' – marinated, tartare and smoked – each with emphatic sauces, and smoked wild boar with green tomato chutney and olive oil. Much of the *carte* is about such pronounced flavours: soy and ginger with scallops and tuna from the chargrill, or hot 'essence' (soup) of mussels with cumin and coriander. Equally, herbs get their proper outing in the meat cookery of the main dishes, although readers have sometimes found dishes presupposing strength, such as hare hotpot, actually lacking in flavour. Puddings do not let the side down: warm savarin, with berries and clotted cream; hot soufflés, with matching ice-creams; iced pear soufflé with red wine and cinnamon. The coffee is excellent, as are the truffles. There is universal irritation at the now discountenanced 'suggested gratuity' of 15 per cent, which renders apparent bargains less so and is not helped by occasional culinary lapses. Several good wines by the glass and some decent half-bottles go some way to relieve the pocket, as do six carefully chosen house wines. Otherwise this is a wine list of good to excellent quality with mark-ups bordering on the rapacious: Cloudy Bay at £34 must be some sort of record. Reports as we went to press suggest that the originality of the kitchen may be on the wane. Progress needs to be monitored.

CHEFS: David Lewis and Lee Bearnan PROPRIETORS: Andrew Leeman, Simon Lowe and Howard Malin OPEN: all week MEALS: 12.30 to 2.15, 7 to 9.45 PRICES: £25 (£37), Set L £16.50 (£25), Set D £19.50 (£28). Service 15%. Card slips closed CARDS: Access, Amex, Diners, Visa SEATS: 60. Private parties: 36 main room, 40 private room. Children's helpings. No cigars/pipes in dining-room. Wheelchair access. Music. Fax: (0993) 813158 ACCOMMODATION: 17 rooms, all with bath/shower. B&B £75 to £125. Children welcome. Baby facilities. Pets welcome. Afternoon teas. Garden. TV. Phone. Scenic. Doors close at 11.30 (*Which? Hotel Guide*)

WOOLLEY GREEN Wiltshire map 2

▲ *Woolley Grange* **NEW ENTRY**

Woolley Green,
Bradford-on-Avon BA15 1TX
BRADFORD-ON-AVON (022 16) 4705 COOKING 3
on B3105, 1m NE of Bradford-on-Avon COST £20–£49

Woolley Green is an almost unidentified hamlet to the north of Bradford-on-Avon. (You are advised to ask for directions when booking.) The Grange is a seventeenth-century manor set behind high walls in a fine garden; do not miss your footing on the way in or you could end up in a pond. On one side there is a conservatory for drinks, lunches or open-air dining in imperial planter style. The roof timbers come from the Royal Albert Dock in Liverpool. The rest of the interior, although seventeenth-century, was done over in Victorian times, and some of it, therefore, is on the heavy side. But it sparkles with attention from the Chapman family, whose taste in pictures gives verve to the dullest panelling – the etchings by Gerard Bellaart are worth a second look. The Grange was dropped from last year's edition because Ian Mansfield took the kitchen over as we were in the press. There was a hiccup at the time, but things have settled down famously. Although the menu is not so overtly fashionable as it was at the time of opening, its ideas are certainly trendy enough for anyone and the skills mobilised are very steady. Service is exceptionally solicitous. 'It says something for our lunch here that after three weeks we still remember every feature,' comments a reader. At dinner there are two set-price options; at lunch, a variety of lighter things may be eaten, as well as a short choice at full price. Dishes include such things as quail salad with foie gras and artichokes; a nage of weaver fish and broad beans; grilled tuna with a pepper dressing; poussin with chicory and Sauternes; apricot parfait with hot apricots; and apple and pecan tart with maple syrup and pecan ice-cream; with good bread, decent coffee, excellent pastry, and fair vegetables. This may develop very well. The hotel is proclaimed paradise for children, and Sunday lunch, with nanny and nursery, is witness to that. A very adequate if very overpriced wine list is expected to have been augmented with some fine Italian bottles by the time the *Guide* appears. With hardly a bottle below £15, all mark-ups beyond many expected in the capital and few half-bottles, this is a list for the prodigal. House wine is £9.85.

CHEF: Ian Mansfield PROPRIETORS: Nigel and Heather Chapman OPEN: all week MEALS: 12 to 2, 7 to 10 PRICES: L £12 (£20), Set L £25 (£33), Sun L £16 (£23), Set D £25 (£33) to £32 (£41). Card slips closed CARDS: Access, Amex, Diners, Visa SEATS: 54. 5 tables outside Private parties: 30 main room, 14 and 22 private rooms. Car park, 40 places. Vegetarian meals. Children's helpings. Wheelchair access (1 step; also WC). No music ACCOMMODATION: 20 rooms, all with bath/shower. B&B £80 to £158. Children welcome. Baby facilities. Pets welcome. Afternoon teas. Garden. Swimming-pool. Tennis. Snooker. TV. Phone. Scenic (*Which? Hotel Guide*)

Card slips closed *in the details at the end of an entry indicates that the totals on the slips of credit cards are closed when these are handed over for signature.*

WOOTTON **Isle of Wight** map 2

▲ *Lugleys*

Staplers Road,
Wootton Common PO33 4RW — COOKING 3
NEWPORT (0983) 882202 — COST £17–£38

'Keeping open has been as much of a challenge as aiming for perfection in my cooking' is Angela Hewitt's modest self-assessment. She occupies a remote detached Victorian house on the common, next to Butterfly World. Not much in the décor matches, but all is individual and has character, as does the garden – definitely not suburban – and the pasture beyond. Everything is very much Angela's own: the kitchen, the ambience and, above all, the food offered on a short menu of perhaps three choices at each course. The menu lengthens unexpectedly with impromptu complimentaries turning up between courses. The food is tied in to supplies of materials, as, of course, is everyone's, but Angela Hewitt tends to make more effort than most of her colleagues on the island. The food also seems strongly related to the flower garden and the fields – reminiscent of Constance Spry in her heroic period during the Second World War. Angela Hewitt would admit to being a 'British' cook; in other words she does not aim at creating some small Mediterranean patch in an English meadow. This would explain meals like old-English oyster stew, confit of duck leg with duck breast and caper sauce, port and plum jelly with lavender flower ice-cream, baked egg and haddock en cocotte, venison with lentils bean and shallot sauce, and coffee mousse with chocolate sorbet and warm chocolate sauce. This is a remarkable venture; may it survive many more recessions ('I am through my third since opening'). The prices at least deserve an award for even-handedness. The wine list is tailored to islanders' tastes, with small bursts of greater extravagance for the short summer season. House Bergerac is £7.45.

CHEF/PROPRIETOR: Angela E. Hewitt OPEN: Tue to Sat, D only (Mon and Sun D and L by arrangement) CLOSED: 4 weeks winter MEALS: 7 to 9.30 PRICES: £22 (£30), Set L £12 (£17) to £20 (£26), Set D £18 (£24) to £25 (£32). Minimum £11.95 SEATS: 16. 5 tables outside. Private parties: 16 main room. Car park, 12 places. No children under 12. No cigars in dining-room. No music ACCOMMODATION: Self-contained flat for 3, £30 a night

WORCESTER **Hereford & Worcester** map 2

Brown's

24 Quay Street, Worcester WR1 2JJ — COOKING 2
WORCESTER (0905) 26263 — COST £20–£42

Brown's is housed in a fine converted cornmill open to the high ceiling, with a mezzanine bar area and views on to the broad and gentle river. The decoration is modern conservationist: stainless steel chairs, much brick, girders and railings setting off good pictures and prints. The cooking is of a piece with this: modern, sometimes rough-edged, avoiding old tricks of display and elaboration. 'Stylish food with splashes of refinement' was how one inspector described it. The most consistent problem is the price. Worcester is not so metropolitan as to take kindly to a meal charge of £30 even if it does include service. Sunday lunch, by contrast, is more realistically priced. The dinner menu offers a choice of six for each course, though beef fillet carries a supplement of £2.50, and exemplar dishes are matelote of fish with aïoli; creamed eggs with wild mushrooms in a pastry crust; salmis of squab with red wine; and chicken with fresh noodles, white wine, cream and Parmesan. Desserts may include a rhubarb crumble, a meringue with ginger ice-cream, or a fruit terrine. People usually find the tastes clear and pronounced. This is a great recommendation. The wine list is always interesting, though largely French. House wines are £9.

CHEFS: W.R. Tansley and S. Meredith PROPRIETORS: W.R. and P.M. Tansley OPEN: all week, exc Sat L and Sun D CLOSED: bank hols, 1 week Christmas MEALS: 12.30 to 1.45 (2 Sun), 7.30 to 9.30 PRICES: Set L £15 (£20), Set D £30 (£35). Net prices, card slips closed CARDS: Access, Amex, Diners, Visa SEATS: 80. Private parties: 80 main room. Vegetarian meals. No children under 10. Wheelchair access (also WC). No music

Il Pescatore NEW ENTRY

34 Sidbury, Worcester WR1 2HZ COOKING 1
WORCESTER (0905) 21444 COST £14–£38

The cosy half-timbered building was originally a tea-room, but now operates as an Italian restaurant with an amiable atmosphere, a fondness for fish, and a British streak expressing the chef's personality. The dining-room is elegantly decorated in pink and grey with exposed brickwork and original paintings (by the proprietor) on display. English chef Adrian Clement makes his own pasta and offers a fixed menu of Continental stalwarts – minestrone, cannelloni, saltimbocca alla romana and bistecca al Barolo – backed up by more enterprising daily specials such as wild rabbit sausage with mustard sauce, fillet of lamb with redcurrant and mint sauce, and fillet steak with distinctive wild mushrooms. Ingredients are fresh, presentation is attractive. Fish might include marinated salmon with orange vinaigrette, grilled hake, lobster thermidor or 'sinfonietta di pesce' – a mix of species poached in wine, garlic and parsley. Specialities include tagliatelle in a seafood sauce and ravioli stuffed with shellfish. Vegetables are crisp and colourful. There is usually a choice of around six home-made desserts, such as Italian trifle. Forty wines are dominated by familiar Italian names. House wine is £6.45.

CHEF: Adrian Clement PROPRIETOR: Giuliano Ponzi OPEN: Tue to Sat CLOSED: first 2 weeks Aug MEALS: 12 to 2, 6.45 to 10 PRICES: £23 (£32), Set L £8.50 (£14), Set D £12.50 (£18) CARDS: Access, Visa SEATS: 40. Private parties: 40 main room. Vegetarian meals. Children's helpings. Smart dress preferred. Wheelchair access (1 step). Music

'My husband and I arrived about 7.20pm, saw the waiter laying up a table and waited for our friends who were driving in from Kent. By the time they had found a parking place it was 7.40pm and we walked up to the restaurant and found it in darkness and closed. We were horrified and could just read a note on the door which said that owing to a "gas leak" the restaurant was closed.' On eating, or not eating, in London

WORLESTON Cheshire map 5

▲ *Rookery Hall*

Worleston, nr Nantwich CW5 6DQ
NANTWICH (0270) 610016 COOKING 3
on B5074, off A51 COST £28–£60

There has been quite a change here. The tranquil Hall was surrounded for the best part of last year by a building site and many readers expressed concern that planned extensions would shatter the peace. The conference and banqueting facilities are now fully operational and recent reports have failed to note any marked change in the welcoming reception and attentive service. One couple arriving for Sunday lunch appreciated a large log fire on an otherwise dreary day. Other readers have commented on the magnificent furnishings and the fine garden view from the mahogany-panelled dining-room. The food, handled in a light, subtle manner, allows the produce to shine. Reports on meals eaten in the spring highlighted the quality of the lamb, particularly that of tender best end topped with a brioche crust and served on a bed of creamed leeks. Fish is also well handled, cautiously reflecting modern trends by using red wine sauces and, as in roasted sea bass on red cabbage with a cider fondue, employing bold accompaniments. The apparent care taken in the blending of flavours and textures has led some to comment on lacklustre food ('a salmon mousse was a bit too creamy and bland') and there has been the odd niggle about less than generous quantities, but the consensus is one of satisfaction. Desserts are well liked; a spring fruit sabayon with vanilla ice-cream was given added richness by being served on a bed of dark chocolate mousse. Cheeses are well kept. Lunch is noticeably cheaper than dinner but the charging of £2.50 for coffee and petits fours against a £16.50 set lunch menu has been singled out for repeated comment. With half-bottles of champagne at prices similar to those charged for whole bottles at some restaurants, be careful to check who is footing the wine bill. Quality, however, is fine. House wine is £13.75. As we went to press the proprietors were in receivership, but the Hall continues to trade with an eye to eventual sale.

CHEF: Christopher Phillips PROPRIETORS: Select Country Hotels plc OPEN: all week OPEN: all week MEALS: 12.15 to 2.15, 7 to 9.30 PRICES: £36 (£50), Set L £16.50 (£28). Minimum £15 CARDS: Access, Amex, Diners, Visa SEATS: 60. Private parties: 40 main room, 20 private room. Car park, 150 places. Children welcome. Jacket and tie. No smoking in dining-room. Wheelchair access (also WC). No music. Fax: (0270) 626027 ACCOMMODATION: 45 rooms, all with bath/shower. Rooms for disabled. Lift. B&B £87 to £245. Chidren welcome. Afternoon teas. Garden. Tennis. Fishing. TV. Phone. Scenic (*Which? Hotel Guide*)

Prices quoted in the Guide *are based on information supplied by restaurateurs. The figure in brackets below an entry is the average for a three-course meal with service, coffee and half a bottle of house wine, as calculated by computer. The prices quoted at the top of an entry represent a range, from the lowest average meal price to the highest; the latter is inflated by 20 per cent to take account of the fact that very few people eat an average meal, and also that prices are likely to rise during the year of the* Guide.

WRIGHTINGTON Lancashire map 5

High Moor

Highmoor Lane, Wrightington WN6 9QA COOKING 2*
APPLEY BRIDGE (02575) 2364 COST £16–£36

The road passes a few feet from the front door of these half-timbered cottages; the car park is set in a field of rape. The tall, once inside, should watch the low beams but admire the view of moorland with lights twinkling in the distance. The dining-room is perhaps more attractive than the three linked salons where aperitifs are drunk and menus perused. There has been this year comment about the service: too many young and inexperienced slither bumpily between tables; second orders are imperfectly registered, even accidents are glossed over with faint concern. The food has also occasioned mixed response. Surprisingly, even quantities have been deemed too small – and this in Lancashire, home of the big eater. The *carte* shows enterprise: sea bass, scallops and Thai prawns are served with lemon grass and Shaoxing wine; poussin is roasted with Chinese mushrooms, spring onion, ginger and soy. The extravagant can indulge in luxuries for fair prices: a first course of lobster with an anisette and a mayonnaise, or beef with a potato and truffle cake and truffle butter sauce. People have spoken warmly of meals that might include a salad of wood pigeon with quails' eggs, red fruits in elderflower jelly, and sweetbreads in tomato and basil sauce. Not so much fun was a Peking duck in soggy pancake, and overcooked loin of lamb saved by the pea tartlet but lost again by a metallic reduction of a tarragon mustard sauce. Puddings can be 'over-elaborate' to the faint-hearted, who are consoled, however, by the excellent cheeses, while others get excited by things like Irish whiskey crème caramel, bourbon crème brûlée, and pink grapefruit and maple syrup salad. High Moor should be supported for its attempt to keep prices within the bounds of everyman's pocket. The wine list might need Superman's bank balance but that is only if he insists on claret or burgundy; the choice of New World and other wines is very budget-conscious and pays due attention to quality. House wines are from £7.90.

CHEF: James Sines PROPRIETOR: John Nelson OPEN: all week, D only, and Sun L MEALS: 12 to 2, 7 to 9 PRICES: £22 (£30), Set Sun L £10.75 (£16). Service 10%. Card slips closed CARDS: Access, Amex, Diners, Visa SEATS: 95. Private parties: 80 main room. Car park, 35 places. Vegetarian meals. Children welcome. Wheelchair access. Music. Air-conditioned

WYE Kent map 3

Wife of Bath

NEW ENTRY

4 Upper Bridge Street, Wye TN25 5AW COOKING 1
WYE (0233) 812540 and 812232 COST £19–£32

John Morgan took over this long-established but sadly out-of-tune restaurant in 1990 and is trying hard. The short menu is a mixture of ideas. Deep-fried Brie and avocado with an onion sauce represents a fairly hefty approach while king prawns wrapped in bacon and baked with garlic and rosemary has a dated bistro appeal. Other dishes sound more interesting – say, slices of smoked duck with a warm potato salad and veal kidneys with sage and Meaux mustard on a bed of home-made noodles. Effects are robust rather than exact. Vegetables are a strong point. Details – the bread and butter, for instance – could be improved. The wine list has its good points – it is not expensive and includes a good selection of house wines and half-bottles. House wine is £7.95.

CHEF: Robert Hymers PROPRIETOR: John Morgan OPEN: Tue to Sat CLOSED: 1 week Christmas to New Year MEALS: 12 to 2.30, 7 to 10 (10.30 with reservation) PRICES: Set L £10.75 (£19) to £16.75 (£25), Set D £19.25 (£27) CARDS: Access, Visa SEATS: 50. Private parties: 60 main room, 20 private room. Car park, 12 places. Children's helpings L. No pipes in dining-room. Wheelchair access. Music.

WYLAM Northumberland map 7

▲ *Laburnum House*

Wylam NE41 8AJ COOKING 1
WYLAM (0661) 852185 COST £32

'It would be so easy to walk past this former shop not realising the delights inside' was the comment of a satisfied summer visitor who chose smoked pheasant, duck with raspberries and crème brûlée from a blackboard menu. The repertoire is so slow-moving that they could carve the names of dishes in stone, chalking in the prices. It would be contentious to say that Kenn Elliott's creations are so finished they merit no improvement. The short wine list has some good growers and prices are fair. House wines are £7.

CHEF: Kenn Elliott PROPRIETORS: Rowan Mahon and Kenn Elliott OPEN: Tue to Sat, D only (L by arrangement; Sun and Mon D residents only) MEALS: 6.30 to 10 PRICES: £21 (£27) CARDS: Access, Amex, Diners, Visa SEATS: 40. Private parties: 40 main room. Children's helpings. Wheelchair access (1 step; also WC). Music ACCOMMODATION: 4 rooms, all with bath/shower. B&B £40 to £50. Children welcome. Pets welcome. TV. Scenic. Doors close at midnight

---

YATTENDON Berkshire map 2

▲ *Royal Oak*

COUNTY RESTAURANT OF THE YEAR

The Square, Yattendon RG16 0UF COOKING 3
HERMITAGE (0635) 201325 COST £47

In the course of the year this pub-hotel-restaurant has been the subject of a management buy-out. Under Richard and Kate Smith, now exclusively at the Beetle & Wedge, Moulsford (see entry), it had an enviable threefold reputation as a pleasant country hotel of no great pretension, a restaurant serving reliable yet adventurous food, and a pub where the food was of the same character as in the restaurant. Value was great. It was a 'mould-breaker', to use the words of PR hype. The mixture is much as before and many's the traveller who has been given gracious welcome, fed good fish soup and excellent mussels marinière in the lounge, been permitted a snooze undisturbed, then driven on well satisfied. There is a willingness to accommodate. The more formal restaurant – polished furniture, immaculate place-settings – serves dishes which avoid too much complexity, such as a warm salad of scallops, wild mushrooms and pine nuts arranged around a 10-point star of radicchio and endive, and scattered with asparagus for good measure. Alternatively, a magnificently risen cheese soufflé had a wild mushroom sauce poured into a hole excavated in its centre. It was a pity that the cheese was an evanescent flavour, for in all else it was exact. Grilled turbot on a bed of spinach had a trimming of caviare and an excellent light lemon sauce. Lamb, though well-trimmed, did not convince a breeder of Welsh mountain sheep for flavour, but again, execution was good. In the vegetable line, Royal Oak goes for numbers: 10 different things on a plate ('would have done as a stand-alone vegetarian dish,' wrote one). This meal, which is not untypical, had shown few lapses and proper respect for materials, although unfortunately the cheeseboard was too chilled, under-ripe and under-sold, the waitress knowing no more than the names. Some cavil, too, has been made about the prices: do not expect this to be a cheap restaurant even if the bar does offer better value. Restricted virtually to France, the wine list allows much sound drinking at or around £15. Quality is good throughout; the glass award will be maintained only if the buying policies of the previous owners are kept to or improved. Comments about the restaurant should also be read in the context of the bar, still serving bold, inventive cooking, with value a strong point. It gets very busy and the expensive cars litter the village junction – though there is a car park. Locals sometimes fume at the untidiness of it all.

CHEF: Dominique Orizet PROPRIETOR: Julie Huff OPEN: all week (Sun D bar meals only) MEALS: 12 to 2, 7.30 to 10 PRICES: £27 (£39) CARDS: Access, Amex, Visa, Diners SEATS: 30. 10 tables outside. Private parties: 30 main room, 8 private room. Car park, 35 places. Children's helpings. No cigars/pipes in dining-room. Wheelchair access. Music. Fax: (0635) 201926 ACCOMMODATION: 5 rooms, all with bath/shower. B&B £60 to £80. Children welcome. Baby facilities. Pets welcome by arrangement. Afternoon teas. Garden. Fishing. Golf. TV. Phone. Scenic. Doors close at 12.30. Confirm by 6 (*Which? Hotel Guide*)

YORK North Yorkshire map 5

▲ *Ivy Restaurant, Grange Hotel*

NEW ENTRY

Clifton, York YO3 6AA COOKING 2
YORK (0904) 644744 COST £19–£38

The newly opened Grange is a Regency townhouse, but a minute or two from the Minster. People speak well of it as a place to stay; rooms of 'comfy elegance' give a country-house atmosphere. There is a brasserie in addition to the restaurant, the latter the showcase of Cara Baird, a young chef who has been much bruited to the locality as fresh from the Gavroche. Her racy *curriculum vitae* is as thoroughbred as the horses whose pictures cover the restaurant walls – so many are there that the expectation is at least a view of the racecourse from the windows – and her training as *saucier* comes out in the finished dishes. The sceptical say 'everything swimming in sauce', the impressed aver 'the sauces have both purity and quality'. These points were identified in a meal which included saddle of venison with juniper sauce and beef with madeira sauce. Satisfaction has been voiced after a salmon mousse wrapped in a blanched cabbage leaf, a leek and pimento soup, lamb with wild mushrooms, salmon with cucumber and dill, and good ice-cream. The style is one that enjoys pastry and glazing things, sometimes to extinction, under the grill. Cheese has appeared highly refrigerated and served without the waiter knowing what varieties made up the selection. The wine list is adequate but unambitious and offers fair range and decent drinking below £15; thereafter, prices climb steeply. House wine is £9.

CHEF: Cara Baird PROPRIETOR: Jeremy Cassel OPEN: all week, exc Sat L MEALS: 12.30 to 2.30, 7 to 10.15 PRICES: £23 (£32), Set L £12.50 (£19), Set D £20 (£27). Card slips closed CARDS: Access, Amex, Diners, Visa SEATS: 60. Private parties: 60 main room, 30 private rooms. Car park, 26 places. Vegetarian meals. Children's helpings. No pipes in dining-room. Wheelchair access (3 steps; also WC). Music. Fax: (0904) 612453
ACCOMMODATION: 29 rooms, all with bath/shower. Rooms for disabled. B&B £82 to £128. Children welcome. Baby facilities. Pets welcome. Afternoon teas. TV. Phone. Scenic. Confirm by 6 previous day

Kites

13 Grape Lane, York YO1 2HU — COOKING 1
YORK (0904) 641750 — COST £26

Grape Lane is a building site, but when the work is finished it will again be a pleasant alley not far from the Minster. Kites is up a vertiginous staircase, not for the frail, and has a decorative finish called by the charitable 'early days of Habitat' and in need of serious refurbishment. Tables are badly sited, and space is at a premium. Reports are so inconsistent that entry in this *Guide* must express reservation. The strong points are the service – young, inexperienced, but willing and pleasing – and the range of the menu, taking in Thai seasonings, French bourgeois, Japanese sushi and 'modern British'. Boo Orman is an apostle of eclecticism. Prices are not high. Plenty gets recommendation: Thai salad, lamb with sorrel sauce, cod with tomato and pepper salsa, leg of lamb. These can work, they are not expensive and tastes are enjoyable. On the down-side, desserts seem lacklustre and there have been too many disappointments for comfort. Kites could fly, but the breeze of devotion to quality and the determination not to send out less than perfect food needs to blow more constantly. The wine list is inventive and informed; house wine is £7.50.

CHEFS: Belinda Roper and Pauline Waines PROPRIETOR: Boo Orman OPEN: Mon to Sat, D only, and Sun L MEALS: 12 to 2, 6.30 to 10.30 (6 to 11 Sat) PRICES: £14 (£22) CARDS: Access, Visa SEATS: 48. Private parties: 30 main room. Vegetarian meals. Children's helpings. No-smoking area. Music

Melton's

COUNTY RESTAURANT OF THE YEAR — NEW ENTRY

7 Scarcroft Road, York YO2 1ND — COOKING 2*
YORK (0904) 634341 — COST £18–£28

This small restaurant in an unremarkable area about one mile from the city centre, part of a Victorian terrace, has already earned residents' and visitors' affection. Michael Hjort worked for the Roux brothers for some years and his own inventive style of cooking reflects their influence. But, above all, he has assessed his market sensitively and provides good food at very fair all-in prices. Reports are both consistent and insistent on the reliability and effort of the kitchen. Dishes such as Jerusalem artichoke mousse, rack of lamb with parsley and breadcrumbs, and sea bass with baked fennel have been heartily endorsed. Portions are generous and attention to detail is close: vegetables are linked to each main course and chosen to complement; mineral water, coffee and petits fours are free; bread and pasta are home-made. Chocolate truffle and the interesting selection of well-kept British and Irish cheeses have been recommended. The French, Italian and antipodean wine list is as fairly priced as the food, with a good dozen bottles under £10 and a decent selection of halves.

CHEF: Michael Hjort PROPRIETORS: Michael and Lucy Hjort OPEN: Tue to Sat, D only (L by arrangement) CLOSED: 3 weeks from 24 Dec, Good Fri, 1 week from Aug bank hol MEALS: 7 (5.30 by arrangement) to 10 PRICES: £19 (£23), Set L £14 (£18) to £14.50 (£19). Net prices, card slips closed CARDS: Access, Visa SEATS: 40. Private parties: 30 main room, 12 private room. Vegetarian meals. Children welcome. Wheelchair access (1 step). Music

▲ *Middlethorpe Hall*

Bishopthorpe Road, York YO2 1QP — COOKING 2
YORK (0904) 641241 — COST £20–£53

'A spectacular converted Queen Anne house next to the race course' is a reader's description that hardly does justice to the grandeur of this lordly hotel catering for well-heeled tourists, business people and – no doubt – devotees of the Sport of Kings. The kitchen ducks and dives between global modernity and British revivalism. Sea bass baked in vodka cream garnished with caviare, and tortellini of chicken and wild mushrooms with a vegetable, tomato and mustard-flavoured olive oil, share the bill with venison and rabbit pudding with Worcestershire sauce and turned vegetables. Complexity is everywhere: whole boned quail is wrapped in smoked bacon, garnished with collops of vension and served on a lentil and wild mushroom sauce. Neat arrangements of vegetables might include snow peas with ginger as well as swede purée. To finish, a glazed fresh fruit platter with japonaise meringue and vanilla ice-cream 'looked and tasted excellent', although the toasted muesli ice-cream accompanying a poached peach 'was not a good idea'. No wine list was sent this year. A glass award was given in 1991 and the owners remain the same.

CHEF: Kevin Francksen PROPRIETORS: Historic House Hotels Ltd OPEN: all week MEALS: 12.30 to 1.45, 7.30 to 9.45 PRICES: £32 (£44), Set L £14.90 (£20) to £16.90 (£22), Set D £29.25 (£35). Net prices, card slips closed CARDS: Access, Amex, Diners, Visa SEATS: 60. Private parties: 40 main room, 14, 20 and 40 private rooms. Car park, 70 places. No children under 8. Jacket and tie. Smoking after meal only. No music ACCOMMODATION: 30 rooms, all with bath/shower. Lift. B&B £92.50 to £134. No children under 8. Afternoon teas. Garden. TV. Phone. Scenic (*Which? Hotel Guide*)

19 Grape Lane

19 Grape Lane, York YO1 2HU — COOKING 2
YORK (0904) 636366 — COST £21–£38

'A phoenix risen from the ashes' is one reader's verdict, a year after a disastrous fire temporarily closed the restaurant. Last year's intelligence was understandably sparse; this year's crop of reports is unanimous in praise. Although the setting is still cramped, horizontally as well as vertically, and certainly lacking in privacy, the cooking scores because the use of ingredients is designed to display individual tastes and qualities; sauces complement rather than mask or overpower. Simplicity is a keynote in presentation and concept, the latter being modern but not adventurous. Collops of beef with a shallot sauce, medallions of hare with field mushrooms, and pork in a grainy mustard sauce are praised, as are traditional English puddings of Yorkshire treacle tart and Eve's pudding. Light lunches as well as a sample of the more substantial evening *carte* are now available, with both options reasonably priced. Generous pricing and an abundance of halves should encourage experiment from the succinct, intelligent and monthly French wine list. Paillard champagne at £21.50 is a bargain unlikely to see the end of 1992. House wine is £8.75.

CHEFS: Michael Fraser and Robert Laing PROPRIETORS: Gordon and Carolyn Alexander OPEN: Tue to Sat CLOSED: 2 weeks Feb, 2 weeks Sept/Oct MEALS: 12.30 to 1.45, 7.30 to 10.30 PRICES: £23 (£32), light L £14 (£21), Set D £17.95 (£25) SEATS: 34. Private parties: 20 main room. Children welcome. Wheelchair access (1 step). Music

Scotland

ABERDEEN Grampian map 8

Faraday's

NEW ENTRY

2 Kirk Brae, Cults, Aberdeen AB1 9SQ
ABERDEEN (0224) 869666

COOKING 1
COST £20–£37

A converted nineteenth-century hydroelectric sub-station is the unlikely setting for this restaurant in a suburb of Aberdeen. Outside is stark grey stone, inside is pure Victoriana, with high beams, long windows, patterned wallpaper and even a gallery over the bar. Ham and haddie with eggs, casserole of venison with mealie and 'chappit tatties' are rooted in Scotland, otherwise the kitchen plunders the globe for inspiration: satay, tagliatelle carbonara, barbecued spare ribs with teriyaki sauce, for instance. This approach can produce unexpected ideas, such as stir-fried scallops with paella, but readers enjoy the unusual combination of flavours. Good dishes have included smoked chicken and sweetcorn soup, black pudding with Bramley sauce, poached turbot with shrimp sauce, and chocolate mousse with coffee sauce. Pork Stroganoff is regularly praised, along with chicken tikka masala, and home-made honey and brandy ice-cream. Herbs are grown in a neighbour's garden, and bread is baked locally. A decent list of around 40 wines provides some reasonably priced drinking. House French is £10.90 a litre.

CHEF/PROPRIETOR: John Inches OPEN: Mon to Sat, exc Mon L CLOSED: first 2 weeks Jan MEALS: 12.15 to 2, 7 to 9.30 PRICES: L £11 (£20), D £16 (£26), Set D Fri and Sat £22.50 (£31). Service 10%. Card slips closed. CARDS: Access, Visa SEATS: 42. Private parties: 32 main room. Car park, 12 places. Vegetarian meals with prior notice. Children's helpings L. Wheelchair access (also WC). Music. Air-conditioned

Silver Darling

Pocra Quay, Footdee, Aberdeen AB2 1DQ
ABERDEEN (0224) 576229

COOKING 2
COST £20–£40

'Incredible' is how one inspector described this restaurant, the first building on the quay, with spectacular views of the sea and close-ups of fishing boats leaving the harbour. Inside, the small dining-room is 'heavy with French accents, coupled with equally heavy Aberdonian tones'. The menu is all about fish, and Didier Dejean makes the best of the local catch, often marinating and barbecuing it in the style of his native Provence. There are numerous combinations of monkfish, scallops and langoustines; grilled sea trout is served with fresh fennel and shallot butter; papillote of red mullet, sole and turbot comes tinged with a provençal sauce flavoured with tomato and basil; brochette of seafood is served on a pool of beurre nantais. Readers have also praised salmon and crab terrine, salad of warm scallops and langoustines with hazelnut dressing, and crawfish tails and monkfish in saffron and mussel cream. Portions are ample. Sweets are thoroughly Gallic: hot apple tart with a sabayon; Grand Marnier soufflé served on a crêpe with orange butter sauce. Some reporters, however, have found prices excessive, cooking inconsistent and service slack, particularly on Sundays. But bear in mind the lack of food of comparable quality in the area. The wine list is exclusively French and mark-ups are high. House Côtes du Rhône is £8.75. There are plans to open a new Aberdeen brasserie in late autumn 1991 where Didier Dejean hopes to be chef. We hope his proposed departure does not affect the standards here.

CHEF: Didier Dejean PROPRIETORS: Didier Dejean, Norman Faulks and Catherine Wood OPEN: all week, exc Sat L and Sun L, and Sun D Christmas to Easter CLOSED: 2 weeks from Christmas MEALS: 12 to 2, 7 to 10 PRICES: £24 (£33), Set L £12.50 (£20) to £18 (£25) CARDS: Access, Amex, Visa SEATS: 35. Private parties: 35 main room. Car park. Children welcome. Wheelchair access (1 step; also WC). Music

ABERFELDY Tayside map 8

▲ *Atkins at Farleyer House*

Aberfeldy PH15 2JE
ABERFELDY (0887) 20332
from Aberfeldy take B846 to Kinloch Rannoch for 2m

COOKING 3*
COST £24–£53

Farleyer House started life in the sixteenth century as a croft. Enlarged after the '45 to a bailiff's house, the addition of an east wing saw it turned into the main residence of the Menzies. Despite its age and history the house has a suburban air, its disparate features brought together by white rendering and the draught-proof plate-glass windows. The interior decoration, however, is all comfort and warmth, and the scenery is magnificent. Frances Atkins, who arrived with her husband Bill in 1989, continues to oversee the kitchen, making the most of local produce. This is British cooking interpreted in an original manner, with composed dishes juxtaposing flavours, textures and tastes, especially sweet and sour. A winter dish of mignons of marinated hill venison, venison sausage and crisp potatoes in a mustard sauce, served with apple and sage jelly, shows some of these ideas at work. Adjustments still need to be made in the balancing; a lime sauce accompanying ravioli filled with lobster and langoustine was too intrusive, killing the delicate flavours of the shellfish and some heavy-handed salting of wild mushrooms marred an otherwise enjoyable dish of venison and fillet steak with a rich port sauce. But there is still a body of opinion that suggests the kitchen can do no wrong. Main courses of breast of duck with a filo basket of leek, orange and foie gras and poached halibut with a ragoût of mussels and samphire have been very well received. Baking, soups and ices are strengths. Invention continues to the dessert stage: cold rhubarb soufflé, 'with the rhubarb picked from the garden that afternoon', had just the right measure of tartness. Breakfasts are reported 'superb'. The proprietors say they plan to 'open a café-bistro in October '91 to serve residents, non-residents and children. Thus we will accept family bookings in the hotel.' Careful buying from good wine merchants brings many fine bottles on to the list. France is treated handsomely and beyond that, selection is cleverly edited but catholic. There are many good bottles below and around £15; thereafter pricing policy is less kind, putting too much mid-quality wine into a luxury bracket. House French is £9.50.

CHEFS: Frances Atkins and Tony Heath PROPRIETORS: Gerald and Frances Atkins OPEN: all week, exc Mon L MEALS: 12.30 to 1.30, 7.30 to 8.30 PRICES: Set L £17.50 (£24) to £25 (£33), Set D £27.50 (£35) to £35 (£44) CARDS: Access, Amex, Visa SEATS: 30. Private parties: 30 main room, 12 private room. Car park, 14 places. No children under 10. Smart dress preferred. Wheelchair access (also WC). Music. Fax: (0887) 29430
ACCOMMODATION: 11 rooms, all with bath/shower. Rooms for disabled. D,B&B £90 to £200. Deposit: £25. No children under 10. Garden. Fishing. Golf. TV. Phone. Scenic. Doors close at midnight. Confirm by noon previous day (*Which? Hotel Guide*)

ABERFOYLE Central map 8

Braeval Old Mill

By Aberfoyle, Stirling FK8 3UY
ABERFOYLE (087 72) 711 COOKING 3*
on A81, 1m from Aberfoyle COST £21–£44

The spartan grey stone of this lovingly restored mill is foil to the vibrant colours of the pictures, collages and other decorative touches in this most personal and impressive restaurant. The common denominator of all reports this year, and last, is improvement. People return repeatedly. 'Since my last visit the standard of cooking has again moved up noticeably and compares favourably with the best in Scotland.' Lunch is now served through the week, measure perhaps of growing recognition. The format is disarmingly simple: a choice of four dishes at dinner, two or three at lunch. Readers are struck by the consistency across the range: 'Each of my three courses pleased enormously – a smoked salmon and avocado soufflé was cooked exactly and had flavour; halibut on a bed of spinach with shellfish sauce and several scallops as garnish was well-judged and again passed the flavour test.' Dessert of a bramble sorbet within a tuile basket on a passion-fruit coulis was a fitting conclusion. The success of the cooking seems to rest on its understatement, which masks extreme skill in composition of sauces as well as accurate cooking. Fiona Nairn runs the front-of-house and her presence is always appreciated – 'good food, charming people too', was one reaction. A fairly priced house selection of 16 bottles, from £8 to £12.50, sets the tone for the entire wine list: catholic in range and even-handed between the Old and New Worlds. It would be invidious to select, but the burgundies, Australians and Italian reds show faultless attention to growers and vintages. Almost anything from the list could be chosen with confidence. A bottle is awarded this year, for intelligence and approachability. CELLARMAN'S CHOICE: St-Véran 1988, Vincent, £17; Chivite Gran Reserva 1981, £15.

CHEF: Nick Nairn PROPRIETORS: Nick and Fiona Nairn OPEN: Tue to Sun, exc Sun D CLOSED: 2 weeks Feb, 1 week May to June, 2 weeks Nov MEALS: 12 to 1.30, 7 to 9.30 PRICES: Set L £15 (£21) to £17.50 (£24), Set D £28 (£35) to £30 (£37). Card slips closed CARDS: Access, Visa SEATS: 34. Private parties: 34 main room. Car park, 16 places. No children under 10. Smart dress preferred. No cigars/pipes in dining-room. Wheelchair access (1 step; also WC). No music

ACHILTIBUIE Highland map 8

▲ *Summer Isles Hotel* 🍷

Achiltibuie IV26 2YG COOKING 2*
ACHILTIBUIE (085 482) 282 COST £43

The directions need clarifying, as the hotel brochure explains: 'Ten miles north of Ullapool turn along the twisting single-track road that skirts lochs Lurgain, Baddagyle and Osgaig. Fifteen miles later you will come upon a straggle of white cottages gazing over the bay. This is Achiltibuie.' Dinners are served almost exclusively to residents who stay usually for several nights, enjoying the civilised remoteness of the place, or indulging passions for walking and birdwatching. Although the five-course dinner menu offers no choice other than for pudding, Mark Irvine is happy to discuss alternative dishes where necessary. The style is dictated by local produce, backed up by vegetables from the Irvines' solar-powered hydroponicum. One meal in September began with sorrel soup, followed by Stilton soufflé, then a main course of halibut with asparagus and vermouth served with a salad of tomato, melon and basil. Butterscotch ice-cream to finish was memorable. On other days there might be haunch of roe deer with smoked bacon and juniper berries, or roast best end of black-faced lamb with braised lettuce and honey. This is cooking firmly set in its home country. Mark Irvine serves and explains the cheeses, which always include several Scottish locals, and is knowledgeable about his wines. This wine list is a gem, although clarity is a weak point: in the best represented areas, Burgundy and Bordeaux, closely typed names arranged only approximately in price order, may confuse the reader. A pity, since there are many fine bottles, although prices look daunting. Closer inspection reveals good value: Fronsac la Rivière 1979 at £17.50, Ch. Potensac 1987 at £12 and a Savigny from Tollot-Beaut for £17.50. Alsace is strong and prices are almost generous. No house wines, but there are recommendations each evening. CELLARMAN'S CHOICE: Riesling Réserve Personelle 1985, Kuentz-Bas, £14; Châteauneuf-du-Pape, Ch. de Beaucastel 1981, £20.

CHEF: Chris Firth-Bernard PROPRIETORS: Mark and Geraldine Irvine OPEN: all week, D only CLOSED: mid-Oct to Easter MEALS: 8 PRICES: Set D £28 (£36) SEATS: 28. Private parties: 8 main room. Car park, 24 places. Vegetarian meals. No children under 8. No smoking in dining-room. No music. One sitting ACCOMMODATION: 12 rooms, all with bath/shower. B&B £39 to £79. No children under 8. Pets welcome. Fishing. Scenic. Doors close at 10.30. Confirm by 6 (*Which? Hotel Guide*)

The Guide *is totally independent, accepts no free hospitality, and survives on the proceeds from copies sold each year.*

ANSTRUTHER Fife map 8

Cellar

24 East Green, Anstruther KY10 3AA
ANSTRUTHER (0333) 310378

COOKING 3
COST £20–£38

The good news is that Peter Jukes has opened another fish restaurant, called the Lindsay Room, on the Kilconquhar Estate at Colinsburgh, Fife. Here, a protegé cooks in similar vein to Peter Jukes himself, giving some hope to those who can't get into the Cellar. But the best news is that the Cellar is as good as ever in providing very fresh fish, accurately and directly cooked and served in unassuming yet pleasant surroundings. You pass through a courtyard, some 50 yards up a hill at the north end of the harbour, and enter a rough-stone and tiled restaurant with exposed beams and low ceilings. It feels as right as the cooking. At lunch there is an inexpensive and short *carte*, at dinner a four-course set-price menu with choices and, on midweek winter evenings, a 'supper' menu which keeps the prices even nearer the pinched pockets of the Neuk of Fife. Pinched pockets may also be the reason that several reports have noticed portions getting smaller this year. The menu progresses in stately fashion, and changes on it could be described as subtle rather than earth-shattering. Grilled halibut with hollandaise, and turbot and scallops with Chardonnay sauce are mentioned with frequency, as are the crayfish and mussel bisque served as a second course and the quiche of lobster and smoked sea trout. Service is invariably pleasant. People wonder if more change would be a good thing, but who wishes to rock a boat sailing so true? The wine list offers remarkable value and quality over a long range that takes in as much from the New World as from the classic regions. The cellar is bought so that comparative study is a simple thing to arrange. Go in a large party and extract the most from it. House wines are £8.50 and tipping is mercifully discouraged.

CHEF: Peter Jukes PROPRIETORS: Peter and Vivien Jukes OPEN: Tue to Sat, D; Fri and Sat L (Mon D July to Oct) CLOSED: 2 weeks Christmas and New Year, 1 week May MEALS: 12.30 to 1.30, 7 to 9.30 PRICES: £13 (£20), Set D £15 (£21) to £25 (£32). Card slips closed CARDS: Access, Amex, Visa SEATS: 32. Private parties: 32 main room. No children under 5. No smoking. Wheelchair access (also WC). Music

ARISAIG Highland map 8

▲ *Arisaig House* NEW ENTRY

Beasdale, By Arisaig PH39 4NR
ARISAIG (068 75) 622
on A830, 3m E of Arisaig village

COOKING 1
COST £17–£54

1990 was a year of adjustment for the Smithers, owners of this fine hunting lodge set in magnificent scenery – hills, beach, burn, woods and meadows – and surrounded at closer quarters by excellent gardens. The grand, ostensibly formal hotel absorbed a new chef in Matthew Burns. Reports since have been mixed. High prices inevitably set up expectations (even a bowl of soup, sandwich and coffee in the bar at lunchtime may cost up to £18 for two), and visitors who come for the food alone also find the menus unpriced. These two facts may contribute to some hard words about variable flavours and execution: a carrot and orange soup that tasted principally of ginger, a blackcurrant coulis like 'battery acid', and strawberry mille-feuille with which one diner played 'hunt the strawberry'. On the other hand, the set menu of five courses, with a couple of alternatives if you don't fancy the chef's selection, has been praised for materials – especially fish – and good cooking of dishes like scallops with a fresh herb butter, chicken mousse with fine and intense wild mushrooms and salmon with a dill sauce. Sauces are not well reported, and banana fritters were 'large balls of batter with minimal banana'. The selection of wines is fine and predominantly French but relentless application of a standard mark-up makes most of the wines pricier than might be expected. The few wines below £15 are of good provenance and are fair value.

CHEF: Matthew Burns PROPRIETORS: Ruth and John Smither OPEN: all week CLOSED: early Nov to early Mar MEALS: 12.30 to 2, 7.30 to 8.30 PRICES: Set L £7.50 (£17) to £15 (£26), Set D £33 (£45). Card slips closed CARDS: Access, Visa SEATS: 34. 5 tables outside. Private parties: 8 main room. Car park, 15 places. Vegetarian meals. No children under 10. Jacket and tie. No smoking in dining-room. Wheelchair access (1 step). No music ACCOMMODATION: 15 rooms, all with bath/shower. D,B&B £79.50 to £215. Deposit: £50. Rooms for disabled. No children under 10. Afternoon teas. Garden. Snooker. TV. Phone. Scenic. Doors close at midnight. Confirm by 4.30 (*Which? Hotel Guide*)

AUCHMITHIE Tayside map 8

But 'n' ben

Auchmithie DD11 5S0 COOKING 1
ARBROATH (0241) 77223 COST £12–£20

Auchmithie, a working coastal village, is both difficult to find (follow the A92 northwards until the village is signposted) and has small claim on the affections of outsiders except for this small restaurant. Proclaim it they should. 'Thank goodness we booked. It was packed for lunch on a late October Thursday,' a reader wrote. Traditional Scottish cooking at three meals, lunch, high tea and dinner, unites the best local produce: fish from the Arbroath boats, vegetables and herbs from the garden, seasonal game as hunters supply it. The local speciality is Arbroath smokie served hot and buttered. A platter of fish and shellfish 'is quite an experience...fresh from the sea with a plentiful supply of plain cooked vegetables'. Monkfish is cooked in a fennel and white wine sauce, fresh squid in a ragoût. Lobsters can be a bargain. 'My son was allowed a whole lobster on the premise that at £11 per creature they must be small. Not so.' A smoky atmosphere has marred for some the enjoyment and taste of fresh food. House wine from Bordeaux is £5.50.

CHEFS: Margaret and Angus Horn PROPRIETORS: Margaret, Iain and Angus Horn OPEN: all week, exc Tue, and Sun D CLOSED: 26 Dec to Jan 3 MEALS: 12 to 2.30, 7.30 to 9.30 (high tea 4 to 5.30) PRICES: £18 (£12), D £12 (£17). Card slips closed CARDS: Access, Visa SEATS: 34. 2 tables outside. Private parties: 40 main room. Car park, 10 places. Vegetarian meals. Children's helpings. No smoking. Wheelchair access (also WC) No music

BALLATER Grampian map 8

▲ *Tullich Lodge*

Ballater AB3 5SB
BALLATER (033 97) 55406
on A93 1m E of Ballater

COOKING 2
COST £11–£35

'Little remains of the village of Tullich,' says the brochure, 'though it was once the oldest Royal Burgh on Deeside and a settlement since Pictish times.' The Lodge is a pink granite Victorian mansion, full of 'an eclectic mixture of interesting pieces', according to one report. Neil Bannister and Hector Macdonald are seasoned campaigners in the crusade for better food and hospitality. Lunch is three courses, dinner runs to four and menus read like a litany of British food: terrine of hare with rowan jelly, cream of cauliflower soup, baked fillet of sole with shrimps, Scottish strawberries and Scottish cheeses made up one July dinner. October might bring braised lentils and liver, or pork, apple and celery soup, filleted Dover sole and chocolate soufflé – a sign that the kitchen can look further afield for inspiration. The overall enterprise and activity is impressive, taking in home-baked breads, home-smoked fish and – provided there is a resident gardener – home-grown vegetables. Neil Bannister has wise thoughts on healthy eating, and voices them in a pleasantly understated way. Cream appears less than it once did, pastry is made with a mixture of flour and ground almonds or hazelnuts to reduce the fat levels; olive oil often replaces butter, sweets are low in sugar. The 50-bottle wine list is an intelligent spread of carefully chosen wines and prices are fair. France continues to dominate. There are good half-bottles. House wine is £8.

CHEF: Neil Bannister PROPRIETORS: Hector Macdonald and Neil Bannister OPEN: all week CLOSED: mid-Dec to end Mar MEALS: 1, 7.30 to 8.30 PRICES: Set L £6 (£11), Set D £22 (£29). Card slips closed CARDS: Access, Amex, Diners, Visa SEATS: 26. Private parties: 10 main room. Car park. Vegetarian meals. Children's helpings L. Jacket and tie. No smoking in dining-room. Wheelchair access (also WC). No music. One sitting. Fax: (033 97) 55397 ACCOMMODATION: 10 rooms, all with bath/shower. D,B&B £88 to £176. Children welcome. Baby facilities. Pets welcome. Garden. Fishing. Golf. TV. Phone. Scenic. Confirm by 5 (*Which? Hotel Guide*)

BIGGAR Strathclyde map 8

▲ *Shieldhill Hotel*

NEW ENTRY

Quothquan, Biggar ML12 6NA
BIGGAR (0899) 20035
from Biggar, take B7016 towards Carnwath
for 2m, then left on Shieldhill Road for 1m

COOKING 1
COST £41

Few country hotels can boast they were established in 1199. However, the present owners have made extensive renovations to bring the grey stone house firmly into the late-twentieth century. Open fires, wood panelling, Laura Ashley drapes, subdued lighting and crested carpets aim for elegance. The menu, changing daily with four choices per course, plays with local Scottish produce: steamed Oban mussels, noisettes of Lanarkshire lamb, tournedos of

Scotch beef fillet. Dishes are elaborately constructed and fashionable: a crispy basket of creamy wild mushrooms with breasts of wood pigeon on a blueberry and thyme essence; venison with a raspberry and rosemary jus lié topped with a ginger cream, the ginger successfully cutting through the gamey richness of the meat. The ambition and adventure coming from the kitchen have resulted in some satisfactory meals, though marked by lapses: a roast leg of pigeon topping a filo parcel of partridge was overcooked whilst the accompanying blueberry sauce was too sweet; an orange and chive sauce judged too harsh for scallops. Home-made bread comes in four guises. Staff are eager to please. The wine list concentrates on France with forays into the New World and prices are fair. House wine is £8.50.

CHEF: David Cleunas PROPRIETORS: Jack Greenwald and Christine Dunstan OPEN: all week D, Fri to Sun L MEALS: 12 to 2, 7 to 9 PRICES: £25 (£34) CARDS: Access, Amex, Diners, Visa SEATS: 30. Private parties: 32 main room, 12 private room. Car park, 50 places. Vegetarian meals. Children's helpings. Smart dress preferred. No smoking in dining-room. Wheelchair access. Music. Fax: (0899) 21092 ACCOMMODATION: 11 rooms, all with bath/shower. B&B £88 to £100. Deposit: 50%. Children welcome. Baby facilities. Garden. TV. Phone. Scenic. Doors close at midnight

BLAIRGOWRIE Tayside map 8

▲ *Kinloch House Hotel*

Blairgowrie PH10 6SG
ESSENDY (025 084) 237 COOKING 2
on A923, 3m W of Blairgowrie COST £9–£30

'Twenty-five acres of wooded policies and parkland', wide-horned Highland cattle and fine views are external characteristics of this Edwardian house that has been done out within to preserve the illusion of the good old days of lairds, guns and ghillies. Some may call it pretentious, but most consider the Shentalls' enthusiasm genuine, the place comfortable and the cooking for the pleasantly decorated dining-room satisfactory. The fixed-price *carte* changes all the time, but is buttressed by a semi-permanent, short list of luxury items: venison, prawns, Barbary duck and steaks. The style sometimes harks back to the days of tropical fruit: one spring menu kicked off with a melon, citrus, kiwi fruit and grape salad on a raspberry coulis, with champagne sorbet and mint before a middle course of chilled avocado and strawberry soup. For the rest, it is country-house cooking of acceptable standard, although not without lapses. Best reports are for the straight cooking of Scottish raw materials: game and shellfish. You may never progress beyond the bar: the number of malts on offer seems to grow each year and a kilted David Shentall will act as eager guide. The list is strongest in a flight of clarets (not cheap) and has well-bred burgundies both red and white. House wines are £7.90.

'I have just returned from a three-day stay at a restaurant-with-rooms where all 10 diners (the maximum seating available) had come through The Good Food Guide.*'*
On eating in Yorkshire

CHEF: Bill McNicoll PROPRIETORS: David and Sarah Shentall OPEN: all week MEALS: 12.30 to 2, 7 to 9.15 PRICES: Set L £5.50 (£9) to £13.50 (£17), Set D £20.75 (£25). Net prices, card slips closed CARDS: Access, Amex, Diners, Visa SEATS: 60. Private parties: 30 main room, 25 and 30 private rooms. Car park, 40 places. No children under 7. Jacket and tie. No smoking in dining-room. Wheelchair access. No music. Fax: (025 084) 333 ACCOMMODATION: 21 rooms, all with bath/shower. Rooms for disabled. D,B&B £69.75 to £132. Baby facilities. Pets welcome (some rooms). Garden. Fishing. TV. Phone. Scenic. Doors close at midnight (*Which? Hotel Guide*)

CAIRNDOW Strathclyde map 8

Loch Fyne Oyster Bar

Clachan Farm, Cairndow PA26 8BH COOKING 2
CAIRNDOW (049 96) 217 and 264 COST £24

'We were delighted to find the restaurant in the middle of a hailstorm at lunchtime. The food was first-class, such a surprise in such a location, and so reasonable.' This judgement from a reader is shared by most of those who go to this simple café-cum-restaurant, smokehouse and produce shop at the head of the loch. Comfort is adequate but expect no luxury – someone suggested it was too cool in January! Just enjoy the oysters, shellfish and smoked fish or meats. The menu is served all day, every day. Service is ever amiable, the wine list is fine for Fyne. House white is £5.95. Were more cooking done, this place would deserve higher marks each year; it does its job with remarkable accuracy.

CHEF: Greta Cameron PROPRIETORS: Loch Fyne Oysters Ltd OPEN: all week MEALS: 9 to 9 PRICES: £14 (£20). Card slips closed CARDS: Access, Amex, Visa SEATS: 90. 10 tables outside. Private parties: 55 main room. Car park, 80 places. Vegetarian meals. Children's helpings on request. Wheelchair access (also WC). Music. Fax: (049 96) 234

CALLANDER Central map 8

▲ *Roman Camp Hotel* NEW ENTRY

off Main Street, Callander FK17 8BG COOKING 2*
CALLANDER (0877) 30003 COST £24–£46

Designed as a hunting lodge for the Dukes of Perth in 1625, this hotel takes its name from a more ancient site nearby. Clipped yews stand like sentinels against the improbably pink walls, and the grey slate roof is broken by a turret over the chapel. 'Such an elegant and enchanting hotel deserves a fine standard of cooking.' Perhaps with the same thought in mind, the owners have acquired chef Simon Burns from Cromlix House, Kinbuck (see entry), several glens away. His sophisticated but florid fixed-price menu changes daily, depending on the availability of ingredients. Salmon is from the river, game from local shoots, herbs and salads from the hotel garden. The result is classy, up-market hotel cooking, which comes, as usual, at a price. Dishes show that the kitchen aims high: Dover sole mousse 'freckled with lumpfish roe', parsnip consommé, warm duck salad pointed up with slices of pickled apple, venison with raspberry sauce. Main courses are preceded by a complimentary sorbet. Other recommendations have included terrine of Mallaig fish with steamed asparagus and beetroot-scented jus ('almost ethereal, it might have levitated off the plate'); pot-roast spring lamb with whole garlic cloves; and fillet of Angus beef served on dauphinois potatoes with Dijon mustard and spring onion sauce. The feeling is that this is a kitchen on the way up, although themes and elements are reiterated rather too often and desserts can be no more than adequate. A single cheese, such as Bonchester, is offered each evening with warm oatcakes. Service is efficient. A wide-ranging wine list has house French at £9.

CHEF: Simon Burns PROPRIETORS: Farquhar Mathieson Hotels Scotland OPEN: all week MEALS: 12 to 2, 7 to 9 PRICES: Set L £17 (£24), Set D £30 (£38). Card slips closed CARDS: Access, Amex, Diners, Visa SEATS: 45. Private parties: 47 main room, 32 private room. Car park, 30 places. Children's helpings (L only). No children under 5. Smart dress preferred. No smoking in dining-room. Wheelchair access (also WC). No music. Air-conditioned. Fax: (0877) 31533 ACCOMMODATION: 14 rooms, all with bath/shower. Rooms for disabled. B&B £75 to £110. Deposit: £30. Children welcome. Baby facilities. Pets welcome. Afternoon teas. Garden. Fishing. TV. Phone. Scenic. Doors close at 11. Confirm by 6 (*Which? Hotel Guide*)

CANONBIE Dumfries & Galloway map 8

▲ *Riverside Inn*

Canonbie DG14 0UX COOKING 2
CANONBIE (038 73) 71512 and 71295 COST £18–£30

Recommendations for the bar meals balance those for the restaurant in this picture-book inn: 'Canonbie is straight from the set of Brigadoon, and the welcome is better than any in Europe; no effusiveness, just great hospitality, an uncanny feeling of belonging.' The bar food offers a choice of four or five pâtés, soup and excellent value in fish (haddock) and chips, or salmon and salad which 'would have made an ample lunch for two and still be good value at twice the price'. The restaurant menu, changing every day, keeps choice fairly short but shows the virtues of good buying, and of making the most of decent materials in dishes such as poached bantam egg in a madeira jelly, and farm duck roasted crisp, with a sage pudding, apples with calvados and a ginger and orange gravy. Vegetables (try the deep-fried cauliflower) are always plentiful. Value in the restaurant, where the price is for a five-course meal and coffee, is as palpable as in the bar. The wine list is by no means 'doctrinaire French', offering a whole-world view of wine production. Prices are again fair. Makers include serious people such as de Villaine, Vacheron, Mitchell in Clare Valley and João Pires. House wines are £6.75.

CHEFS/PROPRIETORS: Robert and Susan Phillips OPEN: Mon to Sat CLOSED: 2 weeks Feb and Nov MEALS: 12 to 2, 7.30 to 8.30 PRICES: £12 (£18), Set D £19.50 (£25). Card slips closed CARDS: Access, Visa SEATS: 28. 4 tables outside. Private parties: 28 main room. Car park, 25 places. Children's helpings. No smoking in dining-room. Wheelchair access (also WC). No music ACCOMMODATION: 6 rooms, all with bath/shower. Rooms for disabled. B&B £57 to £67. Deposit: £15. No children under 10. Garden. Fishing. TV. Scenic. Doors close at midnight. Confirm by 5 (*Which? Hotel Guide*)

CRINAN Strathclyde map 8

▲ *Lock 16 Seafood Restaurant, Crinan Hotel*

Crinan PA31 8SR COOKING 1*
CRINAN (054 683) 261 COST £53

Crinan is a tiny village at the top end of the canal connecting Loch Fyne to the Atlantic. Nick and Frances Ryan's hotel stands right by the water's edge and the views are spectacular. On the top floor is a glazed dining-room, as if a studio, simply furnished and with views of the setting sun for wallpaper. This is Lock 16, a seafood restaurant serving a set menu of the freshest produce as and when it is available. Recommendations are more emphatic than for the mainstream cooking in the hotel's main dining-room downstairs, to which hotel guests are normally directed. Only when the weather allows and when the local boats are working does Lock 16 open. The catch is landed 50 yards from the kitchen and delivered to the hotel slipway every evening. The five-course dinner has little choice and its centrepieces are always the day's catch (with time of delivery noted on the menu): split Sound of Jura lobster and jumbo Corryvreckan prawns presented with an array of tropical fruit, supplemented by Loch Fyne oysters and queenie clams. To start there are normally Galia melon or local mussels, followed by locally smoked wild salmon. To finish there is a dessert and cheese with oatcakes. Enthusiasm for the wine list may be muted by its verbosity and by the mark-ups at the higher end; quality and range, however, are very fine, and while half-bottles are limited, many carefully chosen bottles below £16 offer enjoyment and economy. House wine is £9.50. There are special dinner, bed and breakfast prices in winter.

CHEF: Nick Ryan PROPRIETORS: Nick and Frances Ryan OPEN: Tue to Sat, D only (L by arrangement) CLOSED: 5 days Christmas MEALS: 8 PRICES: Set D £35 (£44). Card slips closed CARDS: Access, Visa SEATS: 24. Private parties: 24 main room. Car park, 30 places. Vegetarian meals. Children welcome. Jacket and tie. Wheelchair access (also WC). One sitting. Fax: (054 683) 292 ACCOMMODATION: 22 rooms, all with bath/shower. Rooms for disabled. Lift. B&B £65 to £110. Deposit: £50. Children welcome. Baby facilities. Pets welcome. Afternoon teas. Garden. Fishing. Golf. TV. Phone. Scenic. Confirm by 6 (*Which? Hotel Guide*)

CROMARTY Highland map 8

Thistles

20 Church Street, Cromarty IV11 8XA COOKING 2*
CROMARTY (038 17) 471 COST £29

Le Chardon was anglicised as Thistles when the Wilkinsons came over from Arisaig House to set up their own shop here in a former pub. The west coast may be all holidays and fishing, but here the serious drilling side of Scotland's economy should provide the means to keep the restaurant going. David Wilkinson offers a short dinner menu of five choices at each course, served and interpreted with discreet style by his wife Alison. The cooking shows promise.

It encompasses the classical in dishes like sole Véronique, and toys with adventure in its tomato sorbet with melon, paw-paw with avocado and tapénade for a vegetarian dish, and by using coriander with chicken or with saddle of lamb first marinated in lime and garlic. The wine list, now at a 100-plus bottles, offers a fine range, albeit dominated by classic French areas. Selection is intelligent with Alsace well-represented and there is a decent spread of clarets. Prices throughout are fair. House wine is £8.40.

CHEF: David Wilkinson PROPRIETORS: Alison and David Wilkinson OPEN: Tue to Sat D and Sun L (L by arrangement on other days) MEALS: 12 to 2, 7.30 to 9 PRICES: £17 (£24). Card slips closed CARDS: Access, Visa SEATS: 26. Private parties: 30 main room. Vegetarian meals. Children's helpings. No smoking. Music

CUPAR Fife map 8

Ostlers Close

25 Bonnygate, Cupar KY15 4BU COOKING 3
CUPAR (0334) 55574 COST £19–£36

The consensus is that James Graham's small family-run restaurant is going from strength to strength. Menus follow the seasons, with faith firmly placed in local produce. Fish from the Pittenween boats is at its best between spring and autumn; game from nearby estates comes to the fore in winter. Ragoût of seafood in pesto sauce and roast breasts of partridge on a bed of lentils with coriander sauce are typical specialities defining the clearcut approach. Flavours are more important than fussy presentation. Supplies are backed up by the abundant output of the kitchen and garden: breads, pasta, ice-cream, herbs, jellies and chutneys are all home-produced. Reporters have been impressed with wild mushrooms in puff pastry, roast saddle of lamb with madeira sauce and half a dozen vegetables, sticky toffee pudding and iced meringue with passion-fruit sauce. Sauces obtain their character from stock reductions and alcohol, with sweetness provided by fruit jellies; butter and cream are not used extensively. Elsewhere menus have featured compote of fruits with sweet Muscat and garden rhubarb sorbet; pan-fried venison livers with hazelnut vinaigrette; fillet of halibut with local asparagus and fresh herb sauce; and honey, Drambuie and oatmeal ice-cream. The wine list is well-spread and includes a decent showing of half-bottles. House French is £6.90.

CHEF: James Graham PROPRIETORS: Amanda and James Graham OPEN: Tue to Sat CLOSED: 1 week Jun, 1 week Nov MEALS: 12.15 to 2, 7 to 9.30 (10 Fri and Sat) PRICES: L £13 (£19), D £22 (£30). Minimum £10. Card slips closed CARDS: Access, Visa SEATS: 28. Private parties: 22 main room. Children's helpings. No children under 6 D. No smoking during meals. Wheelchair access (1 step). No music

The 1993 Guide *will be published before Christmas 1992. Reports on meals are most welcome at any time of the year, but are extremely valuable in the spring. Send them to* The Good Food Guide, *FREEPOST, 2 Marylebone Road, London NW1 1YN. No stamp is needed when posting in the UK.*

DRUMNADROCHIT Highland map 8

▲ *Polmaily House Hotel*

Drumnadrochit IV3 6XT — COOKING 2*
DRUMNADROCHIT (045 62) 343 — COST £26–£42

The paintbrush and wallpaper-paste make stately progress through this improving house where the cooking of a pair of nightly set-dinner menus shows every sign of not being constrained by Highland location. The culinary intelligence ranges far over Europe, even if the materials are locally obtained and all the better for it. Fish and shellfish are especially remarked upon, but praise is also given to the degree of variety that is on offer to residents who stay more than one night. Braised veal with red pimentos, chillies and almonds, and baked chicken with tomato, garlic and armagnac were two springtime offerings, while salmon came with cucumber spaghetti, and there were fresh langoustines en brochette or crab salad with fennel and grapefruit. The large grounds, inhabited by bats at twilight, provide a civilised cordon against the sweeping plunges of the Highlands around; the packed lunches and first-rate breakfasts give stomach to cope with the hills' rigours. Fair range and fair prices make a very acceptable wine list. Good names are scattered liberally and there are decent half-bottles. House wines are from £7.50.

CHEFS: Alison Parsons and Barbara Drury PROPRIETORS: Alison and Nick Parsons OPEN: all week, D only CLOSED: end Oct to end Mar MEALS: 7.30 to 9.30 PRICES: Set D £20 (£26) to £28 (£35). Card slips closed CARDS: Access, Visa SEATS: 30. Private parties: 12 main room. Car park, 20 places. Vegetarian meals with prior notice. Children's helpings on request. No smoking in dining-room/bar area. Wheelchair access. No music ACCOMMODATION: 9 rooms, 7 with bath. B&B £45 to £100. Deposit: £25. Children welcome. Baby facilities. Garden. Swimming-pool. Tennis. Scenic. Doors close at midnight. Confirm by 4 (*Which? Hotel Guide*)

DRYBRIDGE Grampian map 8

Old Monastery

Drybridge AB5 2JB
BUCKIE (0542) 32660 — COOKING 1
2m S of junction A98 and A924 — COST £32

Once a monastic retreat (Gothic arches are pervasive), this is now a refuge for tired urbanites; the views and situation are sensational. 'We sampled perhaps the best chips in Scotland, and courgettes fried in batter that I have been unable to emulate,' wrote one correspondent who was more impressed by the meat (especially the lamb) than the first courses and who notes that when the dessert is said to be '"flavoured with Drambuie", you better make sure someone else is driving home'. The repertoire is conservative (for instance, garlic mushrooms, prawns and melon cubes, and pheasant and pistachio terrine), which puts the emphasis on the materials – good venison, salmon, beef and lamb. Results are often satisfying. The Grays are welcoming hosts, the cushion of warmth amidst the structural austerity. They report having tamed the vegetable garden this year. There is a decent, general-purpose list of wines, amply supplied with halves, and at fair prices. House wines start at £7.

CHEF: Douglas Gray PROPRIETORS: Douglas and Maureen Gray OPEN: Tue to Sat CLOSED: 2 weeks Nov, 3 weeks Jan MEALS: 12 to 1.45, 7 to 9.30 (10 Sat) PRICES: £19 (£27). Card slips closed CARDS: Access, Amex, Visa SEATS: 45. 2 tables outside. Private parties: 45 main room. Car park, 28 places. Children's helpings. No children under 8. No smoking. Wheelchair access (1 step). No music

DUNKELD Tayside map 8

▲ *Kinnaird House*

Kinnaird Estate,
By Dunkeld PH8 0LB
BALLINLUIG (079 682) 440
on B898, 4m NW of Dunkeld

COOKING 4
COST £23–£54

'Are all the houses in Perthshire awash in pale green paint?' asked a traveller from the far north. But he had no cavil with either the standards of decoration and housekeeping or the remarkable value of the luncheon served in this grandly furnished country-house hotel. Consider being delivered nuts and olives with drinks; canapés of cheese and herbs, a tiny sage and sausage turnover, and a pastry case with fish mousse; a hot appetiser of mousseline of lamb; a first course (first!) of mixed lettuces with fried quails' eggs and smoked venison before the main dish of grilled salmon stuffed with diced apples and basil, accompanied by turnip pâté, roast potatoes, a ring of carrot with green beans and courgettes filled with tomato. Excellent bread, and butter from Philippe Olivier, then coffee (decaffeinated has been criticised) and petits fours of candied Cape gooseberries, three sorts of chocolate and nougat completed the picture. John Webber invests a lot of effort in his cooking and the feeling is that the journey to Kinnaird House is worth the detour. Some of the meals are almost too elaborate – a gastronomic affair of several courses nearly came to a halt with too large a portion of wood pigeon *before* the roast lamb and *after* the monkfish – and it has been suggested that Webber retains too great an affection for strong reduction sauces. But simpler styles, with cleaner tastes, are available in dishes like a true pot-au-feu or sole fillets braised in cider and served with cabbage, smoked bacon and a thyme sauce. Dining is in grand style and can reach great heights, though a valley on one Sunday night was put down to Webber's absence. Service is exemplary. The 'Kinnaird suggestions' heading the wine list provide help for the uncertain. Generous provision of half-bottles is not matched, however, by the pricing; with little below £15, temptation to experiment may be dampened. A page of good French country wines showing careful choice provides some relief. Easing the gradient on the mark-up could encourage the award of a glass to an otherwise good list. House wine is £11. CELLARMAN'S CHOICE: Mercurey, Les Ormeaux 1987, Protheau, £22; Montrose, Cabernet/Merlot 1986, £25.

The Guide *office can quickly spot when a restaurateur is encouraging customers to write recommending inclusion – and sadly, several have been doing this in 1991. Such reports do not further a restaurant's cause. Please tell us if a restaurateur invites you to write to the* Guide.

CHEF: John Webber PROPRIETOR: C.C. Ward OPEN: all week CLOSED: Feb MEALS: 12.30 to 2, 7.30 to 9.15 PRICES: Set L £17.50 (£23) to £22 (£28), Set D £34.50 (£40) to £39 (£45). Net prices, card slips closed SEATS: 35. Private parties: 25 main room, 25 private room. Car park, 50 places. No children under 12. Jacket and tie. No smoking in dining-room. Wheelchair access (also WC). Music. Fax: (079 682) 289 ACCOMMODATION: 9 rooms, all with bath/shower. Rooms for disabled. Lift. B&B £85 to £130. No children under 12. Garden. Tennis. Fishing. Billiards. TV. Phone. Scenic. Confirm by 6 (*Which? Hotel Guide*)

DUNVEGAN Highland map 8

▲ *Harlosh Hotel* NEW ENTRY

By Dunvegan, Isle of Skye IV55 8ZG
DUNVEGAN (047 022) 367 COOKING 1
off A863, 3m S of Dunvegan COST £32

A half-dozen rooms and a score of seats (some can be breezy) in the dining-room make for a small yet mostly cosy hotel, in a very isolated position. The reader who noted that the same sheep was in the same place on the return journey after dinner was relying on shifting navigational sands. What is encouraging is that Peter Elford does care about what he cooks and battles against evident difficulties of supplies with determination and some success. Flavours come through in their own gravlax, strong soups such as celeriac and nutmeg, lamb with madeira sauce, turbot with red pimento sauce, and good ice-creams or hot filo parcels of pear, banana and cinnamon. The cooking is modern restaurant, not Scots ethnic – down to the faggots of French beans. Fish is perhaps the most interesting thing to explore: langoustines with ginger and coriander, and skate with black butter are noted examples. Booking is essential. The wine list is short indeed, with a paucity of halves. Malts may fill the gap. House wine is £6.75.

CHEF: Peter Elford PROPRIETORS: Peter and Lindsey Elford OPEN: all week, D only CLOSED: end Oct to Easter MEALS: 7 to 8.30 PRICES: £20 (£27). Minimum £10 CARDS: Access, Visa SEATS: 18. Private parties: 18 main room. Car park, 10 places. Vegetarian meals with prior notice. Children's helpings (early D only). No smoking in dining-room. Wheelchair access (1 step). Music ACCOMMODATION: 6 rooms, 5 with bath/shower. B&B £75 (doubles only). Deposit: £10. Children welcome. Baby facilities. Garden. Scenic. Doors close at 12.30am. Confirm by 5

Three Chimneys

Colbost, Dunvegan,
Isle of Skye IV55 8ZT
GLENDALE (047 081) 258 COOKING 2
on B884, 4m W of Dunvegan COST £21–£40

The awards that have come Three Chimneys' way in the past year have been merited for determination and enthusiasm alone. The isolated setting may be picturesque, but the croft is not *grande luxe* – low ceilings, small rooms and a tiny wine shop next door. Glittering prizes have reinforced the note of self-satisfaction sounded in the menu: 'Not many restaurants are as famous for their puddings as we are...' They may also be justification for spiky defence in response to any criticism or observation. The quality of Three Chimneys lies in the raw materials to hand, of which fish and shellfish are the best, followed by soft fruit in season, followed by meats. The seafood platter is the best way to sample the shellfish, even if it is expensive; other fish, wild salmon for instance, may come with an unexpected recipe, in one case strawberries and champagne sauce. Or, particularly on the lunch menu, it may be offered in some more obviously regional way, such as partan (crab) pie. Puddings are many; some are hot and substantial, others involve ice-cream. Prices may have risen beyond their natural level; surroundings cost little and service may be lugubrious and slow. Bread is good. A carefully chosen wine list ranges from Simi in the USA, Penfolds in Australia, and Stoneleigh Marlborough in New Zealand to good-class French at moderate prices. House French and Australian are from £7.95, and also available by the glass.

CHEF: Shirley Spear PROPRIETORS: Eddie and Shirley Spear OPEN: Mon to Sat CLOSED: Nov to end Mar MEALS: 12.30 to 2, 7 to 9 PRICES: L £16 (£21), D £26 (£33). Minimum £2.50 L, £15 D. Net prices CARDS: Access, Visa SEATS: 35. 2 tables outside. Private parties: 24 main room. Car park, 30 places. Vegetarian meals. Children welcome. No smoking. Music

EDINBURGH Lothian map 8

L'Auberge 🍷 NEW ENTRY

56 St Mary Street, EH1 1SX COOKING 2
031-556 5888 COST £14–£47

'It feels like provincial France in a nice unambitious way,' comments an inspector about this well-established restaurant in a street off the Royal Mile. Recently the kitchen has been given a boost with the arrival of William Reid – ex-Roux brothers, ex-Box Tree, Ilkley (see entry). 'The results are still uneven, but given what else is on offer, this is a blessing for Edinburgh.' He cooks a classy modern menu, with French influences and a loyalty to high-quality Scottish produce. Grilled crottin is perfectly judged with toasted almonds and a 'casually elegant little salad'; mousseline of seafood gets a yoghurt and herb dressing; suprême of pigeon is served on a heap of braised cabbage with red wine and shallot sauce. Otherwise, there might be roast guinea-fowl with calvados and tarragon, and escalope of salmon with vermouth butter sauce and braised lentils. Vegetables are outstanding: dainty new potatoes and elegantly strewn mixtures of mange-tout, beans and carrots. Some have found the sweets ordinary and the cheese in poor condition, but there is praise for the home-made breads. In addition to the *carte* there are business lunches, plus a four-course 'menu dégustation' on Friday evenings. Six grand cru and premier cru Chablis indicate the depth of the wine list, while a fine collection of petits châteaux, some from older years, shows readiness to lower the sights. It is at this lower end that decent value is found; mark-ups above £20 appear grasping. An abundance of half-bottles, especially dessert wines, and a page of regional wines allow some economy. House wine is £7.65.

Report forms are at the back of the book; write a letter if you prefer.

CHEF: William Reid PROPRIETOR: Daniel Wencker OPEN: Tue to Sun CLOSED: 2 weeks Jan, 1 week Easter MEALS: 12.15 to 2, 6.30 to 9.30 (10 Sat) PRICES: £27 (£39), Set L £8.95 (£14) to £11.95 (£17), Set Sun L £14.25 (£20), Set D £18.85 (£25) CARDS: Access, Amex, Diners, Visa SEATS: 50. Private parties: 30 main room, 25 private room. Vegetarian meals. Children's helpings. No cigars/pipes in dining-room. Wheelchair access (1 step). Music. Air-conditioned

Chinese Home Cooking

21 Argyle Place, EH9 1JJ
031-229 4404

COOKING 1
COST £7–£10

A modest converted shop, 'rather like a working-man's cafe', providing ample, familiar Cantonese food to the students and local inhabitants of Edinburgh's bed-sit land. Crisp pancake rolls, beef with green peppers and black-bean sauce, and stir-fried dishes have been commended. This is basic, honest, no-frills cooking offered in a relaxed atmosphere and providing excellent value for money. Unlicensed, but there is no corkage if you bring your own.

CHEF/PROPRIETOR: Steven Chan OPEN: all week, D only MEALS: 5.30 to 11 PRICES: £5 (£8), Set D £6 (£7). Unlicensed, but bring your own: no corkage SEATS: 40. Private parties: 30 main room. Children welcome. No music

Denzler's 121

NEW ENTRY

121 Constitution Street, EH6 7AE
031-554 3268

COOKING 1*
COST £14–£31

Behind a handsome classical doorway extends this new enterprise of the Denzler family – long known to Edinburgh, having opened their first place nearly two decades ago. The restaurant specialises in Swiss cookery, although once through the air-dried beef, the Gruyère soufflé and the spätzli there is not a whole lot of Swissness about veal and mushrooms, chicken with a light curry sauce or guinea-fowl with honey. Rather, the cooking is what we used to know and love twenty years ago, but done carefully using fresh ingredients and presented in a locale – painted pink-peach, with bleached wood and brass fittings – that will offend no one even if it does not arrest. A meal was taken this summer: centrepiece was a dish of three escalopes of Angus beef fillet coated conservatively (i.e. meagrely) with black peppercorns and accompanied by potatoes berrichonne (a standby of the house) and a tomato filled with béarnaise sauce. The fillet was well-hung and flavoursome, the cooking was accurate. Ancillaries, with the exception of the milk bread, were in need of greater attention. The Denzlers themselves afford a warm and attentive welcome, their staff require more training. 'A comfortable, relaxing place; competent and reassuring compared with so much nonsense elsewhere,' was the verdict of one visitor who went through a dozen Edinburgh and Glasgow restaurants in as many days. The unambitious wine list has too few annotations to command great confidence. House wines are £9.50 a litre.

The Guide *always appreciates hearing about changes of chef or owner.*

CHEFS: Sämi Denzler and Richard Winnick PROPRIETORS: Sämi and Pat Denzler OPEN: Tue to Sat, exc Sat D CLOSED: 2 weeks July, 2 weeks Jan MEALS: 12 to 2, 6.30 to 10 PRICES: L £18 (£24), Set L £9.50 (£14) to £13.50 (£18), Set D £15.50 (£20) to £21 (£26). Net prices, card slips closed CARDS: Access, Visa SEATS: 65. Private parties: 65 main room. Vegetarian meals with prior notice. Children welcome. No music

Indian Cavalry Club

3 Atholl Place, EH3 8HP — COOKING **2**
031-228 3282 — COST £10–£26

A discreet frontage and a light-toned, draped interior give this Indian restaurant a classy feel. The paramilitary uniforms of the waiting staff reinforce this, though Mr Chowdhury's tailor seems as approximate in his sizing as an army quartermaster. The Club has attempted a blend of brasserie and Indian restaurant, resulting in a helpful and informative menu. 'This is not the place to order a curry after 10 pints of lager and a romp round the town,' says a reader. The cooking is approved with fresh spice/herb flavours working their way through to the fore, properly supported by decent nans, varied side dishes (built into the menu as suggested accompaniments to principal curries) and excellent lemon rice. Inconsistency may sometimes be reflected, but this is an occupational hazard of places that run all week, twice daily. The 'concept' has now been franchised: Edinburgh's Indian restaurants are remarkably on the ball. The wine list (closely matched to the menu – and a lot of the spicing is light enough to encourage a change to wine) is a cut above many. House French from Ropiteau is £6.90.

CHEF: Bilquis Chowdhury PROPRIETORS: Shahid and Bilquis Chowdhury OPEN: all week MEALS: 12.30 to 2.30, 5.30 to 12 PRICES: £16 (£22), Set L £5.95 (£10) to £13.95 (£19), Set D £8.95 (£14) to £13.95. Minimum £5 CARDS: Access, Amex, Diners, Visa SEATS: 73. 20 tables outside. Private parties: 80 main room, 50 private room. Vegetarian meals. Children's helpings (weekends only). Smart dress preferred. No-smoking area. Wheelchair access (2 steps; also WC). No music

Kalpna

2–3 St Patrick Square, EH8 9EZ — COOKING **2***
031-667 9890 — COST £8–£19

'When we return (which we plan to do) we'll book, take more time, and order more dishes.' Kalpna is on a good streak, its Gujarati vegetarian cooking (more dairy than vegan dishes since it first opened) deservedly popular, so a reservation is indeed wise forethought. 'Brown stew and curry powder' was a style of Indian cooking in the early days that places like Kalpna set determinedly to exorcise. Dishes like khumb masala (mushrooms, green pepper, tomato and peas in a coconut sauce – 'a lovely, rich, slightly sweet dish with a good combination of textures and subtle flavouring'), tarka dhal ('the yellow split beans kept their texture rather than going to a mush, the main flavouring seemed to be well-fried garlic') and a mildly spiced bhindi bhaji are examples of a sophisticated cuisine interpreted with care and intelligence. Breads are good, so is the rice, and the thali is a bargain that shows off the skills. As another observed, 'hunger is a good sauce', and it was well satisfied on this occasion. Service is informed and chatty and the restaurant is resolutely no-smoking. Edinburgh is fortunate in its Indian restaurants and this is a gem in its diadem. Briefly admonishing the 'conventional wisdom that wines do not go well with Indian food', the compact list of decent growers, including Ryman's la Jaubertie, Saget Loires and a Pinot Blanc from Ostertag, shows a sure hand. Prices are very fair with little on offer over £10. House wine is £6.50. CELLARMAN'S CHOICE: Pinot Blanc 1988, Dom. Ostertag, £8.50; Bonarda Oltrepò Pavese 1987, Castello di Luzzano Fugazza, £10.

CHEF: Ajay Bharatdwaj PROPRIETORS: M.E. Jogee, Mrs Mehta, E. Barton and Ajay Bharatdwaj OPEN: Mon to Sat, exc Sat L MEALS: 12 to 2.30, 5.30 to 11.30 PRICES: £9 (£16), Set L £3 (£8) to £5 (£10), Set D £6 (£10) to £10 (£15). Service 10%. Card slips closed CARDS: Access, Visa SEATS: 60. Private parties: 40 main room, 30 private room. Vegetarian meals. Children's helpings. No smoking. Wheelchair access. Music

Kelly's

46 West Richmond Street, EH8 9DZ — COOKING 1
031-668 3847 — COST £28

Once a baker's shop, Kelly's is now a small (very small) restaurant, decently appointed and offering a rather more genteel approach to reasonably priced eating out than the rumbustious style of Pierre Victoire (see entry) in the same city. A short set-price menu, none the less with a couple of supplements, runs through an Anglo-French repertoire with most emphasis on modern Britain in dishes such as salmon with ginger and sultana butter, noisettes of lamb with a coriander crust, or a combination of pork, scallops and red pepper, basil and olive oil sauce. Jacquie Kelly has help in the kitchen now, but it does not detract from the very personal ambience of the place which might, after all, be someone's front room. The no-nonsense wine list, at fair prices, is at one with the food. House French is £6.50.

CHEFS: Jacquie Kelly and Nicholas Carnegie PROPRIETORS: Jacquie Kelly and Jeff Kelly OPEN: Tue to Sat, D only CLOSED: 3 to 25 Sept MEALS: 6.45 to 9.45 PRICES: Set D £16.75 (£23). Card slips closed CARDS: Access, Amex, Visa SEATS: 32. Private parties: 28 main room. Vegetarian meals. Children's helpings. No smoking before 9pm. Wheelchair access (1 step; also WC). Music

Marché Noir 🍷

2–4 Eyre Place, EH3 5EP — COOKING 1
031-558 1608 — COST £15–£31

'Le Lunch' and 'Le Diner' are offered in uncompromising French, but staff translate extensively. Two set-price daily menus are offered at each meal; among them the less expensive offering at lunch is especially good value. The food itself, also uncompromisingly French on the whole, is served cheerfully. There is a suspicion of 'chef's brown sauce' with several meat dishes, but 'it's meaty and often slightly fruity', while vegetables and salads are 'average'. Feuilleté with chicken livers, onion tart, fish soup, *côtes d'agneau au cassis*, chicken provençale, and seafood crêpe with pastis, are standard offerings from a slowly changing repertoire. Puddings have pleased, especially the ice-cream – coffee and walnut, strawberry and coconut. House wine is £7.

CHEFS: Robert Struthers and Stephen Simpson PROPRIETOR: Malcolm Duck OPEN: all week, exc Sat L and Sun L MEALS: 12 to 2.30, 7 to 10 (9.30 Sun, 10.30 Fri and Sat) PRICES: Set L £10 (£15) to £14.50 (£20), Set D £14.50 (£20) to £20.50 (£26) CARDS: Access, Visa SEATS: 45. Private parties: 45 main room. Vegetarian meals. Children's helpings. No cigars/pipes in dining-room. Wheelchair access (1 step). Music

Martins 🍷

70 Rose Street, North Lane, EH2 3DX — COOKING 3
031-225 3106 — COST £18–£41

'Anyone who tries so hard at everything deserves to do well' was a verdict on Martin Irons by a customer who found someone had taken his wife's coat by mistake. 'Martin identified the culprit and set off in hot pursuit. A shocked Swedish lady was roused from her bed in a nearby hotel and the coats exchanged. Finally, a triumphant and panting restaurateur returned with the missing garment.' This approach marks that of the whole meal. Witness one account of a magnificent board of Scottish (with maybe a few Irish) cheeses. 'I tried about eight, including what I was informed was the last slice ever of one, as the maker had retired.' The effect of this manner is invigorating rather than smothering. The change of chef during 1991 has not diminished commitment or standards, though some suggest that the cooking is quieter and lacks a slight edge. Happy, though, are many readers with the extremely fair-value lunch menu and evening *carte*. The latter is not cheap but offers properly cooked and very properly bought food in dishes such as a first course of braised squid and monkfish with a warm nutty dressing, monkfish and scallops with bacon and leeks, and even decent soups – for instance tomato, cumin and potato, and mushroom, cucumber and blue cheese. Martins used to offer mildly unreconstructed nouvelle cuisine; it is no longer so, though some remark that portions are not large. Main courses may number two fish and two meat dishes: among these have been sea bass with yellow peppers and saffron; mullet with fennel and pimento coulis; duck breast with bramble vinegar; and tender lamb with a garlic sauce that excited the eater and never repelled the other party. Vegetables are fresh and seasonal – swede, red cabbage and celery in May, for example. Desserts are simple but good. Everyone loves the goats' cheese and spring onion tart served as an appetiser too. You may start in the pleasing but spare bar before passing on to the Habitatish eau-de-nil dining-room – light, clean and glowing. Do not worry about the approach through deserted streets at night, but ask directions if you have not been before. Martins is no more than a stone's throw from Princes Street, between Frederick and Castle Street, but it is easy to get enmeshed in wrong turnings. The excellent wine list, always being updated, includes great makers at reasonable prices – Avril, Florentin, Balgownie and Selaks, for example. House French is £8.80. CELLARMAN'S CHOICE: Riesling, Silberberg 1987, Rolly Gassmann, £12.50; Rioja Viña Amezola 1987, £13.20.

CHEFS: Forbes Stott, Christopher Colverson and Stephen Paterson PROPRIETORS: Martin and Gay Irons OPEN: Tue to Sat, exc Sat L CLOSED: 4 weeks from 25 Dec MEALS: 12 to 2, 7 to 10 PRICES: £23 (£34), Set L and D £9.95 (£18) to £13.95 (£21). Minimum £9.75 L. Service 10% on parties of 6 or more CARDS: Access, Visa SEATS: 28. Private parties: 34 main room, 10 private room. Children's helpings on request. No smoking. Wheelchair access (2 steps). No music

Pierre Victoire

10 Victoria Street, EH1 2HG — COOKING 2
031-225 1721 — COST £9–£19

Pierre Levicky continues to take Edinburgh by storm for sensational-value food that is often generous and imaginative. The feeling is that the Victoria Street and Grassmarket (38 Grassmarket, EH1 2TU, Tel: 031-226 2442) branches are better than the Union Street one (8 Union Street, EH8 9LU, Tel: 031-557 8451), even if the latter has slightly more room. This may be because the owner is more likely to be cooking at them on one night or another. The style is generous and full of panache: a fish soup loaded with chunks of at least four different sorts of fish as well as mussels, the rich broth flavoured with basil; a huge portion of tender roast beef; warm smoked salmon with mushrooms and a mint hollandaise; chicken with mange-tout and ginger; desserts such as chocolate roulade, strawberry and almond savarin and lemon meringue pie. Prices are give-away for the quantities of prime materials, which include even lobster on good days. Cooking can be very approximate and reminiscent of old-style bistros, but the value induces tolerance. Conditions of comfort are also basic. In the Victoria Street branch, seats are so serried that movement and exit are very difficult indeed. Popularity may also cause great serving delays and hiccups in reservations. Normally, however, goodwill (on both sides) makes light of these limitations. Taking a broader view, the real value of these restaurants is that they introduce new customers to the delight of good food, acting as a step on a ladder that should be found more often in Britain. There is a short and fast-changing wine list. House wines are £5.60.

CHEF/PROPRIETOR: Pierre Levicky OPEN: Mon to Sat, Sun Jun to Aug CLOSED: 2 days Christmas, 2 days New Year MEALS: 12 to 4, 6 to 11 (all day during Edinburgh Festival) PRICES: £11 (£16), Set L £4.90 (£9). Card slips closed CARDS: Access, Visa SEATS: 65. Private parties: 65 main room. Vegetarian meals. Children's helpings. Wheelchair access (1 step). Fax: 031-557 5216

Shamiana

14 Brougham Street, EH3 9JH — COOKING 1*
031-228 2265 — COST £14–£30

Reporters rate this smartly decorated restaurant among the top three Indians in Edinburgh. Chef/proprietor Khalil Mansoori offers a short, distinctive menu of tandooris and curries with specialities from Kashmir and other parts of the subcontinent. Methi chaman gosht is lamb with spinach and fenugreek; Hyderabadi murgh is chicken with peanut, cashew-nut and poppy seed sauce; saali boti khumbani is a Parsi wedding dish of lamb cooked with dried apricots and spices. More familiar items include chicken tikka, rogan josh, well-liked dhal gosht and vegetable pilau. Breads continue to please. The wine list is impressive and wide-ranging by Indian standards, and there are helpful suggestions for bottles to suit specific dishes – Hill Smith Old Triangle Riesling with shashlik kebab, for example. House French is £6.25.

CHEF/PROPRIETOR: Khalil Mansoori OPEN: all week, exc Sat L and Sun L CLOSED: 25 Dec and 1 Jan MEALS: 12 to 2, 6 to 11.30 PRICES: £12 (£25), Set L £9 (£14) to £12 (£18), Set D £12 (£18) to £18 (£25). Service 12.5% D only. Card slips closed CARDS: Access, Amex, Diners, Visa SEATS: 42. Private parties: 18 main room. Vegetarian meals. Children's helpings. No cigars/pipes in dining-room. Wheelchair access (1 step). No music

Shore

NEW ENTRY

3 The Shore,
Leith, EH6 6QW
031-553 5080

COOKING 1
COST £26

Once a rough bar for sailors and their hangers-on and retaining its original decorative character, the pub has gained 'a brilliantly sunny restaurant' and is haven for Edinburgh's socially mobile. Leith waterfront restaurants may be much of a muchness, and do not rise to great heights, but they have hit upon a good formula and an interesting location. Here fish is the thing – on a changing blackboard menu, though many old favourites turn up with regularity – and is enjoyably cooked, for instance monkfish with black pepper and cream, and halibut with a herb crust, served with simple vegetables. First courses such as grilled avocado with ham and goats' cheese (an unexpected success), merguez sausages, and calamares with tomato sauce are trendy enough; desserts have had less attention. Cheese, though a small choice, is acceptable. Service is very laid-back.

CHEF: Ian Burdall PROPRIETORS: Phillipa Cruinkshank and Simon Eddington OPEN: all week MEALS: 12 (12.30 Sun) to 2.30, 6.30 to 10 PRICES: £16 (£22). Minimum £5 L, £10 D SEATS: 38. Private parties: 40 main room. Vegetarian meals. Children restricted. No smoking while others are eating. Wheelchair access (1 step; also WC). Music

Szechuan House

95 Gilmore Place, EH3 9NU
031-229 4655

COOKING 1
COST £13–£26

Chao-Gang Liu is from Szechuan and the kitchen strives for an authentic version of food from his native province. Around a hundred dishes include classics such as steamed lamb, duck roll, squid with crispy rice and tomato sauce, and Ma Po bean curd. Some readers have found flavours dull and the results mediocre, but there is a consensus on the quality of deep-fried sweet potatoes, quick-fried prawns with ginger and garlic, Szechuan noodles, and crispy jiang jin beef with water chestnuts. Home-smoked duck is served authentically with Chinese bread. Vegetarians have plenty of choice, ranging from Szechuan-style aubergines to gluten and mixed vegetables. The owners' warmth and friendliness more than compensate for any starkness in the décor, and there is no pressure to leave in a hurry, even when the dining-room is full. House Italian is £6.50 a litre.

CHEF: Chao-Gang Liu PROPRIETORS: Hsueh-Fen Liu and Chao-Gang Liu OPEN: Tue to Sun, D only CLOSED: 2 weeks summer MEALS: 5.30pm to midnight PRICES: £13 (£22), Set D £8.70 (£13) to £10.50 (£15) CARDS: Access, Visa SEATS: 40. Private parties: 24 main room, 12 private room. Vegetarian meals. Children welcome. Music

Vintners Rooms

87 Giles Street, Leith, EH6 6BZ
031-554 6767

COOKING 3*
COST £16–£36

Over time, Edinburgh has taken the Cummings to its heart. Certainly, some of the best food in the city is being produced here, in most sympathetic surroundings. The Leith warehouse's high wall and gates, enclosing a forecourt, kept out eighteenth-century robbers. In the basement vaults, once used for storing the claret that was Leith's principal trade, the flora is the same moulds as those found in Bordeaux. On the ground floor there are two rooms. The first is a high functional space, candle-lit, a fire at one end, a bar down one side, warm plaster, stone and wood giving varied natural tones. The second, smaller and ornately plastered at the end of the seventeenth century, served as the wine auction room. You may eat in either. The smaller is more constricted and more formal; those with more expansive natures may prefer to spread out before the fire. A daily menu, with extra consideration given to lighter luncheon dishes, gives much space to fish. Tim Cummings has not deserted the repertoire he elaborated during his earlier years in Salisbury and at the Hole in the Wall in Bath. Cooking is still presented naturally rather than artlessly, tastes are subtle yet generous, and he has avoided the mimsy and waywardness of kitchen modernism while absorbing some of the better ideas of flavour combinations. There have been moments of absent-mindedness, made the more heinous in Edinburgh eyes by the relatively high cost of some meals here, but they are overshadowed by the determination to obtain good produce, especially fish, and the underlying genuine approach to eating and drinking. The feeling for quality may also be vitiated by hesitant or reticent service; at times people feel there should be more joy in the house. Dishes that have been praised include fettucine with pesto and mushrooms, turbot marinated with lemon and basil, queen scallops and almonds, plump black olives and pastries for aperitif, sardines with tomato and herbs, plaice and prawns with sorrel, venison with cranberry, monkfish au poivre, monkfish with coriander ('the best fish I have tasted even if the herb could have been more generous' was one report), guinea-fowl with chanterelles and tarragon, usually simple vegetables – sometimes thought perfunctory, St Emilion au chocolat, and pear, almond and armagnac tart. Wines are choice: burgundies are particularly strong but the Rhônes and Italians show an unfailing eye for quality, all at fair prices. A bottle is awarded for intelligence, brevity and generosity. House wines are from £8. CELLARMAN'S CHOICE: Coteaux des Baux, Dom. de Trévallon 1988, £20; Seville Estate, Chardonnay 1988, £19.75.

CHEF: Tim Cumming PROPRIETORS: Tim and Sue Cumming OPEN: Mon to Sat CLOSED: 2 weeks Christmas MEALS: 12 to 2.30, 6.30 to 10.30 PRICES: £22 (£30), Set L £9 (£16) to £12 (£19) CARDS: Access, Amex, Visa SEATS: 65. Private parties: 40 main room. Car park, 3 places. Vegetarian meals. Children's helpings. No smoking. Wheelchair access (2 steps). No music. Air-conditioned

Waterfront Wine Bar

1C Dock Place, Leith, EH6 6LU COOKING 1
031-554 7427 COST £19

'The conservatory must be one of the most delightful places to eat lunch in Edinburgh when the sun is shining,' writes one reporter, who also approved of the extended lunchtime hours during the Festival. The re-vamped kitchen delivers freshly cooked food from a daily-changing menu. Chicken tikka and smoked trout mousse with tomato concassé are well-reported starters. Fish features strongly: poached halibut with fennel sauce and samphire, grilled John Dory with provençal sauce, and unadorned fillet of plaice with fresh vegetables have all been recommended. Alternatives might be aubergine and chickpea curry and grilled lamb chops with lemon and coriander sauce. Cheeses come with oatcakes; otherwise there are fruit salads and excellent plum and almond pudding. Occasional gripes about aerated cream and irrelevant salad garnishes never blur overall positive impressions. The value for money extends to the wine list, which has house vin de pays at £6.70. Evening beer drinkers should seek out organic Golden Promise from the local Caledonian Brewery.

CHEFS: Helen Ruthven, Robin Bowie, Jenny McCrea and Heather McKendrick PROPRIETORS: Helen and Ian Ruthven, Sarah Reid and Robin Bowie OPEN: Mon to Sat, and Sun L MEALS: 12 (12.30 Sun) to 2.30 (3.30 Fri, 3 Sat), 6 to 9.30 (10 Fri and Sat) PRICES: £11 (£16). Minimum £5 in conservatory SEATS: 110. 19 tables outside. Private parties: 100 main room. Vegetarian meals. No children under 5. Wheelchair access (1 step; also WC). Music

ERISKA Strathclyde map 8

▲ *Isle of Eriska Hotel*

Eriska PA37 1SD
LEDAIG (063 172) 371 COOKING 2
off A828, 12m N of Oban COST £49

The hotel is a towered and turreted grey-stone mansion standing proud and dominating the 250-acre island. Visitors making the trek treat it as house and home, according to the Buchanan-Smiths. Sheena Buchanan-Smith has taken full control of the kitchen, but the formula of a five-course dinner, plus coffee, remains unchanged. A March menu shows the style: terrine of vegetables or mousseline of chicken with lobster sauce, before cream of mushroom soup, then poached Loch Creran salmon with hollandaise or breast of duck with sauce bigarade. To finish, there are a trolley of sweets, a savoury such as Scotch woodcock, and perhaps some cheese. Service is young, but attentive. The list of more than 150 wines is heavy on classy clarets and burgundies with famous names to the fore. There is also a small contingent from Germany, Australia, Portugal and Chile among others. House wines are £6.90.

CHEF: Sheena Buchanan-Smith PROPRIETORS: Robin and Sheena Buchanan-Smith OPEN: all week, D only CLOSED: Dec to Mar MEALS: 7.30 to 9 PRICES: Set D £33 (£41). Card slips closed CARDS: Access, Amex, Visa SEATS: 40. Private parties: 10 main room, 12 private room. Car park, 50 places. Children's helpings. Children under 10 high tea only. Jacket and tie. Wheelchair access (also WC). No music. Fax: (063 172) 531
ACCOMMODATION: 16 rooms, all with bath/shower. Rooms for disabled. B&B £73 to £140. Deposit: £50. Children welcome. Baby facilities. Pets welcome. Garden. Tennis. Fishing. TV. Phone. Scenic. Confirm by noon (*Which? Hotel Guide*)

FORT WILLIAM Highland map 8

Crannog

Town Pier, Fort William PH33 7NG COOKING 2
FORT WILLIAM (0397) 703919 and 705589 COST £18–£29

'A wonderful find, great seafood in the summer' is a view echoed by other reporters who have ventured to this restaurant at the end of the pier overlooking Loch Linnhe. The success story began when a group of fishermen formed Crannog Scottish Seafoods to market the catch from their boat *Our Tracy Jane*. In 1989 they opened this restaurant in their converted bait store. There is nothing elaborate about the décor or the menu, merely an emphasis on prime quality and fresh seafood. Huge platefuls of 'fantastic' langoustines with garlic butter are a speciality, 'superb' bouillabaisse is packed with good things, and the menu also features oysters, gravlax, pickled herrings and dishes such as salmon in filo pastry and trout baked with spring onions and ginger. The owners cure salmon, eels, mussels and now Cheddar cheese in their own smokehouse. Some good desserts are offered, including a best-selling Cranachan laced with whisky. The service is excellent. Modest, good-value wines include house white at £6.95.

CHEF: Susan Trowbridge PROPRIETORS: Crannog Ltd OPEN: all week (restricted in winter) CLOSED: Nov MEALS: 12 to 2.30, 6 to 10 PRICES: L £12 (£18), D £17 (£24). Card slips closed CARDS: Access, Visa SEATS: 50. Private parties: 50 main room. Car park, 15 places. Children's helpings. No-smoking area. Wheelchair access (also WC). Music. Fax: (0397) 705026

▲ *Inverlochy Castle* 🍷

Fort William PH33 6SN
FORT WILLIAM (0397) 702177 COOKING 3
3m N of Fort William on A82 COST £28–£70

Monster piles of luxury had a jittery time of it at the beginning of 1991: customers simply disappeared, but overheads rolled on and on. At Inverlochy the problems were compounded: it spent some of 1990 on the market and changed its chef into the bargain. Yet it continues as luxuriously and stylishly as ever, calling for a degree of self-assurance to cope with constant attention from servitors: 'You cannot go to the lavatory without one waiting outside for you to open the door to the dining-room to let you back in, another waiting to ease you into your chair, while a third has replaced your napkin (the second in only two courses) and the manager rushes around adjusting the lampshades,' reported one inspector. Against such surroundings, in the plumpest and most enjoyable grand taste, the food served is predictably fancy but regrettably predictable. The spark of invention is faint. Instead, we have conventional grand cooking: lunch, for example, includes a choice of salad, gravlax, smoked salmon, steak, omelette, grilled fish, and best end of lamb. This is fine when executed without fault, even at £18.50 for the lamb alone or £45 for a meal such as melon and raspberries, tomato soup, rack of lamb with dauphinois, cheese, white chocolate mousse and coffee. No wonder there are many staff and extra napkins. Execution is often skilled; for instance rack of lamb had fine flavourful meat and the sauce, though a simple gravy, was an exact accompaniment; and a dish of langoustines, salmon and scallops, fresh and melting was given life by a lobster sauce of fine judgement. Not so good were a dry lobster and avocado salad with indistinct walnut dressing, and a dessert of caramel bavarois. The star of the evening, a hot orange soufflé, needed ordering one hour in advance. As with so many very grand hotels, you need to be sure you know what you are paying for and that you don't mind. If you do, don't go. Wines are predictably exalted and generally very expensive. Exploration uncovers many half-bottles and some decent value; Bourgogne Aligoté from Tollot-Beaut and a Côtes du Rhône from Meffre show careful attention to provenance. Quality throughout is assured, as is a high bill. House wine is £16.60.

CHEF: D. Whiffin PROPRIETOR: Grete Hobbs OPEN: all week CLOSED: mid-Nov to mid-Mar MEALS: 12.30 to 1.45, 7.30 to 9 PRICES: £31 (£46), Set L £17.50 (£28) to £22 (£33), Set D £39 (£52) to £44 (£58). Card slips closed CARDS: Access, Visa SEATS: 36. Private parties: 18 main room. Car park, 10 places. Children welcome. Jacket and tie. No smoking in dining-room. No music ACCOMMODATION: 16 rooms, all with bath/shower. B&B £132 to £275. Children welcome. Garden. Tennis. Fishing. Snooker. TV. Phone. Scenic. Doors close at midnight (*Which? Hotel Guide*)

GLASGOW Strathclyde map 8

Amber Regent NEW ENTRY

50 West Regent Street, G2 2QZ COOKING 1
041-331 1655 and 1677 COST £14–£35

This is one of a trio of upmarket Chinese restaurants under the 'Amber' banner. Owner Andy Chung clearly knows what his Glaswegians want, aiming at a comfortable bourgeois clientele who would rather not eat birds' nests, but who are capable of enjoying a certain freshness in presentation and above-average sauces. The menu takes in a fashionable mix of Canton, Peking and Szechuan, with satays and grilled and barbecued specialities backing up a strong showing of appetisers and seafood. Some dishes are dramatic, photogenic conversation pieces. Deep-fried 'crystal king prawn' comes perched rakishly beside a spiky half red pepper filled with a light lemon sauce and, in general, there is much decorative cutting and chopping of onions, radishes and carrots. Crispy 'seaweed', Buddha vegetables and ho-fun noodles with bean sprouts have all been good; readers also praise the aromatic crispy lamb. Service is fast, and the chef is noted for his virtuoso performances, and sometimes invites people into the kitchen. The wine list has a creditable showing of bottles from the New World. House wine is £8.50.

CHEF: Tommy Ho PROPRIETOR: Andy Chung OPEN: Mon to Sat MEALS: 12 to 2.15, 6 to 11.30 (midnight Fri and Sat) PRICES: £17 (£29), Set L £6.95 (£14), Set D £18.50 (£25) CARDS: Access, Amex, Diners, Visa SEATS: 90. Private parties: 100 main room, 15 private room. Vegetarian meals. No children under 10. Smart dress preferred. Music. Air-conditioned. Fax: 041-353 3398

Buttery

COUNTY RESTAURANT OF THE YEAR

NEW ENTRY

652 Argyle Street, G3 8UF — COOKING 3
041-221 8188 — COST £19–£37

Set in the middle of a motorway sprawl dotted with Wimpey houses, the Buttery has ecclesiastical overtones in its benches and dark mahogany bar area. Ritual, however, is restricted to the ceremonial lifting of domes. Jim Wilson (General Manager) and Stephen Johnson have succeeded in keeping this among the busiest 'establishment' restaurants in the city: 'Lawyers love it; *very* full indeed,' reported one inspector. They do it by offering full-scale modern cooking at fair prices, with professional service. At an inspection meal, which ranged over the *carte* with about eight choices at each course rather than the short set-price lunch menu, certain proclaimed ingredients, such as the herbs in the polenta (apparently restricted to a sprig of rosemary popped on top), and the dill in a dill cream sauce with excellent mussels, were hard to detect. But the cooking, apart from the tired nouvelle-style vegetables, showed assurance and, in the case of loin of venison with bacon skirlie and madeira jus, great taste attack. Fashion has certainly reached here: beef comes with a brown lentil sauce and red lentil cream, and salmon comes with red cabbage. Similar experiment across the sweet dishes suggested that more work was needed in this department. Reliance on a few big names in Burgundy invites suspicion that wine is not a high priority here. Selection is decent enough and so are the prices; the Rhône valley is a good bet. House wine is £8.95.

CHEF: Stephen Johnson PROPRIETORS: Alloa Brewery Co Ltd OPEN: Mon to Sat, exc Sat L MEALS: 12 to 2.30, 7 to 10.30 PRICES: £20 (£31), Set L £14.25 (£19). Service 10% (net prices Set L). Card slips closed CARDS: Access, Amex, Diners, Visa SEATS: 50. Private parties: 45 main room, 8 private room. Car park, 25 places. Vegetarian meals. Children welcome. Smart dress preferred. Wheelchair access (also men's WC). Music. Air-conditioned. Fax: 041-204 4639

Café Gandolfi

64 Albion Street, G1 1NY — COOKING 1
041-552 6813 — COST £19

Located in Glasgow's newly revived Merchant City (an area of restored warehouses), this bistro-type café has given a new lease of life to a sturdy, wood-panelled Victorian pub. All-day eating from a menu mostly limited to salads and light meals appeals to meat-eaters and vegetarians alike. Dishes of the day could include scallops in filo pastry with a ginger sauce, while Finnan haddock with potatoes is the most substantial main course. Cold baked Cumbrian ham, New York pastrami on rye and smoked venison and gratin dauphinoise are some of the alternatives. Good ingredients are consistently employed, but the kitchen often fails to achieve the right balance of flavours and blandness is a recurring criticism. Six decent, inexpensive wines are offered by the glass or bottle, together with the original Czech Budweiser, the strong Scottish Traquair House ale, home-made lemonade and espresso. House wine is £7.10.

CHEFS: Maggie Clarence and Karen Hepburn PROPRIETOR: Iain M. Mackenzie OPEN: Mon to Sat CLOSED: bank hols MEALS: 9.30am to 11.30pm PRICES: £10 (£16). Service 10% for parties of 6 or more SEATS: 60. Private parties: 12 main room. Vegetarian meals. Children's helpings. Wheelchair access (2 steps). Music

Colonial India

25 High Street, G1 1LX — COOKING 1
041-552 1923 and 6782 — COST £7–£30

Karahi dishes are flamed with spirit here – not very Muslim, but some sense of theatre – while décor bangs the colonial drum and service is of the colonial best. Karahi cooking is good, so is the baking, and the vegetarian side has also been well-reported – examples are turka dhal, Bombay aloo and mushroom bhaji. The wine list is above average and there are lots of beers.

CHEF: Tauquir Malik PROPRIETORS: Satty Singh, Tauquir Malik and Tariq Iqbal OPEN: all week, exc Sun L MEALS: noon to 11.30 (midnight Fri and Sat) PRICES: £13 (£25), Set L £3.50 (£7) to £5.95 (£10), Set D £10 (£14) CARDS: Access, Amex, Diners, Visa SEATS: 45. Private parties: 25 main room. Vegetarian meals. Children's helpings. Smart dress preferred. Wheelchair access. Music. Air-conditioned

October 🍷

128 Drymen Road, Bearsden, G61 3RB — COOKING 3
041-942 7272 — COST £15–£42

Ferrier Richardson's avowed intent of 'elimination of all pretentious ingredients and the use of fresh seasonal produce' informs the direct style of the cooking and is reflected in the distinguished look of the restaurant itself: a fine shop-front, then a reception area, before the clean lines of the dining-room, slabs of colour from modern Scottish paintings, depth of tone from dark-blue carpet and upholstery. 'The paintings are a delight; there was no sense of the place being taken over by the smart set of Glasgow yuppies.' This same man likened the mood to Sutherlands in Soho (see entry) – 'Perhaps the bright young staff made me feel this way.' Prices, it should be stressed, are at least a third less than most of Soho's; the short lunch menu is a true bargain. The cooking has panache. Main courses are more than mere protein and sauce: chicken comes with a potato and onion galette and root vegetables; parcels of leek and monkfish with a mousseline of scallops; duck with a pile of deep-fried celeriac. This may make the extra cost of vegetables (on occasion branded as boring) superfluous. The fish is good: soup with a soufflé topping, haddock in an egg and leek tart, mussels from Oban with garlic and white wine, and scallop mousse with a chive beurre blanc. Desserts may also be enjoyed, either a grand selection, or modern combinations of fruit, gratin and ice-creams (cardamom or honey, for instance). Blandness, as in a Drambuie and almond soufflé, may come from the materials chosen. Although 'pretentious ingredients' are eschewed, there is no doubt that fashion is embraced. Bread is good, and the coffee is decent. When on form, this is the most vigorous Glasgow restaurant, with energy enough to hive off into the café society (see entry below). Fifty-odd wines take in Australia, Portugal and Italy as well as the major French regions, with provençal Mas de la Rouvière and the dry Semillon of Peter Lehmann from the Barossa the bright spots in a sound list. Growers are named erratically and Italy should have a more confident showing. Pricing hits the top end hard, but good-value drinking under £20 abounds. There are useful suggestions for dessert wines by the glass and the 'hidden cellar' is worth more than a glance. House wine is £7.95. CELLARMAN'S CHOICE: Chardonnay 1989, Montrose Winery, £15.95; Marcilly 1985, £18.95.

CHEFS: Ferrier Richardson and Derek Blair PROPRIETORS: Premiere Cuisine Ltd OPEN: Tue to Sat CLOSED: 1 week Easter, first 2 weeks Aug MEALS: 12 to 2, 7 to 10 PRICES: £23 (£35), Set L £9.95 (£15) to £11.95 (£18). Card slips closed CARDS: Access, Visa SEATS: 48. Private parties: 52 main room. Children welcome. Wheelchair access (also WC). Music. Air-conditioned. Fax: 041-942 9650

October Café

NEW ENTRY

The Rooftop, Princes Square,
Buchanan Street, G1 3JX — COOKING **2**
041-221 0303 — COST £19–£29

On the site of the old Penguin Café, partners Ferrier Richardson and Hugh McShannon have taken the plunge into popular catering. This is the place to go in Princes Square ('bears as much relation to the Arndale Centres as Armani does to Marks,' according to one inspector). Here, it's style wars all the way in the glass-fronted lift to the bar and brasserie that skirts the top level of the huge atrium and perches under an immense skylight. 'The effect is of a '30s ocean liner meeting Raffles Hotel.' The bar serves simpler food and sandwiches until six o'clock; the brasserie does two meals a day with a menu that obviously enjoys East-meets-West flavours as well as serving up good steak, mussels, soups and salmon. Early reports have spoken well of the stir-fried prawns and chicken with chilli and egg noodles, the steak with celeriac chips and a mustard butter, and grilled spiced chicken. Even vegetables have been good, though the walnut dressing on a salad was skimped. There is not quite such enthusiasm for the sweet tarts and the crème brûlée, but the chocolate terrine is a knock-out. Quality is high, prices are not. The deal is a fair one, and the operation deserves to succeed.

CHEF: George Craig PROPRIETORS: Premiere Cuisine Ltd OPEN: Mon to Sat MEALS: 12 to 2.30, 7 to 11 (café 12 to 6) PRICES: restaurant £16 (£24), café £11 (£19) CARDS: Access, Visa SEATS: 50 (restaurant), 200 (café). Private parties: 200 main room, 120 private room. Vegetarian meals. Children welcome. Wheelchair access. Music. Air-conditioned

▲ *One Devonshire Gardens* NEW ENTRY

1 Devonshire Gardens, G12 0UX — COOKING 2*
041-339 2001 and 334 9494 — COST £28–£49

This luxurious hotel, in a tree-lined Victorian terrace (10 minutes from the city centre), oozes wealth with its mirrors, wallcoverings and squishy settees. 'Fashionably modern and urbane', from one report, sums up the fixed-price menu, which has included salad of langoustines with lentils and soya vinaigrette, roast fillet of brill on a bed of fresh noodles garnished with scallop ravioli, and peach and strawberry gratin with glazed saké sabayon. There is visual drama on the plate, which inspires effusive comments: terrine of sole, turbot and mussels with saffron vinegar is modelled on a draughts board; tournedos Rossini towers high above a jammy burgundy sauce. The quality of the raw materials shows in the marinated scallops, the crisp-skinned duck breast and the poached salmon. Vegetables deserve to be eaten as a course in their own right: pencil-thin asparagus tips glistening with butter; dark green, barely cooked savoy cabbage. Young, confident staff are full of 'eager zeal'. David Cowan has joined the hotel from the Triangle, now no more. It is early days to know the consistency of output, hence the rating. A big, upper-crust wine list includes a useful showing of half-bottles, some organics, plus representatives from around the world. House Ch. Bonnet 1988 is £14.

CHEF: David Cowan PROPRIETOR: Ken McCulloch OPEN: all week, exc Sat L MEALS: 12 to 2, 7 to 10.30 PRICES: Set L £18 (£28), Set D £30 (£41). Card slips closed CARDS: Access, Amex, Diners, Visa SEATS: 54. Private parties: 10, 14 and 30 private rooms. Car park, 12 places. Vegetarian meals. Children's helpings. Smart dress preferred. No-smoking area. Music. Fax: 041-337 1663 ACCOMMODATION: 27 rooms, all with bath/shower. B&B £110 to £140. Children welcome. Pets welcome. TV. Phone (*Which? Hotel Guide*)

Rogano

11 Exchange Place, G1 3AN — COOKING 1
041-248 4055 — COST £47

Punkahs, potted ferns, shades of art deco abounding – and 'interminable' 1940s music – are leitmotifs of a Glasgow institution. It is large, invariably busy, and the visual experience worth the visit, although opinions vary on whether the food is as good. Competence is agreed – 'chef's food', one reader called it – but while the food is 'acceptable regarding freshness, appearance and quality, cooking lacks flair, particularly in the sauces'. Prices may demand more than sturdy journeyman stuff. The menu offers fair range, with fish the centrepiece: first courses such as feuilleté of lobster and mussels, gravlax, smoked salmon, oysters, sashimi, and fish soup; main dishes of salmon, sole, lobster, brill, scallops and langoustines. Methods are usually straightforward, scallops wrapped in mashed sweet potato, fried and served with a chilli tomato sauce being among the most complex on the menu offered one day. Sauces, therefore, need to be assured, to keep the dish in the memory; so, too, do the vegetables, which generally are not reported with enthusiasm and are charged at a substantial £3.25 for a selection. Quality of supplies is as it should be, although, to one party from Wales, the Anglesey boats brought better and the lamb 'with a fresh herb crust' (actually a round of pastry which appeared to have been popped on as an afterthought) was in fact the best raw material offered in the evening. Service has to be well-drilled to cope with the numbers; on occasion the efficiency is at the expense of warmth. The wine list is not long, but offers adequate range. Sources are mainstream, white Loires and Alsaces being most worthy of exploration. House wines (Loires from Rémy Pannier at £7.95), have not always impressed. Café Rogano often gets more positive response than the restaurant, perhaps because the price/value ratio is more clearly perceptible with main dishes between £6 and £9. Certainly there is praise for the cheerful service, and the modern bistro menu, with dishes fairly spread between fish, meat and vegetarian options.

CHEF: James Kerr PROPRIETORS: Alloa Brewery OPEN: all week MEALS: 12 to 2.30, 6.30 to 10.30 PRICES: £27 (£39). Service 10%. Card slips closed CARDS: Access, Amex, Diners, Visa SEATS: 100. Private parties: 25 main room, 14 private room. Children welcome. Music. Air-conditioned. Fax: 041-248 2608

Ubiquitous Chip

12 Ashton Lane, G12 8SJ — COOKING 3
041-334 5007 — COST £35

The first impression on visiting 'UB Chip', as locals call it, is of a hothouse with a glazed atrium covered with an abundance of cascading greenery. The converted warehouse lends itself admirably to a very informal atmosphere; even the waitresses' dress style is clearly flexible, and there is 'lots of action and laughter'. The dedication to Scottish produce is strongly felt in a daily-changing menu drawing on a well-established repertoire: oak-smoked Loch Fyne kipper pâté, fillets of Ayr-landed cod, breast of Perthshire woodpigeon, marinated haunch of Inverness-shire venison, tails of Oban-landed monkfish. The kitchen draws on the past for some satisfying dishes: braised oxtail ragoût, and a slow-braised silverside of Scotch beef in a rich gravy. Modern ideas permeate others: haggis can be vegetarian, cod is served on a bed of clapshot with roasted and chillied sweet red peppers, monkfish on a bed of cracked wheat flavoured with ginger and saffron. Consistency is not a strong point and the cooking does not always live up to the expectations prompted by price. Upstairs has been developed as a modestly priced separate restaurant offering a simple menu of fresh fish, excellent Ayrshire ham, rare-roast Scotch beef, casseroles and stews. Sensible and fair pricing on the wine list encourages adventurous drinking – the 'Chip' must be as good a place as any to indulge. Prices at the higher reaches are fair, not give-away, but the choice under £20 is bliss. The only complaint is too much choice. Quality is consistently high, the range is wide and there are decent half-bottles. Two pages of single malts. House wines are from £7.

CHEF/PROPRIETOR: Ron Clydesdale OPEN: all week MEALS: 12 to 2.30 (12.30 to 4 Sun), 5.30 to 11 (6.30 to 11 Sun) PRICES: £19 (£29) CARDS: Access, Amex, Diners, Visa SEATS: 100. 12 tables outside. Private parties: 60 main room, 40 private room. Vegetarian meals. Children's helpings. Wheelchair access (also WC). No music. Fax: 041-337 1302

See the back of the Guide *for an index of restaurants listed.*

GULLANE Lothian map 8

La Potinière

Main Street, Gullane EH31 2AA
GULLANE (0620) 843214

COOKING 4
COST £22–£37

People remark upon the flowers: anemones in the lavatory, a great bowl of white and yellow irises and lilies in the centre of the restaurant, a vase of white tulips at the side. La Potinière may be small, almost a chalet from the outside, but it is perfectly formed. Attention to detail is everywhere. The same might be said of Hilary Brown's cooking. The menu is no-choice; the repertoire may grow but it still includes lots of long-runners. Here are two glowing reports: 'How can each course be so good?', 'Left us feeling delightfully full with a sensation of goodwill and happiness.' Brown-watchers – and they are many – comment in this fashion: 'There are definitely more distinctive flavours than there once were, no doubt partly because there is less cream throughout than there was. There has also been less inhibition about producing clear tastes in a set meal, for instance by use of spices.' Recitation of favourite dishes can go on from one year to the next. A winter meal ran as follows. First, there was a rich, thick red pepper soup, the peppers tasting slightly sweet, with a hint of tomato and a decoration of cream and parsley. With it came crusty white and an excellent brown walnut bread with a sweet tinge to it. The next course was soufflé aux courgettes ('How does she get 20 soufflés all looking identical, all at the same time?'). It came to table having just risen, light and fluffy, browned on top. Minuscule pieces of courgette could be tasted as well as seen, lending their texture, flavour and colour. The main dish was pheasant in Norman style – apples, calvados and cream, garnished with sweet chestnuts and a little round of potatoes dauphinois. The juices of the pheasant had been absorbed by the chestnuts. To accompany this was a fine salad, one of the few items that gets a note of reservation from those who like their roughage hot. Dessert was a masterpiece: triangles of puff stuffed with rum and almond sweetmeat, a light custard given edge by a raspberry coulis, the textures boosted by toasted flaked almonds over the top. Hilary Brown seems to have perfect pitch. Of the new departures this year that have received constant accolade, one, a crisped fillet of salmon with morels and cream, has been especially successful. But fear not; the chicken with tarragon, the soufflés sweet and savoury, the Brie and apples, and the amazing value of it all are still there. May it last many years. The wines, chosen and served by David Brown, match the food completely (a glass of Recioto dei Capitelli Anselmi with the sweet course, was, for one reader, 'exactly right for the dish'). The wine list itself is but a starting point to a discussion, if desired, with the intending diner. There are plenty of vintages and regions not yet even noted in writing. This is one of those places where comparative drinking is a must: such prices, such choice, such chances. House wine is £7.75.

CHEF: Hilary Brown PROPRIETORS: David and Hilary Brown OPEN: L Mon, Tue, Thur and Sun; Fri and Sat D CLOSED: 1 week June, Oct MEALS: 1, 8 PRICES: Set L £15.75 (£22), Set Sun L £16.75 (£23), Set D £24.50 (£31) SEATS: 32. Private parties: 30 main room. Car park, 10 places. Children welcome. Smoking after meal only. Wheelchair access. No music. One sitting

HADDINGTON Lothian — map 8

▲ *Browns Hotel*

1 West Road, Haddington EH41 3RD
HADDINGTON (062 082) 2254

COOKING 2
COST £20–£32

The house is classically Georgian with pillars at the doorway and an elegant dining-room full of plants and paintings by modern Scottish artists. Most visitors approve of the congenial atmosphere, although the policy of serving all diners at the same time is too restricting for some. Colin Brown's cooking remains careful and classic, although he is moving towards lighter sauces based on good stocks. Top-quality produce is still the key to his success. Meals are based around fixed-price menus with little choice: coulibiac, lettuce soup, medallions of venison with game sauce, chocolate and Grand Marnier bavarois is a typical choice. Readers have praised monkfish tortellini, veal in tarragon sauce and duck with blackcurrant sauce. Beef en croûte with sauce Robert is a firm favourite. Opinion is divided about the sweets, although there is praise for poached pear in chocolate sauce. Cafetière coffee comes with home-made chocolates. A list of around 60 wines provides decent drinking at reasonable prices. House wines are from £6.50.

CHEF: Colin Brown PROPRIETORS: Colin Brown and Alex McCallum OPEN: all week, D only, and Sun L MEALS: 12.30 for 1, 7.30 for 8 PRICES: Set Sun L £14.90 (£20), Set D £21 (£27) CARDS: Access, Amex, Visa SEATS: 38. Private parties: 38 main room. Car park, 10 places. Vegetarian meals. Children's helpings. Wheelchair access (also WC). Music. One sitting ACCOMMODATION: 6 rooms, 5 with bath/shower. B&B £51.25 to £66.60. Deposit: £20. Children restricted. Baby facilities. Garden. TV. Phone. Scenic. Doors close at midnight. Confirm by 6

HAWICK Borders — map 6

Old Forge 🍷

Newmill-on-Teviot, nr Hawick TD9 0JU
HAWICK (0450) 85298
4m S of Hawick, on A7

COOKING 1
COST £17–£23

A long white-stone building just outside Hawick, the Old Forge carries relics of its past functions, overlaid with impediments often found in craft and gift shops. The stone may chill the marrow of early visitors, but if the place fills up there is almost too much for Bill Irving to attend to in a reasonable time. Economy thus noticed in staffing has also been suggested with reference to the cooking of the imaginative menu – how many places in the Borders knock out tortellini with smoked sausage and a basil cream of a Tuesday night? Pity the sausage wasn't better, or its taste better amalgamated with the other ingredients. That the skill is sometimes blurred by press of business, but exists none the less, may be evidenced by the first-rate bread. The Irvings deserve success, not least for the excellent wines, stored at points around the restaurant. Lengthy notes on each wine make for much page-turning, but the persistent are rewarded with a remarkable selection of pedigree growers from around the world. Prices are very reasonable and half-bottles abound. House wine is £7.95 a litre.

CHEF: Margaret Irving PROPRIETORS: Bill and Margaret Irving OPEN: Tue to Sat, D only CLOSED: first 2 weeks May, first 2 weeks Nov MEALS: 7 to 9.30 PRICES: Set D £11.25 (£17) to £13.25 (£19). Card slips closed CARD: Access, Visa SEATS: 28. Private parties: 30 main room. Car park, 10 places. Vegetarian meals. Children's helpings. Wheelchair access. No music

INVERNESS Highland

map 8

▲ *Culloden House*

Inverness IV1 2NZ
INVERNESS (0463) 790461
off A96, 3m E of Inverness

COOKING 2
COST £21–£44

A stately pile not far from the site of Bonnie Prince Charlie's sad defeat – turned into twentieth-century victory by all the Scotticisms of the tourist industry. You will find kilts here, though guests' accents may be international. International, too, is the cooking, though materials – Dunsyre blue cheese, smoked halibut, haddock, game and whisky in abundance – may lend a Scottish air. The style is elaborate: a five-course meal with silver domes and a buffet of desserts and cheese. This may be successful, though lapses into formula have been reported. The McKenzie family and their staff are solicitous, with a positive warmth that is found refreshing in so apparently stately an establishment. Care has gone into the selection of wines. Fine, classic French wines, at matching prices, are nicely balanced by well-chosen, more modest Italian, French regional and New World bottles. There are good half-bottles.

CHEF: Michael Simpson PROPRIETORS: Ian and Marjory McKenzie OPEN: all week MEALS: 12.30 to 2, 7 to 9 PRICES: £20 (£29), Set L £15 (£21) to £25 (£32), Set D £19.50 (£26) to £29.50 (£37). Card slips closed CARDS: Access, Amex, Diners, Visa SEATS: 50. 3 tables outside. Private parties: 50 main room, 25 private room. Car park, 50 places. Vegetarian meals. Children's helpings. Jacket and tie. No smoking in dining-room. No music. Fax: (0463) 792181 ACCOMMODATION: 23 rooms, all with bath/shower. B&B £95 to £165. Deposit: 1 night. No children under 10. Pets welcome. Afternoon teas. Garden. Sauna. Tennis. Snooker. TV. Phone. Scenic. Doors close at midnight

▲ *Dunain Park*

Inverness IV3 6JN
INVERNESS (0463) 230512

COOKING 1
COST £30

'Mrs Nicoll is a marvel,' wrote one satisfied visitor. 'She deserves recognition for the food produced at this hotel,' commented another. The stately old country house – with its recently completed extension – provides a fine setting for Ann Nicoll's menu, which is now à la carte rather than fixed-price. Local ingredients and fresh fish show up well, sauces are 'beautifully prepared' and soups are regularly mentioned in reports. There have been recommendations for saddle of lamb with tawny port sauce; pigeon breast stuffed with pecan nuts, apples and dates in pastry; and sole in Noilly Prat sauce. The help-yourself buffet of sweets often seems dull and lacklustre by comparison. The wine list is well spread, with a strong French contingent, but no house wine.

CHEF: Ann Nicoll PROPRIETORS: Ann and Edward Nicoll OPEN: all week, D only MEALS: 7 to 9 PRICES: £18 (£25). Card slips closed CARDS: Access, Amex, Diners, Visa SEATS: 36. Private parties: 6 main room. Car park, 20 places. Children's helpings. Smart dress preferred. No smoking in dining-room. Wheelchair access. No music. Fax: (0463) 224532 ACCOMMODATION: 14 rooms, all with bath/shower. Rooms for disabled. B&B £58 to £130. Deposit: £50. Children welcome. Pets welcome, exc in public rooms. Afternoon teas. Garden. Swimming-pool. Sauna. TV. Phone. Scenic. Doors close at midnight (*Which? Hotel Guide*)

ISLE ORNSAY Highland map 8

▲ *Kinloch Lodge*

Isle Ornsay, Isle of Skye IV43 8QY
ISLE ORNSAY (047 13) 214 and 333
off A851 between Broadford and Armadale

COOKING 2
COST £32–£44

'This is the place for people who abhor "smart" hotels. A real country-house atmosphere in enchanting surroundings, comfortable rooms and the best breakfast in Britain. Our hosts were welcoming without being intrusive.' So went one report. To describe this large shooting lodge – with woods (and chanterelles) at beck and call – as laid-back would be anachronistic (its attitudes pre-date Californian mellowness) and a social solecism (its happy sense of relaxation stems from different sets of values). Yet the net effect is the same. Making guests relaxed requires work and this there is aplenty in the kitchen, which is self-supporting as far as it can and needs to be at the end of tenuous lines of supply. Dinners here run through five courses, with a choice of two dishes when it counts. The savoury alternatives will usually be fish or meat. The style takes small account of *nuova cucina*, nouvelle cuisine, Pacific-rim cooking, mother's pride back-to-the-land, or any other buzz phrases. Roast rib of beef, roast leg of lamb, kidneys with port and mustard, and smoked trout with horseradish fit within context and are the things for which people come. Visitors are frequently satisfied and come back the next year. It may be readily imagined that desserts – sticky toffee, almond and coffee meringue – are red hot. Evidence of careful buying abounds on the wine list, although annotation is uneven. Prices are fair, with decent Australasians and petits châteaux nicely balanced by a few classy bottles. House wines are from £8.

CHEFS: Lady Macdonald, Peter Macpherson, Millie Maclure and Sharon Dowie PROPRIETORS: Lord and Lady Macdonald OPEN: all week, D only CLOSED: 1 Dec to mid-Mar MEALS: 8 PRICES: Set D £25 (£32) to £30 (£37) CARDS: Access, Visa SEATS: 25. Private parties: 8 main room. Car park, 25 places. No children under 10. One sitting. Fax: (047 13) 277 ACCOMMODATION: 10 rooms, all with bath/shower. B&B £40 to £100. Deposit: £50. Children by arrangement. Baby facilities. Pets welcome. Afternoon teas. Garden. Fishing. Scenic. Confirm by 3 (*Which? Hotel Guide*)

'The only memorable moment in the meal came as I approached the bottom of a pallid minestrone and was at last able to utter the immortal line, "Waiter, there's a fly in my soup".' On eating in Derbyshire

KENTALLEN Highland map 8

▲ *Ardsheal House* 🍷

Kentallen PA38 4BX
DUROR (063 174) 227

COOKING 2
COST £12–£46

The house itself is mightily impressive, standing white against the blue of Loch Linnhe at the end of a long and picturesque private approach. The impression of 'country house' is fostered actively by the Taylors, giving vicarious pleasure to many casual visitors who enjoy the long, yet limited in choice, dinner menus thought up by George Kelso. Such places can be addictive and testament is recorded of one couple who have made an annual visitation since 1984. Their verdict? That Ardsheal goes from strength to strength and George Kelso's sojourn in the kitchen has been to everyone's benefit. The cooking has London leanings, informed by west coast supplies. Thus venison comes with a wild mushroom marmalade and port and rosemary sauce, and scallops appear with cucumber spaghetti and saffron butter sauce. Bread-and-butter pudding is 'absolutely wonderful' and guests concur. They also praise the cheese (Stilton), the fruit bowl and the gentle pacing of the whole. Prices, as in so many Highland country houses, are positively metropolitan. Good names are scattered liberally through the wine list and prices are fair. Petits châteaux with some age and fine Alsaces stand out. A glass is awarded this year for sound selection and decent value, but there could be a wider range of half-bottles. House wine is £7.50. CELLARMAN'S CHOICE: Médoc, Ch. La Cardonne 1986, £12.50; Graves, Ch. La Louvière 1986, £16.

CHEF: George Kelso PROPRIETORS: Jane and Robert Taylor OPEN: all week CLOSED: early Nov to Easter MEALS: 12.30 to 2, 8.30 PRICES: Set L £7.50 (£12) to £16.50 (£22), Set D £31 (£38) SEATS: 40. Private parties: 38 main room. Car park, 20 places. Children's helpings. Smart dress preferred. No smoking in dining-room. Wheelchair access (also WC). Music. One sitting D. Fax: (063 174) 342 ACCOMMODATION: 13 rooms, all with bath/shower. D,B&B £82 to £165. Children welcome. Baby facilities. Pets welcome. Afternoon teas. Garden. Tennis. Snooker. Phone. Scenic. Doors close at midnight. Confirm by 6 (*Which? Hotel Guide*)

KILLIECRANKIE Tayside map 8

▲ *Killiecrankie Hotel*

Killiecrankie PH16 5LG
PITLOCHRY (0796) 3220,
changes to (0796) 473220 Jan 1992

COOKING 2
COST £31

Killiecrankie Pass is fairly breathtaking, though stronger epithets might have been used by defeated Englishmen forced to retreat by Jacobite Highlanders in 1689. Today this small hotel is a staging-post for a more peaceful invasion, more international too, and the Andersons smother you with kindness (it must have been an aggressive invader who once found them 'dour') rather than sticking your torso with a claymore. Paul Booth remains as chef, though with a new team to help; the feeling of one veteran campaigner is that his cooking becomes more imaginative by the year, even if this does mean indulging a passion for filo pastry. The short menu is carefully split between adventure (scallops cooked with herbs, garlic and cream, served with shitake mushrooms and fresh pasta) and convention – a daily dose of smoked salmon or soup. This seems a fair compromise. Cooking is accurate and mobilises a good range of flavours, even if fruit occasionally wins the day. Bar meals are very well reported. There is a decent merchant's wine list, with no outrageous mark-ups and a fair crack of halves. House wines are from £7.55.

CHEFS: Paul Booth and Guy Jacques PROPRIETORS: Colin and Carole Anderson OPEN: all week CLOSED: Jan and Feb MEALS: 12.30 to 2, 7 to 8.30 PRICES: Set D £20 (£26). Card slips closed CARDS: Access, Amex, Visa SEATS: 70. Private parties: 34 main room. Car park, 30 places. Vegetarian meals. Children's helpings. No children under 5 D. No smoking in dining-room. Wheelchair access (also WC). No music. Fax: (0796) 472451 ACCOMMODATION: 11 rooms, all with bath/shower. Rooms for disabled. B&B £34.75 to £43.85. Children welcome. Baby facilities. Pets welcome. Afternoon teas. Garden. TV. Scenic. Doors close at midnight. Confirm by 6

KINBUCK Central map 8

▲ *Cromlix House* 🍷

Kinbuck FK15 9JT COOKING 3*
DUNBLANE (0786) 822125 COST £30–£49

One overnight visitor listed things that struck him about Cromlix: 'The wonderful breakfasts; the cutlery; the huge suite; the friendly service; the friendly owner; the beautiful estate; the packed lunch that included a game terrine en croûte.' He might also have mentioned the dinners (and lunches by arrangement) which are served to residents and to outsiders who telephone first. The estate bulks large in any view: 'Faculties are softened by the approach through fields of Jacob lambs, strutting pheasants, acres of daffodils, raked gravel, to a courteous reception by name, even if the staff is new.' Everything about the house sounds forbiddingly grand, but reports unite in praising the open attitudes of the staff and management. The routine for dinner is that the no-choice four-course menu is recited and you are asked for any objections; there is a fallback alternative dish for each course but not everyone will discover this. In effect, therefore, the kitchen offers a no-choice dinner. New chef Ian Corkhill seems to have taken over a 'house' repertoire but inspectors have noticed a new discretion in his cooking – omitting 'fussy garnishings in which they once would have revelled' – and accuracy. This is good news, as is the technical assurance of his mainstream modern British production: monkfish larded with pimentos on mange-tout with orange butter sauce, asparagus soup with chicken quenelles, sole with lemon butter sauce, and venison with raspberry sauce are examples of the output. Vegetables continue as micro-tastes of many, though nowadays people want more of one. Desserts continue the good work, though cheese is not always in evidence. Rhapsodies about strawberries in pistachio-sugared fritters, hot prune and armagnac soufflé, and chocolate pyramid with mango ice-cream abound. A page of bottles from Romanée Conti and a page of Krug make clear that we are on serious wine territory; Gaja Barbaresco and Penfolds Grange are confirmation. Decent house wine selections and a neat package of three wines to accompany a meal – a half-bottle of white, a bottle of claret and two glasses of dessert wine or port, all for £28 – afford some economy, but this remains essentially a well-chosen and expensive list. House wine is £10.50.

CHEF: Ian Corkhill PROPRIETOR: The Hon Ronald Eden OPEN: all week CLOSED: 2 weeks Feb MEALS: 12 to 2.30, 7 to 10 PRICES: Set L £22 (£30), Set D £32 (£41). Card slips closed CARDS: Access, Amex, Diners, Visa SEATS: 60. 4 tables outside. Private parties: 30 main room, 12, 16 and 24 private rooms. Car park, 30 places. Vegetarian meals. Children's helpings. No smoking in dining-room. Wheelchair access (also WC). No music. Fax: (0786) 825450 ACCOMMODATION: 14 rooms, all with bath/shower. B&B £100 to £210. Deposit: £100. Children welcome. Baby facilities. Pets welcome. Afternoon teas. Garden. Tennis. Fishing. TV. Phone. Scenic. Doors close at midnight (*Which? Hotel Guide*)

KINGUSSIE Highland map 8

▲ *The Cross*

25–27 High Street, Kingussie PH21 1HX COOKING 3*
KINGUSSIE (0540) 661762 and 661166 COST £32–£47

'The British Rail (Kingussie) Pipe Band strutted and blew joyously as we sipped pre-dinner drinks. The town was getting set for gala and guests were abandoned in the establishments across the road as staff crowded to look,' a reader writes. The Cross is a tiny restaurant with rooms slap on the main street and the Hadleys have made it a place of pilgrimage, pipe band or no. Experience and practice have had their effect, creating a more *soigné* ambience, softening some of the angles of service and improving the presentation. What they have not done is taken the edge off Ruth Hadley's cooking, or put the prices beyond the reach of enthusiastic everyman. A set-price menu offers a choice of three at each stage, with a soup served at second course. On Saturdays, the choice remains for the first and main courses, but around these the soup, fish dish, pre-main course sorbet, cheeseboard and dessert are all set. This extravaganza is remarkable value. English restaurants should blush. As one reporter said, 'After some disappointing Cumbrian evenings this winter, it was refreshing to find Scotland in great fettle.' Ruth Hadley has avoided the pitfall of sophistication through elaboration. There are terrines, and occasional stuffings, but in the main it is raw material plus a sauce. When dishes are 'made' the touch is light, as, for instance, in the mousseline of scallops with a prawn sauce, and smoked salmon parcels with a mousse filling ('balanced and cool, not cloying and creamy at all'). Materials – venison, say, or halibut – are excellent: 'the halibut steak was huge, tender, melting in an exact mustard-sherry sauce, the star of the evening, but even the duck was neither soggy nor fatty, *echt* duck indeed.' Soups are good here, so are vegetables, and so are the lovingly tended cheeses. Puddings may be rich, sometimes, then regretted as 'sighs of delight' over a brittle, sharp blackcurrant tart are heard from the next table. This is cooking of great assurance. Guidance through the very long wine list is readily to hand. Usual constraints such as a search for economy are irrelevant, with mark-ups barely detectable from prices that might be expected in many retail outlets; the problem here is an embarrassment of affordable riches. Mercurey from Juillot at £18.60 or a Rolly Gassmann Gewurztraminer Réserve for £14.80 are snips. Australasia and the Loire are very strong but Italy remains unexplored. Of the many half-bottles, the dessert wines are especially notable. CELLARMAN'S CHOICE: Cloudy Bay Sauvignon 1990, £15.85; Côtes du Rhône Villages, Ch. de la Gardine 1983, £11.60.

CHEF: Ruth Hadley PROPRIETORS: Tony and Ruth Hadley OPEN: Tue to Sat, D only CLOSED: 3 weeks May, first 3 weeks Dec MEALS: 6.30 to 9.30 PRICES: Set D £23.50 (£32) to £29.50 (£39). Card slips closed SEATS: 20. Private parties: 18 main room. Vegetarian meals. No children under 12. No smoking in dining-room. Wheelchair access. No music. Fax: (0540) 661080 ACCOMMODATION: 3 rooms, all with bath/shower. D, B&B £50 to £120. Deposit: £25. No children under 12 (*Which? Hotel Guide*)

LINLITHGOW Lothian map 8

Champany Inn ▲

Champany Corner, Linlithgow EH49 7LU
PHILPSTOUN (050 683) 4532 and 4388
2m NE of Linlithgow at junction of A904 and A803

COOKING 4
COST £47

The Champany continues on a steady course under the watchful eyes of the Davidsons. It achieves, with a style all its own, precisely the ends it has set itself. Beef, lamb, lobster and salmon are cooked, mostly on the charcoal grill, on a scale that enables the restaurant to control its own supplies. The raw materials are matchless. Some would dispute the year-round use of Shetland farmed salmon, though few return from eating it saying it lacked flavour or texture. The beef is hung until dark as dark; the lobsters are kept, and cleansed, in a live tank until ordered; the lamb is only new season's. Customers participate in this provisioning exercise: they choose their steaks raw, they see their lobster or crayfish, they are shown their vegetables, they go to the salad bar or the cheese table. The setting is as definitely Champany as the food, luxurious, thoroughly thought through and unlike anywhere else in Scotland: vivid monogrammed carpet, raw stone, timbered roof and a wine cage. Other things exist on the menu, none of them very complex, but all good: caviare, chicken liver pâté, gravlax, a soup or two. These, however, are apostrophes to the main business. If the list of spirits is longer than most restaurant's wine lists, the wine list itself might intimidate all but the most robust. A dozen 'own label' wines offer help, but the undaunted are faced with a massive volume of finely chosen bottles. France, especially Burgundy, dominates. Good bottles at affordable prices from the Rhône and Bordeaux right-bank, as well as California and Australia, are also in reasonable force. But the thrust here is towards the expensive, and mark-ups do not encourage experiment once the £25 barrier is breached.

CHEFS: David Gibson and Clive Davidson PROPRIETORS: Clive and Anne Davidson OPEN: Mon to Sat, exc Sat L CLOSED: 3 weeks from 24 Dec MEALS: 12.30 to 2, 7.15 to 10 PRICES: £26 (£39). Minimum £12.50. Service 10%. Card slips closed CARDS: Access, Amex, Diners, Visa SEATS: 50. 13 tables outside. Private parties: 50 main room. Car park, 100 places. No children under 8. Smart dress preferred. Wheelchair access. No music. Fax: (050 683) 4302

▲ *This symbol means that accommodation is available.*

MARKINCH Fife map 8

▲ *Balbirnie House*

Balbirnie Park, Markinch KY7 6NE COOKING 2
GLENROTHES (0592) 610066 COST £16–£38

The classical Greek-style mansion is a cracker; so, too, is the park with woods, endless rhododendrons and a golf course lapping the lawns. Discreetly restored, the interiors are grand in scale and keep the clean lines of the original. There may be a serious pitch to the corporate market, but the private customer is not omitted from a wide range of special offers for accommodation, breaks and the like. Similarly, the cooking can be on the corporate side, but it also gives satisfaction. A terrine of fish with dill and lime sauce, bearing a garnish of mussels, prawns, oysters and scallops, leek and asparagus soup, beef with madeira and port sauce and horseradish dumplings, and duck with calvados sauce and apples done in calvados have been good dishes. Less impressive were the vegetables (Scotland in the lean months of early spring) and desserts. Service has mechanical efficiency. Breakfasts are enjoyed. The wine list is ambitious, with wide terms of reference and a fair range of prices. House wine is £9.75.

CHEF: George Mackay PROPRIETORS: Balbirnie House Hotel Ltd OPEN: all week MEALS: 12.30 to 2, 7 to 9.30 PRICES: L £16 (£25), Set L £9.50 (£16) to £12.50 (£19), Set D £24.50 (£32). Card slips closed CARDS: Access, Amex, Diners, Visa SEATS: 45. Private parties: 60 main room, 16 and 60 private rooms. Car park, 100 places. Vegetarian meals. Children's helpings. Smart dress preferred. No cigars/pipes in dining-room. Wheelchair access (also WC). Music ACCOMMODATION: 30 rooms, all with bath/shower. Rooms for disabled. B&B £69 to £140. Children welcome. Baby facilities. Pets welcome. Afternoon teas. Garden. Golf. Snooker. TV. Scenic. Doors close at midnight. Confirm by 6

MOFFAT Dumfries & Galloway map 8

▲ *Beechwood Country House Hotel*

NEW ENTRY

Moffat DG10 9RS COOKING 1
MOFFAT (0683) 20210 COST £16–£28

The hotel is a few sharp turns out of this small country town renowned for a hard toffee sweet. Find the church and school at the north end of the high street and take the road between them. Beechwood was once a house in the country but is now perilously near being engulfed by Moffat Academy, golf greens and other aspects of suburbia. The welcome from Lynda and Jeff Rogers is hearty and you may be seated in modern conservatory, formal dining-room, or in bar lounge if coffee or a daytime snack is all that is wanted. There is no country-house hauteur in either the decoration or the friendliness of the staff. Carl Shaw cooks a bold dinner from a monthly-changing menu that constitutes excellent value and contains dishes and ingredients of originality. One visitor to this corner of Scotland became convinced that the British classic of prawn cocktail, steak, and Black Forest gâteau still held utter dominion. Support the likes of Mr Shaw, therefore. Cooking is not necessarily complex: saucing is not invariable, some items like excellent smoked salmon and a fine home-made dill mayonnaise may outshine made dishes such as terrines. But vegetables are well treated, cooking of meats and fish is careful, and sweet things seem to get extra-special attention. The largely Justerini wine list is decently chosen and never overpriced. House wines start at £6.95.

CHEF: Carl Shaw PROPRIETORS: Lynda and Jeffrey Rogers OPEN: all week CLOSED: 4 Jan to 8 Feb MEALS: 12 to 2, 7.30 to 9 PRICES: Set Sun L £10.50 (£16), Set D £16.85 (£23), Snacks Mon to Sat from £2. Card slips closed CARDS: Access, Amex, Visa SEATS: 26. 2 tables outside L. Private parties: 26 main room. Car park, 15 places. Vegetarian meals. Children welcome. Children's helpings. No smoking in dining-room. Wheelchair access (2 steps). Music. Fax: (0683) 20889 ACCOMMODATION: 7 rooms, all with bath/shower. B&B £45 to £64. Children welcome. Baby facilities. Pets welcome. Afternoon teas. Garden. TV. Phone. Scenic. Doors close at midnight (*Which? Hotel Guide*)

▲ *Well View Hotel*

COUNTY RESTAURANT OF THE YEAR

NEW ENTRY

Ballplay Road, Moffat DG10 9JU
MOFFAT (0683) 20184

COOKING 1*
COST £11–£26

'The decoration is as undemonstrative as the food is imaginative' may sound snooty, but emphasises that this small hotel, 'as green as the fennel and Pernod soup served at my dinner', offers food of quality and value. Janet Schuckardt's daily menus give limited choice, perhaps of three dishes at each course, with extra courses of cheese – of a very high standard for the district – and soup. An inspector's meal comprised a Brie and filo parcel with intense redcurrant sauce; the aforementioned green soup; chicken breast, wrapped in smoked bacon and filled with smoked Orkney cheese, which had a leek butter sauce that might have had more impact; cheeses; then an Ecclefechan pie (shortcrust pastry with candied peel and fruit and nuts). Vigour in the cooking showed through small things like anchovy tarts as an appetiser, finely diced ratatouille as vegetable, and decent truffles and fudge. The price is something to write home about, so is the wine list with good names and fair prices – Guigal Hermitage 1982 at £17.95 should go fast. House wine is £5.80.

CHEF: Janet Schuckardt PROPRIETORS: Janet and John Schuckardt OPEN: all week CLOSED: first week Jan, 1 week Nov MEALS: 12.15 to 1.15, 6.30 to 8.30 PRICES: Set L £7.50 (£11) to £8.50 (£13), Set D £15 (£20) to £17.50 (£22). Card slips closed CARDS: Access, Visa SEATS: 24. Private parties: 24 main room, 8 private room. Car park, 8 places. Vegetarian meals with prior notice. Children's helpings. Smart dress preferred. No smoking in dining-areas. Wheelchair access (2 steps; also WC). No music ACCOMMODATION: 7 rooms, 5 with bath/shower. D,B&B £45.50 to £106. Deposit: £10. Children welcome. Baby facilities. Pets by arrangement. Garden. TV. Scenic. Doors close at 11.30. Confirm by 5.30

Prices quoted in the Guide *are based on information supplied by restaurateurs. The figure in brackets below an entry is the average for a three-course meal with service, coffee and half a bottle of house wine, as calculated by computer. The prices quoted at the top of an entry represent a range, from the lowest average meal price to the highest; the latter is inflated by 20 per cent to take account of the fact that very few people eat an average meal, and also that prices are likely to rise during the year of the* Guide.

MUIR OF ORD Highland

map 8

▲ *Dower House* 🍷

Highfield, Muir of Ord IV6 7XN
MUIR OF ORD (0463) 870090
on A862, 1m out of Muir of Ord

COOKING 2
COST £32–£42

Robyn and Mena Aitchison's delightful eighteenth-century dower house maintains, through an abundance of bric-à-brac, plants and flowered chintz, the semblance of a private house. Guests who find themselves dining alone in the formal dining-room may find the silence bothersome. The food is widely praised for presentation, sauces and vegetables. The concept is unusual, but it works. 'Things we expected to be hot were cold (like the excellent garlic soup) and, likewise, cold were hot, like the fruit salad for dessert,' ran one pleasantly surprised report. The four-course set-price dinner menu offers simple choices, such as chicken livers with ginger butter sauce or langoustine vinaigrette, turbot coated in sesame seed with sorrel sauce or venison with juniper and rowan-berry sauce. To finish, there may be toffee pudding with caramel sauce or a passion-fruit roulade. Desserts, both hot and cold, have been specially remarked. Coffee comes with home-made truffles. Buying from impeccable sources guarantees quality in the wine list. With a collection of halves that should be the envy of many, and prices that seem fair throughout, pleasure is not held hostage to extravagance. House wine is £11. CELLARMAN'S CHOICE: Rioja Blanco Crianza, Monteliva 1988, £13.50; Chinon, Clos des Folies 1986, Dom. du Roncée, £17.50.

CHEF: Robyn Aitchison PROPRIETORS: Robyn and Mena Aitchison OPEN: all week, D only (L by arrangement) MEALS: 7.30 for 8 PRICES: Set D £23.50 (£32) to £26 (£35). Card slips closed CARDS: Access, Amex, Visa SEATS: 20. 3 tables outside. Private parties: 20 main room. Car park, 20 places. Vegetarian meals. Children's helpings. No smoking in dining-room. Wheelchair access (also WC). No music. One sitting. Fax: (0463) 870090 ACCOMMODATION: 5 rooms, all with bath/shower. Rooms for disabled. B&B £45 to £100. Deposit: 25%. Children welcome. Baby facilities. Pets by arrangement. Garden. Fishing. Golf. TV. Phone. Scenic. Doors close at 11.30. Confirm by 4

NEWTONMORE Highland

map 8

▲ *Ard-Na-Coille Hotel* 🍾

Kingussie Road, Newtonmore PH20 1AY
NEWTONMORE (054 03) 214, changes to (0540) 673214 in Autumn 1991

COOKING 3
COST £35

'Placing more importance on the food than the bed, we found ourselves here. But the room was really comfortable, the "refurbishment, which is needed", seemed fully carried out. They have apparently reduced the number of rooms in order to concentrate on the food – commendable. As we sat down to dinner, their devotion was immediately apparent,' went one report. The menu is on show in the corridor downstairs from tea-time and those who care will catch an early glimpse so they can order their wine up from the cellar. This is a treasure-house: of wine, of unembellished food where 'vegetables looked and tasted like vegetables not artistic creations', and of enthusiastic hospitality. The academic background of both Barry Cottam and Nancy Ferrier comes out in the informative notes to the wine list. It also means they are amateurs in the pure sense of the word. The five-course menu has the merit of economy by contrast to some Highland extravaganzas yet the standard of materials is never lower, nor the cooking less skilful. Barry Cottam is becoming more artful (more mousses, more stuffings), yet the purity of the original intentions shines through. A spring meal began with a pastry case filled with turbot with a ginger and coriander sauce, then a courgette, lemon and thyme soup, followed by fillet steak fried to order, with a Meaux mustard sauce. Excellent vegetables, a fine, carefully constructed choice of cheese, then crème brûlée completed the picture – not over-complex, but to the point. A determination to extend the geographical boundaries of the wine list has resulted in disillusion; customers stick to what they know. So this year, while the very generous and sensible fixed-price rather than percentage mark-up is maintained, any expansion of the less popular areas is halted. However, some judicious pruning may render the consumers' decision less awesome. This remains a fine list, as remarkable in its provision of exceptional growers as in its kindness to the pocket. House wines are from £11. CELLARMAN'S CHOICE: Riesling, 'Pflaenzereben' 1985, Rolly Gassmann, £16.50; Chambolle Musigny 1984, Roumier, £14.50.

CHEF: Barry Cottam PROPRIETORS: Barry Cottam and Nancy Ferrier OPEN: all week, D only CLOSED: mid-Nov and Dec MEALS: 7.45 PRICES: Set D £23.50 (£29). Card slips closed CARDS: Access, Visa SEATS: 18. Private parties: 18 main room. Car park, 20 places. Children's helpings on request. No smoking in dining-room. No music. One sitting. Fax: (0540) 673453 ACCOMMODATION: 7 rooms, all with bath/shower. D, B&B £50 to £120. Children welcome. Baby facilities. Pets welcome. Garden. Phone. Scenic. Doors close at 11.30. Confirm by 4 (*Which? Hotel Guide*)

NORTH BERWICK Lothian map 8

Harding's 🍷

2 Station Road,
North Berwick EH39 4AU — COOKING 2*
NORTH BERWICK (0620) 4737 — COST £13–£31

Sitting between station and housing estate, and described by one reporter as a 'shack' and another as 'more fitting for a thatched than a slated roof', Christopher Harding's restaurant serves unexpectedly good food in neat surroundings of tongued-and-grooved boards, rugs on the walls and chequered tablecloths. He cooks, washes up, plans the daily-changing menu and chooses excellent Australasian wines for a surprising list. The repertoire is steady: an avocado salad with walnut dressing, sole with (dryish) prawns in a choux bun and lemon butter sauce, fillets of lamb with red wine and tarragon sauce, good (and generous) cheeses, and hot pear and praline soufflé have been remarked upon this year. The fair coffee, good chocolates and poor vegetables have also been noted. Service is smiling though a mite perfunctory when it comes to the wine: P(our) Y(our) O(wn) rather than B(ring) Y(our) O(wn). There are two routes into the long wine list: turn to the last page for a dozen French, all carefully chosen and fairly priced or, more interestingly, take up Christopher Harding's offer to select an Australian bottle. Prices are modest throughout, and quality of growers and some attention paid to older wines are reassuring. Penfolds Grange comes in four vintages and there are good ranges of '86 and '85 whites. House wine is £7.20. CELLARMAN'S CHOICE: Dalwhinnie Chardonnay 1988, £16.60; Lake's Folly, Cabernet Sauvignon 1988, £19.50.

CHEF/PROPRIETOR: Christopher Harding OPEN: Wed to Sat MEALS: 12 to 2, 7.30 to 9 PRICES: Set L £7.75 (£13) to £10.50 (£16), Set D £17.95 (£24) to £19.70 (£26) SEATS: 24. Private parties: 24 main room. Car park, 3 places. Children's helpings. No smoking. Wheelchair access (also WC). Music

OBAN Strathclyde

map 8

▲ *Knipoch Hotel*

Oban PA34 4QT
KILNINVER (085 26) 251

COOKING 2*
COST £48

Scotland gets right the conjunction of hills, woods, water and the odd hotel popped in the middle of it more often than most British regions. Knipoch is a fair example. What is more, it is occupied by the Craig family, who take seriously food and wine, particularly its production and sourcing. So the diner may rest quiet that much preliminary work has been done to ensure the Muscovy duck was happy before it ended in the oven, and that the bottle came from the right supplier by the right route – just as with the same care, the coffee is roasted on site. The five-course dinner menu (with no choice) is dear for Scotland, but quantities are generous and meals well balanced. If anything is unacceptable to diners, there is a short list of alternatives *in extremis*. Cooking combines the traditional, such as chateaubriand béarnaise, with the enterprising, such as home-smoked local scallops with a lemon mayonnaise, and fruit meringues with a Beaujolais sauce. Mr Craig is an enthusiast and it shows. Our complaint about the confused listing of the wines still stands. But so, also, does our praise for the quality and range offered. Every major area receives even-handed treatment and prices throughout are very fair. House wine is £8.50. CELLARMAN'S CHOICE: New Zealand, Marlborough Sauvignon Blanc 1988, Stoneleigh, £11; Chile, Cabernet Sauvignon 1987, Santa Rita, £9.90.

CHEFS: Colin and Jenny Craig PROPRIETORS: the Craig family OPEN: all week, D only (L by arrangement) CLOSED: mid-Nov to mid-Feb MEALS: 7.30 to 9 PRICES: Set D £33 (£40). Card slips closed CARDS: Access, Amex, Diners, Visa SEATS: 46. Private parties: 24 main room. Car park, 40 places. Children's helpings. No music. Fax: (085 26) 249
ACCOMMODATION: 17 rooms, all with bath/shower. B&B £56 to £112. Children welcome. Afternoon teas. Garden. TV. Phone. Scenic. Doors close at 11. Confirm by 6
(*Which? Hotel Guide*)

'My biggest disappointment over the past 10 years is how little the general eating-out population has changed. I was once asked for everything without sauce. Totally fed up, I refused. The customer's overheard comment was: ''It has to come with sauce because it comes out of the bag like that.'' What surprised me was that he was quite happy to accept this.' On cooking in the South of England

PEAT INN Fife map 8

▲ *Peat Inn*

Peat Inn KY15 5LH
PEAT INN (033 484) 206
at junction of B940 and B941,
6m SW of St Andrews

COOKING 4
COST £23–£53

The Peat Inn gives its name to the settlement, but its character is not grand – from the outside at least. Once you go through the door, surprise may overtake you for the decoration of the first room is striking, the three dining-rooms that follow have overtones of grand French restaurants rather than homely Scots cottages, and the accommodation in the Residence behind is luxurious to a fault. The Wilsons' creation is unique. The steady development of David Wilson's cooking has also captivated a large audience north and south of the border. It has become more artful over the years, entering strongly the mainstream of European fashion even if the regular use of the best local ingredients – fish, shellfish and game – marks it as of its place. One change has been that of fussiness and elaboration. The style of cooking has always steered away from too many mousses and fillings, but plates are none the less littered with small piles which often frustrate those in search of, for instance, more potatoes than 'two the size of a thimble' or more beans 'than three each cut into three pieces'. This development does seem to have vitiated the impact of the cooking and there have been many reports expressing disappointment: having travelled for flavour and art, diners have found only the second. The menus offered include a *carte*, a menu of the day at set price, and a tasting menu at a higher price to be taken by the whole table. An exemplary meal included dishes from the first two menus: a fricassee of artichoke heart, lobster and wild mushrooms; pigeon breast in a pastry case with wild mushrooms; fillet of sole with a sweet pepper sauce; medallions of venison with a port and red wine sauce; and a ragoût of turbot, lobster, sole, brill and langoustine 'so wonderful,' according to one reporter, 'we were sorry to finish it'. Here the sauces had clarity and depth, and the great quality of the principal ingredients both shone through and was enhanced by the accompaniments. Desserts such as a caramelised sandwich of pastry and apple with a strong caramel sauce, and a pineapple and grenadine sorbet with the entire range of exotic fruits available in Fife arranged around it have impressed: 'The smooth sorbet would have been a delight on its own, and the galaxy of fruits made it into a banquet.' A number of readers this year have found the welcome less effusive than before; this may be when the Wilsons are away. The wine list (a refreshing balance of the modest and the grand, all chosen with care) continues to impress with its clarity. It is worth digging deeper in the pocket here since the mark-ups reflect quality very fairly; a large wine bill here could be worth it. Among the clarets the 'super seconds' are much in evidence, and there is a fine collection of 'Cabernets from other countries'. Enthusiasm is manifest throughout but burgundies are especially favoured. CELLARMAN'S CHOICE: Tokay d'Alsace Réserve 1986, Dopff au Moulin, £16; Givry, Clos Marceaux 1988, Juillot, £17.

CHEF: David Wilson PROPRIETORS: David and Patricia Wilson OPEN: Tue to Sat CLOSED: 2 weeks Jan and Nov MEALS: 1 to 2.30, 7 to 9.30 PRICES: £29 (£37), Set L £16.50 (£23), Set D £28 (£34) to £38 (£44). Net prices, card slips closed CARDS: Access, Amex, Diners, Visa SEATS: 48. Private parties: 24 main room, 12 private room. Car park, 24 places. Children's helpings. No smoking during meals. Wheelchair access (also WC). No music. Fax: (033 484) 530 ACCOMMODATION: 8 rooms, all with bath/shower. Rooms for disabled. B&B £95 to £115. No children under 12. Garden. Fishing. Golf. TV. Phone. Scenic. Confirm by 4 (*Which? Hotel Guide*)

PEEBLES Borders map 8

▲ *Cringletie House*

Eddleston, Peebles EH45 8PL
EDDLESTON (072 13) 233
on A703, 2m N of Peebles

COOKING 1
COST £18–£36

A whole lotta turrets, even more dormers, a croquet lawn, a winding drive through daffodils and strutting pheasants: all in all, Cringletie offers atmosphere. The Maguires' hotel is often enjoyed, for its informality and lack of pretension – qualities that the architecture and setting may not at once imply. The cooking has been described as 'solid, pleasant, country-style', but Aileen Maguire injects invention into recipes often enlivened by spices or herbs. Nor is it standard country-style inasmuch as choice is built into the four-course, set-price dinner (soup comes second). When everything runs smoothly, many concur about dishes such as curried chicken salad, courgette and mint timbale, lamb's liver and onions, halibut with ginger and chive sauce, or chicken with mango and coriander. Sweets are on the trolley and may suffer from this fact. With a touch more weight, at no cost to brevity, the wine list could be an award-winner. The range is catholic; the wines are chosen intelligently and show concern for economy. House wine is £9 a litre. CELLARMAN'S CHOICE: Savennières, Clos du Papillon 1988, Baumard, £11.75; Ch. La Tour St Bonnet 1982, £14.50.

CHEFS: Aileen Maguire and Sheila McKellar PROPRIETORS: Mr and Mrs Stanley Maguire OPEN: all week CLOSED: Jan and Feb MEALS: 1 to 1.45, 7.30 to 8.30 PRICES: L £10 (£18), Set Sun L £13.50 (£20), Set D £22.50 (£30). Minimum £5. Alc L only. Card slips closed CARDS: Access, Visa SEATS: 56. Private parties: 30 main room. Car park, 40 places. Vegetarian meals. Children's helpings. No smoking in dining-room. No music. Fax: (072 13) 244 ACCOMMODATION: 13 rooms, all with bath/shower. Lift. B&B £44 to £80. Children welcome. Baby facilities. Pets welcome. Afternoon teas. Garden. Tennis. TV. Phone. Scenic. Doors close at 11. Confirm by 5 (*Which? Hotel Guide*)

'When I am charged £9 for a half-bottle of Gewurztraminer, I do not expect the wine waiter to ask me for the number on the list (it was in fact the Cellarman's Choice) if there is only one Gewurz. I do not then expect a second waiter to come and check that I ordered a Sauvignon. Lastly, I do not expect the bottle to be put in an ice bucket at the other end of the room and then all the staff to run and hide so that I can't have a second glass without attracting the stares of a roomful of men. Never again!' On eating in Manchester

PERTH Tayside map 8

Timothy's

24 St John Street, Perth PH1 5SP COOKING 1
PERTH (0738) 26641 COST £22

A hundred yards from the River Tay, this all-day café-bistro runs a long list of Danish-inspired open sandwiches buttressed by seafood, meat and vegetable salads. Come mealtimes, there are daily specials, savoury and sweet: asparagus, sea trout and steamed sponge pudding with a fudge sauce are mentioned with enthusiasm. The Laings have been here for more than 20 years – 'the mixed assembly of balloon-backed and Windsor chairs, various tables and the hessian on the walls all add to the mellow atmosphere, cosy and restful.' House French is £6.30 and akvavit is kept in the freezer.

CHEF: Caroline Laing PROPRIETORS: Caroline and Athole Laing OPEN: Tue to Sat CLOSED: 3 weeks summer MEALS: 12 to 2.30, 7 to 10.15 (post-theatre menu by arrangement) PRICES: £13 (£18) Minimum £5.50 after 9.30. Card slips closed CARDS: Access, Visa SEATS: 54. Private parties: 20 main room. Vegetarian meals. Children's helpings. Wheelchair access. Music D. Air-conditioned

PORT APPIN Strathclyde map 8

▲ *Airds Hotel*

Port Appin PA38 4DF COOKING 4
APPIN (063 173) 236 COST £50

The cooking at this deceptively unassuming house by Loch Linnhe is triumphant justification for a simple, accurate and direct approach. So many meals are over-priced and over-dressed, even today. It is always distressing knowing what they could have been if only priorities were set differently. No such trouble exists here. What is true of the dining-room is true of the hotel too: sophistication without flash. The house may look modest, but inside is all proud Scottish from red, thistled carpet to plaid ribbons on the napkins and Eric Allen's kilt. Housekeeping is of a high order: flowers are good, antiques well-polished, the staff impeccable in motivation and performance. The short menu is available early so that guests may pick their meal and their wine by 7.30pm. As one reader expressed it: 'The menu is tied directly to the seasons, the cooking appears simple, but this masks well-judged complexities carrying vivid flavour. Portions are not intimidating.' A spring visit produced such dishes as smoked salmon wrapping a smoked salmon mousse flanked by a mustard and fresh dill sauce, topped by a dab of caviare; a rich terrine of chicken livers with Cumberland sauce to give balance; a cauliflower soup that did not taste of last week's washing; turbot on a bed of spinach ('outstandingly good') with a mustard sauce that almost took the fish over; vegetables, with celeriac with pine kernels, scrubbed new potatoes and broccoli; lobster and scallop risotto as good as any in Italophile London; breast of pigeon ('pink, slightly livery, earthy') with a madeira and juniper sauce; lamb with an onion marmalade; a very fine lemon tart; and a jelly of orange and Grand Marnier in two layers, one red, one orange. Saucing is so well thought out that simplicity of concept is forgotten in the balance and counterpoint of centrepiece and support. That, joined with the impeccable ingredients, is the strength of this place. The wine list is a beacon of excellence and fair-minded generosity. France (burgundies are notable) predominates, but the same care goes into California, Italy and Australia. Prices look high but only because quality is exceptional. Many half-bottles, a house selection and finely chosen Loires all afford more thrifty alternatives. House wine is £10.50.

CHEFS: Betty Allen, Graeme Allen and Moira Thompson PROPRIETORS: Eric, Betty and Graeme Allen OPEN: all week MEALS: 12.30 to 1.30, 8 for 8.30 PRICES: Set D £33 (£42), Snacks from £2 SEATS: 40. Private parties: 40 main room, 8 private room. Car park, 30 places. Children's helpings. Smart dress preferred. No smoking in dining-room. No music. One sitting. Fax: (063 173) 535 ACCOMMODATION: 14 rooms, all with bath/shower. B&B £72 to £132. Deposit: £100. Children welcome. Afternoon teas. Garden. TV. Phone. Scenic. Doors close at 11.30. Confirm by 4 (*Which? Hotel Guide*)

PORTPATRICK Dumfries & Galloway map 8

▲ *Knockinaam Lodge*

Portpatrick DG9 9AD
PORTPATRICK (077 681) 471 COOKING 3
off A77, S of Portpatrick COST £25–£46

Drive over open lanes through scrubland and down the glen to a sudden vista of civilisation: a Victorian granite house surrounded by lawns and flowerbeds – then the sea. A private bay is an enviable possession. Once through the door, country-house civilisation continues: Colefax and Fowler and the odd copy of Debrett in the reception rooms or bar, but a pronounced switch to France in the dining-room. Menu, food, style, materials: all is French, much of it (butter, cheese) imported direct. Lunch can be had here, bookings only, but is slightly abbreviated and seems a less satisfactory meal, though cheaper, than the three-course dinner, with coffee. One reader described 'seven evening meals, all of excellent quality, demonstrating how it is possible to produce different menus each day, and give the client a feeling that each evening is a new occasion of good eating.' Trimmings for the dinners are good too: canapés in the bar may include grilled chicken wings, smoked salmon rounds, caviare, and bouchés of sweetbreads. Daniel Galmiche's cooking is undeniably modern, and sometimes veers on the side of parsimony when appetites fired by the day's walking need satisfying, but is also considered: different vegetables are served with different main courses. The sort of dishes offered are salmon marinated with chives and coriander, sweetbreads with truffle on a bed of bacon and watercress, pigeon with peas and a thyme gravy, brill with a purée of potatoes spiked with garlic and curry, and pears on a pastry base with vanilla and calvados sauce. The serious intentions of the restaurant have survived its relative isolation. The Frichots have lasted some years now; long may they continue. On the wine list, fine clarets start a canter through the main wine countries of the world. Burgundy is a weak spot showing over-reliance on big houses. There is a reasonable spread of half-bottles; prices throughout are fair. House wines are from £9.

CHEF: Daniel Galmiche PROPRIETORS: Marcel and Corinna Frichot OPEN: all week CLOSED: 4 Jan to 14 Mar MEALS: 12.30 to 2, 7.30 to 9 PRICES: Set L £18 (£25), Set D £30 (£38). Card slips closed CARDS: Access, Amex, Diners, Visa SEATS: 28. Private parties: 40 main room. Car park, 25 places. Children under 12 high teas only. Jacket and tie. No smoking in dining-room. Wheelchair access (1 step; also WC). No music. Fax: (077 681) 435 ACCOMMODATION: 10 rooms, all with bath/shower. D,B&B £92.50 to £152. Deposit: £100. Children welcome. Baby facilities. Pets welcome. Afternoon teas. Garden. Fishing. Snooker. TV. Phone. Scenic. Doors close at midnight. Confirm 7 days ahead (*Which? Hotel Guide*)

SCONE Tayside map 8

▲ *Murrayshall Hotel*

County Restaurant of the Year

Scone PH2 7PH COOKING 3*
SCONE (0738) 51171 COST £20–£49

Murrayshall is magnificently placed, high above Perth, with panoramic views of the surrounding countryside. Inside, it is thickly carpeted and oozes comfort. Some visitors come for the golf, others for the scenery, the low-key luxury and the food. Taking its cue from its location, the kitchen focuses on Scottish produce: Finnan haddock (poached for breakfast, transformed into a chowder with leeks, green lentils, horseradish and saffron for dinner), Perthshire venison and pigeon, West Coast scallops, Tay salmon and, of course, beef, backed up by fish from the market. The result is cuisine of a high order. Bruce Sangster cooks five-course fixed-price dinners with several choices at each stage; dishes are often complex, as in brace of boneless quail carved and served on a bed of sweet-and-sour cabbage with an essence of madeira and mushrooms. One recorded summer meal showed all the hallmarks of serious intent: freshness and variety, 'a galaxy of tastes and textures', outstanding sauces, perfect timing and artful but unmannered presentation. Hot timbale of field mushrooms and chives with glazed apples came as a soft black mousse with a pretty green peppercorn sauce; fish and shellfish soup with star anise and garlic rouille was reported as a 'strong brew with a fresh aroma of the open sea'. Highlights from the main courses were a brandy, ginger and shellfish sauce accompanying medallion of veal, and perfectly pink loin of marinated lamb with tarragon mousse wrapped in caul fat and served with roasted shallots. To finish, lemon tart with its own sorbet on an orange and pineapple coulis had just the right balance of sweetness and astringency. Other meals have consistently met the same standards and the details and incidentals are well up to the mark too: decent breads, Scottish cheeses served with celery and grapes, good coffee and petits fours, and a multitude of malt whiskies at the bar. Service is naturally polished, but slightly aloof at times. The quality of the wine list is very fine, but there is little on offer below £15. Half-bottles are in profusion, which offers some relief to the high mark-up on more exalted bottles. California and Australia show well, but classic French bottles dominate.

CHEF: Bruce Sangster PROPRIETORS: Macolsen Ltd OPEN: all week, D only, and Sun L MEALS: 12 to 2, 7 to 9.30 PRICES: Set Sun L £13.50 (£20), Set D £32.50 (£41). Card slips closed CARDS: Access, Amex, Diners, Visa SEATS: 60. Private parties: 20 main room, 70 private room. Car park. Vegetarian meals. Children welcome. Jacket and tie. No smoking in dining-room. Wheelchair access. Music. Fax: (0738) 52595 ACCOMMODATION: 19 rooms, all with bath/shower. B&B £70 to £125. No children under 10. Pets welcome. Afternoon teas. Garden. Tennis. Golf. TV. Phone. Scenic. Confirm by 6 (*Which? Hotel Guide*)

STEWARTON Strathclyde map 8

▲ *Chapeltoun House* 🍷

Stewarton KA3 3ED
STEWARTON (0560) 82696
2m from Stewarton, on B769
towards Irvine

COOKING 2
COST £22–£37

Originally a solid turn of the century house, this small country-house hotel is heavily and formally furnished inside to match. Fortunately, though, the food is on another tack. 'Servings are of a reasonable size so that one does not feel bloated at the end but just pleasantly satisfied,' wrote one reader. The set-price menu offers reasonable choice at each of three courses, with an option on a fourth middle dish – perhaps clear duck consommé with beetroot and spring vegetables, or steamed West Coast mussels with a cider and apple sauce – for a supplementary price. Elaborate ideas can fall down on heavy technique or sauces. Salmon wrapped in a puff pastry lattice filled with sultanas and orange was served with an over-creamy, bland chervil and Muscadet sauce. Better executed were monkfish tails in asparagus sauce with chervil and crayfish, and a first-course terrine of lamb fillets 'woven into a creamy, light savoury custard'. Basic materials are not always as good as they should be; vegetables especially have come in for criticism, on one occasion notably lacking freshness. Desserts do not light fires of enthusiasm, coffee and petits fours could be improved. The clear, concise wine list encompasses good range; quality is high throughout, with fine Rhônes and Californians and a generous spread of clarets. Prices are fair and many decent half-bottles reinforce the good sense and generosity of the place. House wines are from £7.80. CELLARMAN'S CHOICE: Vouvray, Ch. de Gaudrelle 1985, £16.10; St Julien, Ch. Candulon 1983, £18.60.

CHEF: Tom O'Donnell PROPRIETORS: Colin and Graeme McKenzie OPEN: all week MEALS: 12 to 2, 7 to 9.15 PRICES: Set L £15 (£22), Set D £22.50 (£29) to £25.40 (£31). Card slips closed CARDS: Access, Amex, Visa SEATS: 55. Private parties: 35 main room, 20 and 55 private rooms. Car park, 50 places. Vegetarian meals. No children under 12. Smart dress preferred. No smoking in dining-room. Wheelchair access (3 steps; also WC). No music. Fax: (0560) 85100 ACCOMMODATION: 8 rooms, all with bath/shower. B&B £69 to £124. No children under 12. Pets by arrangement. Afternoon teas. Garden. Fishing. TV. Phone. Scenic. Doors close at midnight. Confirm by 1 (*Which? Hotel Guide*)

Card slips closed *in the details at the end of an entry indicates that the totals on the slips of credit cards are closed when these are handed over for signature.*

SWINTON Borders map 8

▲ *Wheatsheaf Hotel*

Swinton TD11 3JJ COOKING 3
SWINTON (089 086) 257 COST £23

Alan and Julie Reid are members of that small but growing band of publican/hoteliers who serve good food in bar and restaurant. So true is this in the case of the Wheatsheaf that there is no effective distinction between the menus on offer in dining-room, central lounge or recent (no-smoking) sun-lounge extension. Instead, there is on the one hand a long seasonal list of staples – mushroom, bacon and prawn pancake; chicken liver pâté; prawn cocktail; braised beef with real ale sauce; lamb and vegetable pie – and on the other, a daily blackboard à la carte of a dozen items such as tiger prawns with garlic butter, avocado Marie Rose, red mullet with basil, and tortellini bolognese. Prices are very fair indeed. A certain balance is struck between things that go down well in the Borders and more adventurous ideas. The larger of the two constituencies is impressed by the immediacy of the cooking, the bustling atmosphere and the 'quality craftsmanship that defies more expensive and pretentious competitors'. The wine list is conscious of price and quality and sacks the world to get 40 fair bottles and a dozen halves. Any pub that stocks Billecart-Salmon champagne must know something about taste. House wines are from £5.95.

CHEFS: Alan Reid and George Robertson PROPRIETORS: Alan and Julie Reid OPEN: Tue to Sun CLOSED: 25 Dec, 1 Jan, 2 weeks Feb, 1 week Oct MEALS: 11.45 to 2, 6 to 10 PRICES: £13 (£19). Card slips closed CARDS: Access, Visa SEATS: 20. Private parties: 20 main room, 28 and 28 private rooms. Vegetarian meals. Children's helpings. Smart dress preferred. No cigars/pipes in dining-room. Wheelchair access (1 step; also WC) ACCOMMODATION: 3 rooms. B&B £22 to £34. Children welcome. Baby facilities. Pets welcome. Garden. TV. Scenic. Doors close at midnight. Confirm by 6

TIRORAN Strathclyde map 8

▲ *Tiroran House*

Tiroran, Isle of Mull PA69 6ES COOKING 2
TIRORAN (068 15) 232 COST £15–£37

'It is natural, in traversing this gloom of desolation,' wrote Dr Johnson of a journey across Mull, 'to inquire whether something may not be done to give nature a more cheerful face.' Go to Tiroran House. Local visitors seem reticent letter writers and the *Guide* gets too few reports of insular excursions. But no doubt is thrown on Sue Blockey's talents as a fine natural cook or her husband's cosseting management of the house-party atmosphere. Dinner is for residents only, unless there is space for outsiders, the menu offering a small choice either side of a single main dish. The cooking is not old-fashioned 'Cordon Bleu', even if Sue Blockey does use an Aga as her main instrument. Dishes such as devilled crab puffs with a watercress sauce; leeks, tomato and black olives served with garlic bread; avgolemono soup; and good gravlax with a potato and chive salad and a cucumber dressing, show an alert culinary intelligence. Sweet things like peppered strawberries with orange shortbread, Guards' pudding and hot plum and marzipan pie form ample conclusions to meals. The main dish may be a roast, or perhaps a breast of chicken with leek and cheese stuffing or lamb shoulder stuffed with oysters. The Blockeys comment that too many dismiss roasts as 'simple roasts', pointing out not only the variety of cut, but also the immensely different means taken to prepare each joint for the oven. House wine is £7.75.

CHEF: Sue Blockey PROPRIETORS: Robin and Sue Blockey OPEN: all week, D only (L residents only) CLOSED: Oct to end May MEALS: 7.45 PRICES: Set L £11.50 (£15), Set D £27.50 (£31) SEATS: 20. Private parties: 6 main room. Car park, 20 places. No children under 10. Smart dress preferred. No smoking in dining-room. No music. One sitting ACCOMMODATION: 9 rooms, all with bath/shower. B&B £79 to £196. Deposit: £50. No children under 10. Pets by arrangement. Garden. Fishing. Scenic. Confirm previous day

TROON Strathclyde map 8

▲ *Highgrove House* **NEW ENTRY**

Old Loans Road, Troon KA10 7HL COOKING 1
TROON (0292) 312511 COST £20–£30

Fashions, culinary or health, are not noticed here on a hill overlooking the Firth of Clyde. Instead, Highgrove House offers solid creature comforts in a conventional setting and large portions of well-sauced food served by amiable if uninformed staff. Smoking is popular, especially in the dining-rooms, according to one report by a guest who complained ('waitress looked quite amazed: we are not far from the heart and cancer capital of Europe and I was letting the side down'). Neither the set-price four-course dinner nor the lengthy *carte* holds any surprises, Bill Costley sagely playing to the tastes of the largely local clientele with plain grills of beef and lamb, suprême of chicken with Swiss cheese, beef Stroganoff and poached langoustine. There is an overdose of dairy produce throughout: cheese or cream come with the gratin of mushrooms, in a glaze over the steamed Scottish salmon, on top of potatoes, as part of the sauce for the langoustine, and mussels, and so on. Ingredients are fresh although one reader complained that 'the salmon was the only produce on the menu the waitress could assure me was locally procured'. Desserts are excellent, especially a 'delicate and accomplished' chocolate torte. Coffee is dire. The wine list is fairly priced, with house wine at £8.75.

CHEF: William Costley PROPRIETORS: William and Catherine Costley OPEN: all week MEALS: 12 to 2.30, 7 to 9.30 PRICES: £13 (£20), Set L £15 (£21), Set D £18.50 (£25). Card slips closed CARDS: Access, Amex, Visa SEATS: 80. 8 tables outside. Private parties: 50 main room, 30 and 50 private rooms. Car park, 60 places. Vegetarian meals. Children welcome. Smart dress preferred. Wheelchair access (also WC). Music. Fax: (0292) 318228 ACCOMMODATION: 9 rooms, all with bath/shower. B&B £49 to £59. Children welcome. Baby facilities. Afternoon teas. Garden. TV. Phone. Scenic. Doors close at 1am. Confirm 48 hours ahead

The Guide *relies on feedback from its readers. Especially welcome are reports on new restaurants appearing in the book for the first time.*

UIG Western Isles map 8

▲ *Baile-na-Cille* NEW ENTRY

Timsgarry, Uig,
Isle of Lewis PA86 9JD
TIMSGARRY (085 175) 242
B8011 to Uig, then right down track on shore

COOKING 1
COST £24

'A really delightful place to stay and eat,' writes one visitor, 'indeed the only place to eat in the Outer Hebrides.' The setting is a converted eighteenth-century manse that has been fully modernised by Richard and Joanna Gollin, who run the hotel as an extension of their own home. Ringed by mountains and moorland, sitting on a long white-sand beach, it is ideal for birdwatching, hiking and quiet retreat. The atmosphere is good-humoured, idiosyncratic and informal. Mealtimes 'are a cross between dinner parties and the very best school dinners'. Joanna Gollin is a self-taught cook who turns her hand to substantial dishes built mostly around regional produce. Four-course dinners are along the lines of vegetable soup with pine-kernel dumplings; baked salmon with cucumber and dill sauce; roast haunch of island venison; and fresh strawberries with raspberry and cassis sauce. Vegetables are abundant and the Anglo-Scottish cheeseboard is strengthened by good Lanark Blue. Breads and oatcakes are home-baked. House wine is £8.50; other bottles – mostly from the Loire and Alsace – are priced at £12.50. Splendid breakfasts are crowned by superb kippers and Stornaway black pudding, 'which has acquired mythic status here'.

CHEF: Joanna Gollin PROPRIETORS: Richard and Joanna Gollin (Baile-na-Cille Ltd) OPEN: all week CLOSED: Oct 15 to Mar 1 MEALS: 9.30 to 5 snacks, 7.30 PRICES: Set D £16 (£20), Snacks from £2. Net prices SEATS: 30. Private parties: 30 main room. Car park, 10 places. Vegetarian meals. Children's helpings. No smoking in dining-room. No music. One sitting D. Fax: (085 175) 241 ACCOMMODATION: 13 rooms, 9 with bath/shower. B&B £19 to £56. Deposit: £20 to £50. Children welcome. Baby facilities. Pets welcome. Afternoon teas. Garden. Fishing. Scenic (*Which? Hotel Guide*)

ULLAPOOL Highland map 8

▲ *Altnaharrie Inn* 🍷

COUNTY RESTAURANT OF THE YEAR

Ullapool IV26 2SS
DUNDONNELL (085 483) 230

COOKING 5
COST £54

As is now well known, Gunn Eriksen's and Fred Brown's inn is reached by launch: a small motor boat comes to pick up guests from the harbour at Ullapool. In wild weather this trip may alarm the halt and querulous, as do the paths at the inn itself. A more robust view, from one reader, is that the trip 'tends to create close bonds between the guests (the group jeopardy situation) before they even set foot in the hotel; an unfair advantage perhaps.' Certainly, a sense of calm satisfaction settles on those who stay here. Altnaharrie has restrained taste, it is comfortable, the isolation imparts *de facto* exclusivity (the price may help too). The reverse of the coin – there always has to be one – is that should this mood or situation not captivate, it may grate. The dinner is set, apart from a choice of desserts. Three savoury courses are followed by the produce of two *maîtres fromagers*, as well as fine British cheeses. This effort to buy cheeses from France for a remote Highland spot exemplifies the spirit of the kitchen and dining-room. Effort shows in everything. Gunn Eriksen is faithful to her locality: wild sorrel goes into a soup; fish and shellfish bought off the quay may encompass humble as well as noble varieties. At the same time her cooking is part of a European continuum, and has been increasingly so over the years. There are some who regret this. While the watercress and wild sorrel soup was served tepid and foamy, with a sensual texture, achieved sublime simplicity; the following course of a ravioli stuffed with guinea-fowl forcemeat, decorated with strips from the breast and served with an intense sauce of wild mushrooms and madeira, was, for one reader, 'a dish that left me thinking that it must have been a lot of work for what was a foil to a first-rate sauce'. In like manner, red fish, witch and scallops came with two sauces, one from the corals of the scallops and the other a veal jus. The conception was fine, though complex, and the flavours seemed in need of edge (seasoning) and depth (from a meatier style of fish). The elaboration and great care carries through: potatoes are cooked in their skin in stock, sliced then baked to crispen the skin; just as desserts, for instance a tart encasing a rhubarb mousseline or coffee ice with meringues, candied coffee beans and cherry sauce, are light and inspired. Altnaharrie does seem to produce the comment 'the best meal of our lives' more frequently than most; Gunn Eriksen works a magic. Fred Brown is a knowledgeable host. Wine prices here perhaps reflect popularity more than quality, since Alsaces look particularly good value while many of the burgundies, albeit from fine growers, show no regard for the customer's pocket. Generally the quality here is very high, with careful selection from Italy and California matching pedigree properties in Bordeaux. Pricing defies analysis.

CHEF: Gunn Eriksen PROPRIETORS: Fred Brown and Gunn Eriksen OPEN: all week, D only CLOSED: late Oct to Easter MEALS: 8 PRICES: Set D £40 (£45). Net prices SEATS: 16. Private parties: 14 main room. Car park, 20 places. Vegetarian meals. No children under 10. No smoking in dining-room. No music. One sitting ACCOMMODATION: 8 rooms, all with bath/shower. D,B&B from £100 per person in double. Deposit: £75. No children under 10. Garden. Fishing. Scenic. Confirm by 4 (*Which? Hotel Guide*)

▲ *Morefield Motel*

Ullapool IV26 2TH
ULLAPOOL (0854) 612161

COOKING 1
COST £26

The décor gives new meaning to the word undistinguished. The seafood gives new meaning to the word fresh. Do not go for the ambience, do not go for fancy cooking, go for the product of the motel's own trawler. Every week, says David Smyrl, 'We cook and sell 100 lobsters, dress 100 crabs, boil and peel 4 stone of fresh local langoustines.' There is a short wine list with house wine at £6.50 a litre.

CHEF: Steven Kenyon and Tracy Cockhill PROPRIETORS: David Smyrl and David Courtney Marsh OPEN: all week MEALS: 12 to 2, 6 to 9.30 PRICES: £17 (£22) Card slips closed CARDS: Access, Amex, Visa SEATS: 106. 6 tables outside. Private parties: 40 main room. Car park, 35 places. Children's helpings. No-smoking area. Wheelchair access (also WC). Music. Fax: (0854) 2870 ACCOMMODATION: 11 rooms, all with bath/shower. Rooms for disabled. B&B £25 to £40. Children restricted. Baby facilities. Afternoon teas. Scenic. Doors close at midnight. Confirm by 6

WALLS Shetland map 8

▲ *Burrastow House*

Walls ZE2 9PB
WALLS (059 571) 307 COOKING 2
3m W of Walls COST £15–£29

This remote eighteenth-century house combines peace and informality. Furniture and fittings are products of earlier Shetland domestic bliss rather than part of a country-house interior created by West End designers or the antiques trade. Assurance and skills have been learned from the need of regular and consistent output. Materials, perforce, are local if not home-grown: smoked salmon, Shetland lamb, garden vegetables and, of course, the fish. A short set-price dinner menu shows that inspiration is more far-flung. Smoked salmon purée on potato choux pastry; hummus, carrot and dill timbales with sour cream and mange-tout julienne; garlic-stuffed squid with tomato sauce; and desserts such as tourinois (a chestnut and chocolate log) or ricotta with stewed plums are examples of springtime meals. Vegetarianism, hardly a Shetland norm, is constantly represented. The wine list is spectacularly fair-priced. If you want to watch eagles and other happy fauna, what a place to go!

CHEF/PROPRIETOR: Bo Simmons OPEN: all week (bookings only) CLOSED: Jan and Feb, mid-Oct to end Nov MEALS: 12.30 to 2.30, 7.30 to 9 PRICES: £10 (£15), Set D £18.50 (£24) SEATS: 20. Private parties: 16 main room. Car park, 5 places. Vegetarian meals. Children's helpings. No smoking in dining-room. Music ACCOMMODATION: 3 rooms, 2 with bath/shower. D,B&B £43.50 to £92. Baby facilities. Pets welcome. Afternoon teas. Garden. Fishing. Golf. Snooker. TV. Scenic. Confirm by 6

WHITEBRIDGE Highland map 8

▲ *Knockie Lodge*

Whitebridge IV1 2UP
GORTHLECK (045 63) 276 COOKING 2
on B862, 8m N of Fort Augustus COST D,B&B FROM £70

The Lodge serves food to residents only, offering a no-choice dinner menu of some sophistication, which gives pleasure for its accuracy of execution and avoidance of elaboration. The location is in its favour, even if it makes for lengthy shopping trips. 'Being in the wilds, yet providing comfort and good cooking, its homeliness is very compelling. The Milwards are pleasant and friendly.' Thus reported intrepid walkers who needed decent fuel. Dishes such as tartlets of mushroom with smoked salmon and dill, pistou soup or green pea soup with a light curry flavour, good Scottish beef, pigeon with madeira and port sauce, one substantial or one ethereal dessert and fine cheeses have given pleasure. The wine list is more than adequate, with fair prices. Decent clarets share the space with a short but sound choice from New World wine-makers. House wines are £7.

CHEF: Chris Freeman PROPRIETORS: Brenda and Ian Milward OPEN: all week, D only (residents only) CLOSED: end Oct to end Apr MEALS: 8 PRICES: D,B&B £70 to £174 CARDS: Access, Amex, Visa SEATS: 22. Private parties: 12 main room. Car park, 30 places. No children under 10. Smart dress preferred. No music. One sitting. Fax: (045 63) 389 ACCOMMODATION: 10 rooms, all with bath/shower. D,B&B £70 to £174. Deposit: £50. No children under 10. Pets by arrangement. Garden. Fishing. Snooker. Scenic. Confirm booking by 6 (*Which? Hotel Guide*)

Wales

ABERAERON Dyfed map 4

Hive on the Quay

Cadwgan Place, Aberaeron SA46 0BT COOKING 1
ABERAERON (0545) 570445 COST £23

The converted coal wharf sits between the two harbours of Aberaeron: one half is a whitewashed café/restaurant; the other is a modern conservatory overlooking the water. The enterprise is owned by the Holgate family (of honey fame), and it includes a honey-bee exhibition and shop. Margaret and Sarah Holgate are loyal to local and organic produce. During the day there is a snack menu of soup, salads, wholemeal bread with farmhouse cheeses, ham and pâté, fruit pies and speciality honey ice-creams, supplemented by a self-service buffet at lunchtime. A touch more formality appears in the evening, when dinners feature the likes of vegetable hotpot, grilled Welsh lamb with laverbread sauce, oxtail stew and poached sewin with sorrel sauce. Children get a mini-menu of grown-ups' food. To drink there is Hugh Rock's elderflower wine, Weston's cider, Ruddles bitter, three organic wines and four house wines at £6.75.

CHEF: Sarah Holgate PROPRIETORS: Margaret and Sarah Holgate OPEN: all week CLOSED: end Sept to spring bank hol MEALS: 12 to 2, 6 to 9.30 PRICES: £13 (£19). Service 10% D. Card slips closed CARDS: Access, Visa SEATS: 55. 2 tables outside. Vegetarian meals. Children's helpings. Wheelchair access. Music. Self-service L

ABERDOVEY Gwynedd map 4

Old Coffee Shop

13 New Street, Aberdovey LL35 0EH COOKING 1
ABERDOVEY (0654) 767652 COST £10–£19

Alan and Susan Griffiths succeed because they put their trust in fresh ingredients and proper home cooking. Most seaside coffee-shops could learn a lot from their efforts. The style could not be simpler: snacks, sandwiches and home-baked cakes backed up by wholesome no-nonsense meals during a long lunch-hour. Salads dominate during the summer months; at other times the choice might range from venison in red wine with chestnuts and tenderloin of pork with apples and cider to leek, cheese and potato bake. Sunday lunch is an excellent roast. To drink there are teas, coffees, milkshakes and juices.

CHEF: Susan Griffiths PROPRIETORS: Alan and Susan Griffiths OPEN: Tue to Sun, daytime only, Fri and Sat D (summer only) MEALS: 10 to 5.30 (L 12 to 3), 7 to 9 PRICES: £9 (£11), Set L £7.50 (£10), Set D (summer Fri and Sat) £12.75 (£16). Unlicensed, but bring your own: corkage £1.50 SEATS: 30. Private parties: 30 main room. Vegetarian meals. Children's helpings. No-smoking area. No music

▲ *Penhelig Arms Hotel* 🍷

Aberdovey LL35 0LT — COOKING 2
ABERDOVEY (0654) 767215 — COST £13–£25

'Within the two rather annoying constraints of a £14.95 menu (of which £2.50 is VAT) and the often difficult task of obtaining fresh herbs and interesting vegetables, we still endeavour to provide the best possible food in good quantities for reasonable cost.' So writes Robert Hughes of the harbourside hotel he runs with his wife Sally. Reports are enthusiastic, applauding the value and commitment shown in both the daytime menu served in the bar or dining-room and the set-price dinner menu in the restaurant alone. A praised bar lunch included a carrot, tomato and lemon soup followed by fresh local crab sandwiches, while Sunday lunch of roasts (beef and pork) were found to be 'tender, (with) enormous portions and lashings of good vegetables'. It is at dinner that Sally Hughes shows her skilful blending of modern ideas – guinea-fowl with a redcurrant and juniper berry sauce, and hake wrapped in bacon and served with a green peppercorn and garlic hollandaise – with the more conventional beef en croûte with béarnaise sauce, and rack of lamb. Flavours in these are well-balanced and unusual combinations show assured handling. A page of exciting house wines, mostly well under £12, is followed by careful selections from California, Rhône, Alsace and many smaller Burgundian growers. Italy is a special enthusiasm. There are good half-bottles. Penhelig receives a bottle award for diligence, generosity and sheer vitality. House wine is £6.90. CELLARMAN'S CHOICE: Rully, premier Cru 1988, Dury, £14.90; Gigondas, Dom. les Pallières 1985, £14.50.

CHEFS: Sally Hughes and Jane Howkins PROPRIETORS: Robert and Sally Hughes OPEN: all week MEALS: 12 to 2, 7 to 9 PRICES: L £9 (£13), Set L £8.75 (£15), Set D £14.95 (£21). Card slips closed CARDS: Access, Visa SEATS: 42. Private parties: 24 main room. Car park, 12 places. Children's helpings. Music. Fax: (0654) 767690 ACCOMMODATION: 11 rooms, all with bath/shower. B&B £34 to £74. Deposit: £20. Children welcome. Pets welcome. Afternoon teas. TV. Scenic. Doors close at midnight. Confirm by 6 (*Which? Hotel Guide*)

ABERSOCH Gwynedd — map 4

▲ *Porth Tocyn Hotel*

Abersoch LL53 7BU — COOKING 2
ABERSOCH (075 881) 3303 — COST £18–£34

The glorious setting overlooking Cardigan Bay has drawn visitors to this family-run hotel for more than 30 years. Like the views, the standards of hospitality and cooking are unchanging and readers still report enthusiastically. The daily-changing dinner menu runs to five courses, with a soup following the starter. Dishes from one evening in March show the style: smoked goose with pear and celery salad; carrot and orange soup; poached salmon with grapes and white wine sauce; rhubarb crumble with nutmeg custard. Cheeses have a local flavour and coffee comes with home-made petits fours. 'Excellent in every way, beautiful food and so well presented' was one verdict. Everyone praises the Fletcher-Brewers' personal and courteous service. There are light meals and snacks at lunchtime and a well-organised buffet on Sunday. The wine list has improved largely because of new links with Reids and Haughtons; there is more range and a bigger showing of half-bottles.

CHEFS: E.L. Fletcher-Brewer and Sue Bower PROPRIETORS: the Fletcher-Brewer family OPEN: all week MEALS: 12.30 to 2, 7.30 to 9.30 PRICES: Set Sun L £12.75 (£18), Set D £16.50 (£23) to £21 (£28). Card slips closed CARD: Access SEATS: 60. 12 tables outside. Private parties: 60 main room. Car park, 60 places. Children's helpings (Sun L only). No children under 5. Smart dress preferred. Wheelchair access (1 step; also WC). No music
ACCOMMODATION: 17 rooms, all with bath/shower. Rooms for disabled. B&B £29 to £78. Children welcome. Baby facilities. Pets welcome but not in public rooms. Afternoon teas. Garden. Swimming-pool. Tennis. TV. Phone. Scenic. Doors close at midnight
(*Which? Hotel Guide*)

▲ *Riverside Hotel*

Abersoch LL53 7HW — COOKING 1
ABERSOCH (075 881) 2419 and 2818 — COST £14–£34

This hotel, between river and harbour, is geared to water and holidays. This is a challenge to the hotelier. The Bakewells not only make the world welcome and comfortable but cook a decent menu to boot, not stinting on home-baking or other self-sufficiencies: marmalade, yoghurt and ice-creams, for instance. Portions are tailored to appetites sharpened by the Welsh outdoors. Food is available in the bar at lunch, but the restaurant (reached by spiral staircase) offers a five-course dinner in surroundings as redolent of the Mediterranean as Cardigan Bay. Good words have been spoken of crab tartlets, paupiettes of smoked salmon and cucumber, curried parsnip soup, Lady Llanover's salt duck, fresh fish such as plaice with pesto and scallops with lime and ginger, Welsh cheeses and a well-laden sweets trolley. The wine list comes in two parts: general and particular, the latter from Haughtons with some good choices of estate-bottled wines. None is over-priced, and the New World items are very interesting. House wines are £9.

CHEFS/PROPRIETORS: John and Wendy Bakewell OPEN: all week CLOSED: Nov to Mar MEALS: 12 to 2, 7.30 to 9.30 PRICES: £11 (£18), bar L £7 (£14), Set D £21 (£28). Card slips closed CARDS: Access, Amex, Visa SEATS: 34. Private parties: 34 main room. Car park, 30 places. Children welcome. Smart dress preferred. No smoking in dining-room. Music
ACCOMMODATION: 12 rooms, all with bath/shower. D,B&B £55 to £110. Deposit: £30. Children welcome. Baby facilities. Afternoon teas. Garden. Swimming-pool. TV. Phone. Scenic. Doors close at midnight. Confirm by 4

▲ *This symbol means that accommodation is available.*

BEAUMARIS Gwynedd map 4

▲ *Ye Olde Bulls Head Inn* 🍷

COUNTY OF THE YEAR RESTAURANT

Castle Street, Beaumaris,
Anglesey LL58 8AP — COOKING 3
BEAUMARIS (0248) 810329 — COST £34

A seventeenth-century inn with a restaurant that owners Keith Rothwell and David Robertson have firmly established as one of the leaders of the Gwynedd league. As pub, hotel and restaurant, offering quality at a sensible price, it has weathered the recession well. The bar provides snacks, while the restaurant is a place to satisfy a real appetite. 'The plates are hot and loaded with excellence,' enthused one reader. 'An exceptional culinary experience for this area,' commented another. Local produce extends from turbot, brill or sole to roast Anglesey woodcock, Welsh lamb and Anglesey scallops. The treatment is modern: a ragoût of lambs' kidneys is accompanied by a tartlet of onion and fresh sorrel; roast saddle of venison by cassis and fresh figs; breast of guinea-fowl by hazelnut mousseline. Saucing is spot on, as in fresh asparagus en croûte with a perfect sauce Maltaise, and steamed fillet of halibut with a light herb butter sauce. Desserts maintain standards with a tarte Tatin made with a buttery *pâte brisée* and strong endorsements for the almond praline ice-cream. All the world resorts here, from babes in arms to octagenarians, from locals to travellers. Social tolerance is *de rigueur*. Château Siran 1970 at £24.95 sets the tone for the fair-priced and astutely selected wine list. Half-bottles have been intelligently augmented, ambition and enthusiasm shine throughout. Italy and New World receive fine treatment. House wine is £9.50. CELLARMAN'S CHOICE: Condrieu, Côteau de Chéry 1989, £25.95; Cape Mentelle, Cabernet Sauvignon 1988, £15.75.

CHEFS: Keith Rothwell and Anthony Murphy PROPRIETORS: Rothwell and Robertson Ltd OPEN: all week MEALS: 12 to 2.30, 7.30 to 9.30 PRICES: £19 (£28), bar snacks from £1.50 CARDS: Access, Visa SEATS: 70. Private parties: 70 main room, 40 private room. Car park, 15 places. Children's helpings. No children under 7. No music. Fax: (0248) 811294 ACCOMMODATION: 11 rooms, all with bath/shower. B&B £38 to £63. Baby facilities. Phone. Scenic. Doors close at 1am. Confirm by 6 (*Which? Hotel Guide*)

BROAD HAVEN Dyfed map 4

▲ *Druidstone Hotel*

Broad Haven SA62 3NE — COOKING 1*
BROAD HAVEN (0437) 781221 — COST £22

Since 1972, Rod and Jane Bell have run this family hotel as a 'Rule Free Zone'. 'It is like being in a time warp,' wrote one reader, 'somewhere in the '60s. Most of the locals, and the owners, summon up memories of flower-power.' Their tolerance – of dogs, of assorted happy running children, of smoking, of doing your own thing – is remarkable. It is joined to an engaged view of food and materials: good meat soundly treated, organic produce, a genuine eclecticism. The most is made of the location: an unspoilt stretch of Welsh coast, wild cliff walks and 22 acres of gardens, no telephones or televisions. Chef Chris

Tancock has 'brought a new breath of spring to the place', his vivid cooking taking on board anything from Cajun to Catalan overtones. The results are generous, wholesome, sometimes heavy-handed, but excellent value overall. Typically there might be mussel soup, king prawns with herb and butter sauce, Indonesian satays, Spanish lamb chops with preserved peppers, beef vindaloo or scallops milanese. Vegetarians get plenty of choice, ranging from beansprout and smoked tofu salad to Sante Fe fast-baked vegetables. Sweets are in similar vein. Meals are served in the rustic dining-room and the downstairs bar opening on to the garden. During the winter there is jazz once a month at Sunday lunch. The short, adequate wine list includes a few organics. House French is £5.50.

CHEFS: Chris Tancock, Rod and Jane Bell PROPRIETORS: Rod and Jane Bell
OPEN: all week CLOSED: Nov 4 to Dec 13, Jan 6 to Feb 13 (exc parties of 10 or more by arrangement) MEALS: 12.30 to 2.30, 7.30 to 9.30 PRICES: £13 (£18). Card slips closed
CARDS: Access, Amex, Visa SEATS: 36. 8 tables outside. Private parties: 50 main room, 10 private room. Car park, 40 places. Vegetarian meals. Children's helpings. Wheelchair access (also WC) ACCOMMODATION: 9 rooms and 4 cottages. Rooms for disabled. B&B £19.50 to £49. Deposit: £20. Children welcome. Baby facilities. Pets welcome. Afternoon teas. Garden. Scenic. Doors close from midnight

CAPEL COCH Gwynedd map 4

▲ *Tre-Ysgawen Hall* **NEW ENTRY**

Capel Coch, Llangefni,
Anglesey LL77 7UR COOKING 3
BANGOR (0248) 750750 COST £15–£40

The hall is an impressively restored nineteenth-century country house set in three thousand acres of woodland and landscaped gardens created by the new owners. Beyond are views of Snowdonia. Inside it has been refurbished in the grand manner and boasts comfortable lounges and expansive conference facilities as well as an extravagantly decorated conservatory/dining-room full of mighty plants. Raymond Duthie's cooking matches up to the setting: it is very modern and very elaborate with the emphasis on top-hole presentation. There is a choice of menus (table d'hôte, fixed-price, à la carte, gourmand) and reporters speak with one voice about high standards across the board. A meal started with a pâté of chicken breast and livers marinated in port, speckled with green peppercorns, simply presented with salad leaves; alongside that a puff pastry shell shaped like a chicken came filled with 'exquisitely correct' scrambled eggs and smoked salmon. Main courses are concealed under silver domes. Boneless chicken leg stuffed with calves' sweetbreads in a truffled forcemeat sits on a simple cream sauce on which floated 'an armada of turned baby vegetables'. Desserts such as tarte au citron and fresh strawberry cheesecake are as immaculately visual as stained-glass. Other visitors have praised warm duck salad with hazelnuts, casserole of pheasant with wild mushrooms, rack of lamb on a bed of rösti potatoes, and steamed chocolate pudding. The quality of raw materials is evident, and details such as the home-made rolls and petits fours show that this is a serious enterprise. Service is punctiliously correct, yet friendly. The long international wine list hops haphazardly from Ch. Pétrus to Mateus Rosé. House French is £8.80.

CHEF: Raymond Duthie PROPRIETORS: Mr and Mrs Ray Craighead OPEN: all week MEALS: 12 to 2.30, 7 to 9.30 PRICES: £21 (£33), Set L £9 (£15) to £13 (£19), Set D £16.50 (£23) to £23.50 (£30) CARDS: Access, Amex, Visa SEATS: 84. Private parties: 120 main room, 6, 12 and 30 private rooms. Car park, 150 places. Vegetarian meals. Children's helpings. Jacket and tie. Wheelchair access (also WC). Music. Fax: (0248) 750035 ACCOMMODATION: 19 rooms, all with bath/shower. Rooms for disabled. B&B £78.50 to £107.50. Deposit: £60. Children welcome. Baby facilities. Pets welcome. Afternoon teas. Garden. Swimming-pool. TV. Phone. Scenic. Confirm by noon (*Which? Hotel Guide*)

CARDIFF South Glamorgan map 4

Armless Dragon

97 Wyeverne Road, Cathays,
Cardiff CF2 4BG COOKING 2
CARDIFF (0222) 382357 COST £32

This is a university restaurant in more ways than one: geographically, for its relaxed informality, and for its generous eclecticism. A stable menu offering five ways with fish, three with fillet steak, and a quartet of beginnings – including laverballs – is given a daily gloss by whiteboards running through the available fish and what has been cooking in the kitchen. This will probably include some vegetarian dishes as well as substantial, robust things like 'our cassoulet', venison with port and redcurrant, and home-made sausages with lentils. There is a direct line of colourful spicing ('crispy winglets, Chinese five-spice') and creative use of rice and pulses that shows Dave Richards' antecedents. It can be busy here and little is made of ceremony. They do, however, care. The fast-changing wine list, summary though it is, contains interesting choices and is not dear. House wine is £6.70.

CHEFS: David Richards and Debbie Coleman PROPRIETOR: David Richards OPEN: Tue to Sat, exc Sat L CLOSED: Christmas to New Year MEALS: 12.30 to 2.15, 7.30 to 10.30 (11 Sat) PRICES: £20 (£27) CARDS: Access, Amex, Visa SEATS: 50. Private parties: 50 main room. Vegetarian meals. Children welcome. Wheelchair access. Music

Bo Zan

78 Albany Road, Roath,
Cardiff CF2 3RS COOKING 1
CARDIFF (0222) 493617 COST £17–£28

'A perfectly good little Chinese restaurant that happily lacks the garish excesses of many other places,' writes one reporter about this modest venue in a suburb of Cardiff. The 80-dish menu is dominated by Szechuan specialities, although regulars have noted the recent disappearance of a few favourites. Even so, it still delivers skilful versions of Ma Po bean curd, aromatic Szechuan duck, crispy fried beef with chilli and carrots, and 'sea-spice chicken'. The menu also takes in dishes such as Mongolian lamb, double-cooked pork with green peppers, and stir-fried beans with garlic and chilli. House fried rice is served in lotus leaves. Meat is good quality, and vegetables, according to a report, are always 'fresh, colourful and snappy'. Drink saké or Tsing Tao beer. House French is £6.50.

CHEF: Kim-Lam Fung PROPRIETORS: Kim-Lam and Emma Fung OPEN: all week, exc Sat L and Sun L MEALS: 12 to 2.30, 6 to 11 PRICES: £13 (£23), Set L and D £11.50 (£17) to £16.75 to (£23). Minimum £8 CARDS: Access, Amex, Diners, Visa SEATS: 60. Private parties: 35 main room, 25 private room. Vegetarian meals. Children's helpings. Wheelchair access (1 step). Music

La Brasserie

60 St Mary Street, Cardiff CF1 1FE — COOKING 1
CARDIFF (0222) 372164 — COST £25

This lively eating-place out of the same stable as Champers and Le Monde (see entries) has a French bias on a menu built essentially around grills and fish, backed up by an increasing choice of seasonal game. The Gallic influence shows in mussels provençal, game pâté, sea bass in rock salt and stuffed chicken breast wrapped in bacon, while wild Scotch salmon and crisp honeyed duck add an international flourish to the menu. Garlic bread, French cheeses and a decent list of carefully selected wines from most French growing regions complete the picture. House Blanc de Blanc is £6.25.

CHEF: Franco Peligno PROPRIETOR: Benigno Martinez OPEN: Mon to Sat MEALS: 12 to 2.30, 7 to 12.15 PRICES: £15 (£21). Card slips closed CARDS: Access, Amex, Diners, Visa SEATS: 75. Private parties: 75 main room. Vegetarian meals. Children welcome. Smart dress preferred. Music

Le Cassoulet

5 Romilly Crescent, Canton,
Cardiff CF1 9NP — COOKING 1*
CARDIFF (0222) 221905 — COST £15–£34

A reporter sets the scene: 'Behind a shop-front in newly gentrified...Canton is a stage-set bistro, all red tablecloths and black gloss paint. The waiters are authentically French, however, in speech, appearance and professionalism, serving mainstream French cuisine of sound quality.' Gilbert Viader offers a blackboard lunch menu with a *plat du jour*, plus a regularly changing *carte* for dinner. Wholesome broccoli soup is served with garlic croûtons, and tarte de légumes is rich in leeks and complemented by carrot sauce ('a sensibly restrained nod in the direction of nouvelle cuisine'). Diners have been less convinced by the main courses: good salmon with an unsuitable curry sauce, rather tough rib of beef in country wine and mushroom sauce, while the eponymous cassoulet has been well filled out with white beans but low in meat. There is praise for robust vegetables, desserts and well-kept French cheeses with excellent baguette bread, but not for the surprisingly weak coffee. Meals can be very slow. A short wine list is backed up by some interesting Armagnacs. House French is £6.75.

CHEF: Gilbert Viader PROPRIETORS: Gilbert and Claire Viader OPEN: Tue to Sat, exc Sat L CLOSED: Christmas 1 week, summer 1 month MEALS: 12 to 2, 7 to 10 PRICES: £21 (£28), Set L £8.50 (£15) CARDS: Access, Visa SEATS: 45. Private parties: 45 main room, 16 private room. Children's helpings. Wheelchair access (1 step). Music

Champers

61 St Mary Street, Cardiff CF1 1FE — COOKING 1
CARDIFF (0222) 373363 — COST £24

If its neighbour La Brasserie (see entry) has a French slant, Champers is decidedly Spanish. The bodega-style wine bar has two great attractions: excellent chargrilled meats and a stupendous list of vintage Riojas. The menu takes in hefty, protein-laden steaks, kebabs and chops, backed up by Spanish-style king prawns, chicken with 'salsa picante', hot shrimps, venison pâté and a seafood mix. Salads and garlic bread form the supporting cast. House Rioja is £6.25.

CHEFS: Antonio Louis and Chris Koukaras PROPRIETOR: Benigno Martinez OPEN: all week, exc Sun L MEALS: 12 to 2.30, 7 to 12.15 PRICE: £14 (£20). Card slips closed CARDS: Access, Amex, Diners, Visa SEATS: 70. Private parties: 70 main room. Vegetarian meals. Music

La Chaumière

44 Cardiff Road, Llandaff,
Cardiff CF5 2DP — COOKING 2
CARDIFF (0222) 555319 — COST £17–£32

'Some restaurants survive by reputation and recommendation,' observes an inspector. La Chaumière is a case in point. It is in a poky little building, unmarked, hidden behind The Maltsters' Arms on the Cardiff Road. Yet reports suggest that it has the makings of a good restaurant. New proprietors Karen Duncan and Rory Garvey worked for the original owners, but have quickly stamped their mark on the place and put the kitchen into higher gear. Mussel and leek soup with a herb croûton, spiced marinated chicken rolled in oatmeal, and good-quality pan-fried fillet of beef with an intense onion and bacon sauce have all been out of the top drawer. Other dishes have been layered terrine of red bream, roast monkfish with basil purée and oyster mushrooms, and saddle of venison with honey-roasted parsnips. There is no fading towards the end, with good cheeses (including some Welsh varieties) and desserts such as iced pistachio nut parfait with lemon shortcake, and brandied bananas in a warm tart with a crumble topping. Karen Duncan's flair in the kitchen is matched by Rory Garvey's consistent attention and good service. A short but rather wordy wine list shows careful selection. Good half-bottles and fair prices. House wines are from £6.25.

CHEF: Karen Duncan PROPRIETORS: Karen Duncan and Rory Garvey OPEN: Tue to Sun, exc Sat L and Sun D MEALS: 12.30 to 2, 7.30 to 10 PRICES: £20 (£27), Set L from £12.50 (£17) CARDS: Access, Amex, Visa SEATS: 34. Private parties: 30 main room. Car park, 36 places. Vegetarian meals. Children's helpings (Sun L only)

Indian Ocean

290 North Road, Gabalfa,
Cardiff CF4 3BN — COOKING 1
CARDIFF (0222) 621152 and 621349 — COST £17–£29

Smart pinks and blues, smart cocktails, including 'Raj Rascal' and 'Raja's Ransom', and smart north Indian cookery that draws praise for dishes such as prawns saagwala (with spinach), lamb pasanda and chicken tikka masala.

CHEF: Abdul Kadir PROPRIETORS: Abdul Muhim and Abdul Kadir OPEN: all week CLOSED: 25 Dec MEALS: 12.15 to 2.30, 6.15 to 11.30 PRICES: £13 (£21), Set L £11.95 (£17) to £15.95 (£22), Set D £15.95 (£22) to £17.95 (£24) CARDS: Access, Amex, Diners, Visa SEATS: 60. Private parties: 50 main room, 8 private room. Vegetarian meals. Children welcome. Smart dress preferred. Wheelchair access (1 step; also WC). Music. Air-conditioned

Le Monde

60 St Mary Street, Cardiff CF1 1FE — COOKING 1
CARDIFF (0222) 387376 — COST £26

Le Monde, on the first floor above La Brasserie, next door to Champers, and related to both (see entries), stays with the well-tried formula of fish and grills, fish dominating proceedings. 'We receive fresh fish every day from all over the world,' says the owner. The list might include sea bass, halibut, parrot fish, daurade, Arctic char, pomfret, crawfish and many more – depending on the market. Meat-eaters are offered steaks, chops and kebabs. All main dishes are served with chips or jacket potatoes and a wide variety of sauces are available. To start there might be fish soup, gravlax or prawns with samphire; to finish there is cheese. Well-chosen French and Spanish wines. House Rioja is £6.25.

CHEFS: Andrew Jones and Genaro Sandonato PROPRIETOR: Benigno Martinez OPEN: Mon to Sat CLOSED: 25 Dec, 1 Jan MEALS: 12 to 3, 7 to 12.15 PRICES: £16 (£22). Card slips closed CARDS: Access, Amex, Diners, Visa SEATS: 86. Private parties: 80 main room. No children under 10. Smart dress preferred. Music. Air-conditioned

Quayles — NEW ENTRY

6–8 Romilly Crescent, Canton,
Cardiff CF1 9NR — COOKING 2
CARDIFF (0222) 341264 — COST £17–£28

Irene Canning has emerged after a long-running family saga with a brand new enterprise, a different restaurant name (formerly Gibsons) and an 'utterly modern' eclectic menu. The restaurant itself has been expanded, taking over the delicatessen which was once part of the original set-up. Now the dining-room is on two levels, with folding shutter screens over the windows, a tiled floor and Japanese-style fretwork dividers between the tables. Three flying 'quayles' are highlighted on the woodwork. Chargrilling, a strong Californian strand, Sunday brunch and visits from guest chefs have been grafted on to Irene Canning's traditional French approach. The results are confident and vivid even while one is still experimenting: warm chicken liver, bacon and spinach salad; chargrilled marinated prawns in a pool of spicy sauce with wild rice; marinated venison with grain mustard sauce; brill stuffed with smoked sewin in shrimp sauce. Nicely dressed salads and vegetables are supplemented by mashed potatoes and chips. Vegetarians might be offered aubergine caviare, spinach and cheese cannelloni, and mushroom roast with tamari sauce. Sweets have included excellent hot lemon tart and old-fashioned ginger and marmalade steamed sponge pudding. Sunday brunch stretches from the expected (a pair of Manx kippers) to the surprising (foie gras and mushroom omelette). House Beaujolais is £8.75.

CHEFS: Irene Canning, Matthew Canning and John Khalid PROPRIETORS: Canning and Co Ltd OPEN: all week, exc Sun D CLOSED: bank hols MEALS: 12 to 2.30, 7.30 to 10.30 PRICES: £14 (£23), Set L £9.85 (£17). Service 10% for parties of 10 or more. Card slips closed CARDS: Access, Amex, Diners, Visa SEATS: 48. Private parties: 50 main room. Car park, 5 places. Vegetarian meals. Children's helpings. No-smoking area. Wheelchair access (also WC). Music. Air-conditioned

CHIRK Clwyd map 4

▲ *Starlings Castle*

Bronygarth, nr Chirk SY10 7NU
OSWESTRY (0691) 72464 COOKING 3
5m NW of Oswestry COST £30

This is difficult to find, right on the Welsh border. 'We ended up stuck in a field and had to be hauled out by tractor the next morning (all arranged by our patient hosts, who even re-opened the kitchen for us). I still don't know exactly where it is!' comments one visitor. 'Impossible without an Ordnance Survey map,' says another. The best advice is to obtain directions from the owners and follow them to the letter. 'Castle' is something of a misnomer: the building is actually a converted eighteenth-century sandstone farmhouse with dramatic views. Antony and Jools Pitt run the place as a restaurant-with-rooms, keeping prices affordable, but sacrificing nothing in atmosphere, congeniality or personal attention. After a promising start the kitchen has lost none of its impetus and this year's postbag has yielded an abundant crop of recommendations. Antony Pitt changes his short menu every day, but there are noticeable themes and signatures: cured and smoked specialities among the starters, a healthy showing of fish (especially salmon), poultry and game paired with fruity alcoholic sauces, an undercurrent of French provincial cooking with some fashionable modern touches. Many specific dishes stand out: smoked salmon and mozzarella cheese omelette; marinated smoked haddock in cider with apple salad; salmon coulibiac with a 'truly resonant' hollandaise; turbot with king prawns and seafood sauce; hare casserole with cassis; grilled duck breast with plum sauce; loin of pork with prune and madeira sauce; peach and brandy ice-cream; chilled lime and lemon meringue gâteau. Readers regularly mention the bread rolls and farmhouse butter. The wine list, compiled with the help of Haughton Fine Wines, includes some organics and a few bottles from the New World. House vin de pays is £6.75.

CHEF: Antony Pitt PROPRIETORS: Antony and Jools Pitt OPEN: all week, D only, and Sun L (other days L by arrangement) MEALS: 12 to 2.30, 7 to 9.30 (10 Fri and Sat) PRICES: £18 (£25) CARDS: Access, Visa SEATS: 30. Private parties: 30 main room, 30 private room. Car park, 25 places. Vegetarian meals. Children's helpings. No cigars/ pipes in dining-room. Wheelchair access (also WC). Music ACCOMMODATION: 8 rooms. D,B&B £33.50 to £95. Children welcome. Baby facilities. Pets welcome. Afternoon teas. Garden. TV. Scenic (*Which? Hotel Guide*)

COLWYN BAY Clwyd map 4

Café Niçoise **NEW ENTRY**

124 Abergele Road, Colwyn Bay LL29 7PS COOKING 2
COLWYN BAY (0492) 531555 COST £26

The North Wales Expressway has overtones of the *autoroute* along the Côte d'Azur, and here is a little bit of Nice to fill out the illusion. Yet the converted shop done out in browns and peach, the curtains hanging modestly from a rail across the eye-line of the window, does not smell of garlic. Nor is the cooking just bistro fare, even if prices are for the moment in that bracket. Carl Swift is a hotel professional, and it shows on his blackboard menu and in salad of pigeon with raspberry sauce, accurately rendered salmon with scallops and a butter sauce, and a dish of monkfish with mustard sauce and a pike mousseline. Desserts have been enjoyed too: an amaretti and almond mousse flanked by peach and raspberry sauces was a particular success. Bread is home-made and the people of Colwyn Bay may have themselves a more than useful local resource. The wine list is both cheap and sensible, its range more than adequate. House wines are from £5.30.

CHEF: Carl Swift PROPRIETORS: Carl Swift and Lynne Curtis OPEN: Mon to Sat, exc Mon L CLOSED: first week Jan, first week Nov MEALS: 12 to 2, 7 to 10 PRICES: £16 (£22). Minimum £5.25 D. Card slips closed CARDS: Access, Visa SEATS: 32. Private parties: 30 main room. Vegetarian meals. No children under 3. Smart dress preferred. Music

DINAS Dyfed map 4

Rose Cottage

Dinas SA42 0XD COOKING 1
DINAS CROSS (034 86) 301 COST £23

Rose Cottage is an old stone, end-of-terrace house that was once a pub. Drive past quickly and you may easily miss it. A modern side-extension houses the entrance and bar with its rose-pink, chintz, and leather chesterfields. In the old house proper the style changes to beamed ceiling and plaster walls. Olwen and Gareth Thomas' cooking has a strong following. The emphasis is on local produce with a modern slant exemplified by a first course of sautéed slices of Pencarreg organic soft cheese and redcurrant sauce. The menu also mixes Continental ideas with a more traditional approach: halibut cooked with lemon slices, tomatoes and olive oil; locally reared venison cooked in red wine under a pastry crust; Welsh lamb steaks with Cumberland sauce. Local fish is excellent when available, otherwise recourse is had to Greenland. Supply lines in winter seem difficult to maintain. One February diner wondered why frozen peas were offered when other vegetables were available; Brussels sprouts were over-cooked and over-warmed. Welsh farmhouse cheeses and locally made ice-cream supplement strawberry pavlova and apricot and amaretto trifle. There are several house wines, and some organics, on a low-key but thoughtful wine list. House wine is £6.50.

CHEFS/PROPRIETORS: Olwen and Gareth Thomas OPEN: Tue to Sat D, Sun L CLOSED: Tue and Wed Oct to May MEALS: 12 to 1.30, 7 to 9.30 PRICES: £13 (£19) SEATS: 30. Private parties: 30 main room. Car park, 15 places. Vegetarian meals. Children's helpings. Wheelchair access (also WC). No music

DINAS MAWDDWY Gwynedd map 4

Old Station Coffee Shop

Dinas Mawddwy SY20 9LS COOKING 1
DINAS MAWDDWY (065 04) 338 COST £11

This simply decorated self-service coffee-shop, at the entrance to the Meirion Woollen Mill (a local tourist attraction which provides most of the custom), is housed in the solid greystone and slate railway station. Eileen Minter's highly rated cooking is mainly vegetarian and anything but fancy. What she does she does very well: bowls of piping hot soup – parsnip and apple or mushroom – accompanied by excellent wholemeal bread, cauliflower cheese, vegetarian cottage pie and jacket potatoes. There is some notable baking, especially of savoury flans, pizzas, cheese scones and bara brith (Welsh fruit loaf). Smokers are restricted to the tables on the verandah. There is a good range of speciality and herb teas. House wine is £5.

CHEF/PROPRIETOR: Eileen M.A. Minter OPEN: all week, daytime only CLOSED: mid-Nov to mid-Mar MEALS: 9.30 to 5 (4.30 Mar and Nov) PRICES: £5 (£9) SEATS: 52. 6 tables outside. Private parties: 20 main room. Car park, 80 places. Vegetarian meals. Children's helpings. No smoking. Wheelchair access (also WC). No music. Self-service

DOLGELLAU Gwynedd map 4

▲ *Dolmelynllyn Hall* 🍷

Ganllwyd, Dolgellau LL40 2HP COOKING 2
GANLLWYD (034 140) 273 COST £28

The original 'Old Hall', dating back to 1550, has been completely restored and now forms an extra dining-room. Otherwise Dolmelynllyn still feels as cosseted and relaxed as an Edwardian country house. Joanna Barkwith's cooking is 'an adventure in flavours' according to one summer visitor: 'The emphasis is put on taste rather than volume, which is in any case a relief by the time the fifth course arrives.' The set-dinner menu changes every day and takes its cue from local ingredients and traditional ideas, often given a new cosmopolitan twist. Broccoli and Pencarreg cheese pancakes come with sour cream and chive sauce; best end of spring lamb is crusted with pine nuts, garlic and parsley; roast leg of pork gets a watercress and hazelnut forcemeat and an apricot sauce. Desserts continue the theme, and cheeses are heroically British. French regional wines figure large on the 'house selection' of 15 modestly priced and interesting wines. Chorey-lès-Beaunes 1983 at £15.25 and Sancerre at £11.95 are indicative of the fair pricing throughout. Top quality is provided by Châteauneuf-du-Pape, Ch. de Beaucastel 1986, Martinborough New Zealand Chardonnay and several wines from David Wynn. There are good half-bottles. CELLARMAN'S CHOICE: Coonawarra, Chardonnay 1988, Hollick, £13.95; St-Joseph, Clos de l'Arbalestrier 1985, £15.85.

CHEF: Joanna Barkwith PROPRIETORS: Jonathan and Joanna Barkwith OPEN: all week, D only (L by arrangement) CLOSED: Dec to end Feb MEALS: 7.30 to 8.30 PRICES: Set D £17.75 (£23). Card slips closed CARDS: Access, Amex, Visa SEATS: 24. Private parties: 44 main room, 40 private room. Car park, 25 places. Vegetarian meals. No children under 8. Smart dress preferred. No smoking in dining-room. Wheelchair access (2 steps). No music ACCOMMODATION: Feb to May, Oct to Nov only. 11 rooms, all with bath/shower. D,B&B £42.50 to £105. Deposit: £25. No children under 8, exc by arrangement. Pets welcome. Afternoon teas. Garden. Fishing. TV. Phone. Scenic. Doors close at midnight. Confirm by 6

Dylanwad Da

2 Smithfield Street,
Dolgellau LL40 1BS — COOKING 2
DOLGELLAU (0341) 422870 — COST £22

'The lucky people of Dolgellau,' writes an admirer from Essex. 'Such a restaurant in London could deservedly charge half as much again and all would be most satisfied.' The secret of Dylan Rowlands' success appears to be his 'lack of fancy trimmings or ceremony' and his emphasis on taste and value for money. The cooking is generous, wholesome and substantial, and happily mixes Welsh ingredients, vegetarian dishes and old-style bistro favourites such as chicken, leek and tarragon soup, rabbit stew, and pasta and chilli bean bake. Reporters have praised chicken and apple turnovers with fruit sauce, pork in pear brandy, 'huge' sirloin steak with tomato and madeira sauce, and hot honey sponge. Vegetables are generally spot-on and the cheeses are Welsh. Service is pleasant, although a bit brisk for some. The principle of value for money extends to the wine list, which has around 30 well-chosen wines, with few over £10. House French is £6.40.

CHEF/PROPRIETOR: Dylan Rowlands OPEN: D only; all week Easter and Whitsun, July to Sept; Thur to Sat winter CLOSED: Feb MEALS: 7 to 9.30 PRICES: £12 (£18) SEATS: 30. Private parties: 30 main room. Vegetarian meals. Children's helpings. Music

EGLWYSFACH Powys — map 4

▲ *Ynyshir Hall*

Eglwysfach SY20 8TA — COOKING 1
GLANDYFI (0654) 781209 — COST £32

Physical improvements have continued at the Hall as well as in the gardens, which the Reens are 'fighting to restore to their former glory'. Reports concur on comfort, and approval of the bold decoration – not for nothing is Rob Reen an artist, whose paintings are on many walls – and the stamp of personality on the place. David Dressler has been cooking here for some years, yet his performance is still felt to be improving, not least because of a shift in emphasis from vans delivering goods from Manchester to the use of local produce. Tastes, as in a light roulade of spinach, smoked salmon and chicken, or fillet of pork with apples and lavender sauce have proved delicate where they might be lumpish, though an excessively sweetened sauce with roast mallard was regretted one November night. Fruit is still much favoured as an accompaniment or sauce-base for meats and, indeed, fish, as in smoked salmon tulips with a gooseberry sauce. The set-price menu offers a choice of six dishes at each course. Desserts are often enjoyed, be they puddings or lighter concoctions. Welsh cheeses have been in good condition. Wines, from Tanners of Shrewsbury, include reliable bottles, the great majority French but not omitting other sources (even if no American). Prices are fair. House French is £7.50.

CHEF: David Dressler PROPRIETORS: Joan and Rob Reen OPEN: all week MEALS: 12.30 to 1.30, 6.30 to 8.30 PRICES: Set L and D £19.50 (£27). Card slips closed CARDS: Access, Amex, Visa SEATS: 24. Private parties: 30 main room, 20 private room. Car park, 15 places. No smoking in dining-room. Music ACCOMMODATION: 9 rooms, all with bath/shower. Rooms for disabled. B&B £45 to £120. Deposit: 10%. No children under 9. Pets by arrangement. Afternoon teas. Garden. TV. Phone. Scenic

FISHGUARD Dyfed map 4

Farmhouse Kitchen

Glendower Square, Goodwick,
Fishguard SA64 0BP
FISHGUARD (0348) 873282

COOKING 1
COST £11–£24

A 500-yard sprint brings you to the ferry terminal. This rustic parlour of a café – on two floors – will deliver fuel enough for a voyage. The food is all things to all men (snacks, lunches, dinners and suppers) at low prices and made with honest ingredients. There is still time enough for annual visitors to be greeted like old friends and 'made to feel like club members'. A *carte* is made to seem longer by working variations on a set number of themes: four steaks, with five sauce options on top; 22 first courses, but four of them are avocado-based, four mushroom, four egg and so on. A table holds a heavy weight of sweet cakes. A short range of wines starts with £5.75 for house wine.

CHEF: Barbara Harvey PROPRIETORS: Norman and Barbara Harvey OPEN: all week, exc Mon L MEALS: 12 to 2, 7 to 9.30 PRICES: £15 (£20), Set L from £6.25 (£11) SEATS: 38. Private parties: 24 main room, 24 private room. Vegetarian meals. Children's helpings. Wheelchair access. Music

'Immediately after a table next to us had been vacated, a small cockroach appeared on the cloth. Although he may have been house-trained to perform the task of cleaning the debris, I do not think this appropriate to a restaurant of this standing.'
On eating in South London

▲ *Three Main Street*

NEW ENTRY

3 Main Street, Fishguard SA65 9HG
FISHGUARD (0348) 874275

COOKING 1
COST £15–£25

Formerly the Great Western Railway Hotel, the Georgian building has been carefully restored. The décor is understated: polished boards, muted colours, period light fittings, a display of second-hand chairs and tables. An evening *carte* offers a wide choice: gravlax, mushrooms dauphinoise, fillet of beef (with Dijon mustard and rosemary), turbot with hollandaise. There is little regional identity, apart from the occasional offering of local sewin and Welsh lamb. But one meal struck a reader as being exactly right: a mackerel mousse was served with home-made wholemeal rolls, an enticing mixed leaf salad resembling a 'peony in full bloom' and a good warm vinaigrette; then a delicately spiced chicken Simla and finally a faultless almond basket filled with kiwi fruit sorbet and fresh raspberry purée. Although immediacy and freshness are important characteristics of the kitchen, slavish devotion to this has resulted in under-done vegetables and too much emphasis on the look of the food on the plate. Lunch brings lighter dishes and the place is open for morning coffee and afternoon tea. House French is £6.95.

CHEFS: Marion Evans and Marcus Williams PROPRIETORS: Marion Evans and Inez Ford
OPEN: all week, exc Sun D MEALS: 12 to 2.30, 7 to 9.30 PRICES: £15 (£21), Set Sun L £9.95 (£15) SEATS: 24. Private parties: 24 main room. Vegetarian meals. Children's helpings. No smoking in dining-room. No music. Wheelchair access ACCOMMODATION: 3 rooms, all with bath/shower. B&B £30 to £40. Children welcome. Baby facilities. Pets welcome. Afternoon teas. TV

FORDEN Powys map 4

▲ *Edderton Hall*

Forden SY21 8RZ
FORDEN (093 876) 339 and 410
off A490, 4m S of Welshpool

COOKING 1
COST £17–£30

Nothing by way of human habitation is close to the Georgian hotel on top of a hill. Only sheep dot the views down the valley to distant hilltops. Inside, all is personally furnished with antiques and semi-antiques, making a homely and comfortable impression. The cooking is uneven. 'We came to the conclusion,' writes one reader who stayed four nights, 'that Mrs Hawksley is an accomplished but essentially amateur cook.' But the cooking is not without interest and a few consistent fortes: home-baked bread, whether wholemeal, walnut or brioche, is outstanding; the array of vegetables from the hotel garden has notably fine flavours; hot puddings are a star turn. The menu includes Welsh and traditional British dishes and, although occasionally over-ambitious, avoids major disappointments. In meat dishes, blandness is often spared by the use of alcohol. 'The meat juices which accompanied a lamb steak were enriched, powerfully, with port. The cream sauce with a breast of pheasant contained a substantial shot of calvados,' went one report. Desserts could include a spicy treacle pudding ('not at all heavy') and a moist, light steamed lemon pudding, plus good home-made ice-cream. Service can be slow.

There is a well-spread wine list of some 50 labels, supplemented by Mr Hawksley's auction purchases. House French is £7.75.

CHEF: Evelyn Hawksley PROPRIETORS: Evelyn and Warren Hawksley OPEN: all week, D only, and Sun L (otherwise L by arrangement) MEALS: 12 to 2, 7.30 to 9.30 PRICES: Set L £10.95 (£17), Set D £18.95 (£25) CARDS: Access, Amex, Diners, Visa SEATS: 34. Private parties: 25 main room, 65 private room. Car park, 45 places. Children's helpings. Jacket and tie. Wheelchair access (1 step; also WC). Music. Fax: (093 876) 452
ACCOMMODATION: 8 rooms, all with bath/shower. B&B £22 to £85. Deposit: £20. Children welcome. Pets welcome. Afternoon teas. Fishing. TV. Phone. Scenic. Confirm by 1

GLANWYDDEN Gwynedd map 4

Queen's Head

Glanwydden LL31 9JP COOKING 2
LLANDUDNO (0492) 546570 COST £23

'Still the best pub food we've come across,' writes one loyal supporter of this hostelry in the middle of the village. Lunch has produced rich chicken liver pâté, cream of celery soup, liver and bacon, and steak and mushroom pie. To finish, chocolate brandy trifle was 'well up to its alcoholic standard'. The kitchen moves up a gear for a slightly more ambitious evening menu, taking in specials such as smoked goose breast with kiwi fruit, seafood cassoulet, chicken in filo pastry with mushroom and tarragon sauce, as well as steaks, Conway mussels with garlic butter and salmon salad. Noisettes of Welsh lamb with port and plum sauce is a speciality. The wine list may be short, but it provides interesting, good-value drinking. House Sansovino is £7.50.

CHEFS: Robert F.W. Cureton and Neil McKenzie PROPRIETOR: Robert F.W. Cureton OPEN: all week MEALS: 12 to 2.15, 6.30 (7 Sun) to 9 PRICES: £13 (£19). Card slips closed CARDS: Access, Visa SEATS: 120. 12 tables outside. Private parties: 26 main room. Car park, 25 places. Vegetarian meals. No children under 7. Music

HARLECH Gwynedd map 4

▲ *Cemlyn*

High Street, Harlech LL46 2YA COOKING 3*
HARLECH (0766) 780425 COST £29

While the current edition was being written, news reached us that Ken Goody wished to sell up and retire. It is possible, therefore, that this frog – Cemlyn is Welsh for frog – will have turned into a prince of leisure before the next *Guide* appears. Ring first to establish the truth. It must be hoped that the view of the castle can be enjoyed for a few more months. The informal hospitality, generosity and value of the whole venture, to say nothing of the food and drink itself, deserves preserving in aspic. Ken Goody's cookery is simple, but not plain. He comments that 'much fancy cooking is only designed to conceal things that on their own might not be as good'. However, he does not eschew sauces or combinations himself: Yunnan-style ham braised with soy, sherry and spices; a gratin of shellfish and avocado, chicken with cumin, coriander and cardamom; chicken and hare terrine with onion marmalade. Flavours are stand-up, often expressed in relishes and piquant accompaniments rather than in bland little scoops of mousses or stuffings. Ken Goody was a pioneer of serious food production in the north-west for discriminating restaurants. It shows in what he cooks. The wine list, clear in presentation and very fair in its mark-ups, is a delight. There is intelligent and careful choice throughout, but Alsaces, Loires and Rhônes deserve particular mention. Good house wines start at £6.50.

CHEF/PROPRIETOR: Ken Goody OPEN: all week, D only (L by arrangement) CLOSED: Nov to Easter MEALS: 7 to 9.30 PRICES: £17 (£24) CARDS: Access, Visa SEATS: 55. 3 tables outside. Private parties: 40 main room, 10 private room. Vegetarian meals. Children's helpings. No smoking in 1 dining-room. Wheelchair access (also WC) ACCOMMODATION: 1 room, with bath/shower. B&B £20 to £35. No children under 8. Fishing. Golf. TV. Scenic. Doors close at midnight. Confirm by 6

Llew Glas

NEW ENTRY

Plas-y-Goits, High Street,
Harlech LL46 2YA
HARLECH (0766) 780700

COOKING 2
COST £12–£28

The 'Blue Lion' was once a stable block, complete with granary. When Trevor Pharoah, who made himself a good reputation at Maes-y-Neuadd, Talsarnau (see entry), first struck out on his own here there was a faltering, hence his absence from last year's edition. Variation in quality may have sprung from doing too much too soon, for the block accommodates tea-room, delicatessen and bread shop in addition to the restaurant upstairs. The blackboard menu makes no concession to populism, offering black pudding and peas, red mullet and ratatouille, quail on turnip sauerkraut, and salmon and monkfish on spinach spätzlis. Sunday lunch, cheaper than an already fair-priced dinner, keeps the modern complexity alongside traditional roast beef and Yorkshire pudding. Desserts may be a lemon tart with a strawberry sauce or pistachio ice-cream with a 'soup' of plums. Not all the wrinkles have been ironed out in the kitchen: a dish of fish seemed hard-surfaced as if reheated in some way, and the amiable dining-room service may be slow, even during a quiet meal. One opinion was that financial constraints can cause diminution in quality, but that skill sufficient to make simple pasta and pesto, a complex fish terrine with quails' eggs and caviare, or accurate calf's liver with onion and mushroom should be encouraged. Pies and cakes are in the café. Marj Pharoah is an accomplished hostess. A short wine list is headed by house bottles at £6.95.

CHEF: Trevor Pharoah PROPRIETORS: Trevor and Marj Pharoah OPEN: all week, exc D Sun to Wed Nov to Feb CLOSED: Nov to Feb (exc Christmas) MEALS: 10 to 4, 7 to 10 PRICES: £7 (£12), Set D £13.50 (£19) to £16.50 (£23), Snacks from £1.50 CARDS: Access, Visa SEATS: 30. 5 tables outside. Private parties: 40 main room. No children under 7 D. No smoking. Wheelchair access (4 steps). Music

The text of entries is based on unsolicited reports sent in by readers, backed up by inspections conducted anonymously. The factual details under the text are from questionnaires the Guide *sends to all restaurants that feature in the book.*

HAVERFORDWEST Dyfed map 4

Jemima's

Nash Grove, Freystrop,
Haverfordwest SA62 4HB
HAVERFORDWEST (0437) 891109 COOKING 2
on the Burton road S of Haverfordwest COST £12–£31

Gratin of home-cured ham with leeks and Llangloffan cheese is a dish which says much about the philosophy employed in Ann Owston's converted house on a hill: freshness, self-sufficient enterprise, and local ingredients. Ann makes everything from bread to ice-cream; her large garden provides fruit, vegetables and a formidable range of herbs grown in polytunnels. Fish is from Milford Haven, wild salmon comes out of the River Cleddau, and milk-fed pork is from a local farm: other things come from organic producers in the area. Despite the recession, resolution puts paid to compromise. One reporter's meal shows this: strong wild boar pâté, salmon with herbs and cream, superlative young vegetables, then summer pudding with Jersey cream. Otherwise, there might be Jerusalem artichoke and lovage soup, home-made brawn, salt cod with tomato and fennel sauce, and Welsh black beef with red wine and mushrooms. There is always something for vegetarians. Wendy Connelly has just completed a wine diploma, and the extraordinarily cheap list of two dozen well-chosen wines is likely to receive a facelift. House wine is £6.50.

CHEF: Ann Owston PROPRIETORS: Ann Owston, Wendy and April Connelly OPEN: Tue to Sun, exc Sat L and Sun D MEALS: 12 to 2, 7 to 9 PRICES: £19 (£26), Set L £6 (£12) to £8 (£14), Set D £12 (£18). Card slips closed CARDS: Access, Visa SEATS: 20. Private parties: 26 main room. Car park, 10 places. Children welcome. No smoking. No music

LLANBERIS Gwynedd map 4

Y Bistro

43–45 High Street, Llanberis LL55 4EU COOKING 1
LLANBERIS (0286) 871278 COST £25–£34

A long-standing favourite: a goal at the end of a scenic drive, though the atmosphere in the dining-room has been variously described by readers as 'office-like' and gaining from the 'splash of colour of the fire extinguisher'. There is Welsh in the bilingual menu, but the repertoire is pure bistro with but few signs of Snowdonia (suet pudding with bacon and raisins, Welsh cheeses) among such dishes as carrot and coriander soup, duck with plum sauce and home-made ice-creams. An inspection meal showed a number of bad habits creeping into the cooking, perhaps suffering from an excess of large parties. For sure, timing was not impressive; sauce technique smacked too much of pre-preparation; and tastes were neither interesting nor very considered. The 80-strong wine list tours the world reliably and at modest cost to the customer. House wines are £6.80.

See the back of the Guide *for an index of restaurants listed*.

CHEF: Nerys Roberts PROPRIETORS: Danny and Nerys Roberts OPEN: Tue to Sat, D only CLOSED: Christmas week MEALS: 7 to 9.30 PRICES: Set D £19 (£25) to £22 (£28). Card slips closed CARDS: Access, Visa SEATS: 48. Private parties: 36 main room, 20 private room. Vegetarian meals. Children welcome. Smart dress preferred. No smoking. Wheelchair access (2 steps). Music. Air-conditioned

LLANDEWI SKIRRID Gwent map 4

Walnut Tree Inn

Llandewi Skirrid NP7 8AW
ABERGAVENNY (0873) 2797 COOKING 4
on B4521, 2m NE of Abergavenny COST £48

The pub grew: a whitewashed stone building above a steep car park with a bar holding no more than 15 people; then a bistro, tight-packed tables, light on comforts; a restaurant, with a drawing of a spaghetti tree by Apicella, and a little more comfort; finally, a terrace for summer eating. The kitchen, too, grew, beginning with Franco Taruschio in a room; now it is a series of spaces and maybe four chefs, all working in pregnant silence, cooking the Italian food informed by the materials and resources of the Welsh marches that Franco has made his own. 'The total lack of pretension is almost frightening' was an apt comment on the powerful flavours and direct cooking which have made the Walnut Tree celebrated. The place has its critics. It must be approached with a willingness to enjoy, and if you think double-figure prices demand a tablecloth (rather than good cooking), go elsewhere. Prices do not match the spartan surroundings or the straightforward, but so pleasant, service. There may also be occasions of unevenness, a lot of meals are served and, very occasionally, disaster strikes. It needs to be stressed that the Taruschios have maintained their enthusiasm and bursting hospitality for decades, and that the Walnut Tree is unique. The menu is long, with regulars as well as seasonal appearances. Among the first are the crispy crab pancakes, bresaola, Thai pork appetizer, carré of lamb with garlic and shallots, seafood platters (the 'Italian' version including tiny clams with a spicy tomato sauce) and a long list of desserts – the fruit terrine has sometimes been lacklustre but the granita is pure fruit in ice form. Among the seasonal appearances in the spring were grilled radicchio with fresh truffle, scallops with garlic and coriander, and salmon with rhubarb and ginger. The Italian love of *agro-dolce* comes out in a number of things: the pasta with hare sauce, pork with orange and coriander, liver with sweet-and-sour onions, and fillet steak with pepper and onions. This is one of the benchmarks of public cooking in the '80s and '90s. On the wine list the sweep in quality and price is remarkably wide, allowing something for all tastes and pockets. Although this is a place to experiment with Italian excellence at affordable prices, France, and especially the Rhône, with fine older vintages, is not ignored. House wine is £9.50.

CHEFS: Franco Taruschio and Nigel Ramsbottom PROPRIETORS: Franco and Ann Taruschio OPEN: Tue to Sat CLOSED: 12 to 24 Feb MEALS: 12 to 2.30, 7.15 to 10 PRICES: £30 (£40) SEATS: 80. 5 tables outside. Private parties: 30 main room. Car park, 60 places. Vegetarian meals. Children's helpings. Wheelchair access (also WC). No music. Air-conditioned

LLANDRILLO Clwyd map 4

▲ *Tyddyn Llan*

Llandrillo LL21 0ST
LLANDRILLO (049 084) 264
on B4401, at end of Llandrillo village

COOKING 2
COST £18–£41

Extension to the dining-room, nearly doubling the space, has meant greater pressure on the kitchen and fears that the kindly welcome extended by the Kindreds to their guests would be diluted. No such thing has happened: 'An almost perfect Mother's Day lunch was enhanced by the surroundings.' The only possible consequence may be detected in references to leisurely service. On the other hand, Tyddyn Llan was always meant as a place to retreat to and its leisurely nature may be merely a way to enhance that sense of withdrawal from hustle and bustle. The house, set amidst lawns covered with flowers, is an ideal centre for walks across the Berwyns – less strenuous than Snowdonia, and probably more peaceful. The decoration avoids frills and flounces yet provides comfort within clean lines. A set-price menu offers half a dozen choices within each course and demonstrates a liking for fruit in first courses such as pigeon with blackcurrant and aniseed sauce and melon with smoked salmon and prawns, and in main dishes such as grilled sole fillets with banana and a red wine sauce. Within this kind of complication, elements may occasionally conflict. Comments this year have waxed more lyrical as the end of the meal approaches: cheeses, rich bread-and-butter pudding or chocolate pot, excellent sticky toffee pudding or lemon cream with white chocolate sauce are but prelude to good coffee and first-rate petits fours. The wine list is notable for good choice among the lower-priced bottles. There is not much to offer on half-bottles but a dozen wines are in the house selection with prices starting at £7.

CHEF: Paul Whitecross PROPRIETORS: Peter and Bridget Kindred OPEN: all week, exc Mon L MEALS: 12.30 to 2, 7 to 9.30 PRICES: L £10 (£18), Set L £12 (£20) to £15 (£23), Set D £19 (£28) to £25 (£34). Card slips closed CARDS: Access, Visa SEATS: 60. Private parties: 45 main room. Car park, 25 places. Vegetarian meals. Children's helpings. Smart dress preferred. Wheelchair access. Music ACCOMMODATION: 10 rooms, all with bath/shower. B&B £42.50 to £70.35. Deposit: 15%. Children welcome. Baby facilities. Afternoon teas. Garden. Fishing. Phone. Scenic. Doors close at midnight. Confirm by 6 (*Which? Hotel Guide*)

LLANDUDNO Gwynedd map 4

▲ *Bodysgallen Hall* 🍷

Llandudno LL30 1RS
DEGANWY (0492) 584466
from A55 join new A470 and follow Llandudno signpost, hotel 1m on right

COOKING 3
COST £19–£41

This is a fine house, encompassing the centuries, with views as wide as the stones are old. The gardens, too, are worth a visit; Historic House Hotels has done an immaculate job of restoration, as at Middlethorpe Hall (see entry, York) and Hartwell House (see entry, Aylesbury). Reports from here are very consistent. People like the service: punctilious, willing, only occasionally too young or apprentice. They also like the economy: lunches are especially fair value, but there are 'events', too, that offer good deals; dinner is less conspicuously cheap. In most instances, people enjoy Martin James' cooking: a big menu, changing every day, although with constants in the repertoire that long-term visitors must find familiar. Some of these are the raw materials themselves: Carmarthen ham, Conwy salmon, Welsh lamb, local cheeses. The style is quite light; a lot of tropical fruit pops up through most menus – less local than the lamb, but this ties the style into mainstream country-house-hotel cooking executed carefully and consistently. High prices, with commensurate quality, on the main list of around 250 wines are partly offset by modestly priced house wines, a collection of Bordeaux petits châteaux and 'Cellarman's Choice', a dozen wines mainly from south and south-west France. Elsewhere, pedigree names abound: Clos du Val in the Napa Valley, Te Mata from New Zealand and the provençal Dom. de Trévallon. A range of enviable clarets is matched by burgundies from well-established names. Quality is almost as assured with the 90 half-bottles. There is also a bin-end list. House wines are from £10.50. CELLARMAN'S CHOICE: Gigondas, Dom. de St Gayan 1985, £20.70; Corbières, Dom. des Arbres Blancs 1989, £11.35.

CHEF: Martin James PROPRIETORS: Historic House Hotels OPEN: all week MEALS: 12.30 to 2, 7.30 to 9.30 PRICES: Set L £12.90 (£19) to £14.90 (£21), Set D £28 (£34). Net prices, card slips closed CARDS: Access, Amex, Diners, Visa SEATS: 40. Private parties: 48 main room, 2 private room. Car park, 50 places. No children under 8. Jacket and tie. No cigars/pipes in dining-room. Music. Fax: (0492) 582519 ACCOMMODATION: 28 rooms, all with bath/shower. B&B £99 to £140. No children under 8. Pets welcome. Afternoon teas. Garden. Tennis. TV. Phone. Scenic. Confirm by 5 (*Which? Hotel Guide*)

Richard at Lanterns

NEW ENTRY

7 Church Walks, Llandudno LL30 2HD — COOKING 1
LLANDUDNO (0492) 877924 — COST £22–£28

Richard Hendey moved from Caesar's, Llangollen to open this chintzy restaurant with a bistro downstairs. There is loyal support for his cooking. 'He deserves to succeed on personality, tenacity and acceptable cooking' was one reader's endorsement. The menu, emblazoned with the title 'A Great British Menu', is a mix of traditional and modern British dishes based on local ingredients with occasional foreign influences. 'Roast beef', for example, is fillet steak carved and served with horseradish cream and 'choux pastry' Yorkshire pudding. Watercress soup, black pudding with apples, venison cooked with port and blackberry wine, and roast loin of spring lamb share the bill with Scottish salmon terrine with spinach, and crisp Gressingham duck with strawberries. Dishes often come with powerful, richly reduced sauces – as in a mixture of seafood and shellfish in puff pastry or sautéed pigeon breasts with Dubonnet and juniper berries. Sweets and cheeses can vary from the excellent to the indifferent. Sally Hendey runs the front-of-house with determination. The uncertainty of business in Llandudno may be a reason for unpredictability in accuracy and panache at the stove, as noticed by intrepid winter visitors from across Snowdonia who found meal number two a poor reflection of excellent meal number one. The wine list is a well-chosen selection of Richard's personal favourites; a new British section is planned and there are regular bin-ends. House Rioja is £6.95.

CHEF/PROPRIETOR: Richard Hendey OPEN: Tue to Sun, D only, Mon D summer MEALS: 6.30 to 10 PRICES: £18 (£23), Set D £18.95 (£22). Net prices, card slips closed CARDS: Access, Visa SEATS: 24. Private parties: 24 main room. Vegetarian meals. Children's helpings. Music

▲ *St Tudno Hotel*

North Parade, Llandudno LL30 2LP COOKING 2*
LLANDUDNO (0492) 874411 COST £15–£35

The façade of St Tudno's fits well into the mould of a solid seafront hotel in a classic Victorian seaside town. But the Blands' style of hotel-keeping is distinctive and visitors are grateful, indeed surprised, to find such quality. 'One is always struck by the consistency of this place and its value.' David Harding continues to be in charge of the kitchen, planning daily menus with a seasonal bent. To simplify matters the *carte* has been dropped in the evenings and just a set-price menu offered. The traditional seaside hotel approach of chilled fruit juices and melon, steaks and cold-meat platters are permanent features, but alongside are up-to-date dishes – a hotpot of local seafood in a white wine and fennel sauce, collops of beef with a juniper sauce and pickled walnuts, and saddle of Welsh lamb with anchovies, garlic and noisette potatoes – which provide the real interest. Desserts are usually rich with cream: chocolate pie, honey and walnut syllabub, praline and brandy tart with a fresh egg-custard sauce. A selection of Welsh farmhouse cheese is also served. Service is attentive and tipping is not encouraged. There is fair range on the wine list, prices are very reasonable but selection is uneven. House wines start at £8.50.

CHEF: David Harding PROPRIETORS: Martin and Janette Bland OPEN: all week MEALS: 12.30 to 2, 6.45 to 9.30 (9 Sun) PRICES: L £15 (£22), Set L £9.50 (£15) to £12.50 (£18), Set D £17.50 (£24) to £22.50 (£29). Card slips closed CARDS: Access, Amex, Visa SEATS: 60. Private parties: 45 main room. Car park, 10 places. Vegetarian meals. Children's helpings. Smart dress preferred. No smoking in dining-room. Wheelchair access. Air-conditioned. No music. Fax: (0492) 860407 ACCOMMODATION: 21 rooms, all with bath/shower. Lift. B&B £55.50 to £115. Deposit: £25. Children welcome. Baby facilities. Afternoon teas. Swimming-pool. Air-conditioned. TV. Phone. Scenic. Doors close at midnight (*Which? Hotel Guide*)

LLANGAMMARCH WELLS Powys map 4

▲ *Lake Hotel*

NEW ENTRY

Llangammarch Wells LD4 4BS COOKING 1
LLANGAMMARCH (059 12) 202 COST £19–£38

The lake is a private one, set in the hotel's extensive rough parkland. The interior of the hotel offers comfort rather than elegance, and a relaxed atmosphere. The menu is short, four first courses, three main, four or five desserts, 'but that's perhaps no wonder,' wrote an inspector, 'when one sees what effort the chef has put into a poor fillet of Dover sole before it is let loose on an unsuspecting customer.' Much is rolled, wrapped or stuffed. It is wise to stick to the simpler dishes ('everything that was straightforward was good'), in which clear flavours can come through. Hence loin of Welsh lamb flavoured with wholegrain mustard and thyme, and served on a rösti potato with a red wine sauce, was exemplary, simply conceived and executed with fine blending of flavours. Less satisfactory was timbale of monkfish filled with white crabmeat, tarragon and lemon, on a lemon, cucumber and mint yoghurt. Incidentals are as uneven as the cooking: good home-made bread, butter and coffee, poor amuse-gueules and petits fours. The predominantly French wine list makes few concessions to economy. In the classic areas there is unfailing taste in properties and vintages, the Rhône offers good value and there are more than token offerings from Spain, Italy, Bulgaria and the New World. There is an interesting and economical French regional page with much around £12. House wine is £8.75.

CHEF: Richard Arnold PROPRIETORS: Jean-Pierre and Jan Mifsud OPEN: all week, D only, and Sun L (Mon to Sat L bookings only) CLOSED: Jan MEALS: 1 to 2.15, 7.30 to 9 PRICES: Set L £12.50 (£19), Set D £22.50 (£32). Card slips closed CARDS: Access, Amex, Visa SEATS: 38. Private parties: 70 main room. Car park, 30 places. Vegetarian meals. Children's helpings with prior notice. No children under 8. Jacket and tie. No smoking in dining-room. Wheelchair access (also WC). No music. Fax: (059 12) 457 ACCOMMODATION: 19 rooms, all with bath/shower. Rooms for disabled. B&B £65 to £85. Deposit: £30. Children welcome. Baby facilities. Pets welcome. Afternoon teas. Tennis. Fishing. Golf. Snooker. TV. Phone. Scenic (*Which? Hotel Guide*)

LLANGOLLEN Clwyd map 4

▲ *Gales* 🍷

18 Bridge Street, Llangollen LL20 8PF COOKING 1
WREXHAM (0978) 860089 and 861427 COST £15

'Before lunch,' wrote a couple from Birkenhead, 'we spent two wonderful hours shopping at Llangollen's traditional butchers, bakers and greengrocers...With an afternoon walking the Denbigh moors, Gales will, for us, have a special place for future regular luncheon visits. For a wine bar, the table service was near perfect.' Richard and Gillie Gale's town-centre wine bar plus B&B attracts visitors because of its good-value food and memorable wine list. A blackboard menu of soups, first-class salads, quiches and cheeses is backed up by hot specials such as Somerset pork casserole or prawn and vegetable risotto. Sweets are mainly cheesecakes and ice-creams. The wine list has a host of remarkable wines at prices which alone would justify a journey; the 'supplementary New World wine list' is the equal of any for range and quality. House wine is £6.25.

CHEFS: Jenny Johnson, Mandy Astbury, John Gosling and Gillie Gale PROPRIETORS: Richard and Gillie Gale OPEN: Mon to Sat CLOSED: Christmas to New Year MEALS: 12 to 2, 6 to 10.15 PRICES: £7 (£12) CARDS: Access, Visa SEATS: 50. 6 tables outside. Private parties: 8 and 12 private rooms. Vegetarian meals. Children welcome. Wheelchair access. Music. Fax: (0978) 861313 ACCOMMODATION: 8 rooms, all with bath/shower. B&B £27.50 to £46. Deposit: 10%. Children welcome. TV. Phone. Scenic. Doors close at 10.15. Confirm by 6 (*Which? Hotel Guide*)

LLANRWST Gwynedd map 4

▲ *Meadowsweet Hotel*

Station Road, Llanrwst LL26 0DS COOKING 2*
LLANRWST (0492) 640732 COST £17–£38

Visitors to John and Joy Evans' modest, privately owned hotel are generally full of praise for the high standard of cooking, excellent wine list and homely comforts. John Evans has reorganised the dinner menu into a five-course *carte* with several choices at each stage. Guests can order any number or variety of courses, or choose the full menu for a fixed price. The kitchen makes good use of local ingredients, especially fish and game. Examples from an April menu show the style: rillettes of pork, jellied salmon soup with caviare, breast of chicken poached in vin jaune with ceps, and raspberry parfait with raspberry and kirsch coulis. Reporters have liked the gravlax, the fillet of beef and the Welsh lamb. 'The current economic climate has also persuaded us to open for lunch this year,' say the Evans, who now provide a good-value set menu during the summer season. For the curious there are many 'older vintages and odds and ends' on the wine list. More mainstream tastes are catered for in style. Clarets are of fine pedigree, burgundies are less ambitious, while the Rhône, Alsace and Loire are treated handsomely. There are a few good older vintages in Italy, while Spain and Australasia receive fine showings. Prices are very fair throughout, but half-bottles are relatively scanty. House wine is £8.50. CELLARMAN'S CHOICE: Sancerre 1989, Reverdy, £15.75; St-Joseph 'Le Grand Pompée' 1985, Paul Jaboulet Ainé £15.95.

CHEF: John Evans PROPRIETORS: John and Joy Evans OPEN: all week, D only, Sun L in summer MEALS: 6.30 to 9.30 PRICES: £19 (£28), Set L £8.95 (£17), Set D £25 (£32). Minimum £12. Card slips closed CARDS: Access, Visa SEATS: 36. Private parties: 50 main room. Car park, 10 places. Vegetarian meals. Children's helpings. Smart dress preferred. No smoking in dining-room. Music ACCOMMODATION: 10 rooms, all with bath/shower. B&B £19 to £65. Deposit: £5. Children welcome. Baby facilities. Pets welcome. Afternoon teas. TV. Phone. Scenic. Doors close at midnight. Confirm by 6

LLANSANFFRAID GLAN CONWY Gwynedd map 4

▲ *Old Rectory*

Llansanffraid Glan Conwy LL28 5LF COOKING 3
LLANDUDNO (0492) 580611 COST £37

Views of mountain and estuary wrap around this small hotel with a restaurant that will hold but few people beyond the residents – telephone first; and have a hill-climbing car to negotiate the drive to the plateau. The menu has four courses, cheese and coffee, with a choice offered only at dessert stage. Wendy Vaughan is a very assured cook: pecan and wild mushroom mousse in savoy cabbage, salmon in puff pastry with a green herb sauce, breast of pheasant with spinach and peas, with either apple cranberry pie or hazelnut and pineapple roulade to finish, makes a substantial winter dinner that mobilises serious and professional techniques. This is not a guesthouse playing at dinner-party cookery but a careful match of ability and a particular type of business. The repertoire is modern, drawing on developments of the '70s and '80s rather than some Franco-Italian dream: pear, spinach and watercress soup with lavender and rosemary scones, turbot in puff pastry with spiced sauce, lamb with red pepper tart and artichokes stuffed with asparagus is a meal that exemplifies these sources, just as it puts local materials in the frame (all beef and lamb is from the district). There are some arch aspects that may not always appeal to visitors wanting a less personal experience: a harpist may give gathering diners a burst before commencement of the meal and residents may eat at a communal table. The Rectory is popular with touring Americans, who are attracted also by the no-smoking policy throughout the house and the sophisticated, yet domestic, scale of decoration and furnishings. The wine list gives ample choice and is almost exclusively French. Its strongest area is Burgundy, though there are some useful German bottles. Prices are not high. House Ch. Jaubertie is £10.90.

CHEF: Wendy Vaughan PROPRIETORS: Michael and Wendy Vaughan OPEN: all week, D only CLOSED: 7 Dec to 1 Feb MEALS: 7.30 for 8 PRICES: Set D £23 (£31). Card slips closed CARDS: Access, Visa SEATS: 16. Car park, 10 places. Vegetarian meals. No children under 10. Jacket and tie. No smoking. No music. One sitting. Fax: (0492) 584555 ACCOMMODATION: 4 rooms, all with bath/shower. D,B&B £85 to £135. Deposit: 10%. No children under 10. Garden. TV. Phone. Scenic. Doors close at midnight (*Which? Hotel Guide*)

LLYSWEN Powys map 4

▲ *Llangoed Hall* 🍷

COUNTY RESTAURANT OF THE YEAR

NEW ENTRY

Llyswen LD3 0YP
BRECON (0874) 754525
on A470 2m N of Llyswen

COOKING 3
COST £17–£53

To the east, the flat-topped Black Mountains form an English rampart, supporting a weight of eternal cloud. To the south, piny forest starts out in regimented rows towards the Brecon Beacons. The Hall itself sits in flat land – the valley of the Wye. Clough Williams Ellis was the architect of the re-born house and he did a fine job of it, leaving the original Jacobean porch to stand, still proud. Sir Bernard Ashley undertook the task of restoration in the 1990s. The new work does not always sit happily in the old frame: it seems self-consciously stained and varnished. The underlying ideal of the hotel, to 're-create the atmosphere of an Edwardian house party', is also fairly self-conscious. According to Sir Bernard, guests arrive 'tired from their travels and the workaday world, to be greeted and cared for by their hosts as if they were indeed guests and not people simply renting rooms and patronising the restaurant.' This is an endemic problem with the English country-house hotel; it grates when it doesn't work. Here, by and large, it seems to. One of the best things is the collection of early twentieth-century English paintings that can be seen by the curious visitor. The dining-room is one of the most striking interiors: a pared-down modern classicism in a shade of primrose yellow (the original colour scheme) with full-scale columns and cornice. It makes an attractive frame for Mark Salter's modern classical cooking, which itself tends towards the elaborate – neither pared-down nor country-simple. A towering main dish comprised crumbed and fried calf's liver, layers of artichoke, leeks and coriander, and a slice of veal fillet surrounded by a shallow moat of madeira sauce. The plate was dotted with a piece of cauliflower, a sprig of broccoli, some French beans, some mange-tout, and two discs of mashed potato, each topped by a pair of braised onions. The combination did not work: the liver was too richly cooked, the veal was poorly cooked, the artichoke was tasteless, and the result was boring. A more robust and direct mobilisation of home-grown flavours could stop country-house kitchens appearing to be the same from top to bottom of the kingdom. Such criticism does not mean that the kitchen cannot deliver. The five-course no-choice dinner (there is a *carte* for those who want to choose differently) has pleased many visitors; the short menu offered at lunch, though cheaper, does not offer cheapskate cooking; the Sunday lunches, with a roast of course, are enjoyed. Dishes such as celery and Stilton soup with butter dumplings and toasted almonds (other times with wild-rice pancake and chicken quenelles), salad of pigeon breast with a tempura of vegetables and braised lentils, fillet of beef topped with a lentil purée, panaché of Cornish fish with fresh pasta and a champagne sauce, raspberry and other soufflés, and a pancake filled with glazed apple and served with maple syrup ice-cream have been mentioned with enthusiasm. Service is mustard-keen. It makes a restful stop in a day's touring, or a sybaritic stopover on a longer haul. Prestigious names, aphorisms and misspellings abound on the wine list, which is long and expensive. An Hautes Côtes de Nuits, the cheapest burgundy at £18.50, sets the tone. Fine Italian, Australian and Alsace wines provide a good foil to the clarets. Less space devoted to vacuous notes, and more to a layout affording greater legibility of the wines themselves, would be welcomed. House wine is £9.50.

CHEF: Mark Salter PROPRIETOR: Sir Bernard Ashley OPEN: all week MEALS: 12.15 to 2.15, 7.15 to 9.30 PRICES: £33 (£44), Set L £10.50 (£17) to £16.50 (£23), Set D £35.50 (£44). Card slips closed CARDS: Access, Amex, Diners, Visa SEATS: 48. Private parties: 10 main room, 16 and 26 private rooms. Car park, 60 places. Vegetarian meals. Children's helpings (early D only). No children under 8. Jacket and tie. No smoking in dining-room. Wheelchair access (2 steps; also female WC). No music. Fax: (0874) 754545
ACCOMMODATION: 23 rooms, all with bath/shower. B&B £95 to £185. Deposit: £50. No children under 8. Baby facilities. Afternoon teas. Garden. Tennis. Fishing. Snooker. TV. Phone. Scenic (*Which? Hotel Guide*)

MATHRY Dyfed map 4

Ann FitzGerald's Farmhouse Kitchen

Mabws Fawr, Mathry SA62 5JB COOKING 3
CROESGOCH (0348) 831347 COST £17–£34

'Ann FitzGerald runs a tight ship, with cooking that shows flair and great concentration of flavour in well-presented Welsh bourgeois dishes: an outstanding fish soup with loads of fresh bits of fleshy fish and crustacea; bread rolls of great weight and wheaty flavour; salmon with chives and cream sauce (simple, direct and full of taste); tender guinea-fowl and a tangy "autumn" pudding of the darker berries.' Such was a report from a visiting Londoner. A couple from the North-West remarked that the neighbouring caravan site would give them a chance of eating here every day, an opportunity to sample the product of this 'capable, maybe inspired, hardworking cook'. The dining-room is large and could 'in greedier hands' seat nearly twice the usual number. As it is, there is often a line of applicants for tables. 'Farmhouse' describes location and surroundings but not, to many, the ambience, which another visitor put as more sophisticated and more luxurious than the folksy name might imply. So, too, the good-value cooking, which uses a wide range of raw materials from both locals and from further afield, and shows a desire to cook without the flounce that sometimes goes with modern restaurants, but not without an awareness of current tendencies. 'As you'll have gathered, we liked it here. An air of open-handed generosity pervaded everything.' (And the cheeseboard contained some dozen interesting and well-conditioned items, which people can go at again and again.) The wine list has hit a century of bottles. The selection, especially outside the classic regions, offers interest and value: Italy and Australia are very strong. Prices are fair to generously random and there are bargains for the eagle-eyed. House wine is £6.50. CELLARMAN'S CHOICE: Alsace, Pinot Blanc 1989, Turckheim, £9; Dolcetto d'Acqui 1989, Acquese, £8.

CHEFS: Lionel and Ann FitzGerald PROPRIETOR: Ann FitzGerald OPEN: all week CLOSED: L Christmas to Easter MEALS: 12 to 2, 7 to 9 PRICES: £21 (£28), Set Sun L £12 (£17), Set D £8.50 (£24) SEATS: 40. 4 tables outside. Private parties: 40 main room. Car park, 40 places. Vegetarian meals. Children's helpings. No children under 9. Wheelchair access. Music

NEWPORT Dyfed map 4

▲ *Cnapan* 🍷

East Street, Newport SA42 0WF COOKING 1
NEWPORT (0239) 820575 COST £26

This is a friendly (some have found it zany), small, family-run guesthouse, full of knick-knacks and books, serving simple and unpretentious, yet invariably honest and fair-valued food. There are those who find it too simple, the presentation too unstudied, but the horseradish sauce is home-made, the Yorkshire pudding is light, and the gravy thick and full of taste on the Sunday joint. The vegetarian cookery is wholesome and imaginative; the servings are generous. An intelligent wide range of style and flavour is encompassed within the 40-bottle wine list. Prices are very fair, grandeur eschewed, but good names are everywhere – David Wynn from Australia, Michel from Chablis. House wine is £6.25. CELLARMAN'S CHOICE: New Zealand, Matua Valley Sauvignon 1988, Brownlie, £10.45; South Australia Cabernet Sauvignon 1983, Krondorf, £12.10.

All details are as accurate as possible at the time of going to press, but chefs and owners often change, and it is wise to check by telephone before making a special journey. Many readers have been disappointed when set-price bargain meals are no longer available. Ask when booking.

CHEFS: Eluned Lloyd and Judi Cooper PROPRIETORS: Eluned and John Lloyd, Judi and Michael Cooper OPEN: all week, exc Tue (Fri and Sat D and Sun L only, Nov to Mar) CLOSED: Feb MEALS: 12 to 2.30, 7 to 9 PRICES: £16 (£22), light L from £6. Card slips closed CARDS: Access, Visa SEATS: 34. 4 tables outside. Private parties: 36 main room. Car park, 6 places. Vegetarian meals. Children's helpings. No smoking in dining-room. Wheelchair access (also WC). Music ACCOMMODATION: 5 rooms, all with bath/shower. B&B £25 to £40. Deposit: £20. Children in family-room only. Baby facilities. TV. Scenic. Doors close at midnight. Confirm 3 days ahead (*Which? Hotel Guide*)

NORTHOP Clwyd map 4

▲ *Soughton Hall*

Northop CH7 6AB
NORTHOP (035 286) 811 **COOKING 2**
off A5119, Northop to Mold **COST £24–£52**

The Rodenhursts' dedication to their restored mansion and gardens is palpable. Welcome is personal and made to be felt. The intention is that meals here should be an event, down to the harpist's recitals in the evenings. The architecture – a remarkable amalgam of Georgian, Jacobethan, Victorian and even Islamic – lives up to the intent and the interiors have something to offer in addition to the late twentieth-century formalism associated with dining in the country. A new chef has not meant a great hiccup, nor a radical shift in style. That is still as complicated as some of the prose on the menu, with execution, in the views of readers, often more successful. Not much comes with just one modifier: salmon is topped with a sole mousse and sauced with a saffron and chive cream; sweetbreads and liver are in a puff pastry case, with wild mushrooms and a port sauce; beef comes with bone marrow and peppercorns, then a basil-flavoured hollandaise, then a red wine sauce. The cooking matches the Victorian decoration and the table settings. In the evening there are three set-price menus, at lunch a table d'hôte and light lunch *carte*. The wine list is ample in length, though it depends on négociants and shippers rather than a wide variety of growers. Price range is kept sensible by admission of Italy, Spain and the New World. House wine is £9.50.

CHEF: Mark Fletcher PROPRIETORS: John and Rosemary Rodenhurst OPEN: all week, D only, and Sun L (L Mon to Sat by arrangement) MEALS: 12 to 2, 7 to 9.30 (10 Sat, 8 Sun) PRICES: L £16 (£24), Set L £15.50 (£24), Set D £21.50 (£31) to £33.95 (£43). Card slips closed CARDS: Access, Amex, Visa SEATS: 50. Private parties: 56 main room, 22 private room. Car park, 50 places. Vegetarian meals. No children under 12. Jacket and tie. No cigars/pipes in dining-room. Fax: (035 286) 382 ACCOMMODATION: 12 rooms, all with bath/shower. B&B £80 to £116. Deposit: 25%. No children under 12. Afternoon teas. Garden. Tennis. Snooker. TV. Phone. Scenic (*Which? Hotel Guide*)

'After 30 minutes the waitress came out and asked at reception the whereabouts of another couple who were in the lounge bar. We heard the lady of that couple referred to as "the fat lady in the pink". They duly went to eat. Five minutes later we heard ourselves referred to as "the stroppy couple from Room 3"–we appeared to be invisible.'
On staying in (Wester Ross) Scotland

PONTFAEN Dyfed map 4

▲ *Gelli Fawr Country House*

Pontfaen SA65 9TX
NEWPORT (0239) 820343
off B4313 to Fishguard

COOKING 2
COST £10–£29

A handsome Victorian farmhouse, wild scenery and splendid views provide the backdrop to Frances Roughley's varied cooking. Deep-fried samosas with raita, substantial soups or straightforward liver and brandy pâté precede duck with honey, orange and cloves, chicken breast with mild curry sauce, and Welsh lamb with apricot and celery sauce. Generous attention to small details can be seen in the whole loaf served to each table, home-baked and streaked with layers of white, brown and herbed doughs and a line of tomato in the middle; the Nevern Dairy butter, reminding one reader of the butter his mother produced on their farm many years ago; and the quantities of fresh vegetables served with the main course. Desserts run to locally made ice-cream, fruit pies, sticky toffee pudding and chocolate pots – plus an excellent Welsh cheeseboard. Cheaper bar lunches provide a good-value sample of the cooking style. The wine list is French-dominated but given breadth by some attention to the New World and Wales, all well described. There is a good selection of organic house wines at £6.75.

CHEF: Frances Roughley PROPRIETORS: Ann Churcher and Frances Roughley OPEN: all week MEALS: 12 to 2.30, 7.30 to 10 PRICES: £18 (£24), Set L £5 (£10) to £10 (£16), Set D £16.50 (£23) to £18 (£24). Card slips closed CARDS: Access, Visa SEATS: 45. 4 tables outside. Private parties: 60 main room. Car park. Vegetarian meals. Children's helpings. Wheelchair access. Music. Air-conditioned ACCOMMODATION: 10 rooms, 5 with bath/shower. B&B £23.50 to £53. Deposit: 10%. Children welcome. Baby facilities. Pets welcome. Afternoon teas. Garden. Swimming-pool. Fishing. Scenic

▲ *Tregynon Country Farmhouse Hotel* 🍷

Pontfaen SA65 9TU
NEWPORT (0239) 820531
take B4313 towards Fishguard, then first right, and right again for ½m

COOKING 1
COST £17–£25

'The cooking at Tregynon underlines the joy of pure, fresh wholefood,' wrote one reporter about Jane and Peter Heard's isolated country hotel, which has a waterfall and Iron Age fort in the extensive grounds. The philosophy is admirable: home-cooking dictated by fresh local supplies, vegetables genuinely cooked to order and, above all, variety. Menus are planned to guests' requirements, dishes are seldom repeated over a two-week period and the kitchen takes full account of special dietary needs. Reports have praised the excellent, totally vegetarian soups, main dishes including lamb in filo pastry, and the superb ice-creams made without eggs. Home-smoked gammon, cured the traditional way, has been described as 'out of this world'. The kitchen's repertoire also includes hot Pencarreg cheese salad with apple and sloe jelly, Huntingdon fidget pie, chicken with apricots and brandy, butter-bean and cider casserole, and vegan mincemeat tart. Breads are baked on the premises and the cheeseboard features some local speciality vegetarian cheeses. An enthusiast has composed the wine list, providing detailed notes to each bottle. Buying is intelligent with interest spread far and wide – Drouhin Meursault, Metaireau Muscadet and Petersons Hunter Valley Shiraz; price range is also extensive and mark-ups fair. House wine is £6.50. CELLARMAN'S CHOICE: New Zealand Chardonnay 1987, Morton Estate, £15.50; Ch. Loudenne 1986, £12.25.

CHEFS/PROPRIETORS: Jane and Peter Heard OPEN: all week, D only MEALS: 7.30 to 8.45 PRICES: Set D £12.25 (£17) to £16.25 (£21) SEATS: 28. Private parties: 16 main room. Car park, 30 places. Vegetarian meals. Children restricted. No smoking in dining-room. Music ACCOMMODATION: 8 rooms, all with bath/shower. Rooms for disabled. B&B £20 to £25.50 per person. Deposit: 25%. Children welcome. Afternoon teas. Garden. TV. Scenic

PORTHGAIN Dyfed map 4

Harbour Lights

Porthgain SA62 5BW COOKING 2
CROESGOCH (0348) 831549 COST £28

Anne Marie Davies and her sister run the kitchen whilst her mother, mother-in-law and husband help out. Vegetables and crabs come from her father-in-law, lobster and crayfish from people in the village. Such a cottage industry has its own style: good cooking based on the best the area can provide, including organic meat of prime quality. Unexpected flavour combinations are built around this apparent simplicity. This is seen in dishes such as laverbread with bacon and wild garlic, marinated salmon with Pembrokeshire honey and mustard sauce, crab served hot in the shell with a mild Llangollen cheese sauce. Sensitive handling of vegetables (one of the sisters is vegetarian) is a strength, and prompted one reader to write, 'I would have been satisfied with the variety of vegetables as a main course in themselves.' A meal taken in the spring showed an abundance of fresh fish handled confidently: cockle soup, local salmon with a butter mint sauce and seafood thermidor. Desserts range from lime pie to sticky toffee pudding. The short wine list is carefully chosen and fairly priced. House wine is £7.50.

CHEFS: Anne Marie Davies and Bernadette Barker PROPRIETOR: Anne Marie Davies OPEN: Mon to Sat, D only CLOSED: Jan MEALS: 7 to 9.30 PRICES: Set D £17.50 (£23). Card slips closed CARDS: Access, Visa SEATS: 30. 6 tables outside. Private parties: 25 main room. Car park, 100 places. Vegetarian meals. Children's helpings. Wheelchair access. Music

All entries in the Guide *are rewritten every year, not least because restaurant standards fluctuate. Don't trust an out-of-date* Guide.

denotes an outstanding wine cellar; *denotes a good wine list, worth travelling for.*

PORTHKERRY **South Glamorgan** map 4

▲ *Egerton Grey Country House Hotel*

Porthkerry CF6 9BZ
RHOOSE (0446) 711666

COOKING 1
COST £18–£31

The lack of a reception makes for uncomfortable moments on arrival at the outset of a quiet summer's evening. But once you are in the hands of the Pitkins and spy the furniture and antiques ('worth a visit for these alone') things look up. The formal clerestoried dining-room sees cookery of the once modern sort served at table d'hôte lunches and dinners: salad of smoked duck breast with orange and raspberry coulis; mushroom and walnut soup; salmon with hazelnuts and prawns, on a saffron and ginger sauce; fillet steak with wild mushrooms and a brandy and horseradish sauce; and glazed strawberries with shortcake. Experiences have been like the curate's egg – apt for this former rectory – and although the cooking is adequate, there have been mistakes in conception and execution. The wine list, from Tanners, offers a decent range and is not overpriced. House wines are £8.50.

CHEF: Stewart Marchington PROPRIETORS: Anthony and Magda Pitkin OPEN: all week MEALS: 12 to 1.45, 7 to 9.45 PRICES: Set L £12.50 (£18), Set D £19.50 (£26) CARDS: Access, Amex, Visa SEATS: 50. 2 tables outside. Private parties: 35 main room. Car park, 40 places. Children's helpings. No smoking in dining-room. Wheelchair access (also WC). Music. Fax: (0446) 711690 ACCOMMODATION: 10 rooms, all with bath/shower. B&B £50 to £120. Deposit: £25. Children by arrangement. Baby facilities. Afternoon teas. Garden. Tennis. TV. Phone. Scenic. Doors close at midnight (*Which? Hotel Guide*)

PORTMEIRION **Gwynedd** map 4

▲ *Hotel Portmeirion* 🍷

Portmeirion LL48 6ET
PORTHMADOG (0766) 770228

COOKING 1
COST £19–£36

Portmeirion is paradise. Whether angels think the hotel provides adequate sustenance is another matter. Readers are in some doubt. As with the rest of the village, the visuals – the mirrors, colours, columns, views, plants, statues – help colour the acceptability of the food. Harp or piano music float through from the bar. It helps, too, that *hoi polloi* tramping round the village are kept firmly out of the hotel itself. Popular the dining-room certainly is: the Sunday buffets are crowded, and appreciated for their general profusion, their roasts, and crème brûlée among myriad other sweet things. The cooking itself goes up and down, and so does the service. There is estimable emphasis on local fish, given equal space with meats on the main course, and the repertoire has a certain sophistication in dishes such as monkfish with ginger and oyster sauce, tartare of salmon with white wine and basil, and lamb with aniseed. This may be vitiated, as on the day when it was remarked by one reader that 'all sauces here bear similarities to each other'. More extreme comments have also been received, indicating that intentions run ahead of execution. Wines are chosen with a sure eye for quality; there is as much of interest from the New World as from the classic areas. Italy is a high spot. Prices are fair and reflect quality and cost faithfully, with mark-ups easing on the classier bottles. House wine is £9. CELLARMAN'S CHOICE: Tocai Friulano, 'Collio' 1989, Puiatti, £14.50; Chianti Rufina Selvapiana 1987, £11.50.

CHEF: Hefin Williams PROPRIETORS: Portmeirion Ltd OPEN: all week, exc Mon L CLOSED: 3 weeks Jan to Feb MEALS: 12.30 to 1.45, 7 to 9.30 PRICES: Set L £12.50 (£19) to £14.50 (£21), Set D £23 (£30). Card slips closed CARDS: Access, Amex, Diners, Visa SEATS: 120. 8 tables outside. Private parties: 100 main room, 8 and 30 private rooms. Car park, 100 places. Children's helpings. Smart dress preferred. No smoking in dining-room. Fax: (0766) 771331 ACCOMMODATION: 34 rooms, all with bath/shower. Rooms for disabled. B&B £48 to £83. Deposit: £20. Children welcome. Baby facilities. Garden. Swimming-pool. Tennis. Golf. TV. Phone. Scenic. Doors close at midnight. Confirm by 6 (*Which? Hotel Guide*)

PWLLHELI Gwynedd map 4

▲ *Plas Bodegroes*

Pwllheli LL53 5TH
PWLLHELI (0758) 612363 and 612510 COOKING 4
on A497, 1m W of Pwllheli COST £26–£36

Reports are very enthusiastic. 'An annual hymn of praise may become boring, but this place gets better and better.' 'Apart from the environment and the delicious food, it was the welcome and attention given by Gunna á Trodni before and during the meal and Christopher Chown thereafter that stood out; this was the quintessence of personal service.' 'The house is very comfortable, lots of homely sofas and lamps, magazines and books; the L-shaped dining-room has plenty of windows so tables seem private; on the walls is an odd, eclectic collection of prints, paintings and holiday snaps.' There are changes afoot here: a growing-tunnel is coming onstream for more herbs and vegetables; a private house is under construction so that more guest rooms can be commissioned; fish seems to be gaining in importance as a vehicle for Chris Chown's skills. The menu is set-price and five courses long. There is proper emphasis on local materials and the style is modern without showing worrying modishness; this is not a kitchen captured by peasant revolutionaries. A reported summer meal may give some idea of the range. First, a tartare of wild salmon with cucumber and potato salad, surrounded by slithers of smoked salmon, or medallions of guinea-fowl with cider, hazelnuts and red pepper chutney, then steamed Dover sole served with a lime sauce, or salmon with ginger and asparagus cut in thin strips into a fine sauce. Both people opted for the same main dish: lamb kebabs with little sage forcemeat balls, served with courgettes, garlic and a rosemary sauce. Thin-cut roast potatoes made the most of the sauce. Welsh cheeses followed, before a gratin of summer berries with an elderflower champagne sauce and sorbet. Bread was good; lovely tartlets of wild mushroom were served with pre-dinner drinks; and only an odd number of petits fours for an even-numbered party prompted bickering. This is good cooking, never too heavy, showing proper judgement of when flavour should be strong, when delicate. Wine-loving restaurateurs please note this statement from Plas Bodegroes: 'To avoid confusion we will not be increasing the overall number of wines any further' – the collector's instinct tamed. Instead, there is a fine selection of bottles of impeccable pedigree paying as much attention to the modest as to the exalted. On the one hand there is a Montepulciano d'Abruzzo at £9.50, on the other the magnificent Barolo Monprivato, 1982, by Mascarello for £29.50. The intelligent 'house selection' of 20 wines heads the list, while an enthusiast or an explorer may choose from four hundred – each one a winner. Half-bottles are scattered generously and notes are mercifully succinct. A model wine list. House wine is £9. CELLARMAN'S CHOICE: Tokay Réserve Personnelle 1985, Hugel, £20; Dom. de Chevalier Blanc 1984, £37.

CHEF: Christopher Chown PROPRIETORS: Christopher Chown and Gunna á Trodni
OPEN: Tue to Sun, D only (also bank hol Mons) CLOSED: 1 Nov to 28 Feb MEALS: 7 to 9
PRICES: Set D £21 (£26) to £25 (£30). Net prices, card slips closed CARDS: Access, Visa
SEATS: 45. Private parties: 60 main room, 18 private room. Car park, 25 places. Children's helpings. No smoking in dining-room. Wheelchair access (1 step; also WC). Music. Fax: (0758) 701247 ACCOMMODATION: 8 rooms, all with bath/shower. B&B £45 to £80. Deposit: 10%. Children welcome. Baby facilities. Pets welcome. Garden. Golf. TV. Phone. Scenic (*Which? Hotel Guide*)

ST BRIDE'S-SUPER-ELY South Glamorgan map 4

Bardells

St Bride's-super-Ely CF5 6EZ COOKING 1
PETERSTON-SUPER-ELY (0446) 760534 COST £18–£31

Turn up a long drive alongside the M4, over cattle-grids and through fields of sheep to reach this 1972 'Lutyens-style' house with views of the Glamorgan countryside. Knock on the front door to gain entrance. The atmosphere inside is reserved, almost like that of a private house. This is a family enterprise: Jane Budgen and her two daughters cook, while son-in-law Panikos Antoni runs the front-of-house attentively. The short, fixed-price menu shows careful planning, but results can be uneven. On the plus side, reporters have enjoyed gazpacho mousse with red pepper coulis, excellent fillet of salmon in pastry with lemon butter and marjoram, and rhubarb and ginger ice-cream with shortbread. Main dishes come with bowls of buttery vegetables. Reservations about the freshness of some ingredients and 'too many missed targets' have influenced this year's rating. Thirty well-chosen wines include house French at £6.25.

CHEFS: Jane and Emma Budgen and Lucy Antoni PROPRIETOR: Jane Budgen
OPEN: Tue to Sat, D only and Sun L (other days by arrangement) CLOSED: Mon
MEALS: 12.30 to 1.30, 7.30 to 9.30 PRICES: Set L £13.50 (£18), Set D £20.50 (£26). Card slips closed CARDS: Access, Diners, Visa SEATS: 30. 4 tables outside. Private parties: 30 main room. Vegetarian meals. Children's helpings. No smoking. Music

All letters to the Guide *are acknowledged with an update on latest sales, closures, chef changes and so on.*

Cellarman's Choice: a wine recommended by the restaurateur, normally more expensive than house wine.

SWANSEA West Glamorgan map 4

Annie's

56 St Helen's Road, Swansea SA1 4BE COOKING 1
SWANSEA (0792) 655603 COST £18–£26

The setting is a converted Victorian terraced house in a quiet area of town, but Ann Gwilym's informal bistro has a distinctly Gallic feel: stripped-pine and mirrors, French music in the background, and the food firmly in the French mould. Hot ragoût of seafood with fennel and Pernod, salmon with dill and saffron sauce share the stage with fillet of beef with a herb crust and venison casserole with red wine, chestnuts and baby onions. There is usually something for vegetarians, such as nut and tofu burger with red pepper and tomato chutney. To finish, fruit crumble and passion-fruit sorbet have both been satisfying. Cheeses are patriotically Welsh: Llanboidy, Penbryn, organic Pencarreg. There is a café-bar in the basement. The 30-strong wine list has sound quality and fair prices. House wine is £6.90.

CHEFS: Ann Gwilym and Stephane Rivier PROPRIETOR: Ann Gwilym OPEN: Tue to Sat, D only (plus Mon in summer) MEALS: 7 to 10.30 PRICES: £18 (£22), Set D £13.80 (£18). Net prices, card slips closed CARDS: Access, Visa SEATS: 56. Private parties: 34 main room, 22 private room. Vegetarian meals. Children's helpings on request. Music

La Braseria

28 Wind Street, Swansea SA1 1DZ COOKING 1
SWANSEA (0792) 469683 COST £25

This restaurant (two floors of Spain in Swansea) follows the formula of La Brasserie, Champers and Le Monde in Cardiff (see entries). Opinions vary on whether it is a place to go for a restful dinner out: crowded, noisy, reduced to essentials. The essence of the cooking, which is worth pursuit, is fresh and simply cooked fish, including bass, salmon and turbot. Meats are grilled as well. There are Spanish wines on the list, and other heavyweights that may need calm to appreciate. House wines are from £6.25.

CHEF: M. Tercero PROPRIETORS: Iceimp Ltd OPEN: Mon to Sat MEALS: 12 to 2.30, 7 to 12 PRICES: £14 (£21). Card slips closed CARDS: Access, Amex, Diners, Visa SEATS: 180. Children welcome. Smart dress preferred. Wheelchair access (1 step; also WC). Music

Happy Wok

22A St Helen's Road, Swansea SA1 4AP COOKING 1*
SWANSEA (0792) 466702 and 460063 COST £9–£30

A shop-front, bright neon, then a long, stylish room, though the dim green/red lighting 'may not assist the appetite'. Press on for Swansea's best-rated Peking and Szechuan cooking, with sizzling dishes aplenty from a stable menu that some regulars would like to see change more often – the set meals especially. Cooking avoids greasiness and heaviness; tastes and textures remain gratifyingly distinct. 'The quality of materials is excellent and the cooking sensitive enough to warrant upgrading.' It gets popular and tables are 'turned round' of an evening; occasionally therefore, there can be an urgency to the service. House wine is £6.

CHEFS: C.C. Yuen and K.W. Yuen PROPRIETORS: I.M. Diu, K.W. Yuen and C.C. Yuen OPEN: Tue to Sun CLOSED: 4 days Christmas MEALS: 12 to 2.30, 6.30 to 11.30 PRICES: £19 (£25), Set L £4.50 (£9), Set D £10.50 (£16) to £13.50 (£19). Minimum £7 CARDS: Access, Amex, Diners, Visa SEATS: 55. Private parties: 60 main room. Children welcome. Smart dress preferred. Music. Air-conditioned

Keenans

82 St Helen's Road, Swansea SA1 4BQ COOKING 2
SWANSEA (0792) 644111 COST £28

A French café-style front distinguishes this shop conversion in a street of restaurants. 'The main change,' writes Chris Keenan, 'is simply that I now change my menus...at least three times a week, instead of monthly. These almost spontaneous menus give me far greater satisfaction, and freedom, and also please my customers.' His cooking style is often original, but approached from a strong classical base. One reported meal gives an idea of the range: a coarse and flavoursome game terrine, smoked pigeon breast with fennel and green lentils, pork paprika with a julienne of leeks and a port, garlic and cream sauce, and lamb's liver with roast pepper. There is an emphasis on clear tastes. Melon and orange with elderflower and blackcurrant sauce was refreshing, while a trio of salmon, hake and Dover sole with a pink grapefruit reduction and saffron sauce showed understanding and good handling of fresh fish. Cheese is kept in fine condition. Some note has been taken of last year's comments on service and, judging by recent reports, appears to have been tightened up. The succinct wine list arranged approximately by grape variety, offers a wide and interesting choice. Quality ranges from good to excellent, and prices are fair throughout. House French is £6.95.

CHEF: Chris Keenan PROPRIETORS: Chris and Lynda Keenan OPEN: Tue to Sat, exc Sat L CLOSED: 24 Dec to 2 Jan MEALS: 12.30 to 2, 7 to 10 PRICES: £16 (£23) CARDS: Access, Amex, Visa SEATS: 26. Private parties: 35 main room, 20 private room. Vegetarian meals. Children welcome. Wheelchair access (1 step). Music

Roots

2 Woodville Road, Mumbles,
Swansea SA3 4AD COOKING 1
SWANSEA (0792) 366006 COST £16

Do ecclesiastical touches to the furnishings imply evangelical zeal for vegetarianism and organic materials? Certainly Roots practises what it preaches: wild foods, organics, bio-dynamic cheeses and free-range eggs figure on a menu that leans on the Mediterranean and the Orient for inspiration. Dishes might be chickpea and aubergine samosas, Chinese stir-fried vegetable pancakes with bean curd and sweet-and-sour hot sauce, and wild mushrooms and basil and walnut pesto with fresh pasta. Puddings are puddings. A tendency to heaviness is more evident in eating the food than reading the menu, and sometimes flavours, which need to be upstanding in cooking of this sort, are not proud enough. Prices are fair, the informality is pleasing, and the place is open all day. A new ban on smoking on Fridays will be extended through the week if it works well.

CHEF: Judith Rees PROPRIETORS: Judith Rees and Andrew Castell OPEN: Tue to Sat MEALS: 11 to 9 (5 Tue winter) PRICES: £11 (£13). Unlicensed, but bring your own: corkage £1 SEATS: 38. 1 table outside. Private parties: 50 main room. Vegetarian meals. Children's helpings. No-smoking area. Wheelchair access (1 step). Music

TALSARNAU Gwynedd map 4

▲ *Maes-y-Neuadd*

Talsarnau LL47 6YA
HARLECH (0766) 780200 COOKING 2
off B4573, 1m S of Talsarnau COST £18–£40

'Mansion in a Meadow' might be a translation of the name. The meadow is on a hillside, and the views are sensational. So are the combination of raw stone and cut grass in the setting of the house itself, and the contrast of stone and rich textures in some of the interiors. The hotel thrives on counterpoint. Visitors will doubtless attempt to descry a twin vein of taste in the choice of pictures: which the Slatters', which the Horsfalls'? Just so are the happy opposites of the polished, plastered dining-room and the cosy snug of an oak-beamed bar. Andy Taylor cooks a set-price, five-course dinner, with an alternative first course and two or three main courses. Results have lacked neither skill nor impact in fish dishes such as monkfish with spinach and garlic and a basil cream sauce, and 'squeaky fresh' lemon sole with a julienne of vegetables in an olive oil and tarragon emulsion. Meats might be honey-glazed duck with sauerkraut and orange and Grand Marnier sauce, and discs of rack of lamb with a mixture of shallot, leek and caraway in a dark tomato and rosemary sauce. Details have not always been exact – a lacklustre soup, tepid food, undercooked potatoes – though the cheeseboard (Welsh) is exemplary and the service by girls in flowered skirts and black waistcoats is unhurried and smiling, even if forgetful of the wine. All the changes of the last two years 'have been absorbed', in the words of the owners, and the hotel runs very smoothly. The wine list is extensive, though a copy was not sent to us this year. House wine is £7.50.

CHEF: Andrew Taylor PROPRIETORS: Michael and June Slatter, Malcolm and Olive Horsfall OPEN: all week CLOSED: 6 to 22 Dec MEALS: 12.15 to 1.45, 7.30 to 9 PRICES: Set L £12.50 (£18) to £14.50 (£20), Set D £24 (£33). Card slips closed CARDS: Access, Amex, Diners, Visa SEATS: 46. Private parties: 50 main room, 16 private room. Car park, 50 places. Vegetarian meals. Children's helpings. No children under 7. No smoking in dining-room. Wheelchair access. Music. Fax: (0766) 780211 ACCOMMODATION: 16 rooms, all with bath/shower. Rooms for disabled. B&B £43 to £36. Deposit: £50. No children under 7. Pets welcome. Afternoon teas. Garden. TV. Phone. Scenic. Doors close at midnight. Confirm by 5 (*Which? Hotel Guide*)

Report forms are at the back of the book; write a letter if you prefer.

TALYLLYN Gwynedd map 4

▲ *Minffordd Hotel*

Talyllyn LL36 9AJ
CORRIS (0654) 761665 COOKING 1
at junction of A487 and B4405 COST £23

The local population in this part of Gwynedd is small, so the Pickles family relies on visitors from many miles away. This centuries-old beamed hotel is full of attributes and residents tend to return. 'Country fresh from the Aga,' says a note above the menu, and Jonathan Pickles keeps faith with good ingredients and simple cooking, perhaps sometimes too simple for unreserved recommendation. Dinner is a limited fixed-price *carte* running to four courses. The centrepiece is normally a roast or fish: thick slices of Welsh lamb, guinea-fowl with sauce Normande, poached salmon with Lady Llanover's Sauce (dating from 1867), marinated swordfish steak with apple sauce. Vegetables might feature 'Prince of Wales' potatoes, baked with cream and leeks. Starters are along the lines of spicy carrot soup or garlic mushrooms; sweets have included a massive bread-and-butter pudding. Cheeses are from Old Cardiganshire; the coffee is pure Arabica. Residents wax lyrical about the splendid breakfasts. A short list of 35 wines from Haughton Fine Wines has a few organics and a single Welsh representative. House French is £6.90.

CHEF: Jonathan Pickles PROPRIETORS: Bernard and Jessica Pickles OPEN: Tue to Sat, D only CLOSED: Jan and Feb MEALS: 7.30 to 8.30 PRICES: Set D £15.50 (£19). Net prices, card slips closed CARDS: Access, Diners, Visa SEATS: 28. Private parties: 28 main room. Car park, 12 places. Vegetarian meals. Children's helpings. No children under 3. Smart dress preferred. No smoking in dining-room. Wheelchair access. No music ACCOMMODATION: 6 rooms, all with bath/shower. B&B £57 to £94. Deposit: 10%. No children under 3. Garden. Fishing. Phone. Scenic. Doors close at 11. Confirm by 6 (*Which? Hotel Guide*)

THREE COCKS Powys map 4

▲ *Three Cocks Hotel*

Three Cocks LD3 0SL
GLASBURY (049 74) 215,
changes to (0497) 847215 Nov 1991 COOKING 2*
on A438 between Brecon and Hay-on-Wye COST £24–£34

The Black Mountains, Brecon Beacons and Offa's Dyke are equidistant from this hotel, a fine centre for walking on Wales' finest. It is pure British: old stone, cobbles, courtyards, ivy, the lot. But there is a certain flavour of Belgium, Mrs Winstone's native land, evinced in fine Ardennes ham with honey-pickled onions, dishes such as asparagus 'à la Flamande' or lambs' kidneys with juniper and gin, as well as the range of Belgian beers in the bar. Everyone likes the second helpings of soups – shellfish bisque being a favourite, helped by a well-spiked mayonnaise – and the tactic whereby you get seconds of meat rather than overburdening the plate at first go. Vegetables in profusion are enjoyed as well. The dessert that gets most comment is a goats' cheese with a raspberry and honey sauce – 'it goes well with port'. Most agree that value is considered by the Winstones, pointing out the quality of the bread, the appetisers and the petits fours that are included in the price. 'On the hottest day of the year, after an exhausting afternoon ... at Hay-on-Wye, arriving at the Three Cocks is like going abroad. The ivy-covered inn, the search for shade in the car park, the imaginative menu, and the warm welcome.' The wine list is sensibly short and fairly priced. It has no truck with much that isn't French but has a useful clutch of clarets, burgundies from Drouhin and a trio of decent red Rhônes. House Duboeuf is £8.

CHEF: M.E. Winstone PROPRIETORS: Mr and Mrs Winstone OPEN: Wed to Mon, exc Sun L CLOSED: Dec and Jan MEALS: 12 to 1.30, 7 to 9 PRICES: £23 (£28), Set L and D £20 (£24), Set D £20 (£24). Net prices, card slips closed CARDS: Access, Visa SEATS: 35. Private parties: 35 main room. Car park, 30 places. Children welcome. Smart dress preferred. Music ACCOMMODATION: 7 rooms, all with bath/shower. B&B £53. Children welcome. Baby facilities. Garden. Scenic. Doors close at midnight. Confirm by 5 (*Which? Hotel Guide*)

TREFRIW Gwynedd map 4

Chandler's

Trefriw LL27 0JH COOKING 2
LLANRWST (0492) 640991 COST £28

'Don't be misled by the uninviting exterior,' writes one, 'we thought the place had closed down, but were delighted to find that all is still well in the Rattenbury kitchen and garden: freshly baked bread started the meal, home-grown strawberries completed it.' But the converted chandler's shop does not charm everybody; some visitors dislike the hard, cushionless schoolroom benches in the slate-floored dining-room. 'If they are going to charge serious prices, they must add some dimension of comfort. A comfortable bar or lounge would be a truly welcome addition.' The kitchen continues to deliver from a short inventive menu that can take in Thai fruit salad and roast rack of Welsh lamb with onion sauce. Hot goats' cheese with sage dressing is a perennial favourite, fresh tomato and basil soup is perfectly seasoned, and fillet of beef comes with cream and mustard sauce and capers. Blackboard specials, such as steamed fillet of grey mullet with soy, ginger and spring onion, or almond and peanut bake with barbecue sauce, add further variety. Main courses come with a tureen of colourful vegetables. The pudding list is impressive. There are some decent New World wines on the rather haphazard list; a new list is on its way as we go to press. House French is £7.45.

CHEF: Adam Rattenbury PROPRIETORS: Adam and Penny Rattenbury and Tim Kirton OPEN: Tue to Sat, D only MEALS: 7 to 10 PRICES: £16 (£23). Card slips closed CARDS: Access, Visa SEATS: 36. Private parties: 36 main room. Car park, 10 places. Vegetarian meals. Children welcome. No smoking. Music

Net prices *in the details at the end of an entry indicates that the prices given on a menu and on a bill are inclusive of VAT and service charge, and that this practice is clearly stated on menu and bill.*

WHITEBROOK Gwent map 4

▲ *Crown at Whitebrook* NEW ENTRY

Whitebrook NP5 4TX
MONMOUTH (0600) 860254
on narrow lane running between A466 and B4293, 5m S of Monmouth

COOKING 1
COST £20–£37

The converted village inn is set on a steep hill in a wild and woody part of Wales. Roger Bates provides an enthusiastic welcome to those who try his wife's cooking, offered as a fixed-price menu written in French with English subtitles. Reports of meals have spoken well of boned quail stuffed with livers and wild rice, pork tenderloin filled with pistachio mousse in a port sauce, breast of duck cooked in honey with an apricot sauce, and a sausage made from the leg and thigh. The conception of the dishes is elaborate, and not all ideas work: a complicated pâté of smoked trout, involving hazelnuts, mange-tout, carrot and whisky ended up too bland; mussels baked in a basil crust on a bed of mushrooms in a sherry and cream sauce 'would have made two quite nice little dishes', but were not so good together. Even vegetables are served in fancy numbers: 11 different varieties appeared with one meal – 'yes, I counted twice'. Offering less choice on what amounts to a long menu for such a small kitchen would help tighten things up. House wine is £7.50. A hundred-odd-bottle wine list offers good range and fair prices. Over-reliance on a few big names, especially in Burgundy, deflects total confidence in the choice of wine merchants.

CHEF: Sandra Bates PROPRIETORS: Roger and Sandra Bates OPEN: all week, exc Mon L; Sun D residents only CLOSED: 2 to 3 weeks Jan, 2 weeks Aug MEALS: 12 to 2, 7 to 9.30 PRICES: Set L £14.25 (£20), Set D £24.50 (£31). Card slips closed CARDS: Access, Amex, Carte Blanche, Diners, Visa SEATS: 30. 6 tables outside. Private parties: 24 main room, 10 and 24 private rooms. Car park, 30 places. Vegetarian meals. Children's helpings. No cigars or pipes in dining-room. No-smoking area. Wheelchair access (1 step). Fax: (0600) 860607 ACCOMMODATION: 12 rooms, all with bath/shower. Rooms for disabled. B&B £48 to £76. Children welcome. Baby facilities. Pets welcome. Garden. TV. Phone. Scenic (*Which? Hotel Guide*)

WOLF'S CASTLE Dyfed map 4

▲ *Stone Hall* NEW ENTRY

Welsh Hook, Wolf's Castle SA62 5NS
LETTERSTON (0348) 840212
off A40, between Letterston and Wolf's Castle

COOKING 2
COST £19–£25

The ancient core of this remote building, hidden in a wooded valley, is a fourteenth-century manor house with slate floors and rough oak beams. Extended over time, it has been run by the Watsons as a country restaurant-with-rooms since 1984. Alan Watson's wife and the new chef are both French, and a Gallic atmosphere pervades the dining-room. The cooking is entrenched in the classic tradition: sautéed chicken livers with mushrooms, fillet of Dover sole with chive sauce, and chicken with tarragon sauce, to quote a few dishes, although there are some innovative touches. Chargrilled prawns with Ricard, excellent scallops in flaky pastry with garlic and cream, and 'slightly overcooked' lamb cutlets with shallots and grain mustard sauce have all worked well. Flavours are assertive, though sauces can occasionally be too intense. Ingredients are well-chosen: fish is from Milford Haven, ducks are from Somerset ('because the Welsh ones aren't big enough to take the breasts off,' according to one inspector). Profiteroles with home-made vanilla ice-cream and coffee parfait in a tulip biscuit have benefited from good chocolate sauce. Mrs Watson serves 'with the ease of any Frenchwoman in a family restaurant'. The wine list majors in French vintages and includes a few organics. House wine is £7.40.

CHEF: Pascal Deliant PROPRIETORS: Alan and Martine Watson OPEN: Tue to Sun, D only (L by arrangement) MEALS: 7 to 9.30 PRICES: £15 (£21), Set D £13 (£19) to £13.50 (£20) CARDS: Access, Amex, Visa SEATS: 54. Private parties: 45 main room, 20 private room. Car park, 50 places. Vegetarian meals. Children's helpings. No cigars/pipes in dining-room. No music. Fax: (0348) 840815 ACCOMMODATION: 5 rooms, all with bath/shower. B&B £37 to £49. Deposit: £20. Children welcome. Baby facilities. Garden. TV. Scenic. Doors close at 11.45. Confirm by 7

Isle of Man

DOUGLAS **Isle of Man** map 4

▲ *Boncomptes* — NEW ENTRY

Admiral House,
Loch Promenade, Douglas
DOUGLAS (0624) 629551

COOKING 1
COST £16–£37

Jamie and Jill Boncompte moved their restaurant from Onchan to the first floor of a Victorian hotel on the sea-front at Douglas. Inside, the high-ceilinged rooms have been decorated to create a leisurely elegant atmosphere reminiscent of a country house, and well-spaced tables in the dining-room allow for easy movement of the laden sweets trolley. The handwritten menu puts its faith in fresh fish, steaks and flambés, with the addition of a few predictable exotica such as smoked chicken with mango and curried vegetables in a fresh pineapple. Whitebait, steak chasseur and a rendezvous of seafood have all been good, although the home-smoked salmon has tasted 'insipid' and the giant grilled prawns have needed a more powerful injection of garlic. Desserts are unashamedly calorific, but irresistible. Locals consider the service to be good. The wine list is varied and respectably priced. House French is £8.50.

CHEF: Michael Ashe PROPRIETORS: Jamie and Jill Boncompte OPEN: Mon to Sat, exc Sat L CLOSED: 25 Dec MEALS: 12.30 to 2, 7.30 to 10 PRICES: £21 (£31), Set L £10.50 (£16) CARDS: Access, Diners, Visa SEATS: 80. Private parties: 80 main room. Car park, 6 places. Children's helpings. Smart dress preferred. No cigars/pipes in dining-room. Wheelchair access (also WC). Music. Fax: (0624) 675021 ACCOMMODATION: 12 rooms, 10 with bath/shower. Rooms for disabled. Lift. B&B £50 to £70. Children welcome. Baby facilities. TV. Phone. Scenic

RAMSEY **Isle of Man** map 4

Harbour Bistro — NEW ENTRY

5 East Street, Ramsey
RAMSEY (0624) 814182

COOKING 1
COST £30

After a spell away, when standards slipped, Karl and Linda Meier are back at this long-established bistro and 'working hard'. Reports suggest that they are succeeding. The simply furnished dining-room overlooks the harbour and freshly caught fish feature strongly on the menu. Fisherman's pie topped with mashed potato, salmon and mushroom casserole and paupiettes of plaice stuffed with prawns have been recommended. The extensive menu also takes in hot, crisp avocado slices with chilli sauce, guinea-fowl with mustard sauce, chicken Stroganoff and lemon mousse. 'Karl's Heart' is a confection of meringues, strawberry ice-cream and kiwi sorbet sitting on a liqueur sauce. Service is welcoming. A well-spread wine list has plenty of half-bottles; prices are fair. House wine is £8 a litre.

CHEF/PROPRIETOR: Karl Meier OPEN: all week, exc Sun D CLOSED: 2 weeks Jan, 4 days Christmas MEALS: 12 to 2.15, 6.30 to 10.30 PRICES: £16 (£25) CARDS: Access, Visa SEATS: 40. Private parties: 40 main room. Children's helpings. Wheelchair access (also WC). Music

Channel Islands

ROZEL Jersey map 1

Apple Cottage

NEW ENTRY

Brecque Du Sud, Rozel Bay — COOKING 1
JERSEY (0534) 61002 — COST £12–£26

Grandma's cottage to look at: roses round the door, exposed beams and stone walls, wooden furniture, red frilly lampshades and more. The menu is a long repertory of old favourites, the meat dishes are steak-house in style. Go for the fish, especially the seafood platter. This can be very good. It is a busy place, popular with locals and visitors alike. 'Book from the mainland, before you leave' is a reader's advice. The wine list is rather like the menu, but mark-ups are gentler than in England, or at least the tax is lower.

CHEF: S.C. Pozzi PROPRIETORS: Mr and Mrs S.C. Pozzi OPEN: Tue to Sun, exc Sun D CLOSED: Jan MEALS: 12 to 2.15, 7 to 9.30 PRICES: £16 (£22), Set L £8.50 (£12) to £9 (£12). Card slips closed CARDS: Access, Visa SEATS: 65. 15 tables outside. Private parties: 55 main room. Car park, 15 places. Children's helpings. Smart dress preferred. No cigars/pipes in dining-room. Wheelchair access (1 step; also WC). Music

Granite Corner

Rozel Harbour, Rozel — COOKING 3
JERSEY (0534) 63590 — COST £15–£35

'A little piece of France comes to Jersey, and about time too,' wrote one man with relief. Rozel is a picturesque harbour village at the bottom of a steep and narrow approach. Granite Corner is a cottage. Some craft, however, has been displayed in the pale blue and yellow interior dotted with nautical prints and objects. It may be small – no bar etc. – but it has style. Jean-Luc Robin doggedly pursues his search for materials; he even has a two-way radio in the kitchen to talk directly to the fishermen as they work. He continues to present Périgord specialities – bloc de foie gras and confit de canard, for instance – in tandem with fish from the Channel Islands. Meals thus take shape: say, scrambled eggs with a lingering after-taste of truffles; Jersey asparagus with hollandaise; carré of lamb with rosemary sauce; a mixture of mullet, brill, sea bass and salmon in a saffron sauce. Cheeses are unpasteurised, bread is crusty. It would be wrong to say that every meal is consistent with the last; error seems to creep in during high season. However, the restaurant resists (as too many do not) raking it in with the help of freezer-and-plastic-bag meals for the holiday trade. Set meals are notably inexpensive. The wine list is a short canter round France, with not many pauses in the south-west to partner the food. Prices are not too high. House French is £6.50.

CHEF: Jean-Luc Robin PROPRIETORS: Jean-Luc and Louise Robin OPEN: all week, exc Mon L and Sun D CLOSED: 2 weeks Jan MEALS: 12.30 to 1.30, 7.45 to 9 PRICES: £24 (£29), Set L £9.50 (£15). Net prices, card slips closed CARDS: Access, Amex, Diners, Visa SEATS: 24. Private parties: 24 main room. Children welcome. Jacket and tie. Music

ST SAVIOUR Jersey map 1

▲ *Longueville Manor*

St Saviour COOKING 3
JERSEY (0534) 25501 COST £23–£52

Most people on the Channel Islands come in for criticism of one sort or another from readers. The culprits are variously too many tourists, or too rich a home-based clientele, or simply those guilty of inadequacy in the kitchen, showing a happy insouciance about quality materials, even though so much should be available. This is not true, however, at Longueville Manor: 'This is a place I really found difficult to fault.' The Lewises and the Duftys rarely put a foot wrong. The house is well furnished, picturesque, comfortable and in a pleasing setting. Housekeeping is good. The restaurant, with Andrew Baird into his third year in the kitchen, continues to provide modern neo-classical food of very sound technique. Wayward tastes are not catered for, but it is never old-fashioned in presentation or composition. Dishes that have been recommended include wild mushroom consommé scattered with tarragon, galantine of duck, goats' cheese Pithivier with tomato and basil salad; red mullet with fennel and vegetables en papillote; duck with peaches; calf's liver with onion confit and bacon; banana and mango en papillote; and good sorbets and ice-creams. Service is highly effective, although a visitor last summer did wonder at laying breakfast before 11pm in so expensive a dining-room. Maybe it was a hint. The wine list takes in the world, even if the bulk is French. The prices are not as low as on other parts of the island. House Patriarche is £6.50.

CHEF: Andrew Baird PROPRIETORS: the Lewis family and the Dufty family OPEN: all week MEALS: 12.30 to 2, 7.30 to 9.30 PRICES: £37 (£43), Set L £19 (£23), Set D £27 (£31). Net prices, card slips closed CARDS: Access, Amex, Carte Blanche, Diners, Visa SEATS: 65. 8 tables outside. Private parties: 75 main room, 20 private room. Car park, 30 places. Vegetarian meals. Children restricted. Smart dress preferred. Wheelchair access (also WC). Air-conditioned. No music. Fax: (0534) 31613 ACCOMMODATION: 32 rooms, all with bath/shower. Rooms for disabled. Lift. B&B £76 to £250. Deposit: £50. No children under 7. Pets welcome. Afternoon teas. Garden. Swimming-pool. TV. Phone. Scenic

Northern Ireland

BALLYNAHINCH Co Down map 9

Woodlands

29 Spa Road, Ballynahinch BT24 8PT COOKING 1
BALLYNAHINCH (0238) 562650 COST £29

The small eighteenth-century house surrounded by deep, quiet grounds looking out over rolling countryside is a restaurant for three nights a week. Alison Sandford cooks a short set-price menu from a repertoire at once British (spinach roulade with smoked haddock filling) and bourgeois French (pork with prune and apple stuffing and a calvados cream sauce). The style, whatever the source, is substantial, followed by dinner-party desserts – maybe a dacquoise or ice-cream cake. The menu works a regular change through a limited number of dishes. David Sandford is a gentle host. The wine list is mainly French; growers and makes such as Duboeuf, Jaboulet, Drouhin and Guigal figure. Prices are fair. House wines are £7.50.

CHEF: Alison Sandford PROPRIETORS: Alison and David Sandford OPEN: Thurs to Sat, D only; private parties at other times by arrangement MEALS: 7.30 to 9.30 PRICES: Set D £19.95 (£24). Net prices, card slips closed CARDS: Access, Visa SEATS: 45. Private parties: 45 main room; 14 private room. Car park, 20 places. Children welcome. No cigars/pipes in dining-room. Music

BELFAST Co Antrim map 9

Belfast Castle

NEW ENTRY

Antrim Road, Belfast BT15 5GR COOKING 1
BELFAST (0232) 776925 COST £11–£30

The nineteenth-century castle was restored by the City Council in 1988 for use as function rooms and restaurants. House and grounds are a pleasure. The most-used restaurant is the bistro downstairs, where anything from prawn and melon cocktail to chicken tikka is served seven days a week. The Ben Madigan restaurant opens on three evenings and supplies more elaborate food in modern mode: salmon on spinach with a saffron glaze; lamb with a raspberry gravy; chicken with deep-fried beetroot and a basil and tomato sauce. Desserts go wild on presentation. The fair-priced wine list is adequate, though there are few half-bottles. House wine is £6.50.

CHEF: Carl King PROPRIETORS: Belfast City Council OPEN: Thur to Sat, D only, and Sun L (restaurant); all week, exc Sun L (bistro) MEALS: 12 to 2.30, 7.30 to 10 (bistro 5 to 10) PRICES: restaurant £16 (£25); bistro L £7 (£11), D £11 (£16) CARDS: Access, Amex, Diners, Visa SEATS: 50 restaurant, 100 bistro. 12 tables outside (bistro). Private parties: 50 main room, 30, 50 and 150 private rooms. Car park, 50 places. Vegetarian meals. Children welcome. Children's helpings (bistro). Smart dress preferred. No-smoking area. Wheelchair access (also WC). Music. Air-conditioned (bistro). Fax: (0232) 370228

La Belle Epoque

NEW ENTRY

103 Great Victoria Street,
Belfast BT7 1PT
BELFAST (0232) 323244

COOKING 2
COST £25

This handsome restaurant, 200 yards from the Europa and the spectacular Crown Bar, clad in extraordinary mosaics and offering French food with an Irish accent, has received more positive reports this year. The opening of new Belfast restaurants has perhaps put La Belle Epoque on its mettle. The classic dishes – lots of hollandaise in evidence and a good modern repertoire with few surprises – can be well executed, as in a meal of watercress soup; smoked pigeon breast fanned out on a garlic cream sauce; pork medallions with a raspberry vinegar reduction sauce; fillet steak béarnaise; beef with ginger and bean sprouts; decent sorbets; iced raspberry terrine; and a rich praline cream sandwiched between two almond biscuits, on an almond sauce and decorated with toasted almonds – a nut concerto. Prices are fair, the atmosphere is happy and service good. House wine is £5.95 and Sancerre is still (just) in single figures.

CHEFS: Alan Rousse and Chris Fitzgerald PROPRIETORS: J. Delbart, Alan Rousse, Chris Fitzgerald, G. Sanchez and J. Lindsay OPEN: Mon to Sat, D only CLOSED: 25 and 26 Dec MEALS: 6 to 11.30 PRICES: £14 (£21) CARDS: Access, Diners, Visa SEATS: 80. Private parties: 40 main room. Vegetarian meals. Music

Manor House

NEW ENTRY

43–47 Donegall Pass,
Belfast BT7 1DQ
BELFAST (0232) 238755 and 238739

COOKING 1
COST £8–£25

Some say this is *the* Belfast Chinese restaurant. Certainly, its growth in recent years would indicate popularity for a long Cantonese menu, acceptably cooked.

CHEF: Joyce Wong PROPRIETOR: Joe Wong OPEN: all week MEALS: noon to 11.30pm PRICES: £13 (£21), Set L £4.50 (£8), Set D £12.50 (£17) to £15 (£20). Service 10% CARDS: Access, Diners, Visa SEATS: 120. 25 tables outside. Private parties: 80 main room, 50 private room. Vegetarian meals. Children welcome. Wheelchair access. Music. Air-conditioned

The Guide *office can quickly spot when a restaurateur is encouraging customers to write recommending inclusion – and sadly, several have been doing this in 1991. Such reports do not further a restaurant's cause. Please tell us if a restaurateur invites you to write to the* Guide.

Nick's Warehouse

35–39 Hill Street, Belfast BT1 2LB — COOKING 2
BELFAST (0232) 439690 — COST £24

This is an enterprising wine bar and restaurant spread over two floors in a warehouse conversion. Downstairs, the wine bar has a bistro-style menu at lunch and offers a wider range of food in the evening. Upstairs, the restaurant is open for lunch, with more formal cooking, and can be hired for private parties in the evening. Eclecticism is the word for the wine bar: from samosas to pasta, to lamb chops or prawns with garlic mayonnaise. The restaurant is not expensive and shows some talented cooking of dishes such as loin of pork with fresh plum sauce, monkfish on pesto and steak with onion and horseradish sauce. It is a lively place and well-run. The wine list is short, changes quickly, and offers very fair value, with world-wide choice from fashionable and good makers.

CHEFS: Nick Price, Simon Toye and John Stephens PROPRIETORS: Nick and Kathy Price OPEN: Mon to Fri MEALS: restaurant 12.30 to 2.30; wine bar 12 to 3, 6 to 9 PRICES: £15 (£20) CARDS: Access, Diners, Visa SEATS: 50. Private parties: 50 main room, 45 private room. Vegetarian meals. No children under 18 in wine bar. Wheelchair access (also WC). Air-conditioned. Music

Roscoff — NEW ENTRY

Unit 7, Lesley House, Shaftesbury Square,
Belfast BT2 7DB — COOKING 3*
BELFAST (0232) 331532 — COST £17–£42

While people scoff at Ulster restaurants, the few places that are good are full and buzzing. The fault is not wholly in the clientele, therefore. Roscoff is the latest star in the heavens. Paul Rankin, a classically trained chef (Roux brothers) who returned to his native turf after travels through California and Australia (which have their influence, too), has created a sparkling modern dining-room with food to match. Denizens of Belfast call it pricey; anyone from the mainland might think it the bargain of the year. It has the style to reproduce the Raymond Blanc chocolate cup of coffee (at less than £5) and the invention to serve smoked salmon with a sesame oil and ginger vinaigrette. There is a certain nautical theme to the decoration – a deck-like floor, sails puffing in the wind in the tented ceiling, and portholes in the room dividers. Fish is not the speciality, but its quality, and the way in which turbot, for instance, may be presented as a breaded escalope with sorrel sauce one week, or with a red wine sauce with leeks, potatoes and wild mushrooms another, might cause one to attend for fish alone. Wild salmon, scallops and a symphony of seafood with fennel and a gâteau of wild rice have also come in for praise. A speciality that has been enjoyed in the summer has been 'trio of chicken', where the drumstick is served as if in coq au vin, the thigh is stuffed with spinach, mushrooms, sweetbreads and chicken mousse and the breast is sautéed. High fashion, and the ability to work beyond it, have arrived in Belfast. The *carte* is supplemented by a very fairly priced set menu in the evening and an even cheaper meal at lunchtime. This is backed up by a cellar that must be larger than most in the province. Nor does it stop at France, though the clarets are a fine collection at affordable prices. Names like Clos du Val, Penfolds, Guigal, Marquès de Riscal, Jaboulet, Drouhin and Bürklin-Wolf show the cellar's pedigree, even if sources cannot be as varied as on the mainland. House wines start at £8.95. Jeanne Rankin supervises the front-of-house and from erratic beginnings this too shows relaxed efficiency. Lucky old Belfast.

CHEF: Paul Rankin PROPRIETORS: Paul and Jeanne Rankin OPEN: Mon to Sat, exc Sat L CLOSED: 12 and 13 July, Christmas MEALS: 12.30 to 2, 6.30 to 10.30 PRICES: £23 (£35), Set L £10.95 (£17), Set D £15.95 (£22). Service 10% CARDS: Access, Amex, Diners, Visa SEATS: 65. Private parties: 25 main room. Vegetarian meals. Children welcome. No-smoking area. Wheelchair access (also WC). Music

Strand

12 Stranmillis Road, Belfast BT9 5AA — COOKING 1
BELFAST (0232) 682266 — COST £18

Ten years on, and this wine bar/restaurant close to the Hester Museum still attracts a crowd. The secret of its success is a wide-ranging, eclectic menu that is excellent value for money. The menu changes every month, but there is a consistently middle-of-the-road bistro feel to the mix of old and new, home and abroad: devilled kidneys, goats's cheese tartlets, calf's liver Stroganoff and oriental honeyed pork figured on a May menu with a choice of some dozen first courses and as many main dishes. At lunchtime there are single-dish meals such as fisherman's pie and Greek feta cheese salad. There are around 60 well-spread, fair-priced wines. House French is £5.80.

CHEFS: M. McAuley and Bill Bailey PROPRIETOR: Anne Turkington OPEN: all week MEALS: noon to 11 PRICES: £10 (£15) CARDS: Access, Amex, Diners, Visa SEATS: 80. Private parties: 25 private room. Vegetarian meals. Children welcome. Music. Air-conditioned

BELLANALECK Co Fermanagh — map 9

Sheelin

Bellanaleck
FLORENCECOURT (036 582) 232 — COOKING 1
4m from Enniskillen — COST £11–£26

The Sheelin functions first and foremost as a bakery, with a licensed restaurant providing sustenance for tourists and summer visitors. Teas, high teas and a salad buffet are the stock in trade. The kitchen moves up a gear on Saturday evening, when there is a five-course extravaganza based on a well-tried format. A mixed antipasto is followed by stuffed pancakes, then a sorbet. Main courses might range from roast duckling with Cointreau sauce and chicken à la King to wild salmon in filo pastry. Meals finish on a high note with a resplendent sweets trolley loaded with pavlova, cheesecake, mille-feuilles, tartes and fruity confections. The wine list, aimed at economy, has carefully chosen bottles among more predictable ones. House French is £5.25.

CHEF: Marion Cathcart PROPRIETOR: Arthur Cathcart OPEN: all week Jun to end Aug, Sun L Apr to end Sept, Fri and Sat D all year MEALS: 12.30 to 2.30, 7 to 9.30 PRICES: £13 (£19), Set L £7.50 (£11) to £9.50 (£13), Set D £13 (£17) to £17 (£22). Service 10%. Card slips closed CARDS: Access, Amex, Visa SEATS: 30. Private parties: 24 main room. Car park, 30 places. Vegetarian meals. Children's helpings. Smart dress preferred. No music

COLERAINE Co Derry map 9

▲ *Macduff's*

112 Killeague Road, Blackhill,
Coleraine BT51 4HH COOKING 1
AGHADOWEY (0265) 868433 COST £26

The Erwins' modest hotel is a green-painted Georgian rectory set in two acres of landscaped gardens. Inside, it has been richly decorated and embellished with antiques and greenery. Margaret Erwin now runs the kitchen, but the menu follows a well-tried eclectic path, taking in Stilton puffs with sweet-and-sour sauce, rack of lamb with mulled wine sauce, curries, Athol brose and Jamaican bananas. Visitors have enjoyed asparagus wrapped in ham with cheese sauce, monkfish with tomato and garlic sauce and escalopes of veal. Carragheen – a traditional Irish jellied dessert set by prepared seaweed – is served with whiskey syrup and fresh cream. Coffee comes with home-made petits fours. Service is friendly and attentive. The wine list is well-spread geographically and fairly priced. House French is £6.50.

CHEF: Margaret Erwin PROPRIETORS: Joseph and Margaret Erwin OPEN: Tue to Sat, D only MEALS: 7 to 9.30 PRICES: £14 (£22). Card slips closed CARDS: Access, Visa SEATS: 34. Private parties: 34 main room, 16 private room. Car park, 30 places. No children under 10. No music ACCOMMODATION: 6 rooms, 5 with bath/shower. B&B £25 to £45. No children under 10. Garden. Swimming-pool. TV. Scenic. Doors close at 1am. Confirm by 6

PORTRUSH Co Antrim map 9

Ramore

The Harbour, Portrush BT56 8DQ COOKING 2*
PORTRUSH (0265) 824313 COST £31

The views over the harbour and West Bay make this a doubly handsome place to eat. George McAlpin's cooking will ensure that a modern gloss is put upon fine materials, especially fish and meat, even if vegetables and fruits are harder to come by. He has the technical assurance to bring off dishes such as chicken breast wrapped in caul, stuffed with scampi and bound with leeks and wild mushrooms; or to make appetising filo purses holding garlic to accompany the rack of lamb glazed with ratatouille. The *carte* is inexpensive for the quality of the cooking, with home-made breads, pasta and petits fours giving foundation to a menu that runs from chicken liver pâté, through a version of soufflé suissesse, to mushrooms with garlic cream sauce flanked by quenelles of snails and chicken for first courses; and for main courses, from salmon and monkfish with saffron sauce, or pork with pineapple and a coriander and ginger sauce, to duck breast wrapped in filo, lined with a mousseline from the leg and served

with an orange sauce. The wine list has sufficiently classy names and makers to be a fair partner to the food; it is not expensive. House wines start at £6.50.

CHEF: George McAlpin PROPRIETORS: John and Joy Caithness, and George and Jane McAlpin OPEN: wine bar L Mon to Sat, restaurant D Tue to Sat CLOSED: last 2 weeks Jan MEALS: 12.30 to 2.30, 7 to 10 PRICES: £16 (£26). Card slips closed CARD: Visa SEATS: 55. Private parties: 60 main room. Car park, 8 places. Children welcome. Music

Republic of Ireland

The following entries are the result of our appeal for more reports in last year's *Guide*. Reporting still falls far short of the numbers and density achieved on the mainland of Britain, but we hope that this list will form a solid foundation for further expansion. We are grateful to those of you who have helped in this particular aspect, and would appeal to any who are intending a trip to the Republic this year that they bear us in mind. We would like to hear about your experiences.

It is quite clear that the Irish have a great gift for hospitality and, in many cases, an equal one for cooking, whether it be the simple conversion of matchless raw ingredients, more sophisticated modern cookery alive to current tendencies in Europe, or food in the tradition of the Anglo-Irish country house.

Prices quoted are in Irish punts. As we are still feeling our way, we have not given ratings for cooking as in the British Isles.

To telephone the Republic from mainland Britain, dial 010 353, followed by the area code and number we have listed dropping, however, the initial zero (0).

ADARE Co Limerick map 9

▲ *Adare Manor*

Adare
LIMERICK (061) 396566 COST £49

'The beds are seven feet wide' was the report sent by an incredulous English visitor who had gone to see the work of Ian McAndrew at this large country-house hotel. If recent signs are anything to go by, this chef's individual style has been somewhat tamed to suit the market, but here will be found extremely competent modern cooking, backed up by a classic wine list.

CHEF: Ian McAndrew PROPRIETORS: Mr and Mrs Tom Kane OPEN: all week MEALS: 12.30 to 2.30, 7 to 10 PRICES: £27 (£41). Service 15%. Card slips closed CARDS: Access, Amex, Diners, Visa SEATS: 70. Private parties: 100 main room, 30, 60 and 150 private rooms. Car park, 40 places. Vegetarian meals. Children's helpings. Jacket and tie. No-smoking area. Wheelchair access (also WC). Music ACCOMMODATION: 64 rooms, all with bath/shower. Rooms for disabled. Lift. B&B £150 to £180. Deposit: 1 night. Children welcome. Baby facilities. Afternoon teas. Garden. Swimming-pool. Sauna. Fishing. Golf. TV. Phone. Scenic. Confirm by 6

Healthy eating options *in the details at the end of an entry signifies that a restaurant marks on its menu, in words and/or using symbols, low-fat dishes or other healthy eating choices.*

AHAKISTA Co Cork map 9

▲ *Shiro* NEW ENTRY

Ahakista
BANTRY (027) 67030 COST £44

'Quite how a restaurant with two tables manages to make any money is something of a mystery, even if it is run by a husband and wife team. Past experience of eating Japanese food has been confined to London establishments and dishes which always seemed shy of the real thing. We were in for a surprise.' The Pilzes came over from Germany. Food is as authentic as it can be. The dining occurs in private rooms, Japanese-style. Each party has its room for the evening. Early booking is essential. A rare experience.

CHEF: Kei Pilz PROPRIETORS: Kei and Werner Pilz OPEN: all week, D only CLOSED: Jan to end Feb MEALS: 7 to 9 PRICES: Set D £30 (£37). Minimum £30. 5% charge for credit cards. Net prices CARDS: Access, Amex, Diners, Visa SEATS: 12. Private parties: 12 main room, 8 private room. Car park, 8 places. Vegetarian meals. No children under 12. Music ACCOMMODATION: 1 room with bath/shower. Children welcome. Pets welcome. Garden. Fishing. TV. Scenic. Doors close at 10. Confirm by 3

BALLINA Co Mayo map 9

▲ *Mount Falcon Castle*

Ballina
BALLINA (096) 21172 COST £29

A classic old-style country house where simple and wholesome food is served to guests seated round one great table.

CHEF/PROPRIETOR: Constance Aldridge OPEN: all week, D only CLOSED: 3 days Christmas, Feb to Mar (open Easter) MEALS: 8 PRICES: Set D £17.50 (£24). Service 10%. Card slips closed CARDS: Access, Amex, Diners, Visa SEATS: 22. Private parties: 7 main room. Car park, 20 places. Vegetarian meals with prior notice. Children's helpings with prior notice. No-smoking area. One sitting ACCOMMODATION: 10 rooms, all with bath/shower. B&B £40 to £80. Deposit: 25%. Children welcome. Baby facilities. Pets welcome. Garden. Tennis. Fishing. Scenic. Doors close at midnight. Confirm by 2

BALLYDEHOB Co Cork map 9

Annie's

Main Street, Ballydehob
BALLYDEHOB (028) 37292 COST £13–£31

'A delicious quick lunch of fresh scones, soup, excellent mussels and aromatic coffee' was a meal enjoyed by a reader in the warm, friendly and cheerful atmosphere of Annie's. 'Very good seafood: you can add a dimension to the experience by going across the road to the Levis sisters' pub and order a drink, chat a bit, then Annie will come over and take your order.' The cooking is not elaborate, but the food is very fresh.

CHEF/PROPRIETOR: Anne Ferguson OPEN: Tue to Sat CLOSED: first 3 weeks Oct, 25 and 26 Dec MEALS: 12.30 to 2.30, 6.30 to 9.30 PRICES: £19 (£26), Set L £7 (£13), Set D £19 (£26) CARDS: Access, Visa SEATS: 24. Children welcome. No cigars/pipes in dining-room. Wheelchair access. Music

BALLYLICKEY Co Cork map 9

▲ *Sea View House Hotel*

Ballylickey
BANTRY (027) 50073 and 50462 COST £15–£31

There are great views indeed from this Victorian manor house that is a useful place to stay at and offers traditional hotel cooking and excellent service. Not a place for the culinary adventurous, but it is reliable and popular. 'The meal took us by surprise – the quality was excellent' is the right sort of response from an unexpected visitor.

CHEF/PROPRIETOR: Kathleen O'Sullivan OPEN: all week, D only, and Sun L MEALS: 1 to 2, 7 to 9.30 PRICES: £13 (£21), Set Sun L £9 (£15) to £10 (£17), Set D £17.50 (£25) to £18.50 (£26). Service 10%. Card slips closed CARDS: Access, Amex, Diners, Visa SEATS: 45. Private parties: 16 main room. Car park, 30 places. Vegetarian meals. Children's helpings. No cigars/pipes in dining-room. Wheelchair access (also WC). No music. Fax: (027) 51555 ACCOMMODATION: 17 rooms, all with bath/shower. Rooms for disabled. B&B £35 to £80. Children welcome. Baby facilities. Pets welcome. Afternoon teas. Garden. TV. Phone. Scenic. Doors close at midnight. Confirm by 6

BALLYVAUGHAN Co Clare map 9

▲ *Gregans Castle*

Ballyvaughan
ENNIS (065) 77005 COST £21–£48

Acceptable cooking, strong on fresh fish and seafood, is on offer in this hotel that gets unreserved endorsement as a beautiful location and enjoyable place to stay at.

CHEFS: Peter Haden and Margaret Cronin PROPRIETORS: Peter and Moira Haden OPEN: all week CLOSED: end Oct to end Mar MEALS: 12 to 3, 7 to 8.30 PRICES: bar L £13 (£21), restaurant Set D £23 (£33) to £30 (£40). Service 10% alc, 12.5% set. Card slips closed CARDS: Access, Visa SEATS: 50. Private parties: 80 main room. Car park, 24 places. Vegetarian meals. Children's helpings. Smart dress preferred. No cigars/pipes in dining-room. Wheelchair access (also WC). No music ACCOMMODATION: 22 rooms, all with bath/shower. Rooms for disabled. B&B £65 to £110. Deposit: £50. Children welcome. Baby facilities. Afternoon teas. Garden. Phone. Scenic. Doors close at 11.30. Confirm by 5

Dining-rooms where live and recorded music are not be played are signalled by No music *in the details at the end of an entry.*

Card slips closed *in the details at the end of an entry indicates that the totals on the slips of credit cards are closed when these are handed over for signature.*

BLACKROCK Co Dublin map 9

Colin O'Daly, the Park Restaurant

40 The Mews, Main Street, Blackrock
DUBLIN (01) 2886177 COST £19–£48

Colin O'Daly offers modern cooking in modern surroundings, with an eye for presentation, a pleasure in luxury ingredients and a perception of modern fashion in dishes like saddle of rabbit with black olives and mustard sauce, pigeon with foie gras and a sherry sauce, and a plate of lamb and its offal. Prices are high and some meals reported have not matched the evident ambitions of the place. The wine list is dear, too.

CHEF/PROPRIETOR: Colin O'Daly OPEN: Mon to Sat, exc Sat L MEALS: 12.30 to 1.45, 7.30 to 9.45 PRICES: £29 (£40), Set L £12 (£19), Set D £24 (£32) CARDS: Access, Amex, Carte Blanche, Diners, Visa SEATS: 70. Private parties: 50 main room, 20 private room. Vegetarian meals. Children's helpings. Smart dress preferred. No-smoking area. Music. Air-conditioned. Fax: (01) 2834365

BRAY Co Wicklow map 9

Tree of Idleness NEW ENTRY

Seafront, Bray
DUBLIN (01) 2863498 and 2828183 COST £23–£42

On the seafront, this Greek-Cypriot restaurant does not flaunt its Hellenic character all over the walls or on the Muzak machine – a mercy for some. The menu mixes Greek and international gourmet dishes: fillet with red wine and truffle sauce sits next to lamb stuffed with feta cheese and olives. The service is fast and friendly. The wine list has a remarkable set of clarets, and covers classic regions and auction rarities such as the Crimean fortified wine from Massandra.

CHEF: Akis Courtellas PROPRIETORS: Akis and Susan Courtellas OPEN: Tues to Sun, D only CLOSED: Christmas, first 2 weeks Sept MEALS: 7.30 to 11 (10 Sun) PRICES: £24 (£35), Set D £15 (£23) to £19 (£28). Service 10%. Card slips closed CARDS: Access, Diners, Visa SEATS: 50. Private parties: 18 main room. Vegetarian meals. No children under 12. No-smoking area on request. Wheelchair access (also WC). Music

CASHEL Co Tipperary map 9

Chez Hans

Rockside, Cashel
CASHEL (062) 61177 COST £41

'I must be among those "whose god is the belly", as St Paul wrote to the Philippians, for I found this converted chapel an excellent place of worship,' reported one reader. The dining-room has the open roof of the original chapel, plenty of flowers, religious paintings, plates and lots of Victoriana. This may not sound convivial, but it is. Really sound classic cooking in generous quantity has produced recommendations for home-made soups and consommés, rack of lamb with a herb crust, a spectacular mound of seafood and fish in a simple cream sauce, excellent vegetables ('very tasty mashed potato'), as well as blockbusting sweet things like a strawberry cheesecake and apple and loganberry tart. A consistent restaurant.

CHEF/PROPRIETOR: Hans-Peter Matthiä OPEN: Tue to Sat, D only CLOSED: first 3 weeks Jan MEALS: 6.30 to 10 PRICES: £25 (£34). Card slips closed CARDS: Access, Visa SEATS: 60. Private parties: 60 main room. Car park, 10 places. Vegetarian meals with prior notice. Children's helpings. No-smoking area. Wheelchair access (also WC). Music

CASHEL Co Galway map 9

▲ *Cashel House Hotel*

Cashel
CLIFDEN (095) 31001 COST £24–£42

The McEvillys do not enthuse about 'one-night business' and certainly do not hold with groups, conferences or functions. Their hotel is for 'relaxers'. One such visited for a meal, the only non-resident, but found the welcome as warm as hot mustard. 'We regretted missing breakfast.' Dinner is set-price, but there is plenty of choice within a five-course format (soup at second, sorbet at third). Lobster is a near-constant, and there is as much or more fish as meat as main-course options. The fish is of fine quality, for example ray with lemon and cream sauce, brill with two pepper sauces and salmon with sorrel sauce or stuffed with scallops. This is good country-house cooking in a firmly country-house setting.

CHEFS: Dermot McEvilly, Patrick Hernandez and Meta O'Malley PROPRIETORS: Dermot and Kay McEvilly OPEN: all week CLOSED: 15 Nov to 20 Dec MEALS: 12.30 to 2, 7.30 to 8.45 PRICES: L £13 (£24), Set D £21 (£30) to £25 (£35). Service 12.5%. Card slips closed CARDS: Access, Amex, Visa SEATS: 70. 4 tables outside. Car park, 40 places. Vegetarian meals. No children under 5. Jacket and tie. No-smoking area. Wheelchair access (also WC). No music ACCOMMODATION: 32 rooms, all with bath/shower. Rooms for disabled. B&B £48 to £96. Deposit: £100. No children under 5. Pets welcome. Afternoon teas. Garden. Tennis. Fishing. Golf. TV. Phone. Scenic

CLIFDEN Co Galway map 9

O'Grady's

Market Street, Clifden
CLIFDEN (095) 21450 and 21437 COST £14–£32

This is a family business. The older generation have a B&B in the town and have ceded much of the running of the restaurant to the sons. Having their own trawler ensures the materials are in prime condition. Bouillabaisse is enjoyed, as is the seafood chowder, on a menu offering maybe eight dishes at each course. Although this is a self-proclaimed seafood restaurant, meat gets a fair outing. Connemara scallops with bacon, mushrooms and a brandy cream, brill with lemon butter as well as noisettes of lamb with rosemary jus have been recommended. Reports of puddings are mixed. The style is by no means artless – more restaurant than that of just a fish place.

CHEF: Raymond Collet PROPRIETORS: Jack and Marion O'Grady OPEN: Mon to Sat CLOSED: 16 to 30 Dec, 12 Jan to 12 Mar MEALS: 12.30 to 2.30, 6.30 to 10 PRICES: £18 (£27), Set L £7.95 (£14) to £10.50 (£17), Set D £17.50 (£24). Minimum £8. Service 10%. Card slips closed CARDS: Access, Visa SEATS: 50. Private parties: 10 main room, 8 private room. Vegetarian meals. Children restricted D. Smart dress preferred. No-smoking area. Music

CLONAKILTY Co Cork map 9

Dunworley Cottage NEW ENTRY

Butlerstown, Clonakilty
BANDON (023) 40314
on coast between Clonakilty and Bandon COST £23–£30

A taxi will take you miles into a remote and poetic landscape where this distinguished country restaurant is run by Katherine Norén and her family. The produce is eloquent, the Swedish accent makes it the more interesting and the surroundings give the feeling that dinner is part of a Cocteau film, so cut off and surreal do you feel. A spot to treasure, especially for the Dunworley pig party in May and the black and white puddings, mussel soup and rhubarb tarts. Finish with Mrs Norén's akvavits.

CHEF: Michael Olsson PROPRIETOR: Katherine Norén OPEN: Wed to Sun CLOSED: 6 Jan to 17 Mar MEALS: 1 to 3, 6.30 to 9 PRICES: £16 (£23), Set L and D £17 (£25) CARDS: Access, Amex, Diners, Visa SEATS: 45. Private parties: 20 main room, 15 and 20 private rooms. Vegetarian meals. Healthy eating options. Children's helpings. No-smoking area. Wheelchair access. No music

COLLOONEY Co Sligo map 9

▲ *Knockmuldowney Restaurant*

Markree Castle, Collooney
SLIGO (071) 67800
1m off N4, E of Collooney COST £17–£32

The castle has to be seen to be believed, featuring even in Lord Clark's TV series *Civilisation*. The Coopers are of the family that built it, so not only is the 'experience' authentic, but the prices are lower than at many of Ireland's castle hotels. Fairly straightforward cooking of a daily menu, with a reality that encompasses lead shot in the pigeon terrine, runs through dishes such as beef goulash, salmon with sorrel sauce, duck with orange, and parfaits and mousses at dessert. The vegetables are not good; the wine list is wide-ranging and inexpensive.

CHEF: Mary Cooper PROPRIETORS: Charles and Mary Cooper OPEN: all week CLOSED: 3 days Christmas, mid-Jan to end Feb MEALS: 1 to 2.30, 7.30 to 9.30 PRICES: Set L £10.50 (£17), Set D £16.50 (£24) to £19.50 (£27) CARDS: Access, Amex, Carte Blanche, Diners, Visa SEATS: 80. Private parties: 60 main room, 25 private room. Car park, 40 places. Vegetarian meals on request. Children's helpings. No smoking in dining-room. Fax: (071) 67840 ACCOMMODATION: 15 rooms, all with bath/shower. B&B £42 to £84. Deposit: £20. Children welcome. Pets welcome. Afternoon teas. Garden. Fishing. TV. Phone. Scenic. Doors close from 11.30. Confirm by 5

CONG Co Mayo map 9

▲ *Ashford Castle*

Cong
CLAREMORRIS (092) 46003 COST £29–£76

The Connaught Room is the flagship restaurant of this enormous castle hotel by the shores of Lough Corrib. Denis Lenihan cooks neo-classical French food in conditions of extreme luxury. The other hotel restaurant, the George V Room, is not so satisfactory when viewed in terms of value for money. The atmosphere of the place fair takes one aback, so massive, grand and panelled is it. The building itself is worth the detour.

CHEF: Denis Lenihan PROPRIETOR: Rory Murphy OPEN: all week CLOSED: Jan and Feb MEALS: 1 to 2.30, 7 to 9.45 PRICES: Connaught £40 (£63); George V Set L £18 (£29), Set D £32.50 (£46). Service 15%. Card slips closed CARDS: Access, Amex, Diners, Visa SEATS: 40. Private parties: 40 main room. Car park, unlimited. Vegetarian meals. No children under 8. Jacket and tie. No-smoking area. Wheelchair access. Music. Air-conditioned. Fax: (092) 46260 ACCOMMODATION: 83 rooms, all with bath/shower. Rooms for disabled. Lift. B&B £178 to £189. Deposit: 10%. Children restricted. Baby facilities. Afternoon teas. Garden. Tennis. Fishing. Golf. TV. Phone. Scenic. Doors close at midnight. Confirm by 11

CORK Co Cork map 9

▲ *Arbutus Lodge*

Middle Glanmire Road,
Montenotte, Cork
CORK (021) 501237 COST £16–£46

A town house, once the residence of the mayors of Cork, which is now a fine small hotel with the Ryan family very much in charge. Links with Ireland and its cooking have not been entirely submerged by European influences and wider fame. Bacon and cabbage, Arbutus-style, nettle or lovage soups, salmon on a sorrel and nettle sauce and Cork crubeens are instances of that, just as chargrilled polenta with Mediterranean vegetables of lambs' kidneys with a ginger salad go further afield. The wine list is also very fine with some great runs of claret, good Californians and stylish Italians. Wine service is impeccable, showing care for the cellar and customer alike. Those meals taken on behalf of the *Guide* this year have shown more faults than usually experienced here. It is normally an exact kitchen with fine materials and impressive recipes. One has to add, 'not invariably'. Lunches in the bar are ambitious and yet much cheaper than in the restaurant.

CHEF: Michael Ryan PROPRIETORS: the Ryan family OPEN: Mon to Sat CLOSED: 24 to 29 Dec MEALS: 1 to 2 (12.30 to 3 bar lunches), 7 to 9.30 PRICES: £25 (£38), Set L £15.75 (£23), bar L £10 (£16), Set D £19.75 (£27), Snacks from £1.75 CARDS: Access, Amex, Diners, Visa SEATS: 60. 8 tables outside (bar food only). Private parties: 8 main room, 50 private room. Car park, 40 places. Vegetarian meals. Children's helpings. No cigars/pipes in dining-room. Wheelchair access (3 steps; also WC). Air-conditioned. Fax: (021) 502893 ACCOMMODATION: 20 rooms, all with bath/shower. B&B £38.50 to £105. Children welcome. Baby facilities. Garden. Tennis. Air-conditioned. TV. Phone. Scenic

Clifford's

18 Dyke Parade, Mardyke, Cork
MARDYKE (021) 275333 COST £19–£40

Housed in what was formerly Cork County Library, Clifford's is a fine Georgian building Michael and Deirdre Clifford have had the nous to decorate with modern art, soft furnishings and a great sense of style. The two styles mix well. Michael Clifford is a very fine chef who has moved effortlessly into the stronger flavours and more robust presentation of *cuisine grand'mère*, leaving nouvelle cuisine gasping in the hedgerow. Clonakilty black pudding, smoked beef and great fish lead the evident local input, while materials such as lentils, fresh pasta and cabbage show modern tendencies. A remarkable restaurant. The wine list is exceptionally well chosen, without excessive length.

CHEF: Michael Clifford PROPRIETORS: Michael and Deirdre Clifford OPEN: Mon to Sat, exc L Mon and Sat MEALS: 12.30 to 2.30, 7.30 to 10.30 PRICES: Set L £11.50 (£19), Set D £24.50 (£33) CARDS: Access, Amex, Diners, Visa SEATS: 50. Private parties: 50 main room, 35 private room. Vegetarian meals. Children's helpings. Jacket and tie. No-smoking area. No music. Air-conditioned

Crawford Gallery, Municipal Art Gallery

Emmet Place, Cork
CORK (021) 274415 COST £16–£28

A café/restaurant outpost of Ballymaloe House, situated in the main art gallery in Cork. It is a good place for lunch, for Irish stew and Irish rhubarb cake, and not too expensive for dinner. 'On several visits we had fresh salmon open sandwich, smoked salmon open sandwich, salad with home-made mayonnaise, delectable coffee ice-cream with meringues and fine gooseberry fool. The coffee is better than in most places in Ireland. A blissful place for a light lunch.'

CHEFS: Myrtle and Fern Allen and Rosie Mcleod PROPRIETORS: Myrtle and Fern Allen OPEN: Mon to Sat L, Wed to Fri D CLOSED: 24 Dec for 2 weeks MEALS: 10.30 to 5 (L 12 to 2.30), 6.30 to 9.30 PRICES: L £9 (£16), D £16 (£23) CARDS: Access, Visa SEATS: 70. Private parties: 70 main room. Vegetarian meals. Children's helpings. No-smoking area. Music

DINGLE Co Kerry map 9

▲ *Doyle's*

4 John Street, Dingle
TRALEE (066) 51174 COST £30

This is the place to go in Dingle. It has bedroom accommodation as well, all done out in a relaxed country fashion. The very good, very fresh fish is cooked with style, not just plain. 'A rumbustious experience, no English reserve here, but it is very well run,' says a reader. Hot trout smokie, grilled clams with lots of garlic, a large crayfish and turbot with a thick tartare sauce made a most satisfactory meal. Another reader enthuses: 'This must be the best restaurant ever for lobster' and proceeds to report on two lobster meals taken there in the same day.

CHEF: Stella Doyle PROPRIETORS: John and Stella Doyle OPEN: Mon to Sat CLOSED: mid-Nov to mid-Mar MEALS: 12.30 to 2.15, 6 to 9 PRICES: £18 (£25). Service 10%. Card slips closed CARDS: Access, Amex, Diners, Visa SEATS: 45. Private parties: 28 main room. Children's helpings. No-smoking area. Wheelchair access (1 step; also WC) ACCOMMODATION: 8 rooms, all with bath/shower. Rooms for disabled. B&B £35 to £55. Deposit: 1 night. Children welcome. Baby facilities. TV. Phone. Doors close at 11. Confirm by 6

Half Door

John Street, Dingle
TRALEE (066) 51600 COST £34

Another spot in Dingle that serves lobster dinners, now under the new ownership of the O'Connors. Whether it will continue to be a *close* second to Doyle's (see entry, above) has yet to be seen. Dennis O'Connor's style is more elaborately 'restaurant' than his predecessor's, but the shellfish are still all there.

CHEF: Denis O'Connor PROPRIETORS: Denis and Teresa O'Connor OPEN: all week, exc Tue Sept to June CLOSED: Jan to 17 Mar MEALS: 12.30 to 2.30, 6 to 10 PRICES: £19 (£28) CARDS: Access, Diners, Visa SEATS: 52. Private parties: 30 main room. Vegetarian meals. No-smoking area. Wheelchair access (also WC). No music. Air-conditioned. Fax: (066) 51210

DOUGLAS Co Cork map 9

Lovetts

Churchyard Lane,
off Well Road, Douglas
CORK (021) 294909 and 362204 COST £20–£36

The ground floor of a secluded Georgian house is given over to a restaurant specialising, but not exclusively, in fish. Lovetts is popular with businesses, and can sometimes produce very good meals. Game is a strong point. Informal bar lunches, also with an emphasis on shellfish and fish, are an innovation this year.

CHEF: Greg Dawson PROPRIETORS: Dermod and Margaret Lovett OPEN: Mon to Sat, exc Sat L MEALS: 12.30 to 2, 7 to 10 PRICES: £21 (£30), Set L £12.65 (£20), Set D £18.75 (£27). Service 12.5%. Card slips closed CARDS: Access, Amex, Diners, Visa SEATS: 40. Private parties: 40 main room, 25 private room. Car park, 20 places. Vegetarian meals. Children's helpings. No-smoking area. Wheelchair access (also WC). Music. Fax: (021) 508568

DUBLIN Co Dublin **map 9**

Coq Hardi

35 Pembroke Road,
Ballsbridge, Dublin 4
DUBLIN (01) 689070 and 684130 COST £26–£60

Classical French cooking by John Howard and a classic wine list, particularly for clarets, with a spectacular run of the 1970 vintage and most years of Mouton Rothschild on show, if not on sale. This is pre-eminently a place for the establishment and the world of finance, with prices and standards to match.

CHEFS: John Howard and James O'Sullivan PROPRIETORS: John and Catherine Howard OPEN: Mon to Sat, exc Sat L CLOSED: 2 weeks Christmas, 2 weeks Aug MEALS: 12.30 to 2.30, 7 to 11 PRICES: £31 (£50), Set L £16 (£26). Service 12.5%. Card slips closed CARDS: Access, Amex, Diners, Visa SEATS: 50. Private parties: 50 main room, 4, 10 and 20 private rooms. Car park, 20 places. Children welcome. Jacket and tie. No-smoking area. No music. Air-conditioned. Fax: (01) 689887

Eastern Tandoori

34–35 South William Street, Dublin 2
DUBLIN (01) 710428 and 710506 COST £13–£32

An Indian restaurant for those who hanker for a curry. The food is satisfactory. There is another branch in Blackrock.

CHEFS: Henry Paul and Olli Ullah PROPRIETORS: Mr and Mrs Feroze Khan OPEN: all week, exc Sun L MEALS: 12 to 2.30, 6 to 11.30 PRICES: £15 (£27), Set L £6.95 (£13) to £7.50 (£14), Set D £13.50 (£20) to £15 (£22). Minimum £7.50. Service 12.5%. Card slips closed CARDS: Access, Amex, Diners, Visa SEATS: 74. Vegetarian meals. Children's helpings. No-smoking area. Wheelchair access (2 steps). Music. Air-conditioned. Fax: (01) 779232

Kapriol

45 Lower Camden Street, Dublin 2
DUBLIN (01) 751235 and 985496 COST £43

This is Dublin's favourite Italian restaurant, with Egidia Peruzzi doing the cooking and Giuseppe working the front-of-house. The menu is classic Italian, uninfluenced by the waves of farmhouse cooking now washing on British shores. This is a real gem, with a wonderful welcome and ambience; open late.

CHEF: Egidia Peruzzi PROPRIETORS: Egidia and Giuseppe Peruzzi OPEN: Mon to Sat, D only (L by arrangement) CLOSED: bank hols, 3 weeks Aug MEALS: 7.30 to 12 PRICES: £24 (£37). Service 12.5% CARDS: Access, Amex, Diners, Visa SEATS: 30. Private parties: 36 main room. Vegetarian meals. Children's helpings. Smart dress preferred. Wheelchair access (1 step). Music

Locks

1 Windsor Terrace, Portobello,
Dublin 8
DUBLIN (01) 543391 and 538352 COST £20–£41

The area is run-down enough to require grilles on all the windows, but the canalside location has its advantages. Sound cooking extends from crisp potato skin filled with prawns, smoked salmon, cabbage and a hollandaise or pasta with smoked fish, to spiced rack of lamb with port jus or roast duck with apple and caramel sauce.

CHEF: Brian Buckley PROPRIETOR: Claire Douglas OPEN: Mon to Sat, exc Sat L CLOSED: 1 week Christmas, bank hols MEALS: 12.30 to 2, 7.15 to 11 PRICES: £23 (£34), Set L £12.95 (£20), Set D £18.95 (£27). Service 12.5% CARDS: Access, Amex, Diners, Visa SEATS: 50. Private parties: 15 main room, 8 and 22 private rooms. Children's helpings. Wheelchair access. No music

Patrick Guilbaud

46 James's Place, Dublin 2
DUBLIN (01) 764192 COST £25–£50

Some of the best food in Ireland is served here. The restaurant has been thought to be still improving – not bad after 10 years. The cooking is unreservedly modern in style: home-made ravioli with langoustines and a tomato butter sauce, salmon with potato blinis and caviare, salmon with spices, and duck with ceps sauce and sweet potatoes are some of the current offerings. 'Quite excellent on all counts. Very succulent gravlax; thin, pink calf's liver, with nouvellish vegetables as well as a baked potato with a celery filling; a grand cheeseboard.'

CHEF: Guillaume Lebrun PROPRIETOR: Patrick Guilbaud OPEN: Tue to Sat CLOSED: bank hols MEALS: 12.30 to 2, 7.30 to 10.15 PRICES: £29 (£42), Set L £15.50 (£25), Set D £25 (£36). Service 15% CARDS: Access, Amex, Diners, Visa SEATS: 85. Private parties: 85 main room, 30 private room. Car park, 6 places. Vegetarian meals. Children's helpings. Smart dress preferred. No-smoking area. Wheelchair access (1 step). Fax: (01) 601546

Prices quoted in the Guide *are based on information supplied by restaurateurs. The figure in brackets below an entry is the average for a three-course meal with service, coffee and half a bottle of house wine, as calculated by computer. The prices quoted at the top of an entry represent a range, from the lowest average meal price to the highest; the latter is inflated by 20 per cent to take account of the fact that very few people eat an average meal, and also that prices are likely to rise during the year of the* Guide.

DUN LAOGHAIRE Co Dublin map 9

Digby's

5 Windsor Terrace, Dun Laoghaire
DUBLIN (01) 2804600 and 2809147 COST £17–£42

A well-established restaurant and wine bar that has views across the bay and cooking of some finesse. Much of the repertoire is fish (and game in winter): plaice stuffed with herbs, mussels in a garlic sauce and brill with mussel and saffron sauce are items warmly mentioned. There is a strong line of Mediterranean fashion in current menus: aubergine cake; calamares with olive oil, garlic and lime; and sea bass with balsamic vinegar are examples. 'The wine bar in the restaurant's full title implies a casual atmosphere. Not the case, a very good and very stylish restaurant.' The wine list is certainly not at wine bar price levels.

CHEF: Paul Cathcart PROPRIETORS: Paul and Jane Cathcart OPEN: all week D, exc Tue, and Sun L CLOSED: bank hols MEALS: 12.30 to 3, 7 to 11 PRICES: £25 (£35), Set L £10.50 (£17), Set D £18.50 (£26). Service 12.5%. Card slips closed CARDS: Access, Amex, Diners, Visa SEATS: 50. Private parties: 53 main room. Vegetarian meals. Children's helpings L. No-smoking area. Music

Restaurant Na Mara

Dun Laoghaire Harbour, Dun Laoghaire
DUBLIN (01) 2806767 and 2800509 COST £20–£48

A railway restaurant, owned by Irish Rail, set in a glorious building overlooking Dun Laoghaire harbour that was part of the original railway terminal. It specialises in fish, mainly cooked in classical style. 'We went there 10 years ago and it was memorable. This year it was even better,' ran a report. Quenelles of sole with lemon and sorrel sauce; seafood and saffron consommé; turbot on a bed of leeks, in a pastry shell, with an orange sauce; and snowy eggs with Bailey's Irish Cream sauce were part of the meal. Presentation is a strong point.

CHEF: Derek Dunne PROPRIETORS: Irish Rail Co OPEN: Mon to Sat CLOSED: 1 week Christmas, 1 week Easter MEALS: 12.30 to 2.30, 7 to 10.30 PRICES: £29 (£40), Set L £12.75 (£20), Set D £22 (£31). Service 15%. Card slips closed CARDS: Access, Amex, Diners, Visa SEATS: 75. Private parties: 45 main room, 30 private room. Vegetarian meals. Children welcome. Smart dress preferred. No-smoking area. Wheelchair access (2 steps). Music. Fax: (01) 844649

'Tables crushed cheek-by-jowl so you had to share your neighbour's pleasures, no problem with smoke, but dear me the singing. I wish the Guide *would get up a campaign against the perils of passive singing in pizzerias. Also in fine voice was the maestro, a diminutive dome-head, juggling dough and cheese inches from us and shouting orders across the room, like Italy's answer to the Mekon. Service was slick, as it needed to be in that busy atmosphere.'* On eating in Yorkshire

DUNDALK Co Louth map 9

Cellars

Backhouse Centre, Clanbrassil Street,
Dundalk
DUNDALK (042) 33745 COST £13

Here is home cooking with daily menus and a vegetarian emphasis. Salads are the thing, plus soups and major-league desserts. Open only for lunch.

CHEFS/PROPRIETORS: Alison and George O'Shea OPEN: Mon to Fri L MEALS: 12.30 to 2 PRICES: £6 (£11) SEATS: 150. Private parties: 100 main room, 24 private room. Car park, 140 places. Vegetarian meals. Children's helpings. No-smoking area. Music. Air-conditioned

DURRUS Co Cork map 9

Blair's Cove House

Durrus
BANTRY (027) 61127 COST £38

A great position above the sea, where a simple menu is cooked mainly on a wood-fired grill in the dining-room. Fish is obviously a strong point. The cooking is not elaborate, but that is a quality not a fault.

CHEF: Sabine de Mey PROPRIETORS: Philippe and Sabine de Mey OPEN: Tue to Sat, D only, plus Mon D July and Aug CLOSED: Nov to Feb MEALS: 7.30 to 9.30 PRICES: Set D £22 (£32). Service 10%. Card slips closed CARDS: Access, Amex, Diners, Visa SEATS: 70. 8 tables outside. Private parties: 35 main room. Car park, 20 places. Vegetarian meals. Children's helpings. No-smoking area. Wheelchair access. Music

GOREY Co Wexford map 9

▲ *Marlfield House* **NEW ENTRY**

Courtown Road, Gorey
GOREY (055) 21124 COST £23–£43

This is a small Georgian mansion with fine gardens and displaying a taste for interior design. The dining-room takes in a grand Victorian conservatory – lunch here is a pleasure. There is good cooking of excellent materials, found in such things as orange-flavoured potato cakes with lambs' sweetbreads and kidneys, and chicken breast with sesame seeds and leeks.

CHEF: Rose Brannoch PROPRIETORS: Mary and Ray Bowe OPEN: all week MEALS: 12.30 to 2, 7.15 to 9.30 PRICES: Set L £16.50 (£23) to £17.50 (£24), Set D £26.50 (£34) to £28.50 (£36). Service 10%. Card slips closed CARDS: Access, Amex, Visa SEATS: 60. Private parties: 60 main room, 25 private room. Car park, 45 places. Vegetarian meals with prior notice. Children's helpings L. Smart dress preferred. No cigars/pipes in dining-room. Wheelchair access. No music. Fax: (055) 21572 ACCOMMODATION: 19 rooms, all with bath/shower. Rooms for disabled. B&B £75 to £127. Children welcome. Afternoon teas. Garden. Sauna. Tennis. TV. Phone. Scenic. Doors close at midnight. Confirm by 5

HOWTH Co Dublin map 9

King Sitric

East Pier, Harbour Road, Howth
DUBLIN (01) 325235 and 326729 COST £29–£44

The key words here are 'fresh fish'. It was king of the Dublin region but has started to have some competition. The fresh fish is still very fine, using many classic haute cuisine recipes, but not overloaded with ornament or complexity. There is a classic and fine wine list, with Chablis and white burgundies given a strong outing.

CHEF: Aidan MacManus PROPRIETORS: Aidan and Joan MacManus OPEN: Mon to Sat, D only CLOSED: 10 days Christmas and Easter, bank hols MEALS: 6.30 to 11 PRICES: £27 (£37), Set D £21 (£29). Card slips closed CARDS: Access, Amex, Diners, Visa SEATS: 70. Private parties: 48 main room, 24 private room. Vegetarian meals. Children's helpings. No-smoking area. Wheelchair access. Fax: (01) 392442

KANTURK Co Cork map 9

▲ *Assolas Country House*

Kanturk
KANTURK (029) 50015
signposted from N72, NE of Kanturk COST £37

This lovely house is in a remarkable setting close to a river: manicured rusticity. The same might be said of Hazel Bourke's cooking. There is a daily four-course meal, with no choice and usually a roast as centrepiece, and there is a 'menu of the season' with slightly more choice, the virtue of which lies in the materials and relatively straightforward manner in which they are treated.

CHEF: Hazel Bourke PROPRIETORS: the Bourke family OPEN: all week, D only CLOSED: 1 Nov to 14 Mar MEALS: 7 to 8.30 (8 Sun) PRICES: Set D £25 (£31). Net prices, card slips closed CARDS: Access, Diners, Visa SEATS: 30. Private parties: 8 main room, 18 private room. Car park, 20 places. Vegetarian meals. No children under 10. Jacket and tie. No cigars/pipes in dining-room. Wheelchair access. Music. Fax: (029) 50795
ACCOMMODATION: 9 rooms, all with bath/shower. B&B £50 to £106. Deposit: £100. Children welcome. Garden. Tennis. Fishing. Golf. Phone. Scenic. Doors close at 11.30. Confirm by 6

KENMARE Kerry map 9

Lime Tree

Shelbourne Street, Kenmare
KENMARE (064) 41225 COST £37

An informal cottage-like restaurant, converted from an old schoolhouse, using pottery at table and showing decent pictures on the walls. Acceptable cooking features good fish soup, and a marriage of traditions in potato pancakes with garlic butter. 'We have eaten here, on visits, over the past four years and have found the fish cookery imaginative and of good materials. The day's catch is constantly changing' was a report. Crab claws with ginger sauce, sea bass with red pepper and basil sauce, and turbot with mustard sauce were some choices on offer in spring.

CHEF: Maura Foley PROPRIETORS: Tom and Maura Foley OPEN: Mon to Sat, D only CLOSED: 1 Nov to Easter MEALS: 6 to 9.30 PRICES: £23 (£31). Card slips closed SEATS: 50. Private parties: 25 main room. Car park, 20 places. Vegetarian meals. Children's helpings. No-smoking area. Wheelchair access (side entrance). Music

▲ *Park Hotel*

Kenmare

KILLARNEY (064) 41200 COST £25–£65

Francis Brennan keeps the Park up to the mark: constant refurbishment, antiques everywhere, a magnificent setting and every possible diversion if required. The food is diversion enough for most people and is part of the European culinary continuum – no Irish provincialism here – in dishes such as a parcel of sea trout and turbot filled with braised shallots; calf's sweetbreads and wild mushrooms in a tart case with a calvados sauce; and lamb with oysters and a walnut stuffing. There is, of course, lots of fish. Service and welcome are impeccable. The wine list has expanded firmly into California.

CHEF: Matthew Darcy PROPRIETOR: Francis Brennan OPEN: all week CLOSED: mid-Nov to 23 Dec, 2 Jan to Easter MEALS: 1 to 2, 7 to 9 PRICES: £35 (£51), Set L £16.50 (£25) to £22 (£31), Set D £35 (£44) to £45 (£54). Net prices set meals. Card slips closed CARDS: Access, Visa SEATS: 90. Private parties: 60 main room, 40 private room. Car park, 60 places. Vegetarian meals. Healthy eating options. Children's helpings L. Jacket and tie. Wheelchair access (also WC). Fax: (064) 41402 ACCOMMODATION: 50 rooms, all with bath/shower. Rooms for disabled. Lift. B&B £95 to £226. Deposit: £100. Children welcome. Baby facilities. Afternoon teas. Garden. Tennis. Fishing. Golf. TV. Phone. Scenic. Confirm 2 weeks ahead

KILKENNY Co Kilkenny map 9

▲ *Lacken House*

Dublin Road, Kilkenny

KILKENNY (056) 61085 and 65611 COST £28–£36

Eugene McSweeney's cooking depends on his suppliers. The style is by no means over-complex or straining for effect, but nor is it old-fashioned. It lets the sole, shellfish, poultry and vegetables speak for themselves. 'Service is beyond compare' was the comment of one traveller who found the whole package of meal, bed and breakfast irresistible. The wine list is none too long, but the sources are upper-crust 'and we were guided through it most delightfully'. A small restaurant that transparently cares.

Net prices *in the details at the end of an entry indicates that the prices given on a menu and on a bill are inclusive of VAT and service charge, and that this practice is clearly stated on menu and bill.*

CHEF: Eugene McSweeney PROPRIETORS: Eugene and Breda McSweeney OPEN: Tue to Sat, D only CLOSED: 25 Dec MEALS: 7 to 10 PRICES: £21 (£30), Set D £19.50 (£28). Service 10%. Card slips closed CARDS: Access, Amex, Diners, Visa SEATS: 35. Private parties: 40 main room, 10 private room. Car park, 20 places. Vegetarian meals. Children's helpings. Smart dress preferred. No-smoking area. No music. Air-conditioned. Fax: (056) 62435 ACCOMMODATION: 8 rooms, all with bath/shower. B&B £31 to £55. Deposit: £10. Children welcome. Garden. TV. Phone. Scenic. Confirm by 6

KINSALE Co Cork map 9

▲ *Blue Haven*

3 Pearse Street, Kinsale
CORK (021) 772209 COST £24–£38

A small hotel, bar and restaurant in the centre of Kinsale. It positively heaves at busy times, and small wonder, particularly for the shellfish. A complete service that is performed pleasantly and with style.

CHEF: Brian O'Donoghue PROPRIETORS: Brian and Anne Cronin OPEN: all week CLOSED: 25 Dec MEALS: 12.30 to 3, 7 to 10.30 PRICES: £21 (£31), Set D £16.50 (£24) to £23 (£32). Service 10%. Card slips closed CARDS: Access, Amex, Diners, Visa SEATS: 70. 7 tables outside. Private parties: 45 main room, 22 private room. Vegetarian meals. Children's helpings. No-smoking area. Wheelchair access (also WC). Music. Air-conditioned ACCOMMODATION: 10 rooms, 7 with bath/shower. B&B £43 to £66. Deposit: £30. Children welcome. Baby facilities. Afternoon teas. Garden. TV. Phone. Scenic. Doors close at midnight. Confirm by 6

LETTERFRACK Co Galway map 9

▲ *Rosleague Manor*

Letterfrack
CLIFDEN (095) 41101 COST £11–£38

'Paddy Foyle buys excellent ingredients and realises his main responsibility is not to spoil them,' goes a report. His forte is the main course, conservatively and tactfully cooked, with such dishes as brill Véronique, beef fillet béarnaise and salmon hollandaise. 'Simple cooking of a high and dependable order.' Certain other things, soups and desserts for instance, may not be as steady. The Manor is an addictive place to stay: 'Our ninth visit since 1978 and we hope not our last.' Views of the bay and the mountains from the Regency house are narcotic.

CHEF: Patrick Foyle PROPRIETORS: Anne and Patrick Foyle OPEN: all week CLOSED: Nov to Easter MEALS: 1 to 2.30, 8 to 9.30 PRICES: £21 (£32), Set L £5 (£11) to £15 (£22), Set D £21.50 (£29). Card slips closed CARDS: Access, Visa SEATS: 70. Private parties: 70 main room. Car park, 30 places. Vegetarian meals. Children's helpings. Smart dress preferred. No smoking in dining-room. Wheelchair access (2 steps; also WC) ACCOMMODATION: 20 rooms, all with bath/shower. Rooms for disabled. B&B £25 to £110. Deposit: £25. Children welcome. Pets by arrangement. Afternoon teas. Garden. Sauna. Tennis. Snooker. Phone. Scenic. Doors close at midnight. Confirm by 5

MALLOW Co Cork map 9

▲ *Longueville House*

Mallow
MALLOW (022) 47156 COST £23–£50

The Georgian manor overlooks the Blackwater and the ruins of Dromineen Castle; it is surrounded by 500 acres of working farm, with its own vineyard. Dining is in the ornate Presidents' Restaurant and, in summer months, in the Victorian conservatory. William O'Callaghan has worked for Raymond Blanc so the cooking is sophisticated enough to carry a fine ragoût of mussels and monkfish in saffron sauce, a fricassee of chicken legs with wild mushrooms and modern classic desserts such as a gratin of raspberries and floating islands. The basics are well executed, too. Warmth and hospitality in a very grand setting.

CHEF: William O'Callaghan PROPRIETORS: the O'Callaghan family OPEN: all week CLOSED: 20 Dec to 1 March MEALS: 12.45 to 2, 7 to 9 (9.45 Sat) PRICES: £22 (£33), Set L £13 (£23) to £15 (25£), Set D £20 (£31) to £30 (£42). Card slips closed CARDS: Access, Amex, Diners, Visa SEATS: 50. 8 tables outside. Private parties: 16 main room, 16 private room. Car park, 30 places. Vegetarian meals. Children's helpings. Smart dress preferred. No smoking in dining-room. No music. Fax: (022) 47459 ACCOMMODATION: 16 rooms, all with bath/shower. B&B £50 to £130. Afternoon teas. Garden. Fishing. Golf. Snooker. TV. Phone. Scenic. Doors close at midnight. Confirm by 6

MAYNOOTH Co Kildare map 9

▲ *Moyglare Manor*

Moyglare, Maynooth
DUBLIN (01) 6286351
on N4, 2km W of Maynooth COST £19–£38

A place that offers luxury and antiques and an aristocratic wine list. The cooking is solid and reliable from a traditional repertoire ranging from baked Irish wild salmon in a cream of bay leaves to a brace of quail in a burgundy sauce.

CHEF: Jim Cullinane PROPRIETOR: Nora Devlin OPEN: all week, exc Sat L CLOSED: 24 to 26 Dec MEALS: 12.30 to 2.30, 7 to 9.30 (11.30 Sat) PRICES: £19 (£32), Set L £9.95 (£19), Set D £18.50 (£28). Service 12.5%. Card slips closed CARDS: Access, Amex, Diners, Visa SEATS: 160. Private parties: 90 main room, 35 and 90 private rooms. Car park, 100 places. Vegetarian meals. No children under 12. Smart dress preferred. No smoking in dining-room. Wheelchair access (also WC). Music. Fax: (01) 6285405 ACCOMMODATION: 17 rooms, all with bath/shower. Rooms for disabled. B&B £75 to £110. Deposit: £50. No children under 12. Garden. Tennis. TV. Phone. Scenic. Doors close at 11.30. Confirm by 6

'The staff is younger than ever, all smiles and exhortations. "Have a nice walk?" "Did you enjoy your walk?" "Did you enjoy your dinner?" "Have you had a nice afternoon?" They were like eager budgerigars.' On eating in West Sussex

MIDLETON Co Cork map 9

Farm Gate

The Coolbawn, Midleton
MIDLETON (021) 632771 COST £16–£31

Here is a report that sums the place up: 'We called here for morning coffee and were quite impressed. It is located in a most unlikely place, with no clear sign of a restaurant on the outside. Walk through the delicatessen with its array of freshly baked cakes, Irish farm cheeses, wines, greengrocery etc. to reach the interesting dining-room at the back, with its flagstone floor, pine tables, blackboard menu, large pots of fresh flowers and grand piano. Lovely odours of fresh cooking come from the kitchen, and there is a friendly, informal atmosphere. Cheesecakes, scones etc. are brought from the kitchen to the large table in the middle of the room.'

CHEF/PROPRIETOR: Máróg O'Brien OPEN: Mon to Sat L, Thur to Sat D CLOSED: 25 and 26 Dec, Good Fri MEALS: 12 to 3.30, 7 to 9.45 PRICES: £18 (£26), L £9 (£16), Set D £15 (£22). Card slips closed CARDS: Access, Visa SEATS: 60. 6 tables outside. Private parties: 60 main room. Vegetarian meals. Children's helpings. No-smoking area. Wheelchair access (also WC). Music. Air-conditioned

MOYCULLEN Co Galway map 9

Drimcong House

Moycullen
GALWAY (091) 85115 and 85585 COST £24–£42

More exciting and more eclectic cooking than most that is found on the west coast, for example baked oysters with turbot mousse and fennel sabayon; confit of duck with pineapple and cassis sauce; and rabbit and pigeon with carrot and parsley sauces. Yet there is no preciousness about it, or turning away from simple presentation when it is called for. Nor is good Irish cooking ignored in black and white puddings with sweet-and-sour cabbage or rack of mutton with gravy. There are recommendations for the fish cookery as in salmon with spinach sauce and brill in lobster sauce, as well as an excellent shellfish platter. Drimcong is isolated, a noble gesture. As Gerry Galvin observes: 'This year we are ambitious, we hope to make some money.' They deserve to. The wine list is very good.

CHEF: Gerry Galvin PROPRIETORS: Gerry and Marie Galvin OPEN: Tue to Sat, D only CLOSED: Christmas to Mar MEALS: 7 to 10.30 PRICES: £26 (£35), Set D £16.95 (£24). Card slips closed CARDS: Access, Amex, Diners, Visa SEATS: 50. Private parties: 50 main room, 12 private room. Car park, 40 places. Vegetarian meals. Children's helpings. No-smoking area. Wheelchair access (3 steps; also WC). Music

The text of entries is based on unsolicited reports sent in by readers, backed up by inspections conducted anonymously. The factual details under the text are from questionnaires the Guide *sends to all restaurants that feature in the book.*

NEWMARKET-ON-FERGUS Co Clare map 9

▲ *Dromoland Castle*

Newmarket-on-Fergus
LIMERICK (061) 368144 COST £28–£58

The sister of Ashford Castle (see Cong entry), Dromoland is owned by a New York-based company. It goes without saying that it is magnificent and has a golf course, plus a lot, lot more. The kitchen here is wholly professional, producing food without much personal identity but much finesse (and silver domes). It never helps when sauces on two main courses seem the same, but that is a consequence of 'finesse'.

CHEF: Jean-Baptiste Molinari PROPRIETORS: Ashford Hotels Ltd OPEN: all week MEALS: 12.30 to 2.30, 7 to 9.30 PRICES: £33 (£48), Set L £18 (£28), Set D £29 (£41). Service 15%. Card slips closed CARDS: Access, Amex, Diners, Visa SEATS: 90. 4 tables outside. Private parties: 120 main room, 20 and 60 private rooms. Car park, 250 places. Vegetarian meals. Children's helpings. Jacket and tie. No-smoking area. Wheelchair access. Music. Fax: (061) 363355 ACCOMMODATION: 73 rooms, all with bath/shower. Rooms for disabled. B&B £110 to £367. Deposit: 100%. Children welcome. Baby facilities. Afternoon teas. Garden. Swimming-pool. Sauna. Tennis. Fishing. Golf. Snooker. TV. Phone. Scenic

NEWPORT Co Mayo map 9

▲ *Newport House*

Newport
NEWPORT (098) 41222 COST £36

This Georgian mansion overlooks river and quay. A place for fishermen, it does hedonists well, too, with impressive interiors – note the staircase – and pleasantly informal welcome. Cooking is sound and satisfactory rather than inspired, but quality is shown in producing mainstream dishes such as salmon en croûte, beef with a béarnaise sauce and crème brûlée, with good materials and accuracy to the fore. The wine list is serious. Light lunches are served during the winter months.

CHEF: John Gavin PROPRIETORS: Kieran and Thelma Thompson OPEN: all week CLOSED: 30 Sept to 20 Mar (exc for light L) MEALS: 12.30 to 2, 7.30 to 9.30 PRICES: Set D £25 (£30). Net prices, card slips closed CARDS: Access, Amex, Diners, Visa SEATS: 38. Private parties: 28 main room. Car park, 40 places. Children's helpings. No smoking in dining-room. Wheelchair access (3 steps). No music ACCOMMODATION: 20 rooms, all with bath/shower. B&B £40 to £96. Children welcome. Baby facilities. Afternoon teas. Garden. Fishing. Snooker. Phone. Scenic. Confirm by 6

All details are as accurate as possible at the time of going to press, but chefs and owners often change, and it is wise to check by telephone before making a special journey. Many readers have been disappointed when set-price bargain meals are no longer available. Ask when booking.

OUGHTERARD Co Galway map 9

▲ *Currarevagh House*

Oughterard
GALWAY (091) 82312
4m NW of Oughterard on Hill of
Doon Lakeshore road COST £26

The house sits 100 yards from Lough Corrib, in the middle of 150 acres of woodland. A haven for the fisherfolk, others can ride, putt or walk. A daily no-choice dinner menu, cooked by June Hodgson, restores the bodies wasted by hours of casting for trout. Currarevagh is not open to non-residents except by prior reservation. One visitor writes: 'It is rather like entering a time warp – any time during the first half of this century. The spirit quails at the massive tiger skin on the wall above the stairs, but the hospitality and atmosphere are very warm and overcome any fears. Food is served in Edwardian proportions and refreshingly lacks any of those "Country House Hotel" pretensions.' A meal may work through a herby pâté, trout hollandaise, roast beef, caramel oranges and good cheese to coffee. It is not dear.

CHEF: June Hodgson PROPRIETORS: Harry and June Hodgson OPEN: all week, D only CLOSED: Oct to Mar MEALS: 8 PRICES: Set D £16 (£22). Service 10%. Card slips closed SEATS: 30. Private parties: 10 main room. Car park, 40 places. Vegetarian meals. Children welcome. Smart dress preferred. No smoking in dining-room. No music. One sitting. Fax: (091) 82313 ACCOMMODATION: 15 rooms, all with bath/shower. Rooms for disabled. B&B £35 to £70. Deposit: £20. Children under 12 by arrangement. Pets by arrangement. Garden. Tennis. Fishing. Scenic. Doors close at 12.30am. Confirm by midday

RATHNEW Co Wicklow map 9

▲ *Hunter's Hotel*

Newrath Bridge, Rathnew
WICKLOW (0404) 40106 COST £18–£29

It has been in the same family for five generations, is a great place to stop for tea after the Usher gardens and serves good plain food. 'Mushroom soup, fish pie, crème caramel in a William Trevor ambience' was the report of one who found it more than satisfactory.

CHEF: John Sutton PROPRIETOR: Maureen Gelletlie OPEN: all week MEALS: 1 to 3, 7.30 to 9.30 PRICES: Set L £12 (£18), Set D £18 (£24). Card slips closed CARDS: Access, Amex, Diners, Visa SEATS: 54. Private parties: 20 main room, 12 private room. Car park, 30 places. Vegetarian meals. Children's helpings. Wheelchair access (also WC). Vegetarian meals. Children's helpings. Wheelchair access (also WC). Fax: (0404) 40338 ACCOMMODATION: 18 rooms, 10 with bath/shower. Rooms for disabled. B&B £35 to £70. Deposit: 25%. Children welcome. Baby facilities. Pets by arrangement. Afternoon teas. Garden. Fishing. Phone. Scenic. Doors close at 12.30am. Confirm by 6

If a restaurant is new to the Guide *this year (did not appear as a main entry in the last edition)* NEW ENTRY *appears opposite its name.*

ROSSNOWLAGH Co Donegal map 9

▲ *Sand House Hotel*

Rossnowlagh
DONEGAL (072) 517777 COST £15–£29

A large seaside hotel, right on the beach of Donegal Bay, that is open from Easter until October. The menu has an emphasis on shellfish direct from the Brittons' son's fish farm. A set-price meal gives four courses and coffee, with dishes such as cheese beignets with mustard sauce, crab and spinach roulade, turbot with sorrel sauce and ham glazed with honey with an orange and ginger sauce. This is sound holiday cooking with some ambition.

CHEF: Liam Quinn PROPRIETORS: Vim and Mary Britton OPEN: all week CLOSED: Oct to Easter MEALS: 1 to 2.30, 7 to 9 PRICES: £15 (£24), Set L £9.95 (£15) to £10.50 (£16), Set D £15 (£21) to £18.50 (£25). Service 10%. Card slips closed CARDS: Access, Amex, Diners, Visa SEATS: 80. Private parties: 60 main room, 20 private room. Car park, 30 places. Children's helpings. Children restricted. No-smoking area. Wheelchair access (3 steps). No music. Fax: (072) 52100 ACCOMMODATION: 40 rooms, all with bath/shower. B&B £40 to £90. Deposit: £30. Baby facilities. Pets by arrangement. Afternoon teas. Garden. Sauna. Tennis. Fishing. Golf. Snooker. Phone. Scenic. Doors close at 11. Confirm by 6

SHANAGARRY Cork map 9

▲ *Ballymaloe House*

Shanagarry, Midleton
CORK (021) 652531 COST £21–£44

Hotel, restaurant, cookery school, TV programmes, cookery books all begin from this country house famous beyond its borders. Yet the root of it, as with so many Irish country places, was the farm and estate. It is this close link with the countryside that is the chief strength of the cooking; and it is the sense of fusion with the community that makes Irish hospitality, nowhere better expressed than here, so remarkable. The house is grander than some may expect, with a series of rooms used for dining – the two main saloons and some smaller spaces – and a conservatory for drinks or overflow. Pictures and tapestries of a very high calibre are all around you; the decoration is calm yet enlivening. There is no sense that this house is a cute restoration, unlike what is found in so many country houses, here and in Britain. Food ranges from the near homely to quite fancy. In prime position are the materials, all of which are chosen with care and some of which are very distinguished. There is sometimes a buffet of first courses, which gives a chance to sample, but on no account miss the fish and shellfish, or the vegetables, or the cheeses or some of the sweet sweets. A number have noted a heavy hand with the salt pot. Staying here is recommended. The staff are magic and breakfast – all that porridge and breads – is a delight.

'We asked the waitress what the gâteau was. She said, ''I don't know, it looks like choux pastry and cold custard and looks revolting!''' On eating in Cumbria

CHEFS: Paddy Cullinane and Myrtle Allen PROPRIETORS: Ivan and Myrtle Allen OPEN: all week CLOSED: 24 to 26 Dec MEALS: 1 to 2, 7 to 9.30 PRICES: Set L £14 (£21), Set D £28 (£37) CARDS: Access, Amex, Diners, Visa SEATS: 90. Private parties: 35 main room, 10, 18 and 30 private rooms. Car park, 100 places. Vegetarian meals. Children's helpings D. No-smoking area. Wheelchair access (also WC). Fax: (021) 652021 ACCOMMODATION: 30 rooms, all with bath/shower. Rooms for disabled. B&B £74 to £107. Deposit: £30. Children welcome. Baby facilities. Garden. Swimming-pool. Tennis. Golf. Phone. Scenic

WATERFORD Co Waterford map 9

Dwyers

8 Mary Street, Waterford
WATERFORD (051) 77478 COST £19–£30

Martin Dwyer was ill during 1991 and a reader remarked how well the staff coped in his absence. It is, however, evidently better when he has full control: his personality is magnetic and his skill great. A short *carte* is supplemented by a two-choice set-price menu of very good value. The cooking is pleasantly impervious to recent fashion, yet execution is exact enough for no one to feel in the presence of a survivor. Lambs' kidneys with mustard sauce, brill with a tomato butter sauce and beef Wellington were 'perfect, excellent – as were the vegetables (without going overboard on al dente) and desserts such as lemon crêpe soufflé' to a seasoned visitor of many to Ireland's best.

CHEF/PROPRIETOR: Martin Dwyer OPEN: Mon to Sat, D only (L by arrangement) CLOSED: 3 days Christmas, 5 days Nov MEALS: 6 to 10 PRICES: £17 (£25), Set D £12 (£19). Card slips closed CARDS: Access, Amex, Diners, Visa SEATS: 42. Private parties: 32 main room, 10 private room. Children's helpings on request. No-smoking area. Wheelchair access (also WC). Music

WICKLOW Co Wicklow map 9

▲ *Old Rectory*

Wicklow
WICKLOW (0404) 67048 COST £27–£38

The large garden and Victorian rectory are run by Paul and Linda Saunders with great style. The restaurant is not large, though a new conservatory (Victorian Gothic) is coming on stream late in 1991. The meal is long and no-choice but does not leave you prostrate with feeding. The pace is skilfully managed by Paul Saunders, and Linda Saunders makes some play not only of local materials, but also good herbs, flowers and saladings. Coffee is very good. Dishes such as courgette and lovage soup; chicken stuffed with mushrooms and herbs, with a wild mushroom sauce; quail stuffed with grapes on a red pimento sauce; a mid-meal blackcurrant sorbet laced with Châteauneuf-du-Pape; and a sponge Swiss roll with marzipan with frosted violas and mint leaves, chocolate thimbles and a red fruit coulis have been enthusiastically recommended.

CHEF: Linda Saunders PROPRIETORS: Paul and Linda Saunders OPEN: all week, D only CLOSED: mid-Oct to Easter MEALS: 8 PRICES: £24 (£32), Set D £21.50 (£27). Card slips closed CARDS: Access, Amex, Diners, Visa SEATS: 12. Car park, 20 places. Vegetarian meals. Children's helpings. Smart dress preferred. No smoking in dining-room. Music. One sitting. Fax: (0404) 69181 ACCOMMODATION: 5 rooms, all with bath/shower. B&B £52 to £74. Deposit: £15. Children welcome. Baby facilities. Garden. TV. Phone. Scenic. Doors close at 2am. Confirm by 6

YOUGHAL Co Cork map 9

Aherne's

163 North Main Street, Youghal
YOUGHAL (024) 92424 and 92533 COST £18–£41

Simply excellent shellfish and fish are served proficiently and with great wamth in pleasant surroundings that do not jar with the atmospheric fishing town of Youghal. Supply lines are matchless. Eat a range of oysters, hot crab with rosemary sauce, turbot with herb butter, or shellfish cooked in olive oil and their own juices. Ten guest bedrooms are planned for completion by March 1992.

CHEF: David Fitzgibbon PROPRIETORS: the Fitzgibbon family OPEN: Tue to Sun, exc Sun L (also Mon summer) CLOSED: 4 days Christmas, Good Fri MEALS: 12.30 to 2, 6.30 to 9.30 PRICES: £25 (£34), Set L £10.50 (£18), Set D £17.50 (£25), bar menu £11 (£19). Service 10%. Card slips closed CARDS: Access, Visa SEATS: 50. 4 tables outside. Private parties: 40 main room, 30 private room. Car park, 15 places. Children welcome. Smart dress preferred. No-smoking area. Wheelchair access (also WC). Music

County round-ups

Each year we offer a revised selection of round-up entries. All the eating-places listed below have been recommended by readers but for one reason or another have not graduated to the main listings. They are not places that simply failed at inspection. We hope the list will be especially useful for anyone travelling around Britain. All reports on these places would be most welcome.

England

Avon

Bath *Circus* 34 Brock Street, (0225) 330208. Popular place, competent cooking, interesting menu.
Sally Lunn's House 4 North Parade Passage, (0225) 461634. Medieval bakehouse famous for its buns; eat with savoury toppings or as part of a cream tea.
Bristol *Arnolfini* 16 Narrow Quay, (0272) 279330. Dockside café in the arts complex; inventive menu, stylish surroundings.
Glass Boat nr Bristol Bridge, Welsh Back, (0272) 290704. Maritime cooking at this mooring; can be expensive.
Hinton Charterhouse *Homewood Park Hotel* (0225) 723731. Comfortable hotel outside Bath with good restaurant although bringing in mixed reports.

Bedfordshire

Aspley Guise *Moore Place Hotel* The Square, (0908) 282000. Full-bodied soups and game casseroles, alongside salads and champagne sorbets.
Milton Ernest *The Strawberry Tree* 3 Radwell Road, (023 02) 3633. Take afternoon tea under the thatch: home-made cakes, scones and creamy gâteaux, also light lunches.
Woburn *Black Horse* 1 Bedford Street, (0525) 290210. Pub specialising in steaks, cooked on the grill.

Berkshire

Cookham *Alfonso's* 19–21 Station Hill Parade, (062 85) 25775. Popular restaurant with unchanging menu of international favourites.
Bel and the Dragon (062 85) 21263. Anglo-French; once a tourist-trap, now changed for the better.
Cookham Dean *Jolly Farmer* Church Road, (0628) 482905. Generously portioned bar meals; good for Sunday lunch.
Eton *Eton Wine Bar* 82–83 High Street, (0753) 854921. Blackboard menu and friendly atmosphere, sometimes spoiled by over-loud music.
Inkpen *Swan Inn* Lower Inkpen, (048 84) 326. Incongruous English pub setting for South East Asian cooking. A new chef.
Pangbourne *Copper Inn* Church Road, (0734) 842244. The specials board has more to interest than the menu, though all is well executed.
Taplow *Cliveden* (062 86) 68561. Wonderful house, simpler hotel food better than Waldo's Restaurant. Not cheap.
West Ilsley *Harrow* (063 528) 260. Pub opposite the village cricket pitch. Rabbit pie the speciality, though vegetarians are well catered for.

Buckinghamshire

Beaconsfield *China Diner* 7 The Highway, Station Road, (0494) 673345 and 678346. Lively atmosphere but minimalist décor; Peking and Szechuan the style.
Leigh House 53 Wycombe End, (0494) 676348. Chinese; go for the good crispy duck.
Great Missenden *George* 94 High Street, (024 06) 2084. Couscous, stews and sandwiches are the main staples.
Rising Sun Little Hampden, nr Great Missenden, (0494) 488393. Inventive pub cooking, high on quality.
Long Crendon *Angel Inn* Bicester Road, (0844) 208268. A frequently changing menu biased towards fish and ambitious desserts. Quaint surroundings, real ales.
Speen *Old Plow Inn* Flowers Bottom Lane, Flowers Bottom, (0494) 488300. Housed in a green hollow; home-cooking with ambience to match.
Woburn Sands *Spooners* 61 High Street, (0908) 584385. Above a china shop; jacket potatoes, fresh pasta, fish.

Cambridgeshire

Cambridge *Browns* 23 Trumpington Street, (0223) 461655. American-style venue with atmosphere; food is fun and attracts a popular following.
Café Français 53 Castle Street, (0223) 60723. Intimate surroundings for authentic bistro cooking and a mostly student clientele.
Free Press 7 Prospect Row, (0223) 68337. Locally made pies are popular at this charming pub.
Sala Thong 35 Newnham Road, (0223) 323178. Thai; popular with students.

Ely *Peking Duck* 26 Fore Hill, (0353) 662063. A choice of more than one fowl or fish at this Chinese.
Dominique's 8 St Mary's Street, (0353) 665011. Good home cooking encompassing casseroles, filled jacket potatoes and attractive cakes and pastries.
Fowlmere *Chequers Inn* High Street, (0763) 208369. Attractive sixteenth-century coaching-inn, equipped with log fires and garden. Both restaurant and bar meals are good.
Huntingdon *Old Bridge Hotel* 1 High Street, (0480) 52681. Handsome hotel, prettily placed by the Ouse. The menu manages old and new; excellent wine list.

Cheshire

Bickley Moss *Cholmondeley Arms* (0829) 720300. Victorian schoolhouse conversion, the menu more brasserie than pub.
Bollington *Randalls* 22 High Street, Old Market Place, (0625) 575058. Bistro-style; the menu has ambitions and prose to match, though content sometimes defeats concept.
Chester *Franc's* 14A Cuppin Street, (0244) 317952. Fashionable French café with a lively atmosphere; lots of choice, from crêpes to cassoulet.
Cotebrook *Alvanley Arms* (0829) 760200. Reliable pub in a quiet area, good bar food.
Macclesfield *Flora Tea Room* Flora Flower Gift & Garden Centre, Henbury, nr Macclesfield, (0625) 422418. After scrutinising seed packets, pots of tea and fresh snacks revive.
Prestbury *Steak and Kabab Restaurant* New Road, (0625) 829640. The menu takes in more than the name of the place suggests: chicken tikka, nut terrine and roulades all feature.
Tarporley *Churtons* 55 High Street, (0829) 732483. Old shop, stylishly converted into country wine bar.
Warrington *Lord Daresbury Hotel* Daresbury, off the A56, (0925) 67331. Worth it for the buffets; generous affairs with good salads and cold meats.
Wilmslow *Stanneylands Hotel* Stanneylands Road, (0625) 525225. Professional cooking for international business clientele, ambitious and extensive menu, good service.

Cleveland

Stockton-on-Tees *Waiting Room* 9 Station Road, Eaglescliffe, (0642) 780465. Vegetarian restaurant and wholefood shop, strong on baking.

Cornwall

Constantine *Trengilly Wartha Inn* Nancenoy, nr Constantine, (0326) 40332. Small hotel with strong talents in marinades and grilled lobster.
Falmouth *Cornish Kitchen* 28 Arwenack Street, (0326) 316509. Self-styled bistro specialising in seafood and fresh fish.
Gerrans Bay *Pendower Beach House* Ruan High Lanes, (0872) 501241. Fair hotel food on the Roseland peninsular.
Gweek *Mellanoweth* (032 622) 271. Friendly setting for good home cooking.
Mullion *Polurrian Hotel* Polurrian Bay, (0326) 240268. Clifftop position affording fine views; fresh local fish and smooth sorbets.
Mylor Bridge *Pandora Inn* Restronguet Creek, (0326) 72678. Tucked away, overlooking a tidal creek, this old thatched pub is suited to summer days; seafood and nursery puddings.
Penzance *Harris's* 46 New Street, (0736) 64408. Rich country cooking and puddings to please.
St Austell *Clarets* Trethowel House, Bodmin Road, (0726) 67435. Bar snacks and a restaurant menu of English and French origins: snails, frogs' legs and seafood.
St Dominick *Cotehele Barn* Cotehele Estate, (0579) 50652. Medieval manor, run by the National Trust, housing a lunchtime restaurant; home-spun fare, Cornish cream teas.
Tideford *Heskyn Mill* (0752) 851481. A simple *carte* with more interesting specials; recent reports suggest flavours may have faded.
Tintagel *Old Millfloor* Trebarwith Strand Road, (0840) 770234. Tudor house down by the millstream, cooking time-honoured dishes. Booking essential.
Tregony *Kea House* 69 Fore Street, (087 253) 642. A friendly, unhurried place; Fowey sea trout and vegetables are good.
Tresco *New Inn* Isles of Scilly, (0720) 22844. Plain cooking, fair prices.

County Durham

Barnard Castle *Market Place Teashop* 29 Market Place, (0833) 690110. Tea in silver pots, traditional lunches with some vegetarian offerings, backed up by popular fruit pies and cakes.
Burnopfield *Fairways* Hobson Golf Centre, (0207) 70941. A far cry from a simple sandwich at the nineteenth; pub and restaurant providing imaginative cooking at fair prices.
Crook *Duke of York* Fir Tree, (0388) 762848. Consistent cooking in pleasant pub surroundings.
Darlington *Eastern Bamboo* 194 Northgate, (0325) 461607. Chinese; dim-sum, strong on seafoods.
Durham *And Albert* 17 Hallgarth Street, 091-384 1919. Popular restaurant behind the prison. Décor is pure Victoriana, bistro cooking is big on puddings.
Middleton in Teesdale *Teesdale Hotel* Market Place, (0833) 40264. Old Pennine coaching-inn, still with cobbled courtyard but comfortably renovated.

Cumbria

Ambleside *Wateredge Hotel* Borrans Road, (053 94) 32332. Light lunches or six-course set dinners; the former work best.
Appleby *Royal Oak* Bongate, (076 83) 51463. Stone pub; local specialities – Cumberland sausage and potted shrimps – and international dishes share menu space.
Bowland Bridge *Masons Arms* Strawberry Bank, Cartmel Fell, (044 88) 486. Hard to find but worth the journey; real ales, casseroles and kormas.
Broughton in Furness *Beswicks* The Square, (0229) 716285. Georgian house of character; the kitchen too has an eye for detail.
Carlisle *Franco's* 28 Castle Street, (0228) 34084. Italian with Swiss overtones: pan-fried lamb, cabbage with bacon, good espresso.
Sun Inn Red Dial, Wigton, (069 73) 42167. Pub with good selection of hand-pulled beers; bar meals.
Grasmere *Baldry's* Red Lion Square, (096 65) 301. Café frequented by fell-walkers; organic flour and vegetables are favoured, ham and bread are home-baked. Tempting Cumbrian puddings.
Kendal *Posh Nosh* Yard 11, Stramongate, (0539) 725135. Hidden away down a yard; hearty soups, casseroles, bakes and indulgent desserts.
Keswick *La Primavera* Greta Bridge, High Hill, (07687) 74621. Traditional Italian handy for Lakeland holidaymakers; fresh fish and pasta.
Maryport *Retreat* Birkby, nr Maryport, (0900) 814056. Smart bar and restaurant providing a friendly reception and careful cooking.
Seatoller *Yew Tree* Borrowdale, (076 87) 77634. Cottage conversion in a remote and lovely spot. Fell Farmer's lunch, local ham and sticky toffee pudding are all typically Cumbrian.
Skinburness *Skinburness Hotel*, nr Silloth, (069 73) 32332. Feast eyes on the views across the Solway Firth whilst enjoying hearty bar meals.
Watermillock *Leeming House Hotel* (076 84) 86622. An atmosphere combining charm with opulence; luxury ingredients on the menu.
Windermere *Holbeck Ghyll* Holbeck Lane, (053 94) 32375. Hotel and restaurant with a warm welcome and log fires. Gentle cooking,

Derbyshire

Ashbourne *Beresford Arms Hotel* Station Road, (0335) 300035. Interesting menu taking in East European and Belgian influences.
Ashford *Riverside Country House Hotel* Fennel Street, (062 981) 4275. Charming situation, attractive atmosphere, adventurous nouvelle cuisine.
Bakewell *Biph's* Bath Street, (0629) 812687. Busy restaurant with bistro attached. Good home-cooking and reasonable prices, though its popularity means service can be slow.
Baslow *Cavendish Hotel* (0246) 582311. Fancy hotel on the Chatsworth estate; lovely surroundings, less good service.
Belper *Mixing Place* Dannah Farm, Bowman's Lane, Shottle, nr Belper, (077 389) 630. Farmyard barn now reaping rewards as a restaurant; home-made bread, calorific and creamy puddings.
Matlock *Hodgkinson's Hotel* 150 South Parade, Matlock Bath, (0629) 582170. Sheltering up against the rock-face; small menu, delicate sauces, good desserts.

Devon

Ashprington *Maltsters Arms* Tuckenhay, nr Ashprington, (080 243) 350. Keith Floyd changes his chef regularly, but the cooking is ideal for Sunday lunch.
Branscombe *Masons Arms* (029 780) 300. Standards are being revived by a new regime; restaurant and bar meals.
Dartmouth *Ford House* 44 Victoria Road, (0803) 834047. Comfortable B&B, good cooking.
Taylors 8 The Quay, (0803) 832748. Fish and more overlooking the harbour; all is fresh with seasonings that suit.
Dittisham *Fingals* Old Coombe Manor, (080 422) 398. Laid-back to a fault, a sympathetic holiday-spot for London trend. Cooking can be good, can be dear, can be extremely sociable.
Gittisham *Combe House* (0404) 42756. Flamboyant Elizabethan mansion in rolling parkland, though the cooking is not so lush.
Holbeton *Alston Hall* Alston Cross, (075 530) 555. Edwardian manor; its flower motif is reflected in the delicate cuisine.
Kingsteignton *Old Rydon Inn* Rydon Road, (0626) 54626. Thatched pub with a pretty garden; an adventurous menu includes Indonesian and Chinese alongside English.
Lustleigh *Primrose Cottage* (064 77) 365. A picture-postcard setting for traditional teas; cakes and scones of the highest calibre, also light lunches.
Modbury *Modbury Pippin* 35 Church Street, (0548) 830765. Butcher's shop conversion bearing traces of its honest origins; home-made pâtés, potted crab and fresh fish.
Peter Tavy *Peter Tavy Inn* (0822) 810348. Wholefood on the edge of Dartmoor; homity pie, quiches and meat and potato pasty pull in the crowds.
Plymouth *Trattoria Pescatore* 36 Admiralty Street, Stonehouse, (0752) 600201. Authentic Italian with a cheerful ambience and some courtyard tables.
Princetown *Prince Hall Hotel* (082 289) 403. The Denats' latest venture, a country-house hotel in the heart of Dartmoor; French country cooking, plenty of wines.
Sourton *Collaven Manor Hotel* (083 786) 522. Fifteenth-century stone house with two dining-rooms and set menus. New chef and owners.
Tavistock *Neil's* 27 King Street, Taylor Square, (0822) 615550. A small place that's big on quality; fresh ingredients, tempting puddings, good value.
Teignmouth *Thomas Luny House* Teign Street, (0626) 772976. Small, family-run hotel and restaurant; fresh produce and stalwart English cooking.
Torquay *Vaults* 23 Victoria Passage, (0803) 212059. Harbourside cellar bistro with fair cooking and reasonable prices. Fish and first courses better than puddings.

Dorset

Bournemouth *Chez Fred* 10 Seamoor Road, Westbourne, nr Bournemouth, (0202) 761023. Fish and chip shop where a fresh catch of the day features.
Bridport *George Hotel* 4 South Street, (0308) 23187. Bar meals include fresh local fish, Welsh rarebit and home-made pies; espresso coffee.

Marsh Barn Burton Road, (0308) 22755. Restaurant and tea-room in old barn conversion; home-cooking. Check opening times first.
Dorchester *Yalbury Cottage* Lower Bockhampton, nr Dorchester, (0305) 262382. Thatched restaurant with rooms. Single sitting and single-choice set menu.
East Lulworth *Weld Arms* (092 941) 211. Nautical paraphernalia behind the bar, confident home cooking from the kitchen.
Piddletrenthide *Old Bakehouse* (03004) 305. Cosy restaurant-with-rooms, and some four posters. Light cooking, marvellous sweet and savoury mousses.
Poole *Allan's* 8 Bournemouth Road, Lower Parkstone, (0202) 741489. Unpretentious seafood restaurant; well-run, with pleasant service.
Barrie's 292 Sandbanks Road, Lilliput, (0202) 708810. Seafood restaurant with a bright atmosphere and a strong French flavour.
Shaftesbury *Old Bakery* 14 Salisbury Street, (0747) 52069. The owner cooks all on the short menu, often serving it too, so unbooked callers are out of the question. Unpretentious; good sauces.
Symondsbury *Ilchester Arms* (0308) 22600. Ploughman's, pigeon, fresh fish, treacle tart and clotted cream; picnic tables and a stream.
Tarrant Monkton *Langton Arms* (025 889) 225. Good bar food and blackboard specials under the thatch; theme nights are a feature.
Weymouth *Hamilton's* 5 Brunswick Terrace, (0305) 789544. On the seafront, by the shingle and sand. Basic décor but better menu: pasta, seafood, espresso.

East Sussex

Alfriston *Drusillas Thatched Barn* Drusillas Corner, (0323) 870234. Inside a family theme park and zoo, this is definitely child-oriented: fish and chips, Sussex sausage and dairy ice-cream.
Moonrakers High Street, (0323) 870472. Prettily located restaurant that's certainly popular. A short set-price menu of outdated style keeps regulars happy, though recent reports suggest slipping standards.
Sussex Ox Milton Street, (0323) 870840. Country pub that copes well with children; good-value bar meals.
Brighton *Al Forno* 36 East Street, (0273) 24905. Italian trattoria with some tables for outdoor eating; pizza, pasta and profiteroles.
La Caperon 113 St Georges Road, Kemp Town, (0273) 680317. Good-value lunches include soups, roast meats and vegetarian dishes.
Clarence Wine Bar Meeting House Lane, (0273) 720597. Popular food in a lively, young atmosphere.
English's Oyster Bar 29–31 East Street, (0273) 27980. Fresh fish, shellfish and chowders; surroundings can be smoky.
Latin in the Lane 10 King's Road, (0273) 28672. Busy Italian; home-made pasta and tiramisù have pleased.
Muang Thai 77 St James's Street, (0273) 605223. Fair Thai food.
Eastbourne *Bosworth's* 8 Bolton Road, (0323) 23023. Blackboard menu big on chargrilling. Excellent wine list, many wines by the glass.
Justin's 9 Compton Street, (0323) 22828. Bistro, run by husband and wife team.
Firle *Ram* (0273) 858222. Untouched seventeenth-century inn where fresh and free-range produce rules. Good traditional puddings.

Hove *Classique* 37 Waterloo Street, (0273) 734140. French neighbourhood restaurant with potential. Pleasing food, extrovert service.
Rolling Clock Whitehaven Hotel, 34 Wilbury Road, (0273) 731177. Ambitious, seaside restaurant, popular with business types. Good puddings.
Mayfield *Rose & Crown* Fletching Street, (0435) 872200. Pretty pub with extensive menus. Good desserts include banoffi pie.
Rye *Flushing Inn* 4 Market Street, (0797) 223292. Large portions of fish and shellfish; friendly service.
Ticehurst *Bull* Three-legged Cross, (0580) 200586. Low beams, old floors and in winter, a roaring fire. Good bar meals; book for the evening.
Wilmington *Crossways* Lewes Road, (0323) 482455. Restaurant and hotel that takes some trouble; fair value.

Essex

Burnham-on-Crouch *Polash* 169 Station Road, (0621) 782233/784930. Consistent high-street tandoori.
Castle Hedingham *Old Moot House* 1 St James Street, Castle Hedingham, (0787) 60342. Elizabethan-built restaurant near the castle. Family-run; competent cooking.
Clavering *Cricketers* (0799) 550442. Popular pub, enjoyed for its monthly-changing menu; crab bisque, tandoori chicken and summer pudding have featured.
Dedham *Marlborough Head Hotel* Mill Lane, (0206) 323124. A large menu and portions to match; soups and sandwiches to more serious dishes. Try the treacle tart.
Gosfield *Green Man* (0787) 472746. Extensive lunchtime buffet, evening menu.
Great Dunmow *Chapslee* 27A High Street, (0371) 873299/875891. Small Indian tandoori with a short, sound menu; excellent thalis and Sunday lunch buffet.
Hatfield Peverel *Scotts* Hatfield Cottage, The Street, (0245) 380161. Home cooking using fresh, seasonal produce.
Horndon on the Hill *Hill House* High Road, (0375) 642463. Pretty restaurant with accommodation; interesting menu using best ingredients.
Maldon *Wheelers* 13 High Street, (0621) 853647. Long-established, quality fish and chips restaurant and take-away. Large portions.
Southend-on-Sea *Alvaro's* 32–34 St Helen's Road, Westcliff-on-Sea, (0702) 335840. Genuine Portuguese cooking supplemented by steaks every which way. Service can be slow.
Oldham's 13 West Road, Westcliff-on-Sea (0702) 346736. Fresh fish, non-greasy chips, Formica fittings.
Witham *Crofters* 25 Maldon Road, (0376) 511068. Wine bar with blackboard menus; seafood crumble, Persian lamb, vegetarian dishes.
Woodford Green *Pizzeria Bel-Sit* 439 High Road, 081-504 1164. Worth a visit for the fine pizzas.

Gloucestershire

Bibury *Bibury Court* (028 574) 337. Jacobean country-house hotel, with restaurant in a stables conversion.
Blockley *Crown Hotel* High Street, (0386) 700245. Old coaching-inn; fancy fish and game on the menu.
Cheltenham *Finns* 143 Bath Road, (0242) 232109. Modern menu of mostly fish. Conservatory addition.
Cowley *Green Dragon Inn* Cockleford, (024 287) 271. Old cider house, now selling real ales. A menu encompassing Guinness casserole and African and Indian influences.
Eastington *Saddlers* Eastington Grange, (0453) 791511. Modern English cooking in country-house surrounds. Fine ingredients and presentation, sometimes let down by inexpert service.
Gloucester *Brasseria* 157 Southgate Street, (0452) 506046. Grilled steaks, oysters, Parrot fish and sea bass in rock salt.
Painswick *Painswick Hotel* Kemps Lane, (0452) 812160. Refurbished old rectory, comfortable rooms, careful cooking.
Tetbury *Close Hotel* 8 Long Street, (0666) 502272. Refurbished town mansion with ambitious neo-English kitchen. Service needs tightening up, but new chef as we went to press means no full entry. Reports, please.
Winchcombe *Pilgrims Bistro* 6 North Street, (0242) 603544. Wayfarers in Winchcombe will be rewarded with an imaginative and regularly changing menu.
Woodchester *Ram Inn* (0453) 873329. A terrace and views for summer, open fires for winter. Good bar food and real ales.

Greater Manchester

Altrincham *French* 24 The Downs, 061-941 3355. Bustling brasserie with some atmosphere; traditional dishes, generously portioned.
Manchester *Bella Napoli* 6A Booth Street, 061-236 1537. Good-value Italian; keen service.
Café Primavera 48 Beech Road, Chorlton, 061-862 9934. Meals in Mediterranean mode; cooking can struggle to keep up with the concept.
Cromptons Brittannia Hotel, Portland Street, 061-228 2288. Friendly service, fresh soups, good vegetables.
Etrop Grange Outward Lane, Etrop Green, 061-437 3594. Stylish hotel, close to the airport. Ambitious menu; not cheap.
Hopewell City 45–47 Faulkner Street, 061-236 0091. Cantonese; large basement, long menu, fresh fish, cool service.
Isola Bella Dolefield, Crown Square, 061-831 7099. Routine Italian: a plethora of prawns and creamy sauces.
Royal Oak Hotel 436 Wilmslow Road, Didsbury, 061-445 3152. Regal pub with a grand choice of cheeses – English and French – with wholemeal bread.
Steak and Kabab 846 Wilmslow Road, Didsbury, 061-445 2552. Popular for its extensive menu and value. Basically bistro, with a few pretensions.
Teppan-Yaki 58 George Street, 061-228 2219. Japanese; smart décor, small menu, sizzling dishes.

Wong Chu 63–63A Faulkner Street, 061-236 2346. Cantonese; good for cheap plate meals and a range of roasts.
Rochdale *Tony's* 417 Oldham Road, (0706) 42975. Popular fish and chip shop giving good value and large portions.
Salford *Mark Addy* Stanley Street, 061-832 4080. Wharfside pub where cheeses are the thing; hearty helpings.
Training Restaurant Salford College of Technology, Frederick Road, 061-736 6541. Cheap meals cooked by catering students. Booking essential.
Stockport *Sawasdee* 12A Churchgate, 061-429 0488. Thai; soups, satays and sweet bananas.

Hampshire

Basingstoke *Hee's* 23 Westminster House, Town Centre, (0256) 464410 and 460297. Peking and Szechuan in the main; good cooking though sometimes rushed service.
Beaulieu *Montagu Arms* Palace Lane, (0590) 612324. Beautiful setting, attractive presentation though uneven cooking, good breads.
Gosport *Pebble Beach* Stokes Bay Road, (0705) 510789. Small restaurant and bar standing on the shingle; steaks, mussels and lemon pavlova.
Grateley *Plough Inn* (026 488) 221. Good bar meals backed up by blackboard specials.
New Alresford *Old School House* 60 West Street, (0962) 732134. Nice atmosphere, regularly changing menu with imaginative touches.
Steep *Harrow Inn* (0730) 62685. Old, atmospheric pub with simple home cooking and real ales.
Winchester *Brann's* 9 Great Minster Street, The Square, (0962) 64004. Busy wine bar with upstairs restaurant; dishes reveal a tendency to prettify.

Hereford & Worcester

Bewdley *L'Ile de France* 61 Load Street, (0299) 400040. French cooking but English variety of success.
Broadway *Coach House* The Green, (0386) 853555. Brash barn restaurant catering for tourist types; long menu; breakfasts, roasts, cream teas; large portions.
Dormy House Willersey Hill, (0386) 852711. Luxurious former farmhouse enjoying panoramic views. Ambitious menu, good presentation.
Goblets Wine Bar Lygon Arms, High Street, (0386) 852255. Old inn-style wine bar creating English country dishes.
Chaddesley Corbett *Brockencote Hall* (0562) 777876. Jacobean-style house in fine surroundings; short menus at set prices, from simple French to luxury levels. A new chef as we went to press.

Evesham *Riverside* The Parks, Offenham Road, (0386) 446200. High on a hill, with views and garden down to the River Avon. Variable menu, good desserts and wine list.
Glewstone *Glewstone Court* (098 984) 367. Country house with an all-pervading informality. Fresh ingredients, cheap wines.
Kidderminster *La Brasserie* 5 Lower Mill Street, (0562) 744976. Reconstituted rustic surrounds; fresh fish dominates a blackboard menu, also steaks and salads.
Martley *Talbot Hotel* Knightwick, nr Martley, (0886) 21273. A rural location, by the River Teme, and an imaginative menu. Everything is home-made, including bread.
Ross-on-Wye *Cloisters* 24 High Street, (0989) 67717. Wine bar with small menu, using fresh produce.
Meader's 1 Copse Cross Street, (0989) 62803. Authentic and hearty Hungarian cuisine; soul-satisfying soups, goulash, stuffed pancakes and strudel.
Wharton Lodge Weston-under-Penyard, (0989) 81795. New and handsome country-house conversion, the cooking as yet uneven and not cheap. The table d'hôte is the best bet.
Vowchurch *Croft Country House* (0981) 550226. Guesthouse set in beautiful gardens, with good food sensibly priced. No smoking throughout. Booking essential.
Whitney *Rhydspence Inn* (049 73) 262. Remote pub with an over-long menu, which should mean something for vegetarians. Choose carefully.

Hertfordshire

Berkhamsted *Cooks Delight* 360–364 High Street, (0442) 863584. Green principles are the order of the day at this tea-room-cum-restaurant; much is macrobiotic, vegan or simply organic.
Burnham Green *White Horse* White Horse Lane, (043 879) 416. Friendly pub for good home cooking and tempting desserts.
Hemel Hempstead *Gallery Coffee Shop* Old Town Hall Arts Centre, High Street, (0442) 232416. Not just for snacks, this first-floor café offers hot dishes and good beers. Excellent desserts include bread-and-butter pudding.
St Albans *Alban Tandoori* 145 Victoria Street, (0727) 862111. Conveniently placed curry house, close to the railway station. Some worthwhile specialities in addition to the standard range.
Garibaldi 61 Albert Street, (0727) 55046. Popular pub; Italian chicken, pasta and decent salads.
Langtrys Fish Restaurant London Road, (0727) 861848 and 866878. Menu of all-encompassing length, yet fresh-tasting mussels, monkfish and halibut.
Marmaris 128 London Road, (0727) 40382. Good-value Turkish restaurant; familiar menu features taramasalata, stuffed aubergine, kebabs and moussaka.
Watton-at-Stone *George & Dragon* High Street, (0920) 830285. Both bar meals and restaurant; a strong emphasis on seafood, smoked salmon, home-made pâté.

Humberside

Barton-upon-Humber *Elio's* 11 Market Place, (0652) 635147. Friendly trattoria; the long menu takes in pasta, pizza and meat but favours fish.
Grimsby *Danish Mission* 2 Cleethorpes Road, (0472) 342257. Christian mission for Scandinavian sailors, also open to the public. Good smorgasbord, hot meals, coffee and pastries.
Granary 1st Floor, Haven Mill, Garth Lane, (0472) 346338. Not a wholefood restaurant, but an old grain-mill conversion. Mostly seafood, with other blackboard choices.
Hull *Le Bistro* 400 Beverley Road, (0482) 43088. Small restaurant in an unlikely position; half the menu is vegetarian.
Scunthorpe *Giovanni's* 44 Oswald Road, (0724) 281169. Popular Italian with a long list of pastas, decent pizzas and a few daily specials.

Isle of Wight

Seaview *Seaview Hotel and Restaurant* High Street, (0983) 612711. Cheerful seaside hotel, bar food, sea views, bustling.

Kent

Barham *Old Coach House* Dover Road, (0227) 831218. Comes close to a French transport café; nothing nouvelle but substantial servings: charcuterie, bouillabaisse, steaks.
Broadstairs *Marchesi Bros* 18 Albion Street, (0843) 62481. Family-run restaurant and hotel; friendly service, good vegetables, delicious desserts.
Canterbury *Sully's* County Hotel, High Street, (0227) 766266. Smart surroundings, modish combinations, good wines.
Chiddingstone *Castle Inn*, (0892) 870247. A property owned by the National Trust; pub and restaurant meals, local beers on draught.
Eastry *Coach & Horses* Lower Street, (0304) 611692. Meals must be ordered a day in advance; home cooking, comfortable surroundings.
Folkestone *India* 1 Old High Street, (0303) 59155. French/Bengali; mostly curries and tandooris but with some European dishes added for good measure.
Hadlow *La Crémaillère* The Square, (0732) 851489. Old-fashioned French.
Ivy Hatch *Plough* Coach Road, (0732) 810268. A chef from Alsace producing superior pub food. More reports, please.
Lamberhurst *Brown Trout* (0892) 890312. Pub; blackboard menu with much fish, try the seafood platter.
Newnham *George Inn* 44 The Street, (079 589) 237. Imaginative bar meals; lamb-filled aubergine, fish soup, vegetable terrine.
Tunbridge Wells *Eglantine* 65 High Street, (0892) 24957. Pastel décor, short menu, young chef/patronne striving to succeed.

Lancashire

Bolton by Bowland *Copy Nook* (020 07) 205. Pub, popular for its home cooking.
Crawshaw Booth *Valley Restaurant* 542 Burnley Road, (0706) 831728. Straightforward cooking, set menu, fresh ingredients.
Garstang *El Nido* Whinney Brow Lane, A6 Forton, (0524) 791254. Spanish; good atmosphere, specialises in seafood.
Goosnargh *Solo* Goosnargh Lane, (0772) 865206. The menu sounds alarming, but the materials are good, even if fine detail is lacking. Prices are high.
Lancaster *Dukes* Dukes Play House, Moor Lane, (0524) 843215. Theatre restaurant open for both lunches and pre-performance meals.
Libra 19 Brock Street, (0524) 61551. Share a table for virtuously healthy vegetarian food.
Whitewell *Inn at Whitewell* Forest of Bowland, (020 08) 222. Charming pub; Cumberland sausage, farmhouse cheeses and sticky toffee pudding.

Leicestershire

Grimston *Olde Stocks* Main Street, (0664) 812255. Seventeenth-century surroundings plus competent cooking and friendly service.
Leicester *Bread and Roses* 70 High Street, (0533) 532448. Full Middle Eastern menu in this wholefood café, below a radical bookshop.
Sayonara 49 Belgrave Road, (0533) 665888. Recently arrived vegetarian thali restaurant, looking for Western custom and a reputation.
Water Margin 76–78 High Street, (0533) 516422. The best place in Leicester for lunchtime dim-sum and one-plate dishes in the old Cantonese style. Western dishes are less reliable.
Loughborough *Angelo's* 65 Woodgate, (0509) 266704. Relaxing Italian; the pasta pleases.
Stretton *Ram Jam Inn* Great North Road, (0780) 410776. Alternative roadside refreshment; good breakfasts, imaginative modern menu, espresso coffee.
Uppingham *Lake Isle* 16 High Street East, (0572) 822951. Nice rooms, grand wine list, variable cooking in a 'French provincial' mode.
Walcote *Black Horse* Lutterworth Road, (0455) 552684. Authentic Thai incongruously set in an English country pub.

Lincolnshire

Doddington *Littlehouse Restaurant* Doddington Hall, (0522) 690980. in attractive hall grounds; good for Sunday lunch, less so for dinner.
Gedney Dyke *Chequers* Main Street, (0406) 362666. Popular pub restaurant; long menu supplemented by specials of fresh fish.
Horncastle *Mantles* 19 Lawrence Street, The Market Place, (0507) 526726. Sophisticated seafood, fish and chips.
Lincoln *Moulin Maison* Mill House, Cliff Top, Ingham, (0522) 730130. Converted millhouse cooking to Lincolnshire acclaim. Improving.
Louth *Mr Chips* 17–21 Aswell Street, (0507) 603756. Large, family-run fish and chip establishment.
Newton *Red Lion* (052 97) 256. Quality cold table and local specialities.

Merseyside

Hoylake *Lino's* 122 Market Street, 051-632 1408. Small restaurant with an Italian influence.

Liverpool *Everyman Bistro* 9–11 Hope Street, 051-708 9545. Inventive bistro cooking beneath the theatre. Leave room for the excellent desserts.

Jenny's Old Ropery, Fenwick Street, 051-236 0332. Some fresh fish dishes on an otherwise uninspiring menu: stay with the simplest, skip the sweets trolley.

Shangri La Ashcroft Buildings, 37 Victoria Street, 051-255 0708. Cantonese; smart décor and a business crowd, seafood specials.

Yuet Ben 1 Upper Duke Street, 051-709 5772. Long-standing Peking-style restaurant; lengthy menu mixing genuine and European.

Norfolk

Blickling *Buckinghamshire Arms* (0263) 732133. English country cooking close to Blickling Hall. Local game and freshly grown produce.

Castle Acre *Ostrich Inn* Stocks Green, (076 075) 5398. Friendly pub for freshly made pizzas, ploughman's and pasta.

Diss *Weaver's Wine Bar* Market Hill, (0379) 642411. Home cooking beneath the beams; start with the Brancaster mussels.

Guist *Tollbridge* Dereham Road, (036 284) 359. Idyllic riverside setting on the Wensum, stamped with Liberty style. Straightforward cooking; good puddings.

North Wootton *Red Cat* Station Road, (0553) 631244. Newly opened restaurant in old hotel; careful cooking, imaginative sauces, good wines.

Norwich *Andersens* 52 St Giles Street, (0603) 617199. Old town house with courtyard delivering genuine Danish cooking: smorgasbord, frikadeller, beers.

Upper Sheringham *Red Lion Inn* (0263) 825408. Traditional pub fare takes in crab salad and bread-and-butter pudding.

Wereham *Howards* School Lane, (0366) 500450. Fine ingredients accurately cooked, pleasant surroundings.

West Runton *Mirabelle* 7 Station Road, (026 375) 396. Honest cooking, strong on seafood and game.

Northamptonshire

Crick *Edwards of Crick* The Wharf, (0788) 822517. Coffee-house and restaurant in a canalside conversion. Satisfying snacks downstairs, pricier menu above.

East Haddon *Red Lion* (0604) 770223. Choice lunchtime menu taking in stockpot soup, curries and traditional puddings.

Easton on the Hill *Exeter Arms* Stamford Road, (0780) 57503. Pub serving simple English food with a few foreign influences.

Kilsby *Hunt House* High Street, (0788) 823282. Seventeenth-century hunting lodge now cooking for the locals. Good ingredients though heavy on the wine sauces and cream.

Northampton *Ristorante Ca' d'Oro* 334 Wellingborough Road, (0604) 32660. Home-made pasta and regional Italian cooking. Good espresso.

Oundle *Ship Inn* West Street, (0832) 273918. An honest hostelry: gutsy soups, good pies and gravies, old-fashioned puddings, real ales.
Stoke Bruerne *Bruerne's Lock* The Canalside, (0604) 863654. Canalside cottage that comes alive in the evenings; waterside surroundings for well-presented dishes.

Northumberland

Berwick-upon-Tweed *Rob Roy* Dock Road, Tweedmouth, (0289) 306428. Excellent seafood and fresh fish, though sometimes spoilt by heavy alcohol and herb flavours.
Blanchland *Lord Crewe Arms* (0434) 675251. Competent cooking, decent wines.
Corbridge *Watling Coffee House* The Watling, (0434) 633095. Ambrosial cakes that include scones, apple tart and cappuccino flan; handy for hungry border-crossers.
Seaton Sluice *Waterford Arms* Collywell Bay Road, 091-237 0450. Fish is the thing here, and all is fresh and large-portioned: seafood platter, swordfish, poached salmon, pies.
Warkworth *Jackdaw* 34 Castle Street, (0665) 711488. Small café/restaurant that hauls in fresh fish from the local harbour.

North Yorkshire

Askrigg *Rowan Tree* Market Place, (0969) 50536. Popular restaurant in *All Creatures Great and Small* town. Reservations essential.
Bolton Abbey *Devonshire Arms* (075 671) 441. Former coaching-inn now lovingly restored with antiques and paintings from Chatsworth. Both bar food and a restaurant.
East Witton *Blue Lion* (0969) 24273. Country pub with ambitious cooking; beautiful presentation, fresh fish is a feature.
Harrogate *Bettys* 1 Parliament Street, (0423) 502746. The original Bettys, now part of a chain of traditional tea-rooms. Good baking, cream teas, light meals.
Lords 8 Montpelier Street, (0423) 508762. Wine bar with a cricketing theme.
William & Victoria 6 Cold Bath Road, (0423) 506883. Basement bar with a blackboard menu: poached salmon, aubergine and tomato bake, rice pudding.
Hawes *Simonstone Hall* (0969) 667255. Sound hotel cooking in comfortable and welcoming surroundings of a former shooting lodge.
Helmsley *Black Swan* Market Place, (0439) 70466. New chef making an impression.
Leyburn *Golden Lion Hotel* Market Place, (0969) 22161. Friendly pub, fresh fish, good vegetables.
Northallerton *Bettys* 188 High Street, (0609) 775154. A smaller branch of this illustrious chain, so be warned of queues for tempting tea-breads and cakes.
Pickering *Forest & Vale* Malton Road, (0751) 72722. Friendly hotel, varied menu, catering for all tastes.
Ripon *Old Deanery* Minster Road, (0765) 603518. French cooking in beautiful surroundings.

Scorton *St Cuthberts Inn* Station Road, (0748) 811631. Extensive menu for bar and dining-room that makes much use of sauces. Excellent vegetables, real ales.
Skipton *Oats* Chapel Hill, (0756) 798118. Modern menu and luxury ingredients.
Staithes *Endeavour* 1 High Street, (0947) 840825. Careful cooking of quality ingredients; local fish is good.
Thirsk *Abbey Inn* Byland Abbey, Coxwold, nr Thirsk, (034 76) 204. Atmospheric pub producing premium cooking: venison, home-made ices.
York *Bettys* 6–8 St Helen's Square, (0904) 659142. The most stylish of the Bettys chain. Speciality teas, rare coffees, late breakfasts and light meals.

Nottinghamshire

Nether Langwith *Goff's* Langwith Mill House, Langwith Road, (0623) 744538. Fresh ingredients and ambitious combinations sometimes let down by slack service.
Nottingham *Le Tetard* 10 Pilcher Gate, (0602) 598253. Professional bistro cooking; good sauces and presentation.
Truffles 43 Broad Street, (0602) 472857. Small menu with much to interest, sparse décor.
Southwell *Broadwalk Café* 1 Westgate, (0636) 815619. Regularly changing menu and good views of the Minster by night.

Oxfordshire

Brightwell Baldwin *Lord Nelson Inn* (049 161) 2497. Seventeenth-century stone pub serving seriously large portions; Welsh rarebit, salads, fresh fettuccine.
Kingham *Mill House Hotel & Restaurant* (0608) 658188. Light, colourful cooking in a Cotswold setting. Smart dress preferred.
Marsh Baldon *Seven Stars* (086 738) 255. Village pub with an imaginative menu: chicken wings in chilli and garlic, feuilleté of prawns and Stilton, Sunday roasts.
Oxford *Blue Coyote* 36–37 St Clements Street, (0865) 241431. Stylish Tex-Mex crawling with cacti; grilled chicken and enchiladas from the American continent.
Browns 5–11 Woodstock Road, (0865) 511995. Large and lively American-style restaurant popular with students and their families. No booking, long queues.
Café Français 146 London Road, Headington, nr Oxford, (0865) 62587. Simple French, variable cooking.
Old Parsonage 1 Banbury Road, (0865) 310210. Pretty town-house hotel with combined bar and restaurant. Refurbished rooms and a small-scale operation high on quality.
Shrivenham *Thatchers* (0793) 783848. Fresh ingredients and first-rate presentation from a husband and wife team.
Wallingford *Trapp's Table* The Cellars, Lamb Arcade, (0491) 39606. Old wine vaults, now with pine tables and a daily-changing menu. Try the home-made chocolate brownies.

Waterperry *Waterperry Gardens Teashop* Waterperry Gardens, nr Wheatley, (0844) 339226. Vast choice of cakes and some savouries to be taken inside, or on the spacious lawn. Off A418 N of M40 junction 8.

Shropshire

Acton Scott *Historic Working Farm Café* nr Church Stretton, (069 46) 30617. Part of a historical working farm, providing suitable turn-of-the-century country cooking.
Easthope *Wenlock Edge Inn* Hilltop, (074 636) 403. Old quarryman's cottage now operating as a pub. Savoury pies, pâtés, nursery puddings and real ales.
Hopton Castle *Park Cottage* (054 74) 351. Wonderful location, some homely rooms, and good-value food from the Aga.
Ironbridge *Olivers* 33 High Street, (0952) 433086. Vegetarian food amongst Victorian décor.
Shrewsbury *Goodlife* 73C Barracks Passage, Wyle Cop, (0743) 350455. Cramped wholefood/vegetarian restaurant; worth tackling the crowds for healthy home- cooking and organic baking.
Worfield *Old Vicarage Hotel* (074 64) 497. Harsh brick country-house hotel with useful restaurant serving 'modern' British food, slightly sweet-toothed, with flourishes.

Somerset

Brent Knoll *Goat House Café* Bristol Road, (0278) 760995. Goods on sale – clothing, cheese and ice-cream – are all from goats. The café fare is not so exclusive.
Bridgwater *Nutmeg House* 8–10 Clare Street, (0278) 457823. Café-cum-restaurant; daily roasts, decent lunches, dinner at weekends.
Monksilver *Notley Arms* (0984) 56217. Pleasant village pub; home-made pasta, Chinese-style pork.
North Perrott *Manor Arms* (0460) 72901. Simple bar meals and a more ambitious restaurant menu; good value.
Taunton *Capriccio* 41 Bridge Street, (0823) 335711. Authentic and fairly priced Italian.
Wellington *Hartleys* 41 High Street, (0823) 667646. Go for the simpler dishes, especially the shellfish and home-smoked fish. Interesting and cheap wines.
Withypool *Royal Oak* (064 383) 506 and 507. Good bar food, less good restaurant. Sometimes excellent cheeses, nice location.
Yeovil *Yeovil Court* West Coker Road, (093 586) 3746. Steaks served seven different ways, also more imaginative salmon, sole and lamb.

South Yorkshire

Sheffield *Fat Cat* 23 Alma Street, (0742) 728195. Pub serving wholesome bar meals, real ales.

Just Cooking 16–18 Carver Street, (0742) 727869. Queue at the counter for cold meats, salads and luscious desserts.
Nirmal's 189–193 Glossop Road, (0742) 724054. Warm welcome from Nirmal Gupta; cooking has been less consistent of late.
Tickhill *Forge* 1 Sunderland Street, (0302) 744122. The sheer number of combinations, sauces and flavourings in this small restaurant astounds. Nouvelle cuisine tendencies.

Staffordshire

Burton upon Trent *Dovecliff Hall* Stretton, (0283) 31818. Short set menu lists the likes of scrambled eggs with prawns and smoked salmon, fillet of lamb, good crème brûlée.
Leek *Carriage* 69 Haywood Street, (0538) 386372. A florid menu that's modern Anglo-French.
Lichfield *Pig Barn* Heart of the Country, Swinfen, nr Lichfield, (0543) 480307. Converted barn; blackboard menu, bring your own, booking advisable.
Eastern Eye 19B Bird Street, (0543) 254399. Indian with a local following, some regional dishes, good-value thalis.
Penkridge *William Harding's House* Mill Street, (0785) 712955. Fine ingredients though cooking of variable quality. Good, inexpensive wines.
Rolleston on Dove *Brookhouse Hotel* Brookside, (0283) 814188. Restaurant with accommodation; smart surroundings, cooking standards can waver.
Weeford *Old Schoolhouse* (0543) 480009. Very popular and large restaurant with better cooking than either menu or looks would imply. More reports, please.

Suffolk

Aldeburgh *Aldeburgh Fish & Chip Shop* 226 High Street, (0728) 452250. Fresh fish, great chips and home-smoked salmon.
Boxford *Fleece* (0787) 210247. Country pub; home cooking includes steak and kidney pie and steaks.
Bury St Edmunds *Angel Hotel* Angel Hill, (0284) 753926. Famous hostelry mentioned in *Pickwick Papers*, still cooking such stalwarts as roasts and cream-laden desserts.
Dunwich *Flora Tea Rooms* Dunwich Beach, (072 873) 433. Sit in the sand dunes or inside this former beach hut to enjoy memorable fish and chips.
Ship St James Street, (072 873) 219. Inn, popular perhaps for its salt-marsh location but more probably for its locally caught fish and pleasing puddings.
Horringer *Beehive* (0284) 735260. Pub food par excellence; not a chip in sight but comforting, hot dishes, cold meats and salmon.
Ixworth *Pickerel at Ixworth* High Street, (0359) 30398. Old pub; the Pickerel Pie is packed with fish.
Lavenham *Swan Hotel* High Street, (0787) 247477. Imaginative menu that's also vegetarian-friendly.
Laxfield *Kings Head* Gorams Mill Lane, (0986) 798395. Atmospheric Tudor pub; plain home cooking, real ales.

Long Melford *Chimneys* Hall Street, (0787) 79806. Elegant surroundings for ambitious cooking that costs.
Countrymen Black Lion, The Green, (0787) 79951 and 312356. Family-run hotel; fair cooking, good wines, friendly service.
Rede *Plough* (028 489) 208. Good for garden eating; venison, turkey with all the trimmings, excellent desserts.
Snape *Golden Key* Priory Road, (072 888) 510. Pretty pub with a good line in pies and quiches. Puddings include treacle and walnut tart.
Westleton *Crown* nr Saxmundham, (072 873) 273 and 777. Mostly fish, all fresh. Smokers are segregated in dining areas.
Woodbridge *Royal Bengal* 4–6 Quay Street, (0394) 387983. An established reputation for good curries, sheek kebabs and Indian breads.

Surrey

Chiddingfold *Crown* (0428) 682255. Quality ingredients, subtle flavours, extensive wine list.
Cobham *Cedar House* Mill Road, (0932) 863424. Stately house with a hushed atmosphere and a fine minstrels' gallery; imaginative cooking, sophisticated desserts.
Croydon *Willow* 88 Selsdon Park Road, Addington, nr Croydon, 081-657 4656. Chinese; Peking cuisine with the odd glance at spicier regions. Can be expensive.
Ewhurst *Windmill Inn* Pitch Hill, (0483) 277566. Views of the South Downs from the re-vamped bar, conservatory and gardens. Both bar meals and a more expensive menu.
Farnham *Krug's* 84 West Street, (0252) 723277. Austrian restaurant, open only for dinner. Live accordion music on Fridays.
Godalming *Inn on the Lake* Ockford Road, (0483) 415575/415576. Hotel and restaurant set in landscaped grounds; ambitious menu, large portions, though expensive.
Guildford *Rumwong* 16–18 London Road, (0483) 36092. Thai; the intention of creating an exotic atmosphere is somewhat at the expense of the cooking, which has been variable.
Hampton Wick *Dijonnais* 35 High Street, 081-977 4895. Relocated from Croydon, unassuming French, sound Burgundian cooking.
Hersham *Dining Room* 10–12 Queens Road, (0932) 231686. Friendly, neighbourhood restaurant with a mostly traditional menu.
Kingston upon Thames *Dining Hall* Griffin Passage, Market Square, 081-547 1696/1656. Rococo surrounds and food at reasonable prices; choices include chicken, trout and wood pigeon.
Lemongrass 54 Fife Road, 081-546 8221. Simple, small Thai; delicate noodles, spicy red curry, good value.
Richmond *Refectory* 6 Church Walk, 081-940 6264. Keenly priced English food in an eighteenth-century setting.
South Godstone *Bonne Auberge* Tilburstow Hill, (0342) 893184. Fashionably French; peasant-style food but not peasant portions or prices.

Tyne & Wear

Gateshead *Marquis of Granby* Streetgate, Sunniside, 091-488 7813. Pub restaurant with a regularly changing menu; finish with the nursery puddings.
La Piazza 596 Durham Road, Low Fell, 091-487 5810. Bustling Italian; cooking more than just pizzas and pasta. Booking advisable.
Newcastle upon Tyne *Eastern Taste* 277 Stanhope Street, Fenham, 091-273 9406. Good-value Indian, huge choice of tandooris and curries.
Roman Way Pizzeria 429A Westgate Road, 091-273 1991. Young, lively atmosphere, freshly topped pizzas, pasta and several Middle Eastern dishes.
North Shields *Kristian* Fish Quay, 091-258 5155. Queue on the quay for freshest fish and greaseless chips.

Warwickshire

Alderminster *Bell Inn* (0789) 450414. Imaginative bar food using quality ingredients. Booking advisable in evenings.
Barford *Glebe Hotel* Church Street, (0926) 624218. English cooking; standard formula but good value.
Bidford-on-Avon *White Lion* High Street, (0789) 773309. Prettily placed by the river; spacious restaurant specialising in fresh fish.
Ryton-on-Dunsmore *Ryton Gardens Café* National Centre for Organic Gardening, Wolston Lane, (0203) 303517. An organic gardening centre with café to match: home-grown produce becomes healthy meals.
Stratford-upon-Avon *Opposition* 13 Sheep Street, (0789) 269980. English cooking, pleasant service.

West Midlands

Birmingham *Franzl's* 151 Milcote Road, Bearwood, 021-429 7920. Austrian cooking, complete with cow-bells; large portions though recent reports suggest variable standards.
Punjab Paradise 377 Ladypool Road, 021-449 4110. Balti house; fresh flavours, vivid spicing, low prices.
Coventry *Brooklands Grange Hotel* Holyhead Road, (0203) 591248. Countrified hotel catering for business types; contemporary menu, plush prices.
Stourbridge *French Connection* 3 Coventry Street, (0384) 390940. Good-value bistro; fresh ingredients, friendly service.
Mr Dave's 15 High Street, Lye, nr Stourbridge, (0384) 393698. High-street balti house; food comes in cast-iron skillets, to be mopped up with Indian breads.
Wolverhampton *Bilash Tandoori* 2 Cheapside, (0902) 27762. Family-run curry house; Bangladeshi dishes, Kashmiri baltis, thalis.

West Sussex

Ardingly *Oak Inn* Street Lane, (0444) 892244. Old pub with renovated barn restaurant; good home cooking, blackboard menu.
Chichester *St Martin's Tea Rooms* 3 St Martin's Street, (0243) 786715. All is vegetarian, save for wild smoked salmon, and much is organic. For the conscientious, ingredients of dishes are listed at the counter. Garden eating area.
Shoreham-by-Sea *La Gondola* 90 High Street, (0273) 463231. Italian; spaghetti, veal and chicken all come recommended.
Storrington *Old Forge* 6A Church Street, (0903) 743402. A friendly place for imaginative home cooking; ambitions sometimes outrun results.
West Hoathly *Cat Inn* North Lane, (0342) 810369. Old smugglers' inn with a stash of good recipes.

West Yorkshire

Elland *Berties Bistro* 7–10 Town Hall Buildings, (0422) 371724. Busy bistro; grilled black pudding and, for dessert, Berties Bombe.
Ilkley *Bettys* 34 The Grove, (0943) 608029. A branch of the famous tea-shop chain; home baking, ice-creams and a light supper menu.
Rombalds West View, Wells Road, (0943) 603201. Restaurant-with-rooms; sound cooking with good attention to detail.
Hebden Bridge *Watergate* 11 Bridge Gate, (0422) 842978. Friendly café with a great line in cakes. Also a light-meals menu.
Huddersfield *Ramsden's Landing* Aspley Wharf, Wakefield Road, (0484) 544250. Large brasserie with a busy bar; French-style food.
Leeds *Brasserie Forty Four* 42–44 The Calls, (0532) 343232. New and smartly renovated restaurant; good cooking, Christmas pudding all the year round.
Darbar 16–17 Kirkgate, (0532) 460381. Tandoori; lots of lamb dishes, all tenderly cooked.
Grillade Wellington Street, (0532) 459707. City-centre brasserie, good grills but generally inconsistent. Useful, better at night than lunch.
Jumbo Chinese 120 Vicar Lane, (0532) 458324. Ever-popular Chinese, despite indications of drab décor and sloppy service. Dim-sum are good.
Olive Tree Oaklands, Radley Lane, (0532) 569283. Hard-to-find Greek; standard menu, extra-sweet pastries, bazouki evenings.
Salvo's 115 Otley Road, Headingley, (0532) 755017. Italian, highly regarded for its caring service, good pizzas and shark steak.
Ripponden *Over the Bridge* Millfold, (0422) 823722. Converted weavers' cottages showing a set-price menu, with some modern flourishes. Decent wines, including a selection of half-bottles.

Wiltshire

Aldbourne *Raffles* 1 The Green, (0672) 40700. Bistro cooking; better to stay with simpler combinations.

Avebury *Stones* High Street, (067 23) 514. Forward-thinking vegetarian restaurant close to the stone circle; mostly organic produce, self-service.
Brinkworth *Three Crowns* (066 641) 366. Rich sauces, fresh fish, good vegetables, cheap wines.
Lacock *At the Sign of the Angel* Church Street, (0249) 730230. Half-timbered, in a National Trust Village; traditional roasts, fresh fish, though recent reports suggest variable cooking and slow service.
Marlborough *Polly Tea Rooms* 26–27 High Street, (0672) 512146. Traditional teas, light lunches, hand-made chocolates and ice-creams.
Salisbury *Just Brahms* 68 Castle Street, (0722) 328402. Wine bar offering main meals or a simpler snack menu; decent vegetables and home-made desserts.
Michael Snell Tea Rooms 8 St Thomas's Square, (0722) 336037. Proper patisserie, savoury flans and light lunches.
Warminster *Thatches* 103 High Street, Codford St Peter, nr Warminster, (0985) 50267. Small menu, good value, open for dinner.

Scotland

Aberlour (Grampian) *Archiestown Hotel* by Aberlour, (034 06) 218. Small but excellent menu, comfortable rooms.
Alexandria (Strathclyde) *Cameron House Hotel* Loch Lomond, (0389) 55625. Luxury menus on the banks of the loch: lobster, duck, veal, Scottish cheeses, good wines.
Alyth (Tayside) *Lands of Loyal Hotel* Loyal Road, (082 83) 3151. Popular for good plain cooking: game pâté en croûte, flambé lamb, pavlova.
Arbroath (Tayside) *Gordon's* 32 Main Road, Inverkeilor, nr Arbroath, (024 13) 364. Arbroath is home to the smokie; here expect fresh fish, seafood and friendly service.
Carnan (Western Isles) *Orasay Inn* Loch Carnan, South Uist, (087 04) 298. Primitive building in a bleak location, but useful. Fresh fish, good seafood platters.
Craigellachie (Grampian) *Craigellachie Hotel* (0340) 881204. Sporting hotel; falls between haute cuisine and honest sportsman's fare.
Crail (Fife) *T. Reilly* The Harbour. Fresh shellfish sold from the sea-front; no frills.
Edinburgh (Lothian) *Cellar No 1* 1A Chambers Street, 031-220 4298. Wine bar worth seeking out for good-value meals: burgers, gnocchi, wild Scottish smoked salmon, cheerful puddings, espresso.
Cibo 109 Hanover Street, 031-226 6990. Smartly decorated Italian cooking soups, pasta and pizza.
Doric Tavern 15 Market Street, 031-225 1084. Eclectic and sound cooking: from couscous merguez to monkfish. Cheap wines.
Loon Fung 32 Grindlay Street, 031-229 5757. Chinese; go for the dim-sum.
Marrakech Marrakech Hotel, 30 London Street, 031-556 7293. Subterranean restaurant run by Moroccans; spicy soups, couscous, fragrant pastries. Unlicensed, but bring your own.

Raj 91 Henderson Street, 031-553 3980. Genteelly decorated Indian; cooking draws from north India, also Bangladesh and Bengal.
Skippers Bistro 1A Dock Place, 031-554 1018. Go for the fresh fish and seafood, skip the puddings. Can be expensive.
Szymanski Bristol Place, 031-226 2309. Polish cooking at its heartiest: potato pancakes, dumplings, stuffed cabbage and sweet puddings.
Tinelli 139 Easter Road, 031-652 1932. Traditional Italian where the pastas and professional service continue to please.
Waterloo Place 29 Waterloo Place, 031-557 0007. New restaurant with a short menu in an assured, modern style. Reports, please.
Whighams Wine Cellars 13 Hope Street, 031-225 8674. Lunchtimes only and full of business suits; short menu strong on seafood.
Fort William (Highland) *Factor's House* Torlundy, nr Fort William, (0397) 705767. Belonging to Inverlochy Castle, restaurant-with-rooms offering a simpler alternative to the castle's catering and accommodation. A new chef; more reports, please.
Glasgow (Strathclyde) *Balbir's Ashoka* 108 Elderslie Street, 041-221 1761. Balbir Sing's middle-range restaurant; good curries.
La Bavarde 19 New Kirk Road, Bearsden, 041-942 2202. Great value for interesting ideas: grilled herrings with oatmeal, pigeon and date pie, tripe Italian-style, home-baked bread.
Mai Thai 415 Sauchiehall Street, 041-332 4996. Basic Thai; decent satays but other dishes indicate shortcuts.
Mitchell's 157 North Street, 041-204 4312. Fresh fish, game and organic vegetables from an Arran freeholding, cooked to above local standards.
Peking Inn 191 Hope Street, 041-332 8971. Szechuan with a good line in set meals.
Two Fat Ladies 88 Dumbarton Road, 041-339 1944. Bingo references end with the address; a blackboard menu that takes in shellfish and Eastern influences. Booking essential.
Innerleithen (Borders) *Traquair Arms Hotel* Traquair Road, (0896) 8302299. Good-value bar meals and also a restaurant; some Scottish dishes, excellent breakfasts.
Kentallen (Highland) *Holly Tree Hotel* (063 174) 292. Good home cooking: rabbit hotpot, sticky toffee pudding.
Kilfinan (Strathclyde) *Kilfinan Hotel* (070 082) 201. Careful cooking and excellent value at this old coaching-inn, set in rural isolation. A new chef as we went to press.
Kinross (Tayside) *Croft Bank House Hotel* Station Road, (0577) 63819. Victorian villa with an extravagant menu, fresh ingredients and full of frills. More reports please.
Lochmaddy (Western Isles) *Langass Lodge* Langass, by Loch Maddy, North Uist, (087 64) 285. In fishing and shooting territory; dated menu so choose carefully, local trout the best.
Oban (Strathclyde) *Glenfeochan House* Kilmore, nr Oban, (063 177) 273. Country-house hotel with produce from the estate.
Staffin (Highland) *Flodigarry Country House Hotel*, Isle of Skye, (047 052) 203. New management, good value, worth a visit for Scottish home cooking.

Strachur (Strathclyde) *Inver Cottage* Strathlachlan, nr Strachur, (036 986) 396. Open for the summer season; beautiful setting, fresh fish, good vegetables.
Ullapool (Highland) *Ceilidh Place* 14 West Argyle Street, (0854) 612103. Arts-centre café; budget lunchtime offerings or more pricey dinner menu.

Wales

Aberdovey (Gwynedd) *Maybank Hotel* 4 Penhelig Road, (0654) 767500. Friendly hotel overlooking the harbour.
Abergavenny (Gwent) *Ant & Rubber Plant* 7 Market Street, (0873) 855905. Honest bistro cooking in a relaxed atmosphere.
Borth-y-Gest (Gwynedd) *Blossoms* 4 Ivy Terrace, (0766) 513500. Harbour-front bistro serving snacks and an evening menu.
Cardiff (South Glamorgan) *Caramella's* 116 Salisbury Road, Cathays, (0222) 238348. Traditional Italian embracing pizza, pasta and polenta. Warning: a karaoke machine may appear.
Orient Rendezvous Westgate House, 15–23 Westgate Street, (0222) 226901. Some consider this the best Chinese in Cardiff; extensive menu, dim-sum, courteous service.
Taste of Asia 236 City Road, Roath, (0222) 493994. Indian tandoori offering other regional dishes.
Cilgerran (Dyfed) *Castle Kitchen* High Street, (0239) 615055. Good home cooking in comfortable surroundings.
Cowbridge (South Glamorgan) *Basil's Brasserie* 2 Eastgate, (0446) 773738. Bistro with a blackboard menu concentrating on fish.
Criccieth (Gwynedd) *Blue China Tearooms* Lon Felin, (0766) 523239. Stands by the sea with views from the sheltered garden; home-made scones, cakes, soups and salads.
Crickhowell (Powys) *Bear Hotel* High Street, (0873) 810408. Old coaching-inn; the dining-room is useful for its large portions, low prices and sensible menu.
Harlech (Gwynedd) *Castle Cottage* Pen Llech, (0766) 780479. Hotel and restaurant with a friendly welcome, careful cooking, good breakfasts and fair value.
Yr Ogof High Street, (0766) 780888. Bistro with a menu bearing global influences: Brazilian cod in coconut-milk, bean goulash, tagliatelle and simpler staple dishes.
Hay-on-Wye (Powys) *Oscars* High Town, (0497) 821193. Popular with Hay's second-hand bookshoppers; toasted sandwiches, curries, salads and cakes.
Laleston (Mid Glamorgan) *Great House* High Street, (0656) 657644. A menu of different styles, though recent reports suggest a drop in standards.
Letterston (Dyfed) *Something's Cooking* The Square, (0348) 840621. Fish and chips are the thing here.
Llanddowror (Dyfed) *Old Rectory* (0994) 230030. Interesting menu, popular for Sunday lunch, friendly to children.
Llandovery (Dyfed) *Drovers Restaurant* 9 Market Square, (0550) 21115. Good-value home cooking in welcome surroundings.

Llandudno (Gwynedd) *Number One Food and Wine Bar* 1 Old Road, (0492) 875424. Wine bar with a strong local following; fresh fish, relaxing atmosphere.
Llandybie (Dyfed) *Cobblers* 3 Church Street, (0269) 850540. Local produce and fashionable ideas; Welsh cooking with a difference. Some inconsistencies, reservation recommended.
Llanrwst (Gwynedd) *Tu Hwnt I'r Bont* (0492) 640138. Charming, creeper-clad cottage close to the river; good baking includes bara brith, cream teas and light lunches.
Llanwddyn (Powys) *Lake Vyrnwy Hotel*, Lake Vyrnwy, (069 173) 244. Popular with shooting and fishing parties. Go for the views, the (no-smoking) conservatory and choose from the simpler dishes.
Llanynys (Clwyd) *Cerrigllwydion Arms* (074 578) 247. Out-of-the-way, ancient pub with panelling and beams. Hearty cooking includes home-baked ham and treacle and walnut tart.
Llyswen (Powys) *Griffin Inn* (0874) 754241. Good pub food in an old-fashioned inn: Wye salmon, game, organic produce when available.
Mold (Clwyd) *Chez Colette* 56 High Street, (0352) 759225. Family-run bistro serving good-value French meals.
Nantgaredig (Dyfed) *Cwmtwrch Farmhouse Hotel* (0267) 290238. Good home cooking, especially the puddings. Conservatory dining-room.
Narberth (Dyfed) *Robeston House* Robeston Wathen, (0834) 861195. Old, rambling building in several acres; sound cooking, good views.
Newcastle Emlyn (Dyfed) *Felin Geri* (0239) 710810. Japanese; authentic food.
Penmaenpool (Gwynedd) *George III Hotel* (0341) 422525. Despite sluggish service, a good bet for the bar food and Sunday lunch.
Pontypridd (Mid Glamorgan) *John & Maria's* 1–3 Broadway, (0443) 402977. Italian; fresh fish, spaghetti and home-made zabaglione.
Portfield Gate (Dyfed) *Sutton Lodge* (0437) 768548. Four-course and no-choice menu, may include local lamb or pan-fried smoked goose. Twenty-four hours' advance booking necessary.
Pwllheli (Gwynedd) *Glynllifon Country House* Llanbedrog, (0758) 740147. Indian tandoori in acres of grounds; short menu, friendly reception.
Swansea (West Glamorgan) *Barrows* 42 Newton Road, Mumbles, (0792) 361443. Good-value wine bar with a great atmosphere; try the seafood salad.
P.A.'s 95 Newton Road, Mumbles, (0792) 367723. Simple but much-liked bistro; has a fine new wine list.
Windsor Lodge Mount Pleasant, (0792) 652744. Small but stylish family-run hotel; sound cooking concentrates on game.
Tenby (Dyfed) *Penally Abbey* Penally, (0834) 3033. Fine Gothic house in the abbey grounds; a husband and wife team cooking honest food to a set-price menu.
Trelleck (Gwent) *Village Green* (0600) 860119. Restaurant and brasserie offering fair value and acceptable cooking, though standards may have slipped recently.
Tywyn (Gwynedd) *Proper Gander* Cambrian House, High Street, (0654) 711270. Proper cream teas, home-cooked lunches, roasts on Sundays.
Usk (Gwent) *Beaufort Arms* Monkswood, (049 528) 215. Pleasing pub food, good for Sunday lunch.

Wolf's Castle (Dyfed) *Wolfscastle Country Hotel* (043 787) 225. A friendly place for good, plain cooking. Puddings are particularly successful.

Isle of Man

Ballasalla *La Rosette* Main Road, (0624) 822940. Small restaurant run by a husband and wife team.
Silverburn Lodge (0624) 822343. Good cooking in lovely surroundings, friendly service.
Castletown *Chablis Cellar* 21 Bank Street, (062 482) 3527. Waterside restaurant where the prices are low, the mood informal, the food unfussy.
Douglas *Bowery* 4 Athol Terrace, Queen's Promenade, (0624) 628082. Tex-Mex cooking in a happy atmosphere: burritos, burgers, tacos, nachos, steaks and salads.
Rafters Peter Louis Department Store, 9 Duke Street, (0624) 672344. On the third floor, open daytime hours for breakfast, lunch and afternoon tea.
Onchan *Top Table* King Edward Road, (0624) 675626. The menu has fish, seafood and game, and can be expensive. Occasional live pianist or table magician.
Ramsey *Gophers* 2 West Quay, (0624) 815562. Quayside coffee-shop with a speedy turnover, popular for its decent snack menu.

Channel Islands

Gorey (Jersey) *Jersey Pottery Restaurant* (0534) 51119. When you've watched the wheel and spent on souvenirs, sample superior seafood and fine French pastries. Booking advisable.
St Peter Port (Guernsey) *L'Alchimie* Market Street, (0481) 720963. Local scallops and roast ribs of beef figure, though vegetarians are well-catered for.
Chinese Gourmet The Royal Hotel, Glategny Esplanade, (0481) 723921. Consistently good Chinese, now at a new address. Presentation and seafood have been praised.
Da Nello 46 Pollet Street, (0481) 721552. Friendly and popular Italian; fresh local seafood, fair-value.
San Lorenzo 42–44 Fountain Street, (0481) 722660. Authentic Italian run by a young and keen team; wines are imported directly from Italy.

Northern Ireland

Bangor (Co Down) *Bryansburn* 151 Bryansburn Road, (0247) 270173. Favourable reports have mentioned good soups, sauces, 'sensible' vegetables and speedy service.
Holywood (Co Down) *Culloden Hotel* 142 Bangor Road, Craigavad, (023 17) 5223. Luxury surroundings, sound cooking.

Of women, waiters and the single table

Gone are the days when the 'gentleman' always picked up the bill. Many women pay their own way; they have jobs, careers, travel on business, take clients out to lunch. Attitudes in restaurants have had to change to reflect this, but bad treatment and prejudices still persist. **Elizabeth Carter** (food journalist, restaurant inspector and Editor of the *Guide*'s sister publication, *Out to Eat*) looks into the perils facing women eating out and also the problems faced by the person eating alone.

'What on earth comes over wine waiters when they take the orders of a woman entertaining another woman in a restaurant?' demanded Elizabeth David in a 1962 *Spectator* article. Her complaint was that waiters always assumed that a half-bottle was being ordered: 'Like the steward on the Edinburgh-London express a few years ago who yelled at me across the rattling crockery and two other bemused passengers, "A bottle, madam? A *whole* bottle? Do you know how large a whole bottle is?"'

Have times changed? The advertisement promotions manager of *Marie Claire* would argue that some waiters have simply adjusted their prejudices to suit the times. Her most common complaint is that even after she has wrested the wine list from her male guest, to whom it has been handed by the waiter, and ordered the wine, it is invariably the man who is asked to do the tasting. Then there are the waiters who are still generally confused about who gets the bill, even when it is requested specifically by a woman. 'We never give ladies the bill' was one patronising retort from a waiter when confronted.

Is there anything in the fact that all these waiters were from countries where women may be treated differently? Or is there simply a lack of thought on the part of the management who fail to train their staff correctly? I have never forgotten paying a very substantial bill at one of London's top restaurants. The English waiter turned to my male colleague and remarked, 'You're a lucky man.'

One food writer readily admits to a dislike of eating alone, although her job sometimes makes this necessary. During filming in Birmingham for a TV programme she was booked into a large, modern hotel. Unfortunately, she felt too self-conscious to enter the dining-room of the hotel and only braved the bar once. Both places were overtly male preserves, to the extent that she felt far too uncomfortable to sit alone in them and relied on room service for evening meals. She noted that other women were staying on their own, and how studiously business-like they appeared at all times – wearing suits, clutching briefcases and apparently always immersed in work, even at breakfast. This was an act she was not prepared to ape.

Perhaps because a modern business hotel is noted for its impersonal style (although the management would have you believe otherwise), the above story casts shame on the hotel for failing to identify the needs of a particular group of customers, but is not untypical. The experience of a young research assistant relates to an exclusive hotel where individual guests' needs are paramount. Due to a mix-up she found herself waiting for over an hour one lunchtime in one of London's most exclusive hotels. Despite the outwardly correct attitude of the staff, she was made to feel distinctly uncomfortable – 'as if I could have been from an escort agency'. Why, she wanted to know, did all the other guests waiting in the small salon get offered drinks at once, while she had to summon a waiter after 40 minutes? For this sort of discrimination age is no barrier. The manager of a top Bath hotel must have been extremely surprised to receive a complaint from a mature, self-possessed and quietly dressed woman (a very experienced *Good Food Guide* inspector) who, while dining at the restaurant, had been so upset by the bad treatment meted out by the maître d' that days later, still smarting, she went back and complained. She had been left in no doubt that the man in question thought she was there to be 'picked up'. This sort of treatment is insulting and no amount of protestation by management that it values the single-woman guest can make amends for the inability to pass this enlightenment on to staff.

Eating alone is not a lonely process: it involves the active participation of other people. Attitude is all-important. I am convinced, after five years inspecting restaurants on my own, that either the diner feels uncomfortable with the situation and vulnerable enough to feel easily slighted by the smallest thing, or arrives relaxed and happy and comes smack up against the restaurant approach – not always positive – to the single diner. Women invariably suffer worse treatment than men. But does anyone actually enjoy eating out alone? Most of the people I talked to claimed they did not and ate alone only out of necessity. Although men can dislike dining alone as much as women, and feel they have not been made as welcome as they would have liked, women have to contend with much more. Whatever her feelings, the worst aspect of dining alone for a woman is the attitude of the staff towards her. How about this overheard comment from a

French waiter serving the first course to a single woman: 'Isn't anyone joining you?' That must have really put her in her place. And why are single diners *per se* regarded as second-class citizens? Restaurants should be more sensitive to their needs and show a degree of tact. After all, even a single diner is capable of spreading word-of-mouth recommendations to friends. While every person I spoke to could vividly recall the restaurants where they had had a bad experience, they would also speak glowingly of restaurants where, when alone, they had been treated with understanding. Just the offer of a newspaper and a well-lit table to read it by can be a start. The journalist Frances Edmonds maintains that the best solo lunch she ever had was in the chain restaurant TGI Friday in Covent Garden. Why? Because the (American) staff went out of their way to look after her; it was obviously restaurant policy.

It is hard to feel comfortable when eating alone, and most of us hide behind a newspaper or a book. A journalist and a food commentator (both male) told me that they feel that for single dining you can't beat an Indian or Chinese restaurant. It offers the most relaxing atmosphere and you are rarely made to feel awkward, even when the place is busy. Women should avoid Italian trattorias. The number of times I've entered one to the cry of 'Signorina eating alone?' puts me in mind of the Steve Martin film *The Lonely Guy*. Steve enters a restaurant and requests a single table. Immediately the room falls silent. A spotlight plays on him as he is escorted to a centre table laid for four. The three unwanted place-settings are then removed ostentatiously and noisily while all around groups of diners stare open-mouthed.

The aforementioned male journalist has noticed that when he books for one, the restaurant manager may suggest in his or her attitude that it would be preferable not to take the booking. Some restaurants make sure there is no booking. One female restaurant inspector, when making a reservation for a Saturday evening, has been told by a restaurant manager on several occasions (as soon as it is realised the booking is for one) that no tables are available. On a quiet Monday also, she has been refused a table point blank on the grounds that no one else was booked in and the restaurant was not prepared to take a single booking.

A positive approach is essential when you are being shown to your table. A single diner is rarely given a good table, as a report to *The Good Food Guide* noted: 'I took an instant dislike to the waiter. There was only one table occupied but he insisted on putting me on the smallest table he could find.' Whatever your sex, however empty the restaurant, the only way to a better-lit, more spacious table is to be assertive. I can recall a situation when I failed that test miserably. I was fairly new to restaurant inspecting and had booked for lunch at the rooftop restaurant at the Royal Garden Hotel, Kensington. The restaurant was fairly empty when I arrived and there were a number of coveted window tables free. I stupidly assumed that they were booked, as I was shown to a table for four against an inside wall. Only one other booking arrived after me, and I became quite resentful of the fact that the restaurant must have suspected a quiet lunch and I could have had a better table.

Eating out should not be a conflict. In Britain, a pretentious restaurant – of which there are many – offers a contest from the beginning between the waiter and the maître d' on the one hand, and the customer on the other, to establish authority. The waiting staff, through subtle and not so subtle movements, asserts immediate authority via presumably superior knowledge. The satisfied customer is usually one who has learned early on in the dining game that he or she is the one paying the bill and is not to be cowed into base subjection.

According to a former chief inspector with *The Good Food Guide* (who reckons she was patronised by middle-aged waiters – 'the Italian ones were hellish' – throughout the '70s), attitudes towards women have improved over the years. There are well-run restaurants and hotels where all, regardless of status, are made welcome. Therefore the shock of discrimination, the bad table, the indifferent or patronising service, the general lack of approbation by the staff, is made worse because it is usually unexpected and can strike in the unlikeliest of places – an exclusive hotel, a charming country restaurant or a smart cosmopolitan one. Surprisingly, pubs, especially the sort that get into food guides, are rarely guilty of such attitudes. In all the years that I have inspected alone in hotels, restaurants and pubs I can honestly say that I have received some of the friendliest service in pubs – once the most male of all preserves.

Whilst men can lose esteem in the eyes of the waiter for being alone – the waiter may surmise that they are from out of town and therefore not worth cultivating in terms of tips or return visits – women are often regarded with downright suspicion. As one very experienced female restaurant inspector put it: 'You are either there to be picked up or you are a guide inspector.' In a way, the situation of the single diner is like that of the disabled person 20 years ago. Special legislation and handling have improved the lot of the disabled person, while for single diners a radical reassessment of their needs by restaurant management is seemingly not yet on the agenda. As soon as hotels and restaurants realise this, the faster complaints will be turned into praise and increased custom. After all, single diners, male or female, do not always eat alone.

Educating the palate

Joanna Blythman, food journalist (*Scotland on Sunday, The Independent*), broadcaster, one-time delicatessen-owner, and mother of two, casts a critical eye over the eating habits of British children.

It is a harsh reality of contemporary life that most children emerge from their formal education at school, and nurturing in the home environment, without reasonable proficiency in life's most basic activity – how to feed oneself properly.

Until recently, the eating habits of British children were seen largely as a domestic problem for individual households – write to your agony aunt or magazine doctor if you are unduly worried. This is typical of the self-defeating fatalism which dominates Britain's attitudes to 'children's food'. Parents may moan, but within a framework that children are, by nature, conservative little monsters, with a penchant for everything that is bad and resistance to anything that is good. No surprise, then, that gravitation towards a no-effort, high-fat, high-sugar diet is seen as inevitable.

But while in Britain a certain amount of tolerant neglect in our attitudes to food has traditionally been acceptable, across the Channel a similar state of affairs is viewed almost as a major crisis. A national campaign has been launched to save the good name and reputation of French cuisine. The French, not known to be backward on gastronomic matters, are facing the problem head-on because, despite France's vanguard position among nations in fostering and cherishing a good-food culture, there are signs that all is not well there either. Britain tops the Euro-league of high spenders on fast food, but France is close behind in third position. So concerned is the French consumer about the impact of over-processed junk food on the diet of French children (63 per cent of French people polled said they felt that their 'culinary heritage' was under threat), that the ministries of Education and Culture have swung into action and added a food appreciation course to the curriculum in 200 primary schools thoughout Paris and the provinces. According to Jacques Lang, the government minister who has labelled cuisine as an official branch of French culture, the palates of young French people are also desperately in need of education. 'The struggle for quality is something important for a country which wants to preserve its traditions...traditions which are important for the economy, agriculture, gastronomy and many other elements of culture.' So France's best chefs, boulangers, fromagers and pâtissiers have been drafted into schools to give the pupils a 'leçon de goût'.

Chefs of the standing of Joël Robuchon, of the legendary Jamin restaurant in Paris, arrive with first-class produce in tow. Children are encouraged to take time to smell, taste and touch food and assess its quality beyond any pure cosmetic appeal. Our basic tastes – acid, salty, bitter and sweet – are explored using a small array of food on the desk before each child. Children taste lemon juice with and without sugar, bread with and without salt, and learn that a pot of yoghurt can be made to taste sweet just as well with one spoonful of sugar as half a dozen. By the end of the course, parents and educators hope that their children will be able to tell the difference, say, between a hand-made croissant from a local craft baker and its factory-produced counterpart from the nearest *hypermarché*, and appreciate the characteristics of a ripe Brie de Meaux when compared with the refrigerated and pasteurised equivalent. Next, the children learn to cook a meal and after that, who knows? French children might begin to realise how life-enhancing really good food can be, just as their forebears have always done.

Back in Britain, sensory awakening in the domain of taste is not top of any political or educational agenda. In schools, the dominant message that children are likely to pick up about food is in the dinner hall, where baked beans, low-grade meat products, chips and synthetic mousse desserts are often the order of the day. In Britain, despite the protestations of nutritionists and health activists, there are no nutritional guidelines set by government for school meals. Compulsory Competitive Tendering (CCT) has been introduced into the school meals service. The firm which comes up with the relevant number of meals at the lowest unit cost wins the contract – not necessarily the firm which takes delicious or nutritious food to heart. And with the exception of a token number of home economics and nutrition classes taken in the first two years of secondary school, formal culinary education is an optional part of the school curriculum – not the core subject that many campaigners for better food in Britain would like it to be.

One-off initiatives from outside the formal education system, however, suggest that contrary to the mythology which characterises children as instant gastronomic morons, interested only in food as fuel, there is in fact a massive reserve of enthusiasm for food and cooking just waiting to be tapped. The 'FutureCooks' competition, for instance, sponsored by Sainsbury, challenges children between the ages of 9 and 15 to create an imaginative meal (main course and pudding, to be cooked in 90 minutes and within a modest budget) for the cook, chef or cookery writer of their choice. FutureCooks is in its tenth year and adult judges continue to be amazed at the tangible degree of commitment and enthusiasm for food that contestants display. Recent finalists, some as young as 10, have shown themselves to be accomplished and capable, offering highly palatable offerings such as chickpea curry with naan bread, chicken roulade with sole mousseline, fish curry with lime and coconut and such desserts as glazed lemon flan, caramelised pears in raspberry sauce and exotic fruit brûlée.

These children are the lucky ones. For an ever-growing number of British children staggered eating has become normal; the family table an ever-receding memory. With this comes convenience food for children – breadcrumbed, burger-shaped, always highly processed – shamelessly hyped by the flickering screen. Where once a child might pick up basic cooking procedures and the pleasure of food by a process of absorption, the most exciting procedures to be witnessed in many kitchens nowadays are the loading of the dishwasher or the programming of the microwave.

This growing gastronomic illiteracy in Britain is coming home to roost, and is beginning to look like a massive dead hand which blocks the development of any good-food culture in Britain. It becomes an obstacle, with octopus-like tentacles, which touches almost all spheres of food-related activity. The wet-fishmonger finds that clients don't like to touch fish, preferring the uniform, sanitised fish finger. The butcher complains that the modern consumer is scared of cooking a joint of meat and relies instead on cook-chill lasagne which comes out of the freezer, goes into the microwave and lands on the table in under 15 minutes. Restaurateurs view with growing cynicism the public's ability to appreciate quality. Why go to the bother of making a chocolate mousse cake with expensive bitter chocolate when the majority of your customers can't tell it apart from a commercial concoction of vegetable fat, cocoa powder and sugar?

In black moments, stuck perhaps at a supermarket checkout between typically British trolley-loads of highly processed and adulterated food – with never a piece of fresh fruit, fish, vegetable or wholegrain in sight – it is easy to give into gloomy predictions. Does anyone do any real cooking any more? Is cooking your own food as rare as making your own clothes? Will it be capsules and cubes of food come 2001? If more children were FutureCooks, our culinary culture would be in good hands. But for most children, nothing can be taken for granted. A major initiative to educate the palates of future generations is required, and it's up to today's adults – parents, politicians, nutritionists, chefs, food producers, teachers – to provide it.

Inspectors of floors and walls

The inspection of food premises work of Environmental Health Officers

Tom Jaine

When the general public is quizzed about why they eat out and what they look for in a restaurant, the quality of food and cooking is always well down the list. Readers of *The Good Food Guide* doubtless operate to another set of rules; their meals are hardly enforced fuelling stops at which sustenance takes precedence over enjoyment. However, the constant winner in surveys is cleanliness. Hygiene, safety and health are important to everyone: a bad meal in crumbless surroundings is obviously preferable to a good dinner, no matter how attractive, in an ambience of haze and dirt. None the less, dirty restaurants, grubby kitchens and unsound practices persist. Partly, it is that eating is sometimes a 'distress activity', i.e. you have no choice about where you eat, but eat you must; partly, too, it is that many of us are short-sighted and we need eyes, and ears, to assess cleanliness on our behalf. Enter the Environmental Health Officer.

Many readers think *The Good Food Guide* and its inspectors should act as vigilante in these matters. A pleasant dream, but one that is impracticable. To see just how unrealistic, I spent some time with the Environmental Health departments of the City of Westminster and Bristol District Council in the county of Avon. Were readers to appreciate the level of expertise and amount of time taken in inspection of food premises, they too would see that no guide can undertake independent checks of any validity.

Concern with food-related infections and illness has been growing apace for the last five years. There is little point in rehearsing the scandals here. The most obvious development in catering has been the growth in the number of restaurants and eating-houses and the tremendous increase, throughout Britain, in the number of meals consumed outside the home. These statistics alone would be sufficient to account for much of the apparent rise in food-related sickness. Add to that changes in technology such as freezing, cook-chill and microwaves, as well as the difficulties experienced in production of 'chicken' and 'beef', and the potential for disaster is great.

Natural optimists counter that the jeremiahs always deal in 'potential' and rarely in past fact. 'We have always made our mayonnaise like this, we never refrigerate it, we always add the old to the new as we remake it in the morning, and we've never had any complaints,' might go the caterer's cry. Well, there was an airport kitchen that did just that, and its home-made mayonnaise added class to the sandwiches. But, one day, it all went horribly wrong and a plane-load of holidaymakers fetched up in their hotel with a major outbreak of salmonella poisoning. The assumption was that 'the foreigners had caused it', but eventually it was traced back to that mayonnaise. A one-off, perhaps, but accidents need preventing by sound practice, and accidents are on the increase.

With cases like this in mind, the government finally introduced the Food Safety Act and the Food Hygiene (Amendment) Regulations, which came into force at the beginning of 1991. Many campaigners have said they do not go far enough: for instance, the food temperature regimes are needlessly complicated (they ultimately impose two different temperatures, depending on foodstuff), thus rendering them more difficult to enforce. That said, they have strengthened the hand of the officers – if only there were more of them – and should result in an improvement over time.

EHOs sometimes admit that they are called 'inspectors of floors and walls' because they spend a deal of time, when visiting premises, on their knees, torch in hand, looking at those grubby corners, that junction of floor and skirting, which kitchen porters shrink from exploring on a daily, or even weekly, basis. At just those fault-lines, dirt builds up, the envelope that should surround the kitchen is punctured, rodents and insects feed, lurk and enter. It is a tell-tale zone, one which will indicate sound performance of daily tasks or alert the officer to a lack of routine and defective management.

Downcast restaurateurs, thinking that EHOs are sent to plague them in the innocent pursuit of their occupation, reckon that they concern themselves only with externals – hence the rather dismissive appellation above. Dismissal sometimes turns to fury, even violence (we crossed the street at least once in our tour of Westminster to avoid potential outburst from 'wronged victims of the establishment'). But these externals do matter, for the obvious reasons – how, for example, would the 'health' food shop proprietor in Bristol explain away mouse droppings mingling with open sacks of provender in filthy storerooms? – and because the EHO is looking for signs of good regimes in cleaning, food storage, food use and food service.

I had not realised how far along this road the Environmental Health service had travelled. The main aims of its work, beyond enforcement of regulations, are education and the raising of management standards. Environmental Health departments run their own food-handling courses, or combine with other public and private bodies to do so. Basic training in food handling will become universal: leaflets in Chinese and other minority languages, as well as oral instruction, are extending the message throughout the restaurant community. This programme, to be compulsory by 1992, may not amount to a high-level degree course, but some advice does stick and the general effect should be of improved kitchen practice.

In very similar fashion, inspections of a catering premises will include enquiries about the cleaning routine (if it's written down, at least it's being thought about, even if someone forgets to get out the mop and bucket); the written record of refrigerator temperatures; the record of rodent-control visits; and the means by which stock rotation is ensured. Add to this a concern for staff safety – the existence of a first-aid box is always a bugbear – which has a knock-on effect on good hygiene, as well as being part of the EHO's statutory remit.

The immediate reason for this concern with systems, as well as particular instances of bad practice, is that the Food Safety Act allows a defence of 'due diligence' to transgressors of the provisions. In other words, some mitigation may be allowed if a producer can show all reasonable precautions against contamination or disaster were taken.

No one pretends that sound management routines are the whole answer, but their existence is advantageous. Nor is massive investment in new plant and equipment always a guarantee of cleanliness – there have been notorious cases of infestation in premises recently kitted out – though it does help. Equipment on wheels so that cleaning can be rapid and complete, and walls and floors constructed using modern materials that can be washed repeatedly without deterioration, will always make the task easier, although in my tour of Westminster it was notable that the restaurant with concerned management and equipment installed 20 years ago outperformed the stainless steel wonder with sloppy staff at every turn.

Although food premises have only to be registered with, not licensed by, the Environmental Health Department, which means that the EHO does not have the power of anticipation (by refusing a licence) but only of enforcement (after registration), there are some useful developments in the Food Safety Act. One is strategic. A regime of management is being imposed on the EHOs themselves through 'risk assessment'. This means that all food premises are given points according to their nature and their performance. High scores demand frequent visits. It is a way of envisaging the whole brief that may impose its own discipline on enforcement, and act as a measure of performance from year to year. Another is more specific. EHOs now have the power of summary closure. Before, they had to apply first to a magistrate – allowing three days' grace. This power has long been needed, and will be used to consumers' benefit. The means of day-to-day enforcement have also been formalised and strengthened by the introduction of Improvement Notices. These formal notifications of works required to bring premises up to scratch do away with much less satisfactory, and necessarily informal, letters and conversations that made enforcement in the courts even more difficult than it might have been.

Food poisoning is not on the way out, but it is worth noting the existence of a body of people who are committed to seeing it disappear wherever possible. In large part, their attentions are not frivolous – there is too much work on hand to waste time pursuing minutiae. It will be through them that improvement comes and we should support their work at all turns. It is, after all, our stomachs that pray for survival.

Musical meals

Tom Jaine

This year, we have responded to readers' letters and reports by indicating more clearly where it is possible to eat a meal without being bothered by music. Aural invasion is much the same as any other social pollution, such as smoking or bad smells. There is no escaping it, you are not consulted about it and it may affect your simple enjoyment of conversation, eating and drinking – or even thinking – to a greater degree than the person bopping away to the beat can even begin to imagine. Recorded music in public places has become too prevalent, and is probably too much liked ever to be banned – though victims will recall with joy the cancellation of London Underground's crackly canned-music experiment on Tottenham Court Road station. The point of *The Good Food Guide*, however, is to inform about options. We built a specific enquiry into this year's questionnaire to establishments, which sought a categorical statement that music is *never* played in the dining-room. Where we were given such assurances we are now indicating this in the rubric by the words 'no music'.

As a general rule, music in metropolitan and big-city restaurants is restricted to the cheaper, faster-turnover places that are often aiming for a younger market. True, many large hotels seem convinced that even a lift-ride cannot be undertaken without musical accompaniment, but a lot of good restaurants seem happy to accept the buzz of conversation and the bustle of waiters delivering food as sufficient chords of content. The problem lies more in the country.

Music has been accepted by market researchers and time-and-motion experts as a potent weapon. 'Music while you work' was a devilish scheme of wartime broadcasters to keep operatives happy and increase productivity – along the same behaviourist lines as the correlation between higher light intensity in factories and greater output. Shops were persuaded too that the right sort of music would help sales. Either the customer feels happy and therefore spends more (the incessant pop music of fashion boutiques supposedly encourages this) or the trolley-pusher is tempted to linger a few more minutes in each supermarket aisle, producing more shopping opportunities. The arguments are not quite the same in restaurants, but they are still potent enough to persuade many owners to spend good money on licences from the Performing Rights Society and Phonographic Performance Limited.

The main plank of the music supporters' defence is that quiet restaurants are boring, if not horrid, and that music serves as 'white noise' to dull the clanks and clatters of the staff; to allow people to speak at more than a whisper without being overheard; and to paper over the cracks in a couple's moribund conversational skills. This is the school that asks: after 20 years of marriage, what is there left to talk about? The arguments for music can be persuasive. Many country restaurants can be deathly quiet; many staff do clatter in an unprepossessing way; the design of many restaurants – mere adaptations of private houses – is inadequate for promoting a sense of occasion, of society and of enjoyment. If you are stuck in a small dining-room with three other tables for two people and no view beyond the patch of hydrangeas (fast fading in the gloaming), no choice on the menu and no sense of being part of a larger unit, then you may start praying for Rachmaninov to come to the rescue.

Pro-music people might stand on firmer ground if they paid attention to certain weaknesses in what music is chosen. Taste differs. It is not a question of 'better' or 'worse' music, though many supporters would make a pitch for that. It is one of incompatability. Someone who likes Strauss may hate Handel; Mantovani is not an adequate substitute for early Rolling Stones; traditional jazz may distress beboppers. What often follows from this is that the establishment plays safe and sticks to the 'old favourites'. If it's classical, it has to be Vivaldi or the Brandenburgs; if it's modern, it may be some nameless orchestra doing old favourites. That's when the aural wallpaper begins: the worst thing of all.

The second group of problems, inadequately addressed by so many places, concerns how the music is presented. It is not good enough for managers, in response to a complaint, to shrug their shoulders and claim that the volume cannot be reduced; it is, to say the least, stupid to confess that the CDs are stacked six-high on an autochanger and the sequence cannot be interrupted; it would help if the same piece were not put on endless loops to repeat the evening through; it would also improve everyone's enjoyment if the climax of one work were not interrupted by the introduction of another because the staff, who weren't listening anyway, got bored.

These are some, just some, reasons why silence is golden: why more of us should ask for the music to be turned down or off; why we should talk to each other more, even shout and scream; and why restaurant owners should not think of music as a prop, but consider instead how better to design their dining-rooms so that they are interesting, enlivening and enjoyable places in which to be.

Just so that the *Guide* is not accused of blind prejudice, it should be admitted that some restaurateurs seem able to use music as an enriching element to the entertainment mix of a meal out. There are comparisons with medieval minstrels in their galleries, and many other historical links of music to formal, celebratory dining. Country dinners do have that 'event' aspect that a city business meal does not share. One former restaurateur wrote to us with a defence of her musical activities. Her first essays with a reel-to-reel tape recorder – 'threading it again while the veg burned was a real hassle' – were in the '60s. 'We had a resident who had something the matter with her neck, so she was forced to sit unbending and erect. This apparent hauteur had such an effect on other diners that they ate gingerly in total silence, punctuated by the odd whispered request. So I gave in to music. I recorded extracts from piano concertos and symphonies which I thought suitable.' Would that everyone took such care. For those readers in the capital who can't bear music with *anything*, a new guide, *Muzak-Free London* (Kogan Page) gives the low-down on quiet shops, quiet cafés, quiet everything.

What to drink in 1992

Here are some pointers to help you through a wine list and come out smiling. The advice is not comprehensive; it could not be without filling page after page with figures and notations. It does, however, encourage exploration of areas neglected by customers, though often generously stocked by restaurants; offer brief notes on the classic regions; and suggest broad avenues of approach to other regions and wine-producing countries.

Recommendations have to take into account the immense gulf that separates the good restaurant from the barely competent. In so many instances, wise words fall on stony ground because the list, summary in the extreme, has been put together by people who know and care little about wine, whose advice would not be worth listening to, and whose motives are profit and simplicity of administration. Everything comes from a single wholesaler; everything has a name recognisable to the most inexperienced wine-drinker; everything is cheap but probably heavily marked-up. Not much better are those lists composed by people who again care little about the wine itself, but think a lot about prestige. The names will sound good, but either the year or the source will be suspect. A cellar may be non-existent, the stock a single bottle of each 'bin', ready to serve. The profit margins will be high.

The good lists (the best get our bottle or glass awards) will show real enthusiasm. Wines will be chosen because they offer good value and because they taste excellent, not on name alone. Value does not always mean economy; quality costs. Often, more than one merchant will be used – though a 'tied' house is not necessarily a bad thing, since a good merchant can make a restaurant worth visiting.

When buying a wine in a restaurant, it is worth bearing in mind that most places will be doubling the price, as well as adding VAT. This means that a £6 bottle will have started off as a very cheap drink. If you take away distribution, bottling, tax and duty from that first price, the wine itself may be worth no more than a few pence. It is, therefore, worth paying a bit more than the minimum, especially in a place that cares about wine. After £25, fashion and rarity may start affecting value.

While many restaurant proprietors impose a percentage mark-up across their whole range of wine, there are others that attempt a sliding scale. If the bottle costs the proprietor £50, he or she looks for a standard gross profit and adds VAT. This is better than doubling the cost price, and much better than the London norm of trebling it – both practices effectively put fine wines within reach of only corporate purses. In the *Guide*, we usually identify within an entry those places that use a sliding scale. When discussing the vexed question of mark-up, the moralists – outraged at the sight of a bottle that they bought in the supermarket last week at £6.50 reposing on the list at £18 – need to remember that a restaurant requires a certain revenue to survive. How that money is extracted from the customer is to an extent within the discretion of the proprietor. If he or she chooses to levy a lot from wine-drinkers, the eaters among us may profit from lower food prices. It is, however, particularly hard for makers of fine wine whose product is made the more exclusive by across-the-board percentage mark-ups.

If you feel confidence in the wine list, it is worth placing a similar trust in the man or woman who composed it. This person should know what each bottle tastes like. If you have never heard of many of the alternatives, do not flinch from asking advice. A good restaurant will often introduce you to new and exciting regions and wine-makers.

Two unjustly neglected wine regions: Alsace and the Rhône

Pleading for France may seem misplaced, but these two areas are special cases. The affection of restaurateurs for them is manifested by the disproportionate number of Rhônes and Alsaces on good lists, reflecting their good value and high quality. Paradoxically, this enthusiasm is sometimes reciprocated by neglect on the part of the customers.

Alsace is a safe bet. Dullness can be a fault in Alsace wines, but generally they are dry, characterful and skilfully made. Small vineyards and part-time growers abound in the region so co-operative wineries prevail and are reliable. Current favourite co-ops in the UK are Turckheim and Pfaffenheim. Equally, large companies with vineyards of their own, such as Hugel and Trimbach, produce delightful wine of fine value, some of it outstanding. New names appear with regularity, especially on good lists; these are individual growers, sought out by adventurous wine merchants. Such names include Rolly Gassmann, Kreydenweiss, Cattin and Stentz. Don't be disconcerted by unfamiliar names; in a good list they are almost guaranteed to please. Alsaces offer so much more personality per pound sterling than a lacklustre Chardonnay from Burgundy at the same price or higher.

With reservations for 1987, recent years in Alsace have been good to excellent. Anything from a *grand cru* vineyard needs two or three years in bottle; *vendange tardive* (which may be sweet or dry) may need up to a decade to give of its best.

Châteauneuf-du-Pape and Côte Rôtie share a river – the Rhône – but are 100 miles apart. They also share the neglect of the British customer. A new generation of wines from Hermitage and Côte Rôtie can be expected to mature, or certainly make attractive drinking, earlier and more reliably than they used to, while still being robust. Lesser appellations of the northern Rhône, for instance St-Joseph and Crozes Hermitage, may often come from large producers, yet they are meaty, peppery wines that will be ready a year or two from vintage at modest price. Recent vintages are sound to excellent. More exalted bottles need time, but wines from 1987 may be offered and may be ready. 1986 was variable and advice should be sought. The excellent 1985s are still too young from the best appellations; 1984 or 1983 will be more satisfying. Prices closely reflect quality. Top growers such as Jamet, Clape and Chave command high prices, but are still good value. Less well-known growers in a good list are often a bargain.

Of white northern Rhônes, Condrieu is perhaps the most reliable. Lately many smaller growers have been sought out. Drink within three years of vintage (recent years have all been good). Unless struck by curiosity, avoid the most famous name from this village, Ch. Grillet. Its celebrity has made its price unrealistic. White Hermitage, by contrast, is hostage to unpredictability; it can be fine, and fair value, but it may be wise to seek advice.

Further south, Châteauneuf, Gigondas and many wines under the humble Côtes du Rhône appellation have benefited from modern practices. Allied with respect for tradition, quality is rising fast. In a good list, there should be a number of choices from this area. Gigondas often represents the best value. The southern Rhône has seen a run of good vintages, apart from 1987 when many of the better growers did not bottle. The reputation of these wines for ageing seems sometimes misplaced. Some Châteauneuf growers have great skill in making for long maturity, and older bottles from Jaboulet often repay dividends handsomely, but in 1992 you may want reassurance before ordering anything older than 1981.

Some up-and-coming wine regions: Italy, Jerez (sherry), Provence and south-west France, New Zealand, the upper Loire

Every year, a new wine-producing region, or even country, begins to figure on UK shippers' lists. We should pride ourselves on the extraordinarily wide range of wines available at any moment for purchase and experiment. It is certainly greater than in almost any other developed country. A contradiction, perhaps, is that restaurant wine lists have ever been monuments to conservatism. The endless roll-call of Chablis, Sancerre and Nuits-St-Georges is stultifying; the wines seem bought by name alone, their presence justified by the fact that the customer will recognise them – let the quality go hang. All this is beginning to change. Regulations in the country of origin have made look-alike and sound-alike wines more difficult to produce, thus increasing the cost of the real thing. The value and quality of new alternatives are so transparent that even the most ignorant of wine-buyers will give a novelty a chance. Customers are being educated. Simultaneously, there is ferment among the wine-makers and the consequences of experiment and new initiatives are sensational.

The following paragraphs merely identify a very few regions which have begun to receive due credit on British wine lists and whose bottles you should seriously consider buying.

Italy

The perseverance of a bunch of Italophile wine merchants has shifted the balance of Italian wine available here from awful to excellent. Choosing Italian is now less of a lottery. Apart from the exceptional year, the lacklustre efforts of the past are being replaced by satisfyingly fruity wines retaining the steely Italian core that makes them such good partners of food. Bargains are unlikely, but value is assured, especially on a good list which will probably carry fine examples of familiar names such as Barolo, Barbaresco, Valpolicella and Chianti. These make a real alternative to a classic French.

Italy has also seen the emergence of high-class table wines – vini da tavola. Wine-makers who wish to experiment with noble grape varieties, particularly from France, are unable to satisfy the regulations that govern the production of the traditional names. They are therefore constrained to call their wines 'table wine'; but these wines are more than this, and cost more too. Of stunning depth and complexity, with names that sound more like dogs (la Poja, Balifico or Gri) their value is still good. However, many wines younger than 1987 are probably not worth the inevitably high price; these bottles need age.

Several recent books provide listings of Italian growers and estates. Consign some names to memory. In Piedmont, many of the top producers make simple varietal wines – Nebbiolo del Langhe and Dolcetto, for example – while in Chianti a *normale* from the best estates can be a snip, even though we are conditioned to esteem *riservas* more highly.

Of recent vintages, 1986 produced good, forward wines across northern Italy. 1985 will be attractive but the best should stay in the cellar. In Piedmont and Tuscany, 1982 resulted in high quality, but earlier vintages may sometimes present something of a gamble. Since 1985, vintages have been good or excellent for all the simpler wines.

Jerez

The sale of sherry to the British public has been a no-growth problem for some years. Jerez is suffering from over-production. Yet the fact is that quality has been improving dramatically. This may be linked to the growth of export of specialist sherries, begun by Bodegas Lustau in the 1980s. In good restaurants, vibrant manzanillas and finos are finding their way off the aperitif shelf and on to the wine list, making fine accompaniments to first courses. Although they are still dry, extraordinarily rich and nutty olorosos and amontillados can score with desserts.

Provence, south-west France and the Midi

An arc across southern France, from Gascony to the west, to Aix in the east, takes in a host of small appellations. The central area, from Cahors to the Rhône, used to be the source of France's wine lake: undifferentiated liquids good only for getting drunk cheaply or for distilling. The only way out for ambitious growers was to go for quality: to try new and nobler grape types and brush up their wine-making practices. Good low-priced wines from the ubiquitous Ugni Blanc grape in Gascony, and many decently made reds from new plantings of Cabernet in areas like Corbières are the staple for enjoyable house wines. Many restaurants with exalted wine lists offer interest and economic relief with house selections drawing from these areas. Serious and good growers are found, some following Italian practice and experimenting with wholly new sorts of wine for their area (such as the Cabernet from the Dom. de Trévallon) or deepening and improving existing characteristics (like the Bandols from Mas de la Rouvière on the Côte d'Azur). The downside of this new development is that dull wines are still coming our way and some knowledge on the part of the buyer is necessary.

New Zealand

A partnership of inspired wine-making and a sympathetic government has brought us remarkable wines. Sharing the generosity of fruit of their Australian cousins, they have qualities of their own: further dimensions of complexity and natural balance (invidious comparisons when Australians such as Coonawarra, Margaret River and Piper's Brook come to mind) give the Sauvignon grape a character quite apart from that achieved in the Loire. Big growers like Nobilo and Montana produce reliable and modestly priced wines, frequently seen on good wine lists; prices of Cloudy Bay strain credibility but wines from many smaller growers remain fine value. Some delectably rich dessert wines are now appearing.

Sancerre substitutes

You may have noticed that a Sancerre is no longer priced in single figures. Even so, it remains one of the most popular restaurant wines. For a lot less money, that wonderful fix of exuberant freshness and gooseberry flavour can still be found. The Sauvignon Blanc grape is used in the villages of Menetou-Salon, Reuilly and Quincy. They measure up to much of the output of Sancerre, even if not to the better growers. Wine merchants with a taste for adventure, and an interest in lesser-known appellations, have been stocking them for some years and generally have no truck with indifferent growers. So you can expect fair value if you find them on a list. Drink them young.

The classic areas

Burgundy

The good vineyards of Burgundy occupy a tiny area by comparison with those of Bordeaux. That profusion of petits châteaux which provides a price buffer before you hit the classified heights of claret has no equivalent in Burgundy. For reliable, mid-priced Pinot Noir and Chardonnay, growers and merchants follow two courses. On the Cote d'Or many of the best growers make 'village wines' with an appellation such as Côte de Nuits Villages or just straight AC Bourgogne. Made from the fruit of young vines or grown on less expensive patches of soil they may lack finesse; made under the eye of an expert they are a good way to sample Pinot Noir and Chardonnay. The Hautes Côtes offer similar economy.

Searching out modestly priced Chardonnay of Burgundian provenance is any spirited wine merchant's goal. Chablis prices lurch wildly: at the moment the wine is good value, but recent extensions to the vineyard area that can obtain *appellation contrôlée* status have meant that more indifferent wine has found its way on to lists. In a good list, a straight Chablis should be reliable in 1992.

To the south, the Mâconnais has been yielding some very fine wines from growers new to the English market. Unfortunately, dullness is still a problem with Mâcon from big shippers. It is less so with Pouilly-Fuissé and its cheaper neighbour St-Véran, but Fuissé is not always worth the premium for the name. The wines of Ch. Fuissé are an exception; they may cost as much as a fine Côte de Beaune white, but quality is very fine.

The adage 'look to the grower' not the village, applies with particular force in Burgundy. Too many bottles promise more than they deliver. Grand village and vineyard names may delude the unwary, so always be sure to have confidence in the grower or négociant before spending large sums.

As a last resort, here is some very general comment on burgundy vintages. For red wines, 1980 and 1982 are good, the best of 1983 is not yet ready, but 1984 and 1985 are good, especially from the best growers. Avoid 1986 from Côte de Beaune, but the Côte de Nuits vintage was acceptable. All subsequent years have been good, though the best wines need longer to mature. 1989 could be especially appealing for lower-priced wines.

For white wines, all but 1982 should be at least acceptable, although lesser wines, such as 1985 from the Mâconnais may be past their best. Wines that cost more than, say, £20 should be left for a year or two longer if the vintage offered is 1988 or 1989. Restaurants and merchants make no bones about selling completely immature wines (as well as Muscadets or other *vins courants* well over the hill). A Pouilly Fuissé, or a White Rully or Mercurey from the Côte Chalonnaise, from 1987 or 1988 could be a satisfactory choice. 1989 Chablis is fine but is so uncharacteristically fruity that an Australian Chardonnay may serve as well, and cost less.

Bordeaux

Among 3,600 unclassified properties in the Bordeaux region there is a good collection of petits châteaux, crus bourgeois and wines from appellations such as Fronsac, the outlying areas of St-Emilion and Pomerol, and the Côtes de Bourg and Blaye. These provide reliable and enjoyable drinking and should be priced between £10 and £15. In a good list an unknown Médoc is likely to be well-chosen and a bargain. UK wine merchants work hard to locate decent, low-priced clarets and the best succeed. However, there is much that is indifferent and this is bought by less scrupulous merchants and stocked by lacklustre restaurants. Where you have little confidence in the wine-buying skills of the house, a New World Cabernet will be a safer bet. On poor lists, avoid 1980 and 1984 clarets. These 'off-vintages' did yield decent wine in skilled hands and it will then be good value.

Classified growths command high prices and it is a waste of time to drink wines of vintages more recent than 1983, except for 1984 and 1987, which are both forward. Lesser wines, especially those under about £12, make enjoyable, robust drinking two or three years from vintage. Recent years have been good without exception. Pre-1980, unless you are familiar with the property or have a sound recommendation, should be the preserve of the classified. Here, 1979s are attractive and need drinking up; hence they may be at favourable prices. 1978 and 1970 command exceptionally high prices. For differing reasons, any wines from 1971, 1975 and 1976 should be treated with caution: ask first. 1973, 1974 and 1977 can be ignored.

Champagne

Much youthful, disappointing champagne is sold. In a good restaurant a roll-call of the Grandes Marques – Veuve Clicquot, Bollinger and the rest – will be offered. The first name in the list, however, will probably be unfamiliar. Take it; many genuine finds of small, high-quality producers, free from heavy marketing costs, provide excellent value. A good restaurant should have chosen a decent example. In a place not so enthusiastic about its wines, reverse the procedure. That unfamiliar name will be a cover for deserved obscurity. Unless it is the cheap, cheerful and reliable Asti Spumante, other bubblies are best treated with caution, though a good list may have come up with a good-value Australian, Vouvray or Crémant d'Alsace. It is worth trying Australian and New Zealand sparklers made in co-operation with a French house, such as Mumm or Deutz.

In brief

England

Wine-making has come a long way in the last few years, helped greatly by two hot summers. Good wine lists have occasionally excellent examples of the breed and it is worth experimenting. English wines are not long keepers.

Spain

An uncertain patch for Riojas is perhaps overcome, and reservas are again good value. The Toro region is very good, especially inexpensive examples. Murrieta and possibly CVNE white Rioja apart, Spanish whites can be decent enough but not worth a high price.

Australia

Western Australia, Coonawarra and Tasmania are worth searching out. In a good restaurant quality from Australia should be remarkable; many well-trained wine-makers and a firmer grip on the use of new oak make almost anything worth trying. Semillons have particularly pleased. Prices reflect quality; it is worth spending more rather than less. Even from a poor list, Australia can be a good, cheap, safe choice.

Germany

Traditional late-picked examples – Spätlese and above – from good names are reliable and fairly priced, but newer-style dry and half-dry wines have yet to convince resoundingly. Prices are too high for dull wines.

Chile

Lower-priced wines are competent but unexciting; on a good list the middle-priced are worth trying.

Central Europe

Bulgaria, especially Cabernet and Merlot of reserve quality, are meaty and good value. The cheapest of these wines are unreliable, with too much variation in batches.

USA

California wine-makers have relaxed and are producing wines less likely to deliver a knock-out. Good 'second wines' are coming in from top wineries and represent fine value. Up-and-coming are Washington State and Oregon, especially their Pinot Noirs. These are worth trying in a good list; cheaper examples tend to dullness, just as very cheap Californians are not worth buying.

Loire valley

There is fine, steady value here. Many inexpensive and distinctive reds from the Cabernet Franc grape have begun to be stocked. They make refreshing drinking, sometimes distinguished, especially in good, hot, years. Loire reds in a bad year are awful.

Austria

Dessert wines are especially fine value.

Portugal

Sturdy wines from local grape varieties should be mid-priced. Unless they have been recommended, avoid older years which may be dried out.

Your rights in restaurants

A restaurant is legally obliged to provide you with a meal and service which are of a reasonable standard, and failure to do so may give you the right to sue for breach of contract. However, it is important to remember that the reasonableness or otherwise of both the meal and the service must be judged on the type of restaurant in question.

Dining out should be a pleasurable experience. None the less, it is as well to be aware of your basic legal rights just in case you find yourself in an awkward situation, like one of these:

You book a table in advance but when you arrive the manager says there's been a mistake and there's no room.
When you book, you're making a contract with the restaurant and it must give you a table, in reasonable time. If it doesn't, it's in breach of contract and you can claim a reasonable sum to cover any expenses you had as a result, e.g. travelling costs.

You go into a restaurant and, as you sit and look at the menu, you realise the meal is going to be much more expensive than you thought.
A restaurant must display a menu and a wine list outside, or immediately inside the door – so check the prices before you sit down. Prices shown must be inclusive of VAT. If they aren't, tell the local Trading Standards Officer (see 'The law enforcers', below).

The restaurant says it doesn't serve children. Can you insist it does so?
No – however unfair it may seem. A restaurant can turn away anyone, without giving a reason, except on grounds of sex, race, colour or ethnic origin.

You only want a cup of coffee but the waiter tells you there's a minimum charge of £3 per person.
A restaurant must display any minimum charge or cover charge outside or immediately inside the door. If no charge is indicated, tell the local Trading Standards Officer. You do not have to pay the charge if it is not displayed. Under a new Code of Practice (see below) menus are supposed to show cover and minimum charges as prominently as any other charges.

The bill comes to quite a bit more than you expected and has had 10 per cent service charge added. Do you have to pay this?
As with the minimum charge, the restaurant must display outside or immediately inside the door any service charge to be automatically included in the bill. If it is displayed, you should pay it unless there was something specifically wrong with the service. But if a service charge is not

clearly indicated, you don't have to pay – it's up to you whether to tip and, if you do, by how much.

A Code of Practice, introduced in March 1989 under the Consumer Protection Act, says restaurants should include any compulsory service charges *within* the price for each item (rather than adding a percentage to the total bill). This would make it easier for customers to see at a glance how much they'll have to pay. But restaurants only have to do this 'wherever practicable'. The Code also recommends that restaurants do not suggest optional sums for service or other items, so menus and bills should not say, 'We suggest an optional 10 per cent gratuity'.

The Code is not legally binding, although if the restaurant is prosecuted the court will take into account whether it has been followed.

You go into a restaurant because your favourite dish is on the menu. But the waitress says it's 'off' today. Your second choice isn't available either.
A restaurant doesn't have to be able to serve all items on the menu, although it should have most. If you think the restaurant is genuinely trying to mislead people, tell the local Trading Standards Officer.

You order 'fresh fruit salad', yet it's obviously out of a tin.
Under the Trade Descriptions Act, a restaurant must provide food and drink as described on the menu or by the waiter. If you think what you're served doesn't match the description, don't start eating. Complain immediately and ask for something else. You could also tell the local Trading Standards Officer that the restaurant is misleading customers.

Your fish arrives not properly cooked – it's still cold in the middle.
Under the Supply of Goods and Services Act (and under common law in Scotland), restaurants must prepare food with reasonable care and skill. If this does not appear to be the case, do not eat the dish you have been served and then complain. If you don't manage to get things put right, you can deduct what you think is a fair sum from the bill (see 'Claiming your rights', below). Alternatively, make it clear that you are paying 'under protest', so you can claim compensation later.

You get a nasty stomach upset after eating out at a restaurant. You think the lamb hotpot was to blame.
If you think your illness is a result of a restaurant meal, tell your doctor and the local Environmental Health Officer (see 'The law enforcers', below). The EHO can investigate the incident and may decide to prosecute; under the Food Act, it's a criminal offence for a restaurant to serve food unfit for human consumption. If it can be proved that the restaurant caused your illness – which can be difficult – it could be fined and made to compensate you. In serious cases, it may be worth getting legal advice about suing the restaurant yourself.

You're kept waiting an hour before the waiter takes your order. When you complain, the waiter is rude to you.
A restaurant must give you a reasonable standard of service. If it doesn't, you can refuse to pay all or part of the service charge, even if it's automatically included in the bill.

The waitress drops a dish and the food goes all over your new suit.
If it's the restaurant's fault that you've had food or drink spilled on you, you can claim the cost of cleaning. If the article of clothing can't be cleaned, you can claim the cost of a new one.

You've come out for a leisurely evening but the waiter has different ideas. He whips dishes away before you've finished eating and then presents you with the bill.
A restaurant must give you reasonable time to finish your meal and have a cup of coffee, bearing in mind the type of restaurant and what time it is. If you think you've been unreasonably rushed, complain and don't pay part or all of the service charge.

The people on the next table are smoking. The smoke's wafting in your direction and is spoiling your meal. Can you get the manager to tell them to stop?
The manager can't insist on people not smoking, unless it's specifically a no-smoking restaurant or a no-smoking area. If it is, smokers could be asked to leave if they don't stop. If it's important to you, check beforehand what the smoking arrangements are.

You're short of cash so you ask if you can pay by credit card. The restaurant says 'no'.
A restaurant doesn't have to accept payment by credit card – or even by cheque – unless it had agreed to do so beforehand, or there's a sign on the door. So check first.

You're paying by credit card. When the waiter gives you the voucher to sign you see the total has been left blank, presumably in the hope you'll add something extra for service. Do you have to pay?
Be careful – you could end up paying for service twice. Check whether service is compulsory and, if it is, whether the charge has already been added to the bill. If it has, then there's no reason why you should add anything extra. We think it's misleading of restaurants to present vouchers in this way when service is already included, although it's not illegal, and we indicate at the end of a *Good Food Guide* entry whether credit cards are presented 'closed' (with the total entered). If the service charge is not compulsory, then it's up to you whether you add any more and, if so, how much.

You give your coat to the waitress to hang up. By the time you leave, it has disappeared.
A restaurant must take reasonable care of your belongings if they're left in a cloakroom. If it doesn't you may claim compensation for any damage or loss. Notices limiting the restaurant's liability are valid only if they're

reasonable and prominently displayed. If there's no cloakroom, make sure you ask staff to put your coat or other belongings in a safe place, otherwise you won't be entitled to any compensation.

Claiming your rights

1. Try to sort out your problem on the spot. Ask to speak to the manager, explain what the problem is and say what you want done, for instance, a substitute dish provided. Don't be afraid to make a fuss.
2. If you're not able to come to an agreement with the manager, then you have two options: to deduct a suitable amount from the bill (it's then up to the restaurant to sue you for the balance if it doesn't agree); or to make any payment you're not happy about 'under protest' (put this down in writing when you make the payment). That way you can try to claim it back later by suing under the small claims procedure (see below).
3. If you're still not happy, get advice on your legal position. You can get free advice from Citizens Advice Bureaux, Law Centres and Consumer Advice Centres. The Trading Standards department of the restaurant's local authority may also be able to help. If you go to a solicitor, check first how much it's likely to cost you. Many solicitors offer a half-hour interview for a fixed fee of £5. Or you can join **Which? Personal Service**, which gives advice and help to individual members (write to Which? Personal Service, Consumers' Association, 2 Marylebone Road, London NW1 4DX for details).
4. When you've found out where you stand, write to the restaurant, stating what the problem was and what you want done about it.
5. If you have no success, and think you have a strong case, you can sue under the small claims procedure in the county court. In England, Wales and Northern Ireland, the maximum you can claim is £500. You won't need a solicitor. Just issuing a summons may spur the restaurant into action. In Scotland, claims of under £750 are heard under the small claims procedure of the Sheriff Court.

The law enforcers

The job of enforcing many of the laws affecting restaurants, and which protect consumers' rights, is not done by the police but by officials employed by the local authority. **Environmental Health Officers** enforce food hygiene laws and regulations. They investigate complaints by the public and make routine visits to restaurants – although they're very overstretched and these visits are far fewer in number than is desirable given the immense increase in the number of eating establishments over the last decade.

Trading Standards Officers enforce the law about factual descriptions of goods and services. They will investigate complaints about false or misleading claims made by restaurants, or misleading indications of prices.

If EHOs or TSOs have enough evidence that restaurants have committed a criminal offence, they can prosecute. If found guilty, restaurants can be fined and the customer awarded compensation.

Restaurants' rights

You book a table for four at a country restaurant. But the car won't start and you decide not to go.
If you book a table at a restaurant, you must turn up in reasonable time. If you don't keep your booking, or are very late, you're in breach of contract and the restaurant could sue you for compensation. Let the restaurant know as soon as possible if you can't make it, so the restaurant can reduce its loss by re-allocating the table. Some restaurants now take customers' credit card numbers when they book, and warn them that if they don't turn up a charge will be made. As long as they tell you beforehand, restaurants are within their rights to do this. But the charge should only be reasonable compensation for their loss of profit, not a penalty.

You go out for a meal with relatives but a row develops between feuding members of the family. The manager says the shouting is disturbing other customers and asks you to leave.
You must behave reasonably in a restaurant, otherwise the restaurant may refuse to serve you and ask you to leave.

You can't be bothered to change out of your old gardening clothes before going out for Sunday lunch. The manager refuses to give you a table.
If you are not dressed suitably, the restaurant may refuse to give you a table, even if you've booked.

You've just had the worst meal of your life – it was inedible. Do you have to pay?
You must pay the bill unless you have genuine cause for complaint, in which case you may deduct what you think is a fair amount as compensation. Explain exactly why and, if asked, leave your correct name and address. It's then up to the restaurant to sue you to recover the money. Don't be put off by threats to call the police. They have no right to intervene unless you intended to leave without paying for no genuine reason, or if you caused a violent scene, which could be a criminal offence.

Based on an article that appeared in *Which?* in November 1989.

General lists

London restaurants by cuisine

AFGHAN
Buzkash, SW15
Caravan Serai, W1

ARAB & MID-EASTERN
Adams Café, W12
Al Hamra, W1
Efes Kebab House, W1
Laurent, NW2
Maroush III, W1

AFRICAN/ CARIBBEAN
Bambaya, N8

BURMESE
Mandalay, SE10

CHINESE
Dorchester Hotel, Oriental, W1
Dragon's Nest, W1
Fung Shing, WC2
Jade Garden, W1
Mandarin Kitchen, W2
Mayflower, W1
Mr Kong, WC2
New World, W1
Now & Zen, WC2
Panda Si Chuen, W1
Poons, WC2
Royal China, SW15
Zen W3, NW3

FRENCH
L'Arlequin, SW8
Les Associés, N8
Auberge de Provence, St James's Court Hotel, SW1
Au Bois St Jean, NW8
Au Jardin des Gourmets, W1
Le Chausson, SW11
La Croisette, SW10
La Dordogne, W4
Le Gavroche, W1
Gavvers, SW1
Lou Pescadou, SW5
Mijanou, SW1
Mon Petit Plaisir, W8
Mon Plaisir, WC2
Le Muscadet, W1
Oak Room, Le Meridien Hotel, W1
St Quentin, SW3
Soulard, N1
Le Suquet, SW3
Tante Claire, SW3
La Truffe Noire, SE1

GREEK
Kalamaras, W2
Nontas, NW1

HUNGARIAN
Gay Hussar, W1

INDIAN
Bayleaf Tandoori, N6
Bombay Brasserie, SW7
Ganpath, WC1
Gopal's of Soho, W1
Great Nepalese, NW1
Gurkha Brasserie, NW11
Haandi, NW1
Lal Qila, W1
Ragam, W1
Sree Krishna, SW17
Tandoori Lane, SW6
Veeraswamy, W1

INDIAN VEGETARIAN
Diwana Bhel-Poori, NW1
Kastoori, SW17
Mandeer, W1
Rani, N3
Sabras, NW10
Suruchi, N1
Surya, NW6

INDONESIAN/ STRAITS
Melati, W1
Singapore Garden Mayfair, W1
Singapore Garden Restaurant, NW6

ITALIAN
Alba, EC1
Casale Franco, N1
Cibo, W14
Eleven Park Walk, SW10

Florians, N8
L'Incontro, SW1
Neal Street Restaurant, WC2
Orso, WC2
Osteria Antica Bologna, SW11
Il Passetto, WC2
Pizzeria Castello, SE1
Pizzeria Condotti, W1
Riva, SW13
River Café, W6
Sabatini, SW1

JAPANESE

Ikkyu, W1
Isohama, SW1
Kagura, N3
Mitsukoshi, SW1
Miyama, W1
Nakano, SW3
Neshiko, N1
Suntory, SW1
Tatsuso, EC2
Wakaba, NW3
Yoisho, W1

KOREAN

Arirang, W1
Bu San, N7
Jin, W1

MAURITIAN

Chez Liline, N4
La Gaulette, W1

POLISH

Wódka, W8

SPANISH

Los Remos, W2
Meson Don Felipe, SE1

SWEDISH

Anna's Place, N1

THAI

Bahn Thai, W1
Bedlington Café, W4
Blue Elephant, SW6
Chiang Mai, W1
Khun Akorn, SW3
Sri Siam, W1
Thailand, SE14
Topsy-Tasty, W4
Tui, SW7
Tuk Tuk, N1

London restaurants with tables outside

Al Hamra, W1
Anna's Place, N1
Blueprint Café, SE1
Bombay Brasserie, SW7
Casale Franco, NW1
Chanterelle, SW7
Le Chausson, SW11
Cherry Orchard, E2
Christian's, W4
Connolly's, SW15
La Croisette, SW10
La Dordogne, W4
Eagle, EC1
Emile's, SW6
La Fin de la Chasse, N1
Florians, N8
Frith's, W1
Gilbert's, SW7
Joe's Café, SW3
Lou Pescadou, SW5
Mandeer, W1
Maroush III, W1
Mijanou, SW1
Mon Petit Plaisir, W8
Nichol's, NW6
Nontas, NW1
192, W11
Poissonnerie de l'Avenue, SW3
River Café, W6
Soulard, N1
Le Suquet, SW3
Tuk Tuk, N1

Restaurants with rooms (6 bedrooms or fewer)

England

Abingdon, Thame Lane House
Barnstaple, Lynwood House
Barwick, Little Barwick House
Baslow, Fischer's at Baslow Hall
Birdlip, Kingshead House
Blandford Forum, La Belle Alliance
Bradfield Combust, Bradfield House
Bradford, Restaurant 19, Belvedere Hotel
Brimfield, Poppies, The Roebuck
Calstock, Danescombe Valley Hotel
Cartmel, Uplands
Cleeve Hill, Redmond's
Clun, Old Post Office
Croyde, Whiteleaf at Croyde
Dallington, Little Byres
Dartmouth, Billy Budd's
Dent, Stone Close
Diss, Salisbury House
Dorrington, Country Friends
Drewsteignton, Hunts Tor House
Dulverton, Ashwick House
East Buckland, Lower Pitt
Eyton, Marsh
Fletching, Griffin
Glastonbury, No. 3
Harwich, Pier at Harwich
Haworth, Weavers
Hastingleigh, Woodmans Arms Auberge
Helford, Riverside
Holdenby, Lynton House
Kintbury, Dundas Arms
Kirkby Lonsdale, Lupton Tower
Langho, Northcote Manor
Lavenham, Great House
Leck, Cobwebs
Little Walsingham, Old Bakehouse
Lower Brailes, Feldon House
Lympstone, River House
Manchester, Moss Nook
Mary Tavy, Stannary
Montacute, Milk House
Oakhill, Oakhill House

Pool in Wharfdale, Pool Court
Poughill, Reeds
Powerstock, Three Horseshoes
Redlynch, Langley Wood
Richmond, Howe Villa
Shepton Mallet, Bowlish House
Shipton-under-Wychwood, Lamb Inn
Spark Bridge, Bridgefield House
Staddlebridge, McCoy's
Stoke-by-Nayland, Angel Inn
Storrington, Manleys
Swinton, Wheatsheaf Hotel
Tavistock, Horn of Plenty
Thornton-Cleveleys, Victorian House
Torquay, Mulberry Room
Waterhouses, Old Beams
Weobley, Jules Café
Whimple, Woodhayes
Winteringham, Winteringham Fields
Wylam, Laburnum House
Yattendon, Royal Oak

Scotland

Canonbie, Riverside Inn
Dunvegan, Harlosh Hotel
Haddington, Browns Hotel
Kingussie, The Cross
Muir of Ord, Dower House
Swinton, Wheatsheaf Hotel
Walls, Burrastow House

Wales

Cemlyn, Harlech
Cnapan, Newport
Minffordd Hotel, Talyllyn
Old Rectory, Llansanffraid Glan Conwy
Stone Hall, Wolf's Castle
Three Main Street, Fishguard

Northern Ireland

Coleraine, Macduff's

Republic of Ireland

Ahakista, Shiro
Wicklow, Old Rectory

Service charges

These restaurants state that they include the service charge as part of the net price shown on the menu and the bill. They also have stated that they close the total on the credit card slip before presenting it to the customer (save for those very few places, of course, that do not accept credit cards). WATCH THIS SPACE.

London

L'Arlequin, SW8
Capital Hotel, SW3
Chez Nico, W1
Clarke's, W8
Dorchester, W1
Four Seasons, Inn on the Park, W1
Gavvers, SW1
Leith's, SW1
Rani, N3
Simply Nico, SW1
Suntory, SW1
Villandry Dining Room, W1

England

Abingdon, Thame Lane House
Aylesbury, Hartwell House
Berwick-upon-Tweed, Funnywayt'mekalivin
Bishop's Tachbrook, Mallory Court
Blandford Forum, La Belle Alliance
Box, Clos du Roy at Box House
Bradfield Combust, Bradfield House
Brimfield, Poppies, The Roebuck
Bristol, Markwicks
Chagford, Gidleigh Park
Cleeve Hill, Redmond's
Cosham, Barnards
Dartmouth, Carved Angel
Eastbourne, Byrons
Eversley, New Mill
Evesham, Cedar Restaurant, Evesham Hotel
Eyton, Marsh
Hambleton, Hambleton Hall
Hintlesham, Hintlesham Hall
Holdenby, Lynton House
Horton, French Partridge
Malvern Wells, Croque-en-Bouche
Mary Tavy, Stannary
New Milton, Marryat Room, Chewton Glen Hotel
Oakhill, Oakhill House
Oxford, Restaurant Elizabeth
Petworth, Soanes
Roade, Roadhouse Restaurant
Rochford, Renoufs
Rye, Landgate Bistro
St Leonard's, Röser's
Shipton Gorge, Innsacre
South Molton, Whitechapel Manor
Ston Easton, Ston Easton Park
Sturminster Newton, Plumber Manor
Thornbury, Thornbury Castle
Thornton-Cleveleys, Victorian House
Thundridge, Hanbury Manor
Tunbridge Wells, Sankey's
Tunbridge Wells, Thackeray's House
Ullswater, Sharrow Bay
Wickham, Old House
Worcester, Brown's
York, Melton's
York, Middlethorpe Hall

Scotland

Dunkeld, Kinnaird House
Edinburgh, Denzler's 121
Peat Inn, Peat Inn

Uig, Baile-na-Cille
Ullapool, Altnaharrie Inn

Wales
Llandudno, Bodysgallen Hall
Pwllheli, Plas Bodegroes
Swansea, Annie's
Talyllyn, Minfordd Hotel
Three Cocks, Three Cocks Hotel

Channel Islands
Rozel, Granite Corner
St Saviour, Longueville Manor

Northern Ireland
Ballynahinch, Woodlands

Republic of Ireland
Kanturk, Assolas Country House
Kenmare, Park Hotel (set meals only)
Newport, Newport House

Restaurants with no music

London
Bedlington Café, W4
Bibendum, SW3
Boyd's, W8
Chanterelle, SW7
Chez Moi, W11
Chez Nico, W1
Clarke's, W8
Connaught, W1
Dorchester, the Oriental, W1
Frith's, W1
Le Gavroche, W1
Gavvers, SW1
Gay Hussar, W1
Gilbert's, SW7
Grahame's Seafare, W1
Greenhouse, W1
Hiders, SW6
Hilaire, SW7
Isohama, SW1
Ivy, WC2
Launceston Place, W8
Laurent, NW2
Leith's, W11
Lou Pescadou, SW5
Le Mesurier, EC1
Mijanou, SW1
Mr Kong, WC2
Monkeys, SW3
Museum Street Café, WC1
Neal Street Restaurant, WC2
Odette's, NW1
190 Queensgate, SW7
Orso, WC2
Pizzeria Condotti, W1
Poissonnerie de l'Avenue, SW3
Poons, Lisle Street, WC2
Quality Chop House, EC1
River Café, W6
St Quentin, SW3
Savoy, Grill Room, WC2
Simply Nico, SW1
Sree Krishna, SW17
Surinder's, W2
Tui, SW7
Upper Street Fish Shop, N1
Veeraswamy, W1
Villandry Dining Room, W1

England
Abberley, Elms Hotel
Abingdon, Thame Lane House
Ambleside, Rothay Manor
Amersham, King's Arms
Ashbourne, Callow Hall
Barnstaple, Lynwood House
Barwick, Little Barwick House
Baslow, Fischer's at Baslow Hall
Bath, Priory Hotel
Beaminster, Bridge House
Billesley, Billesley Manor
Birmingham, Adil
Blackwater, Long's
Box, Clos du Roy at Box House
Brampton, Farlam Hall
Bristol, Lettonie
Bristol, Markwicks
Broadhembury, Drewe Arms
Bruton, Truffles
Burford, Lamb
Burnham Market, Fishes'
Bury St Edmunds, Mortimer's
Calstock, Danescombe Valley Hotel
Cambridge, Midsummer House
Cheltenham, Epicurean
Cirencester, Tatyans
Cleeve Hill, Redmond's
Colchester, Warehouse Brasserie
Corse Lawn, Corse Lawn House Hotel
Crudwell, Crudwell Court
Cuckfield, Jeremy's at the King's Head
Dartmouth, Carved Angel
Dedham, Le Talbooth
Dorking, Partners West Street
Dorrington, Country Friends
Drewsteignton, Hunts Tor House
Dulverton, Ashwick House
East Grinstead, Gravetye Manor
Edenbridge, Honours Mill
Ely, Old Fire Engine House
Erpingham, Ark
Evershot, Summer Lodge
Evesham, Cedar Restaurant, Evesham Hotel
Felsted, Rumbles Cottage
Flitwick, Flitwick Manor
Fowey, Food for Thought
Gillingham, Stock Hill House
Goring, Leatherne Bottel
Grasmere, Michael's Nook
Grasmere, White Moss House
Great Gonerby, Harry's Place
Great Milton, Le Manoir aux Quat' Saisons
Grimston, Congham Hall
Harrogate, Drum and Monkey
Haslemere, Morels
Hastingleigh, Woodmans Arms Auberge
Haydon Bridge, General Havelock Inn
Helford, Riverside
Hintlesham, Hintlesham Hall

Hockley Heath, Nuthurst Grange
Holdenby, Lynton House
Holt, Yetman's
Hunstrete, Hunstrete House
Ipswich, Mortimer's on the Quay
Ixworth, Theobalds
Kenilworth, Restaurant Bosquet
Keyston, Pheasant Inn
Kintbury, Dundas Arms
Langley Marsh, Langley House Hotel
Ledbury, Hope End
Lewdown, Lewtrenchard Manor
Lincoln, Wig & Mitre
Lower Beeding, South Lodge
Lower Brailes, Feldon House
Lympstone, River House
Malvern Wells, Croque-en-Bouche
Manchester, Moss Nook
Manchester, Quan Ju De
Mawnan Smith, Nansidwell Country House
Melmerby, Village Bakery
Middle Wallop, Fifehead Manor
Midhurst, Maxine's
Montacute, Milk House
Moreton-in-Marsh, Marsh Goose
Moulton, Black Bull
Nailsworth, Flynns
Nayland, Martha's Vineyard
Newcastle upon Tyne, 21 Queen Street
New Milton, Marryat Room, Chewton Glen Hotel
North Huish, Brookdale House
Norwich, Adlard's
Nottingham, Les Artistes Gourmands
Oakhill, Oakhill House
Old Burghclere, Dew Pond
Oxford, Cherwell Boathouse
Oxford, Munchy Munchy
Oxford, Restaurant Elizabeth
Padstow, Seafood Restaurant
Pinner, La Giralda
Pool in Wharfedale, Pool Court
Poughill, Reeds
Pulborough, Stane Street Hollow
Roade, Roadhouse Restaurant
Romsey, Old Manor House
Rowde, George & Dragon
St Keyne, Well House
St Margaret's at Cliffe, Wallett's Court
Sheffield, Greenhead House
Shepton Mallet, Bowlish House
Shinfield, L'Ortolan
Shipton-under-Wychwood, Lamb Inn
South Molton, Whitechapel Manor
Southwold, Crown
Spark Bridge, Bridgefield House
Stamford, George
Ston Easton, Ston Easton Park
Storrington, Abingworth Hall
Stroud, Oakes
Stuckton, Three Lions
Sudbury, Mabey's Brasserie
Tavistock, Horn of Plenty
Thundridge, Hanbury Manor
Tunbridge Wells, Cheevers
Tunbridge Wells, Thackeray's House
Uckfield, Horsted Place
Ulverston, Bay Horse Inn and Bistro
Underbarrow, Tullythwaite House
Wells-next-the-Sea, Moorings
Weobley, Jules Café
West Mersea, Le Champenois, Blackwater Hotel
Wethersfield, Dicken's
Whitby, Magpie Café
Wickham, Old House
Williton, White House Hotel
Windermere, Gilpin Lodge
Woolley Green, Woolley Grange
Wootton, Lugleys
Worcester, Brown's
Worleston, Rookery Hall
York, Middlethorpe Hall

Scotland

Aberfoyle, Braeval Old Mill
Achiltibuie, Summer Isles Hotel
Arisaig, Arisaig House
Auchmithie, But'n'ben
Ballater, Tullich Lodge
Blairgowrie, Kinloch House Hotel
Callander, Roman Camp Hotel
Canonbie, Riverside Inn
Cupar, Ostlers Close
Drumnadrochit, Polmaily House Hotel
Drybridge, Old Monastery
Edinburgh, Chinese Home Cooking
Edinburgh, Denzler's 121
Edinburgh, Indian Cavalry Club
Edinburgh, Martins
Edinburgh, Shamiana
Edinburgh, Vintners Rooms
Eriska, Isle of Eriska Hotel
Fort William, Inverlochy Castle
Glasgow, Ubiquitous Chip
Gullane, La Potinière
Inverness, Culloden House
Inverness, Dunain Park
Killiecrankie, Killiecrankie Hotel
Kinbuck, Cromlix House
Kingussie, The Cross
Linlithgow, Champany Inn
Moffat, Well View Hotel
Muir of Ord, Dower House
Newtonmore, Ard-Na-Coille Hotel
Oban, Knipoch Hotel
Peat Inn, Peat Inn
Peebles, Cringletie House
Port Appin, Airds Hotel
Portpatrick, Knockinaam Lodge
Stewarton, Chapeltoun House
Tiroran, Tiroran House
Uig, Baile-na-Cille

Ullapool, Altnaharrie Inn
Whitebridge, Knockie Lodge

Wales

Aberdovey, Old Coffee Shop
Abersoch, Porth Tocyn Hotel
Beaumaris, Ye Olde Bulls Head Inn
Dinas, Rose Cottage
Dinas Mawddwy, Old Station Coffee Shop
Dolgellau, Dolmelynllyn Hall
Fishguard, Three Main Street
Haverfordwest, Jemima's
Llandewi Skirrid, Walnut Tree Inn
Llandudno, Richard at Lanterns
Llansanffraid Glan Conwy, Old Rectory
Llyswen, Llangoed Hall
Talyllyn, Minffordd Hotel
Wolf's Castle, Stone Hall

Channel Islands

St Saviour, Longueville Manor

Northern Ireland

Bellanaleck, Sheelin
Coleraine, Macduff's

Republic of Ireland

Ballylickey, Sea View House Hotel
Ballyvaughan, Gregans Castle
Cashel, Cashel House Hotel
Clonakilty, Dunworley Cottage
Cork, Clifford's
Dingle, Half Door
Dublin, Coq Hardi
Dublin, Locks
Gorey, Marlfield House
Kilkenny, Lacken House
Mallow, Longueville House
Newport, Newport House
Oughterard, Currarevagh House
Rossnowlagh, Sand House Hotel

The Good Food Club 1991

Many thanks to all the following people who contributed, in one way or another, to this year's Guide...

Miss C. Abbott
Ismail Abdulla
Dr Sidney Abrahams
Mr R. Abrams
Joseph Abramsky
Ms Heather Acton
Stephen C.F. Adams
Robert Adams
M.A. Ahad
Dr J.B. Ainscough
John R. Aird
Sir Lawrence Airey
E. and J.L. Albarn
Mrs C. Alblas
Mr and Mrs David Alcock
N.S. Alcock
A.H. Alexander
Mrs J R Alexander
Ms Yvonne Alexander
Montague Alexander
Minda and Stanley Alexander
Dr and Mrs A.A. Alibhai
Jeremy Allen
Leon Allen
W.R. Allen
Mr R.G. Allen
Donald W.S. Alloway
Mr D. Allsebrook
Mrs N. Allwood
Mrs G. Allwright
Sir Anthony Alment
Ms Patricia Almond
John Alston
Leonard Amborski
Chris Anderson
S. Andresier
Mrs Ruth Andrews
Lee Andrews
Gwen and Peter Andrews
Mrs Joyce B. Andrews
Mrs G.C. Andrews
Mr E.I. Andrews
Mr D.A. Angless
Sir Michael Angus
David W. T. Angwin
Anthony Ansell
Mrs B. Anthony
Mr and Mrs John Appleton
Mrs Cynthia Archer
Mr and Mrs F. Armstrong
Mr B.J. Armstrong
Hugo Arnold
Mr and Mrs A.E. Arris
Sir Norman Arthur
Mr D.A. Ash
John Ashby
Philip Ashley
Mr and Mrs Douglas Aspinall
Ms Elizabeth Assheton
Mrs Hazel Astley
Adrian Aston
Ms Nikkie Atad
N. Atchley
Mr J.B. Atherton
Mrs M.M. Atherton
Mrs P.M. Atkin
Julian Atkinson
Brian and Ann Atkinson
Mrs J. Atkinson
J.B. Atkinson
G. Atkinson
Mr Atkinson
Mr and Mrs Paul Auchterlonie
N.C. Avery
John and Sue Aylward
Derek Ayres
Mr and Mrs V. Bach
Dr J.R. Backhurst
Cynthia Bacon
Mr D.I. Baddeley
R. Baggallam
Kenneth Bagnall
Lady Bailey
Mrs A. Bailey
Andrew Bailey
P. Bailey
Jane and Martin Bailey
Ian C. Baillie
Ronald W. Bain
Ronald J. Baker
Mrs Julia Baker
Mr and Mrs I. Balaam
Dr P.E. Baldry
I. Baldwin
Mitzi Bales
Prof J.M. Ball
S.K. Ball
G.W. Ballard
C.D. Bamber
C.J. Bancroft
A.H.M. Bankes-Jones
Peter A. Banks
B.G. Banks
Brian Bannatyne-Scott
D.T. Bannister
Neil Bannister
Tony and Sally Banwell
Richard D. Banz
Ms Michelle Barber
H.F.H. Barclay
Mrs Carmel Bardsley
D.G.W. Barham
Dr J.A. Barley
Tim Barlow
R.P. Barlow
Rev D. Barnes
David Barnes
Mrs K. Barnett
Jill and Ray Barnett
C. Barney
Peter Barnsley
Allan Barr
Geoff Barratt
Mrs Julia Barrell
F.J. Barrington
Mr and Mrs George Barry
Matthew Bartlett
Mr Bartlett
Tony Barton
Mrs E.A. Barwood
Mrs M.A. Batchelor
Sir Dawson Bates
Hugh W.T. Bates
Mr and Mrs John Bates
Mrs M. Bates
Dr John R. Batty
Mr W. Batty-Smith
Mr H.G. Baulcombe
Mr R.T. Bayes
D.J. Bayfield
Conrad Bayliss
Dr S.B. Bayly
Mrs G.B. Beachy
Miss L.A. Beaman
Mark and Maire Beaman
Dr A. Beaton
Joseph Beattie
Stephen Beaumont
F.R. Beckett

Mr and Mrs Beckford
H.H. Beckingsale
D. Bedford
Mr and Mrs G. Bedser
Mr D.D. Beevers
Mr E.C.M. Begg
Mrs J. Beggs
Dr F. Bell
Mrs Hilary Bell
Geoffrey Bell
Mrs A. Bellerby
Mrs D. Bellerby
R.K. Bennett
Ms Lindsay A. Bennett
Russell K. Bennett
Bruce Bennett
Mrs Lilian Bent
S.E. Bentley
Anne and Martin Benton
William Bentsen
Stephen Beresford
Dr Jurgen Bergmann
P.D.E. Bergqvist
Mrs V. Berkeley
Mr and Mrs H.I. Berkeley
Mrs Gabriele Berneck
Edward A.M. Berry
Mr and Mrs E. Berry
P.E. Berry
M.J. Berry
J. Berry
Miss D. Best
Mrs F. Best
Miss S. Betteridge
Mrs L. Beaulah
Ms J. Bewick
Sukhina Bhullar
Dr D.R. Bickerton
J.M. Bignell
Mr and Mrs Ernest Bill
John Binnie
Dr G.G. Birch
E.R. Birch
George A.R. Bird
M.R. Bishop
Dr J.M. Bishop
Mr and Mrs B.J. Blackburn
Anthony Blackstock
Simon Blackwell
William M. Blair
Giles Blair
Mr P.A. Blake
Timothy Blake
R.A. Blakemore
Mrs A. Blakey
J.A. Bland
Mrs J.A. Blanks
Mr and Mrs Blatch
Mrs H. Blazey
Edward Blincoe
Dr M.P. Blinston Jones
Mr and Mrs S. Bliss
Jay and Fiona Bluck
Dr S.M. Blunden
Alan Blyth
K.W. Bogle
Mrs Ann L. Bolton
Maurice Bonnor
Mr E. Bonnor-Maurice
Mrs J. Booth
Ms Yvonne M. Booth
Martin and Elaine Borish
Dr P.M.J. Borland
Catherine Borley
Ms Joan Borley
Mrs S.A. Borley
Mrs D. Borrill
Michel Boulesteix
T.P. Boulton
Mr and Mrs James Bourn
Mrs B. Bourne
B.N. Bowcock
P.M. Bowen
W.M. Bowen
Mrs Claire Bowman
Michael Bowyer
Major Roy Boxall
Ms Belinda Brackley
Mrs P. Bradley
Mr M.D. Bradley
J.G. Bradley
Peter Bradshaw
R.G. Bradshaw
Angus Bramwell
Ms Mary Brandt
N.S. Brann
John Brant
Baron Forbes à Brassard
Ms Jane Bray
Mrs Patricia Brazil
John Brebner
Ms Kim Breckon
M.J. Brett
P. Breward
Ms Hilary Bridewell
Robert O. Bridges
Ms Sue Bridgwater
J.B. Brierley
Mr and Mrs D.J. Brine
Miss M.C. Brinton
Mr and Mrs D.M. Briscoe
B.J. Britton
Maurice Broady
Mrs J.W. Brock
Roy Y. Bromell
Mr C.M. Brook
Dr O.G. Brooke
S.T. Brookes
Rachel Brookes
Tom Brooks
Miss Bonny and Miss Whisper Brooks
Mrs D. Brotherston
Dr and Mrs D.G. Brown
Mrs M. Brown
Rev Richard Brown
Mr D.C.A. Brown
A.J. Brown
Mr J.R. Brown
Nick Browne
K.H. Browning
Ms Avril Bruce
D.W.K. Bruce
Terence Bryan
David E H Bryan
Ian Bryant
John Bryant
Grant Buck
R.G. Buckland
Judith Bulger
Ian and Angela Bull
Dave Bullen
F.E. Bullock
Mrs Daphne Bullock
Mrs H.M. Bunch
Herrick Bunney
David V. Burchfield
Norman Burden
G.J. Burgess
James P.C. Burgess
Paul R. Burn
Mr D.R. Burnes
Mrs W. H. Burnett
David Burrows
C. Burton
Mrs K.B. Bushen
Mervyn Buston
Paul and Christine Butler
D. Butterfield
Peter Bye
Malcolm Cade
Prof Robert Cahn
Mr M. Cairney
Dr and Mrs A.G. Cairns Smith
David Calder
Donald and Sylvia Cammack
Malcolm Campbell
Dr Brian C. Campbell
Dr and Mrs. R.W.B. Campbell
R.D. Campbell
Mr and Mrs Allan Campbell
G.A. Cape
Mr M.M. Capey
Betty Carey
Mr and Mrs Carlisle
Miss C.A. Carlton
Miss Y. Carpenter
P. Carpenter
M.B. Carpenter
Richard Carpenter
Ms Sarah Carr
Mrs Patricia Carr
Mr D.L. Carr
Lt Cdr G. Carr
Susan A. Carrier
Miss Patricia Carroll
B.J. Carroll
R. Carsberg
J.S. Carter
David M. Carter
Philip Carter
Mr N. Carter
Mr P.E. Carter
Mrs B. Carter
Miss Sally Carter
Mrs S. Cartlidge
R. Carty
Ms Diane Cass
Sarah Cassidy
Ms Jennie Cassidy
Mr R. Castle
R.E. Catlow
Leslie Caul
B.I. Caulfield
George C. Cernoch
Mr and Mrs R. Chadwick
Mrs Susan Chait
Mrs P.H. Challens
M.A. Chamberlain
Mr and Mrs M. Chamberlain
Philip Chan
A.F. Chapman
Mrs B. Chapman
P. Chapman
Chris Chapman
Shona Adam and Keith Chapman
Mrs M. Chapman
Brian Chapman
Nigel Chapman

Mr and Mrs E.J. Chappell
Mr and Mrs. Chard
Mr S. Charles
Tim Charlesworth
Mr and Mrs W. Charlesworth
David Charlesworth
N. Charlesworth
Piers Chater Robinson
Derek Cheesbrough
Rev M. Child
Ms Jennifer Child
Bellone Christian
Mrs Elisabeth Christopher
Miss S.J. Church
Norman Civval
Mr D.H. Clark
G.R. Clark
Mrs V.J. Clarke
Ms D. Clarke
Mrs M. Clarke
V. Clarke
A. Class
R.S. Clayton
Mrs A.J.B. Cleave
Terence Clegg
Mrs N.E. Cliff
Mr C. Clifford-Jones
K.C. Clinch
Lady Clitheroe
I.P. Clough
George S. Clyne
Dr B. Coghlan
F.N. Cogswell
Mr and Mrs David Cohen
Mr and Mrs Harold Cohen
Mr J. Cohen
Mrs Heather Colbeck
Lois Cole
Mr and Mrs Tarquin Cole
Adrian Cole
Mr W. Colfer
Janet Collett
Prof Leslie Collier
M.L. Collier
Paul Collins
Mrs Rosemary Collins
Ms Pamela Colman
R.T. Combe
Richard Comben
Toby M.S. Comerford
Mr M. Comninos
Peter A. Connell
Sean Connolly
Ms Jillian Cook
Mrs J. Cook
Godfrey J. Cook
Mr D.H. Cook
Mrs Brenda Cooke
A. Cooke
Mrs J Cookson
B.E. Coombs
P.J. Cooper
Mrs C. Cooper
Mrs Marianne Cooper
Nick Coote
Alan and Patricia Copley
Mr J. Corbluth
N.B. Corner
Mr and Mrs Bernard Cosgrove
Mrs Hannah Cotton
Mr R.H. Couchman
Mr and Mrs Clive Coultass
C.J. Coulter
Mr and Mrs D. Couperthwaite
Robert Court
Christopher and Jean Cowan
Mrs S.M. Cowen
Derek Cowlin
Ms Jeanette Cox
D.P.A. Cox
Prof A.P.M. Coxon
R.M. Cozens
Ms S. L. Crabtree
David Cramb
Mr and Mrs Ian Crammond
R.D. Cramond
Mr and Mrs Peter Crane
T.J. Craven
Dr K.W.E. Craven
Mr G. Crawford
Mr and Mrs M.W. Crawshaw
William C. Craze
Mrs Kathleen Creighton
Mr D.J. Creman
Mrs Clarice Cresswell
Dr G.S. Crockett
S.J.M. Cromie
Mr T.E. Crompton
Mrs J.H. Crook
Ms Helen Crookston
Mr G.B. Cross
Kate Cross
Rodney Cross
Mr G.B. Crosthwaite
Mr and Mrs M.R. Crowder
Mrs M.D. Crowther
Michael Crowther-Watson
George Cruddas
Dr S.N. Crutchley
Tim and Gill Culley
Kevin Cully
John Culshaw
Frank Cummins
Dr R. Cundall
David M. Cundy
Dr James Stevens Curl
Ms Carol Ann Curran
Steve Currid
Miss K. Curryer
Mr and Mrs S. Curtis
Ms Margaret Curtis
John Curtis
Moira da Costa
W.J.A. Dacombe
Ronan Daffey
Dr M.M. Dale
Mr K.W. Daley
Mrs Isobel D. Dalling
M.J. Daly
T.D. Dampney
Gerry A. Danby
M. Daneshvar
Dr V.J. Daniel
L. and P. Darby
C.J. Darkens
David Darley
Mr and Mrs David Darrah
Dr Papiya Das
Dr P.J. Dash
Adam J. Daszkiewicz
D. Davies
J.L. Davies
D.E. Davies
Dr David Davies
Maurice R. Davies
Dr R.J. and Mrs K.B. Davies
Sydney G.C. Davies
Mrs D.M. Davies
Dr D. Wynne Davies
C.V. Davies
R. Davies
Emily Davies
Andrew Davis
R.M. Davis
Brian Davis
A.M. Davis
Lynn Davis
Dr G. Davison
J. Davison
Bill Davy
Mr and Mrs S.W. Daw
Mr G.H. Daw
Dr and Mrs R.P.R. Dawber
Mr and Mrs Keith Dawson
C.F. Dawson
B. De Capell Brooke
Mrs J.A. De Groot
Emanuel de Kadt
F.C. de Paula
David de Saxe
Mr and Mrs J.I. de Villiers
W.P. De Winton
Nigel Deacon
John Deacon
A. Dean
Mr and Mrs Keith J. Dean-Orange
J.W. Deane
Mr P.V. Deeney
Mrs D.E. Defer-Wyatt
Ms B. Deinhardt
Mr C.R.L. Delaney
Mr and Mrs Michael Denison
N.J. Desmond
Conal Devitt
G. Dewar
I.C. Dewey
Charles J. Dick
Ms Fiona Dick
Mr and Mrs J.K. Dick
Rev A.W. Dickinson
Mr and Mrs. Dilks
Mrs G.M. Dickson
Ms Sheila Dillon
Mr and Mrs Robert Dillon
Mr S. Dingle
A.R. Dingwall
John Dixon
Ms A. Dixon
Mrs S.E. Dixon
Mr and Mrs J. Dobris
Charles Dobson
A. Docherty
Miss Alison Dockree
Mr and Mrs J. Dodd
Ms M.S. Dodkins
Peta Dollar
John Dominic
Colin Donald

Michael Donne
Ms Elizabeth Ann Dorman
T.S. Dorsch
James and Mary Douglas
A.J. Dourleyn
Mrs Pat Downes
Mrs Erica M. Downie
A. Downs
Mr R.H. Downs
Sidney Downs
P.B. Dowsett
Stephen Doyle
Dr R.J. Draper
John Drayson
Garth Drinkwater
Mr P. Driscoll
Jeff Driver
Bernard Driver
Capt S.H. Drummond
Joseph Dryden Blinco
Ms P. Dryhurst
Dr W.R. Drysdale
J.H. Du Bois
John Ducker
Ms Antonia Dudgeon
Mr and Mrs.R. Duggan
Mr C. Duggan
Richard Duggleby
Mr and Mrs D. Dulson
Mrs J. Dundas
Hugo and Alice Dunn-Meynell
Susan Dunnett
David Dunnett
Mrs Kay Dunton
Denis Durno
Mrs Janet M. Durrant
Dr W.H. Duthie
Mr and Mrs N.R. Dutson
Mrs S. Dutton
Mr and Mrs M. Dutton
Paul Dwyer
Gerry Dwyer
Mr and Mrs V. Dyke
Mrs Mary Earle
Mrs C.E. Earp
Harold East
Mrs C. Easthaugh
Don Easton
Dr S. Eden
John Edington
Neil Edkins
Mr and Mrs R. Edmondson
P.G. Edwards
John R. Edwards
E. Eisenhandler
John Elder
Myra and Ray Elderfield
D.M. Elliott
Mr and Mrs P. Elliott
R.G. Ellis
D.R. Ellis
Mrs M. Ellis
Paul Ellis-Howe
J.J. Elreston
C.W. Elston
Mrs D.M. Emanuel
Roger Emmott
Michael and Anita Emmott
Mrs Ann C. Emsley
Mrs B.P. Endean
Ms Emma England
Mr C.C. English
Robert Entwistle
Jeremy Eppel
Dr Edgar Ernstbrunner
David Erskine
C.G. Erwin
Maurice Eslow
Dr C.S. Evans
Mrs D. Evans
T.G. Evans
J.L.D. Evans
Mrs Veronica Evans
Barry Evans
J.S. Evans
P.M. Eyre
Adrian Faiers
Mrs A. Faiman
I. Fair
Mrs M. Fairall
Miss Irene F. Fairey
Mrs Helen Fairley
Mr J. Fairley
Ms Judith Fairlie
R.B. Fairweather
Jed Falby
Mr R.A.Farrand
Eric F. Farrer
Ms Ann Farrow
P.F.M. Featherby
Peter Feeley
J.G. Ferguson
Mr and Mrs Fergusson
M.L. Ferrar
Dr Eric Ferraris
Mrs J. Ferrett
S.J. Few
Alan Field
Mrs Helen E. Fielder
R.J. Fieldhouse
Mrs K.J. Filby
Mario Fillo
Mrs Julie Finch
Sir Geoffrey Finsberg
P.C. Firmin
Mr and Mrs D. Fisher
Dr F. Fisher
A.R. Fisher
Mr I.N. Fishman
Ms S. Fitzgerald
T.C. Flanagan
Clare Fletcher
A.T.R. Fletcher
J. Fletcher-Watson
Marcy Flicker
Mr M. Flinn
Mrs Susan Russell Flint
V.R. Flint
Roy Flood
Mrs M.A. Floyer
R.S.A Fontyn
Hazel H. Forbes
Mr P. Forbes
Ray Ford
Ms R. Ford
J.C. Ford
Susan Foreman
Ms Sally L. Forman
P.J. Forrest
Alan J. Forrest
Michael Forsbrey
Mr B.W. Forster
A.P. Forster
Mrs Christina Forster
Alan J. Fortune
E.T. Foulds
John C. Foulkes
M et Mme Fournel
R.J.N. Fowler
Mrs S. Fowler
Mrs Foxandrews
Dr A. Frank
R. Frankenburg
R. Frankland
R.S and S. Frapwell
C. Fraser
Dr Fraser
Paul Fraser
R.H. Fraval
A.L. Freedman
S. Freedman
M.R. Freeman
B. Freemantle
Tony Freeth
D.G.J. Frewin
Anthony Froggatt
Prof Victoria A. Fromkin
Jonathan Fry
Mr and Mrs D. Fryer
Ms Barbara Fryman
Ms Susan Fumo
Davina Furnval
Mrs A.M. Furst
Dr and Mrs R. Gadsby
John Gagg
Ms Patricia Galvan
Mr and Mrs Tony Gamble
J.H. Gandon
R.P. Gapper
Mrs N.W. Gardiner
Mr and Mrs Gardner
Mrs M.S. Gardner
Mrs S. Gardner
Mr H. Garner
Amanda Garrett
Mr C.D.F. Gaskill
P.J. Gater
Mrs J.J. Gaunt
Cathy Gayner
N.C. Gaywood
David Gearing
Mrs B. Gebhardt
Mrs Ann M. Geen
B. Gell
Mr and Mrs G.N. Georgano
Keith George
Mrs J. Gerrard
Mrs Renee Gerson
Mrs A.M. Geeson
S. Geston
Mr and Mrs Sadaqat H. Ghori
Mr and Mrs Austin Gibbons
Mr.R.W. Gibling
Richard J Gibson
W. Gibson
Miss Mary Gibson
Ms Pamela Gibson
Ms Gibson
D.S. Gilbert
B.L. Gilbert
Christopher Giles
J.S. Gilks
Jonathan Gill
Dr Jonathan H. Gillard
Mr M.E. Gilleland
Mrs A.F. Gillon
Ms Susan Gillotti
Anthony Gilmartin
Ms Nicola Ginesi

J.A. Given
H.C. Gladstone
Prof Duncan Glen
Mrs D. Gloster
Mrs Barbara Glover
R.J.N. Glover
Mrs P.M. Glover
Mrs Joy Glover
B.M. Glover
A.J. Goater
Mr P. Goddard
Ms Marlene Godfrey
Mr and Mrs J.C. Godfrey
John Godfrey
Mrs Lynne Goff
Mr and Mrs J.D. Gold
Arnold Goldman
Joy and Raymond Goldman
L.A. Goldsmith
Nicholas Goldwyn
Cdr Gomersall
Mr R.F. Gompertz
M.E. Gooch
Norman Goodchild
Stephen Goode
W.G and S.O. Goodwin
Brian Goodwin
Mrs Sandra Goodwin
Tony Gordon
David Gordon
Mr and Mrs I.C. Gordon
Mr and Mrs J.J. Gordon
David Gordon Smith
Mrs E. Gordon-Smith
D.B. Gorst
Dr J.R. Gosden
Mrs P. Gosen
Ms Sally Goss
V. Gotts
Mrs Chris Gould
John B. Goulding
Mr R J Goundry
Mr D.G. Graham
Hugh Graham
Mr and Mrs L.J. Grant
Mr J.D. Grant
Mr R.L. Grant
Mrs Moira Grattidge
K. Gray
Mrs D.M. Gray
Simon Gray
Dr T.S. Gray
Mrs Veronica Gray
Dr M.J. Grayson
Anthony V. Green
Mrs J.R. Green
R.P. Green
Mrs P.A. Green
Mr and Mrs J. Green
Mr and Mrs M. Green
Mrs D. Green-Armytage
H.I. Greenfield
Stephen Greensted
N.D.A. Greenstone
Mr and Mrs K. Greenwood
Mr A. Greenwood
Mr J. Greenwood
J.D. Greenwood
J. Gregory
Conal R. Gregory
Dr P.R. Gregor
James Greig
Dr and Mrs A.R. Griew
Mrs S. A. Griffin
M.K. Griffith
W.T.G. Griffiths
William Griffiths
P. Grimsdale
Nigel Grimshaw
Mr N.M. Grimwood
Don Grisbrook
Miss Louise Grove-White
Mr R. Grover
A.D. Grumley-Grennan
Mr and Mrs R.K. Guelff
D.H. Guilford
Mr B.A. Gunary
Rosalind Gunning
Alexander P. Gunning
Mr R.K. Gupta
Dr J.D. Guthrie
Pamela and Raymond Guy
B.S. Gylee
Michele Hagard
Mrs T. Haile
Mr and Mrs P Haines
Austin J. Haines
Mr R.Hainsworth and Ms C.Craig
Mrs D. Haire
Mr I. Hall
Mrs R. Hall
Mr and Mrs W.G. Hall
Ms Caroline Hall
W.J. Hallett
Mrs G. Hallsworth
Tom Halsall
Ms Abigail Hamilton
Ms Kate Hamlyn
Mr D.H.C. Hampshire
Ronnie Hampson
Ms Alison Hancock
Mr and Mrs K.B. Hancock
Dr N.E. Hand
M.R. Handcock
Capt E. Handley
Mr and Mrs Handley
Sir Michael Hanley
T.B.G. Hanlon
Kelvin Hard
Mr and Mrs J. Harding
Mrs Marjorie Harding
Mrs Jane M. Hargraves
B. Hargrove
Christopher Harlow
Mr R.W. Harries
Mr and Mrs C.E. Harris
Raymond Harris
Katy Harris
R.J.D. Harris
Mr and Mrs Harris
Bruce Harris
John Harris
Mrs Joan Harris
Mr J. Harris
Malcolm Harris
Mr and Mrs J. Harris
James Harris
Vincent Harrison
Gordon Harrison
Andrew Harrison
Mrs B. Harrison
Ms I. Hart
Miss W. Hart
J.D. Hartley
Ms S. Hartley
Donald Hartog
C.I. Harvey
Dr Peter Harvey
Jennifer Harvey
Mrs Harwood
Mrs P. Haselden
E. Hastings
Ms A.C. Hatt
Mr J.G. Hattner
Peter and Nita Hauser
Mrs S. Haward
Mrs J.P. Hawken
Mr R.G.P. Hawkins
Mr A.S. Hawkins
Ms K. Susanna Hayward
Donald Haywood
Dennis W. Hazell
D.A. Headley
Greg Heah
Mrs A.B. Heal
J.David Healey
J.D. Healey
D.J. Heap
Barry Heasman
A.V. Heath
J.H.D. Heath
Rev N.C. Heavisides
Mr and Mrs Heber-Percy
Richard Heieh
S. Height
A.D. Hein
A. Hemmant
Mr and Mrs M. Hemming
K.B. Hemming
Mrs Phil Hemmings
Mrs W.A. Henderson
Dr and Mrs A.F. Henderson
Benet Hennessey
N.J. Hennessy
Mr T.F. Henshaw
R.A. Hepher
S.G. Heritage
Philip Herlihy
J. Hermans
Garth Heron
Andrew Herxheimer
Roland and Anna Mae Herzig
Gad Heuman
Mrs Jill Hewitson
Mrs A.E. Hewitt
William B. and Laura M. Hewitt
Mr B.G. Heydecker
Mr and Mrs R. Heyne
E.V. Hibbert
C.N.G. Hicks
Michael S. Hicks
Mrs D. Highton
Mrs S. Highton
M.R. Hill
Mr and Mrs A.V. Hill
Miles Hill
Mrs A.E. Hill
Wendy Hillary
Ms Disma Hills

Mr and Mrs D.W. Hills
Ronald and Maureen Hinde
Mr E. Hinds
Dr T.C. Hindson
Jennifer Hinton
Joan Hoar
Dr Stephen Hoare
P.A. Hoare
David D. Hobbs
Mr and Mrs R.F. Hobbs
Michael Hobsley
Miss P.J. Hodge
Mr B.J. Hodges
Malcolm C. Hodgson
J.S. Hodgson
Jonathan Hoffman
Ms Bridget Hogan
Michael Hogg
Mr and Mrs C. Hogg
David Holbrook
R.H. Holland
Edward Holland
Mrs D. Holliday
Dr M.H. Holloway
Mr J.F. Holman
J.S and J. Holmes
Mr and Mrs Holmes
Mr and Mrs B Holmes
Mike Holt
F.J. Homer
V. Hope
S.J. Hopkinson
Mr A.V. Hopkinson
Lt Col and Mrs F.T. Hopkinson
Chris Hopson and Sabrina Elias
Mrs. H. Horn
Mrs R.N. Horne
Mr P.R. Hornsby
Air Marshal Sir Peter Horsley
Darrin Hosegrove
John Hoskins
Ms Jane Hoskyns
Sarah E. Hotchkiss
Mr and Mrs.R. Hotopf
Dr Keith Hotten
Dr R.A. Houston
Mr and Mrs John Howarth
Andrew Howe
Ms Dorothy Howe
Geoffrey Howell
Mr and Mrs J. Howell
John I. Howells
Mr and Mrs D.R. Howells
Mrs G. Howey
Nicholas Huber
David G.T. Hudd
John and Barbara Huddart
A.M. Hudson
Joan and Peter Hudson
Mrs R. Hughes
Mr C. Hughes
Dr Louis Hughes
Mrs C.A. Hughes
Ms M. Huhtala
Mr and Mrs Hummer
Ms S.C. Humphreys
J.R. Humphreys
P.W. Humphreys
Dr B.J. Hunt
T.V. Hunt
J.B. Hunt
Alan Hunter
Mr I.D. Hunter-Craig
Sue Hurt and Chris Harris
John C. Husband
Mrs D.M. Hutchinson
M. Hutchinson
Miss M. Hutchinson
Mike Hutton
N.R.P. Hutton
H. Hyde
Mrs E.H. Hyde
Mr T.J. Hypher
Dr Frank Hytten
Mrs V.A. Iddon
Mrs A.R. Inglis
Mrs J. Ingram
Brian Ingram
C.S. Innocent
Ms Sally Irvine
Major and Mrs M.D. Isherwood
E.J.F. Isherwood
Dr H.R.S. Jack
Mrs E.A. Jackson
Mr Jackson
James McG. Jackson
P. Jackson
Mrs E.S. Jackson
H.C. Jackson
B. Jackson
Susan B. Jackson
Ms Maggie Jackson
Eric Jaffe
Mrs C. James
S.M. James
A.M. Jameson
Mr M.D. Janson
Moira Jarrett
Alan Jarrett
Mr and Mrs M. Jarvis
Mrs R. Jarvis
The Rt.Hon Lord Jauncey
Mrs O. Jeacock
Michael Jefferson
Ronald Jeffery
Drs Howard and Pat Jenkins
A.D. Jenkins
Richard M. Jenkins
Mr C.R. Jenkinson
B.H. Jenkinson
J.C. Jennings
Mrs M.M.G. Jennings
David Jervois
Peter Jessop
Ms V. Joel
C.M. John
G.K. Johns
Adrianna and Keith Johnson
Iris Johnson
Mr and Mrs M.H. Johnson
Ms F. Johnson
M. Johnson
Mrs J.K. Johnson
H. A. and C. Johnson
Dr I.H.D. Johnston
Andrew Johnston
Captain and Mrs J.R.C. Johnston
Mr and Mrs E.A. Jones
Ian Jones
Mr and Mrs T.O. Jones
Sheilagh Jones
Mr W.C.M. Jones
Michael Jones
Dr Gill Jones
Mr and Mrs W. Morris Jones
C.D.A. Jones
Mrs M.J. Jones
Mr P.G. Jones
Colin Jones
Mr and Mrs J.A.L. Jones
Dr Simon Jones
Mr and Mrs L.H. Jones
David Bellington Jones
Dr J. Barrie Jones
D.W.H. Jordan
Charles Joseph
C.S. Joseph
Mr G.A. Jowitt
Mr and Mrs M. Joyce
Ms Louise Jukes
Mr A. Kalsi
A.K. Kameen
N.L. Kaphan
Esther Kaposi
Mr and Mrs Richard Kaufman
Dr Leon Kaufman
Dr Dina Kaufman
Ms Dinah Keal
Miss R. Keane
G. Keating
Geoffrey Keen
Ms Sheila Keene
I.C. Keizner
M.V. Kelher
Allan Kelly
Mrs K. Kelly
Anthony Kendall
Michael Kent
W.J. Kent
Mrs J. Kent
Neville Kenyon
A.J.F. Kenyon
K.L.S. Beauchamp Kerr
Mr and Mrs B.M. Kettle
Ms Sheila Kidd
J.H. Kilby
Mr and Mrs J. Kilner
Mrs Joyce E. Kimber
Ms Sue Kinch
C.F. King
Sarah King
W.M. Kingston
James Kingston-Stewart
J.C. Kingswood
Mr and Mrs Robert Kinnon
Mrs E. Kirby
W.J.S. Kirton
Sylvia Knapp
P.M. Knatchbull-Hugessen
F.W. Knight
Mr A.J. Knights
Susan Knights
N.F. Knollys
Mrs N. Knoop
Mrs J. Knox
Martin Kochanski
Andreas Koulouris

Ms Judith Kramer
Ms H. Kroll
Robert Kuehn
D.S. Kyle
Dr D.W. Kyle
Dr Ilias Kyriazakis
Jenny and Peter Ladefoged
Lady Kirkhill
Mr I. Laidlaw-Dickson
Simon Lait
Susan R. Laithwaite
Mrs B.G. Laker
Ms H. Lambert
R.E. Lambert
Mrs A.C. Lambirth
Gordon Lammie
Mr J. Lancaster
Lady Lancaster
Anthony Land
Mrs A. Lander
M.D. Lane
Mr R.C. Lang
Dr Bernard W. Langley
Mr R.D. Langran
Mr A.T. Langton
Mrs D. Langton
Ms Shirley Lanigan
Ms N. Lank
Mr and Mrs A. Lanzl
Ms Karen Larkin
Peter Larkworthy
Dr R.D. Last
P.D.N. Laurie
H.M.P. Lawford
Chris Lawrance
Mrs M.E. Lawrence
Steven Lawrence
Mr T.W. Lawrence
Mr A.L. Laws
Neil Lawson-May
David Lea
R.J.R. Lea
Dr and Mrs R. Leach
J. Ledbury
T.J. Ledger
Mr and Mrs T. Lee
Geoffrey Lee
N. Leeming
Mr P.C.S. Lees
Ms Paula Leigh
Mrs A.A. Lenanton
Barbara Leonard
P.L. Leonard
Mrs Joy Levene
Ms E. Lever
Mrs Marilyn Levi
Mr A. S. Levitt
James Lewis
Mrs W. Lewis
Mr I.T. Lewis
Mr D.J.B. Lewis
D.G. Lewis
M.J. Lewis
Mrs Maggie Lewis
Peter Lewis
Mrs Anne Lewis-Smith
Mrs J. Leyland
Harold Lievesley
Dr R. Lincoln
Katherine Lindap
Ms Zena Linfield
Donald C. Lindon
Rev J.D.A. Linn
D.R. and A.J. Linnell
Miss E.A. Linton
Mr Lipton
B.T.E. Livesey
Dr R.S. Lloyd
Miss B. Loader
Mrs Lockwood
David Logan
Ms Victoria Logue
Dr S. Lomax
Sheila M. Longbottom
Fiona Longmore
Andrew Lonsdale
Mr G.W.M. Loveitt
R.F. Lovelock
Gareth Lovett Jones
P.A. and J.B. Lowater
Robert Lowther
Mr S. Luiggi
Mr D.F. Lyle
Mrs T. Lynch
Jan Lyons
Diane Maby
Ian Macaulay
J.A. Macdonald
R.G. Mace
Miles C.M. Maceacharn
Dr J.M. MacFie
R.B. MacGeachy
Walter MacGregor
Mrs Margaret M. Macintosh
J. Gordon Macintyre
Mrs J.A. Mackenzie
Mrs H.K. Mackett
Mr D.B. Mackie
Dr and Mrs M.D. Mackinnon
Neil Mackintosh
Allan Macleod
Ms Karen MacLeod
Neil and Ros Macmillan
Ms Morag MacMillan
Ms Ella Macpherson
Mrs S. Magee
Aubrey Magnus
Professor I.A. Magnus
Mrs Janice Magnus
Dr W. Maguire
P.J. Mahaffey
Mr and Mrs Maheson
C.R. Mains
Peter Mair
M.J. Mallett
Robbie Malloy
E. Maloney
Marianne Malonne
S.R. Mamdani
Mrs B.J. Manchester
Stuart Manger
Trevor Manhire
Ms Deborah Manley
A.J. Manning
Laurence Manning
Michael Manser
E.J.D. Mansfield
Jeremy Mansfield
Ms Karen A. Mansfield
Ray March
Darryl Marks
J.P. Marland
Mr R. Marleyn
P.K. Marlow
Leonard Marlow
Mrs J. Marriott
R.H. Marsden
Sharon Marsh
Mrs P.J. Marshall
Richard J. Marshall
Mrs M.G.R. Marshall
Mr and Mrs T.F. Marshall
Tony and Valerie Marshall
R.O. Marshall
P.R. Marshall
C.P. Marshall
Mrs Rosamond Marshall-Smith
Sally Martin
Miss P.M. Martin
Mr and Mrs Martin
Jurek Martin
Mr J.S.Martin
J. Martineau
J.R. Martyn
Mrs Yvonne Mason
Ms Laura Mason
Mrs J. Mason
Christopher Mason-Watts
Ms Patricia I. Massey
Paul Mather
Mr and Mrs Mathias
Alan G. Matthews
Patrick Matthiesen
Peter Mauger
P.J. Maughan
Ian May
Lester May
Mrs J. Mayringer
M.D. Maythorn
Mr and Mrs D.G. McAdam
Mr H.D. McBeath
Major M.C. McCabe
Dr and Mrs Colin McCance
Dr Graham McCann
Mrs A. McClurkin
Mr and Mrs G.A. McConnell
J.B. McCormack
Mr and Mrs I. McCutcheon
Dr and Mrs G. McDade
Kate McDowall
Mrs Julie McDowall
Prof and Mrs I.D. McFarlane,
Mr C.J. McFeeters
Colin and Lilian McGhee
Dr Ian McGill
Bob McGuire
O.D. McKay
Mr and Mrs A.L.G. McKee
Kevin McKeen
Mr and Mrs K. McKeown
J.A. McKinnell
John G. McLennan
Peter McLeod
Mrs E. McLoughlin
G.M.K. McLoughlin
R. McLoughlin
Stan McNellan
Mr and Mrs John Mead
M.R. Medcalf
Mrs E.P. Medgitt
Ms Joanna Melhuish
Ms S. Melling
W.K. Mendenhall
Dr and Mrs A.P. Mercer
Ms Diane Mercer

Miss C.A. Merrett
Richard and Mary Merritt
I.D. Merry
John Messer
Mr C.J. Messer
Hilary Meth
Dr Alex Mezey
Ms Elizabeth M. Middleton
Peter Middleton
Robin Middleton
R.T. Middleton
Ms Caroline Midmore
W.G. and M.I. Miles
Peter Miles
Julian Miller
D.J. Miller
Dr B. Miller
Kevin Miller
Mrs D.E. Mills
Mrs Jose Mills
Mr and Mrs P. Millward
Mr H.G. Millward
Mrs F. Millward
P.W. Milne
Miss D.F. Milroy
Mrs J. Milton
B.J.S. Minson
Mr C.J.W. Minter
Robert Mitchell
Mr I.W. Mitchell
E. Mitchell
John Mitchell
Ms Ruth Mitchell
Mrs D. Mitchell
J.D. Mitchell
Mrs Annette Molesworth
Dr and Mrs A. Moliver
Dr J. Mollon
C.J. Monk
Janet Monk
Edward Monro
Mrs J.F. Montagu
Mrs Julia Montague
N. Moody
Francis Mooney
Eric Moonman
Mrs C. Moore
Mr H.J. Moore
Craig Jonathan Moore
Alan Brooks Moore
Michael J. Moran
Dr A. Mordue
David R. Moreton
Simon Morford Gravett
Rhian Morgan and David Bishop
Mr M.J.L. Morgan
Dr B. Morgan
C.R. Morgan
P.A. Morgan
Mr and Mrs David Morgan
Neil Morisetti
Mrs L. Morland
Mr F. Morrell
Mr and Mrs John Morrell
D. Morris
J.V.H. Morris
Mrs G. Morris
R.M. Morris
Aubrey Morris
P.I. Morris
Mr V.G.F. Morris
Mr J. Morrison and Ms J. Lee
Mustafa Morrison
Mrs W.D. Morrison
David Mort
Simon Mortimer
Alex and Mai Moss
Mrs N.J. Moss
Joe and Richard Moss-Norbury
P. Mott
Mr and Mrs B. Mottershead
Gillian I. Moussa
Richard F. Moy
Mrs Jane Moyle
Robert Muller
Ms Debra Mumford
A. Mumford
Ms Toni Mundel
Peter Munnoch
Graeme Munro
Mrs M.A. Munro Glass
Mr and Mrs Ken Munroe
David Murdoch
A.D. Murfin
Mr M. Murgatroyd
Mr and Mrs Raymond Murmann
M.C. Murphy
Captain John Murray
Mrs M.L. Murray Smith
Mr R. Murray-Leach
D.M. Musitano
John and Margaret Myring
Mrs C.M. Napier
Tom and Anne Nellist
Jennifer Nelson
Tim Nelson
C. Netting
Julia Neuberger
Ms Susan Neve
Michael Neve
Mr P.A. Newell
Charles and Valerie Newey
Philip Newfield
Ms Jennifer Newman
John Newson
Mr A. Newton
Mr D.R. Nicholas
Tom Nicholls
David Nicholls
Dr C.W. Nicholls
Mr H.W. Nichols
S.J. Nickson
Mrs Alison Niman
Joyce Nixon
P.J. Noble
Mr and Mrs Max Nocton
Dr John Nocton
Geoff Normile and Pat Pavitt
Roger Norrington
Mr J.G. Norris
Peter W. Northey
M. Northover
Mr and Mrs Steve Norton
Graham Norwood
Mr P. Nowak
David Nutt
A.M. Nutting
Mr D.E. Nye
Mrs Sylvia O'Brien
Adrian O'Donovan
Ms Amanda O'Leary
Ms Margaret O'Neill
W.B. O'Neill
Gavin O'Nians
Mrs Ashling O'Reilly
D.H. O'Shaughnessy
Mrs J.M. Oakes
A.P. Oakley
Charles Oatwig-Thain
John Oddey
R.A.L. Ogston
H.N. Olden
Dr B. Olding
Mr N.J. Oldnall
J.N. Oldroyd
Miss C. Oliver
J.M. Oliver
Dr C.J.R. Oliver
Mr G.E. Oliver
Mr D.C. Oliver
Mr and Mrs Dino Olmi
Michael Olpin
Steve Ongeri
Ms Janet Orchard
Ms Loretta Ordewer
Edmond Orkin
Mrs A. Orton
Mrs Frances E. Osborn
Mrs S.E. Osborne,
Mr and Mrs R.E. Osborne
Clarke A. Osborne
Mrs Daphne Osmond
B.T. Overall
Ms Carrie Owen
Rhian Forrest Owen
B.W. Page
Ms Jacqueline Page
Mr and Mrs D.E. Pain
Nadia Pallatt
Mark Palmer
Colin B. Parfitt
Richard Parish
Stephen Parish
Ms Elaine Park
Mr W.E. Parker
J.M. Parker
Mrs Janet Parker
Dr R.B. Parker
Mr T.R. Parker
Dr D. Parker
Sally Parker
Ms Kathleen Parkinson
Martin Parr
Mr J. Parr
Miss P.A. Parsons
D.A. Passey
R.H. Passmore
Stephen Paterson
Mr and Mrs Frank Paterson
Ms Madeline Paterson
Mrs D.S. Paterson-Fox
Mark Patrick
Mr G.M. Patrick
Michael Pattison
John Pattisson
Ms Diana Paulson
T.D. Payton
A. and R. Peace
Mrs J. Pearce
Norman Pearse

Andrew Pearson
Dr R. Pearson
Dr R.M. Pearson
Mrs M.J.T. Peaston
Anthony Peck
P. Peers
Sandra Pegg
Stephen Pegler
Dr and Mrs J.S. Pegum
G.W.Y. Pell
Ms M. Pelling
Mrs J. Pence
Wing Cdr R.A. Pendry
Adrian Penrose
Ms E.A. Percy
Neil and Alison Perkins
Mrs L.J. Perry
Ms Patricia Perry
B. Perryman
David Pert
Helen Peston
Ms Irene Peters
Mr R.C. Petherick
Mr B.W.B. Pettifer
Peter Petts
Anne Phellas
Mr C. Philips
Mr D.R. Philip
Ms C. Phillips
Mr A.P. Phillips
Mr S.L. Phillips
Mr and Mrs C.I. Phillips
Howard Phillips
Mrs I.L. Phillipson
Don Philpott
Ms Susan Pick
Mrs Janice Pickup
A.M. Pickup
W.H. Pierce
L. Pierpont
Richard Piggott
Phil Pilley
Mrs Ann Pilling
Dr and Mrs N.J. Pinfield
Michael Pitel
Hugh Pitt
R.N. Pittman
Dr S. Plant
Mrs J. Plante Cleall
Michele Platman
H.G. Platt
Prof Peter H. Plesch
R. Plumb
Catherine Plummer
R.E. Plunkett
Mr M.D. Pole
Mr D.M. Pollick
Ms Claudia Pollinger
Mrs Lesley A. Pollock
Sir Michael Pollock
David J. Poole
Prof and Mrs Derek Poole
Rosie Porter
Andrew Porter
G.A. Potter
Mr D. Potter
Mr and Mrs A. Powell
Joan A. Powell
Michael Power
Mr and Mrs John Poysden
I. Prackauskas
Helen Preston
N.S. Price
Mrs K. Price
Mrs M. Price
Mr and Mrs J.J.D. Price
R.M. Price
Mr and Mrs J.W. Price
Ms Jane Priddis
Edwin Prince
Peter J. Prior
Captain E.F. Proctor
Mr E. Punchard
R.G. Punshon
R.O. Purcell
Chris Purchase
D.L. Purdy
Stephen J. Purse
C. Purslow
Ms Anna Quick
P.G. Quilliam
Brian Quinn
Mr C.A. Quinn
Harry Rabinowitz
Dr and Mrs Frank Rackow
Christopher J. Rae
Dr Barry S. Ramer
Mr A. Rampton
Dr and Mrs Rampton
Ms Selina Rand
Dr and Mrs D.G.S. Randall
J. Randall
Dr A.M. Rankin
William Rankin
Mrs Caroline Raphael
Mr A.T. Ratcliffe
Mr H.W. Ratcliffe
Mr R. Rava
Marc Rawcliffe
Cdr C.F. Rawnsley
Mrs Patti Raymond
Timothy Raymont
Mr and Mrs Peter Rayner
Martin Rayner
Peter Rea
J.G. Read
Mark Redfern
Andrew Redmond
Alec Reed
W.L. Rees
Ms Phillipa Reeve
Mrs Rupert Reeves
Mrs R.I. Reeves
Miss E. Reeves
Mrs Julie Reid
John Reid
Diana Rendall
Mrs S.E. Rendell
Jill Reumerman
Mr M. Revell
Mr and Mrs Mark Reynolds
R.K. Reynolds
Michael Reynolds
Mrs Siobhan Reynolds
Brian Rice
J.R. Richards
Mrs R.B. Richards
Mr and Mrs David Richards
Jerry Richards
Dr and Mrs K. Richards
David Richards
Mrs H. Richards
Mrs J.D. Richmond
Dr G.S. Riddell
Carol Riddick
John Riddleston
Mrs Gill M. Ridgewell
Frank Ridgway
Dr Ridley Scott
Gordon Ringrose
Dr B. Ritson
Ms Mary Rivers
Richard Robbins
M. Roberts
Michael W. Roberts
Ms Caroline Roberts
A.J. Roberts
Ruth Roberts
Mr A.G. Roberts
Mrs Angela Roberts
Mr and Mrs G. Roberts
Dr A. John Robertson
Ian J. Robertson
Maureen Robertson
Mr C. Robertson
Sheelagh Robertson
N.A. Robinson
Mrs Janine Robinson
Mrs P.N. Robinson
Ivor Robinson
Mrs H.J. Robson
C. Robson
Alan Robson
Mr J. Rochelle
Mr and Mrs Brian Roden
Ms C.J. Rodgers
Mr and Mrs P.N. Rodgers
Neil Lloyd Rogall
Ms Frances M. Rogers
Sir Frank Rogers
Miss A. Rogers
Susan Rollings
Ms Eileen Ronan
Mrs B.S. Rose
Philippa Rose
Mr and Mrs Jeffery Rose
Dr Eric Rose
Daniel Rose
Anthony Rosen
Jonathan Rosenhead
Mrs Lynda N. Ross
Bob Ross
Christopher Ross
Mrs D.S. Ross
Baron von Rothenthal
Mr and Mrs P. Rothwell
R.H. Rowan
Michael Rowland
Mr and Mrs W.R.Rowland
J. Rowland-Entwistle
David and Diana Rowlands
Dr Angela Rowlands
Jill Rowley
Mrs Hilda A. Rowley
I. Roxborough
W.V. Royall
Angela M. Royle
Anthony J. Royle
Rajendra Ruia
Hilary Rubenstein
Mr G. Ruff

Mr and Mrs D E Ruffell
Mr R.J. Ruffell
Mrs S. Rumfitt
John Rumsey
P.W. Runchman
Miss M. Ruparelia
Mr M Rushton
Mr and Mrs R.E.P. Russell
Ms Rosemary Russell
Sue Russell
Dr T. Russell
Alexander B. Russell
Mr D.I. Russell
Mr D. Russell
Mr J.S. Rutter
Mr and Mrs Robert Ryan
Mr and Mrs Rupert Ryle-Hodges
Stephen Ryman
Karen Sadler
Mr L. Saffron
Ron Salmon
Mrs A. Salter
D.E. Samuel
C. Sanderson
Priscilla Sandford
Dr R.J. Sandry
P.E.A.Savage
Mrs M. Savage
Ms M. Savage
G. Sawyer
George Sayer
Ms Sally Saysell
Mrs Helen Scallan
Miss M.D. Scarborough
Ms Emma Scarborough
Andrew F. Scarfe
Prof P.J. Scheuer
Mrs S.E. Schofield
Theo Schofield
Mr R.H. Schofield
Mr K.W. Schofield
Michael Schofield
Miss J. Schroeder
Dr Joseph Schwartz
Dr Stuart Schwartz
Mr R. Schwarz
K.H. Scollay
Mr P.D. Scott
Stella Scott
Adrian E.B. Scott
K.J. Scott
Lady Scott
John U. Scott
Mrs Priscilla Scott
Richard Scott
C.G.P. Scott-Malden
Kenneth H. Scoular
Dr J.W.F. Scrimgeour
Tony Scull
Philip Seaman
Peter Searle
A.G. Searle
N.C. Seddon
Mr Sedgewick
Graham D. Sedgley
Mr and Mrs N.G. Sedgwick
Ms Gillian Seel
B.A. Segal
Mrs F. Segal
Ms Lucy Selby
Mr and Mrs S.A. Seligman
Mrs J. Seller
Ms A. Sennett
Sqdn Ldr J.B. Servant
Dr David and Marlis Sever
J.E. Shackleton
Mrs B.R. Shafer
Mrs D.M. Shalit
Brian Shallom
Mr and Mrs Shamash
Ms Nina Shandloff
Mark Sharman
Mr L.R. Sharman
Dr Clifford Sharp
John A. Sharp
Colin Sharp
Ivor P. Sharpe
Derek Shaw
A. Shaw
H. Shaw
Mr and Mrs Martin Shaw
Miss Nicola Shears
John Sheinman
Harry Sheppard
Nicholas Sheridan
Mr and Mrs P.V. Sherlock
Howard Sherman
S. Sherwood
Mrs E. Sherwood
Miss Rosalind Shields
David Shillitoe
Mr and Mrs Tim Shilton
Mr and Mrs Peter Shimell
Ms Marion Shoard
V. Shofick
Matthew Shore
Ms K. Short
Mr and Mrs D. Shortland
Dr and Mrs T.E. Sicks
Mrs B.A. Silcock
Brian Silverstone
Mr D.A.K. Simmonds
Mr and Mrs Simmons
Ms Josette Simon
R.F. Simons
Mark Simpson
Paul Simpson
Jane Sims
Mr E. Sinclair
Ms Anne Sinclair
Keith Sinclair
R. Sinclair-Taylor
Jeremy Sinden
Arlette and Brian Singleton
S.C. Sixsmith
Mrs P.M. Sizeland
S.J. Skibicki
Peter Skinnard
Mr P.R.Slade
Mr D.A. Slade
Derek Slater
Mrs E.S.Halter
Richard J. Slawson
Rev John E. Slegg
W.L. Sleigh
Ms Susan Small
E.J. Smalley
Colonel D. Smiley
Pat Smith
Mr J.A.R. Smith
Mr and Mrs S.M. Smith
Mr P.E. Smith
Kenneth E. Smith
Dr and Mrs Peter Smith
I.N. Smith
A.F.C. Smith
L.C. Smith
Gary Smith
Mr D.C. Smith
Mrs Penny Smith
Nigel Smith
Mrs L.G. Smith
Mr and Mrs N.L.V. Smith
D.A. Smith
Ian and Sheila Smith
David R. Smith
Ms F.M.K. Smith
T.A. Smith
Mr J.H.B. Smith
Pamela Smith
Mr and Mrs N. Smith
P.A.W. Smith
Mrs Helen R. Smyth
Mr and Mrs John Snelling
Herbert Snoek
D.J. Solly
Zacharo Solomon
Mrs A. Southall
Mrs E. Southorn
Mrs W.S. Soutter
Dr D.S. Sowden
Mrs Stephanie Sowerby
V.G. Spain
Wg Cdr R.M. Sparkes
Ms Alison L. Sparkes
Mr H.H. Sparks
Mr D.H. Sparks
Mrs G.E. Sparrow
Mrs S.M. Spaull
Karen Speed
Mr and Mrs D. Spence
E.A. Spencer
Mr T. Spickett
Mr P.T. Spivey
Colin S. Spotswood
Clive P. Stadler
Cynthia A. Stafford
Mrs B. Staines
Dr and Mrs John Stamford
A.J.W. Stancomb
Frank Stanger
M.G. Staniland
Sybella Stanley
Mr A. Stanton
R.A.J. Starkey
Mr and Mrs Rob Stay
Andrew and Sheena Steed
John Steel
Anthony Steen
Mrs G.M. Stein
Mr F.M. Steiner
M. Stenson
A.J. Stenson
E.M. Stent
Mrs Stephens
Dr and Mrs C.J. Stephens
Mr and Mrs W M Stern
Mrs D. Stevens

Mr and Mrs A.J. Stevens
Mr F. Stevens
Sylvia Stevenson
John Stevenson
Michael Stewart
Captain and Mrs J.S. Stewart
Dr R. Stewart
Paul Stimpson
R.B. Stimpson
A.C. Stoker
Howard Stone
Rod Stoneman and Susan Clarke
D.W. Stooke
Mr and Mrs C.M. Stooke
Mr and Mrs Arthur Storey
M. Stott
Mr L.D. Stovin
Mrs H.A. Stowell
R. Stringer
Hilary and Malcom Strong
C. Stynes
Mr R.M. Summers
Serena Sutcliffe
Ms A.M. Sutcliffe
Miss P. Sutherland
John N. Sutton
Mrs Stella Sutton
Thomas R. Sutton
Mrs Margaret Swain
Mark B. Swindells
A.F. Syed
Ms Brenda Symes
Mrs Elizabeth Syrett
Cdr Patrick Tailyour
Mr and Mr R.M. Talbot
Digby Tantam
Henry Tapper
A. Tarnopolsky
Mr J.A. Tarrant
Mr D.W. Tate
Mr and Mrs M.B. Tate
Dr P.H. Tattersall
Mrs Ann Taurins
Mr T.M. Tayler
A.D. Taylor
Nigel Taylor
Mr A. Taylor
Mrs A.C. Taylor
A.C.G. Taylor
A.R. Taylor
Mrs Wendy Taylor
Dr R.J. Taylor
J.B.C. Taylor
George Taylor
T.W. Taylor
Mrs V. Taylor
S. Taylor
Jean Taylor
P. Teather
John Teenan
Marc K. Temin
Paul Temple
Mr M.T. Temprell
K. Tewsler
Mr J.C. Thackray
Ms Catherine Thanki
A.N. Thatcher
A.D. Thelwall
Russell Thersby
Mrs C. Thomas
Richard and Carol Thomas
Rebecca Thomas
Ms Sophie Thomas
Alan Thomas
Mr and Mrs M. Thomas
J.E. Thomas
R.E. Thomas
Fred Thomas
Ms Gill Thomas
J.E. Thomas
Mr and Mrs Philip Thomas
Miss Emma Thomason
Karen Thompson
Mrs D. Thompson
Mrs J. Thompson
Mrs M. Thompson
J.R. Thompson
Mr and Mrs Peter Thompson
Mr and Mrs Howard Thompson
Dr C.S. Thomson
Tim Thomson
Miss H.A. Thomson
Mrs D.M. Thomson
Mr and Mrs J.C. Thomson
A.R. Thorley
Brian Thorley
J.I. Thorn
Mr D. Thornber
Mr D. Thornton
Mr G. Thwaites
Francis Tibbalds
Capt Sir David Tibbits
T.F. Tiggs
Floyd Timms
Dr P.W. Timms
Mr J. Timms
Mrs Margaret Tipping
Mr and Mrs P. Titcombe
B.A. Tizard
Ms Ruth Tobbell
Dr Jeffrey Tobias
Waldemar Tobolewski
Mr and Mrs T.I.F. Tod
Ms Christine Tollman
Neil Tomkinson
Dr D.R. Tomlinson
Michael Tomlinson
Mrs Susan Tompkins
Mr D.P. Tong
D.F. Tooley
C.G. Toomer
Mrs P.J. Towler
Dr M. Townend
Mr and Mrs R. Towns
Michael Townson
Mr G. Tragen
Dr R.C. Trembath
Mrs S. Trench
Paul Trevisan
Mr and Mrs A.G. Tristram
T. Truran
Fraser Tuddenham
L.K. Tune
Mr D. Tungatt
Mr and Mrs D. Tunnicliffe
Adrian Turner
John R. Turner
Simon Turner
Charles Turner
L.F. Turner
R.K. Turner
David Turner
Mr and Mrs G. Turner
Stuart Turner
Mr B.W.B. Turner
Mr J.S. Turpin
K.C. Turpin
Mr and Mrs R.D. Turvil
Curzon Tussaud
Barbara Tutty
Alan R. Tye
Ms Debbie Tyler
D.R. Tyler
S. Tyndall
Ms Victoria Uden
M.R. Underwood
Adrian Underwood
Mrs R.J. Upchurch
Mrs R. Upson
Mr. R.J. Upward
Dudley Utting
Patricia Valentine
Jo Vanderflier
Yves Vanderweyden
Peter Vanneck
Mr J. Varley
Sue and Alan Vass
Sqdn Ldr.D.G. Vasse
Mrs Monique Venables
A.C. Verdie
A.J.B. Vernon
Andrew C. Vernon
Sir Nigel Vernon
L. Verrico
Mr and Mrs Paul Veysey
C.J. Vezey
Mrs Heather Vidgen
Bosie Vine-Miller
Hon Mrs.A.M. Viney
T.J. Voelcker
Ian Vosper
Michael Wace
Dr M.H.G. Waddington
Peter J. Wade
Sir Ruthven Wade
D.G. Wadsworth
Michael Waggett
Dr B. Waitefield
Russell Wakefield
Mrs Sonia Wakely
Mrs A.M. Walden
Mark Walford
Mrs Elizabeth Walker
C.M. Walker
Mr J. Walker
W.Denis Walker
Ms Corrina Walker
Ian Walker
Michael J. Wall
Marc and Margaret Wall
William Wall
N. Wallace
Mr and Mrs N.E. Wallace
Brian V. Wallace
Dr Robert Waller
D.J. Wallington
Barry Wallwork
Ms Sheila Walsh
Mrs Susan Walsh
John Walsh
Ms Elizabeth Walsh-Heggie

Mr and Mrs D. Walter
Mrs P.R. Walters
Mr and Mrs Peter Warby
Mrs Harriet Warden
Mr A.J. Wardrop
G.M. Wareing
Prof Charles Warlow
Mr and Mrs Warren
Mr and Mrs B. Warren
Major E.M. Warrick
Mr R.A. Wartnaby
Mr D.C.R. Waterfield
Susan Watkin
Denis R. Watkins
R.C. Watkins
Mrs Marion Watkinson
Susan Watsham
Michael Watson
A.P. Watson
Stephen Watson
Mr and Mrs F.B. Watson
Dr.N.P. Watson
Gordon Watt
Mr F.L. Watt
Mr and Mrs E.K. Watts
Mrs N. Webb
Maurice Webb
A.E.P. Webb
Brian Webster
Miss P.M. Webster
Mrs Claire Weeks
Ms Linda L. Welder
Dr Frank O. Wells
Martin F. Wells
Mrs Van Wely
Ms Barbara Wensworth
M.J. West
C.L. West
T.H. West
I.E. West
Mrs D. West
Mrs M. Weston-Smith
S.A. Westrop
Colonel and Mrs. D.C. Whall
F.D. Wharton
Robert Wharton
Ms Mary Wheeler
Ben Whitaker
Dr D.R. Whitbread
Mrs Janet Whitcut
Graham J. White
C.H.J. White
Mrs K.V. White
Mrs J.K. White
E. Clifford White
Drusilla and Colin White
Dr J.E.M. Whitehead
Ms Amanda Whitehead
Jennifer Whitelaw
Paul H. Whiting
Paul Whittaker
Ms Susan M. Whittaker
Stephen and Susan Whittle
Kenneth R. Whitton
Mrs L. S. Whitworth
Ms Carole Whyatt
Mr D.N. Whyte
Miss L. Wickes
P. Widdows
A. Widdup
Gwyneth Wigley
P.G. Wigney
R.N. Wilby
L.J. Wilcocks
Mr K. Wilcox
Mrs Elizabeth Wilcox
Jonathan Wild
Mr and Mrs J.V. Wilde
C.J. Wildt
John B. Wilkin
Ms Clare Wilkins
J.S. and W.V. Wilkinson
W. Wilkinson
Mr P. Willer
Paul Willer
Mrs Alma Williams
Mr M.L.B. Williams
David Williams
Dr and Mrs A M Williams
Peter J. Williams
J.R. Williams
Mr G.L. Williams
Jonathan Williams
Ms Sarah J. Williams
Kieran Williams
Ms Vanessa Williams
C.D. Williams
Barry Williams
N.M. Williamson
Stephen Williamson
Mr and Mrs A.J. Wills
Rev Kenneth C.A. Wills
T.A. Wills
Mr G.D. Wills
Mr and Mrs S.R. Wills
D.C. Wilsdon
Anthony Wilshaw
Cdr G.R.R. Wilson
H. Wilson
C.H. Wilson
Janet Wilson
Mrs S. Wilson
Nicholas J. Wilson
G.D. Wilson
B.M. Wilson
R. Wilson
S. Wilson
Mr D.H. Wilson
Mr R.W. Wilson
Prof P.N. Wilson
J. Wilson Bett
Mrs A.M. Windsor
Ms Emma Windsor
Philippe G. Wines
J.K. Winterbottom
Mr and Mrs Wise
L.M. Wise
Mrs S.V. Wiseman
John Withers
Mr and Mrs T. Withers
D.E. Witts
Mats Wivesson
Mrs M. Wolff
Dr A. Shuk-Yee Wong-Fraser
Hugh Wood
Mrs B. Wood
R. Wood
K.W.J. Wood
Alan Wood
Mrs C.J. Wood
J. Woodall
E.A. Wood
Sir Colin and Lady Woods
J. Woods
Clive P. Woodwards
Barbara M. Wooldridge
R.C. Woolgrove
Mrs J.H.G. Woollcombe
Alan Worsdale
Mr and Mrs P. Wraight
Mr and Mrs A. C. Wright
Duncan Wright
Dennis Wright
Keith Wright
Mr G.L. Wright
Mrs C. Wright
Mr and Mrs Stephen Wright
Mrs C. Wright
D.C. Wright
Alan Wright
Mrs Jill L. Wyatt
J.G. Wyatt
Richard Wyber
Dr and Mrs E. Wyn-Jones
T.J. Wynn-Williams
Mr B.D. Yates
Paul Yeoman
Simon Yorke
P.T. Young
D.E. Young
Mr B. Young
Mr and Mrs R.F. Young
D.F. Young
M.J. Younger
Tasha Yu
Dr J.S. Yudkin
G.B. and I.A Yuille
Dr Peter Zacharias
Mr S. Zammit
Peter and Carola Zentner
Max Zwalf
Ann Zwemmer

Alphabetical list of entries

Abbey Green, Chester, Cheshire
Abingworth Hall, Storrington, West Sussex
Adams Café, London W12
Adare Manor, Adare, Co Limerick
Adil, Birmingham, West Midlands
Adlard's, Norwich, Norfolk
Aherne's, Youghal, Co Cork
Airds Hotel, Port Appin, Strathclyde
Al-Shami, Oxford, Oxfordshire
Alastair Little, London W1
Alba, London EC1
Alfred's, Louth, Lincolnshire
Al Hamra, London W1
Les Alouettes, Claygate, Surrey
Altnaharrie Inn, Ullapool, Highland
Alverton Manor, Truro, Cornwall
Amber Regent, Glasgow, Strathclyde
Angel Inn, Hetton, North Yorkshire
Angel Inn, Stoke-by-Nayland, Suffolk
Ann FitzGerald's Farmhouse Kitchen, Mathry, Dyfed
Anna's Place, London N1
Annie's, Swansea, West Glamorgan
Annie's, Ballydehob, Co Cork
Apple Cottage, Rozel, Jersey
Arbutus Lodge, Cork, Co Cork
Ard-Na-Coille, Newtonmore, Highland
Ardsheal House, Kentallen, Highland
Arirang, London W1
Arisaig House, Arisaig, Highland
Ark, Erpingham, Norfolk
Arkle, Chester Grosvenor Hotel, Chester, Cheshire
L'Arlequin, London SW8
Armadillo, Liverpool, Merseyside
Armenian, Granada Hotel, Manchester, Greater Manchester
Armless Dragon, Cardiff, South Glamorgan
Armstrongs, Barnsley, South Yorkshire
Les Artistes Gourmands/ Café des Artistes, Nottingham, Nottinghamshire
Arundell Arms, Lifton, Devon
Ashford Castle, Cong, Co Mayo
Ashwick House, Dulverton, Somerset
Les Associés, London N8
Assolas Country House, Kanturk, Co Cork
Atkins at Farleyer House, Aberfeldy, Tayside
L'Auberge, Edinburgh, Lothian
Auberge de Provence, St James's Court Hotel, London SW1
Au Bois St Jean, London NW8
Auctioneer, Clitheroe, Lancashire
Auctioneer, Preston, Lancashire
Au Jardin des Gourmets, London W1
Au Provençal, London SE24
Austins, Aldeburgh, Suffolk
Aynsome Manor, Cartmel, Cumbria
Ayudhya, Kingston upon Thames, Surrey
Bahn Thai, London W1
Baile-na-Cille, Uig, Highland
Balbirnie House, Markinch, Fife
Ballymaloe House, Shanagarry, Co Cork
Bambaya, London N8
Bardells, St Bride's-super-Ely, South Glamorgan
Barnards, Cosham, Hampshire
Barretts, Glemsford, Suffolk
Barretts of Princess Street, Plymouth, Devon
Bath Place Hotel, Oxford, Oxfordshire
Baumann's Brasserie, Coggeshall, Essex
Bay Horse Inn and Bistro, Ulverston, Cumbria
Bayleaf Tandoori, London N6
Beadles, Birkenhead, Merseyside
Beaujolais, Bath, Avon
Bedlington Café, London W4
Beechwood Country House, Moffat, Dumfries & Galloway
Beetle & Wedge, Moulsford, Oxfordshire
Belfast Castle, Belfast, Co Antrim
Bell, Aston Clinton, Buckinghamshire
La Belle Alliance, Blandford Forum, Dorset
Belle Epoque, Belfast, Co Antrim
Belle Epoque, Knutsford, Cheshire
Belvedere Hotel, Bradford, West Yorkshire
Le Berger, Bramley, Surrey

Bharat, Bradford, West Yorkshire
Bibendum, London SW3
Billboard Café, London NW6
Billesley Manor, Billesley, Warwickshire
Billy Budd's, Dartmouth, Devon
Bistro Montparnasse, Southsea, Hampshire
Bistro Twenty One, Bristol, Avon
Bistrot 190, London SW7
Black Bull, Moulton, North Yorkshire
Black Chapati, Brighton, East Sussex
Black House, Hexham, Northumberland
Black Swan, Beckingham, Lincolnshire
Blackwater Hotel, West Mersea, Essex
Blair's Cove House, Durrus, Co Cork
Blostin's, Shepton Mallet, Somerset
Blue Elephant, London SW6
Blue Haven, Kinsale, Co Cork
Blueprint Café, London SE1
Bobby's, Leicester, Leicestershire
Bodysgallen Hall, Llandudno, Gwynedd
Bombay Brasserie, London SW7
Boncomptes, Douglas, Isle of Man
Boucha's, London W14
Bowlish House, Shepton Mallet, Somerset
Box Tree, Ilkley, West Yorkshire
Boyd's, London W8
Bozan, Cardiff, South Glamorgan
Bradfield House, Bradfield Combust, Suffolk
Brady's, London SW18
Braeval Old Mill, Aberfoyle, Central
La Braseria, Swansea, West Glamorgan
La Brasserie, Morpeth, Northumberland
La Brasserie, Cardiff, South Glamorgan
Brasted's, Norwich, Norfolk
Breamish House, Powburn, Northumberland
Bridge House, Beaminster, Dorset
Bridgefield House, Spark Bridge, Cumbria
Brookdale House, North Huish, Devon
Brown's, Worcester, Hereford & Worcester
Brown's Bistro, Clitheroe, Lancashire
Browns Hotel, Haddington, Lothian
Brundholme Country House Hotel, Keswick, Cumbria
Bryans, Leeds, West Yorkshire
Buckland Manor, Buckland, Gloucestershire
Burrastow House, Walls, Shetland
Bu San, London N7
But'n'ben, Auchmithie, Tayside
Butley-Orford Oysterage, Orford, Suffolk
Buttery, Glasgow, Strathclyde
Buzkash, London SW15
Byrons, Eastbourne, East Sussex
Café du Marché, London EC1
Café Gandolfi, Glasgow, Strathclyde
Café Istanbul, Manchester, Greater Manchester
Café Niçoise, Colwyn Bay, Clwyd
Café Procope,Newcastle upon Tyne,Tyne & Wear
Café Volnay, Porthoustock, Cornwall
Calcot Manor, Tetbury, Gloucestershire
Callow Hall, Ashbourne, Derbyshire
Capers, Torquay, Devon
Capital Hotel, London SW3
Le Caprice, London SW1
Caravan Serai, London W1
Carl's, Trinity House Hotel, Coventry, West Midlands
Carved Angel, Dartmouth, Devon
Casale Franco, London N1
Cashel House Hotel, Cashel, Co Galway
Le Cassoulet, Cardiff, South Glamorgan
Castle Hotel, Taunton, Somerset
Cavaliers, London SW8
Cedar Restaurant, Evesham Hotel, Evesham, Hereford & Worcester
Cellar, Anstruther, Fife
Cellars, Dundalk, Co Louth
Cemlyn, Harlech, Gwynedd
C'est la Vie, Lytham St Anne's, Lancashire
Cézanne, Twickenham, Greater London
Champany Inn, Linlithgow, Lothian
Le Champenois, Blackwater Hotel, West Mersea, Essex
Champers, Cardiff, South Glamorgan
Le Champignon Sauvage, Cheltenham, Gloucestershire
Chandler's, Trefriw, Gwynedd
Chanterelle, London SW7
Chapeltoun House, Stewarton, Strathclyde
Chapters, Stokesley, North Yorkshire
Charnwood Hotel, Sheffield, South Yorkshire
La Chaumière, Cardiff, South Glamorgan
Le Chausson, London SW11
Chedington Court, Chedington, Dorset
Cheevers, Tunbridge Wells, Kent
Chelsea Room, Hyatt Carlton Tower, London SW1
Cherry Orchard, London E2
Cherwell Boathouse, Oxford, Oxfordshire
Chester Grosvenor Hotel, Chester, Cheshire
Chewton Glen Hotel, New Milton, Hampshire
Chez Hans, Cashel, Co Tipperary
Chez Liline, London N4
Chez Max, Surbiton, Surrey
Chez Moi, London W11
Chez Nico, London W1
Chez Nous, Plymouth, Devon
Chiang Mai, London W1
Chikako's, Bath, Avon

Chinese Home Cooking, Edinburgh, Lothian
Chinon, London W14
Christian's, London W4
Chung Ying, Birmingham, West Midlands
Churchill Hotel, London W1
Cibo, London W14
Claire De Lune, Bruton, Somerset
Clarke's, London W8
Clifford's, Cork, Co Cork
Clos du Roy at Box House, Box, Wiltshire
Cnapan, Newport, Dyfed
Cobbett's, Botley, Hampshire
Cobwebs, Leck, Lancashire
Colin O'Daly, the Park Restaurant, Blackrock, Co Dublin
Collin House, Broadway, Hereford & Worcester
Colonial India, Glasgow, Strathclyde
Congham Hall, Grimston, Norfolk
Connaught, London W1
Connolly's, London SW15
Coq Hardi, Dublin, Co Dublin
Cork & Bottle, London WC2
Corner Cupboard Dining Room, Winchcombe, Gloucestershire
Corse Lawn House Hotel, Corse Lawn, Gloucestershire
Count House, Botallack, Cornwall
Country Club, Harrow, Greater London
Country Friends, Dorrington, Shropshire
La Cour, Nailsea, Avon
Courtney's, Newcastle upon Tyne, Tyne & Wear
Crabwall Manor, Mollington, Cheshire
Crannog, Fort William, Highland
Crawford Gallery, Cork, Co Cork
Crinan Hotel, Crinan, Strathclyde
Cringletie House, Peebles, Borders
La Croisette, London SW10
Cromlix House, Kinbuck, Central
Cromwellian, Kirkham, Lancashire
Croque-en-Bouche, Malvern Wells, Hereford & Worcester
The Cross, Kingussie, Highland
Cross Keys Inn, Delph, Greater Manchester
Crown, Southwold, Suffolk
Crown at Whitebrook, Whitebrook, Gwent
Crowthers, London SW14
Crudwell Court, Crudwell, Wiltshire
Culloden House, Inverness, Highland
Currarevagh House, Oughterard, Co Galway
Danescombe Valley Hotel, Calstock, Cornwall
Days of the Raj, Birmingham, West Midlands
Denzler's 121, Edinburgh, Lothian
Dew Pond, Old Burghclere, Hampshire
Dickens, Wethersfield, Essex
Digby's, Dun Laoghaire, Co Dublin
Diwana Bhel-Poori, London NW1
Dolmelynllyn Hall, Dolgellau, Gwynedd
Dorchester, London W1
La Dordogne, London W4
Dower House, Muir of Ord, Highland
Doyle's, Dingle, Co Kerry
Dragon House, Newcastle upon Tyne, Tyne & Wear
Dragon's Nest, London W1
Drewe Arms, Broadhembury, Devon
Drimcong House, Moycullen, Co Galway
Dromoland Castle, Newmarket-on-Fergus, Co Clare
Druidstone Hotel, Broad Haven, Dyfed
Drum and Monkey, Harrogate, North Yorkshire
Dunain Park, Inverness, Highland
Dundas Arms, Kintbury, Berkshire
Dunworley Cottage, Clonakilty, Co Cork
Dwyers, Waterford, Co Waterford
Dylanwad Da, Dolgellau, Gwynedd
Eagle, London EC1
Eastern Promise, Grampound, Cornwall
Eastern Tandoori, Dublin, Co Dublin
Eastwell Manor, Boughton Lees, Kent
Edderton Hall, Forden, Powys
Efes Kebab House, London W1
Egerton Grey Country House, Porthkerry, South Glamorgan
Eleven Park Walk, London SW10
Elms Hotel, Abberley, Hereford & Worcester
Emile's, London SW6
English Garden, London SW3
Epicurean, Cheltenham, Gloucestershire
Epworth Tap, Epworth, Humberside
Eslington Villa Hotel, Gateshead, Tyne & Wear
Esseborne Manor, Hurstbourne Tarrant, Hampshire
Evesham Hotel, Evesham, Hereford & Worcester
Fanshawe's, Warwick, Warwickshire
Fantails, Wetheral, Cumbria
Faraday's, Aberdeen, Grampian
Farlam Hall, Brampton, Cumbria
Farm Gate, Midleton,Co Cork
Farmhouse Kitchen, Fishguard, Dyfed
Fat Tulip, Hereford, Hereford & Worcester
Faulkner's, London E8
Feathers Hotel, Woodstock, Oxfordshire
Feldon House, Lower Brailes, Warwickshire
Ferns, Louth, Lincolnshire
Fifehead Manor, Middle Wallop, Hampshire

15 North Parade, Oxford, Oxfordshire
La Fin de la Chasse, London N16
First Floor, London W11
Fischer's at Baslow Hall, Baslow, Derbyshire
Fish at Sutton Courtenay, Sutton Courtenay, Oxfordshire
Fisherman's Lodge, Newcastle upon Tyne, Tyne & Wear
Fishes', Burnham Market, Norfolk
Flitwick Manor, Flitwick, Bedfordshire
Floodlite, Masham, North Yorkshire
Florians, London N8
Flynns, Nailsworth, Gloucestershire
Food for Friends, Brighton, East Sussex
Food for Thought, Fowey, Cornwall
Forsters, East Boldon, Tyne & Wear
Fountain House, Dedham, Essex
Four Seasons, Inn on the Park, London W1
Fox and Goose, Fressingfield, Suffolk
French Partridge, Horton, Northamptonshire
Frith's, London W1
Fung Shing, London WC2
Funnywayt'mekalivin, Berwick-upon-Tweed, Northumberland
Gales, Llangollen, Clwyd
Galley, Swanage, Dorset
Gannets Bistrot, Newark, Nottinghamshire
Ganpath, London WC1
Garbo's, King's Lynn, Norfolk
Garlands, Bath, Avon
La Gaulette, London W1
Le Gavroche, London W1
Gavvers, London SW1
Gay Hussar, London W1
Gelli Fawr Country House, Pontfaen, Dyfed
General Havelock Inn, Haydon Bridge, Northumberland
George, Stamford, Lincolnshire
George & Dragon, Rowde, Wiltshire
George Hotel, Dorchester-on-Thames, Oxfordshire
George's Brasserie, Canterbury, Kent
Gidleigh Park, Chagford, Devon
Gilbert's, London SW7
Gilpin Lodge, Windermere, Cumbria
La Giralda, Pinner, Greater London
Gopal's of Soho, London W1
Grahame's Seafare, London W1
Granada Hotel, Manchester, Greater Manchester
Grand Hotel, Eastbourne, East Sussex
Grange Hotel, York, North Yorkshire
Granite Corner, Rozel, Jersey
Gravetye Manor, East Grinstead, West Sussex
Great House, Lavenham, Suffolk
Great Nepalese, London NW1
Green Apple, Bakewell, Derbyshire
Greenhead House, Sheffield, South Yorkshire
Greenhouse, London W1
Greens Seafood, Norwich, Norfolk
Greenway, Shurdington, Gloucestershire
Gregans Castle, Ballyvaughan, Co Clare
Griffin, Fletching, East Sussex
Grosvenor Hotel, Rugby, Warwickshire
Gurkha Brasserie, London NW11
Haandi, London NW1
Half Door, Dingle, Co Kerry
Hambleton Hall, Hambleton, Leicestershire
Hanbury Manor, Thundridge, Hertfordshire
Hansa's, Leeds, West Yorkshire
Happy Wok, Swansea, West Glamorgan
Harbour Bistro, Ramsey, Isle of Man
Harbour Lights, Porthgain, Dyfed
Harding's, North Berwick, Lothian
Harlosh Hotel, Dunvegan, Isle of Skye
Harper's, Salisbury, Wiltshire
Harry's Place, Great Gonerby, Lincolnshire
Hartwell House, Aylesbury, Buckinghamshire
Harveys, London SW17
Harvey's Cathedral Restaurant, Lincoln, Lincolnshire
Heathcote's, Longridge, Lancashire
Henfry's Restaurant, Charnwood Hotel, Sheffield, South Yorkshire
Henrys, Birmingham, West Midlands
Hiders, London SW6
High Moor, Wrightington, Lancashire
Highgrove House, Troon, Strathclyde
Hilaire, London SW7
Hintlesham Hall, Hintlesham, Suffolk
L'Hippocampe, London W1
Hive on the Quay, Aberaeron, Dyfed
Honfleur, Cross Keys Inn, Delph, Greater Manchester
Honours Mill, Edenbridge, Kent
Hope End, Ledbury, Hereford & Worcester
Horn of Plenty, Tavistock, Devon
Horsted Place, Uckfield, East Sussex
Hospitality Inn, Brighton, East Sussex
Hotel Portmeirion, Portmeirion, Gwynedd
Howard's House Hotel, Teffont Evias, Wiltshire
Howe Villa, Richmond, North Yorkshire
Hughenden, Goudhurst, Kent

Hungry Monk, Jevington, East Sussex
Hunstrete House, Hunstrete, Avon
Hunter's Hotel, Rathnew, Co Wicklow
Hunters Lodge, Broadway, Hereford & Worcester
Hunts Tor House, Drewsteignton, Devon
Ikkyu, London W1
L'Incontro, London SW1
Indian Cavalry Club, Edinburgh, Lothian
Indian Ocean, Cardiff, South Glamorgan
Innsacre, Shipton Gorge, Dorset
Inverlochy Castle, Fort William, Highland
Island Hotel, Tresco, Isles of Scilly
Isle of Eriska Hotel, Eriska, Strathclyde
Isohama, London SW1
Ivy, London WC2
Ivy House, Braithwaite, Cumbria
Ivy Restaurant, Grange Hotel, York, North Yorkshire
Jade Garden, London W1
Jameson's, Bristol, Avon
Jemima's, Haverfordwest, Dyfed
Jeremy's at the King's Head, Cuckfield, West Sussex
Jin, London W1
Joe's Café, London SW3
John Blackmore's, Alnwick, Northumberland
Jonathans, Oldbury, West Midlands
Julés Café, Weobley, Hereford & Worcester
Kagura, London N3
Kalamaras, London W2
Kalpna, Edinburgh, Lothian
Kapriol, Dublin, Co Dublin
Kastoori, London SW17
Keenans, Swansea, West Glamorgan
Kelly's, Edinburgh, Lothian
Kensington Place, London W8
Khun Akorn, London SW3
Killiecrankie Hotel, Killiecrankie, Tayside
King Sitric, Howth, Co Dublin
King's Arms, Amersham, Buckinghamshire
Kingshead House, Birdlip, Gloucestershire
Kinloch House Hotel, Blairgowrie, Tayside
Kinloch Lodge, Isle Ornsay, Highland
Kinnaird House, Dunkeld, Tayside
Kinsella's, Ipswich, Suffolk
Kirkstone Foot Country House Hotel, Ambleside, Cumbria
Kitchen, Polperro, Cornwall
Kites, York, North Yorkshire
Knipoch Hotel, Oban, Strathclyde
Knockie Lodge, Whitebridge, Highland
Knockinaam Lodge, Portpatrick, Dumfries & Galloway
Knockmuldowney Restaurant, Collooney, Co Sligo
Koreana, Manchester, Greater Manchester
Kosmos Taverna, Manchester, Greater Manchester
Kuti's, Southampton, Hampshire
Kwok's Rendezvous, Ipswich, Suffolk
Laburnum House, Wylam, Northumberland
Lacken House, Kilkenny, Co Kilkenny
Lake Hotel, Llangammarch Wells, Powys
Lal Qila, London W1
Lamb, Burford, Oxfordshire
Lamb Inn, Shipton-under-Wychwood, Oxfordshire
Lancrigg, Grasmere, Cumbria
Landgate Bistro, Rye, East Sussex
Langan's Bistro, Brighton, East Sussex
Langan's Brasserie, London W1
Langar Hall, Langar, Nottinghamshire
Langley House Hotel, Langley Marsh, Somerset
Langley Wood, Redlynch, Wiltshire
Lanterna, Scarborough, North Yorkshire
Lanterns, Llandudno, Gwynedd
Latymer, Pennyhill Park Hotel, Bagshot, Surrey
Launceston Place, London W8
Laurent, London NW2
Leatherne Bottel, Goring, Oxfordshire
Leela's, Newcastle upon Tyne, Tyne & Wear
Leith's, London W11
Lettonie, Bristol, Avon
Lewtrenchard Manor, Lewdown, Devon
Liaison, Oxford, Oxfordshire
Lillibet's, Liversedge, West Yorkshire
Lime Tree, Kenmare, Co Kerry
Lime Tree, Manchester, Greater Manchester
Little Barwick House, Barwick, Somerset
Little Byres, Dallington, East Sussex
Little Yang Sing, Manchester, Greater Manchester
Llangoed Hall, Llyswen, Powys
Llew Glas, Harlech, Gwynedd
Loch Fyne Oyster Bar, Nottingham, Nottinghamshire
Loch Fyne Oyster Bar, Cairndow, Strathclyde
Lock 16 Seafood Restaurant, Crinan Hotel, Crinan, Strathclyde
Locks, Dublin, Co Dublin
Lodge Hotel, Huddersfield, West Yorkshire
Lombard Room, King's Norton, West Midlands
Long's, Blackwater, Cornwall
Longueville House, Mallow, Co Cork
Longueville Manor, St Saviour, Jersey
Los Remos, London W2

Lou Pescadou, London SW7
Lovetts, Douglas, Co Cork
Lower Pitt, East Buckland, Devon
Lowman, Tiverton, Devon
Lucknam Park, Colerne, Wiltshire
Lugleys, Wootton, Isle of Wight
Lupton Tower, Kirkby Lonsdale, Cumbria
Lychgates, Bexhill, East Sussex
Lygon Arms, Broadway, Hereford & Worcester
Lynton House, Holdenby, Northamptonshire
Lynwood House, Barnstaple, Devon
Mabey's Brasserie, Sudbury, Suffolk
Macduff's, Coleraine, Co Derry
Maes-y-Neuadd, Talsarnau, Gwynedd
Magpie Café, Whitby, North Yorkshire
Magpies, Horncastle, Lincolnshire
Maharaja, Birmingham, West Midlands
Mallards, St Michael's on Wyre, Lancashire
Mallory Court, Bishop's Tachbrook, Warwickshire
La Malmaison, Hersham, Surrey
Man Ho, Leicester, Leicestershire
Mandalay, London SE10
Mandarin Kitchen, London W2
Mandeer, London W1
Manleys, Storrington, West Sussex
Le Manoir aux Quat'Saisons, Great Milton, Oxfordshire
Manor, Chadlington, Oxfordshire
Manor Hotel, West Bexington, Dorset
Manor House, Belfast, Co Antrim
Manor House Inn, Kiln Pit Hill, Northumberland
Manzi's, London WC2
Marché Noir, Edinburgh, Lothian
Marco's, Norwich, Norfolk
Market Restaurant, Manchester, Greater Manchester
Markwicks, Bristol, Avon
Marlfield House, Gorey, Co Wexford
Maroush III, London W1
Marryat Room, Chewton Glen Hotel, New Milton, Hampshire
Marsh, Eyton, Hereford & Worcester
Marsh Goose, Moreton-in-Marsh, Gloucestershire
Martha's Vineyard, Nayland, Suffolk
Martin's, London NW1
Martins, Edinburgh, Lothian
Mary's, Walberswick, Suffolk
Mauro's, Bollington, Cheshire
Maxine's, Midhurst, West Sussex
Mayflower, London W1
Mayflower, Cheltenham, Gloucestershire
McClements, Twickenham, Greater London
McCoy's, Staddlebridge, North Yorkshire
Meadowsweet Hotel, Llanrwst, Gwynedd
Melati, London W1
Melbournes, Bristol, Avon
Melton's, York, North Yorkshire
Le Meridien Hotel, London W1
Meson Don Felipe, London SE1
Le Mesurier, London EC1
Michael's Nook, Grasmere, Cumbria
Michels', Ripley, Surrey
Middlethorpe Hall, York, North Yorkshire
Midsummer House, Cambridge, Cambridgeshire
Mijanou, London SW1
Milk House, Montacute, Somerset
Miller Howe, Windermere, Cumbria
Miller Howe Café, Windermere, Cumbria
Millers, Harrogate, North Yorkshire
Mims, Barnet, Hertfordshire
Minffordd Hotel, Talyllyn, Gwynedd
Mirabelle, Grand Hotel, Eastbourne, East Sussex
Mr Kong, London WC2
Mr Kuks, Manchester, Greater Manchester
Mr Underhill's, Stonham, Suffolk
Mitsukoshi, London SW1
Miyama, London W1
Mock Turtle, Dorchester, Dorset
Mon Petit Plaisir, London W8
Mon Plaisir, London WC2
Le Monde, Cardiff, South Glamorgan
Monkeys, London SW3
Moon, Kendal, Cumbria
Moorings, Wells-next-the-Sea, Norfolk
Morefield Motel, Ullapool, Highland
Morels, Haslemere, Surrey
Mortimer's, Bury St Edmunds, Suffolk
Mortimer's on the Quay, Ipswich, Suffolk
Moss Nook, Manchester, Greater Manchester
Mount Falcon Castle, Ballina, Co Mayo
Moyglare Manor, Maynooth, Co Kildare
Mulberry Room, Torquay, Devon
Munchy Munchy, Oxford, Oxfordshire
Murrayshall Hotel, Scone, Tayside
Le Muscadet, London W1
Muset, Bristol, Avon
Museum Street Café, London WC1
Nakano, London SW3
Nansidwell Country House, Mawnan Smith, Cornwall
Neal Street Restaurant, London WC2
Neshiko, London N1
New Mill, Eversley, Hampshire
New World, London W1

Newport House, Newport, Co Mayo
Nichol's, London NW6
Nick's Warehouse, Belfast, Co Antrim
Café Niçoise, Colwyn Bay, Clwyd
Nightingales, Taunton, Somerset
19 Grape Lane, York, North Yorkshire
Nippon Kan, Old Thorns, Liphook, Hampshire
La Noblesse, Hospitality Inn, Brighton, East Sussex
Nontas, London NW1
Normandie, Birtle, Greater Manchester
Northcote Manor, Langho, Lancashire
Now & Zen, London WC2
No. 3, Glastonbury, Somerset
No. 28, Standon, Hertfordshire
Nunsmere Hall, Northwich, Cheshire
Nuthurst Grange, Hockley Heath, West Midlands
O'Grady's, Clifden, Co Connemara
Oak Room, Le Meridien Hotel, London W1
Oakes, Stroud, Gloucestershire
Oakhill House, Oakhill, Somerset
Ocean City, Nottingham, Nottinghamshire
Ockenden Manor, Cuckfield, West Sussex
October, Glasgow, Strathclyde
October Café, Glasgow, Strathclyde
Odettes, London NW1
Old Bakehouse, Little Walsingham, Norfolk
Old Beams, Waterhouses, Staffordshire
Old Coffee Shop, Aberdovey, Gwynedd
Old Fire Engine House, Ely, Cambridgeshire
Old Forge, Hawick, Borders
Old Hall, Threshfield, North Yorkshire
Old Hoops, Saffron Walden, Essex
Old House, Wickham, Hampshire
Old Manor House, Romsey, Hampshire
Old Monastery, Drybridge, Grampian
Old Post Office, Clun, Shropshire
Old Rectory, Campsea Ash, Suffolk
Old Rectory, Llansanffraid Glan Conwy, Gwynedd
Old Rectory, Wicklow, Co Wicklow
Old Station Coffee Shop, Dinas Mawddwy, Gwynedd
Old Thorns, Liphook, Hampshire
Old Vicarage, Witherslack, Cumbria
Old Vicarage, Ridgeway, Derbyshire
Old Woolhouse, Northleach, Gloucestershire
Olivers, Staple Cross, East Sussex
One Devonshire Gardens, Glasgow, Strathclyde
192, London W11
190 Queensgate, London SW7
Orient Rendezvous, Bristol, Avon
Orso, London WC2
L'Ortolan, Shinfield, Berkshire
Osteria Antica Bologna, London SW11
Ostlers Close, Cupar, Fife
Pailin, Lewes, East Sussex
Panda Si Chuen, London W1
Paris, Leeds, West Yorkshire
Paris House, Woburn, Bedfordshire
Paris II, Huddersfield, West Yorkshire
Park Hotel, Kenmare, Co Kerry
Parrock Head Hotel, Slaidburn, Lancashire
Partners West Street, Dorking, Surrey
Il Passetto, London WC2
Patrick Guilbaud, Dublin, Co Dublin
Pavilion, Consett, Co Durham
Peat Inn, Peat Inn, Fife
Pebbles, Aylesbury, Buckinghamshire
Penhelig Arms Hotel, Aberdovey, Gwynedd
Pennyhill Park Hotel, Bagshot, Surrey
Pennypots, Blackwater, Cornwall
Penrhos Court, Kington, Hereford & Worcester
Peppers, Manchester, Greater Manchester
Perkins Bar Bistro, Plumtree, Nottinghamshire
Il Pescatore, Worcester, Hereford & Worcester
Le Petit Canard, Maiden Newton, Dorset
Le Petit Pierrot, Claygate, Surrey
La Petite Auberge, Great Missenden, Buckinghamshire
Pheasant Inn, Keyston, Cambridgeshire
Pier at Harwich, Harwich, Essex
Pierre Victoire, Edinburgh, Lothian
Pizzeria Castello, London SE1
Pizzeria Condotti, London W1
Les Plantagenêts, Leamington Spa, Warwickshire
Planters, Malvern Wells, Hereford & Worcester
Plas Bodegroes, Pwllheli, Gwynedd
Plumber Manor, Sturminster Newton, Dorset
Poissonnerie de l'Avenue, London SW3
Pollyanna's, London SW11
Polmaily House Hotel, Drumnadrochit, Highland
Pool Court, Pool in Wharfedale, West Yorkshire
Poons, London WC2
Pophams, Winkleigh, Devon
Poppies, The Roebuck, Brimfield, Hereford & Worcester

Porth Tocyn Hotel, Abersoch, Gwynedd
Porthole Eating House, Bowness-on-Windermere, Cumbria
Hotel Portmeirion, Portmeirion, Gwynedd
La Potinière, Gullane, Lothian
Le Poussin, Brockenhurst, Hampshire
Powdermills, Battle, East Sussex
Priory Hotel, Wareham, Dorset
Priory Hotel, Bath, Avon
Le Provençale, Whitley Bay, Tyne & Wear
Provence, Lymington, Hampshire
Puckrup Hall, Tewkesbury, Gloucestershire
Quality Chop House, London EC1
Quan Ju De, Manchester, Greater Manchester
Quayles, Cardiff, South Glamorgan
Queen's Head, Glanwydden, Gwynedd
Quince and Medlar, Cockermouth, Cumbria
Quincy's, Seaford, East Sussex
Ragam, London W1
Ramore, Portrush, Co Antrim
Rampsbeck Country House Hotel, Watermillock, Cumbria
Rani, London N3
Rankins, Sissinghurst, Kent
Read's, Faversham, Kent
Redmond's, Cleeve Hill, Gloucestershire
Reeds, Poughill, Cornwall
Regatta, Aldeburgh, Suffolk
Renoufs, Rochford, Essex
Restaurant Bonnet, Cranleigh, Surrey
Restaurant Bosquet, Kenilworth, Warwickshire
Restaurant Elizabeth, Oxford, Oxfordshire
Restaurant Na Mara, Dun Laoghaire, Co Dublin
Restaurant 19, Belvedere Hotel, Bradford, West Yorkshire
Restaurant Peano, Barnsley, South Yorkshire
Restaurant Roger Burdell, Loughborough, Leicestershire
Riber Hall, Matlock, Derbyshire
Richard at Lanterns, Llandudno, Gwynedd
Rise of the Raj, Leicester, Leicestershire
Ritcher's, Wells, Somerset
Riva, London SW13
River Café, London W6
River House, Poulton-le-Fylde, Lancashire
River House, Lympstone, Devon
Riverside, King's Lynn, Norfolk
Riverside, Helford, Cornwall
Riverside Hotel, Abersoch, Gwynedd
Riverside Inn, Canonbie, Dumfries & Galloway
Riverside Café and Restaurant, West Bay, Dorset
Roadhouse Restaurant, Roade, Northamptonshire
Rocher's, Milford-on-Sea, Hampshire
Rocinante's, Bristol, Avon
Rogano, Glasgow, Strathclyde
Roger's, Windermere, Cumbria
Roman Camp Hotel, Callander, Central
Rondelle, Birkenhead, Merseyside
The Roebuck, Brimfield, Hereford & Worcester
Rookery Hall, Worleston, Cheshire
Roots, Swansea, West Glamorgan
Roscoff, Belfast, Co Antrim
Rose Cottage, Dinas, Dyfed
Röser's, St Leonard's, East Sussex
Rosleague Manor, Letterfrack, Co Galway
Rothay Manor, Ambleside, Cumbria
Rotisserie, London W12
Royal China, London SW15
Royal Crescent Hotel, Bath, Avon
Royal Oak, Yattendon, Berkshire
RSJ, London SE1
Rue St Jacques, London W1
Rumbles Cottage, Felsted, Essex
Rupali, Newcastle upon Tyne, Tyne & Wear
Saagar, Nottingham, Nottinghamshire
Sabatini, London SW1
Sabras, London NW10
St Quentin, London SW3
St Tudno Hotel, Llandudno, Gwynedd
Salisbury House, Diss, Norfolk
Sanam, Manchester, Greater Manchester
Sand House Hotel, Rossnowlagh, Co Donegal
Sankey's, Tunbridge Wells, Kent
Saverys, Frampton on Severn, Gloucestershire
Savoy Grill and River Restaurant, London WC2
Sea View House Hotel, Ballylickey, Co Cork
Seafood Restaurant, Great Yarmouth, Norfolk
Seafood Restaurant, Padstow, Cornwall
September Brasserie, Blackpool, Lancashire
Severn Tandoori, Stourport-on-Severn, Hereford & Worcester
Shamiana, Edinburgh, Lothian
Sharrow Bay, Ullswater, Cumbria
Sheelin, Bellanaleck, Co Fermanagh
Sheila's Cottage, Ambleside, Cumbria
Shieldhill Hotel, Biggar, Strathclyde
Shiro, Ahakista, Cork
Shoes, High Ongar, Essex
Shore, Edinburgh, Lothian
Siam Orchid, Manchester, Greater Manchester
Silver Darling, Aberdeen, Grampian

Silver Plough, Pitton, Wiltshire
Simply Nico, London SW1
Singapore Garden Mayfair, London W1
Singapore Garden Restaurant, London NW6
Singing Chef, Ipswich, Suffolk
Sir Charles Napier Inn, Chinnor, Oxfordshire
Sir Edward Elgar, Swallow Hotel, Birmingham, West Midlands
Sir Toby's, Stratford-upon-Avon. Warwickshire
Slassor's, Southend-on-Sea, Essex
Sloans, Birmingham, West Midlands
Smithfield, Manchester, Greater Manchester
Soanes, Petworth, West Sussex
Soho Soho, London W1
Sonny's, London SW13
Sonny's, Nottingham, Nottinghamshire
Sophisticats, Bournemouth, Dorset
Le Soufflé, Inter-Continental Hotel, London W1
Soughton Hall, Northop, Clwyd
Soulard, London N1
Sous le Nez, Ilkley, West Yorkshire
South Lodge, Lower Beeding, West Sussex
Spencers, Emsworth, Hampshire
Spindlewood Hotel, Wadhurst, East Sussex
Sportsman's Arms, Wath-in-Nidderdale, North Yorkshire
Sree Krishna, London SW17
Sri Siam, London W1
Stane Street Hollow, Pulborough, West Sussex
Stannary, Mary Tavy, Devon
Stapleford Park, Stapleford, Leicestershire
Starlings Castle, Chirk, Clwyd
Starr, Great Dunmow, Essex
Stephen Bull, London W1
Stile, Willington, Co Durham
Stock Hill House, Gillingham, Dorset
Ston Easton Park, Ston Easton, Somerset
Stone Close, Dent, Cumbria
Stone Hall, Wolf's Castle, Dyfed
Stonor Arms, Stonor, Oxfordshire
Stour Bay Cafe, Manningtree, Essex
Strand, Belfast, Co Antrim
Sud Ouest, London SW3
Summer Isles Hotel, Achiltibuie, Highland
Summer Lodge, Evershot, Dorset
Sundial, Herstmonceux, East Sussex
Suntory, London SW1
Le Suquet, London SW3
Surinder's, London W2
Suruchi, London N1
Surya, London NW6
Sutherlands, London W1
Swallow Hotel, Birmingham, West Midlands
Swan Hotel, Leighton Buzzard, Bedfordshire
Swan, Southwold, Suffolk
Swinfen Hall Hotel, Lichfield, Staffordshire
Sykes House, Halford, Warwickshire
Szechuan House, Edinburgh, Lothian
Table, Babbacombe, Devon
Le Talbooth, Dedham, Essex
Tandoori Lane, London SW6
Tante Claire, London SW3
Tarts, Bath, Avon
Tatsuso, London EC2
Tatyans, Cirencester, Gloucestershire
Thackeray's Ho Tunbridge W
Thailand, Londo
Thame Lane Hou Abingdon, Oxf
That Café, Manche , Greater Manchester
Theobalds, Ixworth, Suffolk
34 Surrey Street, Croydon, Surrey
36 on the Quay, Emsworth, Hampshire
Thistells, London SE22
Thistles, Cromarty, Highland
Thompsons, Chichester, West Sussex
Thornbury Castle, Thornbury, Avon
Three Chimneys, Dunvegan, Isle of Skye
Three Cocks Hotel, Three Cocks, Powys
Three Horseshoes, Powerstock, Dorset
Three Lions, Stuckton, Hampshire
Three Main Street, Fishguard, Dyfed
Timothy's, Perth, Tayside
Tiroran House, Tiroran, Isle of Mull
Topo's, Macclesfield, Cheshire
Topsy-Tasty, London W4
Tre-Ysgawen Hall, Capel Coch, Gwynedd
Tree of Idleness, Bray, Co Wicklow
Tregynon Farmhouse, Pontfaen, Dyfed
Trenchers, Whitby, North Yorkshire
Trinity House Hotel, Coventry, West Midlands
La Truffe Noir, London SE1
Truffles, Bruton, Somerset
Truffles, Portman Inter-Continental Hotel, London W1
Tui, London SW7
Tuk Tuk, London N1
Tullich Lodge, Ballater, Grampian
Tullythwaite House, Underbarrow, Cumbria
Tung Fong, Manchester, Greater Manchester
Turner's, London SW3
21 Queen Street, Newcastle upon Tyne, Tyne & Wear
Twenty Two, Cambridge, Cambridgeshire
Tyddyn Llan, Llandrillo, Clwyd
Ubiquitous Chip, Glasgow, Strathclyde
Uplands, Cartmel, Cumbria

Upper Street Fish Shop, London N1
Veeraswamy, London W1
Victorian House, Thornton-Cleveleys, Lancashire
Victor's, Darlington, Co Durham
Village Bakery, Melmerby, Cumbria
Village Restaurant, Ramsbottom, Greater Manchester
Villandry Dining Room, London W1
Vintners Rooms, Edinburgh, Lothian
Wakaba, London NW3
Wallett's Court, St Margaret's at Cliffe, Kent
Walnut Tree Inn, Llandewi Skirrid, Gwent
Warehouse Brasserie, Colchester, Essex
Waterfront Wine Bar, Edinburgh, Lothian
Waterside Inn, Bray, Berkshire
Weavers, Haworth, West Yorkshire
Weavers Shed, Golcar, West Yorkshire
Well House, Watlington, Oxfordshire
Well House, St Keyne, Cornwall
Well View, Moffat, Dumfries & Galloway
Wheatsheaf Hotel, Swinton, Borders
White Horse Inn, Chilgrove, West Sussex
White House, Prestbury, Cheshire
White House Hotel, Williton, Somerset
White Moss House, Grasmere, Cumbria
Whitechapel Manor, South Molton, Devon
Whiteleaf at Croyde, Croyde, Devon
Wickens, Northleach, Gloucestershire
Wife of Bath, Wye, Kent
Wig & Mitre, Lincoln, Lincolnshire
Will's, Bridport, Dorset
Wiltons, London SW1
Windmill, Burgh le Marsh, Lincolnshire
Wine Bar, Woodbridge, Suffolk
Wing Ki, Edgware, Greater London
Wings, Barnet, Hertfordshire
Winteringham Fields, Winteringham, Humberside
Wódka, London W8
Woodhayes, Whimple, Devon
Woodlands, Ballynahinch, Co Down
Woodlands, Manchester, Greater Manchester
Woodmans Arms Auberge, Hastingleigh, Kent
Woods, Bath, Avon
Woods Place, Grayshott, Hampshire
Woolley Grange, Woolley Green, Wiltshire
Wyck Hill House, Stow-on-the-Wold, Gloucestershire
Y Bistro, Llanberis, Gwynedd
Yang Cheng, Plymouth, Devon
Yang Sing, Manchester, Greater Manchester
Ye Old Bulls Head Inn, Beaumaris, Gwynedd
Yetman's, Holt, Norfolk
Yeung's, Gloucester, Gloucestershire
Ynyshir Hall, Eglwysfach, Powys
Yoisho, London W1
Zen W3, London NW3

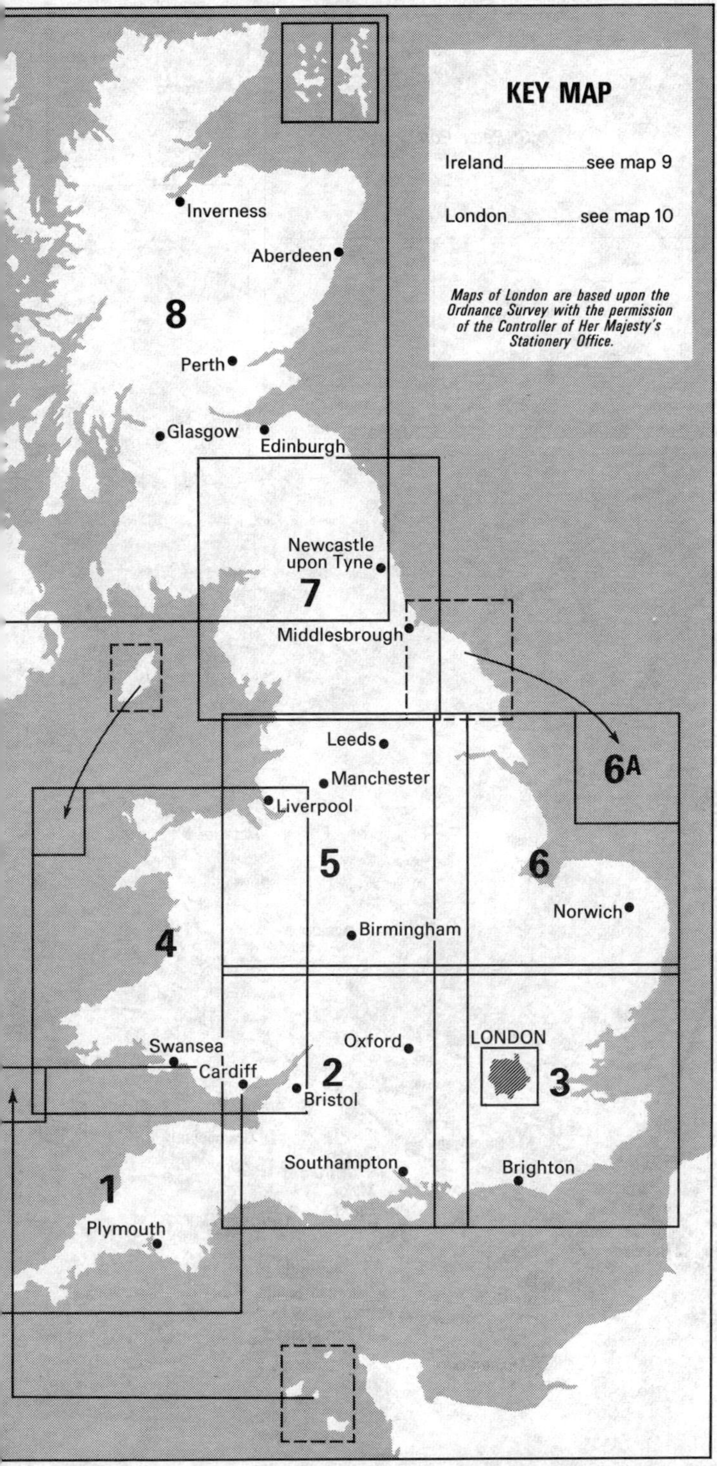
KEY MAP
Ireland see map 9
London see map 10
Maps of London are based upon the Ordnance Survey with the permission of the Controller of Her Majesty's Stationery Office.
8
Inverness
Aberdeen
Perth
Glasgow
Edinburgh
Newcastle upon Tyne
7
Middlesbrough
6A
Leeds
Manchester
Liverpool
5
6
Norwich
4
Birmingham
Oxford
LONDON
3
Swansea
Cardiff
2
Bristol
Southampton
Brighton
1
Plymouth

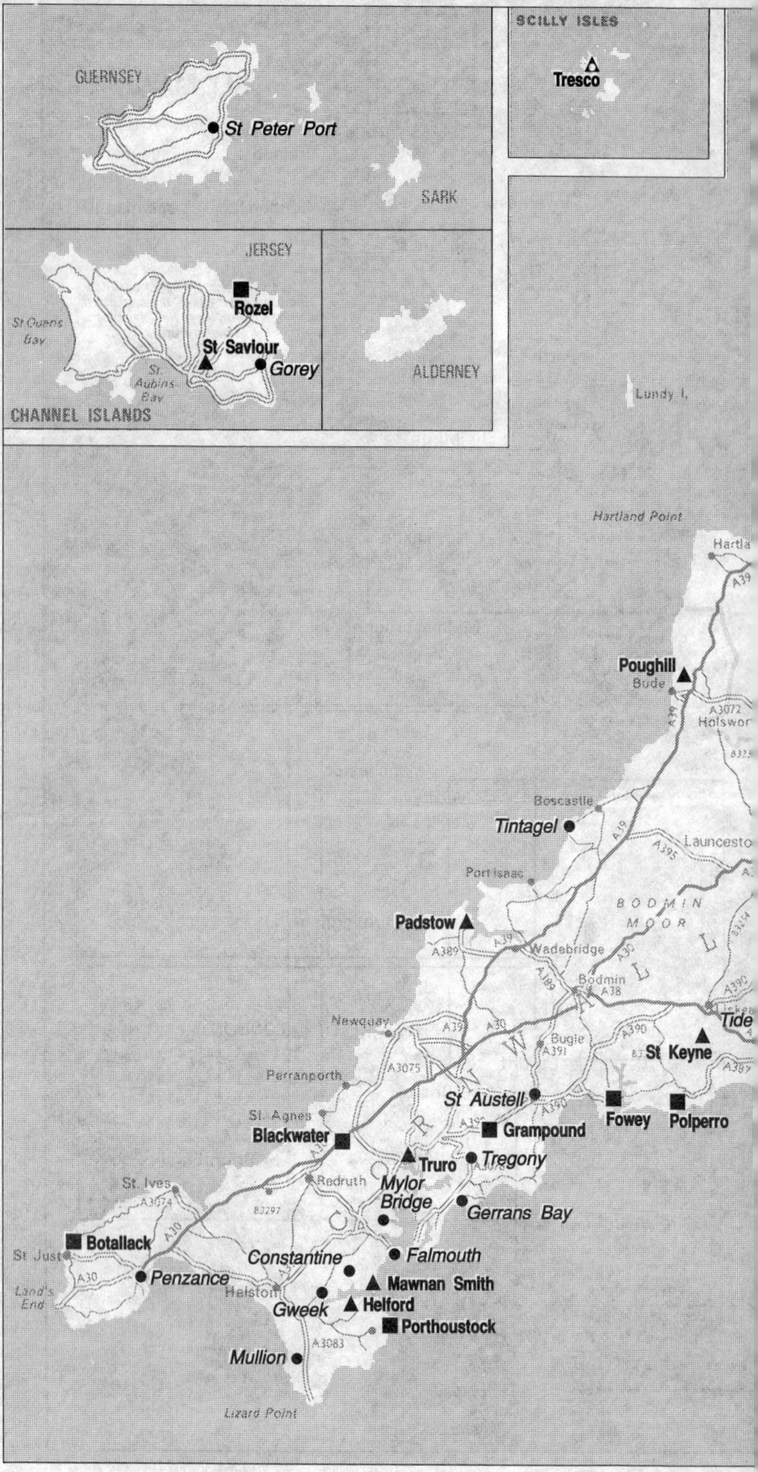

SCILLY ISLES
Tresco
GUERNSEY
St Peter Port
SARK
JERSEY
Rozel
St Ouens Bay
St Saviour
Gorey
St. Aubins Bay
CHANNEL ISLANDS
ALDERNEY
Lundy I.
Hartland Point
Poughill
Bude
Holsworthy
Boscastle
Tintagel
Launceston
Port Isaac
BODMIN MOOR
Padstow
Wadebridge
Bodmin
Newquay
Bugie
St Keyne
Perranporth
St Austell
Fowey
Polperro
St. Agnes
Grampound
Blackwater
Truro
Tregony
St. Ives
Redruth
Mylor Bridge
Gerrans Bay
Botallack
St Just
Constantine
Falmouth
Penzance
Land's End
Helston
Mawnan Smith
Gweek
Helford
Porthoustock
Mullion
Lizard Point

1

DEVON and CORNWALL

CHANNEL ISLANDS

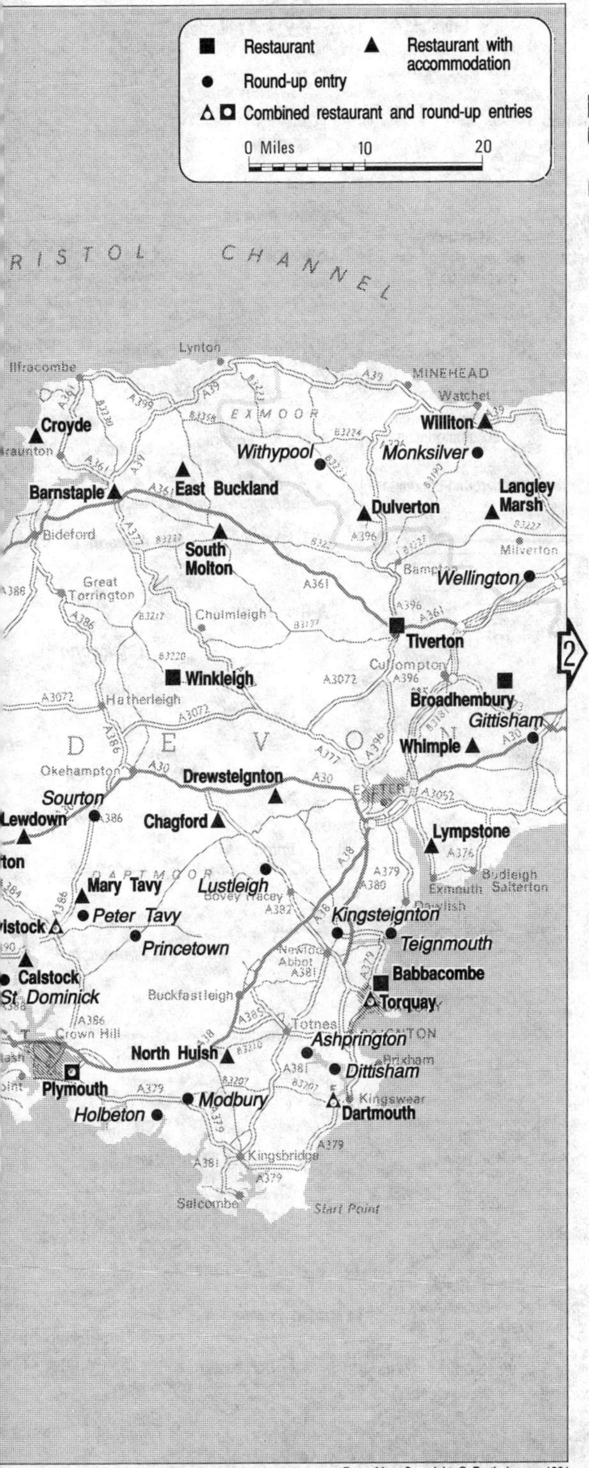

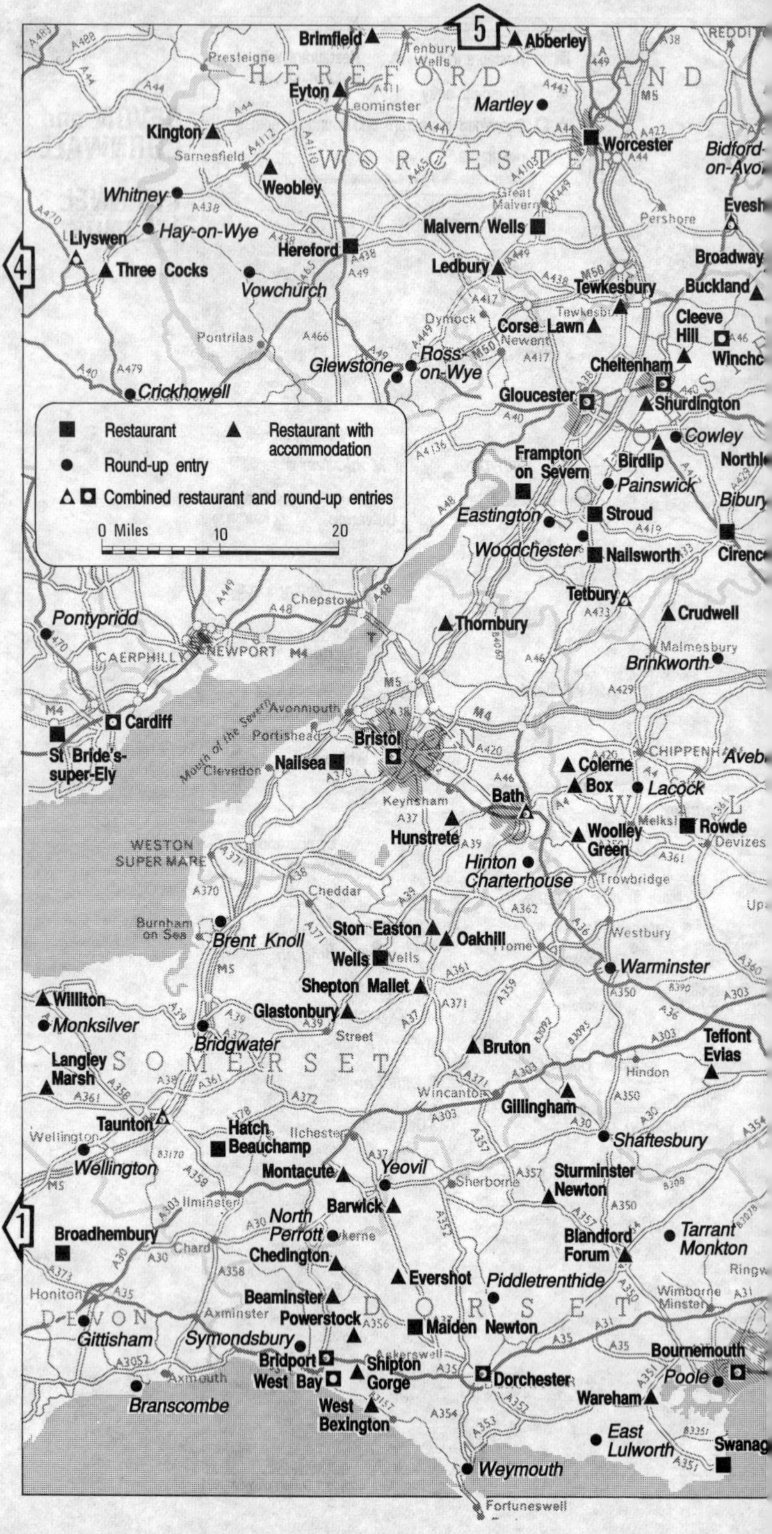
5
4
1
Restaurant
Restaurant with accommodation
Round-up entry
Combined restaurant and round-up entries
0 Miles
10
20
HEREFORD AND WORCESTER
SOMERSET
DORSET
DEVON
Brimfield
Abberley
Presteigne
Tenbury Wells
Eyton
Leominster
Martley
Kington
Sarnesfield
Weobley
Worcester
Bidford-on-Avon
Whitney
Great Malvern
Pershore
Evesham
Llyswen
Hay-on-Wye
Malvern Wells
Three Cocks
Hereford
Broadway
Vowchurch
Ledbury
Tewkesbury
Buckland
Dymock
Corse Lawn
Cleeve Hill
Newent
Pontrilas
Winchcombe
Glewstone
Ross-on-Wye
Cheltenham
Crickhowell
Gloucester
Shurdington
Cowley
Frampton on Severn
Birdlip
Painswick
Northleach
Bibury
Eastington
Stroud
Woodchester
Nailsworth
Cirencester
Tetbury
Chepstow
Crudwell
Pontypridd
Thornbury
Malmesbury
CAERPHILLY
NEWPORT
Brinkworth
Avonmouth
Cardiff
Mouth of the Severn
Portishead
Bristol
St Bride's-super-Ely
Nailsea
Clevedon
CHIPPENHAM
Avebury
Colerne
Box
Lacock
Bath
Keynsham
Melksham
Rowde
Devizes
Hunstrete
Woolley Green
WESTON SUPER MARE
Hinton Charterhouse
Trowbridge
Cheddar
Burnham on Sea
Ston Easton
Oakhill
Westbury
Brent Knoll
Frome
Wells
Warminster
Shepton Mallet
Williton
Glastonbury
Monksilver
Street
Bridgwater
Bruton
Teffont Evias
Langley Marsh
Hindon
Wincanton
Gillingham
Taunton
Wellington
Hatch Beauchamp
Ilchester
Shaftesbury
Montacute
Yeovil
Sturminster Newton
Sherborne
Ilminster
Barwick
North Perrott
Crewkerne
Broadhembury
Chard
Tarrant Monkton
Blandford Forum
Chedington
Evershot
Piddletrenthide
Honiton
Beaminster
Wimborne Minster
Axminster
Powerstock
Maiden Newton
Gittisham
Symondsbury
Bridport
Bournemouth
Poole
Axmouth
West Bay
Shipton Gorge
Dorchester
Branscombe
Wareham
West Bexington
East Lulworth
Swanage
Weymouth
Fortuneswell

2

ENGLAND: SOUTH WEST

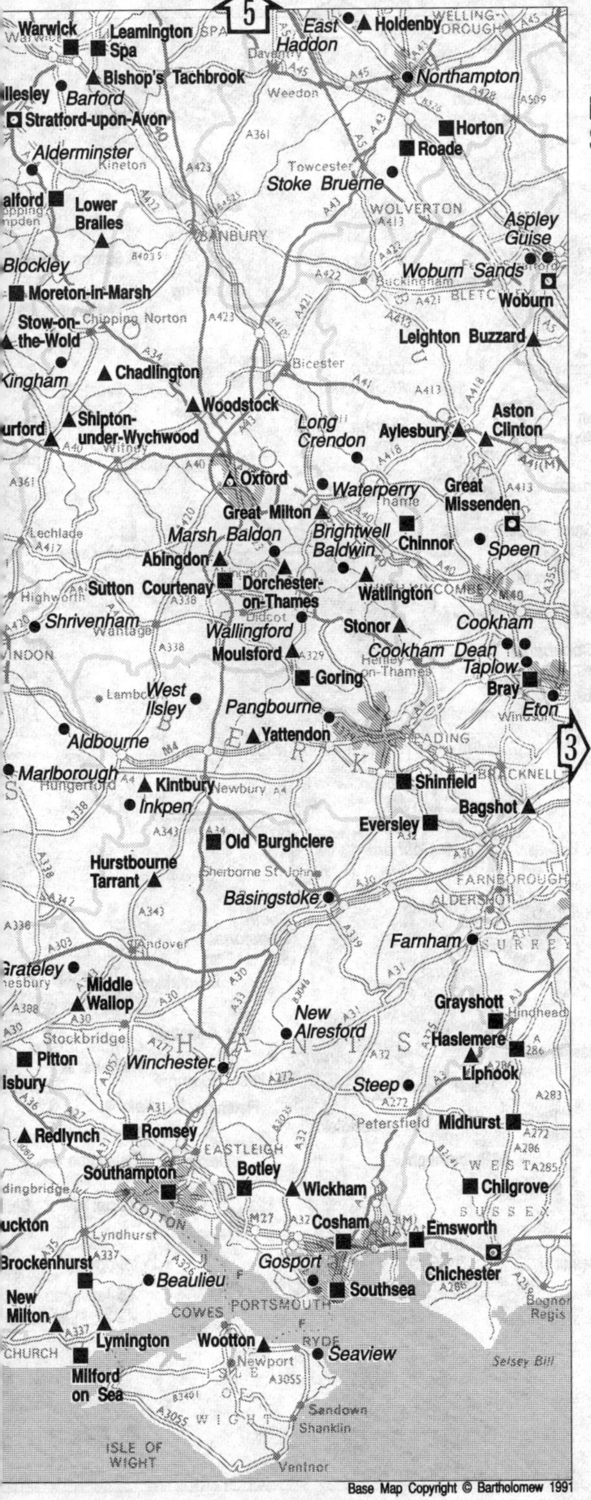

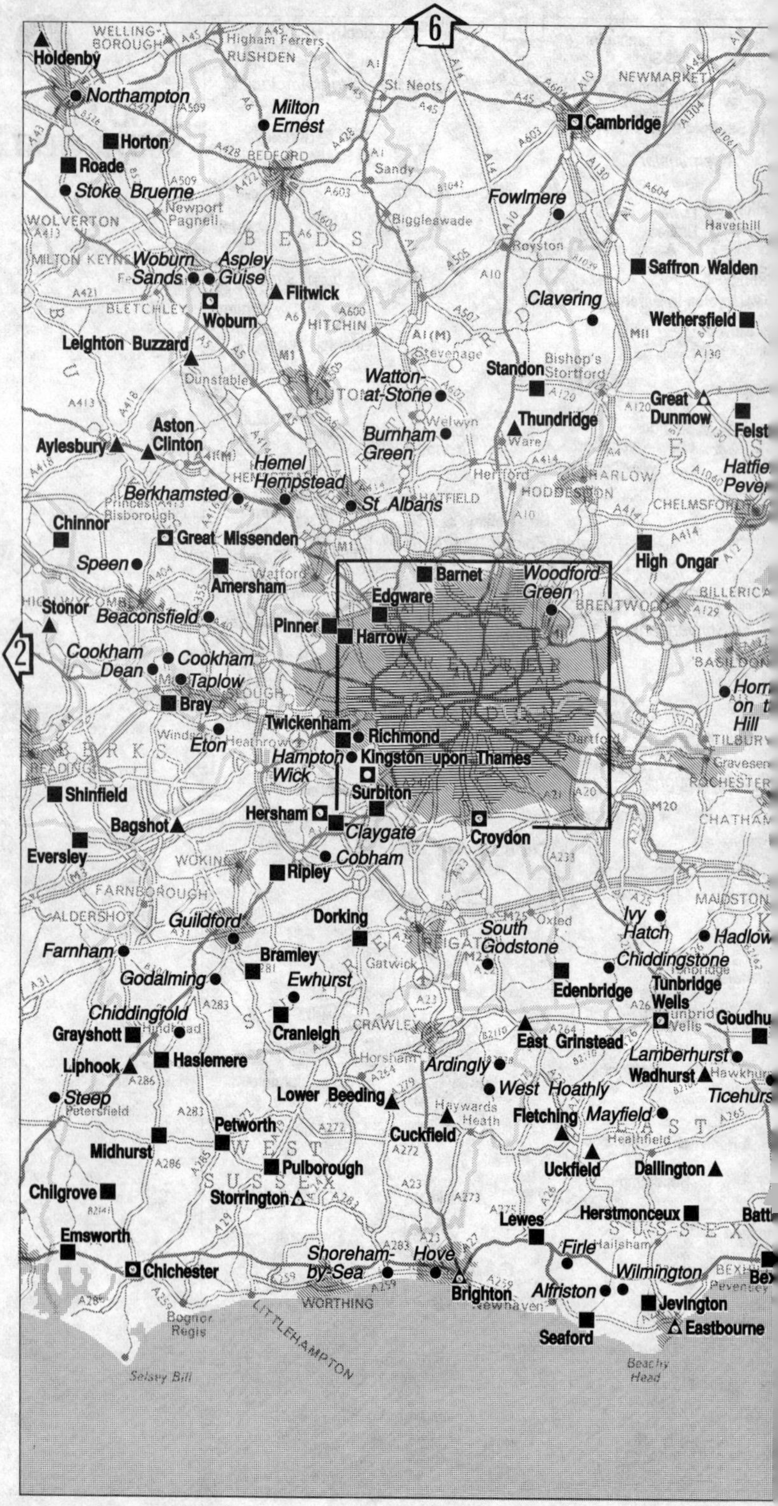
6
2
Holdenby
Northampton
Milton Ernest
Cambridge
Horton
Roade
Stoke Bruerne
Fowlmere
Woburn Sands
Aspley Guise
Flitwick
Woburn
Saffron Walden
Clavering
Wethersfield
Leighton Buzzard
Standon
Watton-at-Stone
Great Dunmow
Thundridge
Felst
Aston Clinton
Aylesbury
Burnham Green
Hemel Hempstead
Berkhamsted
St Albans
Hatfie
Pever
Chinnor
Great Missenden
High Ongar
Speen
Amersham
Barnet
Woodford Green
Edgware
Stonor
Beaconsfield
Pinner
Harrow
Cookham Dean
Cookham
Taplow
Horn on the Hill
Bray
Twickenham
Richmond
Eton
Hampton Wick
Kingston upon Thames
Shinfield
Surbiton
Hersham
Bagshot
Claygate
Croydon
Eversley
Cobham
Ripley
Guildford
Dorking
South Godstone
Ivy Hatch
Hadlow
Farnham
Bramley
Chiddingstone
Godalming
Ewhurst
Edenbridge
Tunbridge Wells
Chiddingfold
Goudhu
Grayshott
Cranleigh
East Grinstead
Lamberhurst
Liphook
Haslemere
Ardingly
Wadhurst
Steep
Lower Beeding
West Hoathly
Ticehurs
Fletching
Mayfield
Petworth
Cuckfield
Midhurst
Pulborough
Uckfield
Dallington
Chilgrove
Storrington
Herstmonceux
Batt
Lewes
Emsworth
Firle
Chichester
Shoreham-by-Sea
Hove
Wilmington
Brighton
Alfriston
Jevington
Bex
Seaford
Eastbourne
WELLINGBOROUGH
Higham Ferrers
RUSHDEN
St. Neots
NEWMARKET
BEDFORD
Sandy
Newport Pagnell
WOLVERTON
Biggleswade
Haverhill
Royston
MILTON KEYNES
BLETCHLEY
HITCHIN
Stevenage
Bishop's Stortford
Dunstable
Welwyn
Ware
Hertford
HARLOW
HODDESDON
HATFIELD
CHELMSFORD
Princes Risborough
Watford
BRENTWOOD
BILLERICAY
BASILDON
Windsor
Heathrow
Dartford
TILBURY
READING
Gravesend
ROCHESTER
CHATHAM
WOKING
FARNBOROUGH
ALDERSHOT
MAIDSTONE
Oxted
Gatwick
CRAWLEY
Horsham
Haywards Heath
Petersfield
Heathfield
Hailsham
WORTHING
Newhaven
Bognor Regis
LITTLEHAMPTON
Selsey Bill
Beachy Head
BEDS
HERTS
BERKS
SURREY
WEST SUSSEX
EAST SUSSEX
ESSEX
LONDON

ENGLAND: SOUTH EAST

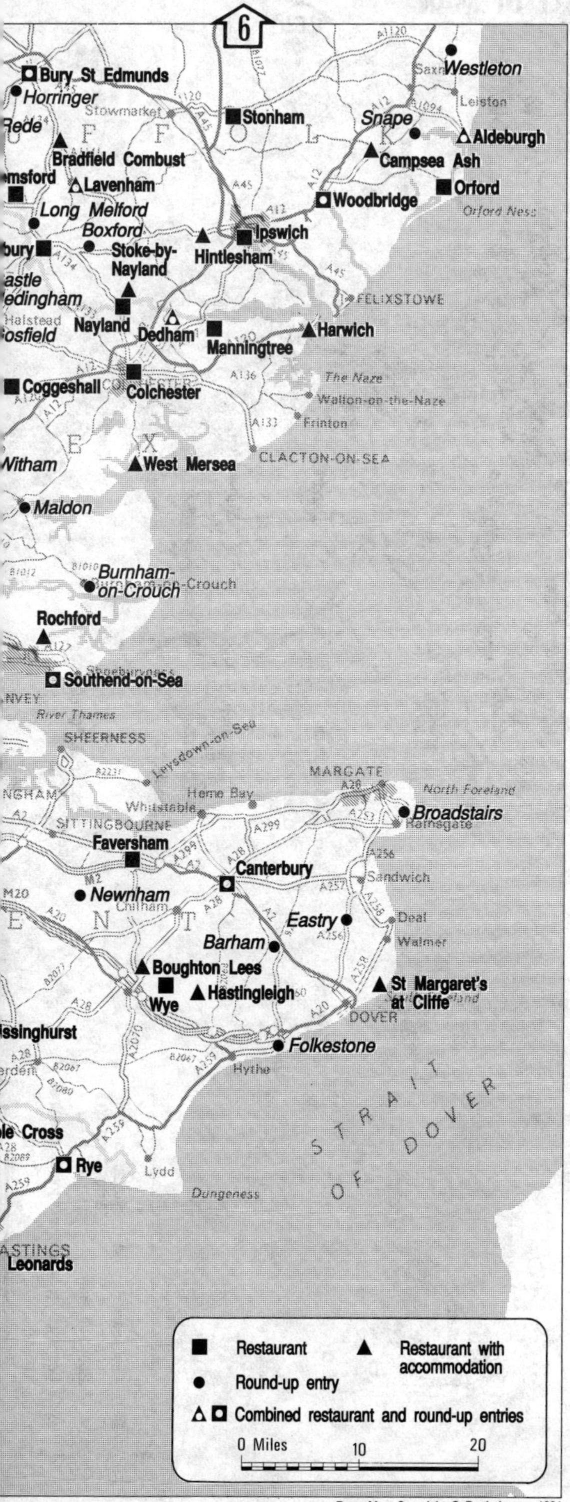

Base Map Copyright © Bartholomew 1991

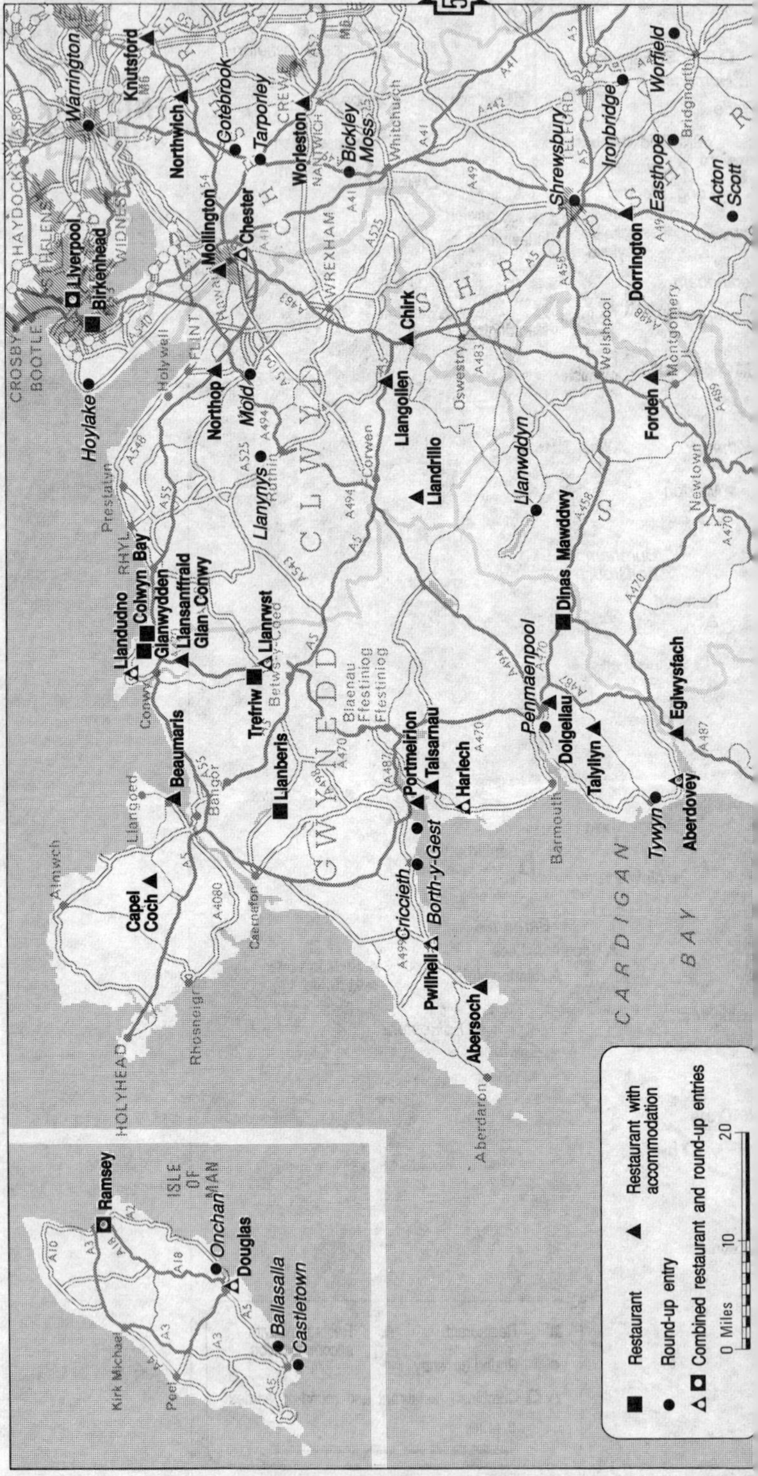
5
Warrington
Knutsford
Northwich
Cotebrook
Tarporley
Worleston
Bickley Moss
Liverpool
Birkenhead
Mollington
Chester
Hoylake
Northop
Mold
Llanynys
Chirk
Llangollen
Llandrillo
Llanwddyn
Dinas Mawddwy
Shrewsbury
Ironbridge
Worfield
Easthope
Acton Scott
Dorrington
Forden
Llandudno
Colwyn Bay
Glanwydden
Llansanffraid Glan Conwy
Llanrwst
Trefriw
Beaumaris
Llanberis
Portmeirion
Talsarnau
Harlech
Penmaenpool
Dolgellau
Talyllyn
Eglwysfach
Tywyn
Aberdovey
Capel Coch
Criccieth
Borth-y-Gest
Pwllheli
Abersoch
CARDIGAN BAY
Ramsey
Onchan
Douglas
Ballasalla
Castletown
ISLE OF MAN
Restaurant
Round-up entry
Restaurant with accommodation
Combined restaurant and round-up entries
0 Miles 10 20

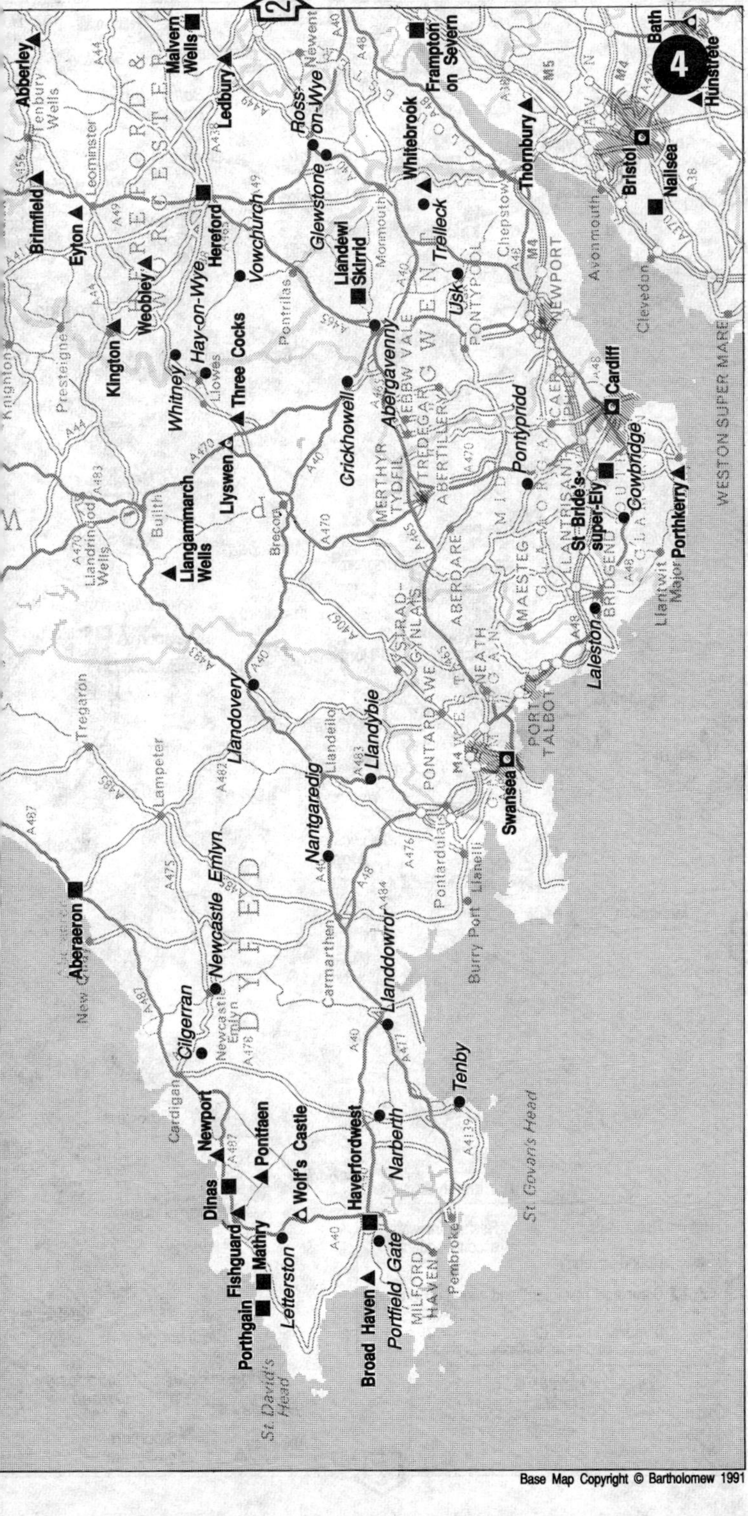
2
4
Abberley
Malvern Wells
Ledbury
Brimfield
Eyton
Weobley
Hereford
Kington
Hay-on-Wye
Whitney
Three Cocks
Llyswen
Llangammarch Wells
Vowchurch
Ross-on-Wye
Glewstone
Llandewi Skirrid
Crickhowell
Abergavenny
Whitebrook
Trelleck
Usk
Frampton on Severn
Thornbury
Bath
Hunstrete
Bristol
Nailsea
Cardiff
Pontypridd
St Bride's-super-Ely
Cowbridge
Porthkerry
Laleston
Swansea
Llandovery
Llandybie
Nantgaredig
Aberaeron
Newcastle Emlyn
Cilgerran
Llanddowror
Tenby
Narberth
Newport
Pontfaen
Wolf's Castle
Haverfordwest
Dinas
Fishguard
Mathry
Porthgain
Letterston
Broad Haven
Portfield Gate
St David's Head
St Govan's Head
WESTON SUPER MARE

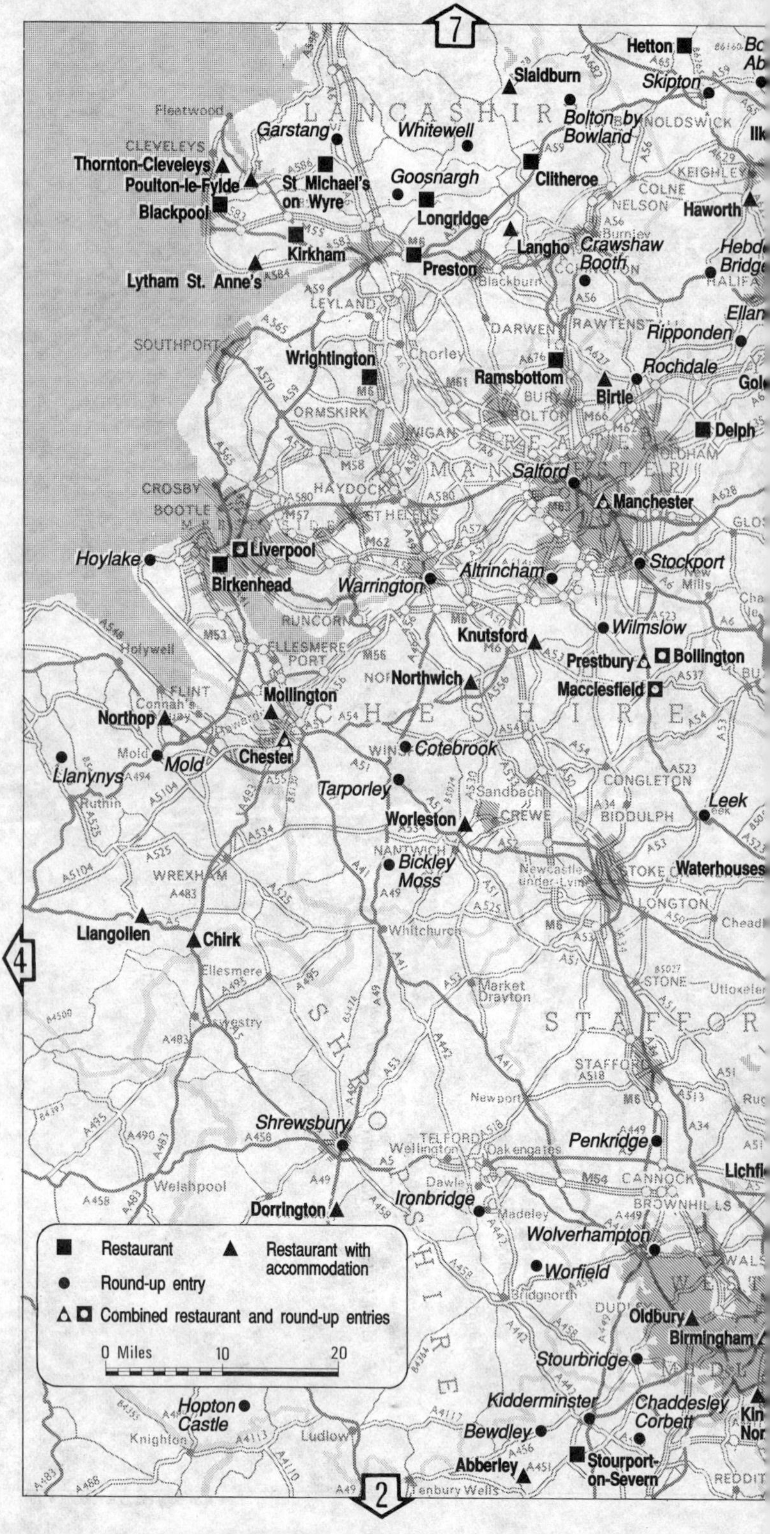
7
Hetton
Skipton
Slaidburn
LANCASHIRE
Fleetwood
CLEVELEYS
Thornton-Cleveleys
Poulton-le-Fylde
Blackpool
Garstang
Whitewell
Bolton by Bowland
Clitheroe
St Michael's on Wyre
Goosnargh
Longridge
Kirkham
Preston
Langho
Crawshaw Booth
Haworth
Hebden Bridge
Lytham St. Anne's
LEYLAND
Blackburn
DARWEN
RAWTENSTALL
Ripponden
SOUTHPORT
Wrightington
Chorley
Ramsbottom
Rochdale
Birtle
ORMSKIRK
WIGAN
BOLTON
BURY
Delph
OLDHAM
GREATER MANCHESTER
Salford
Manchester
CROSBY
BOOTLE
HAYDOCK
ST HELENS
Liverpool
Hoylake
Birkenhead
Warrington
Altrincham
Stockport
New Mills
RUNCORN
Wilmslow
Holywell
ELLESMERE PORT
Knutsford
Prestbury
Bollington
Macclesfield
FLINT
Northwich
Mollington
Connah's Quay
Northop
CHESHIRE
Chester
Mold
Llanynys
Ruthin
Cotebrook
Tarporley
Sandbach
CONGLETON
Leek
CREWE
BIDDULPH
Worleston
NANTWICH
Bickley Moss
WREXHAM
Newcastle-under-Lyme
STOKE ON TRENT
Waterhouses
LONGTON
Llangollen
Chirk
Whitchurch
Ellesmere
Market Drayton
STONE
Uttoxeter
Oswestry
SHROPSHIRE
STAFFORD
Newport
Shrewsbury
TELFORD
Wellington
Oakengates
Penkridge
CANNOCK
Lichfield
Welshpool
Dawley
Ironbridge
Madeley
BROWNHILLS
Dorrington
Wolverhampton
WALSALL
Worfield
Bridgnorth
DUDLEY
Oldbury
Birmingham
WEST MIDLANDS
Stourbridge
Kidderminster
Chaddesley Corbett
Hopton Castle
Knighton
Ludlow
Bewdley
Abberley
Stourport-on-Severn
Tenbury Wells
REDDITCH
4
2
Restaurant
Restaurant with accommodation
Round-up entry
Combined restaurant and round-up entries
0 Miles 10 20

5

ENGLAND: MIDLANDS and NORTH WEST

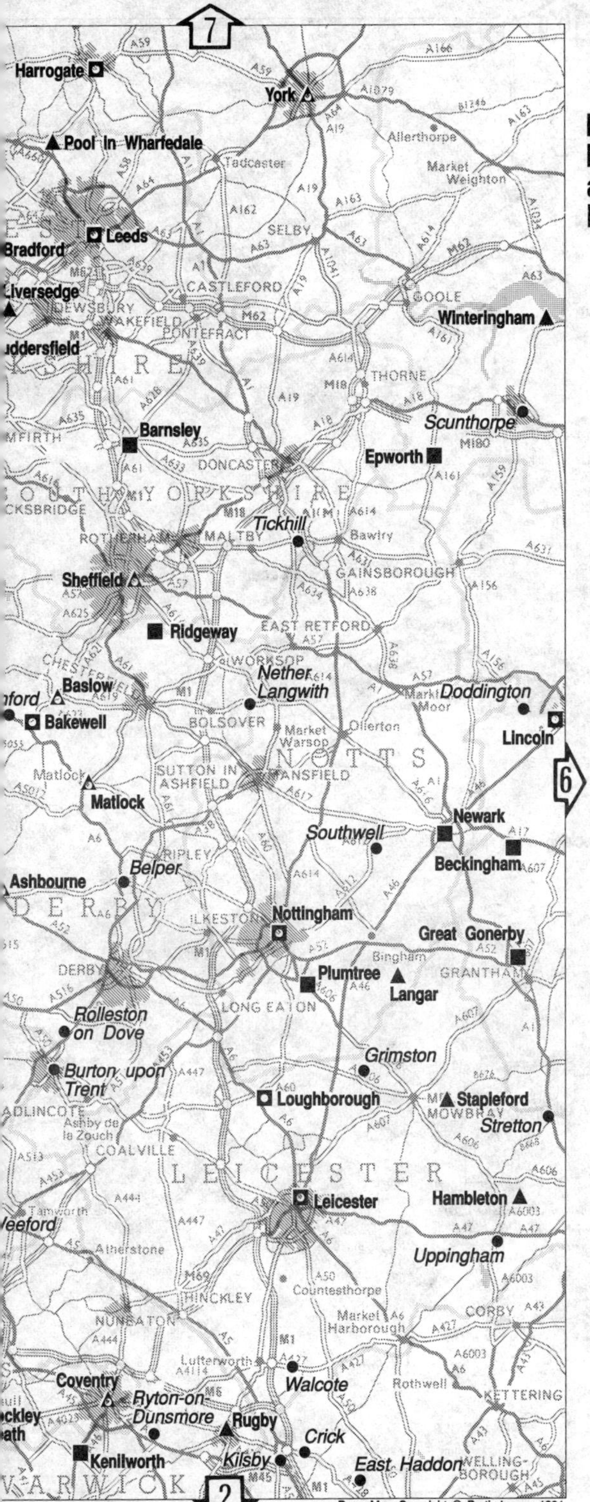

Base Map Copyright © Bartholomew 1991

6A
5
3
HUMBERSIDE
LINCOLN
NORTHANTS
CAMBRIDGE
Great Driffield
Allerthorpe
Market Weighton
BEVERLEY
HESSLE
Hull
Withernsea
GOOLE
Winteringham
Barton-upon-Humber
Grimsby
Cleethorpes
Spurn Head
Scunthorpe
Epworth
Brigg
Caistor
GAINSBOROUGH
Louth
Mablethorpe
Alford
Markham Moor
Doddington
Lincoln
Horncastle
Burgh le Marsh
Spilsby
SKEGNESS
Newark
Beckingham
Sleaford
BOSTON
THE WASH
Hunstanton
Bingham
Great Gonerby
Langar
GRANTHAM
Newton
Gedney Dyke
Holbeach
Long Sutton
North Wootton
SPALDING
King's Lynn
Stapleford
MOWBRAY
Bourne
Stretton
Oakham
Hambleton
Stamford
Market Deeping
WISBECH
Downham Market
Easton on the Hill
Uppingham
PETERBOROUGH
March
Wereham
CORBY
Oundle
Market Harborough
Rothwell
KETTERING
Thrapston
Chatteris
Ramsey
Littleport
Ely
Keyston
Huntingdon
Mildenhall
WELLINGBOROUGH
Irthlingborough
Higham Ferrers
Godmanchester

6

ENGLAND: EAST

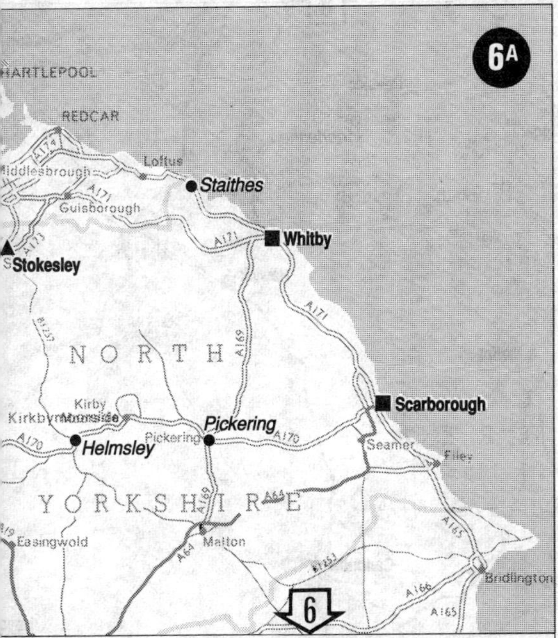

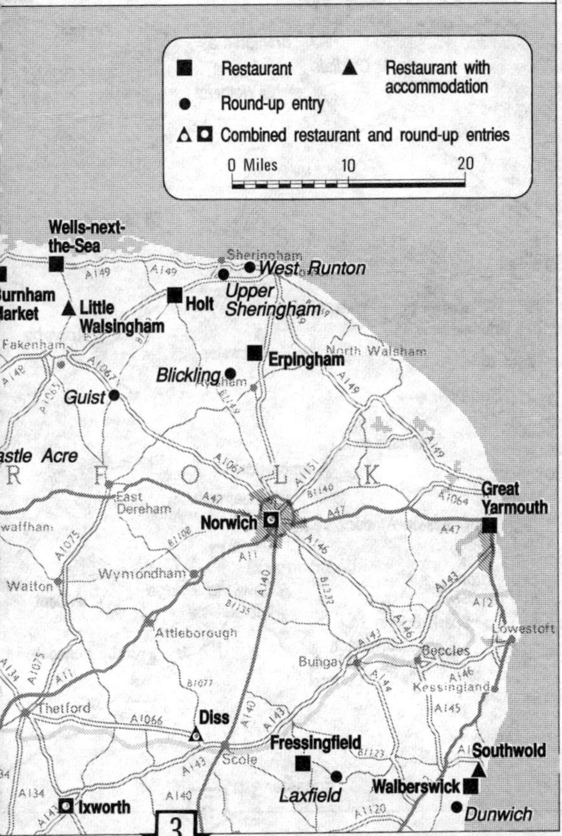

Base Map Copyright © Bartholomew 1991

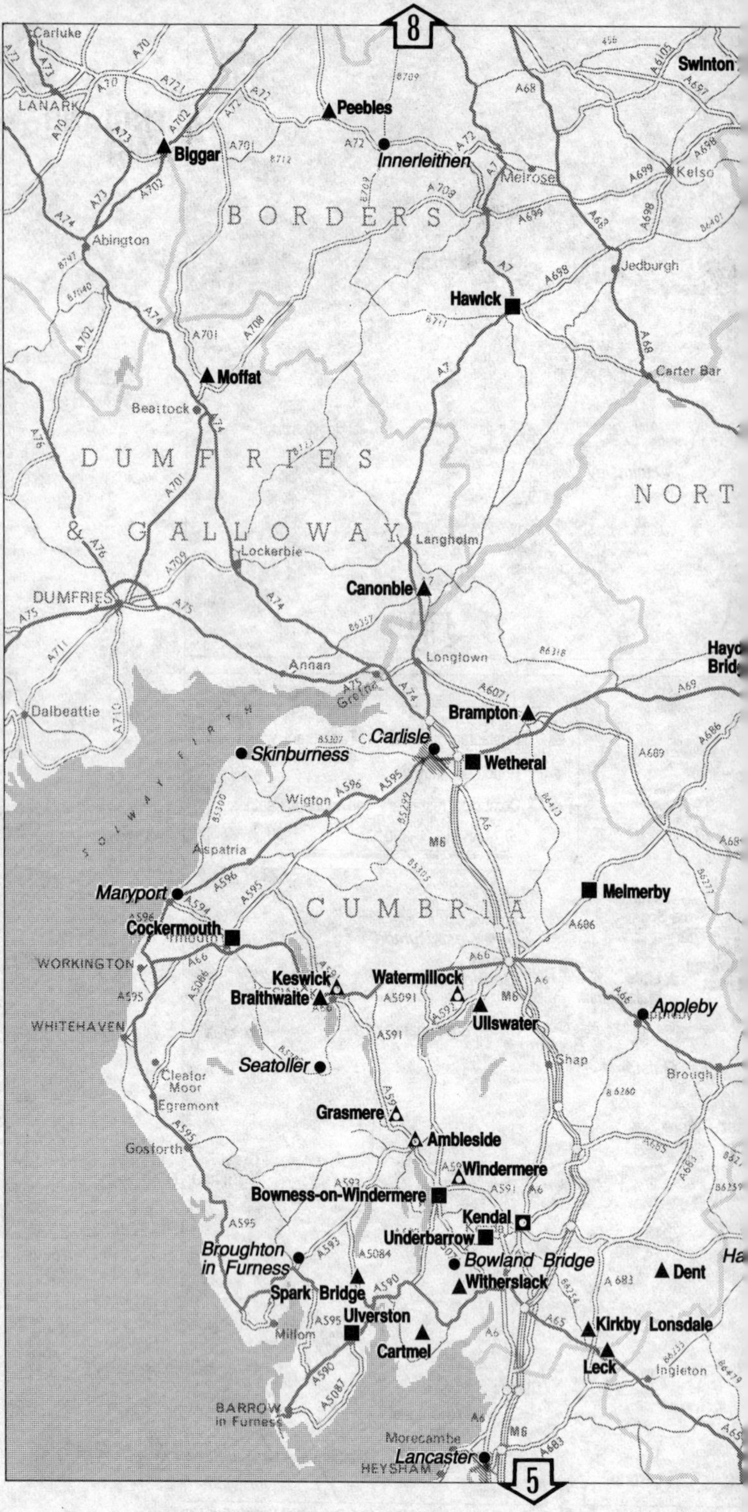
8
5
BORDERS
DUMFRIES & GALLOWAY
CUMBRIA
NORT
SOLWAY FIRTH
Carluke
LANARK
Peebles
Biggar
Innerleithen
Swinton
Melrose
Kelso
Jedburgh
Abington
Hawick
Moffat
Carter Bar
Beattock
Langholm
Lockerbie
DUMFRIES
Canonbie
Annan
Longtown
Gretna
Hayd Bridg
Dalbeattie
Brampton
Carlisle
Wetheral
Skinburness
Wigton
Aspatria
Maryport
Melmerby
Cockermouth
WORKINGTON
Keswick
Watermillock
Braithwaite
Ullswater
Appleby
WHITEHAVEN
Seatoller
Shap
Cleator Moor
Brough
Egremont
Grasmere
Ambleside
Gosforth
Windermere
Bowness-on-Windermere
Kendal
Underbarrow
Broughton in Furness
Bowland Bridge
Dent
Spark Bridge
Witherslack
Ulverston
Kirkby Lonsdale
Millom
Cartmel
Leck
Ingleton
BARROW in Furness
Morecambe
Lancaster
HEYSHAM
M6

ENGLAND: NORTH

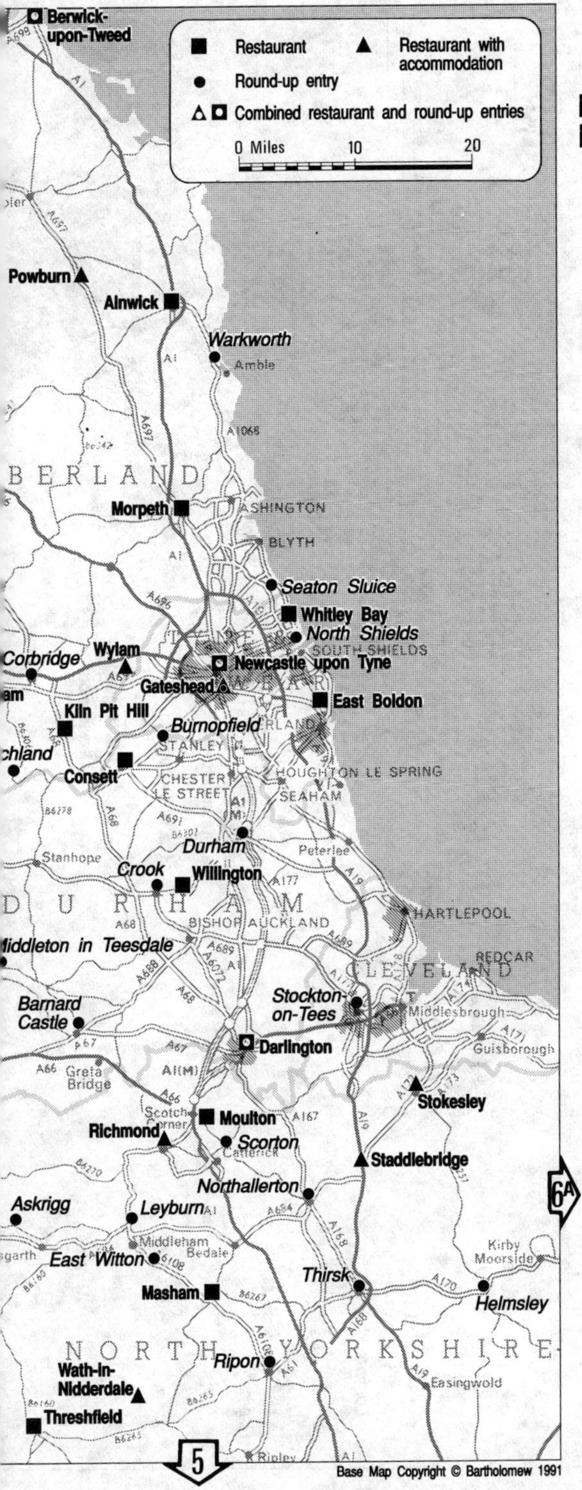
Restaurant
Restaurant with accommodation
Round-up entry
Combined restaurant and round-up entries
0 Miles 10 20
Berwick-upon-Tweed
Powburn
Alnwick
Warkworth
Amble
BERLAND
Morpeth
ASHINGTON
BLYTH
Seaton Sluice
Whitley Bay
North Shields
SOUTH SHIELDS
Corbridge
Wylam
Newcastle upon Tyne
Gateshead
East Boldon
Kiln Pit Hill
Burnopfield
STANLEY
Consett
CHESTER LE STREET
HOUGHTON LE SPRING
SEAHAM
Durham
Peterlee
Stanhope
Crook
Willington
DURHAM
HARTLEPOOL
BISHOP AUCKLAND
Middleton in Teesdale
CLEVELAND
REDCAR
Barnard Castle
Stockton-on-Tees
Middlesbrough
Darlington
Guisborough
Greta Bridge
Stokesley
Scotch Corner
Moulton
Richmond
Scorton
Catterick
Staddlebridge
Northallerton
Askrigg
Leyburn
Middleham
East Witton
Bedale
Kirby Moorside
Thirsk
Masham
Helmsley
NORTH YORKSHIRE
Ripon
Wath-in-Nidderdale
Easingwold
Threshfield
Ripley
6A
5

Base Map Copyright © Bartholomew 1991

SCOTLAND

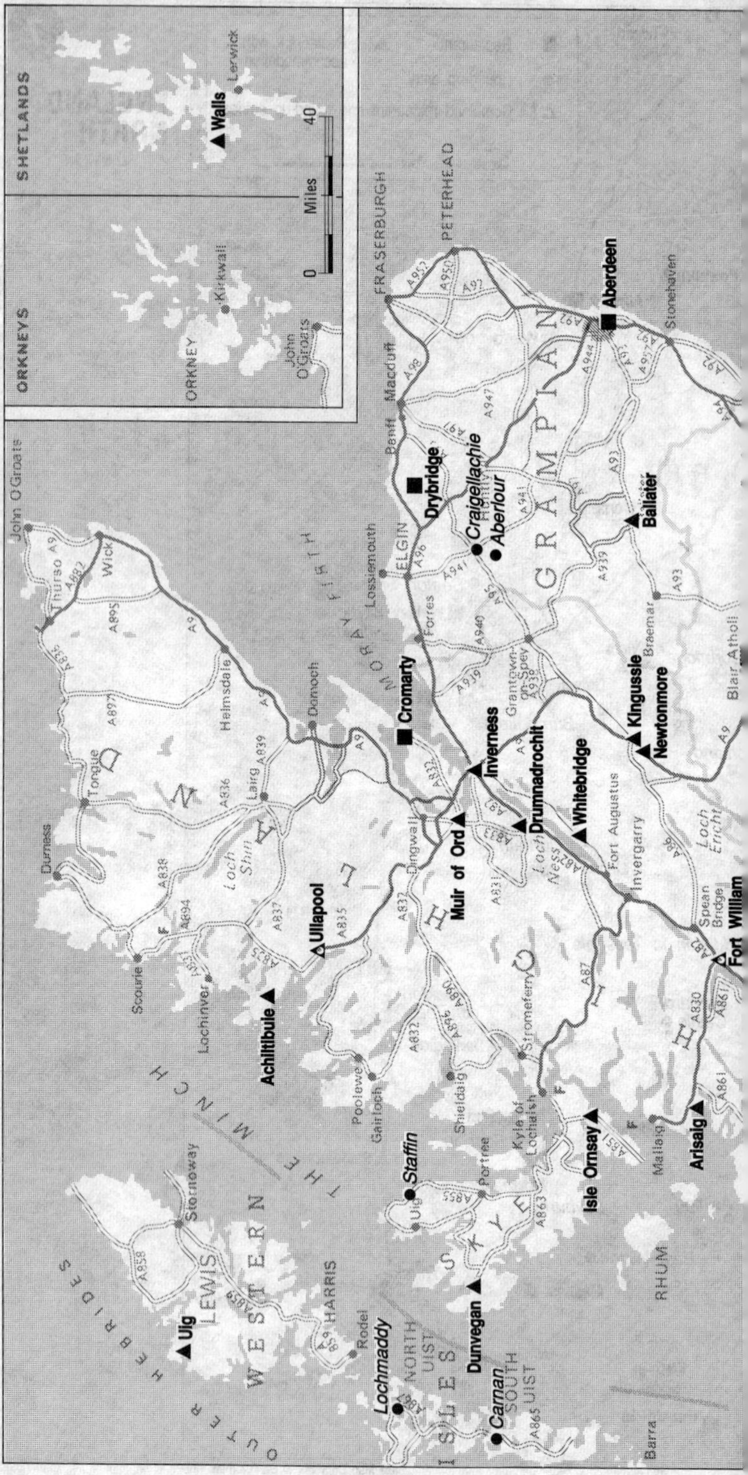

SHETLANDS
Walls
Lerwick
ORKNEYS
ORKNEY
Kirkwall
John O'Groats
Miles
0
40
FRASERBURGH
PETERHEAD
Aberdeen
Stonehaven
Macduff
Banff
Drybridge
Craigellachie
Aberlour
Ballater
Braemar
Blair Atholl
GRAMPIAN
Lossiemouth
ELGIN
Forres
MORAY FIRTH
Cromarty
Grantown-on-Spey
Kingussie
Newtonmore
Inverness
Drumnadrochit
Whitebridge
Fort Augustus
Invergarry
Loch Ness
Loch Ericht
Spean Bridge
Fort William
Muir of Ord
Dingwall
Dornoch
Helmsdale
Wick
Thurso
John O'Groats
Tongue
Lairg
Loch Shin
Durness
Scourie
Lochinver
Ullapool
Achiltibuie
Poolewe
Gairloch
Shieldaig
Stromeferry
Kyle of Lochalsh
Isle Ornsay
Mallaig
Arisaig
HIGHLAND
THE MINCH
Stornoway
LEWIS
HARRIS
Uig
Rodel
Staffin
Uig
Portree
Dunvegan
SKYE
RHUM
Lochmaddy
NORTH UIST
Carnan
SOUTH UIST
Barra
WESTERN ISLES
OUTER HEBRIDES

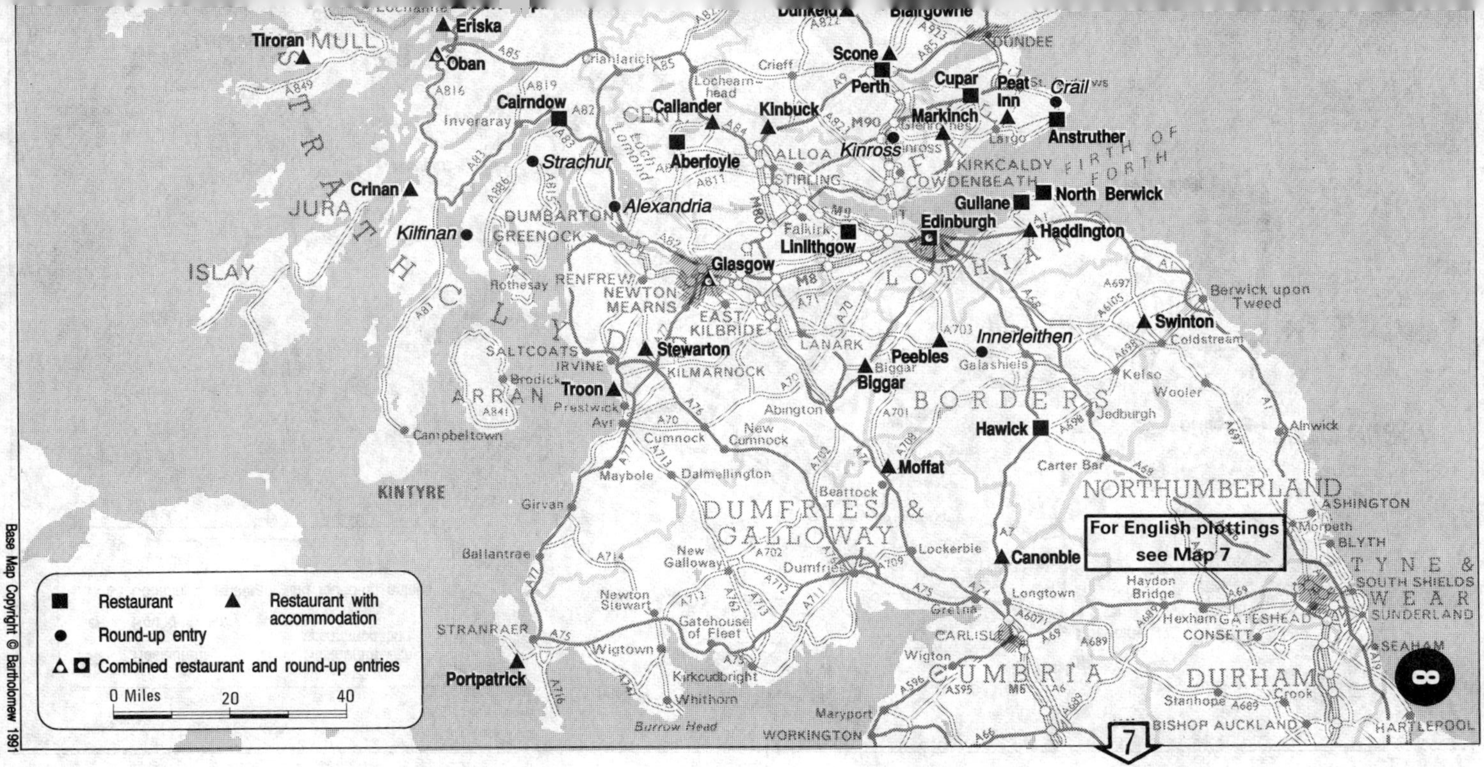
8
Tiroran
Eriska
Oban
Cairndow
Strachur
Crinan
Kilfinan
Alexandria
Callander
Aberfoyle
Kinbuck
Scone
Perth
Cupar
Peat Inn
Crail
Markinch
Anstruther
Kinross
North Berwick
Gullane
Edinburgh
Haddington
Linlithgow
Glasgow
Stewarton
Troon
Biggar
Peebles
Innerleithen
Swinton
Hawick
Moffat
Canonbie
Portpatrick
For English plottings see Map 7
7
Restaurant
Restaurant with accommodation
Round-up entry
Combined restaurant and round-up entries
0 Miles
20
40

IRELAND

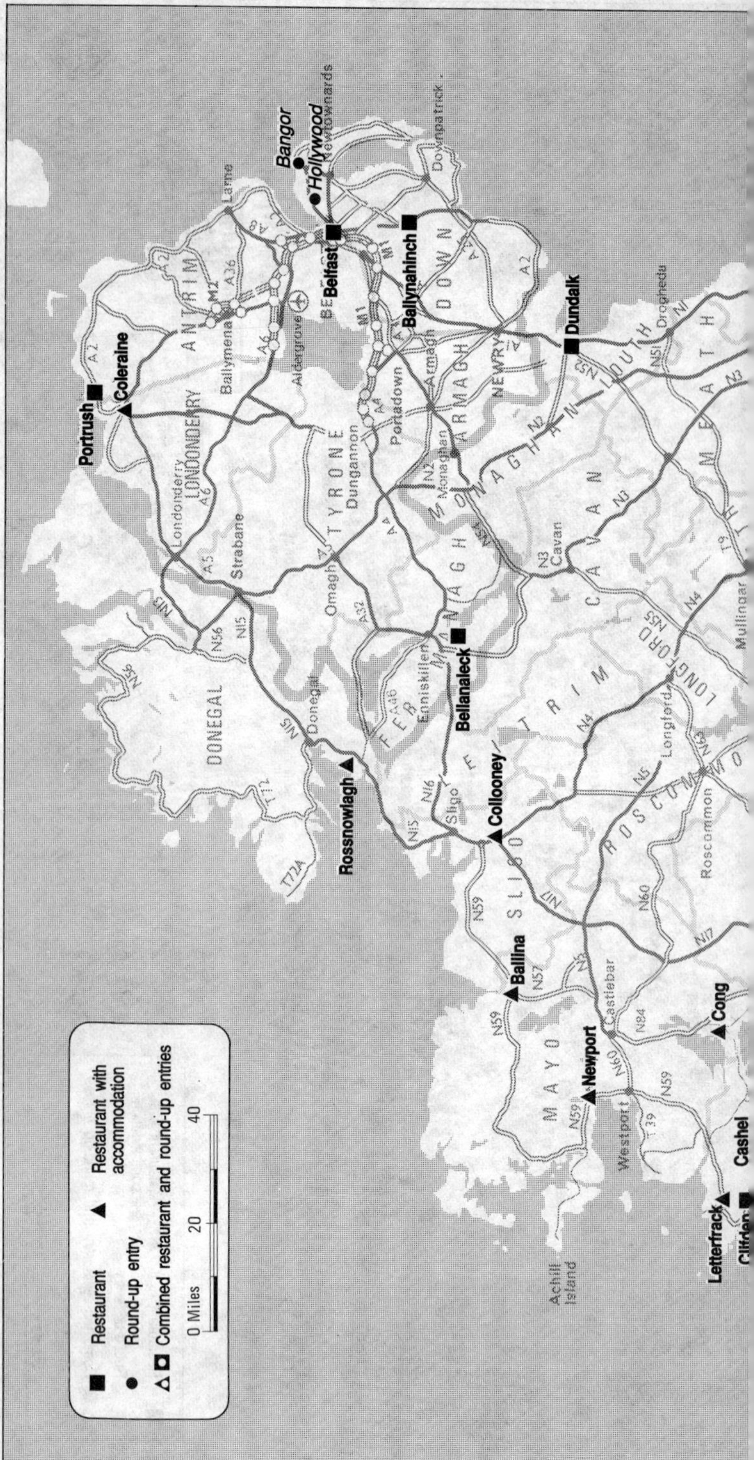
Restaurant
Round-up entry
Combined restaurant and round-up entries
Restaurant with accommodation
0 Miles 20 40
Portrush
Coleraine
Bangor
Hollywood
Newtownards
Downpatrick
Larne
Belfast
Ballynahinch
Dundalk
Drogheda
Aldergrove
Ballymena
Londonderry
Strabane
Omagh
Dungannon
Portadown
Armagh
Newry
Monaghan
Cavan
Enniskillen
Bellanaleck
Donegal
Rossnowlagh
Sligo
Collooney
Longford
Mullingar
Roscommon
Ballina
Castlebar
Westport
Newport
Cong
Cashel
Letterfrack
Achill Island
ANTRIM
LONDONDERRY
TYRONE
DOWN
ARMAGH
MONAGHAN
CAVAN
LOUTH
MEATH
DONEGAL
FERMANAGH
LEITRIM
LONGFORD
SLIGO
ROSCOMMON
MAYO

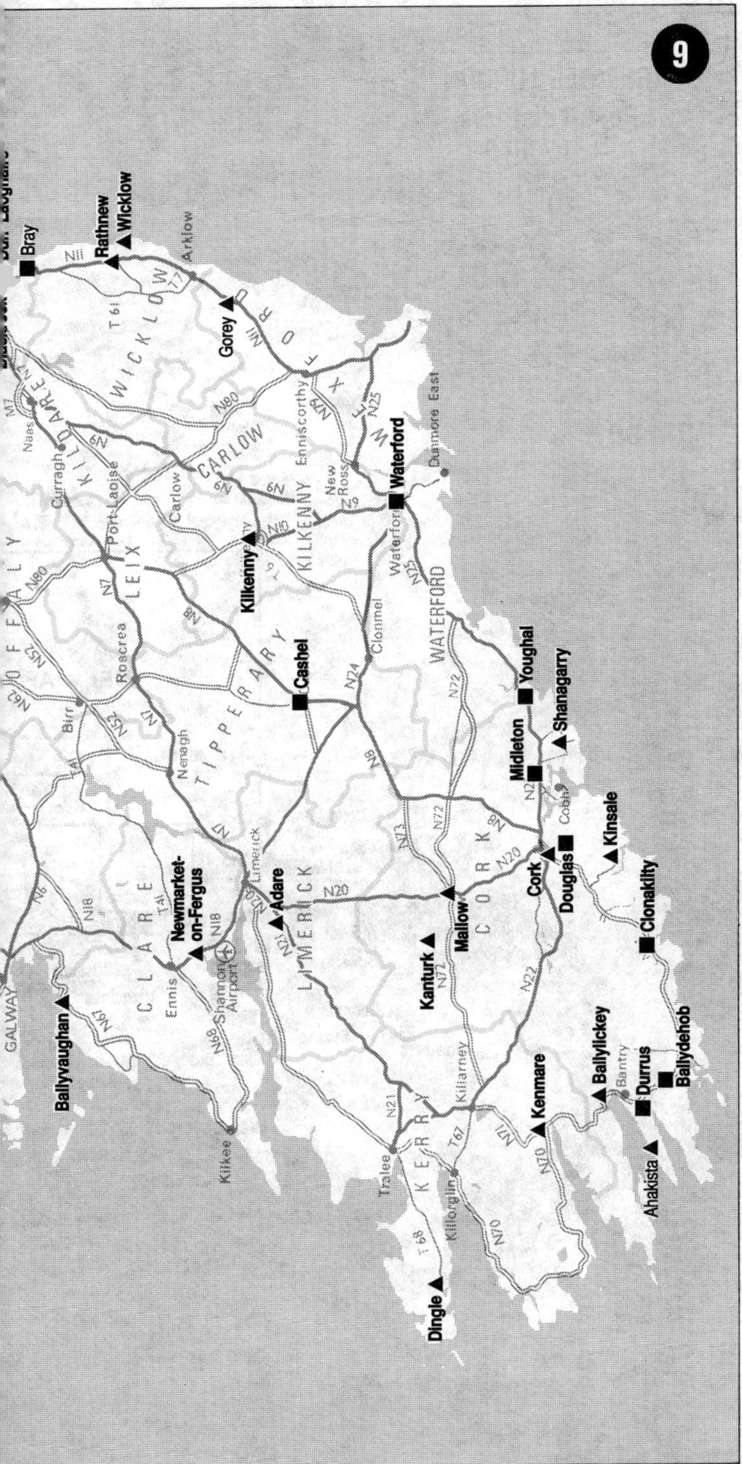
9
Bray
Rathnew
Wicklow
Arklow
Gorey
WICKLOW
WEXFORD
CARLOW
KILDARE
Naas
Curragh
Port Laoise
Carlow
Enniscorthy
New Ross
Waterford
Dunmore East
Kilkenny
KILKENNY
LEIX
OFFALY
Roscrea
Birr
Nenagh
TIPPERARY
Cashel
Clonmel
WATERFORD
Youghal
Shanagarry
Midleton
Cobh
Cork
Douglas
Kinsale
Clonakilty
Mallow
Kanturk
CORK
LIMERICK
Limerick
Adare
Newmarket-on-Fergus
Shannon Airport
Ennis
CLARE
GALWAY
Ballyvaughan
Kilkee
Tralee
KERRY
Killarney
Killorglin
Dingle
Kenmare
Ballylickey
Bantry
Durrus
Ballydehob
Ahakista

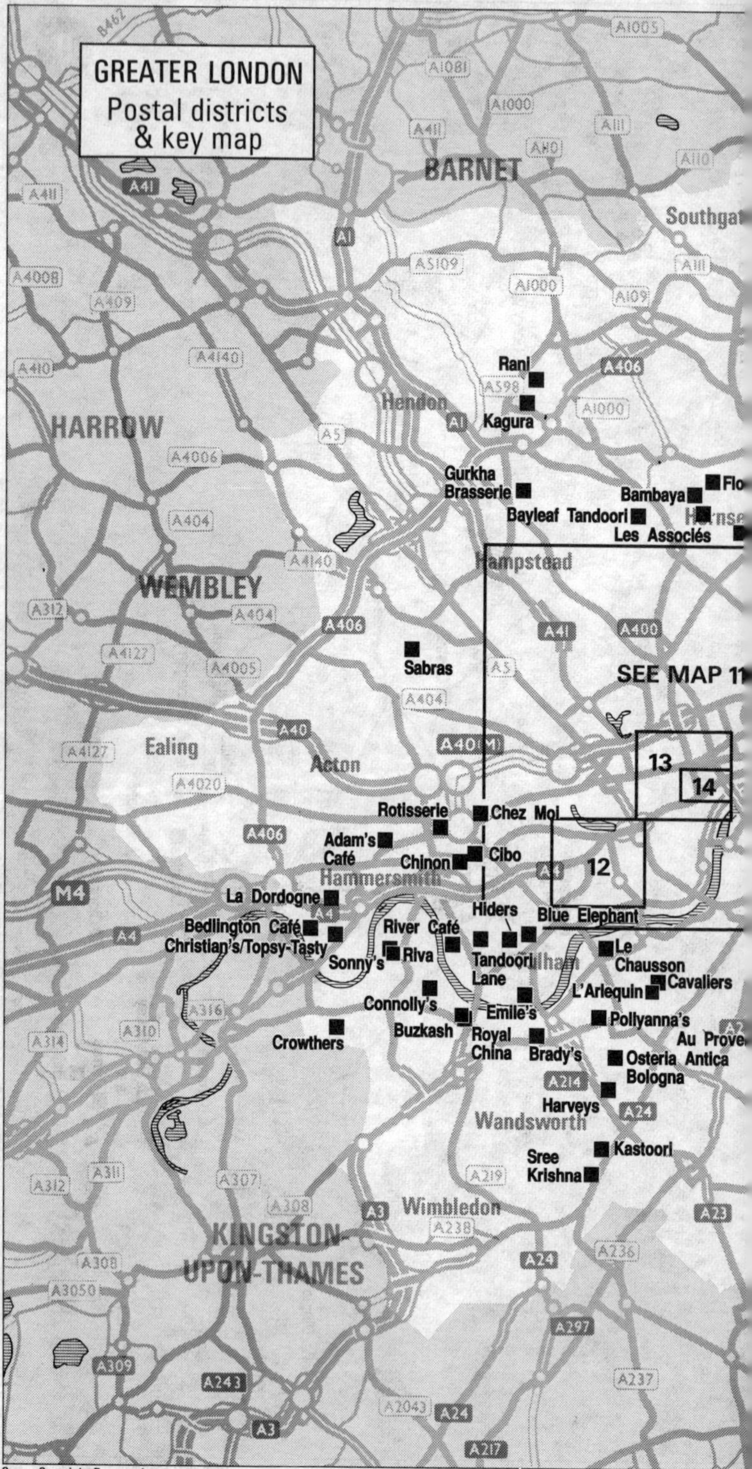
GREATER LONDON
Postal districts
& key map
BARNET
Southgat
HARROW
WEMBLEY
Hendon
Hampstead
Ealing
Acton
Hammersmith
Wandsworth
Wimbledon
KINGSTON-
UPON-THAMES
SEE MAP 11
13
14
12
Rani
Kagura
Gurkha
Brasserie
Bambaya
Flo
Bayleaf Tandoori
Les Associés
Sabras
Rotisserie
Chez Moi
Adam's
Café
Chinon
Cibo
La Dordogne
Bedlington Café
Christian's/Topsy-Tasty
Sonny's
Riva
River Café
Hiders
Blue Elephant
Tandoori
Lane
Le
Chausson
Cavaliers
L'Arlequin
Connolly's
Emile's
Buzkash
Royal
China
Brady's
Pollyanna's
Au Prove
Osteria Antica
Bologna
Crowthers
Harveys
Kastoori
Sree
Krishna
M4
A1
A3
A4
A24
A40
A40(M)
A41
A400
A406
A5
A23
A214
A217
A243
A297
A309
A1000
A1005
A1081
A411
A110
A111
A109
A5109
A598
A4008
A409
A4140
A410
A4006
A404
A312
A4127
A4005
A4020
A316
A310
A314
A311
A307
A308
A3050
A219
A238
A236
A237
A2043
B462

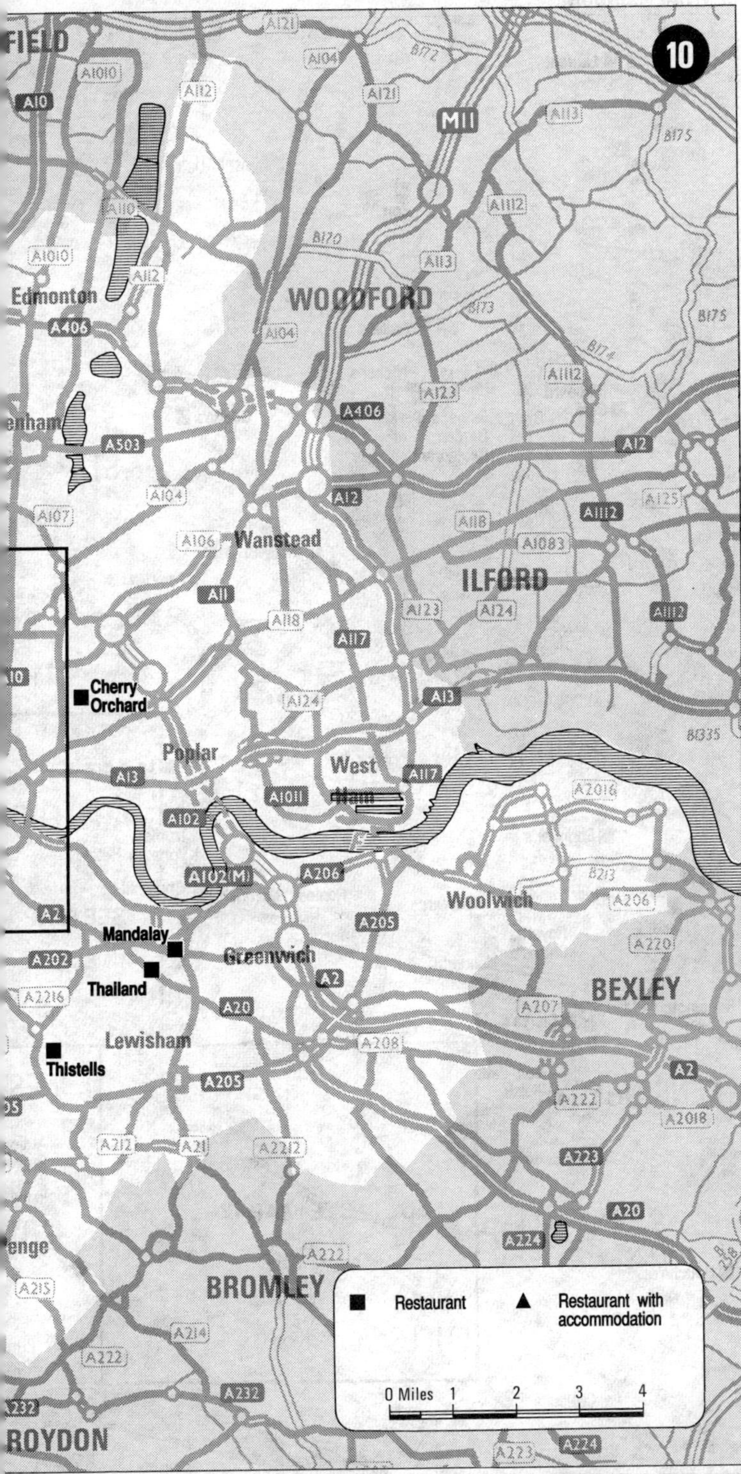

Base Map Copyright © Bartholomew 1991

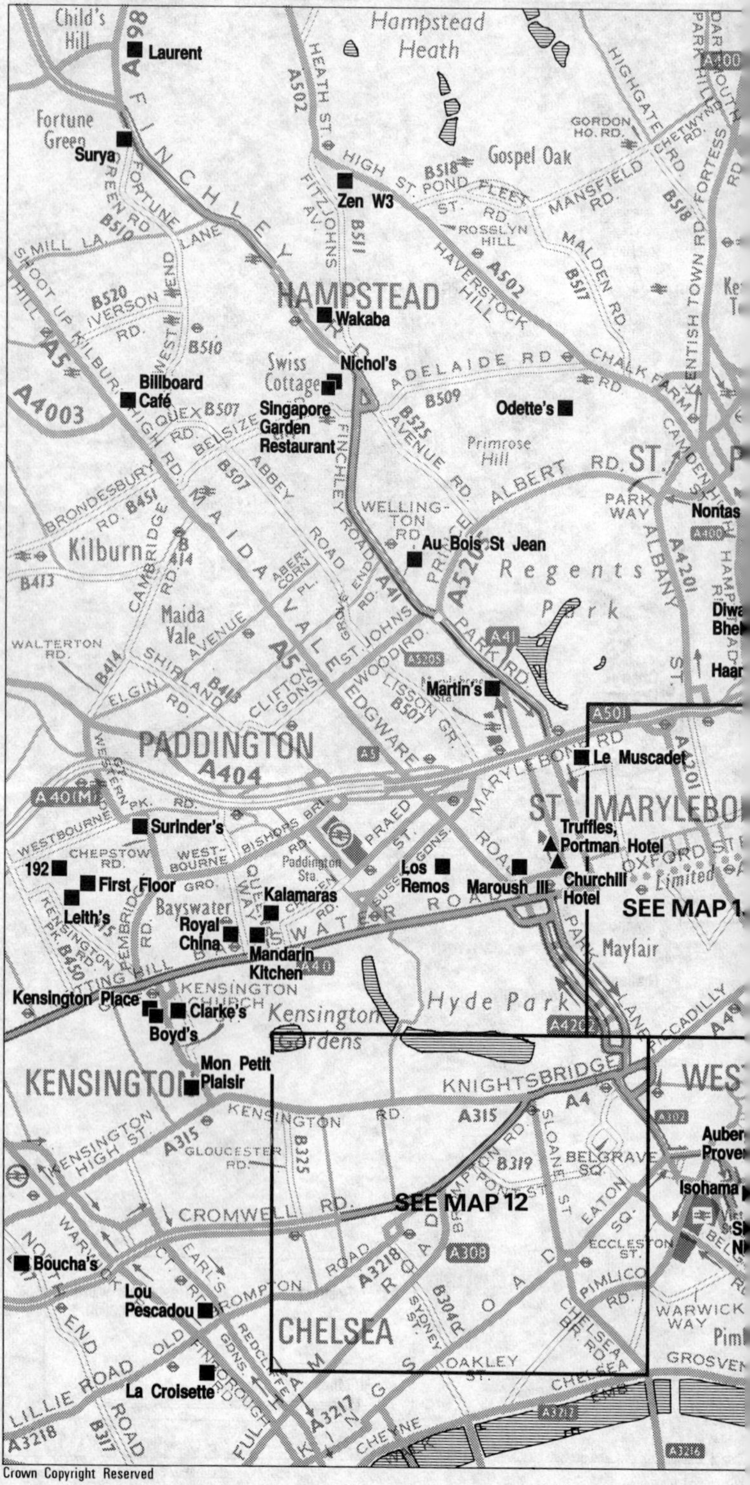

Child's Hill

Laurent

Hampstead Heath

Fortune Green

Surya

Zen W3

Gospel Oak

HAMPSTEAD

Wakaba

Nichol's

Swiss Cottage

Billboard Café

Singapore Garden Restaurant

Odette's

Primrose Hill

ST.

Kilburn

Nontas

Au Bois St Jean

Regents

Park

Maida Vale

Diwa Bhe

Haar

PADDINGTON

Martin's

Le Muscadet

ST MARYLEBO

Surinder's

Truffles, Portman Hotel

192

First Floor

Leith's

Los Remos

Marqush III

Churchill Hotel

SEE MAP 1

Kalamaras

Bayswater

Royal China

Mandarin Kitchen

Mayfair

Hyde Park

Kensington Place

Clarke's

Boyd's

Kensington Gardens

KENSINGTON

Mon Petit Plaisir

KNIGHTSBRIDGE

WES

Auber Prove

Isohama

SEE MAP 12

BELGRAVE SQ.

Boucha's

Lou Pescadou

CHELSEA

SH N

La Croisette

GROSVEN

Pim

Crown Copyright Reserved

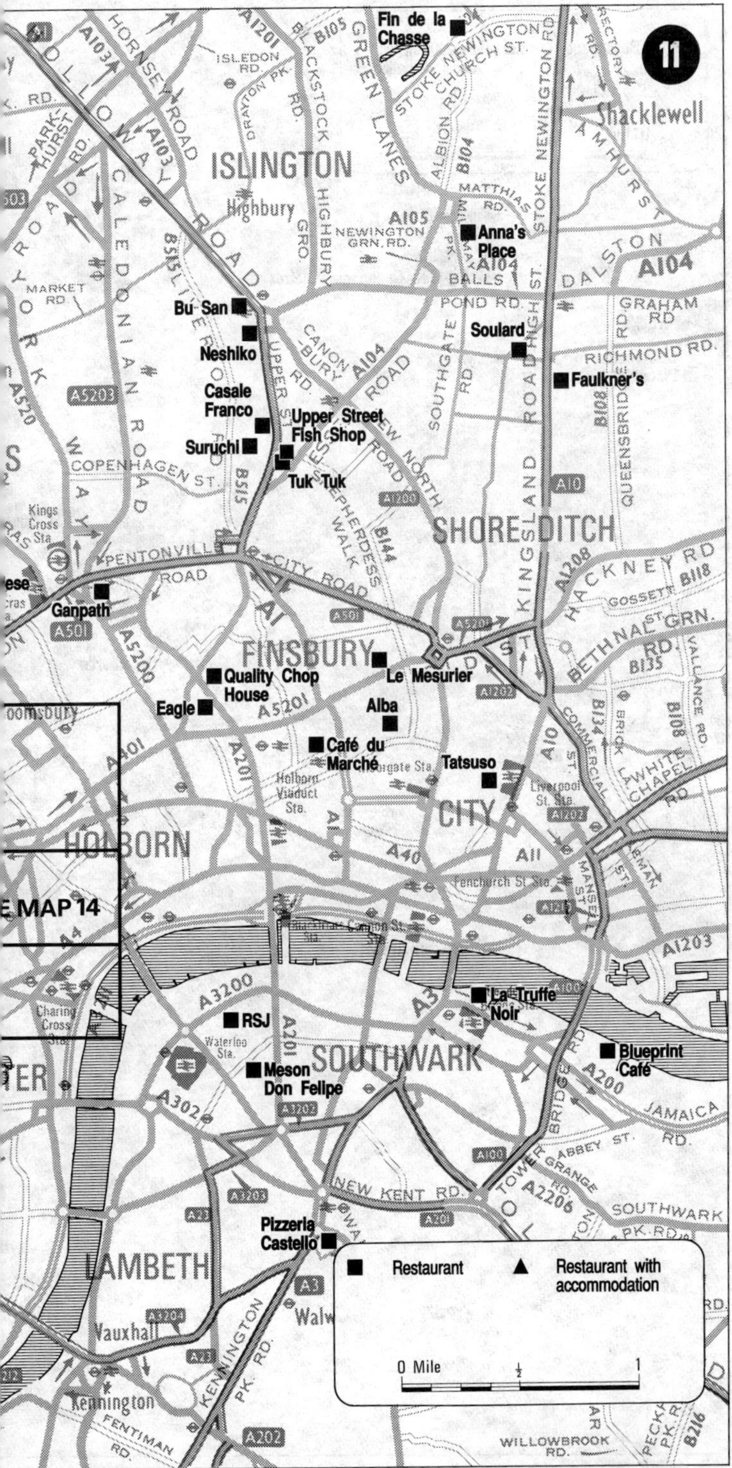

Fin de la Chasse

Shacklewell

ISLINGTON

Highbury

Anna's Place

Bu San

Soulard

Neshiko

Faulkner's

Casale Franco

Upper Street Fish Shop

Suruchi

SHOREDITCH

Tuk Tuk

Ganpath

FINSBURY

Quality Chop House

Le Mesurier

Eagle

Alba

Café du Marché

Tatsuso

CITY

HOLBORN

SEE MAP 14

11

La Truffe Noir

RSJ

SOUTHWARK

Blueprint Café

Meson Don Felipe

Pizzeria Castello

LAMBETH

Vauxhall

Walw

Kennington

| ■ Restaurant | ▲ Restaurant with accommodation |

0 Mile ½ 1

Base Map Copyright © Bartholomew 1991

CENTRAL LONDON: South-West

Restaurant
Restaurant with accommodation
0 Mile
¼
South Carriage
Kensington Rd.
Kensington Gore
Royal College of Art
Royal Albert Hall
190 Queensgate/Bistrot 190
Imperial College
Prince Consort Road
Wódka
Kensington Gate
Launceston Place
Royal College of Music
City & Guilds College
Queen's Gate Ter.
Petersham Pl.
Imperial College Rd.
Holy Trinity Church
Elvaston Place
Royal College of Science
Science Museum
Geological Museum
Victoria & Albert Museum
Brompton Oratory
St Quentin
Natural History Museum
Southwell Gdns.
Cromwell Road
Tui
Thurloe Place
Gilbert's
French University College
Gloucester Road
Harrington Rd.
South Kensington
Bombay Brasserie
Stanhope Gdns.
Pelham Street
Hilaire
Onslow Square
Old Brompton Road
Chanterelle
Brompton Hospital
Royal Marsden Hospital
Chelsea Hospital for Women
Drayton Gardens
The Boltons
Little Boltons
Chelsea Polytechnic
Fulham Road
Sydney Street
Beaufort St.
Eleven Park Walk
St. Stephen's Hospital
Hollywood Road
Redcliffe Rd.
Fawcett Street
Gloucester Road
Exhibition Road
Queen's Gate
Ennismore Gardens
Princes Gardens
Onslow Gardens
Elm Park Gardens
Park Walk
Gilston Road
Tregunter Road
Carlyle Square
The Vale
Mulberry Walk
Mallord St.
Paultons Square
Glebe Pl.

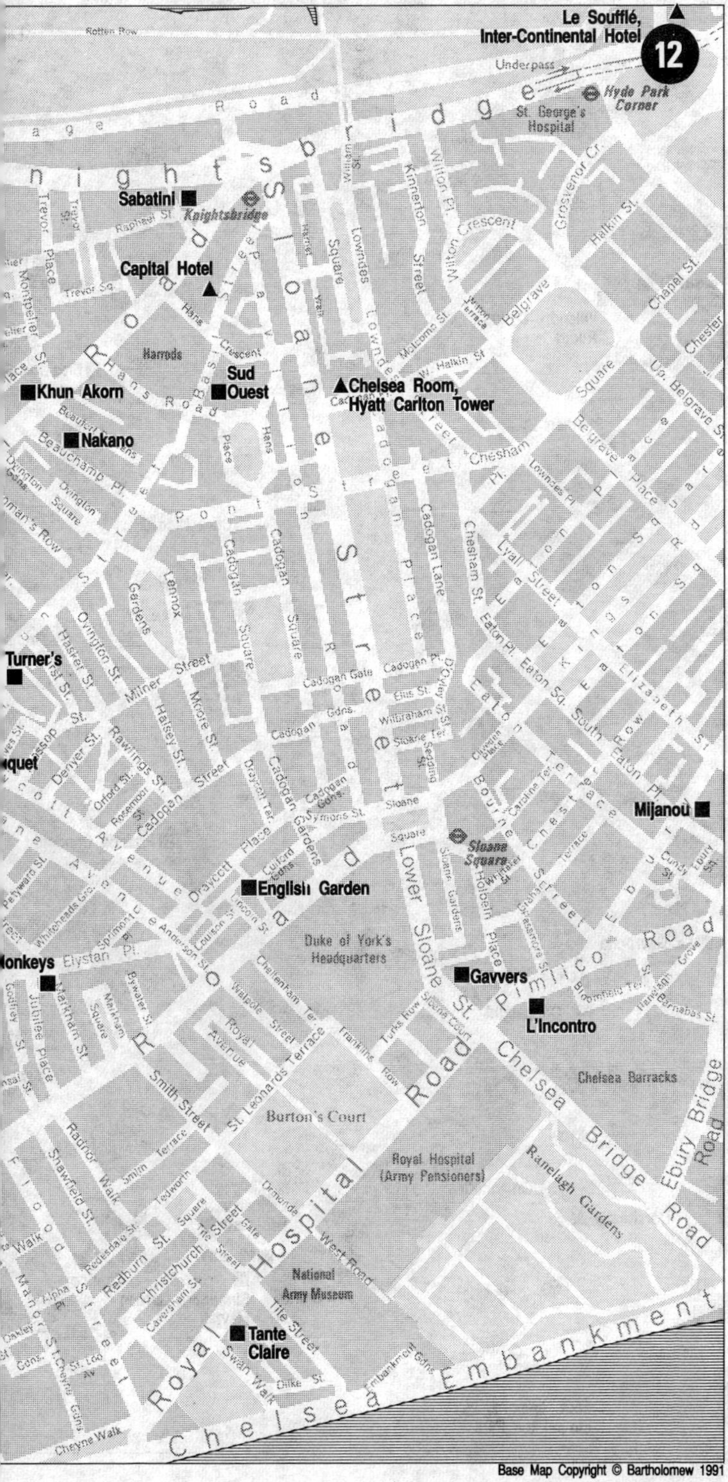
Le Soufflé,
Inter-Continental Hotel
12
Underpass
Hyde Park Corner
St. George's Hospital
Rotten Row
Knightsbridge
Sabatini
Knightsbridge
Capital Hotel
Harrods
Sud Ouest
Khun Akorn
Nakano
Chelsea Room,
Hyatt Carlton Tower
Sloane Street
Turner's
Mijanou
English Garden
Duke of York's Headquarters
Sloane Square
Gavvers
L'Incontro
Chelsea Barracks
Burton's Court
Royal Hospital (Army Pensioners)
Ranelagh Gardens
National Army Museum
Tante Claire
Royal Hospital Road
King's Road
Pimlico Road
Chelsea Bridge Road
Ebury Bridge Road
Chelsea Embankment
Lower Sloane St.
Cadogan Square
Cadogan Place
Cadogan Lane
Lowndes Square
Lowndes Street
Kinnerton Street
Wilton Crescent
Wilton Pl.
Belgrave Square
Grosvenor Cr.
Halkin St.
Chapel St.
Chesham Pl.
Chesham St.
Lyall Street
Eaton Place
Eaton Square
Elizabeth St.
Beauchamp Pl.
Ovington Square
Ovington St.
Milner Street
Moore St.
Halsey St.
Lennox Gardens
Pont Street
Hans Road
Hans Crescent
Draycott Avenue
Draycott Place
Elystan Pl.
Smith Street
St. Leonards Terrace
Franklins Row
Turks Row
Holbein Place
Radnor Walk
Flood Street
Christchurch Street
Tite Street
Swan Walk
Dilke St.
Cheyne Walk
West Road
Jubilee Place
Markham Square
Walpole Street
Royal Avenue
Cheltenham Terrace
Bourne Street
Chester Row
Ebury Street
Cundy St.
Sloane Gardens
Sloane Terrace
Wilbraham Pl.
Ellis St.
Cadogan Gate
Symons St.
Culford Gdns.
Lincoln St.
Walton St.
Trevor Place
Trevor Sq.
Montpelier St.
Raphael St.
Basil Street
William St.
Harriet Walk
Motcomb St.
W. Halkin St.
Up. Belgrave St.
Bloomfield Ter.
Ranelagh Grove
St. Barnabas St.
Ormonde Gate
Tedworth Square
Redesdale St.
Redburn St.
Shawfield St.

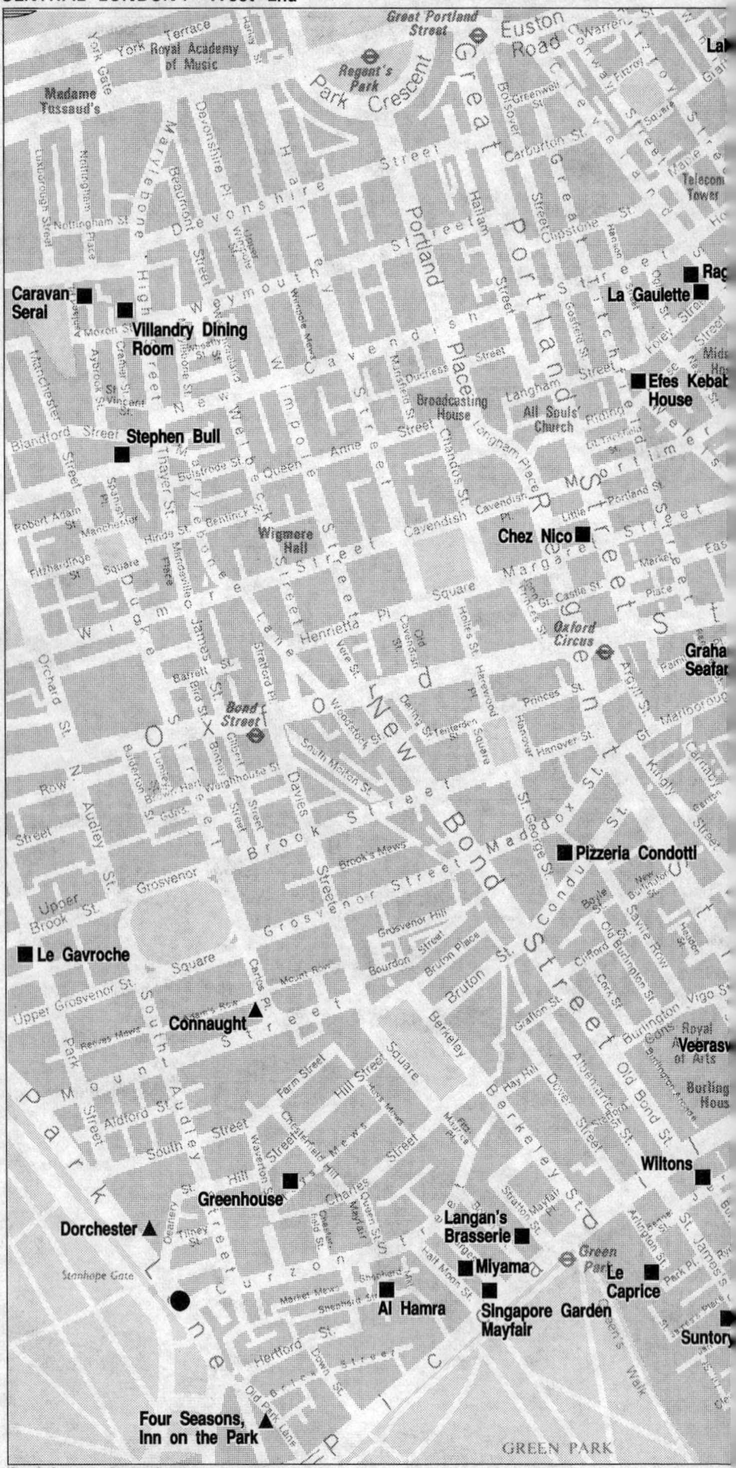
Great Portland Street
Euston Road
Royal Academy of Music
Regent's Park
Park Crescent
Madame Tussaud's
York Gate
York Terrace
Devonshire Street
Weymouth Street
Harley Street
Wimpole Street
Portland Place
Great Portland Street
Carburton St.
Clipstone St.
Marylebone High Street
Nottingham Pl.
Luxborough Street
Caravan Serai
Villandry Dining Room
La Gaulette
Efes Kebab House
Telecom Tower
Broadcasting House
All Souls' Church
Langham Place
New Cavendish Street
Mortimer Street
Stephen Bull
Blandford Street
Manchester Square
Wigmore Hall
Wigmore Street
Cavendish Square
Chez Nico
Margaret Street
Oxford Circus
Regent Street
Henrietta Pl.
Oxford Street
Bond Street
New Bond Street
Orchard St.
North Audley St.
Duke Street
James St.
Davies Street
South Molton St.
Brook Street
Hanover Square
Princes St.
Pizzeria Condotti
Maddox St.
Conduit Street
Grosvenor Square
Grosvenor Street
Upper Brook St.
Upper Grosvenor St.
Le Gavroche
Connaught
Mount Street
Bruton St.
Berkeley Square
Savile Row
Old Bond St.
Vigo St.
Royal Academy of Arts
Burlington House
Park Street
South Audley Street
South Street
Hill Street
Farm Street
Dover Street
Albemarle Street
Berkeley St.
Wiltons
Greenhouse
Dorchester
Langan's Brasserie
Miyama
Al Hamra
Singapore Garden Mayfair
Le Caprice
Green Park
Curzon Street
Park Lane
Piccadilly
Stanhope Gate
Hertford St.
Four Seasons, Inn on the Park
GREEN PARK

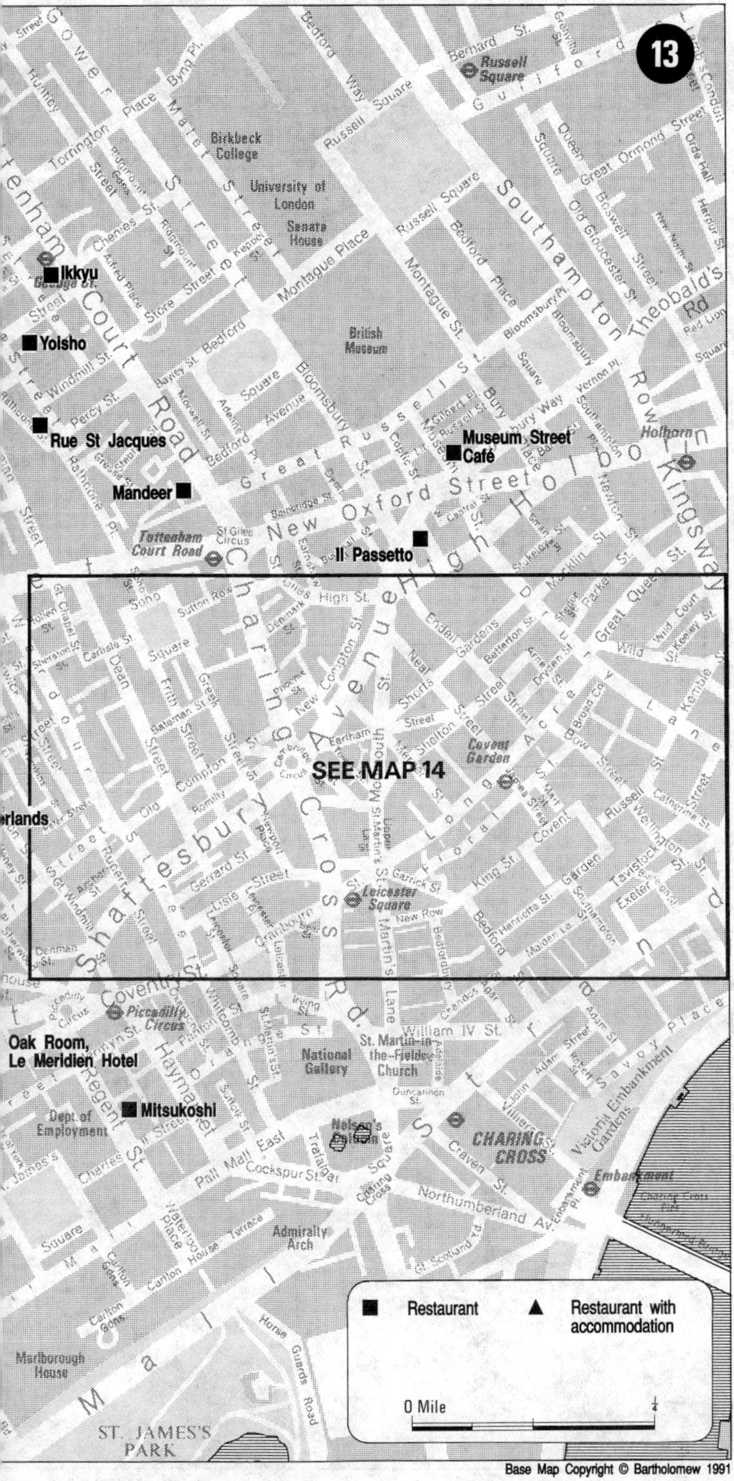
13
Ikkyu
Yoisho
Rue St Jacques
Mandeer
Museum Street Café
Il Passetto
Oak Room, Le Meridien Hotel
Mitsukoshi
SEE MAP 14
Birkbeck College
University of London
Senate House
British Museum
Russell Square
Tottenham Court Road
Holborn
Covent Garden
Leicester Square
Piccadilly Circus
National Gallery
St. Martin-in-the-Fields Church
Nelson's Column
CHARING CROSS
Embankment
Admiralty Arch
Dept of Employment
Marlborough House
ST. JAMES'S PARK
Restaurant
Restaurant with accommodation
0 Mile
¼

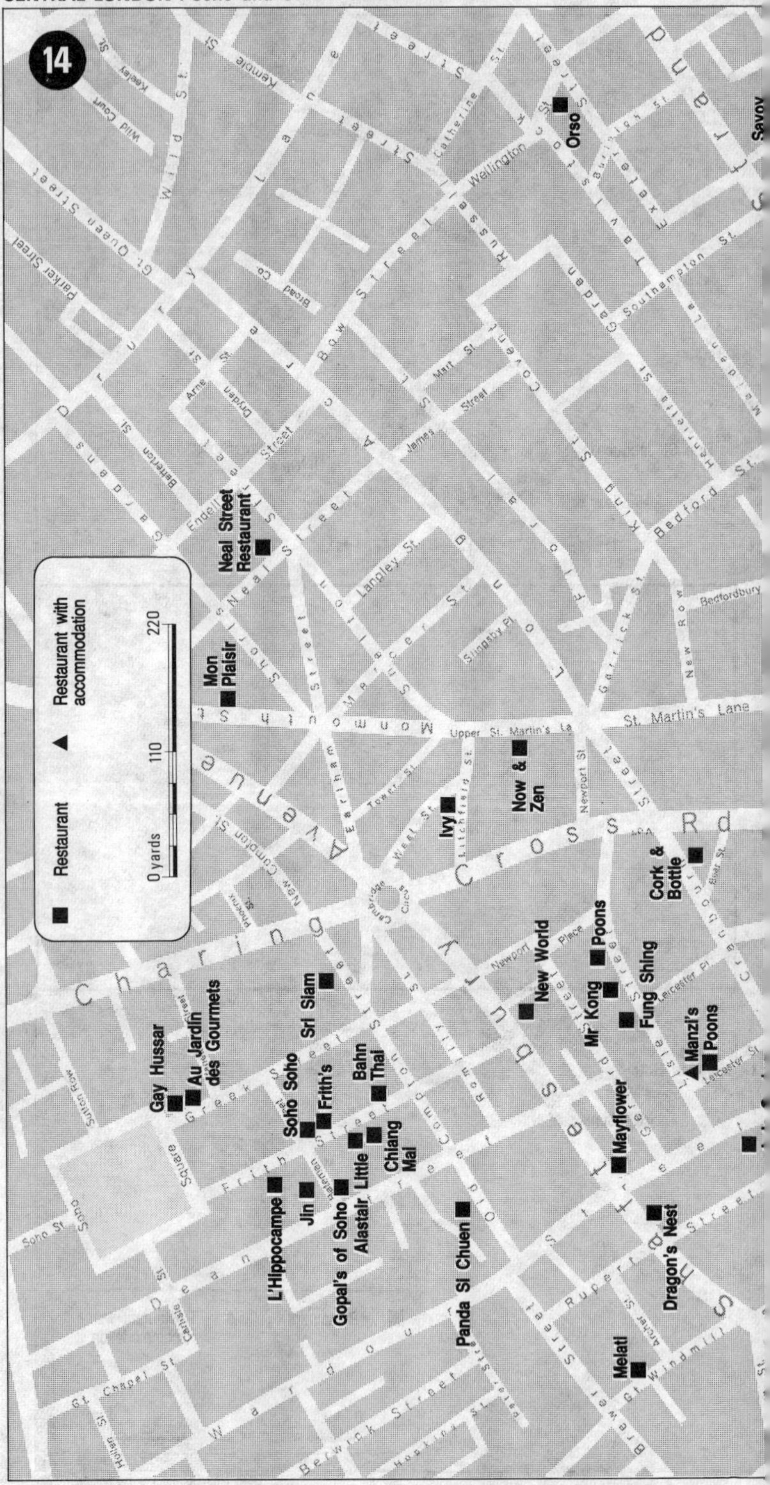
14
Restaurant
Restaurant with accommodation
0 yards
110
220
Neal Street Restaurant
Mon Plaisir
Orso
Now & Zen
Ivy
Cork & Bottle
Poons
New World
Mr Kong
Fung Shing
Manzi's
Poons
Gay Hussar
Au Jardin des Gourmets
Sri Siam
Soho Soho
Frith's
Bahn Thai
Chiang Mai
Little
Alastair
Gopal's of Soho
Jin
L'Hippocampe
Panda Si Chuen
Mayflower
Dragon's Nest
Melati
Savoy
Charing Cross Rd
Shaftesbury Avenue
Long Acre
Drury Lane
Bow Street
Neal Street
Monmouth St
Shorts Gardens
Endell Street
Earlham Street
Wardour Street
Dean Street
Frith Street
Greek Street
Old Compton Street
Gerrard Street
Lisle Street
Leicester Sq
St. Martin's Lane
Upper St. Martin's La
Garrick St
King Street
Henrietta St
Bedford St
Southampton St
Wellington St
Russell Street
Floral St
Covent Garden
Soho Square
Cambridge Circus
Berwick Street
Rupert Street
Brewer Street
Gt. Windmill St
Gt. Chapel St
Carlisle St
Soho St
Sutton Row
Newport Place
Newport St
Litchfield St
West St
Tower St
New Compton St
Phoenix St
Langley St
Slingsby Pl
Mercer St
James Street
Mart St
Arne St
Dryden St
Betterton St
Broad Ct
Gt. Queen Street
Parker Street
Wild St
Wild Court
Keeley St
Kemble Street
Catherine St
Exeter St
Burleigh St
Maiden La
Bedfordbury
New Row
Bateman St
Archer St
Hopkins St
Hollen St

Report Form

To the Editor *The Good Food Guide*
FREEPOST, 2 Marylebone Road, London NW1 1YN

From my personal experience the following establishment should/should not be included in the *Guide*.

____

____

Telephone______________

I had lunch/dinner/stayed there on ______________ 19____

I would rate this establishment _____ out of five.

please continue overleaf

My meal for ____ people cost £____________ *attach bill where possible*

☐ Please tick if you would like more report forms

I am not connected in any way with management or proprietors.
Name and address (BLOCK CAPITALS)

Signed ____________

Report Form

To the Editor *The Good Food Guide*
FREEPOST, 2 Marylebone Road, London NW1 1YN

From my personal experience the following establishment should/should not be included in the *Guide*.

Telephone

I had lunch/dinner/stayed there on 19

I would rate this establishment ____ out of five.

please continue overleaf

My meal for ____ people cost £ ______________ *attach bill where possible*

☐ Please tick if you would like more report forms

I am not connected in any way with management or proprietors.
Name and address (BLOCK CAPITALS)

Signed ____________________

Report Form

To the Editor *The Good Food Guide*
FREEPOST, 2 Marylebone Road, London NW1 1YN

From my personal experience the following establishment should/should not be included in the *Guide*.

Telephone__________________

I had lunch/dinner/stayed there on __________________ 19____

I would rate this establishment _____ out of five.

please continue overleaf

My meal for ____ people cost £ ____________ *attach bill where possible*

☐ Please tick if you would like more report forms

I am not connected in any way with management or proprietors.
Name and address (BLOCK CAPITALS)

Signed ____________

Report Form

To the Editor *The Good Food Guide*
FREEPOST, 2 Marylebone Road, London NW1 1YN

From my personal experience the following establishment should/should not be included in the *Guide*.

____

____

Telephone______________

I had lunch/dinner/stayed there on ______________ 19___

I would rate this establishment ____ out of five.

please continue overleaf

My meal for ____ people cost £____________ *attach bill where possible*

☐ Please tick if you would like more report forms

I am not connected in any way with management or proprietors.
Name and address (BLOCK CAPITALS)

Signed ____________

Report Form

To the Editor *The Good Food Guide*
FREEPOST, 2 Marylebone Road, London NW1 1YN

From my personal experience the following establishment should/should not be included in the *Guide*.

____

____

Telephone____________________

I had lunch/dinner/stayed there on ____________________ 19____

I would rate this establishment _____ out of five.

please continue overleaf

My meal for ____ people cost £ ______________ *attach bill where possible*

☐ Please tick if you would like more report forms

I am not connected in any way with management or proprietors.
Name and address (BLOCK CAPITALS)

Signed ______________________________

Report Form

92

To the Editor *The Good Food Guide*
FREEPOST, 2 Marylebone Road, London NW1 1YN

From my personal experience the following establishment should/should not be included in the *Guide*.

Telephone________________

I had lunch/dinner/stayed there on ________________ 19___

I would rate this establishment _____ out of five.

please continue overleaf

My meal for ____ people cost £ ____________ *attach bill where possible*

□ Please tick if you would like more report forms

I am not connected in any way with management or proprietors.
Name and address (BLOCK CAPITALS)

Signed ________________

Report Form

To the Editor *The Good Food Guide*
FREEPOST, 2 Marylebone Road, London NW1 1YN

From my personal experience the following establishment should/should not be included in the *Guide*.

Telephone__________________

I had lunch/dinner/stayed there on __________________ 19____

I would rate this establishment _____ out of five.

please continue overleaf

My meal for ____ people cost £ ______________ *attach bill where possible*

☐ Please tick if you would like more report forms

I am not connected in any way with management or proprietors.
Name and address (BLOCK CAPITALS)

Signed ______________________________

Which?

Published once a month, *Which?* gives you comparative reports on the merits and value for money of many products and services that you buy for yourself, your family and your home.

Because Consumers' Association is an independent organisation our product testing is completely unbiased, so you can be sure you are getting the facts.

Which? is not sold by newsagents or on bookstalls. It is available only on subscription, with copies sent direct to your address. To make sure you get your copy, fill in the form opposite.

To claim your free trial subscription to *Which?* just complete and return the form opposite. No action is necessary if you wish to continue after your free trial: your subscription will bring you *Which?* for £12.75 a quarter until you cancel by writing to us (and to your bank to cancel your Direct Debiting Mandate), or until we advise you of a change in price. Your subscription becomes due on the first of the month, three months after the date on the mandate. If you do not wish to continue beyond the trial period, simply write and let us know before your first payment is due.

Gardening from Which?

Published 10 times a year with bumper issues in spring and autumn, this magazine aims to help you in your gardening by sharing the results of our thorough research and the experience of our gardening experts.

Every issue of *Gardening* contains something for everyone; from beginner to expert. The magazine's 80 or so comparative reports a year look at a wide variety of subjects from shrubs, flowers and cacti, fruit and vegetables to tools, techniques and equipment. So whether you've got a few window boxes, a lawn, well-established ornamental borders or a greenhouse, *Gardening* will help you to find ways of improving what you have and save you time and money.

To claim your free trial subscription to *Gardening from Which?* just complete and return the form opposite. No action is necessary if you wish to continue after your free trial: your subscription wili bring you *Gardening from Which?* for £11.75 a quarter until you cancel by writing to us (and to your bank to cancel your Direct Debiting Mandate), or until we advise you of a change in price. Your subscription becomes due on the first of the month, three months after the date on the mandate. If you do not wish to continue beyond the trial period, simply write and let us know before your first payment is due.

Which? way to Health

This lively and authoritative magazine will help you and your family stay healthy. You'll find articles on staying fit, eating the right foods, early detection of any health problems, health products and how to get the best from the NHS.

This magazine is published every two months and, like *Which?*, is completely independent – bringing you unbiased facts about health in Britain today. The magazine takes a close look behind the scenes exposing bad practice and harmful products to help prevent you, the consumer, being deceived. We also report on any medical breakthroughs which could bring relief or cure for victims.

To claim your free trial subscription to *Which? way to Health* just complete and return the form opposite. No action is necessary if you wish to continue after your free trial: your subscription will bring you *Which? way to Health* for £5.75 a quarter until you cancel by writing to us (and to your bank to cancel your Direct Debiting Mandate), or until we advise you of a change in price. Your subscription becomes due on the first of the month, three months after the date on the mandate. If you do not wish to continue beyond the trial period, simply write and let us know before your first payment is due.

Consumers' Association, Castlemead, Gascoyne Way, Hertford X, SG14 1LI

FREE TRIAL ACCEPTANCE

Please send me free the next 3 issues of *Which?* as they appear. I understand that I am under no obligation. If I do not wish to continue with *Which?* after the free trial, I can cancel this order at any time before payment is due on the 1st of the month three months after the date shown. But if I decide to continue I need do nothing – my subscription will bring me *Which?* for the current price of £12.75 a quarter.

☐ Tick here if you do not wish your name and address to be added to a mailing list to be used by ourselves or third parties for sending you further offers.

KE_

DIRECT DEBITING MANDATE

I/We authorise you until further notice in writing to charge to my/our account with you unspecified amounts which may be debited thereto at the instance of Consumers' Association by Direct Debit. Originator's Ref. No. 992338

Signed	Today's date
Bank account in the name of	
Bank account number	
Name and address of your bank	
	Postcode

Banks may decline to accept instructions to charge direct debits to certain types of account other than current accounts.

YOUR NAME AND ADDRESS

Name	
Address	
	Postcode

FREE TRIAL ACCEPTANCE

Please send me free the next 3 issues of *Gardening* as they appear. I understand that I am under no obligation. If I do not wish to continue with *Gardening* after the free trial, I can cancel this order at any time before payment is due on the 1st of the month three months after the date shown. But if I decide to continue I need do nothing – my subscription will bring me *Gardening* for the current price of £11.75 a quarter.

☐ Tick here if you do not wish your name and address to be added to a mailing list to be used by ourselves or third parties for sending you further offers.

L_J

DIRECT DEBITING MANDATE

I/We authorise you until further notice in writing to charge to my/our account with you unspecified amounts which may be debited thereto at the instance of Consumers' Association by Direct Debit. Originator's Ref. No. 992338

Signed	Today's date
Bank account in the name of	
Bank account number	
Name and address of your bank	
	Postcode

Banks may decline to accept instructions to charge direct debits to certain types of account other than current accounts.

YOUR NAME AND ADDRESS

Name	
Address	
	Postcode

FREE TRIAL ACCEPTANCE

Please send me free the next 2 issues of *Which? way to Health* as they appear. I understand that I am under no obligation. If I do not wish to continue with *Which? way to Health* after the free trial, I can cancel this order at any time before payment is due on the 1st of the month three months after the date shown. But if I decide to continue I need do nothing – my subscription will bring me *Which? way to Health* for the current price of £5.75 a quarter.

☐ Tick here if you do not wish your name and address to be added to a mailing list to be used by ourselves or third parties for sending you further offers.

E_XQ

DIRECT DEBITING MANDATE

I/We authorise you until further notice in writing to charge to my/our account with you unspecified amounts which may be debited thereto at the instance of Consumers' Association by Direct Debit. Originator's Ref. No. 992338

Signed	Today's date
Bank account in the name of	
Bank account number	
Name and address of your bank	
	Postcode

Banks may decline to accept instructions to charge direct debits to certain types of account other than current accounts.

YOUR NAME AND ADDRESS

Name	
Address	
	Postcode

Which? – details overleaf

Consumers' Association, Castlemead,
Gascoyne Way, Hertford X, SG14 1LH.

Gardening from Which? – details overleaf

Consumers' Association, Castlemead,
Gascoyne Way, Hertford X, SG14 1LH.

Which? way to Health – details overleaf

Consumers' Association, Castlemead,
Gascoyne Way, Hertford X, SG14 1LH.